INTRODUCTION TO EMPLOYEE BENEFITS LAW

POLICY AND PRACTICE

Fourth Edition

■ ■ ■

by

Colleen E. Medill

Robert and Joanne Berkshire
Family Professor of Law
University of Nebraska-Lincoln College of Law

AMERICAN CASEBOOK SERIES®

Mat #41381181

American Casebook Series is a trademark registered in the U.S. Patent and Trademark Office.

© West, a Thomson business, 2004, 2007
© 2011 Thomson Reuters
© 2015 LEG, Inc. d/b/a West Academic
    444 Cedar Street, Suite 700
    St. Paul, MN 55101
    1-877-888-1330

West, West Academic Publishing, and West Academic are trademarks of West Publishing Corporation, used under license.

Printed in the United States of America

ISBN: 978-0-314-28654-3

PREFACE TO THE FOURTH EDITION

The world of employee benefits law is constantly changing. Since the third edition of this casebook was published in 2011, pension assets have increased to record levels as the equity markets have recovered from the 2008 crash. The Departments of Labor, Treasury, and Health and Human Services have printed thousands of pages in the Federal Register as part of the administrative implementation of the Affordable Care Act (ACA). Meanwhile, the Supreme Court has decided important new cases on the ACA, fiduciary duties under the Employee Retirement Income Security Act of 1974 (ERISA), and private claims and remedies under ERISA.

Today, more than ever, employee benefits law issues are part of the everyday practice of law. Although the subject matter can be daunting at times, the goal of this casebook is to make the study of employee benefits law exciting and enjoyable, both for the professor to teach, and for the student to learn.

Unlike a traditional casebook on pension law, this book provides a more extensive treatment of defined contribution plans (particularly 401(k) plans) and health care plans. To accommodate an expanded discussion of these topics, the casebook has a streamlined and simplified discussion of defined benefit plans and nonqualified plans. The casebook describes the current state of federal law as of August 1, 2014. The past history of the Internal Revenue Code requirements for qualified plans has been eliminated in an effort to simplify the material for the student.

The casebook relies heavily on real life illustrations and emphasizes solving hypothetical client problems. There are problems throughout each chapter to review and reinforce the subject matter. Discussion questions, found at the end of each chapter, require the student to draw upon material from throughout the chapter to analyze either a sophisticated client problem or a significant public policy issue.

The casebook generally relies on narrative text to introduce each new concept and to summarize the fundamental principles of employee benefits law. Where possible, the casebook reproduces ERISA's legislative history to explain the policy objectives and purposes of the law. The narrative text, problems and discussion questions in the casebook provide frequent opportunities for the students to rise above the technical details of the material and instead focus more broadly on the policy objectives and implications of the law. Often, these policy-oriented problems and questions do not have a "correct" answer. Rather, they are designed to engage the students in a lively discussion of the many significant public policy issues that underlie this field of federal law.

The presentation in the casebook is organized around the statutory structure of Title I of ERISA. Title I of ERISA has seven parts. The casebook generally follows ERISA's seven part structure. This order of presentation also naturally coincides with the typical student experience concerning employee benefit plans, and with the sequence of events that follow the establishment of an employee benefit plan by the employer.

Most students first encounter an employee benefit plan when their employer hands them a summary plan description. Chapter Two of the casebook introduces the concept of a plan that is subject to regulation under ERISA and discusses the reporting and disclosure requirements of Part 1 of Title I. Chapter Three of the casebook covers qualified retirement plans and incorporates both the requirements of Part 2 of Title I concerning employee pension plans and the Code requirements for qualified plans. Chapter Four covers welfare benefit plans, with a primary emphasis on health care plans. Chapters Five, Six and Seven of the casebook cover ERISA fiduciary responsibilities (Part 4 of Title I), civil enforcement actions (Part 5 of Title I), and preemption of state laws (Part 5 of Title I), all of which apply to both pension plans and welfare benefit plans.

The casebook reproduces or discusses in the narrative text all of the major modern Supreme Court opinions concerning ERISA. To accommodate the expanded scope of coverage and still keep the course to a manageable length, only a select number of lower federal court opinions are reproduced in the casebook. Many of the leading lower federal court precedents in the field are described in the narrative text or in the notes and questions following related judicial opinions.

In editing material for inclusion in the casebook, the overarching principle has been to avoid distracting the reader. Cases, statutes and footnotes referenced in judicial opinions reproduced in the book have been deleted without so indicating. Other deleted material in judicial opinions or in material written by others is indicated by " * * * ". Citations have been conformed to the following standardized citation forms: ERISA § ___ (substituted for citations to Title 29 of the United States Code); DOL Reg. § ___ (substituted for citations to Title 29 of the Code of Federal Regulations): Code § ___ (substituted for citations to Title 26 of the United States Code); and Treas. Reg. § ___ (substituted for citations to Title 26 of the Code of Federal Regulations). When a footnote in a judicial opinion has been retained, the text contains the original footnote number from the opinion. Editor's footnotes are alphabetized and run consecutively from the beginning of each chapter. Rather than liberally using the [sic] editing convention, in reproducing the material of others I have occasionally made minor spelling or grammar changes to conform the text to Standard English.

The fourth edition of the casebook retains the general organizational structure of the third edition. Older Supreme Court cases have been edited to make room for the latest Supreme Court decisions. For those instructors who previously used the third edition, the accompanying Teacher's Manual contains a detailed chapter-by-chapter listing of the changes made in the fourth edition.

I would like to thank Dean Susan Poser for supporting this project, and my Employee Benefits Law students at the University of Nebraska College of Law, whose energy and enthusiasm make teaching delightful. My secretary, Vida Eden, has been a true partner in this project by providing invaluable assistance in preparing the manuscript. Finally, I would like to thank my husband, Steven J. Medill, who kept our household running smoothly and our four children happy while I completed this book.

COLLEEN E. MEDILL

August 1, 2014

SUMMARY OF CONTENTS

TABLE OF CONTENTS

TABLE OF CASES

The principal cases are in bold type.

───────────

TABLE OF STATUTES

INTRODUCTION TO EMPLOYEE BENEFITS LAW

POLICY AND PRACTICE

Fourth Edition

CHAPTER 1

INTRODUCTION TO EMPLOYEE BENEFITS LAW

■ ■ ■

A. EMPLOYEE BENEFITS LAW IN YOUR FUTURE PRACTICE

Health care and retirement issues frequently are in the news. Consider the following examples:

Will The Supreme Court's Contraceptive Decision Affect Coverage Of Other Drugs?, FORBES, June 30, 2014.

AOL CAVES: Tim Armstrong Restores 401(k) Plans for Employees, BUSINESS INSIDER, Feb. 8, 2014.

Boeing to End Traditional Pension Plans for Nonunion Workers, ST. LOUIS BUSINESS JOURNAL, Mar. 6, 2014.

Local Companies Promote Wellness to Lower Insurance Costs, DAYTON DAILY NEWS, June 28, 2014.

Millennials (With Jobs) Are Super Saving Their Way to Retirement, TIME.COM, July 14, 2014.

For most workers, retirement and health care security is achieved through an employer-sponsored benefit plan. Whatever the nature of your future legal practice, you are likely to encounter employer-sponsored benefit plans and the body of federal law that regulates them. In a 1997 speech at the dedication of the Harrison Law Grounds at the University of Virginia Law School, former United States Supreme Court Chief Justice William H. Rehnquist described the importance of studying employee benefits law:

> If one examines the current offerings of the University of Virginia Law School, one learns that this year there are some 160 courses offered, and some 90 seminars. This is an intellectual feast that stands in sharp contrast, certainly, to the offerings of my law school when I attended long ago. When one looks further, one sees that there are at least three courses offered just on the First Amendment to the United States Constitution. By contrast, there seems to be no course offering devoted to federal regulation of employer-employee benefit and retirement plans—an area of the law which is much less

1

glamorous, receives much less media attention, but the ramifications of which have a far greater effect on the daily lives of people than do the nuances of First Amendment law. Surely practitioners are much more likely to have clients with pension and benefit plan problems than with separation of church and state problems.

Chief Justice William H. Rehnquist, Address at the Dedication of the David A. Harrison II Law Grounds, University of Virginia (Nov. 8, 1997).

Of course, at the time Chief Justice Rehnquist could not foresee that the First Amendment (specifically, the Free Exercise Clause) would become the basis for employers to challenge federally-mandated health care plan benefits! E.g., Hobby Lobby Stores, Inc. v. Sebelius, 870 F. Supp. 2d 1278 (W.D. Okla. 2012) (denying request for preliminary injunction). Nevertheless, the broader point of his remarks continues to ring true, namely that employee benefits law is of practical importance in the everyday practice of law. (By the way, today the University of Virginia Law School does offer an employee benefits law course.)

This casebook has been written with two goals in mind. First, the casebook introduces the types of employee benefits law issues that are likely to arise in legal practice, whether that practice lies in the areas of litigation, corporate law, tax law, labor and employment law, family law, or estate planning. Second, the casebook introduces the major public policy issues that permeate this area of federal law and encourages you to think about and debate these issues with your classmates.

The casebook is organized into seven chapters. The remainder of Chapter One summarizes the history of the federal regulation of employee benefit plans and describes several of the major public policy issues that underlie this body of federal law. Chapter Two describes the types of plans subject to ERISA and the federal law requirements for plan operation and administration. Chapter Three focuses on the Code requirements that govern employer-sponsored retirement plans. Welfare benefit plans, including health care plans, are discussed in Chapter Four. Fiduciary responsibilities, the types of ERISA claims that may be brought by private litigants, and ERISA remedies are covered in Chapters Five and Six. The topic of ERISA preemption of state law is explored in Chapter Seven.

B. HISTORICAL BACKGROUND

1. HISTORY OF THE REGULATION OF EMPLOYEE BENEFIT PLANS[a]

Pre-ERISA

Over the course of the 20th century, the regulation of employee benefit plans has progressed from a few measured steps in the early 1920s to an accelerating march of increasingly complex and comprehensive regulation. Before 1921 there were few, if any, federal or state laws with respect to employee benefits generally. Employers that sponsored such plans for their employees generally did so without an incentive or a compulsion from federal or state law.

In 1921, Congress for the first time encouraged companies to establish retirement programs for their employees by providing a tax deduction for employers who contributed to employee pension plans. The Revenue Acts of 1926 and 1928 brought further encouragement, providing for tax-exempt trusts and the shielding of employees from income taxation because of contributions by employers on their behalf. The 1926 Act allowed contributions to be made to a trust that would accumulate income free of tax until distributed in the form of benefits to covered employees. The 1928 Act permitted additional deductible contributions in amounts actuarially determined to provide benefits based on service prior to adoption and to amortized benefit increases.

Some companies took advantage of these tax incentives by providing contributions disproportionately for executives and other highly compensated employees. In the Revenue Acts of 1938 and 1942, Congress conditioned the tax incentives by requiring that, in order to be tax-qualified, pension, profit-sharing, or stock bonus plans may not discriminate in favor of the highly compensated in their benefits or eligibility. These basic principles are still contained in the Internal Revenue Code today.

In the midst of the Depression, Congress in 1935 passed the Social Security Act. The old age and survivor benefits initially provided under that law were relatively modest compared to the breadth and size of today's Social Security benefits. The Social Security Act, however, evidenced Congress' growing awareness of the need for programs that would contribute to the retirement income security of the population.

---

[a] Reprinted with permission from Chapter 1, pages 1–6, "Brief History of the Regulation of Employee Benefits," from EMPLOYEE BENEFITS LAW, Second Edition, by The American Bar Association. Copyright © 2000 by The American Bar Association, Chicago, IL 60611. Published by The Bureau of National Affairs, Inc., Arlington, VA 22202. For copies of Bloomberg BNA Books publications call toll free 1-800-960-1220 or visit www.bnabooks.com. The footnotes in the original text have been omitted.

Also in 1935, the National Labor Relations Act (NLRA) was enacted. The NLRA provided a basic framework for the regulation of relations between organized labor and management and provided a framework of collective bargaining that would be held to encompass pension and welfare plans as "terms and conditions of employment." During World War II, labor relations were heavily regulated by the War Labor Board, which was vested with extensive authority to maintain peace in the labor force so that the war effort would continue unabated. The War Labor Board, like the National Labor Relations Board, helped to foster a collective bargaining environment that could give rise to employee benefit plans. In addition, under its authority to impose terms in labor disputes, the War Labor Board mandated the establishment of new retirement plans.

As company-sponsored pension plans were becoming more commonplace in the decades of the 1930s and 1940s, many workers were still without coverage, especially in industries characterized by a mobility of workers between relatively small employers. Because of their size, the conditions and traditions of their industries, and the transience of their work forces, these companies were slower to establish employee benefit plans. Many of these companies were in businesses known as "trades" (e.g., construction, needlework and garment manufacturing, dairies, confectionery, and retailing). In many areas, their employees were organized by unions, which, beginning after World War II and accelerating in the 1950s, moved to fill the pension and health and welfare coverage void. The same lack of employer-sponsored plans in the coal mining industry had earlier led to formulation of a pension and health and welfare plan by the United Mine Workers (UMW), which succeeded in obtaining collective bargaining agreements with mining employers under which contributions were made to the UMW plans on a cents-per-ton-of-coal-mined basis.

In 1947, two major developments significantly affected employee benefits. The first was the Seventh Circuit decision in *Inland Steel v. NLRB,* 170 F.2d 247 (7th Cir. 1948), holding that pension benefits were a mandatory subject of collective bargaining. The second major development was enactment of the Labor Management Relations Act of 1947 (LMRA or Taft-Hartley Act). Responding to concerns that the United Mine Workers plan might be used as a "war chest" to finance strike activity and, more generally, that a lack of regulation over union-sponsored plans allowed too many opportunities for abuse, Congress imposed a series of requirements on union-sponsored plans financed with employer contributions.

Accordingly, Section 302 of the Taft-Hartley Act made it a criminal violation for an employer to provide anything of value to a representative of employees. Among the exceptions to this rule was one for employer contributions to employee benefit plans that met the conditions specified in Section 302(c)(5). Chief among these was the requirement that the plan be administered by a joint board of trustees with equal representation of management and labor. Thus began the jointly administered Taft-Hartley plan. The LMRA also required that there be provision for the breaking of deadlocks through the appointment of either an impartial trustee or other decision maker, and that contributions be made pursuant to a written instrument and used for the exclusive benefit of plan participants and beneficiaries. An extensive case law was developed under Section 302(c)(5) that, among other things, established certain principles of fiduciary responsibility for the administration of these plans and the investment of their assets.

In the post-World War II economic expansion, employer sponsorship of retirement and welfare plans grew rapidly. In response to certain inadequacies in protection of plan participants and beneficiaries, the Welfare and Pension Plans Disclosure Act (WPPDA) was enacted in 1958. It required limited reporting to the U.S. Department of Labor (DOL) by private sector plans and disclosure of certain information to their participants, and specified certain behavior relating to employee benefit plans as criminal felonies, subject to fine and imprisonment. In 1962, the WPPDA was amended to require bonding of all persons who handled plan assets and to provide limited investigatory and enforcement powers for the DOL.

While the federal government was expanding its involvement with retirement and welfare plans, the states were also playing a role. Various states enacted laws dealing with disclosure, collection of delinquent contributions, and the assertion of claims by plan participants. State insurance commissioners took an increasingly active role in the regulation of plans. Plan sponsors—companies and unions alike—in particular were increasingly concerned about having to deal with different and sometimes inconsistent state laws. For example, in *State v. Monsanto Co.,* 517 S.W.2d 129 (Mo. Sup. Ct. 1974), the Missouri State Insurance Commissioner successfully asserted that a self-insured plan constituted insurance and was subject to his jurisdiction. The impact of this decision was a key motivation for Congress to include strong preemption rules in ERISA, largely precluding states from regulating benefit plans.

Enactment of ERISA

By the 1960s, a consensus began to form that existing federal and state regulation of employee benefit plans did not sufficiently protect the interests of participants and beneficiaries. Through the years, examples were reported in the media of employees putting in long years of service and not receiving pension benefits because of lengthy vesting requirements and harsh break in service rules. One occurrence that shaped public opinion was the demise of the Studebaker Company. Employees of Studebaker lost not only their jobs, but also the vast bulk of their pensions, even though Studebaker had complied with all then-existing laws and tax-qualification rules. Another source of widespread negative publicity was certain pension funds, especially the Central States, Southeast and Southwest Areas Pension Fund (Central States Teamsters Plan), in which there were repeated allegations of organized crime influence leading to questionable investment activity.

The effort to enact comprehensive employee benefit regulation started in earnest in 1963, when a study was initiated by President Kennedy. Its report, issued in 1965, recommended most of the reforms that were enacted nine years later as part of ERISA. In 1967, Senator Jacob Javits (R-N.Y.) introduced a relatively modest bill that would have imposed certain standards relating to eligibility, vesting, and funding. Hearings on this and later bills laid the foundation for the subsequent comprehensive pension legislation. By 1971, Senator Harrison Williams (D-N.J.), Chairman of the Senate Labor and Human Resources (then Labor and Public Welfare) Committee, and Congressman John Dent (D-Pa.), Chairman of the House Education and Labor Committee's Subcommittee on Employment Standards, had become sufficiently interested in the subject of pension reform to spearhead major efforts to enact a bill.

In 1973, comprehensive legislation was introduced in both the Senate and the House by Senators Williams and Javits and Congressman Dent. The legislation formed the basis for what was to become ERISA. The House Labor Committee acted first on the legislation and was followed by the Senate Labor Committee. Although initially reluctant, the Senate Finance Committee and the House Ways and Means Committee actively participated in the development of the legislative proposals. By the spring of 1974, both the Senate and the House had passed bills, and after a lengthy period of conference, a bill acceptable to both houses was passed, and was signed on Labor Day of 1974 by President Ford.

2. LEGISLATIVE HISTORY OF ERISA

House of Representatives Report No. 93–533 (1973)

The Committee on Education and Labor, to whom was referred the bill (H.R. 2) to revise the Welfare and Pension Plans Disclosure Act, having considered the same, report favorably thereon with an amendment and recommend that the bill, as amended, do pass.

Synopsis

The Employee Benefit Security Act as reported by the Committee is designed to remedy certain defects in the private retirement system which limit the effectiveness of the system in providing retirement income security. The primary purpose of the bill is the protection of individual pension rights, but the committee has been constrained to recognize the voluntary nature of private retirement plans. The relative improvements required by this Act have been weighed against the additional burdens to be placed on the system. While modest cost increases are to be anticipated when the Act becomes effective, the adverse impact of these increases has been minimized. Additionally, all of the provisions in the Act have been analyzed on the basis of their projected costs in relation to the anticipated benefit to the employee participant. In broad outline, the bill is designed to:

(1) establish equitable standards of plan administration;

(2) mandate minimum standards of plan design with respect to the vesting of plan benefits;

(3) require minimum standards of fiscal responsibility by requiring the amortization of unfunded liabilities;

(4) insure the vested portion of unfunded liabilities against the risk of premature plan termination; and

(5) promote a renewed expansion of private retirement plans and increase the number of participants receiving private retirement benefits.

Provision is made for the imposition of criminal penalties on those willfully violating their duties under the Act. The Labor Department is given primary authority to administer the provisions of the Act, but the Committee has placed the principal focus of the enforcement effort on anticipated civil litigation to be initiated by the Secretary of Labor as well as participants and beneficiaries.

Background

The private pension system is a relatively modern economic institution tracing its role as an important social and economic factor only from the mid 1940's. A variety of converging financial and social trends in our society has created a favorable environment for the growth and expansion of private deferred compensation schemes and retirement programs in general. As our economy has matured, an ever increasing number of employers have recognized their responsibility for the physical and economic welfare of their employees, even for the years beyond retirement. Its development parallels and is a response to the transition of the American life style from its rural agrarian antecedents into its present urbanized, wage earner society. The dynamic asset growth necessary to meet its responsibilities has placed the private pension system in a position to influence the level of savings, the operation of our capital markets, and the relative financial security of millions of consumers, three of the fundamental elements of our national economic security.

The growth of the private pension movement in the United States proceeded slowly until the years preceding World War II. As the full implications of the economic changes sweeping the nation were felt, American beliefs and attitudes regarding retirement security changed. The passage of the Railroad Retirement Act and the Social Security Act marked the turning point in American thinking, and dissatisfaction with those early governmental programs contributed to an accelerated interest in private retirement plans. The wage freezes imposed during World War II and the Korean conflict focused increased attention on the deferred component of compensation as a means of avoiding the freeze restrictions.

In 1947 a series of administrative proceedings and court decisions under the National Labor Relations Act of 1935 held that pensions were a form of remuneration for the purposes of that Act, and they accordingly became mandatory subjects of collective bargaining. Inland Steel Company v. NLRB, 170 F.2d 247 (7th Cir. 1948), cert. denied, 336 U.S. 960 (1949). In the same time period a Presidential fact finding commission in presenting its report on the steel industry labor dispute in 1949 stated that:

> We think all industry, in the absence of adequate Government programs, owes an obligation to workers to provide for maintenance of the human body in the form of medical and similar benefits and full depreciation in the form of old age retirement—in the same way as it now does for plant and machinery.

In 1940, an estimated four million employees were covered by private pension plans; in 1950, the figure had increased to almost 10 million, and in 1960, over 21 million were covered. Currently, over 30 million employees or almost one half of the private non-farm work force are covered by these plans. This phenomenal expansion of coverage has been matched by an even more startling accumulation of assets to back the benefit structure. Today, in excess of $150 billion in assets are held in reserve to pay benefits credited to private plan participants.

This rapid growth has constituted the basis for legislative efforts at both the federal and state levels to assure equitable and fair administration of all pension plans.

Various aspects of pension plans have been affected to some degree by most of the major labor legislation of the twentieth century, including the National Labor Relations Act (1935), the Labor Management Relations Act (1947), and the Labor Management Reporting and Disclosure Act (1959). However, not until 1958, with the enactment of the Welfare and Pension Plans Disclosure Act, was legislation effected which was specifically designed to exercise regulatory controls over pension and welfare funds. Based upon disclosure of malfeasance and improper activities by pension administrators, trustees, or fiduciaries, the Act was amended in 1962 to designate certain acts of conduct as federal crimes when they occurred in connection with welfare and pension plans. The amendments also conferred investigatory and various regulatory powers upon the Secretary over pension and welfare funds. In the decade since the amendments were enacted, experience has shown that, despite intermittent enforcement of the reporting requirements and the criminal provisions, the protection accomplished by statute has not been sufficient to accomplish Congressional intent.

The Existing Law

The growth and development of the private pension system in the past two decades have been substantial. Yet, regulation of the private system's scope and operation has been minimal and its effectiveness a matter of debate. The assets of private plans, estimated to be in excess of $150 billion, constitute the only large private accumulation of funds which have escaped the imprimatur of effective federal regulation.

At the federal level, there are essentially three federal statutes which, although accomplishing different purposes and vested within different federal departments for enforcement, are all compatible in their regulatory responsibilities. These are the Welfare and Pension Plans Disclosure Act, the Labor Management Relations Act, and the Internal Revenue Code of 1954.

After a comprehensive investigation of abuses in the administration and investment of private fund assets, Congress adopted the Welfare and Pension Plan Disclosure Act in 1958. The policy underlying enactment of this Act was purportedly to protect the interest of welfare and pension plan participants and beneficiaries through disclosure of information with respect to such plans. The essential requirement of the Act was that the plan administrator compile, file with the Secretary of Labor, and send to participants and their beneficiaries upon written request, a description and annual report of the plan. It was expected that the knowledge thus disseminated would enable participants to police their plans. The Act was amended in 1962 to make theft, embezzlement, bribery, and kickbacks federal crimes if they occur in connection with welfare and pension plans. The 1962 amendments also conferred limited investigatory and regulatory powers upon the Secretary of Labor, and required bonding of plan officials.

Experience in the decade since the passage of the above amendments has demonstrated the inadequacy of the Welfare and Pension Plans Disclosure Act in regulating the private pension system for the purpose of protecting rights and benefits due to workers. It is weak in its limited disclosure requirements and wholly lacking in substantive fiduciary standards. Its chief procedural weakness can be found in its reliance upon the initiative of the individual employee to police the management of his plan.

The Labor Management Relations Act provides the fundamental guidelines for the establishment and operation of pension funds administered jointly by an employer and a union. The Act is not intended to establish, nor does it provide, standards for the preservation of vested benefits, funding adequacy, security of investment, or fiduciary conduct.

Tax deduction benefits accruing to employers are prescribed by the Internal Revenue Code under which the employer is granted a deduction within certain limits for contributions made to a qualified plan, and the investment earnings on such plans are made tax-exempt. To attain "qualified status" under the Code, the plan must: (1) be for the exclusive benefit of the participants; (2) be for the purpose of distributing the corpus or income to the participants; (3) be established in such a manner to make it impossible for the employer to use or divert funds before satisfying the plan's liabilities; and (4) not discriminate in favor of officers, stockholders, or highly-compensated or supervisory employees.

The Internal Revenue Code provides only limited safeguards for the security of anticipated benefit rights in private plans since its primary functions are designed to produce revenue and to prevent evasion of tax obligations. The essence of enforcement under the Code lies in the power of the Internal Revenue Service to grant or disallow qualified status to a pension plan, thus determining the availability of statutory tax advantages. The Internal Revenue Service jurisdiction and enforcement capabilities are solely to allow various tax advantages to accrue to employers who establish and maintain pension plans which can qualify for such tax benefit privileges.

In the absence of adequate federal standards, the participant is left to rely on the traditional equitable remedies of the common law of trusts. A few states, including New York, Washington, Wisconsin, Massachusetts, and California have codified existing trust principles and enacted legislation which requires in many instances a degree of disclosure similar to that required by federal statute.

The fact that statutory rules exist says little as to their efficacy in adjusting inequities that are visited upon plan participants, as evidenced by the hearings before this Committee. In almost every instance, participants lose their benefits not because of some violation of federal law, but rather because of the manner in which the plan is executed with respect to its contractual requirements of vesting or funding. Courts strictly interpret the plan indenture and are reluctant to apply concepts of equitable relief or to disregard technical document wording. Thus, under present law, accumulated pension credits can be lost even when separated employees are within a few months, or even days, of qualifying for retirement.

The proposed bill would, therefore, establish minimum standards of vesting, funding, and fiduciary and a system of compulsory benefit insurance to protect the security of pension rights.

As suggested by the President's Cabinet Committee Report of 1965, "[a]s a matter of equity and fair treatment an employee covered by a pension plan is entitled, after a reasonable period of service, to protection of his future retirement benefit against any termination of his employment." Concern for loss of benefits by workers after long years of labor through circumstances beyond their control was similarly expressed by President Richard M. Nixon on December 8, 1971, when, in a message to the Congress he said, "When a pension plan is terminated, an employee participating in it can lose all or a part of the benefits which he has long been relying on, even if his plan is fully vested . . . even one worker whose retirement security is destroyed by the termination of a plan is one too many."

Major Issues

Although the need for legislative reform has been and continues to be widely acknowledged among all persons and sectors affected, federal mandate of essential improvements has been resisted due to the belief that such legislation might impede plan growth. However, the Committee's inquiries have revealed that the costs associated with the vesting and funding proposals in the Act are sufficiently modest as not to constitute a major impediment to plan growth. Additionally, any added cost attributable to the imposition of vesting and funding standards will inure directly to the benefit of the participants in each plan in the form of increased availability of benefits and added security.

The principal issues affecting the vital and basic needs for legislation involve consideration of the essential elements of pensions:

a. Vesting

One of the major private pension plan considerations centers around the concept of vesting. Vesting refers to the nonforfeitable right of interest which an employee participant acquires in the pension fund. The benefit credits may vest in the employee immediately, although in most cases participants do not become eligible for vesting of benefits until a stipulated age or period of service, or a combination of both, is attained.

Upon compliance with the basic requirements of age or service, many places will grant their participants vested rights to those benefits earned to that time. However, should employment terminate prior to such time, the employee will receive no benefits. Some pension plans, however, specify "graded" vesting formulas, whereby only a defined percentage of the accrued benefits earned will vest upon fulfillment of minimum requirements, and such percentage may increase periodically, as the employee continues in his employment and completes additional service.

Despite the recognized and acknowledged need for pension plans to provide for vesting of earned benefits, if pension promises are to be meaningful to workers, there is need for federal statutory requirements which will compel an employer to grant such vesting benefits. The difficulties and hardships resulting from non-existent or inadequate plan provisions for vesting of benefits have been vividly established by the Committee's studies and hearings.

It is noteworthy that in 1965, the President's Commission on Public Policy and Private Pensions, while acknowledging that there had been some improvement in private plans by increased adoption of vesting provisions, nonetheless found and recommended legislation to make minimum vesting provisions mandatory. That Commission concluded that "the degree of retirement protection in private pension plans varies widely and in many cases remains quite inadequate." President's Committee on Corporate Pension Funds and Other Private Retirement and Welfare Programs, Public Policy and Private Pension Programs: A Report to the President on Private Employee Retirement Plans, January, 1965, at 39.

Despite claims by opponents that progress made in pension plan provisions to provide vesting manifests movement toward an eventual voluntary vesting system, plans involving substantial numbers of workers which contain no vesting are still not uncommon. Opponents of mandatory vesting believe that compulsory vesting provisions will discourage development of new plans and impede flexibility and latitude in formulating employee benefits because of excessive costs that are certain to result. However, in the face of Committee findings relative to projected costs to plans for imposed vesting, indications are that the resistance of opponents to universal vesting is essentially structured upon extreme reluctance to submit to governmental regulatory measures concerning pension plan administration and operations. In its final analysis, the issue basically resolves itself into whether workers, after many years of labor, whose jobs terminate voluntarily or otherwise, should be denied benefits that have been placed for them in a fund for retirement purposes.

b. Funding

Another major issue in private pension plans relates to the adequacy of plan funding. Funding refers to the accumulation of sufficient assets in a pension plan to assure the availability of funds for payment of benefits due to the employees as such obligations arise. Today, funding of pension plans for the limited and specific purpose of qualifying for tax benefits permitted by law for contributions made is governed by statutory and regulatory requirements which are under the jurisdiction of the Internal Revenue Service. The minimum funding rules require an employer to make contributions to a pension fund, qualified by the Internal Revenue Service, of amounts at least equal to the pension liabilities being created currently, and the interest due upon those amounts of monies which reflect unfunded accrued liabilities. The inherent weakness of this required minimum funding is that the employer is not required under law to make payments toward the principal of the unfunded accrued liabilities. Without mandatory funding of past service liabilities, a pension plan may never be in a financial posture to meet its pension obligations to its employees. The pension plan which offers full protection to its employees is one which is funded with accumulated assets which at least are equal to the accrued liabilities, and with a contribution rate sufficient to maintain that status at all times. However, since plans are revised and amended to provide new benefits which create new and different liabilities for the plan, opponents of compulsory funding argue that it is unrealistic to expect that plans maintain a full funding status at all times. The same opposition is voiced for new plans, which invariably assume a large unfunded liability at the outset of the plan, due to the granting of credit for past service by employees to the employer.

The ineffectiveness of funding requirements was acknowledged in the President's Cabinet Committee Report of 1965, when it concluded that "the minimum standards for funding under present tax law do not assure adequate funding. The setting of standards for adequate funding therefore becomes an important public concern." Public Policy and Private Pension Programs, 1965, at 50–51. The promise and commitment of a pension can be fulfilled only when funds are available to pay the employee participant what is owed to him. Without adequate funding, a promise of a pension may be illusory and empty.

c.   Fiduciary Responsibility and Disclosure

Another area of concern of the Subcommittee has involved the conduct of administration and operations of pension plans. Of particular interest has been the course of conduct in fund transactions, the degree of responsibility required of the fiduciaries, the types of persons who should be deemed pension "fiduciaries," and the standards of accountability they shall be governed by in the management and disposition of pension funds. The only current federal requirement is that the Secretary of Labor require fiduciaries, trustees, etc., to make disclosure of the provisions and financial operations of the pension plan under the Welfare and Pension Plans Disclosure Act.

An important issue relates to the effectiveness of communication of plan contents to employees. Descriptions of plans furnished to employees should be presented in a manner that an average and reasonable worker participant can understand intelligently. It is grossly unfair to hold an employee accountable for acts which disqualify him from benefits, if he had no knowledge of these acts, or if these conditions were stated in a misleading or incomprehensible manner in plan booklets. Subcommittee findings were abundant in establishing that an average plan participant, even where he has been furnished an explanation of his plan provisions, often cannot comprehend them because of the technicalities and complexities of the language used.

Committee Action

The Committee endorses the concept of a comprehensive private pension reform program. It believes that expeditious enactment of H.R. 2 will institute a program which will achieve a strengthening of the role played by private retirement plans within the fabric of our economic and social structures. Its most important purpose will be to assure American workers that they may look forward, with anticipation, to a retirement with financial security and dignity, and without fear that this period of life will be lacking in the necessities to sustain them as human beings within our society. The enactment of progressive and effective pension legislation is also certain to increase stability within the framework of our nation's economy, since the tremendous resources and assets of the private pension plan system are an integral part of our economy. It will also serve to restore credibility and faith in the private pension plans designed for American working men and women, and this should serve to encourage rather than diminish efforts by management and industry to expand pension plan coverage and to improve benefits for workers. The Committee believes that the legislative approach of establishing minimum standards and safeguards for private pensions is not only consistent with retention of the freedom of decision-making vital to pension plans, but in furtherance of the growth and development of the private pension system. At the same time, the Committee recognizes the absolute need that safeguards for plan participants be sufficiently adequate and effective to prevent the numerous inequities to workers under plans which have resulted in tragic hardship to so many.

The Bill reported by the Committee represents an effort to strike an appropriate balance between the interests of employers and labor organizations in maintaining flexibility in the design and operation of their pension programs, and the need of the workers for a level of protection which will adequately protect their rights and just expectations. In adopting this approach, the Committee believes it has designed a bill, which, like the National Labor Relations Act, the wage-hour laws and other labor standards laws, brings the workers' interests up to parity with those of employers. This legislation strikes an appropriate and equitable balance between two opposing schools of thought—those who advocate complete and stringent control of private pensions and those who oppose any form of government supervisory or regulatory control.

3. PUBLIC POLICY GOALS OF ERISA

ERISA § 2

Findings and Declaration of Policy

(a) The Congress finds that the growth in size, scope, and numbers of employee benefit plans in recent years has been rapid and substantial; that the operational scope and economic impact of such plans is increasingly interstate; that the continued well-being and security of millions of employees and their dependents are directly affected by these plans; that they are affected with a national public interest; that they have become an important factor affecting the stability of employment and the successful development of industrial relations; that they have become an important factor in commerce because of the interstate character of their activities, and of the activities of their participants, and the employers, employee organizations, and other entities by which they are established or maintained; that a large volume of the activities of such plans are carried on by means of the mails and instrumentalities of interstate commerce; that owing to the lack of employee information and adequate safeguards concerning their operation, it is desirable in the interests of employees and their beneficiaries, and to provide for the general welfare and the free flow of commerce, that disclosure be made and safeguards be provided with respect to the establishment, operation, and administration of such plans; that they substantially affect the revenues of the United States because they are afforded preferential Federal tax treatment; that despite the enormous growth in such plans many employees with long years of employment are losing anticipated retirement benefits owing to the lack of vesting provisions in such plans; that owing to the inadequacy of current minimum standards, the soundness and stability of plans with respect to adequate funds to pay promised benefits may be endangered; that owing to the termination of plans before requisite funds have been accumulated, employees and their beneficiaries have been deprived of anticipated benefits; and that it is therefore desirable in the interests of employees and their beneficiaries, for the protection of the revenue of the United States, and to provide for the free flow of commerce, that minimum standards be provided assuring the equitable character of such plans and their financial soundness.

(b) It is hereby declared to be the policy of this Act to protect interstate commerce and the interests of participants in employee benefit plans and their beneficiaries, by requiring the disclosure and reporting to participants and beneficiaries of financial and other information with respect thereto, by establishing standards of conduct, responsibility, and obligation for fiduciaries of employee benefit plans, and by providing for appropriate remedies, sanctions, and ready access to the Federal courts.

(c) It is hereby further declared to be the policy of this Act to protect interstate commerce, the Federal taxing power, and the interests of participants in private pension plans and their beneficiaries by improving the equitable character and the soundness of such plans by requiring them to vest the accrued benefits of employees with significant periods of service, to meet minimum standards of funding, and by requiring plan termination insurance.

NOTES AND QUESTIONS

1.   What were the historical problems with private employer pension plans that Congress intended ERISA to address? How did ERISA attempt to resolve these problems?

2.   *The Studebaker Incident.* One of the key events that galvanized public opinion in favor of the reforms enacted by ERISA was the 1963 closing of the Studebaker Corporation plant in South Bend, Indiana, and the resulting adverse consequences for participants in the company's pension plan. The workers at the Studebaker plant were covered by a pension plan negotiated on their behalf by the United Automobile Workers Union (UAW). When the plant closed, Studebaker and the UAW negotiated an agreement to terminate the pension plan. Under this termination agreement, of the approximately 10,500 retirees and active workers covered by the plan, only 3,600 individuals received their full benefits promised under the terms of the plan. Due to grossly inadequate funding, the remaining plan participants received only part, or none, of their pension benefits. The plight of the Studebaker workers, many of whom had long years of service with the company, was well-publicized by the national media. Studebaker became a public symbol of the insecurity of pension plan benefits and a rallying cry for pension system reform.

Although ERISA enacted minimum standards for the funding of pension plans sponsored by private industry employers, plans sponsored by governmental entities are exempt from these minimum funding requirements. See ERISA § 4(b)(1). Moreover, the independent agency established by ERISA to insure the benefits provided by defined benefit plans in the event of employer insolvency, the Pension Benefit Guaranty Corporation, does not insure retirement benefits provided by governmental plans. When state and municipal governments experience a decline in tax revenues during periods of economic recession, funding shortfalls in pension plans for public sector workers may jeopardize their retirement benefits. Due to the combination of ERISA's minimum funding and PBGC insurance, the employees of private employers enjoy a measure of security regarding their pension benefits that is not available to public sector workers.

3. *ERISA and Participant-Directed 401(k) Plans.* When Congress enacted ERISA in 1974, the participant-directed 401(k) plan did not exist. Employer insolvency (as exemplified by the Studebaker incident) was the major source of insecurity for retirement plan benefits. Today, participants in 401(k) plans face other sources of financial insecurity in addition to the problem of employer insolvency. Workers may invest heavily in company stock through their 401(k) plan, only to find that their employer has become bankrupt. Retirees and workers may invest broadly in the stock market, only to find that stock values decline. Alternatively, retirees and workers can invest in bonds, but the interest income generated may not keep pace with the rate of inflation. Or, retirees and workers may invest in mutual funds, but the fund's fees and expenses may erode their investment returns over time. These issues related to participant-directed 401(k) plans are discussed in Chapter Five of the casebook.

C. EMPLOYEE BENEFIT PLANS IN THE MODERN WORKPLACE

The nature of work and the organization of the modern American workplace have changed significantly since the enactment of ERISA in 1974. Workers today are increasingly mobile and no longer expect to spend their entire career with one employer. The traditional employer-employee relationship that characterized the workplace of the 1960s has evolved into nontraditional forms of employment. Many individuals work as self-employed independent contractors. Other individuals serve as temporary workers whose services are leased to the employer by an employment agency. Employers have become increasingly willing to accommodate the personal needs and preferences of workers. For example, some employers now permit individuals to work a nontraditional three or four day workweek, to work primarily from home, or to job-share a single position.

Despite these changes, employee benefit plans continue to be a fixture of the modern workplace. Since the enactment of ERISA, the design of employee benefit plans and the types of benefits provided by these plans have evolved in response to broad societal, demographic and economic trends. Retirement plans have moved increasingly from a paternalistic, employer-managed system to one where the plan's participants are primarily responsible for funding and managing their own retirement plan assets. Retirement plan benefits are increasingly portable rather than being linked to one employer. In the area of health care benefits, employers have responded to rising costs by replacing the traditional indemnity insurance model, first with employer-insured health care plans and managed care networks, and more recently with high-deductible health care plans coupled with health savings accounts. As the baby boomer generation of workers ages, disability plans designed to replace lost wages in the event an individual becomes unable to work have become an increasingly popular employee benefit.

These trends have caused the roles and responsibilities of persons associated with employee benefit plans—the sponsoring employer, the plan's participants, and the other parties who assist in managing and administering employee benefit plans—to change dramatically. Yet ERISA's core statutory provisions that regulate the conduct of persons associated with employee benefit plans have changed very little since 1974. As a result, federal regulators and the federal courts increasingly have struggled to apply ERISA's statutory language to situations that are produced by the modern workplace.

One of the reasons that many of the key provisions of ERISA have remained unchanged is that the current regulatory structure represents a delicate balancing of competing private interests and public policy objectives. Section D of Chapter One introduces some of the major public policy issues that underlie the federal regulation of employee benefit plans. Periodically throughout this course, pause and consider whether the legal rules you are studying continue to strike the appropriate policy balance. Does ERISA need to be "modernized" to better accommodate changing circumstances in society? If so, what changes would you favor, and why?

D. EMPLOYEE BENEFITS LAW TODAY: PUBLIC POLICY ISSUES

1. FEDERAL TAX POLICY AND EMPLOYEE BENEFIT PLANS

Professor Michael J. Graetz has described the importance of examining federal tax policy in the following terms:

> The tax law . . . is the primary link between the nation's citizens and their government . . . The tax law . . . is a window into the nation's views about justice, about how much economic inequality the society considers appropriate . . . [N]owhere in American law is there a better place to examine carefully . . . the tensions between citizens' insistence that the government perform well its assigned functions, on the one hand, and each person's personal resistance to sacrificing private resources to the public treasury, on the other.

Michael J. Graetz, *2001 Erwin N. Griswold Lecture Before the American College of Tax Counsel: Erwin Griswold's Tax Law-And Ours*, 56 TAX LAW. 173, 174 (2002).

Employee benefit plans and the United States income tax system are deeply intertwined. The income tax system subsidizes health care, retirement, and other types of benefits by providing employers and employees an income tax incentive to sponsor and participate in employee benefit plans. The technical term used to describe this income tax subsidy is a *tax expenditure*. Essentially, a tax expenditure represents revenue that the government does not collect in the form of income taxes because an economic activity receives preferential treatment under the Internal Revenue Code.

For fiscal year 2016, the tax expenditure for health care plans and long-term care plans sponsored by employers is estimated at $161.5 billion. This amount represents the single largest tax expenditure in the federal budget. The tax expenditure for qualified retirement plans in 2016 is estimated at $135.0 billion. This amount represents the second largest tax expenditure in the federal budget. To put these numbers in perspective, in comparison the tax expenditure for the home mortgage interest deduction is estimated to be "only" $79.2 billion in 2016. See JOINT COMMITTEE ON TAXATION, ESTIMATES OF FEDERAL TAX EXPENDITURES FOR FISCAL YEARS 2012–2017 (2013).

Conceptually, a tax expenditure is analogous to other social policy entitlement programs subsidized through direct payments by the federal government. The public policy that underlies the tax expenditure for qualified retirement plans is to encourage employers and employees to save for retirement. As a matter of social policy, we want retired workers to have an additional source of income during retirement other than Social Security benefits. A similar public policy rationale underlies the tax expenditure for health care plans and long-term care plans. As a society, we want to encourage employers and employees to provide for their own health care-related needs, particularly in the years prior to attaining eligibility for the federal Medicare program.

Keep these tax expenditure figures in mind as you study the qualified retirement plan system in Chapter Three and health care and other welfare benefit plans in Chapter Four of the casebook. Who benefits from these tax expenditures? Are these tax expenditures allocated fairly among all segments of society?

2. DEMOGRAPHIC TRENDS: EMPLOYEE BENEFIT PLANS AND PUBLIC BENEFIT PROGRAMS[d]

The aging of the American population and the impending retirement of the baby boomer generation will place significant strains over the next several decades on both Social Security and on retirees' own financial resources. The decline in birth rates since the 1960s, coupled with longer life spans, will result in fewer workers relative to the number of retirees.

---

[d] Based on CONGRESSIONAL RESEARCH SERVICE, REPORT FOR CONGRESS, INCOME OF AMERICANS AGED 65 AND OLDER, 1968 TO 2008 (Nov. 4, 2009), and U.S. SAVINGS FOR RETIREMENT IN 2010 (July 23, 2013).

Consequently, Social Security benefits will have to be financed by a working population that is shrinking relative to the number of retirees. With continued increases in average life expectancies, retirees in the 21st century will have to stretch their savings and other assets over longer periods of retirement than were experienced by their parents and grandparents.

America's Aging Population

Americans are living longer than ever before. The average life expectancy of Americans born in 1968 was 70.5 years. It has been estimated that persons born in 2010 will live for an average of 78.3 years. Women continue to have a longer average life expectancy than men, but both men and women have experienced gains in average life expectancy since the 1960s.

As more people live into old age, the age-profile of the population will shift. In 1968, 18.6 million people in the United States—9.4% of the population—were 65 or older. By 2030, according to projections made by the Census Bureau, there will be 71.5 million people aged 65 and older, comprising 19.7% of the U.S. population.

Table 1.1

Projections of the Resident U.S. Population, by Age

(in thousands, as of July 1 each year)

Age	2010	2012	2030	2040	2050
Under 20	83,236	88,887	95,104	101,625	109,147
20–64	185,456	192,285	197,027	210,270	224,001
65–84	34,120	47,363	61,850	64,640	65,844
85 and older	6,123	7,269	9,603	15,409	20,861
Total	**308,935**	**335,804**	**363,584**	**391,944**	**419,853**
65 and older	**40,243**	**54,632**	**71,453**	**80,049**	**86,705**
% of Total	**13.0%**	**16.3%**	**19.7%**	**20.4%**	**20.7%**

The aging of the population will strain the components of the traditional "three-legged stool" of retirement income: Social Security, pensions, and personal savings. Social Security is the largest source of income among the elderly. Earnings are the second largest source of income among people aged 65 and older, but much of this income is earned by people under 70 years of age. Pensions are the third largest source of income among the elderly, but only about half of all workers in the United States have pension coverage through their jobs, and more employers offer 401(k) plans than traditional pension plans. In a typical 401(k) plan, the worker must elect to participate, decide how much to contribute to the plan, how to invest the funds, and what to do with the account when he or she changes jobs or retires. Workers who do not choose to save, save too little, or make poor investment choices may face difficult financial circumstances in retirement.

Trends in Retirement Plan Design

Since the 1970s, the proportion of workers who participate in employer-sponsored retirement plans has remained relatively stable at approximately half of the workforce. In the early 1980s, however, employers moved away from *defined benefit* (DB) plans to *defined contribution* (DC) plans. Defined benefit plans—what most people think of as traditional pensions—are required by federal law to offer plan participants a retirement benefit in the form of a lifetime annuity. The amount of the annuity typically is based on the employee's length of service and average salary. In the private sector, DB plans usually are funded solely by employer contributions and investment earnings on those contributions. Defined contribution plans, in contrast, are more like savings accounts maintained by employers on behalf of each participating employee. In the most common type of DC plan, the employee defers a portion of his or her salary, which is invested in stocks, bonds, or other assets. The employer often matches some or all of the employee's contribution to the plan. At retirement, the balance in the account is the sum of past contributions plus interest, dividends, and capital gains or losses. The account balance is often distributed to the departing employee as a single lump sum.

One of the key distinctions between a defined benefit plan and a defined contribution plan is that in a DB plan, the employer bears the investment risk. The employer must ensure that the plan has sufficient assets to pay the benefits promised to workers and their surviving dependents. In a DC plan, the worker bears the risk of investment losses. The worker's account balance depends on how much has been contributed to the plan over the years and how the plan's underlying investments have performed.

Retirement Savings

The amounts that Americans have saved for retirement are an important component of evaluating the effectiveness of public policies aimed at achieving retirement income. Despite tax incentives to promote saving for retirement, 57% of Americans surveyed by Gallup in January 2013 reported that they were worried about outliving their savings after they retired. Many factors affect the accumulation of financial and non-financial assets by American households. Some of these factors include: education; income; the number of children in a household; the amount, if any, of non-measured wealth, such as future Social Security or DB pension benefits; and tax policy as established by Congress.

Although workers may retire at any age, ages 62 to 67 might generally be thought of as retirement age. Individuals are eligible to receive reduced Social Security benefits at age 62, are eligible for Medicare at age 65, and are eligible for full Social Security benefits at their normal retirement age (age 67 for individuals born on or after January 1, 1960). In addition, age 65 is often the normal retirement age in private-sector and state and local pension plans. In 2010, for households in which the head of the household was ages 62 to 67, only 57.2% had retirement assets. The table below shows the median and average amounts for retirement assets.

Median and Average Retirement Assets in 2010 Among Households in Which the Head Was Ages 62 to 67

		All Households	Single Households	Married Households
Total Retirement (IRA and DC) Assets	Median	$150,000	$70,000	$178,000
	Average	$341,417	$205,227	$384,000
IRA Assets	Median	$115,000	$50,000	$140,000
	Average	$265,475	$148,792	$307,300
DC Assets	Median	$80,000	$30,000	$100,000
	Average	$246,115	$152,123	$272,761

Source: Congressional Research Service Analysis of the 2010 Survey of Consumer Finances.

Many households have wealth other than retirement accounts on which they will be able to draw during retirement. For example, the most valuable asset owned by many families is their home. The broadest measure of net household wealth—the difference between a household's total assets and total liabilities—is called *net worth*. In 2010, among married households in which the age of the head of the household was younger than 35, 25% had a net worth that was less than or equal to $1,170; 50% had a net worth less than or equal to $15,000 (which was the median net worth for this group); and 75% had a net worth less than or equal to $63,900. Within each age group, median net worth was higher for married households than for single households.

Conclusion

Are Americans saving adequately—and wisely—for retirement? On the one hand, the widespread adoption of tax-favored retirement savings plans over the past 30 years indicates that many workers are taking seriously their responsibility to save for retirement. On the other hand, the balances in these accounts for many persons,—even among those who are near retirement age—are low.

The uncertain future of Social Security and the declining prevalence of defined-benefit pensions that provide a guaranteed lifelong income have put much of the responsibility for preparing for retirement directly on workers. The low rate of personal saving in the United States and the lack of any retirement savings accounts among millions of American households indicate that there is a need for greater awareness among the public about the importance of setting aside funds to prepare for life after they have stopped working. Most workers in the United States will need to begin saving more of their income if they wish to maintain a standard of living in retirement comparable to that which they enjoyed while working. The alternatives would be to work longer or to greatly reduce their standard of living when they retire.

3. THE SCOPE AND COST OF RETIREMENT AND HEALTH CARE PLAN COVERAGE

The modern employee benefits system established by ERISA makes plan sponsorship by an employer voluntary. Given the voluntary nature of the system, the cost of providing retirement, health care, and other benefits to employees is an important factor in the employer's decision whether or not to offer such benefits. The Bureau of Labor Statistics estimates that the total compensation (defined as wages and salaries plus employee benefits) for private industry workers in June of 2013 averaged $29.11 per hour. Of this amount, 70.3% ($20.47 per hour) was attributable to wages and salaries. The remaining 29.7% ($8.64 per hour) represented the employer's cost to provide various types of benefits to employees. See BUREAU OF LABOR STATISTICS, EMPLOYER COSTS FOR EMPLOYEE COMPENSATION—JUNE 2013 (Sept. 11, 2013).

For retirement benefits, 64% of all private industry workers in 2013 had access to an employer-sponsored retirement plan, but only 49% actually participated in their employer's plan. In contrast, 89% of state and local government employees had access to a retirement plan, and 85% of those workers participated in a retirement plan. See BUREAU OF LABOR STATISTICS, EMPLOYEE BENEFITS IN THE UNITED STATES—MARCH 2013 (July 17, 2013). The difference is attributable in part to the type of retirement plan offered by the employer. Private industry employers have shifted heavily toward 401(k) plans, which are funded primarily by employee contributions. In contrast, many state and local governmental employers continue to offer employer-funded defined benefit retirement plans to their workers. The distinctive features of the various types of retirement plans are explained in Chapter Three of the casebook.

With regard to health care benefits, 85% of full-time private industry workers (defined as employees who regularly worked 35 or more hours per week) had access to an employer-sponsored group health plan in 2013. Sixty-four percent (64%) of these full-time workers participated in an employer-sponsored plan. For state and local government workers, 99% of full-time employees had access to a health care plan through their employers, and 84% participated in a plan. In contrast, only 24% of part-time private industry and state and local government workers (defined as regularly working 34 or fewer hours per week) had access to an employer-sponsored group health plan. Of these part-time workers, only 13% in private industry and 17% in state and local government actually participated in the employer's plan. See BUREAU OF LABOR STATISTICS, EMPLOYEE BENEFITS IN THE UNITED STATES—MARCH 2013 (July 17, 2013). Note that these statistics do not fully reflect the scope of health insurance *coverage*, but only measure whether or not a worker had access to and participated in a group health plan sponsored through the workplace. For example, the employee may decline coverage under the employer plan for dependent children. Or, an employee who is under age 26 may decline coverage under his or her employer's plan and elect to continue to be covered under a parent's plan.

On average, in 2013 private industry employers paid 79% of the premium for employee-only coverage and 68% of the premium for family coverage for workers who participated in employer-sponsored group health plans. The comparable percentages for state and local governments were 87% and 70%, respectively. See BUREAU OF LABOR STATISTICS, EMPLOYEE BENEFITS IN THE UNITED STATES—MARCH 2013 (July 17, 2013). As a result of employer cost-sharing, many employees are not aware of the true cost of their health care insurance. Each year, the Kaiser Family Foundation's Health Research and Educational Trust surveys more than 2,000 small and large employers to assess trends in employer-sponsored health care insurance plans. In 2013, this survey found that the average annual total cost of family coverage offered through an employer was $16,351. For individual coverage offered through an employer, the average total cost in 2013 was $5,884. The historical trend shows that the cost of group health plan insurance continues to rise. In 2009, this same survey found that the total cost for employer-sponsored health care insurance was $13,375 for family coverage and $4,824 for individual coverage. See THE KAISER FAMILY FOUNDATION, EMPLOYER HEALTH BENEFITS, 2009 & 2013 ANNUAL SURVEYS.

4. FEDERALISM AND PREEMPTION OF STATE LAW

The limited nature of the claims and remedies available to private litigants under ERISA has proven controversial. Although ERISA often preempts potential state law claims and remedies, the statute may not supply a substitute federal claim or an adequate federal remedy. This result, commonly known as "betrayal without a remedy," has been an ongoing source of both public and judicial frustration. The federal court's reaction in *Suggs v. Pan American Life Insurance Co.*, 847 F.Supp. 1324 (S.D. Miss. 1994), is typical:

> The overriding purpose of the judiciary is to provide justice. When Congress passes legislation and clearly sets out the purposes and intentions of such legislation, "to protect . . . the interest of participants in private pension plans and their beneficiaries," and Courts acknowledge that ERISA "is a comprehensive statute designed to promote the interests of employees and their beneficiaries," and yet the Courts have to say "for what may have been a serious mistake there is no remedy, state or federal" or even worse, ERISA's preemption may leave a victim of fraud or misrepresentation without a remedy, something is wrong. The system isn't working. Either Congress is incapable of writing legislation to accomplish what they plainly say is their intent, or the Courts lack the ability to interpret the statute to do what Congress plainly says it intended to do, or both, or a mixture. In any event, the system fails.

Id. at 1357 (citations omitted). Although consumer advocacy groups lobbied Congress to expand the scope of ERISA claims and remedies as part of the reforms enacted by the Affordable Care Act, the final legislation left ERISA's claims and remedies provisions unchanged. As you study this statutory scheme for federal claims, remedies, and preemption of state laws later in Chapters Six and Seven of the casebook, try to discern who benefits from the status quo. Who would "win" and who would "lose" if the current system is changed?

E. STUDYING AND RESEARCHING EMPLOYEE BENEFITS LAW

Employee benefits law is the product of two distinct federal statutes. The Employee Retirement Income Security Act of 1974, 29 U.S.C. §§ 1001–1461 (ERISA), is the primary federal law that regulates retirement, health care, disability, and other welfare benefit plans sponsored by private employers for their employees. In addition, selected provisions of the Internal Revenue Code of 1986, 26 U.S.C. §§ 1–9833 (Code), establish specific requirements that retirement plans must satisfy to qualify for highly favorable income tax treatment for both the employer who sponsors the plan and the employee who participates in the plan. Retirement plans that satisfy these Code requirements are commonly referred to as qualified plans.

Employee benefits law has a well-deserved reputation among practicing lawyers for being a difficult subject. See Martha Neil, *ERISA*, A.B.A. J. 54 (June 2001) ("Employee benefits law is thorny as ever, and recent changes mean lawyers need to be doubly careful when trekking though the brambles."). This complexity results from several factors:

- The statutory provisions of ERISA have generated a substantial body of federal common law, particularly in the areas of claims, remedies and preemption of state law. Outright conflicts among the federal circuit courts of appeals exist, along with numerous circuit-by-circuit variations in how the federal courts interpret ERISA's statutory language.

- Although the key substantive provisions of ERISA have remained relatively stable since their enactment in 1974, the Code provisions regulating qualified retirement plans have been amended by Congress every few years. Such amendments require employers, in turn, to amend their plans to remain in compliance with the Code's highly technical requirements for qualified retirement plans.

- The statutory numbering system for ERISA is confusing to novices. Title I of ERISA (known as the *labor provisions* of ERISA) is codified in Title 29 of the United States Code. The statutory sections of ERISA do not equate with the section numbers used in the United States Code. For example, ERISA Section 404 is found at 29 U.S.C. § 1104. This casebook follows the convention used by ERISA scholars and practitioners, which is to refer to the original section numbers as enacted by ERISA (e.g., ERISA Section 404), rather than the numbering system used in the United States Code, when citing to a statutory provision. References in this casebook to Code sections are to the corresponding section of the Internal Revenue Code of 1986, as amended, which are codified in Title 26 of the United States Code. Thus, "Code Section 401(a)" refers to 26 U.S.C. § 401(a). Finally, to compound the statutory confusion, some of the

Code requirements for qualified retirement plans are duplicated in ERISA. For example, Code Section 401(a)(13), which provides that plan benefits may not be assigned or alienated, is duplicated in ERISA Section 206(d). Where a dual Code/ERISA provision exists, the convention of this casebook is to provide a dual citation.

- The statutory provisions of both ERISA and the Code are accompanied by numerous and detailed regulations, which are issued by the Department of Labor and the Treasury Department. This casebook refers to Department of Labor regulations codified in Title 29 of the Code of Federal Regulations as "DOL Reg." Similarly, references in this casebook to "Treas. Reg." are to the Treasury Department regulations codified in Title 26 of the Code of Federal Regulations.

- In addition to issuing regulations, both the Department of Labor and the Treasury Department have created another layer of governing legal authority through the issuance of various administrative rulings, announcements, opinion letters, advisory letters and private letter rulings. As a practical matter, this additional body of legal authority is best researched electronically.

- Lawyers who practice in the field of employee benefits law converse using a virtual alphabet soup of acronyms. To the uninitiated, such conversations may sound like a foreign language. The acronyms used by ERISA lawyers typically refer to either major pieces of enacted legislation or technical defined terms used in ERISA or the Code. Appendix H of the casebook contains a list of the most common acronyms associated with employee benefit plans. To familiarize you with this new legal vocabulary, many of these acronyms are used throughout the casebook.

Secondary Sources

This casebook provides an introduction to employee benefits law. It is designed to familiarize you with the key statutory provisions of Title I of ERISA, the primary Code requirements for qualified plans, and the major cases interpreting these statutory provisions. In legal practice, however, familiarity with the basic statutory rules and the major cases usually provides only a starting point for much more detailed research.

There are numerous secondary sources available to assist you in researching employee benefit plan issues. Although the following list is certainly not exhaustive, these secondary sources form the core library for many ERISA practitioners.

AMERICAN BAR ASSOCIATION, EMPLOYEE BENEFITS LAW (3rd ed. 2012) (with cumulative supplements). This book, written by various members of the ABA Section of Employee Benefits Law, is the most authoritative single volume treatise in the field. It is accompanied by an annual supplement containing the most recent developments in the law.

ERISA FIDUCIARY LAW (Susan P. Serota and Frederick A. Brodie (2d. ed. 2007)) (with cumulative supplements). ERISA fiduciary law is the product of a vast body of complex, and often conflicting, federal judicial decisions. This book and its cumulative annual supplement provide an overview of recent judicial trends in the interpretation of ERISA's provisions regulating the conduct of plan fiduciaries.

JAYNE E. ZANGLEIN, LAWRENCE A. FROLIK & SUSAN J. STABILE, ERISA LITIGATION (4th ed. 2011) (with cumulative supplements). Written primarily by three well-known legal scholars in the ERISA field, with additional chapters contributed by specialized ERISA practitioners, this book provides detailed coverage of both the procedural and substantive aspects of ERISA litigation.

DONALD J. MEYERS & MICHAEL B. RICHMAN, ERISA CLASS EXEMPTIONS (4th ed. 2012) (with cumulative supplements). This book describes and reproduces all of the Department of Labor's administrative class exemptions, and also provides an explanation and historical background. It is truly a one-stop shopping guide to the arcane world of ERISA prohibited transaction exemptions.

JEFFREY D. MAINORSKY, HEALTH CARE BENEFITS LAW (2014). Everything you may need to know about health care plans is described in this book. The breadth of coverage includes a more detailed discussion of the federal laws described in Chapter Four of this casebook, with an emphasis on compliance and transactional issues.

BNA TAX MANAGEMENT PORTFOLIO SERIES. Selected portfolios of this series provide a more detailed discussion of many of the topics covered in this casebook.

Internet Resources

The official web sites of the Internal Revenue Service (http://www.irs. gov) and the Employee Benefits Security Administration at the Department of Labor (http://www.dol.gov/ebsa/) contain public education materials, official agency announcements and publications and the various forms used for governmental filings.

For the latest developments, ERISA practitioners rely on the daily postings at the Benefitslink web site (http://www.benefitslink.com), which hyperlinks to all posted material. Benefitslink also provides two daily electronic newsletters—one for retirement plans, one for welfare plans— that summarize the most important news of the day. This newsletter service is free. Try subscribing during your employee benefits law course to supplement and enrich your classroom experience. There also are numerous blogs devoted to employee benefits law topics. Find one or two that you like and check them periodically for commentary and analysis on new developments.

F. DISCUSSION QUESTION FOR CHAPTER ONE

Based on your personal knowledge and experience, have employer-sponsored benefit plans achieved the policy goals described in Section 2 of ERISA? What do you perceive to be the most pressing problems associated with employee benefit plans in today's modern workplace? What reforms do you favor? Why?

CHAPTER 2

PLAN OPERATION AND ADMINISTRATION

■ ■ ■

Chapter Two introduces the fundamental rules that govern the daily operation and administration of employee benefit plans. Section A provides an overview of the statutory structure of ERISA and explains the various federal regulatory agencies and their roles in the regulation of employee benefit plans. Section B explores the types of plans that are subject to regulation under ERISA. ERISA's formal requirements for establishing and amending an employee benefit plan are examined in Section C. Chapter Two concludes with the plan administrator's responsibilities to disclose information concerning the plan and its benefits to federal regulatory agencies and to plan participants.

A. THE STATUTORY STRUCTURE OF ERISA AND ITS REGULATING FEDERAL AGENCIES

ERISA is divided into four Titles. Title I of ERISA, which forms the heart of the regulatory scheme, is divided into seven major parts. Part 1 contains the statutory reporting and disclosure requirements for all employee benefit plans. Parts 2 and 3 contain the minimum participation, vesting, benefit accrual and funding rules applicable to employee pension plans. Part 4 contains the rules that govern fiduciaries of employee benefit plans. Part 5 contains the mechanisms for enforcing the requirements of Title I of ERISA through civil litigation. Part 5 also provides for the preemption of state law. Parts 6 and 7 of Title I, which were added later by Congress, contain special rules applicable to employer-sponsored group health care plans.

Title II of ERISA originally amended the Internal Revenue Code of 1954 so that the Code's requirements for participation, vesting, benefit accrual and funding of qualified retirement plans reflected the rules established in Parts 2 and 3 of Title I of ERISA. Congress subsequently amended the 1954 Code on several occasions before enacting the Internal Revenue Code of 1986, which governs qualified retirement plans today.

Title III of ERISA established the authority of the Department of Labor and the Department of the Treasury to enforce the provisions of Titles I and II of ERISA. Title IV of ERISA addressed the specific problem of inadequately funded defined benefit plans by creating a federal program of plan termination insurance and a new federal agency, the Pension Benefit Guaranty Corporation, to administer the insurance system. Congress later amended Title IV to address the problem of chronic underfunding in multiemployer defined benefit pension plans and abusive practices in the termination of defined benefit plans sponsored by single employers.

As originally enacted, the Department of Labor and the Treasury Department had dual authority over certain areas of the statute to interpret and enforce ERISA's requirements. Predictably, this dual regulatory structure led to conflicting interpretations of the statute by these federal agencies. To improve the regulatory administration of ERISA President Carter proposed, and Congress approved, a revised plan for the division of regulatory authority between the Department of Labor and the Treasury Department. See Reorg. Plan No. 4 of 1978, 43 Fed. Reg. 47,713 (1978).

Today, the Department of Labor has primary jurisdiction over the areas of reporting and disclosure, fiduciary responsibility (including prohibited transactions), and administration and enforcement under Title I of ERISA. These regulatory functions are performed by the Employee Benefits Security Administration (formerly known as the Pension and Welfare Benefits Administration), which operates as a division of the Department of Labor. The Treasury Department has primary jurisdiction over the standards for employee pension plans in Parts 2 and 3 of Title I of ERISA and the independent Code requirements for qualified plans. The Pension Benefit Guaranty Corporation has primary jurisdiction over matters falling within Title IV of ERISA.

B. TYPES OF PLANS SUBJECT TO ERISA

The key to determining the types of plans subject to ERISA lies in navigating the statute's labyrinth of defined terms. These defined terms are listed in Section 3 of ERISA. In general, Title I of ERISA applies to any employee benefit plan maintained by an employer or an employee organization whose activities affect interstate commerce. ERISA § 4(a). ERISA Section 3(3) defines an employee benefit plan as including an employee welfare benefit plan or an employee pension benefit plan. These terms are defined in ERISA Sections 3(1) and 3(2) as arrangements which provide certain types of benefits, enumerated in the statute, to a participant, beneficiary, or employee. The definitions of a participant and a beneficiary, found in Sections 3(7) and 3(8), circle the reader back to two critical terms—the definition of a plan in ERISA Section 3(3), and the definition of an employee as any individual employed by an employer in ERISA Section 3(6).

In short, the statutory definitions of ERISA do not provide meaningful definitions of a "plan," a "participant," or an "employee." The criteria the federal courts use to determine when a plan exists, and whether an individual is an employee, are explored in Section B of

Chapter Two. These terms often are crucial to determining whether an individual has a claim under Title I of ERISA, and whether the individual's potential claims and remedies under state law are preempted by ERISA.

Distinguishing Between Pension and Welfare Benefit Plans

The distinction between pension plans and welfare benefit plans is significant because the principal protections offered to plan participants in Parts 2 and 3 of Title I of ERISA—namely the participation, vesting, benefit accrual and funding requirements—apply only to pension plans. The nature of the benefits provided by the plan is usually self-evident from the plan. A pension plan is designed to provide retirement income to the employee or results in a deferral of income by the employee until the termination of employment or beyond. Welfare benefit plans are designed to provide other types of benefits to the employee, such as health care benefits or benefits in the event of sickness, accident, disability, death or unemployment. See ERISA § 3(1)–(2).

pension plans covered by Part 2 and 3

Pension plan v. Welfare Benefit Plan

A severance pay plan illustrates the situation where the distinction between a pension plan and a welfare plan may not be obvious. Severance pay plans provide payments to former employees when the employer involuntarily terminates their employment. Department of Labor regulations provide that a severance pay plan will be deemed to be a welfare plan, and not a pension plan, if the plan payments are not contingent on the employee's retirement, the payments do not exceed twice the employee's annual salary, and the payments cease within twenty-four months of termination of employment. See DOL Reg. § 2510.3–2(b).

Severance Plans

A high-ranking executive of a corporation may participate in a plan where the payment of part of the executive's compensation is deferred until the executive terminates employment. These executive-only plans, which are commonly known as *top hat plans*, may appear to be similar to a severance pay plan. If the top hat plan is more generous in terms of either the amount or the duration of payments than the Department of Labor regulations permit, the top hat plan may be classified as a pension plan under ERISA Section 3(2).

Top Hat Plan OR non qualified plans

Top hat plans also are known as *nonqualified plans* because they do not receive the favorable tax treatment reserved for qualified retirement plans that satisfy the requirements of Code Section 401(a). These Code requirements, and the tax treatment of nonqualified and qualified retirement plans, are discussed in Chapter Three of the casebook.

Plans Excluded from Coverage Under ERISA

The significance of whether a plan is excluded from coverage under Title I of ERISA lies primarily in the types of claims and potential remedies that may be asserted in connection with the plan and persons who are closely associated with the plan's operation and administration. If the plan is regulated under Title I of ERISA, a potential plaintiff generally is limited to the claims and remedies available under ERISA. See ERISA § 502(a). Potential state law claims and remedies, including punitive damages, are preempted by federal law. See ERISA § 514. Conversely, if the plan is not subject to ERISA, state law claims and remedies may be asserted.

Certain types of plans are expressly excluded from coverage under Title I of ERISA. The following types of plans are not subject to ERISA's requirements:

- Governmental plans (defined in ERISA Section 3(32));
- Church plans (defined in ERISA Section 3(33));
- Plans maintained by an employer solely to comply with state workmen's compensation, unemployment compensation, or disability insurance laws;
- Plans maintained outside of the United States primarily for the benefit of persons who are nonresident aliens; or
- Unfunded excess benefit plans (defined in ERISA Section 3(36)).

See ERISA § 4(b). The Department of Labor by regulation excludes from the definition of an employee pension plan:

- Plans having as participants only the partners of a partnership;
- Plans having as a participant only the sole proprietor of a trade or business; or
- Plans having as participants only an individual and the individual's spouse, where the trade or business that sponsors the plan is wholly owned by the individual or by the individual and the spouse.

See DOL Reg. § 2510.3–3. The statutory basis for these regulatory exceptions is that an individual cannot simultaneously be both the "employer" who establishes and maintains the plan and the sole "employee" who receives retirement benefits under the plan. See Matinchek v. John Alden Life Ins. Co., 93 F.3d 96, 101 (3d Cir. 1996) ("Congress clearly intended 'employer' and 'employee' to be mutually exclusive definitions under ERISA."). From a policy perspective, the regulatory exception is based on the premise that "when the employee and the employer are one and the same, there is little need to regulate plan administration." Meredith v. Time Ins. Co., 980 F.2d 352, 358 (5th Cir. 1993).

The Department of Labor also excludes by regulation certain *payroll* [*other exclusion*] *practices* where the employer continues to pay compensation, out of the employer's general assets, to employees who are absent from work due to illness, vacation, jury duty, active military duty, or educational sabbatical. See DOL Reg. § 2510.3–1. This regulation also excludes several benefits that are commonly provided to employees, such as maintaining recreational, dining, or first-aid facilities on or near the employer's premises for employees to use, providing holiday gifts to employees, giving employees a discount on the purchase of the employer's goods or services, providing flowers or other remembrance contributions at the death of an employee or an employee's family member, or tuition and education expense reimbursement programs where the payments are made from the employer's general assets. See id.

Single Employer Plans, Multiemployer Plans and Multiple Employer Plans

Many employee benefit plans subject to regulation under ERISA are sponsored by a single employer. ERISA also regulates an employee benefit plan that is sponsored by more than one employer. A plan that is [*multi-employer plan*] sponsored by more than one employer pursuant to a collective bargaining agreement is called a *multiemployer plan.* See ERISA § 3(37). Multiemployer plans are plans established for workers who are part of a collective bargaining unit that are operated in accordance with Section 302 of the Labor Management Relations Act of 1947, also known as the Taft-Hartley Act. See 29 U.S.C. § 186. These so-called Taft-Hartley Act plans are administered by a board of trustees comprised of an equal number of representatives from management and labor.

Occasionally, more than one unrelated employer maintains a plan, [*multiple employer plan*] but the employers do not maintain the plan pursuant to a collective bargaining agreement under the Taft-Hartley Act. In this situation, the resulting plan is called a *multiple employer plan.* Multiple employer plans today generally are multiple employer welfare benefit plans, or *MEWAs* for short.

1. WHAT IS A "PLAN"?

Contrary to popular belief, an ERISA "plan" is not always found in a single written document. Indeed, there may be no writing at all that [*ERISA plan definition*] evidences the plan. Rather, an ERISA plan is simply an "inchoate group of rights, benefits and procedures (literally, a 'plan') established by an employer to create pension or welfare benefits." Orth v. Wisconsin State Employees Union Council 24, 500 F.Supp.2d 1130, 1140 (E.D. Wis. 2007).

The next case, *Donovan v. Dillingham,* involved a famous lawsuit brought by the Secretary of Labor under Title I of ERISA against the trustees of a group trust. The group trust offered participating small employers health insurance coverage for their employees at more favorable rates than the rates offered by insurers—in other words, the group trust was operating as a MEWA. The defendant trustees in *Donovan v. Dillingham* argued unsuccessfully that the group trust arrangement was not a "plan" subject to regulation under Title I of ERISA. Today, the criteria the Eleventh Circuit relied upon to determine that the group trust arrangement was in fact a "plan" subject to ERISA are known as the *Dillingham* factors.

DONOVAN V. DILLINGHAM

United States Court of Appeals, Eleventh Circuit, 1982.
688 F.2d 1367.

[handwritten: look for the (Dillingham factors)]

The Secretary of Labor, pursuant to his authority under ERISA § 502(a), brought this action against the trustees of Union Insurance Trust (UIT) and businesses owned and operated by them, alleging they are fiduciaries subject to the fiduciary responsibility provisions contained in Part 4 of Title I of ERISA. Fiduciary duties under ERISA, however, arise only if there are employee benefit plans as defined by the Act.

[handwritten: when fiduciary duties arise under]

[The district court dismissed the case for lack of federal question subject matter jurisdiction on the ground that an employee benefit "plan" subject to regulation under Title I of ERISA did not exist. The Secretary of Labor appealed.]

[handwritten: dist. ct. → D not a 'plan' as defined by ERISA]

I

Congress enacted ERISA to protect working men and women from abuses in the administration and investment of private retirement plans and employee welfare plans. Broadly stated, ERISA established minimum standards for vesting of benefits, funding of benefits, carrying out fiduciary responsibilities, reporting to the government and making disclosures to participants.

[handwritten: Legislative Purpose and main focus areas of ERISA]

With a few specific exceptions not pertinent to this decision, Title I of ERISA applies to any "employee benefit plan" if it is established or maintained by any employer or employee organization engaged in commerce or in any industry or activity affecting commerce, or by both an employer and an employee organization. ERISA § 4(a). "Employee benefit plan" or "plan" means an "employee welfare benefit plan" or an "employee pension benefit plan" or a plan which is both a welfare plan and a pension plan. ERISA § 3(3).

[handwritten: what Title I of ERISA applies to]

UIT is a group insurance trust, commonly known as a multiple employer trust ("MET"), whose purpose is to allow employers of small numbers of employees to secure group health insurance coverage for their employees at rates more favorable than offered directly by an insurer. UIT obtained a group health insurance policy from Occidental Life Insurance Company of California to furnish specified insurance benefits.

Employers and various employee organizations "subscribe" to UIT to receive the coverage of the blanket Occidental Life policy. Appellees contend that ERISA does not apply because there is involved only the "bare purchase of health insurance" and that no employee welfare benefit plans are implicated. The parties have debated whether UIT is a fiduciary and how that status or lack thereof bears on the presence of an employee welfare benefit plan. We agree with the Secretary that whether UIT merely sells insurance or is a fiduciary does not determine whether employee welfare benefit plans exist. Likewise, we agree with appellees that the existence of appellees' management of the trust or their falling within ERISA's fiduciary definition (which they challenge) does not necessarily mandate a finding that employee welfare benefit plans exist.

Appellee's Argument

neither of these factors are dispositive

II

ERISA § 3(1) defines "employee welfare benefit plan" or "welfare plan" as any plan, fund, or program which was heretofore or is hereafter established or maintained by an employer or by an employee organization, or by both, to the extent that such plan, fund, or program was established or is maintained for the purpose of providing for its participants or their beneficiaries, through the purchase of insurance or otherwise, (A) medical, surgical, or hospital care or benefits, or benefits in the event of sickness, accident, disability, death or unemployment, or vacation benefits, apprenticeship or other training programs, or day care centers, scholarship funds, or prepaid legal services, or (B) any benefit described in § 302(c) of the Labor Management Relations Act, 1947 (other than pensions on retirement or death, and insurance to provide such pensions).[4]

definition of emp. welfare benefit plan

By definition, then, a welfare plan requires (1) a "plan, fund, or program" (2) established or maintained (3) by an employer or by an employee organization, or by both, (4) for the purpose of providing medical, surgical, hospital care, sickness, accident, disability, death, unemployment, or vacation benefits, apprenticeship or other training programs, day care centers, scholarship funds, prepaid legal services or severance benefits (5) to participants or their beneficiaries.

elements of welfare plan

A

Prerequisites (3), (4) and (5) are either self-explanatory or defined by statute. A plan, fund, or program must be established or maintained "for the purpose of providing for its participants or their beneficiaries, through the purchase of insurance or otherwise," health, accident, disability, death, or unemployment or vacation benefits or apprenticeship

---

[4] The ERISA definition refers to benefits in Section 302(c) of the Labor Management Relations Act, 1947 (codified at 29 U.S.C. § 186(c)). The Secretary in regulations says § 302 duplicates to a large extent the benefits enumerated in ERISA § 3(1)(A) except that § 302 adds holiday and severance benefits. DOL Reg. § 2510.3–1(a)(3).

or other training programs, day care centers, scholarship funds, prepaid legal services or severance benefits.

The gist of ERISA's definitions of employer, employee organization, participant, and beneficiary is that a plan, fund, or program falls within the ambit of ERISA only if the plan, fund, or program covers ERISA participants because of their employee status in an employment relationship, and an employer or employee organization is the person that establishes or maintains the plan, fund, or program. Thus, plans, funds, or programs under which no union members, employees or former employees participate are not employee welfare benefit plans under Title I of ERISA.

* * *

B

Not so well defined are the first two prerequisites: "plan, fund, or program" and "established or maintained." Commentators and courts define "plan, fund, or program" by synonym-arrangement, scheme, unitary scheme, program of action, method of putting into effect an intention or proposal, design-but do not specify the prerequisites of a "plan, fund, or program." At a minimum, however, a "plan, fund, or program" under ERISA implies the existence of intended benefits, intended beneficiaries, a source of financing, and a procedure to apply for and collect benefits.

"Established or maintained" appears twice in the definition of an employee welfare benefit plan: first, an employer or employee organization or both must establish or maintain a plan, fund, or program, and, second, the plan, fund, or program must be established or maintained for specified purposes. In many instances a plan is established or maintained, or both, in writing. It is obvious that a system of providing benefits pursuant to a written instrument that satisfies ERISA §§ 102 and 402 would constitute a "plan, fund or program."

ERISA does not, however, require a formal, written plan. ERISA's coverage provision reaches "any employee benefit plan if it is *established or maintained*" by an employer or an employee organization, or both, who are engaged in any activities or industry affecting commerce. ERISA § 4(a) (emphasis added). There is no requirement of a formal, written plan in either ERISA's coverage section, ERISA § 4(a), or its definitions section, ERISA § 3(1). Once it is determined that ERISA covers a plan, the Act's fiduciary and reporting provisions do require the plan to be established pursuant to a written instrument, ERISA §§ 102 and 402, but clearly these are only the responsibilities of administrators and fiduciaries of plans covered by ERISA and are not prerequisites to coverage under the Act. Furthermore, because the policy of ERISA is to safeguard the well-being and security of working men and women and to apprise them of their rights and obligations under any employee benefit plan, see ERISA § 2, it would be incongruous for persons establishing or maintaining informal or unwritten employee benefit plans, or assuming the responsibility of safeguarding plan assets, to circumvent the Act merely because an administrator or other fiduciary failed to satisfy reporting or fiduciary standards.

The Secretary contends that "establish" means no more than an ultimate decision by an employer or an employee organization to provide the type of benefits described in ERISA § 3(1). This sweeps too broadly. A decision to extend benefits is not the establishment of a plan or program. Acts or events that record, exemplify or implement the decision will be direct or circumstantial evidence that the decision has become reality— e.g., financing or arranging to finance or fund the intended benefits, establishing a procedure for disbursing benefits, assuring employees that the plan or program exists—but it is the reality of a plan, fund or program and not the decision to extend certain benefits that is determinative.

In determining whether a plan, fund or program (pursuant to a writing or not) is a reality a court must determine whether from the surrounding circumstances a reasonable person could ascertain the intended benefits, beneficiaries, source of financing, and procedures for receiving benefits. Some essentials of a plan, fund, or program can be adopted, explicitly or implicitly, from sources outside the plan, fund, or program—e.g., an insurance company's procedure for processing claims— but no single act in itself necessarily constitutes the establishment of the plan, fund, or program. For example, the purchase of insurance does not conclusively establish a plan, fund, or program, but the purchase is evidence of the establishment of a plan, fund, or program; the purchase of a group policy or multiple policies covering a class of employees offers substantial evidence that a plan, fund, or program has been established.[11]

C

In summary, a "plan, fund, or program" under ERISA is established if from the surrounding circumstances a reasonable person can ascertain the intended benefits, a class of beneficiaries, the source of financing, and procedures for receiving benefits. To be an employee welfare benefit plan, the intended benefits must be health, accident, death, disability, unemployment or vacation benefits, apprenticeship or other training programs, day care centers, scholarship funds, prepaid legal services or

---

[11] Department of Labor regulations recognize that an employer may be involved in a plan, fund, or program without establishing or maintaining it. See DOL Reg. § 2510.3–1(j). According to the regulation, the term "employee welfare benefit plan" does not include group insurance if the sole functions of the employer are, without endorsing the program, to permit an insurer to publicize a program to employees, to collect premiums through payroll deductions, and to remit the premiums to the insurer, and the employer does not contribute premiums to the insurer or make a profit from the program.

severance benefits; the intended beneficiaries must include union members, employees, former employees or their beneficiaries; and an employer or employee organization, or both, and not individual employees or entrepreneurial businesses, must establish or maintain the plan, fund, or program.

III

[The court analyzed the facts and circumstances and concluded the "numerous subscribers to UIT established employee welfare benefit plans; with respect to each of these, ERISA conferred subject matter jurisdiction on the district court."]

* * *

We hold only that the district court had subject matter jurisdiction over this case. We have not determined how many subscribers established or maintained plans or if any defendant is a fiduciary to any plan. The judgment of the district court dismissing the case is REVERSED and the case is REMANDED for proceedings not inconsistent with this opinion.

NOTES

1. In *Dillingham*, the Secretary of Labor argued that a plan was "established" within the meaning of ERISA Section 4(a) if an employer or an employee organization has decided to provide benefits to employees. Did the Eleventh Circuit agree with this interpretation? What are the four *Dillingham* factors that indicate the existence of a plan? What evidence is necessary to prove these factors?

2. *A Fifth Factor.* In *Fort Halifax Packing Co. v. Coyne,* 482 U.S. 1 (1987), the Supreme Court stated that one of the hallmarks of an ERISA plan was the need for "ongoing plan administration," such as determining eligibility for benefits, calculating benefit amounts, and monitoring the funding of the plan to ensure that the funding level is adequate to pay the promised benefits. Id. at 9. *Fort Halifax* was an ERISA preemption case in which the Court held that a Maine statute requiring employers to make a one-time severance payment to employees in the event of a plan closure did not require the creation of an ERISA "plan." Since *Fort Halifax*, the federal courts have looked to whether the alleged ERISA "plan" has the hallmarks of an ongoing administrative scheme in addition to considering the four *Dillingham* factors.

———————

The case below, *Musmeci v. Schwegmann Giant Super Markets, Inc.*, involves a dispute over whether a voucher program established by a grocery store chain to provide discounts on food for its retired employees should be characterized as a pension plan or as a welfare benefit plan. Parts 2 and 3 of Title I of ERISA impose vesting and funding requirements on pension plans that are intended to protect the security of promised pension benefits. In contrast, welfare benefit plans are exempt from these requirements. See ERISA §§ 201(1), 301(a)(1). Consequently, the characterization issue in *Musmeci*—pension plan or welfare benefit plan—determines whether the grocery store chain can terminate its voucher program.

MUSMECI V. SCHWEGMANN GIANT SUPER MARKETS, INC.

United States Court of Appeals, Fifth Circuit, 2003.
332 F.3d 339.

Defendants, Schwegmann Giant Super Markets, Inc. (SGSM, Inc.), Schwegmann Giant Super Markets Pension Plan (SGSM Pension Plan), John F. Schwegmann, Sr. (Mr. Schwegmann), G.G. Schwegmann Co. (G.G.Schwegmann), John Schwegmann, Jr. Trust Estate (Schwegmann Trust) (collectively the "Schwegmann Defendants"), and United States Fidelity & Guaranty Company (USF & G) (collectively the "Defendants"), appeal the district court's adverse money judgment, in favor of the Plaintiff class, holding, inter alia, that a grocery Voucher Plan established by Schwegmann Giant Super Market Partnership (SGSM) was a pension benefit plan under the Employee Retirement Income Security Act of 1974 (ERISA) and that the Plaintiffs were entitled to monetary relief. * * * We agree with the district court. * * *

I

Until 1997, SGSM operated a chain of over forty grocery stores, employing over 5000 employees, primarily in the New Orleans, Louisiana area. SGSM is a partnership comprised of SGSM, Inc., G.G. Schwegmann, and Schwegmann Trust. SGSM, Inc. owned a seventy percent interest in the partnership and was its managing partner. Mr. Schwegmann was the majority stockholder of SGSM, Inc. and its chief executive officer. As such, Mr. Schwegmann was responsible for the daily operations of SGSM and was the primary policy maker for the partnership.

Mr. Schwegmann conceived a plan for SGSM to give its retirees groceries and other goods free of charge. Mr. Schwegmann then worked with Mr. Sam Levy, president of SGSM, Inc., and Mr. Joe Warnke, SGSM director of human resources, to create a voucher program for long-term SGSM employees at their retirement. In 1985, SGSM implemented this grocery voucher plan (the "Voucher Plan") designed to supply SGSM retirees with a portion of their monthly food needs. Under this plan, SGSM issued vouchers to retirees, and these vouchers could then be used in lieu of cash to purchase goods in SGSM stores. It is this Voucher Plan which is the subject of this lawsuit.

In 1985, Joe Warnke prepared a memorandum memorializing the eligibility requirements for participation in the Voucher Plan. To qualify for the vouchers, an employee must have completed twenty years of service with SGSM, have reached the age of sixty, and have been employed in a supervisory position for at least one year at the time of retirement. SGSM informed qualifying employees of the program at the time of their retirement. Each month, SGSM sent qualifying employees a set of four vouchers worth a total of $216. These vouchers were valid for a period of thirty days, redeemable only at SGSM stores and could not be transferred. Although SGSM intended the vouchers to be used only for in-kind purchases with no cash redemption, store personnel, including managers, were largely unaware of this proscription, and retirees were often given change in cash when using the vouchers for grocery purchases.

SGSM had no written procedures for administering the Voucher Plan. The Voucher Plan was nonetheless run in a systematic manner. When a manager or supervisor retired, the SGSM human resources department prepared a form with information used to determine whether the employee qualified for the Voucher Plan. The form was then sent to Sam Levy who reviewed the form and decided whether a retiree qualified for the program. Levy would sign the forms of qualified retirees and forward the forms to the SGSM controller, Gene Lemoine, who issued the vouchers. Lemoine performed this task two to three days before the month in which they were to be used. Once used, the vouchers were routed back to Lemoine, who retained them for five years.

SGSM did not set up a trust to fund the Voucher Plan. Rather, the Voucher Plan was funded out of the partnership's general revenue. Each year, SGSM deducted the total face value of the vouchers as a business expense on its tax returns under the category of "retirement plans, etc." SGSM also issued an Internal Revenue Service form 1099–R to every retiree receiving vouchers, reflecting the face value of the vouchers received by the retiree that year.

By the early 1990's, SGSM experienced declining profits due to competition from well-financed national supermarket chains. In 1995, Mr. Schwegmann decided to aggressively expand SGSM to compete with these stores. SGSM acquired the 28-store National Tea Company chain and, in doing so, undertook a sizable debt. After this acquisition, SGSM continued to suffer from financial losses, and in 1997, it sold the business. A week before the sale, Mr. Schwegmann sent a letter to all voucher recipients informing them that they would no longer receive vouchers because of the sale of the business. Because Mr. Schwegmann considered the Voucher Plan a gratuity subject to termination at will, he made no provision for the continuation of the Voucher Plan after the sale.

* * *

After being informed of the termination of the Voucher Plan, Plaintiffs filed this suit on behalf of themselves and other similarly situated individuals under ERISA and Louisiana state law claiming that they were vested in a pension benefit plan. Plaintiffs are former employees of SGSM who were adversely affected by the termination of the grocery Voucher Plan when SGSM sold its business in February 1997. The matter was certified as a class action, defining the plaintiff class as:

> Those individuals who were SGSM employees and (1) who were retired and receiving grocery vouchers when SGSM stopped the program, or (2) who, although not retired or receiving grocery vouchers at the time SGSM stopped the grocery program, were (i) supervisors for at least one year before retirement, and (ii) had at least 20 years experience with SGSM.

After a bench trial, the court dismissed the Plaintiffs' state law claims. After taking the remaining claims under advisement, the court issued findings of fact and conclusions of law, ruling that the grocery Voucher Plan was a pension benefit plan under ERISA, that SGSM breached its fiduciary duty under ERISA, that Mr. Schwegmann was liable as a fiduciary to the plan, and that the Plaintiffs were entitled to monetary relief for benefits denied after SGSM's sale. * * * The Defendants lodged a timely appeal, urging various grounds for reversal. We address each of the Defendants' arguments in turn.

II

While not disputing the underlying facts, USF & G first argues that the district court committed legal error in concluding that the in-kind Voucher Plan constituted a pension benefit plan under ERISA. The Schwegmann Defendants have adopted USF & G's argument by reference. Specifically, the Defendants contend that ERISA does not apply to any program providing a non-cash benefit. This court reviews legal challenges de novo.

ERISA does not regulate all benefits paid by an employer, but only those paid pursuant to an "employee benefit plan." ERISA § 4. Two different types of benefit programs are regulated by ERISA: welfare plans and pension plans. ERISA § 3. The district court determined that the Voucher Plan was a pension benefit plan and not a welfare benefit plan. The Plaintiffs have not challenged this ruling. The Defendants, however, challenge the district court's determination that it is a pension benefit plan.

To determine whether ERISA applies to the Voucher Plan, we begin our analysis with an examination of the language of the statute itself. ERISA defines an "employee pension benefit" plan as:

> any plan, fund, or program which was heretofore or is hereafter established or maintained by an employer or by an employee organization, or by both, to the extent that by its express terms

or as a result of surrounding circumstances such plan, fund, or program . . . provides retirement income to employees . . . ERISA § 3(2)(A)(i).

The parties agree that SGSM established a "program." Thus, the primary issue this court must resolve is whether the vouchers issued pursuant to SGSM's Voucher Plan provided the Plaintiffs with "retirement income."

Neither ERISA's statutory provisions nor the federal regulations define the term "income." However, they do not affirmatively require that the pension benefit be paid in cash. Moreover, the Department of Labor (DOL) refused to declare as a general policy whether in-kind benefits are regulated by ERISA. We have likewise found no controlling case law directly addressing the issue.

Relying on the definition of "income" used for the purposes of determining taxable income under the Internal Revenue Code (IRC), the district court found that the grocery vouchers constituted retirement income. We believe that the district court's analysis is sound given the close connection between ERISA and the IRC.

Congress dedicated Title II of ERISA entitled "Amendments to the Internal Revenue Code Relating to Retirement Plan" (Title II), to addressing taxation of retirement plans. Title II amends provisions of the IRC and sets forth guidelines and standards governing the establishment and operation of pension plans qualified for favorable tax treatment. Title I sets out guidelines and standards governing the establishment and operation of pension plans. Title I, which defines "employee benefit plan," was drafted in concert with Title II. Much of Title I of ERISA was duplicated in Title II, indicating that overlapping terms should be consistently defined in both. See, e.g., Code § 411(a)(7) and ERISA § 3(23) (same definition of "accrued benefit"); Code § 411(a)(8) and ERISA § 3(24) (same definition of "normal retirement age"); Code § 411(a)(9) and ERISA § 3(22) (same definition of "normal retirement benefit").

We acknowledge that courts generally do not look to other statutes to determine the meaning of a term where an act has left that term undefined. In such instances, courts rely on common usage to give the term meaning. However, in this instance, we believe that the interconnection between ERISA and the IRC reflects an intent to use common terminology.

This court has interpreted the term income broadly under the IRC to include anything that can be valued in terms of currency. The district court was entitled to infer that when SGSM deducted the vouchers' face value as a business expense on its tax returns under the category of "retirement plans" and issued Internal Revenue Service form 1099–R's to the recipients of the vouchers, SGSM considered the vouchers as income under the IRC. The cash value of the grocery vouchers is readily ascertainable from the face of the vouchers. The district court correctly concluded that the vouchers constitute income and the Voucher Plan is governed by ERISA.

Even if we were to adopt the plain or ordinary meaning of "income," our conclusion would be the same. As noted by the Supreme Court in *Lukhard v. Reed*, the term "income" is commonly understood to mean a "gain or recurrent benefit usually measured in money." Lukhard v. Reed, 481 U.S. 368, 374 (1987). Because the vouchers provided a gain or benefit to SGSM employees and could readily be measured in money, they would constitute income as the term is generally understood.

NOTES AND QUESTIONS

1.   The parties in *Schwegmann* agreed that the Voucher Plan was a "plan" under Title I of ERISA. What facts were critical to the court is conclusion that the benefits provided by the Voucher Plan constituted "income" to retired employees?

2.   *ERISA "Plans" and Employer Fiduciary Liability.* The facts in *Schwegmann* illustrate the potential peril for an employer who does not realize that it has established an ERISA plan, and therefore fails to operate the plan in accordance with ERISA's requirements, including the provisions that regulate the conduct of plan fiduciaries. In a later part of the *Schwegmann* opinion, the Fifth Circuit affirmed the district court's conclusion that Mr. Schwegmann personally was a plan fiduciary and, as such, was liable along with the other *Schwegmann* defendants for $5,127,587.36 in damages based on plan benefits, $267,032.71 in prejudgment interest, and the plaintiffs' attorney fees. See Musmeci v. Schwegmann Giant Super Markets, 27 E.B.C. 1717 (2002), aff'd in part, 332 F.3d 339, 355–56 (5th Cir. 2003). The Fifth Circuit dismissed the employer's insurance company, United States Fidelity & Guaranty Co., as a defendant in the case because under the terms of the employer's insurance policy, each individual plaintiff's claim fell below the employer's $250,000 policy deductible. See Musmeci, 332 F.3d at 352–55 (5th Cir.2003). Consequently, the *Schwegmann* defendants were jointly and severally responsible for paying the entire amount of the judgment.

2.   WHO IS AN EMPLOYEE?

NATIONWIDE MUTUAL INSURANCE CO. v. DARDEN
United States Supreme Court, 1992.
503 U.S. 318, 112 S.Ct. 1344, 117 L.Ed.2d 581.

JUSTICE SOUTER delivered the opinion of the Court.

In this case we construe the term "employee" as it appears in § 3(6) of the Employee Retirement Income Security Act of 1974 (ERISA), and read it to incorporate traditional agency law criteria for identifying master-servant relationships.

I

From 1962 through 1980, respondent Robert Darden operated an insurance agency according to the terms of several contracts he signed with petitioners Nationwide Mutual Insurance Co. et al. Darden promised to sell only Nationwide insurance policies, and, in exchange, Nationwide agreed to pay him commissions on his sales and enroll him in a company retirement scheme called the "Agent's Security Compensation Plan" (Plan). The Plan consisted of two different programs: the "Deferred Compensation Incentive Credit Plan," under which Nationwide annually credited an agent's retirement account with a sum based on his business performance, and the "Extended Earnings Plan," under which Nationwide paid an agent, upon retirement or termination, a sum equal to the total of his policy renewal fees for the previous 12 months.

Such were the contractual terms, however, that Darden would forfeit his entitlement to the Plan's benefits if, within a year of his termination and 25 miles of his prior business location, he sold insurance for Nationwide's competitors. The contracts also disqualified him from receiving those benefits if, after he stopped representing Nationwide, he ever induced a Nationwide policyholder to cancel one of its policies.

In November 1980, Nationwide exercised its contractual right to end its relationship with Darden. A month later, Darden became an independent insurance agent and, doing business from his old office, sold insurance policies for several of Nationwide's competitors. The company reacted with the charge that his new business activities disqualified him from receiving the Plan benefits to which he would have been entitled otherwise. Darden then sued for the benefits, which he claimed were nonforfeitable because already vested under the terms of ERISA.

Darden brought his action under ERISA § 502(a), which enables a benefit plan "participant" to enforce the substantive provisions of ERISA. The Act elsewhere defines "participant" as "any employee or former employee of an employer . . . who is or may become eligible to receive a benefit of any type from an employee benefit plan. . . ." § 3(7). Thus, Darden's ERISA claim can succeed only if he was Nationwide's "employee," a term the Act defines as "any individual employed by an employer." § 3(6).

It was on this point that the District Court granted summary judgment to Nationwide. * * * [T]he court found that "the total factual context of Mr. Darden's relationship with Nationwide shows that he was an independent contractor and not an employee."

The United States Court of Appeals for the Fourth Circuit vacated. Darden v. Nationwide Mutual Ins. Co., 796 F.2d 701 (1986). After observing that "Darden most probably would not qualify as an employee" under traditional principles of agency law, id. at 705, it found the traditional definition inconsistent with the "declared policy and purposes" of ERISA, id. at 706, and specifically with the congressional statement of purpose found in § 2 of the Act, ERISA § 2.[1] It therefore held that an ERISA plaintiff can qualify as an "employee" simply by showing "(1) that he had a reasonable expectation that he would receive [pension] benefits, (2) that he relied on this expectation, and (3) that he lacked the economic bargaining power to contract out of [benefit plan] forfeiture provisions." 922 F.2d 203, 205 (4th Cir. 1991) (summarizing 796 F.2d 701). The court remanded the case to the District Court, which then found that Darden had been Nationwide's "employee" under the standard set by the Court of Appeals. 717 F.Supp. 388 (E.D.N.C. 1989). The Court of Appeals affirmed. 922 F.2d 203 (4th Cir. 1991).

In due course, Nationwide filed a petition for certiorari, which we granted on October 15, 1991. We now reverse.

II

We have often been asked to construe the meaning of "employee" where the statute containing the term does not helpfully define it. Most recently we confronted this problem in *Community for Creative Non-Violence v. Reid*, 490 U.S. 730 (1989), a case in which a sculptor and a nonprofit group each claimed copyright ownership in a statue the group had commissioned from the artist. The dispute ultimately turned on whether, by the terms of § 101 of the Copyright Act of 1976, the statue had been "prepared by an employee within the scope of his or her employment." Because the Copyright Act nowhere defined the term "employee," we unanimously applied the "well established" principle that

> [w]here Congress uses terms that have accumulated settled meaning under . . . the common law, a court must infer, unless the statute otherwise dictates, that Congress means to incorporate the established meaning of these terms. . . . In the past, when Congress has used the term 'employee' without defining it, we have concluded that Congress intended to describe the conventional master-servant relationship as understood by common-law agency doctrine.

[handwritten margin note: when act doesn't define 'employee' is well est. principle]

---

    [1]   The Court of Appeals cited Congress's declaration that "many employees with long years of employment are losing anticipated retirement benefits," that employee benefit plans "have become an important factor affecting the stability of employment and the successful development of industrial relations," and that ERISA was necessary to "assur[e] the equitable character of such plans and their financial soundness." 796 F.2d at 706, quoting ERISA § 1. None of these passages deals specifically with the scope of ERISA's class of beneficiaries.

490 U.S. at 739–740. While we supported this reading of the Copyright Act with other observations, the general rule stood as independent authority for the decision.

ERISA's definition of employee is circular and useless

So too should it stand here. ERISA's nominal definition of "employee" as "any individual employed by an employer," ERISA § 3(6), is completely circular and explains nothing. As for the rest of the Act, Darden does not cite, and we do not find, any provision either giving specific guidance on the term's meaning or suggesting that construing it to incorporate traditional agency law principles would thwart the congressional design or lead to absurd results. Thus, we adopt a common-law test for determining who qualifies as an "employee" under ERISA, a test we most recently summarized in *Reid*:

common law test for employee

> In determining whether a hired party is an employee under the general common law of agency, we consider the hiring party's right to control the manner and means by which the product is accomplished. Among the other factors relevant to this inquiry are the skill required; the source of the instrumentalities and tools; the location of the work; the duration of the relationship between the parties; whether the hiring party has the right to assign additional projects to the hired party; the extent of the hired party's discretion over when and how long to work; the method of payment; the hired party's role in hiring and paying assistants; whether the work is part of the regular business of the hiring party; whether the hiring party is in business; the provision of employee benefits; and the tax treatment of the hired party.

490 U.S. at 751–752. Cf. Restatement (Second) of Agency § 220(2) (1958) (listing nonexhaustive criteria for identifying master-servant relationship); Rev. Rul. 87–41, 1987–1 C.B. 296, 298–299 (setting forth 20 factors as guides in determining whether an individual qualifies as a common-law "employee" in various tax law contexts). Since the common-law test contains "no shorthand formula or magic phrase that can be applied to find the answer, . . . all of the incidents of the relationship must be assessed and weighed with no one factor being decisive." NLRB v. United Ins. Co. of America, 390 U.S. 254 (1968).

* * *

III

While the Court of Appeals noted that "Darden most probably would not qualify as an employee" under traditional agency law principles, it did not actually decide that issue. We therefore reverse the judgment and remand the case to that court for proceedings consistent with this opinion.

NOTES AND QUESTIONS

1.   In *Darden*, the Supreme Court adopted the multiple-factor test developed under the common law of agency for determining whether an individual qualifies as an employee under Title I of ERISA. How relevant are these common law agency factors in today's modern workplace environment?

2.   *Determining Participant Status.* The Supreme Court addressed the question of who is a participant under ERISA Section 3(7) in *Firestone Tire & Rubber Co. v. Bruch*, 489 U.S. 101 (1989). In *Firestone*, the plaintiffs were a class of former employees who claimed they were entitled to benefits under the employer's severance pay plan. The plaintiffs made a request for information concerning the plan to the plan's administrator under ERISA Section 104(b)(4). The plan administrator claimed that the former employees were not entitled to receive information concerning the plan because they were not "participants." The Supreme Court described the test for determining a participant as follows:

> Congress did not say that all "claimants" could receive information about benefit plans. To say that a "participant" is any person who claims to be one begs the question of who is a "participant" and renders the definition set forth in § 3(7) superfluous. * * *

> In our view, the term "participant" is naturally read to mean either "employees in, or reasonably expected to be in, currently covered employment," or former employees who "have . . . a reasonable expectation of returning to covered employment" or who have "a colorable claim" to vested benefits. In order to establish that he or she "may become eligible" for benefits, a claimant must have a colorable claim that (1) he or she will prevail in a suit for benefits, or that (2) eligibility requirements will be fulfilled in the future. This view attributes conventional meanings to the statutory language since all employees in covered employment and former employees with a colorable claim to vested benefits "may become eligible." A former employee who has neither a reasonable expectation of returning to covered employment nor a colorable claim to vested benefits, however, simply does not fit within the [phrase] "may become eligible."

Firestone, 489 U.S. at 117–18 (quotations and citations omitted). The question of participant status frequently arises in the context of claims brought by terminated employees under ERISA Section 510 for interference with or retaliation for the exercise of rights under an employee benefit plan. Section 510 claims are discussed in Chapter Six of the casebook.

3.   *Working Owners as Participants.* The shareholder of a professional corporation, a general partner of a partnership, or a sole proprietor may both own and work in the business. Such individuals are known as *working owners*. Under Department of Labor regulations, if the only persons who are eligible for benefits from the plan are the partners of or the sole proprietor of

the business (or their spouses), the plan has no "employees." Therefore, the employer's plan is not subject to regulation under Title I of ERISA as an employee pension plan. See DOL Reg. § 2510.3–3.

Suppose that instead of providing benefits solely to the working owners of the business, other employees of the business also are eligible to receive benefits under the plan. In this situation, does a working owner of the business who is eligible to receive benefits from the plan qualify as a participant under ERISA Section 3(7)? Or should a working owner be treated as an employer and not receive the protections that Title I of ERISA provides to a participant in an employee benefit plan?

The Supreme Court answered these questions in *Yates v. Hendon*, 541 U.S. 1 (2004). Dr. Yates was the sole shareholder and president of a professional corporation that maintained a profit sharing plan. From its inception, at least one employee of the corporation other than Dr. Yates or his wife had been eligible to receive benefits from the plan as a participant. In 1996, Dr. Yates's creditors filed an involuntary petition against him under Chapter 7 of the federal Bankruptcy Code. Dr. Yates claimed that, because he was a participant in the plan, his account under the plan was protected from the claims of creditors under the anti-alienation rule of ERISA Section 206(d). (ERISA Section 206(d) provides that a participant's interest in an employee pension plan cannot be involuntarily assigned or alienated.) The bankruptcy trustee argued that Dr. Yates was not a participant in the plan within the definition of ERISA Section 3(7) because as the owner of the corporation that sponsored the plan, Dr. Yates was an employer, not an employee.

The Supreme Court held that a working owner in Dr. Yates's situation qualified as a participant under ERISA Section 3(7):

> If the plan covers one or more employees other than the business owner and his or her spouse, the working owner may participate on equal terms with other plan participants. Such a working owner, in common with other employees, qualifies for the protections ERISA affords plan participants and is governed by the rights and remedies ERISA specifies. In so ruling, we reject the position, taken by the lower courts in this case, that a business owner may rank only as an "employer" and not also as an "employee" for purposes of ERISA-sheltered plan participants.

541 U.S. at 6. What policy objectives are served by providing working owners the same protections under Title I of ERISA as the law provides to other participants in the plan?

4. *Misclassification of Independent Contractors. Vizcaino v. Microsoft Corp.*, 120 F.3d 1006 (9th Cir. 1997), illustrates the ERISA issues that may arise if an employer misclassifies workers as independent contractors. At various times prior to 1990, Microsoft Corporation (Microsoft) entered into individualized contracts with freelance computer programmers (free lancers). Under these contracts, the free lancers were paid higher hourly wages than

Microsoft employees, but were responsible for payment of their own Social Security, Medicare, and income taxes as independent contractors. As part of their contracts, the free lancers also acknowledged that they were not eligible for Microsoft's employee benefit plans. These plans included one plan subject to ERISA—the company's 401(k) plan, which provided for an employer matching contribution based on employee salary deferral contributions.

Although the free lancers were hired by Microsoft to work on specific projects, they were integrated into the Microsoft workforce. The free lancers worked on teams along with regular Microsoft employees, shared the same supervisors, performed similar functions to regular employees and worked the same core hours. The free lancers received admittance card keys to the Microsoft work premises, and received office equipment and supplies from the company. Unlike regular Microsoft employees, however, the free lancers were not paid through Microsoft's payroll department. Instead, the free lancers submitted invoices to and were paid through the accounts payable department.

The Internal Revenue Service examined Microsoft's records for 1989 and 1990 and determined that for purposes of Social Security, Medicare, and income taxes Microsoft should have treated the free lancers as regular Microsoft employees. Microsoft acquiesced in the Service's determination and made the necessary corrections by issuing W-2 forms to the free lancers and paying the employer's share of the taxes to the government. Microsoft then hired some of the free lancers as regular Microsoft employees, and arranged for other free lancers to become employees of a temporary employment agency. Eight of the free lancers later sued Microsoft, alleging that as employees they should have been allowed to participate in Microsoft's employee benefit plans, including the 401(k) plan.

The Ninth Circuit found that the contracts between Microsoft and the free lancers were the product of a "mutual mistake" and therefore not determinative of whether the free lancers should have been allowed to participate in the Microsoft 401(k) plan. Microsoft argued that the free lancers were not eligible to participate in the 401(k) plan because the plan limited the group of persons who were eligible to participate as "any common-law employee . . . who is on the United States payroll of the employer." Thus, even assuming that the free lancers were "common-law employees," the plan language itself arguably excluded the free lancers, who were not paid through the Microsoft payroll department during the years at issue. In a fractured en banc opinion, a majority of the judges on the Ninth Circuit ruled that the terms of the plan were ambiguous concerning the question of eligibility, and ordered the case remanded back to the 401(k) plan's administrator to construe the plan's eligibility criteria and determine whether the free lancers were eligible to participate in the 401(k) plan.

The risks associated with misclassifying an employee as an independent contractor have become even more significant due to the requirements of the Affordable Care Act. Misclassification issues under the ACA can arise in two ways. First, the employer may, depending on the number of its full-time equivalent "employees," be required to offer minimum essential coverage of health care services to its full-time "employees." Second, the penalty for noncomplicance by an employer with the requirements of the ACA is assessed on a per "employee" basis. These ACA requirements are discussed later in Chapter Four of the casebook.

5. *Waiver of Right to Participate in the Employer's Plan.* ERISA does not prohibit an individual from waiving his or her right to participate in an employee benefit plan. To be valid, the waiver must be "knowing and voluntary." E.g., Rodriguez-Abreu v. Chase Manhattan Bank, 986 F.2d 580, 587 (1st Cir. 1993). This determination is made by the court based on the totality of the circumstances. E.g., Leavitt v. Northwestern Bell Tel. Co., 921 F.2d 160 (8th Cir. 1990). In reviewing the circumstances surrounding the waiver, the federal courts generally focus on the following factors: (1) the individual's education, business experience, and sophistication; (2) the parties' respective roles in deciding the final terms of the waiver agreement; (3) the clarity of the waiver agreement; (4) the amount of time the individual had to study the waiver agreement before executing it; (5) whether the individual had independent advice from legal counsel; and (6) the nature of the consideration the individual received in exchange for the waiver. E.g., Laniok v. Advisory Comm. of the Brainerd Mfg. Co. Pension Plan, 935 F.2d 1360 (2d Cir. 1991).

3. WHO IS A SPOUSE?

Although ERISA grants numerous specific rights to the spouse of an employee who participates in an employee benefit plan, the statute itself does not define the term "spouse." In 1996, Congress enacted a federal definition of the terms "marriage" and "spouse" pursuant to Section 3 of the Defense of Marriage Act (DOMA). Section 3 of DOMA provided that for purposes of all federal statutes, "the word 'marriage' means only a legal union between one man and one woman as husband and wife, and the word 'spouse' refers only to a person of the opposite sex who is a husband or a wife." In *United States v. Windsor*, 133 S. Ct. 2675 (2013), the Supreme Court ruled in a 5–4 decision that Section 3 of DOMA "is unconstitutional as a deprivation of the liberty of the person protected by the Fifth Amendment of the Constitution." Id. at 2695.

As a result of the *Windsor* decision, the individual states now define "marriage" (and the related term "spouse"). See id. at 2689–90. At the time of the *Windsor* decision, 12 states and the District of Columbia recognized same-sex marriages. Under Section 2 of DOMA, which was not challenged in the *Windsor* litigation, the individual states are allowed to refuse to recognize same-sex marriages performed under the laws of another state. This situation created difficult issues for employers who sponsor ERISA plans for employees who are domiciled in different states, some of which may recognize same-sex marriage, and some of which may not.

In Technical Release 2013–14, the Department of Labor announced that for purposes of ERISA:

> the term "spouse" will be read to refer to any individuals who are lawfully married under any state law, including individuals married to a person of the same sex who were legally married in a state that recognizes such marriages, but who are domiciled in a state that does not recognize such marriages. Similarly, the term "marriage" will be read to include a same-sex marriage that is legally recognized as a marriage under any state law.

In adopting this position, the Department of Labor rejected an alternative interpretation of the terms "marriage" and "spouse" for purposes of ERISA based on the state law of the employee's place of domicile. The Department of Labor determined that:

> [a] rule for employee benefit plans based on [an employee's] state of domicile would raise significant challenges for employers that operate or have employees (or former employees) in more than one state or whose employees move to another state while entitled to benefits. Furthermore, substantial financial and administrative burdens would be placed on those employers, as well as the administrators of employee benefit plans. For example, the need for and validity of spousal elections, consents, and notices could change each time an employee, former employee, or spouse moved to a state with different marriage recognition rules. To administer employee benefit plans, employers (or plan administrators) would need to inquire whether each employee receiving plan benefits was married and, if so, whether the employee's spouse was the same sex or opposite sex from the employee. In addition, the employers or plan administrators would need to continually track the state of domicile of all same-sex married employees and former employees and their spouses. For all of these reasons, plan administration would grow increasingly complex, administrators of employee benefit plans would have to be retrained, and systems reworked, to comply with an unprecedented and complex system that divided married employees according to their sexual orientation. In many cases, the tracking of employee and spouse domiciles would be less than perfectly accurate or timely and would result in errors or delays.
>
> Such a system would be burdensome for employers and would likely result in errors, confusion, and inconsistency for employers, individual employees, and the government. In addition, given the interconnectedness of statutory provisions affecting employer benefit plans, recognition of marriage based on domicile could prevent qualification for tax exemption, lead to

> loss of vested rights if spouses move, and complicate benefits determinations if spouses live in different states. All of these problems are avoided by the adoption of a rule that recognizes marriages that are valid in the state in which they were celebrated. That approach is consistent with the core intent underlying ERISA of promoting uniform requirements for employee benefit plans.

DOL Technical Release 2013–14 at 2 (footnotes omitted). Consistent with the position taken by the Internal Revenue Service post-*Windsor*, marriages validly performed under the laws of a foreign jurisdiction are recognized for purposes of spousal plan benefits, but civil unions and domestic partnerships are not treated as "marriages" for purposes of qualifying for benefits as the "spouse" of a plan participant. See IRS Rev. Ruling 2013–17.

C. PLAN DOCUMENTS, TRUST REQUIREMENTS AND AMENDMENT PROCEDURES

1. PLAN DOCUMENTS AND THE WRITTEN INSTRUMENT RULE

ERISA Section 402 describes the formal requirements for an employee benefit plan. Section 402(a) requires that the plan must be established and maintained pursuant to a written instrument that provides for one or more named fiduciaries. This requirement is commonly referred to as the *plan document* or *written instrument* rule. The legislative history of ERISA explains the purpose of the written instrument rule.

> Under [ERISA Section 402], every covered employee benefit plan (both retirement and welfare plans) is to be established and maintained in writing. A written plan is to be required in order that every employee may, on examining the plan documents, determine exactly what his rights and obligations are under the plan. Also, a written plan is required so the employee may know who is responsible for operating the plan. Therefore, the plan document is to provide for the "named fiduciaries" who have authority to control and manage the plan operations and administration. A named fiduciary may be a person whose name actually appears in the document, or may be a person who holds an office specified in the document, such as the company president. A named fiduciary also may be a person who is identified by the employer or union, under a procedure set out in the document. For example, the plan may provide that the employer's board of directors is to choose the person who manages or controls the plan. In addition, a named fiduciary

> may be a person identified by the employers and union acting
> jointly. For example, the members of a joint board of trustees of
> a Taft-Hartley plan would usually be named fiduciaries.

H.R. Conf. Rep. No. 93–1280 (1973). Rather than naming an individual or
individuals, the plan document may identify the named plan fiduciary as
a committee or as the company that sponsors the plan. See DOL Reg.
§ 2509.75–5, FR–1–FR–3.

More recently, the Supreme Court has emphasized the policy
importance of the written instrument rule as a cost-containment
safeguard for employers:

> Once a plan is established, the administrator's duty is to see that
> the plan is "maintained pursuant to [that] written instrument."
> ERISA § 402(a)(1). This focus on the written terms of the plan is
> the linchpin of "a system that is not so complex that
> administrative costs, or litigation expenses, unduly discourage
> employers from offering plans in the first place." Varity Corp. v.
> Howe, 516 U.S. 489, 497 (1996).

Heimeshoff v. Hartford Life & Accident Ins. Co., 134 S. Ct. 604, 612
(2013). See also US Airways v. McCutchen, 133 S. Ct. 1537, 1548 (2013)
("The plan, in short, is at the center of ERISA.").

Donovan v. Dillingham, reproduced in Section B of Chapter Two, is
often cited for the proposition that the federal courts will recognize the
existence of an employee benefit plan that is not established in writing if
the plan has the characteristics of an employee benefit plan. Most
employers, however, prefer to establish their employee benefit plans in
writing so that the benefits provided under the plan and the identity and
fiduciary functions of the various persons involved in administering the
plan are clearly delineated. In addition, the existence of a written plan
document often precludes claims by plan participants that oral
statements by a plan fiduciary have "amended" the terms of the plan.
This type of participant claim is discussed in the Note on Estoppel Claims
in Section D of Chapter Two.

ERISA Section 402(b) lists the mandatory provisions that must
appear in the plan document. Every plan subject to ERISA must:

- Provide a procedure for establishing and carrying out a
  funding policy;
- Describe the procedure for allocating and delegating
  fiduciary responsibilities for the management and
  administration of the plan;
- Describe the procedure for amending the plan, including the
  identity of the person or persons who have authority to
  amend the plan; and

- Specify the basis on which payments are made to and from the plan.

ERISA Section 402(c) lists optional plan features that are not required, but that must appear in the plan if the plan fiduciaries intend to take advantage of these features. As a practical matter, these optional features are viewed as desirable and are usually incorporated into the plan document. These optional fiduciary features are:

- A provision authorizing a person or persons to serve in more than one fiduciary capacity with respect to the plan (such as serving as both the plan's trustee and administrator);

- A provision authorizing a fiduciary to employ advisors to assist the fiduciary in carrying out his or her responsibilities; and

- A provision authorizing a named plan fiduciary who is responsible for the plan's assets to appoint an investment manager to manage all or part of the assets of the plan.

Although ERISA Section 402(a) refers to a "written instrument," it is not uncommon for the plan to consist of a collection of one or more written documents. For example, many employers use *prototype plans* as the written instrument establishing their pension plans. A prototype plan consists of two documents, a *prototype plan document* and the employer's *adoption agreement*. The prototype plan document contains the boilerplate language required by Code Section 401(a) for a qualified retirement plan. The adoption agreement contains the employer's individual choices concerning various optional design features for qualified retirement plans. A sample employer adoption agreement for a prototype plan is contained in Appendix A at the end of the casebook.

When plan benefits are provided through insurance, such as for health care or disability benefits, the "written instrument" governing the plan usually consists of more than one document. In this situation, the written instrument establishing the welfare plan typically consists of the insurance policy together with another document designed to satisfy ERISA's written plan document content requirements. For multiemployer pension and welfare benefit plans, the plan's written instrument typically is the collective bargaining agreement.

2. TRUST REQUIREMENT FOR PLAN ASSETS AND TYPES OF TRUSTEES

ERISA Section 403(a) requires that the assets of an employee benefit plan generally must be held in trust by one or more trustees. ERISA Section 403(b) lists various exemptions to this trust requirement. Each trustee must be named in the plan document or in the plan's trust agreement if separate plan and trust documents are used. Alternatively, the named plan fiduciary may appoint the trustee(s).

ERISA Section 403(a) authorizes two types of trustees. A *discretionary trustee* has exclusive authority and discretion to manage, invest, and control the assets of the plan. In contrast, a *directed trustee* is subject to the directions of a named plan fiduciary (the *directing fiduciary*) with respect to the management and investment of the plan's assets. The directing fiduciary cannot be another trustee, but can be the sponsoring employer, a properly designated investment manager, or (as is the case for the typical 401(k) plan) the plan participants themselves. See ERISA § 403(a)(1)–(2).

ERISA Section 403(a)(1) requires that a directed trustee must follow the "proper" directions of the directing fiduciary, so long as those directions are "made in accordance with the terms of the plan" and are "not contrary to" the requirements of Title I of ERISA. See ERISA § 403(a)(1). Although the functions of a directed trustee are narrowly circumscribed by ERISA Section 403(a)(1), in performing these functions the directed trustee nevertheless is a fiduciary. According to the Department of Labor, a directed trustee has residual fiduciary responsibility for determining whether a given direction is proper and whether following the direction would result in a violation of ERISA. See DOL Op. Ltr. 97–15A, n. 6.

The scope of a directed trustee's duties under Section 403(a)(1) has proven controversial in recent years, particularly in the context of plans where the company that sponsors the plan directs the trustee concerning the plan's investment in company stock. The root of the controversy stems from the absence of guidance in the statute concerning what degree of investigation the directed trustee must undertake to ascertain whether the direction provided by the directing fiduciary is "proper" and is "in accordance with" the provisions of ERISA. See DOL Field Assistance Bulletin No. 2004–3 (describing the fiduciary duties of directed trustees); Colleen E. Medill, *The Law of Directed Trustees Under ERISA: A Proposed Blueprint for the Federal Courts*, 61 MO. L. REV. 825 (1996).

3. PLAN AMENDMENT PROCEDURES

In *Curtiss-Wright Corporation v. Schoonejongen*, the company had the authority to amend the plan, but the plan document did not specify an amendment procedure. As you read this case, consider what language in the plan document could have avoided this lawsuit.

CURTISS-WRIGHT CORP. V. SCHOONEJONGEN

United States Supreme Court, 1995.
514 U.S. 73, 115 S.Ct. 1223, 131 L.Ed.2d 94.

JUSTICE O'CONNOR delivered the opinion of the Court.

Section 402(b)(3) of the Employee Retirement Income Security Act of 1974 (ERISA) requires that every employee benefit plan provide "a procedure for amending such plan, and for identifying the persons who have authority to amend the plan." This case presents the question whether the standard provision in many employer-provided benefit plans stating that "The Company reserves the right at any time to amend the plan" sets forth an amendment procedure that satisfies § 402(b)(3). We hold that it does.

I

For many years, petitioner Curtiss-Wright voluntarily maintained a postretirement health plan for employees who had worked at certain Curtiss-Wright facilities; respondents are retirees who had worked at one such facility in Wood Ridge, New Jersey. The specific terms of the plan, the District Court determined, could be principally found in two plan documents: the plan constitution and the Summary Plan Description (SPD), both of which primarily covered active employee health benefits.

In early 1983, presumably due to the rising cost of health care, a revised SPD was issued with the following new provision: "TERMINATION OF HEALTH CARE BENEFITS. . . . Coverage under this Plan will cease for retirees and their dependents upon the termination of business operations of the facility from which they retired." The two main authors of the new SPD provision, Curtiss-Wright's director of benefits and its labor counsel, testified that they did not think the provision effected a "change" in the plan, but rather merely clarified it. Probably for this reason, the record is less than clear as to which Curtiss-Wright officers or committees had authority to make plan amendments on behalf of the company and whether such officers or committees approved or ratified the new SPD provision. In any event, later that year, Curtiss-Wright announced that the Wood-Ridge facility would close. Shortly thereafter, an executive vice president wrote respondents a series of letters informing them that their post-retirement health benefits were being terminated.

Respondents brought suit in federal court over the termination of their benefits, and many years of litigation ensued. The District Court ultimately rejected most of respondents' claims, including their contention that Curtiss-Wright had bound itself contractually to provide health benefits to them for life. The District Court agreed, however, that the new SPD provision effected a significant change in the plan's terms and thus constituted an "amendment" to the plan; that the plan documents nowhere contained a valid amendment procedure, as required by § 402(b)(3); and that the proper remedy for the § 402(b)(3) violation was to declare the new SPD provision void ab initio. The court eventually ordered Curtiss-Wright to pay respondents $2,681,086 in back benefits.

On appeal, Curtiss-Wright primarily argued that the plan documents did contain an amendment procedure, namely, the standard reservation clause contained in the plan constitution and in a few secondary plan documents. The clause states: "The Company reserves the right at any time and from time to time to modify or amend, in whole or in part, any or all of the provisions of the Plan." In Curtiss-Wright's view, this clause sets forth an amendment procedure as required by the statute. It says, in effect, that the plan is to be amended by "*[t]he Company*."

The Court of Appeals for the Third Circuit rejected this argument, as well as all other arguments before it, and affirmed the District Court's remedy. See 18 F.3d 1034 (1994). It explained: "A primary purpose of § 402(b)(3) is to ensure that all interested parties [including beneficiaries] will know how a plan may be altered and who may make such alterations. Only if they know this information will they be able to determine with certainty at any given time exactly what the plan provides." Id. at 1038. And the court suggested that § 402(b)(3) cannot serve that purpose unless it is read to require that every amendment procedure specify precisely "what individuals or bodies within the Company c[an] promulgate an effective amendment." Id. at 1039. In the court's view, then, a reservation clause that says that the plan may be amended "by the Company," without more, is too vague. * * *

In a footnote, the court related the concurring views of Judge Roth. Id. at 1039 n.3. According to the court, Judge Roth thought that the notion of an amendment "by the Company" should be read in light of traditional corporate law principles, which is to say amendment "by the board of directors or whomever of the company has the authority to take such action." Id. And read in this more specific way, "by the Company" indicates a valid amendment procedure that satisfies § 402(b)(3). She concurred rather than dissented, however, because, in the court's words, "neither [Curtiss-Wright's] board nor any other person or entity within [Curtiss-Wright] with the power to act on behalf of 'the Company' ratified [the new SPD provision]." Id.

Curtiss-Wright petitioned for certiorari on the questions whether a plan provision stating that "[t]he Company" reserves the right to amend the plan states a valid amendment procedure under § 402(b)(3) and, if not, whether the proper remedy is to declare this or any other amendment void ab initio. We granted certiorari on both.

II

In interpreting § 402(b)(3), we are mindful that ERISA does not create any substantive entitlement to employer-provided health benefits or any other kind of welfare benefits. Employers or other plan sponsors are generally free under ERISA, for any reason at any time, to adopt, modify, or terminate welfare plans. Nor does ERISA establish any minimum participation, vesting, or funding requirements for welfare plans as it does for pension plans. Accordingly, that Curtiss-Wright amended its plan to deprive respondents of health benefits is not a cognizable complaint under ERISA; the only cognizable claim is that the company did not do so in a permissible manner.

A

The text of § 402(b)(3) actually requires *two* things: a "procedure for amending [the] plan" *and* "[a procedure] for identifying the persons who have authority to amend the plan." With respect to the second requirement, the general "Definitions" section of ERISA makes quite clear that the term "person," wherever it appears in the statute, includes companies. See ERISA § 3(9) ("The term 'person' means an individual, partnership, joint venture, corporation, mutual company, joint-stock company, trust, estate, unincorporated organization, association, or employee organization"). The Curtiss-Wright reservation clause thus appears to satisfy the statute's identification requirement by naming "[t]he Company" as "the perso[n]" with amendment authority.

The text of § 402(b)(3) speaks, somewhat awkwardly, of requiring a *procedure* for identifying the persons with amendment authority, rather than requiring identification of those persons outright. Be that as it may, a plan that simply identifies the persons outright necessarily indicates a procedure for identifying the persons as well. With respect to the Curtiss-Wright plan, for example, to identify "[t]he Company" as the person with amendment authority is to say, in effect, that the procedure for identifying the person with amendment authority is to look always to "[t]he Company." Such an identification procedure is more substantial than might first appear. To say that one must look always to "[t]he Company" is to say that one must look *only* to "[t]he Company" and *not* to any other person-that is, not to any union, not to any third party trustee, and not to any of the other kinds of outside parties that, in many other plans, exercise amendment authority.

The more difficult question in this case is whether the Curtiss-Wright reservation clause contains a "procedure for amending [the] plan." To recall, the reservation clause says in effect that the plan may be amended "by the Company." Curtiss-Wright is correct, we think, that this states an amendment procedure and one that, like the identification procedure, is more substantial than might first appear. It says the plan may be amended by a unilateral company decision to amend, and only by such a decision—and not, for example, by the unilateral decision of a third-party trustee or upon the approval of the union. Moreover, to the extent that this procedure *is* the barest of procedures, that is because the Curtiss-Wright plan is the simplest of plans: a voluntarily maintained single-employer health plan that is administered by the employer and funded by the employer. More complicated plans, such as multiemployer plans, may have more complicated amendment procedures, and § 402(b)(3) was designed to cover them as well.

In any event, the literal terms of § 402(b)(3) are ultimately indifferent to the level of detail in an amendment procedure, or in an identification procedure for that matter. The provision requires only that there *be* an amendment procedure, which here there is. A "procedure," as that term is commonly understood, is a "particular way" of doing something, Webster's Third New International Dictionary 1807 (1976), or "a manner of proceeding," Random House Dictionary of the English Language 1542 (2d ed.1987). Certainly a plan that says it may be amended only by a unilateral company decision adequately sets forth "a particular way" of making an amendment. Adequately, that is, with one refinement.

In order for an amendment procedure that says the plan may be amended by "[t]he Company" to make any sense, there must be some way of determining what it means for "[t]he Company" to make a decision to amend or, in the language of trust law, to "sufficiently manifest [its] intention" to amend. Restatement (Second) of Trusts § 331, Comment c (1957). After all, only natural persons are capable of making decisions. As Judge Roth suggested, however, principles of corporate law provide a ready-made set of rules for determining, in whatever context, who has authority to make decisions on behalf of a company. Consider, for example, an ordinary sales contract between "Company X" and a third party. We would not think of regarding the contract as meaningless, and thus unenforceable, simply because it does not specify on its face exactly who within "Company X" has the power to enter into such an agreement or carry out its terms. Rather, we would look to corporate law principles to give "Company X" content. See 2 W. Fletcher, Cyclopedia of Law of Private Corporations § 466, 505 (rev. ed. 1990) ("[A] corporation is bound by contracts entered into by its officers and agents acting on behalf of the corporation and for its benefit, provided they act within the scope of their express or implied powers."). So too here.

In the end, perhaps the strongest argument for a textual reading of § 402(b)(3) is that to read it to require specification of individuals or bodies within a company would lead to improbable results. That is, it might lead to the invalidation of myriad amendment procedures that no one would think violate § 402(b)(3), especially those in multiemployer plans—which, as we said, § 402(b)(3) covers as well. For example, imagine a multiemployer plan that says, "This Plan may be amended at any time by written agreement of two-thirds of the participating Companies, subject to the approval of the plan Trustees." This would seem to be a fairly robust amendment procedure, and we can imagine numerous variants of it. Yet, because our hypothetical procedure does not specify who within any of "the participating Companies" has authority to enter into such an amendment agreement (let alone what counts as the "approval of the plan Trustees"), respondents would say it is insufficiently specific to pass muster under § 402(b)(3). Congress could not have intended such a result.

B

Curtiss-Wright's reservation clause thus satisfies the plain text of both requirements in § 402(b)(3). Respondents nonetheless argue that, in drafting § 402(b)(3), Congress intended amendment procedures to convey enough detail to serve beneficiaries' interest in knowing the terms of their plans. Ordinarily, we would be reluctant to indulge an argument based on legislative purpose where the text alone yields a clear answer, but we do so here because it is the argument the Court of Appeals found persuasive.

Section 402(b)(3)'s primary purpose is obviously functional: to ensure that every plan has a workable amendment procedure. This is clear from not only the face of the provision but also its placement in § 402(b), which lays out the requisite functional features of ERISA plans. ERISA § 402(b) (every ERISA plan shall have, in addition to an amendment procedure, "a procedure for establishing and carrying out a funding policy and method," "[a] procedure under the plan for the allocation of responsibilities for the operation and administration of the plan," and "[a] basis on which payments are made to and from the plan").

Requiring every plan to have a coherent amendment procedure serves several laudable goals. First, for a plan *not* to have such a procedure would risk rendering the plan forever unamendable under standard trust law principles. See Restatement (Second) of Trusts § 331(2). Second, such a requirement increases the likelihood that proposed plan amendments, which are fairly serious events, are recognized as such and given the special consideration they deserve. Finally, having an amendment procedure enables plan administrators, the people who manage the plan on a day-to-day level, to have a mechanism for sorting out, from among the occasional corporate communications that pass through their offices and that conflict with the existing plan terms, the bona fide amendments from those that are not. In fact, plan administrators may have a statutory responsibility to do this sorting out. See ERISA § 404(a)(1)(D) (plan administrators have a duty to run the plan "in accordance with the documents and instruments governing the plan insofar as such documents and instruments are consistent with the provisions of [the statute]," which would include the amendment procedure provision). That Congress may have had plan administrators in mind is suggested by the fact that § 402(b)(3), and § 402(b) more generally, is located in the "fiduciary responsibility" section of ERISA. See ERISA §§ 401–414.

Respondents argue that § 402(b)(3) was intended not only to ensure that every plan has an amendment procedure, but also to guarantee that the procedure conveys enough detail to enable beneficiaries to learn their rights and obligations under the plan at any time. Respondents are no doubt right that one of ERISA's central goals is to enable plan beneficiaries to learn their rights and obligations at any time. But ERISA already *has* an elaborate scheme in place for enabling beneficiaries to learn their rights and obligations at any time, a scheme that is built around reliance on the face of written plan documents.

The basis of that scheme is another of ERISA's core functional requirements, that "[e]very employee benefit plan shall be established and maintained *pursuant to a written instrument*." ERISA § 402(a)(1) (emphasis added). In the words of the key congressional report, "[a] written plan is to be required in order that every employee may, *on examining the plan documents*, determine exactly what his rights and obligations are under the plan." H.R. Rep. No. 93–1280, 297 (1974) (emphasis added). ERISA gives effect to this "written plan documents" scheme through a comprehensive set of "reporting and disclosure" requirements, see ERISA §§ 101–111, of which § 402(b)(3) is not part. One provision, for example, requires that plan administrators periodically furnish beneficiaries with a Summary Plan Description, see ERISA § 104(b)(1), the purpose being to communicate to beneficiaries the essential information about the plan. Not surprisingly, the information that every SPD must contain includes the "name and address" of plan administrators and other plan fiduciaries, but not the names and addresses of those individuals with amendment authority. ERISA § 102(b). The same provision also requires that plan administrators furnish beneficiaries with summaries of new amendments no later than 210 days after the end of the plan year in which the amendment is adopted. See ERISA § 104(b)(1). Under ERISA, both Summary Plan Descriptions and plan amendment summaries "shall be written in a manner calculated to be understood by the average plan participant." ERISA § 102 (a)(1).

More important, independent of any information automatically distributed to beneficiaries, ERISA requires that every plan administrator make available for inspection in the administrator's "principal office" and other designated locations a set of all currently operative, governing plan documents, see § ERISA 104(b)(2), which necessarily includes any new, bona fide amendments. See also ERISA

§ 104(b)(4) (requiring plan administrators, upon written request, to furnish beneficiaries with copies of governing plan documents for a reasonable copying charge). As indicated earlier, plan administrators appear to have a statutory responsibility actually to run the plan in accordance with the currently operative, governing plan documents and thus an independent incentive for obtaining new amendments as quickly as possible and for weeding out defective ones.

This may not be a foolproof informational scheme, although it is quite thorough. Either way, it is the scheme that Congress devised. And we do not think Congress intended it to be supplemented by a far away provision in another part of the statute, least of all in a way that would lead to improbable results.

In concluding that Curtiss-Wright's reservation clause sets forth a valid amendment procedure, we do not mean to imply that there is anything wrong with plan beneficiaries trying to prove that unfavorable plan amendments were not properly adopted and are thus invalid. This is exactly what respondents are trying to do here, and nothing in ERISA is designed to obstruct such efforts. But nothing in ERISA is designed to facilitate such efforts either. To be sure, some companies that have plans with the standard reservation clause may want to provide greater specification to their amendment procedures precisely to avoid such costly litigation. Or they may want to retain the flexibility that designating "[t]he Company" (read in light of corporate law) provides them. But either way, this is simply a species of a larger dilemma companies face whenever they must designate who, on behalf of the company, may take legally binding actions that third parties may later have an interest in challenging as unauthorized. It is not a dilemma ERISA addresses. ERISA, rather, follows standard trust law principles in dictating only that whatever level of specificity a company ultimately chooses, in an amendment procedure or elsewhere, it is bound to that level.

III

Having determined that the Curtiss-Wright plan satisfies § 402(b)(3), we do not reach the question of the proper remedy for a § 402(b)(3) violation. On remand, the Court of Appeals will have to decide the question that has always been at the heart of this case: whether Curtiss-Wright's valid amendment procedure—amendment "by the Company"— was complied with in this case. The answer will depend on a fact-intensive inquiry, under applicable corporate law principles, into what persons or committees within Curtiss-Wright possessed plan amendment authority, either by express delegation or impliedly, and whether those persons or committees actually approved the new plan provision contained in the revised SPD. See 2 W. Fletcher, Cyclopedia of the Law of Private Corporations § 444, 397–98 (1990) (authority may be by express delegation or it "may be inferred from circumstances or implied from the acquiescence of the corporation or its agents in a general course of business"). If the new plan provision is found not to have been properly authorized when issued, the question would then arise whether any subsequent actions, such as the executive vice president's letters informing respondents of the termination, served to ratify the provision ex post. See id. § 437.10, at 386.

The judgment of the Court of Appeals is reversed, and the case is remanded for further proceedings consistent with this opinion.

NOTES AND QUESTIONS

1. Do you agree with the Supreme Court's characterization in *Curtiss-Wright* of ERISA Section 402(b)(3) as primarily functional? Is this characterization consistent with the policy that underlies ERISA's written instrument rule?

2. *Oral or Informal "Amendments" to Written Plan Documents.* Section 402's written instrument rule modifies general contract law principles:

> An ordinary contract can be modified by subsequent dealings that give rise to an inference that the parties agreed, even if just tacitly, to the modification. . . . But because ERISA plans must be "maintained pursuant to a written instrument," only modifications of such plans in writing are enforceable, and so it would seem that the principle that contracts can be modified by the subsequent conduct of the parties is inapplicable to ERISA plans unless the conduct is proved by a writing.

Orth v. Wisconsin State Employees Union, 546 F.3d 868, 872 (7th Cir. 2008). The federal courts generally read the written instrument rule of ERISA Section 402 in conjunction with *Curtiss-Wright* as requiring that any amendment to the plan must be in writing *and* in accordance with the plan's specified amendment procedure. Thus, the written instrument rule of ERISA Section 402 precludes both oral modifications to the terms of the plan as well as informal written modifications that fail to comply with the plan's formal amendment procedure. See Livick v. Gillette Co., 524 F.3d 24, 31 & n.7 (1st Cir. 2008).

3. *The Settlor Function Doctrine and the Employer's Ability to Amend Plan Terms.* In *Curtiss-Wright*, the Supreme Court recognized that an employer is "generally free under ERISA, for any reason at any time, to adopt, modify, or terminate welfare plans." 514 U.S. at 78. This right of the employer to amend or terminate an employee benefit plan is known as the *settlor function doctrine*. The employer's right to amend or terminate a plan is more constrained in the context of qualified retirement plans due to the vesting and benefit accrual requirements of the Code and ERISA. These requirements are examined in Chapter Three of the casebook. In contrast, ERISA does not place constraints on an employer's ability to amend the terms of a welfare benefit plan, other than requiring that the amendment procedure as specified in the plan document must be followed.

D. PLAN REPORTING AND DISCLOSURE REQUIREMENTS

A working knowledge of ERISA's reporting and disclosure requirements is useful in many situations in the general practice of law. For example, suppose you are approached by an individual whose health care plan has denied a claim for medical treatment. Whether you decide to represent this individual is likely to depend on the merits of the individual's claim for benefits under the health care plan, which in turn will depend on the language of the plan document itself. How can your potential client obtain a copy of the plan document and a summary of its relevant provisions for you to review? The answer lies in ERISA's reporting and disclosure requirements, which are found in Part 1 of Title I of ERISA.

For estate planning lawyers, retirement plan benefits are among their clients' largest assets. In planning a client's estate, you would certainly want to know the amount of your client's retirement plan benefits and the client's options for the distribution of these benefits. Some clients may know this information, but others will not, or they will not be confident they know all of the relevant details of the employer's retirement plan. Again, in this situation it would be very helpful if your client could obtain a copy of the plan document and a summary of its relevant provisions for you to review.

A basic understanding of ERISA's reporting and disclosure requirements also is important for lawyers who represent corporate clients in business transactions. Suppose your corporate client has engaged you to represent the client in negotiations to acquire another company. As part of this engagement you will be required to investigate and identify any potential liabilities associated with the soon-to-be acquired company. An important component of your due diligence investigation will be to evaluate the company's employee benefit plans. Part of this task includes determining whether the company's employee benefit plans are in compliance with ERISA's reporting and disclosure requirements.

1. LEGISLATIVE HISTORY AND POLICY OBJECTIVES

The precursor to ERISA, the Welfare and Pension Plans Disclosure Act of 1958, contained only limited disclosure requirements. When these requirements proved inadequate, Congress concluded that more rigorous standards were necessary under ERISA.

> The underlying theory of the Welfare and Pension Plans Disclosure Act (WPPDA) to date has been that reporting of generalized information concerning plan operations to plan participants and beneficiaries and to the public in general would,

by subjecting the dealings of persons controlling employee benefit plans to the light of public scrutiny, insure that the plan would be operated according to instructions and in the best interests of participants and beneficiaries. The Secretary of Labor's role in this scheme was minimal. Disclosure has been seen as a device to impart to employees sufficient information and data to enable them to know whether the plan was financially sound and being administered as intended. It was expected that the information disclosed would enable employees to police their plans. But experience has shown that the limited data available under the WPPDA is insufficient. Changes are therefore required to increase the information and data required in the reports both in scope and detail. Experience has also demonstrated a need for a more particularized form of reporting so that the individual participant knows exactly where he stands with respect to the plan—what benefits he may be entitled to, what circumstances may preclude him from obtaining benefits, what procedures he must follow to obtain benefits, and who are the persons to whom the management and investment of his plan funds have been entrusted. At the same time, the safeguarding effect of the fiduciary responsibility section will operate efficiently only if fiduciaries are aware that the details of their dealings will be open to inspection, and that individual participants and beneficiaries will be armed with enough information to enforce their own rights as well as the obligations owed by the fiduciary to the plan in general.

H.R. Rep. No. 93–533 (1973).

Congress addressed these perceived deficiencies under existing federal law by enacting new reporting and disclosure requirements in Part 1 of Title I of ERISA. ERISA requires the plan administrator to furnish a number of different disclosures and notices to plan participants or federal regulators. The primary reporting and disclosure documents prepared by the plan administrator are:

- A summary plan description;
- A summary of material modifications made to the plan;
- An annual report for the plan;
- A summary annual report or an annual funding notice for the plan;
- A periodic benefit statement;
- Advance notice of a blackout period when the participant's rights to his plan account are suspended;

- Notice when the participant has the right to diversify contributions invested in publicly traded employer securities; and

- Other specific information, if requested by a plan participant or the Secretary of Labor.

As you review ERISA's reporting and disclosure requirements, consider whether these rules achieve the twin policy objectives of providing sufficient information to participants so that they can "self-police" the administration of their employee benefit plans and deterring fiduciary misconduct. If not, how should ERISA's reporting and disclosure requirements be changed to accomplish these policy objectives?

2. GENERAL REPORTING AND DISCLOSURE REQUIREMENTS

ERISA's major reporting and disclosure requirements for employee benefit plans are summarized in Table 2.1. Each of these requirements is discussed in the reading material following Table 2.1. A willful violation of ERISA's reporting and disclosure requirements is subject to potential criminal sanctions. See ERISA § 501.

Table 2.1

Reporting and Disclosure Requirements

Requirement	Nature of Disclosure	Timing	Penalty for Nondisclosure
SPD	• Summary of key provisions of the plan • Provided to participants	• New plan = 120 days • New participant = 90 days • Updated SPD = every 5th year	• None
SMM	• Summary of amendment(s) to plan • Provided to participants	• Material reduction in health plan services/ benefits = 60 days before reduction is effective • Other amendments = 210 days after end of plan year	• None

Annual Report	• Form 5500 • Filed with DOL	• 210 days after end of plan year	• Civil monetary penalty (ERISA §502(c)(2))
SAR	• Description of plan's finances and funding mechanism • Provided to participants in retirement plans and welfare plans	• 210 days after end of plan year	• None
Annual Funding Notice	• Description of plan's funding status, assets and liabilities • Provided to participants in defined benefit plans	• 120 days after end of plan year (plans with more than 100 participants) • 210 days after end of plan year (plans with 100 or fewer participants)	• Federal court has discretion to award daily penalty (ERISA §502(c)(1)) • Penalty paid to each participant who is not given timely notice
Periodic Benefit Statement	• Description of vested accrued benefits under the plan • Provided to participants in pension plans	• Varies by type of retirement plan	• Civil monetary penalty (ERISA §502(c)(1)) • Penalty paid to each participant who is not given a timely statement
Blackout Period Notice	• Advance notice of period during with participants cannot direct or diversity investments	• At least 30 days prior to start of blackout period	• Civil monetary penalty (ERISA §502(c)(7))

Diversification Notice	• Notice that participant has right to diversity contributions invested in publicly traded employer securities	• At least 30 days prior to when participant's diversification rights commence	• Civil monetary penalty (ERISA §502(c)(7))
Information Provided "Upon Request"	• Documents requested in writing under ERISA §104(b)(4)	• 30 days after request is made	• Federal court has discretion to award daily penalty (ERISA §502(c)(1) • Penalty paid to each participant who is not given requested information within 30 days of request

Summary Plan Description and Summary of Material Modifications

The plan administrator must furnish a summary plan description (SPD) and a summary of any material modifications made to the plan (SMM) to each plan participant and each beneficiary who is receiving benefits under the plan. ERISA § 102(a). Although there is no precise format, the statute requires that the SPD and SMM "shall be written in a manner calculated to be understood by the average plan participant, and shall be sufficiently accurate and comprehensive to reasonably apprise such participants and beneficiaries of their rights and obligations under the plan." See ERISA § 102(a). Consistent with this standard, if the SPD is written in English, the plan administrator may be required to provide assistance to participants who are not literate in the English language. See DOL Reg. § 2520.102–2.

As a general rule, the SPD must accurately convey the contents of the plan. ERISA Section 102(b) describes, in a summary fashion, the basic information that must be contained in the SPD:

- The plan's eligibility requirements for participation;
- A description of the plan's benefits;

- Circumstances that may result in disqualification, ineligibility, or denial or loss of benefits, including the termination of the plan;

- The relevant provisions of any applicable collective bargaining agreement;

- For retirement plans, the plan rules for benefit accrual, vesting and distribution of benefits;

- The procedures for filing a claim for benefits under the plan, along with the procedures for appeal of a denied claim;

- The names and addresses of various plan fiduciaries, along with the name and address of the agent for service of process; and

- The Department of Labor office where participants may seek assistance or information concerning their rights under ERISA.

Department of Labor regulations describe in detail the content requirements for summary plan descriptions for pension and welfare benefit plans. See DOL Reg. § 2520.102–3. The plan administrator may provide the SPD using electronic media, such as posting these documents on a readily accessible web site, or by e-mail. See DOL Reg. § 2520.104b–1(c).

Curiously, ERISA does not impose a civil penalty on a plan administrator who fails to comply with the SPD and SMM notice requirements for disclosures to plan participants and beneficiaries. As a practical matter, enforcement of these requirements is accomplished primarily through ERISA's fiduciary responsibility provisions. As a fiduciary under ERISA, the plan administrator is required to discharge his or her duties in a prudent manner, which includes compliance with the statutory requirements for disclosures to plan participants. See ERISA § 404(a)(1)(B). If the SPD or SMM is inaccurate, incomplete, or misleading, a plan participant may allege that the plan and its administrator are estopped from denying a claimed benefit, or that the plan administrator has breached the fiduciary duty to inform plan participants concerning their plan benefits. Claims based on plan disclosures are discussed in the Note on Estoppel Claims at the end of Chapter Two. ERISA's fiduciary responsibility provisions, including a fiduciary's duty to inform, are discussed in Chapter Five of the casebook.

Annual Report

ERISA Section 103(a) requires the plan administrator to prepare and file an annual report for each employee benefit plan that is subject to Title I of ERISA. Plan administrators refer to the annual report as *Form 5500* after the government-assigned number of the form that is filed.

Form 5500 is accompanied by a lengthy list of schedules for various types of plans and the different types of plan funding mechanisms. A sample of Form 5500 is contained in Appendix B of the casebook.

Annual reports must be filed electronically. See ERISA § 104(b)(5); DOL Reg. § 2520.104a–2. Filing Form 5500 with the Department of Labor satisfies the annual reporting requirement to the Treasury Department under Code Section 6058(a) for qualified plans and funded deferred compensation plans. Filing Form 5500 with the Department of Labor also satisfies the reporting requirements to the Pension Benefit Guaranty Corporation under ERISA Section 4065 for defined benefit plans covered by plan termination insurance. Certain one-participant retirement plans having less than $250,000 in assets are exempt from the annual reporting requirement, and plans with fewer than 25 participants are subject to simplified annual reporting requirements.

Top hat plans may comply with the annual reporting requirement by taking advantage of a simplified reporting mechanism. In lieu of annually filing Form 5500, the plan administrator may elect to file a one-time statement with the Department of Labor. The contents of this statement are prescribed by regulation. See DOL Reg. § 2520.104–23. The plan administrator must file this one-time statement within 120 days after the plan becomes effective. If the plan administrator fails to file this one-time statement within the regulatory time period, Form 5500 reports must be filed annually for the top hat plan.

In general, the annual report must be filed within 210 days after the close of the plan year. See ERISA § 104(a)(1)(A); DOL Reg. § 2520.104b–10. In contrast to the SPD and SMM, substantial monetary penalties may be imposed if the plan administrator fails to comply with the requirements for filing and furnishing annual reports. Effective for plan years beginning in 1988, ERISA Section 502(c)(2) authorizes the Secretary of Labor to impose a civil penalty for each day that the annual report is delinquent. The maximum daily penalty amount is $1,100. The IRS also has authority to assess a penalty of $25 per day, with a maximum penalty of $15,000, for failure to file an annual report for a qualified retirement plan. See Code §§ 6058; 6652(e).

To encourage plan administrators to comply with the annual reporting requirements, in 1995 the Department of Labor created the Delinquent Filer Voluntary Compliance Program (DFVCP) for employee benefit plans that are subject to Title I of ERISA. This program is available to all plan sponsors who have failed to file a required annual report for plan years beginning on or after January 1, 1988, and who have not received a notice of delinquency from the Department of Labor for failure to file. Under the DFVCP, the plan administrator who voluntarily files a delinquent annual report is subject to substantially reduced penalties. See generally 67 Fed. Reg. 15,052 (March 28, 2002) (describing the purposes and history of the DFVCP).

Summary Annual Report and Annual Funding Notice

The annual report data is used by the plan administrator to produce either the summary annual report (SAR) or the annual funding notice. The SAR must be furnished to each plan participant and each beneficiary in a defined contribution plan or a welfare plan. ERISA §§ 101(a)(2); 104(b)(3). SARs and annual funding notices may be distributed to participants and beneficiaries using electronic media. Department of Labor regulations describe the requirements for the format and contents of the SAR. See DOL Reg. § 2520.104b–10. The content of the typical SAR for a defined contribution plan is minimal—a basic financial statement, a description of the minimum funding standards (if any) for the plan, and a statement of the participant's right to additional information. For welfare plans, the SAR includes insurance information, if applicable.

The annual funding notice must be provided to each participant and each beneficiary in a defined benefit plan. ERISA § 101(f)(1). The annual funding notice provides detailed information concerning the plan's funding status, assets and liabilities, the investment allocation of plan assets and the projected financial effect of any plan amendment or scheduled benefit increase. In addition, the annual funding notice must provide a description of ERISA's rules concerning plan termination and the plan benefits that are insured by the Pension Benefit Guaranty Corporation. See ERISA § 101(f)(2). Violation of the annual funding notice requirement subjects the plan administrator to a potential civil penalty, assessed by the federal courts, of up to $100 per day for each plan participant or beneficiary who was not given a timely notice. See ERISA § 502(c)(1).

Periodic Benefit Statement

ERISA Section 105 requires the plan administrator to provide a periodic benefit statement to participants in employee pension plans. Violation of the requirements for periodic benefit statements subjects the plan administrator to a potential civil penalty, assessed by the federal courts, of up to $100 per day for each plan participant who was not given a timely statement. See ERISA § 502(c)(1).

Every periodic benefit statement must describe the value of the participant's total accrued benefit under the pension plan and the participant's nonforfeitable portion of that accrued benefit. If the participant's accrued benefits are forfeitable, the statement must inform the participant of the earliest date at which his accrued benefits will become nonforfeitable. See ERISA § 105(a)(1)–(2).

For defined contribution plans, the benefit statement must include additional information concerning the value of each investment that is part of the participant's individual plan account. The statement must provide an explanation, written in a manner calculated to be understood by the average plan participant, of the importance of a well-balanced and diversified investment portfolio. The statement must provide a notice directing the participant to an internet web site sponsored by the Department of Labor for additional information on retirement investing. The statement further must contain an explicit warning that concentrating more than 20% of the participant's plan investments in a single investment, such as employer securities, may not be adequately diversified. See ERISA § 105(a)(2)(B).

These disclosure requirements are in response to research studies concerning the investment behavior of participants in 401(k) plans. These research studies, which are described in more detail later in Chapter Five, have found that some participants in 401(k) plans use retirement investment strategies that are likely to result in either excessive investment losses or less than a market rate of investment return over time.

Blackout Period Notice

ERISA Section 101(i) requires the plan administrator to provide at least thirty days' advance notice to all participants and beneficiaries of any blackout period during which the individual's right to direct or diversify investments, obtain a loan, or receive a distribution under the plan is temporarily suspended. A blackout period notice is not required to be given for certain one-participant retirement plans. See ERISA § 101(i)(8).

Congress enacted ERISA Section 101(i) in response to the plight of participants in the Enron Corporation 401(k) plan, who were unable to sell their holdings of Enron stock during a period of falling share prices while the plan was changing plan administrators. The purpose of the blackout period notice is to give plan participants and beneficiaries the opportunity to take appropriate actions with respect to their plan accounts in anticipation of a blackout period. Violation of the blackout notice requirement subjects the plan administrator to a potential civil penalty, assessed by the Secretary of Labor, of up to $100 a day for each plan participant who was not given a timely notice. See ERISA § 502(c)(7); DOL Reg. § 2560.502c–7.

Diversification Notice

Many publicly traded employers make matching and other employer contributions to the accounts of participants in defined contribution plans in the form of company stock. Under ERISA, participants with three years or more of service are permitted to diversify employer contributions to their plan accounts that are invested in publicly traded employer securities. See ERISA § 204(j)(3). Employee contributions to a defined contribution plan that are invested in publicly traded employer securities can be diversified by the participant at any time. See ERISA § 204(j)(2).

ERISA Section 101(m) requires the plan administrator to notify participants of these diversification rights. The plan administrator must provide each participant who is entitled to exercise a diversification right with a notice informing the participant of the right to diversify contributions that are invested in publicly traded employer securities at least 30 days prior to the commencement of the diversification right. ERISA § 101(m)(1). The diversification notice also must explain the importance of diversifying the investment of retirement plan assets. ERISA § 101(m)(2). Violation of the diversification notice requirement subjects the plan administrator to a potential civil penalty, assessed by the Secretary of Labor, of up to $100 per day for each plan participant who was not given a timely notice. See ERISA § 502(c)(7).

"Upon Request" Disclosures and Other Information

ERISA Section 104(b)(4) requires the plan administrator to furnish to any participant who makes a written request "the latest updated summary plan description, and the latest annual report, any terminal report, the bargaining agreement, trust agreement, contract, or other instruments under which the plan is established or operated." A similar request may be made by the Secretary of Labor, often on behalf of a plan participant. See ERISA § 104(a)(6); DOL Reg. § 2520.104a–8.

The plan administrator has up to 30 days to furnish the requested information. This requirement is satisfied if the plan administrator mails the requested materials to the last known address of the participant or beneficiary within 30 days of receiving the request. If the plan administrator fails to furnish the requested information within this 30-day period, ERISA Section 502(c)(1) gives the federal courts discretion to declare the plan administrator personally liable in an amount of up to $100 per day to each participant who requested the information. The Secretary of Labor may assess a penalty of up to $100 a day (not to exceed $1,000 per request) if the plan administrator fails to provide requested plan information to the Department of Labor within 30 days. ERISA § 502(c)(6). *Glocker v. W.R. Grace & Co.*, reproduced below, is typical of situations where the federal courts impose a penalty on the plan administrator under ERISA Section 502(c)(1).

GLOCKER V. W.R. GRACE & CO.

United States Court of Appeals, Fourth Circuit, 1995.
19 Employee Benefits Cas. 2227.

Elma A. Glocker appeals from the district court's award of summary judgment to W.R. Grace & Company and Aetna Insurance Company (collectively, Grace) on her claims for failure to pay medical benefits and for a civil penalty. We affirm the denial of benefits, reverse the district court's refusal to award a civil penalty, and remand for assessment of a reasonable penalty.

I

The facts pertinent to this appeal are set forth in our opinion in *Glocker v. W.R. Grace & Co.*, 974 F.2d 540, 542 (4th Cir.1992) (*Glocker I*), and we summarize them here.

Edwin Glocker retired from Grace in 1973 and was entitled to medical benefits under a Medicare Supplemented Benefit-I Plan, which, taken together with a Comprehensive Medical Expense Benefits-VI Plan, constitute Grace's Plan. Mr. Glocker was hospitalized in 1988 with advanced prostate cancer. While in the hospital, he employed several private-duty nurses. His physician, Dr. Schirmer, recommended the employment of nurses to ensure that Mr. Glocker not choke on his saliva or phlegm, remove intravenous tubes, or increase the risk of pneumonia by lying on his back. The nurses were also to notice any instances of apnea and to monitor his supply of oxygen. Dr. Schirmer did not think the staff nurses could adequately guard against these risks because of their workload.

After Mr. Glocker died, Mrs. Glocker filed a claim seeking reimbursement for the cost of the private-duty nurses. Grace denied the request on the basis that the nurses provided custodial care, which was not covered by the Plan.

Mrs. Glocker sued Grace, charging that it had improperly denied benefits and that it had violated the disclosure provisions of ERISA by failing to supply her with portions of the Plan in a timely manner. The district court granted summary judgment to Grace, finding that it had not abused its discretion in denying benefits and that civil penalties were not appropriate.

In *Glocker I* we vacated the district court's order and directed the court to consider the denial of benefits de novo, rather than under an abuse of discretion standard. We also directed the court to reconsider Mrs. Glocker's claim for civil penalties.

Reviewing Grace's denial of benefits de novo on remand, the district court again granted summary judgment to Grace, finding that the provisions of the Plan did not cover the care for which expenses were incurred. The court also denied Mrs. Glocker's claim for civil penalties, finding that any delay in producing documents did not prejudice her.

II

The general provisions of the Plan exclude from coverage expenses for custodial nursing care. Because Mr. Glocker was eligible for Medicare, he received benefits under Grace's Medicare Supplement Benefits-I plan. That plan states: "No Medicare Supplement Benefits are provided under the plan for charges for custodial care." Custodial care is defined as follows:

> Custodial care is care which consists of services and supplies, including board and room and other institutional services, furnished to an individual primarily to assist him in activities of daily living, whether or not he is disabled. These services and supplies are custodial care regardless of the practitioner or provider who prescribed, recommended or performed them.

> When board and room and skilled nursing services must be combined with other necessary therapeutic services and supplies in accordance with generally accepted medical standards to establish a program of medical treatment, they will not be considered custodial care. However, to meet this test they must be provided to an individual in an institution for which coverage is available under the plan and the program of medical treatment must be one which can reasonably be expected to substantially improve the individual's medical condition.

After examining the depositions of Dr. Schirmer and the private duty nurses, the court found that the primary function of the nurses was to assist Mr. Glocker in the tasks of everyday living by giving him baths, helping him brush his teeth, performing motion exercises with him, shaving his face when he could not, and so forth. The court concluded that the care provided was custodial in nature.

Next, the court found that the custodial care was not part of a program of treatment reasonably expected to substantially improve Mr. Glocker's condition. The court emphasized Dr. Schirmer's testimony that, because of the advanced stage of his cancer, no treatment could have improved Mr. Glocker's condition by the time he was admitted to the hospital. Relying on Dr. Schirmer's testimony, the court rejected Mrs. Glocker's argument that the term "substantial improvement" should be interpreted to include intermediate improvements such as diminution in pain.

The nurses who cared for Mr. Glocker testified that their primary function was to provide companionship and daily assistance to Mr. Glocker during his stay in the hospital. Dr. Schirmer, who was Mr.

Glocker's treating physician, stated repeatedly that Mr. Glocker's condition could not be "substantially improved," only moderated. We agree with the district court's analysis and affirm its judgment on this issue.

III

Under ERISA, a plan administrator must "upon written request of any participant or beneficiary, furnish a copy of the latest updated summary plan description, plan description ... contract, or other instruments under which the plan is established or operated." ERISA § 104(b)(4). Failure to comply with such a request within 30 days may, in the court's discretion, be punished by sanctions of up to $100 per day of delay. ERISA § 502(c)(1).

As early as June 19, 1989, Mrs. Glocker's attorney asked Grace in writing to supply "the whole policy." Sixteen repeated requests followed in subsequent months. The correspondence indicates rising levels of frustration on both sides; apparently, Grace had difficulty gathering all the pertinent documents from its voluminous files without undertaking an extensive process of review. On November 5, 1990, after Mrs. Glocker's attorney had filed a motion to compel and amended the complaint to include a count for civil penalties under ERISA, Grace provided the requested documents.

In declining to impose penalties, the district court placed great emphasis on its finding that Mrs. Glocker suffered no prejudice from Grace's delay. * * *

While prejudice is a factor to be considered, it is not an absolute requirement for imposing penalties under ERISA. In *Daughtrey v. Honeywell, Inc.*, 3 F.3d 1488, 1494–95 (11th Cir.1993), the court awarded penalties for an unexplained twelve-month delay by an employer. The court stated that a showing of prejudice to the claimant was not necessary, noting that the penalty provision of ERISA § 502(c) is unrelated to any injury suffered by the plan participant. Accord Moothart v. Bell, 21 F.3d 1499, 1506 (10th Cir.1994); Gillis v. Hoechst Celanese Corp., 4 F.3d 1137, 1148 (3d Cir.1993); Rodriguez-Abreu v. Chase Manhattan Bank, N.A., 986 F.2d 580, 588 (1st Cir.1993).

Where prejudice consists mainly of aggravation and frustration for the requesting party, courts have awarded penalties in the range of $10 to $30 per day. See, e.g., Moothart, 21 F.3d at 1506 (affirming district court's award of $30 per day where no substantial prejudice was shown); Daniel v. Eaton Corp., 839 F.2d 263, 268 (6th Cir.1988) (affirming district court's award of $25 per day where delay resulted from neglect or misfeasance and no prejudice was shown); Paris v. F. Korbel & Brothers, Inc., 751 F.Supp. 834, 839–40 (N.D. Cal.1990) (awarding $10 per day for technical violation where no prejudice was shown); Dehner v. Kansas City

Southern Ind., 713 F.Supp. 1397, 1401–02 (D. Kan.1989) (awarding $20 per day for delay, despite unreasonableness of plaintiff's initial request for documents); Porcellini v. Strassheim Printing Co., 578 F.Supp. 605, 614 (E.D. Pa.1983) (awarding $25 per day for unexcused three-month delay resulting from administrator's indifference to claimant's requests).

The district court found that Mrs. Glocker was not prejudiced because she was timely furnished relevant portions of the handbook and pages of the MSB-I pertaining to custodial care. It found that the Comprehensive Medical Expense Benefit-VI (CMEB-VI), which pertains to employees not entitled to Medicare, and the Medicare Supplemental Benefit (MSB-I), which pertained to Mr. Glocker, were not timely provided. The district court concluded that the defendant's delay in furnishing CMEB-VI did not cause prejudice because it did not apply to Mr. Glocker. With respect to MSB-I, the court found no prejudice because Grace timely provided the pages of this document pertaining to custodial care.

Actually, Mrs. Glocker did suffer some prejudice from Grace's delay. She was unable to firmly establish her cause of action until she possessed all the documents she had requested. As we noted in *Glocker I*, Mrs. Glocker was unable to determine that she was entitled to de novo review until she had received the entire Plan. 974 F.2d at 544.

Moreover, the district court's observation that Mr. Glocker was not covered by CMEB-VI is only partially accurate. MSB-I states that Medicare and the Plan will "provide a level of benefits at least as high as that previously provided by the Plan alone." MSB-I also states that benefits under Medicare are those which "Medicare will actually pay." Since Medicare does not pay for private-duty nursing, Mrs. Glocker needed CMEB-VI to ascertain what her previously provided benefits would be if she prevailed on her claim for reimbursement.

Grace points out that it acted in good faith in responding to Mrs. Glocker's requests. It explains that its failure to produce the Plan was hampered by its voluminous files and was inadvertent. While the absence of bad faith is a factor in determining whether penalties are warranted, it does not of itself exonerate the failure to provide a timely statement of benefits. Section 502(c)(1) excuses failure to comply with a request for information if it results "from matters reasonably beyond control of the administrator." Certainly, Grace's inadvertence and the complexities of its filing system were not beyond its control. Congress intended the ERISA disclosure provisions to ensure that "the individual participant knows exactly where he stands with respect to the plan. . . ." Firestone Tire & Rubber Co. v. Bruch, 489 U.S. 101, 118 (1988) (quoting H.R. Rep. No. 93–533, p. 11 (1973)). Only by receiving Grace's entire Plan, including CMEB-VI and MSB-I, could Mrs. Glocker know all pertinent information about her procedural rights and Mr. Glocker's benefits.

The purpose of the civil penalty provision is to encourage otherwise reluctant employers to provide beneficiaries with documents without undue delay, and to punish those who remain intransigent in the face of requests for information. The delay in this case calls for the assessment of penalties.

* * *

We remand the case with directions to the district court to award a civil penalty in a manner consistent with this opinion. The district court should take into account, among other factors, Grace's lack of bad faith, the prejudice to Mrs. Glocker, the length of the delay, the time and expense incurred by Mrs. Glocker's attorneys in their efforts to obtain Grace's Plan, and the amount needed to suitably punish Grace.

NOTES AND QUESTIONS

1. Was Mrs. Glocker prejudiced by the company's failure to provide the plan document? How? Did W.R. Grace & Co. gain a strategic advantage in the litigation by an 18 month delay in furnishing the plan document? Why or why not? If you were the district court judge on remand, what penalty amount would you assess against the employer under ERISA Section 502(c)(1)?

2. *Judicial Discretion in Awarding Statutory Penalties.* As indicated in *Glocker*, the district courts have wide latitude in assessing statutory penalties under Section 502(c)(1) against a plan administrator who fails to comply in a timely manner with a request for plan documents under Section 104(b)(4). Even if the plaintiff prevails on the underlying substantive ERISA claim, the district court may, in its discretion, refuse to award a statutory penalty or may award a nominal amount. Compare Nair v. Pfizer, Inc., 47 Empl. Benefits Cas. (BNA) 1074 (D.N.J. 2009) (awarding summary judgment for plaintiff on claim for plan benefits, but denying request for statutory penalties because "Plaintiff was not diligent in pursuing the documents"), with Arnone v. CA, Inc., 46 Empl. Benefits Cas. (BNA) 1076 (S.D.N.Y. 2009) (awarding judgment for plaintiff on claim for plan benefits, but finding that a statutory penalty of $10,000 for a delay of over a year in providing requested plan documents was "sufficient to deter similar misconduct in the future").

Should the district court consider the ability of the defendant to pay in deciding whether to award statutory penalties under Section 502(c)(1)? In *Leister v. Dovetail, Inc.,* 546 F.3d 875 (7th Cir. 2008), the district court found that the individual defendants, who were plan fiduciaries as well as the owners of the business, had breached their fiduciary duties by pocketing the plaintiff's salary deferral contributions to her 401(k) plan account and failing to make required employer matching contributions. The district court refused to award a statutory penalty under Section 502(c)(1) based on the "precarious financial condition" of the defendants. The Seventh Circuit reversed the district court's refusal to award a statutory penalty as an abuse of discretion:

The aim of penalties, whatever form they take (fines, punitive damages, or, as in this case, statutory penalties), is to deter; and the poorer the defendant, the lower the penalty can be set and still deter wrongdoers in the same financial stratum. Picking the right penalty in light of such considerations, like picking a federal criminal sentence within a statutory range, inescapably involves judgment, and so judicial review of the trial judge's determination is light. . . .But given the willful character of the defendants' breach. . .the award of zero penalties was unreasonable.

It is true that "many courts have refused to impose any penalty at all under § 502(c)(1) in the absence of a showing of prejudice or bad faith." Bartling v. Fruehauf Corp. 29 F.3d 1062, 1068–69 (6th Cir. 1994). But in this case there was both prejudice and bad faith. The failure to award penalties was, in the circumstances, an abuse of discretion.

Leister, 546 F.3d at 883–84 (other citations omitted). Upon remand, the district court awarded statutory penalties totaling $377,600 against the individual defendants, who were jointly and severally liable along with the company for the penalty amount.

3. NOTE ON REPORTING AND DISCLOSURE REQUIREMENTS UNIQUE TO HEALTH CARE PLANS

The Affordable Care Act created additional reporting and disclosure requirements that are unique to group health plans for employees. These requirements supplement ERISA's general reporting and disclosure requirements. In part because the ACA requirements also apply to governmental and church plans that are not subject to Title I of ERISA, Congress enacted these requirements as amendments to the Public Health Services Act, 42 U.S.C. § 300gg et seq. (PHSA), and incorporated these requirements by reference into ERISA and the Code. See ERISA § 715 (incorporating by reference the requirements of part A of title XXVII of the PHSA for group health plans, with limited exceptions for self-insured plans).

Disclosures to Plan Participants

Plan administrators for all group health plans must notify participants no later than 60 days *before* any material modification in the terms or coverage of the plan. ACA § 1001 (adding PHSA § 2715(d)(4)). This requirement supersedes ERISA Section 104(b)(1), which requires that a summary of material modifications must be provided to the participants in a group health plan within 60 days *after* the modification is implemented. See ERISA § 104(b)(1); DOL Reg. § 2520.104b–3(d).

In addition to the general SPD requirements of ERISA Section 104, participants in all group health plans must receive a second, more concise summary of plan benefits and coverage in accordance with regulations issued by the Department of Health and Human Services (HHS). The *HHS summary of benefits and coverage* must contain:

- Uniform definitions of insurance and medical terms;
- A description of the scope of coverage and any participant cost-sharing requirements for each category of essential health benefits or other benefits provided under the plan;
- Exceptions, reductions and limitations in coverage;
- Provisions describing the terms and conditions for renewability and continuation of coverage;
- Illustrations of coverage under common benefits scenarios;
- A statement concerning whether the plan meets the federal standard for minimum individual coverage required for individuals beginning in 2014 under the Affordable Care Act;
- A warning that the HHS summary of benefits and coverage is only an outline and that the participant should consult the actual plan or policy language;
- A web site address where the actual plan or policy language may be found; and
- A contact number that participants in the plan may call for additional information.

See ACA § 1001 (adding PHSA § 2715); 77 Fed. Reg. 8668 (Feb. 14, 2012).

The HHS summary of benefits and coverage cannot exceed four pages in length or be written in print that is smaller than 12 point font. The summary must be "presented in a culturally and linguistically appropriate manner" and utilize "terminology understandable by the average plan enrollee." ACA § 1001; PHSA § 2715(b)(1)–(2). The penalty for a willful failure to provide the HHS summary of benefits and coverage in accordance with HHS regulations is up to $1,000 per enrollee in the plan. ACA § 1001; PHSA § 2715(f).

Reporting to Federal Agencies

Many of the provisions of the Affordable Care Act distinguish between grandfathered plans and non-grandfathered plans. A *grandfathered plan* is one that was in existence on March 23, 2010, and that subsequently has not been changed in a way that causes the plan to lose its grandfathered status. A *non-grandfathered plan* is either a new plan that is established after March 23, 2010, or a preexisting plan that has lost its grandfathered status due to changes made to the plan after March 23, 2010. The distinctions between grandfathered and non-grandfathered plans are described in more detail later in Chapter Four of the casebook.

For purposes of reporting to federal agencies, the ACA establishes new annual reporting requirements for group health plans regarding the quality of care provided to plan participants. The content of these quality of care reports, which are to be submitted to the HHS, differ for grandfathered and non-grandfathered group health plans. Enforcement of these new annual reporting requirements, which were to become effective in 2012, has been suspended until further regulatory guidance is issued.

Once regulatory guidance is issued, non-grandfathered group health plans must provide an annual report to the HHS that provides information on the quality of care provided by the plan. The annual *HHS quality of care report* must include information concerning whether the plan:

- Improved health outcomes through activities such as quality reporting, case management, care coordination, and chronic disease management;
- Implemented activities to prevent hospital readmission, improve patient safety, and reduce medical services; and
- Implemented wellness and health promotion activities.

See ACA § 1001 (adding PHSA § 2717). The plan administrator must provide the plan's participants with a copy of the HHS quality of care report.

Non-grandfathered group health plans also must report to the HHS and make available to the public additional information, including:

- Claims payment policies and practices;
- Periodic financial disclosures;
- Enrollment and disenrollment data;
- Data on the number of denied claims;
- Data on rating practices; and
- Information on participant cost-sharing and payments made for out-of-network coverage.

See ACA § 1001 (adding PHSA § 2715A).

The Affordable Care Act requires in general that every individual must have *minimum essential coverage* of health care services or else pay a tax penalty. This individual coverage mandate was held to be constitutional by the Supreme Court in *NFIB v. Sebelius*, 132 S. Ct. 2566 (2012). To make minimum essential coverage more available and affordable for individuals, the ACA requires employers with 50 or more full-time equivalent employees to either provide minimum essential coverage to their full-time employees at an affordable premium price for coverage under a plan that provides at least 60% minimum actuarial value or else pay a tax penalty for noncompliance. Premium assistance tax credits are available for qualifying low-income persons to use to offset the cost of purchasing an individual health insurance policy through an on-line health insurance marketplace (officially known as the "American Health Benefit Exchanges" or just an "Exchange" for short). Finally, the ACA expands the scope of Medicaid coverage by requiring the states to provide Medicaid coverage to adults with incomes of up to 133% of the federal poverty level. This expansion of Medicaid was rendered optional for state governments as a result of the Supreme Court's decision in *NFIB v. Sebelius*. The employer mandate, the Exchange system, and the Supreme Court's decision in *NFIB v. Sebelius* are explained in more detail later in Chapter Four of the casebook.

To assist the Internal Revenue Service in administering and enforcing the individual coverage mandate, the ACA requires all employers who provide minimum essential coverage for their employees to report information concerning the employees who are covered under the group health plan and the premiums charged by the plan. Under the ACA, the Internal Revenue Service is authorized to disclose individual income tax information to the HHS and state-sponsored Medicaid programs to verify an individual's income eligibility for assistance in obtaining minimum essential coverage, either by qualifying for a state-operated Medicaid program or by using a premium assistance tax credit to purchase an individual health insurance policy on an Exchange.

On July 2, 2013, the Treasury Department announced that enforcement of the employer mandate and all related reporting requirements would not begin to be phased in until 2015, with full implementation to begin in 2016. This delay did not, however, affect access to the premium assistance tax credits available to qualifying individuals to offset the cost of purchasing an insurance policy through an Exchange.

One reporting requirement for employers that remained in effect is the requirement that employers who sponsor group health plans must report the cost of plan coverage for each employee to the Internal Revenue Service on Form W-2. The cost of plan coverage is based on the premium amount that would be charged for plan continuation coverage under the Consolidated Omnibus Budget Reconciliation Act of 1985 (COBRA). See ACA § 9002 (amending Code § 6051(a)). Although required to be reported on Form W-2, the cost of plan coverage that is paid by the employer is excluded from the gross income of the employee and is not subject to federal or state income taxation. Employers who file fewer than 250 Form W-2's and plan administrators for multiemployer plans are not required to report the cost of plan coverage until further regulatory guidance is issued by the Internal Revenue Service. See IRS Notice 2012–9.

4. NOTE ON ESTOPPEL CLAIMS

Estoppel claims typically arise when a plan participant or beneficiary expects, based on written or oral representations made by the plan administrator, to receive a certain benefit under the plan. When the participant or beneficiary later receives a less generous benefit than the individual anticipated (or no benefit at all), the individual seeks to force the plan and its administrator to furnish the expected benefit under the equitable doctrine of estoppel. Estoppel cases often arise when a conflict exists between the terms of the plan and the SPD, or when a participant or beneficiary asks the plan administrator to provide an oral explanation of an ambiguous provision in the plan or the SPD.

Estoppel is not authorized expressly as a statutory claim under ERISA. See ERISA § 502(a). Rather, it is a claim that has been recognized by the federal courts under their authority to develop a body of federal common law governing the rights and obligations under ERISA-regulated plans. See Franchise Tax Bd. v. Construction Laborers Vacation Trust, 463 U.S. 1, 24 n. 26 (1983).

In developing the federal common law of estoppel under ERISA, the federal courts have balanced competing policy concerns. First, the written instrument rule of ERISA Section 402(a)(1) emphasizes the importance of abiding by the terms of the written plan document. Second, the requirement under ERISA Section 402(b)(3) that the plan document must specify a formal procedure for amending the terms of the plan deters the allegation that other "informal" writings or oral statements amended the plan's written terms. Third, under the settlor function doctrine "plan sponsors are generally free under ERISA, for any reason at any time, to adopt, modify, or terminate welfare plans." Curtiss-Wright Corp. v. Schoonejongen, 514 U.S. 73, 79 (1995). This right of the plan sponsor also extends to the modification or termination of future accrued benefits offered under a pension plan. See Hughes Aircraft Co. v. Jacobson, 525 U.S. 432, 443–44 (1999). Balanced against these policy concerns, which generally favor the employer in estoppel litigation, are ERISA's overall purpose of protecting the rights of plan participants and beneficiaries concerning plan benefits, and the important role that ERISA's disclosure requirements, particularly the SPD, play in effective enforcement of these rights.

Due to its nature as a federal common law claim and remedy, a considerable degree of variation exists among the federal circuits concerning the required elements for a valid estoppel claim and the factors that the court will consider when determining whether the plaintiff should prevail. As you read the description of these variations below, try to identify the underlying policy or policies that are at stake. Do you agree with the balancing of policy interests that the requirement or factor represents? If not, how would you change the law to strike a more appropriate balance?

Basic Elements Required for Estoppel

To assert estoppel, the plaintiff generally must prove the following elements:

- A misrepresentation of material fact;
- Actual and reasonable reliance on the misrepresentation; and
- Detriment to the individual resulting from reliance on the misrepresentation.

Beyond these common elements, each circuit has developed its own particular requirements necessary to establish a claim for estoppel. These requirements vary depending on the circumstances that give rise to the plaintiff's estoppel claim. Estoppel claims typically arise in two types of factual situations. In situation one, the SPD provides more generous benefits than the terms of the written plan document. In situation two, a plan fiduciary has made other written or oral representations that are inconsistent with the plan's written terms.

As a general rule, an estoppel claim is more likely to prevail if the statements relied upon by the plaintiff were contained in the formal SPD (situation one) than if the claim is based on other informal written or oral statements made to the plaintiff (situation two). Numerous circuit-specific nuances have evolved in addressing estoppel claims in each of these two situations.

Situation One: Estoppel Claims Based on the Summary Plan Description

When the terms of the plan document are unambiguous, but the SPD provides a more generous benefit, awarding the more generous benefit described in the SPD would be contrary to the terms of the written plan document. Nevertheless, in this situation the federal courts routinely award the more generous SPD benefit to the plaintiff under an estoppel theory. E.g., Washington v. Murphy Oil USA, Inc., 497 F.3d 453, 456 (5th Cir. 2007); Burstein v. Retirement Account Plan for Employees of Allegheny Health Education and Research Foundation, 334 F.3d 365, 377–78 & n.18 (3d Cir. 2003) (adopting the rule embraced by numerous other circuits that in the event of conflict between the plan and the SPD, the SPD controls). Awarding the more generous SPD benefit is viewed as furthering "Congress's desire that the SPD be transparent, accurate, and comprehensive." Burstein, 334 F.3d at 378. The plaintiff's estoppel claim based on the representations in the SPD is even more compelling when the terms of the plan document itself are ambiguous or silent. See Hansen v. Continental Ins. Co., 940 F.2d 971, 982 (5th Cir. 1991) ("Any burden of uncertainty created by careless or inaccurate drafting of the [SPD] must be placed on those who do the drafting, and who are most able to bear that burden, and not on the individual employee, who is powerless to affect the drafting of the [SPD] * * * and ill equipped to bear the burden of the financial hardship that might result from a misleading or confusing document.").

Prior to the Supreme Court's decision in *Cigna Corp. v. Amara*, 131 S. Ct. 1866 (2011), the federal circuits disagreed concerning whether the plaintiff had to demonstrate actual reliance on the statements made in the SPD. See Washington, 497 F.3d at 458 (describing the divisions among the circuits); Burstein, 334 F.3d at 380–82 (same). Some circuits required the plaintiff to show actual reliance on the terms of the SPD, along with resulting prejudice or detriment to the plaintiff. E.g., Collins v. American Cast Iron Pipe Co., 105 F.3d 1368, 1371 (11th Cir. 1997) (plaintiff failed to establish reliance element of estoppel claim because he admitted he had not read the SPD). Other circuits viewed an estoppel claim based on the terms of the SPD as essentially contractual in nature and did not require proof of actual reliance on the SPD's terms. E.g., Burstein, 334 F.3d at 381. In *Cigna Corp. v. Amara*, the Supreme Court held that when the plaintiff makes an estoppel claim based on the more generous terms of the SPD, the claim is one for "appropriate equitable relief" under Section 502(a)(3) of ERISA. The *Amara* Court further held that proof of actual reliance by the plaintiff on the terms of the SPD is necessary for an estoppel claim:

> [W]hen equity courts used the remedy of *estoppel*, they insisted upon a showing akin to detrimental reliance, i.e., that the defendant's statement in truth, influenced the conduct of the plaintiff, causing prejudice. Accordingly, when a court exercises its authority under § 502(a)(3) to impose a remedy equivalent to estoppel, a showing of detrimental reliance must be made.

131 S. Ct. at 1881 (emphasis in original, quotations and citations omitted). The full opinion in *Amara* is reproduced later in Chapter Six of the casebook. The practical effect of the Supreme Court's ruling in *Amara* is the elimination of class action claims based on an estoppel theory due to the required showing of actual and detrimental reliance.

To prevent estoppel claims based on the terms of the SPD, employers often insert a disclaimer clause in the SPD, stating that in the event the provisions of the SPD conflict with the plan document, the terms of the plan document will control. The circuits are divided concerning whether such disclaimers are enforceable against plan participants and beneficiaries. Some courts view the existence of the disclaimer as rendering the plaintiff's reliance on the SPD terms unreasonable, thereby precluding an estoppel claim. E.g., Pisciotta v. Teledyne Indus., 91 F.3d 1326, 1331 (9th Cir. 1996); de Nobel v. Vitro Corp., 885 F.2d 1180, 1195

(4th Cir. 1989). Courts refusing to recognize a disclaimer provision generally do so based on the policy rationale that enforcing the disclaimer would undermine the purpose of the SPD. As the Eleventh Circuit explained in *McKnight v. Southern Life & Health Insurance Co.*, 758 F.2d 1566 (11th Cir. 1985), "[i]t is of no effect to publish and distribute a plan summary booklet designed to simplify and explain a voluminous and complicated document, and then proclaim that any inconsistencies will be governed by the plan. Unfairness will flow to the employee for reasonably relying on the summary booklet." Id. at 1570.

Numerous estoppel cases involve a "vested" benefits claim where the plaintiff believes that the plaintiff has a nonforfeitable right to benefits under a welfare plan under the terms of the SPD, and the employer later modifies or terminates the plaintiff's welfare plan benefits. Many of these cases involve health care or other insurance benefits provided to retirees. Such cases often turn on whether the plan document contains a clause that unambiguously reserves to the employer the right to modify or terminate the benefits provided by the welfare benefit plan. For example, in *In re Unisys Corp. Retiree Medical Benefit ERISA Litigation*, 58 F.3d 896 (3d Cir. 1995), the SPD stated that retiree medical benefits would be available "for life." The retiree medical plan itself, however, unambiguously reserved the employer's right to modify or terminate the benefits provided by the retiree medical plan "at any time" and "for any reason." When the employer terminated the retiree medical plan, the retirees who had been receiving benefits under the plan, brought suit arguing that the employer was estopped from terminating the plan by the guarantee of "for life" made in the SPD. The Third Circuit ruled that this unambiguous reservation of rights clause in the plan document rendered the plaintiffs' reliance upon on the SPD's guarantee of benefits "for life" unreasonable as a matter of law. See id. at 903–04. Given that any future change or reduction in a retiree's benefits is likely to trigger an estoppel claim, employers today routinely include a reservation of rights clause in the SPD of every plan (whether a pension plan or a welfare plan) to preclude such claims in the event the plan is later amended or terminated.

Situation Two: Estoppel Based On Other Informal Written or Oral Representations

When the plaintiff's estoppel claim is based on representations other than the written terms of the SPD, such as written correspondence or oral communications between the plan administrator and individual plan participants, the federal courts generally are much more reluctant to permit estoppel. Permitting estoppel based on informal written or oral statements undermines the integrity of the written plan document's formal amendment procedures and ERISA's mandatory form of formal disclosure—the SPD. For this reason, most circuits require that the plaintiff must demonstrate "extraordinary circumstances" to establish an estoppel claim based on informal written or oral statements. See, e.g., Mello v. Sara Lee Corp., 431 F.3d 440, 444–45 (5th Cir. 2005). Although the Supreme Court in *Amara* did not address lower court decisions applying the "extraordinary circumstances" criteria, the *Amara* Court did note in dicta that the scope of "appropriate equity relief" available under Section 502(a)(3) could include "reformation of the terms of the the the plan, in order to remedy the false or misleading information [that the employer] provided." Amara, 131 S.Ct. at 1879. Thus, the "extraordinary circumstances" line of precedent appears to be consistent in principle with the *Amara* decision (at least until the Supreme Court indicates otherwise)

Extraordinary circumstances exist where there is an affirmative act of fraud or deception, a pattern or practice of making misrepresentations to participants over an extended period of time, or an intentional misrepresentation designed to induce the participant to take some action. Mere injustice or prejudice to the plaintiff does not give rise to extraordinary circumstances. See, e.g., Bloemker v. Laborers' Local 265 Pension Fund, 605 F.3d 436 (6th Cir. 2010) (extraordinary circumstances existed where plan administrator certified erroneous early retirement pension amount as correct and paid incorrect amount to participant for 22 months); Pell v. E.I. DuPont de Nemours & Co., Inc., 539 F.3d 292 (3d Cir. 2008) (extraordinary circumstances existed where benefit plan administrator repeatedly misrepresented amount of participant's pension benefit); Schonholz v. Long Island Jewish Med. Ctr., 87 F.3d 72 (2d Cir. 1996) (extraordinary circumstances existed where employer promised a severance benefit to employee to induce employee's voluntary termination of employment and then terminated severance plan so that ex-employee would not receive the severance benefit); Smith v. Hartford Ins. Group, 6 F.3d 131 (3d Cir. 1993) (extraordinary circumstances existed where employer repeatedly misrepresented that the employer's new health insurance plan would cover medical treatment needed by participant's wife).

Defining the parameters of "extraordinary circumstances" has proven difficult for the federal courts. For example, do extraordinary circumstances exist where an employer intentionally promises lifetime life insurance benefits to lure employees from other firms paying higher salaries, and later reduces the plan's life insurance benefits? Should it make a difference whether or not the employer reserved its right to amend the insurance plan benefits in the SPD? Compare Devlin v. Empire Blue Cross & Blue Shield, 274 F.3d 76 (2d Cir. 2001) (extraordinary circumstances necessary to support estoppel claim may exist where employer did not reserve right to change "lifetime" life insurance benefits in the SPD) with Abbruscato v. Empire Blue Cross and Blue Shield, 274 F.3d 90 (2d Cir. 2001) (extraordinary circumstances necessary to support estoppel claim may exist where SPD reserved employer's right to change benefits).

When informal communications are the basis for the plaintiff's claim, some circuits draw a sharp distinction between a pension plan and a welfare plan, and between a single employer plan and a multiemployer plan. In *Black v. TIC Investment Corp.*, 900 F.2d 112 (7th Cir. 1990), the Seventh Circuit explained the reasons for drawing these distinctions:

> [E]ven among courts that recognize the availability of estoppel in ERISA cases, there is real resistance to the use of that doctrine. The reason ordinarily cited for this reluctance (and for earlier refusals to allow estoppel at all) is a concern for the actuarial soundness of the ERISA plan. There are two types of ERISA plans: pension plans, which are funded and have strict vesting and accrual requirements; and welfare plans such as the one involved in this case, which have no such requirements. In the case of an unfunded welfare plan, there is no particular fund which is depleted by paying benefits. Thus, there is no need for concern about the plan's actuarial soundness.

> One scholar, noting the trend toward allowing use of estoppel in ERISA cases, has noted that where estoppel is disallowed, the pension plan involved is ordinarily a multiemployer plan. The reason for reluctance in such cases is the fact that the plan has multiple fiduciaries with control over a common fund. To allow one employer to bind the fund to pay benefits outside the strict terms of the plan would be to make all the employers pay for one employer's misrepresentations, and to the extent that such payments damage the actuarial soundness of the plan, it hurts all the employees as well. It could even encourage employers to make intentional misrepresentations so as to bind the plan to make improper payments in favor of their own employees.

Id. at 115 (citations omitted). Are the distinctions described in *Black* relevant when an estoppel claim is made against a health care plan that is funded by a combination of employer and employee contributions? Against a health care plan that provides benefits through a policy of insurance? As a practical matter, who ultimately bears the costs of the misleading communications with the plaintiff if the estoppel claim prevails?

In addressing estoppel situations based on oral statements, the federal courts draw a sharp line between circumstances where the oral statement is contrary to the unambiguous terms of the written plan document or SPD, and circumstances where the oral statement can be characterized as merely a verbal interpretation of an ambiguous provision in the plan document or SPD. When the written plan terms are unambiguous, the federal courts generally will not allow an oral statement to modify the terms of the plan through an estoppel claim. In this circumstance, permitting estoppel would contradict the statutory requirement that the plan terms (and any amendments) must be in writing. E.g., Ladouceur v. Credit Lyonnais, 584 F.3d 510, 512–13 (2d Cir. 2009); Perreca v. Gluck, 295 F.3d 215, 225 (2d Cir. 2002) (oral promises cannot vary the written terms of an ERISA plan); Slice v. Sons of Norway, 34 F.3d 630, 634 (8th Cir. 1994); Smith v. Dunham-Bush, Inc., 959 F.2d 6, 7, 10 (2d Cir. 1992) ("The writing requirement [of ERISA Section 402(a)(1)] protects employees from having their benefits eroded by oral modifications to the plan.") Rejecting estoppel based on oral misrepresentations also furthers the policy purpose of encouraging participants and beneficiaries to rely on the terms of the written plan document and its accompanying SPD. See Frahm v. Equitable Life Assurance Soc'y, 137 F.3d 955, 961 (7th Cir. 1998) (holding that bad advice delivered orally does not entitle an individual to whatever the oral statement promised when the written documents provided accurate information).

When the written terms of the plan or the SPD are ambiguous, judicial concern over preserving the integrity of written plan terms is no longer a determinative factor. Where the plan document or SPD provides incomplete or ambiguous information, the plan administrator's oral statements are likely to be characterized as an "interpretation" of the written terms. In these oral interpretation cases, the plan administrator's verbal explanation can form the basis for an estoppel claim and remedy without undermining ERISA's policies concerning written plan terms and disclosures. E.g., Bowerman v. Wal-Mart Stores, Inc., 226 F.3d 574, 588–90 (7th Cir. 2000).

Given this strong judicial reluctance to recognize estoppel based on oral statements, after the Supreme Court's decision in *Varity Corp. v. Howe*, 516 U.S. 489 (1996), plaintiffs have tended to rely on the fiduciary's duty to inform rather than a theory of estoppel in situations involving oral misrepresentations. The fiduciary duty to inform is discussed Chapter Five of the casebook.

E. DISCUSSION QUESTIONS FOR CHAPTER TWO

QUESTION ONE

Your firm's client, a large corporation, has just hired a new company vice-president for operations. The company's president and the incoming vice-president have orally agreed to a substantial severance package for the new vice-president, "just in case things don't work out." Under this oral understanding, the new vice-president will receive her salary for a period of five years if her employment is terminated "for any reason whatsoever, or no reason at all."

The company president has asked you to memorialize this agreement in writing. Based on the reading material in Chapter Two, what ERISA issues should you consider in preparing this severance agreement?

QUESTION TWO

Discuss what documents you would want to examine and how you would acquire these documents in each of the following situations:

A. Your client Alex comes to you and asks you to represent him in negotiations to acquire all of the stock of Nox Company. Alex tells you that he is a little concerned about the potential liability associated with the Nox Company Retirement Plan, which "hasn't been run too well in the last several years."

B. Your client Barbara comes to you and asks you to represent her. Barbara's child Cathy has a rare form of cancer. Cathy's doctor has told Barbara that the Mayo Clinic has developed a new treatment for this type of cancer, and the preliminary results are promising. The treatment costs $450,000 if it is not covered by the patient's health insurance policy. Barbara has family coverage under a group insurance policy through her employer, Echo Company. Barbara spoke to the Echo Company human resources manager about whether the plan would pay for Cathy's treatment under the Mayo Clinic program. The response of the human resources manager was "I doubt it—it sounds experimental to me. Our health insurance plan doesn't cover experimental treatments." Barbara is concerned about "making a big deal of this at work by bringing a lawyer into it," but nevertheless wants you to advise her concerning her rights under her health insurance plan.

QUESTION THREE

A. Refer to the facts in Part A of Question Two above. Assume that instead of cooperating with your request for documents as part of your due diligence efforts, the human resources manager of Nox Company calls the company president, who tells you to "get out of here and don't come back!" Back at your office, you receive a phone call from your client Alex. Alex tells you that "he really wants this deal to go through" and he "doesn't mind that risky retirement plan." What should you do to:

- Protect yourself from a future malpractice liability lawsuit?
- Protect your client through language in the agreement for the acquisition of Nox Company?

B. Assume that your client Alex acquires Nox Company. A few weeks later, the human resources manager of Nox Company (the same one who kicked you out of his office) calls and tells you, "Now that you're my lawyer, I need you to help me fix a couple of problems with our retirement plan."

Who is your client in this situation? Nox Company? The human resources manager? Why might this matter?

QUESTION FOUR

The Pension Protection Act of 2006 required that periodic benefit statements must include a notice referring plan participants to a Department of Labor site on retirement planning and investment diversification. Is referring plan participants to a web site sufficient? Should employers be required to provide more information on retirement savings and related investment practices directly to plan participants?

QUESTION FIVE

As you review the subject matter of each chapter in this casebook, it is helpful to compile your own personal list of issues that are likely to arise in the course of your future practice. For example:

A. If you are a future litigator, what have you learned so far in this course that may prove useful in litigating issues involving employee benefit plans?

B. If you are a future corporate lawyer or in-house corporate counsel, what have you learned concerning your corporate client's legal duties concerning the establishment and administration of its employee benefit plans?

Repeating this exercise on your own at the end of every chapter will help you to learn this field of law and to more easily identify the connections among the topics covered in the subsequent chapters of the casebook.

CHAPTER 3

QUALIFIED RETIREMENT PLANS

■ ■ ■

Chapter Three provides an introduction to qualified retirement plans sponsored by private employers. The term *qualified retirement plan or qualified plan* refers to an employee pension plan under ERISA that also complies with the requirements of Section 401(a) of the Internal Revenue Code (Code). In other words, qualified plans are a subset of the larger universe of employee pension plans regulated by Title I of ERISA.

QRP's are employee pension plans under ERISA that conform to 40 1(a) of IRC

According to the Investment Company Institute, assets held in qualified plans sponsored by private employers totaled over *eight trillion dollars* at the end of the first quarter in 2014. Given the significant amount of money at stake, it is not surprising that qualified plans are regulated heavily under federal law. The resulting legal labyrinth presents a daunting challenge for those lawyers who specialize in the field of federal regulation and taxation of qualified plans. Among practitioners, lawyers who practice in this highly technical field are known as "ERISA tax" or "pension tax" lawyers.

Chapter Three is not intended to make you an ERISA tax lawyer. Rather, the purpose of Chapter Three is to present the various contexts in which issues concerning qualified plans arise in the general practice of law. The materials contained in Chapter Three are designed to give you a basic understanding of the fundamental legal rules that govern qualified plans and an appreciation of the public policies that underlie these rules. Your primary objective in studying this material should be to learn to recognize relevant issues.

Chapter Three begins by discussing the significance of qualified plans for national retirement policy and for the general practice of law. Section B introduces the basic concepts and vocabulary associated with qualified plans. Section C describes the distinct types and characteristics of qualified plans. Sections D and E address the duplicate requirements of the Code and ERISA for eligibility, vesting, and benefit accrual for participants in qualified plans. Section F explains the major design features of qualified plans that are required by the Code's nondiscrimination rules. Chapter Three concludes by focusing on several areas of private legal practice where qualified plan issues often arise. Section G looks at qualified plan issues in the context of bankruptcy and divorce. Section H discusses several important issues involving qualified plans that may arise in the representation of corporate clients.

A. PERSPECTIVES ON QUALIFIED RETIREMENT PLANS

1. NATIONAL RETIREMENT POLICY: THE TWIN PROBLEMS OF ELDERLY POVERTY AND RETIREMENT PLAN COVERAGE

The Problem of Elderly Poverty

National retirement policy seeks to mitigate the pressing social problem of elderly poverty for future generations of retirees. In 2012, there were 43.1 million persons age 65 and older (the elderly or elderly persons). Elderly persons represented 13.7% of the United States population in 2012. By 2040 the elderly population in the United States is projected to increase to 79.1 million persons. See U.S. DEPT. OF HEALTH AND HUMAN SERVICES, ADMINISTRATION ON AGING, A PROFILE OF OLDER AMERICANS: 2013.

The median income of elderly persons in 2012 was $27,612 for males and $16,040 for females. Over 3.9 million elderly persons were below the poverty level in 2012. Another 2.4 million or 5.5% of the elderly were classified as "near-poor" (income between the poverty level and 125% of the poverty level). For all elderly persons who reported their income in 2012 (41.8 million), 17% reported less than $10,000 and 41% reported $25,000 or less. Elderly women had a higher poverty rate (11%) than elderly men (6.6%). Elderly persons living alone were much more likely to be poor (16.8%) than were elderly persons living with families (5.4%). The highest poverty rates were experienced by elderly Hispanic women (41.6%) and elderly Black women (33%) who lived alone. See PROFILE OF OLDER AMERICANS: 2013.

The lower an elderly person's income, the less likely the elderly person is receiving retirement benefits from a qualified plan. Low-income elderly persons are heavily dependent on Social Security benefits. For elderly persons in the lowest income quintile, Social Security accounted for 82.5% of income as compared to 16.1% for those in the highest income quintile. See AARP Policy Inst. Sources of Income for Older Americans, 2012 Fact Sheet.

Public Attitudes and Preparedness for Retirement

The Retirement Confidence Survey (Survey) annually assesses public attitudes and preparedness for retirement. The Survey results consistently have shown that a majority of Americans are cautiously optimistic that they will have enough money to live comfortably during retirement, despite (or perhaps because of) widespread ignorance and apathy concerning retirement financial planning.

false hope

The 2014 Survey found that 18% of workers were "very confident" and 37% were "somewhat confident" they would have enough money to live comfortably in retirement. Twenty-four percent of workers were "not at all confident" that they would have enough money to live comfortably during retirement.

In the 2014 Survey, 64% of current workers reported they and/or their spouses had personally saved for retirement. Most workers, however, appear to be saving blindly without a goal in mind. Only 44% of current workers indicated that they and/or their spouses have ever tried to calculate how much money they will need to have saved by the time they retire to live comfortably in retirement. Workers with higher household incomes or more formal education were much more likely to have attempted this calculation.

In short, many Americans lack a realistic understanding of retirement savings. After reviewing recent research studies on public perceptions concerning retirement savings, a panel of experts concluded that many American workers have one or more of the following misperceptions about their income needs during retirement:

1. **Saving too little.** Most people have not tried to estimate how much money they will need for retirement. Moreover, those who have calculated this amount often underestimate it.

2. **Not knowing when retirement will occur.** Many workers will retire before they expect to, and before they are ready.

3. **Living longer than planned.** As individuals learn to manage their own retirement funds, they may not understand that life expectancy is a very limited planning tool. In fact, some retirees will live long beyond their life expectancy, with a substantial risk of outliving their savings.

4. **Not facing facts about long-term care.** Many people underestimate their chances of needing long-term care. Relatively few people either own long-term care insurance or can afford to self-insure an extended long-term care situation.

5. **Trying to self-insure against long life.** Although people find guaranteed lifetime income attractive, in practice they usually will choose to receive retirement plan benefits in a lump sum form. They pass up opportunities to obtain a lifetime pension or annuity, failing to recognize the difficulty of self-insuring their longevity. *taking lump sum instead of lifetime pen*

6. **Not understanding investments.** Due to the growth of individual account-based retirement plans, workers are now responsible for managing investments for retirement. Many

workers misunderstand investment returns and how investment vehicles work.

7. **Relying on poor advice.** A significant portion of retirees and pre-retirees do not seek the help of a qualified professional. Yet they indicate a strong desire to work with a financial professional.

[handwritten: seek professional help]

8. **Not knowing sources of retirement income.** Workers misunderstand what their primary sources of income will be in retirement, and may be disappointed when trying to live on the actual income that is available.

9. **Failing to deal with inflation.** Inflation is a fact of life that workers usually deal with through pay increases. But after retirement, few people can increase their income to keep pace with inflation.

[handwritten: income needs to keep pace of inflation]

10. **Not providing for a surviving spouse.** Many married couples fail to plan for the eventual death of one spouse before the other. This can have serious consequences, especially when the survivor is the wife.

[handwritten: don't depend on two person income, spouse could die]

These experts concluded that "[c]leaning up these misperceptions will be essential for people to fulfill their dreams of a comfortable retirement." PUBLIC MISPERCEPTIONS ABOUT RETIREMENT SECURITY 6–7 (2005) (special report commissioned by the Society of Actuaries Committee on Post-Retirement Needs and Risks).

The Scope of Qualified Plan Coverage

Qualified plans form a key component of national retirement policy by providing a source of income during retirement in addition to Social Security benefits and personal savings. Federal income tax policy provides incentives, for both private employers to sponsor and for workers to participate in qualified plans. The price tag for the qualified plan tax subsidy is a steep one. In 2014, the federal tax expenditure for qualified retirement plans was estimated to be $108.0 billion. See JOINT COMMITTEE ON TAXATION, ESTIMATES OF FEDERAL TAX EXPENDITURES FOR FISCAL YEARS 2012–2017 (2013).

[handwritten: tax policy provides incentives to participate in qualified plans]

The sheer magnitude of the tax expenditure for qualified plans raises significant social policy issues. Unfortunately, the quality of political debate over the tax expenditure for employer-sponsored retirement plans often is simplistic. Supporters of the tax expenditure for qualified plans justify the amount as a means to mitigate the problem of elderly poverty. Critics cite the statistic that just under half (49%) of all private industry workers participated in a qualified plan in 2013, and further argue that higher income taxpayers disproportionately benefit from the qualified plan tax subsidy. A closer examination of the coverage statistics presented in Table 3.1 reveals a much more complex pattern of coverage under the qualified plan system.

Table 3.1

Percentage of Private Industry Workers
Participating in Qualified Plans

Characteristics	% Participating
All Employees	49
By Occupation	
Management/Professional	68
Service	21
Sales/Office	51
Natural Resources/Construction	53
Production/Transportation	51
By Employer Size:	
1 to 99 workers	35
100 or more workers	65
By Employment Status:	
Full-time	59
Part-time	20
By Union Status:	
Union workers	86
Nonunion workers	45
By Wage Percentile:	
Lowest 25 percent	18
Highest 25 percent	75
By Type of Industry:	
Goods-Producing	62
Services-Producing	46

Source: U.S. DEP'T OF LABOR, EMPLOYEE BENEFITS IN THE UNITED STATES, MARCH 2013.

The data in Table 3.1 present an overview of which workers are most likely to participate in a qualified plan. Understanding exactly *why* the coverage data appear as they do, however, requires a much more in-depth analysis. Some of the relevant economic and social factors that influence the coverage data results are outside the scope of an introductory course in employee benefits law. But certainly one crucial factor is how the tax laws influence the scope of qualified plan coverage. For the curious, a few questions concerning the role the tax laws might play in producing these statistics are obvious. For example, why is there a difference in the scope of qualified plan coverage between small and large employers? Between full-time and part-time workers? Between higher and lower wage earners? If the tax laws governing qualified plans contribute to these results, how might the tax laws be reformed to broaden the scope of coverage in these areas?

Proposed legislation to change the tax laws governing qualified plans is frequently introduced in Congress. To evaluate the potential impact of these proposals on national retirement policy, a basic understanding of the current rules governing qualified plans is necessary. As you study the detailed and technical rules for qualified plans presented in Chapter Three, it is natural at times to feel "lost in the forest." When this occurs, step back for a moment and regain perspective by asking yourself how the particular technical rule you are studying (a "tree limb" or perhaps even a "tree twig") may be contributing, directly or indirectly, to the coverage statistics presented in Table 3.1.

2. QUALIFIED PLANS IN YOUR FUTURE PRACTICE

If your future legal career lies in litigation, you are certain to run into qualified plan issues, particularly in the area of employment litigation. As you study the material in Chapter Three, notice how the benefits provided by a qualified plan are tied to an employee's compensation. Suppose your client has been wrongfully discharged from employment, or suffered from employment discrimination that resulted in a lower amount of compensation over many working years. What remedy should you seek that will make your client truly whole? Is it sufficient to just focus on your client's lost wages? If your client participated in a qualified plan, part of your client's remedy should include the restoration of lost retirement benefits.

Perhaps your client believes that the client has been wrongfully excluded from participation in an employer's qualified plan. To evaluate whether your client has a valid claim, you would need to know the federal laws that limit the employer's ability to exclude employees from participation in a qualified plan. If a violation has occurred, you also would need to know whether your client has a private civil cause of action and a remedy under ERISA.

Another area of qualified plan litigation involves corporate restructurings and associated layoffs. Suppose your client has been terminated from employment as the result of a plant closing or a downsizing of the employer's workforce. Is your client receiving all of the retirement benefits that the client is entitled to receive under federal law? A related area of litigation involves plan amendments designed to reduce the cost of the plan for the employer. Suppose your client is an older worker employed by a company that has decided to reduce the cost of its traditional pension plan by amending the plan's benefit structure. As a result, your client will receive a lesser amount of benefits at retirement than the client anticipated receiving. Is the employer's amendment to the plan legal under federal law? Responding to these questions requires a basic knowledge of the vesting and benefit accrual rules for qualified retirement plans.

The above issues are not just the domain of the plaintiff's litigation lawyer. If your future career lies in representing employers, knowledge of these rules is essential when advising corporate clients how best to minimize the threat of potential litigation over qualified plan benefits. If litigation does occur, the corporate client will require a lawyer who understands these rules to defend the client's actions concerning the qualified plan.

If your future legal practice lies in counseling small businesses (or in owning a small business yourself), you may be called upon to suggest an appropriate retirement plan for the business. Your answer will depend on many factors, such as the financial condition of the business, how many employees the plan must cover, and how much in benefits the highly paid employees of the business would like to receive under the plan. The client also may have questions concerning the tax consequences of the plan, both from the perspective of the employer and the perspective of the participating employees. Again, responding to these questions requires a fundamental understanding of the Code provisions governing qualified plans.

Lawyers who represent large corporations often encounter qualified plan issues in the course of negotiating a merger or asset acquisition. An important aspect of due diligence in any proposed business combination is the impact of the merger or acquisition on the qualified retirement plans sponsored by the parties to the transaction. Liability issues are particularly acute if a corporate transaction potentially affects employee participation in a multiemployer plan for union workers.

A growing number of publicly traded corporations today include their own company stock as an investment option in their qualified retirement plans. If your future career lies in representing publicly traded corporations, a basic knowledge of how the company's qualified plan operates is essential to advising your client on matters that may affect the value of company stock held by the corporation's qualified plan.

Qualified retirement plan issues also arise frequently in estate planning and family law. One of the most significant assets in a client's future estate is likely to be the individual's retirement plan benefits. An integral function of the modern estate planning lawyer is to assist clients in the tax-efficient consumption of qualified plan assets during retirement and to facilitate the transfer of accumulated pension wealth at death. This type of sophisticated estate planning requires knowledge of the Code rules governing the timing and taxation of distributions from qualified plans. For the family law lawyer, qualified plan benefits often are one of the most significant assets the parties must agree to divide as a part of the property settlement in a divorce. One of the best ways for a family law lawyer to secure financial support for a former spouse or minor children involved in a divorce is to obtain a court-ordered assignment of the other spouse's retirement plan benefits. Again, effective representation of your client in family law situations requires knowledge of the federal laws governing qualified plans.

Chapter Three also contains information that you are likely to find useful in your personal life. Your employer's qualified plan benefits are an important part of your compensation. Before accepting an offer of employment, you should always assess the value of the prospective employer's qualified retirement plan as part of your total compensation package. Is the plan funded solely by employer contributions, your own salary deferral contributions, or a combination of both? How long must you be employed to participate in the plan and to vest fully in the plan's benefits? Can you access your qualified plan benefits prior to retirement and, if so, under what circumstances? And finally, if you later terminate employment, what will happen to your qualified plan benefits? The material in Chapter Three addresses these very practical personal questions.

B. INTRODUCTION TO QUALIFIED RETIREMENT PLANS

1. COMPARISON OF THE CODE AND ERISA REQUIREMENTS FOR QUALIFIED PLANS

An employee pension plan will not receive favorable income tax treatment as a qualified plan unless the plan satisfies the requirements listed in Code Section 401(a). Some of the Code Section 401(a) requirements overlap with the requirements of ERISA, but other provisions do not. Why is the treatment of employee pension plans under ERISA and the Code not uniform? The answer lies in the different policy purposes that ERISA and the Code are designed to serve.

Fundamentally, ERISA's requirements for employee pension plans *different* are designed to protect and secure the assets of the plan and the benefits *goals of* promised to the plan's participants. In contrast, the provisions of Code *ERISA and* Section 401(a) represent a compromise between two competing policy *§401(a)* goals. On the one hand, as a matter of social policy we want to encourage employers voluntarily to sponsor qualified plans so that workers will have a source of income (other than Social Security benefits) during *IRC is balancy* retirement. The favorable income tax treatment of qualified plans is *no P.P.* designed to encourage this type of behavior among employers. On the *problems* other hand, the resulting drain on the national budget created by the federal tax expenditure for qualified plans is difficult to justify unless qualified plan coverage and benefits are broadly available to all workers, and do not disproportionately favor higher income workers. Many of the Code's unique provisions for qualified plans, discussed in Section F of Chapter Three, are designed to distribute this federal tax expenditure, in the form of qualified plan coverage and benefits, broadly among workers of all income levels.

Table 3.2 lists the major Code Section 401(a) requirements for qualified plans that are discussed in this casebook. Most of these requirements are discussed in Chapter Three, although a few are presented in Chapters Two and Five.

If ERISA contains a dual provision, the corresponding ERISA section is noted in Table 3.2. Whether a Code provision has an ERISA corollary is significant because only an ERISA provision can be enforced by the plan participants and beneficiaries, a plan fiduciary, or by the Department of Labor through civil litigation. See generally ERISA § 502(a). Violation of *penalty for* a Code requirement does not give rise to a private cause of action. *failure to* Instead, the penalty for failing to comply with a Code requirement is *comply w/* forfeiture of the favorable income tax treatment of the plan and its *IRC is forfeiture* benefits. *of favorable income tax treatment*

Table 3.2

Major Code and ERISA Requirements for Qualified Plans

Code Section	Description	ERISA Corollary	Casebook Discussion
401(a); Treas. Reg. §1.401–1(a)(2)	Written Plan Document Requirement	402(a)(1)	Chapter Two, Section C
401(a)(1),(3),(5)	Trust Requirement	403(a)	Chapter Two, Section C
401(a)(3); 411(a)	Age and Service Rules	202	Chapter Three, Section D
401(a)(7); 411(a)	Vesting Rules	203	Chapter Three, Section D
401(a)(7) 411(d)(6)	Anti-Cutback Rule	204(g)	Chapter Three, Section E
401(a)(7); 401(a)(35); 411(b)	Benefit Accrual Rules	204	Chapter Three, Section E
401(a)(3); 410(b);	Minimum Coverage Rules	None	Chapter Three, Section F
401(a)(26)	Minimum Participation Rule	None	Chapter Three, Section F
401(k); 401(m)	Special Nondiscrimination Rules for 401(k) Plans	None	Chapter Three, Section F
401(a)(4)	Nondiscrimination in Plan Contributions or Benefits	None	Chapter Three, Section F
401(a)(10); 416	Top Heavy Rules	None	Chapter Three, Section F
401(a)(16),(17), (30); 402(g)(1); 404; 415	Limitations on Contributions, Benefits, and Deductions	None	Chapter Three, Section F

401(a)(31)	Direct Rollover Rules	None	Chapter Three, Section F
401(a)(9)	Required Minimum Distribution Rules	None	Chapter Three, Section F
401(a)(11); 417	Spousal Annuity Rules	205	Chapter Three, Section F
401(a)(13)	Anti-Alienation Rule	206(d)	Chapter Three, Section G
401(a)(12); 414(*l*)	Plan Merger Rules	208	Chapter Three, Section H
411(d)(3)	Vesting for Plan Terminations	None	Chapter, Three Section H
401(a); 401(a)(2)	Exclusive Benefit Rule	404(a)(1)(A); 403(c)(1)	Chapter Five, Section C

The presentation of the major Code rules for qualified plans in Chapter Three necessarily has been simplified to focus on fundamental principles. A close reading of the statutory Code requirements governing qualified plans and the accompanying Treasury Department regulations will reveal the complexity of these rules. Such complexity makes it difficult for many employers—both large and small—to administer their qualified plans in compliance with the Code requirements. It also virtually guarantees full employment for ERISA tax lawyers!

2. VOCABULARY AND BASIC TAXATION PRINCIPLES

The reading material in this section focuses on the following questions:

- What makes a plan *qualified*? What is a *nonqualified* plan? What are the significant differences between qualified and nonqualified plans?
- What are the income tax advantages of a qualified plan for the employer? For the plan's participants?
- What are the non-tax advantages of a qualified plan for the plan's participants?

a. Qualified Retirement Plans Versus Nonqualified (Top Hat) Plans

A *qualified plan* is a retirement plan that satisfies the requirements of Code Section 401(a). As a result of satisfying these requirements, a qualified plan receives favorable income tax treatment under the Code. A *non-qualified plans*

nonqualified plan, also known as a *deferred compensation agreement,* is a plan providing retirement benefits that does not meet the requirements of Code Section 401(a). A nonqualified plan receives less favorable income tax treatment than a qualified plan. The details of the different tax attributes of qualified and nonqualified plans are discussed later in this section.

Qualified plans and nonqualified plans not only differ in their tax attributes under the Code, but also in terms of compliance with numerous requirements of Title I of ERISA. ERISA generally requires that all employee pension plans must satisfy certain standards governing participant eligibility, vesting, benefit accrual and funding. Normally, a nonqualified plan that satisfies the definition of an employee pension plan under ERISA Section 3(2)(A) would be subject to these ERISA standards.

nonqualified ERISA exemption

TOP HAT PLANS

ERISA expressly exempts, however, any pension plan that is "unfunded and. . .maintained by an employer primarily for the purpose of providing deferred compensation for a select group of management or highly compensated employees" from the participant eligibility, vesting, benefit accrual and funding requirements. See ERISA §§ 201(2); 301(a)(3); 401(a)(1). Nonqualified plans that satisfy this ERISA exemption are known as *top hat plans.*

There are many reasons why companies adopt nonqualified plans for their executive employees that are classified as exempt top hat plans under ERISA:

reasons for adopting a Top HAT plan

- The employer may want to limit eligibility to participate in the plan to executive employees and exclude rank and file employees. This type of limited eligibility usually is not possible under the Code requirements for qualified plans. See Code § 410(b).

- The employer may want to provide its executives with a greater amount of retirement benefits than are permitted under the Code limitations on contributions to and benefits from qualified plans. See Code § 415. (This type of nonqualified plan is referred to as a *supplemental executive retirement plan,* or SERP).

- The employer may desire to retain the use of the funds that represent the employee's deferred compensation under the plan until the future when the benefits from the plan are paid to the employee. This is not possible unless the plan is exempt from ERISA's funding, exclusive benefit and trust requirements as a top hat plan. See ERISA §§ 301–305; 403(a); 403(c)(1); 404(a)(1)(B).

- The employer may desire to use the future benefits promised under the plan as both an incentive for future performance and as a penalty for certain undesirable conduct. For example, the plan may tie the amount of the executive's deferred compensation to certain performance goals, such as an increase in corporate earnings or stock price. The plan also may be used to impose "golden handcuffs" on the executive by providing that deferred compensation benefits under the nonqualified plan will be forfeited if the executive fails to remain with the employer for a certain number of years, or if the executive is subsequently employed by a competitor. These types of performance incentive and forfeiture provisions are prohibited by ERISA's eligibility, vesting and benefit accrual rules unless the plan is an exempt top hat plan. See ERISA §§ 202; 203; 204.

In short, it is precisely because a top hat plan *avoids* many of ERISA's requirements that the employer may want to sponsor a nonqualified plan that is also qualifies as a top hat plan for purposes of ERISA.

[handwritten margin note: ER's csc top hat plans b/c they skirt ERISA regs.]

Top hat plans are subject to Parts 1 and 5 of Title I of ERISA. Consequently, a top hat plan must satisfy ERISA's reporting and disclosure requirements, and any claims concerning plan benefits must be litigated under ERISA's civil enforcement provisions. See ERISA § 502(a)(1)(B). State law claims that relate to a top hat plan (e.g., breach of contract claims) generally are preempted by ERISA. See ERISA § 514(a).

One particular type of nonqualified plan, the *unfunded excess benefit plan*, is exempt from all of the provisions of Title I of ERISA, including the reporting and disclosure requirements contained in Part 1 of Title I. See ERISA § 4(b)(5). An excess benefit plan is "a plan maintained by an employer solely for the purpose of providing benefits for certain employees in excess of the limitations on contributions and benefits imposed by section 415 of the Internal Revenue Code of 1986." ERISA § 3(36). Today, few nonqualified plans satisfy the definition of an excess benefit plan exempt from regulation under Title I of ERISA because such plans typically are not maintained "solely" for this purpose. See Kathryn J. Kennedy, *A Primer on Taxation of Executive Deferred Compensation Plans*, 35 J. MARSHALL L. REV. 487, 499–500 (2002).

If the employer establishes a top hat plan, only to have a federal court later determine that the plan fails the statutory criteria for an exempt top hat plan under ERISA, the financial consequences to the employer can be catastrophic. The litigation over the employer's top hat plan in *Carrabba v. Randalls Food Markets, Inc.* illustrates this situation. In *Carrabba*, the original employer, Cullum Companies, Inc. (Cullum), created a plan in 1974 to provide death and retirement benefits to some of its managerial employees. Selected managers were invited to participate in the plan by the plan's administrative committee. In 1992, Cullum was acquired by Randalls Food Markets, Inc., and the plan was terminated.

See Carrabba v. Randalls Food Markets, Inc., 38 F.Supp.2d 468, 470–71 (N.D. Tex. 1999) (Carrabba I).

At the time the plan was terminated, 244 employees were participating in the plan. See Carrabba v. Randalls Food Markets, Inc., 145 F. Supp. 2d 763, 782–85 (N.D. Tex. 2000) (Carrabba II). The plan's participants included management employees at every level of the employer's business operations, including persons in positions as low as the manager of an individual department within a single store. See Carrabba I, 38 F. Supp. 2d at 474–75. Although all of these employees were classified as managers by the employer, the district court found that the breadth of participation meant that the participants in the plan could not be characterized as a "select" group, and therefore the plan failed to qualify as a top hat plan under ERISA. The court made this finding even though the employer clearly had intended the plan to be a top hat plan and the employer had believed in good faith that the plan in fact was a top hat plan. See Carrabba I, 38 F. Supp. 2d at 478. Because the plan failed ERISA's statutory criteria for a top hat plan, the court ordered that the employer's plan had to comply retroactively with ERISA's vesting, benefit accrual and funding rules. See Carrabba II, 145 F. Supp. 2d at 768. The court ordered the employer to pay $6,745,409 to the participants in vested plan benefits. In addition, the court awarded the participants $3,801,454.42 in prejudgment interest on their benefits, and $3,078,810.40 in attorneys' fees. See Carrabba II, 145 F. Supp. 2d at 781–85.

b.   Statutory Criteria for a Top Hat Plan Under ERISA

Carrabba illustrates the importance of compliance with ERISA's statutory definition of a top hat plan when the employer enters into a nonqualified deferred compensation agreement with managerial or executive employees. The statutory definition of a top hat plan has three key components. First, the plan must be *unfunded*. Second, the plan must be maintained *primarily* for the top hat group. Third, the plan must provide deferred compensation for a *select group of management or highly compensated employees*. See ERISA §§ 201(2); 301(a)(3); 401(a)(1).

An "unfunded" plan is a term of art. This term means that the employer's promise to pay plan benefits is unsecured and payable solely out of the employer's general assets. In the event of employer insolvency, the participant in an unfunded top hat plan must have the same priority status as any other general unsecured creditor of the employer. E.g., Demery v. Extebank Deferred Compensation Plan, 216 F.3d 283, 287 (2d Cir. 2000).

Simply because ERISA requires that a top hat plan must be unfunded does not mean that the employer is prohibited from setting aside funds to pay the benefits promised under the terms of the deferred compensation agreement. The Internal Revenue Service has approved a technique by which employers may place funds in a separate trust to pay the benefits promised under the top hat plan, so long as the assets in the trust remain subject to the claims of general creditors of the employer. This technique originated when a congregation established such a trust to pay retirement benefits to its rabbi. The name of the technique, a *rabbi trust*, is a short-hand reference to the private letter ruling issued by the Internal Revenue Service that approved the congregation's trust arrangement with the rabbi. See IRS Private Letter Ruling 8113107. Today, pension tax lawyers who create rabbi trusts rely on a model form of trust agreement that has been approved by both the Treasury Department and the Department of Labor as satisfying the requirement for an unfunded top hat plan. See Rev. Proc. 92–64, 1992–2 C.B. 422.

The second component of ERISA's definition of a top hat plan involves the meaning of the word "primarily." To illustrate the issue that arises under this second component, assume that the employer establishes a top hat plan for the top nineteen managerial employees on the employer's organizational chart out of a total workforce of 500 employees. In addition, the plan also includes the long-time personal secretary to the company president. Given these facts, it may seem that the plan is being maintained "primarily" for a select group of managerial employees because nineteen out of the twenty participants in the plan are top ranking executives of the company. The Department of Labor, however, construes the meaning of "primarily" in a different manner as modifying the words "deferred compensation." According to the Department of Labor, the term "primarily" refers to the "purpose of the plan (i.e., the benefits provided) and not the participant composition of the plan. Therefore, a plan that extends coverage beyond a 'select group of management or highly compensated employees' would not constitute a 'top hat' plan." DOL Adv. Op. Ltr. 90–14A, n. 1. In other words, having just one participant in the plan who is not a bona fide member of the select group, such as the president's secretary in the illustration, causes the entire plan to fail to satisfy the statutory definition of a top hat plan.

The third component of the top hat plan definition, the determination of the "select" group, is potentially confusing because it incorporates the same terminology, the phrase *highly compensated employee*, that is used as part of the Code requirements for qualified plans. These Code requirements generally define a highly compensated employee solely in terms of the amount of the employee's annual compensation. See Code § 414(q). In contrast, the Department of Labor applies a functional approach to the meaning of a "select group of management or highly compensated employees," stating that "[i]t is the view of the Department that in providing relief for 'top hat' plans from the broad remedial provisions of ERISA, Congress recognized that certain individuals, by virtue of their position or compensation level, have the ability to affect or substantially influence, through negotiation or otherwise, the design and operation of their deferred compensation plan, taking into consideration any risks attendant thereto, and, therefore, would not need the substantive rights and protections of Title I [of ERISA]." DOL Adv. Op. Ltr. 90–14A. Unlike the Code requirements for qualified plans, annual compensation alone is not the litmus test for highly compensated employee status as a participant in a top hat plan under ERISA. Rather, the employee must have sufficient bargaining strength when negotiating the terms and benefits of the deferred compensation arrangement with the employer that the protections normally offered by ERISA to participants in employee pension plans are unnecessary.

The federal courts do not always give deference to the Department of Labor's interpretation of the statutory criteria for a top hat plan. For example, in *Dependahl v. Falstaff Brewing Corp.*, 653 F.2d 1208 (8th Cir. 1981), the Eighth Circuit interpreted the concept of an unfunded plan quite differently, stating that "[f]unding implies the existence of a res separate from the ordinary assets of the corporation. . . . The employee may look to a res separate from the corporation in the event the contingency occurs which triggers the liability of the plan." Id. at 1214.

The Second Circuit also has disagreed with the Department of Labor's interpretation of the statutory criteria for a top hat plan. In *Demery v. Extebank Deferred Compensation Plan*, 216 F.3d 283 (2d Cir. 2000), the Second Circuit pointedly disagreed with the Department of Labor's interpretation of the word "primarily" in DOL Advisory Opinion Letter 90–14A:

> [W]e think it significant that the statute defines a top hat plan as "primarily" designed to provide deferred compensation for certain individuals who are management or highly compensated employees. * * * It suggests that if a plan were principally intended for management and highly compensated employees, it would not be disqualified from top hat status simply because a very small number of the participants did not meet these criteria, or met one of the criteria but not the other. * * * Therefore, we do not find plaintiffs' focus on the two or three employees who are arguably not "highly compensated" or a "select group of management" to be dispositive.

Id. at 289. In *Demery*, the court found that the employer's nonqualified deferred compensation plan, which covered 15.34% of the company's employees, nevertheless satisfied ERISA's statutory criteria for an exempt top hat plan.

c. The Income Tax Treatment of Qualified Plans and Nonqualified (Top Hat) Plans

Employer compliance with the Code requirements for qualified plans is administratively burdensome and costly. Why would an employer bother? The rewards for compliance with Code Section 401(a) are significant income tax advantages for the employer and the plan's participants. These tax benefits occur because the normal rules of income taxation are suspended for qualified plans. The easiest way to grasp the income tax advantages of qualified plans is to examine first how the normal rules of income taxation operate, and then compare how qualified plans are treated for purposes of income taxation.

Several fundamental concepts underlie the normal rules of income taxation. Under the *matching principle*, the employer's tax deduction must "match up" with a like amount included in an employee's gross income. Normally, the matching principle would prevent the employer from claiming a tax deduction for the employer's contribution to the plan until the amount attributable to the contribution is included in the gross incomes of the plan's participants. See Code § 404(a)(5); Albertson's Inc. v. Commissioner, 42 F.3d 537 (9th Cir. 1994) (discussing the Code Section 404 matching principle in the context of qualified and nonqualified plans). An employer's contribution to a qualified plan is exempt from the matching principle. As a result of this exemption, the employer may claim a current income tax deduction for a contribution to a qualified plan, even though this contribution will not be included in the gross income of a participant until a future time when the participant receives a distribution from the plan. See Code § 404(a)(1)–(3).

Normally, an individual taxpayer is taxed on compensation (whether in the form of cash or other property having an economic value) in the year of receipt. If an individual has an unrestricted right to compensation that is not subject to a substantial risk of forfeiture, and the individual can control the timing of its receipt, the *doctrine of constructive receipt* applies to include the compensation in the taxpayer's gross income. Under the doctrine of constructive receipt, an individual must include in gross income both compensation the individual actually received during the year, and compensation that is deemed to be "constructively" received because the individual can control the timing of receipt of the compensation.

Applying the doctrine of constructive receipt to a qualified plan would mean that once a plan participant's benefit became vested, the amount of the benefit would be included in the gross income of the participant and subject to immediate taxation. This result would be highly undesirable because the benefit from a qualified plan is not paid until the participant retires or terminates employment (possibly many years later). Vested benefits from a qualified plan are exempt from the doctrine of constructive receipt. The amount of the participant's vested accrued benefit under a qualified plan is not included in the participant's gross income until the participant receives payment of the benefit (in technical terms, the participant receives a *distribution* from the plan).

Finally, under the normal rules of income taxation the investment earnings generated by the assets held in the plan's trust would be subject to taxation. Such earnings might be taxed as income to the trust, or as income to the plan participants. The trust of a qualified plan is not subject to income tax on the undistributed earnings from trust assets. Most importantly, a participant in a defined contribution plan is not taxed on investment earnings from the assets held in the individual's qualified plan account until a distribution from the account is made to the participant.

All of the general principles of income taxation described above apply to nonqualified plans. In addition, a separate set of special rules apply to the taxation of deferred compensation benefits under a nonqualified plan. These special rules, which were enacted as part of the American Jobs Creation Act of 2004, Pub. L. No. 108–357, § 885, 118 Stat. 1418 (2004), are contained in Code Section 409A.

Under Code Section 409A, all amounts deferred under a nonqualified deferred compensation plan that are not subject to a substantial risk of forfeiture are included in the gross income of the employee who is the beneficiary of the plan, unless the nonqualified plan satisfies a litany of statutory requirements. These statutory requirements generally restrict the employee's ability to control the timing or form of payments from the nonqualified plan. If the nonqualified plan fails to satisfy the statutory requirements of Code Section 409A, then all of the employee's deferred compensation under the nonqualified plan is immediately taxable, even if the deferred compensation has not yet been paid to the employee. Code Section 409A further imposes a 20% additional tax on the deferred compensation amounts from the nonqualified plan that are included in the employee's gross income.

d.   Another Advantage of Qualified Plans: Benefit Security

The deferral of income taxation is not the only advantage associated with benefits from a qualified plan. Recall that under ERISA, the assets of a nonqualified top hat plan must be subject to the claims of general creditors of the employer. This rule applies even if the assets of the nonqualified plan are held in a rabbi trust. Another significant advantage of a qualified plan is that the assets held in the trust of a qualified plan are not subject to the claims of creditors of the employer in the event of the employer's insolvency or bankruptcy. In the past, the perceived risk of employer bankruptcy associated with nonqualified plans was low. As a practical matter, executives of large and well-established companies who participated in nonqualified plans were not concerned with the risk of employer insolvency. Today, this attitude has changed and virtually no employer is considered to be "bankruptcy proof." The assets held in the trust of a qualified plan are secure from general creditors of the employer and can be used only for the exclusive purpose of providing benefits to the plan's participants and beneficiaries. Subject to certain limited exceptions, a participant's benefits from a qualified plan also are secure from creditors of the plan participant until the benefits are distributed from the plan to the participant. This principle, known as the *anti-alienation rule*, is discussed in Section G of Chapter Three.

e. Other Tax-Deferred Vehicles for Retirement Savings

The Code provides several other vehicles for the deferred taxation of retirement savings. Two of the these vehicles, the *403(b) plan* and the *457 plan*, are sponsored by the employer for the benefit of its employees. A third vehicle, the *individual retirement account* or *individual retirement annuity* (IRA) is maintained by the individual taxpayer. Finally, the *simplified employee pension* (SEP) and its more recent incarnation, the *SIMPLE IRA*, allow an employer to make deductible contributions directly to an account established by the employer for each employee.

403(b) and 457 Plans

Both the 403(b) plan and the 457 plan derive their names from the Code sections that authorize these types of plans. Both 403(b) and 457 plans offer the same income tax advantages as qualified plans. Rather than being designed to comply with the requirements of Code Section 401(a), however, 403(b) plans and 457 plans are designed to satisfy the requirements of Code Section 403(b) or Code Section 457.

Sponsorship of 457 plans is limited to employers who are state or local governments or employers who are tax-exempt organizations. A 457 plan sponsored by a state or local government employer is not subject to ERISA. See ERISA § 4(b)(1). Sponsorship of 403(b) plans is limited to employers who are either public educational organizations (schools, colleges, and universities) or who are tax-exempt organizations. Whether a 403(b) plan is subject to regulation under Title I of ERISA as an employee pension plan depends on the nature of the employer who sponsors the 403(b) plan. For example, a 403(b) plan for employees of a public state university would be exempt from regulation under Title I of ERISA as a governmental plan. See ERISA § 4(b)(1). In contrast, a 403(b) plan for employees of a private secular university would be regulated under Title I of ERISA as an employee pension plan. See ERISA § 4(a).

Traditional and Roth (Nondeductible) IRAs

There are two types of IRAs. The *traditional IRA* is authorized under Code Section 408. The *Roth (nondeductible) IRA* is authorized under Code Section 408A. The individual's annual contribution to a traditional IRA may be deductible from the individual's gross income, subject to certain income limits. A contribution to a Roth IRA is not deductible by the individual and also is subject to certain income limits. The individual's total contribution to traditional and Roth IRAs each year cannot exceed the dollar limitation established by Code Section 219(b)(5)(A) for IRA contributions. In 2014, this dollar limit for individuals under age 50 was $5,500. For individuals age 50 and older, the dollar limit in 2014 for annual IRA contributions was $6,500.

Amounts distributed from a traditional IRA are included in the taxpayer's gross income in the year of distribution. Contributions and investment earnings from a Roth IRA may be withdrawn tax-free by the taxpayer, subject to certain conditions and restrictions. Traditional and Roth IRAs are not subject to ERISA when they are established by the individual taxpayer and not by his or her employer. See ERISA § 4(a); DOL Reg. § 2510.3–2(d).

SEPs and SIMPLE IRAs

SEPs and SIMPLE IRAs are designed to combine the tax incentives of qualified plans with the simplicity of administration offered by IRAs. Employers who otherwise might be discouraged by the complicated rules governing the design and administration of qualified plans may find that a SEP or SIMPLE IRA offers a less cumbersome alternative.

SEPs are authorized under Code Section 408(k). A SEP generally is funded by employer contributions to participant accounts. SIMPLE IRAs are authorized under Code Section 408(p). A SIMPLE IRA permits only employee salary deferral contributions and employer matching contributions. The employer who sponsors a SIMPLE IRA cannot sponsor any other type of qualified plan for its employees. See Code §§ 408(p)(1)(B); (2)(D). The rules governing traditional IRAs generally govern distributions, rollovers and penalties for early withdrawals from SEPs and SIMPLE IRAs.

SEPs are the retirement plan of choice for many individuals who are self-employed (or who have self-employment income), but who do not have other employees. A self-employed individual having no other employees may contribute up to 25% of compensation to the individual's SEP account, up to the maximum amount authorized for annual additions to a participant's qualified plan account under Code Section 415(c) ($52,000 in 2014). See Code § 402(h)(2). In contrast, employee salary deferral contributions to a SIMPLE IRA are subject to a much lower maximum dollar limit ($12,000 in 2014). See Code § 408(p)(2)(E).

A Historical Footnote: The H.R. 10 (Keogh) Plan

Prior to 1962, self-employed individuals (e.g., partners and sole proprietors) were not allowed to participate in qualified plans because they were considered to be owners, not employees. This rule was particularly irritating to the partners of large law and accounting firms that were organized as old-fashioned partnerships. (Recall that during this period, the limited liability company, the limited liability partnership, and the professional corporation forms of business entity were not yet widely available.) In 1962, Congress amended the Code to allow self-employed individuals to participate in qualified plans. See Code § 401(c)(1).

Today, a qualified plan that includes partners or sole proprietors as participants is still occasionally referred to as an *H.R. 10 plan* or *Keogh plan* after the legislation and sponsor, respectively, of this 1962 amendment to the Code. An H.R. 10 plan or a Keogh plan is not a unique type of qualified plan. Rather, it is merely a historical reference to the 1962 Code amendment that brought these plans into the Code's qualified plan system.

3.   INVESTMENT FUNDAMENTALS

Qualified plans are built upon several fundamental principles of investing:

- The time value of money;
- The magic of compounded investment earnings over time (magnified by the deferred taxation of investment earnings); and
- Investment diversification.

The reading material in this subsection describes and illustrates each of these fundamental investment principles.

a.   The Time Value of Money

Which would you prefer—to have $100 today, or $100 ten years from now? If you responded that you would rather have $100 today, you intuitively grasp the concept of the time value of money.

Why is $100 today more valuable to you than $100 ten years from now? You can immediately spend $100 if you have $100 today. If you have $100 today, you also can put the money in a bank account and earn interest on it. Alternatively, you can invest the $100 and, if the investment performs well, receive investment earnings. In ten years, you will have *more than $100. You will have your original $100, plus any interest or investment earnings accumulated over ten years.*

Which would you rather have—$100 today, or $150 ten years from now? To answer this question, you would need to know the value in today's dollars (in technical terms, the *present value*) of receiving $150 ten years from now. Calculating the present value of receiving $150 ten years from now is the only way you can do an "apples-to-apples" comparison with receiving $100 today. If the present value of $150 ten years from now is more than $100, you will be better off (in an economic sense) choosing to receive $150 ten years from now. If the present value of $150 ten years from now is less than $100, you will be better off choosing to receive $100 today.

How do you calculate the present value today of receiving a specified amount of money in the future? The answer depends on two factors: (1) *time* (how many years in the future until you will receive the money); and (2) *the discount rate* (the technical term for the average annual rate of investment return you assume you will receive if you invest the money today). In this example, the time factor is known. You will receive $150 ten years from now. The second factor, the discount rate, seems impossible to know. After all, who can predict what money invested today will earn in the future? No one really can, but the science of economics certainly tries. To determine the second factor, the discount rate, you must make a simplifying assumption. You assume that the discount rate is equivalent to one of today's interest rates.

Numerous interest rates are commonly used in society at any given time. Typical examples include the interest rates on one-year United States Treasury bonds and thirty-year United States Treasury bonds, the prime lending rate charged by commercial lenders, and the prime rate plus an additional percentage amount, such as the prime rate plus 2%. In this example, you may select as the discount rate the interest rate that best reflects your personal preferences. In the context of qualified plans, federal law regulates the discount rate.

Assume that you select a discount rate of 10%. Using a 10% discount rate, the present value of receiving $150 ten years from now is $57.83. To easily perform this calculation yourself, refer to Table C.1, Present Value of $1 Tomorrow, in Appendix C of the casebook. Using this table, the present value is computed by multiplying $150 times 0.385543 (the discount factor at a 10% discount rate for ten years). Given a choice between $100 today or $150 in ten years (worth $57.83 in today's dollars), naturally you decide to take $100 today.

Suppose that your discount rate is 5% instead of 10%. Using a 5% discount rate, the present value of receiving $150 ten years from now is $92.08. You would still be slightly better off in an economic sense by deciding to take $100 today.

This example illustrates the fundamental investment principle that *the lower the discount rate, the higher the present value will be.* Stated in the converse, *the higher the discount rate, the lower the present value will be.*

Suppose that instead of receiving $150 ten years from now, you will receive $150 five years from now. How does the present value of $150 change? At a 10% discount rate, the present value of receiving $150 in five years is $93.14. At a 5% discount rate, the present value of receiving $150 in five years is $117.53.

This example illustrates the fundamental investment principle that, for a given discount rate, *the shorter the period of time, the higher the present value will be.* Stated in the converse, for a given discount rate, *the longer the period of time, the lower the present value will be.*

The concept of the time value of money arises frequently in the operation of qualified plans. For example, assume that the qualified plan promises to pay a specific monthly amount to a plan participant, commencing at retirement, for the remainder of the participant's life. In technical terms, this form of payment is called an *annuity.* Generally, the plan satisfies this benefit obligation by purchasing an annuity from an insurance company. When the plan purchases the annuity from the insurance company, the plan pays a lump sum amount to the insurance company, and in exchange the insurance company agrees to pay the monthly benefit amount to the retired participant for the remainder of the participant's life.

How does the insurance company determine how much to charge the plan for the participant's annuity contract with the insurance company? The insurance company selects an appropriate discount rate and determines the present value of paying the monthly amounts to the participant over the course of the participant's estimated life expectancy. The insurance company then adds an additional amount representing its business risk and profit margin, and arrives at a lump sum amount (measured in today's dollars) as the price for the annuity contract.

Suppose that the plan offers the participant the option of selecting either an annuity form of benefit or a lump sum amount representing the present value of the annuity benefit. How does the plan determine the amount of the lump sum equivalent of the annuity in today's dollars? Here, the plan document and federal law determine the discount rate. The plan administrator uses this discount rate and the participant's average life expectancy to calculate the lump sum equivalent of the lifetime annuity benefit in accordance with federal law.

It may have occurred to you that the plan's discount rate may be higher or lower than the participant's personal discount rate. Moreover, the participant's actual life expectancy may be longer or shorter than the average life expectancy used in the plan administrator's calculation. If you wondered how these variables may play into the participant's decision whether to elect the annuity or lump sum form of retirement benefits from the plan, you are beginning to appreciate the nuances of the time value of money.

The concept of the time value of money also underlies the federal law requirements imposed on an employer for funding certain types of qualified plans. These minimum plan funding requirements operate as a safeguard for the plan's participants. They ensure that the plan is adequately funded today so that the plan will be able to pay the level of retirement benefits promised to participants in the future.

b.   The Magic of Compounded Investment Earnings

To illustrate the magical effect of compounded investment earnings over time, consider the following example from *The Complete Idiot's Guide to 401(k) Plans*. The particular plan used in the example, a *401(k) plan*, is a variation of a broad category of qualified plans known as *defined contribution plans*. The fundamental characteristic of a defined contribution plan is that each participant in the plan has an individual plan account. (The characteristics of defined contribution plans are described in more detail later in Section C of Chapter Three.)

> George and Maria are both age 20. Maria decides to save $2,500 [in her 401(k) plan account] each year for 10 years. George, on the other hand, says, "I'll wait. I'm young and have plenty of time." (Sound familiar?) So he saves nothing.
>
> At age 30, they reverse roles. Maria stops saving and George starts to save $2,500 a year [in his 401(k) plan]. They continue this strategy for the next 35 years, with each earning an 8% annual return on their money. Our question for you: Who has more money at age 65? George or Maria?
>
> You would think it's George. After all, he saved over three times what Maria did—$87,500 versus $25,000. But Maria's ahead at age 65. She has over $114,000 more ($535,472) than George does ($430,792), even though she saved $62,500 less. How did this happen, you ask? The power of compounding.

WAYNE G. BOGOSIAN & DEE LEE, THE COMPLETE IDIOT'S GUIDE TO 401(K) PLANS 43 (1998).

Several fundamental investment principles underlie this "magic." First, both Maria and George benefitted from a *compounded rate of investment return*. A compounded rate of investment return occurs when an investor chooses to reinvest his or her investment earnings rather than withdrawing them. In the example, Maria and George both chose to leave the investment earnings in their accounts and reinvest the earnings. As a result, the amount in their accounts that earned an average annual return of 8% grew larger, year by year, not only as a result of additional contributions, but also as a result of accumulated investment earnings. The net effect was to increase the compounded rate of investment return to far more than 8% for both Maria and George.

To determine what the compounded rate of investment return will be for a given period of time and average annual rate of investment return, refer to Table C.2, Compound Amount of $1, in Appendix C of the casebook. Table C.2 illustrates the fundamental investment principle that *the longer the amount of time invested, the greater the compounded rate of investment return will be.* Maria fared better than George because even though they both earned an 8% average rate of investment return, Maria's compounded rate was much higher because her amounts were invested for a longer period of time.

To illustrate, consider the first $1 that Maria invested at age twenty. This investment earned an 8% average annual rate of return for forty-five years until Maria reached age sixty-five. Referring to Table C.2, you can see the multiplying factor (31.9204) that corresponds to investing just $1 for forty-five years at an average annual return of 8%. By age sixty-five, the first $1 Maria invested at age twenty had grown to $31.92!

Table C.2 also illustrates what is commonly known as the *Rule of 72.* To estimate how long it will take an investment to double in amount as a result of compounded investment earnings, simply divide 72 by the anticipated average annual rate of return. The result will be the approximate number of years it will take the investment to double at the assumed rate of return. For example, at an average annual rate of return of 6%, it will take between eleven and twelve years for an investment of $1 to become $2.

Obviously, if Maria or George had chosen to withdraw any part of their 401(k) plan savings, the long-term negative impact on the account balance at retirement would be much more than simply the amount withdrawn early. They also would lose the benefit of compounded investment earnings on the withdrawn funds.

Another fundamental investment principle at work in the example of Maria and George is the economic effect of deferred taxation on the investment earnings generated by the assets held by a qualified plan. If George or Maria had to pay income tax on their investment earnings each year, their after-tax average annual rate of investment return would have been less than 8%. Rather than paying a portion of their investment earnings to the government in the form of taxes, Maria and George kept this amount, reinvested it in their 401(k) plan accounts, and consequently enjoyed a higher compounded rate of investment return. The deferred taxation of investment earnings inside a qualified plan accelerates the economic benefit of compounded investment earnings. Of course, the higher the individual's income tax bracket, the more significant the economic benefit of deferred taxation of investment earnings will be.

Maria and George each benefitted from deferred taxation in another way. The payment of income tax on the amounts they contributed to their 401(k) plan accounts is deferred until they receive the amounts in their accounts in the form of a distribution. Again, the higher the individual's income tax bracket, the more significant the economic benefit of deferred taxation of contributions to the 401(k) plan will be.

When will Maria and George have to pay income taxes? Not until the money in their 401(k) plan accounts is distributed out to them. If they wait until their retirement years to withdraw the money from their accounts, they may be in a lower income tax bracket than they are today. If so, they will pay less in income tax in the future (measured as a present value) than they would pay in income tax today.

Again, if Maria or George had chosen to withdraw any part of their 401(k) plan savings, the long-term negative impact on their account balance at retirement would be much more than simply the amount of the withdrawn funds. Not only would they lose the benefit of compounded investment earnings on the withdrawn amount, the negative economic effect would be magnified because their deferral period for income taxation of contributions and related investment earnings would cease. They would have to pay income tax on the amounts withdrawn.

To summarize, Maria and George illustrate the following conventional words of wisdom for investment success through a qualified plan:

- Invest as early as you can;
- Invest as much as you can;
- Avoid paying income tax on your retirement investment and related earnings for as long as you can; and
- If you must take a distribution that triggers payment of income tax, minimize the tax paid by controlling the timing or amount of the distribution so that you are in the lowest possible income tax bracket.

The final "secret" for investment success in a qualified plan is investment diversification. Investment diversification is such an important fundamental investment principle that the next section is devoted solely to this concept.

c. Investment Diversification

The fundamental concept of investment diversification can be reduced to the following sage advice: *Don't put all of your (retirement nest) eggs in one basket.* A diversified investment portfolio is one in which the assets are invested broadly across the spectrum of the national (or even the world) economy. When one industrial sector is languishing, another is thriving. When one nation's economy is sluggish, the economy of another country is growing. If one company fails, many others are doing well. When corporate earnings generally are lackluster due to an economic recession, bonds issued by the United States Treasury, state and local governments, and private corporations provide a steady stream of interest income.

A diversified investment portfolio accomplishes two things. First, a diversified investment portfolio *maximizes* the average rate of investment return over time. Second, a diversified investment portfolio *minimizes* the risk of catastrophic investment losses. Everyone understands the benefit of minimizing catastrophic investment losses. Many individual investors, however, do not fully appreciate the dramatic effect of increasing the average annual rate of investment return—even by a small percentage— over a long period of time.

To illustrate this point, assume that you invest $100 in your 401(k) plan account at age twenty. If your investment earns an average annual rate of return of 6%, when you retire at age seventy your $100 investment will have become $1,842.02. Not bad, you think. But consider what will happen to your $100 investment if, by adopting a diversified investment strategy for your 401(k) plan account, you are able to increase your average annual rate of investment return over a fifty-year investment period from 6% to 7%. If you earn an average annual return of 7%, at age seventy your $100 investment will have grown to $2,945.70, or $1,103.68 more! (To calculate these numbers yourself, refer to Table C.2, Compound Amount of $1, in Appendix C of the casebook. Multiply $100 times the factors for 6% and 7% for a period of fifty years and compare the results.)

Why the substantial difference? The 1% increase in the average annual rate of investment return, *compounded over fifty years,* yields a much higher overall rate of investment return. In other words, the magical principle of compounded investment earnings over time is at work.

Professional investment managers with substantial assets under management can achieve investment diversification by investing in the stock of many different individual companies. The individual investor with smaller sums to invest can achieve investment diversification by buying shares in a mutual fund, the assets of which are invested in a diversified manner by the investment manager for the fund. Virtually all 401(k) plans today offer mutual funds as part of their menu of investment options.

The economic benefit of investment diversification appears obvious. Yet some individuals who direct the investment of their 401(k) plan accounts ignore this fundamental investment principle. The Employee Benefit Research Institute (EBRI) has studied the investment decisions of 401(k) plan participants for many years. See EMPLOYEE BENEFIT RESEARCH INST., ISSUE BRIEF NO. 394, 401(K) PLAN ASSET ALLOCATION,

ACCOUNT BALANCES, AND LOAN ACTIVITY IN 2012 (DEC. 2013). FOR 2012, the EBRI study consisted of 64,619 plans with 24.0 million participants and $1.536 trillion in assets. The EBRI study found that slightly more than 10% of 401(k) plan participants in the study *were zero percent invested in in any type of equity investment.* Thirty-six percent (36%) of the 401(k) plan participants in the study participated in a 401(k) plan that offered the company stock of the employer as an investment option. Approximately 7% of participants in these 401(k) plans *had more than 80% of their 401(k) plan account balance invested in company stock.* In short, the EBRI study found that some 401(k) plan participants make investment choices that are likely either to reduce their average rate of investment return over time by failing to invest in the stock market, or place themselves at risk of suffering a catastrophic investment loss by investing in company stock.

PROBLEMS ON INVESTMENT FUNDAMENTALS

PROBLEM ONE

In the example of Maria and George, Maria had accumulated $535,472 in 401(k) plan retirement savings by the time she was ready to retire. This may seem like a substantial sum of money. But is it really? Select a reasonable discount rate and determine the *present value* of receiving $535,472 as a lump sum in forty years. (Hint: Use Table C.1, Present Value of $1 Tomorrow, in Appendix C of the casebook to calculate the present value of $535,472 received forty years from now.)

If you were to retire today, would you consider this present value amount adequate for a financially secure retirement?

PROBLEM TWO

Assume that Maria wants to retire today and she has accumulated $535,472 in her 401(k) plan account. Rather than purchasing an individual annuity contract from an insurance company, Maria decides to "self annuitize" her retirement savings. Maria determines that she will need to withdraw $25,000 each year for the next twenty years to supplement her other sources of retirement income. If Maria anticipates an average annual return on her retirement investments of 6%, how much should she set aside today to be able to make annual withdrawals of $25,000 for the next twenty years? (Hint: Use Table C.3, Present Value of Annuity of $1, in Appendix C of the casebook to calculate this "set aside" amount. To determine the amount that Maria should set aside, multiply the factor that corresponds to 6% and twenty years times $25,000.)

If you were to retire today, how much money would you need to provide yourself with a comfortable annual income during the next twenty years of retirement?

C. TYPES AND CHARACTERISTICS OF QUALIFIED PLANS

1. DEFINED CONTRIBUTION (INDIVIDUAL ACCOUNT) PLANS AND DEFINED BENEFIT PLANS

Qualified plan sponsorship by the employer is voluntary. The employer is likely to sponsor a qualified plan only if the plan is affordable for the employer, suitable for its business and workforce, and will serve as an attractive recruiting and retention tool for its employees. When an employer considers whether to sponsor a qualified plan, the threshold question in the employer's mind is, "What type of plan best suits my business?"

The Code and ERISA divide the universe of employee pension benefit plans into two categories: (1) defined contribution plans (also known as individual account plans); and (2) defined benefit plans. As discussed below, the name for each category is derived (literally) from how the plan document is written to define the nature of the sponsoring employer's obligation concerning the benefits provided by the plan. Within each of these two categories, various plan design alternatives are possible. These design variations give rise to the commonly used names for the different types of qualified plans.

The characteristics of defined contribution plans and defined benefit plans are quite different. As you read the description of these characteristics, consider what types of businesses would find each characteristic advantageous or disadvantageous when deciding what type of qualified plan to sponsor.

Defined Contribution Plans

In a defined contribution plan, the plan document *defines the amount of the contribution* the employer must make to the plan each year. The employer's funding obligation under a defined contribution plan is limited to this plan-defined contribution amount. In a defined contribution plan, the employer's contribution to the plan is allocated among each participant's account according to the allocation formula described in the plan document. This system of individual accounts is the hallmark of a defined contribution plan.

A participant's benefit at retirement under a defined contribution plan consists of the *nonforfeitable* (or *vested*) balance in the individual's account, which includes both contributions to the account and accumulated investment earnings. Thus, it is the amount of contributions to the individual's account, plus the investment earnings on account assets over time, that ultimately determine the amount of the participant's benefit at retirement. A defined contribution plan does not guarantee that the participant will receive a specified amount as a benefit at retirement.

The various types of defined contribution plans are characterized by the nature of the contribution that the employer makes to the plan. In a *profit sharing plan*, the amount of the employer's annual contribution is left to the discretion of the employer. The profit sharing plan originally derived its name from the requirement that the employer had to earn an accounting profit in order to make a contribution to the plan. Although this requirement was repealed in 1986, see Code § 401(a)(27), the name remains, and the term profit sharing plan is used to describe any defined contribution plan where the employer has discretion to determine the amount of its annual contribution to the plan.

In a profit sharing plan, the employer may choose to contribute a specified percentage of each participant's compensation to the individual's plan account. Alternatively, the employer may choose to contribute a lump sum amount to the profit sharing plan as a symbolic gesture, with the lump sum contribution representing the employees' collective share of the employer's profits for the year. A lump sum contribution is allocated among the individual participant accounts in the plan according to the allocation formula described in the profit sharing plan document.

In contrast to the financial flexibility for the employer offered by a profit sharing plan, in a *money purchase pension plan* the amount of the employer's annual contribution obligation is fixed by a formula under the terms of the plan. The typical money purchase pension plan requires that the employer must contribute a predetermined percentage of each participant's compensation to the participant's individual plan account each year. (A variation of the money purchase pension plan, known as the *target benefit plan*, uses a contribution formula that is actuarially designed to produce a specific account balance at retirement.) Unlike the profit sharing plan, a money purchase pension plan is subject to the minimum funding requirements of the Code, which impose an excise tax penalty on the employer if the employer's contribution to the plan is less than the amount dictated by the terms of the plan document. See Code §§ 412(a); 4971.

In a traditional *401(k) plan,* also known as a *cash or deferral arrangement* or *CODA,* the plan participants individually direct the employer to contribute part of their current compensation to their plan accounts rather than receiving this amount as present compensation. Although the employer is not required to make a contribution to a 401(k) plan, many employers voluntarily make *employer matching contributions* up to a certain percentage or amount of each participant's salary deferral contributions to the 401(k) plan. These employer matching contributions provide an incentive for employees to make salary deferral contributions in the 401(k) plan.

The 401(k) plan did not exist when ERISA originally was enacted in 1974. Rather, the 401(k) plan came into existence in 1980 as the result of technical changes made by Congress to the Code. Today's 401(k) plan derives its name from Code Section 401(k), which expressly authorizes this type of defined contribution plan. Many employers today sponsor a profit sharing plan with a 401(k) feature.

Prior to the enactment of Code Section 401(k), employers sponsored so-called *thrift savings plans*. Historically, employers sponsored thrift savings plans so that employees could make after-tax contributions, usually in the form of a periodic payroll deduction, to the employee's plan account. In essence, thrift savings plans operated as employer-sponsored savings accounts for employees. After the enactment of Code Section 401(k), employers converted their thrift savings plans into 401(k) plans so that employees could make pre-tax contributions to their plan accounts. In some instances, however, the employer may have retained the original name of the plan. Hence, you may occasionally come across a 401(k) plan today that is still designated as the "Company Thrift Savings Plan."

From the employer's perspective, a 401(k) plan is perceived as desirable because the plan is funded by the employees themselves through voluntary salary deferral contributions. Another perceived advantage of the 401(k) plan from the perspective of both employers and employees is that, unlike other types of plans, the 401(k) plan provides flexibility in the employer's overall compensation (wages plus benefits) package. The 401(k) plan allows each individual worker to choose between deferring receipt of part of the worker's wages to save for retirement, or to receive all of the worker's compensation as current income. For every other type of pension plan, the employer's contribution to the plan is a form of "forced" retirement savings for those participants who may have preferred to receive higher current wages instead.

The individual account system inherent in any defined contribution plan shifts the *risk of investment loss* to the plan's participants, whose ultimate retirement benefit will depend in large part on the investment earnings generated by the assets in their accounts. Although the employer may continue to assume responsibility for investing the assets in a defined contribution plan, the growing trend among employers is to allow participants, who bear the risk of investment loss, to direct the investment of the assets in their accounts. This is particularly true in the context of 401(k) plans, where the participants generally both finance and direct the investment of their own 401(k) accounts.

From the perspective of the employee, one key advantage of a defined contribution plan is the *portability* of the individual's account. If a participant changes jobs, the participant can always transfer (in technical terms, *rollover*) the nonforfeitable balance of the participant's account to an IRA. In addition, the participant may be able to rollover the nonforfeitable account balance to the retirement plan sponsored by the participant's new employer.

Defined contribution plans also offer continued income tax advantages to the participant during the participant's retirement years. Almost all profit sharing plans and 401(k) plans pay the participant's benefit at retirement in the form of a lump sum, which may be rolled over to an IRA and withdrawn as needed by the participant during retirement. So long as the money remains in the IRA, the participant continues to defer income taxation of contributions and accumulated investment earnings. The participant will pay income tax only when amounts are distributed from the IRA. This continuation of deferred taxation provides a significant investment advantage, particularly if the participant will spend many years in retirement and does not need an immediate distribution from the IRA to provide retirement income.

A defined contribution plan that pays retirement benefits in a lump sum rather than in the form of an annuity transfers the risk of living a very long life, and thereby outliving one's retirement savings, to the retiree. This risk is known as the *risk of longevity*. The corresponding trade-off for assuming the risk of longevity is that, unlike benefits from a qualified plan that are paid in an annuity form, the portion of a lump sum retirement benefit that is not consumed during life is transferrable to the beneficiaries designated by the participant. If no beneficiaries are designated, the remaining amount becomes part of the deceased participant's estate.

Defined Benefit Plans

In a defined benefit plan, the plan document *defines the amount of the benefit* that will be paid by the plan to the participant at retirement. The benefit amount is typically determined by a formula based on a combination of the participant's earnings and years of service with the employer. A defined benefit plan formula usually provides the most generous benefits to workers who have long years of service with the employer.

The employer's funding obligation under a defined benefit plan is to make certain that the plan will have sufficient assets in the future to provide the retirement benefits promised under the plan's formula. Federal law requires a minimum level of funding for a defined benefit plan. The purpose of this minimum funding requirement is to ensure that the plan has adequate assets today so that, given investment earnings over time, the plan will be able to pay the promised level of benefits to the plan's participants tomorrow. Specialized pension plan actuaries assist the employer in determining the funding status of the defined benefit plan each year under federal law. If the assets of the plan fall below the federal minimum funding standard, the employer is obligated to contribute an amount to the plan sufficient to bring the plan's total assets up to the federal minimum funding standard.

Compared with the defined contribution plan, the defined benefit plan imposes greater fiscal and fiduciary responsibility on the employer, who is responsible for funding the plan and investing the plan's assets. The employer's required funding contribution to the defined benefit plan under the federal minimum funding rules can vary dramatically from year to year due to unanticipated investment losses or changes in the interest rates used to determine the minimum funding level under federal law. Particularly for smaller and less established companies with variable earnings, the financial unpredictability associated with a defined benefit plan may make the employer reluctant to sponsor a defined benefit plan.

The various types of traditional defined benefit plans are commonly referred to by their benefit formulas. In a *flat benefit formula plan*, the plan formula provides that a fixed dollar amount will be paid for every year of service. In a *career average formula plan*, the plan formula provides a benefit equal to a fixed percentage of the participant's compensation, multiplied by the participant's years of service. The percentage may be calculated on each year's compensation, or the plan may use the participant's average compensation calculated over the entire period of service. A *final pay formula plan* is similar to the career average formula plan, except that the compensation figure used is the average compensation measured over the period at the end of the participant's career (typically the last five or ten years) when presumably the participant's earnings are at the highest level.

A defined benefit plan provides that the plan will pay the participant a specific amount upon attaining normal retirement age under the plan. If the participant terminates employment prior to attaining normal retirement age, in a single-employer plan the participant's accrued benefits under the plan cannot be transferred to a new employer. Unless waived by the participant (and if the participant is married, the participant's spouse), the benefits from a defined benefit plan are paid at retirement in the form of a monthly annuity for the life of the participant or the joint lives of the participant and the participant's spouse. Payment of benefits in the form of a lifetime annuity is designed to give the participant a dependable source of retirement income, no matter how long the participant lives. Defined benefit plans typically transfer the risk of longevity associated with lifetime annuity benefits by using plan assets to purchase annuity contracts for retired participants from an insurance company.

Unlike defined contribution plans, the retirement benefits provided by defined benefit plans are federally insured by the Pension Benefit Guaranty Corporation. In the event of insolvency, the Pension Benefit

Guaranty Corporation will pay the plan's promised benefits to each plan participant, up to the limit established under federal law.

Hybrid Plans

A hybrid plan is a defined benefit plan that simulates a defined contribution plan by presenting the value of each participant's retirement benefit under the plan as the lump sum balance of a hypothetical individual account. A hybrid plan is technically classified as a defined benefit plan, despite this hypothetical account feature, because the employer remains responsible for investing the plan's assets and must make contributions to the plan sufficient to comply with the minimum funding rules for defined benefit plans.

The most common type of hybrid plan is the *cash balance plan*. In a cash balance plan, each participant's benefit is presented as the balance of a hypothetical account. The benefit formula for the cash balance plan typically requires the employer to contribute annually to each participant's account an amount equal to a specified percentage of the participant's pay, plus an assumed rate of investment return on the account.

For example, the plan's formula may provide that each participant's hypothetical account will be credited annually with an amount equal to 5% of the participant's compensation. This credit amount further will be credited with an annual rate of return equal to the rate of return on a thirty-year United States Treasury bond. Based on this formula, a participant with annual compensation of $50,000 would have $2,500 credited to the participant's hypothetical account each year. This $2,500 amount in the hypothetical account (and contributions in subsequent years) would be credited with interest at the plan's assumed rate for each year until the participant terminated employment or commenced receiving benefits under the plan at retirement.

As with a defined benefit plan, the employer retains investment responsibility and assumes the risk of investment loss for the assets of the cash balance plan. If the plan's investments underperform the assumed rate of interest credited for each account, the employer remains responsible for funding the hypothetical account balance promised under the terms of the cash balance plan. Conversely, if the plan's investment returns exceed the plan's assumed rate of credited interest, the superior investment performance reduces the amount of the employer's minimum funding obligation for the next year. If the investment returns from the plan's assets significantly exceed the plan's assumed rate of credited interest, the employer may enjoy a "contribution holiday"—a period of time during which, under minimum funding rules, the employer is not required to make any contributions to the plan because the plan already is adequately funded as a result of the superior investment returns.

Another type of hybrid plan is the *pension equity plan*. In a pension equity plan, the benefit formula defines each participant's benefit as a lump sum equal to a percentage of the participant's final compensation, multiplied by the participant's number of years of service. To illustrate, assume that the pension equity plan provides for a benefit equal to 20% of the participant's final compensation times the participant's number of years of service. Under this formula, a participant whose final compensation was $50,000 who retired after 25 years of service would receive a benefit with a lump sum value of $250,000.

Viewed from the perspective of plan participants, hybrid plans appear to be defined contribution plans because each participant's benefit is presented as the balance of a hypothetical account. Hybrid plans often are designed so that the participant has the choice of receiving the distribution of plan benefits either as a lump sum or as an annuity. This distribution feature makes the plan's benefits portable if the participant terminates employment prior to attaining normal retirement age under the plan.

Employee Stock Ownership Plans

Although an *employee stock ownership plan* (ESOP) is a type of defined contribution plan, its objective is not simply to provide a source of retirement income to plan participants. An employer may desire to establish an ESOP as a financing mechanism for a corporate acquisition. An employer also may decide to establish an ESOP as part of the overall estate plan for the owner of a privately held business.

An ESOP is a defined contribution plan that is designed to invest primarily in *qualifying employer securities*. See Code §§ 409; 4975(e). An ESOP's concentrated investment in employer stock is permissible because an ESOP is exempt from the normal rule under ERISA that the assets of a plan must be prudently diversified. See ERISA § 404(a)(2). In general, qualifying employer securities include the publicly traded stock of the employer or, if the employer's stock is privately held, the common stock of the employer having the greatest voting power and dividend rights. See Code § 409(*l*)(1)–(2). If the company stock held by the ESOP is not publicly traded, a participant who receives his ESOP retirement benefit in the form of a distribution of the stock from his account must be given the option to sell the stock back to employer (in technical terms, a *put option*) for its fair market value. See Code § 409(h).

As a corporate finance tool, so-called *leveraged ESOPs* are unique among qualified plans in that the ESOP is permitted to borrow money from the sponsoring employer (or have the sponsoring employer guarantee a loan to the ESOP from a commercial lender) if the loan proceeds are used to purchase qualifying employer securities. Ordinarily, such a loan or loan guarantee would be prohibited. See ERISA § 406; Code § 4975(c).

In a leveraged ESOP, the qualifying employer securities held by the ESOP are pledged as collateral for the loan that is used to acquire the employer securities as part of a corporate acquisition. As the loan is repaid, the pledged shares of stock are released and allocated to the accounts of the ESOP participants. Prior to 1996, Code Section 133 encouraged commercial lenders to make loans of leveraged ESOPs by allowing the lender to exclude from its taxable income 50% of the interest received from the ESOP loan. This provision was repealed for loans made after August 20, 1996. See Small Business Jobs Protection Act of 1996, Pub. L. No. 104–188, § 1602(a), 110 Stat. 1755. Many ESOPs in existence today were established prior to the repeal of Code Section 133's tax incentive for loans to ESOPs.

ESOPs also are used as an estate planning tool when the shareholder of a privately held business desires to sell his stock and defer recognition of capital gains for income tax purposes. The founder of a successful company is likely to have a large percentage of the assets of his future estate concentrated in company stock. The founder also is likely to have a very low basis in his company stock. Thus, diversifying the founder's assets by selling the stock of the company is likely to trigger a substantial capital gains tax. By selling at least 30% of the ownership of the company to an ESOP and purchasing *qualifying replacement property,* the founder of the company can simultaneously defer capital gains tax on the sale of the company stock while diversifying his investment portfolio. See Code § 1042.

The specialized uses of ESOPs for purposes other than providing workers with retirement benefits make a detailed discussion of ESOPs unsuitable for an introductory course on employee benefit plans. The technical requirements for the operation and administration of ESOPs are found in Code Sections 409, 4975(d)(3) and 4975(e)(7), and accompanying Treasury Department regulations.

PROBLEMS ON TYPES OF QUALIFIED PLANS

PROBLEM ONE

Identify the type of qualified retirement plan from the following plan document language:

A. Contributions to the Plan shall be made at the discretion of the Employer. Contributions shall be allocated to Participant Accounts pro rata based on Plan Compensation.

B. The Accrued Benefit of a Participant shall be equal to 35% of the Participant's Final Average Compensation.

C. The Employer shall make an annual contribution to the Plan equal to 10% of each Participant's Plan Compensation.

D. The Employer shall contribute to the Plan an amount equal to 2% of the amount of each Participant's Salary Deferral Election.

PROBLEM TWO

For each type of retirement plan described below, what characteristics of the employer would be important factors in determining whether or not the plan would be a suitable choice for the adoption by the employer?

A. Defined benefit plan

B. Money purchase pension plan

C. Profit sharing plan

D. 401(k) plan

2. THE GROWTH OF DEFINED CONTRIBUTION PLANS

Since the enactment of ERISA in 1974, there has been a shift in the type of qualified plan favored by employers. Tables 3.3 through 3.5 below provide the raw data documenting the growing trend among employers favoring the defined contribution plan in general, and the 401(k) plan in particular.

Table 3.3

Number of Pension Plans

Year	Total	DB Plans	DC Plans	401(k) Plans
1980	488,901	148,096	340,805	—
1985	632,135	170,172	461,963	29,860
1990	712,308	113,062	599,245	97,614
1995	693,404	69,492	623,912	200,813
2000	735,651	48,773	686,878	348,053
2005	679,095	47,614	631,481	436,207
2007	707,787	48,982	658,805	490,917
2009	706,667	47,137	659,530	512,464
2011	683,647	45,526	638,380	513,496

Source: U.S. Dep't of Labor, Private Pension Plan Bulletin Historical Tables and Graphs (June 2013).

Table 3.4

Number of Active Participant in Pension Plans (in thousands)

Year	Total	DB Plans	DC Plans	401(k) Plans
1980	48,986	30,100	18,886	–
1985	62,064	28,895	33,168	10,315
1990	61,545	26,205	35,304	19,466
1995	65,599	23,395	42,203	27,759
2000	73,092	22,218	50,874	39,847
2005	82,665	20,310	62,355	54,623
2007	86,280	19,407	66,873	59,566
2009	90,105	18,111	71,994	60,285
2011	90,175	16,507	73,668	61,371

Source: U.S. Dep't of Labor, Private Pension Plan Bulletin Historical Tables and Graphs (June 2013).

Table 3.5

Assets of Pension Plans (in millions of dollars)

Year	Total	DB Plans	DC Plans	401(k) Plans
1980	563,551	401,455	162,096	–
1985	1,252,739	826,117	426,622	–
1990	1,674,139	961,904	712,236	384,854
1995	2,723,735	1,402,079	1,321,657	863,918
2000	4,202,672	1,986,177	2,216,495	1,724,549
2005	5,061,622	2,254,032	2,807,590	2,395,792
2007	6,090,473	2,646,603	3,443,870	2,981,522
2009	5,511,060	2,193,983	3,317,076	2,784,064
2011	6,345,595	2,516,109	3,829,487	3,145,851

Source: U.S. Dep't of Labor, Private Pension Plan Bulletin Historical Tables and Graphs (June 2013).

The story of the modern pension system is the story of the emergence of the 401(k) plan. When Congress enacted ERISA in 1974, the 401(k) plan did not exist. The 401(k) plan began to grow in popularity after

Congress amended the pension tax rules by adding Code Section 401(k). The subsequent effect on the pension system has been dramatic, as evidenced by the data in Tables 3.3, 3.4 and 3.5.

The reasons for this dramatic shift in the pension system are complex. One explanation attributes this shift to underlying structural change in the United States economy and labor workforce away from traditional large firms and unionized manufacturing industries, where defined benefit plans are more common, toward smaller firms and non-unionized industries, particularly in the services sector, where defined contribution plans, and 401(k) plans in particular, are the most popular. Another explanation is that the relative cost of plan sponsorship and administration for the employer is higher for defined benefit plans than for defined contribution plans. This cost differential was exacerbated in the 1980s, when Congress enacted changes to the pension tax laws that reduced the tax incentives for small and medium-sized employers to sponsor defined benefit plans. A third explanation is that as job insecurity and mobility increased, workers preferred the portability of retirement benefits provided by individual account plans. Finally, as the United States stock market experienced strong investment gains during the 1990s and again from 2002 to 2007, workers increasingly demanded 401(k) plans to reap the benefits of a rising stock market.

From a policy perspective, the employer-controlled defined benefit and the participant-directed 401(k) plan represent two distinct models for the future of the pension system. The defined benefit plan represents a *paternalistic model.* Under this paternalistic model, employers bear the funding cost and investment risk of providing retirement benefits to their workers. In contrast, the participant-directed 401(k) plan represents an *individual responsibility model*, where each individual worker is responsible for funding and investing his or her own retirement benefit.

Experts disagree concerning whether participants in 401(k) plans can accumulate sufficient retirement savings to provide an adequate income during retirement. In Chapter Two of their book, *Coming Up Short: The Challenge of 401(k) Plans,* Alicia Munnell and Annika Sundén present the results of a simulation study showing that if certain key assumptions are satisfied, it is possible for an individual covered continuously by a 401(k) plan to accumulate even more retirement wealth than the individual would have received from a traditional defined benefit plan. These assumptions include:

(1) a constant contribution rate from employee contributions and employer matching contributions of 9% of compensation (which the authors admit may be "somewhat optimistic");

(2) the individual begins contributing to the 401(k) plan before age 40, and does so continuously until retirement age;

(3) the assets in the 401(k) plan earn a constant nominal (before inflation) annual rate of investment return of at least 7.6%; and

(4) the individual does not make any withdrawals from the 401(k) plan until retirement.

In the remainder of their book, Munnell and Sundén discuss numerous research studies suggesting why, for a variety of reasons, many individuals likely will fail to satisfy these assumptions and therefore may find themselves "coming up short" for an adequate retirement income based on their 401(k) plan retirement savings. See generally ALICIA MUNNELL & ANNIKA SUNDÉN, COMING UP SHORT: THE CHALLENGE OF 401(K) PLANS (2004). In particular, two important factors that affect a participant's ability to save for retirement are earnings variability and job mobility. Why would these factors be important in determining an individual's accumulated 401(k) plan savings over the course of the individual's career?

Research studies indicate there are two significant obstacles workers face in trying to achieve retirement income security through a 401(k) plan. First, beginning early in their careers, workers must regularly contribute sufficient amounts to the 401(k) plan. Second, workers must invest their 401(k) plan accounts wisely to maximize investment returns and minimize catastrophic investment losses. Pension system reform proposals seek to encourage this type of investment behavior among workers. Proposals for reform focus primarily on investment education and investment advice for 401(k) plan participants, and greater government regulation of the investment options available to 401(k) plan participants. These issues are explored in more detail in Chapter Five of the casebook.

D. AGE, SERVICE AND VESTING REQUIREMENTS

1. INTRODUCTION

The Code and ERISA contain duplicate age, service and vesting requirements for participants in qualified plans. These requirements address two fundamental questions. First, what is the *maximum amount of time* an employer can exclude an otherwise eligible new employee from participating in the employer's qualified plan based on a minimum age requirement or a prerequisite period of service with the employer? Second, if a plan participant terminates employment, *how much*, if any, of the participant's accrued benefit under the plan can be *forfeited*? The answers to these questions are found in Code Sections 410(a) and 411(a), which are duplicated in ERISA Sections 202 and 203.

As a prelude to examining the age, service and vesting requirements in detail, it is important to note the limited function of these rules. The age, service and vesting rules protect only employees who have already been designated by the employer as *eligible to participate* in the employer's qualified plan. These rules do *not* prevent the employer from designating certain groups of employees—based on neutral business criteria—as ineligible to participate in the plan. For example, a plan may designate as ineligible for participation all hourly employees, or the employees who work in a certain division, facility or geographic location.

The employer's ability to exclude employees from participation in a qualified plan is constrained by a different set of Code requirements, known as the *minimum coverage rules*. The minimum coverage rules, which are unique to the Code and are not duplicated by ERISA, are discussed in Section F of Chapter Three.

2. AGE AND SERVICE RULES FOR ELIGIBILITY

The employer may require that an employee who is otherwise eligible to participate in the qualified plan must attain a certain minimum age before becoming a participant in the plan. A qualified plan's minimum age requirement for participation generally cannot exceed age 21. See Code § 410(a)(1)(A)(I); ERISA § 202(a)(1)(A)(i). An individual also cannot be excluded from participating in a qualified plan because the individual *exceeds* a specified age. This rule prevents an employer from discriminating against older employees by excluding them from participating in the plan merely on the basis of age. See Code § 410(a)(2); ERISA § 202(a)(2).

In addition to a minimum age requirement, the employer may require that a newly hired eligible employee must perform a prerequisite period of service for the employer before being admitted as a participant in the employer's qualified plan. This service period generally cannot exceed one *year of service*. See Code § 410(a)(1)(A)(ii); ERISA § 202(a)(1)(A)(ii). A year of service is defined as a twelve consecutive month period during which an employee has worked at least 1,000 *hours of service*. See Code § 410(a)(3)(A); ERISA § 202(a)(3)(A). Regulations issued by the Department of Labor provide the following guidance to employers concerning how these statutory requirements are to be implemented.

- **When does the twelve consecutive month period begin?**

For new employees, the twelve consecutive month period begins on the date employment commenced. If a new employee fails to obtain 1,000 hours of service during the first year of employment, the plan may continue to measure hours of service required for eligibility to participate in the plan using the individual's employment commencement date, or the plan may switch to a calendar year measure (so long as the calendar year includes the first anniversary of the employee's commencement date). See DOL Reg. § 2530.202–2(a)–(b).

- **Does the employee have to work continuously during the eligibility year of service period?**

No. The employee can work intermittently during the twelve consecutive month period rather than working continuously for twelve months. As long as the individual has worked 1,000 hours during the course of the consecutive twelve month period, the individual must be given credit for an eligibility year of service. See DOL Reg. § 2530.200b–1(b).

- **What is an hour of service, and how does the employer determine an individual's number of hours of service?**

An hour of service is more than just simply the employee's regularly scheduled working hours. As a general rule, an hour of service is *every hour for which the employee has received or is entitled to receive compensation*. An hour of service includes unscheduled or irregular work periods and overtime hours. An hour of service also includes periods during which no work is performed, but the employee is still being paid (so-called paid passive hours of service). Paid passive hours of service include time for paid vacation, paid holidays, paid time off for jury duty, paid sick leave or paid disability leave, paid time off for military leave, and periods of employment for which a court has awarded damages in the form of back pay. See DOL Reg. § 2530.200b–2(a).

Some employers may prefer not to keep track of each employee's work using an hour by hour standard of measurement. The employer is permitted to use alternative methods to measure hours of service. See DOL Reg. § 2530.200b–3 (authorizing three alternative equivalency methods in addition to the actual method option).

- **Can the employer exclude a group of employees from participating in the plan solely because they are classified by the employer as "part-time" or "temporary" workers?**

No. Excluding a group of employees *solely* on the basis that they are classified as "part-time" or "temporary" or "seasonal" workers is tantamount to a disguised service requirement that violates the minimum service requirements of Code Section 410(a) and ERISA Section 202(a). Under a plan with this type of exclusion, an otherwise eligible employee may exceed 1,000 hours of service, which is generally the maximum prerequisite period of service that a qualified plan can impose before admitting the employee as a participant in the plan. See IRS Employee Plans Determinations Quality Assurance Bulletin, Part-Time Employees Revisited, Feb. 14, 2006; IRS Field Directive dated Nov. 24, 1994.

- **Can the employer exclude individuals from participating in the plan because they are classified by the employer as independent contractors and not as regular employees?**

Yes, but the classification may later be subject to challenge based on the facts and circumstances. The *Darden* factors described in Chapter Two are used to determine whether or not an individual should have been classified by the employer as a regular employee and therefore eligible to participate in the plan.

- **Can the plan have more generous rules than the minimum age and service requirements of the Code and ERISA?**

Yes. The age and service requirements are the maximum restrictions the plan can impose to exclude an otherwise eligible employee from participating in the employer's qualified plan. The employer's qualified plan can always establish rules that allow for the earlier participation of eligible employees in the plan. For example, some 401(k) plans allow eligible employees to enroll immediately in the plan and begin making salary deferral contributions from the first day of employment. Other 401(k) plans impose a three month or six month period of service before new employees can participate in the 401(k) plan.

- **How soon must the employee become a participant in the plan after satisfying the plan's age and service requirements?**

The statutory requirement for the latest point in time when an eligible employee must be admitted to the plan as a participant after satisfying the plan's age and service requirements essentially creates a logic puzzle. See Code § 410(a)(4); ERISA § 202(a)(4). Employers generally solve this logic puzzle by having two plan entry dates, set six months apart, for eligible employees who have satisfied the plan's age and service requirements. Once a new eligible employee has satisfied the plan's minimum age and service requirements, the employee must be admitted to the plan as a participant on the next available plan entry date. Even if the employee has completed 1,000 hours of service before the initial twelve consecutive month period of service has ended, the employer's plan can delay the employee's participation in the plan until the next available plan entry date *after* the twelve consecutive month period has been completed.

As with the year of service requirement for participation in a qualified plan, this rule represents the maximum period of time the qualified plan can delay the employee's participation in the plan after satisfying the plan's minimum age and service requirements. The employer is free to design the terms of the qualified plan so that its employees enter the plan as participants at an earlier time, such as immediately upon completing the plan's minimum age and service requirements for participation.

Minimum Service Requirements and the Accumulation of Retirement Savings

Many employers require some minimum service period before a new employee is admitted as a participant in the employer's qualified plan. For a worker who frequently changes jobs, a one year of service requirement for participation in a qualified plan can significantly reduce the amount of retirement savings accumulated over the course of the worker's career. An employee who has not yet been admitted as a participant in the employer's defined contribution plan does not share in any employer contributions made to the plan. Requiring a year of service prior to participation is less detrimental to a participant in a defined benefit plan because the employee's period of service prior to becoming a plan participant still counts as service for purposes of vesting. See Code § 411(a)(4); ERISA § 203(b)(1). The vesting rules are discussed in the next section.

Minimum service requirements vary widely for 401(k) plans, ranging from immediate eligibility to one year of service. The potential reduction in future accumulated retirement savings resulting from a one year of service requirement is particularly significant for participants in 401(k) plans. For example, a 22-year-old who contributes $4,000 each year to a 401(k) plan until age 62 will have accumulated $1.1 million in retirement savings, assuming an eight percent compounded annual rate of return. But if that worker changes jobs seven times during the course of a career and must sit out a year each time before becoming eligible to participate in the employer's 401(k) plan, the worker will have accumulated just $534,000 in retirement savings through 401(k) plans by age 62. See Jeannie Mandelker, *Empowered Employees*, CFO, April 1999, at 74. The difference, much more than merely the $28,000 in lost contributions, is attributable to the lost economic benefit of pre-tax compounded investment earnings inside the 401(k) plan over a long period of time.

3. VESTING RULES

The vesting rules become significant when a participant terminates employment. If the participant's benefits under the employer's qualified plan are fully (100%) vested, the benefits cannot be forfeited if the participant terminates employment.

Code Section 411(a) and ERISA Section 203 establish the maximum amount of time the employer can delay a participant from fully vesting in the participant's benefit under a qualified plan. For purposes of the reading material that follows, you should assume that references to a plan "benefit" mean the participant's *accrued benefit* under the plan. The concept of an accrued benefit in the context of a defined contribution plan and a defined benefit plan is explained more fully in Section E of Chapter Three. For a defined contribution plan, the participant's accrued benefit is the total balance (combining both vested and any nonvested portions) of the participant's plan account. For defined benefit plans, the concept of an accrued benefit is much more complex. For simplicity's sake, at this point you should think of the participant's accrued benefit from a defined benefit plan as the monthly annuity amount the participant will receive if the participant continues employment until attaining normal retirement age under the plan.

Two factors determine the degree of vesting in the benefits provided by a qualified plan: (1) the applicable *vesting schedule* under the terms of the plan and (2) the participant's number of *years of vesting service*. Each of these factors is discussed below.

Determining the Applicable Vesting Schedule

There are seven possible vesting schedules that may apply to benefits from a qualified plan. For benefits from a traditional defined benefit plan, the employer may choose either *five-year cliff vesting* or *seven-year graduated vesting*. For employer contributions to a defined contribution plan (including employer matching contributions to a 401(k) plan), the employer may choose either *three-year cliff vesting* or *six-year graduated vesting*. In the event the plan becomes *top heavy*, a fifth type of vesting schedule must be used. A special vesting rule applies if a *plan termination* has occurred. Finally, hybrid forms of defined benefit plans, such as cash balance plans, have a unique vesting rule.

Defined Benefit Plan Vesting Schedules

For defined benefit plans, the employer may select either a five-year cliff or a seven-year graduated vesting schedule. The five-year cliff vesting schedule is described in Code Section 411(a)(2)(A)(ii). Under a five-year cliff vesting schedule, the participant is not vested in any portion of the participant's benefit under the plan until the participant has attained five years of vesting service. Upon attaining five years of vesting service, the participant immediately becomes fully (100%) vested in the benefit under the plan. See Code § 411(a)(2)(A)(ii); ERISA § 203(a)(2)(A)(ii).

The seven-year graduated vesting schedule, which is set forth in Table 3.6, is found in Code Section 411(a)(2)(A)(iii) and ERISA Section 203(a)(2)(A)(iii).

Table 3.6

Defined Benefit Plans
Seven-Year Graduated Vesting Schedule

Years of Service	Nonforfeitable % of Benefit
3	20
4	40
5	60
6	80
7 or more	100

Under a seven-year graduated vesting schedule, the participant becomes partially vested (20%) in the participant's benefit after attaining three years of vesting service. For each subsequent year of vesting service attained, the participant becomes vested in a progressively higher percentage of the benefit under the plan until finally becoming fully (100%) vested after attaining seven years of vesting service. See Code § 411(a)(2)(A)(iii); ERISA § 203(a)(2)(A)(iii).

Defined Contribution Plan Vesting Schedules

An employee's salary deferral contributions to a 401(k) plan (and any related investment earnings) are immediately and fully vested. See Code § 401(k)(2)(C). For employer contributions to a participant's individual account under a defined contribution plan (including employer matching contributions), the employer may select either a three-year cliff or a six-year graduated vesting schedule. The three-year cliff vesting schedule is described in Code § 411(a)(2)(B)(ii). Under a three-year cliff vesting schedule, the participant is not vested in any portion of the employer contributions to the account until the participant has attained three years of vesting service. Upon attaining three years of vesting service, the participant immediately becomes fully (100%) vested in the employer contributions to the participant's account. See Code § 411(a)(2)(B)(ii); ERISA § 203(a)(2)(B)(ii).

The six-year graduated vesting schedule, which is set forth in Table 3.7, is found in Code Section 411(a)(2)(B)(iii) and ERISA Section 203(a)(2)(B)(iii).

Table 3.7

Defined Contribution Plans
Six-Year Graduated Vesting Schedule

Years of Service	Nonforfeitable % of Benefit
2	20
3	40
4	60
5	80
6 or more	100

Under a six-year graduated vesting schedule, the participant becomes partially vested (20%) in employer contributions to the participant's individual account under the plan after attaining two years of vesting service. For each subsequent year of vesting service attained, the participant becomes vested in a progressively higher percentage of the employer contributions to the account until finally becoming fully (100%) vested after six years of vesting service. See Code § 411(a)(2)(B)(iii); ERISA § 203(a)(2)(B)(iii).

Vesting Schedules for Top Heavy, Terminated and Hybrid Defined Benefit Plans

A special accelerated vesting schedule, found in Code Section 416, applies to a qualified plan that is top heavy. This special vesting schedule and the criteria for determining when a qualified plan is top heavy are discussed in Section F of Chapter Three.

The special vesting schedule that applies in the event of a plan termination is unique to the Code. Under Code Section 411(d)(3), upon the termination of a qualified plan those participants whose employment was previously terminated may be immediately and fully vested in their plan benefits, regardless of their actual number of years of vesting service at the time when their employment was terminated. A plan termination that triggers immediate and full vesting can include a *partial termination*. Whether a partial termination has occurred is determined under "all the facts and circumstances in a particular case." See Treas. Reg. § 1.411(d)–2. Plan terminations and the factual criteria for determining whether a partial termination has occurred are discussed in more detail in Section H of Chapter Three.

Hybrid defined benefit plans, such as cash balance plans, have their own unique vesting rule. When a defined benefit plan computes the participant's accrued benefit under the plan by reference to a hypothetical account, the plan must use a three-year cliff vesting schedule. See Code § 411(a)(13)(B).

Determining Years of Vesting Service

The general rule when counting years of vesting service is that the plan must count *all* years of service for vesting. See Code § 411(a)(4); ERISA § 203(b)(1). A year of vesting service is defined as a twelve consecutive month period during which the participant has 1,000 hours of service. See Code § 411(a)(5)(A); ERISA § 203(b)(2)(A). Hours of service for purposes of determining vesting generally are counted in the same manner as hours of service for purposes of determining eligibility to participate in the plan. See Code § 411(a)(5)(B); ERISA § 203(b)(2)(B). The computation period for a vesting year of service may differ, however, from the computation period used to determine an eligibility year of service. Recall that when determining eligibility, the computation period for a new employee must begin on the date the new employee begins employment. If the employee fails to complete an eligibility year of service during this first computation period, the plan may then switch to a calendar or plan year for measuring subsequent attempts to earn an eligibility year of service. In contrast, for purposes of vesting the plan may elect to use a calendar year, plan year, or other twelve consecutive month period to measure vesting years of service. See Code § 411(a)(5)(A); ERISA § 203(b)(2)(A). Consequently, it is possible for a participant already to have earned a year of vesting service *before* entering the plan as a participant. This situation is illustrated by the following example:

> ABC Company sponsors a profit sharing plan (Plan) for its employees. The Plan requires an employee to have obtained one year of eligibility service before becoming a participant in the Plan. The Plan has two entry dates, January 1 and July 1. The Plan measures years of vesting service based on calendar years.

> Employee X commences employment with ABC Company on January 15, 2015, and completes 1,000 hours of service by July 2, 2015. X completes his eligibility year of service on January 14, 2016. X will become a participant in the Plan on July 1, 2016, which is the next plan entry date following completion of X's eligibility year of service. Because the Plan measures vesting years of service on a calendar year basis, when X enters the Plan as a participant on July 1, 2016, X will already have earned one year of vesting service. X earned 1,000 hours of vesting service during the 2015 calendar year. If X earned 1,000 hours of vesting service between January 1, 2016, and July 1, 2016, X already will have earned a second year of vesting service for the 2016 calendar year.

NOTES

1. *Plans Excluded from the Age, Service and Vesting Requirements.* ~~ERISA $201~~ ERISA Section 201 specifies the types of employee benefit plans that are subject to the age, service and vesting rules, as well as the benefit accrual rules discussed in Section E of Chapter Three. The two most significant exclusions from Part 2 of Title I of ERISA are *for welfare benefit plans* and *top hat plans.* See ERISA §§ 201(1); (2). Exempting welfare benefit plans from the age, service and vesting requirements of Part 2 of Title I of ERISA is highly significant because these plans are not subject to ERISA's restrictions on the employer's ability to amend the plan to reduce or eliminate plan benefits. In the context of a top hat plan, this employer right of amendment and termination generally is negotiated and may be restricted by the contractual terms of the deferred compensation agreement between the employer and the employee. Because welfare benefit plans and top hat plans are exempt from regulation under Part 2 of Title I, the employer may design the plan so that benefits can be changed or eliminated, as in the case of health care plans, or impose a forfeiture clause for certain misconduct by the participant, such as clauses not to compete or other forfeiture clauses commonly found in top hat plans.

2. *Exceptions to the Age and Service Requirements.* Several statutory exceptions to the age and service requirements exist. One exception is for plans sponsored by educational institutions. Under this exception, the minimum age requirement can be set at age 26 instead of age 21. See Code § 410(a)(1)(B)(ii); ERISA § 202(a)(1)(B)(ii). Why did universities lobby for this special rule?

Another exception exists for qualified plans that immediately and fully (100%) vest plan benefits once an employee enters the plan as a participant. Such plans can require up to two years of service before a new employee becomes a participant in the plan. See Code § 410(a)(1)(B)(i); ERISA § 202(a)(1)(B)(i).

3. *Administrative Simplification Through Cash Out Distributions.* Many plan participants are at least partially vested in their plan benefits when they terminate employment. The vested benefit amounts of some former participants may be quite small, particularly for those individuals who worked only a few years for the employer.

To reduce the administrative burden associated with retaining small vested benefit amounts in the plan, a qualified plan is permitted to make a *cash out distribution.* A cash out distribution allows the plan to distribute the vested portion of the former participant's benefit without the participant's consent. See Code § 411(a)(11); ERISA § 203(e)(1). The specific criteria for when the plan administrator may make a cash out distribution are discussed in Section F of Chapter Three.

4. *Special Rules for Rehired Employees.* Determining eligibility and years of vesting service for an employee who once worked for the employer, terminated employment, and later is reemployed by the same employer can

be administratively burdensome. As a general rule, the plan must take into account all prior years of service by a rehired employee when determining whether the rehired employee has satisfied a year of service for eligibility and when counting years of vesting service. See Code §§ 410(a)(5)(A); 411(a)(4); ERISA §§ 202(b)(1); 203(b)(1).

Plans with a one year of service requirement for eligibility may, but are not required to, adopt one of two statutory exceptions to this general rule when determining the eligibility of a rehired employee to participate in the plan. These statutory exceptions are known as the *one year holdout rule* and the *rule of parity*.

Under the one year holdout rule, the plan may disregard a rehired employee's prior service if the rehired employee has incurred a *one-year break in service*, which is defined as a calendar year, plan year, or other twelve consecutive month period defined by the plan during which the employee has not completed at least 501 hours of service. See Code § 411(a)(6)(A); ERISA § 203(b)(3)(A). If the rehired employee completes a year of service after being rehired, then under the one year holdout rule the plan must take into account the rehired employee's prior service. See Code § 410(a)(5)(C); ERISA § 202(b)(3). The effect of the one year holdout rule is temporary—the plan may only "holdout" the rehired employee from participating in the plan until the rehired employee completes a "new" year of eligibility service.

The rule of parity permits the plan permanently to disregard a rehired employee's prior years of service for purposes of determining eligibility to participate in the plan. Under the rule of parity, the plan may disregard the rehired employee's prior service only if, at the time the employee terminated employment, the employee was both (1) "nonvested" (i.e., 0% vested) under the plan, and (2) the rehired employee has incurred five consecutive one-year breaks in service. See Code § 410(a)(5)(D); ERISA § 202(b)(4).

A different set of statutory exceptions apply to determine when the plan can disregard a rehired employee's prior years of vesting service. See Code § 411(a)(4); ERISA § 203(b). Qualified plans also may use the rule of parity to disregard a rehired employee's prior years of vesting service. See Code § 411(a)(6)(D); ERISA § 203(b)(3)(D).

When calculating one-year breaks in service under these statutory exceptions, the plan must count as hours of service the hours of an employee who is absent from work on unpaid leave due to pregnancy, adoption, and related maternity or paternity leave, up to a total of 501 hours in a twelve month period. See Code §§ 410(a)(5)(E); 411(a)(6)(E); ERISA §§ 202(b)(5)(A); 203(b)(3)(E). The plan must count both hours of service attributable to unpaid leave under the Family and Medical Leave Act and hours of service during a period of qualifying military service by a reemployed veteran under the Uniformed Services Employment and Reemployment Rights Act. See 29 C.F.R § 825.215(d)(4) (FMLA); Code § 414(u)(8)(A) (USERRA). The Family and Medical Leave Act and the Uniformed Services Employment and Reemployment Rights Act are discussed in Chapter Four.

PROBLEMS ON THE AGE, SERVICE AND VESTING REQUIREMENTS

PROBLEM ONE

Mirox Company (Mirox) sponsors the Mirox Company Retirement Plan (Retirement Plan) for its employees. The Retirement Plan is a calendar year plan with plan entry dates of January 1 and July 1. The Retirement Plan uses calendar years to determine years of service for purposes of vesting. Mirox employees become eligible to participate in the Retirement Plan after completing one year of service and attaining age twenty-one. The Retirement Plan is a defined benefit plan that has a five-year cliff vesting schedule. The Retirement Plan also has adopted the rule of parity for purposes of excluding prior years of vesting service.

In addition to the Retirement Plan, Mirox sponsors two other employee benefit plans. The Mirox Employee Health Care Plan (Health Plan) is available for employees who are regularly scheduled to work thirty or more hours per week. Mirox sponsors the Mirox Company Nonqualified Deferred Compensation Plan (Deferred Comp Plan) for the company president. Under the terms of the Deferred Comp Plan, upon attainment of age 65 Mirox will pay the president $8,000 per month for life. If the president terminates employment prior to age 65 and is employed by a competitor of Mirox within two years of termination of employment, no benefits will be paid to the president from the Deferred Comp Plan.

A. The vice-president of sales, who has worked at Mirox as a full-time employee for three years, learns of the Deferred Comp Plan. He demands to be admitted to the Deferred Comp Plan as a participant. Must Mirox include the vice-president as a participant in the Deferred Comp Plan?

B. The president terminates employment with Mirox to go to work *Terminated DX plan?* for Mirox's closest competitor, Xorim Corporation. At age 65, the former Mirox president demands that her benefits commence under the Deferred Comp Plan. Must the Deferred Comp Plan pay the promised benefits?

C. Sally, age 23, is a part-time word processor for Mirox. Sally begins employment on February 1, 2015. Sally is regularly scheduled to work 100 hours per month. By November 30, 2015, Sally has completed 1,000 hours of service. She demands to be admitted as a participant in the Retirement Plan and the Health Plan. Is Sally entitled to participate in these employee benefit plans? If so, when? (Answer and explain with respect to each plan.)

D. Sam, age 62, is a part-time janitor for Mirox. Sam begins employment on March 1, 2015. Sam is regularly scheduled to work 80 hours per month. During the twelve month period after his employment commencement date, Sam works his eighty regularly scheduled hours each month. In addition, Sam works twenty overtime hours in April and June, and receives payment for sixteen hours of vacation time in August. Is Sam eligible for the Retirement Plan? If so, when will Sam become a participant in the Retirement Plan?

E.   Refer to the facts regarding Sam in Question D above. Assume that Sam has these hours of service for the following years:

$$2016 = 960$$

$$2017 = 960$$

$$2018 = 1,020$$

$$2019 = 1,050$$

$$2020 = 1,015$$

$$2021 = 1,025$$

Sam terminates employment on January 1, 2022. What percentage of Sam's benefit is vested under the Retirement Plan's five-year cliff vesting schedule?

F.   Shoo begins employment with Mirox on February 1, 2015, and has 2,000 hours of service as of January 31, 2016. Shoo terminates employment with Mirox on October 1, 2016. As of the date of Shoo's termination of employment, Shoo has over 1,000 hours of service in 2016.

On March 1, 2021, Shoo is reemployed by Mirox. Shoo has 1,000 hours of service in 2021, 2022 and 2023. On January 15, 2024, Shoo terminates employment with Mirox. Is Shoo entitled to a benefit from the Retirement Plan?

G.   How would your answer in Question F. above change if Shoo had not been reemployed by Mirox until March 1, 2022?

PROBLEM TWO

GRITT Corporation sponsors the GRITT Corporation Profit Sharing and 401(k) Salary Deferral Plan (Plan) for its employees. The Plan is a fiscal year plan with a plan year commencing on April 1 and ending on March 31. The Plan's entry dates for new participants are April 1 and October 1. The Plan uses calendar years to determine years of service for purposes of vesting. GRITT Corporation employees are eligible to participate in the Plan after completing one year of service and attaining age 21. The Plan has a six-year graduated vesting schedule for employer contributions to the Plan.

Jack Jones, age 32, begins employment with GRITT Corporation on January 1, 2015. He is regularly scheduled to work 40 hours each week throughout 2015 and he does so. On January 1, 2016, Jack becomes temporarily disabled and is unable to work. In accordance with company policy, Jack is paid by the company for his regularly scheduled hours during this period of temporary disability. Jack returns to work on November 15, 2016, and resumes his regular work schedule of 40 hours per week.

In 2017 and 2018 Jack has over 1,000 hours of service. Jack terminates his employment with GRITT Corporation on January 1, 2019. At that time, Jack's 401(k) salary deferral account balance is $50,000, his employer matching contribution account balance is $3,000, and his profit sharing account balance is $20,000.

A. As of what date did Jack become a participant in the Plan?

B. At the time of Jack's termination of employment on January 1, 2019, how many years of vesting service does Jack have?

C. At the time of Jack's termination of employment on January 1, 2019, what is the amount of Jack's nonforfeitable accrued benefit from:

- his 401(k) salary deferral account?
- his employer matching contribution account?
- his profit sharing account?

E. BENEFIT ACCRUAL REQUIREMENTS

Imagine this telephone call. A business consultant for your financially distressed client has been working closely with the client to find ways to reduce the cost of doing business. The consultant has proposed a possible amendment to the client's retirement plan that will reduce the client's expenses associated with maintaining the plan by a projected $2 million over the next several years. At the last minute the client has decided to consult you concerning the consultant's proposed plan amendment. The client asks you whether "there are any legal issues floating out there" that the client should consider in reviewing the consultant's proposal. How will you respond?

The benefit accrual requirements of the Code and ERISA discussed in Section E provide the foundation for your legal advice. The first part of Section E provides an overview of the rules governing plan amendments that affect accrued benefits under a qualified plan. The second part of Section E examines the application of these rules in the particular context of conversions of defined benefit plans to cash balance plans.

The reading material in Section E focuses on the following two questions:

- What constraints does federal law place on the employer's ability to alter the benefits offered under a qualified plan?

- What protections does federal law provide to plan participants concerning the benefits promised to them under a qualified plan?

1. PLAN AMENDMENTS, ACCRUED BENEFITS AND THE ANTI-CUTBACK RULE

An amendment to a qualified plan cannot reduce a participant's *accrued benefit* under the plan or eliminate an *optional form of benefit* available under the plan. See Code § 411(d)(6)(A)–(B); ERISA § 204(g)(1)– (2). The purpose of this prohibition, known as the *anti-cutback rule*, is to ensure that the plan's sponsor cannot use a plan amendment to retroactively repeal or reduce a participant's benefit once it has accrued according to the terms of the plan. The anti-cutback rule plays a crucial role in ensuring the integrity of the vesting rules for qualified plans. Without the anti-cutback rule, the concept of vesting would be meaningless because a participant's accrued benefit could be taken away by the employer through an amendment to the plan before the participant had an opportunity to vest in these benefits.

When discussing proposed plan amendments with their clients, ERISA tax lawyers customarily refer to accrued benefits protected by the anti-cutback rule as *411(d)(6) benefits* as a shorthand reference to the Code section that protects and preserves these benefits. If a plan amendment violates the anti-cutback rule, ERISA Section 204(g), which duplicates Code Section 411(d)(6), provides the basis for the plan's participants to bring a private civil action challenging the plan amendment under ERISA.

The anti-cutback rule also protects early retirement benefits. Code Section 411(d)(6) and ERISA Section 204(g) state that a plan amendment that has the effect of "eliminating or reducing an early retirement benefit or a retirement-type subsidy . . . with respect to benefits attributable to service before the amendment shall be treated as reducing accrued benefits." Code § 411(d)(6)(B); ERISA § 204(g)(2). The protection provided by the anti-cutback rule for early retirement benefits is particularly significant if the early retirement benefit is *subsidized*. A subsidized early retirement benefit is not actuarially reduced to account for the commencement of benefit payments before the participant attains normal retirement age under the terms of the plan. Consequently, a subsidized early retirement benefit is more valuable to the participant, and more costly for the plan to offer, than the comparable accrued benefit that would be paid once the participant attains normal retirement age. Subsidized early retirement benefits may be the target of a plan amendment designed to reduce the costs of sponsoring the plan by reducing or eliminating the subsidy for early retirement benefits.

In *Central Laborers' Pension Fund v. Heinz*, 541 U.S. 739 (2004), the Supreme Court addressed the application of the anti-cutback rule in the specialized context of early retirement benefits provided by a multiemployer plan that contained a *suspension of benefits clause*. ERISA permits a multiemployer plan to suspend a retired participant's benefits if the participant accepts employment "in the same industry, in the same trade or craft, and the same geographic area covered by the plan." ERISA § 203(a)(3)(B). The Congressional intent behind permitting a multiemployer plan to adopt a suspension of benefits clause is "to protect participants against their pension plan being used, in effect, to subsidize low-wage employers who hire plan [early] retirees to compete with, and undercut the wages and working conditions of employees covered by the [multiemployer] plan." 120 Cong. Rec. 29930 (1974) (statement of Sen. Williams concerning ERISA § 203(a)(3)(B)). The particular suspension of benefits clause at issue in *Heinz* prohibited a participant who was receiving an early retirement pension from engaging in certain types of "disqualifying employment" after the participant retired. Under the suspension of benefits clause, the plan suspended the monthly early retirement benefit payments of any participant who had accepted "disqualifying employment" until the participant stopped performing the prohibited work.

When the plaintiffs in *Heinz* retired in 1996 and began receiving payment of their early retirement benefits, the plan defined "disqualifying employment" as any job as a union or nonunion construction worker, but did not include employment in the construction industry in a supervisory capacity. When the *Heinz* plaintiffs accepted employment as construction supervisors after retiring, the plan continued to pay their early retirement benefits. In 1998 the plan was amended to expand the definition of disqualifying employment to include any job in the construction industry, including supervisory work. Applying this new definition, the plan suspended payment of the early retirement benefits to the *Heinz* plaintiffs.

The *Heinz* plaintiffs challenged the 1998 plan amendment as a violation of the anti-cutback rule. The Supreme Court in *Heinz* held that the 1998 amendment was invalid based on the anti-cutback rule:

> [D]id the 1998 amendment to the Plan have the effect of "eliminating or reducing an early retirement benefit" that was earned by service before the amendment was passed? The statute, admittedly, is not as helpful as it might be in answering this question; it does not explicitly define "early retirement benefit," and it rather circularly defines "accrued benefit" as "the individual's accrued benefit determined under the plan. . . ." § 3(23)(A). Still, it certainly looks as though a benefit has suffered under the amendment here, for we agree with the

Seventh Circuit that, as a matter of common sense, "[a] participant's benefits cannot be understood without reference to the conditions imposed on receiving those benefits, and an amendment placing materially greater restrictions on the receipt of the benefit 'reduces' the benefit just as surely as a decrease in the size of the monthly benefit payment." 303 F.3d at 805. Heinz worked and accrued retirement benefits under a plan with terms allowing him to supplement retirement income by certain employment, and he was being reasonable if he relied on those terms in planning his retirement. The 1998 amendment undercut any such reliance, paying retirement income only if he accepted a substantial curtailment of his opportunity to do the kind of work he knew. We simply do not see how, in any practical sense, this change of terms could not be viewed as shrinking the value of Heinz's pension rights and reducing his promised benefits.

541 U.S. at 744–45.

a. Benefits Protected by the Anti-Cutback Rule

The Concept of an Accrued Benefit

The starting point for determining whether a proposed plan amendment runs afoul of the anti-cutback rule is with the statutory definition of an accrued benefit. For individual account plans, a participant's accrued benefit is the total balance (combining both vested and any nonvested portions) of the participant's individual account under the plan. See Code § 411(a)(7)(A)(ii); ERISA § 3(23)(B). The following example illustrates the concept of an accrued benefit in the context of an individual account plan, and the distinction between a permissible *forfeiture* under the vesting rules and a prohibited *cutback* of an accrued benefit.

Assume that Employee X is a participant in the ABC Company Profit Sharing Plan. The Plan has a six-year graduated vesting schedule for employer contributions to the Plan. ABC Company makes a contribution in the amount of $5,000 each year to X's Plan account. After one year, X's account balance (including investment earnings) is $5,200. X's accrued benefit under the Plan is $5,200. Even though X is not yet vested in any portion of X's accrued benefit under the Plan, ABC Company cannot amend the Plan to decrease the amount held in X's account. Under the anti-cutback rule, X must be given the opportunity to vest in this accrued benefit through the passage of time.

X later terminates employment with ABC Company with four years of vesting service and an account balance of $22,000. At the time of termination, X's *nonforfeitable* (i.e., vested) *accrued benefit* is $13,200

(60% times $22,000). Although X forfeits the nonvested portion of the account ($8,800), this forfeiture is not a prohibited cutback of X's accrued benefit under the Plan. Why? The "reduction" of X's accrued benefit (from an account balance of $22,000 while employed to a nonforfeitable benefit of $13,200 upon termination of employment) did not occur as the result of a plan amendment. Rather, it occurred as the result of application of the plan's vesting rules when X terminated employment.

For defined benefit plans, the definition of an accrued benefit is a more complex concept. Federal law provides that a participant's accrued benefit under a defined benefit plan "is determined under the plan and. . .expressed in the form of an annual benefit commencing at normal retirement age." Code § 411(a)(7)(A)(i); ERISA § 3(23)(A). The formula used by defined plan to determine a participant's accrued benefit must satisfy one of three benefit accrual methods defined in the statute. See generally Code § 411(b); ERISA § 204. The purpose of these statutory benefit accrual methods, which are described in more detail below, is to prohibit the practice of backloading benefits under a defined benefit plan. Prior to the enactment of ERISA, it was not uncommon for the benefit formula under a defined benefit plan to be structured so that a participant would not accrue substantial benefits under the plan until the last few years before retirement. If the participant terminated employment prior to attaining normal retirement age, such a backloaded defined benefit plan provided only nominal benefits to the participant. The purpose of the statutory benefit accrual methods is to ensure that a participant in a defined benefit plan accrues benefits more proportionately over the course of the participant's period of employment.

Statutory Benefit Accrual Methods for Defined Benefit Plans[a]

The three permissible accrual methods are: (1) the *133-1/3% method*; (2) the *fractional method*; and (3) the *3% method*. Most defined benefit plans use the 133-1/3% method or the fractional method. The purpose common to all three methods is to ensure that participants accrue benefits proportionately across their period of service for the employer.

Under the *133-1/3% method*, the accrued benefit payable at normal retirement age must equal the normal retirement benefit under the plan, and the annual rate at which any individual who is or could be a participant can accrue the retirement benefits payable at normal retirement age for any plan year cannot be more than 133-1/3% of the annual rate at which he or she can accrue benefits for any earlier plan year. For example, if the plan provides that a participant accrues a benefit of 1.5% of compensation for each year of service up to 20, and 2% of compensation for each year of service in excess of 20, the plan satisfies

---

[a] Excerpted from Joint Committee on Taxation, Present Law and Background Relating to Employer-Sponsored Defined Benefit Plans (June 18, 2002).

the requirements of the 133-1/3% method. However, a benefit that accrues at the rate of 1% of compensation for each year of service up to 20, and 1.5% of compensation for each year of service in excess of 20, does not satisfy the requirements of the 133-1/3% method.

Under the *fractional method*, the accrued benefit to which a participant is entitled at any time must equal or exceed the participant's "fractional rule benefit," multiplied by a fraction (not exceeding one), the numerator of which is the participant's total years of participation in the plan, and the denominator of which is the total number of years of plan participation the participant would have if he or she separated from service at normal retirement age. A participant's "fractional rule benefit" is the normal retirement benefit to which the participant would be entitled under the plan if the participant attained normal retirement age on the date the benefit is being determined (i.e., based on the participant's current amount of compensation and years of service).

The fractional method is illustrated by the following example. Suppose a plan provides a normal retirement benefit at age 65 of 2% of compensation for each year of service up to 30 years, so that a participant with 15 years of service has a fractional rule benefit of 30% of compensation (determined as if the participant attained normal retirement age on the date the benefit is being determined). For a participant who began participation in the plan at age 21 and is now age 36, the participant's accrued benefit under the fractional method is the participant's fractional rule benefit (30% of compensation), multiplied by the fraction 15/44 (i.e., the participant's 15 years of participation over the participant's projected years of plan participation at normal retirement age of 65) or 10.22% of compensation. For a participant who began participation in the plan at age 35 and is now age 50, the participant's accrued benefit under the fractional method is the participant's fractional rule benefit (30% of compensation), multiplied by the fraction 15/30 (i.e., the participant's 15 years of participation over the participant's projected years of plan participation at normal retirement age of 65) or 15% of compensation.

Under the *3% method*, the accrued benefit to which each participant is entitled (computed as if the participant separated from the service as of the end of the plan year) must be at least 3% of the "three-percent method benefit," multiplied by the participant's years of plan participation as of the end of the year (but not more than 33-1/3 years). A participant's "three-percent method benefit" is the normal retirement benefit to which the participant would be entitled if he or she began participation at the earliest age possible under the plan and participated in the plan continuously until the earlier of age 65 or the normal retirement age under the plan.

The fractional method and the 3% method provide the minimum rate at which a participant's benefit must accrue. A plan may use an accrual method under which participants' accrued benefits exceed the minimum, provided that no participant's accrued benefit can be less than the minimum.

Optional Forms of Benefits

The anti-cutback rule also prohibits the elimination of an *optional form of benefit*. Treasury Department regulations describe an optional form of benefit as any form in which accrued benefits under the plan may be distributed to a participant, including such features as the payment schedule, timing, commencement, medium of distribution (i.e., in cash or in-kind), the portion of the benefit to which the distribution feature applies, and the participant's right to elect among different forms and features of distributions. See Treas. Reg. § 1.411(d)–4, Q & A–1(b). The various types of optional forms of benefits include the option to choose between a lump sum distribution or an annuity, the option to choose among annuities with different payout amounts and features, and the right for a participant to receive in-service distributions from his account under a profit sharing plan. Under the anti-cutback rule an optional form of benefit generally cannot be made subject to the exercise of employer discretion. For example, an employer cannot make the option to receive a distribution of benefits in the form of a lump sum conditional upon the consent of the employer. See Treas. Reg. § 1.411(d)–4, Q & A–4–Q & A–7.

The anti-cutback rule does not apply to plan features that are characterized as *ancillary benefits* or *administrative features* of the plan. The Treasury Department regulations list the following examples of types of ancillary plan benefits or administrative features that are not protected by the anti-cutback rule and therefore can be modified or eliminated:

- Ancillary life insurance protection.
- Accident or health insurance benefits.
- Certain social security supplements described in Code Section 411(a)(9).
- The availability of loans (other than the distribution of an employee's accrued benefit upon default under a loan).
- The right to make after-tax employee contributions or elective deferrals described in Code Section 402(g)(3).
- The right to direct investments.
- The right to a particular form of investment (e.g., investment in employer stock or securities or investment in certain types of securities, commercial paper, or other investment media).
- The allocation dates for contributions, forfeitures and earnings.

- The time for making contributions (but not the conditions for receiving an allocation of contribution forfeitures for a plan year after such conditions have been satisfied).

- The valuation dates for account balances.

- Administrative procedures for distributing benefits, such as provisions relating to the particular dates on which notices are given and by which elections must be made.

- Rights that derive from administrative and operational provisions, such as mechanical procedures for allocating investment experience among accounts in defined contribution plans.

Historically, the prohibition against elimination of an optional form of benefit meant that if the plan had at any time offered a particular form of distribution, this form of distribution could never be eliminated with respect to benefits that had already accrued while the optional form of distribution was available under the plan. This rule made the administration of the plan more complex because optional forms of benefits that were unwanted (and therefore not used by plan participants and beneficiaries) nevertheless could not be eliminated. The prohibition on elimination of optional forms of benefits also made plan administration more difficult when, as the result of a corporate merger or acquisition, two or more dissimilar employer plans were merged. For example, assume that one party to the merger sponsors a money purchase pension plan containing numerous types of annuity distribution forms. The other party to the merger sponsors a profit sharing plan that only offers distributions in the form of a lump sum. If the two plans are merged, each of the annuity options in the money purchase pension plan must be "grandfathered" into the resulting combined plan. Accordingly, the plan administrator must keep track of the benefits accrued by each participant in the money purchase plan pension up to the date of plan merger, and continue to offer all of the annuity distribution forms that were available under the money purchase pension plan with respect to the benefits previously accrued under the money purchase pension plan.

As a result of the administrative difficulties caused by application of the anti-cutback rule to optional forms of benefits, Congress has authorized several statutory exceptions to the anti-cutback rule. These exceptions allow plan administrators of defined contribution plans to eliminate optional forms of benefits, such as annuity distribution form options, if certain statutory criteria are satisfied. See Code § 411(d)(6)(D)–(E); ERISA § 204(g)(4)–(5); Treas. Reg. § 1.411(d)–4, Q & A–2(e).

Special Restrictions for Underfunded Defined Benefit Plans

Special restrictions apply to defined benefit plans sponsored by single employers that are less than fully funded under the minimum funding rules. See generally ERISA § 303, Code § 430. If the plan is less than 80% funded under the minimum funding rules, the plan may not be amended to increase benefits. If the plan is less than 60% funded, benefit accruals must cease and the plan may not make a lump sum benefit payment in an amount over $5,000. See generally ERISA § 206(g); Code § 436. Similar restrictions apply to underfunded multiemployer defined benefit plans. See generally ERISA §§ 304, 305; Code §§ 431, 432.

b. Plan Amendments Reducing the Rate of Future Benefit Accrual

The anti-cutback rule does not prohibit an employer from amending the plan prospectively to reduce the participant's rate of future benefit accrual, or to eliminate an optional form of benefit with respect to benefits yet to be accrued under the plan. Participants in a defined benefit plan (including a cash balance plan) or a money purchase pension plan must receive written notice of a plan amendment that significantly reduces the rate of future benefit accrual under the plan, including an amendment that significantly reduces early retirement subsidies. See Code § 4980F(e)–(f); ERISA § 204(h). This notice is often referred to as a *Section 204(h) notice* as a shorthand reference to the ERISA section containing the notice requirement.

In general, for a single-employer plan a Section 204(h) notice must be provided at least 45 days before the plan amendment takes effect to every individual whose benefit may be affected by the amendment. See 26 C.F.R. §§ 1.411(d)–3; 54.4980F–1, Q & A–9(a). For small plans having fewer than 100 participants and multiemployer plans, the notice period is reduced to 15 days. See 26 C.F.R. § 54.4980F–1–, Q & A–9(b)–(c). Like a summary plan description, a Section 204(h) notice must be written in a manner calculated to be understood by the average plan participant and provide sufficient information to allow participants to understand the effect of the amendment. In the event of an egregious failure to comply with the Section 204(h) notice requirements, individuals who are entitled to benefits under the plan will receive the greater of their preamendment benefits or their benefits under the plan as amended. Failure to comply with the advance written notice requirement does not, however, result in disqualification of the plan.

c. Diversification Rights for Accounts Invested in Company Stock

Although the right to a certain type of investment is not protected by the anti-cutback rule, the Pension Protection Act of 2006, Pub. L. No. 109–280, 120 Stat. 780 (Pension Protection Act), created new diversification rights for participants in defined contribution plans that hold company stock as an investment option. A participant in a defined contribution plan must have the right to diversify immediately any salary deferral contributions to a 401(k) plan that are invested in company stock. Once the participant has attained at least three years of service, the participant must be permitted to diversify all employer contributions to the participant's plan account that are invested in company stock. See Code § 401(a)(35); ERISA § 204(j). The plan must offer at least three alternative investment options for the participant to choose from to diversify the participant's investment in company stock. Each alternative investment option must be diversified (i.e., be a mutual fund), and must offer materially different risk and return characteristics. See Code § 401(a)(35)(D); ERISA § 204(j)(4). Significantly, these diversification rights apply even if the participant is only partially vested in the employer contributions to the participant's plan account because the plan uses a six-year graduated vesting schedule.

Years of service for purposes of this diversification right are measured similarly to years of vesting service, and include years of service prior to the enactment of the Pension Protection Act. See Code § 401(a)(35)(G)(vi); ERISA § 204(j)(6)(F). Traditional employee stock ownership plans are exempt from these diversification requirements. See Code § 401(a)(35)(E)(ii); ERISA § 204(j)(5)(B).

d. Eligibility, Vesting and Benefit Accrual During Periods of Active Duty Military Service

The Uniformed Services Employment and Reemployment Rights Act of 1994, Pub. L. No. 103–353, 108 Stat. 3150 (1994) (USERRA) is designed to protect the plan benefits of employees who are called to active duty military service. USERRA is codified in Sections 4301 through 4333 of Title 38 of the United States Code. The protections of the USERRA are activated when an employee is called to active duty military service and, after being discharged from active duty military service, the individual is reemployed by the same employer within the statutory time periods proscribed by the USERRA.

With respect to benefits under a qualified plan, the USERRA requires that the reemployed veteran's period of active duty military service must be credited for purposes of eligibility to participate in the plan, vesting and benefit accrual. For a defined benefit plan, the plan must treat the reemployed veteran as receiving compensation during the period of active duty military service that is equal to the compensation the employee otherwise would have received from the employer during the period as if the employee had not been called to active duty military service. For employer contributions to a defined contribution plan that are based on compensation, the same rule concerning equivalent compensation applies. If the employer's contribution to the plan is dependent on employee contributions (as in a matching contribution to a 401(k) plan), the reemployed veteran must be given at least three (but no more than five) years to make up employee salary deferral contributions for the period of active duty military service. If the reemployed veteran makes up salary deferral contributions for the period of active duty military service, the employer is obligated to make corresponding matching contributions. Under no circumstances, however, is the employer required to make up the reemployed veteran's lost investment earnings in a defined contribution plan. See generally 20 C.F.R. § 1002.

PROBLEM ON BENEFIT ACCRUAL REQUIREMENTS

For each of the following plan amendments, discuss the following:

- Whether the amendment violates the anti-cutback rule if applied retroactively;

- Whether the amendment, if prospective in effect, requires a Section 204(h) notice; and

- Any additional notice or disclosure requirements under Part 1 of Title I of ERISA that are triggered by the amendment.

A. An amendment eliminating vision care benefits for adults from a health care plan.

B. An amendment changing the benefit formula in a defined benefit plan from 50% of final average compensation to 35% of final average compensation.

C. An amendment eliminating employer matching contributions to a 401(k) plan.

D. An amendment limiting loan amounts from a 401(k) plan to $10,000.

E. An amendment changing the mutual fund investment options available to participants in their 401(k) plan.

2.   NOTE ON CASH BALANCE PLANS

During the mid-to-late 1990s, many large employers converted their traditional defined benefit plans into cash balance plans. There were several motivating factors behind this trend. First and probably foremost, the employer's minimum funding obligation under a cash balance plan is less volatile than for a defined benefit plan. Second, the pattern of benefit accrual under a cash balance plan is more attractive to an increasingly mobile workforce. Third, the "hybrid" feature of the cash balance plan—the presentation of the participant's accrued benefit as the present value of a hypothetical account—is more favorably perceived by workers who have grown accustomed to individual account plans. See generally GEN. ACCT. OFF., PRIVATE PENSIONS: INFORMATION ON CASH BALANCE PLANS (2005).

Cash balance plan conversions proved controversial with older workers due to the differences in the pattern of benefit accrual between a traditional defined benefit plan and a cash balance plan. When a defined benefit plan is converted into a cash balance plan, older workers usually accrue lesser future retirement benefits under the cash balance plan than they anticipated receiving under the formula used by the employer's defined benefit plan. In contrast, younger workers often immediately accrue greater retirement benefits under the cash balance plan than they would have accrued under the employer's defined benefit plan. This difference in the pattern of benefit accrual occurs because in a traditional defined benefit plan, the participant's accrued benefit is backloaded (subject, of course, to the restrictions imposed by the three statutory benefit accrual methods for defined benefit plans discussed earlier in Section E of Chapter Three).

A participant's accrued benefit in a defined benefit plan represents the plan's promise to pay a fixed monthly annuity amount in the future when the participant attains normal retirement age under the plan. For a younger participant, this normal retirement age date for the commencement of benefits is further in the future than for a similarly situated older worker. As a result, the present value of the younger worker's accrued benefit under a defined benefit plan will be less than the present value of the accrued benefit of a similarly situated older worker who has fewer years until normal retirement age. Under the system of benefit accrual in a defined benefit plan, the greatest benefits are accrued in the later years of the participant's career with the employer.

In contrast, under a cash balance plan the present value of the participant's accrued benefit in any given year is unrelated to the time remaining until the participant attains normal retirement age under the plan. Instead, the benefit formula for a cash balance plan typically requires the employer to contribute annually to each participant's account an amount equal to a specified percentage of the participant's pay, plus an assumed rate of investment return on the account. Consequently, benefits under a cash balance plan accrue at a more consistent rate over time than under a defined benefit plan. This pattern of benefit accrual under a cash balance plan tends to favor younger and more mobile workers, who will accrue greater benefits immediately in the early years of participation in the employer's cash balance plan.

Older workers were disappointed they received much less as a retirement benefit under the cash balance plan than they would have received under the benefit formula of the employer's defined benefit plan. This disappointment translated into a series of high-profile legal challenges to cash balance plan conversions.

The legal challenges to cash balance plan conversions coalesced into two main lines of cases. One line of cases challenged the plan's method of calculating the present lump sum value of the accrued benefit when a participant terminated employment prior to attaining normal retirement age under the plan. See, e.g., West v. AK Steel Corp., 484 F.3d 395 (6th Cir. 2007); Berger v. Xerox Corp. Ret. Income Guar. Plan, 338 F.3d 755 (7th Cir. 2003); Esden v. Bank of Boston, 229 F.3d 154 (2d Cir. 2000); Lyons v. Georgia-Pacific Corp. Salaried Employees Ret. Plan, 221 F.3d 1235 (11th Cir. 2000). These cases involve the *whipsaw calculation* problem described below. The other line of cases challenged the rate of benefit accrual under the cash balance plan as a prohibited form of age discrimination. See, e.g., Hurlic v. Southern Cal. Gas Co., 539 F.3d 1024 (9th Cir. 2008); Hirt v. Equitable Ret. Plan for Employees, Managers and Agents, 533 F.3d 102 (2d Cir. 2008); Drutis v. Rand McNally & Co., 499 F.3d 608 (6th Cir. 2007); Register v. PNC Fin. Servs. Group, Inc., 477 F.3d 56 (3d Cir. 2007); Cooper v. IBM Personal Pension Plan, 457 F.3d 636 (7th Cir. 2006); Campbell v. BankBoston, N.A., 327 F.3d 1 (1st Cir. 2003).

Congress addressed the whipsaw calculation problem and the problem of age discrimination in the design of cash balance plans in the Pension Protection Act of 2006, Pub. L. No. 109–208, 120 Stat. 280 (Pension Protection Act). To understand the rules for benefit accruals enacted by the Pension Protection Act, it is necessary to understand the historical problems the rules were designed to address.

The Whipsaw Calculation Problem

In *West v. AK Steel Corp.*, 484 F.3d 395 (6th Cir. 2007), the Sixth Circuit described how the whipsaw calculation problem may arise when a participant in a cash balance plan terminates employment prior to attaining normal retirement age:

> The most litigated aspect of cash balance plans has proven to be the so-called "whipsaw calculation." This calculation arises when participants opt to "cash out" their hypothetical accounts before they reach normal retirement age. To comply with ERISA, lump sum payments such as the ones received by the plaintiffs in the present case must be the actuarial equivalent of the normal accrued pension benefit. The actuarial equivalent is calculated in two steps. First, a participant's hypothetical account balance is projected forward to normal retirement age-in the AK Steel Plan, age 65-using the rate at which future interest credits would have accrued if the participant had remained in the AK Steel Plan until that time. Second, that projected amount is discounted back to its present value on the date of the actual lump sum distribution.

> If the interest rate used in Step 1 is greater than the discount rate used in Step 2, the amount of the participant's

lump sum disbursement will be larger than his or her hypothetical account balance. This two-step process is commonly referred to as the "whipsaw calculation." In the present case, Opening Accounts receive interest credits at a minimum annual rate of 7.5%, while the statutory discount rate for calculating the present value of a lump sum distribution has been invariably lower (5.1% in 2002, for example). This causes the value of the pension benefit under the whipsaw calculation to be greater than the simple value of the account balance at the time of the lump sum distribution. The IRS provides a useful example of the whipsaw effect:

A cash balance plan provides for interest credits at a fixed rate of 8% per annum that are not conditioned on continued employment, and for annuity conversions using the Code Section 417(e) applicable interest rate and mortality table. A fully vested employee with a hypothetical account balance of $45,000 terminates employment at age 45 and elects an immediate single sum distribution. At the time of the employee's termination, the Section 417(e) applicable interest rate is 6.5%.

The projected balance of the employee's hypothetical account as of normal retirement age is $209, 743. If $209,743 is discounted to age 45 at 6.5% (the Section 417(e) applicable interest rate), the present value equals $59,524.

Accordingly, if the plan paid the hypothetical account balance of $45,000, instead of $59,524, the employee would receive $14,524 less than the amount to which the employee is entitled. IRS Notice 96–8, 1996–1 C.B. 359.

The plaintiffs argue that ERISA mandates the whipsaw calculation-in other words, a payout of $59,524 in the example cited above-and that AK Steel's failure to calculate lump sum distributions in this manner constitutes a statutory violation of ERISA. AK Steel responds by arguing that, under the plain language of the AK Steel Plan, the plaintiffs received exactly the lump sum distribution to which they were entitled-the value of each participant's hypothetical account at the date of termination ($45,000 in the example above).

Cash balance plans are typically designed to pay accrued benefits to participants upon the termination of their employment. ERISA, however, was not designed with cash balance plans in mind and, instead, is premised on the notion that in a defined benefit plan, the benefit due is an annuity beginning at the normal retirement age, typically age sixty-five. Until August of 2006, ERISA enforced this annuity obligation through several interrelated provisions. The net result of this enforcement scheme was that a cash balance plan such as the AK Steel Plan would be required to use the whipsaw calculation in order to comply with ERISA.

Partly to address the treatment of cash balance plans under the ERISA statutory scheme, Congress passed the Pension Protection Act of 2006. The Pension Protection Act created special rules for cash balance plans, among them the provision that defined benefit plans shall not be treated as failing to meet the requirements of ERISA solely because the present value of an accrued benefit is deemed equal to the amount expressed as the balance in a participant's hypothetical account. These rules apply to distributions made after August 17, 2006. In effect, the Pension Protection Act establishes on a prospective basis that the whipsaw calculation is not required.

West, 484 F.3d at 400–02 (citations and quotations omitted). The relevant provisions of the Pension Protection Act that eliminated the whipsaw calculation problem are found in Code Section 411(a)(13)(A).

Age Discrimination in Plan Design

ERISA Section 204(b)(1)(H)(i) provides in relevant part that "a defined benefit plan shall be treated as not satisfying the requirements of [ERISA's benefit accrual requirements] if, under the plan, an employee's benefit accrual is ceased, or *the rate of an employee's benefit accrual is reduced*, because of the attainment of any age." Prior to the enactment of the Pension Protection Act, this provision sparked numerous claims that the rate of benefit accrual inherent in the design of a cash balance plan discriminated against older workers. This argument was based on the fact that, although the terms of the cash balance plan purported to be age-neutral, as a practical matter younger workers received projected interest rate credits on their account balances for more years (because they had more years until attaining normal retirement age) than did older workers.

In *Cooper v. IBM Personal Pension Plan*, 457 F.3d 636 (7th Cir. 2006), the Seventh Circuit rejected this argument, reasoning:

This approach treats the time value of money as age discrimination. Yet the statute does not require that equation.* * *Nothing in the language or background of [Code Section] 204(b)(1)(H)(i) suggests that Congress set out to legislate against the fact that younger workers have (statistically) more time left before retirement, and thus a greater opportunity to earn interest on each year's retirement savings. Treating the time value of money as a form of [age] discrimination is not sensible. Cf. Hazen Paper Co. v. Biggins, 507 U.S. 604, 611 (1993) (variable correlated with age must be kept "analytically distinct" from age when searching for discrimination).

Id. at 638–39. Other federal circuits agreed with *Cooper*. See, e.g., Hurlic v. Southern Cal. Gas Co., 539 F.3d 1024 (9th Cir. 2008); Hirt v. Equitable Ret. Plan for Employees, Managers and Agents, 533 F.3d 102 (2d Cir. 2008); Drutis v. Rand McNally & Co., 499 F.3d 608 (6th Cir. 2007); Register v. PNC Fin. Servs. Group, Inc., 477 F.3d 56 (3d Cir. 2007). The Pension Protection Act resolved the type of age discrimination claim described in *Cooper* by expressly addressing the concept of age discrimination in the context of a cash balance plan. Today, a cash balance plan does not violate the age discrimination rules of ERISA Section 204(b)(1)(H) if the plan satisfies certain requirements for the interest rate used to credit amounts to participant accounts and adopts a vesting schedule where participants are fully vested after three years of service. See ERISA §§ 203(f); 204(b)(5); Code §§ 411(a)(13); 411(b)(5).

Prior to the enactment of the Pension Protection Act, a second type of age discrimination claim arose when, in conjunction with converting a traditional defined benefit plan into a cash balance plan, the employer imposed a *wear away provision* on the converted plan. *Campbell v. BankBoston, N.A.*, 327 F.3d 1 (1st Cir. 2003), explains how a wear away provision operates:

> If begun from scratch, cash balance plans would not be terribly controversial. The controversy engenders from the transition from traditional defined benefit plans. Older workers, such as Campbell, expected to see their pension benefits rise dramatically as a result of their service just before retirement. Instead, as a result of their companies' adoption of cash balance plans, their pension increases under the old plans ceased.

> Under some plans, these workers whose traditional benefits have ceased to accrue are at least entitled to cash balance plan benefits. However, some transition schemes, including that employed by BankBoston, include a "wear away" provision. This provision specifies that employees' pension entitlement does not grow until their pension benefits, as calculated under the new cash balance system, equal their actual accrued benefits under the old system. Benefits already earned under an old plan may not be taken away, see Code § 411(d)(6)(A); ERISA § 204(g), but benefits expected but not yet accrued are not similarly protected. The result is that for many workers, including Campbell, their pension benefits stop accruing completely in their final years of service, when their expectation was that during those years, the benefits would build up the most.

Id. at 8. The Pension Protection Act resolved the wear away provision issue by mandating that cash balance plans that were converted on or after June 29, 2005, are prohibited from imposing wear away periods for the accumulation of accrued benefits following the conversion. When a defined benefit plan is converted into a cash balance plan, each participant in the defined benefit plan must receive an accrued benefit, after the conversion, that is not less than the sum of the participant's accrued benefit for years of service under the defined benefit plan prior to the amendment, *plus* the participant's accrued benefit for years of service under the cash balance plan after the amendment. See Code § 411(b)(5)(B)(iii); ERISA § 204(b)(5)(B)(iii). The plan also may be required to credit the value of an early retirement subsidy to the participant's accrued benefit under the defined benefit plan. See Code § 411(b)(5)(B)(iv); ERISA § 204(b)(5)(B)(iv).

F. CODE REQUIREMENTS FOR QUALIFIED RETIREMENT PLANS

The Code requirements for qualified plans described in Section F do not have duplicate requirements under ERISA. Consequently, a violation of these unique Code requirements for qualified plans does not give rise to a private cause of action by a plan participant under ERISA. The enforcement mechanism for these Code requirements is primarily one of deterrence. If the employer's plan fails to satisfy any one of these requirements, the Internal Revenue Service may deem the plan to be disqualified, and the income tax advantages associated with the plan will be lost to the employer and the plan's participants.

Section F is divided into four subsections. Section F.1 is devoted to the various nondiscrimination requirements for qualified plans. Section F.2 explains the different ways the Code seeks to limit the tax expenditure for qualified plans by limiting benefit and contribution amounts. Section F.3 provides an overview of the Code rules governing distributions, direct rollovers and loans from qualified plans. Section F.4 concludes with a discussion of the administrative and regulatory mechanisms that are commonly used to prevent plan disqualification.

1. THE NONDISCRIMINATION REQUIREMENTS

ERISA tax lawyers specialize in expertly navigating (some might say "manipulating") the legal labyrinth known as the *nondiscrimination requirements* of the Code for qualified plans. Although the policy objectives that underlie the nondiscrimination rules are straightforward, the implementation of these objectives has resulted in a notoriously technical regulatory scheme.

This regulatory complexity results from the inherent tension between the tax and social policy objectives of the qualified plan system. As a matter of tax policy, Congress has decided to grant highly favorable income tax treatment to qualified plans to encourage employers voluntarily to sponsor these plans for their employees. As a matter of social policy, tax-favored qualified plans must benefit not only the highest paid employees of the employer, but also the rank and file employees. The Code nondiscrimination requirements serve this social policy objective of the qualified plan system.

no significant constraints

The Code nondiscrimination requirements impose two significant constraints on the employer's voluntary decision to sponsor a qualified plan. First, the nondiscrimination requirements establish minimum standards for *how many* of the employer's rank and file employees must be participants in the qualified plan. Second, the nondiscrimination requirements influence *how much* in benefits or contributions the employer's plan must provide to those rank and file employees who are participants in the plan.

Although these two constraints further the social policy objective of the qualified plan system, the constraints also are in tension with the voluntary nature of qualified plan sponsorship. This tension arises because if the employer perceives that the cost of including rank and file employees in the employer's qualified plan is too high, the employer may choose not to sponsor a qualified plan at all.

The nondiscrimination requirements of the Code historically have attempted to strike an appropriate policy balance between the tax incentives for voluntary plan sponsorship and the social policy goal of ensuring that the employer's rank and file employees benefit from the employer's qualified plan. Congress first encouraged employers to sponsor retirement plans for their employees in the Revenue Act of 1921 by authorizing an income tax deduction for employer contributions to pension plans. In taking advantage of this tax deduction, employers generally allowed only company executives to participate in these early pension plans. By 1942, rising personal income tax rates had made employer-sponsored pension plans an attractive device for high income employees to avoid payment of income taxes. In the Revenue Act of 1942, Congress inaugurated the policy concept of nondiscrimination by requiring that a qualified plan had to cover a minimum number of rank and file employees, and that contributions to or benefits provided under the plan could not discriminate in favor of officers, shareholders, supervisors, or highly compensated employees of the employer. See Revenue Act of 1942, Pub. L. No. 758, § 162(a), 56 Stat. 798.

From its origin in the Revenue Act of 1942, the Code principle of nondiscrimination has evolved from a malleable set of requirements that were heavily dependent on facts and circumstances to a sophisticated combination of mechanical numerical tests and *safe harbor* plan designs. If the employer adopts a safe harbor plan design, the plan is deemed automatically to satisfy, or is exempted from, various Code nondiscrimination requirements and associated numerical testing.

The Code nondiscrimination requirements effective for qualified plans today primarily are the product of the Tax Reform Act of 1986, Pub. L. No. 99–514, 100 Stat. 2085, and its implementing Treasury Department regulations. Subsequent legislation enacted by Congress has simplified the application of several Code nondiscrimination requirements, but the fundamental character of these requirements essentially has remained unchanged since 1986.

The material that follows introduces the four most important, and most commonly encountered, Code nondiscrimination requirements for qualified plans:

- The *minimum coverage requirements* of Code Section 410(b);
- The prohibition of Code Section 401(a)(4) against *discrimination in favor of highly compensated employees with respect to benefits or contributions provided under the plan*;
- The special nondiscrimination requirements of Code Sections 401(k) and 401(m) for employee salary deferral contributions and employer matching contributions to 401(k) plans (known as the *actual deferral percentage test* and the *actual contribution percentage test*); and
- The requirements of Code Section 416 for *top heavy* plans.

The presentation of the Code nondiscrimination requirements in this section reflects the state of the law as of August 1, 2014. The presentation has been simplified to facilitate an understanding of the basic concepts and policy choices that underlie the requirements. To further simplify the presentation, special rules applicable only to multiemployer plans generally have been omitted.

a. Definitions

The Code nondiscrimination requirements share several common definitions. These definitions form the foundation for the subsequent application of the various Code nondiscrimination requirements to qualified plans.

The Concept of Discrimination and Highly Compensated Employees

For testing purposes, Code Sections 410(b), 401(a)(4), 401(k) and 401(m) rely on two interrelated terms of art—the Code's concept of *discrimination*, and the meaning of a *highly compensated employee*. When used in the context of a qualified plan, discrimination is a specialized term disconnected from its ordinary connotations of prejudice based on race, religion, gender or national origin. As used in the Code, a qualified plan is discriminatory if it favors highly compensated employees in excess of the numerical testing limits established under the relevant Code provision. In other words, Code Sections 410(b), 401(a)(4), 401(k) and 401(m) all *permit* a certain amount of discrimination in favor of highly compensated employees, but only up to a specified numerical limit.

To determine if a qualified plan impermissibly discriminates, the Code divides the universe of employees into two mutually exclusive categories: *highly compensated employees* (HCEs) and *nonhighly compensated employees* (NHCEs). Any employee who does not qualify as a HCE is classified as a NHCE. Code Section 414(q) defines a HCE as any employee:

- who was more than a 5% owner during the present or prior year (known as the *5% ownership test*), or

- who earned annual compensation from the employer during the prior year in excess of $80,000 (an amount that is indexed annually for inflation and set at $115,000 in 2014) (known as the *annual compensation test*).

For purposes of the 5% ownership test, an individual is considered to own any stock owned directly or indirectly by his or her spouse, children, grandchildren or parents. This family aggregation rule applies even if the other family member or members are not associated in any capacity with the employer. See I.R.S. Notice 97–45, 1997–2 C. B. 296 (explaining that Code Section 414(q)(2)'s reference to Code Section 416(i)(1) incorporates by reference the family aggregation rules of Code Section 318). Code Section 414(q) itself does not describe the details of the 5% ownership test, or how the 5% ownership test applies to corporations with more than one class of stock, or to business entities other than corporations. Rather, the 5% ownership test of Code Section 414(q) incorporates by reference the statutory criteria for a 5% owner under the top heavy rules of Code Section 416. See Code § 414(q)(2).

who are HCE and loopholes

The Internal Revenue Service annually publishes the dollar amount for the annual compensation test in the late fall of the year preceding the year when the new dollar limit will take effect. The employer may limit the number of individuals who qualify as HCEs under the annual compensation test by making an election in the original plan document itself or by a subsequent plan amendment. This election, which is known as the *top-paid group election*, is authorized by Code Section 414(q)(3). If the plan makes a top-paid group election, only those employees who earn in excess of the Code Section 414(q) annual compensation test *and* who are among the top 20% of employees when ranked by compensation are counted as HCEs. See Code §§ 414(q)(1)(B); 414(q)(3); I.R.S. Notice 97–45, 1997–2 C.B. 296 (explaining how the top-paid group election is made by the plan). Under the top-paid group election, any employees who earn in excess of the annual compensation test, but who are not among the top 20% of employees when ranked by compensation "drop down" into the pool of NHCEs and are counted as NHCEs for testing purposes.

The top-paid group election is particularly significant for smaller employers who sponsor qualified plans. For example, assume that the employer, ABC Corporation, has a total of ten employees. Employee 1 owns 100% of the stock of ABC Corporation. Each of the ten employees of ABC Corporation earned the following compensation amounts in 2014:

Employee	Compensation
#1	$200,000
#2	$150,000
#3	$145,000
#4	$140,000
#5	$130,000
#6	$ 50,000
#7	$ 30,000
#8	$ 25,000
#9	$ 18,000
#10	$ 18,000

In this example, Employee #1 is an HCE under both the 5% ownership test and the annual compensation test. Employees #2 through #5 also are HCEs under the annual compensation test (set at $115,000 in 2014). If a top-paid group election is not made, ABC Corporation has a total of five HCEs (Employees #1 through #5) and five NHCEs (Employees #6 through #10).

If ABC Corporation makes a top-paid group election, there will be only two HCEs, Employees #1 and #2, who are in the top 20% of all employees of ABC Corporation ranked on the basis of compensation. Employees #3, #4, and #5 will become part of the NHCE group of employees. As a result of making the top-paid group election, ABC Corporation will have two HCEs and eight NHCEs for testing purposes instead of having five HCEs and five NHCEs.

Why might a small employer choose to make a top-paid group election? Quite simply, sometimes making a top-paid group election will enable a small employer's qualified plan to satisfy the Code's nondiscrimination requirements. This situation is illustrated in Problem One following the discussion of the Code Section 410(b) minimum coverage rules.

Determining the "Employer" and "Employees" for Testing Purposes

Under certain circumstances, different entities must be aggregated and their employees treated as the employees of a single employer for purposes of nondiscrimination testing under Code Sections 410(b), 401(a)(4), 401(k), 401(m) and 416. The purpose of these *employer aggregation rules* (also known descriptively as the *controlled group rules*) relates back to the fundamental social policy objective that underlies the Code nondiscrimination requirements. Without the employer aggregation rules, an employer could easily circumvent the Code nondiscrimination requirements.

To illustrate this point using a dramatic example, assume that Company A owns 100% of its subsidiary, Company B. Absent the employer aggregation rules, the workers employed by Company A and Company B could be arranged so that only HCEs are employed by Company A and only NHCEs are employed by Company B. Company A could sponsor a qualified plan for the Company A employees (all of whom are HCEs). Company B would not sponsor any qualified plan for the Company B employees (all of whom are NHCEs). The employer aggregation rules are designed to prevent this and other similar scenarios by requiring that certain types of related business entities who are part of a controlled group must be treated as a single employer.

The employer aggregation rules are triggered if related business entities are:

(1) *members of a controlled group of corporations* under Code Section 414(b);

(2) *trades or businesses under common control* under Code Section 414(c); or

(3) *members of an affiliated service group* under Code Section 414(m).

Under rule (1) above, companies that share at least 80% common ownership are deemed to be members of a controlled group of corporations and are treated as one employer. When the members of a controlled group of corporations are treated as a single employer, the employees of each member corporation are counted as employees of this single employer. To illustrate, assume that Company A has two subsidiaries, Company B and Company C. Company A owns 100% of the stock of Company B, but only 50% of the stock of Company C. Company A and Company B are members of a controlled group of corporations and therefore are treated as a single employer. The employees of Company A and Company B (but not the employees of Company C) are counted as the employees of this single employer for nondiscrimination testing purposes. As a result, if Company A employs five HCEs and Company B employs one HCE and twenty-five NHCEs, Company A and Company B are treated as one employer who has a total of six HCEs and twenty-five NHCEs.

What about the employees of Company C? In this example, Company C is not a member of the Company A-Company B controlled group of corporations. Rather, Company C is treated as a separate employer for purposes of testing under the Code nondiscrimination requirements. Consequently, Company C's decision concerning whether to sponsor a qualified plan for Company C employees will have no impact on whether a qualified plan for the employees of Company A and Company B satisfies the Code nondiscrimination requirements. Conversely, the decisions made by Company A and Company B concerning whether to sponsor a qualified plan for their employees will not affect whether Company C's qualified plan satisfies the Code nondiscrimination requirements.

The 80% or more common ownership test for members of a controlled group of corporations is the most simple of the employer aggregation rules to apply. It is also the rule most frequently encountered in private legal practice. Employer aggregation rule (2) for trades or businesses under common control applies to unincorporated business entities, such as partnerships, sole proprietorships or trusts. Rule (2) operates using principles similar to the 80% common ownership test for controlled corporations. Employer aggregation rule (3) for members of an affiliated service group generally applies when an organization has as its principal business the performance of services or management functions for third parties, and regularly uses other affiliated organizations to provide these services or management functions to third parties.

For purposes of nondiscrimination testing under Code Sections 410(b), 401(a)(4), 401(k), 401(m) and 416, an individual's status as an "employee" of the employer is determined using the *Darden* factors for common law employee status discussed in Chapter Two. Mistakenly classifying a bona fide employee as an independent contractor can, depending on how close the numerical testing results are, cause a qualified plan to fail a nondiscrimination test once the employee is properly classified and the plan is retested.

Special Rules for Leased Employees

An employer may decide to use temporary workers provided through an employment agency. From the employer's perspective, a temporary worker generally is not viewed as an "employee." Rather, the employer leases the services of the temporary worker from the worker's "real" employer, who is the employment agency.

Code Section 414(n) creates a special vocabulary to describe these temporary worker situations. In the parlance of Code Section 414(n), the employment agency is called a *leasing organization*. The temporary worker may, if certain statutory criteria are satisfied, be deemed a *leased employee*. Code Section 414(n) defines a leased employee as any person

- who is not otherwise an employee of the employer for whom the leased employee performs services; and

- who has provided services for the employer on a substantially full-time basis for a period of at least one year pursuant to an agreement between the employer and a leasing organization; and

- whose services for the employer are performed under the primary direction or control of the employer.

See Code § 414(n)(2). If the temporary worker satisfies these statutory criteria for a leased employee, the temporary worker must be counted as an employee of the employer when testing the employer's qualified plan under the Code nondiscrimination requirements. See Code § 414(n)(1), (3).

This special rule for temporary workers who qualify as leased employees prevents employers from circumventing the fundamental social policy objective that underlies the Code nondiscrimination requirements. The typical temporary worker does not earn sufficient compensation to qualify as a HCE. Without the special rule of Code Section 414(n) for long-term temporary workers, the employer could "lease" the services of numerous rank and file workers for a period of more than one year, effectively supervise those workers as if they were employees, and yet never count these workers when testing the employer's qualified plan for compliance with the Code's nondiscrimination requirements.

For employers who routinely use temporary workers, criteria (2) for leased employee status—that the individual must have provided services for the employer on a substantially full-time basis for at least a year— provides clear guidance. If the employer regularly uses temporary workers, but the employer does not want to count any of its temporary workers as employees when conducting nondiscrimination testing of the employer's qualified plan, the employer should not lease the services of any individual worker for more than one year.

If the employer leases the services of a temporary worker on a substantially full-time basis for more than one year, the employer may attempt to prove that the temporary worker fails criteria (3) for leased employee status. Criteria (3) for leased employee status, known as the *primary direction or control test*, is inherently circumstantial. The legislative history of Code Section 414(n) describes the factors used to determine whether primary direction or control by the employer exists:

> Whether services are performed by an individual under primary direction or control by the [employer] depends on the facts and

circumstances. In general, primary direction and control means that the [employer] exercises the majority of direction and control over the individual. Factors that are relevant in determining whether primary direction or control exists include whether the individual is required to comply with instructions of the [employer] about when, where, and how he or she is to perform the services, whether the services must be performed by a particular person, whether the individual is subject to the supervision of the [employer], and whether the individual must perform services in the order or sequence set by the [employer]. Factors that generally are not relevant in determining whether such direction or control exists include whether the [employer] has the right to hire or fire the individual and whether the individual works for others.

H.R. Rep. No.104–586 (1996).

Code Section 414(n) provides for one exception where a temporary worker who otherwise satisfies the definition of a leased employee is not counted as an employee of the employer. If the leasing organization itself provides the temporary worker with a money purchase pension plan and the leasing organization contributes at least 10% of the temporary worker's compensation to the worker's account under the plan, the temporary worker is not counted as a leased employee of the employer. See Code § 414(n)(5). This exception rarely applies in practice because few leasing organizations provide such a money purchase pension plan for their workers.

[handwritten margin note: exception to general leased Eemployee rule]

Leased employees also present a potential trap for the unwary employer when a leased employee is subsequently hired by the employer as a regular employee. Rather than treating the former leased employee as a newly hired employee, under Code Section 414(n) the employer is required to count the individual's prior period of service as a leased employee for purposes of eligibility, vesting and benefit accrual. See Code §§ 414(n)(1); (3); 414(n)(3); 414(n)(4)(B).

[handwritten margin note: treat temp time as real Emp time for qualification purposes]

Leased employee status under Code Section 414(n) can significantly impact the number of HCEs and NHCEs of the employer. The following example illustrates how HCEs and NHCEs are counted for an employer whose workforce consists of a high percentage of temporary workers.

Assume that ABC Corporation has a total of ten employees, two of whom are HCEs, and eight of whom are NHCEs. Of these eight NHCEs, one NHCE is a receptionist, two NHCEs are clerical workers, and one NHCE is a bookkeeper. Temp Workers, Inc., an employment agency, approaches the owner of ABC Corporation and proposes that ABC Corporation can reduce its labor costs by replacing the four NHCEs with temporary workers leased from Temp Workers, Inc. ABC Corporation terminates the employment of four NHCEs and enters into the proposed leasing arrangement with Temp Workers, Inc.

For the first year the leasing arrangement is in effect, ABC Corporation has a total of six employees, two HCEs and four NHCEs. The four other NHCEs of ABC Corporation have been replaced by four full-time temporary workers (each earning less than the annual compensation test for HCE status) who have been leased from Temp Workers, Inc. For the first year, these temporary workers are not counted as leased employees of ABC Corporation under Code Section 414(n).

After the leasing agreement for these four individuals has been in effect for over one year, the four temporary workers will become leased employees of ABC Corporation under Code Section 414(n) (assuming that the primary direction and control test is satisfied). If the four temporary workers continue to perform services for ABC Corporation on a substantially full-time basis for more than one year, for purposes of nondiscrimination testing ABC Corporation again will have a total of ten employees. ABC Corporation will have two HCEs and eight NHCEs because the four leased employees must be counted as NHCEs of ABC Corporation under Code Section 414(n).

b. Code Section 410(b): The Minimum Coverage Rules

The minimum coverage rules dictate how many of the employer's NHCEs can be excluded from benefitting as participants in the employer's qualified plan based on neutral, business-related criteria. For example, the employer may decide to include only salaried employees in the qualified plan and exclude hourly workers, or the employer may decide to limit participation in the plan to only those employees who work at a certain business facility or location. To satisfy the minimum coverage rules, a qualified plan must pass one of three alternative tests established by Code Section 410(b). Ranked in order of complexity, the three alternative tests for satisfying the minimum coverage rules are

- The *percentage test* of Code Section 410(b)(1)(A);
- The *ratio test* of Code Section 410(b)(1)(B); or
- The *average benefits test* of Code Section 410(b)(1)(C).

Generally, the average benefits test will be used only if the plan cannot satisfy either the percentage test or the ratio test. The average benefits test is described in the Notes after the Problems for this subsection.

The Code Section 410(b) tests are based on the number of participants who *benefit* under the plan. Whether a plan "benefits" an individual is a term of art that varies according to the type of qualified plan. An employee is deemed to benefit under a defined contribution plan (other than a 401(k) plan) if an employer contribution amount or a forfeiture amount has been allocated to the employee's plan account during the testing year. An employee is deemed to benefit under a defined benefit plan if the employee has accrued a benefit under the plan during the testing year. Employees are deemed to benefit under a 401(k) plan if they are eligible to make salary deferral contributions to the 401(k) plan, regardless of whether they actually do so. See Treas. Reg. § 1.410(b)–3.

The Percentage Test

The plan satisfies the percentage test if the plan benefits at least 70% of all NHCEs of the employer. The percentage test is illustrated by the following example: *How to pass percentage test*

> ABC Corporation has a total of ten employees, consisting of two HCEs and eight NHCEs. Of the eight NHCEs, seven NHCEs are participants who benefit under the ABC Corporation Profit Sharing Plan. The eighth NHCE is a temporary worker who qualifies as a leased employee under Code Section 414(n) (and therefore must be counted as a NHCE). The Profit Sharing Plan expressly excludes a leased employee from participation in the Plan.

> Does the Profit Sharing Plan satisfy the percentage test? Yes, because 87.5% of all NHCEs of ABC Corporation (7 ÷ 8 = 87.5%) benefit under the Profit Sharing Plan.

The Ratio Test

The plan satisfies the ratio test if the plan benefits a percentage of NHCEs of the employer that is at least 70% of the percentage of HCEs who benefit under the plan. The ratio test consists of several computational steps:

Step One: Calculate the percentage of HCEs who benefit under the plan during the testing year.

Step Two: Multiply the HCE percentage calculated in Step One times 70%. The resulting product is the minimum percentage of NHCEs who must benefit under the plan for the plan to satisfy the ratio test.

Step Three: Calculate the percentage of NHCEs who benefit under the plan during the testing year.

Step Four: Compare the percentage in Step Two with the percentage in Step Three. If the percentage in Step Two is less than the percentage in Step Three, the plan satisfies the ratio test. If the percentage in Step Two is more than the percentage in Step

Three, the plan fails the ratio test.

Illustration of the Ratio Test

The computational steps of the ratio test are illustrated by the following example. Assume that XYZ Corporation sponsors a retirement plan (Plan) for its employees. For purposes of nondiscrimination testing under Code Section 410(b), XYZ Corporation has ten HCEs and 500 NHCEs. Of the ten HCEs, the company president has her own nonqualified deferred compensation agreement with XYZ Corporation and does not participate in the Plan. The other nine HCEs of XYZ Corporation benefit under the Plan during the testing year.

Of the 500 NHCEs employed by XYZ Corporation, 140 work at Plant A, which makes ping pong balls. The remaining 360 NHCEs work at Plant B, which makes soccer balls. The market for ping pong balls is highly competitive. To reduce the labor costs at Plant A, XYZ Corporation excludes the 140 NHCEs who work at Plant A from participation in the Plan. The other 360 NHCEs of XYZ Corporation who work at Plant B benefit under the Plan during the testing year.

Based on these factual assumptions, does the Plan satisfy the ratio percentage test?

Step One:	Nine of the ten HCEs benefit under the Plan during the testing year. Therefore, the HCE percentage for the Plan is 90%.
Step Two:	The minimum percentage of NHCEs who must benefit under the Plan is 63% (90%, as determined in Step One, times 70% equals 63%).
Step Three:	The percentage of NHCEs who benefit under the Plan during the testing year is 360 divided by 500, or 72%.
Step Four:	The Plan satisfies the ratio test because the percentage of NHCEs who benefit under the Plan under Step Three (72%) is more than the minimum percentage determined under Step Two (63%).

Employees Not Counted When Conducting Code Section 410(b) Testing

When testing a qualified plan for compliance with the minimum coverage rules of Code Section 410(b), the following categories of employees are excluded from consideration when performing the testing calculation.

- Employees who have not satisfied the plan's minimum age *Employees not* and service requirements for eligibility to participate in the *considered* plan. See Code § 410(b)(4).

- Union employees who are subject to a collective bargaining unit agreement, where retirement benefits were the subject of good faith collective bargaining with the employer. See Code § 410(b)(3)(A).

- Nonresident aliens who receive no United States earned income from the employer. See Code § 410(b)(3)(C).

These exclusions are applied before the employer begins testing the plan under Code Section 410(b). The following example illustrates how excluding these categories of employees prior to testing can dramatically reduce the number of employees who are counted for testing purposes.

Assume that the employer, U & O Textile Corporation, operates three facilities: a manufacturing plant in Mexico (Plant 1); a manufacturing plant in North Carolina (Plant 2); and a manufacturing plant in Arizona (Plant 3). Before eliminating workers who fall in one of the three exclusion categories, U & O Textile Corporation has the following numbers of HCEs and NHCEs:

Facility	HCEs	NHCEs
Plant 1	0	489
Plant 2	3	687
Plant 3	5	356
Total	8	1,532

All of the employees at Plant 1 are nonresident aliens who receive no United States earned income. All of the NHCEs employed at Plant 2 are members of a collective bargaining unit where retirement benefits were the subject of good faith collective bargaining. Of the employees at Plant 3, one HCE and three NHCEs are newly hired employees who have not yet satisfied the one year of service requirement for participation in the qualified plan sponsored by U & O Textile Corporation.

Prior to testing its qualified plan for compliance with the minimum coverage rules, U & O Textile Corporation may exclude the following groups of employees for testing purposes:

- All NHCEs employed at Plant 1 as nonresident aliens who received no United States earned income.

- All NHCEs employed at Plant 2 as union employees subject to a collective bargaining agreement where retirement benefits were the subject of good faith collective bargaining.

- One HCE and three NHCEs employed at Plant 3 as employees who have not satisfied the plan's minimum service requirement for eligibility.

After U & O Textile Corporation excludes these employees, the company's qualified plan will be tested for compliance with the minimum coverage rules of Code Section 410(b) based on a total of seven HCEs and 353 NHCEs.

Summary of Procedures for Code Section 410(b) Testing

To summarize, testing a qualified plan for compliance with the minimum coverage rules of Code Section 410(b) requires the following procedures:

1.   Determine who the "employer" is by applying the Code's employer aggregation rules.

2.   Eliminate from consideration all employees of the employer (as determined in Procedure 1) who are not counted because they are excluded from testing under one of the three exclusion categories described in Code Sections 410(b)(3)–(4).

3.   Add to the number of employees remaining after Procedure 2 any temporary workers who must be counted as leased employees of the employer under Code Section 414(n).

4.   Based on the results from Procedures 2 and 3 above, determine the number of HCEs and NHCEs of the employer, taking into account the effect of a top-paid group election, if such an election was made by the plan.

5.   Using the numbers of HCEs and NHCEs determined under Procedure 4, perform minimum coverage testing using one of the tests described in Code Section 410(b).

Problems One and Two below provide an opportunity for you to practice performing the procedures required to test a qualified plan for compliance with the percentage test and the ratio test of Code Section 410(b).

*PROBLEMS ON CODE SECTION 410(*b*)*

PROBLEM ONE

Analyze the facts presented below to determine if the plan satisfies the minimum coverage requirements of Code Section 410(b). In analyzing Questions A, B and C, assume that the employer's plan has not made a top-paid group election and use the 2014 dollar amount ($115,000) to determine HCE status.

Med Associates, P.C. is a small physicians group. The company has a total of nine employees, consisting of four physicians (earning $200,000,

$185,000, $170,000, and $165,000, respectively, in annual compensation), one insurance billing coordinator (earning $45,000 in annual compensation), two nurses (earning $35,000 each in annual compensation), one receptionist (earning $18,000 in annual compensation) and one part-time medical records clerk (earning $8,000 in annual compensation).

Med Associates, P.C. sponsors a profit sharing plan for its employees (Plan). All of the employees of Med Associates, Inc. have satisfied the Plan's minimum age (21) and service (one year) requirements for eligibility as specified in Section 2.1 of the Plan document.

A. Assume that the Plan document reads as follows:

¶ 2.2 Participation. All employees of Med Associates, P.C., who have satisfied the minimum age and service requirements of Section 2.1 shall be participants in the Plan.

Does the Plan satisfy the percentage test or the ratio test of Code Section 410(b)?

B. Assume that the Plan document reads as follows:

¶ 2.2 Participation. All full-time employees of Med Associates, P.C., who have satisfied the minimum age and service requirements of Section 2.1 shall be participants in the Plan.

As a result of this provision, the medical records clerk is excluded from participating in the Plan. Does the Plan satisfy the percentage test or the ratio test of Code Section 410(b)? What other Code qualification requirement does the Plan violate?

C. Assume the medical records clerk: (1) is an employee of a temporary employment agency who has worked at Med Associates, P.C., for two years; (2) the medical records clerk works under the "primary direction and control" of the insurance billing coordinator for Med Associates, P.C.; and (3) the leasing organization does not provide any retirement plan benefits for the medical records clerk.

Further assume that the Plan document reads as follows:

¶ 2.2 Participation. All employees (excluding leased employees under Code § 414(n)) of Med Associates, P.C., who have satisfied the minimum age and service requirements of Section 2.1 shall be participants in the Plan.

Does the Plan satisfy the percentage test or the ratio test of Code Section 410(b)?

D. Assume the same facts as in Question C above. In addition to the medical records clerk, assume that the receptionist also is a leased employee within the definition of Code Section 414(n), and that her leasing organization does not provide her with a retirement plan. Does the Plan satisfy the percentage test or the ratio test of Code Section 410(b)? How would your testing result in Question D change if the Plan has made a top-paid group election?

PROBLEM TWO

Ranoy Corporation (Ranoy) has 1200 employees, including 800 collective bargaining unit employees who are employed in Ranoy's manufacturing facility. Of the remaining employees who are not part of the collective bargaining unit, there are 300 salaried and 100 hourly employees.

A.   Assume that the Retirement Plan for Salaried Employees of Ranoy Corporation (Plan) reads as follows:

> **¶ 2.2 Participation. All salaried employees (excluding leased employees, employees of any subsidiary corporation, and collective bargaining unit employees) of Ranoy Corporation who satisfy the minimum age and service requirements of Section 2.1 shall be participants in the Plan.**

> Of the 300 salaried employees, there are fifteen HCEs. The number of NHCEs who benefit under the Plan is 280. Five salaried employees have not satisfied the minimum age and service requirements of Section 2.1 of the Plan and therefore are not yet eligible to participate in the Plan. There are no HCEs among Ranoy's 100 hourly employees.

> Does the Plan satisfy the percentage test or the ratio test of Code Section 410(b)?

B.   Assume that Ranoy Corporation acquires a 100% owned subsidiary, Subroy, Inc. (Subroy). Subroy has 21 salaried employees and no hourly employees. The president of Subroy is added to the payroll of Ranoy as a salaried employee and thus participates in the Plan as a salaried Ranoy employee.

> Assume the Subroy president is a HCE of the Ranoy-Subroy controlled group of corporations. In the Ranoy-Subroy controlled group, there are now sixteen HCEs, 321 salaried employees, and 1,221 total employees. The twenty salaried employees of Subroy are all NHCEs of the controlled group who are excluded from participating in the Ranoy Plan under the language of Section 2.2 of the Plan document. Thus, the number of NHCEs who benefit under the Plan remains at 280.

> Does the Plan satisfy the percentage test or the ratio test of Code Section 410(b)?

C.   Refer to the facts in Question B above. Assume that three years have passed since the acquisition of Subroy by Ranoy. Subroy has expanded its operations and hired an additional twenty salaried

NHCEs, all of whom have satisfied the minimum age and service requirements of Section 2.1 of the Plan by the end of the third Plan year after the initial acquisition of Subroy. The workforce demographics of Ranoy are unchanged from the circumstances described in Question A above.

On January 1 of the fourth Plan year following the acquisition of Subroy, does the Plan satisfy the percentage test or the ratio test of Code Section 410(b)?

NOTES

1.   *Demonstrating Compliance with Code Section 410(b).* The majority of qualified plans satisfy the minimum coverage rules of Code Section 410(b) by passing either the percentage test or ratio test. The Internal Revenue Service permits the employer to demonstrate compliance with the minimum coverage rules by conducting periodic *snapshot testing.* See Rev. Proc. 93–42. When snapshot testing is used, the employer selects a single day during the plan year that is reasonably representative of the employer's workforce and plan coverage during the plan year. If the employer uses snapshot testing, the Internal Revenue Service may require that the plan must benefit a slightly higher percentage of NHCEs than the 70% required under the statutory provisions of Code Section 410(b). See Rev. Proc. 93–42 (snapshot testing may require 73.5% rather than 70% to adjust for employee turnover).

2.   *The Average Benefits Test of Code Section 410(b).* If the employer's qualified plan fails both the percentage test and the ratio test, the plan may still satisfy the minimum coverage rules by passing the average benefits test. The average benefits test has two components. These components are known as the *nondiscriminatory classification test* and the *average benefits percentage test.* See Code § 410(b)(2).

Under the nondiscriminatory classification test, the plan must benefit employees who qualify for participation based upon a classification system that does not discriminate in favor of HCEs. See Code § 410(b)(2)(A)(i). Under the average benefit percentage test, the average benefit percentage for NHCEs of the employer must be at least 70% of the average benefit percentage for HCEs of the employer. See Code §§ 410(b)(2)(A)(ii); (B)–(C). These two components of the average benefits test are fleshed out in detailed Treasury Department regulations. See Treas. Reg. §§ 1.410(b)–4 (nondiscriminatory classification test); 1.410(b)–5 (average benefit percentage test).

3.   *The Minimum Participation Requirement of Code Section 401(a)(26) for Defined Benefit Plans.* Code Section 401(a)(26) establishes a special minimum participation rule for qualified defined benefit plans. A defined benefit plan must benefit the lesser of:

(1) fifty employees of the employer; or

(2) the greater of (i) 40% of all of the employer's employees, or (ii) two employees (one employee if the employer has only one employee).

The purpose of Code Section 401(a)(26) is to curb the practice among employers of adopting a defined benefit plan solely for the benefit of certain older HCEs. Code Section 401(a)(26) does not apply to defined contribution plans.

4. *Employees of a Qualified Separate Line of Business.* Employers with a division or subsidiary having at least fifty employees can exclude these employees from the testing calculation under Code Section 410(b) if the division or subsidiary satisfies the requirements for a *qualified separate line of business* (QSLOB). See Code §§ 410(b)(5); 414(r). If the QSLOB entity offers a separate qualified plan limited solely to the employees of the QSLOB entity, the QSLOB is treated as a separate employer and the plan for the QSLOB employees is tested under Code Section 410(b) accordingly. The requirements for QSLOB status are detailed in Treasury Department regulations. See Treas. Reg. § 1.414(r).

From a policy perspective, the QSLOB exemption is justified as necessary to preserve flexibility and competitiveness for larger employers with multiple lines of business. Depending on the nature of the QSLOB's business and industry practice, the QSLOB entity may not be able to afford a qualified plan because its competitors do not offer retirement benefits to their workers. Conversely, the QSLOB entity may need to offer a separate, more lucrative qualified plan to attract and retain workers because industry competitors are providing lucrative retirement plan benefits for their workers.

5. *Exemptions for Governmental Plans and Multiemployer Plans.* Qualified plans sponsored by governmental employers are exempt from the minimum coverage rules of Code Section 410(b). See Code § 410(c)(1)(A). Defined benefit plans sponsored by state and local government employers are exempt from the minimum participation requirements of Code Section 401(a)(26). See Code § 401(a)(26)(H). Multiemployer plans benefitting only collective bargaining unit employees are exempt from the minimum coverage rules and the minimum participation requirements for defined benefit plans. See Treas. Reg. § 1.410(b)–2(b)(7); Code § 410(a)(26)(E).

6. *Transition Period for Changes in the Aggregated Employer Group.* The workforce demographics of an aggregated employer group may change over time due to corporate mergers and acquisitions. For example, the members of a controlled group of corporations may sell a subsidiary, buy another subsidiary, or merge with another corporation. A special transition period rule, described in Code Section 410(b)(6)(C), applies in situations where the members of an aggregated employer group change. Under this transition rule, if the employer's qualified plan satisfied the requirements of Code Section 410(b) immediately before the change in the aggregated employer group, the plan is deemed to satisfy Code Section 410(b) during the

transition period following the change. The transition period begins on the date of the change in the members of the aggregated employer group and ends on the last day of the first plan year that begins after the date of the change. The purpose of this transition period rule is to provide adequate time to amend the employer's qualified plan so that the amended plan will continue to satisfy the minimum coverage rules of Code Section 410(b).

The transition period rule can pose a potential trap for the unwary employer precisely because the rule removes the urgency of amending the employer's qualified plan after a significant corporate disposition, acquisition, or merger. The transition period can be as short as one year and one day, or as long as two years minus one day, depending on the point during the plan year when the change in the aggregated employer group occurred. The longer the duration of the transition period, the greater the temptation to ignore the sometimes difficult issues associated with amending the coverage of the employer's qualified plan.

7. *Penalty for Failure to Satisfy the Code's Minimum Coverage and Participation Requirements.* Unlike the other Code requirements for qualified plans, a special rule applies if the plan fails to satisfy Code Section 410(b). This special rule also applies to defined benefit plans that fail to satisfy Code Section 401(a)(26). Normally, if a qualified plan fails to satisfy a Code requirement, all participants in the plan suffer the adverse income tax consequences of plan disqualification. Under the special rule for plans that fail to satisfy Code Sections 410(b) or 401(a)(26), only the HCEs who participate in the plan are penalized. Each HCE must include in his gross income the total amount of his vested accrued benefits under the plan for the taxable year during which the qualification failure occurs. See Code § 402(b)(4)(A). The vested accrued benefits of the NHCEs who participate in the plan are not subject to income taxation. See Code § 402(b)(4)(B).

This special rule is justified by the social policy objective that underlies Code Sections 410(b) and 401(a)(26). The purpose of these Code requirements is to ensure that a certain number of NHCEs benefit under the employer's qualified plan so that, as retirees, these workers will receive retirement income from the plan. Thus, penalizing NHCEs for the plan's failure to comply with these Code requirements by taxing their vested accrued benefits under the plan would be contrary to the social policy goal Congress intended the requirements to serve.

c. **Code Section 401(a)(4): Nondiscrimination in Benefits or Contributions**

Code Section 401(a)(4) performs a very different function than Code Section 410(b). Code Section 410(b) dictates *how many* NHCEs must benefit under the employer's qualified plan. In contrast, Code Section 401(a)(4) dictates *how much* each NHCE who participates in the employer's qualified plan must receive in benefits or contributions.

Viewed in light of the social policy objective that underlies the Code nondiscrimination requirements, Code Section 401(a)(4) operates as a necessary corollary to Code Section 410(b). Without Code Section 401(a)(4), employers easily could thwart the intended purpose of the minimum coverage rules of Code Section 410(b). To illustrate this point, assume for a moment that Code Section 401(a)(4) did not exist. The employer could permit all employees to participate in the employer's qualified plan, thereby satisfying the minimum coverage rules of Code Section 410(b). Absent the requirements of Code Section 401(a)(4), the employer could contribute a mere .01% of compensation for each NHCE who participates in the plan, and at the same time contribute a much higher percentage of compensation for each HCE who participates in the Plan. It is the nondiscrimination requirement of Code Section 401(a)(4) that prevents employers from adopting this form of qualified plan design.

The statutory language of Code Section 401(a)(4) is deceptively simple. A qualified plan and its accompanying trust are nondiscriminatory "if the contributions or benefits provided under the plan do not discriminate in favor of highly compensated employees." Code § 401(a)(4). Although this statutory language has remained unchanged since the enactment of ERISA in 1974, its implementation through Treasury Department regulations has had a torturous history.

The Treasury Department formulated the current version of the regulations implementing Code Section 401(a)(4) in the wake of the Tax Reform Act of 1986, Pub. L. No. 99–514, 100 Stat. 2085. See generally Treas. Reg. § 1.401(a)(4) (Code 401(a)(4) Regulations). The Code 401(a)(4) Regulations are effective for plan years beginning on or after January 1, 1994. The issuance of the Code 401(a)(4) Regulations marked a significant change in the Treasury Department's approach to the concept of nondiscrimination in benefits or contributions for qualified plans. Under prior regulations, the Treasury Department used a much more flexible facts and circumstances approach to identify individuals designated as HCEs and to measure discrimination in benefits or contributions. Over time, this regulatory flexibility was perceived as providing opportunities for manipulation that undermined the social policy objective of using qualified plans to provide a source of retirement income to rank and file employees. The Tax Reform Act of 1986 substituted a much more objective standard for the determination of a highly compensated employee under Code Section 414(q). (These original objective criteria were later simplified, resulting in the current test for HCE status described earlier in Section F.1 of Chapter Three.) In keeping with Congress's more objective approach to the concept of nondiscrimination reflected in the Tax Reform Act of 1986, the Treasury Department promulgated the Code 401(a)(4) Regulations to reduce the level of subjectivity in their application and to provide a more objective set of criteria to measure discrimination in benefits or contributions.

The Code 401(a)(4) Regulations rely on a combination of safe harbor plan designs and the heavily quantitative general test for plans that do not satisfy a safe harbor plan design. See generally Treas. Reg. § 1.401(a)(4). The Code 401(a)(4) Regulations create various safe harbor plan designs for defined contribution and defined benefit plans. See Treas. Reg. §§ 1.401(a)(4)–2(b) (defined contribution plan safe harbors); 1.401(a)(4)–3(b) (defined benefit plan safe harbors). If the design of the employer's plan satisfies the safe harbor criteria, the plan is deemed automatically to satisfy Code Section 401(a)(4). Thus, the employer may avoid costly numerical testing for prohibited discrimination under Code Section 401(a)(4) if the employer adopts a safe harbor plan design.

The safe harbor plan design for defined contribution plans that is most frequently used allocates employer contributions to the plan so that each participant receives the same percentage of the participant's compensation as an allocation to the participant's account. See Treas. Reg. § 1.401(a)(4)–2(b)(2)(i). This safe harbor plan design is commonly referred to as *pro rata based on compensation* (or just *pro rata*, for short).

For example, an employer who sponsors a profit sharing plan may decide to make a contribution to the plan equal to 10% of each participant's compensation. This type of employer contribution clearly satisfies the pro rata safe harbor because each participant's account will receive an allocation that is equal to 10% of the participant's compensation.

Alternatively, the employer may decide to make a discretionary contribution to the profit sharing plan in the form of a lump sum dollar amount. The following simplified example illustrates how the pro rata plan design would allocate the employer's lump sum contribution among the participants' accounts so that each participant receives the same percentage of compensation as an allocation.

Assume that Company A makes a discretionary contribution to its Profit Sharing Plan (Plan) in the lump sum amount of $10,000. The Plan uses a pro rata allocation formula for employer contributions. There are five participants in the Plan, each earning the following annual compensation amounts:

Employee #1 =	$120,000
Employee #2 =	$ 60,000
Employee #3 =	$ 50,000
Employee #4 =	$ 40,000
Employee #5 =	$ 30,000

How should the $10,000 employer contribution be allocated so that each participant receives an allocation amount that is the same percentage of compensation for all participants? In real life, this computation would be performed using specialized computer software. To perform this calculation manually, the first step is to add the compensation of all of the Plan's participants. In this example, the total compensation of all of the Plan's participants is $300,000. Next, each participant's proportionate share of total Plan compensation is determined by dividing the individual's compensation by the amount of total Plan compensation. This process illustrates why the safe harbor plan design is described as pro rata based on compensation. Performing this calculation results in the following pro rata compensation percentages for each Plan participant.

Employee #1 =	$120,000/$300,000 =	40%
Employee #2 =	$60,000/$300,000 =	20%
Employee #3 =	$50,000/$300,000 =	16.67%
Employee #4 =	$40,000/$300,000 =	13.33%
Employee #5 =	$30,000/$300,000 =	10%

The second step is to determine each participant's share of the $10,000 employer contribution by multiplying the individual's pro rata compensation percentage by $10,000. This calculation results in the following dollar allocation amounts for each participant's Plan account.

Employee #1 =	40% x $10,000 =	$4,000
Employee #2 =	20% x $10,000 =	$2,000
Employee #3 =	16.67% x $10,000 =	$1,667
Employee #4 =	13.33% x $10,000 =	$1,333
Employee #5 =	10% x $10,000 =	$1,000

The third and final step (because this is a manual calculation) is to check to see if the safe harbor criteria—that each participant must receive the same percentage of his or her compensation as an allocation—has been satisfied. This step is performed by dividing each participant's dollar allocation amount by the individual's compensation. In the example, the safe harbor criteria are satisfied because each participant in the Plan has received a contribution equal to 3.33% of the individual's compensation, as demonstrated below:

Employee #1 =	$4,000/$120,000 =	3.33%
Employee #2 =	$2,000/$60,000 =	3.33%
Employee #3 =	$1,667/$50,000 =	3.33%
Employee #4 =	$1,333/$40,000 =	3.33%
Employee #5 =	$1,000/$30,000 =	3.33%

The above example of the Company A Profit Sharing Plan illustrates a key policy point. Nondiscrimination in contributions or benefits under Code Section 401(a)(4) permits wide variations in how HCEs and NHCEs may fare under the employer's qualified plan. In the example of the Company A Profit Sharing Plan, the highest paid employee received an allocation of $4,000, whereas the lowest paid employee received an allocation of just $1,000. Measured in absolute dollar terms, Code Section 401(a)(4) permits HCEs to receive a much higher contribution or benefit amount than the NHCEs who participate in the employer's qualified plan.

The example of the Company A Profit Sharing Plan also illustrates a second key policy point. Fundamentally, qualified plan contributions and benefits are intertwined with compensation. Consequently, the higher one's compensation, the greater one's retirement benefits from a qualified plan will be.

Given the tax and social policy objectives that underlie the Code nondiscrimination requirements, both of these key policy points merit further exploration. Rank and file workers, who earn lesser compensation amounts during their working years, are more likely than HCEs to need substantial levels of qualified plan benefits to obtain an adequate level of income during their retirement years. The Code requirements for qualified plans contain several mechanisms that limit, either directly or indirectly, the dollar amount of benefits or contributions for HCEs who participate in the plan. These mechanisms are described in Section F.2 of Chapter Three.

Plan Compensation

In the example of the Company A Profit Sharing Plan, the problem was simplified by providing the annual compensation amounts used by the plan to determine each participant's allocation. There are two ways in which a participant's *plan compensation*, defined as the compensation amount used for purposes of the qualified plan, may differ from the actual compensation amount paid to the participant by the employer. First, a qualified plan may use one of several options for defining a participant's plan compensation. See Code § 414(s); Treas. Reg. § 1.414(s)–1(c)–(d). For example, the plan may elect to use an alternative definition of plan compensation and exclude overtime pay, shift differential premiums and bonuses. This alternative definition is permitted if the plan can demonstrate, through additional numerical testing, that the alternative definition does not discriminate in favor of HCEs. See Treas. Reg. § 1.414(s)–1(d)(3). The plan must use the same definition of plan compensation for all of the participants in the plan.

Second, the amount of a participant's plan compensation may differ from the actual compensation amount paid by the employer due to the limit on a participant's plan compensation imposed by Code Section 401(a)(17). Under Code Section 401(a)(17), the plan cannot take into account annual compensation that exceeds $200,000. This dollar amount, like other dollar limits in the Code provisions governing qualified plans, is indexed for inflation and periodically adjusted upward by the Treasury Department. In 2014, the Code Section 401(a)(17) limit on plan compensation was $260,000. The Code Section 401(a)(17) limit on an individual's plan compensation is one of the ways the Code indirectly limits the amount of benefits or contributions provided under the plan for HCEs.

Code Section 401(a)(17) indirectly limits benefits or contributions for HCEs because a qualified plan may not take into account compensation in excess of the Code Section 401(a)(17) limit when applying the plan's formula for the accrual of benefits or the allocation of employer contributions. Moreover, the plan may not consider compensation in excess of the Code Section 401(a)(17) limit when conducting nondiscrimination testing under other Code provisions. These provisions include testing under Code Section 401(a)(4), the average benefits test of Code Section 410(b)(2), and the special nondiscrimination tests for 401(k) plans under Code Sections 401(k) and 401(m).

The dollar amount at which Congress sets the Code Section 401(a)(17) limit has significant policy consequences. The higher the plan compensation limit, the larger the benefits or contributions a qualified plan will be able to provide to HCEs. The tax policy implications of a higher or lower dollar amount under Code Section 401(a)(17) are explored in the Problem on Code Sections 401(a)(4) and 401(a)(17) at the end of this subsection.

To simplify the reading material, references in the text to "compensation" in the remainder of Chapter Three refer to plan compensation as determined under Code Section 401(a)(17) rather than the actual compensation of the employee, unless the discussion clearly indicates otherwise. The various Code dollar amounts in effect for 2014 referred to in the remainder of Chapter Three are summarized in Appendix E. For years after 2014, consult Appendix E in the current student supplement to the casebook.

PROBLEM ON CODE SECTIONS 401(a)(4) AND 401(a)(17)

Company A sponsors a profit sharing plan (Plan) for its employees. The Plan uses a pro rata allocation formula for employer contributions to the Plan. There are five participants in the Plan in 2014, each earning the following compensation amounts:

Employee #1 =	$300,000
Employee #2 =	$ 60,000
Employee #3 =	$ 50,000
Employee #4 =	$ 40,000
Employee #5 =	$ 30,000

Company A makes a discretionary contribution to the Plan in 2014 of $75,000.

A. How much of the employer's $75,000 contribution to the Plan is allocated under the pro rata allocation formula to each participant's account?

B. Assume that in 2014 the plan compensation limit under Code Section 401(a) (17) is only $150,000. How would your answer to Question A change?

NOTES

1. *The General Test Under Code Section 401(a)(4).* The general test for nondiscrimination in benefits or contributions is an alternative to using a safe harbor plan design. The general test requires the services of a skilled pension actuary to perform. The Code 401(a)(4) Regulations describe the general test. See Treas. Reg. §§ 1.401(a)(4)–2(c); 1.401(a)(4)–3(c). The basic approach underlying the general test is to divide the plan's participants into rate groups based on each participant's rate of contribution allocations (under a defined contribution plan) or rate of accrued benefits (under a defined benefit plan). The plan demonstrates compliance with Code Section 401(a)(4) by showing that each rate group independently satisfies one of the minimum coverage tests under Code Section 410(b). From a policy perspective, requiring that each rate group independently must satisfy the Code Section 410(b) minimum coverage requirements ensures that the rate groups having the highest rates of contributions or benefits are not dominated by HCEs, and that the rate groups having the lowest rates are not dominated by NHCEs.

2. *Permitted Disparity (Integration for Social Security) Under Code Section 401(l).* A qualified plan that is *integrated* for Social Security takes into account the employer's payment of taxes for each employee under the Federal Insurance Contributions Act (FICA). FICA requires both the employer and the employee to each pay a tax equal to 6.20% of the employee's

compensation up to a dollar amount set by the Social Security Administration for each year. This dollar amount, officially known as the Social Security taxable wage base, is indexed for inflation.

Under an integrated plan, the employer is allowed to increase contributions or benefits for participants who earn over the Social Security taxable wage base amount. Consequently, an integrated plan creates a disparity in the benefits or contributions the plan provides for HCEs, who are likely to earn more than the Social Security taxable wage base amount. Such disparity in benefits or contributions for HCEs is permitted under Code Section 401(a)(4) if the plan satisfies the safe harbor under Code Section 401(*l*). If the plan's integration formula does not satisfy the Code Section 401(*l*) safe harbor, the plan may demonstrate compliance with Code Section 401(a)(4) through the general test.

Integrated plans have been criticized as inconsistent with the social policy objective of the qualified plan system. Workers earning below the Social Security taxable wage base, who are receiving lesser benefits or contributions under an integrated plan, are the very individuals most likely to suffer from inadequate income during their retirement years. For a comprehensive analysis and critique of the history and social policy consequences of integrated plans, see Patricia E. Dilley, *The Evolution of Entitlement: Retirement Income and the Problem of Integrating Private Pensions and Social Security*, 30 LOY. L.A. L. REV. 1063 (1997).

3. *Nondiscrimination in Other Benefits, Rights, and Features of the Plan.* The Code 401(a)(4) Regulations require that the benefits, rights and features of the plan must be both currently and effectively available on a nondiscriminatory basis. See Treas. Reg. § 1.401(a)(4)–4(a)–(c). The currently available requirement is satisfied if the group of employees to whom the benefit, right or feature is available satisfies the ratio percentage test of Code Section 410(b). See Treas. Reg. § 1.401(a)(4)–4(b). The effectively available requirement is satisfied if, based "on all of the relevant facts and circumstances, the group of employees to whom a benefit, right or feature is effectively available [does not] substantially favor HCEs." Treas. Reg. § 1.401(a)(4)–4(c).

To illustrate these requirements, assume that the Company A Retirement Plan requires distributions from the Plan to be in the form of an annuity and does not allow for distributions in the form of a lump sum. On June 30, 2015, Company A amends the Retirement Plan to permit a lump sum form of distribution for participants who terminate employment between June 30, 2015, and July 31, 2015. The only employee of Company A who terminated employment during this period is a HCE. Although this lump sum distribution feature is currently available to all HCEs and NHCEs alike, under these circumstances the feature is not effectively available (and therefore is discriminatory under Code Section 401(a)(4)). The lump sum distribution feature is discriminatory because the feature substantially favors only one participant, who is a HCE. See Treas. Reg. § 1.401(a)(4)–4(c)(2), Example 3.

4. *"Cross-Tested" Plans*. To satisfy the requirements of Code Section 401(a)(4), the plan must demonstrate nondiscrimination in *either* benefits *or* contributions. Defined contribution plans usually satisfy this requirement with respect to contribution amounts, whereas defined benefit plans usually satisfy this requirement with respect to benefits. So-called *cross-tested plans* deviate from this norm. A cross-tested defined contribution plan demonstrates compliance with Code Section 401(a)(4) by showing that the benefits each participant receives at normal retirement age are nondiscriminatory under Code Section 401(a)(4). A cross-tested defined benefit plan demonstrates that the employer contributions to the plan for each participant are nondiscriminatory under Code Section 401(a)(4). Cross-testing often is performed by a specialized pension actuary. The practice of demonstrating compliance with Code Section 401(a)(4) using cross-testing has provoked controversy. Cross-testing is predominantly used by cash balance plans and age-weighted profit sharing plans.

5. *Plan Forfeitures*. When a participant in a defined benefit plan terminates employment prior to becoming fully vested, the forfeiture amount remains part of the assets held in the plan's trust. Thus, in a defined benefit plan forfeitures help to fund the accrued benefits of the other plan participants.

Forfeitures in a defined contribution plan also help to fund the accrued benefits of the other plan participants. When a participant in a defined contribution plan incurs a forfeiture, the forfeited portion of the participant's account remains in the plan's trust. In a profit sharing plan that uses a safe harbor allocation formula, the forfeiture amount eventually will be allocated among the accounts of other participants in the plan pro rata based on plan compensation.

d. Code Sections 401(k) and 401(m) Tests

The popularity of the 401(k) plan presents Congress with a policy dilemma. In a 401(k) plan, the participants finance their own retirement benefits. Each participant directs the employer to contribute part of the participant's current compensation (known as a *salary deferral contribution*) to the participant's account in the 401(k) plan. The amount of the participant's salary deferral contribution is not included in the participant's gross income. Naturally, the higher the level of the participant's compensation, the more likely the participant will be able to afford to make salary deferral contributions to the 401(k) plan. In addition, the higher the level of the participant's compensation, the greater the participant's income tax savings will be if the participant makes a salary deferral contribution to the 401(k) plan.

The special nondiscrimination tests for 401(k) plans are necessary in part because the minimum coverage requirements of Code Section 410(b) do not prohibit large disparities in the salary deferral contribution amounts made by the HCEs and NHCEs to a 401(k) plan. Recall that for purposes of testing under the minimum coverage rules of Code Section 410(b), an employee is treated as "benefitting" under a 401(k) plan so long as the employee is *eligible* to make a salary deferral contribution to the 401(k) plan. This special rule under Code Section 410(b) applies even if the employee chooses not to make a salary deferral contribution to the 401(k) plan. Thus, under the minimum coverage tests of Code Section 410(b), those NHCEs who do not make salary deferral contributions to the 401(k) plan nevertheless are counted as "participants" in the 401(k) plan. See Treas. Reg. § 1.410(b)–3.

The special nondiscrimination tests for 401(k) plans are designed to address the potential inequities in employee salary deferral contributions and employer matching contributions that may arise between HCEs and NHCEs in a 401(k) plan. These tests focus specifically on the salary deferral contributions made by the HCEs and NHCEs to the 401(k) plan and related matching contributions made to the 401(k) plan by the employer. Code Section 401(k) describes the *actual deferral percentage* (ADP) test, which focuses on employee salary deferral contributions. See Code § 401(k)(3); Treas. Reg. § 1.401(k)–1(a)(4)(iv). If the 401(k) plan also provides for employer matching contributions, the plan must satisfy an additional nondiscrimination test, known as the *actual contribution percentage* (ACP) test. The ACP test is functionally similar to the ADP test. See Code § 401(m); Treas. Reg. § 1.401(m)–1(a).

In the real world, 401(k) plan nondiscrimination testing is performed using computer software. ADP testing is an additional administrative cost for the employer who sponsors a traditional 401(k) plan that is subject to ADP testing. Employers who wish to avoid this administrative cost may adopt safe harbor design features for their 401(k) plans. These safe harbor design features are described in the Notes following the Problem on ADP Testing and Code Section 401(a)(17) at the end of this subsection.

The Actual Deferral Percentage Test

To perform the ADP test, the first step is to calculate the ratio (expressed as a percentage) for each individual employee who is eligible to participate in the plan of the individual's salary deferral contribution to the individual's compensation. This ratio is called the *actual deferral percentage*. For example, if an employee has compensation of $120,000 and makes a salary deferral contribution to the 401(k) plan of $12,000, the employee's actual deferral percentage is $12,000 ÷ $120,000, or 10%. If an employee is eligible to participate in the 401(k) plan, but chooses not to make a salary deferral contribution, the employee's actual deferral percentage is zero.

The second step in performing the ADP test is to calculate the average of all of the individual actual deferral percentages for the group of HCEs and the group of NHCEs. The example below illustrates these first two steps.

Assume that Company A sponsors a 401(k) plan (Plan). All five employees of Company A are eligible to participate in the Plan. The compensation, salary deferral contribution amounts, and actual deferral percentages in 2014 for each individual employee of Company A are as follows:

Employee	Compensation	Salary Deferral Contribution	Actual Deferral Percentage
#1	$160,000	$16,000	10.00%
#2	$120,000	$ 7,200	6.00%
#3	$ 50,000	$ 4,000	8.00%
#4	$ 40,000	0	0%
#5	$ 30,000	0	0%

In this example, the two HCEs (Employee #1 and #2) together have an average actual deferral percentage of 8%. To determine the average actual deferral percentage of the NHCEs as a group, the "zeros" of Employees #4 and #5 are counted. As a result, the average actual deferral percentage for the NHCE group is reduced to 2.67%.

The third step of the ADP test is compare the average for the HCE group to the average for the NHCE group using the statutory criteria. See Code § 401(k)(3)(A)(ii)(I)–(II). A 401(k) plan satisfies the ADP test if one of two testing options is satisfied:

Testing Option (1): The average percentage for the group of HCEs does not exceed the average percentage for the group of NHCEs multiplied by 1.25; or

Testing Option (2): The amount by which the average percentage for the group of HCEs exceeds the average percentage for the group of NHCEs is not more than two percentage points, *and* the average percentage for the group of HCEs is not more than the average percentage for the group of NHCEs multiplied by two.

In this example, the Plan does not satisfy either testing option. Under testing option (1), the average percentage for the NHCE group (2.67%) multiplied by 1.25 is only 3.34%, much less than the average percentage (8%) for the HCE group. Under testing option (2), the average percentage for the HCE group exceeds the average percentage for the NHCE group by much more than two percentage points (8% minus 2.67% equals 5.33%).

Illustration of Correction Method for Failing the ADP Test

For the Company A 401(k) Plan to remain qualified, the employer must use one of several possible correction methods that will enable the Plan to pass the ADP test. From a policy perspective, these correction methods generally operate either to reduce the benefits of the HCEs under a 401(k) plan, or to increase the benefits of the NHCEs under a 401(k) plan.

One correction method is for the employer to reduce the salary deferral contributions of the HCEs until the ADP test is satisfied. Under this correction method, the plan administrator distributes the excess salary deferral amounts (and any related investment earnings) to the HCEs. The plan administrator reports these distribution amounts as part of each HCE's gross income.

To illustrate this correction method, assume that the administrator for the Company A 401(k) Plan distributes $10,600 and $6,600 in excess salary deferral contributions back to Employee #1 and Employee #2, respectively. (To simplify the illustration, the distribution of related investment earnings is omitted.) After the distribution, the corrected average actual deferral percentage for the HCE group becomes 4.5%, as demonstrated by the calculations below:

Employee	New Deferral Amount	Compensation	Corrected ADP
#1	$16,000-$10,600 = $7,200	$160,000	$7,200/$160,000=4.5%
#2	$12,000-$6,600 = $5,400	$120,000	$5,400/$120,000=4.5%
			Average = 4.5%

Does the Plan as corrected satisfy either testing option (1) or (2) under the ADP test? Under testing option (1), the average percentage for the HCE group (4.5%) still exceeds the average percentage for the NHCE group multiplied by 1.25 (2.67% times 1.25 equals 3.34%, which is less than 4.5%). As corrected, the Plan does satisfy testing option (2). First, the average percentage for the HCE group does not exceed the average percentage for the NHCE group by more than two percentage points (4.5% minus 2.67% equals 1.83%). Second, the average percentage for the

HCE group does not exceed the average percentage for the NHCE group multiplied by two (2.67% times 2 equals 5.34%, which is more than 4.5%).

The distribution correction method is one of several methods that may be used to redeem a 401(k) plan that initially has failed the ADP test. The potential tax consequences for the employer and the HCEs resulting from the distribution correction method are described in the Notes following the Problem on ADP Testing and Code Section 401(a)(17) at the end of this subsection. The Notes also describe other possible methods for correcting a 401(k) plan that has failed the ADP test.

401(k) Plan Design and the ADP Test: Policy Implications

The example of the Company A 401(k) Plan illustrates the significant constraints that the ADP test places on the ability of HCEs to make salary deferral contributions to a traditional 401(k) plan that is subject to ADP testing. Under the ADP test, the ability of HCEs to make salary deferral contributions to the 401(k) plan is constrained by the salary deferral contributions made by the NHCEs who participate in the 401(k) plan. For this reason, the employer may choose to adopt certain 401(k) plan design features to encourage NHCEs voluntarily to increase their salary deferral contributions to the plan. Employer matching contributions, permitting loans from the employee's 401(k) plan account and permitting early distributions in cases of financial hardship are examples of design features that employers may use to increase the average actual deferral percentage of the NHCE group.

Although these plan design features may boost the salary deferral contributions of NHCEs to the 401(k) plan, two of these features, permitting loans and hardship distributions, potentially undermine the social policy objective of the qualified plan system. Amounts that are withdrawn from a participant's account prior to retirement in the form of a loan or a hardship distribution reduce the participant's ultimate benefit from the 401(k) plan at retirement.

PROBLEM ON ADP TESTING AND CODE SECTION 401(a)(17)

The plan compensation limit of Code Section 401(a)(17) has a significant impact on the results of ADP testing for a 401(k) plan. This problem is designed to illustrate the tax policy implications of Code Section 401(a)(17) for ADP testing.

Company A sponsors a 401(k) plan (Plan) for its five employees. Each employee earned the following actual compensation amounts from Company A and made the following salary deferral contributions to the Plan during the testing year:

Employee	Actual Compensation	Salary Deferral Contribution
#1	$300,000	$13,000
#2	$250,000	$ 6,000
#3	$ 50,000	$ 4,000
#4	$ 40,000	0
#5	$ 30,000	0

The average actual deferral percentage for the NHCEs of Company A (Employees #3, #4 and #5) is 2.67%. Calculate the average actual deferral percentage for the group of HCEs (Employees #1 and #2) assuming that:

A. The Code Section 401(a)(17) plan compensation limit is $300,000; and

B. The Code Section 401(a)(17) plan compensation limit is $150,000.

If Congress chooses to lower the plan compensation limit under Code Section 401(a)(17), what is the ultimate effect on the ability of HCEs to make salary deferral contributions to a traditional 401(k) plan that is subject to ADP testing?

NOTES

1.   *Automatic Enrollment (Negative Election) 401(k) Plans.* Normally, an eligible employee must complete certain administrative paperwork to participate in a 401(k) plan. This administrative paperwork indicates the amount of the employee's salary deferral contribution and the investments for the employee's 401(k) account. By requiring the employee to complete this paperwork before participating in the 401(k) plan, a certain number of eligible employees will fail to act and therefore will not participate in the plan.

Beginning in the late 1990s, employers began adopting an *automatic enrollment* or *negative election* design feature for their 401(k) plans. In an automatic enrollment 401(k) plan, the employer automatically enrolls each eligible employee as a participant in the 401(k) plan and designates the amount of the employee's salary deferral contribution. If the employee does not want to participate in the 401(k) plan, the employee must complete the necessary paperwork to elect out of participation in the plan.

Studies of participation and contribution rates in automatic enrollment 401(k) plans found that 401(k) plans with an automatic enrollment design feature boosted participation and contribution levels among NHCEs. Nevertheless, many employers were reluctant to adopt an automatic enrollment feature due to several legal obstacles. First, the employer's fiduciary responsibilities and liability under ERISA associated with an automatic enrollment feature were unclear. See Colleen E. Medill, *Stock Market Volatility and 401(k) Plans*, 34 MICH. J. L. REFORM. 469, 513–521 (2001). Second, state payroll withholding laws generally required affirmative consent by an employee to any amount withheld from the employee's wages by an employer. Although these state payroll withholding laws arguably were preempted by ERISA, a few states had criminal laws that prohibited an employer from withholding any amount from an employee's wages without the employee's express authorization. Such state criminal laws were not preempted by ERISA. See ERISA § 514(b)(4).

Congress addressed these obstacles to automatic enrollment 401(k) plans in the Pension Protection Act of 2006. All conflicting state laws are preempted as of the effective date of the Pension Protection Act of 2006 (August 17, 2006) for those 401(k) plans with an automatic enrollment feature that meet minimum contribution standards, automatic investment option requirements, and participant notice requirements as prescribed by the Secretary of Labor. See ERISA § 514(e).

2.   *SIMPLE 401(k) Plans for Small Employers.* SIMPLE 401(k) plans were created by Congress to encourage smaller employers to provide retirement plans for their employees. SIMPLE 401(k) plans are authorized under Code Section 401(k)(11), which incorporates by reference the terms and definitions of Code Section 408(p).

SIMPLE 401(k) plans may be sponsored by employers who do not maintain another qualified plan and who have no more than 100 employees earning compensation of $5,000 or more in the preceding plan year. See Code §§ 401(k)(11)(C)(I); 408(p)(2)(C)(i)(I). Two characteristics of SIMPLE 401(k) plans are designed to make these plans attractive to smaller employers. SIMPLE 401(k) plans are less costly to administer because they are exempt from ADP/ACP testing and the requirements for top heavy plans. See Code §§ 401(k)(11)(A); 401(m)(10); 416(4)(G). Due to the exemption from ADP testing, the HCEs of the employer are able to make salary deferral contributions to a SIMPLE 401(k) plan up to the maximum dollar amount permitted under federal law. These two characteristics represent the perceived advantages of a SIMPLE 401(k) plan as compared with a traditional 401(k) plan that is subject to ADP/ACP testing.

SIMPLE 401(k) plans have two perceived disadvantages when compared with a traditional 401(k) plan. First, the salary deferral contribution limit for a SIMPLE 401(k) plan is less than the limit for a traditional 401(k) plan. For example, in 2014 the maximum salary deferral contribution amount for a SIMPLE 401(k) plan was $12,000, whereas the maximum salary deferral contribution amount for a traditional 401(k) plan was $17,500.

Second, the employer who sponsors a SIMPLE 401(k) plan must make contributions to the plan based upon a statutory formula. See Code § 401(k)(11)(B). The employer who sponsors a traditional 401(k) plan is not required to make employer contributions to the plan. Under this statutory formula, the employer has two options for making employer contributions. The employer may make a matching contribution for each participant in the plan that is equal to the participant's salary deferral contribution, up to a maximum employer matching contribution of 3% of compensation for each participant in the SIMPLE 401(k) plan. Alternatively, the employer may make a contribution equal to 2% of compensation for each eligible employee whose annual compensation is at least $5,000, regardless of whether the employee makes salary deferral contributions to the SIMPLE 401(k) plan. All employer contributions to a SIMPLE 401(k) plan must be immediately and fully vested. See Code §§ 401(k)(11)(A)(iii); 408(p)(3).

Although Congress intended the SIMPLE 401(k) plan to boost the rate of qualified plan coverage among employees of smaller employers, the effect of the SIMPLE 401(k) plan has been negligible. Surveys of smaller employers indicate that lower administrative costs are not sufficient to motivate smaller employers to sponsor a qualified plan. Rather, it is primarily business reasons that motivate smaller employers to sponsor qualified plans. Such business reasons include a positive impact on the employer's ability to attract and retain quality employees and a positive impact on the attitude and performance of their employees. See EMPLOYEE BENEFIT RESEARCH INST., THE SMALL EMPLOYER RETIREMENT SURVEY SUMMARY OF FINDINGS (2003).

3. *Safe Harbor 401(k) Plans and Qualified Automatic Enrollment Features.* Code Section 401(k)(12) authorizes the safe harbor 401(k) plan. Like a SIMPLE 401(k) plan, a safe harbor 401(k) plan is exempt from ADP/ACP testing. See Code §§ 401(k)(12)(A); 401(m)(11). A safe harbor 401(k) plan also is exempt from the requirements for top heavy plans. See Code § 416(4)(H).

A safe harbor 401(k) plan has several advantages when compared with a SIMPLE 401(k) plan. First, a safe harbor 401(k) plan is not limited to small employers. Second, the employer who sponsors a safe harbor 401(k) plan also may sponsor another qualified plan. Finally, the maximum salary deferral contribution amount for a safe harbor 401(k) plan is the higher amount that applies to a traditional 401(k) plan that is subject to ADP/ACP testing rather than the lower amount for a SIMPLE 401(k) plan.

A safe harbor 401(k) plan must satisfy three sets of detailed design requirements:

(1) The plan annually must provide a special notice to each employee eligible to participate in the 401(k) plan describing the employee's rights and obligations under the plan. See Code § 401(k)(12)(D). This notice, which may be provided electronically, must be given at least thirty days and no more than ninety days before the beginning of each plan year. See IRS Notice 98–52; IRS Notice 2000–3.

(2) The employer must make employer contributions to the plan using one of two alternative statutory formulas. The employer may make a matching contribution for each NHCE who makes

a salary deferral contribution to the plan. Alternatively, the employer may make a contribution for every NHCE who is eligible to participate in the plan, regardless of whether the individual makes a salary deferral contribution to the plan. If the employer chooses to make matching contributions, the amount of each matching contribution cannot exceed 6% of the employee's compensation. See Code § 401(m)(11)(B). These formulas for mandatory employer contributions to a safe harbor 401(k) plan are defined in detail in the statute and further explained in subsequent Internal Revenue Service notices. See Code §§ 401(k)(12)(B); 401(m)(11)(B); IRS Notice 2000–3 (modifying IRS Notice 98–52).

(3) The employer's contributions to the plan must satisfy special vesting and withdrawal requirements. The employer's contributions must be immediately and fully vested. In addition, the employer's contributions are subject to the same restrictions on distributions that apply to an employee's salary deferral contributions to a 401(k) plan. See Code § 401(k)(12)(E)(i).

Employers who sponsor an automatic enrollment 401(k) plan have a second safe harbor plan design option known as a *qualified automatic enrollment feature*. See generally Code § 401(k)(13). A 401(k) plan with a qualified automatic enrollment feature is deemed to satisfy the ADP/ACP tests and the top heavy rules.

A qualified automatic enrollment feature must satisfy three statutory criteria concerning: (1) the amount of the automatic salary deferral contribution; (2) the amount and vesting of the employer's contributions to the 401(k) plan; and (3) the content of the notice sent to plan participants describing their rights under the qualified automatic enrollment feature. Each of these statutory criteria is described in detail below.

(1) The automatic salary deferral contribution amount for a qualified automatic enrollment feature must be set at not more than 10% and not less than 3% of the employee's plan compensation for the participant's first year. The automatic salary deferral contribution percentage must increase to 4%, 5% and 6% of the participant's plan compensation during the second, third, and fourth years that the employee participates in the 401(k) plan, and must remain at 6% or higher thereafter. See Code § 401(k)(13)(C). This "default" setting for automatic salary deferral contributions may be changed by the employee at any time to a lesser or higher percentage.

(2) The employer who sponsors a 401(k) plan with a qualified automatic enrollment feature must either make a contribution of at least 3% of plan compensation for each NHCE who is eligible to participate in the 401(k) plan's automatic enrollment arrangement, or must make a matching contribution to the

401(k) plan for each NHCE. The matching contribution amount must be equal to 100% of the employee's salary deferral contribution up to 1% of compensation, and 50% of the employee's salary deferral contribution that is more than 1% but not more than 6% of the employee's plan compensation. All employer contributions under a qualified automatic enrollment feature must be fully vested after two years of service, and must be subject to the withdrawal rules that apply to employee salary deferral contributions. See Code § 401(k)(13)(D).

(3) A 401(k) plan with a qualified automatic enrollment feature must provide each employee who is eligible to participate in the 401(k) plan with an annual notice, written in a manner calculated to be understood by the average employee, that explains the employee's rights under the arrangement. The notice must be provided within a reasonable amount of time before the first automatic enrollment salary deferral contribution is scheduled to be made. The notice must explain the employee's right to opt out of the automatic enrollment arrangement and to elect a different salary deferral contribution amount or percentage. The notice also must explain how contributions made under the automatic enrollment feature will be invested if the employee does not affirmatively designate an investment choice for the contributions. See Code § 401(k)(13)(E).

4. *Qualified Roth Election Programs.* Code Section 402A authorizes the *qualified Roth election program* (Roth feature). A 401(k) plan adopting the Roth feature allows employees to designate their salary deferral contributions to the plan as after-tax contributions, much in the same fashion as individuals may choose to make after-tax contributions to a Roth IRA. Roth feature contributions to a 401(k) plan are limited in amount so that the employee's total of pre-tax and after-tax contributions to the 401(k) plan cannot exceed the maximum amount permitted under the federal tax laws for salary deferral contributions to a traditional 401(k) plan. See Code § 402A(c)(2).

An employer is not permitted to establish a 401(k) plan with a Roth feature if the employees only are permitted to make after-tax Roth 401(k) contributions. The employer's 401(k) plan must also permit employees to make pre-tax salary deferral contributions. See Final Regulations, Designated Roth Contributions to Cash or Deferred Arrangements Under Section 401(k), 71 Fed. Reg. 6–11 (Jan. 3, 2006).

After-tax Roth contribution amounts are included in the 401(k) plan participant's income and subject to income and FICA taxes at the time of contribution. The after-tax Roth amount must be irrevocably designated by the 401(k) plan participant at the time the amount is contributed to the 401(k) plan and maintained in a separate account within the 401(k) plan. Pre-tax salary deferral contributions to the 401(k) plan cannot be later redesignated by the 401(k) plan participant as after-tax Roth contribution amounts. Investment gains and losses attributable to Roth contributions must be separately accounted for by the plan administrator. See id.

In a traditional 401(k) plan with a Roth feature, after-tax Roth contributions are combined with the participant's pre-tax salary deferral contributions for purposes of ADP testing. In the event that the 401(k) plan fails the ADP test, the 401(k) plan may permit each HCE to designate whether the excess amount to be distributed should be taken from the HCE's pre-tax salary deferral contribution account, the after-tax Roth contribution account, or allocated between the two accounts. A corrective distribution from the Roth contribution account is not included in the HCE's taxable income, but any related accumulated investment earnings are included.

If a distribution from a Roth account is made due to the participant's disability, death, or attainment of age 59 ½, the distributed investment earnings from a Roth account are tax-free if the distribution occurs at least five years after the first taxable year during which the participant made an after-tax Roth contribution to the 401(k) plan. Roth accounts may be directly rolled over to another 401(k) plan with a Roth feature, or to a Roth IRA. Unlike Roth IRAs, Roth 401(k) accounts are subject to the required minimum distribution rules of Code Section 401(a)(9). See Code §§ 402A; 408A(c)(5)(A); Final Regulations, supra.

Adding a Roth feature to a 401(k) plan is likely to benefit participants who are many years away from retirement, are currently in a low-income tax bracket, and who anticipate that in future years they will be in a higher income tax bracket. For these participants, it is the tax-free accumulation of investment earnings in the Roth account, compounded over many years, that makes the Roth feature financially attractive. Other participants who may benefit from a Roth feature in their employer's 401(k) plan are high-income individuals who are disqualified from making contributions to a Roth IRA because their income exceeds the modified adjusted gross income limitation for contributions to a Roth IRA. In 2013, this limitation was set at $127,000 for an individual taxpayer and $188,000 for married taxpayers who filed a joint return. See Code § 408A(c)(3)(C).

5. *Tax Consequences Associated with Distributing Excess Salary Deferral Contributions.* Tax consequences arise when a traditional 401(k) plan must distribute excess salary deferral contributions to HCEs to enable the plan to pass the ADP test. If excess salary deferral contributions are distributed to a HCE within two and one-half months after the end of the plan year, the distributed amount is included in the gross income of the HCE in the year the distribution is made. See Code § 4979(f)(2).If excess salary deferral contributions are distributed to a HCE later than two and one-half months after the end of the plan year, the distributed amount is included in the gross income of the HCE and the employer is subject to a 10% excise tax penalty on the amount of the excess salary deferral contributions. See Code § 4979(a)–(b). For excess salary deferral contributions to a 401(k) plan with an eligible automatic contribution arrangement (as defined in Code Section

414(w)(3)), the deadline for making corrective distributions is six months after the end of the plan year. See Code § 4979(f)(1).

If excess salary deferral contributions are not distributed within twelve months after the end of the plan year, the 401(k) plan is disqualified for the testing year and for all subsequent years in which the excess salary deferral contributions remain in the plan's trust. See Treas. Reg. § 1.401(k)–1(f)(6)(ii). This rule obviously places a high premium on timely ADP testing and correction of excess salary deferral contributions made by HCEs to a 401(k) plan. To avoid the administrative burden associated with the distribution of excess salary deferral contributions to HCEs, many plans use the ADP test results for the plan's NHCEs from the prior year as a guide to limit the amount of salary deferral contributions by HCEs at the outset of the next plan year. This approach allows the HCEs to know the amount of their salary deferral contribution at the beginning of the plan year, and helps to preempt the need for corrective distributions at the end of the plan year.

6.   *Other ADP Testing Correction Methods.* Rather than distributing excess salary deferral contributions to HCEs, the employer may make additional contributions, known as *qualified nonelective contributions* (QNECs) to the accounts of NHCEs under the 401(k) plan until the plan satisfies the ADP test. QNECs must be immediately and fully vested. If the employer already makes matching contributions to the 401(k) plan and these matching contributions are immediately and fully vested, these contributions, known as *qualified matching contributions*, may be counted for purposes of retesting the plan. See generally Treas. Reg. § 1.401(k)–1(g)(13).

Another possible correction method is to recharacterize a portion of the excess salary deferral contributions made by HCEs as after-tax contributions to the 401(k) plan. The recharacterized amounts are included in each HCE's gross income, but are not included as part of each HCE's salary deferral contributions when the 401(k) plan is retested. See generally Treas. Reg. § 1.401(k)–1(f)(3)(ii)–(iii). As a practical matter, the recharacterization correction method often is of limited utility because when the plan is retested, such recharacterized amounts may cause the plan to fail the ACP test, which counts both employer matching contributions and after-tax employee contributions in performing the test.

e.   Code Section 416: The Top Heavy Rules

Congress enacted the top heavy rules for qualified plans in 1982 as Code Section 416. The top heavy rules potentially affect qualified plans that skew benefits too heavily in favor of the owners and highly paid officers of the employer's business.

The top heavy rules are based on the concept of a *key employee.* Any employee of the employer who is not a key employee under the statutory criteria is deemed a *non-key employee.* A key employee is defined as any individual who satisfies one of the three statutory criteria:

(1) The employee is an officer of the employer whose compensation is more than $130,000 (indexed for inflation and set at $170,000 in 2014);

(2) The employee has more than a 5% ownership interest in the employer; or

(3) The employee has more than a 1% ownership interest in the employer and receives more than $150,000 in compensation.

See Code § 416(i)(1).

Although the definition of a key employee under Code Section 416 differs from the definition of a HCE under Code Section 414(q), in application a large degree of overlap exists between those individuals who are HCEs for purposes of nondiscrimination testing and those individuals who are key employees for purposes of the top heavy rules. The 5% ownership test for a key employee is identical to the 5% ownership test for a HCE. In addition, some HCEs are likely to be officers of the employer earning over the annual compensation test under the top heavy rules and therefore also qualify as key employees. The primary difference between the definitions of a HCE and a key employee is that the annual compensation amount for HCE status ($115,000 in 2014) is less than the annual compensation amount for key employees who are officers or 1% owners ($170,000 and $150,000, respectively, in 2014).

Top Heavy Testing

A defined benefit plan is considered to be top heavy under Code Section 416 if the present value of the cumulative accrued benefits for all key employees is more than 60% of the cumulative accrued benefits for all employees participating in the plan. A defined contribution plan is considered to be top heavy under Code Section 416 if the total value of the accounts of key employees under the plan exceeds 60% of the total value of all accounts of all employees under the plan. See Code §§ 416(g)(1)(A)(i)–(ii). Both the vested and nonvested portions of the accrued benefits or account amounts for the plan's key and non-key employees are counted when testing the plan under the top heavy rules. The following example illustrates how a defined contribution plan is tested for compliance under the top heavy rules.

Company A has sponsored a profit sharing plan (Plan) for many years. Company A has two key employees, Employee #1 and Employee #2. Employee #1 owns 100% of Company A. Employee #2 is an officer of Company A and earns $175,000 in annual compensation. Employees #3, #4 and #5 of Company A are non-key employees.

Each employee's account under the Plan (including both vested and nonvested portions) has the following account value:

Employee	Plan Account Value
#1	$410,000
#2	$220,000
#3	$230,000
#4	$ 90,000
#5	$ 50,000
	$1,000,000

The total value of all accounts under the Plan is $1 million. The total value of the accounts of the Plan's two key employees (Employee #1 and Employee #2) is $630,000. The Plan is top heavy because the total value of the accounts of the Plan's key employees exceeds 60% of the total value of all accounts under the Plan ($630,000 divided by $1,000,000 equals 63%).

Consequences of Top Heavy Status

When a defined benefit plan is top heavy, the plan must satisfy special vesting requirements under Code Section 416. A top heavy defined benefit plan must use an accelerated vesting schedule for determining the nonforfeitable amount of accrued benefits for non-key employees. See Code § 416(b). Under this accelerated vesting schedule, if the defined benefit plan normally uses a five-year cliff vesting schedule, the plan must use a three-year cliff vesting schedule. If the defined benefit plan normally uses a seven-year graduated vesting schedule, the plan must switch to the two- to six-year graduated schedule described in Code Section 416(b)(1)(B), which is summarized in Table 3.8.

Table 3.8

Accelerated Graduated Vesting Schedule for Top Heavy Plans

Years of Vesting Service	Nonforfeitable %
2	20%
3	40%
4	60%
5	80%
6	100%

Notice that both the three-year cliff vesting schedule and the six-year graduated vesting schedule for defined contribution plans are identical to the accelerated top heavy vesting schedules required by Code Section 416(b). Thus, accelerated vesting under the top heavy rules only impacts defined benefit plans.

A top heavy plan must provide a minimum level of contributions or benefits for the plan's non-key employees. See Code Section 416(c). For defined contribution plans that are top heavy, the employer must contribute a minimum of 3% of compensation each year to the account of each non-key employee. (Note: If the highest contribution to a key employee during the plan year as a percentage of compensation is less than 3%, the employer may contribute that lesser percentage amount to the accounts of the non-key employees.) For top heavy defined benefit plans, Code Section 416 describes the minimum annual benefit that must accrue each year for non-key employees so long as the plan is top heavy.

If the employer sponsors more than one qualified plan, complex plan aggregation rules govern how the top heavy rules of Code Section 416 apply to multiple plans. See Code § 416(f), (g)(2); Treas. Reg. § 1.416–1. The policy objective of these plan aggregation rules is to prevent the employer from circumventing the top heavy rules by operating multiple plans.

PROBLEM ON TOP HEAVY PLANS

The law firm of Chance and Chance (C & C) sponsors a profit sharing plan (Plan) for its salaried employees. The Plan uses a six-year graduated vesting schedule.

In 2015, C & C had three key employees (Employees #1, #2 and #3), who were partners of the firm, and six non-key employees (Employees #4 through #9). The value of each employee's account under the Plan in 2015 is set forth below:

Employee	Account Value in 2015
#1	$250,000
#2	$250,000
#3	$160,000
#4	$140,000
#5	$140,000
#6	$100,000
#7	$100,000
#8	$ 90,000
#9	$ 80,000

In 2016, Employee #3 terminated employment with C & C and established her own law firm. Shortly thereafter, Employees #4, #5, #6 and #7 terminated employment at C & C and become employees at the new law firm of Employee #3. During the next two years, C & C hired three new employees (Employees #A, #B and #C) to replace Employees #3, #4, #5, #6 and #7. In 2019, C & C has two key employees (Employees #1 and #2) and five non-key employees (Employees #8, #9, #A, #B and #C). The value of each employee's account under the Plan in 2019 is set forth below:

Employee	Account Value in 2019
#1	$300,000
#2	$300,000
#8	$108,000
#9	$ 96,000
#A	$ 4,000
#B	$ 3,000
#C	$ 2,000

A.   Was the Plan top heavy in 2015?

B.   Is the Plan top heavy in 2019?

C.   In 2020, C & C had lower than projected revenues for the year. The partners of the firm, Employees #1 and #2, have come to you for legal advice. They are considering whether to make a discretionary employer contribution to the Plan for 2020. How would you advise the partners of C & C?

D.   Assume that Employee #A terminates employment with C & C on December 31, 2019, with two years of vesting service. At the time Employee #A terminates employment, his account balance under the Plan is $4,000, and the account values of the other employees are unchanged from the above facts. What is the amount of Employee #A's nonforfeitable accrued benefit under the Plan?

2. LIMITS ON QUALIFIED PLAN BENEFITS FOR INDIVIDUALS AND EMPLOYER DEDUCTIONS

The Code contains rules that limit the amount of benefits or contributions for a participant in a qualified plan (individual limits). The Code also limits the amount the employer may deduct for contributions to a qualified plan (employer limits). These individual and employer limits are the most fluid provisions of the Code requirements for qualified plans. Congress regularly "reforms" (i.e., adjusts) these limits as part of the overall federal budget negotiation process when new tax legislation is enacted. Consequently, the exact dollar amounts of the individual and employer limits described in this casebook today are unlikely to be the dollar limits in effect five or ten years from now. For this reason, the reading material in this subsection emphasizes the policy choices and employer incentives that underlie how Congress selects and structures the individual and employer limits for qualified plans.

Viewed from the tax and social policy objectives that underlie the qualified plan system, the revenue losses attributable to the individual and employer limits present a significant challenge for Congressional lawmakers. On the one hand, the tax expenditure associated with any increase in the individual and employer limits for qualified plans represents lost revenues that could be used to fund other priorities in the federal budget. On the other hand, any reduction in the individual and employer limits for qualified plans becomes counterproductive if employers respond by ceasing to voluntarily sponsor qualified plans for their workers.

As you read the material in this subsection of Chapter Three, imagine that you are the owner of a small business or the president of a large corporation. How might these rules influence the retirement plan benefits that your company provides to its employees?

a. Individual Limits Under Code Section 415

Code Section 415 is the starting point for determining the maximum level of benefits an individual participant may receive from a qualified plan. Table 3.9 below summarizes the individual limits in effect for 2014. These amounts are indexed for inflation in subsequent years. Where a technical term exists for a particular type of individual limit under the Code, the term is in italics. These italicized terms are explained in the reading material following Table 3.9.

Table 3.9

Individual Limits for Qualified Plans

Types of Plan	2014 Limit
Defined Benefit Plan *Annual Benefits*	$210,000
Defined Contribution Plan *Annual Additions*	$52,000
Exclusion Amounts for Traditional or Safe Harbor 401(k) Plans	$17,500
Catch Up Contributions for Traditional or Safe Harbor 401(k) Plans	$5,500
Exclusion Amounts for SIMPLE 401(k) Plans	$12,000
Catch Up Contributions for SIMPLE 401(k) Plans	$2,500

Defined Benefit Plans

For participants in a defined benefit plan, the individual limit is expressed in terms of the maximum *annual benefit* that the plan may pay to the participant in the form of a straight life annuity commencing at age 65. This maximum annual annuity benefit is the lesser of $160,000 (indexed for inflation and set at $210,000 in 2014) or 100 percent of the participant's average compensation for the highest paid three consecutive years. The maximum annual annuity benefit amount is actuarially adjusted if the participant begins receiving the benefit before age 62 or after age 65, or for employees who have less than ten years of participation in the defined benefit plan. If an individual participates in more than one defined benefit plan, the individual limit applies to the combined total of all benefits from all defined benefit plans. See Code § 415(b).

Defined Contribution Plans

For participants in a defined contribution plan, the individual limit is expressed in terms of the maximum *annual addition* that may be made to an individual's plan account. The maximum annual addition amount is the lesser of $40,000 (indexed for inflation and set at $52,000 in 2014) or 100% of the participant's compensation. If an individual participates in more than one defined contribution plan that is a qualified plan under Code Section 401(a), the individual limit applies to the combined total of all annual additions to all of the individual's defined contribution plan accounts. See Code § 415(c).

Annual additions *include*:

- employer contributions;

- employee salary deferral contributions to a 401(k) plan; and

- forfeitures that have been allocated to the participant's account.

Annual additions *do not include*:

- direct rollover amounts from another plan or an IRA;

- assets transferred from the trustee of one plan to the trustee of another;

- plan loan repayments;

- catch up contributions; and

- investment earnings.

Some individuals are fortunate enough to participate in both a defined benefit and defined contribution plan sponsored by their employer. In this situation, special rules govern the maximum amount that the employer may contribute to each plan. See generally Code § 404(a)(7).

401(k) Plans: Exclusion Amounts

Code Section 402(g) places limits on the maximum dollar amount of employee salary deferral contributions that can be made to a 401(k) plan. This limit, known as the *exclusion amount*, determines the maximum amount of salary deferral contributions to a 401(k) plan that can be excluded from the employee's gross income and thereby escape income taxation. (Note: Although the employee's 401(k) salary deferral contributions are not subject to income tax, salary deferral contributions remain subject to the federal FICA payroll tax and do count as part of the employee's wage history for purposes of earning Social Security benefits.) In 2014, the annual exclusion amount for employee salary deferral contributions to a traditional or safe harbor 401(k) plan was set at $17,500. For a SIMPLE 401(k) plan, the annual exclusion amount in 2014 was set at $12,000.

401(k) Plans: Catch Up Contributions

Participants who are age 50 or older may elect to make additional salary deferral contributions to a 401(k) plan. These additional salary deferral contributions, known as *catch up contributions,* are permitted so that older participants will have an opportunity to save additional amounts for retirement. For a traditional or safe harbor 401(k) plan, the maximum annual catch up contribution amount was set at $5,500 in

2014. For a SIMPLE 401(k) plan, the maximum annual catch up contribution amount was set at $2,500 in 2014.

Catch up contributions are not subject to the nondiscrimination requirements of Code Sections 410(b) and 401(a)(4), ADP testing under Code Section 401(k)(3), the top heavy rules of Code Section 416, or the limit on annual additions under Code Section 415(c). See Code § 414(v)(3).

b. Employer Deduction Limits Under Code Section 404

Code Section 404 has two significant functions. First, Code Section 404 determines when the employer may claim a deduction for a contribution to a qualified plan. Second, Code Section 404 determines how much the employer may claim as a deduction for a contribution to a qualified plan.

The Policy Significance of Code Section 404

Code Section 404(a) governs the timing of the employer's deduction by exempting contributions to qualified plans from the *matching principle* of income taxation, which normally would delay the employer's deduction until the contribution amount was included in the gross income of a plan participant. The Ninth Circuit in *Albertson's, Inc. v. Commissioner*, 42 F.3d 537 (9th Cir. 1994), explained the policy significance of Code Section 404 as an incentive for employers to sponsor qualified plans for their employees.

The significance of Section 404's matching principle becomes evident when one compares the treatment of qualified and nonqualified plans under that section. Because Section 404 requires employer deductions for contributions to nonqualified plans to be "matched," an employer cannot take the tax deductions for payments to its employees until the nonqualified plan participants include those payments in their taxable income—that is, until the employees actually receive the compensation promised to them.

Qualified plans, in contrast, are *not* governed by the matching principle and consequently generate concurrent tax benefits to employers. Although employees are not taxed upon the benefits they receive from the plan until they actually receive them, an employer's contributions to a qualified plan are deductible when paid to the trust. Thus, the employer may take an *immediate, unmatched* deduction for any contribution it makes to a qualified plan.

By exempting contributions to qualified plans from the matching principle, Congress compensates employers for meeting the burdensome requirements associated with qualified plans by granting them favorable tax treatment. The current taxation scheme thus creates financial incentives for employers to contribute to qualified plans while providing no comparable benefits for employers who adopt plans that are unfunded or that discriminate in favor of highly compensated employees.

Id. at 543 (emphasis in original). As a result of Code Section 401(a), employer contributions to the plan are excluded from the employee's income for purposes of both the income tax and the federal FICA payroll tax.

Employer Deduction Limit for Defined Contribution Plans

The maximum deduction for total employer contributions to a profit sharing plan, stock bonus plan or money purchase pension plan, and employer matching contributions to a 401(k) plan is 25% of the aggregate plan compensation for all of the participants in the employer's plan(s). See Code § 404(a)(3)(A). Aggregate plan compensation for purposes of calculating the employer deduction limit includes any salary deferral contributions made by participant to a 401(k) plan, even though this amount has been excluded from the participants' gross income. See Code § 404(a)(12); 415(c)(3)(D).

In determining aggregate plan compensation for purposes of calculating the employer deduction limit under Code Section 404, each participant's compensation is subject to the dollar amount limitation of Code Section 401(a)(17). Thus, if an individual participant in a plan earned annual compensation of $400,000 in 2014, when calculating the aggregate plan compensation of all plan participants under Code Section 404, only $260,000 of the individual's compensation would be counted. See Code § 404(l).

The employer deduction limit of Code Section 404(a)(3) for employer contributions to a defined contribution plan is linked to the individual limits of Code Section 415(c) through Code Section 404(j). Under Code Section 404(j), the employer is not permitted to deduct the portion of annual additions to a participant's account that exceeds the individual limit for annual additions under Code Section 415(c).

Employer Deduction Limit for Single Employer Defined Benefit Plans

Code Section 404(o) sets forth a formula to compute the employer's maximum deduction limit for contributions to a defined benefit plan. Greatly simplified, under this formula the employer's deduction limit for a single employer defined benefit plan is the sum of:

(1) the funding target for the plan year; plus

(2) the target normal cost for the plan year; plus

(3) the cushion amount for the plan year, minus

(4) the value of the plan's assets for the year.

The actuarial concepts imbedded in this formula (funding target, target normal cost, and cushion amount) are further defined in Code Section 404(*o*). Code Section 404(*o*) also provides that if the employer's defined benefit plan is required to make a larger contribution under the minimum funding rules of Code Section 430, then the larger minimum funding contribution amount is deductible by the employer. See Code § 404(*o*)(1)(B). The minimum funding rules for defined benefit plans are described in the Notes after the Problem on Code Sections 415 and 404.

c. Illustration: The Hypothetical Small Business Client

Most employers (and some law students) are not keenly interested in a recitation of the technical rules governing individual and employer deduction limits. An employer does, however, expect an ERISA tax lawyer to "show me the money" by applying these limits in the specific context of the employer's business. The following hypothetical client situation is designed to illustrate how the individual and employer deduction limits may influence a small business owner's decision whether to sponsor a qualified plan. In working through this illustration, assume that the Code dollar amount limits in effect for 2014 apply.

The owner and president of Company A (let's call him Al) is interested in sponsoring a profit sharing plan with a 401(k) feature for the employees of Company A. Al's primary objective in establishing the plan is to maximize the annual additions made to the plan for Al. (Recall that for 2014, the annual addition dollar limit for defined contribution plans is $52,000.) Al is concerned, however, about how much Company A will need to contribute to the profit sharing plan for the other employees of Company A.

Assume that the Company A workforce earned the following compensation amounts in 2014. Al is the only HCE of Company A.

Employee	Compensation
Al	$290,000
Employees #1–#30	$1,750,000 (total)

Al's first decision involves what type of 401(k) plan to sponsor. Although Company A is small enough to sponsor a SIMPLE 401(k) plan, the Company cannot sponsor both a SIMPLE 401(k) plan and a profit sharing plan. Thus, Al's choice of a 401(k) plan is limited to a traditional 401(k) plan or a safe harbor 401(k) plan. If Company A sponsors a traditional 401(k) plan, the ADP test is likely to limit the amount of salary deferral contributions that Al may make to the plan. If Company A sponsors a safe harbor 401(k) plan, Al will be able to contribute the maximum exclusion amount annually to the 401(k) plan (set at $17,500 in 2014). But if Company A sponsors a safe harbor 401(k) plan, Company A also will have to make employer contributions to the safe harbor 401(k) plan for the other employees of Company A, who are all NHCEs.

Assume that Al decides Company A should sponsor a safe harbor 401(k) plan. Al further decides that under the safe harbor formula Company A will make an employer contribution for each NHCE that is equal to 3% of each NHCE's compensation. Al has selected one of the two statutory options for employer contributions to a safe harbor 401(k) plan. This particular option, described in Code Section 401(k)(12)(C), means that Company A will make a contribution to the safe harbor 401(k) plan of 3% of each employee's compensation, regardless of whether the employee makes a salary deferral contribution to the 401(k) plan. Based on Company A's workforce compensation in 2014, the estimated amount of Company A's annual contribution to a safe harbor 401(k) plan is 3% times $1,750,000, or $52,500.

Under a safe harbor 401(k) plan, Al may make a $17,500 salary deferral contribution to his account in 2014.[b] Al also will receive a 3% employer safe harbor contribution. How much of Al's actual compensation of $290,000 may be counted for purposes of the safe harbor contribution? Under Code Section 401(a)(17), Al's plan compensation cannot exceed $260,000 in 2014. Therefore, Al will receive an employer 3% safe harbor contribution of $7,800 (3% times $260,000).[c] Al still needs approximately $26,700 in employer contributions to his profit sharing plan account to achieve his primary goal of receiving the maximum annual addition permitted in 2014, which is $52,000. (In the real world, you would advise Al concerning the possibility that annual additions in the form of forfeitures may be allocated to his profit sharing plan account. But because this illustration is a simplified analysis, it ignores the nuances of annual additions in the form of forfeitures.)

Al decides Company A should sponsor a profit sharing plan with a safe harbor allocation formula that allocates employer contributions to the account of plan participants pro rata based on compensation. Recall that under a pro rata allocation formula, each participant in the Company A profit sharing plan must receive an amount that is the same percentage of the participant's plan compensation. For Al to receive an allocation to his profit sharing plan account of $26,700, the Company A contribution to

---

[b]   Although the $17,500 salary deferral contribution will not be subject to income tax, it will remain subject to the federal FICA payroll tax of 15.2% (combined employee and employer rate).

[c]   Note that because the 3% safe harbor amount of $7,800 is an employer contribution, this amount escapes both income tax and the federal FICA payroll tax.

the plan must be a percentage that is equal to $26,700 divided by Al's plan compensation of $260,000, or 10.269%.[d]

Under a pro rata allocation formula, Company A also must contribute 10.269% of compensation for each participant in the profit sharing plan. At this point, Al is faced with an important decision concerning the coverage of the Company A profit sharing plan. If all of the employees of Company A are eligible to participate in the plan, then Company A must make a contribution for employees other than Al equal to 10.269% times $1,750,000 (the total compensation of the other thirty employees of Company A). This results in an estimated cost to Company A for employer contributions to the profit sharing plan for employees other than Al of approximately $179,707 (rounded).

Al could reduce this employer contribution amount by excluding some of his employees from participation in the Company A profit sharing plan. Under either the percentage test or the ratio test of Code Section 410(b), the plan must benefit at least 70% of Company A's thirty NHCEs. Whether Al chooses to make certain NHCEs ineligible for participation in the Company A profit sharing plan is a significant business decision having potential ramifications for employee morale and productivity.

To summarize, if all of the employees of Company A are eligible to participate in the profit sharing plan, Company A must make the following contributions in 2014 in order for Al to maximize his own annual additions under Code Section 415(c):

Plan	Al's Account	Company Contributions for NHCEs
Safe Harbor 401(k)	Al has $17,500 in salary deferral and $7,800 in employer matching contributions	$ 52,500
Profit Sharing	$26,700 Company contribution	$179,707
Total	$52,000	$232,207

Al's reaction to this analysis may be that his company cannot afford to make these contributions for its employees. What other options are available to Al? The above illustration relied upon a safe harbor 401(k) plan and a profit sharing plan with a pro rata allocation formula. The plan designs used in the illustration are the most simple (and therefore the least costly) to administer. Al may want to consult an ERISA tax lawyer for more specialized advice concerning other qualified plan design

---

[d] Actually, 10.269% times $260,000 is $26,699.40, so Al is 60 cents short (but close enough).

options. Other plan design options are likely to be more difficult and costly to administer, but may reduce the amount of Company A's contribution for its NHCEs while still allowing Al to achieve his goal of maximizing the annual additions to his account.

PROBLEM ON CODE SECTIONS 415 AND 404

Assume that the year is 2017. Due to a growing federal budget deficit Congress has reduced the individual and employer deduction limits under the Code. The Code Section 401(a)(17) limit on plan compensation is now $150,000. The Code Section 415(c) limit on annual additions to defined contribution plans has been reduced to $30,000. The exclusion amount for all types of 401(k) plans has been fixed at $10,000. Catch up contributions to 401(k) plans are no longer permitted. The employer deduction limit under Code Section 404 for contributions to defined contribution plans has been reduced to 15% of aggregate plan compensation.

Your client, Smith Animal Clinic (Clinic), is a small veterinary business with three employees. The Clinic is a limited liability corporation owned by the veterinarian, Alicia Smith, who earns annual compensation of $225,000. The other two employees, Joe Stites and Joyce Scamp, earn annual compensation of $25,000 and $35,000, respectively.

After learning of the merits of profit sharing plans by reading a magazine for small business owners, Alicia has come to the conclusion that the Clinic should sponsor a profit sharing plan. Alicia wants all employees of the Clinic to immediately become participants in the profit sharing plan.

Using the above-described dollar amounts in effect for 2017, how much must the Clinic contribute to the profit sharing plan so that Alicia will receive the maximum annual addition of $30,000? (For purposes of this estimate, assume that the profit sharing plan will use a pro rata allocation formula and ignore the possibility of forfeitures.) How much of this contribution will be allocated to the accounts of the Clinic's two other employees under the plan's pro rata allocation formula?

Will the Clinic be able to deduct the full amount of this contribution under the reduced employer deduction limit of Code Section 404? If not, can you propose an alternative that will enable Alicia to receive the maximum annual addition of $30,000?

NOTES

1. *Consequences for Violation of the Employer Deduction Limit.* If the employer makes a contribution to a defined contribution plan in excess of the employer deduction limit established by Code Section 404(a)(3), in certain circumstances the excess contribution amount may be carried forward and deducted in future years. See Code § 404(a)(3)(A)(ii). In contrast, excess annual additions in violation of the individual limit of Code Section 415(c) must be corrected to avoid disqualification of the plan.

With limited exceptions, the employer normally is subject to a 10% excise tax on the amount of an employer contribution to a qualified plan that is not immediately deductible under Code Section 404. See Code § 4972. Because this 10% excise tax is imposed for each subsequent year on the amount of the excess contribution that remains nondeductible, as a practical matter employers are deterred from making nondeductible contributions to their qualified plans.

2. *Stock Market Volatility and Minimum Funding Requirements for Defined Benefit Plans.* The amount of the employer's contribution necessary to maintain adequate funding for a defined benefit plan can vary dramatically from year to year based upon stock market conditions and prevailing interest rates. For example, during the period of a rising stock market in the 1990s, many employers who sponsored defined benefit plans enjoyed a "contribution holiday." During this period, the investment returns of many defined benefit plans were sufficient to maintain adequate funding for the plan under the minimum funding standards that were then in effect under the Code. At the end of 2000, 360 of the 500 companies comprising the Standard and Poor's 500 sponsored a defined benefit plan for their workers. These 360 companies reported a cumulative pension asset surplus of $263 billion. After 2000, as both the stock market and interest rates declined, the result was a dramatic reversal in defined benefit plan funding. By the end of 2002, these same 360 companies reported a cumulative plan funding deficit of $216 billion, despite having voluntarily contributed almost $46 billion to their defined benefit pension plans during 2002.

Congress enacted the Pension Protection Act of 2006 to address the twin problems of substantial underfunding of defined benefit plans and the corresponding growing liabilities of the Pension Benefit Guaranty Corporation. See Pension Protection Act, Pub. L. No. 109–208, §§ 101–102; 111–112, 120 Stat. 780. Ironically, before employers had time to digest the new, more stringent minimum funding rules enacted by the Pension Protection Act, the stock market experienced a dramatic deterioration in the fall of 2008. Employers who sponsored defined benefit plans that previously were fully funded suddenly were being warned by their accountants and actuaries that, as a result of the new minimum funding requirements, they would have to make substantial additional contributions to their defined benefit plans. For defined benefit plans that were already in endangered or critical funding status, particularly multiemployer plans, compliance with the new minimum funding requirements seemed almost impossible. In short, the timing for implementing the Pension Protection Act's new minimum funding requirements could not have been worse as employers struggled to maintain their day-to-day operations in the wake of a deepening economic recession.

Congress responded to the funding crisis by enacting the Worker, Retiree, and Employer Recovery Act of 2008, Pub. L. No. 110–458, 122 Stat. 5092 (WRERA). The WRERA provided relief to defined benefit plans in several ways. Among the changes, small employers were given more flexibility in the use of interest rate assumptions. The more rigorous funding targets enacted by the Pension Protection Act for single employer defined benefit plans were eased, and multiemployer plans in endangered or critical funding status were given additional time to satisfy the funding requirements. In addition, employers were permitted to compute the value of their pension plan assets over a 24 month period for funding purposes, a change that helped to mitigate the sharp downturn in asset values in the fall of 2008. See generally 24 Fed. Reg. 53,004 (Oct. 15, 2009) (explaining final regulations on funding issues under the Pension Protection Act, as amended by the WRERA); CONG. RES. SERV., THE WORKER, RETIREE, AND EMPLOYER RECOVERY ACT OF 2008: AN OVERVIEW (Jan. 29, 2009); JOINT COMM. ON TAXATION, 110TH CONG., GENERAL EXPLANATION OF TAX LEGISLATION ENACTED IN THE 110TH CONGRESS 544–49 (Comm. Print 2009). The minimum funding rules for single employer defined benefit plans are contained in Code Section 412 and ERISA Section 303. The rules for multiemployer defined benefit plans are found in Code Sections 431 and 432 and ERISA Sections 304 and 305.

3. *FAS 158 and Accounting Disclosures for Single Employer Defined Benefit Plans.* For publicly traded companies, an important considerations in sponsoring a defined benefit plan is the potential financial impact of the plan on the company's financial statements. In the past, publicly traded employers were not always required to report the current funding status of a defined benefit plan or to integrate completely the financial effects of the plan into the company's financial statements. Rather, the full picture of the plan's funding status was reported in the notes to the company's financial statements.

Today, under Statement of Financial Accounting Standard No. 158 (FAS 158) a publicly traded company must:

- Recognize in its statement of financial position an asset for a plan's overfunded status or a liability for a plan's underfunded status;

- Measure a plan's assets and its obligations that determine the plan's funded status as of the end of the employer's fiscal year (with limited exceptions); and

- Recognize changes in the funded status of a defined benefit plan in the year in which the changes occur. These changes must be reported in the comprehensive income of a business entity.

FAS 158 was developed in response to concerns that the prior accounting standard for reporting defined benefit plan assets and liabilities lacked transparency. Under the prior accounting standard, employers could delay recognition of changes in plan assets and liabilities that affected the employer's costs associated with sponsoring the defined benefit plan. As a result of FAS 158, stock market swings that make the company's defined benefit plan underfunded or overfunded in any given year are reflected immediately in the company's financial statements.

3. DISTRIBUTIONS, ROLLOVERS AND PARTICIPANT LOANS

There are many ways in which money can "exit" from a qualified plan in the form of a payment. How the payment from the plan is characterized will determine whether the plan may make the payment, the options available to the participant concerning the form of the payment, and the timing rules for when the payment may (or must) be made. The characterization of the payment from the plan also will determine the income tax consequences for the recipient of the payment.

a. The Vocabulary of Payments from Qualified Plans

A *distribution* is a payment of the participant's nonforfeitable accrued benefit under the plan. Distributions typically are either in the form of a *lump sum* or an *annuity*. A lump sum distribution is a single cash payment. An annuity is a stream of fixed periodic payments that is normally based upon the life expectancy of the participant or the joint life expectancies of the participant and a designated beneficiary. An annuity also may be for a fixed term of years.

The amount of a lump sum distribution from a defined contribution plan is determined by the nonforfeitable portion of the participant's plan account. The amount of a lump sum distribution from a defined benefit plan is determined by calculating the present value of the vested accrued benefit the participant would receive if the participant attained normal retirement age under the plan. The interest rate and mortality assumptions used to perform this present value calculation are defined by the Code and ERISA. See Code §§ 415(b)(2)(E)(ii), 417(e)(3); ERISA § 205(g)(3).

Rather than receiving a distribution, upon termination of employment the participant may elect to receive payment from the plan in the form of a *direct rollover*. A direct rollover is a payment of all or part of the participant's vested accrued benefit in a lump sum form that is made directly to the trustee of another tax-favored retirement plan or to the trustee of the participant's IRA. Distributions from a qualified plan made in the form of an annuity payable over ten years or more cannot be rolled over to another plan or an IRA.

A *trustee to trustee transfer* generally involves a plan merger, a transfer of assets and liabilities, or a spin-off of plan assets to another qualified plan. In this situation, the trustee of one plan transfers all or part of the plan's assets to the trustee of another qualified plan. Plan mergers, transfers of assets and liabilities, and spin-offs are discussed in Section H of Chapter Three.

An *in-service distribution* is a lump sum payment made from the participant's plan account while the participant is still employed by the employer who sponsors the plan. A *hardship distribution* is a particular type of in-service distribution that requires the participant to demonstrate an immediate and heavy financial need for the payment from the participant's plan account. In-service distributions and hardship distributions are optional plan design features that an employer may choose to incorporate as a plan design feature. In-service distributions and hardship distributions may be made only from defined contribution plans.

A *phased retirement distribution* is an in-service distribution of benefits from a defined benefit plan to a participant who is age 62 or older. Phased retirement distributions permit older workers to work less than full-time for their employer prior to retirement and supplement their reduced wages by commencing the distribution of their monthly retirement benefits from the employer's defined benefit plan. Like in-service distributions from defined contribution plans, a phased retirement distribution is an optional plan design feature than an employer may incorporate into the design of the defined benefit plan.

A *plan loan* is made from the participant's account in a defined contribution plan. The participant must repay the loan pursuant to a regular repayment schedule. Loan repayments typically are made to the plan through payroll deduction. The participant's loan repayments (principal and interest) are made to the participant's own plan account.

Rules Governing Distributions

The Code rules governing the various types of payments from qualified plans are highly technical. From the perspective of the typical plan participant, the most important issues raised by a payment from a qualified plan are:

- Whether the plan administrator will report the payment as part of the recipient's gross income (with the result that the payment is subject to income taxation); *most important issue only from payment from QP*
- Whether the participant has a choice concerning the timing or form of the payment; and
- Whether the participant must pay an excise tax penalty in addition to any income tax due as a result of the payment.

The reading material in this subsection does not attempt to describe all of the technical rules governing payments from qualified plans. Rather, this subsection focuses on issues that are of most concern to plan participants in the following contexts:

- Distributions and direct rollovers;
- Plan loans;
- Required minimum distributions; and

- Special distribution forms for married participants.

b. Distributions and Direct Rollovers

As a general rule, a distribution to a plan participant is included in the participant's gross income and subject to income tax. (Distribution amounts are not, however, subject to the FICA payroll tax.) For a certain type of distribution, known as an *eligible rollover distribution*, the participant may choose to have the payment sent directly to the trustee of another tax-favored retirement plan or an IRA. A payment from a qualified plan that qualifies as an eligible rollover distribution that is, in fact, actually distributed in the form of a direct rollover is not included in the participant's gross income.

The following types of payments do not qualify as eligible rollover distributions. These payments cannot be made in the form of a direct rollover and must be included in the participant's gross income:

(1) Annuity payments for a period of ten or more years;

(2) Annuity payments for the life of a participant (or the joint lives of the participant and someone else);

(3) Required minimum distributions; and

(4) Hardship distributions.

See Code § 402(c)(4); Treas. Reg. § 1.402(c)–2, Q & A–3—Q & A–8.

A participant in a qualified plan also may make a rollover to the trustee of the participant's Roth IRA if the participant satisfies the income limit for contributions to a Roth IRA. Unlike a direct rollover to an IRA, however, the amount of the rollover to a Roth IRA must be included in the participant's gross income. See Code § 408A(d)(3)(A).

A qualified plan must offer a participant the option of directly rolling over any payment that qualifies as an eligible rollover distribution. See Code § 401(a)(31). If the participant elects to receive a distribution instead of a direct rollover, the plan administrator must withhold 20% of the distribution payment amount for federal income taxes. See Treas. Reg. § 1.402(c)–2, Q & A–1(b)(3). For example, if a participant elects a $100,000 distribution, the plan administrator will make a payment of $80,000 to the participant and withhold and forward $20,000 to the Treasury Department, much like an employer withholds and forwards federal income and payroll taxes from the participant's wages.

The participant who elects to receive a distribution may still rollover all or part of the distribution by making a deposit to an IRA within sixty days of the date the distribution was made. See generally Code § 408(d)(3). This sixty-day limit can be waived for "casualty, disaster or other events beyond the reasonable control of the individual." See Code § 408(d)(3)(I). If the amount deposited is less than the amount of the eligible rollover distribution, the difference is included in the participant's gross income. As a practical matter, it may be difficult for the participant to rollover the full amount of the eligible rollover distribution because the plan administrator will have withheld 20% of the distribution amount for federal income taxes. To avoid paying income tax on the amount withheld by the plan administrator, the participant may deposit other funds equal to the amount withheld in the IRA as part of the rollover.

The surviving spouse of a deceased participant who is the beneficiary of the participant's plan account has all of the rollover rights under the Code that the participant would have. A surviving spouse may elect a direct rollover to any qualified plan in which the surviving spouse is a participant, or to the surviving spouse's IRA. See Code § 402(c)(9).

A deceased plan participant may have designated an individual other than a surviving spouse, such as a child or a domestic partner, as the beneficiary of the participant's plan account. A nonspouse beneficiary may elect a direct rollover of the account to an IRA, but not to another qualified plan in which the nonspouse beneficiary is a participant. See Code §§ 402(c)(11); 402(f)(2)(A). A direct rollover to an IRA enables the nonspouse beneficiary to achieve the same favorable income tax treatment—deferred income taxation of the distribution amount until a distribution is made from the IRA—as the surviving spouse of a deceased participant.

Prior to the Supreme Court's decision in *United States v. Windsor*, 133 S. Ct. 2675 (2013), a surviving same-sex spouse who was the designated beneficiary of a deceased participant's plan account was afforded only the direct rollover rights of a nonspouse beneficiary. This meant that a direct rollover could be made to an IRA, but not to another qualified plan. Post-*Windsor*, a surviving same-sex spouse has spousal direct rollover rights with respective to the deceased participant's account. Therefore, a surviving same-sex spouse may directly rollover the nonforfeitable accrued benefit from the deceased participant's plan account to either an IRA or the surviving spouse's qualified plan. In Technical Release 2013–14, the Department of Labor announced that a designated beneficiary who was not legally married, but who was in a civil union or a domestic partnership with a deceased plan participant, is limited to nonspouse direct rollover rights and may only rollover the nonforfeitable accrued benefit to an IRA.

A qualified plan may distribute a participant's nonforfeitable accrued benefit immediately without the participant's consent when the participant terminates employment using a *cash out distribution*. The plan administrator may make a cash out distribution if the present value of the participant's vested accrued benefit under the plan (excluding any rollover amounts) is $5,000 or less. See Code § 411(a)(11). If the present value of the participant's vested accrued benefit exceeds $5,000, the plan must obtain the participant's consent to make a distribution prior to the time the participant attains normal retirement age under the plan. See Code § 411(a)(11)(A); ERISA § 203(e)(1); Treas. Reg. § 1.411(a)–11(c).

Before making a cash out distribution, the plan administrator must notify the participant of the option to elect a direct rollover in lieu of a cash out distribution. If the plan administrator notifies the participant that a cash out distribution will be made and the participant does not provide affirmative instructions concerning the distribution to the plan administrator, the plan administrator may proceed with the cash out distribution. If the cash out distribution amount is more than $1,000, payment must be made in the form of a direct rollover to an IRA established by the employer for the benefit of the plan participant. See Code § 401(a)(31)(B)(i). Department of Labor regulations provide guidance to employers concerning their fiduciary responsibilities under ERISA in implementing this requirement. See DOL Reg. § 2550.404a–2. The regulations establish a safe harbor for plan administrators to assure compliance with the fiduciary responsibility provisions of Title I of ERISA, particularly with respect to the selection of an IRA provider, the selection of appropriate investments and the assessment of fees and expenses by the IRA provider.

The cash out distribution feature is useful because it reduces the costs associated with administering small benefit amounts. Normally, the plan may not distribute the nonfeitable accrued benefit of a terminated plan participant without the participant's consent until many years later when the participant attains normal retirement age under the plan. A cash out distribution, made immediately when the participant terminates employment, eliminates the burden of managing a small benefit amount over a long period of time and maintaining contact with a former employee over many years.

In addition to being included in the participant's gross income, a distribution from a qualified plan that is made prior to the time the participant attains age 59½ is subject to an excise tax penalty equal to 10% of the distribution amount. See Code 72(t). The excise tax does not apply if:

- The distribution is made to a beneficiary or the participant's estate on account of the participant's death;

- The distribution is being made under the plan because the participant has become disabled;

- The participant has separated from service and has attained age 55;

- The distribution is in the form of an annuity for the life expectancy of the participant or the joint life expectancies of the participant and a beneficiary; or

- The distribution is made to the alternate payee of a qualified domestic relations order.

See Code § 72(t). Alternate payees and qualified domestic relations orders are discussed in Section G of Chapter Three. Special exemptions from the 10% excise tax penalty for distributions prior to age 59½ also apply for reservists called to active military service.

c. Plan Loans

Plan loans typically are offered only by defined contribution plans. Defined contribution plans are not required to make loans available to plan participants. If the employer adopts a plan loan feature, the plan may be designed to permit loans for any reason, or the employer may establish criteria for loans. For example, the plan may limit loans to instances of financial hardship or where the loan proceeds will be used only for selected purposes, such as the purchase of a primary personal residence or the payment of medical or educational expenses for the participant and the participant's family members. Although the concept of a plan loan appears to be simple—borrowing from one's own plan account—a plan loan program requires compliance with several technical sections of the Code and ERISA. These sections include:

- The anti-alienation rule of Code Section 401(a)(13) and ERISA Section 206(d);
- The prohibited transaction exemptions described in Code Section 4975(d)(1) and ERISA Section 408(b)(1); and
- The income tax provisions of Code Section 72(p).

The anti-alienation rule and prohibited transaction exemptions are discussed in Section G of Chapter Three and Section D of Chapter Five. To satisfy these first two requirements, the typical plan loan program is designed so that a plan loan:

- is available to all participants on a reasonably equivalent basis;
- is not available to highly compensated employees, officers or shareholders in an amount greater than the amount made available to other employees;
- is made in accordance with specific provisions regarding loans that are set forth in the plan document;
- bears a reasonable rate of interest; and
- is adequately secured.

If the participant's plan account is used as security for the loan, the loan is treated as adequately secured only if the loan amount is secured by not less than 50% of the participant's nonforfeitable accrued benefit, calculated at the time the loan is made. See DOL Reg. § 2550.408b–1(f)(2).

A plan loan is subject to income taxation as a distribution under Code Section 72(p)(1) unless certain criteria are satisfied. Although a violation of the criteria under Code Section 72(p)(1) will not result in disqualification of the plan, the resulting adverse income tax consequences for the borrower—inclusion in the participant's gross income and a possible excise tax penalty for an early distribution from the plan—are likely to make for an unhappy plan participant. For this reason, plan loan programs are designed to follow the criteria of Code Section 72(p)(1).

Under Code Section 72(p)(1), the loan amount will not be treated as a distribution if the participant's loan balance (including the outstanding balance of any prior unpaid loan or loans from the plan) does not exceed the lesser of: (1) $50,000 or (2) the greater of $10,000 or 50% of the participant's nonforfeitable account balance. See Code § 72(p)(2). Criteria (2) is potentially problematic for the plan's administrator because a minimum loan of $10,000 may not be adequately secured by a participant's nonforfeitable accrued benefit under the plan. To illustrate, assume that a participant has only a $1,000 nonforfeitable accrued benefit under the plan and would like to receive a plan loan. The plan *could* loan the participant up to $10,000 under the "greater of" test of Code Section 72(p)(2), but the participant's nonforfeitable accrued benefit is only $1,000. May the participant supply some other type of collateral so that the plan loan is "adequately secured"?

In theory, the answer is "yes." The plan could accept other collateral as security for the participant's loan of $10,000 if the other collateral is "of a type and amount of security which would be required in the case of an otherwise identical transaction in a normal commercial setting between unrelated parties on arm's-length terms." See DOL Reg. § 2550.408b–1(f)(1).

In practice, allowing other collateral as security for a plan loan greatly increases the burden of administering a plan loan program. If the plan administrator accepts collateral for a plan loan other than up to 50% of the participant's nonforfeitable accrued benefit under the plan, the plan administrator has essentially assumed the role of a commercial lender. Most plan administrators would prefer not to assume this responsibility. Consequently, a plan loan program usually is designed so that the maximum amount of any loan is limited *under the terms of the plan document* to an amount that does not exceed the lesser of $50,000 or 50% of the participant's nonforfeitable accrued benefit under the plan.

To avoid inclusion in the participant's gross income, a plan loan also must:

- be documented by an enforceable loan agreement;

- have a repayment term not exceeding five years (except for loans used to purchase a principal residence—here any "reasonable" repayment period is allowed); and

- provide for at least quarterly payments with level amortization of principal and interest over the repayment term (i.e., no "balloon" payments are permitted).

See Code § 72(p)(2)(B)–(C); Treas. Reg. § 1.72(p)–1, Q & A–3. Failure to comply with any of these criteria subjects the entire amount of the loan to income taxation as a *deemed distribution*. Exceeding the dollar amount restrictions of Code Section 72(p)(2) results in a deemed distribution subject to income taxation of only the amount in excess of the Code Section 72(p)(2) restrictions. If the participant is under age 59½, an additional excise tax penalty of 10% is assessed.

If a participant terminates employment before the plan loan has been fully repaid, the plan may provide that the participant must repay the loan in full within a short period of time, or else the account balance will be reduced (in technical terms, *offset*) to repay the loan. A plan loan offset is treated as a taxable distribution to the participant. See Treas. Reg. § 1.72(p)–1, Q & A–13.

d.   Required Minimum Distributions

A participant in a defined contribution plan may want to delay receiving a distribution as long as possible to continue to receive tax-deferred investment earnings on the assets held in the participant's plan account. The required minimum distribution rules of Code Section 401(a)(9) (RMD rules) dictate the longest period of time that a participant may delay receiving a distribution from the plan. Due to the wealth-creating effect of compounding tax-deferred investment earnings on assets held in a qualified plan account, estate planners and their clients view the RMD requirements as a potential tool for accumulating wealth to transfer to future generations.

The function of the RMD rules is relatively simple: to prevent the accumulation of large amounts of wealth through qualified plans by forcing the annual distribution of a minimum amount once a participant is well into his or her retirement years. In operation, the RMD rules are complex, notwithstanding recent regulatory efforts to simplify their application. See generally Treas. Reg. § 1.401(a)(9).

The RMD rules are built upon two fundamental concepts. The first concept is the date that distributions must commence (known as the *required beginning date*). The second concept is the amount that must be distributed (known as the *required minimum distribution amount*). A participant's required beginning date is April 1 of the calendar year following the calendar year in which the participant attains age 70½. If a participant who owns less than 5% of the employer is still employed at age 70½ by the employer who sponsors the qualified plan, the participant's required beginning date is delayed until the calendar year when the participant retires. If the participant is deceased and has designated a surviving spouse as the account beneficiary, the surviving spouse may delay the commencement of required minimum distributions from the account until April 1 following the calendar year in which the surviving spouse attains age 70½.

For defined contribution plans, the annual required minimum distribution amount is determined by dividing the value of the participant's nonforfeitable accrued benefit by the life expectancy of the participant. If the participant has designated a beneficiary, the annual required minimum distribution amount is determined under life expectancy tables promulgated by the Treasury Department. If the beneficiary is a spouse who is more than ten years younger than the participant, then joint life expectancy may be used to calculate the required minimum distribution amount. The advantage of electing to use a joint life expectancy calculation (in lieu of the participant's life expectancy alone) is to reduce the amount that must be distributed each year pursuant to the RMD rules and subjected to income taxation. Prior to the Supreme Court's decision in *United States v. Windsor*, 133 S. Ct. 2675 (2013), this option to use the more favorable joint life expectancy calculation was not available to a plan participant who had a same-sex spouse. Post-*Windsor*, a plan participant with a same-sex spouse who satisfies the eligibility criteria described above may elect this joint life expectancy distribution option. See generally DOL Technical Release 2013–14.

A failure by a qualified plan to comply with the RMD rules of Code Section 401(a)(9) results in plan disqualification. In addition, if the plan distributes less than the required minimum distribution amount dictated by the Code's formula, the participant is subject to an excise tax penalty of 50% of the deficiency amount. See Code § 4974. The RMD rules (and the 50% excise tax penalty) also apply to traditional IRAs, but not to Roth IRAs while the owner of the Roth IRA is alive. The RMD rules do apply to the beneficiary of the Roth IRA at the owner's death. See Code §§ 408(a)(6); 408A(c)(5)(A). For a Roth 401(k) plan, the RMD rules apply to both the participant and the beneficiary of the Roth 401(k) plan account at participant's death.

The RMD rules have been compared to a great "floodgate" that will control the future flow of the large amounts of pension wealth that have been accumulated by the baby boomer generation through defined contribution plans and IRAs. See Jay A. Soled and Bruce A. Wolk, *The Minimum Distribution Rules and Their Critical Role in Controlling the Floodgates of Qualified Plan Wealth*, 2000 BYU L. REV. 587. One economist has even argued that the income taxation of distributions in future years from qualified plans and IRAs (such distributions having been "forced" in part by the RMD rules) will generate sufficient tax revenues to offset the increased costs of the federal Medicare and Medicaid programs that are projected for the years after the baby boomer generation retires. See ROBERT L. BROWN, QUALIFIED PENSION PLANS AND HEALTH CARE FOR THE ELDERLY: THE PERFECT MACROECONOMIC IMMUNIZED PORTFOLIO (Working Paper, June 2002).

e.   Special Distribution Forms for Married Participants

The Retirement Equity Act of 1984, Pub. L. No. 98–397, 98 Stat. 1426 (REA), created certain safeguards for the spouses of plan participants by requiring special distribution forms for married participants in defined benefit plans and money purchase pension plans. These special distribution forms are the *qualified joint and survivor annuity* (QJSA) for a participant and the participant's spouse or, if the participant has died prior to the commencement of benefits under the plan and has left a surviving spouse, the *qualified preretirement survivor annuity* (QPSA). See Code §§ 401(a)(11); 417; ERISA § 205. As a result of the Supreme Court's decision in *United States v. Windsor*, 133 S. Ct. 2675 (2013), the QJSA and QPSA requirements apply to the same-sex spouse of a deceased plan participant. See generally DOL Technical Release 2013–14.

The REA's special distribution options for married participants are required for all defined benefit plans and money purchase pension plans. Other types of qualified plans may be subject to REA's special distribution options if the plan offers an annuity as a form of distribution. See Code § 401(a)(11)(B)(iii). Qualified plans subject to the REA rules are required to offer a QJSA and a QPSA as their normal (i.e., "default") forms of distribution. For a married participant who survives to the commencement of benefits from the plan, the QJSA must provide a survivor annuity to the spouse at least equal to 50%, but not more than 100%, of the annuity payable during the life of the participant. See Code § 417(b). Plans that are subject to the REA rules also must offer a 75% QJSA. To illustrate, assume that at retirement the participant is married and that the plan pays a monthly annuity benefit of $1,000 to the participant and the participant's spouse. If the participant later dies survived by the spouse, a 50% QJSA must continue to pay $500 each month to the surviving spouse for the spouse's life. A 75% QJSA must continue to pay $750 each month to the surviving spouse for the spouse's life.

The QJSA applies only if the surviving spouse is the same individual to whom the participant was married when the plan commenced benefit payments. For example, assume that Employee A is married to Spouse A at the time Employee A retires and begins receiving the monthly annuity benefit payments from the plan. Spouse A dies and Employee A remarries Spouse B. When Employee A dies, the monthly payments from the plan will cease and will not continue to be made for the life of Spouse B.

If the participant dies before the distribution of benefits under the plan has commenced, the normal form for distribution of the deceased participant's benefit to the surviving spouse is a QPSA. A QPSA is paid for the life of the surviving spouse. The spouse of a participant can waive the right to receive either a QJSA or a QPSA. If a valid waiver is made, the participant's plan benefit will be distributed in the form of a lump sum payment that is the actuarial equivalent of the QJSA or QPSA.

Lorenzen v. Employees Retirement Plan of the Sperry and Hutchinson Co. illustrates several principles that underlie the QJSA and QPSA requirements. As you read *Lorenzen*, consider the legal advice that should be given to any married participant in a defined benefit plan who is considering postponing retirement and delaying the commencement of benefit payments from the plan.

LORENZEN V. EMPLOYEES RETIREMENT PLAN OF THE SPERRY AND HUTCHINSON CO.

United States Court of Appeals, Seventh Circuit, 1990.
896 F.2d 228.

POSNER, CIRCUIT JUDGE.

This is a suit under the Employee Retirement Income Security Act of 1974 (ERISA), by the widow of an employee of S & H, claiming that S & H's Retirement Plan, an ERISA plan, violated its fiduciary duties to her husband and herself, causing a loss of retirement benefits. The district judge granted summary judgment for Mrs. Lorenzen, awarding her some $192,000, and the plan appeals. Mrs. Lorenzen cross-appeals, seeking prejudgment interest.

* * *

Warren Lorenzen, a sales manager and long-time employee of S & H, was eligible to retire on February 1, 1987, having turned 65. As he was in the midst of managing a company project, the company requested him to postpone his retirement until July 1, and he agreed. At the same time he decided that when he did retire he would take his retirement benefits as a lump sum, rather than as a series of monthly payments for his life followed by monthly payments half as large to his wife for her life should she outlive him (the "50 percent joint and survivor option," as it was called). The taking of retirement benefits in a lump sum was an option expressly permitted by the plan, provided the spouse executed a written consent form, which Mrs. Lorenzen did. Since death is not retirement, in order to receive any retirement benefit at all, lump sum or annuity, the employee must live to the date of his retirement. If he dies before then, his spouse is entitled to a preretirement benefit but it is much smaller than the retirement benefit. On June 15, two weeks before his extended retirement date, Lorenzen suffered cardiac arrest and was hospitalized in grave condition. On June 27, he suffered cardiac arrest again and was plugged into life support machinery. His condition was believed to be hopeless and his physicians advised Mrs. Lorenzen to request that the machinery be disconnected. She did so, it was disconnected, and Mr. Lorenzen died that day.

The plan documents do not define death, but the parties and the district judge assume that if Mrs. Lorenzen had not requested the removal of the life support apparatus Mr. Lorenzen would have survived, within the meaning of the plan, until his retirement on July 1. In that event he would have received, pursuant to his earlier election, the lump sum retirement benefit. Assuming he would then have been taken off life support, the lump sum would have passed to his widow either under his will or conceivably as marital property; the parties agree, in any event, that she would have gotten it. And this was the amount the district court ordered the plan to pay her. The plan argues that since Lorenzen died before he retired, the widow is entitled only to the preretirement death benefit—in present value terms and rounded off, $89,000 versus $192,000. Of course if Lorenzen had received the lump sum, frittered it away at the gaming tables, and then died, Mrs. Lorenzen would be even worse off than she is (it is against this possibility that the spouse is required to sign a consent form, as she did), but the plan has not argued this possibility as a ground for reducing her damages.

In holding for Mrs. Lorenzen the district judge appears to have been moved by the human appeal of her case. This is understandable. To have to decide whether to order the removal of life support from a loved one is painful enough without having to incur an enormous financial penalty into the bargain. The equities are not all on one side, however. (They rarely are; the tension between formal justice and substantive justice is often, and perhaps here, illusory.) Life support equipment is expensive and, to a considerable degree, futile and degrading. It should not be used to secure retirement benefits. If the parties to retirement plans envisaged such a use, they probably would define death as inability to "live" without life support machinery—at least if permitted by state law, which might forbid the guardian of a patient even in a hopeless vegetative state to disconnect the patient's life support machinery. By postponing his retirement Mr. Lorenzen took a risk that if he died his widow would obtain less money than if he retired as soon as he was eligible. But he was compensated for bearing this risk by being paid his full salary (which exceeded his retirement benefit, lump sum or annuity, evaluated on a comparable basis, i.e., as a monthly payment) for a longer time, and by having an expectation of slightly increased retirement benefits, for they rose with the length of time that he was employed, although not steeply. This "compensation" was, to be sure, ex ante rather than ex post—had Lorenzen been gifted with prevision he would have retired. But a gamble is not unfair merely because the gambler loses. Nor was the plan unjustly enriched at the Lorenzens' expense. "A pension plan is not 'unjustly enriched' where a pensioner dies early with no benefits payable to his survivor. That eventuality simply offsets cases where a pensioner lives well into old age and more benefits are paid to him than were statistically predictable." Cummings v. Briggs & Stratton Retirement Plan, 797 F.2d 383, 389 (7th Cir. 1986). Finally, the record contains no evidence of what it would have cost Mrs. Lorenzen to maintain her husband on life support machinery for an additional three days. It could have been a considerable sum, depending on the scope and terms of his hospital insurance.

Mrs. Lorenzen had no contractual entitlement to retirement benefits—this much is clear—since her husband did not survive until retirement. ERISA, however, requires that a retirement or welfare plan make clear to the participants what the plan's terms and conditions are. ERISA § 101. Mrs. Lorenzen claims that the plan did not adequately apprise her husband of the consequences of his electing the lump sum rather than annuity form of retirement benefits and of his electing to keep on working rather than retire at the earliest possible opportunity. The first claim is frivolous; regardless of which election Lorenzen would have made if fully informed, his death nullified any retirement benefits to which he and his wife might have been entitled had he lived to retirement. If he had elected the annuity form, then even though Mrs. Lorenzen would have been entitled—had he retired and she outlived him—to an annuity that would outlast his death, this entitlement would have been contingent on his retiring; and before he retired he died.

The second claim is that the plan should have advised Mr. Lorenzen more clearly than it did that if he postponed his retirement he was risking a net loss of benefits, since preretirement death benefits were lower than retirement benefits. There was no want of clarity, however. The plan summary explains that "if you should die either before retirement or after retirement but before benefits begin . . . your spouse or other beneficiary will receive a benefit. . . . [I]f you die after age 55 and your legal spouse is your beneficiary, this benefit will be the larger of 40% of the lump sum equivalent of the benefits you have earned under the plan or the amount he or she [i.e., the legal spouse] would receive if you had retired on the day before your death under the 50% joint-and-survivor option." Mr. Lorenzen could have been under no illusion that if he died before his extended retirement date arrived, his widow would receive 100% of his lump sum retirement benefits rather than 50% of his retirement annuity. The risk he took in not retiring as soon as he could was an informed, a calculated, one.

Mrs. Lorenzen does not argue that the plan was under a duty to monitor Mr. Lorenzen's deteriorating physical condition and advise her not to order the life support machinery disconnected before July 1. Nor does she argue that, supposing the plan became aware of his condition, it should have advised her to elect, on her husband's behalf, immediate retirement. The election would have done the Lorenzens no good. Although Mr. Lorenzen was not contractually obligated to continue working until June 30—and we may assume that, with him unconscious, his wife was empowered to elect retirement on his behalf—the plan made retirement effective on the first day of the month following the decision to retire. That would have been July 1—too late.

Nor does Mrs. Lorenzen argue that the plan summary was defective for failing to advise participants of the consequences of finding themselves on life support machinery shortly before the scheduled date of retirement. She is wise not to make that argument, for the law is clear that the plan summary is not required to anticipate every possible idiosyncratic contingency that might affect a particular participant's or beneficiary's status. If it were, the summaries would be choked with detail and hopelessly confusing. Clarity and completeness are competing goods.

* * *

The judgment is reversed and the case is remanded with directions to award Mrs. Lorenzen only the preretirement death benefit to which she is entitled under her husband's retirement plan * * *. The "victory" is indeed partial, quite apart from the lump sum versus annuity issue, since if she had never brought this suit she would have received the death benefit as soon as it was due and would have had no occasion to seek prejudgment interest on it. The district court will have to decide on remand whether she is entitled to attorney's fees in these unusual circumstances. We vacate the district court's award of costs and attorney's fees to abide the remand, and award no costs in this court.

NOTE

Spousal Waivers of the QJSA and QPSA Requirements. The widow in *Lorenzen* had consented to waive the plan's normal forms of distribution—the QJSA and the QPSA. The rules governing the proper procedures, disclosures and form of a valid spousal waiver of the right to receive a QJSA and a QPSA are described in Treasury Department regulations. See generally Treas. Reg. §§ 1.401(a)–20; 1.417(a)(3)–1. These regulations require the plan administrator to provide a spouse with disclosures concerning the relative values and monthly payment amounts for each of the plan's optional forms of benefits using the plan's QJSA or QPSA as the benchmark. The purpose of this disclosure requirement is to permit the spouse to make a fully informed choice concerning the relative economic values of optional forms of benefits.

The spouse also must consent to the substitution of any nonspouse beneficiary. The consent is personal only to that spouse, and is not binding on a subsequent spouse of the participant. A premarital agreement in which the spouse waives the right to any qualified plan benefits of the participant is not a valid spousal waiver. See Treas. Reg § 1.401(a)–20, Q&A–28. For plans subject to the requirements of the REA that offer plan loans, the participant's spouse must consent to the loan if the security for the loan exceeds $5,000 of the participant's accrued benefit under the plan. See id. at Q&A–24(a)(1).

PROBLEM ON DISTRIBUTIONS, ROLLOVERS, AND PARTICIPANT LOANS

Your client, Smith Animal Clinic (Clinic), is a small veterinary business with three employees. The Clinic is a limited liability corporation owned by the veterinarian, Alicia Smith. Alicia is age 60. The Clinic has two other employees, Joe Stites (age 43) and Joyce Scamp (age 72).

The Clinic sponsors a profit sharing plan (Plan) for its employees. Alicia, Joe and Joyce are all participants in the Plan and currently have the following amounts as nonforfeitable accrued benefits under the Plan:

Participant	Nonforfeitable Benefit
Alicia	$200,000
Joe	$ 90,000
Joyce	$ 20,000

The Plan allows for loans based on the following criteria: (1) the amount of the loan cannot exceed the lesser of $50,000 or 50% of the participant's nonforfeitable accrued benefit; and (2) the loan may be made only for the following purposes:

- Purchase of a principal residence;
- Payment of medical expenses incurred by the participant, a spouse, or dependent child;
- Payment of tuition expenses incurred by the participant, a spouse, or children of the participant or the spouse;
- To prevent a foreclosure of the mortgage on the participant's principal residence;
- Payment of funeral or burial expenses for the participant's deceased parent, spouse, child or dependent; or
- Payment for repairs to the participant's principal residence when the damage qualifies as a casualty loss under the Code.

A. Joe terminates employment and elects a lump sum distribution of his entire nonforfeitable accrued benefit. How much must the Plan administrator withhold from Joe's account balance for federal income tax purposes when making the distribution? How much money will Joe actually receive from the Plan as a distribution? How much money will Joe have left after paying the federal and state income taxes attributable to the distribution?

B. Joe terminates employment at the Clinic and elects a direct rollover of his nonforfeitable accrued benefit. What are the tax consequences of the direct rollover for Joe?

C. When must Joyce begin receiving required minimum distributions under Code Section 401(a)(9) from the Plan? When must Alicia begin receiving required minimum distributions from the Plan?

D. What is the maximum amount Alicia may borrow from the Plan to pay the cost of her daughter's tuition, room, and board at Harvard Medical School for the year? How long will Alicia have to repay this loan?

E. Assuming that Joe is still employed by the Clinic, what is the maximum amount Joe may borrow from the Plan to purchase a principal residence? How long will Joe have to repay this loan?

F. What is the maximum amount Joyce may borrow from the Plan to pay off the outstanding balance of her credit card bills?

4. MECHANISMS TO AVOID PLAN DISQUALIFICATION

An employer's qualified retirement plan must satisfy the requirements of Code Section 401(a) in both *form* and *operation*. A plan is qualified in form if the words of the written plan document comply with Code Section 401(a) and related Treasury Department regulations. A plan is qualified in operation if the plan is administered in compliance with Code Section 401(a), Treasury Department regulations, and the terms of the written plan document.

The Internal Revenue Service has long embraced the philosophy that a qualified plan must adhere strictly to all of the requirements of Code Section 401(a). This regulatory philosophy of strict compliance applies regardless of the size of the plan or the legal sophistication of the employer. A qualified plan sponsored by a small business with five employees is held to the same standards as the qualified plan of a Fortune 100 company with an entire staff devoted to managing the company's employee benefit programs.

If the employer's qualified plan fails to comply with one of the requirements of Code Section 401(a), the plan is *disqualified*. Disqualification means that the favorable income tax treatment of the plan is forfeited, and the plan becomes subject to the general rules of income taxation. Under these general rules, employer contributions to the plan are deductible only when matched with inclusion in the participants' gross incomes. Participants are subject to income tax on plan benefits immediately once the benefits are vested. Investment income earned by the assets held in the plan's trust is no longer exempt from income taxation. A limited exception exists if the plan is disqualified due to a violation of Code Sections 410(b) or 401(a)(26). In these instances, only the highly compensated employees of the plan are penalized by being subject to the normal rules of income taxation for their plan benefits. See Code § 402(b)(4)(A)–(B).

Given the complexity of the requirements for qualified plans, it is inevitable that errors and mistakes will occur. There are two regulatory mechanisms that assist employers in maintaining the qualified status of their plans under Code Section 401(a). These mechanisms are the *determination letter* and the *Employee Plans Compliance Resolution System* (EPCRS).

Determination Letters

The employer who sponsors a qualified plan may submit the written plan document (and any related plan amendments) to the Internal Revenue Service for a determination that the plan satisfies all of the requirements of Code Section 401(a). Although obtaining a determination letter from the Internal Revenue Service is not required for a plan to be qualified, the better practice is for the employer to obtain one. A determination letter assures the employer that the plan document has been written correctly. Moreover, a current favorable determination letter is required for the employer to take advantage of several programs under the EPCRS to correct plan qualification failures.

To obtain a determination letter, the employer must submit the plan document, along with any amendments, to the Internal Revenue Service. The employer selects and submits the appropriate application from the *Form 5300* series along with any schedules required by the form. Form 5300 is reproduced in Appendix D of the casebook.

The Internal Revenue Service accepts applications for determination letters for individually designed qualified plans according to a five-year cycle. The last digit of the employer identification number for the plan's sponsor determines the year within the cycle that the plan must submit a determination letter application.

Employee Plans Compliance Resolution System

The EPCRS has several programs that allow the employer to correct various types of errors that, if left uncorrected, would result in plan disqualification. The programs available under the EPCRS are the *Self-Correction Program* (self-correction), the *Voluntary Correction Program* (VCP), and the *Audit Closing Agreement Program* (Audit CAP). A current favorable determination letter is required for the employer to take advantage of self-correction and to use the VCP.

Using self-correction, the employer who has established an internal procedure to ensure plan compliance may correct insignificant operational defects at any time and without notifying the Internal Revenue Service. The employer also may self-correct significant operational defects if the correction is made within two years following the end of the plan year in which the operational defect occurred. A list of factors, such as the number of times and years in which the defect occurred, the percentage of participants and the percentage of plan assets affected by the operational defect, and the reason the defect occurred (typically, a computer data entry error or a math error) are used to determine whether an operational error is "insignificant" or "significant." See generally Rev. Proc. 2013–12.

The employer must use the VCP to correct certain types of plan qualification failures that cannot be self-corrected. Plan qualification failures that may only be corrected through the VCP include a *plan document failure* (the plan language fails to comply with the current requirements for qualified plans), a *demographic failure* (the plan fails to satisfy the requirements of Code Sections 401(a)(4), 401(a)(26), or 410(b)), or an *employer eligibility failure* (the employer has adopted a type of plan for which it is not eligible). The employer also may use the VCP to correct significant operational defects. The primary advantage of using the VCP over the self-correction method for significant operational defects is that the Internal Revenue Service approves the correction method for defects submitted to the VCP.

To access the VCP, the employer must submit a letter, along with supporting documentation, to the Internal Revenue Service describing the plan's qualification failure and proposing a correction method. For certain types of common failures, the VCP has established standardized correction methods that the employer must follow. See generally Rev. Proc. 2013–12.

The Audit CAP is the correction method of last resort for the employer. If the plan is under examination by the Internal Revenue Service, plan qualification failures may only be corrected through the Audit CAP. An exception applies if the plan already had begun self-correction mechanisms and the corrections were substantially completed before the plan came under audit. Under the Audit CAP, the employer must correct the failure and pay a penalty amount that is negotiated with the Internal Revenue Service. The Audit CAP process is concluded when the employer and the Internal Revenue Service enter into final settlement of the matter, known as a *closing agreement.* The closing agreement describes the corrective steps taken by the employer, the negotiated penalty amount paid by the employer, and any other future requirements for ongoing plan operation and administration imposed by the Internal Revenue Service.

G. QUALIFIED PLAN ISSUES IN BANKRUPTCY AND DIVORCE

Issues involving qualified plans often arise in the context of personal bankruptcy and divorce proceedings. In the bankruptcy context, the creditors of an individual plan participant may seek repayment of the participant's debts by attempting to levy on the participant's qualified plan benefits. In the divorce context, a participant's qualified plan benefits may be part of a negotiated division of the couple's property. The reading material in this section discusses how the rules of the Code and ERISA governing qualified plans operate in these situations.

1. BANKRUPTCY AND THE ANTI-ALIENATION RULE

Code Section 401(a)(13), which is duplicated in ERISA Section 206(d), establishes the *anti-alienation rule* for qualified plans. Under this rule, a qualified plan generally must prohibit the assignment or alienation of a participant's benefits provided under the plan. It is the combination of the anti-alienation rule and ERISA's broad preemption of state law that provides qualified plan participants with an almost impenetrable shield against third party creditors.

The concept of a prohibited assignment or alienation is derived from trust law. Under the common law of trusts, the settlor who established the trust determined the conditions and circumstances under which the trustee could distribute trust assets to a beneficiary of the trust. These terms and conditions were described in the written trust agreement. If the settlor believed that a trust beneficiary was financially irresponsible, the settlor could impose constraints on the trustee's ability to distribute trust assets to creditors of the trust beneficiary. This type of constraint, known as a *spendthrift clause,* usually addressed two distinct situations. First, a spendthrift clause prohibited the trust beneficiary from voluntarily assigning the beneficiary's right to receive payments from the trust to a creditor of the beneficiary. Second, a creditor of the trust beneficiary might obtain a court order directing the trustee to pay part of the trust assets to the creditor in satisfaction of a judgment against the trust beneficiary. A spendthrift clause restricted this type of involuntary alienation of the beneficiary's interest in the trust assets so that the trustee could not be forced by a court order to make a premature payment of trust assets to a judgment creditor of the trust beneficiary. With a spendthrift clause in the trust agreement, the judgment creditor could only receive those trust assets that the trust beneficiary was entitled to receive, and not before such time as the trust beneficiary was entitled to receive the trust assets under the terms of the trust agreement.

The anti-alienation rule for qualified plans expands the common law trust concept of a spendthrift clause in several important aspects. Under the law of trusts, a spendthrift clause was an optional constraint that typically was limited in use to financially irresponsible trust beneficiaries. Absent a spendthrift clause, the beneficiary of a trust was permitted to assign the beneficiary's right to receive trust distributions to a third party creditor as payment for the beneficiary's debt. In contrast, the anti-alienation rule for qualified plans is a mandatory provision that applies to all participants in the employer's qualified plan and prohibits the participants from voluntarily assigning payment of their benefits from the plan to third parties.

Under the law of trusts, a spendthrift clause prohibited a judgment creditor of a trust beneficiary from reaching trust assets prior to the time that a distribution to the trust beneficiary was permitted under the terms of the trust agreement. Thus, if a trust beneficiary was not entitled to receive the assets of the trust until age 50, a court could not order the trustee to use trust assets to pay the creditor directly in satisfaction of the judgment until the trust beneficiary attained age 50. In the qualified plan context, the anti-alienation rule is even more effective against the involuntary alienation of a participant's plan benefit to satisfy the participant's creditors. As a consequence of the anti-alienation rule, the trustee of a qualified plan normally can only pay plan benefits directly to the plan participant (or the participant and the participant's spouse) while the participant is alive. Moreover, any state law mechanism that might override the distribution provisions of the plan, such as an order of garnishment obtained in state court, or an attempt to levy on the participant's plan benefits in satisfaction of a state court judgment against the participant, is preempted by ERISA. See ERISA § 514(a); Mackey v. Lanier Collection Agency & Service, 486 U.S. 825, 837 (1988).

ERISA does not automatically preempt other federal laws, including the federal Bankruptcy Code. See ERISA § 514(d). In *Patterson v. Shumate*, 504 U.S. 753 (1992), the Supreme Court was called upon to reconcile the conflicting provisions and competing policies of ERISA and the Bankruptcy Code. The Supreme Court ruled in favor of ERISA, holding that the benefits from a qualified plan subject to ERISA are excluded from the debtor's bankruptcy estate. The *Patterson* Court found that the anti-alienation rule for qualified plans was a "restriction on the transfer of a beneficial interest of the debtor in a trust" that was "enforceable under applicable nonbankruptcy law" within the meaning of

Section 541(c)(2) of the federal Bankruptcy Code, 11 U.S.C. § 541(c)(2). The Supreme Court in *Patterson* articulated several policy justifications for its holding:

> Our holding * * * gives full and appropriate effect to ERISA's goal of protecting pension benefits. This court has described that goal as one of ensuring that if a worker has been promised a defined pension benefit upon retirement—and if he has fulfilled whatever conditions are required to obtain a vested benefit—he actually will receive it. * * *

> ERISA Section 206(d) reflects a considered congressional policy choice, a decision to safeguard a stream of income for pensioners (and their dependents, who may be, and perhaps usually are, blameless), even if that decision prevents other from securing relief for the wrongs done them. If exceptions to this policy are to be made, it is for Congress to undertake that task. * * *

> Finally, our holding furthers another important policy underlying ERISA: uniform national treatment of pension benefits. Construing "applicable nonbankruptcy law" to include federal law ensures that the security of a debtor's pension benefits will be govern by ERISA, not left to the vagaries of state spendthrift trust law.

Patterson, 504 U.S. at 764–65 (quotations and citations omitted).

After *Patterson v. Shumate*, the federal circuits were divided over whether assets held in the debtor's IRA were part of the debtor's bankruptcy estate and therefore subject to the claims of creditors. In *Rousey v. Jacoway*, 544 U.S. 320 (2005), the Supreme Court held that assets in a traditional IRA are exempt from the debtor's bankruptcy estate under federal bankruptcy law. The Bankruptcy Abuse Prevention and Consumer Protection Act of 2005, Pub. L. No. 109–8, 119 Stat. 23 (Bankruptcy Abuse Prevention Act), later expanded the bankruptcy protection of *Patterson v. Shumate* and *Rousey v. Jacoway* to all employer-sponsored retirement plans that are exempt from taxation (such as 403(b) plans and 457 plans) and to assets held in Roth IRAs. See 11 U.S.C. §§ 522(b)(3)(C), (d)(12). The Bankruptcy Abuse Prevention Act imposed a $1 million limit on the assets held in traditional and Roth IRA accounts that are exempt from the debtor's bankruptcy estate. See 11 U.S.C. § 522(n). The $1 million limit on exempt assets of the debtor does not apply to amounts that have been rolled over to an IRA or a Roth IRA from an employer-sponsored retirement plan. As a result, retirement plan assets rolled to an IRA or a Roth IRA continue to enjoy the same immunity from the claims of creditors in bankruptcy as if such assets had remained in the employer's retirement plan. See 11 U.S.C. § 522(n).

What about IRAs?

Exceptions to the Anti-Alienation Rule

There are four statutory exceptions to the anti-alienation rule for qualified plans. These exceptions are:

(1) A loan by the plan made to a participant from assets held in the participant's plan account. See Code § 401(a)(13)(A); ERISA § 206(d)(2).

(2) A voluntary and revocable assignment made by a participant to a third party of not more than 10% of any benefit payment made to the participant. See Code § 401(a)(13)(A); ERISA § 206(d)(2).

(3) A state or federal court order, judgment, consent decree, or settlement agreement attaching the plan benefits of a participant who is also a fiduciary of the plan, where the fiduciary engaged in a breach of fiduciary duty that caused losses to the plan. See Code § 401(a)(13)(C); ERISA § 206(d)(4).

(4) A payment of the participant's plan benefits to an alternate payee pursuant to a qualified domestic relations order. See Code § 401(a)(13)(B); ERISA § 206(d)(3).

4 statutory Exceptions

Of these statutory exceptions to the anti-alienation rule, plan loans and qualified domestic relations orders are the most commonly encountered. The requirements for a plan loan to be exempt from the anti-alienation rule are described in Section F of Chapter Three. The requirements for a payment to an alternate payee pursuant to a qualified domestic relations order are described in Section G of Chapter Three.

Assignment of Health Care Plan Benefits

The anti-alienation rule does not apply to welfare benefit plans. See ERISA § 201(1). For this reason, health care providers usually require that a patient must assign any benefits provided to the patient under the patient's health care plan to the health care provider. This assignment of benefits is made before health care services are rendered to the patient. With an assignment of benefits in hand, the health care provider may seek to be paid directly by the health care plan for the health care services provided to the participant.

The participant's assignment of benefits under the health care plan to the health care provider also operates to give the health care provider standing under ERISA to sue the plan on behalf of the patient-participant if the plan administrator refuses to pay the participant's claim for health care benefits. Private civil actions under ERISA for the payment of a claim that has been denied by the plan administrator are discussed in Chapter Six of the casebook.

2. QUALIFIED DOMESTIC RELATIONS ORDERS

A *qualified domestic relations order* (QDRO) is commonly used to secure the payment of alimony or child support after a divorce. A QDRO is defined as a judicial judgment, decree, or order made pursuant to state domestic relations law that:

    (1) establishes the right of an alternate payee to receive, or assigns to the alternate payee the right to receive, all or a portion of the benefits payable to a participant under the plan; and

    (2) relates to the provision of child support, alimony payments, or marital property rights of the alternate payee.

See Code § 414(p)(1); ERISA § 206(d)(3)(A)–(B). An *alternate payee* is defined as a spouse, former spouse, child, or other dependent of the participant. See Code § 414(p)(8); ERISA § 206(d)(3)(K). As a statutory exemption to the anti-alienation rule, the plan trustee is permitted to pay the plan benefits described in the QDRO directly to the alternate payee.

The contents of the QDRO must clearly specify a number of items listed in the statute. These items are:

- the name and last known mailing address of the participant and any alternate payee covered by the order;
- the amount or percentage of the participant's benefits to be paid by the plan to each alternate payee, or a description of the method the plan administrator must use to determine such amount or percentage;
- the number of payment to be made to the alternate payee and, if applicable, the period during which the order applies; and
- the name of each qualified plan to which the order applies.

See Code § 414(p); ERISA § 206(d)(3). In drafting the language of the QDRO, the lawyer who represents an alternate payee must be careful to comply strictly with all of the technical requirements listed in the statute. A QDRO cannot require the plan to provide a benefit to the alternate payee in a form that is not authorized under the terms of the plan. A QDRO also cannot require the plan to provide greater benefits to the alternate payee than the plan provides to the participant. See Code § 414(p)(2)–(3); ERISA § 206(d)(3)(C)–(D). A sample form of a QDRO is contained in Appendix F of the casebook.

There are several pragmatic reasons why a lawyer should focus carefully on drafting the terms of the QDRO to satisfy both the statutory requirements and the terms of the qualified plan. If the plan administrator rejects the court's order as an invalid QDRO, the alternate payee is forced to choose among equally undesirable options. The alternate payee may go back to the state court that originally issued the order and request to amend the terms of the court's order. If the alternate payee believes that the plan administrator was wrong in rejecting the order as an invalid QDRO, the alternate payee may attempt to enforce the state court order through the judicial system. The alternate payee in *Dickerson v. Dickerson* elected the second option.

DICKERSON V. DICKERSON

United States District Court, Eastern District of Tennessee, 1992.
803 F.Supp. 127.

EDGAR, DISTRICT JUDGE.

This action involves a demand by plaintiff Janet Dickerson for the immediate alienation and distribution to her of a portion of her former husband's pension assets under the terms of a divorce decree. Plaintiff and defendant Southern Electrical Retirement Fund ("SERF") have filed cross motions for summary judgment. * * *

I.   FACTS

The facts are not in dispute. On January 26, 1990, the Circuit Court of Hamilton County, Tennessee, entered a final decree of divorce which dissolved the marriage of Janet and James Dickerson and divided their marital assets. One of the primary assets accumulated by the parties during their marriage are pension benefits accumulated by James Dickerson as a participant under SERF. Janet Dickerson was granted a judgment against James Dickerson in the amount of $8,000 to be paid out of his pension benefits. In order to aid Janet Dickerson in collecting the $8,000 judgment, the Hamilton County Circuit Court included language in the decree which purports to provide for a qualified domestic relations order ("QDRO"). Paragraph 8 of the divorce decree provides in pertinent part:

8.   *Qualified Domestic Relations Order.* The Husband currently has certain pension benefits in the Southern Electrical Retirement Fund. Pursuant to the parties' division of their marital property rights and interest, and in order to equitably distribute the marital assets of the parties, Wife, Janet Delynn Dickerson is hereby given a judgment against James Allen Dickerson in the sum of $8,000. In order to effectuate the Wife's collection of this judgment amount, the Court orders as follows:

[handwritten margin notes: contents of QDRO · amount ✓ · address ✗ · name of Q plan ✗]

(a) *Application of Retirement Equity Act of 1984.* The Court determines that pursuant to the Retirement Equity Act of 1984 (Act), Public Law 98–397, Section 204, $8,000 of James Allen Dickerson retirement benefits under the Southern Electrical Retirement Fund may be disbursed and distributed to Janet Delynn Dickerson pursuant to this order as soon as administratively possible in the form provided in such respective plan.

* * *

(e) *Southern Electrical Retirement Fund Pension Plan.* Pursuant to T.C.A. § 34–4–121, and the Retirement Equity Act of 1984, the Court determines that all vested benefits to which James Allen Dickerson is entitled as a participant under the Southern Electrical Retirement Fund are marital property subject to equitable division of this Court and further are subject to application by this Court to satisfy the parties' division of marital assets and adjustment of marital rights. As part of the overall equitable division of assets entered into in this case, the Court awards to Janet Delynn Dickerson, as alternate payee, the right to receive $8,000 of those vested benefits to which James Allen Dickerson is entitled as a participant under the Southern Electrical Retirement Fund. Such benefits in the sum of $8,000 shall be distributed to Janet Delynn Dickerson as quickly as administratively possible following the entry of the Final Decree of Divorce. The distribution to Janet Delynn Dickerson shall be in a lump sum payment or other form as provided in the Southern Electrical Retirement Fund.

(f) This Qualified Domestic Relations Order does not require the Southern Electrical Retirement Fund to provide any type or form of benefit not otherwise provided under the Southern Electrical Retirement Fund; nor does this Qualified Domestic Relations Order require the Southern Electrical Retirement Fund to provide increased benefits to the participant or any alternate payee; nor does this Qualified Domestic Relations Order require that payment to an alternate payee of plan benefits which are required to be paid to another alternate payee under another order previously determined to be a qualified domestic relations order.

After entry of the final divorce decree, Janet Dickerson requested SERF to distribute the $8,000 in pension assets to her. SERF refused to comply with the request because SERF contends that such a distribution of pension funds would violate § 206(d) of the Employee Retirement Income Security Act ("ERISA"), and §§ 401(a)(13) and 414(p) of the Internal Revenue Code, which impose strict limitations on the alienation of pension funds.

SERF's argument

The SERF pension plan contains the following provision concerning the alienation and assignment of benefits:

ELIGIBILITY FOR BENEFITS

Normal Retirement

alienation and assignment of SERF plan

Any Employee who retires from Covered Employment and Industry Employment will be eligible for a Normal Retirement benefit upon achieving his 55th (fifty-fifth) birthday.

Disability Retirement

An Employee who leaves Covered Employment and Industry Employment because of Disability shall be eligible for a Disability Retirement benefit.

* * *

earliest age eligible to receive = 55 yrs

Under the SERF plan there are only two benefit options for participants, the normal retirement benefit and the disability retirement benefit. The earliest age that the participant, James Dickerson, is eligible to receive normal retirement benefits is fifty-five, provided he has terminated his employment. According to SERF's records, James Dickerson was born on October 21, 1958, and he will be eligible for normal retirement benefits no earlier than October 21, 2013.

Janet Dickerson filed a motion in the state court to add SERF as a party to the divorce action as a means of challenging SERF's refusal to distribute the pension assets to her and the motion was granted. Janet Dickerson also moved the state court to order SERF to show cause why it should not be held in contempt for failing to comply with the divorce decree requiring SERF to distribute $8,000 in pension assets to her. The state court issued a show cause order to SERF. SERF thereafter removed the case invoking this Court's subject matter jurisdiction under ERISA. SERF essentially requests this Court to issue a declaratory judgment that the divorce decree does not comply with the statutory requirements to constitute a QDRO pursuant to ERISA § 206(d).

II. ANALYSIS

The question to be resolved is whether the divorce decree is a QDRO *issue* within the meaning of ERISA § 206(d), which entitles Janet Dickerson to have SERF disburse $8,000 from the pension plan to her as an alternate payee-beneficiary. After reviewing the plain statutory language and the legislative history of § 206(d), the Court concludes that the divorce decree is not a QDRO and summary judgment will be entered in SERF's favor. *Holding: not an enforceable QDRO*

spendthrift provision of ERISA

ERISA, as originally enacted, contains a spendthrift provision which states that benefits provided under covered retirement pension plans may not be alienated or assigned. ERISA § 206(d)(1). The purpose of the spendthrift provision is to protect and secure the financial well-being of employees and their dependents. Ablamis v. Roper, 937 F.2d 1450, 1453–54 (9th Cir. 1991). However, ERISA was flawed in that it did not clearly delineate a spouse's interest in an employee's pension benefits. "The statutory confusion often left women who worked in the home and contributed significantly to the family's financial security without the ability to obtain any pension benefits upon their husband's death or upon divorce." Id. at 1453. Congress, therefore, enacted the Retirement Equity Act of 1984 ("REA"), Pub. Law 98–397, 98 Stat. 1426 (1984), primarily for the purpose of safeguarding the financial security of widows and divorcees. Id.[2]

purpose of REA and QDRO

In order to protect the interests of women who may suffer inequities as the economic victims of divorce or separation from their wage earning husbands, the REA creates an express statutory exception to the spendthrift provision. ERISA's spendthrift provision does not apply to a QDRO. A court may divide the rights of spouses in pension benefits through a QDRO and award the non-employee spouse her proper share of those benefits.

There is no dispute between Janet Dickerson and SERF about the state court's authority to issue a QDRO. The controversy is that SERF contends the divorce decree is not a QDRO because it seeks to order SERF to pay the $8,000 in pension funds to Janet Dickerson now instead of delaying payment until such time as her former husband becomes eligible at age 55 to receive a regular distribution of benefits under the terms of the SERF plan. Janet Dickerson * * * claims that the divorce decree is a QDRO which entitles her to an immediate distribution of $8,000 to her from SERF even though her former husband is approximately twenty-one years away from being entitled to receive normal retirement benefits under the SERF plan.

claims of each party

* * *

Janet Dickerson contends that ERISA § 206(d)(3)(E)(ii)(I) entitles her to receive an immediate distribution of pension benefits from SERF on the theory that the divorce decree found her to be a "participant" under the SERF plan. She urges the Court to interpret ERISA § 206(d)(3)(E)(ii)(I) to mean that earliest retirement age is the date on which the plan participant, Janet Dickerson, is entitled to a distribution under the pension plan and she contends the divorce decree is a QDRO which provides that she has a right to be paid by SERF "as quickly as

---

[2]   In the legislative history of the REA, it is noted that ERISA was amended to:

provide for greater equity under private pension plans for workers and their spouses . . . by taking into account changes in work patterns, the status of marriage as an economic partnership, and the substantial contribution to that partnership of spouses who work both in and outside the home.

S. Rep. No. 575, 98th Cong.2d Sess. (1984). The Senate Report also observed that "the assignment of [an] alternate payee's rights to the benefits is not considered an assignment or alienation of benefits under the plan if and only if the order is a qualified domestic relations order," and that state law providing these rights under a QDRO would be exempt from federal preemption. Id.

administratively possible." This argument is without merit because the divorce decree never refers to Janet Dickerson as being a "participant" under the SERF plan. The divorce decree states that James Dickerson is the participant and Janet Dickerson is the alternate payee. Moreover, Janet Dickerson is not a "participant" within the meaning of that term as defined under ERISA. As the former spouse of the SERF plan participant, Janet Dickerson is merely an alternate payee or beneficiary.

Janet Dickerson next argues the divorce decree is a valid QDRO under ERISA § 206(d)(3)(E)(i)(II) which provides a QDRO may require that payment of benefits be made to an alternate payee "as if the participant had retired on the date on which such payment is to begin under such order. . . ." She contends that the event which triggers the distribution of SERF pension benefits to her is the divorce decree rather than James Dickerson becoming eligible to receive normal retirement benefits at age fifty-five. The Court disagrees with this reasoning. A self-proclaimed QDRO does not in and of itself create a right in an alternate payee to obtain pension benefits. Rather, the legal sufficiency of the divorce decree is tested by the provisions of ERISA § 206(d) to determine if it meets the statutory requirements to constitute a true QDRO and properly allow access to the participant's pension benefits.

* * *

[T]he intent of Congress in enacting ERISA was to protect the fiscal integrity of covered pension plans for the benefit of *all* of their participants. To this end, Congress imposed strict actuarial planning and reporting requirements along with a prohibition against assignment or alienation of the interests of individual participants. If the courts were to allow divorce decrees of participants entered many years prior to their normal retirement dates to cause sudden, unanticipated and immediate withdrawals from pension funds, it would be in contravention of the fundamental purpose of ERISA. If Congress had intended to make a drastic departure from its previous spendthrift policy when it enacted the REA and provided for the utilization of QDROs, as Janet Dickerson suggests, then the intent should be abundantly clear in both the plain statutory language and the legislative history of the REA. The Court concludes that such intent is not evident in either source.

The operative language in ERISA § 206(d)(3)(E)(i)(II) is "as if the participant had *retired*. . . ." (emphasis added). This subparagraph, when read in context with ERISA § 206(d)(3)(E)(i)(I), presumes that the participant has reached the age where he is eligible to receive retirement benefits under the terms of his pension plan, but he has not actually retired or terminated his employment. This interpretation of the statute is supported by the pertinent legislative history. In its explanation of the intent of Congress with regard to the combined effect of ERISA §§ 206(d)(3)(D) and (E), the Senate Finance Committee reported:

> A domestic relations order is not a qualified order if it (1) requires a plan to provide any type or form of benefit, or any option, not otherwise provided under the plan,. . . . The bill provides that a domestic relations order is not treated as failing the requirements for a qualified domestic relations order merely because the order provides that payments must begin to the alternate payee on or after the date on which the participant attains the earliest retirement age under the plan whether or not the participant actually retires on that date. . . . In the case of an order providing for the payment of benefits *after* the earliest retirement age, the payments to the alternate payee at that time are computed *as if the participant had retired on the date on which benefit payments commence under the order.*

S. Rep. No. 575, 98th Cong.2nd Sess. 1 (1984) (emphasis supplied).

The Court has also considered the following excerpt from the legislative history of the Tax Reform Act of 1986, P.L. 99–514, 100 Stat. 2085 (1986), wherein Congress discussed the REA:

> *Qualified domestic relations orders.*—Under present law, a domestic relations order is not a qualified domestic relations order ("QDRO") if such order requires a plan to provide any type or form of benefit, or any option, not otherwise provided under the plan. Thus, an order generally constitutes a QDRO if it provides that payments attributable to a participant's benefits are to begin before the participant separates from service and becomes eligible for a distribution. *As an exception to the rule, present law provides that a QDRO may require that an alternate payee commence receiving payments on or after the date that the participant attains the earliest retirement age under the plan, even if the participant has not yet separated from service.*

[handwritten margin note: When an order generally constitutes a QDRO]

> Under the conference agreement, the definition of "earliest retirement age" for purposes of the QDRO provisions in the case of a defined contribution plan or a defined benefit plan is the earlier of: (1) the earliest date benefits are payable under the plan to the participant, and (2) the later of the date the participant attains age 50 and the date on which the participant could obtain a distribution from the plan if the participant separated from service.

> For example, in the case of a plan which provides for payment of benefits upon separation from service (but not before then), the earliest date on which a QDRO can require payments to an alternate payee to begin is the date the participant separates from service. A QDRO could also require such a plan to begin payments to an alternate payee when the participant attains age 50, even if the participant has not then separated from service.

The amount payable under a QDRO following the participant's earliest retirement age cannot exceed the amount which the participant is (or would be) entitled to receive at such time. For example, assume that a profit sharing plan provides that a participant may withdraw some, but not all, of the participant's account balance before separation from service. A QDRO may provide for payment to an alternative payee up to the amount which the participant may withdraw.

A plan may provide for payment to an alternate payee prior to the earliest retirement age as defined under the conference agreement.

H.R. Conf. Rep. No. 99–841, 99th Cong.2nd Sess. (1986) (emphasis added).

After reviewing the plain language of ERISA § 206(d) and the pertinent legislative history, the Court concludes that the divorce decree dissolving the marriage of James and Janet Dickerson is not a qualified domestic relations order because it seeks to require SERF to provide a benefit not otherwise permitted under the pension plan and to disburse pension funds to the alternate payee spouse prior to participant James Dickerson reaching age 55, which is the earliest retirement age when he is eligible to begin receiving normal retirement benefits under the terms of the SERF plan.

An order will enter granting summary judgment in favor of SERF. If Janet Dickerson desires to have the terms of her divorce decree modified to provide for a qualified domestic relations order which complies with ERISA § 206(d), it will be necessary for her to initiate proceedings in the Hamilton County Circuit Court.

NOTES

1.   *QDRO Review Procedures.* In reviewing the terms of a court order, the plan administrator is not required to look beyond the face of the order to ascertain the validity of the order under state domestic relations law. The plan administrator is responsible for determining whether a domestic relations order issued by a state court satisfies the statutory requirements for a QDRO. To assist plan administrators in establishing correct procedures for reviewing QDROs, the Department of Labor has issued a monograph providing administrative guidance. See U.S. DEP'T LABOR, QDROS: THE DIVISION OF PENSIONS THROUGH QUALIFIED DOMESTIC RELATIONS ORDERS (1997).

There are two reasons why the plan administrator is cautious when determining whether the order satisfies the statutory requirements for a QDRO. First, if the order is not a QDRO, the assignment of benefits to the alternate payee pursuant to the order will result in disqualification of the plan under the anti-alienation rule. Second, because the anti-alienation rule is duplicated in ERISA, the erroneous assignment and payment of plan benefits to the alternate payee would constitute a breach of fiduciary duty, thereby potentially subjecting the plan administrator to fiduciary liability in a private civil action brought by the plan participant under ERISA. Fiduciary duties and private civil actions under ERISA are discussed in Chapters Five and Six of the casebook.

To avoid disputes concerning whether the language of a domestic relations order is a valid QDRO, many plan administrators prepare model QDRO forms for alternate payees to use. Plan administrators generally will provide these model QDRO forms if a prospective alternate payee requests an example of QDRO language that is acceptable under the terms of the plan.

2. *Income and Gift Tax Consequences of QDRO Distributions.* For purposes of income taxation, when a QDRO distribution is made to an alternate payee who is the former spouse of the participant, the distribution to the alternate payee is included in the alternate payee's gross income. If the QDRO payment qualifies as an eligible rollover distribution, the alternate payee may elect a direct rollover of the QDRO distribution and thereby avoid income taxation. See Code § 402(e)(1). If the alternate payee is a dependent child of the participant, the payment of QDRO benefits to the child is treated as if a distribution has been made to the participant, and the amount of the distribution is included in the participant's gross income.

A QDRO distribution to a former spouse may be deemed a "gift" for purposes of federal gift taxation. See Code §§ 2501(a); 2511(a); 2512(b). A gift to a former spouse does not qualify for the marital deduction for purposes of federal gift taxation. See Code § 2523. To avoid paying a possible gift tax on the amount transferred to the former spouse, the order containing the QDRO must be structured to meet the requirements for a divorce property settlement agreement under Code Section 2516.

3. *Dividing Benefits Under the QDRO.* In dividing the participant's benefits under a qualified plan, the two approaches commonly used are the *shared payment approach* and the *separate interest approach*. See U.S. DEP'T LABOR, QDROS: THE DIVISION OF PENSIONS THROUGH QUALIFIED DOMESTIC RELATIONS ORDERS, Q & A 3–1—3–3 (1997). The shared payment approach generally is used for orders of alimony or child support when the participant has already begun to receive benefits in the form of annuity payments from the plan. Under the shared payment approach, the QDRO directs that a specific dollar amount or percentage of each annuity benefit payment must be paid to the alternate payee. The QDRO further specifies the period during which the alternate payee is to share in the payments. For example, if the payments are for the support of a minor child, the order may require payments to begin immediately and continue until the child attains the age of 18. If the payments are for the support of a former spouse, the order may require payments to continue until the death or remarriage of the former spouse.

The separate interest approach is used to divide the plan benefits as part of a marital property settlement. Under the separate interest approach, the

QDRO divides the entire benefit of the participant into two separate portions so that the alternate payee can receive his or her portion at a different time (typically, as soon as permitted under the plan terms) and in a different form (typically, a lump sum) than the time and form that apply to the plan participant's portion.

For a defined contribution plan, valuing the participant's accrued benefit for purposes of dividing the benefit through a QDRO is simple. The value of the participant's accrued benefit is the balance of the individual's account under the plan. If the participant is less than fully vested in the accrued benefit, the parties may negotiate over the amount to be allocated to the participant's ex-spouse under the terms of the QDRO.

Valuing the participant's accrued benefit from a defined benefit plan is more difficult because the value of the participant's benefit can change over time for many reasons, such as an increase in the participant's compensation, years of service, or a cost of living adjustment. Moreover, the defined benefit plan may have a subsidized early retirement benefit or disability benefit with a greater actuarial value than the actuarial value of the participant's accrued benefit payable at normal retirement age. See U.S. DEP'T LABOR, QDROS: THE DIVISION OF PENSIONS THROUGH QUALIFIED DOMESTIC RELATIONS ORDERS, Q & A 3–4—3–7 & Appendix C (1997). If the participant's accrued benefit under the defined benefit plan is substantial, the alternate payee may hire a pension actuary to provide assistance concerning the actuarial value of various benefit options and how the accrued benefit may be divided.

4.   *Waivers.* Rather than dividing a participant's benefits under a qualified plan through a QDRO, the ex-spouse of the plan participant may attempt to waive any right to the participant's plan benefits. *Kennedy v. Plan Administrator for DuPont Savings and Investment Plan*, 555 U.S. 285 (2009), illustrates this situation and its possible perils.

In *Kennedy*, the employee participated in several retirement plans sponsored by his employer. When the employee married, he named his wife as the beneficiary under these plans. Later, when the employee obtained a divorce, his ex-wife waived "all right, title, interest, and claim" to any of the benefits under the employee's retirement plans as part of the divorce decree. The employee later designated his daughter as the beneficiary for one retirement plan, but failed to change the designation of his ex-wife as the beneficiary for his account under the employer's Savings and Investment Plan (SIP).

When the employee died, his daughter became the executrix for his estate. The daughter demanded that the administrator honor the waiver executed by the ex-wife and distribute the $400,000 balance of the deceased employee's account under the SIP to the estate (the normal procedure when a participant dies without a valid beneficiary designation on file). Instead, the administrator for the SIP distributed the $400,000 to the deceased employee's ex-wife pursuant to the beneficiary designation on file, which had never been

248 QUALIFIED RETIREMENT PLANS CH. 3

revoked or changed while the employee was alive. Incensed, the daughter sued the employer and the SIP administrator on behalf of the estate.

The Supreme Court first determined that the waiver by the ex-spouse was not an impermissible "assignment" of benefits, and therefore was not automatically rendered null and void under the anti-alienation rule. This holding, however, did not result in victory for the daughter. ERISA imposes a statutory fiduciary duty on the plan administrator to "act in accordance with the terms of the plan. . . ." ERISA § 404(a)(1)(D). The terms of the SIP required the plan administrator to pay a deceased employee's benefits according to the most current beneficiary designation on file. The terms of the plan did not permit the plan administrator to honor a waiver of plan benefits by a designated beneficiary. Consequently, the *Kennedy* Court ruled that the SIP administrator had properly paid the SIP benefits to the deceased employee's ex-spouse.

5. *QDROs and Divorce for Same-Sex Spouses.* As a result of the Supreme Court's decision in *United States v. Windsor*, 133 S. Ct. 2675 (2013), the QDRO rules apply to a former same-sex spouse of a plan participant who is named as an alternate payee in a domestic relations order. See generally DOL Technical Release 2013–14. Whether a domestic relations order can be obtained from a state court will depend on the law of the couple's state of domicile. If the couple's state of domicile recognizes same-sex marriages, then a domestic relations order can be obtained pursuant to the state's regular procedures for divorce proceedings in state court. If, however, the state of domicile does not recognize same-sex marriages, then it may be difficult for a same-sex couple to obtain a divorce in that jurisdiction. In this situation, the same-sex couple may be forced to obtain a divorce, and any related QDRO, in another jurisdiction that recognizes the couple's same-sex marriage and will allow a divorce under state law. If a divorce is granted by a court in another jurisdiction, then the plan administrator is required to comply with a valid QDRO that is issued by a state court in another jurisdiction.

PROBLEMS ON THE ANTI-ALIENATION RULE

PROBLEM ONE

You are a commercial loan officer for First City Bank. A bank customer comes to you requesting a loan. The customer has just resigned her position as an officer of ABC Corporation. The customer is seeking a loan of $250,000 to purchase a small business. The customer lists the following assets on her loan application as collateral for the proposed loan:

1. Personal residence ($50,000 net value after the mortgage is deducted);

2. Various stock market investments ($100,000);

3. A fully vested account in the ABC Corporation profit sharing plan ($500,000).

Should you rely on the customer's profit sharing plan benefit as collateral for the proposed loan? Why or why not?

PROBLEM TWO

You are in-house legal counsel to DT Corporation, which sponsors a profit sharing plan and a defined benefit plan for its employees. The profit sharing plan permits loans to plan participants in an amount up to the lesser of $50,000 or 50% of the participant's nonforfeitable accrued benefit. The defined benefit plan provides for a monthly retirement benefit commencing at normal retirement age of 40% of the participant's final average pay, but does not have a plan loan feature.

The president of DT Corporation has just gone through a bitter divorce. The value of the president's account under the profit sharing plan is $250,000. The president is 60% vested in his profit sharing plan benefits. The present lump sum value of the president's nonforfeitable accrued benefit under the defined benefit plan is $200,000. The human resources manager for DT Corporation serves as the plan administrator for both the profit sharing plan and the defined benefit plan. She has asked for your legal advice concerning the following situations.

A.   The president has requested a loan of $150,000 from the profit sharing plan to "help him get back on his feet after the divorce." Can the plan administrator waive the $50,000 limit on plan loans for the president and make the required loan of $150,000 to the president?

B.   The president's former spouse has submitted the domestic relations order issued by the state court in the president's divorce proceeding to the plan administrator for the profit sharing plan and the defined benefit plan. The order provides in relevant part:

7.   [Former spouse] shall receive one-half of all of [president's] retirement benefits.

The lawyer for the president's former spouse is threatening to sue if the plan administrator does not make an immediate payment of one-half of all of the president's retirement benefits. How would you advise the plan administrator to proceed?

H. QUALIFIED PLAN ISSUES IN THE REPRESENTATION OF CORPORATE CLIENTS

In the typical corporate transaction, the deal makers are concerned with evaluating the assets and liabilities of the acquired company, how the acquisition will be structured, and how the surviving company will be managed, among other issues. One area of concern that is frequently ignored until shortly before the deal closes is the evaluation of the employee benefit programs sponsored by the acquired company and the determination of how best to change these programs during and after the transaction. While employee benefits issues will not often scuttle a corporate transaction, they can play a significant role in determining how the transaction must be structured, and they will often impact the costs of the acquisition. Deal makers who ignore employee benefits issues in their transaction do so at their own peril. Participant lawsuits, withdrawal liability, and liability for plan underfunding are only three of the many expensive benefits problems an unwitting corporate suitor may find itself saddled with if it rushes to complete a seemingly attractive acquisition.

Richard D. Nix & Timothy Verrall, *Employee Benefit Issues in Mergers and Acquisitions*, 25 OKLA. CITY U. L. REV. 435 (2000).

1. PLAN MERGERS, ASSET AND LIABILITY TRANSFERS, AND SPIN-OFFS

Plan mergers and consolidations, asset and liability transfers, and spin-offs are a by-product of corporate mergers and acquisitions. To illustrate, assume that two companies, each of which sponsors a qualified plan for its employees, decide to merge. The surviving company after the merger often will encounter legal and practical obstacles if the company continues to operate the qualified plans of the two pre-merger companies as two separate plans. For example, after the transition period of Code Section 410(b)(6)(C) has expired, each plan must separately satisfy the minimum coverage rules of Code Section 410(b). Viewed from a practical perspective, it is cumbersome and costly to continue to administer and operate two separate qualified plans. The solution to these legal and practical problems usually is a plan *merger* or *consolidation*. A plan merger or consolidation occurs when two or more plans are combined into a single plan. See Treas. Reg. § 1.414(*l*)–1(b)(2).

When a company with several operating divisions sells one of its divisions to another company, many of the employees of the division that is sold may continue to be employed by the buyer. The seller usually prefers not to continue to be responsible for the benefits of its former employees (who are now current employees of the buyer) under the seller's ongoing qualified plan. Rather, the seller would prefer that the transferred employees look to the buyer and the buyer's qualified plan in the future for their retirement benefits.

In this situation, the solution is either a *transfer of plan assets and liabilities* to the buyer's qualified plan or a s*pin-off*. A transfer of plan assets and liabilities occurs when the assets or liabilities of one plan are diminished when another plan acquires these assets and assumes these liabilities. A spin-off occurs when a single plan is divided into two or more plans. See Treas. Reg. § 1.414(*l*)–1(b)(3), (4). The difference between a transfer and a spin-off is that in a transfer, the assets and liabilities of the seller's qualified plan are transferred to a qualified plan of the buyer that is already in existence. In a spin-off, the assets and liabilities of the seller's qualified plan attributable to the transferred employees become part of a new qualified plan established by the buyer.

Code Section 414(*l*) addresses plan mergers or consolidations, asset and liability transfers, and spin-offs involving qualified plans. Code Section 414(*l*)(1), which concerns mergers or consolidations and asset transfers, is duplicated in ERISA Section 208. Code Section 414(*l*)(2) governs the allocation of surplus (i.e., overfunded) plan assets in a defined benefit plan when a spin-off occurs.

Both the Code and ERISA establish the general principle that changes involving the structure of a qualified plan cannot adversely impact the accrued benefits of the plan participants. Each plan participant must "receive a benefit immediately after the merger, consolidation, or transfer which is equal to or greater than the benefit he would have been entitled to receive immediately before the merger, consolidation, or transfer (if the plan had then terminated)." Code § 414(*l*)(1); ERISA § 208. Treasury Department regulations elaborate on this general principle by explaining that "[t]his condition requires that each participant receive benefits on a termination basis . . . from the plan immediately after the merger, consolidation or transfer which are equal to or greater than the benefits the participant would receive on a termination basis immediately before the merger, consolidation, or transfer." Treas. Reg. § 1.414(*l*)–1(a)(2)(ii).

The regulatory requirement that participants must receive "benefits on a termination basis" has a specialized meaning. See Treas. Reg. § 1.414(*l*)–1(b)(5). For defined contribution plans involved in a merger, transfer or spin-off, the requirement that participants must receive benefits on a termination basis is satisfied by transferring each participant's entire account balance (including any portion that is not yet vested) to the recipient plan. See Treas. Reg. § 1.414(*l*)–1(d), (m), (o). If the plan restructuring involves two defined benefit plans, or a defined benefit plan and a defined contribution plan, the specialized expertise of a pension plan actuary is necessary to determine how this requirement should be satisfied. See generally Treas. Reg. § 1.414(*l*)–1. Note carefully that Code Section 414(*l*) does *not* require that each participant must be fully and immediately vested in his or her accrued benefit, as is the case when a plan termination has occurred. See Code § 411(d)(3).

Benefits that are the subject of a merger, transfer or spin-off also are protected under the anti-cutback rule. See Code § 411(d)(6); ERISA § 204(g); Treas. Reg. § 1.411(d)–4, Q & A–2(a)(3). Consequently, the recipient plan must preserve all of the optional forms of benefits that were associated with the old plan, unless the new plan qualifies for one of the limited statutory exceptions that permit an optional form of benefit to be eliminated. See Code § 411(d)(6)(D)–(E); ERISA § 204(g)(4)–(5); Treas. Reg. § 1.411(d)–4, Q & A–3(b).

2. PLAN TERMINATIONS

The procedural requirements for the termination of a defined contribution plan and a defined benefit plan are distinctly different. When a defined contribution plan is terminated, the primary requirement is compliance with the special vesting rule of Code Section 411(d)(3). Code Section 411(d)(3) requires that all participants in the terminated plan must be immediately and fully vested in their accrued benefits under the plan.

The special vesting rule of Code Section 411(d)(3) also applies to defined benefit plans. Unlike defined contribution plans, however, the benefits under a defined benefit plan are insured through the federal Pension Benefit Guaranty Corporation (PBGC). For this reason, the termination of a defined benefit plan is governed by an additional set of procedures under Title IV of ERISA:

> One of Congress' central purposes in enacting this complex legislation was to prevent the "great personal tragedy" suffered by employees whose vested benefits are not paid when pension plans are terminated. Congress found "that owing to the inadequacy of current minimum standards, the soundness and stability of plans with respect to adequate funds to pay promised benefits may be endangered; that owing to the termination of plans before requisite funds have been accumulated, employees and their beneficiaries have been deprived of anticipated benefits." Congress wanted to correct this condition by making sure that if a worker has been promised a defined pension benefit upon retirement—and if he has fulfilled whatever conditions are required to obtain a vested benefit—he actually will receive it. The termination insurance program [established by Title IV of ERISA] is a major part of Congress' response to the problem. Congress provided for a minimum funding schedule and prescribed standards of conduct for plan administrators to make as certain as possible that pension fund assets would be adequate. But if a plan nonetheless terminates without sufficient assets to pay all vested benefits, the PBGC is required to pay them—within certain dollar limitations * * *—from funds established by that corporation.

Nachman Corp. v. Pension Benefit Guar. Corp., 446 U.S. 359, 374–75 (1980) (citations omitted).

Today's procedures under Title IV of ERISA for termination of single employer pension plans were established by the Single Employer Pension Plan Amendments Act of 1986 (SEPPAA), Pub. L. No. 99–272, 100 Stat. 237. Two types of single employer plan terminations are permitted under the SEPPAA. A *standard termination* is permitted when the plan has sufficient assets to pay all benefit liabilities. See ERISA § 4041(b). A *distress termination* is permitted only if the employer satisfies certain statutory criteria for employer financial distress, or if the PBGC initiates termination of the plan. See ERISA § 4041(c). The standard termination and the distress termination procedures under Title IV are the sole avenues that an employer may use to terminate a defined benefit plan. See Hughes Aircraft Co. v. Jacobson, 525 U.S. 432, 446 (1999); cf. Beck v. PACE Int'l Union, 551 U.S. 96 (2007) (merger of single employer plan into a multiemployer plan is not a permissible method of plan termination).

The employer's decision whether to terminate its qualified plan is a settlor function rather than a fiduciary act. See Lockheed Corp. v. Spink, 517 U.S. 882, 890–91 (1996). In implementing a plan termination, however, the actions of the plan administrator are subject to scrutiny under the fiduciary responsibility provisions of ERISA. See ERISA § 404(a); Bussian v. RJR Nabisco, Inc., 223 F.3d 286, 292 (5th Cir. 2000).

Highly specialized regulatory procedures apply to the termination of a multiemployer plan, including a multiemployer plan that effectively has been terminated by a mass withdrawal of its participating employers. See ERISA § 4041A; DOL Reg. § 4041A. These elaborate rules and procedures are the province of literally a handful of specialists in a few select labor law firms and at the PBGC.

a. Standard Terminations

To qualify for a standard termination, the employer must demonstrate to the PBGC that the employer's plan has sufficient assets to pay all benefit liabilities. This demonstration is prepared by a pension actuary, who certifies that the statutory criteria for a standard termination are satisfied. In general, the procedures for a standard termination involve completion of the following steps:

(1) The plan administrator gives advance notice to the plan participants of the proposed termination.

(2) The employer files a notice of plan termination with the PBGC and applies to the Internal Revenue Service for a determination that the plan as terminated will satisfy all of the requirements for a qualified plan (known as a *termination determination letter*).

(3) The plan administrator provides an individual benefit statement to each of the plan's participants.

(4) The PBGC reviews and approves the proposed termination.

(5) The plan's trustee distributes benefits to the plan participants.

(6) The employer files a closing statement with the PBGC.

After the plan administrator has distributed all of the benefits owed to plan participants, any surplus assets may revert back to the employer if the plan document provides for such a reversion. The employer must pay the Internal Revenue Service a 50% excise tax penalty on the amount of any surplus plan assets that revert back to the employer. See Code § 4980(d)(1). The purpose of this excise tax penalty on reversions is to prevent employers from terminating their defined benefit plans merely to recapture the surplus plan assets. The excise tax penalty on reversion assets may be reduced to 20% if the employer uses the surplus assets to establish another qualified plan or to increase the benefits paid to participants in the terminating plan. See Code § 4980(d)(1).

If the employer's plan does not have sufficient assets to qualify for a standard termination, but the employer does not meet the financial hardship criteria for a distress termination, the employer may decide to cease future benefit accruals under the plan. This technique is commonly described as "freezing" the plan. Freezing the plan gives the employer time to make additional contributions to the plan until the plan's funding level qualifies for a standard termination. When a defined benefit plan is frozen, the plan's participants are given the opportunity to vest fully under the terms of the plan's vesting schedule in their accrued benefits. A frozen plan must continue to be updated and amended to remain in compliance with the current state of the Code Section 401(a) requirements for qualified plans.

b. Distress Terminations

The procedures for a distress termination are described in ERISA Section 4041(c). To qualify for a distress termination, the employer must satisfy at least one of the following statutory criteria:

(1) Liquidation in bankruptcy or other insolvency proceedings. ERISA § 4041(c)(2)(B)(i).

(2) Reorganization in bankruptcy or other insolvency proceedings where the court finds that the reorganization cannot succeed unless the plan is terminated. ERISA § 4041(c)(2)(B)(ii).

(3) Demonstrated inability to pay debts when due and to continue in business unless the plan is terminated. ERISA § 4041(c)(2)(B)(iii)(I).

(4) A demonstration that the pension costs have become unreasonably burdensome solely as a result of a decline in the employer's workforce. ERISA § 4041(c)(2)(B)(iii)(II).

In a distress termination of a single employer plan, the sponsoring employer (including all members of the employer's controlled group) are jointly and severally liable for the plan's unfunded benefit liabilities. See ERISA § 4062(a). In addition to the general liability claim of the PBGC against the plan's employer for all unfunded benefit liabilities, ERISA Section 4068 creates a statutory lien in favor of the PBGC of up to 30% of the collective net worth of the employer's controlled group.

To avoid large future pension liabilities, the employer may attempt to sell part of its business, such as an unprofitable division or subsidiary, and transfer the associated pension plan liabilities to the buyer. The anticipated outcome of this transaction is that the buyer eventually will become bankrupt, the plan will be terminated in a distress termination, and the PBGC will become responsible for the plan's unfunded benefit liabilities. ERISA Section 4069 is designed to deter such transactions by imposing a *five-year look-back rule* when a distress termination of a defined benefit plan occurs. Under the five-year look-back rule, if a principal purpose of the transaction was for the seller to avoid its pension plan liabilities and the plan terminates within five years of the transaction, then the selling employer (including any members of the employer's controlled group) are subject to liability as if the employer were still the sponsor of the plan.

c.   The Future of the PBGC

The Pension Benefit Guaranty Corporation is an independent federal agency that insures the pension benefits owed by underfunded defined benefit plans that are terminated in a distress termination. The PBGC's insurance program is financed through insurance premiums paid by the sponsors of all defined benefit plans. In addition, the PBGC obtains revenue from investment income on the assets held in the PBGC insurance fund, from the assets of defined benefit plans the PBGC has taken over as trustee, and through collections actions against employers.

For single employer plans covered by PBGC insurance, the employer is required to pay a flat premium fee per participant (set at $49 in 2014, and indexed for inflation in future years) and a variable premium that is based on the amount of vested benefits that are unfunded under the plan. The maximum amount of benefits the PBGC will pay to an individual plan participant under the insurance program is limited by a statutory formula. See ERISA §§ 4022; 4022A; 4022B. For example, in 2014 the maximum annual PBGC insurance payment under the statutory formula for a single-life annuity commencing at age 65 was $59,320.

The insurance premiums charged by the PBGC have increased substantially since 1974, when the per participant rate for single employer plans was $1.00. Nevertheless, insurance premium revenues have been unable to keep pace with the PGBC's pension obligations from insolvent defined benefit plans. As of September 30, 2013, the PBGC's single-employer and multiemployer insurance programs had deficits of $27.4 billion and $8.3 billion, respectively. PENSION BENEFIT GUAR. CORP., ANNUAL REPORT 2013.

Economists Steven Boyce and Richard A. Ippolito have studied the methodology used by the PBGC to determine the appropriate insurance premium amounts needed to fund the insurance program. Unlike the typical insurance scheme, calculating the amount of the premium to be charged by the PBGC is a complicated task.

> The Pension Benefit Guaranty Corporation is a federal agency that insures underfunded defined benefit pension plans that are terminated in bankruptcy proceedings. Given any economic conditions, the pension insurer is susceptible to the possibility that particular firms with pension underfunding will enter bankruptcy, which is firm-specific, or *idiosyncratic*, risk. In addition, since pension underfunding and bankruptcy rates are influenced by systematic changes in economy-wide variables, the pension insurer is also subject to *market risk*.

> Other insurances, such as property insurance in areas prone to flooding or hurricane damage, have an aggregate or systematic component. But as long as these events are uncorrelated with the wealth of the economy, arguably, the pricing problem is strictly actuarial. The premium is simply the discounted value of projected claims where the discount rate is the risk-free rate. The addition of a *catastrophic-risk* element to the insurance (the small chance of very large claims) may change the mechanics of how losses are estimated, but the fundamental pricing problems remain unchanged.

> The market-risk feature makes pension insurance a more challenging contract to price. When there is an economy-wide downturn, pension underfunding and the rate of bankruptcy are expected to increase. This correlation means that investors backing the insurance require a return in excess of the risk-free discount rate, meaning that the cost of the insurance is more than the present value of actuarial losses using the risk-free discount rate. This complication sets pension insurance apart from most other catastrophic insurance coverage.

Steven Boyce and Richard A. Ippolito, *The Cost of Pension Insurance*, 69 J. RISK & INS. 121, 122 (2002) (footnotes omitted) (emphasis in original). Boyce and Ippolito concluded that "the pricing schedule currently enforced by the PBGC only vaguely resembles one that meets a market standard" and that "the overall premiums now collected amount to about 50% of those that would be charged in the private sector for the same coverage." Id. at 124. In other words, Boyce and Ippolito determined that the PBGC's insurance program for defined benefit plans was heavily subsidized by the federal government.

One of the core objectives of the Pension Protection Act of 2006 was to strengthen the PBGC insurance system. To increase PBGC revenues, Congress increased the amount of the flat rate and variable rate insurance premiums and added a new increased plan termination premium (set at $1,250 per participant for most plans). The termination premium must be paid for a total of three years following the termination of the plan. The purpose of the plan termination premium is to penalize employers who file for Chapter 11 bankruptcy, transfer their unfunded pension plan liabilities to the PBGC as part of the bankruptcy process, and later emerge from Chapter 11 bankruptcy. In *PBGC v. Oneida Ltd.*, 562 F.3d 154 (2d Cir. 2009), the Second Circuit held that the plan sponsor's obligation to pay the termination premium is not dischargeable in bankruptcy.

d. Partial Terminations of Single Employer Plans

When a corporation seeks to reduce its operating costs, one way to achieve this objective is through "downsizing" or "right-sizing"—corporate language that signals layoffs and the involuntary termination of employees. In this situation, individuals whose employment has been terminated may resort to litigation to protect and preserve their qualified plan benefits. One legal theory that may be asserted by the plaintiffs is that the plan has suffered a *partial termination*. If a partial termination of the employer's qualified plan has occurred, the accrued benefits of the participants in the plan whose employment was terminated must be fully and immediately vested under the special vesting rule of Code Section 411(d)(3).

A partial termination can occur for either a defined contribution plan or a defined benefit plan. A partial termination of a defined benefit plan is distinguished from a standard or distress termination in that the employer intends to continue sponsoring the plan. Therefore, when a partial termination of a defined benefit plan occurs, the employer is not required to obtain approval of the partial termination from the PBGC.

A partial termination of a defined benefit plan represents a significant liability for the employer because the funding status of the plan is determined in part by the amount of accrued benefits under the plan that are vested. If a partial termination occurs, terminated participants in the plan who were less than fully vested are immediately and fully vested in their accrued benefits. Consequently, the employer may be required immediately to make a substantial unanticipated contribution to the defined benefit plan.

The partial termination of a defined contribution plan is usually less significant from the employer's perspective. Each terminated participant's plan account is already "funded" in the sense that the account already holds the participant's accrued benefit. Consequently, if a court finds that a partial termination has occurred, each affected participant receives the entire balance of the participant's account, rather than receiving nothing as a nonvested participant or only a portion of the account balance as a partially vested participant.

Code Section 411(d)(3), which requires full and immediate vesting of the accrued benefits of participants whose employment has been terminated as a result of a partial plan termination, is a requirement for plan qualification. As a result, every qualified plan document contains the special vesting rule of Code Section 411(d)(3). Plan participants seeking to enforce this plan provision under ERISA must frame their claim as one to enforce their rights under the terms of the plan pursuant to ERISA Section 502(a)(1)(B). See, e.g., Administrative Comm. of the Sea Ray Employees' Stock Ownership and Profit Sharing Plan v. Robinson, 164 F.3d 981 (6th Cir. 1999). Claims by plan participants brought under ERISA Section 502(a)(1)(B) are discussed in Chapter Six.

According to Treasury Department regulations, whether a partial termination of a qualified plan has occurred is determined "with regard to all the facts and circumstances in a particular case." Such facts and circumstances include "the exclusion, by reason of a plan amendment or severance by the employer, of a group of employees who have previously been covered by the plan and plan amendments which adversely affect the rights of employees to vest in benefits under the plan." See Treas. Reg. § 1.411(d)–2(b)(1). The term *vertical partial termination* is used to refer to the situation where a group of employees who previously were covered by the plan are excluded from participation, usually due to the termination of their employment. The term *horizontal partial termination* is used to refer to the situation where there has been a plan amendment or series of amendments that may adversely affect the rights of employees concerning their future accrued benefits. See generally In re Gulf Pension Litigation, 764 F.Supp. 1149 (S.D. Tex. 1991).

Prior to 2007, the opaque regulatory definition of a partial termination left much to be desired in terms of providing meaningful guidance to employers, plan participants and the federal courts. As the Seventh Circuit complained in *Matz v. Household International Tax Reduction Investment Plan*, 265 F.3d 572 (7th Cir. 2001), "the meaning of 'partial termination' is unclear because the statutory language is ambiguous, the Treasury Regulation is not helpful, the statutory framework offers no assistance, and the legislative history provides little more guidance." Id. at 575.

In Revenue Ruling 2007–43, the Internal Revenue Service officially adopted the approach to partial terminations that had been developed by the federal courts. See Matz v. Household Int'l Tax Reduction Inv. Plan, 388 F.3d 570 (7th Cir. 2004); Weil v. Retirement Plan Admin. Comm. of the Terson Co., 933 F.2d 106 (2d Cir. 1991). Under this approach, a rebuttable presumption that a partial termination has occurred arises if the percentage reduction in the number of plan participants is 20% or greater. A decrease of less than 20% generally does not result in a partial termination.

To measure the reduction in the number of plan participants, both vested and nonvested participants are counted. To calculate the percentage reduction, the number of terminated participants (vested and nonvested) is divided by the number of all participants in the plan. The applicable period for performing the calculation generally is the plan year, but may be a longer period if the reduction is due to a series of related events, such as where an employer engages in a series of sales of subsidiaries or divisions of the business.

Revenue Ruling 2007–43 provides the following illustration of a partial termination:

> Employer X maintains Plan A, a defined contribution plan qualified under § 401(a). The plan year for Plan A is the calendar year. The plan participants include both current and former employees. Plan A provides that an employee of Employer X has a fully vested and nonforfeitable interest in his or her account balance upon either completion of 3 years of service or attainment of age 65. The plan also provides for each participant to have a fully vested and nonforfeitable right to his or her account balance upon the plan's termination or upon a partial termination of the plan that affects the participant.

> Employer X ceases operations at one of its four business locations. As a result, 23 percent of the Plan A participants who are employees of Employer X cease active participation in Plan A due to a severance from employment (excluding any severance from employment that is either on account of death or disability, or retirement on or after normal retirement age) during the plan year. Some of these participants are fully vested due to having completed 3 years of service or having attained age 65. Plan A is not terminated.

> In the present case, there is a presumption that a partial termination has occurred because the turnover rate is 20 percent or more. The facts and circumstances support the finding of a

partial termination because the severances from employment occurred as a result of the shutdown of one of the employer's business locations (and not as a result of routine turnover). Therefore, a partial termination of Plan A has occurred.

A partial termination of a qualified plan may occur for reasons other than turnover. For example, a partial termination may result if the plan is amended in a way that adversely affects the ability of employees to vest in their benefits under the plan, excludes a group of employees who were previously covered by the plan, or reduces the rate of future benefit accruals in such a way that a reversion of plan assets may result for the employer. See Rev. Rul. 2007–43.

3. MULTIEMPLOYER PLANS, EMPLOYER WITHDRAWAL LIABILITY AND DELINQUENCY ACTIONS

Congress amended Title IV of ERISA in 1980 to address the problem of significant underfunding in multiemployer defined benefit pension plans established and administered under Section 302 of the Labor Management Relations Act of 1947, 29 U.S.C. § 186 (Taft-Hartley Act). The Multiemployer Pension Plan Amendments Act of 1980, Pub. L. No. 96–364, 94 Stat. 1208 (MPPAA), was designed to protect and promote the financial stability of multiemployer plans. The most controversial feature of the MPPAA was the creation of *withdrawal liability* for the employer who ceases making contributions to a multiemployer plan for its employees. The withdrawal liability provisions of the MPPAA have withstood numerous challenges by employers on various Constitutional grounds. See Connolly v. Pension Benefit Guar. Corp., 475 U.S. 211 (1986); Concrete Pipe & Products v. Construction Laborers Pension Trust, 508 U.S. 602 (1993).

Employer withdrawal liability under the MPPAA is triggered when an employer engages in either a *complete withdrawal* or a *partial withdrawal* from a multiemployer defined benefit plan. See ERISA §§ 4201(a); 4203; 4205. A complete or partial withdrawal may be triggered by a sale of the operating assets of the business to another employer. Employer withdrawal liability also may be triggered if the employer and the local union negotiate a new collective bargaining agreement under which the employer is no longer obligated to make contributions to a multiemployer pension plan for its collective bargaining unit employees. See ERISA § 4204.

If a complete or partial withdrawal occurs, the trustees of the multiemployer plan have a statutory duty to determine the amount of the employer's withdrawal liability, notify the employer of the amount, and collect the amount of withdrawal liability from the employer. See ERISA § 4202. Withdrawal liability may be collected from any member of the employer's controlled group. The special statutory collection procedures used by the trustees of a multiemployer plan to collect the withdrawal liability amount from the employer have been described as "draconian" and "pay now, dispute later."

An employer's withdrawal liability under the MPPAA is based on the employer's share of the plan's unfunded vested benefits. The amount of the employer's withdrawal liability is calculated by the plan trustees using a statutory allocation method. See ERISA § 4211. Significantly, the employer may incur withdrawal liability even through the employer has made all of the contributions to the multiemployer plan required under the collective bargaining agreement with the local union. If the assets held by the multiemployer plan have yielded low investment returns, after several years the plan may become significantly underfunded, and the employer's corresponding share of the plan's unfunded vested benefits in the event of a withdrawal may grow to be substantial in amount.

Another significant reform enacted by the MPPAA was to strengthen the ability of the trustees of a multiemployer plan to collect delinquent contributions to the plan from participating employers. The issues of employer withdrawal liability and delinquent employer contributions to the plan are often linked. When an employer ceases contributions to a multiemployer plan, a typical response by the plan trustees is to audit the employer to ascertain whether the employer has made all of the contributions to the plan that were required under the terms of the collective bargaining agreement.

In the past, it was difficult for an employer who participated in a multiemployer plan to obtain information from the plan's trustees concerning the funding status of the plan and the employer's potential withdrawal liability. The Pension Protection Act of 2006 enhanced the disclosures that the trustees of a multiemployer plan must make annually to each employer who contributes to the multiemployer plan. See ERISA § 104(d)(1). The new disclosure rules require the trustees of a multiemployer plan to disclose annually to each employer information concerning the number of plan participants, the number of employers contributing to the plan, withdrawal liability assessments, and whether the plan is in endangered or critical funding status under the revised minimum funding rules for multiemployer plans enacted by the Pension Protection Act of 2006. Upon the written request of a contributing employer, the plan's trustees must disclose to the employer certain additional financial information, such as actuarial reports and investment manager reports. See ERISA § 101(k)(1).

In *Gerber Truck Service, Inc.*, reproduced below, and *Independent Fruit and Produce Co.*, reproduced after *Gerber*, an unsophisticated employer became the target of a delinquency collection action under the MPPAA by the trustees of the Central States Southeast and Southwest

Areas Pension Fund (Teamsters Fund). The official policy of the board of trustees for the Teamsters Fund (Special Bulletin 90–7) is reproduced following *Independent Fruit*. After you read each of these cases and Special Bulletin 90–7, consider what legal advice the employer should have received before deciding to enter into a collective bargaining agreement with the local union representative.

CENTRAL STATES, SOUTHEAST AND SOUTHWEST AREAS PENSION FUND v. GERBER TRUCK SERVICE, INC.

United States Court of Appeals, Seventh Circuit, 1989.
870 F.2d 1148.

EASTERBROOK, CIRCUIT JUDGE.

We took this case en banc to decide whether, when an employer and union submit to a pension fund documents promising to make contributions on behalf of all employees, understandings and practices that would prevent enforcement of the writings between employer and union also defeat the fund's claims. The answer depends on § 515 of the Employee Retirement Income Security Act (ERISA), which provides:

> Every employer who is obligated to make contributions to a multiemployer plan under the terms of the plan or under the terms of a collectively bargained agreement shall, to the extent not inconsistent with law, make such contributions in accordance with the terms and conditions of such plan or such agreement.

This means, we conclude, that a plan may enforce the writings according to their terms, if "not inconsistent with law." The pension or welfare fund is like a holder in due course in commercial law, or like the receiver of a failed bank—entitled to enforce the writing without regard to understandings or defenses applicable to the original parties. In so concluding, we follow our own opinion in *Robbins v. Lynch*, 836 F.2d 330 (7th Cir.1988), and the unanimous view of the other courts of appeals.

I

James H. Gerber, who operated a trucking service as a proprietorship, wanted to expand his operations. Early in 1981 he bought the assets, including the operating authorities, of Fat's Express Truck Service. He hired its three drivers and other employees. The three new drivers, the "Fat's Three," were members of Teamsters Local 50 and had enjoyed pension and welfare coverage under multiemployer pension and welfare plans established by the Teamsters union and employers throughout the motor carrier business. The Fat's Three—two of whom were close to retirement age—wanted to keep that coverage. Gerber's other employees were not union members, and Gerber had no desire to pay union scale wages to them or to the Fat's Three. He was willing to accommodate their desire to preserve pension and welfare coverage, however.

To achieve this objective, Gerber approached John Gonzales, the business representative of Local 50, with a proposition: Gerber would sign the Teamsters' collective bargaining agreement, if Gonzales would promise not to expect Gerber to do anything beyond making pension and welfare contributions on behalf of the Fat's Three. Gonzales found this acceptable, because it protected three union members who might otherwise get no coverage or have to search for new jobs late in their careers.

Gerber and Gonzales signed the National Master Freight Agreement and its Central States Area Local Cartage Supplemental Agreement, which required Gerber to make pension and welfare contributions on behalf of "all truck drivers, helpers, dockmen, warehousemen, checkers, powerlift operators, hostlers, and such other employees as may be presently or hereafter represented by the Union." Because "representation" in labor law encompasses all bargaining unit employees, this pledge reached well beyond the three who were *members* of the union. Gerber and Gonzales signed a separate "Participation Agreement" requiring Gerber to contribute fixed sums per week to the pension and welfare plans on behalf of all "DRIVERS represented by the Union." "Drivers" was typed into a blank in a preprinted form. The district court found after a bench trial that

> [t]he collective bargaining agreement was modified by an understanding reached between Gonzales and Gerber only to extend Health and Welfare and Pension coverage to three employees. . . . James Gerber and John Gonzales both stated that the sole intent of the parties was to provide benefit coverage to [the Fat's Three]. Gerber and the employees established their own wages and other terms and conditions of employment. The Union did not seek to include any other employees in the [bargaining] Unit.

In other words, Gerber and Gonzales agreed that the documents they signed would not be enforced. They were not enforced. Local 50 treated Gerber as if it were a nonunion firm. We shall assume that these oral understandings and practices would have frustrated any attempt by the Teamsters, or by Gerber's employees, to assert rights under the agreements as contracts.

Gerber and Gonzales did not inform the pension and welfare plans of their arrangement. They sent the collective bargaining and participation agreements to the funds. Gerber began to make contributions on behalf of the three drivers; he did not tell the plans that he employed additional drivers and other workers.

In June 1981 Gerber incorporated Gerber Truck Service, Inc., which assumed Gerber's obligations. Gerber Truck grew but continued to make contributions only on behalf of the Fat's Three. In August 1982 Gerber Truck informed Local 50 that it would not sign another collective bargaining agreement, but it did not send the union a written notice of withdrawal, and it continued making pension and welfare payments on behalf of the Fat's Three. One of the Three retired in September 1983, a second in August 1984. The third resigned from the union in April 1984, apparently because someone at Local 50 called his wife a bad name. Gerber Truck sent the funds a notice of termination and stopped paying.

This caught the attention of the plans, which audited Gerber Truck's books. The plans discovered that Gerber Truck had drivers in addition to the Fat's Three and workers with other duties, a total of 18 additional employees apparently covered by the collective bargaining agreement. They opened pension and welfare accounts on behalf of the other employees, giving them credit for covered employment; the plans also demanded that Gerber Truck make contributions on behalf of these employees from February 1, 1981, when Gerber signed the documents, through March 31, 1985, the first contract anniversary after the written notice of cancellation. Gerber Truck refused, and this litigation followed.

After finding that Gerber and Gonzales agreed that the written documents would be enforced only with respect to the Fat's Three, and then only to the extent they promised pension and welfare coverage—and that this oral restriction had been honored—the district court concluded that the pension and welfare trusts acquired no more than what Gerber and Gonzales had negotiated. The court ordered Gerber Truck to make full payments on behalf of the Fat's Three but otherwise rejected the plans' claims.

II

The pension and welfare plans are not parties to the collective bargaining and participation agreements. Third party beneficiaries usually take contracts as they find them. They get no more than the signatories provided, and if there is a flaw in the formation of the contract the third party beneficiaries get nothing. See Restatement (Second) of Contracts § 309(1) (1981), stating that a voidable contract may not be enforced by the intended beneficiary, and § 309(3), stating that if the contract was properly formed "the right of any beneficiary against the promisor is not subject to the promisor's claims or defenses against the promisee."

Multiemployer pension and welfare plans would be in a bind if this familiar rule applied, so that flaws in the formation cut off third party claims. Plans rely on documents to determine the income they can expect to receive, which governs their determination of levels of benefits.

Multiemployer plans are defined contribution in, defined benefit out. Once they promise a level of benefits to employees, they must pay even if the contributions they expected to receive do not materialize—perhaps because employers go broke, perhaps because they are deadbeats, perhaps because they have a defense to the formation of the contract. If some employers do not pay, others must make up the difference in higher contributions, or the workers will receive less than was promised. Lynch, 836 F.2d at 333. Costs of tracking down reneging employers and litigating also come out of money available to pay benefits. The more complex the litigation, the more the plan must spend. Litigation involving conversations between employers and local union officials—conversations to which plans are not privy—may be especially costly, and hold out especially great prospects of coming away empty-handed. How is a pension fund to overcome a jointly advanced claim that there were oral exceptions to the documents?

Costs of this nature would not be large in an industry populated by a few mammoth firms, for then the funds could participate in the formation of the contracts and observe their performance. Many industries with multiemployer plans, including trucking, construction, and mining, are characterized by thousands of small firms, however. Multiemployer plans cover hundreds of local unions.

Our pattern must be common: An employer wants some of its employees to have pension and health benefits, and others not. Some may be only a few years away from vesting. Pension and welfare trusts, like insurers generally, want to avoid "adverse selection," the dropout of persons safer or younger than the pool's average. Funds insist that members of a group be in or out as a bloc: the fund cannot cover the old and infirm at a rate computed from group averages while receiving nothing on behalf of younger employees. Employers often strongly wish it were otherwise. Local unions may not care about selective inclusion in pension plans (since the costs are borne by employers in other parts of the country), and from their perspective having some workers covered is better than having none. So the local and the employer sign a collective bargaining agreement and send it to the pension and welfare trusts. Seeing documents apparently in order, the plans accept the tendered contributions. Later the plans discover the partial payment and try to recover the balance. The employer resists on the ground that it did not "really" agree to do what the documents say. Or the employer may say that the local union induced its signature by fraud, or did not keep its part of the bargain, or was not authorized to represent the employees, or a dozen other lines of defense.

Early in the history of multiemployer pension and welfare plans, the Supreme Court established that breach by the union would not relieve the employer of its obligation to make pension contributions. Lewis v.

Benedict Coal Corp., 361 U.S. 459, 469–71 (1960). The Court observed that the trusts have independent obligations to workers, and that if one employer drops out on account of a union's misconduct (in *Benedict*, a strike), other employers must make up the difference, or the funds will default. *Lewis* did not address defenses to the formation of the contract, however, and employers continued to press them, putting plans to high costs of litigation and risk of failing to collect.

Congress added § 515 to ERISA in 1980 to deal with these collection problems. Two cases in particular caught the eye of the sponsors: *Washington Area Carpenters' Welfare Fund v. Overhead Door Co.*, 488 F.Supp. 816 (D.D.C.1980), and *Western Washington Laborers-Employers Health & Security Trust Fund v. McDowell*, 103 L.R.R.M. 2219 (W.D. Wash.1979). Each of the employers signed an agreement common in the construction business, promising to recognize the union and adhere to the collective bargaining agreement as soon as it had hired its complement of employees for the job. "Pre-hire" agreements avoid the need to negotiate separately for each project when the employer assembles a new labor force for each site, sometimes from day-to-day. The Supreme Court held in *NLRB v. Bridge Workers*, 434 U.S. 335 (1978), that pre-hire agreements are valid only if a majority of those ultimately hired wish to be represented by the union. Employers predictably repudiated pre-hire agreements for many construction jobs and refused to make pension and welfare contributions. *Overhead Door* and *McDowell* held that because the union's failure to achieve majority status prevented the pre-hire agreement from coming into force, the employer was relieved of obligations to pension and welfare funds. As the court put it in *Overhead Door*, 488 F. Supp. at 819: "These cases [such as *Lewis*] involved collateral defenses to enforcement of agreements. The defense in the instant case, on the other hand, concerns the validity of the very agreement that sought to establish a contractual relationship between Funds and Overhead." *Overhead Door* drew the same distinction as the Restatement (Second) of Contracts between defenses to formation, which cut off third party beneficiaries' claims, § 309(1), and defenses arising out of the course of performance, which do not, § 309(3).

The multiemployer amendments to ERISA in 1980 were enacted without the usual committee reports. The managers of the legislation made up for part of the omission. The manager in the House stated on the floor:

> Because delinquencies of employers in making required contributions are also a serious problem for many multiemployer plans, we wish to make clear the public policy in this area, which this bill is intended to further. Failure of employers to make promised contributions in a timely fashion imposes a variety of costs on plans. . . .

These costs detract from the ability of plans to formulate or meet funding standards and adversely affect the financial health of plans. Participants and beneficiaries of plans as well as employers who honor their obligation to contribute in a timely fashion bear the heavy cost of delinquencies in the form of lower benefits and higher contribution rates. . . .

Recourse available under current law for collecting delinquent contributions is insufficient and unnecessarily cumbersome and costly. Some simple collection actions brought by plan trustees have been converted into lengthy, costly, and complex litigation concerning claims and defenses unrelated to the employer's promise and the plans' entitlement to the contributions. This should not be the case. Federal pension law must permit trustees of plans to recover delinquent contributions efficaciously, and without regard to issues which might arise under labor-management relations law—other than [Section 302 of the Labor Management Relations Act,] 29 U.S.C. 186. Sound national pension policy demands that employers who enter into agreements providing for pension contributions not be permitted to repudiate their pension promises.

In this regard we endorse judicial decisions such as *Lewis v. Benedict Coal Corp.* . . . Cases such as *Western Washington Laborers-Employers Health and Security Trust Fund v. McDowell* . . . and *Washington Area Carpenters' Welfare Fund, et al. v. Overhead Door Company* . . . are considered to have been incorrectly decided and this legislation is intended to clarify the law in this respect by providing a direct, unambiguous ERISA cause of action to a plan against a delinquent employer.

126 Cong. Rec. 23039 (Rep. Thompson). Senator Williams, the manager in the Senate, read into the record the third and fourth paragraphs of Rep. Thompson's statement, id. at 23288. The first three paragraphs of Rep. Thompson's statement appear verbatim in a Senate committee print explaining the scope and effects of the pending bill. Senate Committee on Labor & Human Resources, S. 1076-The Multiemployer Pension Plan Amendments Act of 1980: Summary and Analysis of Consideration, 96th Cong., 2d Sess. 43–44 (April 1980).

The text of § 515 is adapted to its purpose, making promises enforceable "to the extent not inconsistent with law". If the contract provides for the commission of unlawful acts, it will not be enforced. Kaiser Steel Corp. v. Mullins, 455 U.S. 72, 86–88 (1982). If the employer simply points to a defect in its formation—such as fraud in the inducement, oral promises to disregard the text, or the lack of majority support for the union and the consequent ineffectiveness of the pact under labor law—it must still keep its promise to the pension plans.

Anything less may well saddle the plans with unfunded obligations. The pension and welfare trusts involved in this case gave all of Gerber Truck's employees credit for years of service, even though Gerber Truck paid only for the Fat's Three. Pension plans believe that their obligations to employees stem from the terms of the participation agreements, and that employers' failure to fulfill their promises is irrelevant. * * *

Whether or not the plans are obligated to Gerber Truck's workers, nothing in ERISA makes the obligation to contribute depend on the existence of a valid collective bargaining agreement; the repudiation of cases such as *McDowell* and *Overhead Door* shows the opposite. Section 515 interacts with a provision of the labor laws in a way that strengthens its effects. No employer may agree with a union to contribute to a pension plan without a "written agreement" under § 302(a)(5)(B) of the National Labor Relations Act. 29 U.S.C. § 186(c)(5)(B). This need not be a formal collective bargaining agreement. Local 50 and Gerber signed and sent to the plans a participation agreement, separate from the collective bargaining agreement, in which Gerber promised to contribute on behalf of all of its drivers. Section 302(c)(5)(B) of the Labor Management Relations Act, like ERISA § 515, prevents a court from giving force to oral understandings between union and employer that contradict the writings. So ERISA and the Labor Management Relations Act work together rather than at cross purposes.

Gerber Truck asks us to give § 515 the least possible scope because its arrangement with Local 50 so clearly negated the presence of a collective bargaining agreement. It implies that the pension plans would not bear high costs of litigation if they would recognize the obvious and desist from litigating. Costs always can be held down by accepting defeat in advance. But a legal system in which the Gerbers of the world can avoid their commitments creates opportunities for similar firms. One is obvious: write a broad contract and claim later that it "really" meant something else, if employees do not qualify for benefits. If they qualify, the employer pays; if not, it doesn't. This is strategic behavior, and sifting strategic from ingenuous conduct through the tools of litigation will be difficult (and time consuming, and expensive, and error-prone). Defenses based on fraud in the inducement, oral side agreement, course of performance, want of consideration, failure of the union to have majority support—the sort of defenses Gerber Truck's position would make available—are as a class the defenses *most* likely to breed litigation even when asserted in good faith, and they create manifold opportunities for manipulation by crafty operators.

Administrative problems and litigation costs, although stressed in the legislative history, are not the only effects plans fear. Gerber and Gonzales tried to arrange things so that Gerber would not need to make contributions on behalf of employees who did not expect to receive benefits. Gerber would support the expectations of two employees close to retirement but introduce no young employees into the plans. Yet pension and welfare plans are insurance vehicles. Insurers *depend* on receiving contributions from persons who collect far in the future or not at all.

Collective bargaining agreements may call for, say, an annual contribution of $2000 on behalf of each employee for medical coverage.[2] The trust pays only if the employee needs care. Older employees need more care, on average. If employers can put only their oldsters, or those who actually need hospitalization, into the plan, the assumptions do not hold. A retirement plan is the same. A defined benefit plan promises a specified benefit at retirement age after, say, ten years of work. Computations underlying such a plan include two important assumptions: (a) many persons who work in the industry, and have contributions made on their behalf, will never collect because they do not satisfy the vesting rule (they may quit or die before doing so); (b) many persons who qualify for pensions will work more than ten years.[e] These two categories of workers fatten the pot and support the benefit levels. Gerber was trying to have only those who will qualify for pensions contribute to the fund. Yet without contributions on behalf of others, the plan's assumptions are unsound.

In a defined contribution plan, no other employee (or employer) loses anything if a firm such as Gerber Truck neglects to pay. It is easy to match the payments in and the payments out, to say that those who will not receive anything need not pay in. For a defined benefit plan, however, there is no such matching. The scheme works only if the plan receives contributions on behalf of persons who will not get benefits.[3] These characteristics of multiemployer defined benefit plans may well account for the unwillingness of other circuits to allow an employer to achieve partial coverage of its work force, as Gerber Truck frankly wants to do.

Nothing depends on proof that a given plan will be unable to satisfy its obligations if a given employer avoids payment. Actuarial computations are the *reason* plans want to include or exclude bargaining

---

[2]   The participation agreement Gerber signed required it to pay $51.00 per week per employee to the pension fund and $39.50 per week per employee to the health and welfare fund starting April 1, 1981, a total of $4525 per employee per 50 week year. (The weekly contributions before April 1 were slightly lower.) Contributions did not depend on the age or health of the employees.

[e]   At the time, multi-employer plans were permitted to have a ten-year cliff vesting schedule.—Ed.

[3]   The nature of multiemployer plans makes the problem worse. A single employer defined benefit plan has a claim on all of the employer's assets to make good the promised benefits. A multiemployer plan is a defined contribution plan from the employer's perspective (the employer promises to pay so much per week per employee) even though it is a defined benefit plan from the worker's perspective (the plan promises to pay so much per year's employment, whether or not employers as a group contribute enough to make good the promise). The employer, seeing the disjunction between the nature of its promise and the nature of the plans' promise, tries to scrimp on contributions.

units as groups, but this reason is the basis of a rule. A life insurance company may offer a plan for nonsmokers only, computing its rates on the basis of actuarial tables applying to nonsmokers. If a smoker should lie about his habit and enroll in the plan, a court could not permit him to stay—or to require the insurer to pay up—simply because he died in a plane crash rather than from lung cancer, or because payment of his claim would not bankrupt the plan. He would be booted out (or, if he had died, the insurer would be excused from payment) on the ground that he did not meet a contractual requirement of admission. Just *why* the insurer imposed this requirement would not be the measure of its entitlement to enforce its rules. So too with pension and welfare trusts. No matter why the plans have a rule of all-in-or-all-out, they have it, and an employer must play by the rules.

We recognize that the upshot may be harsh. Had Gerber known that Gonzales could not keep his pledge to withhold enforcement, he would not have signed; the cost of covering the Fat's Three would have been too steep. Section 515 does not admit of such an equitable defense; there is a wide gap between an "inequitable" result and an "illegal" one. More, Gerber's position is not all that "equitable." Gerber signed documents promising to make contributions on behalf of all bargaining unit employees (in the collective bargaining agreement) and all "drivers" (in the participation agreement). He knew when he signed that he did not plan to live up to his commitment. Gerber Truck's defense is essentially that if the employer signs with its fingers crossed behind its back, it does not "really" agree to remit, and what it doesn't agree to do it needn't.

If Gerber and Local 50 had approached the pension and welfare trusts and said: "We want to continue the benefits for the Fat's Three, without making contributions on behalf of the current employees of Gerber," the funds would have replied "No."[4] It would be a poor rule that allowed persons to do in secrecy what they could not do openly. Gerber and Gonzales sent the plans two documents containing promises neither intended to honor. The district court allowed the stratagem to succeed *precisely because it was a sham*—because it did not even amount to a collective bargaining agreement. Gerber doubtless acted with the interest of his three older employees at heart. But the employer's wish to set the terms on which he will deal with a pension trust is not a self-fulfilling prophesy.

---

[4]   Whether it would have been impossible to accomplish the arrangement some other way is a tougher question. Perhaps Gerber could have formed a subsidiary and placed the former Fat's employees in it, then negotiated a collective bargaining agreement on behalf of the subsidiary. It is hard to say whether such an arrangement could have succeeded. Using their power under Article IV § 9 of the Pension Fund Trust Agreement, the trustees have declined to "split" bargaining units to allow partial coverage. The Fat's Three might not have been doing distinctive work, preventing Gerber from handling their business as a subsidiary while observing corporate forms, or the National Labor Relations Board might have ruled that they were not a logical collective bargaining unit.

The district court did not address the question whether the reference to "drivers" in the participation agreement establishes the measure of the plans' entitlements, or whether instead the plans could collect contributions on behalf of the larger class of employees mentioned in the collective bargaining agreement. That question is open on remand.

III

The district court held not only that Gerber Truck's obligations were limited to the Fat's Three but also that even with respect to them—and presumably with respect to any others—Gerber Truck's undertaking ended in 1982 when it told Local 50 that it would not sign a new collective bargaining agreement. Both the collective bargaining agreement and the participation agreement permit a party to terminate; both, however, require the notice to be in writing and provide that in the absence of such notice the agreement is automatically extended from year to year. Gerber's statement that he would not sign another agreement, even if taken as a notice of termination of the existing agreement (dubious at best), is ineffectual because not in writing.

The first writing came in May 1984, when Gerber sent the funds a letter stating that because the last of the Fat's Three had resigned from the union, Gerber Truck would make no further contributions. This writing did not purport to cancel the collective bargaining agreement, however, and so it too was ineffectual. In November 1984 Gerber Truck finally gave a notice that complied with the collective bargaining and participation agreements. These provide that cancellation takes effect on an anniversary date, in this case March 31, 1985. Gerber Truck therefore had to contribute to the pension and welfare funds, under the terms of the participation agreement, through the end of March 1985.

One final issue wraps up the case. The plans sought liquidated damages and attorneys' fees on the authority of § 502(g)(2) of ERISA. Although the district court awarded the plans their attorneys' fees, it declined to impose liquidated damages or other penalties because it found that there was a legitimate dispute about the extent of Gerber Truck's obligations. This is not the legal standard established by § 502(g)(2), however. * * * Liquidated damages compensate the plans for delay and give employers an incentive to be forthcoming with payments. The structure of the multiemployer amendments of 1980, of which § 502(g)(2) is a part, is pay-now-argue-later. Even on the district court's view of the case, the pension and welfare trusts were prevailing parties. The district court must add the penalties provided by § 502(g)(2) to whatever sums it ultimately awards to the plans as past due contributions.

The judgment is reversed, and the case is remanded for further proceedings in accordance with this opinion.

CUDAHY, CIRCUIT JUDGE, with whom WOOD, JR., CIRCUIT JUDGE joins, concurring in part and dissenting in part:

The majority opinion is long on legal, economic and actuarial theory and short on facts and a sense of proportion. This case was originally heard by a unanimous panel that required Mr. Gerber to make contributions through the end of March 31, 1985, and to pay liquidated damages and attorneys' fees (as reiterated in Part II of the majority en banc opinion), but confined the required contributions to those on behalf of the "Fat's Three." The panel, however, required Gerber, in order to escape the broader liability now imposed by the en banc court, to prove to the district court that "no employee (other than the Fat's Three) has a colorable potential claim to benefits from the [pension and welfare] Funds and that no employee has ever had a reasonable basis for believing himself entitled to make such a claim." Only if Gerber could make such a difficult and demanding showing, would the panel relieve him of the broader obligations purportedly owed on behalf of the other employees pursuant to the written documents. I rely principally on the panel opinion, 854 F.2d 1074 (7th Cir.1988), as furnishing an alternative—and fairer—solution of this difficult problem. I note that the conditions imposed by the panel opinion are so rigorous and virtually impossible of fulfillment in the general case that it is hardly a precedent for the chicanery the majority purports to foresee.

This case is quite atypical, however. Gerber was a truck driver who acquired Fat's trucking business as a sole proprietor and with it the Fat's Three. Fat's had been a party to the 1979–1982 National Freight Agreement, which, among other things, entitled the Fat's Three, who were members of Teamsters' Local 50, to employer paid health and pension benefits administered by the plaintiff funds. Gerber had no intention of conducting a unionized operation but apparently generously sought to continue pension and health benefits for the Fat's Three (two of whom were approaching retirement age). Gonzales, the union business agent, testified that neither party intended anything but benefits specifically for the Fat's Three. There is no evidence in the record that anyone, including any Gerber employee, had any other understanding.

ERISA does not repeal basic contract law. What was intended and agreed to was not a collective bargaining agreement since it did not give the parties or any employees who knew about it any rights beyond the specific, limited benefits to the Fat's Three. This, of course, does not mean that Gerber did not have problems with the Funds based on ERISA and the written documents which he ill-advisedly signed—on a sort of estoppel principle—but it is simply incorrect to say that the "contract" amounted to anything more than what *both* parties unequivocally intended and to what they testified. In this respect, this case is different than any other I have seen. Typically, in these cases, an employer signs a broad agreement (which is unarguably a "collective bargaining" agreement), the union hopes he will perform and the employer later cuts corners, with or without the union's tacit consent. Here the intention of both union and employer was clear from the very start. The employer reinforced their understanding by securing health insurance for his other employees from another source. The implication of the majority that Gerber acted with sinister motives or possibly engaged in "strategic behavior" is preposterous. Gerber was a truck driver, unassisted by lawyers and accountants, who apparently sought nothing more sinister than to keep in force the pensions of three older employees who came to him from a failed firm. He may have erred in attempting to accomplish this by using the National Master Freight Agreement form, but the district court did not find, nor does the record disclose, that he was attempting to cheat or mislead anyone. And the majority opinion is totally off base in its charge that Gerber failed to "live up to his commitment." In the view of the union and of Gerber's employees, as well as of Gerber himself, his only commitment at any time was to the Fat's Three.

The majority opinion fails to clarify one very puzzling aspect of the written documents. The majority notes the rather broad description of job categories covered by the Master Agreement ("all truck drivers, helpers, dockmen, warehousemen, checkers . . . and such other employees as may be presently or hereafter represented by the Union"). It also notes the much more limited description contained in the Participation Agreement ("DRIVERS represented by the Union"). The latter description was specifically intended to describe the Fat's Three. And it literally does describe them since the union never purported to represent any other drivers. If the district court so finds on remand, the en banc rehearing may result in a nullity. In any event, this discrepancy in description, although patent on the face of the documents, was never noted or questioned by the Funds, whose reliance on documents we are told is so crucial.

I take no issue with the broad purposes of ERISA as described in the majority opinion nor in the need to achieve a match between the contributions to, and the liabilities of, pension and welfare funds. Judge Easterbrook's excellent opinion in *Robbins v. Lynch*, 836 F.2d 330 (7th Cir.1988), was cited and quoted at length in the original panel opinion as an authoritative statement of general principles. But all rules must admit of equitable exception and modification in appropriate cases lest the tyranny of theory over reality bring about obnoxious results. Whatever asymmetries there may be in the funding of pension and welfare plans, it was likely that under the *panel* opinion, where Gerber had to make contributions plus liquidated damages through March 1985, the Plans were more than fully funded with respect to their liabilities for the Fat's Three. To require contributions for all the other employees, who have no corresponding claim for any benefits, is to present the Funds with a fat windfall. Gerber bought health insurance for his other employees from another source which presumably has already covered their health needs. And these other employees can hardly claim pensions they knew neither Gerber nor the union intended to provide them.

Of course, in 99% of the cases it is necessary to enforce the written pension or welfare contribution requirements in order to avoid backsliding by employers—possibly abetted by unions. But here is a case where a minuscule employer's effort to help three superannuated truck drivers has brought down on his head the full fury of a rule that knows no exceptions. A Gerber with his handful of trucks is no match for adversaries with platoons of accountants, actuaries and lawyers out to maximize his liabilities (in a good cause, no doubt). Yet, it seems to me that the Gerbers of the world (as the majority refers to them), starting to build a business beginning with their own single truck, deserve some consideration in preserving a common sense balance.

I respectfully dissent.

CENTRAL STATES, SOUTHEAST AND SOUTHWEST AREAS PENSION FUND v. INDEPENDENT FRUIT AND PRODUCE CO.

United States Court of Appeals, Eighth Circuit, 1990.
919 F.2d 1343.

BEAM, CIRCUIT JUDGE.

In this consolidated appeal, Central States, Southeast and Southwest Areas Pension Fund (Central States) appeals from judgments entered in favor of defendants-employers. Pursuant to sections 502 and 515 of the Employee Retirement Income Security Act, Central States brought separate actions against more than twenty independent produce wholesalers to collect delinquent pension contributions. Central States contended that the produce companies failed to make pension contributions on behalf of certain employees as required by the governing collective bargaining agreements. Central States argued that these employees, whose questionable status was discovered in an audit, were regular employees for whom contributions were due. The employers, however, classified these employees as "casuals" for whom contributions were not required by the collective bargaining agreements. The district court found that the collective bargaining agreements were ambiguous and looked to the intent and past practice of the parties to define "casual employee." The district court held that a "casual employee" is not necessarily a person who works only intermittently or sporadically, as Central States thought, but, instead, includes those employees so designated by the employer, with the consent of the union, regardless of their work schedules. Accordingly, the district court found no contributions owing and entered judgment for defendants. We reverse.

I.   BACKGROUND

Due to their physical proximity on several city blocks in St. Louis, the defendants-employers in these cases, members of the St. Louis Fruit and Produce Association, are collectively known as Produce Row. Most are independently owned, family-run companies, wholesaling fresh fruits and vegetables to small, independent grocers. Central States is an employee benefit fund as defined by ERISA. Central States, which is headquartered in Chicago, receives more than 5,000 collective bargaining agreements for review each year, covering more than 250,000 active participants and 125,000 retired participants. In this case, contributions to the pension fund are governed by collective bargaining agreements negotiated by the employers and Local 688 of the International Brotherhood of Teamsters, Chauffeurs, Warehousemen and Helpers of America.

The collective bargaining agreements at issue cover the years 1973 through 1988 and are dated 1973, 1976, 1979, 1982 and 1985. Because they contain similar provisions on casual employees, the agreements dated before 1982 can be conveniently considered together. The pre-1982 agreements provide in Article IX that casual employees are to be hired subject to need, that their hiring cannot increase "the normal then existing number of working employees," that casuals cannot work more than eighty hours per month, and that casuals are to be used as replacements for regular employees. Article IX was renegotiated in 1982 so that many of these restrictions on the use of casuals were eliminated. Generally, however, all relevant agreements provide that casual employees receive neither fringe benefits nor seniority. At issue is not whether casuals are entitled to benefits, but, rather, which employees are casuals.

The dispute over the meaning of "casual employee" arose from a random audit in October 1983 of Lamperson Fruit and Produce Company. As a result of the audit, which covered September 28, 1980, to September 24, 1983, Central States claimed that Lamperson owed $73,034 for " 'non-reporting of eligible Plan Participants.' " In its audit, Central States discovered employees who worked more or less full-time during the audit period but whom Lamperson classified as casuals. Because it understood casuals to be employees who worked only sporadically or intermittently as needed, Central States contended that these employees were regulars for whom contributions were due. In the resulting action to collect delinquent contributions, Central States requested audits of the Produce Row employers.

On January 16, 1985, the Chief Judge of the Eastern District of Missouri designated the case against Friedmeyer-Sellmeyer Distributing

Company as "the most suitable case to try, brief and decide as a guide in the ultimate trying, briefing and decision in all of the above cases." On January 12, 1987, the district court ordered defendant Friedmeyer-Sellmeyer to submit to an audit of its personnel records from December 28, 1980, to December 31, 1983.The audit was later expanded to cover the years 1979 to 1986. It revealed seven employees who worked essentially full-time for some if not all of the audit period. "[T]he audit report . . . revealed that six of the seven employees included in the report worked virtually every week for over one year and one of these individuals worked all but two weeks during a period of nearly six years." William Kauck, who conducted the audit of Friedmeyer-Sellmeyer, testified that the audit revealed "an inordinate use of what the employer was calling 'casual employees.'" As a result of the audit, Central States claimed that Friedmeyer-Sellmeyer owed $24,774 in delinquent contributions.

At the bench trial, Friedmeyer-Sellmeyer contended that its use of casual employees was consistent with the collective bargaining agreements, that no dispute or misunderstanding about casuals existed between the employer and the union, that none of the casuals were confused about their status as casuals, and that the only party complaining was Central States. The evidence established that it was standard practice for the Produce Row employers to initially hire all employees as casuals, some of whom might later become regulars upon a vacancy. Several witnesses testified that the casuals knew of their status when hired, and that no one "other than Central States ever questioned which employees were casuals versus regulars." Casuals were casuals merely because they were hired as casuals and because they received no benefits.

The evidence is also clear, however, that casuals did the same work as regulars and in some cases worked as many hours as regulars. The testimony of Douglas Brand, the secretary-treasurer of United Fruit and Produce Company, is typical:

Q: Do they have the same hours at work?
A: They may.
Q: They work full-time?
A: They may.
Q: Any difference in the hours of a casual or regular?
A: Not that I know of.

Central States argued to the district court that these facts proved its case: that given the standard meaning of "casual employee"—someone who works sporadically or intermittently as needed—used in the collective bargaining agreement, those employees denominated casuals who worked as many hours as regular employees for a year or more were in fact regular employees.

The district court disagreed with Central States that the term "casual employee" in the collective bargaining agreement meant only those employees who worked sporadically or intermittently. Rather, the district court found the contract term to be ambiguous, and, after examining past hiring practices on Produce Row, held that the collective bargaining agreements had not been violated. "Quite simply, the Produce Row employers acted exactly as they agreed—they contributed to the pension fund on behalf of regular employees, but not on behalf of casual employees." Central States, Southeast & Southwest Areas Pension Fund v. N.E. Friedmeyer-Sellmeyer Distrib. Co., No. 84–1669 C (5), slip op. at 10 (E.D. Mo. April 28, 1989). In essence, the district court held that by "casual employee" the collective bargaining agreement meant whomever the employer so designated. This appeal concerns the correctness of that decision in the context of ERISA.

II. DISCUSSION

Central States brought these actions pursuant to section 515 of ERISA, which provides that:

> Every employer who is obligated to make contributions to a multiemployer plan under the terms of the plan or under the terms of a collectively bargained agreement shall, to the extent not inconsistent with law, make such contributions in accordance with the terms and conditions of such plan or such agreement.

It is clear that this section "creates a federal right of action independent of the contract on which the duty to contribute is based." Bituminous Coal Operators' Ass'n v. Connors, 867 F.2d 625, 633 (D.C. Cir.1989). It is equally clear that Congress intended that this section would simplify actions to collect delinquent contributions, avoid costly litigation, and enhance the actuarial planning necessary to the administration of multiemployer pension plans. See, e.g., Central States, Southeast & Southwest Areas Pension Fund v. Gerber Truck Serv., Inc., 870 F.2d 1148, 1152 (7th Cir.1989).

Prior to the enactment of section 515 in 1980, collection actions brought by plan trustees were often converted into complex and costly litigation involving various contract formation defenses. Collection actions result in lower benefits and higher contribution rates not only because of this cost, but also because any shortfalls in contributions skew the pension fund's actuarial planning.

The actuarial calculations that produce the contribution and payout systems are based on the supposition that the funds will receive full contributions on behalf of all employees covered. If a local union and an employer try to shrink the duty to contribute without notice to the funds and a contraction of the funds' obligations, the fund may end up paying benefits without corresponding contributions.

Robbins v. Lynch, 836 F.2d 330, 333 (7th Cir.1988).[3] Central States claims, for precisely these reasons, that it would not have accepted the plans from Produce Row for participation had it known of the employers' definition of "casual employee." "Because of the actuarial detriment inherent in arrangements that limit contributions to only those employees that are likely to receive benefits, the Pension Fund prohibits the participation of employers who split the bargaining unit for the purpose of pension coverage." Brief for Appellant at 26.[4]

Section 515 deals with these concerns by placing a pension fund in a better position than that which it would otherwise occupy in relation to the collective bargaining agreement. Because a pension fund is not a party to the collective bargaining agreement, it would normally be a third party beneficiary of it. As a third party beneficiary, however, the pension fund would be subject to "any contract defense which the promisor could assert against the promisee if the promisee were suing on the contract." Southwest Adm'rs, Inc. v. Rozay's Transfer, 791 F.2d 769, 773 (9th Cir. 1986). It is these contract defenses—for example, fraud in the inducement, oral side agreements or course of performance—that are most likely to breed litigation. Gerber, 870 F.2d at 1154. As a result, the courts find that section 515 places the pension fund in a better position, analogous to that of a holder in due course or a receiver of a failed bank— "entitled to enforce the writing without regard to understandings or defenses applicable to the original parties." Id. at 1149. "If it means nothing else, section 515 means that ... suit [by a trustee] cannot be thwarted by defenses not apparent from the face of the Agreement." Connors, 867 F.2d at 634. The courts of appeals have been unanimous in so holding. In sum, the courts recognize only two defenses to a collection

---

[3]   The importance of this rationale does not depend on whether any of those employees whom Central States regards as regulars, but whom the employers regard as casuals, actually files a claim against Central States for benefits. "[P]ension and welfare plans are insurance vehicles. Insurers *depend* on receiving contributions from persons who collect far in the future or not at all." Gerber, 870 F.2d at 1154. What matters is not whether the employees at issue ever attempt to collect, but that without contributions from those whom Central States claims are regulars according to the terms of the collective bargaining agreement, its actuarial assumptions are unsound. See id.

[4]   Casuals were not union members until 1982. Indeed, casuals were distinguishable from union employees in part because they did not wear union buttons. Nevertheless, the parties seemed to agree at oral argument that casuals were part of the bargaining unit and that the union acquiesced in their exclusion from pension benefits. The district court rejected any argument based on splitting the bargaining unit, and no such argument has been made on appeal.

action: that the pension contributions are themselves illegal or that the collective bargaining agreement is void.

Through section 515, Congress has decided that a pension fund is entitled to "assume that all participants in a plan are following *the stated terms;* no other approach permits accurate actuarial computations and proper decisions about which claims to pay." Robbins, 836 F.2d at 333 (emphasis added). Thus, whether the employer and union agree in this case that they knew what they meant by "casual employee" is irrelevant if the written agreement unambiguously expresses something other than what they intended. Absent ambiguity in the written agreement, the claims of the Produce Row employers are little different from a side agreement made with the union not to disclose their true intention to the pension plan. Absent ambiguity, it is clear that the employers in this case do not assert a defense apparent from the face of the agreements.

The district court considered the provisions of four collective bargaining agreements, from 1973, 1976, 1979 and 1982. Because the three agreements prior to the 1982 agreement contain similar provisions pertaining to casual employees, the district court referred only to the 1979 and the 1982 agreements. Casual employees are covered in Article IX of the 1979 agreement, which provides:

> Employer may hire, subject to need, persons who will be known as "casual employees (casuals)." Such casuals may be used as follows and subject to the conditions listed:
>
> 1. Casuals may be hired where the normal then existing number of working employees is not thereby increased.
>
> 2. Notwithstanding the limitation in paragraph 1 above, casuals may be hired to work a cumulative maximum of eighty (80) hours during any calendar month for purposes of overflow work.
>
>   . . . .
>
> 4. Fringe benefits shall not be paid on account of casuals . . . and no seniority shall be acquired by such casuals.
>
>   . . . .
>
> 6. Casuals may be used to replace regular employees who are absent for any reason . . . provided, however, casuals will be used to fill vacancies on the shift where the vacancy occurs or exists.

Article IX was changed in the 1982 collective bargaining agreement by eliminating several of the restrictions on the use of casual employees. It still provides that "the Employer may hire, subject to need, persons who will be known as 'casual employees' (casuals)." Similarly, it still provides that casual employees are not entitled to fringe benefits, although it does provide for a separate seniority list for casuals. The provisions restricting hours and hiring such that the "normal then existing number of working employees" is not thereby increased, however, are absent.

Without reference to these differences between the pre-1982 and 1982 agreements, the district court found that "casual employees are specifically defined in the CBAs." Despite its reference to the specific definition, however, the district court found that "[t]he use of the term 'casual employee' in these agreements creates an ambiguity that requires the Court to apply . . . rules of construction." We disagree that any of the agreements are ambiguous.

As with any contract, whether a collective bargaining agreement is ambiguous is a question of law subject to de novo review. The law is clearly established in this circuit that a contract is ambiguous only if it is reasonably susceptible of more than one construction. In ascertaining whether a contract is reasonably susceptible of more than one construction, words are to be given their plain and ordinary meaning as understood by a reasonable, average person. Recourse to the ordinary, dictionary definition of words is not only reasonable, but may be necessary.

Given that the provisions on casual employees in the pre-1982 agreements differ from those in the 1982 agreement, we must consider the agreements separately. Beginning with the pre-1982 agreements, we find no ambiguity. The dictionary contains a standard definition of "casual employment."

> Employment at uncertain or irregular times. Employment for short time and limited and temporary purpose. Occasional, irregular or incidental employment. Such employee does not normally receive seniority rights nor does he normally receive fringe benefits.

Black's Law Dictionary 198 (5th ed. 1979). The auditors for Central States who testified before the district court said that their understanding of "casual employee" was consistent with this definition. Joel Ahrens testified that "[w]e have an understanding or we use an assumption, I guess you would call it, for casual employees, we assume that a casual employee is not an employee who is going to work with any great regularity." Trial Transcript, Vol. 1, at 52–58. William Kauck also testified that he had a general understanding that a "casual employee" worked on a sporadic or infrequent basis, and that his understanding was consistent with the Central States field audit manual. Id. at 147–48. Ahrens further testified that Central States had a general understanding of "casual," id. at 64, and contrasted the employers' use of "casual" with a contract provision providing that people labeled "blue hats" would not receive pension benefits but all other employees would. Ahrens said that in that instance, "[w]e would want to know what a 'blue hat' is. I don't know what a 'blue hat' is." Id. at 63. By implication, Ahrens suggested that if the employers meant by "casual employee" something other than its dictionary definition—indeed, something contrary to its dictionary definition—they could have said so. Central States merely presumed that "casual employee" was used consistently with its dictionary definition.

The record makes clear that Central States thought it knew what the employers meant by "casual employee" because of that term's common meaning. It is also clear that Central States thought the restrictive provisions dealing with casuals contained in the pre-1982 agreements confirmed its understanding. * * * Contrary to the assertion of the employers that "casual employee" is not defined in any of the agreements but is merely subject to various conditions, we think that these conditions help to define the term and do so consistently with the dictionary definition. From the face of the written documents, the pre-1982 agreements are not ambiguous.

It is also clear from the record before the district court that the hiring practices of Produce Row employers did not conform to this unambiguous definition in the pre-1982 agreements. As indicated, several witnesses for the employers testified that it was standard practice to hire all employees as casuals; only some would later become regulars. As for the restrictions in the pre-1982 agreements, the witnesses testified that the agreements were simply ignored. * * *

In essence, the employers argue that "casual employee" means anyone so intended by the employer and the union, even if contrary to the plain meaning of "casual employee" in the written agreement. In *TKO Equipment Co. v. C & G Coal Co.,* 863 F.2d 541 (7th Cir.1988), the Seventh Circuit considered a situation in which a security agreement was written as a lease but contended by the parties to be a sale. The court held that if the parties meant for their agreement to be a sale, they should have said so.

> If [the parties] wish the symbols "one Caterpillar D9G tractor" to mean "500 railroad cars full of watermelons," that's fine—provided parties share this weird meaning. A meaning held by one party only may not be invoked to change the ordinary denotation of a word, however. Intent must be mutual to be effective; unilateral intent does not count. Still less may the parties announce that they "share" an unusual meaning to the detriment of strangers, who have no way of finding out what was in the contracting parties' heads.

Id. at 545 (citation omitted). The employers in this case argue the contrary, that Central States is merely attempting to ascribe to "casual employee" its own meaning, not the meaning intended by the union and the employers, and that Central States cannot do this. "Central States does not have the right to pull up a chair to the bargaining table, long after the bargain has been struck, and tell the employer that the agreement he signed years ago means something other than that which the employer and union intended." Brief for Appellee at 23. Section 515, however, requires that what the parties to the bargaining agreement intended must be made clear from its face.

That intention was not clear in this case, and the testimony at trial confirms that the employers knew both that the meaning they attached to "casual employee" in the written agreements was unusual, and that Central States could not ascertain their meaning from the documents.

* * *

Clearly, the union and the employers attached to "casual employee" a meaning different from its plain meaning and yet did not tell Central States of their intention. For purposes of ERISA, such conduct is no different from when parties orally agree to ignore the unambiguous terms of a written agreement. As indicated, section 515 was intended to preclude such a defense. Gerber, 870 F.2d at 1153. Whatever their intent, given an unambiguous agreement, the parties must follow its terms when dealing with the pension plan.

III. CONCLUSION

The employers in this case argue that the agreements at issue were ambiguous, but not because of any misunderstanding between the parties to the contract. Given the purpose of written contracts and section 515 of ERISA, the parties to a collective bargaining agreement are bound by the terms of their agreement, regardless of their undisclosed intent. By so holding, we merely reaffirm a basic rule of contract interpretation. "A signatory to a contract is bound by its ordinary meaning even if he gave it an idiosyncratic one; private intent counts only if it is conveyed to the other party and shared." Robbins, 836 F.2d at 332. Section 515 of ERISA emphasizes that this is especially true as to third parties obligated to administer a pension fund according to the terms of written agreements. The judgment of the district court is reversed and this matter is remanded for proceedings consistent with this opinion. Given our decision on the merits, the judgment of the district court denying the employers' request for attorneys' fees is affirmed.

Central States Southeast and Southwest Areas Pension Fund, Special Bulletin 90–7

This bulletin has been issued to emphasize the Board of Trustees' long standing policy which prohibits the Pension Fund from participating in collective bargaining arrangements which encourage "adverse selection" and are, therefore, actuarially unsound.

When establishing the contribution rate necessary to support a benefit level, the Trustees rely upon cost estimates of actuaries who assume that all employees of an employer in the same work classification will participate equally in the Pension Fund. However, if in practice the collective bargaining arrangement restricts pension coverage to only those employees likely to receive a benefit and excludes those employees less likely to receive a benefit, then the contribution rate is insufficient to support the benefit level. To protect the financial soundness of the Pension Fund, the Trustees must avoid this type of "adverse selection." Therefore the Trustees will terminate continued participation and reject collective bargaining arrangements which in practice result in adverse selection.

Although not exhaustive, the following examples illustrate actuarially unsound arrangements which may result in contract rejection or termination of continued participation:

1. The collective bargaining agreement covers all of the employees who perform the same type of work (such as drivers), but does not require that contributions be made equally on all of the employees. Such unequal treatment may take the form of:

    (a) some employees participate in the Pension Fund while others do not; or

    (b) all employees participate in the Pension Fund, but at different contribution rates.

2. The collective bargaining agreement requires contributions to the Pension Fund on behalf of all employees, but the agreement in practice does not cover all employees of the employer who perform the same type of work. For example, an agreement might be structured to cover only certain specified individuals, instead of a classification of employment. Alternatively, the employer may establish a non-covered bargaining unit, corporate division or corporation which consists of employees who perform the same type of work as the covered bargaining unit but are generally differentiated from the covered employees based upon any of the following characteristics:

    (a) the age of such employees;

    (b) the length of service or seniority of such employees;

    (c) the employment commencement date of such employees;

    (d) the amount of "Credited Service" (as defined in the Pension Plan) of such employees; or

    (e) the likelihood of such employees to meet any of the prerequisites for any benefits defined in the Pension Plan.

3.   The agreement provides reduced or no pension coverage for employees classified as "casual," "part-time" or "temporary," and in practice the employees are actually full-time, long-term employees.

This discussion is not intended to be an all-inclusive list of unacceptable arrangements. Any collective bargaining arrangement that encourages adverse selection is subject to rejection by the Board of Trustees.

NOTES AND QUESTIONS

1.   In *Gerber Truck Services*, Judge Cudahy characterized the majority opinion as "long on legal, economic and actuarial theory, and short on facts and a sense of proportion." Do you agree?

2.   The Eighth Circuit in *Independent Fruit* concluded that the term "casual employee" as used in the collective bargaining agreement was unambiguous. Do you agree? If the collective bargaining agreement had been written so that a "casual employee" was clearly defined in a manner consistent with the employers' practices, how likely is it that the board of trustees of the Teamsters Fund would have accepted the collective bargaining agreement?

3.   *"Involuntary" Employer Withdrawals.* The phrase "withdrawal liability" suggests a voluntary cessation of contributions to the plan by the employer. Under the MPPAA, however, withdrawal liability can be triggered when the trustees refuse to accept further contributions to the multiemployer plan from the employer. The trustees of the multiemployer plan may refuse to accept the employer's contributions because the employer's collective bargaining agreement with the local union permits adverse selection, or because the employer refuses to make additional contributions to the plan after an audit by the trustees has determined that additional employer contributions to the multiemployer plan are required under the terms of the collective bargaining agreement.

4.   *The MPPAA and Multiemployer Welfare Plans.* ERISA Section 515 concerning delinquent employer contributions applies to multiemployer welfare benefit plans (particularly health care plans) as well as multiemployer pension plans. The employer withdrawal liability provisions of the MPPAA, however, apply only to multiemployer pension plans. Consequently, a multiemployer welfare benefit plan cannot assess withdrawal liability against a participating employer unless the employer has expressly agreed to the assessment of withdrawal liability. In this situation, either the collective bargaining agreement or the trust agreement for the welfare benefit plan must clearly define the circumstances that will trigger the employer's withdrawal liability and the method by which the trustees of the multiemployer plan will determine the amount of the employer's withdrawal liability.

I. DISCUSSION QUESTIONS FOR CHAPTER THREE

QUESTION ONE

Should the pension system continue to be voluntary, or should employers be required under federal law to sponsor a retirement plan for all of their workers?

QUESTION TWO

If you were a business owner, would you voluntarily sponsor a pension plan for your workers? If so, what type? What factors would you consider in making this decision?

QUESTION THREE

In his article, *The Defined Contribution Paradigm*, 114 Yale L.J. 451 (2004), Professor Edward Zelinsky argues that one effect of the growth of defined contribution plans (along with other tax-favored individual account mechanisms to promote savings, such as IRAs, health savings accounts, and education savings accounts) is a distribution of the tax expenditure that is disproportionately skewed in favor of middle-and upper-middle-class taxpayers. Safe harbor options for employers who sponsor 401(k) plans further skew the tax expenditure for qualified plans by permitting highly compensated employees to maximize their salary deferral contributions to a safe harbor 401(k) plan. Should Congress amend the safe harbor options for 401(k) plans so that employers are required to provide a larger contribution for nonhighly compensated employees? Why or why not?

QUESTION FOUR

How do the minimum coverage requirements of Code Section 410(b) contribute to the patterns of qualified plan coverage revealed in the data presented in Table 3.1 (Percentage of Private Industry Workers Participating in Employee Retirement Plans) at the beginning of Chapter Three? Would you favor changing the minimum coverage rules of Code Section 410(b)? If so, what changes would you propose? Can you predict the likely impact of your proposal on the current demographic patterns of retirement plan coverage?

QUESTION FIVE

If the social policy objective that underlies the qualified plan system is to promote retirement income security, why does the law permit a qualified plan to: (1) make a lump sum distribution to a terminated employee at any age; (2) make loans to plan participants; (3) allow participants to delay receiving contributions under the required minimum distribution rules; and (4) make payments pursuant to a QDRO? Can each of these exceptions be justified on other tax policy or social policy grounds?

QUESTION SIX

Should the trustees of a multiemployer plan be required to provide a clear and concise explanation to employers concerning the consequences of not fully reporting the number of collective bargaining unit employees for whom employer contributions are due under the terms of the employer's collective bargaining agreement? Of the financial consequences of withdrawal liability under the Multiemployer Pension Plan Amendments Act? Or should employers be deemed to know federal law?

CHAPTER 4

WELFARE BENEFIT PLANS

■ ■ ■

Chapter Four focuses on welfare benefit plans, and in particular health care plans, sponsored by private employers. When ERISA was originally enacted in 1974, unlike the detailed requirements for eligibility, vesting, benefit accrual and funding for employee pension plans, the provisions of Title I did not contain a single substantive requirement regulating the content of employee welfare benefit plans. Rather, welfare benefit plans were subject only to the requirements of Part 1 of Title I concerning reporting and disclosure, the fiduciary duty provisions of Part 4 of Title I, and rules governing claims and the preemption of state laws established in Part 5 of Title I.

In the years following the enactment of ERISA, Congress passed a series of targeted requirements for employer-sponsored group health care plans. In 1980, Congress gave participants in group health care plans the right to continued coverage under group health plans if their coverage otherwise would terminate due to the occurrence of specified events, such as the termination of employment. Between 1996 and 2010, Congress added a series of narrowly tailored requirements for group health care plans. Finally, in 2010 Congress enacted a comprehensive package of reforms aimed at transforming the national health care system pursuant to the Affordable Care Act.

Chapter Four begins by discussing the role of employer-sponsored group health care plans as a component of national health care policy. Section A presents an overview of the national health care insurance system and the reforms enacted by the Affordable Care Act. Section A concludes with a discussion of the significance of welfare benefit plans in the general practice of law. Section B provides an overview of the various types of welfare benefit plans and the federal income tax treatment of different types of welfare benefit plans. Section C explores the distinction between insured health care plans and health care plans that are self-insured by the sponsoring employer. Section D reviews the specific requirements for group health care plans under ERISA and the Affordable Care Act. Section E addresses the amendment or termination of welfare benefit plans. Section F discusses some of the more prominent points of intersection between welfare benefit plans regulated by ERISA and other federal laws. Chapter Four concludes with a discussion of litigation under ERISA concerning the amendment or termination of retiree health care plans.

A. PERSPECTIVES ON WELFARE BENEFIT PLANS

1. THE NATIONAL HEALTH CARE INSURANCE SYSTEM

The national health care insurance system consists of four fundamental components: (1) the federal Medicare program; (2) the federal Medicaid program; (3) health care policies purchased by private individuals; and (4) group health care plans sponsored by employers. For workers under age 65 and their families who are not eligible for Medicaid, employer-sponsored group health care plans traditionally have been the most likely means of obtaining affordable health care insurance coverage for themselves and their families.

The federal *Medicare* program covers all persons who qualify for Social Security retirement benefits, thereby ensuring nearly universal health care coverage for persons age 65 and older. The federal Medicare program consists of automatic coverage under a basic program (known as Medicare Part A) for hospital services, and some home health care and hospice services. Medicare Part A is financed through payroll taxes paid by the employer and the employee during the employee's working years. The current payroll tax for Medicare is 2.9% (combined employer/employee rate) of the employee's compensation. Unlike the payroll tax for Social Security benefits, which is limited to the taxable wage base amount, there is no dollar limit on the amount of an employee's compensation that is subject to the Medicare payroll tax.

Medicare also offers supplemental medical insurance, known as Medicare Part B, which covers medical services not covered by Medicare Part A. The Medicare Part B program covers outpatient hospital services, physician services, laboratory tests, rehabilitation therapy and the purchase of durable medical equipment. Participants in the Medicare Part B program must pay a minimal (by private sector standards) monthly premium and annual deductible. Significantly, the federal Medicare program does not cover extended skilled nursing home or custodial care (known as *long-term care*). Medicare will cover up to a maximum of 100 days of skilled nursing care following a hospital stay, so long as the individual meets certain requirements. See generally CENTERS FOR MEDICARE & MEDICAID SERVICES, MEDICARE COVERAGE OF SKILLED NURSING FACILITY CARE (Sept. 2007).

By most objective measures, the federal Medicare program has proven highly successful in providing health care services for individuals age 65 and older (so-called "elderly persons"). In 2013, 96% of elderly persons reported that they did have a usual place to go for medical care, and only 2.3% of elderly persons said that they failed to obtain needed medical care during the previous twelve months due to financial barriers.

U.S. DEP'T HEALTH AND HUMAN SERVICES, ADMINISTRATION ON AGING, A PROFILE OF OLDER AMERICANS: 2013, 12.

The federal *Medicaid* program is jointly sponsored and financed by the federal government and each of the fifty states. Medicaid provides health care coverage to low-income persons who satisfy the eligibility criteria established by the person's state of domicile. Some states require that, in addition to meeting income and asset criteria, the individual also must fall within one or more of the following categories: the disabled; the blind; the elderly (e.g., for nursing home care); or families with dependent children. Each state has a measure of discretion to determine the precise Medicaid eligibility criteria for its citizens, with some states providing more generous coverage than others. In 2013, over 62 million persons in the United States had health care coverage through Medicaid. See Kaiser Family Foundation, The Medicaid Program at a Glance (March 2013).

Unlike Medicare, Medicaid covers the cost of long-term care, but only for persons who meet the state program's income and asset criteria. Long-term care is quite expensive if the cost is being paid by the individual and not by Medicaid. Moreover, it is not unusual for an individual to spend several years in long-term care. For this reason, long-term care insurance plans are an increasingly desirable employee benefit among older workers.

For individuals under age 65 who do not qualify for Medicaid, one means of obtaining health care insurance coverage is through their employer or the employer of their spouse or domestic partner. Surveys of employees indicate that a health care insurance plan is the employee benefit that is most valued by employees of all ages. In 2013, 85% of workers in private industry had access to a health care insurance plan offered by their employer, but only 64% of these workers participated in an employer-sponsored plan. BUREAU OF LABOR STATISTICS, EMPLOYEE BENEFITS IN THE UNITED STATES—MARCH 2013 (July 17, 2013). The "gap" between the availability of coverage and actual participation in employer-sponsored health care plans suggests that not all employees who are offered access to health care benefits through their employer can afford the cost of coverage.

Current national expenditures for health care are staggering. Such expenditures are projected to increase in the future as the baby boomer generation continues to age. According to the federal Centers for Medicare and Medicaid Services, national health care expenditures in 2013 were projected to be $2.915 trillion, an amount equal to $9,210 per person and 18% of the Gross Domestic Product. In 2014, total annual expenditures are projected to increase to $3.093 trillion due to implementation of the Affordable Care Act.

According to the Congressional Budget Office, in 2013 a total of 272 million persons under the age of 65 (80% of the non-elderly population) were covered by some form of public or private health care insurance. Approximately 55 million non-elderly persons were uninsured in 2013. Employment-based health care insurance plans accounted for the coverage of more than 158 million individuals under the age of 65 in 2013. Medicaid and the Children's Health Insurance Program covered 36 million persons, with the balance being covered by individual insurance policies. These statistics indicate the significant role that employer-sponsored plans play in national health care policy.

2. HISTORIC NATIONAL HEALTH CARE REFORM

Rising public dissatisfaction with the cost and quality of health care made comprehensive national health care reform a central issue in the United States presidential election of 2008. The election of President Barack Obama, combined with the election of Democratic majorities in both the House of Representatives and the Senate, moved health care reform to the top of the national domestic policy agenda.

After a lengthy incubation period, including town hall meetings around the country to solicit public opinion during the summer of 2009, the House passed health care reform legislation on November 7, 2009. The original House bill included a "public option" that allowed individuals to purchase health care insurance coverage directly from the federal government. The House bill raised income taxes on higher-income taxpayers to pay for the cost of expanded coverage. The House bill also contained a provision, sponsored by Representative Bart Stupak of Michigan, that expressly banned the use of federal funds for abortion (the "Stupak Amendment").

On December 24, 2009, the Senate passed its version of health care reform legislation. The Senate's Affordable Care Act differed in significant respects from the original House bill. The Senate bill did not contain a public option and did not duplicate the language of the Stupak Amendment. The Senate bill raised revenues to pay for expanded coverage primarily through cuts to the federal Medicare program and a variety of tax increases, including a 40 percent tax on so-called "Cadillac" health care plans that charged very high premiums for coverage.

The original Senate bill passed on a party-line vote of 60 to 39. Sixty votes was the minimum number of votes necessary to defeat a threatened filibuster by Republican Senators, who unanimously voted against the bill. To obtain 60 affirmative votes, Democratic leaders included several provisions in the Senate bill that garnered wide-spread media attention. The "Louisiana Purchase"—a special provision in the Senate bill that allocated $300 million in additional federal subsidies to Louisiana's Medicaid program—solidified the vote of Senator Mary Landrieu of Louisiana. The crucial 60th vote was obtained from Senator Ben Nelson of Nebraska. In an arrangement dubbed the "Cornhusker Kickback" by the national media, lawmakers inserted a special provision into the Senate bill guaranteeing that the federal government would pay, in perpetuity, for any additional costs to the State of Nebraska that resulted from the legislation's requirements for expanded Medicaid coverage.

Political insiders expected that the significant differences between the more ambitious House bill and the more modest Senate bill would be reconciled through a Conference Committee bill. An unexpected turn of events occurred on January 19, 2010, when Republican Scott Brown won a special election in Massachusetts for the Senate seat formerly held by the late Senator Edward Kennedy. Brown, who was the first Republican Senator elected in Massachusetts since 1972, opposed the Democratic health care reform legislation. His election meant the loss of the crucial 60th vote that was necessary to approve final health care reform legislation in the form of a Conference Committee bill over unanimous Republican opposition in the Senate.

Unable to use the normal reconciliation procedure of a Conference Committee bill, the Democratic leadership decided to use a somewhat obscure parliamentary process, known as budget reconciliation, to enact final health care reform legislation. Using the budget reconciliation process, only a bare majority of 51 votes in the Senate is necessary to enact legislation that impacts the federal budget. The budget reconciliation process required a two-step procedure. First, the House had to pass the Senate bill without any changes to the bill. Second, both the House and the Senate had to enact a separate series of limited amendments to the Senate bill. This amendment bill became the Health Care and Education Reconciliation Act of 2010.

Although many Democratic members of the House initially balked at the prospect of passing the Senate bill verbatim, eventually they conceded. The last group of Democratic holdouts was led by Representative Bart Stupak. The Stupak group objected to the Senate bill on the ground that it did not contain the original language of the Stupak Amendment that was incorporated into the final House bill. After receiving assurances that President Obama would sign an executive order prohibiting the use of federal funds for abortion, enough members of the Stupak group agreed to vote for the Senate bill to enable its passage in the House.

On March 21, 2010, the House passed both the Senate bill and the amendment bill. President Obama signed the Affordable Care Act, Pub. L. No. 111–148, 124 Stat. 119 (2010) (ACA), into law on March 23, 2010. On March 30, 2010, after a series of back-and-forth votes in the Senate and the House, the Health Care and Education Reconciliation Act of 2010, Pub. L. No. 111–152, 124 Stat. 1029 (HCRA), became law. Together, these two pieces of legislation form what is commonly called the Affordable Care Act (ACA).

The Affordable Care Act enacted systemic-level reforms to the Medicare and Medicaid programs, the market for health insurance policies purchased directly by individuals from insurance company issuers, and employer-sponsored group health plans. In studying national health care reform, it is important to distinguish reforms directed at public programs and the private insurance market from reforms that are specific to employer-sponsored plans. The former are more properly the subject of a course in health care law and public policy; the latter are the focus of this casebook. Nevertheless, an overview of how the major mechanisms of the ACA operate to expand the scope of health insurance coverage is fundamental to understanding the law's impact on employer-sponsored group health plans.

National health care reform under the ACA was designed as a series of three major "waves" of changes implemented over time. (A timeline of the major reforms applicable to employer-sponsored group health plans is contained in Appendix G of the casebook.) For group health plans that operate on a calendar plan year, the first wave of reforms became effective on January 1, 2011. This first wave prohibited lifetime dollar limits and restricted annual dollar limits on essential health benefits offered by the plan, prohibited preexisting condition coverage exclusions for children under age 19, and generally required that adult children must be offered coverage under a parent's plan through age 26. New plans or existing plans that lost their "grandfathered" status after March 23, 2010 (the effective date of the ACA), are subject to additional requirements. These requirements, including the conditions for maintaining grandfathered status, are explained in more detail later in Chapter Four.

The second wave of reforms involved changes to the Internal Revenue Code to raise revenue to pay for the tax-subsidized expansion of health insurance coverage starting in 2014. Beginning in 2013, a new tax of 3.8% was imposed on unearned income for individuals. The Medicare tax on earned income was increased by 0.9% for high-income taxpayers.[a] A new 2.3% tax was imposed on the manufacturers of medical devices. For individuals having health care insurance with high deductible amounts or high out-of-pocket medical expenses, two revenue changes were particularly significant. First, the threshold amount for deducting medical expenses as an itemized deduction for individual taxpayers was increased from 7.5% to 10% of adjusted gross income. Second, the maximum annual contribution amount to a cafeteria plan flexible health spending account for the reimbursement of out-of-pocket medical expenses was capped at $2,500. In addition to new permanent taxes, employer-sponsored group health plans were required to pay two new

---

[a] For purposes of this tax, high-income taxpayers are defined as individuals earning wages of at least $200,000 or married couples filing jointly who earn wages of at least $250,000. These threshold amounts are indexed for inflation in future years.

temporary fees beginning in 2014. The Transitional Reinsurance Fee and the Patient-Centered Outcome Research Institute fees are assessed on a per capita basis and end after 2016.[b] The last revenue provision becomes effective in 2018, when a 40% nondeductible excise tax is imposed on so-called "Cadillac" health insurance plans. A "Cadillac" health care plan is defined as a plan that has annual premiums in excess of $10,200 for single coverage or $27,500 for family coverage (indexed for inflation in future years). The 40% excise tax is assessed only on the portion of the annual premium that exceeds these dollar amounts. For fully insured plans, the issuer of the policy is responsible for paying the tax. For self-insured plan, it is the plan's administrator who must pay the tax. As a practical matter, this tax predominantly impacts multiemployer health insurance plans for workers who are represented by a collective bargaining unit. In these collectively-bargained plans, the employer typically pays most (if not all) of the premium pursuant to the terms of a collective bargaining agreement with the Union.

The third wave of major reforms required individuals to have minimum essential coverage. See generally Code § 5000A. Individual taxpayers without minimum essential coverage (including the dependents of the taxpayer) are subject to a minimum tax penalty under Code Section 5000A. This penalty amount is the greater of a fixed penalty amount or a percentage of a formula amount based on the taxpayer's modified adjusted gross income. The fixed penalty amount is set at $95 in 2014, $325 in 2015, and $695 in 2016. This requirement (known as the *individual mandate*) was upheld by the Supreme Court under the Taxing Clause of the United States Constitution in *NFIB v. Sebelius*, 132 S. Ct. 2566 (2012).

To assist uninsured individuals in obtaining minimum essential coverage, the ACA as originally enacted provided for three assistance mechanisms:

(1) *Expanded coverage through employer-sponsored group health plans.* This requirement (known as the *employer mandate*) imposed penalties on large employers who failed to offer minimum essential coverage to their full-time employees, or who offered coverage to full-time employees that was not *affordable* or that did not provide *minimum*

---

[b]   Under the ACA, the total amount collected by the Transition Reinsurance Fee must be $12 billion in 2014, $8 billion in 2015, and $5 billion in 2016. For 2014, the Department of Health and Human Services determined that the fee should be $63 per plan participant in order to satisfy the $12 billion requirement. The sums collected using the Transition Reinsurance Fee are paid to health insurance issuers participating in the Exchange system to offset the cost of policies sold to individuals with pre-existing conditions who are at risk for higher than average medical costs. The Patient-Centered Outcome Research Institute fee begins at $1 per plan participant in 2014 and increases to $2 in later years.

value to the plan's participants.[c] For purposes of the employer mandate, a "large" employer is defined as an employer who has the equivalent of 50 full-time equivalent employees. An "employer" is defined as including a controlled group of employers under Code Sections 414(b), (c), (m) and (o). See generally Code § 4980H. A "full-time" employee is one who works on average 30 hours of service per week. Hours are counted in the same way as hours of service for purposes of determining eligibility for participation in a qualified retirement plan. The hours worked by part-time or seasonal workers are added together to estimate the number of full-time equivalent employees. See Code § 5000A, 78 Fed. Reg. 218 (Jan. 2, 2013).

(2) *Expanded coverage through individual policies purchased on an Exchange.* The ACA created a system of on-line marketplaces (known as the "American Health Benefit Exchanges" or just the "Exchange" for short) so that insurance companies could market and sell individual health insurance policies that satisfy state and federal standards for the coverage of *essential health benefits.*[d] Policies sold on an Exchange are available only to United States citizens and legal residents.[e] Individual policies sold on an Exchange must cover pre-existing health conditions. The premiums for policies sold on an Exchange are priced according to a community rating (rather than according to the individual health status of the person(s) covered by the policy). The ACA provided that each State may establish an Exchange for the purchase of individual policies by its residents, or may opt to use the federal Exchange created and operated by the Department of Health and Human Services. For individuals and families with incomes between 100% and 400% of the federal poverty level,[f] a premium assistance tax credit is available to reduce the cost of the policy's premium.[g] In addition, the ACA established the

---

[c] These italicized terms have a unique technical meaning, which is explained later in Chapter Four.

[d] Coverage of "essential health benefits" is more extensive than the requirement of "minimum esstenial coverage" for purpose of compliance with the employer and individual mandates. The significance of this distinction is explained in detail later in Chapter Four.

[e] Foreign-born workers who cannot document they are in the United States legally are ineligible to use the Exchange system and cannot receive premium assistance tax credits.

[f] For 2013, 100% of the federal poverty level was $11,490 for a single individual and $23,550 for a family of four. At the 400% level, these figures were $45,960 and $94,200 in 2013. Amounts for Alaska and Hawai'i are slightly higher.

[g] The amount of the premium assistance tax credit is refundable, which means that if the amount of the credit is more than the amount of individual's tax liability, the taxpayer receives the difference as a refund, even if no income tax is owed. The amount of the tax credit is based on the individual's estimated income for the upcoming year. The credit can be paid in advance if the

Small Business Health Options Program (SHOP) for "small" employers (defined as employers having fewer than 50 full-time equivalent employees). Under the SHOP, an employee of a small employer can access the Exchange and select from a range of plans according to the employee's individual needs and budget. The employer remits a single lump sum premium payment, with the Exchange allocating the premium among the various plans selected by the employees. Significantly, premium assistance tax credits are not available to: (1) employees who use the SHOP option; (2) employees who are offered a group health plan by their employer that is affordable and provides minimum value; or (3) individuals who are eligible for Medicaid coverage.

(3) *Expanded coverage through state-operated Medicaid programs.* The ACA expanded the scope of the jointly-funded, but state-operated, federal Medicaid program by requiring each state to provide Medicaid coverage to all adults[h] under the age of 65 with incomes up to 133% of the federal poverty level.[i] The ACA further required that all of these new Medicaid recipients must have a specified package of benefits. This expansion of Medicaid coverage was a significant change in federal health care policy because prior to the enactment of the ACA an individual could not qualify for Medicaid coverage merely on the basis of income. Rather, eligibility for Medicaid coverage was limited to four categories of low-income persons: (1) the disabled; (2) the blind; (3) the elderly; and (4) families with dependent children. Due in part to these additional eligibility restrictions, at the time the ACA was enacted on average the states covered only adults making less than 37% and parents making less than 63% of the federal poverty level. See NFIB v. Sebelius, 132 S. Ct. at 2601. The ACA increased federal Medicaid funding to the states by covering 100% of the additional cost of this expanded Medicaid coverage through 2016, with the additional federal

---

individual desires to use it immediately to offset the cost of the monthly insurance premiums for a policy purchased on an Exchange. If the individual's actual income during the year is more than the estimated amount, the individual must refund to the Treasury Department any excess tax credit that was used during the year to offset monthly insurance premiums for an Exchange policy. This reconciliation occurs when the taxpayer's annual income tax return is filed at the end of the year. See generally http://www.irs.gov/uac/Newsroom/Questions-and-Answers-on-the-Premium-Tax-Credit.

  [h] Dependent children of low-income families can receive health insurance coverage under the state-operated Children's Health Insurance Program (CHIP), even if a parent earns too much income to qualify for Medicaid coverage.

  [i] The text of the ACA states 133%, but provides for a new methodology of calculating income that effectively makes the threshold 138%.

funding for expanded Medicaid coverage gradually decreasing to 90% in subsequent years. If a state failed to provide expanded coverage, the ACA authorized the Secretary of the Department of Health and Human Services to withhold *all* federal Medicaid funds from the state.

The implementation of each of these three assistance mechanisms was delayed, or its impact in terms of expanding health insurance coverage was reduced, by subsequent events. These events began in July of 2013, when the federal government delayed enforcement of the employer mandate, first until January 1, 2015, and later until January 1, 2016 for employers who have between 50 and 99 full-time equivalent employees. The establishment of the Exchange system was made far more difficult when a majority of the states opted not to operate an Exchange and chose to rely instead on the federal Exchange operated by the Department of Health and Human Services.[j] When the Exchanges opened for enrollment on October 1, 2013, the federal Exchange and some state-operated Exchanges suffered well-publicized technical glitches. Some individuals who did successfully navigate the enrollment process were disappointed by the premium prices or the limitations on the network of health care providers available for the less expensive insurance policies offered for sale on the Exchange.

At the same time, during the fall of 2013 many persons who previously had purchased relatively inexpensive individual health insurance policies with limited coverage of health care services and benefits received cancellation notices from their insurance companies. These cancellation notices were required because their policies did not cover the full range of ten essential health benefits without lifetime or annual dollar limits, a requirement that became effective under the ACA in 2014 for individual insurance policies and group insurance policies sold on the small employer market.[k] The SHOP for employees of small

---

[j] States electing to establish and operate their own Exchanges were: California; Colorado; Connecticut; the District of Columbia; Hawai'i; Kentucky; Maryland; Massachusetts; Minnesota; Nevada; New York; Oregon; Rhode Island; Vermont; and Washington. States opting to rely on the federal Exchange were: Alabama; Alaska; Arizona; Arkansas; Delaware; Florida; Georgia; Idaho; Illinois; Indiana; Iowa; Kansas; Louisiana; Maine; Michigan; Mississippi; Missouri; Montana; Nebraska; New Hampshire; New Jersey; New Mexico; North Carolina; North Dakota; Ohio; Oklahoma; Pennsylvania; South Carolina; South Dakota; Tennessee; Texas; Utah; Virginia; Washington; West Virginia; Wisconsin; and Wyoming.

[k] The requirements of the ACA regarding coverage of essential health benefits are discussed in detail later in Chapter Four. In the wake of negative publicity about individuals losing their existing health insurance coverage due to the more stringent benefit requirements of the ACA, the Department of Health and Human Services authorized transitional relief that gave health insurance issuers a temporary exemption from compliance for policies that do not comply with all of the requirements of the ACA. State insurance regulators were encouraged, but not required, to adopt the same transitional policy. Some state insurance commissioners issued transitional relief that would allow the noncompliant insurance policies to continue to be offered to state residents, but others did not. This transitional relief permits policy holders to renew their nonconforming policies for policy years beginning on or before October 1, 2016. See Centers for Medicare and Medicaid Services, Insurance Standards Bulletin Series—Extension of Transitional Policy Through October 1, 2016 (Mar. 5, 2014).

employers, which was to offer a range of insurance policy options, was delayed due to technical difficulties in implementation. Finally, 26 states successfully challenged the mandatory expansion of Medicaid coverage, which the Supreme Court held to be an unconstitutional expansion of Congress's authority under the Spending Clause in *NFIB v. Sebelius*, 132 S. Ct. 2566 (2012). As a result, eligibility for Medicaid coverage based solely on income was not implemented in all states.

This situation created an unanticipated coverage gap for some low-income adults in those states that did not expand Medicaid coverage. Under the statutory language of ACA, persons who earn less than 100% of the federal poverty level are not eligible to purchase an individual insurance policy on the Exchange using premium assistance tax credits. If coverage is not available under Medicaid in the person's state of domicile, these low-income individuals cannot receive federal financial assistance to purchase an health insurance policy on the Exchange. This coverage gap primarily impacts low-income, nonelderly adults who do not have dependent children.

The long-term cost of national health care reform under the Affordable Care Act has proven difficult to estimate. The nonpartisan Congressional Budget Office (CBO) originally estimated that the cost of the ACA over the first ten years would be approximately $940 billion. A few months after the ACA was enacted, the CBO revised its cost estimate upward and projected that the cost of reform would exceed $1 trillion over the first ten years.

Several years later, in July of 2013 the CBO estimated that the total cost of the ACA for the period 2014–2023 at $1.375 trillion. This $1.375 trillion figure reflected the loss of $10 billion in previously anticipated penalty payments by employers that would not be collected in 2014 due to the delay in enforcement of the employer mandate.

In terms of the net increase in health insurance coverage, the CBO calculated the projected number of uninsured nonelderly persons for each year between 2013 and 2023. The table that follows presents the CBO's projections, both in absolute numbers and as a percentage of the population.

CBO's May 2013 Estimate of the Effects of the
Affordable Care Act on Health Insurance Coverage
(in millions of nonelderly persons by calendar year)

	2013	2014	2015	2016	2017	2018	2019	2020	2021	2022	2023
No. of Uninsured Nonelderly People [1]	55	44	37	31	30	30	30	30	31	31	31
Insured Share of the Nonelderly Population [2]	80%	84%	86%	89%	89%	89%	89%	89%	89%	89%	89%
All Residents Excluding Unauthorized Immigrants	82%	86%	89%	91%	92%	92%	92%	92%	92%	92%	92%

1. The count of uninsured people includes undocumented immigrants as well as people who are eligible for, but not enrolled in, a Medicaid program.

2. Figures for the nonelderly population include only residents who are younger than age 65.

QUESTIONS

1. The centerpiece of national health care reform is the individual mandate, which requires all individuals and their dependents to have minimum essential coverage or else pay a tax penalty. Do you agree with this policy approach?

2. Notwithstanding the cost of the ACA, the estimated number of uninsured persons in the future remains significant. Many of the uninsured will be those persons who are not citizens or otherwise legal residents of the United States. Should Congress amend the ACA to cover all persons working and residing in the United States?

3. The Exchange system is designed in essence as a private-public partnership between the federal and state governments and the insurance industry. Is such a partnership too complex to manage and operate efficiently? If the goal is to provide affordable access to health care services, would a single-payer system operated and funded by the federal government be a better approach?

3. WELFARE BENEFIT PLANS IN YOUR FUTURE PRACTICE

The significant role of welfare benefit plans, particularly health care plans, for a specialized career in the ERISA field is obvious. But knowledge of welfare benefit plans also is necessary for lawyers who work in the areas of general corporate law, litigation, estate planning, family law, and employment law.

Private lawsuits brought by individuals whose claims for welfare plan benefits have been denied by a plan administrator represent the largest number of ERISA cases filed in the federal courts today. The tendency of plan participants to pursue litigation when their claims for welfare plan benefits are denied is an indication of just how valuable participants perceive these benefits to be. If your future career lies in general corporate law or litigation, a working knowledge of welfare benefit plans, particularly health care plans, is essential.

If your future career lies in estate planning, whether your client has access to a retiree health care plan or a long-term care insurance plan through an employer will significantly affect the estate planning process. These types of welfare benefit plans play a significant role in financial planning for a client's retirement years and the eventual transfer of accumulated wealth at death. Unanticipated health care and long-term care expenses during retirement can wreak havoc with the client's estate plan by consuming assets that were expected to become part of the client's estate at death.

For lawyers who practice in the area of family law, divorce often represents the potential loss of health insurance coverage for the spouse of the employee and the employee's dependent children. ERISA provides significant protections concerning health insurance coverage for spouses and dependent children in the event of divorce. Understanding how these rules operate is fundamental to the effective representation of clients in divorce matters.

Welfare benefit plans subject to ERISA also raise potential issues under a litany of other federal laws, particularly federal employment laws. If you are a "bilingual" employment lawyer—meaning that you are conversant in *both* ERISA and federal and state employment laws—then you will have a significant competitive advantage in the market for legal services. Section F of Chapter Four highlights some of the more prominent points of intersection between welfare benefit plans subject to regulation under ERISA and other federal laws that regulate the employer-employee relationship.

Finally, the remainder of Chapter Four contains information that you are likely to find useful in your personal life. If you are like the vast majority of working Americans, your health insurance coverage, disability income insurance, long-term care insurance and life insurance will be provided through welfare benefit plans sponsored by your employer. Like the retirement benefits provided by the employer's qualified plan, these welfare plan benefits are an important part of your overall compensation package. Knowing how these plans operate and the benefits they provide will enable you to make informed choices and to protect your rights as a plan participant.

B. INTRODUCTION TO WELFARE BENEFIT PLANS

1. TYPES OF WELFARE BENEFIT PLANS AND OTHER EMPLOYEE BENEFITS

ERISA Section 3(1) broadly defines a welfare benefit plan as:

any plan, fund, or program which . . . is established or maintained by an employer or by an employee organization, or by both, . . . for the purpose of providing for its participants or their beneficiaries, through the purchase of insurance or otherwise, (A) medical, surgical, or hospital care or benefits, or benefits in the event of sickness, accident, disability, death or unemployment, or vacation benefits, apprenticeship or other training programs, or day care centers, scholarship funds, or prepaid legal services, or (B) any benefit described in section 302(c) of the Labor Management Relations Act, 1947 (other than pensions on retirement or death, and insurance to provide such pensions).

The broad scope of this definition makes many types of employee welfare benefit plans possible. As a general rule, the benefit design, coverage and administration of an employer's welfare benefit plan are closely coordinated with the income tax provisions of the Code to achieve the most favorable tax treatment possible for employer contributions to the plan and benefits paid by the plan to its participants and beneficiaries.

Health care plans are designed to provide medical, surgical or hospital benefits. These benefits may be provided in different ways. The employer's plan may consist of coverage under a group insurance policy issued by an insurance company, coverage under a plan that is self-insured by the employer, or group plan coverage via enrollment in a health maintenance organization that provides health care services to its enrollees. Some employers even provide health care benefits through their own on-site medical facilities.

Disability income plans (disability plans) provide payments to replace an employee's lost income when the employee is unable to work due to an illness, disease or injury. *Short-term disability plans* pay income replacement benefits to the employee for a limited period of time (e.g., for six weeks, or 120 days, or one year). If the period of coverage under the short-term disability plan is relatively brief, the benefits under the disability plan may be paid by the employer from its general assets. *Long-term disability plans* generally begin to pay income replacement benefits to the employee after an initial period of disability has transpired and continue to make payments until the employee reaches retirement age or the employee is no longer disabled. Long-term disability plan benefits usually are provided through an insurance policy. In a well-designed disability income program, coverage of employees under the employer's short-term disability and long-term disability plans is coordinated so that when the period of coverage under the short-term plan expires, the employee is eligible to receive disability income payments under the employer's long-term disability plan.

Accidental death plans pay benefits to the employee's surviving spouse and dependents when the employee's death is the result of an accidental injury. *Life insurance plans* pay a benefit to the employee's designated beneficiary in the event of the employee's death, irrespective of the cause of death. Many employers provide $50,000 of death benefit coverage for every employee under a *group term life insurance plan*. An employer also may offer employees the opportunity to purchase additional amounts of individual life insurance coverage from the insurance company that provides the employer's group term life insurance policy.

Long-term care plans provide benefits for nursing home or custodial care. Long-term care plan benefits are provided through insurance contracts designed to satisfy the criteria of Code Section 7702B for *qualified long-term care insurance*. These plans cover *qualified long-term care services* that are not covered by Medicare. Qualified long-term care services include diagnostic, preventive and rehabilitative services, and maintenance and personal care services for a chronically ill individual who is unable to perform daily living activities due to a loss of functional capacity. See Code § 7702B(c).

Educational assistance programs may qualify as a training program under the definition of a welfare benefit plan. An educational assistance program provides employer payments for tuition for courses, fees, books, supplies, equipment and other educational expenses incurred by employees. The employer may limit payments under educational assistance programs to courses that are reasonably related to the business of the employer. Educational assistance programs are usually structured by the employer so that the program payments satisfy the criteria for favorable income tax treatment under Code Section 127(b).

Dependent care assistance programs may qualify as a welfare benefit plan under ERISA. A dependent care assistance program may take the form of a daycare center operated by the employer for the benefit of its employees, or it may be a reimbursement program to assist employees in paying for outside day care services. See Code § 129. Only a select group of typically large and "family friendly" employers nationwide operate day care centers for the children of their employees. An employer's day care assistance program is more likely to pay or reimburse the employee for day care services incurred by the employee.

A *severance pay plan* provides benefits to an employee whose termination of employment from the employer satisfies the eligibility criteria for payments under the terms of the plan. For severance pay plans established by a single employer, plan benefits normally are paid from the general assets of the employer. Whether an employer's severance pay arrangement has the hallmarks of an ongoing administrative scheme will determine if it is subject to regulation as a plan under ERISA.

A *vacation plan* typically provides that the employer will continue to pay the employee's regular compensation during the employee's absence from work for a specified number of days or weeks each year. A *sick leave plan* typically provides that the employer will continue to pay the employee's regular compensation for a specified number of days each year when the employee is absent from work due to illness. The trend among employers is to combine vacation and sick leave plan benefits into a single program, known as *paid leave* or *paid time off*. Such paid leave programs provide that the employer will continue to pay the employee's regular compensation for a specified number of days each year when the employee is absent from work, regardless of the reason for the employee's absence.

Normally, when the employee is absent from work due to vacation, short-term disability, or sick leave, the employer continues to pay the employee's regular compensation out of the general assets of the employer, rather than out of the assets of a separate trust established to fund the plan. When the employee's regular compensation for periods of vacation or sick leave is paid out of the general assets of the employer, the employee's vacation or sick leave "plan" is deemed to be a *payroll practice* that is not subject to regulation under Title I of ERISA. See DOL Reg. § 2510.3–1(b)(2)–(3).

Table 4.1 shows the percentage of workers who participated in various types of welfare benefit plans and other employee benefit programs sponsored by employers in private industry in 2013.

Table 4.1

Percentage of Private Industry Workers

Participating in Welfare Benefit Plans (2013)

Type of Welfare Benefit Plan	All Employees	Full-Time Employees	Part-Time Employees
Health Care	51	64	13
Life Insurance	55	70	12
Paid Holidays	77	90	39
Paid Sick Leave	61	74	24
Paid Vacations	77	91	36

Source: Bureau of Labor Statistics, Employee Benefits in the United States—March 2013.

2. THE INCOME TAX TREATMENT OF WELFARE BENEFIT PLANS

Employer contributions to a health care plan, accidental death plan, disability plan, life insurance plan or long-term care insurance plan normally are deductible by the employer as ordinary and necessary business expenses. See Code § 162(a). Whether employer contributions to the plan or benefits paid from the plan are included in an employee's gross income depends upon the type of plan. Table 4.2 summarizes the employee's income tax consequences for various types of ERISA-regulated welfare benefit plans and employer payroll practices.

Table 4.2

Taxation of Welfare Benefit Plans and Other Employee Benefits

Type of Employee Benefit	Included in Employee Gross Income	Excluded From Employee Gross Income
Health Care Plan		• Employer Contributions to Plan • Benefits Paid from Plan
Accidental Death Plan	• Benefits Paid From Plan	• Employer Contributions to Plan
Disability Income Plan*	• Benefits Paid From Plan	• Employer Contribution to Plan
Qualified Long-Term Care Plan		• Employer Contribution to Plan • Benefits Paid From Plan
Group Life Insurance Plan	• Employer Contributions to Plan (over $50,000 of coverage)	• Employer Contribution to Plan (up to $50,000 of coverage) • Benefits Paid From Plan
Educational Assistance		• Employer Payments (up to $5,250 per year)
Dependent Care Assistance		• Employer Payments (up to $5,000 / $2,500 per year)
Severance Pay	• Payments to Employee	
Sick Leave	• Payments to Employee	
Vacation	• Payments to Employee	

*If the employee pays the premiums for the disability income plan using after-tax dollars, then any benefits paid from the plan if the employee becomes disabled are excluded from the employee's gross income.

Employer contributions to, and benefits paid from, a group health care plan usually are not included in the employee's gross income. See Code §§ 106(a); 105(b); 213(d). This rule applies whether the benefits under the plan are paid pursuant to a group health insurance policy or from the employer's self-insured health care plan. See Code § 105(e)(1). The distinction between an insured health care plan and a self-insured health care plan is explored in Section C of Chapter Four.

Employer contributions to an accidental death plan or a disability plan are not included in an employee's gross income. See Code § 106(a). The benefits paid to the employee under a disability plan (or, in the case of an accidental death plan, to the employee's beneficiary) are included in the employee's gross income if "such amounts . . . are attributable to contributions by the employer which were not includible in the gross income of the employee, or . . . are paid by the employer." Code §§ 104(a)(3); 105(a). For this reason, employers who offer coverage to their employees under an accidental death or disability plan where the benefits are provided through a group insurance policy may choose to structure the plan so that the premium payments are made by the employees themselves using after-tax dollars. If the plan is structured in this way, the benefit payments for disability income (or accidental death) will be excluded from the employee's (or beneficiary's) gross income. See Code § 104(a)(3). Otherwise, the benefits provided by a disability or accidental death plan will be included in the employee's gross income.

Qualified long-term care insurance plans sponsored by an employer are treated similarly to health care plans. See Code § 7702B(a)(1). Employer contributions to a qualified long-term care insurance plan are not included in the employee's gross income. See Code §§ 7702B(a)(3), 106(a). A limited exception applies if the long-term care coverage is provided through a flexible spending arrangement. See Code § 106(c). The benefits paid from a qualified long-term care insurance plan are not included in an employee's gross income so long as the amount of the benefit does not exceed a statutory per diem limit of $175 per day (indexed for inflation). See Code §§ 7702B(a), (d), 105(b), 213(d)(1).

Employer contributions for the first $50,000 of death benefit coverage for each employee under a group term life insurance plan are not included in the employee's gross income. See Code § 79. Employer contributions for death benefit coverage in excess of $50,000 are imputed to the employee and included in the employee's gross income. See Code § 79(a); Treas. Reg. § 1.79–3. The death benefit paid under a life insurance policy on account of the death of the insured generally is not included in the employee's income. See Code § 101(a). The death benefit may be subject to federal estate tax as part of the insured's gross estate. See Code § 2042.

For educational assistance programs, the first $5,250 of benefits paid annually is not included in the employee's gross income, so long as the employer's plan satisfies the criteria of Code Section 127. Similarly, the first $5,000 of benefits provided annually to an employee ($2,500 if the employee is married but files separately) under a dependent care assistance program is not included in the employee's gross income if the employer's plan satisfies the criteria listed in Code Section 129.

Benefits from a severance pay plan, sick leave plan, or vacation benefit plan are considered part of the employee's compensation and are included in the employee's gross income.

3. CAFETERIA (CODE SECTION 125) PLANS

A *cafeteria plan* is not a welfare benefit plan subject to regulation under ERISA. Rather, a cafeteria plan is a financing arrangement created in writing pursuant to the requirements of Code Section 125. A cafeteria plan allows employees to choose between receiving their compensation from the employer in the form of cash or *qualified benefits* offered under the terms of the arrangement. If the employee elects to receive the qualified benefits offered through the cafeteria plan, the value of these qualified benefits is not included in the employee's gross income. See Code § 125.

The menu of qualified benefits the employer may offer through a cafeteria plan arrangement includes group term life insurance, health care expense reimbursement, health care plan premium payments, disability and accidental death benefits, dependent care assistance and vacation benefits. Qualified long-term care benefits cannot be offered through a cafeteria plan.

Health care expense reimbursement and dependent care assistance benefits under a cafeteria plan are usually structured as *flexible spending accounts*. A flexible spending account allows each individual employee to decide how much, if any, of the employee's cash compensation the employer should contribute to the employee's flexible spending account to cover expenses incurred by the employee during a defined period of coverage. From an income tax perspective, participation in a flexible spending account arrangement through a cafeteria plan is desirable because the employee effectively can pay for medical expenses and dependent care expenses using compensation dollars that are not included in the employee's gross income. The employee is reimbursed for qualifying medical expenses that are not otherwise covered by the employee's health care plan from the health care flexible spending account. Similarly, the employee is reimbursed for dependent care expenses from the dependent care flexible spending account.

Under the "use it or lose it" rule, up to $500 that remains in a health care flexible spending account at the end of the coverage period can be carried forward and used for expenses incurred by the employee during a subsequent coverage period. Any remaining funds in excess of $500 are forfeited. See IRS Notice 2013–71. (No funds can be carried forward for dependent care.) If the cafeteria plan provides for a grace period that permits participants to use the funds in a health care flexible spending account remaining from a prior plan year to pay for medical expenses incurred up to two months and fifteen days after the beginning of the next plan year, then this grace period rule precludes application of the $500 carry-forward rule. Complex rules determine the circumstances under which a participant in the cafeteria plan may change an election under the plan during the coverage period. See Treas. Reg. § 1.125–4. As a result, the "use it or lose it" rule requires employees to engage in careful planning when estimating the annual amount to be set aside for qualifying benefits under the cafeteria plan.

The Affordable Care Act made several changes to the rules governing cafeteria plans with respect to the reimbursement of qualifying medical expenses. For calendar year cafeteria plans, the cost of over-the-counter medications (excluding insulin) can no longer be reimbursed through a flexible health care spending account unless the medication is prescribed by a physician. See HCRA § 9003(c) (amending Code § 106(f)). Employers with 100 or fewer employees are permitted to establish cafeteria plans that have relaxed administrative requirements in exchange for employer contributions to the employees' flexible spending accounts under the plan. See HCRA § 9022(a) (amending Code § 125(j)). Finally, the maximum annual amount that can be contributed to a health care flexible spending account for the reimbursement of qualifying medical expenses is limited to $2,500.

4. CODE NONDISCRIMINATION REQUIREMENTS FOR WELFARE BENEFIT PLANS

As compared with a qualified retirement plan, the employer has greater flexibility to design welfare plan benefits so that the plan will favor highly compensated or key employees. Welfare plan benefits are subject to limited nondiscrimination testing requirements. See Code §§ 79(d) (life insurance), 105(h) (health care plans), 127(b) (educational assistance), 129(d) (dependent care), 137(c) (adoption assistance). Cafeteria plans also are subject to limited nondiscrimination testing. See Code § 125(b). Although a complete discussion of the various Code nondiscrimination tests for welfare benefit plans is beyond the scope of an introductory course on employee benefits law, a bit of historical background is useful.

When Congress enacted the current system of nondiscrimination requirements for qualified retirement plans described in Chapter Three, Congress also enacted similar requirements for certain welfare benefit plans based on the qualified plan concept of a highly compensated employee. In an unprecedented act, these nondiscrimination requirements for welfare benefit plans, which were codified as Section 89 of the Code, later were retroactively repealed by Congress:

> Without question, the most controversial benefits provision of [the Tax Reform Act of 1986] was Code Section 89, which imposed mandatory, extraordinarily complex nondiscrimination requirements on health plans and group term life plans. The outpouring of consternation that led to its subsequent repeal is a singular event on the post-ERISA legislative scorecard—the sole instance in which Congress has been forced to backtrack after staking out a position ostensibly in the interests of employees. Ultimately, Congress became convinced that the cost and complexity of the Section 89 rules would not justify the protection against discrimination in favor of the highly compensated that the new rules were intended to effect, but not until plan sponsors had spent many million of dollars to do demographic testing necessitated by the onset of the rules.

AMERICAN BAR ASSOCIATION, EMPLOYEE BENEFITS LAW 12–13 (2d ed. 2000).

The repeal of Section 89 left intact the status quo, which permitted fully insured health care plans to be discriminatory. As a result, it was not uncommon for an employer to provide a select group of executives with a separate plan that offered more generous health care benefits and lower premiums and deductibles than the health care plan provided to rank and file workers. The Affordable Care Act changed the status quo so that both fully insured and self-insured group health plans were subject to the same nondiscrimination testing requirements under Code Section 105(h). See ACA § 1001. Enforcement of Section 105(h) for fully insured group health plans has been suspended until further regulatory guidance is issued. See IRS Notice 2011–1.

5.　THE VOCABULARY OF HEALTH CARE PLANS

Although health care plans can be designed in a variety of ways, in general there are two main factors that determine the plan's design: (1) how the costs of the plan are controlled; and (2) how much freedom of choice the participants have to access health care services and to select their health care providers. These two factors result in a range of plan designs. At one end of the range is the traditional fee-for-service insurance plan. At the opposite end of the range is the health maintenance organization (HMO). In between lie fee-for-service plans with managed care features and preferred provider organizations (PPOs). Each plan's design represents a choice that attempts to balance freedom of choice for the plan's participants and cost-control mechanisms for the employer.

HMOs are designed to provide comprehensive health care services to their enrollees. The HMO contracts with or employ physicians and other health care provides, and also contracts with hospitals to give enrollees access to hospital care. (Some large HMOs even own and operate their own hospitals). In contrast, fee-for-service insurance plans simply reimburse health care providers for services rendered that are covered under the terms of the group insurance policy. Commercial insurers and employer self-insured health plans increasingly use managed care elements to encourage employees to use certain designated health care providers, who have agreed in advance to limit the fee they charge for services in exchange for an increased volume of patients. These designated health care providers form the plan's PPO network, and help to reduce the costs of the plan.

The financial incentives within a health plan can affect a physician's decision-making process. For example, a HMO may tie the amount of the physician's annual bonus directly to the costs of services authorized by the physician from providers outside of the HMO's network, or tie the bonus pool for all of the HMO's physicians to the total expenses incurred by the HMO for patient care. Although these financial incentives can encourage the HMO's physicians to minimize unnecessary health care services and procedures, they also may result in the rationing of care or delays in diagnosis and treatment that adversely impact the health of the HMO's enrollees. *Pegram v. Herdrich*, 530 U.S. 211 (2000), reproduced in Chapter Five, provides one illustration of an adverse patient overcome that resulted from a physician's decision to delay diagnostic treatment. *Aetna Health Inc. v. Davila*, 542 U.S. 200 (2004), reproduced in Chapter Seven, provides an illustration of how cost-driven treatment decisions by HMO administrators can result in serious injuries to their patients.

The PPO has emerged as a strong middle-ground alternative to traditional fee-for-service insurance plans and HMOs. A PPO is a panel of health care providers who individually contract with insurance companies and/or employers to offer health care benefits to their members at a reduced rate. PPO network physicians generally do not assume financial risk for the provision of health care services. Typically, PPOs reimburse their physicians on a negotiated fee schedule or a discounted fee-for-service basis. PPO plans choose physicians to fit geographic and specialty areas, often in response to requests from employers who use the PPO network for their self-insured health care plans. Participants in these employer-sponsored health care plans can receive health care services either from PPO (or in-network) providers or from non-PPO (or out-of-network) providers, but generally must pay more when receiving care from a non-PPO provider.

QUESTION

The two design factors of controlling the costs of the plan and providing participants in the plan with freedom of choice obviously are in conflict. If you were given the option of choosing among the various types of health care plans, what type of plan would you prefer to participate in? How significant would the cost of your premium to participate in the plan or your deductible amount be in influencing your decision?

6.   INNOVATION: CONSUMER-DRIVEN HEALTH CARE

In an effort to reduce rapidly escalating costs, employers have modified their approach to managing employee health care benefits. Terms such as *defined contribution* and *consumer-driven* health care plans have been used to describe these new approaches. These terms generally refer to programs in which employees are the direct purchasers of health care services rather than the indirect beneficiaries of purchases made by the employer. Consumer-driven health care plans are designed so that employees will be more prudent purchasers of health care services.

Employers are interested in consumer-driven health care plans for a number of reasons. First, employers want more cost-effective ways to provide health care benefits for their workers. Second, employers may want to limit their involvement in the plan to contributing a specified amount for health care benefits and letting the employees choose the health care services that they desire. Third, employers may be able to provide workers more choice, control, and flexibility through a consumer-driven approach.

Health Savings Accounts and High-Deductible Health Care Plans

The dominant form of consumer-driven health care plans today is the *health savings account* (HSA), which was authorized by the Medicare Prescription Drug Improvement and Modernization Act of 2003, Pub. L. No. 108–173, § 1201, 117 Stat. 2066. A HSA is a tax-exempt trust or custodial account that is established by an individual for the purpose of paying qualified medical expenses of the account beneficiary. HSAs are regulated by the Internal Revenue Code, most notably Code Section 223 and the prohibited transactions rules of Code Section 4975. See DOL Field Assistance Bulletin 2006–2.

In order for an individual to make contributions to a HSA, the account beneficiary must have health insurance coverage through a *high-deductible health plan* (HDHP). For 2014, a HDHP must have a deductible of at least $1,250 for an individual and $2,500 for family coverage. The maximum out-of-pocket expense for participants in HDHPs in 2014 was $6,350 for individual coverage and $12,700 for family coverage. (These amounts are indexed for inflation in future years.)

The primary attraction of the HDHP for employers is the dramatic lowering of the costs associated with the plan. These lower costs are a direct reflection of the higher deductible amounts for the participants in the plan. When switching from a traditional insured plan to a HDHP, the employer may pass on these cost savings to workers in the form of lower premiums, or the employer may use the savings to reduce its own contributions to the plan.

The cost-saving premise that underlies the consumer-driven approach is based on personal accountability for health care spending. In a HSA/HDHP arrangement, each year the individual must pay, either out-of-pocket or using funds from the HSA, for health care services until the annual deductible amount under the HDHP has been satisfied. This plan design encourages the individual to make prudent spending decisions for health care services and treatment. Surveys of participants in consumer-driven health care plans indicate that they are more cost-conscious in making health care decisions and that they are more willing to participate in a wellness program if their employer offers one.

HSAs that are voluntarily established by employees are not employee welfare benefits plans that are subject to regulation under Title I of ERISA. See DOL Field Assistance Bulletin 2004–1. A HDHP established by the employer is an employee welfare benefit plan that is subject to regulation under Title I of ERISA. See id. The employer may encourage its employees to establish HSAs by selecting a vendor or vendors for employees to use in establishing their HSAs. The employer also may make contributions to the HSAs that are established by its employees.

A HSA is owned by the individual employee and is completely portable when the employee terminates employment. HSA funds can be rolled over to another HSA. Unlike flexible health care spending accounts in a cafeteria plan, funds contributed to the HSA that are not spent in the year of contribution can accumulate in unlimited amounts and may be used to pay for qualifying medical expenses in future years.

Distributions and Contributions

A HSA functions similarly to an IRA. Contributions to the HSA (whether made by the employee or the employer) are deductible from the employee's taxable income. Investment earnings on the funds accumulated in the HSA are tax-deferred. Distributions of HSA funds that are used to pay for qualifying medical expenses (as defined in Code Section 213(d)) are tax-free. Distributions from a HSA that are not used to pay qualifying medical expenses are included in gross income and further subject to an additional excise tax of 20%. This excise tax does not apply, however, if the distribution is made due to the death or disability of the account owner, or if the distribution is made after the account owner attains the age of Medicare eligibility. See Code § 223.

In 2014, the maximum annual deductible contribution to a HSA was $3,300 for individual coverage or $6,550 for family coverage. Catch up contributions to a HSA are permitted for individuals who have attained age 55 by the end of the taxable year. In 2014, the additional catch-up contribution amount was $1,000. (These dollar amounts are indexed for inflation in future years.)

The employer is not required to make contributions to the HSAs of its employees. If the employer does choose to make HSA contributions for its employees, the employer is required to make *comparable contributions.* See generally Treas. Reg. §§ 54.4980G. Employer contributions are considered to be comparable if the employer contributes the same dollar amount or the same percentage of the HDHP amount deductible for all eligible employees who are in the same category of HDHP coverage. For example, an employer may choose to make a $500 contribution for each eligible employee who has individual coverage under the employer's HDHP, and make a $1,000 contribution for each eligible employee who has family coverage.

An employer may have different contribution amounts for full-time and part-time employees, but may not have different contribution amounts based on other job classification criteria, such as distinguishing between salaried and hourly employees. The employer is not required to make comparable HSA contributions for collective bargaining unit employees. When determining the pool of comparable employees, the employer may disregard any employees who are designated as highly compensated employees under Code Section 414(q), and may make larger contributions to the HSAs of nonhighly compensated employees than for highly compensated employees. In administering these comparability rules, the rules for qualified plans that consolidate controlled group members into a single "employer" and a single group of "employees" for testing purposes are used. See generally Treas. Reg. § 54.4980G–2. These controlled group rules, which also apply to qualified retirement plans, are described in Section F of Chapter Three.

Employers who make HSA contributions that are not comparable are subject to an excise tax penalty. The excise tax penalty is 35% of the total amount of all contributions made by the employer to HSAs during the calendar year. See Code § 4980G.

There are legitimate reasons why an employer may desire to make HSA contributions that are not comparable. For example, an employer may desire to condition the employer's HSA contribution on the employee's participation in health promotion programs such as health assessments, disease management programs or wellness programs that are designed to lower the costs of the employer's plan. Under the comparability rules, unless all of the comparable employees satisfy this condition (an unlikely outcome) and thereby earn the employer's HSA additional contribution, the employer's HSA contributions are not comparable and *all* of the employer's HSA contributions for the year will be subject to the 35% excise tax penalty. See Treas. Reg. § 54.4980G–4, Q & A–9.

To avoid violating the comparability rules for employer HSA contributions, the employer may make the HSA contributions though a cafeteria plan. Using the above example, the comparability rules do not apply if, under the written terms of the employer's cafeteria plan, the employees have the right to elect to receive in cash the employer's bonus amount for participation in the employer's health promotion programs, or to elect to have the employer contribute the bonus amount through the cafeteria plan to the employee's HSA account. See Treas. Reg. § 54.4980G–5.

Transfers of HSA Funds

HSAs are designed to be portable. An employee may make a trustee-to-trustee transfer of the balance of a HSA account to another HSA account. Permitted HSA to HSA transfers are unlimited in amount.

An individual may make a one-time trustee-to-trustee transfer to a HSA from an IRA that is established by the individual and not through an employer. The amount of the transfer is limited to the individual's maximum annual HSA contribution amount in effect for the year of the transfer. The funds transferred reduce, dollar for dollar, the contributions that may be made to the individual's HSA for that year.

Employees who participate in a health care flexible spending account through a cafeteria plan with a grace period permitting the reimbursement of medical expenses incurred up to two months and fifteen days after a new plan year begins generally cannot contribute to a HSA until the grace period ends. See IRS Notice 2005–86. This prohibition does not apply if the employee makes a one-time qualifying transfer of the residual balance of the employee's health care flexible spending account at the end of the plan year to a HSA. Such a one-time qualifying transfer to a HSA from a health care flexible spending account does not reduce the maximum annual contribution amount that the individual may make to the HSA during the year the transfer is made.

Public Policy Issues

Consumer-driven health care plans raise significant public policy issues. One public policy debate centers around the potential problem of adverse selection. If an employer offers employees the choice between participating in a HSA/HDHP or a traditional health care plan with lower deductible amounts, healthy workers are likely to prefer the lower cost of the HSA/HDHP arrangement. The result could be a higher concentration of participants with substantial health care expenses in the lower deductible plan, which in turn will result in significantly higher premiums for the lower deductible plan over time.

A second public policy debate concerns the tax expenditure for HSA contributions and how this tax expenditure is distributed among workers of varying income levels. Proponents of HSAs have proposed to increase the maximum annual contribution amount. Opponents argue that such an increase would disproportionately favor higher-income taxpayers, who benefit the most from the tax deduction permitted for HSA contributions.

A third public policy debate concerns whether participants in consumer-driven health care plans have access to the information necessary to make informed decisions about the cost and quality of health care services. Consumer-driven health care plans shift responsibility to the participants in the plan for decisions concerning the utilization of health care services. Without access to reliable information concerning the costs and quality of medical care, skeptics argue that consumer-directed health care plans are unlikely to achieve lower costs.

C. INSURED AND SELF-INSURED HEALTH CARE PLANS

1. THE SAVINGS AND DEEMER CLAUSES OF ERISA SECTION 514

As a consequence of the two Supreme Court decisions reproduced below, *Metropolitan Life Insurance Co. v. Massachusetts* and *FMC Corp. v. Holliday,* health care plans sponsored by private employers today are categorized as either *insured* or *self-insured*. The significance of this distinction is explored in the materials following the two cases.

As you read *Metropolitan Life* and *FMC Corp.*, focus carefully on the Supreme Court's statutory interpretation analysis of ERISA's preemption provision, Section 514. How do the "savings" and "deemer" clauses of ERISA Section 514(b)(2) affect the scope of ERISA Section 514(a), which generally preempts "any and all State laws insofar as they may now or hereafter relate to" an employee benefit plan?

METROPOLITAN LIFE INSURANCE COMPANY v. MASSACHUSETTS

United States Supreme Court, 1985.
471 U.S. 724, 105 S.Ct. 2380, 85 L.Ed.2d 728.

JUSTICE BLACKMUN delivered the opinion of the Court.

A Massachusetts statute requires that specified minimum mental health care benefits be provided a Massachusetts resident who is insured under a general insurance policy, an accident or sickness insurance policy, or an employee health care plan that covers hospital and surgical expenses. The first question before us in these cases is whether the state statute, as applied to insurance policies purchased by employee health care plans regulated by the federal Employee Retirement Income Security Act of 1974, is preempted by that Act. * * *

I

A

General health insurance typically is sold as group insurance to an employer or other group. Group insurance presently is subject to extensive state regulation, including regulation of the carrier, regulation of the sale and advertising of the insurance, and regulation of the content of the contracts. Mandated benefit laws, that require an insurer to provide a certain kind of benefit to cover a specified illness or procedure whenever someone purchases a certain kind of insurance, are a subclass of such content regulation.

While mandated benefit statutes are a relatively recent phenomenon, statutes regulating the substantive terms of insurance contracts have become commonplace in all 50 States over the last 30 years. Perhaps the most familiar are those regulating the content of automobile insurance policies.

The substantive terms of group health insurance contracts, in particular, also have been extensively regulated by the States. For example, the majority of States currently require that coverage for dependents continue beyond any contractually imposed age limitation when the dependent is incapable of self-sustaining employment because of mental or physical handicap; such statutes date back to the early 1960's. And over the last 15 years all 50 States have required that coverage of infants begin at birth, rather than at some time shortly after birth, as had been the prior practice in the unregulated market. Many state statutes require that insurers offer on an optional basis particular kinds of coverage to purchasers. Others require insurers either to offer or mandate that insurance policies include coverage for services rendered by a particular type of health care provider.

Mandated benefit statutes, then, are only one variety of a matrix of state laws that regulate the substantive content of health insurance policies to further state health policy. Massachusetts Gen. Laws Ann., ch. 175, § 47B (West Supp.1985), is typical of mandated benefit laws currently in place in the majority of States. With respect to a Massachusetts resident, it requires any general health insurance policy that provides hospital and surgical coverage, or any benefit plan that has such coverage, to provide as well a certain minimum of mental health protection. In particular, § 47B requires that a health insurance policy provide 60 days of coverage for confinement in a mental hospital, coverage for confinement in a general hospital equal to that provided by the policy for non-mental illness, and certain minimum outpatient benefits.

Section 47B was designed to address problems encountered in treating mental illness in Massachusetts. The Commonwealth determined that its working people needed to be protected against the high cost of treatment for such illness. It also believed that, without insurance, mentally ill workers were often institutionalized in large state mental hospitals, and that mandatory insurance would lead to a higher incidence of more effective treatment in private community mental health centers.

In addition, the Commonwealth concluded that the voluntary insurance market was not adequately providing mental health coverage, because of "adverse selection" in mental health insurance: good insurance risks were not purchasing coverage, and this drove up the price of coverage for those who otherwise might purchase mental health insurance. The legislature believed that the public interest required that it correct the insurance market in the Commonwealth by mandating minimum coverage levels, effectively forcing the good-risk individuals to become part of the risk pool, and enabling insurers to price the insurance at an average market rather than a market retracted due to adverse selection. Section 47B, then, was intended to help safeguard the public against the high costs of comprehensive inpatient and outpatient mental health care, reduce nonpsychiatric medical care expenditures for mentally related illness, shift the delivery of treatment from inpatient to outpatient services, and relieve the Commonwealth of some of the financial burden it otherwise would encounter with respect to mental health problems.

It is our task in these cases to decide whether such insurance regulation violates or is inconsistent with federal law.

B

The federal Employee Retirement Income Security Act of 1974 (ERISA) comprehensively regulates employee pension and welfare plans. An employee welfare benefit plan or welfare plan is defined as one which provides to employees "medical, surgical, or hospital care or benefits, or benefits in the event of sickness, accident, disability [or] death," whether these benefits are provided "through the purchase of insurance or otherwise." ERISA § 3(1). Plans may self-insure or they may purchase insurance for their participants. Plans that purchase insurance—so-called "insured plans"—are directly affected by state laws that regulate the insurance industry.

ERISA imposes upon pension plans a variety of substantive requirements relating to participation, funding and vesting. It also establishes various uniform procedural standards concerning reporting, disclosure and fiduciary responsibility for both pension and welfare plans. It does not regulate the substantive content of welfare benefit plans.

ERISA thus contains almost no federal regulation of the terms of [welfare] benefit plans. It does, however, contain a broad preemption provision declaring that the statute shall "supersede any and all State laws insofar as they may now or hereafter relate to any employee benefit plan." ERISA § 514(a). Appellant Metropolitan argues that ERISA preempts Massachusetts' mandated-benefit law insofar as § 47B restricts the kinds of insurance policies that benefit plans may purchase.

While § 514(a) of ERISA broadly preempts state laws that relate to an employee-benefit plan, that preemption is substantially qualified by an "insurance saving clause," § 514(b)(2)(A), which broadly states that, with one exception, nothing in ERISA "shall be construed to exempt or relieve any person from any law of any State which regulates insurance, banking, or securities." The specified exception to the saving clause is found in § 514(b)(2)(B), the so-called "deemer clause," which states that no employee benefit plan, with certain exceptions not relevant here, "shall be deemed to be an insurance company or other insurer, bank, trust company, or investment company or to be engaged in the business of insurance or banking for purposes of any law of any State purporting to regulate insurance companies, insurance contracts, banks, trust companies, or investment companies." Massachusetts argues that its mandated benefit law, as applied to insurance companies that sell insurance to benefit plans, is a "law which regulates insurance," and therefore is saved from the effect of the general preemption clause of ERISA.

* * *

II

Appellants are Metropolitan Life Insurance Company and Travelers Insurance Company (insurers) who are located in New York and Connecticut respectively and who issue group health policies providing hospital and surgical coverage to plans, or to employers or unions that employ or represent employees residing in Massachusetts. Under the terms of § 47B, both appellants are required to provide minimal mental health benefits in policies issued to cover Commonwealth residents.

In 1979, the Attorney General of Massachusetts brought suit in Massachusetts Superior Court for declaratory and injunctive relief to enforce § 47B. The Commonwealth asserted that since January 1, 1976, the effective date of § 47B, the insurers had issued policies to group policyholders situated outside Massachusetts that provided for hospital and surgical coverage for certain residents of the Commonwealth. It further asserted that those policies failed to provide Massachusetts resident beneficiaries the mental health coverage mandated by § 47B, and that the insurers intended to issue more such policies, believing themselves not bound by § 47B for policies issued outside the Commonwealth.

* * *

[The Supreme Judicial Court of Massachusetts eventually ruled that Section 47B was saved from ERISA preemption as a law regulating insurance.]

III

In deciding whether a federal law preempts a state statute, our task is to ascertain Congress' intent in enacting the federal statute at issue. Preemption may be either express or implied, and "is compelled whether Congress' command is explicitly stated in the statute's language or implicitly contained in its structure and purpose." Shaw v. Delta Air Lines, Inc., 463 U.S. 85, 95 (1983). The narrow statutory ERISA question presented is whether Mass. Gen. Laws Ann., ch. 175, § 47B (West Supp.1985), is a law "which regulates insurance" within the meaning of § 514(b)(2)(A), and so would not be preempted by § 514(a).

A

Section 47B clearly "relate[s] to" welfare plans governed by ERISA so as to fall within the reach of ERISA's preemption provision, § 514(a). The broad scope of the preemption clause was noted recently in *Shaw v. Delta Air Lines, Inc.,* where we held that the New York Human Rights Law and that State's Disability Benefits Law "relate[d] to" welfare plans governed by ERISA. The phrase "relate to" was given its broad common sense meaning, such that a state law "relate[s] to" a benefit plan "in the normal sense of the phrase, if it has a connection with or reference to such a plan." 463 U.S. at 97. The preemption provision was intended to displace all state laws that fall within its sphere, even including state laws that are consistent with ERISA's substantive requirements. Id. at 98–99. "[E]ven indirect state action bearing on private pensions may encroach upon the area of exclusive federal concern." Alessi v. Raybestos-Manhattan, Inc., 451 U.S. 504, 525 (1981).

Though § 47B is not denominated a benefit plan law, it bears indirectly but substantially on all insured benefit plans, for it requires them to purchase the mental health benefits specified in the statute when they purchase a certain kind of common insurance policy. The Commonwealth does not argue that § 47B as applied to policies purchased by benefit plans does not relate to those plans, and we agree with the Supreme Judicial Court that the mandated benefit law as applied relates to ERISA plans and thus is covered by ERISA's broad preemption provision set forth in § 514(a).

B

Nonetheless, the sphere in which § 514(a) operates was explicitly limited by § 514(b)(2). The insurance saving clause preserves any state law "which regulates insurance, banking, or securities." The two preemption sections, while clear enough on their faces, perhaps are not a model of legislative drafting, for while the general preemption clause broadly preempts state law, the saving clause appears broadly to preserve the States' lawmaking power over much of the same regulation. While Congress occasionally decides to return to the States what it has previously taken away, it does not normally do both at the same time.

Fully aware of this statutory complexity, we still have no choice but to "begin with the language employed by Congress and the assumption that the ordinary meaning of that language accurately expresses the legislative purpose." Park 'N Fly, Inc. v. Dollar Park and Fly, Inc., 469 U.S. 189, 194 (1985). We also must presume that Congress did not intend to preempt areas of traditional state regulation. See Jones v. Rath Packing Co., 430 U.S. 519, 525 (1977).

To state the obvious, § 47B regulates the terms of certain insurance contracts, and so seems to be saved from preemption by the saving clause as a law "which regulates insurance." This common sense view of the matter, moreover, is reinforced by the language of the subsequent subsection of ERISA, the "deemer clause," which states that an employee benefit plan shall not be deemed to be an insurance company "for purposes of any law of any State purporting to regulate insurance companies, *insurance contracts*, banks, trust companies, or investment companies." § 514(b)(2)(B) (emphasis added). By exempting from the saving clause laws regulating insurance contracts that apply directly to benefit plans, the deemer clause makes explicit Congress' intention to include laws that regulate insurance contracts within the scope of the insurance laws preserved by the saving clause. Unless Congress intended to include laws regulating insurance contracts within the scope of the insurance saving clause, it would have been unnecessary for the deemer clause explicitly to exempt such laws from the saving clause when they are applied directly to benefit plans.

The insurers nonetheless argue that § 47B is in reality a health law that merely operates on insurance contracts to accomplish its end, and that it is not the kind of traditional insurance law intended to be saved by § 514(b)(2)(A). We find this argument unpersuasive.

Initially, nothing in § 514(b)(2)(A), or in the "deemer clause" which modifies it, purports to distinguish between traditional and innovative insurance laws. The presumption is against preemption, and we are not inclined to read limitations into federal statutes in order to enlarge their preemptive scope. Further, there is no indication in the legislative history that Congress had such a distinction in mind.

Appellants assert that state laws that directly regulate the insurer, and laws that regulate such matters as the way in which insurance may be sold, are traditional laws subject to the clause, while laws that regulate the substantive terms of insurance contracts are recent innovations more properly seen as health laws rather than as insurance laws, which § 514(b)(2)(A) does not save. This distinction reads the saving clause out of ERISA entirely, because laws that regulate only the insurer, or the way in which it may sell insurance, do not "relate to" benefit plans in the first instance. Because they would not be preempted by § 514(a), they do not need to be "saved" by § 514(b)(2)(A). There is no indication that Congress could have intended the saving clause to operate only to guard against too expansive readings of the general preemption clause that might have included laws wholly unrelated to plans. Appellants' construction, in our view, violates the plain meaning of the statutory language and renders redundant both the saving clause it is construing, as well as the deemer clause which it precedes, and accordingly has little to recommend it.

Moreover, it is both historically and conceptually inaccurate to assert that mandated benefit laws are not traditional insurance laws. As we have indicated, state laws regulating the substantive terms of insurance contracts were commonplace well before the mid-70's, when Congress considered ERISA. * * *

* * *

Nothing in the legislative history of ERISA suggests a different result. There is no discussion in that history of the relationship between the general preemption clause and the saving clause, and indeed very little discussion of the saving clause at all. In the early versions of ERISA, the general preemption clause preempted only those state laws dealing with subjects regulated by ERISA. The clause was significantly broadened at the last minute, well after the saving clause was in its present form, to include all state laws that relate to benefit plans. The change was made with little explanation by the Conference Committee, and there is no indication in the legislative history that Congress was aware of the new prominence given the saving clause in light of the rewritten preemption clause, or was aware that the saving clause was in conflict with the general preemption provision. There is a complete absence of evidence that Congress intended the narrow reading of the saving clause suggested by appellants here. Appellants do call to our attention a few passing references in the record of the floor debate to the "narrow" exceptions to the preemption clause, but these are far too frail a support on which to rest appellants' rather unnatural reading of the clause.

We therefore decline to impose any limitation on the saving clause beyond those Congress imposed in the clause itself and in the "deemer clause" which modifies it. If a state law "regulates insurance," as mandated benefit laws do, it is not preempted. Nothing in the language, structure, or legislative history of the Act supports a more narrow reading of the clause, whether it be the Supreme Judicial Court's attempt to save only state regulations unrelated to the substantive provisions of ERISA, or the insurers' more speculative attempt to read the savings clause out of the statute.

We are aware that our decision results in a distinction between insured and uninsured plans, leaving the former open to indirect regulation while the latter are not. By so doing we merely give life to a distinction created by Congress in the "deemer clause," a distinction Congress is aware of and one it has chosen not to alter. We also are aware that appellants' construction of the statute would eliminate some of the disuniformities currently facing national plans that enter into local markets to purchase insurance. Such disuniformities, however, are the inevitable result of the congressional decision to "save" local insurance regulation. Arguments as to the wisdom of these policy choices must be directed at Congress.

* * *

FMC CORP. v. HOLLIDAY

United States Supreme Court, 1990.
498 U.S. 52, 111 S.Ct. 403, 112 L.Ed.2d 356.

JUSTICE O'CONNOR delivered the opinion of the Court.

This case calls upon the Court to decide whether the Employee Retirement Income Security Act of 1974 (ERISA) preempts a Pennsylvania law precluding employee welfare benefit plans from exercising subrogation rights on a claimant's tort recovery.

I

Petitioner, FMC Corporation (FMC), operates the FMC Salaried Health Care Plan (Plan), an employee welfare benefit plan within the meaning of ERISA that provides health benefits to FMC employees and their dependents. The Plan is self-funded; it does not purchase an insurance policy from any insurance company in order to satisfy its obligations to its participants. Among its provisions is a subrogation clause under which a Plan member agrees to reimburse the Plan for benefits paid if the member recovers on a claim in a liability action against a third party.

Respondent, Cynthia Ann Holliday, is the daughter of FMC employee and Plan member Gerald Holliday. In 1987, she was seriously injured in an automobile accident. The Plan paid a portion of her medical expenses. Gerald Holliday brought a negligence action on behalf of his daughter in Pennsylvania state court against the driver of the automobile in which she was injured. The parties settled the claim. While the action was pending, FMC notified the Hollidays that it would seek reimbursement for the amounts it had paid for respondent's medical expenses. The Hollidays replied that they would not reimburse the Plan, asserting that § 1720 of Pennsylvania's Motor Vehicle Financial Responsibility Law, 75 Pa. Cons. Stat. § 1720 (1987), precludes subrogation by FMC. Section 1720 states that "[i]n actions arising out of the maintenance or use of a motor vehicle, there shall be no right of subrogation or reimbursement from a claimant's tort recovery with respect to. . .benefits. . .payable under section 1719." Section 1719 refers to benefit payments by "[a]ny program, group contract or other arrangement."

Petitioner, proceeding in diversity, then sought a declaratory judgment in Federal District Court. The court granted respondent's motion for summary judgment, holding that § 1720 prohibits FMC's exercise of subrogation rights on Holliday's claim against the driver. The United States Court of Appeals for the Third Circuit affirmed. 885 F.2d 79 (1989). The court held that § 1720, unless preempted, bars FMC from enforcing its contractual subrogation provision. According to the court, ERISA preempts § 1720 if ERISA's "deemer clause," ERISA § 514(b)(2)(B), exempts the Plan from state subrogation laws. The Court of Appeals determined that "the deemer clause [was] meant mainly to reach back-door attempts by states to regulate core ERISA concerns in the guise of insurance regulation." 885 F.2d at 86. Pointing out that the parties had not suggested that the Pennsylvania antisubrogation law addressed "a core type of ERISA matter which Congress sought to protect by the preemption provision," the court concluded that the Pennsylvania law is not preempted. The Third Circuit's holding conflicts with decisions of other Courts of Appeals that have construed ERISA's deemer clause to protect self-funded plans from all state insurance regulation. We granted certiorari to resolve this conflict, and now vacate and remand. * * *

II

In determining whether federal law preempts a state statute, we look to congressional intent. Preemption may be either express or implied, and "is compelled whether Congress' command is explicitly stated in the statute's language or implicitly contained in its structure and purpose." Shaw v. Delta Air Lines, Inc., 463 U.S. 85, 95 (1983). Three provisions of ERISA speak expressly to the question of preemption:

Except as provided in subsection (b) of this section [the saving clause], the provisions of this subchapter and subchapter III of this chapter shall supersede any and all State laws insofar as they may now or hereafter relate to any employee benefit plan. ERISA § 514(a) (preemption clause).

Except as provided in subparagraph (B) [the deemer clause], nothing in this subchapter shall be construed to exempt or relieve any person from any law of any State which regulates insurance, banking, or securities. ERISA § 514(b)(2)(A) (saving clause).

Neither an employee benefit plan . . . nor any trust established under such a plan, shall be deemed to be an insurance company or other insurer, bank, trust company, or investment company or to be engaged in the business of insurance or banking for purposes of any law of any State purporting to regulate insurance companies, insurance contracts, banks, trust companies, or investment companies. ERISA § 514(b)(2)(B) (deemer clause).

We indicated in *Metropolitan Life Ins. Co. v. Massachusetts*, 471 U.S. 724 (1985), that these provisions "are not a model of legislative drafting." Id. at 739. Their operation is nevertheless discernible. The preemption clause is conspicuous for its breadth. It establishes as an area of exclusive federal concern the subject of every state law that "relate[s] to" an employee benefit plan governed by ERISA. The saving clause returns to the States the power to enforce those state laws that "regulat[e] insurance," except as provided in the deemer clause. Under the deemer clause, an employee benefit plan governed by ERISA shall not be "deemed" an insurance company, an insurer, or engaged in the business of insurance for purposes of state laws "purporting to regulate" insurance companies or insurance contracts.

III

Pennsylvania's antisubrogation law "relate[s] to" an employee benefit plan. We made clear in *Shaw v. Delta Air Lines*, that a law relates to an employee welfare plan if it has "a connection with or reference to such a plan." 463 U.S. at 96–97. We based our reading in part on the plain language of the statute. Congress used the words " 'relate to' in § 514(a) [the preemption clause] in their broad sense." 463 U.S. at 98. It did not mean to preempt only state laws specifically designed to affect employee benefit plans. That interpretation would have made it unnecessary for Congress to enact ERISA § 514(b)(4), which exempts from preemption "generally" applicable criminal laws of a State. We also emphasized that to interpret the preemption clause to apply only to state laws dealing with the subject matters covered by ERISA, such as reporting, disclosure, and fiduciary duties, would be incompatible with the provision's legislative history because the House and Senate versions of the bill that became

ERISA contained limited preemption clauses, applicable only to state laws relating to specific subjects covered by ERISA. These were rejected in favor of the present language in the Act, "indicat[ing] that the section's preemptive scope was as broad as its language." Shaw v. Delta Air Lines, 463 U.S. at 98.

Pennsylvania's antisubrogation law has a "reference" to benefit plans governed by ERISA. The statute states that "[i]n actions arising out of the maintenance or use of a motor vehicle, there shall be no right of subrogation or reimbursement from a claimant's tort recovery with respect to . . . benefits . . . paid or payable under section 1719." 75 Pa. Cons. Stat. § 1720 (1987). Section 1719 refers to "[a]ny program, group contract or other arrangement for payment of benefits." These terms "includ[e], *but [are] not limited to*, benefits payable by a hospital plan corporation or a professional health service corporation." § 1719 (emphasis added).

The Pennsylvania statute also has a "connection" to ERISA benefit plans. In the past, we have not hesitated to apply ERISA's preemption clause to state laws that risk subjecting plan administrators to conflicting state regulations. See, e.g., Shaw v. Delta Air Lines, 463 U.S. at 95–100 (state laws making unlawful plan provisions that discriminate on the basis of pregnancy and requiring plans to provide specific benefits "relate to" benefit plans); Alessi v. Raybestos-Manhattan, Inc., 451 U.S. 504, 523–26 (1981) (state law prohibiting plans from reducing benefits by amount of workers' compensation awards "relate[s] to" employee benefit plan). To require plan providers to design their programs in an environment of differing state regulations would complicate the administration of nationwide plans, producing inefficiencies that employers might offset with decreased benefits. See Fort Halifax Packing Co. v. Coyne, 482 U.S. 1, 10 (1987). Thus, where a "patchwork scheme of regulation would introduce considerable inefficiencies in benefit program operation," we have applied the preemption clause to ensure that benefit plans will be governed by only a single set of regulations. Id. at 11.

Pennsylvania's anti-subrogation law prohibits plans from being structured in a manner requiring reimbursement in the event of recovery from a third party. It requires plan providers to calculate benefit levels in Pennsylvania based on expected liability conditions that differ from those in States that have not enacted similar anti-subrogation legislation. Application of differing state subrogation laws to plans would therefore frustrate plan administrators' continuing obligation to calculate uniform benefit levels nationwide. * * *

There is no dispute that the Pennsylvania law falls within ERISA's insurance saving clause, which provides, "*[e]xcept as provided in [the deemer clause]*, nothing in this subchapter shall be construed to exempt or relieve any person from any law of any State which regulates insurance," ERISA § 514(b)(2)(A) (emphasis added). Section 1720 directly controls the terms of insurance contracts by invalidating any subrogation provisions that they contain. See Metropolitan Life Ins. Co. v. Massachusetts, 471 U.S. at 740–41. It does not merely have an impact on the insurance industry; it is aimed at it. See Pilot Life Ins. Co. v. Dedeaux, 481 U.S. 41, 50 (1987). This returns the matter of subrogation to state law. Unless the statute is excluded from the reach of the saving clause by virtue of the deemer clause, therefore, it is not preempted.

We read the deemer clause to exempt self-funded ERISA plans from state laws that "regulat[e] insurance" within the meaning of the saving clause. By forbidding States to deem employee benefit plans "to be an insurance company or other insurer . . . or to be engaged in the business of insurance," the deemer clause relieves plans from state laws "purporting to regulate insurance." As a result, self-funded ERISA plans are exempt from state regulation insofar as that regulation "relate[s] to" the plans. State laws directed toward the plans are preempted because they relate to an employee benefit plan but are not "saved" because they do not regulate insurance. State laws that directly regulate insurance are "saved" but do not reach self-funded employee benefit plans because the plans may not be deemed to be insurance companies, other insurers, or engaged in the business of insurance for purposes of such state laws. On the other hand, employee benefit plans that are insured are subject to indirect state insurance regulation. An insurance company that insures a plan remains an insurer for purposes of state laws "purporting to regulate insurance" after application of the deemer clause. The insurance company is therefore not relieved from state insurance regulation. The ERISA plan is consequently bound by state insurance regulations insofar as they apply to the plan's insurer.

Our reading of the deemer clause is consistent with *Metropolitan Life Ins. Co. v. Massachusetts*. That case involved a Massachusetts statute requiring certain self-funded benefit plans and insurers issuing group health policies to plans to provide minimum mental health benefits. 471 U.S. at 734. * * * We concluded that the statute, as applied to insurers of plans, was not preempted because it regulated insurance and was therefore saved. Our decision, we acknowledged, "results in a distinction between insured and uninsured plans, leaving the former open to indirect regulation while the latter are not." Id. at 747. "By so doing, we merely give life to a distinction created by Congress in the 'deemer clause,' a distinction Congress is aware of and one it has chosen not to alter." Id.

* * *

Respondent resists our reading of the deemer clause and would attach to it narrower significance. According to the deemer clause, "[n]either an employee benefit plan . . . nor any trust established under such a plan, shall be deemed to be an insurance company or other insurer, bank, trust company, or investment company or to be engaged in the business of insurance or banking for purposes of any law of any State *purporting* to regulate insurance companies [or] insurance contracts." ERISA § 514(b)(2)(B) (emphasis added). Like the Court of Appeals, respondent would interpret the deemer clause to except from the saving clause only state insurance regulations that are pretexts for impinging upon core ERISA concerns. The National Conference of State Legislatures as amici curiae in support of respondent offer an alternative interpretation of the deemer clause. In their view, the deemer clause precludes States from deeming plans to be insurers only for purposes of state laws that apply to insurance as a business, such as laws relating to licensing and capitalization requirements.

These views are unsupported by ERISA's language. Laws that *purportedly* regulate insurance companies or insurance contracts are laws having the "appearance of" regulating or "intending" to regulate insurance companies or contracts. Black's Law Dictionary 1236 (6th ed.1990). Congress' use of the word does not indicate that it directed the deemer clause solely at deceit that it feared state legislatures would practice. Indeed, the Conference Report, in describing the deemer clause, omits the word "purporting," stating, "an employee benefit plan is not to be considered as an insurance company, bank, trust company, or investment company (and is not to be considered as engaged in the business of insurance or banking) for purposes of any State law that regulates insurance companies, insurance contracts, banks, trust companies, or investment companies." H.R. Conf. Rep. No. 93–1280, p. 383 (1974).

Nor, in our view, is the deemer clause directed solely at laws governing the business of insurance. It is plainly directed at "any law of any State purporting to regulate insurance companies, insurance contracts, banks, trust companies, or investment companies." ERISA § 514(b)(2)(B). Moreover, it is difficult to understand why Congress would have included *insurance contracts* in the preemption clause if it meant only to preempt state laws relating to the operation of insurance as a business. To be sure, the saving and deemer clauses employ differing language to achieve their ends—the former saving, except as provided in the deemer clause, "any law of any State which regulates insurance" and the latter referring to "any law of any State purporting to regulate insurance companies [or] insurance contracts." We view the language of the deemer clause, however, to be either coextensive with or broader, not narrower, than that of the saving clause. Our rejection of a restricted reading of the deemer clause does not lead to the deemer clause's engulfing the saving clause. As we have pointed out, the saving clause retains the independent effect of protecting state insurance regulation of insurance contracts purchased by employee benefit plans.

* * * Our interpretation of the deemer clause makes clear that if a plan is insured, a State may regulate it indirectly through regulation of its insurer and its insurer's insurance contracts; if the plan is uninsured, the State may not regulate it. As a result, employers will not face "conflicting or inconsistent State and local regulation of employee benefit plans." Shaw v. Delta Air Lines, Inc., 463 U.S. at 99. A construction of the deemer clause that exempts employee benefit plans from only those state regulations that encroach upon core ERISA concerns or that apply to insurance as a business would be fraught with administrative difficulties, necessitating definition of core ERISA concerns and of what constitutes business activity. It would therefore undermine Congress' desire to avoid "endless litigation over the validity of State action," see 120 Cong. Rec. 29942 (1974), and instead lead to employee benefit plans' expenditure of funds in such litigation.

In view of Congress' clear intent to exempt from direct state insurance regulation ERISA employee benefit plans, we hold that ERISA preempts the application of § 1720 of Pennsylvania's Motor Vehicle Financial Responsibility Law to the FMC Salaried Health Care Plan. We therefore vacate the judgment of the United States Court of Appeals for the Third Circuit and remand the case for further proceedings consistent with this opinion.

JUSTICE STEVENS, dissenting.

The Court's construction of the statute draws a broad and illogical distinction between benefit plans that are funded by the employer (self-insured plans) and those that are insured by regulated insurance companies (insured plans). Had Congress intended this result, it could have stated simply that "all State laws are preempted insofar as they relate to any self-insured employee plan." There would then have been no need for the "saving clause" to exempt state insurance laws from the preemption clause, or the "deemer clause," which the Court today reads as merely re-injecting into the scope of ERISA's preemption clause those same exempted state laws insofar as they relate to self-insured plans.

From the standpoint of the beneficiaries of ERISA plans—who after all are the primary beneficiaries of the entire statutory program—there is no apparent reason for treating self-insured plans differently from insured plans. Why should a self-insured plan have a right to enforce a subrogation clause against an injured employee while an insured plan may not? The notion that this disparate treatment of similarly situated beneficiaries is somehow supported by an interest in uniformity is singularly unpersuasive. If Congress had intended such an irrational result, surely it would have expressed it in straightforward English. At least one would expect that the reasons for drawing such an apparently irrational distinction would be discernible in the legislative history or in the literature discussing the legislation.

The Court's anomalous result would be avoided by a correct and narrower reading of either the basic preemption clause or the deemer clause.

* * *

NOTES AND QUESTIONS

1.   *The Significance of Insured Versus Self-Insured Health Care Plans.*

One consequence of ERISA's Title I preemption provisions, as interpreted and applied by the Supreme Court in *Metropolitan Life Insurance Co. v. Massachusetts* and in *FMC Corp. v. Holliday*, was the de facto creation of two categories of private health care plans under ERISA. "Insured" health care plans provide health care benefits to plan participants through the purchase of health care insurance. Because ERISA does not preempt state laws regulating insurance, insurance companies selling health care insurance policies (and, thus, indirectly the policy benefits to plan participants) are subject to regulation by state insurance laws. In particular, state insurance laws mandate and regulate the types of benefits that must be included in health insurance policies.

"Self-insured" or "self-funded" health care plans provide health care benefits to plan participants from a fund comprised of employer or employee contributions, or both, or out of the general assets of the employer. State laws attempting to regulate employee health care plans as "insurance" are preempted by ERISA and, therefore, do not apply to self-insured health care plans. The preemption of state laws with respect to self-insured private health care plans has been criticized often in the scholarly literature. Specifically, critics have argued that, due to ERISA's lack of substantive coverage and benefits requirements for private health care plans, such preemption in effect allows self-insured plans to operate in a regulatory void.

Colleen E. Medill, *HIPAA and Its Related Legislation: A New Role for ERISA In the Regulation of Private Health Care Plans?*, 65 TENN. L. REV. 485, 491–92 (1998) (citations omitted).

The Affordable Care Act addressed this regulatory void by enacting a number of benefits requirements that are applicable to both insured and self-insured health care plans. These requirements are discussed in detail later in Chapter Four. The ACA did not, however, completely eliminate the distinctions between insured and self-insured plans. Moreover, grandfathered self-insured plans remain exempt from many of the ACA's substantive coverage and benefits requirements. Thus, the characterization of a group health care plan as either insured or self-insured remains an important factor in the regulation of group health plans.

2. *The Significance of Self-Insured Health Care Plans.* In 2013, sixty-one percent of workers with health insurance were covered by an employer plan that was self-insured. Workers in large firms having 200 or more workers are much more likely to be in a self-insured plan (83%) than workers in small firms with fewer than 200 workers (16%). See KAISER FAMILY FOUNDATION, EMPLOYER HEALTH BENEFITS 2013 ANNUAL SURVEY 176.

3. *State Laws "Regulating Insurance" Under Section 514(b)(2)(A).* In omitted portions of *Metropolitan Life* and *FMC Corp.*, the Supreme Court relied upon prior judicial decisions under the McCarran-Ferguson Act to interpret the statutory language of ERISA Section 514(b)(2)(A). The McCarran-Ferguson Act provides that "[n]o Act of Congress shall be construed to invalidate, impair, or supersede any law enacted by any State for the purpose of regulating the business of insurance." 15 U.S.C. § 1012(b). In *Kentucky Association of Health Plans, Inc. v. Miller*, 538 U.S. 329 (2003), the Supreme Court later jettisoned the approach used in *Metropolitan Life* and replaced it with a two-factor test for determining when a state law "regulates insurance" within the meaning of Section 514(b)(2)(A). *Miller* is reproduced in Chapter Seven of the casebook.

4. *The Supreme Court's Influence on National Health Care Policy.* *Metropolitan Life* and *FMC Corp.* provide one prominent example of the influence that the Supreme Court has had on the structure of the health care insurance system and the delivery of health care services. Other examples are found later in Chapter Four and Chapters Five, Six and Seven of the casebook, which cover the topics of ERISA fiduciary responsibilities, civil claims and remedies, and the preemption of state laws. As you read these landmark Supreme Court decisions in forthcoming chapters, consider whether Congress in 1974 awarded too much discretion to the federal judiciary regarding interpretation and enforcement of ERISA's provisions. Does the Supreme Court have too much influence over national health care policy?

2. HOW SELF-INSURED HEALTH CARE PLANS WORK (AND WHY THEY COST LESS)

In an insured health care plan, the insurance company assumes the financial risk that the premium amount charged for coverage may be inadequate to cover all of the claims for benefits under the terms of the plan. Therefore, when determining the amount of the premium the insurance company must charge an additional amount to account for this financial risk. If the insurance company desires to make a profit on its policy, the premium charged will be increased accordingly.

When an employer sponsors a self-insured plan, the employer effectively acts as its own insurer and assumes the financial risk of catastrophic claims. The employer uses the premiums that would have been paid to the insurance company and places these funds in a separate trust. The plan administrator processes claims for plan benefits, and the trustee of the trust disburses the trust funds to pay for plan benefits. A self-insured plan generally is less costly than an insured plan with comparable coverage and benefits features because the employer's premium calculation does not include additional amounts for financial risk and profit. In addition, under the Affordable Care Act, self-insured plans are not required to provide comprehensive coverage of the ten essential health benefits listed in the statute. See ACA § 1302(b). Offering a lesser package of benefits results in further cost savings for self-insured plans.

To protect against the risk of catastrophic health care claims, the employer who sponsors a self-insured health care plan may purchase *stop-loss insurance*. Stop-loss insurance policies provide that the stop-loss insurer will pay for claims made by participants in the self-insured plan that exceed a specified dollar amount. This dollar amount is known as the policy's *attachment point*. As the attachment point under stop-loss insurance policy declines, a self-insured health care plan may begin to resemble an insured health care plan in the sense that the employer is assuming very little financial risk.

In *American Medical Security, Inc. v. Bartlett,* the technical issue before the Fourth Circuit was whether ERISA preempted a Maryland insurance regulation directed at stop-loss insurance policies. As you read the case, notice how the preemption of state insurance laws under ERISA's deemer clause provides yet another economic incentive for employers to sponsor self-insured health care plans.

AMERICAN MEDICAL SECURITY, INC. V. BARTLETT
United States Court of Appeals, Fourth Circuit, 1997.
111 F.3d 358.

NIEMEYER, CIRCUIT JUDGE:

We must decide whether the Employee Retirement Income Security Act of 1974 ("ERISA") preempts a Maryland insurance regulation that fixes the minimum attachment point for stop-loss insurance policies issued to self-funded employee benefit plans covered by ERISA. See Code of Maryland Regulations § 9.31.02 (hereafter "COMAR"). The state regulation is designed to prevent insurers and self-funded employee benefit plans from depriving plan participants and beneficiaries of state mandated health benefits.

* * *

Because the purpose and effect of Maryland's regulation is to force state mandated health benefits on self-funded ERISA plans when they purchase certain types of stop-loss insurance, we hold that § 514(a) of ERISA preempts the regulation, and, therefore, we affirm.

I

Client First Brokerage Services, Incorporated; Maran, Incorporated; and Trio Metal Products Company, Incorporated, are Maryland employers sponsoring self-funded employee health benefit plans subject to ERISA. Each has purchased stop-loss insurance from United Wisconsin Life Insurance Company ("United Wisconsin Life") and has engaged American Medical Security, Inc. ("AMS") as administrator of their plans. These Maryland employers purchased stop-loss insurance to cover their plans' benefit payments above an annual $25,000 per-employee level, known as the "attachment point." United Wisconsin Life was also agreeable to a lower attachment point, insuring a greater portion of the plans' payments, if requested to do so by the plans' sponsors. The stop-loss insurance afforded by United Wisconsin Life protected the plans themselves and not their participants or beneficiaries.

The employee benefit plans sponsored by these three Maryland employers contained substantially fewer benefits than the 28 mandated by Maryland for health insurance policies regulated by the Maryland Insurance Commissioner. The benefit plans sponsored by these Maryland employers did not, for example, include benefits for skilled nursing facility services, outpatient rehabilitative services, and certain organ transplants, all of which are mandated for inclusion in Maryland health insurance policies.

In the course of its review of United Wisconsin Life stop-loss policies in the fall of 1994—insurance companies issuing policies to Maryland residents are required to obtain prior approval for their policies—the Maryland Insurance Agency disapproved United Wisconsin Life's stop-loss policies issued to the Maryland employers in this case because the attachment point was set informally at $25,000 and could be reduced at the employer's request. Since the policy could have an attachment point below $25,000 (the then mandated minimum), it was considered a policy of health insurance and, as such, was required to include mandated health benefits. Subsequently, the Maryland Insurance Commissioner dropped the minimum attachment point for stop-loss insurance to $10,000 of benefits paid to any single beneficiary annually. The Commissioner also imposed a minimum aggregate attachment point of 115% of total benefit payments expected to be paid to all plan beneficiaries.

The Maryland employers, United Wisconsin Life, and AMS filed suit seeking a declaratory judgment that the regulations are not enforceable and an injunction against their enforcement. They alleged that Maryland's insurance regulations—which (1) establish a minimum attachment point for stop-loss insurance, and (2) deem stop-loss insurance policies with lower attachment points to be health insurance policies—improperly sought to regulate employee benefit plans in violation of ERISA's preemption provision. On cross motions for summary judgment, the district court agreed with the plaintiffs and declared that ERISA preempts Maryland's regulations. This appeal followed.

II

This case presents the tension between Maryland's effort to guarantee through its regulation of insurance that employee benefit plans offer at least 28 state-mandated health benefits, and Congress' preemption, through ERISA, of any state regulation that "relates to" an employee benefit plan.

ERISA is a comprehensive federal statute regulating private employee benefit plans, including plans maintained for the purpose of providing medical or other health benefits for employees. To assure national uniformity of federal law, ERISA broadly preempts state law and assures that federal regulation will be exclusive. Section 514(a) provides that ERISA "shall supersede any and all State laws insofar as they may now or hereafter relate to any employee benefit plan" as defined by ERISA. The courts have interpreted this clause broadly to carry out Congress' purpose of displacing any state effort to regulate ERISA plans. See, e.g., FMC Corp. v. Holliday, 498 U.S. 52, 58 (1990) ("The preemption clause is conspicuous for its breadth"). Thus, any law that "relates to" a plan is preempted by § 514(a), and the phrase "relates to" is given its common sense meaning, as having "[1] connection with or [2] reference to such a plan." Shaw v. Delta Air Lines, 463 U.S. 85, 96–97 (1983).

Although ERISA's preemptive scope is broad, the "savings clause" explicitly saves from ERISA's preemption those state laws that regulate insurance. See ERISA § 514(b)(2)(A). At the same time, however, the "deemer clause" provides that state insurance laws are not saved from preemption if they deem an employee benefit plan to be an insurance company in order to regulate it. See ERISA § 514(b)(2)(B). Thus, a preempted law is saved from preemption if it regulates insurance and does not deem ERISA plans to be insurers for purposes of the state regulation of insurance. But at bottom, state insurance regulation may not directly or indirectly regulate self-funded ERISA plans. See FMC, 498 U.S. at 62. Accordingly, although plans that provide benefits in the form of insurance may be indirectly regulated through regulation of that insurance, plans that are self-funded or self-insured may not themselves be regulated as insurance companies even if the self-funded or self-insured plan purchases stop-loss insurance to cover losses or benefits payments beyond a specified level.

Stop-loss insurance provides coverage to self-funded plans above a certain level of risk absorbed by the plan. It provides protection to the plan, not to the plan's participants or beneficiaries, against benefits payments over the specified level, called the "attachment point." Attachment points may be "specific" or "aggregate." Specific attachment points define the level of benefits paid to individual beneficiaries beyond which the insurance company will indemnify the plan. Aggregate attachment points define the total amount of benefits paid to all participants or beneficiaries beyond which the insurance company will indemnify the plan. Stop-loss insurance is thus akin to "reinsurance" in that it provides reimbursement to a plan after the plan makes benefit payments.

The State of Maryland regulates health insurance, requiring that health insurance policies afford at least 28 specified benefits. Apparently not wishing to be subject to state-mandated health benefits, insurance companies and their ERISA plan clients have entered into arrangements under which plans self-fund benefits and purchase stop-loss insurance to insure themselves against benefits paid beyond designated attachment points. A stop-loss policy does not itself provide coverage for benefits. Since such a policy insures only those benefits defined and actually paid by the plan, the ERISA plan's sponsor, not state health insurance regulations, dictates the range of benefits provided. Thus, by absorbing a minimal amount of initial risk and insuring the remainder through stop-loss insurance, plans are able to provide health benefits of a kind or at a level different from what state law requires of health insurance.

Recognizing that such arrangements bypass Maryland's regulations for health insurance and intending to prevent such arrangements, the Maryland Insurance Commissioner adopted regulations that require plans to absorb the risk of at least the first $10,000 of benefits paid to each beneficiary. As the regulations' statement of purpose notes, the Commissioner seeks to protect Maryland residents "against acts by persons and insurers which deprive them of mandated health benefits." 22 Md. Reg. 913 (1995). Justifying the regulation and explaining how low attachment points permit self-funded ERISA plans to bypass state mandates, the Insurance Commissioner stated in his order:

> At very low attachment points, however, a "stop loss" policy is merely a substitution for health insurance. It does not insure only against catastrophic loss. The self-funded health benefit plan is not regulated by the Insurance Commissioner and is not required to provide any of the state-mandated benefits. The goal is obvious: As policies become available with attachment points lower than many deductibles, it became an increasingly attractive option to "self-insure" a health plan, but to continue to

shift the majority of the risk to the insurance carrier by purchasing "stop loss" coverage.

The regulations accordingly provide that any stop-loss insurance policy with a specific attachment point below $10,000 is deemed to be a health insurance policy for purposes of Maryland's health insurance regulations and must therefore contain mandated benefits. On the other hand, if the specific attachment point is above $10,000 and the policy provides for payment only to the plan, and not to its participants and beneficiaries, it is considered to be traditional stop-loss insurance that essentially reinsures the risks defined by the plan. See id.

In summary, on one side of the issue before us, the Maryland Insurance Commissioner seeks to take advantage of his right under ERISA's savings clause to regulate the business of insurance. And on the other side, the insurance companies seek to take advantage of ERISA's preemption and deemer clauses to remove self-funded plans from the reach of state insurance regulation.

III

We begin the analysis with the question of whether Maryland's regulations "relate to" ERISA employee benefit plans and thus whether they fall within ERISA's preemptive scope. See ERISA § 514(a). A regulation relates to an employee benefit plan when it has a "connection with or reference to such a plan." Shaw, 463 U.S. at 96–97. The Maryland Insurance Commissioner wisely concedes that the regulations at issue do "relate to" ERISA plans. By their own terms, the stop-loss insurance regulations apply to "an employer's health plan," i.e., an ERISA health plan. See COMAR § 09.31.02.02(4). * * *

Even though Maryland's regulations relate to ERISA plans, they nevertheless may be saved from preemption if they constitute a law that "regulates insurance," see ERISA § 514(b)(2)(A), without deeming an ERISA plan to be an insurance company or other insurer, see ERISA § 514(b)(2)(B). * * *

We recognize that the regulations are carefully drafted to focus directly on insurance companies issuing stop-loss insurance and not on the employee benefit plans themselves. Thus, the regulations purport to define stop-loss *insurance* as health insurance subject to state regulation if the stop-loss *insurance* meets specific criteria. Notwithstanding the regulations' wording, however, their purpose and effect are directed at self-funded employee benefit plans that attempt to provide fewer health benefits to Maryland residents than state law mandates for health insurance policies. The state asserts a need for this regulation because, in its absence, the loophole would allow every self-funded plan to provide coverage for fewer health benefits than state law mandates for health insurance policies. It argues that absorbing a minimal risk is simply a sham to circumvent state insurance regulation, the area carved out by ERISA in which states may act. But in seeking to address this perceived loophole, the state in fact ends up regulating self-funded employee benefit plans that are exclusively subject to ERISA.

In seeking to require self-funded plans to offer coverage consistent with state insurance law, Maryland crosses the line of preemption. Even though the regulatory language targets stop-loss insurance policies, the Commissioner's stated purpose is to protect Maryland residents from self-funded ERISA plans and insurers "which deprive them of mandated health benefits." 22 Md. Reg. 913 (1995). The regulations thus use stop-loss insurance policies as a vehicle to impose the requirements of Maryland health insurance law on self-funded ERISA plans. By aiming at the plan-participant relationship, Maryland law violates the ERISA provision that no ERISA plan "shall be deemed to be an insurance company . . . for purposes of any law of any State purporting to regulate insurance companies [or] insurance contracts." ERISA § 514(b)(2)(B).

The state's fear that plans will circumvent state regulation and offer citizens too few health benefits is understandable. But to state that fear reveals that Maryland is really concerned, not with the business of insurance and its coverage of risks, but with the benefits that ERISA plans can choose to provide their participants and beneficiaries. No matter how understandable this concern may be, only Congress may address it, not the State of Maryland through its insurance regulations. In attempting to address this concern through the regulation of stop-loss insurance, the state blurs the real distinction between self-funded plans, with or without stop-loss insurance, and fully insured plans.

Maryland's regulations distinguish self-funded plans from insured plans solely based on the level of the attachment point of stop-loss insurance. Thus, when the attachment point becomes low, Maryland deems self-funded plans with stop-loss insurance to be insured plans. This distinction overlooks the real risks.

Under a self-funded plan, the employer who promises the benefit incurs the liability defined by the plan's terms. That liability remains the employer's even if it has purchased stop-loss insurance and even if the stop-loss insurer becomes insolvent. Conversely, if the employer becomes insolvent, the solvency of the stop-loss insurer may not benefit plan participants and beneficiaries. This is because their claims against the insurer would be derivative of the plan's claim against the insurer, which arises only after the plan actually makes benefit payments beyond the agreed attachment point. In contrast, when a plan buys health insurance for participants and beneficiaries, the plan participants and beneficiaries have a legal claim directly against the insurance company, thereby securing the benefits even in the event of the plan's insolvency. Participants and beneficiaries in self-funded plans may not have the security of the insurance company's assets because stop-loss insurance insures the plan and not the participants.

The state's regulations fail to recognize that in a self-funded plan, with or without stop-loss insurance and regardless of the attachment point, the provision of benefits depends on the plan's solvency, whereas the provision of benefits in an insured plan depends entirely on the insurer's solvency. It is this fundamental difference that precludes the Maryland Insurance Agency from regulating self-funded plans but permits them to regulate insurance companies that provide health benefits to plans for their participants. While ERISA's savings clause explicitly empowers states to adjust the obligations and incentives which bear on insurance companies' solvency, the combined effect of the preemption and deemer clauses is that ERISA plan solvency is the purview of federal law alone.

Maryland's stop-loss insurance regulations also directly and impermissibly affect ERISA plans' costs and choices in designing their own array of benefits. If a self-funded plan insured by stop-loss insurance having an attachment point of $5,000 provided no benefit for organ transplants, the regulations would either raise plan costs by including unwanted, state-mandated insurance coverage for organ transplants or convert the self-funded plan into a fully insured plan contrary to its preference. These effects impermissibly intrude on the relationship between an ERISA plan and its participants and beneficiaries.

While we recognize that self-funded plans may not be providing Maryland residents with the range of benefits mandated by state law and that such plans' benefits may not always be as secure as those offered by regulated insurance companies, the remedy for any such deficiency must be requested of Congress. When ERISA preempted state law relating to ERISA-covered employee benefit plans, it may have created a regulatory gap, but Maryland is without authority to fill that gap. This is not to say that Maryland may not regulate stop-loss insurance policies. Such regulation is clearly reserved to the states. But because the Maryland regulation before us attempts to mandate the benefits that certain self-insured plans may offer, we affirm the judgment of the district court.

NOTES

1. *"Lasering" Individual Health Care Plan Participants Under Stop-Loss Policies.* Lasering is a technique used by the issuers of stop-loss insurance policies to reduce the cost of coverage for high-risk participants enrolled in the employer's health care plan. When an individual participant is lasered by the stop-loss insurance carrier, the carrier carves out an exception to the employer's stop-loss policy coverage for that individual participant. As a result, the employer who self-insures the plan must bear the risk of large medical bills incurred by a lasered participant. Christopher Windham, *More*

Companies That Self-Insure Get Stuck With Huge Medical Bills As Insurers "Laser" Sickest Workers, WALL ST. J., Sept. 30, 2003, at B1.

Under the amendments made to Title I of ERISA by the Health Insurance Portability and Accountability Act of 1996 (HIPPA), an employer's group health plan is prohibited from charging a plan participant higher premiums or limiting the participant's ability to enroll in the plan due to a health-related factor. See ERISA § 702. Consequently, when a high-risk participant has been lasered by the plan's stop-loss insurance carrier, the employer cannot discriminate against the high-risk participant by singling out that person and charging the individual a higher premium for coverage under the self-insured plan. ERISA Section 702 was not repealed or superseded by the Affordable Care Act and remains in effect for group health plans. The HIPAA rules are discussed in detail in Section D of Chapter Four.

When a stop-loss insurance carrier proposes to laser a high-risk participant, the employer has several options. The employer can agree to exclude all claims made by the high-risk participant under the employer's self-insured plan from coverage under the stop-loss policy, or agree to put a dollar limit on the amount of claims by the high-risk participant that will be paid by the stop-loss policy. These options have become more important for employers to consider due to the requirements of the Affordable Care Act. Beginning in 2014, claims for any essential health benefit offered by the employer's self-insured plan cannot be subject to lifetime or annual dollar limits. Thus, without stop-loss coverage for a high-risk participant's claims, the employer faces potentially unlimited financial liability for claims made by a high-risk participant for essential health benefits that are offered by the plan.

Of course, the employer always has the option of covering the high-risk participant under the general terms of the stop-loss policy and paying the corresponding higher price for the policy demanded by the stop-loss insurance carrier. If the employer passes the increased cost of the stop-loss insurance policy on to the participants in the plan by charging a higher premium amount to all the participants, this option effectively allocates the increased costs of coverage for the high-risk participant among all of the participants in the employer's group health plan.

2. *Regulation of Multiple Employer Welfare Benefit Plans Under State Insurance Laws and ERISA.* ERISA defines a *multiple employer welfare plan* (MEWA) as "an employee welfare benefit plan, or any other arrangement . . . which is established or maintained for the purpose of offering or providing any benefit described in [ERISA Section 3(1)] to the employees of two or more employers (including one or more self-employed individuals), or to their beneficiaries." ERISA § 3(40)(A). A MEWA is different from a multiemployer plan because the arrangement is not established subject to the terms of a collective bargaining agreement under federal labor law.

MEWAs often are used by industry trade associations to offer health care plan coverage to their member employers. If the MEWA is fully insured (defined as insured under a contract of insurance that has been issued by an insurance company licensed to do business in the state where the MEWA is located), then as a practical matter the persons who receive coverage through the MEWA must be limited to residents of that state.

ERISA Section 514(b)(6) establishes a special set of preemption rules concerning the regulation of MEWAs under state insurance laws and ERISA. If the benefits provided by the MEWA are fully insured, (the MEWA is subject only to state insurance laws that govern financial standards, such as the maintenance of financial reserves and requiring a level of member contributions that will be adequate to pay benefits due in full. If the MEWA is not fully insured, then the MEWA is subject to both the provisions of Title I of ERISA *and* any applicable state insurance laws "to the extent" such state insurance laws are "not inconsistent with" Title I of ERISA. See ERISA § 514(b)(6)(A)(i)–(ii).

Under these rules, a MEWA that is not fully insured may potentially be subject to *both* state regulation under applicable state insurance law and regulation under Title I of ERISA. Unscrupulous MEWA operators sometimes attempt to avoid federal and state regulation by simultaneously arguing that the MEWA is not a "plan" (and therefore not subject to Title I of ERISA) and that the MEWA is not an "insurance company" subject to regulation under state insurance laws. (Recall that in *Donovan v. Dillingham,* 688 F.2d 1367 (11th Cir. 1982), which is reproduced in Chapter Two, the operators of the MEWA attempted to argue that it was not a "plan" subject to Title I of ERISA.)

The Affordable Care Act gives the Department of Labor additional enforcement authority over MEWAs. A MEWA that provides medical care benefits must register with the Department of Labor before commencing operations in a state. ERISA § 101(g) (as amended by ACA § 6606). The Department of Labor may issue a cease and desist order to shut down a MEWA that is operating fraudulently, or may seize the assets of a MEWA that is in a financially hazardous condition. ERISA § 521 (added by ACA § 6605(a)). Making false statements or representations in the marketing or sale of a MEWA is now a federal criminal offense. ERISA § 501(b) (as amended by ACA § 6601(a)).

D. THE ALPHABET SOUP REQUIREMENTS FOR GROUP HEALTH CARE PLANS

Section D of Chapter Four describes the ERISA requirements for *group health plans.* These federal requirements for group health plans apply to both insured and self-insured plans. ERISA practitioners refer to these rules collectively as the "alphabet soup" requirements because a convenient way to refer to a particular rule is by reference to the acronym for the federal legislation that created the requirement. The "alphabet soup" requirements discussed in Section D (and their corresponding acronyms) for group health plans are:

- The Consolidated Omnibus Budget Reconciliation Act of 1985, Pub. L. No. 99–272, § 10002(a), 100 Stat. 82 (COBRA);

- The Omnibus Budget Reconciliation Act of 1993, Pub. L. No. 103–66, § 4301(a), 107 Stat. 312 (OBRA);

- The Health Insurance Portability and Accountability Act of 1996, Pub. L. No. 104–191, § 101, 110 Stat. 1936 (HIPAA);

- The Newborns' and Mothers' Health Protection Act of 1996, Pub. L. No. 104–204, § 601, 110 Stat. 2935 (NMHPA);

- The Women's Health and Cancer Rights Act of 1998, Pub. L. No. 105–277, § 901, 112 Stat. 2681 (WHCRA).

- The Genetic Information Nondiscrimination Act of 2008, Pub. L. No. 110–233, § 101, 122 Stat. 881 (GINA);

- The Paul Wellstone and Pete Domenici Mental Health Parity and Addiction Equity Act of 2008, Pub. L. No. 110–343, § 511, 122 Stat. 3765 (MHPAEA); and

- The Patient Protection and Affordable Care Act, Pub. L. No. 111–148, 124 Stat. 119 (2010), as amended by the Health Care and Education Reconciliation Act of 2010, Pub. L. No. 111–152, 124 Stat. 1029 (HCRA) (collectively, the Affordable Care Act or the ACA).

1.   COBRA AND OBRA

The Consolidated Omnibus Budget Reconciliation Act of 1985 (COBRA) created the first federal coverage requirements for group health plans subject to Title I of ERISA. Eight years later, Congress created additional requirements in the Omnibus Budget Reconciliation Act of 1993 (OBRA). The requirements of COBRA and OBRA are contained in Part 6 of Title I of ERISA. The COBRA requirements are set forth in ERISA Sections 601 through 608. OBRA's requirements are found in ERISA Section 609.

a.   Overview of COBRA

COBRA requires that a sponsor of a group health plan must provide each *qualified beneficiary*, who otherwise would lose coverage under the plan due to the occurrence of a *qualifying event*, the opportunity to continue coverage under the plan. ERISA § 601(a). The notice requirements of COBRA are implemented through Department of Labor Regulations. See DOL Reg. § 2590.606–1–.606–4. The maximum period of continuation coverage varies from eighteen to thirty-six months, depending upon the type of qualifying event that triggers COBRA rights.

- **What group health plans are subject to COBRA?**

Group health plans subject to COBRA include both insured and self-insured group health care plans. ERISA § 607(1). If the employer maintaining the plan normally employed fewer than twenty full-time equivalent employees on a typical business day during the prior calendar year, the plan is exempt from COBRA's requirements. ERISA § 601(b). For purposes of this requirement, the employer is determined on a controlled group basis under the same rules used for determining the "employer" for purposes of testing a qualified plan for compliance with the Code's nondiscrimination requirements. See ERISA § 607(4). (The controlled group rules are for qualified plans are described in Section F.1 of Chapter Three of the casebook.) If the plan has fewer than twenty full-time equivalent employees, it may still be subject to state insurance laws that create COBRA-type rights for participants in insured group health care plans.

The statutory criteria for determining whether a group health care plan is subject to COBRA are further defined in Treasury Department regulations. See Treas. Reg. § 54.4980B. Under these regulations, employees of the employer who must be counted for purposes of determining whether COBRA applies include only common law employees of the employer. Self-employed individuals and independent contractors are not counted. See Treas. Reg. § 54.4980B–2, Q & A–5(c). Each full-time employee is counted as one employee. Each part-time employee is counted as a fraction of one employee. This fraction is computed by comparing the number of hours the part-time employee works during a day or a pay period with the number of hours required by the employer to be considered a full-time employee. See Treas. Reg. § 54.4980B–2, Q & A–5(e).

- **Who is a "qualified beneficiary" protected by COBRA?**

A qualified beneficiary includes the employee of the employer who is covered under the plan. If the employee's spouse or any dependent children were covered under the plan on the day before a qualifying event occurs, they too are qualified beneficiaries. If a child is born to or placed for adoption with an employee who is covered under the plan during a period of continuation coverage under COBRA, that child also is a qualified beneficiary. See ERISA § 607(2)–(3).

- **What is a "qualifying event" triggering COBRA rights, and how long is the maximum period of COBRA continuation coverage under the plan?**

A qualifying event occurs when, but for COBRA continuation coverage, the qualified beneficiary would cease to be covered under the plan. Qualifying events under COBRA and the corresponding period of continuation coverage are described in Sections 602 and 603 of ERISA. Table 4.3 on the next page summarizes the types of qualifying events and their corresponding periods of continuation coverage under COBRA. (Note: A "dependent child" for purposes of COBRA is now any child who is under the age of 26 as a result of the Affordable Care Act.)

Table 4.3
COBRA Qualifying Events and Continuation Coverage

Qualifying Event	Qualified Beneficiaries Entitled to COBRA Coverage	Period of COBRA Continuation Coverage
Termination or reduction in hours of the covered employee	Employee Spouse Dependent Child	18 Months
Death of covered employee	Spouse Dependent Child	36 Months
Divorce or legal separation of covered employee	Spouse Dependent Child	36 Months
Covered employee becomes eligible for Medicare benefits	Spouse Dependent Child	36 Months
Ceasing to qualify for coverage as a "dependent child" under the terms of the plan	Dependent Child	36 Months

The employer is not required to offer COBRA coverage if the covered employee's termination of employment was for gross misconduct. ERISA § 603(2). COBRA and its implementing regulations do not define gross misconduct. Therefore, the standard is one that has been developed over time by the federal courts through COBRA litigation. Although the cases on gross misconduct are difficult to generalize, most federal courts require either a criminal act or a showing of intentional misconduct on the part of the terminated employee that would give rise to an intentional tort claim under state law.

Employers who fail to comply with COBRA and are later sued by a terminated employee for a violation of COBRA rights often assert gross misconduct by the terminated employee as a defense. The employer's assertion that the employee engaged in gross misconduct in these cases often is less than credible. See, e.g., Paris v. F. Korbel & Bros., Inc. 751 F. Supp. 834 (N.D. Cal. 1990) (terminated employee breached a confidence that made the pilot of the company's jet angry, thereby risking the safety of company executives who flew with the pilot); Lloyd v. Hanover Foods

Corp., 72 F. Supp. 2d 469 (D. Del. 1999) (terminated employee failed on a single day to add onion powder to the ravioli mix).

A qualifying event occurs regardless of whether the employer involuntarily terminates the employment of an employee who is a qualified beneficiary or the employee voluntarily terminates employment. Many employers require that an employee must regularly work a certain number of hours each week to remain eligible to participate in the employer's group health plan. When the employee switches to a reduced work schedule, the corresponding reduction in the employee's working hours is a qualifying event if the reduction causes the employee to cease to be covered under the plan. If, however, the reduction in hours is due to leave that is permitted under the Family and Medical Leave Act, a qualifying event does not occur. See Treas. Reg. § 54.4980B–10. The interaction of COBRA rights with the rights of employees under the Family and Medical Leave Act is discussed in Section F.3 of Chapter Four in the casebook.

A special rule applies if, at any time during a period of eighteen months of COBRA continuation coverage due to the covered employee's termination of employment or reduction in hours, a qualified beneficiary becomes eligible to receive disability benefits under Social Security. In this situation, the maximum period of COBRA continuation coverage for the disabled qualified beneficiary is extended to twenty-nine months. See ERISA § 602(2)(A).

A corporate merger or acquisition can trigger a qualifying event due to the termination of employment of employees who were covered by the seller's group health plan. Treasury Department regulations address which employer (the seller or the buyer) is responsible for providing COBRA continuation coverage to qualified beneficiaries whose coverage under the seller's group health plan has ceased due to a termination of employment in connection with the corporate transaction. See Treas. Reg. § 54.4980B–9.

An employee who anticipates soon becoming divorced occasionally will direct the plan administrator to stop covering the employee's spouse or dependent children under the employer's group health plan. If the criteria for a qualifying event under the statute were construed strictly, technically a qualifying event would not occur at the time of divorce because the spouse and dependent children would not have been covered by the plan on the day before the qualifying event (the divorce) occurred. In these circumstances, the plan administrator must ignore the elimination of the spouse and dependent children as covered participants from the plan prior to the divorce and offer COBRA coverage to them as qualified beneficiaries. See Rev. Rul. 2002–88, Treas. Reg. § 54.4980B–4, Q & A–1(c).

Phillips v. Saratoga Harness Racing, Inc., 240 F.3d 174 (2d Cir. 2001), illustrates the thorny issues of domestic relations law in which the plan administrator may easily become entangled when dealing with a potential qualifying event under due to a divorce. According to the district court judge who initially heard the case, "[i]n the realm of ERISA suits * * * the factual setting for this case may even pass as sensational and riveting." In *Phillips*, the plaintiff and the employee were married and living in New York. The plaintiff was covered under the employer's group health plan and was receiving treatment for a serious medical condition. When the couple separated, the employee obtained an ex parte divorce decree from the Dominican Republic. Two days later, the employee, "his Dominican judgment of divorce in hand," married his secretary. When the employee returned from his honeymoon, he informed the administrator for the employer's group health plan that he had divorced and remarried, and that he wanted to drop his ex-spouse from medical coverage under the plan. Inexplicably, the plan administrator gave the COBRA notice and other necessary forms to the employee to deliver to his ex-spouse rather than directly mailing the documents to her (the usual procedure for providing a COBRA notice). The plaintiff claimed that she never received the COBRA notice, and continued to undergo expensive treatment for her medical condition. It was only after the plan denied her claims for medical treatment that the plaintiff learned her ex-husband had terminated her health insurance coverage.

The plaintiff sued the employer for failing to provide the COBRA notice, seeking to recover the out-of-pocket costs of her medical treatment. The employer's defense was that a qualifying event under COBRA had not taken place because, two years after the Dominican Republic divorce decree was issued, a New York state court declared the Dominican Republic divorce decree to be invalid. The Second Circuit Court of Appeals dismissed the employer's defense, concluding that "whether or not an invalid divorce is actually a qualifying event under COBRA is not the question. It is the act of the employee telling his employer that the qualifying event has occurred—not the actual occurrence of the qualifying event itself—that triggers the employer's obligations under COBRA." Id. at 178.

When multiple qualifying events occur, under COBRA the maximum total period of continuation coverage cannot exceed thirty-six months. Consequently, a second qualifying event cannot expand the duration of COBRA coverage beyond this maximum thirty-six month period. See Treas. Reg. § 54.4980B–7, Q & A–6. For example, assume that the employment of the covered employee is terminated for reasons other than gross misconduct. The covered employee, spouse, and dependent children all elect COBRA continuation coverage, which begins on January 1, 2014. During the eighteen month period of COBRA continuation coverage, the former employee dies or becomes divorced. So long as the spouse and dependent children are receiving COBRA coverage under the plan at the time the second qualifying event (the employee's death) occurs, they will be entitled to a total of thirty-six months of COBRA coverage, measured from the date that COBRA coverage first began. Thus, in this example the continuation coverage of the spouse and dependent children under COBRA cannot extend beyond December 31, 2016.

- **What is the maximum premium that can be charged for COBRA continuation coverage?**

COBRA continuation coverage is not free to the qualified beneficiary, who may be required by the employer to pay up to 100% of the applicable premium for coverage under the employer's plan, plus an additional 2% administrative fee. ERISA § 602(3)(A). Many employers subsidize participation in a group health plan for current employees by paying a portion of each current employee's premium for coverage under the plan. When a qualified beneficiary elects COBRA coverage, the applicable premium is the *entire* premium required for participation in the plan, not just the amount that a current employee pays for coverage under the plan. Consequently, the cost of COBRA continuation coverage can be significantly more than the subsidized premium amount paid by current employees.

Recognizing the difficulty that unemployed persons may have in paying for health insurance coverage, Congress eliminated the 10% excise tax penalty on distributions from an IRA prior to age 59½ for persons who have received unemployment compensation for twelve consecutive weeks. This excise tax exemption applies only if the IRA distributions are used to pay health insurance premiums, which may include COBRA premiums. See Code § 72(t)(2)(D).

- **How does COBRA continuation coverage compare with purchasing an individual health insurance policy through the Exchange system?**

If the individual qualifies for a premium assistance tax credit, the premium cost of an individual insurance policy purchased on an Exchange may be less expensive than the COBRA premium for continuation coverage under an employer-sponsored group health plan. The network of health care providers offered by policies sold on the Exchange may be different than the network offered under the employer's group health plan. If the qualified beneficiary is or has been seriously ill, he or she may prefer COBRA continuation coverage in order to avoid having to change health care providers.

- **What are the consequences of failing to comply with COBRA?**

The employer who maintains the group health plan is subject to an excise tax penalty of $110 per day, per qualified beneficiary, for each day during the noncompliance period. See Code § 4980B(b)(1). Additional minimum and maximum excise tax penalty limits may apply. See Code § 4980B(b)(3)–(c). The excise tax penalty is paid by the employer to the Internal Revenue Service and is nondeductible.

COBRA rights may be enforced directly by plan participants and beneficiaries through ERISA civil litigation. Under ERISA Sections 502(a)(1)(A) and 502(c), the federal court may order the plan's administrator to pay a civil penalty to the plaintiffs of $110 a day, per qualified beneficiary, for failure to provide the notice of COBRA rights. In addition to seeking a civil penalty, the qualified beneficiary whose COBRA rights have been violated may ask the federal court to award "such other relief as it deems proper." ERISA § 502(c)(1).

Private civil litigation involving COBRA is predictable when a qualifying event occurs, the employer or plan administrator fails to provide the required COBRA notice, and the participant or beneficiary subsequently incurs significant medical bills. The plaintiff's claim in a COBRA case usually is that if the COBRA notice had been provided, the plaintiff would have elected COBRA and the medical bills would have been covered under the employer's group health care plan. *Holford v. Exhibit Design Consultants* illustrates this scenario.

HOLFORD V. EXHIBIT DESIGN CONSULTANTS

United States District Court, Western District of Michigan, 2002.
218 F.Supp.2d 901.

ENSLEN, DISTRICT JUDGE.

This matter is before the Court to consider Plaintiff Lisa Holford's Application for Default Judgment and Corrected Application for Default Judgment. Defendant Exhibit Design Consultants has opposed the relief. Both parties have had multiple opportunities to file briefs and supporting documents. Hearing of the matter is unnecessary in light of the briefing and the issues presented.

BACKGROUND

Default was entered against Defendant by the Clerk for failing to timely answer and defend. Thereafter, by agreement of the parties, the default was set aside except as to Count II of the Complaint. Count II alleges that Defendant violated the Consolidated Omnibus Reconciliation Act, ERISA §§ 601–609 ("COBRA"). COBRA is an amendment to the Employee Retirement Income Security Act of 1974 ("ERISA"). More particularly, Plaintiff alleges that Defendant violated section 606 by failing to provide Plaintiff with written notice of her right to continue health coverage upon termination of her employment. See also ERISA § 502(c) (enforcement provision).

Regarding such claim, Defendant admits that it did not properly notify Plaintiff of her COBRA rights on termination. Nevertheless, it requests that the Court view its noncompliance indulgently because it provided an insufficient COBRA notice in its Employee Handbook (such that it did not act in "bad faith" as to the statutory violation), because of its new-found knowledge and respect for COBRA,[2] and because it is a small employer who has suffered from recent economic downturns. Defendant also asserts that it has attempted to right the situation by offering to Plaintiff COBRA coverage retroactive to the effective date of her separation. Plaintiff has argued that this offer may well not return her to the status quo ante because the offer asserted allows the health insurer to deny coverage as to the retroactive medical expenses and because Defendant's offer would require lump sum payment as opposed to payment over time. Defendant in its Reply Brief, however, argues that Plaintiff has misunderstood the terms of its offer; that is, the offer was not intended to assert any limitations on insurability nor any coverage limitations (other than those that would ordinarily apply to covered employees) and was not intended to demand lump sum payment. Plaintiff seeks actual damages of $16,984.27, consisting of unpaid medical expenses less unpaid premiums. Plaintiff also seeks a statutory penalty of $110 per day between April 9, 2001[3] and August 23, 2002; in other words, $110 for 502 days for a total of $55,220.00. Finally, Plaintiff seeks attorney fees and costs in the amount of $32,406.25.

LEGAL ANALYSIS

Two quotations from the well-tilled ground of COBRA litigation provide an overview of COBRA's notice requirements:

> The notification requirements of COBRA are clear. In the event of a covered employee's termination, an employer must notify the administrator of the group health care plan within thirty days, ERISA § 606(a)(2); the administrator then has fourteen days to notify the qualified beneficiary of her right to continue coverage, and this period may be longer if the plan is a multiemployer group health care plan and it so provides. ERISA § 606(a)(4). An

---

[2]   This determination, though laudable, is not the true test for determining sanctions aimed at deterrence. As in this Court's criminal cases, many defendants express respect and allegiance to the laws of the land while their deeds are being weighed in the balances of justice. The legitimate goal of deterrence (which is the object of the civil fine provision applicable in this case) is to see that litigants will observe the same respect for the laws when the courts are far off and their conduct is hidden.

[3]   Given the date of the termination, April 9, 2001, is the last day which Defendant could have delivered a COBRA notice to Plaintiff under the statute's notice period. Thus, the statutory penalty may not be assessed before that date.

employer or plan administrator who sends proper notice to the covered employee's last known address is deemed to be in good faith compliance with COBRA's notification requirements.

A qualified COBRA beneficiary may elect continuation coverage within sixty days of the qualifying event or of notice of the qualifying event, whichever is later. Continued coverage extends for a maximum period of eighteen months. ERISA § 602(2)(A).

Hubicki v. Amtrak Nat. Passenger R. Co., 808 F. Supp. 192, 196 (E.D.N.Y.1992).

Unfortunately, COBRA contains no specific requirements as to the manner in which notice must be given. . . . [The] courts that have addressed the issue have held that "a good faith attempt to comply with a reasonable interpretation of the statute is sufficient." Courts have generally approved the employer's methods of giving notice where those methods are reasonably calculated to reach the employee. For example, employers have been found in compliance with section 606(a) when they send COBRA notices via first class mail to the last-known address of an employee.

The compulsory character of COBRA's notification requirement has been repeatedly upheld by federal courts, even where the qualified beneficiary had received the initial COBRA notice at the commencement of his/her coverage, or where the employee had personal knowledge of his/her COBRA rights. Even where the former employee's duties during employment included the distribution of COBRA notices, as would have been the case with [the plaintiff], the employer is not excused from providing that employee with the required COBRA notice. "The fact that [a plaintiff] was given notice of [her] COBRA rights at the commencement of [her] insurance plan. . ., in no way relieves the plan administrator of the second round of notice obligations under [COBRA] after a qualifying event. . . . [Plaintiff's] personal knowledge of [her] COBRA rights likewise does not nullify the administrator's statutory duty to give notice upon termination."

Torres-Negron v. Ramallo Bros. Printing, Inc., 203 F. Supp. 2d 120, 124–25 (D. Puerto Rico 2002).

1. Actual Damages

Plaintiff seeks actual damages in the amount of $16,984.27. This amount was calculated by Plaintiff by totaling medical bills incurred during the eighteen month COBRA period and reducing the total amount by Plaintiff's unpaid insurance premiums. It is unclear whether Plaintiff has further reduced the amount to account for deductibles which would apply as to the insurance coverage and, if so, whether the reductions have been appropriate under the coverage language. Defendant has also raised other coverage issues—i.e., whether some of the health care in question was medically necessary such that the COBRA insurance would have covered these expenses.

Defendant has also asserted two other defenses. Defendant argues that Plaintiff has applied for payment of these expenses in a worker's compensation suit such that payment in this suit might cause a double recovery and windfall. This argument is not persuasive in this context. First of all, it is speculative at this point in time. Second, the federal courts, which are duty-bound to enforce COBRA, have frowned on such "windfall" arguments in COBRA cases. The reason is obvious. The employee is paying for the additional insurance and the additional coverage is, typically, not a windfall precisely because the employee's claim to it is supported by premium payments establishing a contract between knowing parties. Therefore, the Court rejects this defense as lacking a sound foundation in either law or fact.

However, Defendant's argument as to duty to mitigate is persuasive. Plaintiff, by virtue of Defendant's offer, has been given an opportunity to insure the COBRA medical expenses retroactively. Should she accept that offer, the medical expenses, if covered, will be paid and she will not incur a loss. Should she decline the offer, the decision would constitute a failure to mitigate damages which would make her ineligible to recover the medical expenses as actual damages. In either case, then, the offer prevents Plaintiff's recovery of the medical expenses as actual damages.

However, while this Court accepts Defendant's argument that medical expenses incurred should not be reimbursed as actual damages, the Court will require one additional condition of Defendant to satisfy the purpose and intent of COBRA. COBRA permits an employee a sixty day period to elect coverage. See ERISA § 602(3). In this case, the notice of the offer given by Defendant was ambiguous and failed to explain the terms of payment (that it would consist of payment of monthly premiums according to a standard schedule), the terms of insurability (that Plaintiff could not be denied coverage), and the terms of coverage (that standard terms of coverage would apply). Because of these ambiguities, the Court will require Defendant to re-extend the COBRA offer with clarifying language for an additional sixty day period. The Court has authority to fashion this equitable remedy under ERISA § 502(c)(1). See Griggs v. E.I. Dupont de Nemours & Co., 237 F.3d 371, 381 (4th Cir.2001) (holding that the reinstatement of the right to an election of benefits may be an appropriate equitable remedy under ERISA § 502(a)(3)).

This equitable remedy also works to the advantage of both of the parties. This is particularly so because it avoids difficult and protracted litigation (including discovery and evidentiary hearing) over the issue of covered medical expenses under two separate insurance policies. Plaintiff will have the benefit, should she elect it, to prompt coverage and payment of medical claims. Defendant will have the benefit of the resolution of time-consuming legal issues in a case in which Defendant is required, statutorily, to finance reasonable attorney services of Plaintiff. This resolution also works to the advantage of the Court-which does not intend to waste public resources for the resolution of manifold and mundane coverage issues when those issues can be resolved privately through ordinary claim procedures.

2. Statutory Damages

As stated above, Plaintiff seeks $110 per day for the statutory violation. Defendants urge that no statutory damages be assessed because of the lack of bad faith in committing the violation-i.e., it mistakenly relied on its Employee Handbook instead of sending the required notice. Plaintiff believes that this conduct evidences bad faith and that it is appropriate to award the maximum amount of statutory damages since she has suffered prejudice, including foregone treatments for serious mental illness and other conditions.

Of course, as recognized by COBRA, the assessment of statutory damages is discretionary and depends in large part on an assessment of pertinent factors including employer bad faith and prejudice to the employee. The whole intent of this discretion is, while avoiding Draconian justice, to construct a remedy which regards the violation with sufficient seriousness that it will not be repeated.

In the instant manner, the Court finds that the statutory violation was committed in bad faith because no reasonable interpretation of the statutory language would permit one to believe that a notice in a plan document (or worse in an employee handbook) satisfied the notification requirement triggered by the employee separation. * * * [T]his case involves both bad faith and prejudice to the employee (i.e., foregone health care treatments).

Nevertheless, such cases as the *Torres-Negron* case (in which a similar violation resulted in statutory damages of $45 per day) make clear that statutory damages are truly discretionary and that the Court need not award the maximum amount of statutory damages for each violation. See also Garred v. General Am. Life Ins. Co., 774 F. Supp. 1190, 1201 (W.D. Ark.1991) (awarding $50 per day for corporation's bad faith conduct); Thomas v. Jeep-Eagle Corp., 746 F. Supp. 863, 864 (E.D. Wis.1990) (awarding $50 per day for corporation's bad faith conduct). In this case, the deterrent purposes of COBRA would be sufficiently served by setting statutory damages at a rate of $55 per day, especially considering the size and fortune of the Defendant company. Therefore, the Court concludes that statutory damages should be assessed at a rate of $55 per day, for a total award of $27,610.00.

* * *

CONCLUSION

For the reasons stated, Plaintiff's Application (and Corrected Application) for Default Judgment will be granted and a judgment shall entered as to Count II of the Complaint. The Partial Judgment shall award equitable relief as described above, statutory damages in the amount of $27,610.00, attorney fees in the amount of $23,730.00, and costs in the amount of $229.25.

b. Overview of OBRA

The Omnibus Budget Reconciliation Act of 1993 (OBRA), codified in ERISA Section 609, has two important requirements aimed at benefits provided to children under a group health plan. First, OBRA makes the *qualified medical child support order* (QMCSO) possible. ERISA § 609(a). Second, OBRA requires that group health plans must provide coverage and benefits for adopted children of plan participants on the same terms and conditions as coverage offered to children who are naturally born to plan participants. ERISA § 609(c).

- **What is a qualified medical child support order, and how does it work?**

A QMCSO requires a parent who is eligible to obtain dependent coverage under the employer's group health plan to enroll a dependent child in the plan and to pay the premium for the dependent child's coverage under the plan. Like a qualified domestic relations order in the context of an employee pension plan, the QMCSO is a common technique used in divorce situations. A QMCSO is sometimes referred to as a "kiddie QDRO" because a QMCSO uses much of the same terminology and operates in a similar fashion to a qualified domestic relations order.

A QMCSO is defined as a judgment, decree, order or settlement agreement that is made pursuant to a state domestic relations law and that requires a group health plan to provide coverage to the child of a plan participant. ERISA § 609(a)(2)(A)–(B). The content of a QMCSO must clearly specify a number of items listed in the statute. These items are:

(1) the name and last known mailing address of the participant and each *alternate recipient* (dependent child) covered by the order;

(2) a reasonable description of the type of coverage to be provided to each alternate recipient, or the manner in which the type of coverage is to be determined; and

(3)   the period to which the order applies (typically until the child attains the age of majority under state law, but can be extended until age 26).

A QMCSO cannot require the group health plan to provide any type of coverage or form of benefit that is not normally offered under the plan. ERISA § 609(a)(4). Once the plan administrator determines that the order satisfies the statutory criteria for a QMCSO, the plan administrator must enroll the dependent child in the plan. Payment for coverage is made by the parent-employee through the plan's usual payment mechanism (typically, payroll deduction).

A *National Medical Support Notice* functions like a QMCSO. A National Medical Support Notice is an order used by state agencies who are charged with administering child support enforcement programs under Part D of Title IV of the Social Security Act. A National Medical Support Notice directs the plan administrator to enroll a child who is a dependent of an employee in the employer's health care plan. If the National Medical Support Notice is appropriately completed, the notice is deemed to satisfy the statutory criteria for a valid QMCSO. ERISA § 609(a)(5)(C).

- **How is a qualified medical child support order enforced?**

ERISA does not preempt a QMCSO. See ERISA § 514(b)(7). Consequently, if the administrator for the group health plan refuses to comply with the terms of the QMCSO, the alternate recipient may attempt to enforce the order through the state courts. A state agency may enforce a National Medical Support Notice by filing a claim directly in federal court under ERISA Section 502(a)(7).

If the parent of the alternate recipient changes employers, the QMCSO must be revised accordingly for the new employer's health care plan and presented to the new employer. In anticipation of a possible future change in employment by the parent-employee, a QMCSO may direct that the parent-employee is required to pay for COBRA coverage of the alternate recipient if a COBRA qualifying event occurs.

- **Does the adoption of a child have to be final under the legal procedures governing adoption before the plan administrator is required to enroll the adopted child as a participant in the plan?**

ERISA Section 609(c)(1) provides that if the group health plan provides coverage for the dependent children of participants in the plan, the plan also must provide benefits to dependent children placed with participants for adoption under the same terms and conditions as in the case of dependent children who are the natural children of participants. This rule applies "irrespective of whether the adoption has become final."

ERISA § 609(c)(1). (ERISA Section 609(c) is reproduced at the end of these Supplemental Materials.) If the participant has assumed a legal obligation for the total or partial support of the child in anticipation of adoption, the child is deemed to have been placed with the participant, and the requirements of ERISA Section 609(c) concerning enrollment of the child apply. ERISA § 609(c)(3)(B). For purposes of ERISA Section 609(c), a child is defined as an individual who has not yet attained age eighteen as of the date of adoption or placement of adoption. ERISA § 609(c)(3)(A).

- **How does the Affordable Care Act impact OBRA's requirements?**

The ACA did not repeal OBRA. The provisions of OBRA regarding coverage of children with pre-existing health conditions who are in the process of being adopted remain in effect. The rules regarding coverage of dependent children under a QMCSO also remain in effect. Due to the requirement under the ACA that a group health plan must offer coverage of adult children up to age 26, a QCMSO can be used to ensure expanded coverage is available to a child of the divorced couple until age 26. Coverage under a parent's plan for an adult child may be less expensive for the adult child than coverage under the plan of the adult child's employer or purchasing an individual insurance policy through the Exchange system.

2.   HIPAA

The Health Insurance Portability and Accountability Act of 1996 (HIPAA) placed restrictions on the ability of a group health plan to impose preexisting condition coverage exclusions on plan participants. The HIPAA also prohibited group health plans from discriminating against individual participants by charging higher premiums or restricting an individual's eligibility to enroll in the plan based on various health-related factors. Although HIPAA's limitations on preexisting condition coverage exclusions are now unnecessary due to changes made by the Affordable Care Act, the law's nondiscrimination requirements remain in effect. The nondiscrimination requirements of HIPPA apply to any group health plan with two or more participants who are current employees. ERISA §§ 706(a); 705(a).

a.   Nondiscrimination Requirements

The HIPAA nondiscrimination provisions are found in ERISA Section 702. Section 702 prohibits a group health plan (including an issuer of a group health insurance policy) from basing eligibility to enroll in a group health plan on any of the following health-related factors.

- Health status
- Medical condition (including both physical and mental illness)
- Claims experience
- Receipt of health care
- Medical history
- Genetic information
- Evidence of insurability
- Disability

ERISA § 702(a)(1)(A)–(H). Congress included evidence of insurability in the above list "to ensure. . .that individuals are not excluded from health care coverage due to their participation in activities such as motorcycling, snowmobiling, all-terrain vehicle riding, horseback riding, skiing and other similar activities." H.R. CONF. REP. No. 104–736 (1996). Department of Labor regulations implementing the HIPAA further clarify that evidence of insurability includes prohibiting an individual from enrolling in the group health plan due to a history of domestic violence. DOL Reg. § 2590.702(a)(2)(I).

The HIPAA prohibits charging an individual more than similarly situated individuals for coverage under a group health plan based on any of these health-related factors. ERISA § 702(b)(1). The legislative history states that a group health plan is permitted to vary benefits available to different groups of employees, such as full-time versus part-time employees or employees in different geographic locations. In addition, a group health plan may have different benefit schedules for different collective bargaining units. See H.R. CONF. REP. NO. 104–736 (1996). Premium discounts, rebates, or reductions in co-payment or deductible amounts are permitted for participation in disease prevention or wellness programs. ERISA § 702(b)(2)(B); DOL Reg. § 2590.702(f).

b. The Role of the HIPAA in National Health Care Reform

Absent ERISA Section 702, the plan's sponsor could discourage a new participant with a preexisting health condition from enrolling in the plan by charging a prohibitively higher premium due to the foreseeable costs of treatment for the preexisting condition. ERISA Section 702(b) prevents such tactics by prohibiting the practice of charging a greater premium to an individual participant as compared to "similarly situated" individuals based on a health-related factor.

Although Congress intended the HIPAA to prohibit premium price discrimination against individuals and their dependents due to health-related factors, the HIPAA did not require a group health plan to provide particular benefits, and it allowed a group health plan to establish limits or place restrictions on the amount, level, extent, or nature of the plan's coverage or benefits, so long as these limits or restrictions applied to all similarly situated individuals enrolled in the plan. Most significantly, the HIPAA did not restrict the premium amount that a group health plan may charge all similarly situated participants for coverage under the plan. The Conference Report accompanying the HIPAA summarized the limited effect of the legislation as follows:

> The conferees intend that these provisions preclude insurance companies from denying coverage to employees based on health status and related factors that they have traditionally used. In addition, this provision is meant to prohibit insurers or employers from excluding employees in a group from coverage or charging them higher premiums based on their health status and other related factors that could lead to higher health costs. This does not mean that an entire group cannot be charged more. But it does preclude health plans from singling out individuals in the group for higher premiums or dropping them from coverage altogether.

H.R. CONF. REP. No. 104–736 (1996).

In retrospect, the HIPAA sparked changes in the design and administration of group health care plans that led eventually to cries for a more comprehensive approach to national health care reform. As explained above, the HIPAA did not attempt to regulate or control rising premium costs charged by group health plans. To control rising costs employers began scrutinizing and reducing the package or benefits being provided by their group health plans. State insurance laws somewhat constrained the employer's ability to reduce the costs of an insured plan by reducing or eliminating the plan's coverage, both in terms of dollar amounts and the types of medical treatments covered. An employer who sponsored a self-insured plan, however, was under no state insurance law constraints.

In response to growing political pressure in the years following the enactment of the HIPPA, Congress enacted a series of targeted federal requirements for both insured and self-insured group health plans. But these additional federal requirements, which are discussed in the next subsection, generally were limited to specific medical conditions or circumstances. Such reforms did not address the three underlying fundamental trends that were changing group health plans as employers tried to slow rising costs. Employers were reducing the package of plan benefits, implementing managed care techniques, and increasingly shifting costs to plan participants in the form of increased premiums, higher deductibles, and higher co-payments. As a result, dissatisfaction among plan participants increased. Their own costs for health care insurance coverage were rising while at the same time more claims for medical treatment were being denied because the requested treatment was not covered under the terms of the employer's plan.

Thus, the HIPAA redirected the impulse for comprehensive national health care reform in two ways. First, a public consensus began to emerge that health care insurance should be required to provide a certain minimum level of coverage and benefits. Second, and most difficult of all to achieve, was the idea that reform should make health care insurance more affordable. Eventually, comprehensive national health care reform, in the form of the Affordable Care Act, attempted to resolve these significant public policy issues.

c. Health Information Privacy

As originally enacted, the HIPAA provided that if Congress did not enact legislation regulating the disclosure of a protected health information by August 21, 1999, the United States Department of Health and Human Services (HHS) was to promulgate regulations governing the privacy of an individual's protected health information. Congress failed to act, and therefore the HHS enacted regulations. HIPAA's privacy regulations are found in Title 45 of the Code of Federal Regulations at Parts 160 and 164.

In general, the HHS regulations require that an individual must consent to the disclosure of protected health information before a covered entity may release the information. The regulations define a covered entity broadly to include health care plans, health care insurance issuers, HMOs, Medicare, Medicaid and other public health programs, church plans and governmental plans that are excluded from coverage under Title I of ERISA, and health care providers.

The HHS regulations deter disclosure violations through civil money penalties and criminal sanctions. In the event of a disclosure breach, the regulations require that the covered entity must mitigate any harmful effect resulting from the breach. The original HHS regulations did not, however, require notification of the breach to the individual whose protected health information had been compromised. In addition, the HHS regulations did not apply to business associates of covered entities, such as third-party plan administrators, benefit consultants, ERISA attorneys, and other plan service providers (although many plans voluntarily imposed similar requirements on their business associates through contractual arrangements).

To address these perceived shortcomings, Congress enacted the Health Information Technology for Economic and Clinical Health Act (HITECH) as Title XIII of the American Recovery and Reinvestment Act of 2009, Pub. L. No. 111–5, 123 Stat. 115. Under the HITECH, the HIPAA privacy requirements now apply directly to business associates of covered entities. The HITECH further requires that if "unsecured" protected health information is accessed, acquired or disclosed and the breach presents a significant risk of harm, then both potentially affected individuals and the HHS must be notified of the breach. If the breach impacts more than 500 individuals, then prominent media outlets serving the affected area also must be notified.

Protected health information held in a paper format is deemed "unsecured" and subject to these notification requirements until it is destroyed. Protected health information held in an electronic format is deemed "unsecured" unless it is encrypted using a process approved by the National Institute of Standards and Technology. By defining "unsecured" protected health information in this manner, the HITECH strongly encourages that medical records and related health information be held in an encrypted electronic format.

Under HITECH, criminal sanctions and civil money penalties potentially apply to violations. Knowing violations with the intent to sell, transfer or use protected health information for commercial advantage, personal gain or malicious harm may result in a criminal fine of up to $250,000 and ten years' imprisonment. The HITECH substantially increased the civil penalties for violations. The penalty amounts now range from up to $25,000 per calendar year for an innocent violation to up to $1.5 million per calendar year for a willful violation that is not corrected. Although affected individuals do not have a private cause of action for violations, the HHS may investigate complaints by individuals and conduct compliance reviews of covered entities.

Problems on COBRA, OBRA, and HIPAA

Timber Company sponsors an insured health care plan (Plan) for its 500 employees. To be eligible for benefits under the Plan, an employee must be regularly scheduled to work thirty or more hours per week. The actual monthly cost for coverage under the Plan is $200 per month for employee-only coverage and an additional $1,000 per month for family coverage. Timber Company contributes $150 of the monthly cost for coverage for all of its employees, so that an employee pays only $50 per month for self-only coverage under the Plan, but pays $1,050 per month for family coverage.

A. Lashauna Dupree, an employee of the Timber Company, has family coverage under the Plan for herself and her husband, Jack. Lashauna and Jack desire to adopt a child and have been working with an adoption agency that specializes in adoptions of infant girls from China. The adoption agency has just informed Lashauna that it has located a possible adoption candidate, a one-month-old girl, Chang Lu. Chang Lu suffers from a heart condition that is correctable by surgery in the United States, but the surgical technique is not available in China.

The Chinese doctor who has treated Chang Lu's condition predicts that if Chang Lu does not have the necessary surgery within six months, her condition will deteriorate and she will die. Because of Chang Lu's serious heart condition, Chang Lu qualifies for an expedited adoption under the Chinese government's adoption procedures. Lashauna and Jack would like to adopt Chang Lu immediately.

How would you advise Lashauna and Jack with respect to the following questions:

1. Must the Plan provide coverage for Chang Lu as an adopted child?

2. Can the Plan require that Chang Lu's adoption must be finalized (a legal process that could take up to one year) before she can be enrolled for family coverage under the Plan?

3. Assuming Chang Lu is enrolled as a participant in the Plan, can the Plan charge a higher monthly premium than $1,050 for family coverage due to her preexisting heart condition?

B. Brad Smith, an hourly employee of the Timber Company, is considering whether to temporarily switch from a regular schedule of forty hours per week to a reduced schedule that requires fewer hours for the next several months. Brad is in the process of writing a novel, and he thinks that working a lesser schedule for several months will enable him to complete his manuscript. Brad is concerned, however, about maintaining his family coverage under the Plan because his spouse was diagnosed with cancer and her doctor is an oncology specialist who practices at a regional cancer center located in another state. The Timber Company Plan includes this oncology specialist and the regional cancer center as part of the plan's network of covered health care providers.

1. Can Brad switch to a reduced work schedule and maintain his family's health insurance coverage under the Timber Company Plan?

2. What factors should Brad consider before reducing the number of hours he works each week?

C. Terry Clerk, a salaried employee of the Timber Company, has family coverage under the Timber Company Plan for his spouse Cherry and their five children. Unknown to Cherry, Terry drops his family coverage under the Plan and files for a divorce one week later. Cherry has come to you for legal representation in her divorce. One of Cherry's concerns is continued health insurance coverage for herself and her five children.

How would you advise Cherry with respect to the following questions:

1. Are Cherry and the five children entitled to receive a COBRA notice? If so, what will be the maximum period of their COBRA continuation coverage under the Timber Company Plan?

2. Can Cherry make certain that—so long as Terry continues to work for the Timber Company for at least thirty hours per week—the five children will receive coverage under the Plan? For how long can the children be covered under the Timber Company Plan?

3. What will happen to the health insurance coverage for the five children under the Timber Company Plan if Terry's regular work schedule at the Timber Company is reduced to less than thirty hours per week? If Terry changes employers? Can you address these possibilities in your representation of Cherry in the divorce proceeding?

3. TARGETED FEDERAL REFORMS: 1996–2008

Between 1996 and 2008, Congress adopted an incremental approach to national health care reform by enacting a series of discrete and narrowly tailored requirements applicable to all insured and self-insured group health plans. Congress left these requirements for group health plans in place when it enacted the Affordable Care Act in 2010.

a. NMHPA

The Newborns' and Mothers' Health Protection Act of 1996 (NMHPA) established minimum federal standards for maternity hospital benefits offered by a group health plan. These requirements, which are found in ERISA Section 711, apply to any group health plan that has at least two participants who are current employees. The NMHPA does not require a group health plan to offer maternity hospital care benefits. Rather, the NMHPA requires that if the plan does provide maternity hospital care benefits, such benefits must meet certain minimum duration of hospital stay requirements. The NMHPA's standards were based on medical practice guidelines that were developed jointly by the American College of Obstetricians and Gynecologists and the American Academy of Pediatrics.

Congress enacted the NMHPA in response to the perception, held by both physicians and the public, that insurers and health care plans were risking the safety of mothers and newborn children by limiting the duration of maternity hospital care as a cost saving measure. See S. REP. NO. 104–326 (1996). Prior to the enactment of the NMHPA, 28 states had adopted state insurance laws establishing minimum hospital care coverage after childbirth for mothers and newborns. These state laws were far from comprehensive, however, because not all states had adopted such laws, and self-insured group health plans were not subject to these state insurance laws by virtue of ERISA preemption.

ERISA Section 711(a) requires that for a normal vaginal delivery, the minimum length of the mother's hospital stay following childbirth must be at least forty-eight hours. The minimum hospital stay after a birth by caesarean section is ninety-six hours. The attending health care provider may, after consultation with the mother, discharge the mother and her newborn child prior to the expiration of these minimum stay requirements. ERISA Section 711(b) prohibits group health plans and health insurance issuers from:

- providing financial incentives to mothers to encourage them to accept less than the minimum hospital stay;
- penalizing physicians when patients utilize the minimum hospital stay; and
- providing incentives to physicians to induce their patients to accept less than the minimum hospital stay.

The NMHPA has special preemption provisions that address the situation where a state has more generous standards for maternity benefits offered by insured plans. Under ERISA Section 711(f), state insurance laws that require a longer minimum hospital stay following childbirth are not preempted, and thus continue to apply to insured group health plans.

b. WHCRA

The Women's Health and Cancer Rights Act of 1998 (WHCRA), codified in ERISA Section 713, requires group health plans and health insurance issuers that provide medical and surgical benefits with respect to a mastectomy to provide certain additional benefits to a mastectomy patient if the patient requests these benefits. These WHCRA-mandated benefits are:

- reconstruction of the breast on which the mastectomy has been performed;
- surgery and reconstruction of the other breast to produce a symmetrical appearance; and
- coverage of prostheses and coverage of physical complications at all stages of the mastectomy.

Group health plans and health insurance issuers may not penalize or provide financial or other incentives to health care providers to encourage them to provide care to the participant that is inconsistent with these WHCRA requirements. See ERISA § 713(c). The preemption provisions of WHCRA operate similarly to the NMHPA, thereby preserving state insurance laws that require more generous coverage by insured plans of the reconstructive breast surgery and related services than are required under the WHCRA. See ERISA § 713(e)(1).

c. GINA

Congress expanded the HIPAA nondiscrimination requirements concerning the use of genetic information in the Genetic Information Nondiscrimination Act of 2008 (GINA). Prior to the GINA, ERISA Section 702(a) prohibited a group health plan (including the issuer of a group health insurance policy) from using genetic information to determine an individual's eligibility to enroll in the plan, to set an individual's premium amount, or to subject an individual to a preexisting condition coverage exclusion. These prohibitions did not prevent group health plans from using genetic information to set group-wide premiums, collecting genetic information, or requiring mandatory genetic testing.

Congress enacted the GINA in response to concerns that persons were refusing to participate in clinical trials or to undergo genetic testing, such as genetic testing for breast cancer, because of the fear that employers or health insurance insurers would discriminate against them or refuse to sponsor or underwrite a group health plan based on the genetic testing results. GINA amended Section 702 of ERISA to:

- prohibit group health plans from adjusting premium or contribution amounts for the group covered by the plan on the basis of genetic information;
- prohibit mandatory genetic testing of plan participants; and
- prohibit the collection of genetic information (including requesting, requiring, or purchasing such information) on plan participants or their family members.

GINA further amended ERISA Section 702 so that the new GINA prohibitions extend to group health plans with only one employee. The GINA contains numerous exceptions and safe harbors, such as for employee wellness programs, requests for Family and Medical Leave, or the monitoring of the biological effects of workplace toxins. See generally ERISA § 702(c)–(f).

d. MHPAEA

The Paul Wellstone and Pete Domenici Mental Health Parity and Addiction Equity Act of 2008 (MHPAEA) was enacted as part of the Emergency Economic Stabilization Act of 2008, Pub. L. No. 110–343, § 512, 122 Stat. 3881. The MHPAEA made permanent and expanded the requirements governing mental health benefits that Congress originally enacted in the Mental Health Parity Act of 1996, Pub. L. No. 104–204, § 701, 110 Stat. 2944 (MHPA). These requirements are codified in ERISA Section 712.

The original MHPA did not require a group health plan to offer any mental health benefits to plan participants. Rather, the MHPA required that if the plan did provide mental health benefits along with medical and surgical care benefits, then the plan could not impose lower aggregate lifetime or annual limits for mental health benefits than for medical or surgical care benefits. The MHPA requirements did not apply, however, to the coverage of treatment for substance abuse or chemical addiction. Moreover, the original MHPA did not require true "parity" between physical and mental health care benefits. Under the original MHPA, a group health plan could impose other restrictions on mental health benefits that would deter plan participants from utilizing mental health services. Such permissible restrictions included limits on the number of visits or days of in-patient hospital coverage and higher participant co-payments. Finally, the original MHPA's requirements were temporary in that the requirements were subject to a sunset provision (which Congress subsequently extended several times).

Like the original MHPA, the MHPAEA does not mandate that a group health plan must provide mental health or substance abuse and chemical addiction benefits. The MHPAEA amended Section 712 of ERISA so that, if a group health plan does offer mental health or substance abuse and chemical addiction benefits, there must be absolute parity with medical and surgical care benefits on all levels. The MHPAEA requires that, in addition to the same aggregate lifetime or annual limits, the co-payments, deductibles, coinsurance, out-of-network coverage, out-of-pocket expenses and other treatment limitations (e.g., caps on number of visits, days, or duration of treatment) must be equivalent.

The MHPAEA applies only to group health plans sponsored by employers having an average of more than fifty employees during the preceding calendar year. Under the MHPAEA, a group health plan may be exempt from the parity requirements if an actuary certifies that the actual total costs of the plan increased by more than 2% in the first year of compliance and by 1% for each subsequent year. As with the HIPAA and the NMHPA, the MHPAEA does not preempt state insurance laws that mandate more generous coverage of mental health or substance abuse and chemical addiction benefits for insured plans.

4. AFFORDABLE CARE ACT

The Affordable Care Act (ACA), as amended by the Health Care and Education Reconciliation Act of 2010 (HCRA) (collectively, the Affordable Care Act or the ACA), became effective on March 23, 2010. The Affordable Care Act created new federal requirements for group health plans. Some requirements of the ACA, however, do not apply to so-called "grandfathered" plans. A *grandfathered plan* is an insured or self-insured plan in existence on March 23, 2010, that does not make a subsequent disqualifying change to the terms of the plan. Table 4.4 summarizes the major ACA requirements that are applicable to grandfathered and non-grandfathered health plans as of January 1, 2014. These requirements are explained in the reading material that follows the table.

Table 4.4

Major ACA Requirements for Group Health Plans

Requirement	Application
Lifetime and annual dollar limits on essential health benefits prohibited; pre-existing condition coverage exclusions prohibited; waiting periods restricted	All Plans
Required coverage of minor children and adult children up to age 26	All Plans
Prohibition on rescission of coverage	All Plans
Automatic enrollment of workers in group health plans sponsored by very large employers (200+ employees)	All Plans
Mandatory coverage with no participant-cost sharing of immunizations and preventive care services	Grandfathered plans exempt
In-network coverage of emergency care services	Grandfathered plans exempt
Patient choice of physicians for maternity and pediatric services	Grandfathered plans exempt
Independent external review of denied claims for plan benefits	Grandfathered plans exempt
Coverage of all ten essential health benefits	All self-insured plans and insured plans in the large employer market are exempt
Limits on maximum out-of-pocket payments by participants	Grandfathered plans exempt

A Preliminary Note About Federalism and Counting Employees

At first glance, the lofty concept of federalism and the mundane task of counting employees to determine whether an employer is classified as "large" or "small" for purposes of the requirements of the Affordable Care Act may seem unrelated. The purpose of this preliminary note is to warn you that counting the number of employees of an employer is not necessarily a simple exercise. The reason, in a nutshell, is federalism.

To understand why federalism complicates what should be a simple task, a brief history lesson is necessary. Starting with the passage of the McCarran Ferguson Act of 1945, 15 U.S.C. §§ 1011–1015, Congress historically has left the regulation of insurance companies and the benefits provided by health insurance policies to the individual states. ERISA's preemption provisions reflect this traditional federal deference to state regulation by providing that state laws regulating insurance are saved from federal preemption. See ERISA § 514(b)(2)(A).

As explained earlier in Section C of Chapter Four, self-insured group health plans are not subject to regulation under state insurance laws. See ERISA § 514(b)(2)(B); FMC Corp. v. Holliday, 498 U.S. 52 (1990). Over time, two regulatory mechanisms evolved for group health plans. Fully insured (or just "insured") plans are the product of a group health insurance policy, the terms of which are regulated by state insurance laws. Self-insured group health plans are regulated solely by federal law requirements.

The ACA attempts to bring a measure of uniformity to group health plans by bridging these two regulatory mechanisms. But due to Congress's lengthy prior history of allowing the individual states to regulate the "business of insurance" under the McCarran Ferguson Act, a problem arose when lawmakers drafted the ACA. Even though it was common for a state to impose different requirements for health insurance policies sold on the large employer market and the small employer market, there was no uniform definition of a "small" and "large" employer. Rather, each state had its own definition.

A second problem arose because under key federal laws—namely the Code and ERISA—the counting of employees had evolved to an art form. For purposes of qualified retirement plans and COBRA coverage under federal law, the "employer" is defined as including all of the members of a controlled group under Code Sections 414(b), (c), (m), and (o). Recall that COBRA continuation coverage must be offered if the employer has 20 or more full-time equivalent employees on a typical business day during the prior calendar year. See ERISA § 601 (a)–(b); IRS Rev. Ruling 2003–7. Part-time employees are counted as fractions of full-time employees based on the number of hours normally worked by full-time employees in the business. For example, if a full-time employee normally works 40 hours a week, the two part-time employees who each work 20 hours in a week are counted as one full-time employee under COBRA's fractional counting method. Although this fractional counting method makes sense to ensure compliance with federal laws, it does not make sense for purposes of coverage under a health insurance policy. An employer can have "partial" (i.e., part-time) workers, but a health insurance policy has to provide coverage to a whole person.

Finally, the sheer number of pages required to draft the ACA created some drafting oversights. The ACA redefined a "small employer" under the Public Health Services Act (PHSA) as one having 100 or fewer employees, but did not make conforming amendments to the definitions under the Code and ERISA, which define a "small employer" as one having 2 to 50 employees. See 78 Fed. Reg. 65,046, 65,049 (Oct. 30, 2013).

This background helps to explain the different ways that a "large" employer and a "small" employer currently are defined under the ACA. When the ACA is addressing market reform requirements for group health insurance policies, the Department of Health and Human Services (now the primary *federal* regulator for health insurance issuers), permits each state in 2015 to elect to define a small employer as one having 50 or fewer employees, and a large employer as one having 51 or more employees. (Some states already have set their dividing line at 100 employees.) Equivalencies are not used in this context for determining whether an employer is classified as large or small. Beginning January 1, 2016, all state insurance markets must use the PHSA definition of a large employer as one having 101 or more employees. See 78 Fed. Reg. at 65,092 (explanation of definitions).

When the ACA is addressing the "large" employer requirements for purposes of triggering the federal employer mandate under Code Section 4980H, the definition used is based on the equivalent of 50 or more full-time employees. The counting method for determining full-time equivalent employees is similar to COBRA's approach, but a full-time employee for purposes of the ACA is defined as one who works an average of 30 or more hours per week. Adding to this complexity, for purposes of *assessing the federal excise tax penalty* for noncompliance with the employer mandate, the equivalence concept is *not* applied, and the Code Section 4980H penalty is assessed only on the basis of *actual* full-time employees. (The technical details of how the employer mandate operates are explained later in this subsection.)

Normally, when Congress enacts major legislation such as the ACA, these sorts of discrepancies and oversights are corrected (or at least clarified) by enacting subsequent technical amendments. Until Congress enacts technical amendments, federal regulators, state insurance commissioners, employers and their legal counsel must adapt to a variable and contextual definition of "large" and "small" employer under the ACA.

a. Requirements for Maintaining Grandfathered Plan Status

As indicated by Table 4.4, grandfathered plans are exempt from many of the Affordable Care Act's requirements. The statutory language of the ACA itself is cryptic concerning the types of changes that will cause a plan to lose its grandfathered status. According to the statute, a plan may enroll family members of existing participants and new employees and their family members in the plan without losing its grandfathered status. For collectively bargained group health plans, grandfathered plan status ends automatically when the collective bargaining agreement under which the plan was established expires. A plan may make amendments to conform to the requirements of state or federal law and may increase the plan's premiums without losing its grandfathered status. See ACA § 1251(a)–(d). Other than these brief statutory provisions, the ACA is silent concerning the requirements for maintaining grandfathered plan status.

Department of Labor regulations implementing the ACA provide more guidance for plan sponsors who desire to maintain grandfathered plan status. See generally 75 Fed. Reg. 34,538 (June 17, 2010), as amended by 75 Fed. Reg. 70,114 (Nov. 17, 2010). The preamble to the Department of Labor's regulations describes the policy balance that Congress attempted to strike by drawing a distinction between grandfathered and non-grandfathered plans:

> In making grandfathered health plans subject to some, but not all, of the health reforms contained in the Affordable Care Act, the statute balances its objective of preserving the ability to maintain existing coverage with the goals of expanding access to and improving the quality of health coverage. The statute does not, however, address at what point changes to a group health plan or health insurance coverage in which an individual was enrolled on March 23, 2010, are significant enough to cause the plan or health insurance coverage to cease to be a grandfathered health plan, leaving that question to be addressed by regulatory guidance.
>
> These [Department of Labor] regulations are designed to ease the transition of the healthcare industry into the reforms established by the [ACA] by allowing for gradual implementation of reforms through a reasonable grandfathering rule.

75 Fed. Reg. at 34,541–2. Although in theory grandfathered plan status may continue indefinitely, the Department of Labor predicted in 2010 that many plans, particularly plans sponsored by small employers, voluntarily would relinquish their grandfathered plan status in future

years. The Department of Labor's projections in June of 2010 for the gradual transition of grandfathered plans into compliance with all of the requirements of the ACA are set forth in Table 4.5.

Table 4.5

Estimates of the Cumulative Percentage of Employer Plans Relinquishing Their Grandfathered Plan Status, 2011–2103

	2011	2012	2013
Low-end Estimate			
Small employer plans (3–99 employees)	20%	36%	49%
Large employer plans (100 + employees)	13%	24%	34%
All employer plans	15%	28%	39%
Mid-range Estimate			
Small employer plans (3–99 full-time employees)	30%	51%	66%
Large employer plans (100+ full-time employees)	18%	33%	45%
All employer plans	22%	38%	51%
High-end Estimate			
Small employer plans (3–99 full-time employees)	42%	66%	80%
Large employer plans (100 + full-time employees)	29%	50%	64%
All employer plans	33%	55%	69%

Source: 75 Fed. Reg. 34,538, 34,553 (June 17, 2010) (definitions of employer size are in the original).

The Department of Labor regulations for maintaining grandfathered status focus on: (1) the benefits package offered by the plan or the insurance policy that constituted the grandfathered plan as of March 23, 2010; (2) the costs (other than premiums) borne by the participants in the grandfathered plan as of March 23, 2010; and (3) the employer contribution to the plan as of March 23, 2010. With limited exceptions, a change in any one of these three areas results in a loss of grandfathered plan status. An insured plan retains its grandfathered status if the employer changes its insurance carrier so long as the new policy does not make any of the above-described changes that would otherwise trigger a loss of grandfathered plan status. See 75 Fed. Reg. at 70,117. Any elimination of benefits to diagnose or treat a particular condition will result in the loss of grandfathered plan status. For changes to cost-sharing by plan participants, the Department of Labor regulations distinguish between co-insurance and fixed-amount cost-sharing. For co-insurance, any percentage increase in the portion the participant must pay is a disqualifying change. For example, if the grandfathered plan required a participant to pay 20% of the cost of benefits and later increases the co-insurance percentage to 30%, the change would cause the plan to lose its grandfathered plan status. For fixed-amount cost sharing, such as co-payments for services such as office visits, a numeric formula permits the plan to increase the fixed amount of the co-payment to maintain pace with medical inflation. For employer contributions, the employer generally cannot decrease its contribution rate for any class of similarly situated individuals by more than 5% below the rate in effect on March 23, 2010.

To maintain grandfathered plan status, additional administrative paperwork is necessary. The plan administrator or the insurance company that issues the plan's policy must provide notice to the participants that the plan is a grandfathered plan. The burden of proof of grandfathered plan status rests with the plan administrator or the policy issuer, who must maintain records and documentation proving that the plan has maintained its grandfathered plan status.

b. Coverage of Essential Health Benefits

Due in part to the fact that the Affordable Care Act applies to governmental plans, which are not subject to regulation under Title I of ERISA, many of the federal requirements described below were enacted as amendments to the Public Health Services Act, 42 U.S.C. § 300gg et seq. (PHSA), and incorporated by reference into ERISA and the Code. See generally ERISA § 715; Code §§ 4980D, 9815. Citations below are to the appropriate section of the ACA or the HCRA that created the requirement.

The ACA requires that only certain types of group health plans must provide coverage of the full range of ten *essential health benefits* beginning in 2014. The ACA's ten essential health benefits are:

- Ambulatory patient services
- Emergency services
- Hospitalization coverage
- Maternity and newborn care services

- Mental health and substance abuse disorder services, including behavioral health treatment
- Prescription drug coverage
- Rehabilitative and habilitative services and devices
- Laboratory services
- Preventive and wellness services and chronic disease management
- Pediatric services, including dental and vision care for children under age 18

ACA § 1302(b); 78 Fed. Reg. 12,834 (Feb. 25, 2013). If a group health plan provided an essential health benefit on March 23, 2010, then the plan is prohibited from imposing lifetime dollar limits or unreasonable annual dollar limits on claims for that essential health benefit. ACA § 1001 (adding PHSA § 2711); HCRA § 2301. As of January 1, 2014, all non-grandfathered insured group health plans sold in the small employer market must provide the complete range of ten essential health benefits without any lifetime or annual limitations. This requirement also applies to any policies sold to individuals through an Exchange, and to Exchange policies purchased by employees of small employers through the SHOP. Insured group health plans sold on the large employer market, self-insured plans sponsored by employers of any size, and grandfathered insured plans are *not* required to offer the full range of ten essential health benefits. Of course, many of these exempt plans do offer most of the essential health benefits voluntarily. Moreover, insured plans may already be required to cover many of the ten essential health benefits under state insurance laws. E.g., Metropolitan Life Ins. Co. v. Massachusetts, 471 U.S. 724 (1985).

Effective in 2014, all group health plans are prohibited from imposing a waiting period for the commencement of benefits under the plan that is longer than 90 days. (Individuals are not penalized for a lack of coverage during the plan's waiting period under the individual mandate.) In addition, all group health plans are prohibited from imposing preexisting condition coverage exclusions on adults. This requirement supersedes Section 701 of ERISA, which previously permitted a group health plan to impose limited preexisting condition coverage exclusions on new enrollees who lacked prior creditable coverage. All non-grandfathered self-insured plans and non-grandfathered insured plans that are sold in the large employer market must set out-of-pocket annual limits for participants that cannot exceed $6,350 for employee-only coverage and $12,700 for family coverage. For non-grandfathered insured plans that are sold in the small employer market, the maximum out-of-pocket limits are $2,000 and $4,000 for employee-only and family coverage, respectively. These dollar amounts are indexed for inflation in future years. The effect of these much lower maximum out-of-pocket amounts is that the insurance issuer must charge a higher monthly premium for an insured plan sold on the small employer market.

Out-of-pocket expenses that must be counted toward the annual maximum limit include deductibles and co-payments, but exclude premiums, non-essential health benefits, and essential health benefits that are provided by medical professionals who are outside of the plan's network. See ACA § 1302(c)(3). Emergency care services always must be treated as in-network and therefore count toward the annual out-of-pocket limit.

c. Coverage Requirements for Dependents and Adult Children

All group health plans are prohibited from imposing a preexisting condition coverage exclusion for minor children under age 19. ACA § 10103(e); HCRA § 2301. In addition, all group health plans are required to offer coverage to an adult child of a plan participant until the child turns age 26, regardless of the child's marital status, full-time student status, or financial support by the parent. ACA § 1001 (adding PHSA § 2714); HCRA § 2301. For administrative convenience, some plans allow a child who turns age 26 to remain on the parent's plan until the end of the month, or even until the end of the plan year. If an adult child is enrolled in the plan and loses coverage due to the attainment of age 26, the loss of "dependent" coverage under the employer's plan is treated as a COBRA qualifying event and the adult child is entitled to up to 36 months of COBRA continuation coverage. A plan cannot charge a separate or higher premium for coverage of an adult child than for a minor child of the parent. Conforming amendments to the Code provide that the employer's contribution to the plan is not treated as taxable income to an adult child who is covered under the plan. See IRS Notice 2010–38.

d. Prohibitions on Rescission of Coverage

All group health plans are prohibited from rescinding coverage once an individual is enrolled in the plan, unless the individual has engaged in fraud or intentional misrepresentation in enrolling in the plan. ACA § 1001 (adding PHSA § 2712); HCRA § 2301. This requirement reinforces the nondiscrimination provisions of ERISA Section 702, which prohibit a group health plan from basing an individual's eligibility to enroll in the plan on a health-related factor. See ERISA § 702(a)(1)(A)–(H). Cancellation of coverage due to the participant's failure to make a timely premium payment is not considered to be a prohibited rescission of coverage.

e. Automatic Enrollment Requirements for Very Large Employers

The ACA requires that very large employers with more than 200 full-time equivalent employees who sponsor a group health plan automatically must enroll new full-time employees in the plan. HCRA § 1511. Employers who offer multiple plans may select a "default" plan for the automatic enrollment of employees. Employees who are automatically enrolled in a group health plan must receive notice of the enrollment and have the ability to opt out of coverage under the plan. Enforcement of this requirement has been suspended until further regulatory guidance is issued to employers. See IRS Notice 2012–17.

f. Additional Requirements for Non-Grandfathered Plans

Immunizations, Preventive Care and Emergency Services

All non-grandfathered group health plans are required to provide first-dollar coverage of all immunizations and preventive care services. The plan cannot require participants to share in the cost of these benefits by subjecting immunizations and preventive care services to deductibles or co-payments. ACA § 1001 (adding PHSA § 2713). With regard to emergency services, non-grandfathered plans cannot require pre-authorization for these services and must treat all emergency services as in-network. ACA § 1001 (making group health plans subject to the requirements of PHSA § 2719A).

The list of preventive services that must be offered by non-grandfathered plans at no cost to the plan's participants includes all FDA-approved contraceptive methods and sterilization procedures for women along with related counseling. After several preliminary attempts at drafting regulatory guidance that would accommodate the objections of business owners with strongly held religious beliefs that guide their business operations, religious groups, and religiously-affiliated employers, the federal government issued final regulations on July 2, 2013. See 78 Fed. Reg. 398, 701 (July 2, 2013) (describing in detail the history of the conflict and prior attempts at accommodations). A few months after the issuance of final regulations, the Supreme Court agreed to hear two cases in which employers challenged the mandatory coverage of certain contraceptive methods on religious grounds. In each case, the owners of a closely-held, for-profit corporation challenged the requirement of mandatory contraceptive coverage as an unconstitutional interference with the free exercise of religion under the First Amendment, and as a violation of the federal Religious Freedom Restoration Act, 42 U.S.C. § 2000bb (RFRA). In *Burwell v. Hobby Lobby Stores, Inc.*, 134 S. Ct. 2751 (2014), the Supreme Court ruled that the contraceptive mandate as applied to the companies was a violation of the RFRA. The Supreme Court did not address the plaintiffs' First Amendment claims, however, because the Court ruled in their favor based on the statutory RFRA claim. (*Hobby Lobby Stores* is reproduced later in this subsection of the casebook.)

Selection of Physicians for Maternal and Pediatric Services

Group health plans with managed care features historically have placed restrictions on the participant's access to treatment by requiring that referrals to other doctors must be made by a designated primary care physician. Under the ACA, a non-grandfathered group health plan that provides for the designation of a primary care physician must permit a child who is covered under the plan to select an available pediatrician as the child's primary care physician. Female participants in the plan must have direct access to obstetrical or gynecological care without having to obtain a referral or an authorization from a primary care physician. ACA § 1001 (making group health plans subject to the requirements of PHSA § 2719A).

Independent External Review of Denied Claims

ERISA established a unique process for a participant to appeal a claim for plan benefits that is denied by the plan's administrator. This process, which is described in more detail later in Chapter Six, requires the participant to appeal the denied claim first through the plan's internal administrative review process. See generally ERISA § 503. Once the internal administrative appeal process has been exhausted, the participant may challenge the plan administrator's decision by filing a claim in federal or state court under ERISA Section 502(a)(1)(B).

In response to concerns about the objectivity of the internal administrative review process, several states enacted independent external review procedures for claims that were denied by insured plans or HMOs. In *Rush Prudential HMO, Inc. v. Moran*, 536 U.S. 355 (2002), the Supreme Court held that these state-operated independent external review processes were not preempted by ERISA Section 514. (*Moran* is reproduced in Chapter Seven of the casebook.) In the wake of the Supreme Court's decision in *Moran*, many more states enacted independent external review programs for denied claims. But these state-based procedural alternatives to ERISA litigation did not exist in every state, and they did not apply to self-insured plans by virtue of ERISA's deemer clause, ERISA § 514(b)(2)(B). See generally FMC Corp. v. Holliday, 498 U.S. 52 (1990).

The ACA gives the option of independent external review of denied claims to participants in all non-grandfathered plans, including non-grandfathered self-insured plans. See ACA § 1001. Grandfathered self-insured plans remain exempt from federal and state independent external review procedures for denied claims.

Prior to the enactment of the ACA, the Uniform Health Carrier External Review Model Act (Model Act) was created by the National Association of Insurance Commissioners to encourage states to enact independent external review programs for insured plans and HMOs, and to create consumer protection standards for such programs. Some states followed the terms of the Model Act closely; others did not. The ACA requires that state-operated independent external review programs must include consumer protection standards that are similar to those set forth in the Model Act. See PPACA § 1001 (adding PHSA § 2719). Under regulatory compliance guidelines issued by the Department of Labor, the states have until January 1, 2016, to implement independent external review programs that parallel the consumer protection standards of the Model Act. See DOL Technical Bulletin 2013–01.

Non-grandfathered self-insured plans can satisfy the independent external review requirement by contracting with at least three accredited private independent review organizations (IROs) and rotating assignments among them. See Group Health Plans and Health Insurance Issuers: Rules Relating to Internal Claims and Appeals of External Review Processes, 76 Fed. Reg. 37,208, 37,211 (June 24, 2011); DOL Technical Bulletin 2010–01, as modified by Technical Release 2011–02. Each state determines the scope of denied claims that are eligible for independent external review under its state-operated process. The scope of denied claims by participants in self-insured plans that are eligible for independent external review by IROs is determined by Department of Labor regulations. See 76 Fed. Reg. at 37,211, 37,216. In general, any claim that involves the exercise of medical judgment is subject to independent external review. See 76 Fed. Reg. at 37,216 (providing examples).

How does the independent external review process for insured plans operate under the consumer protection standards of the Model Act? First, the participant must exhaust the plan's internal administrative appeal procedure and receive a final adverse determination of the claim before seeking independent external review of the plan administrator's decision. Model Act § 7. Next, the participant must file a request for independent external review with the state insurance commissioner. Model Act § 8. Among the consumer protections provided by the Model Act, the independent reviewer must be an expert in the treatment of the participant's medical condition that is the subject of the participant's claim. If a physician serves as an external reviewer, the physician must be currently licensed and be certified by a recognized American medical specialty board in the area or areas that are the subject of the denied claim. Model Act § 13. The participant may submit additional written information to the independent reviewer to support the participant's claim that was not initially submitted to the plan's administrator. In rendering an opinion, the independent reviewer is not bound by the prior judgments or opinions of the plan administrator. The decision of the independent external reviewer is binding on the plan administrator and cannot be appealed through litigation. Model Act § 11.

Similar consumer protection standards apply to the independent review processes operated by accredited IROs for participants in self-insured plans. In the self-insured plan context, however, the request for independent external review is submitted to the plan administrator, who then assigns the claim to one of the plan's IROs for review.

g. Guaranteed Issue and Renewability for Group Health Insurance Policies

To give all employers greater access to group health insurance, the ACA requires that insurance issuers must issue a policy to an employer who applies for a new group health insurance policy. The insurance company also must renew the employer's coverage under a group policy if requested by the employer. The insurance company cannot cancel the employer's group policy based on an adverse claims experience, but the ACA does not restrict the premium amount that the insurance company may charge for the renewed policy.

h. Minimum Essential Coverage and the Employer and Individual Mandates

The ACA requires that, unless an exemption applies, beginning in 2014 all individuals are required to maintain *minimum essential coverage* through a federal or state program, an employer-sponsored group health plan, or an individual health insurance policy for themselves and their dependents. Individuals who fail to maintain minimum essential coverage for themselves and their dependents must pay a tax penalty (the *individual mandate*). See generally Code § 5000A.

As originally enacted, the individual mandate was paired with the *employer mandate*. The individual mandate went into effect as scheduled on January 1, 2014. On July 2, 2013, the Treasury Department announced that it would not enforce the employer mandate until January 1, 2015. Later, the Treasury Department announced that only employers with 100 or more full-time equivalent employers must provide minimum essential coverage in 2015, and that coverage during 2015 only had to be provided to 70% of full-time employees. Employers with 50 or more full-time equivalent employees must provide minimum essential coverage to their full-time employees beginning January 1, 2016. In 2016, minimum essential coverage must be provided to 95% of full-time employees. (This *95% compliance rule* is explained in more detail at the end of this subsection.)

The employer mandate applies only to "large" employers. See Code § 4980H. For purposes of triggering the employer mandate, the ACA defines a large employer as one who employs on average at least 50 or more full-time equivalent employees. To determine large employer status for purposes of the employer mandate, the employer looks backward to the prior calendar year when counting employees and hours of service. A *full-time employee* is defined as one who is regularly scheduled to work 30 or more hours of service per week. To calculate the number of "equivalent" full-time employers, the employer first must count the number of actual full-time employees. Next, the employer must aggregate the number of hours worked by its part-time employees for each month and divide this monthly total by 120 to determine the number of "equivalent" full-time employees for that month. This month by month count of "actual plus equivalent" full-time employees is then totaled and divided by 12 to determine whether or not the employer employed an average of 50 or more full-time equivalent employees during the prior calendar year. If an employer is in business for only part of a calendar year, then the calculation is prorated so that only the operational months are used to determine large employer status. See Code § 4980H(c)(2)(E). A statutory exemption applies for employers who have seasonal workers. See Code § 4980H(c)(2)(B). Hours of service are measured in the same manner as the minimum participation rules for qualified retirement plans. Employees of employers who are part of a controlled group under Code Sections 414(b), (c), (m), or (o) are aggregated to determine large employer status. In addition, leased employees under Code Section 414(n) are counted as employees of the employer.

Employers who employ on average fewer than 50 full-time equivalent employees are classified as "small employers." Small employers are not required to offer minimum essential coverage through a group health plan to their employees.

The employer mandate is set forth in Code Section 49804H. Section 4980H has two components, each with a different employer penalty for noncompliance. The first component, known as the *play or pay penalty*, is set forth in Section 4980H(a). The second component, known as the *free rider penalty*, is found in Section 4980H(b). Each component has its own unique design features, but certain common concepts are fundamental to the operation of each penalty.

Let's begin with the play or pay component of Section 4980H(a), which provides as follows:

(a) Large Employers Not Offering Coverage.

If—

(1) any applicable large employer fails to offer to its full-time employees (and their dependents) the opportunity to enroll in minimum essential coverage under an eligible employer-

sponsored plan (as defined in section 5000A(f)(2)) for any month, and

(2) at least one-full-time employee of the applicable large employer * * * [qualifies and has] enrolled for such month in a qualified health plan [offered through an Exchange] with respect to which an applicable premium tax credit or cost-sharing reduction is allowed or paid with respect to the employee,

then there is hereby imposed on the employer an assessable payment equal to the product of the applicable payment amount [defined under Section 4980H(c)(1) as 1/12 of $2,000, or $2,000 on an annual basis] and the number of individuals employed by the employer as full-time employees during such month.

Although the statutory language of the play or pay penalty is straight-forward, there are several important concepts imbedded in this relatively brief provision. First, the employer is required to offer coverage *only* to its *full-time* employees (defined in Code Section 4980H(c)(4)(A) as those individuals who are regularly scheduled to work at least 30 hours of service per week), even though the calculation of large employer status triggering the employer mandate requires aggregating the hours of service worked by *part-time* employees. This distinction also applies for the purpose of assessing the penalty for noncompliance. The play or pay penalty is triggered only if a *full-time* employee applies for individual coverage through an Exchange *and* qualifies on the basis of income for a premium assistance tax credit. The penalty of $2,000 on an annual basis is assessed based on the *total number of full-time employees* employed by the employer, even if only *one* full-time employee applies for and receives coverage through an Exchange policy and qualifies for a premium assistance tax credit.

In assessing the play or pay penalty, the first 30 full-time employees of the employer are *not* counted. See Code § 4980H(c)(1) (defining penalty), (c)(2)(D) (penalty calculation reduced by 30 full-time employees). In other words, so long as the number of full-time employees is limited to 30 or less, the employer will not be subject to the play or pay penalty for failing to offer minimum essential coverage to its employees. Consequently, the design of the play or pay penalty provides an incentive for employers to restrict the number of their actual full-time employees and to use more part-time workers to operate their businesses.

A second important concept imbedded in the statutory language of Section 4980H is the distinction between coverage offered to the individual employee (known as *employee-only* or *self-only* coverage), coverage offered to the employee's dependents, and coverage offered to an employee's spouse. (*Family coverage* applies to the employee, the employee's spouse, and any dependents.) Section 4980H(a) requires that the employer must offer coverage only to employees *and their dependents.* The employer is *not* required to offer spousal coverage (although many employers are likely to continue to do so voluntarily by offering family coverage). The distinction between self-only coverage and dependent coverage arises again later in the determination of *affordable coverage,* a concept that underlies the free rider penalty component of the employer mandate under Code Section 4980H(b).

The third important concept imbedded in Section 4980H(a) is *minimum essential coverage,* a technical term that only superficially resembles the concept of *essential health benefits.* The concept of minimum essential coverage mirrors the requirement of the individual mandate under Code Section 5000A, which is incorporated by reference in both Sections 4980H(a) and 4980H(b). Code Section 5000A(a) provides as follows:

(a) Requirement to Maintain Minimum Essential Coverage

An applicable individual shall for each month beginning after 2013 ensure that the individual, and any dependent of the individual who is an applicable individual, is covered under minimum essential coverage for such month.

For purposes of both the employer and individual mandates, *minimum essential coverage* is defined in Code Section 5000A(f)(2) as including coverage under an employer-sponsored plan, including a grandfathered plan, that offers more than just "excepted benefits" under Sections 2791(c)(1) through (c)(4) of the Public Health Services Act. According to the Department of Labor's on-line Health Benefits Glossary, "excepted benefits" consist of:

- benefits that are not considered health coverage, such as accidental death and disability income insurance or worker's compensation;

- benefits that are offered separately or are not an integral part of a health plan, such as dental or vision insurance for adults or long-term care insurance;

- benefits that are offered separately and not coordinated with benefits under another group health plan, such as insurance coverage for a specific disease (e.g., cancer) or a fixed indemnity amount for hospitalization; or

- benefits offered as a separate insurance policy and supplemental to Medicare, Armed Forces health care coverage, or (in very limited circumstances) group health plan coverage.

To illustrate, a plan that offers *only* dental or vision care for adults as its benefit would not constitute minimum essential coverage because dental and vision care are excepted benefits. But if a large employer offered a group health plan that provided only preventive care services and immunizations, such a plan *would* qualify as minimum essential coverage under the Code Sections 4980H and 5000A.[1] See 78 Fed. Reg. 218, 220 (Jan. 2, 2013).

Why would a large employer choose to offer a group health plan that provides such a minimal range of benefits? The first incentive is obviously cost-reduction. Although any essential health benefit that is covered by a minimum essential coverage plan cannot be subject to lifetime or annual limits, if the plan's coverage is restricted to only one or a few such benefits, the premium price is greatly reduced. A second (and closely related) employer incentive is to avoid the play or pay penalty component of Section 4980H(a), which is calculated based on the total number of full-time employees. Third, the demographic composition of the employer's workforce may provide an incentive. If the employer's workforce consists of younger or part-time employees (all of whom must satisfy the individual mandate, or else pay a tax penalty under Code Section 5000A), an employer who offers a minimum essential coverage plan at a very low monthly premium may be highly attractive to employees, who can obtain minimum essential coverage at a minimal price.

The play or pay penalty component of the employer mandate alone is not an effective mechanism for achieving the policy goal of universal health insurance coverage. Code Section 4980H(a) does not address whether the minimum essential coverage offered by the employer to its full-time employees is *affordable*, or whether the plan's covered benefits are *adequate*. The concepts of affordable and adequate coverage are addressed by Code Section 4980H(b), which provides as follows:

(b) Large Employers Offering Coverage With Employees Who Qualify For Premium Tax Credits Or Cost-Sharing Reductions

(I) In general

If—

(A) an applicable large employer offers to its full-time employees (and their dependents) the opportunity to enroll in minimum essential coverage under an eligible employer-sponsored plan (as defined in section 5000A (f)(2)) for any month, and

---

[1]   Recall that beginning in 2014 only non-grandfathered insured group health plans sold in the small employer market (and individual health insurance policies) must provide the full range of ten essential health benefits. Given that small employers are exempt from the employer mandate under Code Section 4980H, very small employers who are unable to self-insure may choose not to offer health insurance benefits to their employees due to the cost of an insured group health plan that provides coverage of the ten essential health benefits.

(B) 1 or more full-time employees of the applicable large employer * * * [qualify and are] enrolled for such month in a qualified health plan [offered through an Exchange] with respect to which an applicable premium tax credit or cost-sharing reduction is allowed or paid with respect to the employee,

then there is hereby imposed on the employer an assessable payment equal to the product of the number of full-time employees of the applicable large employer described in subparagraph (B) for such month and an amount equal to 1/12 of $3,000 [or $3,000 on an annual basis].

Section 4980H(b) is known as the free rider penalty because it addresses the policy concern that employers could offer group health coverage to all of their full-time employees (thus satisfying Section 4980H(a)), but at a premium price that would be unaffordable for full-time, but lower income, employees. If the premium charged for coverage under the employer's plan is unaffordable, lower income employees would be better off by purchasing an individual health insurance policy through the Exchange system using premium assistance tax credits. Section 4980H(b) is designed to deter employers from "free-riding" on the Exchange system of premium assistance tax credits available to individuals who have a household income that is between 100% and 400% of the federal poverty level.

The key to Section 4980H(b) is the triggering mechanism for assessment of the penalty, which requires that a full-time employee of the large employer must receive coverage through an Exchange policy *and* must qualify for a premium assistance tax credit. An employee who is eligible for coverage offered through an employer group health plan that provides minimum essential coverage, but who instead purchases an Exchange policy, is *not* eligible for a premium assistance tax credit if: (1) the employer's plan has an actuarial minimum value of at least 60% (as measured by federal regulations); and (2) the employee's share of the premium for *self-only coverage* under the employer's plan does not exceed 9.5% of the employee's *household income*. See Code § 36B(c)(2)(C)(i)–(ii) (defining employer-sponsored minimum coverage that is affordable and provides minimum value); see generally 78 Fed. Reg. 12,834 (Feb. 25, 2013) (proposed regulations for actuarial methods used to determine minimum value); 78 Fed. Reg. 218 (Jan. 2, 2013) (proposed regulations for employer shared responsibility under Code Section 4980H); IRS Notice 2014–69 (plans that fail to provide coverage for in-patient hospitalization services or physician services do not satisfy the minimum value requirement). If an employee or a member of the employee's family enrolls in an employer-sponsored group health plan, then the enrollee cannot qualify for a premium assistance tax credit to purchase additional coverage under an Exchange policy. See Code § 36B(c)(2)(C)(iii). (A grace period to unwind the enrollment applies if the employee has been automatically enrolled in a very large employer's plan. See Treas. Reg. § 1.36B–2(c)(3)(vii)(B).)

Final regulations issued by the Treasury Department took the controversial position that "affordability" is based on the cost of employee-only coverage under the employer's plan. See Treas. Reg. § 1.36B–2(c)(3)(v)(A)(2). This interpretation provides an incentive for employers to reduce the premium for employee-only coverage, but to increase the premiums for required dependent coverage (which must be offered by the employer to children of employees up to age 26) and optional spousal coverage. See 78 Fed. Reg. 218, 231–32, 241 (Jan. 2, 2013). The ACA does not prohibit employers from charging higher premiums for dependent, spousal, or family coverage.

Additional Nuances

Although the above discussion of the employer mandate may seem complex, it is actually a simplified presentation. To wrap up the remaining loose ends, here are four more nuances to consider.

First, to ensure compliance with the play or pay rule of Section 4980(a), the employer may take advantage of the *95% compliance rule*. Under the 95% compliance rule, no penalty is assessed under Section 4980H(a) if the employer offers minimum essential coverage to all but 5% of its full-time employees, or, if greater, five full-time employees. The 95% compliance rule "is designed to accommodate relatively small applicable large employers...[and] applies to the failure to offer coverage to the specified number or percentage of employees (and their dependents), regardless of whether the failure to offer was inadvertent." 78 Fed. Reg. 218, 232–33 (Jan. 2, 2013). In other words, under the 95% compliance rule the employer can designate which full-time employees are to be excluded from coverage under the employer's plan.

Assuming a large employer successfully avoids the play or pay penalty of Section 4980H(a), what is the financial risk associated with the free rider penalty under Section 4980H(b) if the employer's plan is unaffordable for some employees, or the plan fails to provide 60% actuarial minimum value? The potential free rider penalty is limited under Section 4980H(b) to the maximum possible play or pay penalty (which includes the reduction for the first 30 full-time employees of the employer). See Code § 4980H(b)(2)(D)(i). If the employer does not have more than 30 full-time employees who have a household income that is between 100% and 400% of the federal poverty level (thereby qualifying for a premium assistance tax credit to offset the cost of an Exchange policy), the employer will not be penalized at all if the employer's plan is unaffordable or fails to provide minimum value. A second, albeit indirect, limitation on the free rider penalty is the price charged for Exchange policies in the employer's market. Recall that the free rider penalty is assessed only if a full-time employee actually purchases an Exchange policy and qualifies for a premium assistance tax credit based on household income. Some Exchange markets may offer policies at a premium price that, notwithstanding the premium assistance tax credit, exceeds the individual mandate penalty amount under Code Section 5000A. In this situation, the employee may prefer to pay the penalty rather than purchase a health insurance policy through the Exchange.

Third, can an employer who offers a "skinny" minimum essential coverage plan (e.g., a plan that excludes coverage for in-patient hospitalization services) escape the free rider penalty altogether? The allure of a "skinny" minimum essential coverage plan for employers is that the reduced premium charged to employees for coverage under such a plan is more likely to be affordable for lower income full-time employees. The major obstacle to a "skinny" plan under the free rider penalty is the 60% minimum value requirement. The design of the benefits package under the plan and the relative amounts contributed by the employer and the plan's participants will determine whether the plan satisfies the actuarial standard of "minimum value." See generally IRS Notice 2012-31; Patient Protection and Affordable Care Act: Standards Related to Essential Health Benefits, Actuarial Value, and Accreditation-Final Rule, 78 Fed. Reg. 12,834 (Feb. 25, 2013); IRS Notice 2014–69. The short answer is that a plan that covers only preventive care services and immunizations, or excludes coverage of in-patient hospitalization services or physician services (all variations on the "skinny" plan technique), will fail the 60% minimum value requirement.

Finally, how is an employee's household income estimated for purposes of determining whether the employer's plan is affordable under the 9.5% of household income test? Under the individual mandate of Section 5000A, it is household income that determines eligibility for a premium assistance tax credit. Of course, the employer has no reliable way of determining what an employee's household income might be. To assist employers, the Treasury Department has issued proposed regulations that create three safe harbor mechanisms for employers to use in determining whether the plan's premiums are affordable for low-income full-time employees. The most simple safe harbor to apply allows the employer to substitute the employee's wages and other income reported on Form W-2 for the employee's household income when analyzing the affordability of the plan for its full-time workers. See generally 78 Fed. Reg. 218 (Jan. 2, 2013) (adopting IRS Notice 2011–73).

i. Challenges to the Affordable Care Act

Legal challenges to the validity of major social legislation are inevitable. The Affordable Care Act is no exception. Two major Supreme

Court cases—one challenging the individual coverage mandate, and the other challenging the mandatory coverage of all FDA-approved contraceptive methods as preventive care services—are reproduced in this subsection. In *NFIB v. Sebelius*, the Supreme Court upheld the individual mandate under the ACA as a constitutional exercise of Congress's power to "lay and collect Taxes," U.S. Const. Art. I, § 8, cl. 1, but struck down as unconstitutional the mandatory expansion of the state-operated Medicaid system. (The dissenting opinions, which are very long, have been heavily edited in the interests of time and space constraints.) In *Burwell v. Hobby Lobby Stores, Inc.*, which followed *NFIB v. Sebelius*, the Supreme Court ruled that the contraceptive coverage mandate, as applied to the plaintiffs' closely-held corporations, violated the Religious Freedom Restoration Act, 42 U.S.C. § 2000bb.

NATIONAL FEDERATION OF INDEPENDENT BUSINESS V. SEBELIUS

United States Supreme Court, 2012.
132 S. Ct. 2566.

Chief Justice ROBERTS announced the judgment of the Court and delivered the opinion of the Court with respect to Parts I, II, and III-C, an opinion with respect to Part IV, in which Justice BREYER and Justice KAGAN join, and an opinion with respect to Parts III-A, III-B, and III-D.

Today we resolve constitutional challenges to two provisions of the Affordable Care Act of 2010: the individual mandate, which requires individuals to purchase a health insurance policy providing a minimum level of coverage; and the Medicaid expansion, which gives funds to the States on the condition that they provide specified health care to all citizens whose income falls below a certain threshold. We do not consider whether the Act embodies sound policies. That judgment is entrusted to the Nation's elected leaders. We ask only whether Congress has the power under the Constitution to enact the challenged provisions.

* * *

I

In 2010, Congress enacted the Affordable Care Act. The Act aims to increase the number of Americans covered by health insurance and decrease the cost of health care. * * * This case concerns constitutional challenges to two key provisions, commonly referred to as the individual mandate and the Medicaid expansion.

The individual mandate requires most Americans to maintain "minimum essential" health insurance coverage. Code § 5000A. * * * Many individuals will receive the required coverage through their employer, or from a government program such as Medicaid or Medicare. See Code § 5000A(f). But for individuals who are not exempt and do not receive health insurance through a third party, the means of satisfying the requirement is to purchase insurance from a private company.

Beginning in 2014, those who do not comply with the mandate must make a "[s]hared responsibility payment" to the Federal Government. Code § 5000A(b)(1). That payment, which the Act describes as a "penalty," is calculated as a percentage of household income, subject to a floor based on a specified dollar amount and a ceiling based on the average annual premium the individual would have to pay for qualifying private health insurance. Code § 5000A(c). In 2016, for example, the penalty will be 2.5 percent of an individual's household income, but no less than $695 and no more than the average yearly premium for insurance that covers 60 percent of the cost of 10 specified services. * * * The Act provides that the penalty will be paid to the Internal Revenue Service with an individual's taxes, and "shall be assessed and collected in the same manner" as tax penalties, such as the penalty for claiming too large an income tax refund. Code § 5000A(g)(1). The Act, however, bars the IRS from using several of its normal enforcement tools, such as criminal prosecutions and levies. Code § 5000A(g)(2). * * *

On the day the President signed the Act into law, Florida and 12 other States filed a complaint in the Federal District Court for the Northern District of Florida. Those plaintiffs—who are both respondents and petitioners here, depending on the issue—were subsequently joined by 13 more States, several individuals, and the National Federation of Independent Business. The plaintiffs alleged, among other things, that the individual mandate provisions of the Act exceeded Congress's powers under Article I of the Constitution. * * *

The second provision of the Affordable Care Act directly challenged here is the Medicaid expansion. Enacted in 1965, Medicaid offers federal funding to States to assist pregnant women, children, needy families, the blind, the elderly, and the disabled in obtaining medical care. See 42 U.S.C. § 1396a(a)(10). In order to receive that funding, States must comply with federal criteria governing matters such as who receives care and what services are provided at what cost. By 1982 every State had chosen to participate in Medicaid. Federal funds received through the Medicaid program have become a substantial part of state budgets, now constituting over 10 percent of most States' total revenue.

The Affordable Care Act expands the scope of the Medicaid program and increases the number of individuals the States must cover. For example, the Act requires state programs to provide Medicaid coverage to adults with incomes up to 133 percent of the federal poverty level, whereas many States now cover adults with children only if their income is considerably lower, and do not cover childless adults at all. The Act increases federal funding to cover the States' costs in expanding Medicaid coverage, although States will bear a portion of the costs on their own. If a State does not comply with the Act's new coverage requirements, it may lose not only the federal funding for those requirements, but all of its federal Medicaid funds.

* * *

II

Before turning to the merits, we need to be sure we have the authority to do so. The Anti-Injunction Act provides that "no suit for the purpose of restraining the assessment or collection of any tax shall be maintained in any court by any person, whether or not such person is the person against whom such tax was assessed." Code § 7421(a). This statute protects the Government's ability to collect a consistent stream of revenue by barring litigation to enjoin or otherwise obstruct the collection of taxes. Because of the Anti-Injunction Act, taxes can ordinarily be challenged only after they are paid, by suing for a refund. See Enochs v. Williams Packing & Nav. Co., 370 U.S. 1, 7–8 (1962).

The penalty for not complying with the Affordable Care Act's individual mandate first becomes enforceable in 2014. The present challenge to the mandate thus seeks to restrain the penalty's future collection. Amicus contends that the Internal Revenue Code treats the penalty as a tax, and that the Anti-Injunction Act therefore bars this suit.

The text of the pertinent statutes suggests otherwise. The Anti-Injunction Act applies to suits "for the purpose of restraining the assessment or collection of any *tax*." Code § 7421(a) (emphasis added). Congress, however, chose to describe the "[s]hared responsibility payment" imposed on those who forgo health insurance not as a "tax," but as a "penalty." Code §§ 5000A(b), (g)(2). There is no immediate reason to think that a statute applying to "any tax" would apply to a "penalty."

Congress's decision to label this exaction a "penalty" rather than a "tax" is significant because the Affordable Care Act describes many other exactions it creates as "taxes." Where Congress uses certain language in one part of a statute and different language in another, it is generally presumed that Congress acts intentionally. See Russello v. United States, 464 U.S. 16, 23 (1983).

Amicus argues that even though Congress did not label the shared responsibility payment a tax, we should treat it as such under the Anti-Injunction Act because it functions like a tax. It is true that Congress cannot change whether an exaction is a tax or a penalty for *constitutional* purposes simply by describing it as one or the other. Congress may not, for example, expand its power under the Taxing Clause, or escape the Double Jeopardy Clause's constraint on criminal sanctions, by labeling a severe financial punishment a "tax." See Bailey v. Drexel Furniture Co., 259 U.S. 20, 36–37 (1922); Department of Revenue of Mont. v. Kurth Ranch, 511 U.S. 767, 779 (1994).

The Anti-Injunction Act and the Affordable Care Act, however, are creatures of Congress's own creation. How they relate to each other is up to Congress, and the best evidence of Congress's intent is the statutory text. * * *

The Affordable Care Act does not require that the penalty for failing to comply with the individual mandate be treated as a tax for purposes of the Anti-Injunction Act. The Anti-Injunction Act therefore does not apply to this suit, and we may proceed to the merits.

III

The Government advances two theories for the proposition that Congress had constitutional authority to enact the individual mandate. First, the Government argues that Congress had the power to enact the mandate under the Commerce Clause. Under that theory, Congress may order individuals to buy health insurance because the failure to do so affects interstate commerce, and could undercut the Affordable Care Act's other reforms. Second, the Government argues that if the commerce power does not support the mandate, we should nonetheless uphold it as an exercise of Congress's power to tax. According to the Government, even if Congress lacks the power to direct individuals to buy insurance, the only effect of the individual mandate is to raise taxes on those who do not do so, and thus the law may be upheld as a tax.

A

The Government's first argument is that the individual mandate is a valid exercise of Congress's power under the Commerce Clause and the Necessary and Proper Clause. According to the Government, the health care market is characterized by a significant cost-shifting problem. Everyone will eventually need health care at a time and to an extent they cannot predict, but if they do not have insurance, they often will not be able to pay for it. Because state and federal laws nonetheless require hospitals to provide a certain degree of care to individuals without regard to their ability to pay, hospitals end up receiving compensation for only a portion of the services they provide. To recoup the losses, hospitals pass on the cost to insurers through higher rates, and insurers, in turn, pass on the cost to policy holders in the form of higher premiums. Congress estimated that the cost of uncompensated care raises family health insurance premiums, on average, by over $1,000 per year.

In the Affordable Care Act, Congress addressed the problem of those who cannot obtain insurance coverage because of preexisting conditions or other health issues. It did so through the Act's "guaranteed-issue" and "community-rating" provisions. These provisions together prohibit insurance companies from denying coverage to those with such conditions or charging unhealthy individuals higher premiums than healthy individuals.

The guaranteed-issue and community-rating reforms do not, however, address the issue of healthy individuals who choose not to purchase insurance to cover potential health care needs. In fact, the reforms sharply exacerbate that problem, by providing an incentive for individuals to delay purchasing health insurance until they become sick, relying on the promise of guaranteed and affordable coverage. The reforms also threaten to impose massive new costs on insurers, who are required to accept unhealthy individuals but prohibited from charging them rates necessary to pay for their coverage. This will lead insurers to significantly increase premiums on everyone.

The individual mandate was Congress's solution to these problems. By requiring that individuals purchase health insurance, the mandate prevents cost-shifting by those who would otherwise go without it. In addition, the mandate forces into the insurance risk pool more healthy individuals, whose premiums on average will be higher than their health care expenses. This allows insurers to subsidize the costs of covering the unhealthy individuals the reforms require them to accept. The Government claims that Congress has power under the Commerce and Necessary and Proper Clauses to enact this solution.

1

The Government contends that the individual mandate is within Congress's power because the failure to purchase insurance "has a substantial and deleterious effect on interstate commerce" by creating the cost-shifting problem. The path of our Commerce Clause decisions has not always run smooth, but it is now well established that Congress has broad authority under the Clause. We have recognized, for example, that "[t]he power of Congress over interstate commerce is not confined to the regulation of commerce among the states," but extends to activities that "have a substantial effect on interstate commerce." United States v. Darby, 312 U.S. 100, 118–119 (1941). Congress's power, moreover, is not limited to regulation of an activity that by itself substantially affects interstate commerce, but also extends to activities that do so only when aggregated with similar activities of others.

Given its expansive scope, it is no surprise that Congress has employed the commerce power in a wide variety of ways to address the pressing needs of the time. But Congress has never attempted to rely on that power to compel individuals not engaged in commerce to purchase an unwanted product. Legislative novelty is not necessarily fatal; there is a first time for everything. But sometimes "the most telling indication of [a] severe constitutional problem. . .is the lack of historical precedent" for Congress's action. Free Enterprise Fund v. Public Company Accounting Oversight Bd., 130 S. Ct. 3138, 3159 (2010) (internal quotation marks omitted). At the very least, we should "pause to consider the implications of the Government's arguments" when confronted with such new conceptions of federal power. *United States v. Lopez*, 514 U.S. 549, 564 (1995).

The Constitution grants Congress the power to "*regulate* Commerce." Art. I, § 8, cl. 3 (emphasis added). The power to *regulate* commerce presupposes the existence of commercial activity to be regulated. If the power to "regulate" something included the power to create it, many of the provisions in the Constitution would be superfluous. For example, the Constitution gives Congress the power to "coin Money," in addition to the power to "regulate the Value thereof." *Id.* at cl. 5. And it gives Congress the power to "raise and support Armies" and to "provide and maintain a Navy," in addition to the power to "make Rules for the Government and Regulation of the land and naval Forces." *Id.* at cls. 12–14. If the power to regulate the armed forces or the value of money included the power to bring the subject of the regulation into existence, the specific grant of such powers would have been unnecessary. The language of the Constitution reflects the natural understanding that the power to regulate assumes there is already something to be regulated.

Our precedent also reflects this understanding. As expansive as our cases construing the scope of the commerce power have been, they all have one thing in common: They uniformly describe the power as reaching "activity." It is nearly impossible to avoid the word when quoting them. * * *

The individual mandate, however, does not regulate existing commercial activity. It instead compels individuals to *become* active in commerce by purchasing a product, on the ground that their failure to do so affects interstate commerce. Construing the Commerce Clause to permit Congress to regulate individuals precisely *because* they are doing nothing would open a new and potentially vast domain to congressional authority. Every day individuals do not do an infinite number of things. In some cases they decide not to do something; in others they simply fail to do it. Allowing Congress to justify federal regulation by pointing to the effect of inaction on commerce would bring countless decisions an individual could *potentially* make within the scope of federal regulation, and—under the Government's theory—empower Congress to make those decisions for him.

* * *

Indeed, the Government's logic would justify a mandatory purchase to solve almost any problem. To consider a different example in the health care market, many Americans do not eat a balanced diet. That group makes up a larger percentage of the total population than those without health insurance. See, e.g., Dept. of Agriculture and Dept. of Health and Human Services, Dietary Guidelines for Americans 1 (2010). The failure of that group to have a healthy diet increases health care costs, to a greater extent than the failure of the uninsured to purchase insurance. Those increased costs are borne in part by other Americans who must pay more, just as the uninsured shift costs to the insured. See Center for Applied Ethics, Voluntary Health Risks: Who Should Pay?, 6 Issues in Ethics 6 (1993) (noting "overwhelming evidence that individuals with unhealthy habits pay only a fraction of the costs associated with their behaviors; most of the expense is borne by the rest of society in the form of higher insurance premiums, government expenditures for health care, and disability benefits"). Congress addressed the insurance problem by ordering everyone to buy insurance. Under the Government's theory, Congress could address the diet problem by ordering everyone to buy vegetables. See Dietary Guidelines, supra, at 19 ("Improved nutrition, appropriate eating behaviors, and increased physical activity have tremendous potential to. . .reduce health care costs").

People, for reasons of their own, often fail to do things that would be good for them or good for society. Those failures—joined with the similar failures of others—can readily have a substantial effect on interstate commerce. Under the Government's logic, that authorizes Congress to use its commerce power to compel citizens to act as the Government would have them act.

That is not the country the Framers of our Constitution envisioned. James Madison explained that the Commerce Clause was "an addition which few oppose and from which no apprehensions are entertained." The Federalist No. 45, at 293. While Congress's authority under the Commerce Clause has of course expanded with the growth of the national economy, our cases have "always recognized that the power to regulate commerce, though broad indeed, has limits." Maryland v. Wirtz, 392 U.S. 183, 196 (1968). The Government's theory would erode those limits, permitting Congress to reach beyond the natural extent of its authority, "everywhere extending the sphere of its activity and drawing all power into its impetuous vortex." The Federalist No. 48, at 309 (J. Madison). Congress already enjoys vast power to regulate much of what we do. Accepting the Government's theory would give Congress the same license to regulate what we do not do, fundamentally changing the relation between the citizen and the Federal Government.

To an economist, perhaps, there is no difference between activity and inactivity; both have measurable economic effects on commerce. But the distinction between doing something and doing nothing would not have been lost on the Framers, who were "practical statesmen," not metaphysical philosophers. Industrial Union Dept., AFL-CIO v. American Petroleum Institute, 448 U.S. 607, 673 (1980) (Rehnquist, J., concurring in judgment). As we have explained, "the framers of the Constitution were not mere visionaries, toying with speculations or theories, but practical men, dealing with the facts of political life as they understood them, putting into form the government they were creating, and prescribing in language clear and intelligible the powers that government was to take." South Carolina v. United States, 199 U.S. 437, 449 (1905). The Framers gave Congress the power to *regulate* commerce, not to *compel* it, and for over 200 years both our decisions and Congress's actions have reflected this understanding. There is no reason to depart from that understanding now.

* * *

2

The Government next contends that Congress has the power under the Necessary and Proper Clause to enact the individual mandate because the mandate is an "integral part of a comprehensive scheme of economic regulation"—the guaranteed-issue and community-rating insurance reforms. Brief for United States 24. Under this argument, it is not necessary to consider the effect that an individual's inactivity may have on interstate commerce; it is enough that Congress regulate commercial activity in a way that requires regulation of inactivity to be effective.

The power to "make all Laws which shall be necessary and proper for carrying into Execution" the powers enumerated in the Constitution, Art. I, § 8, cl. 18, vests Congress with authority to enact provisions "incidental to the [enumerated] power, and conducive to its beneficial exercise," McCulloch v. Maryland, 4 Wheat. 316, 418 (1819). Although the Clause gives Congress authority to "legislate on that vast mass of incidental powers which must be involved in the constitution," it does not license the exercise of any "great substantive and independent power[s]" beyond those specifically enumerated. Id. at 411, 421. Instead, the Clause is " 'merely a declaration, for the removal of all uncertainty, that the means of carrying into execution those [powers] otherwise granted are included in the grant.' " Kinsella v. United States ex rel. Singleton, 361 U.S. 234, 247 (1960) (quoting VI Writings of James Madison 383 (G. Hunt ed. 1906)).

As our jurisprudence under the Necessary and Proper Clause has developed, we have been very deferential to Congress's determination that a regulation is "necessary." * * * But we have also carried out our responsibility to declare unconstitutional those laws that undermine the structure of government established by the Constitution. Such laws, which are not "consist[ent] with the letter and spirit of the constitution," McCulloch, supra, at 421, are not "*proper* [means] for carrying into Execution" Congress's enumerated powers. Rather, they are, "in the words of The Federalist, 'merely acts of usurpation' which 'deserve to be treated as such.' " Printz v. United States, 521 U.S. 898, 924 (1997) (alterations omitted) (quoting The Federalist No. 33, at 204 (A. Hamilton)).

Applying these principles, the individual mandate cannot be sustained under the Necessary and Proper Clause as an essential component of the insurance reforms. Each of our prior cases upholding laws under that Clause involved exercises of authority derivative of, and in service to, a granted power. * * * The individual mandate, by contrast, vests Congress with the extraordinary ability to create the necessary predicate to the exercise of an enumerated power.

This is in no way an authority that is "narrow in scope," or "incidental" to the exercise of the commerce power. Rather, such a conception of the Necessary and Proper Clause would work a substantial expansion of federal authority. No longer would Congress be limited to regulating under the Commerce Clause those who by some preexisting activity bring themselves within the sphere of federal regulation. Instead, Congress could reach beyond the natural limit of its authority and draw within its regulatory scope those who otherwise would be outside of it. Even if the individual mandate is "necessary" to the Act's insurance reforms, such an expansion of federal power is not a "proper" means for making those reforms effective.

* * *

B

That is not the end of the matter. Because the Commerce Clause does not support the individual mandate, it is necessary to turn to the Government's second argument: that the mandate may be upheld as within Congress's enumerated power to "lay and collect Taxes." Art. I, § 8, cl. 1.

The Government's tax power argument asks us to view the statute differently than we did in considering its commerce power theory. In making its Commerce Clause argument, the Government defended the mandate as a regulation requiring individuals to purchase health insurance. The Government does not claim that the taxing power allows Congress to issue such a command. Instead, the Government asks us to read the mandate not as ordering individuals to buy insurance, but rather as imposing a tax on those who do not buy that product.

The text of a statute can sometimes have more than one possible meaning. To take a familiar example, a law that reads "no vehicles in the park" might, or might not, ban bicycles in the park. And it is well established that if a statute has two possible meanings, one of which violates the Constitution, courts should adopt the meaning that does not do so. Justice Story said that 180 years ago: "No court ought, unless the terms of an act rendered it unavoidable, to give a construction to it which should involve a violation, however unintentional, of the constitution."

Parsons v. Bedford, 3 Pet. 433, 448–449, 7 L.Ed. 732 (1830). Justice Holmes made the same point a century later: "[T]he rule is settled that as between two possible interpretations of a statute, by one of which it would be unconstitutional and by the other valid, our plain duty is to adopt that which will save the Act." Blodgett v. Holden, 275 U.S. 142, 148 (1927) (concurring opinion).

The most straightforward reading of the mandate is that it commands individuals to purchase insurance. After all, it states that individuals "shall" maintain health insurance. Code § 5000A(a). Congress thought it could enact such a command under the Commerce Clause, and the Government primarily defended the law on that basis. But, for the reasons explained above, the Commerce Clause does not give Congress that power. Under our precedent, it is therefore necessary to ask whether the Government's alternative reading of the statute—that it only imposes a tax on those without insurance—is a reasonable one.

Under the mandate, if an individual does not maintain health insurance, the only consequence is that he must make an additional payment to the IRS when he pays his taxes. See Code § 5000A(b). That, according to the Government, means the mandate can be regarded as establishing a condition—not owning health insurance—that triggers a tax—the required payment to the IRS. Under that theory, the mandate is not a legal command to buy insurance. Rather, it makes going without insurance just another thing the Government taxes, like buying gasoline or earning income. And if the mandate is in effect just a tax hike on certain taxpayers who do not have health insurance, it may be within Congress's constitutional power to tax.

The question is not whether that is the most natural interpretation of the mandate, but only whether it is a "fairly possible" one. Crowell v. Benson, 285 U.S. 22, 62 (1932). As we have explained, "every reasonable construction must be resorted to, in order to save a statute from unconstitutionality." Hooper v. California, 155 U.S. 648, 657 (1895). The Government asks us to interpret the mandate as imposing a tax, if it would otherwise violate the Constitution. Granting the Act the full measure of deference owed to federal statutes, it can be so read, for the reasons set forth below.

C

The exaction the Affordable Care Act imposes on those without health insurance looks like a tax in many respects. The "[s]hared responsibility payment," as the statute entitles it, is paid into the Treasury by "taxpayer[s]" when they file their tax returns. Code §5000A(b). It does not apply to individuals who do not pay federal income taxes because their household income is less than the filing threshold in the Internal Revenue Code. Code § 5000A(e)(2). For taxpayers who do owe the payment, its amount is determined by such familiar factors as taxable income, number of dependents, and joint filing status. Code §§5000A(b)(3), (c)(2), (c)(4). The requirement to pay is found in the Internal Revenue Code and enforced by the IRS, which—as we previously explained—must assess and collect it "in the same manner as taxes." This process yields the essential feature of any tax: it produces at least some revenue for the Government. Indeed, the payment is expected to raise about $4 billion per year by 2017. Congressional Budget Office, Payments of Penalties for Being Uninsured Under the Affordable Care Act (Apr. 30, 2010), in Selected CBO Publications Related to Health Care Legislation, 2009–2010, p. 71 (rev. 2010).

It is of course true that the Act describes the payment as a "penalty," not a "tax." But while that label is fatal to the application of the Anti-Injunction Act, it does not determine whether the payment may be viewed as an exercise of Congress's taxing power. It is up to Congress whether to apply the Anti-Injunction Act to any particular statute, so it makes sense to be guided by Congress's choice of label on that question. That choice does not, however, control whether an exaction is within Congress's constitutional power to tax.

* * *

The same analysis here suggests that the shared responsibility payment may for constitutional purposes be considered a tax, not a penalty. First, for most Americans the amount due will be far less than the price of insurance, and, by statute, it can never be more. It may often be a reasonable financial decision to make the payment rather than purchase insurance * * *. Second, the individual mandate contains no scienter requirement. Third, the payment is collected solely by the IRS through the normal means of taxation—except that the Service is *not* allowed to use those means most suggestive of a punitive sanction, such as criminal prosecution. See Code § 5000A(g)(2). * * *

None of this is to say that the payment is not intended to affect individual conduct. Although the payment will raise considerable revenue, it is plainly designed to expand health insurance coverage. But taxes that seek to influence conduct are nothing new. Some of our earliest federal taxes sought to deter the purchase of imported manufactured goods in order to foster the growth of domestic industry. Today, federal and state taxes can compose more than half the retail price of cigarettes, not just to raise more money, but to encourage people to quit smoking. And we have upheld such obviously regulatory measures as taxes on selling marijuana and sawed-off shotguns. See United States v. Sanchez, 340 U.S. 42, 44–45 (1950); Sonzinsky v. United States, 300 U.S. 506, 513 (1937). Indeed, "[e]very tax is in some measure regulatory. To some extent it interposes an economic impediment to the activity taxed as compared with others not taxed." Sonzinsky, supra, at 513. That § 5000A seeks to shape decisions about whether to buy health insurance does not mean that it cannot be a valid exercise of the taxing power.

In distinguishing penalties from taxes, this Court has explained that "if the concept of penalty means anything, it means punishment for an unlawful act or omission." United States v. Reorganized CF & I Fabricators of Utah, Inc., 518 U.S. 213, 224 (1996). While the individual mandate clearly aims to induce the purchase of health insurance, it need not be read to declare that failing to do so is unlawful. Neither the Act nor any other law attaches negative legal consequences to not buying health insurance, beyond requiring a payment to the IRS. The Government agrees with that reading, confirming that if someone chooses to pay rather than obtain health insurance, they have fully complied with the law. Brief for United States 60–61; Tr. of Oral Arg. 49–50 (Mar. 26, 2012).

Indeed, it is estimated that four million people each year will choose to pay the IRS rather than buy insurance. See Congressional Budget Office, supra, at 71. We would expect Congress to be troubled by that prospect if such conduct were unlawful. That Congress apparently regards such extensive failure to comply with the mandate as tolerable suggests that Congress did not think it was creating four million outlaws. It suggests instead that the shared responsibility payment merely imposes a tax citizens may lawfully choose to pay in lieu of buying health insurance.

* * *

Whether the mandate can be upheld under the Commerce Clause is a question about the scope of federal authority. Its answer depends on whether Congress can exercise what all acknowledge to be the novel course of directing individuals to purchase insurance. Congress's use of the Taxing Clause to encourage buying something is, by contrast, not new. Tax incentives already promote, for example, purchasing homes and professional educations. See Code §§ 163(h), 25A. Sustaining the mandate as a tax depends only on whether Congress *has* properly exercised its taxing power to encourage purchasing health insurance, not whether it *can*. Upholding the individual mandate under the Taxing Clause thus does not recognize any new federal power. It determines that Congress has used an existing one.

Second, Congress's ability to use its taxing power to influence conduct is not without limits. A few of our cases policed these limits aggressively, invalidating punitive exactions obviously designed to regulate behavior otherwise regarded at the time as beyond federal authority. More often and more recently we have declined to closely examine the regulatory motive or effect of revenue-raising measures. We have nonetheless maintained that " 'there comes a time in the extension of the penalizing features of the so-called tax when it loses its character as such and becomes a mere penalty with the characteristics of regulation and punishment.'" Kurth Ranch, 511 U.S. at 779 (quoting Drexel Furniture, 259 U.S. at 38, 42).

We have already explained that the shared responsibility payment's practical characteristics pass muster as a tax under our narrowest interpretations of the taxing power. Because the tax at hand is within even those strict limits, we need not here decide the precise point at which an exaction becomes so punitive that the taxing power does not authorize it. It remains true, however, that the "'power to tax is not the power to destroy while this Court sits.'" Oklahoma Tax Comm'n v. Texas Co., 336 U.S. 342, 364 (1949) (quoting Panhandle Oil Co. v. Mississippi ex rel. Knox, 277 U.S. 218, 223 (1928) (Holmes, J., dissenting)).

Third, although the breadth of Congress's power to tax is greater than its power to regulate commerce, the taxing power does not give Congress the same degree of control over individual behavior. Once we recognize that Congress may regulate a particular decision under the Commerce Clause, the Federal Government can bring its full weight to bear. Congress may simply command individuals to do as it directs. An individual who disobeys may be subjected to criminal sanctions. Those sanctions can include not only fines and imprisonment, but all the attendant consequences of being branded a criminal: deprivation of otherwise protected civil rights, such as the right to bear arms or vote in elections; loss of employment opportunities; social stigma; and severe disabilities in other controversies, such as custody or immigration disputes.

By contrast, Congress's authority under the taxing power is limited to requiring an individual to pay money into the Federal Treasury, no more. If a tax is properly paid, the Government has no power to compel or punish individuals subject to it. We do not make light of the severe burden that taxation—especially taxation motivated by a regulatory purpose—can impose. But imposition of a tax nonetheless leaves an individual with a lawful choice to do or not do a certain act, so long as he is willing to pay a tax levied on that choice.

The Affordable Care Act's requirement that certain individuals pay a financial penalty for not obtaining health insurance may reasonably be characterized as a tax. Because the Constitution permits such a tax, it is not our role to forbid it, or to pass upon its wisdom or fairness.

* * *

IV

A

The States also contend that the Medicaid expansion exceeds Congress's authority under the Spending Clause. They claim that

Congress is coercing the States to adopt the changes it wants by threatening to withhold all of a State's Medicaid grants, unless the State accepts the new expanded funding and complies with the conditions that come with it. This, they argue, violates the basic principle that the "Federal Government may not compel the States to enact or administer a federal regulatory program." New York v. United States, 505 U.S. 144, 188 (1992).

There is no doubt that the Act dramatically increases state obligations under Medicaid. The current Medicaid program requires States to cover only certain discrete categories of needy individuals—pregnant women, children, needy families, the blind, the elderly, and the disabled. 42 U.S.C. § 1396a(a)(10). There is no mandatory coverage for most childless adults, and the States typically do not offer any such coverage. The States also enjoy considerable flexibility with respect to the coverage levels for parents of needy families. On average States cover only those unemployed parents who make less than 37 percent of the federal poverty level, and only those employed parents who make less than 63 percent of the poverty line. Kaiser Comm'n on Medicaid and the Uninsured, Performing Under Pressure 11, and fig. 11 (2012).

The Medicaid provisions of the Affordable Care Act, in contrast, require States to expand their Medicaid programs by 2014 to cover *all* individuals under the age of 65 with incomes below 133 percent of the federal poverty line. The Act also establishes a new "[e]ssential health benefits" package, which States must provide to all new Medicaid recipients—a level sufficient to satisfy a recipient's obligations under the individual mandate. The Affordable Care Act provides that the Federal Government will pay 100 percent of the costs of covering these newly eligible individuals through 2016. In the following years, the federal payment level gradually decreases, to a minimum of 90 percent. In light of the expansion in coverage mandated by the Act, the Federal Government estimates that its Medicaid spending will increase by approximately $100 billion per year, nearly 40 percent above current levels. Statement of Douglas W. Elmendorf, CBO's Analysis of the Major Health Care Legislation Enacted in March 2010, p. 14, Table 2 (Mar. 30, 2011).

The Spending Clause grants Congress the power "to pay the Debts and provide for the...general Welfare of the United States." U.S. Const., Art. I, § 8, cl. 1. We have long recognized that Congress may use this power to grant federal funds to the States, and may condition such a grant upon the States' "taking certain actions that Congress could not require them to take." College Savings Bank v. Florida Prepaid Postsecondary Ed. Expense Bd., 527 U.S. 666, 686 (1999). Such measures "encourage a State to regulate in a particular way, [and] influenc[e] a State's policy choices." New York, supra, at 166. The conditions imposed by Congress ensure that the funds are used by the States to "provide for the. . .general Welfare" in the manner Congress intended.

At the same time, our cases have recognized limits on Congress's power under the Spending Clause to secure state compliance with federal objectives. "We have repeatedly characterized ... Spending Clause legislation as 'much in the nature of a *contract.*' " Barnes v. Gorman, 536 U.S. 181, 186 (2002) (quoting Pennhurst State School and Hospital v. Halderman, 451 U.S. 1, 17 (1981)). The legitimacy of Congress's exercise of the spending power "thus rests on whether the State voluntarily and knowingly accepts the terms of the 'contract.' " Pennhurst, supra, at 17. Respecting this limitation is critical to ensuring that Spending Clause legislation does not undermine the status of the States as independent sovereigns in our federal system. That system "rests on what might at first seem a counter-intuitive insight, that 'freedom is enhanced by the creation of two governments, not one.' " Bond v. United States, 131 S. Ct. 2355, 2364 (2011) (quoting Alden v. Maine, 527 U.S. 706, 758 (1999)). For this reason, "the Constitution has never been understood to confer upon Congress the ability to require the States to govern according to Congress' instructions." New York, supra, at 162. Otherwise the two-government system established by the Framers would give way to a system that vests power in one central government, and individual liberty would suffer.

That insight has led this Court to strike down federal legislation that commandeers a State's legislative or administrative apparatus for federal purposes. * * *

Permitting the Federal Government to force the States to implement a federal program would threaten the political accountability key to our federal system. "[W]here the Federal Government directs the States to regulate, it may be state officials who will bear the brunt of public disapproval, while the federal officials who devised the regulatory program may remain insulated from the electoral ramifications of their decision." New York, supra, at 169. Spending Clause programs do not pose this danger when a State has a legitimate choice whether to accept the federal conditions in exchange for federal funds. In such a situation, state officials can fairly be held politically accountable for choosing to accept or refuse the federal offer. But when the State has no choice, the Federal Government can achieve its objectives without accountability * * *. Indeed, this danger is heightened when Congress acts under the Spending Clause, because Congress can use that power to implement federal policy it could not impose directly under its enumerated powers.

* * *

The States, however, argue that the Medicaid expansion is far from the typical case. They object that Congress has "crossed the line distinguishing encouragement from coercion," New York, supra, at 175, in the way it has structured the funding. Instead of simply refusing to grant the new funds to States that will not accept the new conditions, Congress has also threatened to withhold those States' existing Medicaid funds. The States claim that this threat serves no purpose other than to force unwilling States to sign up for the dramatic expansion in health care coverage effected by the Act.

Given the nature of the threat and the programs at issue here, we must agree. We have upheld Congress's authority to condition the receipt of funds on the States' complying with restrictions on the use of those funds, because that is the means by which Congress ensures that the funds are spent according to its view of the "general Welfare." Conditions that do not here govern the use of the funds, however, cannot be justified on that basis. When, for example, such conditions take the form of threats to terminate other significant independent grants, the conditions are properly viewed as a means of pressuring the States to accept policy changes.

* * *

In this case, the financial "inducement" Congress has chosen is much more than "relatively mild encouragement"—it is a gun to the head. Section 1396c of the Medicaid Act provides that if a State's Medicaid plan does not comply with the Act's requirements, the Secretary of Health and Human Services may declare that "further payments will not be made to the State." 42 U.S.C. § 1396c. A State that opts out of the Affordable Care Act's expansion in health care coverage thus stands to lose not merely "a relatively small percentage" of its existing Medicaid funding, but *all* of it. Medicaid spending accounts for over 20 percent of the average State's total budget, with federal funds covering 50 to 83 percent of those costs. See Nat. Assn. of State Budget Officers, Fiscal Year 2010 State Expenditure Report, p. 11, Table 5 (2011); 42 U.S.C. § 1396d(b). The Federal Government estimates that it will pay out approximately $3.3 trillion between 2010 and 2019 in order to cover the costs of *pre-*expansion Medicaid. Brief for United States 10, n. 6. In addition, the States have developed intricate statutory and administrative regimes over the course of many decades to implement their objectives under existing Medicaid. The threatened loss of over 10 percent of a State's overall budget * * * is economic dragooning that leaves the States with no real option but to acquiesce in the Medicaid expansion.

* * *

Here, the Government claims that the Medicaid expansion is properly viewed merely as a modification of the existing program because the States agreed that Congress could change the terms of Medicaid when they signed on in the first place. * * *

The Medicaid expansion, however, accomplishes a shift in kind, not merely degree. The original program was designed to cover medical services for four particular categories of the needy: the disabled, the blind, the elderly, and needy families with dependent children. See 42 U.S.C. § 1396a(a)(10). Previous amendments to Medicaid eligibility merely altered and expanded the boundaries of these categories. Under the Affordable Care Act, Medicaid is transformed into a program to meet the health care needs of the entire nonelderly population with income below 133 percent of the poverty level. It is no longer a program to care for the neediest among us, but rather an element of a comprehensive national plan to provide universal health insurance coverage.

Indeed, the manner in which the expansion is structured indicates that while Congress may have styled the expansion a mere alteration of existing Medicaid, it recognized it was enlisting the States in a new health care program. Congress created a separate funding provision to cover the costs of providing services to any person made newly eligible by the expansion. While Congress pays 50 to 83 percent of the costs of covering individuals currently enrolled in Medicaid, once the expansion is fully implemented Congress will pay 90 percent of the costs for newly eligible persons. The conditions on use of the different funds are also distinct. Congress mandated that newly eligible persons receive a level of coverage that is less comprehensive than the traditional Medicaid benefit package.

As we have explained, "[t]hough Congress' power to legislate under the spending power is broad, it does not include surprising participating States with post-acceptance or 'retroactive' conditions." Pennhurst, supra, at 25. A State could hardly anticipate that Congress's reservation of the right to "alter" or "amend" the Medicaid program included the power to transform it so dramatically.

[The Court's prior precedent] do not attempt to "fix the outermost line" where persuasion gives way to coercion. Steward Machine Co. v. Davis, 301 U.S. 548, 591 (1937). The Court found it "[e]nough for present purposes that wherever the line may be, this statute is within it." Id. We have no need to fix a line either. It is enough for today that wherever that line may be, this statute is surely beyond it. Congress may not simply "conscript state [agencies] into the national bureaucratic army," FERC v. Mississippi, 456 U.S. 742, 775 (1982) (O'Connor, J., concurring in judgment in part and dissenting in part), and that is what it is attempting to do with the Medicaid expansion.

B

Nothing in our opinion precludes Congress from offering funds under the Affordable Care Act to expand the availability of health care, and requiring that States accepting such funds comply with the conditions on their use. What Congress is not free to do is to penalize States that choose not to participate in that new program by taking away their existing Medicaid funding. Section 1396c gives the Secretary of Health and Human Services the authority to do just that. It allows her to withhold *all* "further [Medicaid] payments . . . to the State" if she determines that the State is out of compliance with any Medicaid requirement, including those contained in the expansion. 42 U.S.C. § 1396c. In light of the Court's holding, the Secretary cannot apply § 1396c to withdraw existing Medicaid funds for failure to comply with the requirements set out in the expansion.

That fully remedies the constitutional violation we have identified. The chapter of the United States Code that contains § 1396c includes a severability clause confirming that we need go no further. That clause specifies that "[i]f any provision of this chapter, or the application thereof to any person or circumstance, is held invalid, the remainder of the chapter, and the application of such provision to other persons or circumstances shall not be affected thereby." 42 U.S.C. § 1303. Today's holding does not affect the continued application of § 1396c to the existing Medicaid program. Nor does it affect the Secretary's ability to withdraw funds provided under the Affordable Care Act if a State that has chosen to participate in the expansion fails to comply with the requirements of that Act.

* * *

The question remains whether today's holding affects other provisions of the Affordable Care Act. * * *

We are confident that Congress would have wanted to preserve the rest of the Act. It is fair to say that Congress assumed that every State would participate in the Medicaid expansion, given that States had no real choice but to do so. The States contend that Congress enacted the rest of the Act with such full participation in mind; they point out that Congress made Medicaid a means for satisfying the mandate, Code §5000A(f)(1)(A)(ii), and enacted no other plan for providing coverage to many low-income individuals. According to the States, this means that the entire Act must fall.

We disagree. The Court today limits the financial pressure the Secretary may apply to induce States to accept the terms of the Medicaid expansion. As a practical matter, that means States may now choose to reject the expansion; that is the whole point. But that does not mean all or even any will. Some States may indeed decline to participate, either because they are unsure they will be able to afford their share of the new funding obligations, or because they are unwilling to commit the administrative resources necessary to support the expansion. Other States, however, may voluntarily sign up, finding the idea of expanding

Medicaid coverage attractive, particularly given the level of federal funding the Act offers at the outset.

We have no way of knowing how many States will accept the terms of the expansion, but we do not believe Congress would have wanted the whole Act to fall, simply because some may choose not to participate. The other reforms Congress enacted, after all, will remain * * *. Confident that Congress would not have intended anything different, we conclude that the rest of the Act need not fall in light of our constitutional holding.

* * *

Justice GINSBURG, with whom Justice SOTOMAYOR joins, and with whom Justice BREYER and Justice KAGAN join as to Parts I, II, III, and IV, concurring in part, concurring in the judgment in part, and dissenting in part.

I agree with THE CHIEF JUSTICE that the Anti-Injunction Act does not bar the Court's consideration of this case, and that the minimum coverage provision is a proper exercise of Congress' taxing power. I therefore join Parts I, II, and III-C of THE CHIEF JUSTICE's opinion. Unlike THE CHIEF JUSTICE, however, I would hold, alternatively, that the Commerce Clause authorizes Congress to enact the minimum coverage provision. I would also hold that the Spending Clause permits the Medicaid expansion exactly as Congress enacted it.

* * *

Justice SCALIA, Justice KENNEDY, Justice THOMAS, and Justice ALITO, dissenting.

Congress has set out to remedy the problem that the best health care is beyond the reach of many Americans who cannot afford it. It can assuredly do that, by exercising the powers accorded to it under the Constitution. The question in this case, however, is whether the complex structures and provisions of the Affordable Care Act (Affordable Care Act or ACA) go beyond those powers. We conclude that they do.

* * *

The Court today decides to save a statute Congress did not write. It rules that what the statute declares to be a requirement with a penalty is instead an option subject to a tax. And it changes the intentionally coercive sanction of a total cut-off of Medicaid funds to a supposedly noncoercive cut-off of only the incremental funds that the Act makes available.

The Court regards its strained statutory interpretation as judicial modesty. It is not. It amounts instead to a vast judicial overreaching. It creates a debilitated, inoperable version of health-care regulation that Congress did not enact and the public does not expect. It makes enactment of sensible health-care regulation more difficult, since Congress cannot start afresh but must take as its point of departure a jumble of now senseless provisions, provisions that certain interests favored under the Court's new design will struggle to retain. And it leaves the public and the States to expend vast sums of money on requirements that may or may not survive the necessary congressional revision.

The Court's disposition, invented and atextual as it is, does not even have the merit of avoiding constitutional difficulties. It creates them. * * * Those States that decline the Medicaid Expansion must subsidize, by the federal tax dollars taken from their citizens, vast grants to the States that accept the Medicaid Expansion. If that destabilizing political dynamic, so antagonistic to a harmonious Union, is to be introduced at all, it should be by Congress, not by the Judiciary.

* * *

For the reasons here stated, we would find the Act invalid in its entirety. We respectfully dissent.

[The separate dissenting opinion of Justice Thomas is omitted.]

QUESTIONS

1. *Congressional Intent?* In Part II of the majority opinion, the Supreme Court finds it significant for purposes of the federal Anti-Injunction Act that Congress described the shared responsibility payment under the individual mandate as a penalty and not as a tax. Do you think that Congress had the Anti-Injunction Act in mind when it drafted the language of Code Section 5000A? Why is the shared responsibility payment assessed under Code Section 5000A not a tax for purposes of the Anti-Injunction Act, but yet falls within Congress's power to "lay and collect Taxes"?

2. *The Commerce and Necessary and Proper Clauses.* Five Justices found that the individual mandate could not be sustained on the basis of the Commerce Clause or the Necessary and Proper Clause. The main arguments of the federal government are addressed and rejected in the majority opinion by Chief Justice Roberts. Do you agree with the reasoning of the majority opinion in rejecting these arguments? For purposes of Commerce Clause analysis, is the line drawn by the majority between the regulation of "activity" versus "inactivity" a persuasive distinction?

3. *Future Limitations on Shared Responsibility Penalties.* In Part III.C of the majority opinion, Chief Justice Roberts cautions that "Congress's ability to use its taxing power to influence conduct is not without limits" and that "the power to tax is not the power to destroy while this Court sits." Given this

warning, how much could Congress increase the penalty amounts under the individual and employer mandates in the future if the current penalty amounts do not achieve the desired policy result of nearly universal health insurance coverage?

BURWELL v. HOBBY LOBBY STORES, INC.

United States Supreme Court, 2014.
134 S. Ct. 2751.

JUSTICE ALITO delivered the opinion of the Court.

We must decide in these cases whether the Religious Freedom Restoration Act of 1993 (RFRA), 107 Stat. 1488, 42 U.S.C. § 2000bb et seq., permits the United States Department of Health and Human Services (HHS) to demand that three closely held corporations provide health insurance coverage for methods of contraception that violate the sincerely held religious beliefs of the companies' owners. We hold that the regulations that impose this obligation violate RFRA, which prohibits the Federal Government from taking any action that substantially burdens the exercise of religion unless that action constitutes the least restrictive means of serving a compelling government interest.

In holding that the HHS mandate is unlawful, we reject HHS's argument that the owners of the companies forfeited all RFRA protection when they decided to organize their businesses as corporations rather than sole proprietorships or general partnerships. The plain terms of RFRA make it perfectly clear that Congress did not discriminate in this way against men and women who wish to run their businesses as for-profit corporations in the manner required by their religious beliefs.

Since RFRA applies in these cases, we must decide whether the challenged HHS regulations substantially burden the exercise of religion, and we hold that they do. The owners of the businesses have religious objections to abortion, and according to their religious beliefs the four contraceptive methods at issue are abortifacients. If the owners comply with the HHS mandate, they believe they will be facilitating abortions, and if they do not comply, they will pay a very heavy price—as much as $1.3 million per day, or about $475 million per year, in the case of one of the companies. If these consequences do not amount to a substantial burden, it is hard to see what would.

Under RFRA, a Government action that imposes a substantial burden on religious exercise must serve a compelling government interest, and we assume that the HHS regulations satisfy this requirement. But in order for the HHS mandate to be sustained, it must also constitute the least restrictive means of serving that interest, and the mandate plainly fails that test. There are other ways in which

Congress or HHS could equally ensure that every woman has cost-free access to the particular contraceptives at issue here and, indeed, to all FDA-approved contraceptives.

In fact, HHS has already devised and implemented a system that seeks to respect the religious liberty of religious nonprofit corporations while ensuring that the employees of these entities have precisely the same access to all FDA-approved contraceptives as employees of companies whose owners have no religious objections to providing such coverage. The employees of these religious nonprofit corporations still have access to insurance coverage without cost sharing for all FDA-approved contraceptives; and according to HHS, this system imposes no net economic burden on the insurance companies that are required to provide or secure the coverage.

Although HHS has made this system available to religious nonprofits that have religious objections to the contraceptive mandate, HHS has provided no reason why the same system cannot be made available when the owners of for-profit corporations have similar religious objections. We therefore conclude that this system constitutes an alternative that achieves all of the Government's aims while providing greater respect for religious liberty. And under RFRA, that conclusion means that enforcement of the HHS contraceptive mandate against the objecting parties in these cases is unlawful.

As this description of our reasoning shows, our holding is very specific. We do not hold, as the principal dissent alleges, that for-profit corporations and other commercial enterprises can "opt out of any law (saving only tax laws) they judge incompatible with their sincerely held religious beliefs." Nor do we hold, as the dissent implies, that such corporations have free rein to take steps that impose "disadvantages. . .on others" or that require "the general public [to] pick up the tab." And we certainly do not hold or suggest that "RFRA demands accommodation of a for-profit corporation's religious beliefs no matter the impact that accommodation may have on. . .thousands of women employed by Hobby Lobby." The effect of the HHS-created accommodation on the women employed by Hobby Lobby and the other companies involved in these cases would be precisely zero. Under that accommodation, these women would still be entitled to all FDA-approved contraceptives without cost sharing.

I

A

Congress enacted RFRA in 1993 in order to provide very broad protection for religious liberty. RFRA's enactment came three years after this Court's decision in *Employment Division Department of Human Resources of Oregon v. Smith*, 494 U.S. 872 (1990), which largely repudiated the method of analyzing free-exercise claims that had been used in cases like *Sherbert v. Verner*, 374 U.S. 398 (1963), and *Wisconsin v. Yoder,* 406 U.S. 205 (1972). In determining whether challenged government actions violated the Free Exercise Clause of the First Amendment, those decisions used a balancing test that took into account whether the challenged action imposed a substantial burden on the practice of religion, and if it did, whether it was needed to serve a compelling government interest. Applying this test, the Court held in *Sherbert* that an employee who was fired for refusing to work on her Sabbath could not be denied unemployment benefits. And in *Yoder,* the Court held that Amish children could not be required to comply with a state law demanding that they remain in school until the age of 16 even though their religion required them to focus on uniquely Amish values and beliefs during their formative adolescent years.

In *Smith,* however, the Court rejected "the balancing test set forth in *Sherbert*." 494 U.S. at 883. *Smith* concerned two members of the Native American Church who were fired for ingesting peyote for sacramental purposes. When they sought unemployment benefits, the State of Oregon rejected their claims on the ground that consumption of peyote was a crime, but the Oregon Supreme Court, applying the *Sherbert* test, held that the denial of benefits violated the Free Exercise Clause.

This Court then reversed, observing that use of the *Sherbert* test whenever a person objected on religious grounds to the enforcement of a generally applicable law "would open the prospect of constitutionally required religious exemptions from civic obligations of almost every conceivable kind." 494 U.S. at 888. The Court therefore held that, under the First Amendment, "neutral, generally applicable laws may be applied to religious practices even when not supported by a compelling governmental interest." City of Boerne v. Flores, 521 U.S. 507, 514 (1997).

Congress responded to *Smith* by enacting RFRA. "Laws that are 'neutral' toward religion," Congress found, "may burden religious exercise as surely as laws intended to interfere with religious exercise." 42 U.S.C. § 2000bb(a)(2); see also § 2000bb(a)(4). In order to ensure broad protection for religious liberty, RFRA provides that "Government shall not substantially burden a person's exercise of religion even if the burden results from a rule of general applicability." § 2000bb–1(a).[2] If the Government substantially burdens a person's exercise of religion, under the Act that person is entitled to an exemption from the rule unless the Government "demonstrates that application of the burden to the person— (1) is in furtherance of a compelling governmental interest; and (2) is the

---

[2]   The Act defines "government" to include any "department" or "agency" of the United States. § 2000bb–2(1).

least restrictive means of furthering that compelling governmental interest." § 2000bb–1(b).[3]

As enacted in 1993, RFRA applied to both the Federal Government and the States, but the constitutional authority invoked for regulating federal and state agencies differed. As applied to a federal agency, RFRA is based on the enumerated power that supports the particular agency's work, but in attempting to regulate the States and their subdivisions, Congress relied on its power under Section 5 of the Fourteenth Amendment to enforce the First Amendment. In *City of Boerne,* however, we held that Congress had overstepped its Section 5 authority because "the stringent test RFRA demands" "far exceeded any pattern or practice of unconstitutional conduct under the Free Exercise Clause as interpreted in *Smith.*" Id. at 533–534. See also id. at 532.

Following our decision in *City of Boerne,* Congress passed the Religious Land Use and Institutionalized Persons Act of 2000 (RLUIPA), 114 Stat. 803, 42 U.S.C. § 2000cc et seq. That statute, enacted under Congress's Commerce and Spending Clause powers, imposes the same general test as RFRA but on a more limited category of governmental actions. And, what is most relevant for present purposes, RLUIPA amended RFRA's definition of the "exercise of religion." See § 2000bb–2(4) (importing RLUIPA definition). Before RLUIPA, RFRA's definition made reference to the First Amendment. See § 2000bb–2(4) (1994 ed.) (defining "exercise of religion" as "the exercise of religion under the First Amendment"). In RLUIPA, in an obvious effort to effect a complete separation from First Amendment case law, Congress deleted the reference to the First Amendment and defined the "exercise of religion" to include "any exercise of religion, whether or not compelled by, or central to, a system of religious belief." § 2000cc–5(7)(A). And Congress mandated that this concept "be construed in favor of a broad protection of religious exercise, to the maximum extent permitted by the terms of this chapter and the Constitution." § 2000cc–3(g).[5]

B

At issue in these cases are HHS regulations promulgated under the Affordable Care Act of 2010 (ACA), 124 Stat. 119. ACA generally requires

---

[3]   In *City of Boerne v. Flores,* 521 U.S. 507 (1997), we wrote that RFRA's "least restrictive means requirement was not used in the pre-*Smith* jurisprudence RFRA purported to codify." Id. at 509. On this understanding of our pre-*Smith* cases, RFRA did more than merely restore the balancing test used in the *Sherbert* line of cases; it provided even broader protection for religious liberty than was available under those decisions.

[5]   The principal dissent appears to contend that this rule of construction should apply only when defining the "exercise of religion" in an RLUIPA case, but not in a RFRA case. That argument is plainly wrong. Under this rule of construction, the phrase "exercise of religion," as it appears in RLUIPA, must be interpreted broadly, and RFRA states that the same phrase, as used in RFRA, means "religious exercise as defined in RLUIPA." 42 U.S.C. § 2000bb–2(4). It necessarily follows that the "exercise of religion" under RFRA must be given the same broad meaning that applies under RLUIPA.

employers with 50 or more full-time [equivalent] employees to offer "a group health plan or group health insurance coverage" that provides "minimum essential coverage." 26 U.S.C. § 5000A(f)(2); §§ 4980H(a), (c)(2). Any covered employer that does not provide such coverage must pay a substantial price. Specifically, if a covered employer provides group health insurance but its plan fails to comply with ACA's group health plan requirements, the employer may be required to pay $100 per day for each affected "individual." §§ 4980D(a)–(b). And if the employer decides to stop providing health insurance altogether and at least one full-time employee enrolls in a health plan and qualifies for a subsidy on one of the government-run ACA exchanges, the employer must pay $2,000 per year for each of its full-time employees. §§ 4980H(a), (c)(1).

Unless an exception applies, ACA requires an employer's group health plan or group health insurance coverage to furnish "preventive care and screenings" for women without "any cost sharing requirements." 42 U.S.C. § 300gg–13(a)(4). Congress itself, however, did not specify what types of preventive care must be covered. Instead, Congress authorized the Health Resources and Services Administration (HRSA), a component of HHS, to make that important and sensitive decision. The HRSA in turn consulted the Institute of Medicine, a nonprofit group of volunteer advisers, in determining which preventive services to require. See 77 Fed. Reg. 8725–8726 (2012).

In August 2011, based on the Institute's recommendations, the HRSA promulgated the Women's Preventive Services Guidelines. See id. at 8725–8726, and n. 1; online at http://hrsa.gov/womensguidelines. The Guidelines provide that nonexempt employers are generally required to provide "coverage, without cost sharing" for "all Food and Drug Administration (FDA) approved contraceptive methods, sterilization procedures, and patient education and counseling." 77 Fed. Reg. 8725. Although many of the required, FDA-approved methods of contraception work by preventing the fertilization of an egg, four of those methods (those specifically at issue in these cases) may have the effect of preventing an already fertilized egg from developing any further by inhibiting its attachment to the uterus.

HHS also authorized the HRSA to establish exemptions from the contraceptive mandate for "religious employers." 45 CFR § 147.131(a). That category encompasses "churches, their integrated auxiliaries, and conventions or associations of churches," as well as "the exclusively religious activities of any religious order." See id. (citing 26 U.S.C. §§ 6033(a)(3)(A)(i), (iii)). In its Guidelines, HRSA exempted these organizations from the requirement to cover contraceptive services.

In addition, HHS has effectively exempted certain religious nonprofit organizations, described under HHS regulations as "eligible organizations," from the contraceptive mandate. See 45 CFR § 147.131(b);

78 Fed. Reg. 39874 (2013). An "eligible organization" means a nonprofit organization that "holds itself out as a religious organization" and "opposes providing coverage for some or all of any contraceptive services required to be covered . . . on account of religious objections." To qualify for this accommodation, an employer must certify that it is such an organization. § 147.131(b)(4). When a group health insurance issuer receives notice that one of its clients has invoked this provision, the issuer must then exclude contraceptive coverage from the employer's plan and provide separate payments for contraceptive services for plan participants without imposing any cost-sharing requirements on the eligible organization, its insurance plan, or its employee beneficiaries. § 147.131(c).[8] Although this procedure requires the issuer to bear the cost of these services, HHS has determined that this obligation will not impose any net expense on issuers because its cost will be less than or equal to the cost savings resulting from the services. 78 Fed. Reg. 39877.

In addition to these exemptions for religious organizations, ACA exempts a great many employers from most of its coverage requirements. Employers providing "grandfathered health plans"—those that existed prior to March 23, 2010, and that have not made specified changes after that date—need not comply with many of the Act's requirements, including the contraceptive mandate. And employers with fewer than 50 employees are not required to provide health insurance at all.

All told, the contraceptive mandate "presently does not apply to tens of millions of people." 723 F.3d 1114, 1143 (10th Cir. 2013). This is attributable, in large part, to grandfathered health plans: Over one-third of the 149 million nonelderly people in America with employer-sponsored health plans were enrolled in grandfathered plans in 2013. Brief for HHS in No. 13–354, at 53; Kaiser Family Foundation & Health Research & Educational Trust, Employer Health Benefits, 2013 Annual Survey 43, 221.[10] The count for employees working for firms that do not have to provide insurance at all because they employ fewer than 50 employees is 34 million workers. See The Whitehouse, Health Reform for Small Businesses: The Affordable Care Act Increases Choice and Saving Money for Small Businesses 1.

---

[8] In the case of self-insured religious organizations entitled to the accommodation, the third-party administrator of the organization must "provide or arrange payments for contraceptive services" for the organization's employees without imposing any cost-sharing requirements on the eligible organization, its insurance plan, or its employee beneficiaries. 78 Fed. Reg. The regulations establish a mechanism for these third-party administrators to be compensated for their expenses by obtaining a reduction in the fee paid by insurers to participate in the federally facilitated exchanges. See 78 Fed. Reg. 39893. HHS believes that these fee reductions will not materially affect funding of the exchanges because "payments for contraceptive services will represent only a small portion of total exchange user fees." 78 Fed. Reg. 39882.

[10] While the Government predicts that this number will decline over time, the total number of Americans working for employers to whom the contraceptive mandate does not apply is still substantial, and there is no legal requirement that grandfathered plans ever be phased out.

II

A

Norman and Elizabeth Hahn and their three sons are devout members of the Mennonite Church, a Christian denomination. The Mennonite Church opposes abortion and believes that "[t]he fetus in its earliest stages. . . shares humanity with those who conceived it."[12]

Fifty years ago, Norman Hahn started a wood-working business in his garage, and since then, this company, Conestoga Wood Specialties, has grown and now has 950 employees. Conestoga is organized under Pennsylvania law as a for-profit corporation. The Hahns exercise sole ownership of the closely held business; they control its board of directors and hold all of its voting shares. One of the Hahn sons serves as the president and CEO.

The Hahns believe that they are required to run their business "in accordance with their religious beliefs and moral principles." 917 F. Supp. 2d 394, 402 (E.D. Pa. 2013). To that end, the company's mission, as they see it, is to "operate in a professional environment founded upon the highest ethical, moral, and Christian principles." The company's "Vision and Values Statements" affirms that Conestoga endeavors to "ensure a reasonable profit in a manner that reflects [the Hahns'] Christian heritage."

As explained in Conestoga's board-adopted "Statement on the Sanctity of Human Life," the Hahns believe that "human life begins at conception." It is therefore "against their moral conviction to be involved in the termination of human life" after conception, which they believe is a "sin against God to which they are held accountable." The Hahns have accordingly excluded from the group health insurance plan they offer to their employees certain contraceptive methods that they consider to be abortifacients.

The Hahns and Conestoga sued HHS and other federal officials and agencies under RFRA and the Free Exercise Clause of the First Amendment, seeking to enjoin application of ACA's contraceptive mandate insofar as it requires them to provide health insurance coverage for four FDA-approved contraceptives that may operate after the fertilization of an egg. These include two forms of emergency contraception commonly called "morning after" pills and two types of intrauterine devices.

In opposing the requirement to provide coverage for the contraceptives to which they object, the Hahns argued that "it is immoral and sinful for them to intentionally participate in, pay for, facilitate, or otherwise support these drugs." The District Court denied a preliminary

---

[12] Mennonite Church USA, Statement on Abortion.

injunction, and the Third Circuit affirmed in a divided opinion, holding that "for-profit, secular corporations cannot engage in religious exercise" within the meaning of RFRA or the First Amendment. The Third Circuit also rejected the claims brought by the Hahns themselves because it concluded that the HHS "mandate does not impose any requirements on the Hahns" in their personal capacity.

B

David and Barbara Green and their three children are Christians who own and operate two family businesses. Forty-five years ago, David Green started an arts-and-crafts store that has grown into a nationwide chain called Hobby Lobby. There are now 500 Hobby Lobby stores, and the company has more than 13,000 employees. Hobby Lobby is organized as a for-profit corporation under Oklahoma law.

One of David's sons started an affiliated business, Mardel, which operates 35 Christian bookstores and employs close to 400 people. Mardel is also organized as a for-profit corporation under Oklahoma law.

Though these two businesses have expanded over the years, they remain closely held, and David, Barbara, and their children retain exclusive control of both companies. David serves as the CEO of Hobby Lobby, and his three children serve as the president, vice president, and vice CEO.

Hobby Lobby's statement of purpose commits the Greens to "honoring the Lord in all [they] do by operating the company in a manner consistent with Biblical principles." Each family member has signed a pledge to run the businesses in accordance with the family's religious beliefs and to use the family assets to support Christian ministries. In accordance with those commitments, Hobby Lobby and Mardel stores close on Sundays, even though the Greens calculate that they lose millions in sales annually by doing so. The businesses refuse to engage in profitable transactions that facilitate or promote alcohol use; they contribute profits to Christian missionaries and ministries; and they buy hundreds of full page newspaper ads inviting people to "know Jesus as Lord and Savior."

Like the Hahns, the Greens believe that life begins at conception and that it would violate their religion to facilitate access to contraceptive drugs or devices that operate after that point. They specifically object to the same four contraceptive methods as the Hahns and, like the Hahns, they have no objection to the other 16 FDA-approved methods of birth control. Although their group health insurance plan predates the enactment of ACA, it is not a grandfathered plan because Hobby Lobby elected not to retain grandfathered status before the contraceptive mandate was proposed.

The Greens, Hobby Lobby, and Mardel sued HHS and other federal agencies and officials to challenge the contraceptive mandate under RFRA and the Free Exercise Clause. The District Court denied a preliminary injunction and the plaintiffs appealed, moving for initial en banc consideration. The Tenth Circuit granted that motion and reversed in a divided opinion. Contrary to the conclusion of the Third Circuit, the Tenth Circuit held that the Greens' two for-profit businesses are "persons" within the meaning of RFRA and therefore may bring suit under that law

The court then held that the corporations had established a likelihood of success on their RFRA claim. The court concluded that the contraceptive mandate substantially burdened the exercise of religion by requiring the companies to choose between "compromis[ing] their religious beliefs" and paying a heavy fee—either "close to $475 million more in taxes every year" if they simply refused to provide coverage for the contraceptives at issue, or "roughly $26 million" annually if they "drop[ped] health insurance benefits for all employees."

The court next held that HHS had failed to demonstrate a compelling interest in enforcing the mandate against the Greens' businesses and, in the alternative, that HHS had failed to prove that enforcement of the mandate was the "least restrictive means" of furthering the Government's asserted interests. After concluding that the companies had "demonstrated irreparable harm," the court reversed and remanded for the District Court to consider the remaining factors of the preliminary-injunction test.

III

A

RFRA prohibits the "Government from substantially burdening *a person's* exercise of religion even if the burden results from a rule of general applicability" unless the Government "demonstrates that application of the burden to *the person*—(1) is in furtherance of a compelling governmental interest; and (2) is the least restrictive means of furthering that compelling governmental interest." 42 U.S.C. §§ 2000bb–1(a), (b) (emphasis added). The first question that we must address is whether this provision applies to regulations that govern the activities of for-profit corporations like Hobby Lobby, Conestoga, and Mardel.

HHS contends that neither these companies nor their owners can even be heard under RFRA. According to HHS, the companies cannot sue because they seek to make a profit for their owners, and the owners cannot be heard because the regulations, at least as a formal matter, apply only to the companies and not to the owners as individuals. HHS's argument would have dramatic consequences.

Consider this Court's decision in *Braunfeld* v. *Brown,* 366 U.S. 599 (1961). In that case, five Orthodox Jewish merchants who ran small retail businesses in Philadelphia challenged a Pennsylvania Sunday closing law as a violation of the Free Exercise Clause. Because of their faith, these merchants closed their shops on Saturday, and they argued that requiring them to remain shut on Sunday threatened them with financial ruin. The Court entertained their claim (although it ruled against them on the merits), and if a similar claim were raised today under RFRA against a jurisdiction still subject to the Act (for example, the District of Columbia, see 42 U.S.C. § 2000bb–2(2)), the merchants would be entitled to be heard. According to HHS, however, if these merchants chose to incorporate their businesses—without in any way changing the size or nature of their businesses—they would forfeit all RFRA (and free-exercise) rights. HHS would put these merchants to a difficult choice: either give up the right to seek judicial protection of their religious liberty or forgo the benefits, available to their competitors, of operating as corporations.

As we have seen, RFRA was designed to provide very broad protection for religious liberty. By enacting RFRA, Congress went far beyond what this Court has held is constitutionally required. Is there any reason to think that the Congress that enacted such sweeping protection put small business owners to the choice that HHS suggests? An examination of RFRA's text, to which we turn in the next part of this opinion, reveals that Congress did no such thing.

As we will show, Congress provided protection for people like the Hahns and Greens by employing a familiar legal fiction: It included corporations within RFRA's definition of "persons." But it is important to keep in mind that the purpose of this fiction is to provide protection for human beings. A corporation is simply a form of organization used by human beings to achieve desired ends. An established body of law specifies the rights and obligations of the *people* (including shareholders, officers, and employees) who are associated with a corporation in one way or another. When rights, whether constitutional or statutory, are extended to corporations, the purpose is to protect the rights of these people. For example, extending Fourth Amendment protection to corporations protects the privacy interests of employees and others associated with the company. Protecting corporations from government seizure of their property without just compensation protects all those who have a stake in the corporations' financial well-being. And protecting the free-exercise rights of corporations like Hobby Lobby, Conestoga, and Mardel protects the religious liberty of the humans who own and control those companies.

* * *

B

1

As we noted above, RFRA applies to "a person's" exercise of religion, and RFRA itself does not define the term "person." We therefore look to the Dictionary Act, which we must consult "[i]n determining the meaning of any Act of Congress, unless the context indicates otherwise." 1 U.S.C. § 1.

Under the Dictionary Act, "the word 'person'. . .includes corporations, companies, associations, firms, partnerships, societies, and joint stock companies, as well as individuals." Id. see FCC v. AT & T Inc., 131 S. Ct. 1177, 1182-83 (2011) ("We have no doubt that 'person,' in a legal setting, often refers to artificial entities. The Dictionary Act makes that clear"). Thus, unless there is something about the RFRA context that "indicates otherwise," the Dictionary Act provides a quick, clear, and affirmative answer to the question whether the companies involved in these cases may be heard.

We see nothing in RFRA that suggests a congressional intent to depart from the Dictionary Act definition, and HHS makes little effort to argue otherwise. We have entertained RFRA and free-exercise claims brought by nonprofit corporations, see Gonzales v. O Centro Espírita Beneficiente União do Vegetal, 546 U.S. 418 (2006) (RFRA); and HHS concedes that a nonprofit corporation can be a "person" within the meaning of RFRA.

This concession effectively dispatches any argument that the term "person" as used in RFRA does not reach the closely held corporations involved in these cases. No known understanding of the term "person" includes *some* but not all corporations. The term "person" sometimes encompasses artificial persons (as the Dictionary Act instructs), and it sometimes is limited to natural persons. But no conceivable definition of the term includes natural persons and nonprofit corporations, but not for-profit corporations. Cf. Clark v. Martinez, 543 U.S. 371, 378 (2005) ("To give th[e] same words a different meaning for each category would be to invent a statute rather than interpret one").

2

The principal argument advanced by HHS and the principal dissent regarding RFRA protection for Hobby Lobby, Conestoga, and Mardel focuses not on the statutory term "person," but on the phrase "exercise of religion." According to HHS and the dissent, these corporations are not protected by RFRA because they cannot exercise religion. Neither HHS nor the dissent, however, provides any persuasive explanation for this conclusion.

Is it because of the corporate form? The corporate form alone cannot provide the explanation because, as we have pointed out, HHS concedes that nonprofit corporations can be protected by RFRA. The dissent suggests that nonprofit corporations are special because furthering their religious "autonomy. . .often furthers individual religious freedom as well." But this principle applies equally to for-profit corporations. Furthering their religious freedom also "furthers individual religious freedom." In these cases, for example, allowing Hobby Lobby, Conestoga, and Mardel to assert RFRA claims protects the religious liberty of the Greens and the Hahns.

If the corporate form is not enough, what about the profit-making objective? In *Braunfeld,* 366 U.S. 599, we entertained the free-exercise claims of individuals who were attempting to make a profit as retail merchants, and the Court never even hinted that this objective precluded their claims. As the Court explained in a later case, the "exercise of religion" involves "not only belief and profession but the performance of (or abstention from) physical acts" that are "engaged in for religious reasons." Smith, 494 U.S. at 877. Business practices that are compelled or limited by the tenets of a religious doctrine fall comfortably within that definition. Thus, a law that "operates so as to make the practice of. . .religious beliefs more expensive" in the context of business activities imposes a burden on the exercise of religion. Braunfeld, supra, at 605; see United States v. Lee, 455 U.S. 252, 257 (1982) (recognizing that "compulsory participation in the social security system interferes with [Amish employers'] free exercise rights").

If, as *Braunfeld* recognized, a sole proprietorship that seeks to make a profit may assert a free-exercise claim, why can't Hobby Lobby, Conestoga, and Mardel do the same?

Some lower court judges have suggested that RFRA does not protect for-profit corporations because the purpose of such corporations is simply to make money. This argument flies in the face of modern corporate law. "Each American jurisdiction today either expressly or by implication authorizes corporations to be formed under its general corporation act for *any lawful purpose* or business." 1 J. Cox & T. Hazen, Treatise of the Law of Corporations § 4:1, p. 224 (3d ed. 2010) (emphasis added); see 1A W. Fletcher, Cyclopedia of the Law of Corporations § 102 (rev. ed. 2010). While it is certainly true that a central objective of for-profit corporations is to make money, modern corporate law does not require for-profit corporations to pursue profit at the expense of everything else, and many do not do so. For-profit corporations, with ownership approval, support a wide variety of charitable causes, and it is not at all uncommon for such corporations to further humanitarian and other altruistic objectives. Many examples come readily to mind. So long as its owners agree, a for-profit corporation may take costly pollution-control and energy-conservation measures that go beyond what the law requires. A for-profit corporation that operates facilities in other countries may exceed the requirements of local law regarding working conditions and benefits. If for-profit corporations may pursue such worthy objectives, there is no apparent reason why they may not further religious objectives as well.

HHS would draw a sharp line between nonprofit corporations (which, HHS concedes, are protected by RFRA) and for-profit corporations (which HHS would leave unprotected), but the actual picture is less clear-cut. Not all corporations that decline to organize as nonprofits do so in order to maximize profit. For example, organizations with religious and charitable aims might organize as for-profit corporations because of the potential advantages of that corporate form, such as the freedom to participate in lobbying for legislation or campaigning for political candidates who promote their religious or charitable goals.[24] In fact, recognizing the inherent compatibility between establishing a for-profit corporation and pursuing nonprofit goals, States have increasingly adopted laws formally recognizing hybrid corporate forms. Over half of the States, for instance, now recognize the "benefit corporation," a dual-purpose entity that seeks to achieve both a benefit for the public and a profit for its owners.[25]

In any event, the objectives that may properly be pursued by the companies in these cases are governed by the laws of the States in which they were incorporated—Pennsylvania and Oklahoma—and the laws of those States permit for-profit corporations to pursue "any lawful purpose" or "act," including the pursuit of profit in conformity with the owners' religious principles. 15 Pa. Cons. Stat. § 1301 (2001) ("Corporations may be incorporated under this subpart for any lawful purpose or purposes"); Okla. Stat., Tit. 18, §§ 1002, 1005 (West 2012) ("[E]very corporation, whether profit or not for profit" may "be incorporated or organized. . .to conduct or promote any lawful business or purposes.

* * *

Finally, HHS contends that Congress could not have wanted RFRA to apply to for-profit corporations because it is difficult as a practical matter

---

[24] See, e.g., M. Sanders, Joint Ventures Involving Tax-Exempt Organizations 555 (4th ed. 2013) (describing Google.org, which "advance[s] its charitable goals" while operating as a for-profit corporation to be able to "invest in for-profit endeavors, lobby for policies that support its philanthropic goals, and tap Google's innovative technology and workforce"); cf. 26 CFR § 1.501(c)(3)–1(c)(3).

[25] See Benefit Corp Information Center, online at http://www.benefitcorp.net/state-by-state-legislative-status; e.g., Va. Code Ann. §§ 13.1–787, 13.1–626, 13.1–782 (Lexis 2011) ("A benefit corporation shall have as one of its purposes the purpose of creating a general public benefit," and "may identify one or more specific public benefits that it is the purpose of the benefit corporation to create. . . . This purpose is in addition to [the purpose of engaging in any lawful business]." "'Specific public benefit' means a benefit that serves one or more public welfare, religious, charitable, scientific, literary, or educational purposes, or other purpose or benefit beyond the strict interest of the shareholders of the benefit corporation. . . ."); S. C. Code Ann. §§ 33–38–300 (2012 Cum. Supp.), 33–3–101 (2006), 33–38–130 (2012 Cum. Supp.) (similar).

to ascertain the sincere "beliefs" of a corporation. HHS goes so far as to raise the specter of "divisive, polarizing proxy battles over the religious identity of large, publicly traded corporations such as IBM or General Electric."

These cases, however, do not involve publicly traded corporations, and it seems unlikely that the sort of corporate giants to which HHS refers will often assert RFRA claims. HHS has not pointed to any example of a publicly traded corporation asserting RFRA rights, and numerous practical restraints would likely prevent that from occurring. For example, the idea that unrelated shareholders—including institutional investors with their own set of stakeholders—would agree to run a corporation under the same religious beliefs seems improbable. In any event, we have no occasion in these cases to consider RFRA's applicability to such companies. The companies in the cases before us are closely held corporations, each owned and controlled by members of a single family, and no one has disputed the sincerity of their religious beliefs.[28]

* * *

For all these reasons, we hold that a federal regulation's restriction on the activities of a for-profit closely held corporation must comply with RFRA.

IV

Because RFRA applies in these cases, we must next ask whether the HHS contraceptive mandate "substantially burden[s]" the exercise of religion. 42 U.S.C. § 2000bb–1(a). We have little trouble concluding that it does.

A

As we have noted, the Hahns and Greens have a sincere religious belief that life begins at conception. They therefore object on religious grounds to providing health insurance that covers methods of birth control that, as HHS acknowledges, may result in the destruction of an embryo. By requiring the Hahns and Greens and their companies to arrange for such coverage, the HHS mandate demands that they engage in conduct that seriously violates their religious beliefs.

If the Hahns and Greens and their companies do not yield to this demand, the economic consequences will be severe. If the companies continue to offer group health plans that do not cover the contraceptives at issue, they will be taxed $100 per day for each affected individual. 26

---

[28] To qualify for RFRA's protection, an asserted belief must be "sincere"; a corporation's pretextual assertion of a religious belief in order to obtain an exemption for financial reasons would fail. Cf., e.g., United States v. Quaintance, 608 F.3d 717, 718–719 (10th Cir. 2010).

U.S.C. § 4980D. For Hobby Lobby, the bill could amount to $1.3 million per day or about $475 million per year; for Conestoga, the assessment could be $90,000 per day or $33 million per year; and for Mardel, it could be $40,000 per day or about $15 million per year. These sums are surely substantial.

It is true that the plaintiffs could avoid these assessments by dropping insurance coverage altogether and thus forcing their employees to obtain health insurance on one of the exchanges established under ACA. But if at least one of their full-time employees were to qualify for a subsidy on one of the government-run exchanges, this course would also entail substantial economic consequences. The companies could face penalties of $2,000 per employee each year. § 4980H. These penalties would amount to roughly $26 million for Hobby Lobby, $1.8 million for Conestoga, and $800,000 for Mardel.

B

Although these totals are high, amici supporting HHS have suggested that the $2,000 per-employee penalty is actually less than the average cost of providing health insurance and therefore, they claim, the companies could readily eliminate any substantial burden by forcing their employees to obtain insurance in the government exchanges. We do not generally entertain arguments that were not raised below and are not advanced in this Court by any party and there are strong reasons to adhere to that practice in these cases. HHS, which presumably could have compiled the relevant statistics, has never made this argument—not in its voluminous briefing or at oral argument in this Court nor, to our knowledge, in any of the numerous cases in which the issue now before us has been litigated around the country. As things now stand, we do not even know what the Government's position might be with respect to these amici's intensely empirical argument.[31] For this same reason, the plaintiffs have never had an opportunity to respond to this novel claim that—contrary to their longstanding practice and that of most large employers—they would be better off discarding their employer insurance plans altogether.

Even if we were to reach this argument, we would find it unpersuasive. As an initial matter, it entirely ignores the fact that the Hahns and Greens and their companies have religious reasons for providing health insurance coverage for their employees. Before the advent of ACA, they were not legally compelled to provide insurance, but they nevertheless did so—in part, no doubt, for conventional business

---

[31] Indeed, one of HHS's stated reasons for establishing the religious accommodation was to "encourag[e] eligible organizations to *continue* to offer health coverage." 78 Fed. Reg. 39882 (2013) (emphasis added).

reasons, but also in part because their religious beliefs govern their relations with their employees.

Putting aside the religious dimension of the decision to provide insurance, moreover, it is far from clear that the net cost to the companies of providing insurance is more than the cost of dropping their insurance plans and paying the ACA penalty. Health insurance is a benefit that employees value. If the companies simply eliminated that benefit and forced employees to purchase their own insurance on the exchanges, without offering additional compensation, it is predictable that the companies would face a competitive disadvantage in retaining and attracting skilled workers.

The companies could attempt to make up for the elimination of a group health plan by increasing wages, but this would be costly. Group health insurance is generally less expensive than comparable individual coverage, so the amount of the salary increase needed to fully compensate for the termination of insurance coverage may well exceed the cost to the companies of providing the insurance. In addition, any salary increase would have to take into account the fact that employees must pay income taxes on wages but not on the value of employer-provided health insurance. 26 U.S.C. § 106(a). Likewise, employers can deduct the cost of providing health insurance, see § 162(a)(1), but apparently cannot deduct the amount of the penalty that they must pay if insurance is not provided; that difference also must be taken into account. Given these economic incentives, it is far from clear that it would be financially advantageous for an employer to drop coverage and pay the penalty.

In sum, we refuse to sustain the challenged regulations on the ground—never maintained by the Government—that dropping insurance coverage eliminates the substantial burden that the HHS mandate imposes. We doubt that the Congress that enacted RFRA—or, for that matter, ACA—would have believed it a tolerable result to put family-run businesses to the choice of violating their sincerely held religious beliefs or making all of their employees lose their existing healthcare plans.

C

In taking the position that the HHS mandate does not impose a substantial burden on the exercise of religion, HHS's main argument (echoed by the principal dissent) is basically that the connection between what the objecting parties must do (provide health insurance coverage for four methods of contraception that may operate after the fertilization of an egg) and the end that they find to be morally wrong (destruction of an embryo) is simply too attenuated. HHS and the dissent note that providing the coverage would not itself result in the destruction of an embryo; that would occur only if an employee chose to take advantage of the coverage and to use one of the four methods at issue.[33]

This argument dodges the question that RFRA presents (whether the HHS mandate imposes a substantial burden on the ability of the objecting parties to conduct business in accordance with *their religious beliefs*) and instead addresses a very different question that the federal courts have no business addressing (whether the religious belief asserted in a RFRA case is reasonable). The Hahns and Greens believe that providing the coverage demanded by the HHS regulations is connected to the destruction of an embryo in a way that is sufficient to make it immoral for them to provide the coverage. This belief implicates a difficult and important question of religion and moral philosophy, namely, the circumstances under which it is wrong for a person to perform an act that is innocent in itself but that has the effect of enabling or facilitating the commission of an immoral act by another. Arrogating the authority to provide a binding national answer to this religious and philosophical question, HHS and the principal dissent in effect tell the plaintiffs that their beliefs are flawed. For good reason, we have repeatedly refused to take such a step. See, e.g., Smith, 494 U.S. at 887 ("Repeatedly and in many different contexts, we have warned that courts must not presume to determine. . .the plausibility of a religious claim").

Moreover, in *Thomas v. Review Bd. of Indiana Employment Security Div.,* 450 U.S. 707 (1981), we considered and rejected an argument that is nearly identical to the one now urged by HHS and the dissent. In *Thomas,* a Jehovah's Witness was initially employed making sheet steel for a variety of industrial uses, but he was later transferred to a job making turrets for tanks. Because he objected on religious grounds to participating in the manufacture of weapons, he lost his job and sought unemployment compensation. Ruling against the employee, the state court had difficulty with the line that the employee drew between work that he found to be consistent with his religious beliefs (helping to manufacture steel that was used in making weapons) and work that he found morally objectionable (helping to make the weapons themselves). This Court, however, held that "it is not for us to say that the line he drew was an unreasonable one." Id. at 715.

---

[33] This argument is not easy to square with the position taken by HHS in providing exemptions from the contraceptive mandate for religious employers, such as churches, that have the very same religious objections as the Hahns and Greens and their companies. The connection between what these religious employers would be required to do if not exempted (provide insurance coverage for particular contraceptives) and the ultimate event that they find morally wrong (destruction of an embryo) is exactly the same. Nevertheless, as discussed, HHS and the Labor and Treasury Departments authorized the exemption from the contraceptive mandate of group health plans of certain religious employers, and later expanded the exemption to include certain nonprofit organizations with religious objections to contraceptive coverage. 78 Fed. Reg. 39871. When this was done, the Government made clear that its objective was to "protec[t]" these religious objectors "from having to contract, arrange, pay, or refer for such coverage." * * *

Similarly, in these cases, the Hahns and Greens and their companies sincerely believe that providing the insurance coverage demanded by the HHS regulations lies on the forbidden side of the line, and it is not for us to say that their religious beliefs are mistaken or insubstantial. Instead, our "narrow function. . .in this context is to determine" whether the line drawn reflects "an honest conviction," id. at 716, and there is no dispute that it does.

* * *

V

Since the HHS contraceptive mandate imposes a substantial burden on the exercise of religion, we must move on and decide whether HHS has shown that the mandate both "(1) is in furtherance of a compelling governmental interest; and (2) is the least restrictive means of furthering that compelling governmental interest." 42 U.S.C. § 2000bb–1(b).

A

HHS asserts that the contraceptive mandate serves a variety of important interests, but many of these are couched in very broad terms, such as promoting "public health" and "gender equality." RFRA, however, contemplates a "more focused" inquiry: It "requires the Government to demonstrate that the compelling interest test is satisfied through application of the challenged law 'to the person'—the particular claimant whose sincere exercise of religion is being substantially burdened." O'Centro, 546 U.S. at 430–431 (quoting § 2000bb–1(b)). This requires us to "loo[k] beyond broadly formulated interests" and to "scrutiniz[e] the asserted harm of granting specific exemptions to particular religious claimants"—in other words, to look to the marginal interest in enforcing the contraceptive mandate in these cases. O Centro, supra, at 431.

In addition to asserting these very broadly framed interests, HHS maintains that the mandate serves a compelling interest in ensuring that all women have access to all FDA-approved contraceptives without cost sharing. Under our cases, women (and men) have a constitutional right to obtain contraceptives, see Griswold v. Connecticut, 381 U.S. 479, 485–486 (1965), and HHS tells us that "[s]tudies have demonstrated that even moderate copayments for preventive services can deter patients from receiving those services."

The objecting parties contend that HHS has not shown that the mandate serves a compelling government interest, and it is arguable that there are features of ACA that support that view. As we have noted, many employees—those covered by grandfathered plans and those who work for employers with fewer than 50 employees—may have no contraceptive coverage without cost sharing at all.

HHS responds that many legal requirements have exceptions and the existence of exceptions does not in itself indicate that the principal interest served by a law is not compelling. Even a compelling interest may be outweighed in some circumstances by another even weightier consideration. In these cases, however, the interest served by one of the biggest exceptions, the exception for grandfathered plans, is simply the interest of employers in avoiding the inconvenience of amending an existing plan. Grandfathered plans are required "to comply with a subset of the Affordable Care Act's health reform provisions" that provide what HHS has described as "particularly significant protections." 75 Fed. Reg. 34540 (2010). But the contraceptive mandate is expressly excluded from this subset.

We find it unnecessary to adjudicate this issue. We will assume that the interest in guaranteeing cost-free access to the four challenged contraceptive methods is compelling within the meaning of RFRA, and we will proceed to consider the final prong of the RFRA test, i.e., whether HHS has shown that the contraceptive mandate is "the least restrictive means of furthering that compelling governmental interest." § 2000bb–1(b)(2).

B

The least-restrictive-means standard is exceptionally demanding, see City of Boerne, 521 U.S. at 532, and it is not satisfied here. HHS has not shown that it lacks other means of achieving its desired goal without imposing a substantial burden on the exercise of religion by the objecting parties in these cases.

The most straightforward way of doing this would be for the Government to assume the cost of providing the four contraceptives at issue to any women who are unable to obtain them under their health insurance policies due to their employers' religious objections. This would certainly be less restrictive of the plaintiffs' religious liberty, and HHS has not shown that this is not a viable alternative. HHS has not provided any estimate of the average cost per employee of providing access to these contraceptives, two of which, according to the FDA, are designed primarily for emergency use. Nor has HHS provided any statistics regarding the number of employees who might be affected because they work for corporations like Hobby Lobby, Conestoga, and Mardel. Nor has HHS told us that it is unable to provide such statistics. It seems likely, however, that the cost of providing the forms of contraceptives at issue in these cases (if not all FDA-approved contraceptives) would be minor when compared with the overall cost of ACA. According to one of the Congressional Budget Office's most recent forecasts, ACA's insurance-coverage provisions will cost the Federal Government more than $1.3 trillion through the next decade. See CBO, Updated Estimates of the Effects of the Insurance Coverage Provisions of the Affordable Care Act,

April 2014, p. 2. If, as HHS tells us, providing all women with cost-free access to all FDA-approved methods of contraception is a Government interest of the highest order, it is hard to understand HHS's argument that it cannot be required under RFRA to pay *anything* in order to achieve this important goal.

HHS contends that RFRA does not permit us to take this option into account because "RFRA cannot be used to require creation of entirely new programs." But we see nothing in RFRA that supports this argument, and drawing the line between the "creation of an entirely new program" and the modification of an existing program (which RFRA surely allows) would be fraught with problems. We do not doubt that cost may be an important factor in the least-restrictive-means analysis, but both RFRA and its sister statute, RLUIPA, may in some circumstances require the Government to expend additional funds to accommodate citizens' religious beliefs. HHS's view that RFRA can never require the Government to spend even a small amount reflects a judgment about the importance of religious liberty that was not shared by the Congress that enacted that law.

In the end, however, we need not rely on the option of a new, government-funded program in order to conclude that the HHS regulations fail the least-restrictive-means test. HHS itself has demonstrated that it has at its disposal an approach that is less restrictive than requiring employers to fund contraceptive methods that violate their religious beliefs. As we explained above, HHS has already established an accommodation for nonprofit organizations with religious objections. Under that accommodation, the organization can self-certify that it opposes providing coverage for particular contraceptive services. If the organization makes such a certification, the organization's insurance issuer or third-party administrator must "[e]xpressly exclude contraceptive coverage from the group health insurance coverage provided in connection with the group health plan" and "[p]rovide separate payments for any contraceptive services required to be covered" without imposing "any cost-sharing requirements. . .on the eligible organization, the group health plan, or plan participants or beneficiaries." 45 CFR § 147.131(c)(2); 26 CFR § 54.9815–2713A(c)(2).[38]

---

[38] HHS has concluded that insurers that insure eligible employers opting out of the contraceptive mandate and that are required to pay for contraceptive coverage under the accommodation will not experience an increase in costs because the "costs of providing contraceptive coverage are balanced by cost savings from lower pregnancy-related costs and from improvements in women's health." 78 Fed. Reg. 39877. With respect to self-insured plans, the regulations establish a mechanism for the eligible employers' third-party administrators to obtain a compensating reduction in the fee paid by insurers to participate in the federally facilitated exchanges. HHS believes that this system will not have a material effect on the funding of the exchanges because the "payments for contraceptive services will represent only a small portion of total [federally facilitated exchange] user fees." Id. at 39882; see 26 CFR § 54.9815–2713A(b)(3).

We do not decide today whether an approach of this type complies with RFRA for purposes of all religious claims. At a minimum, however, it does not impinge on the plaintiffs' religious belief that providing insurance coverage for the contraceptives at issue here violates their religion, and it serves HHS's stated interests equally well.

* * *

C

HHS and the principal dissent argue that a ruling in favor of the objecting parties in these cases will lead to a flood of religious objections regarding a wide variety of medical procedures and drugs, such as vaccinations and blood transfusions, but HHS has made no effort to substantiate this prediction. HHS points to no evidence that insurance plans in existence prior to the enactment of ACA excluded coverage for such items. Nor has HHS provided evidence that any significant number of employers sought exemption, on religious grounds, from any of ACA's coverage requirements other than the contraceptive mandate.

It is HHS's apparent belief that no insurance coverage mandate would violate RFRA—no matter how significantly it impinges on the religious liberties of employers—that would lead to intolerable consequences. Under HHS's view, RFRA would permit the Government to require all employers to provide coverage for any medical procedure allowed by law in the jurisdiction in question—for instance, third-trimester abortions or assisted suicide. The owners of many closely held corporations could not in good conscience provide such coverage, and thus HHS would effectively exclude these people from full participation in the economic life of the Nation. RFRA was enacted to prevent such an outcome.

In any event, our decision in these cases is concerned solely with the contraceptive mandate. Our decision should not be understood to hold that an insurance coverage mandate must necessarily fall if it conflicts with an employer's religious beliefs. Other coverage requirements, such as immunizations, may be supported by different interests (for example, the need to combat the spread of infectious diseases) and may involve different arguments about the least restrictive means of providing them.

* * *

HHS also raises for the first time in this Court the argument that applying the contraceptive mandate to for-profit employers with sincere religious objections is essential to the comprehensive health insurance scheme that ACA establishes. HHS analogizes the contraceptive mandate to the requirement to pay Social Security taxes, which we upheld in *Lee* despite the religious objection of an employer, but these cases are quite different. Our holding in *Lee* turned primarily on the special problems associated with a national system of taxation. We noted that "[t]he obligation to pay the social security tax initially is not fundamentally different from the obligation to pay income taxes." 455 U.S. at 260. Based on that premise, we explained that it was untenable to allow individuals to seek exemptions from taxes based on religious objections to particular Government expenditures: "If, for example, a religious adherent believes war is a sin, and if a certain percentage of the federal budget can be identified as devoted to war-related activities, such individuals would have a similarly valid claim to be exempt from paying that percentage of the income tax." We observed that "[t]he tax system could not function if denominations were allowed to challenge the tax system because tax payments were spent in a manner that violates their religious belief." Id.; see O Centro, 546 U.S. at 435.

Lee was a free-exercise, not a RFRA, case, but if the issue in *Lee* were analyzed under the RFRA framework, the fundamental point would be that there simply is no less restrictive alternative to the categorical requirement to pay taxes. Because of the enormous variety of government expenditures funded by tax dollars, allowing taxpayers to withhold a portion of their tax obligations on religious grounds would lead to chaos. Recognizing exemptions from the contraceptive mandate is very different. ACA does not create a large national pool of tax revenue for use in purchasing healthcare coverage. Rather, individual employers like the plaintiffs purchase insurance for their own employees. And contrary to the principal dissent's characterization, the employers' contributions do not necessarily funnel into "undifferentiated funds." The accommodation established by HHS requires issuers to have a mechanism by which to "segregate premium revenue collected from the eligible organization from the monies used to provide payments for contraceptive services." 45 CFR § 147.131(c)(2)(ii). Recognizing a religious accommodation under RFRA for particular coverage requirements, therefore, does not threaten the viability of ACA's comprehensive scheme in the way that recognizing religious objections to particular expenditures from general tax revenues would.

* * *

The contraceptive mandate, as applied to closely held corporations, violates RFRA. Our decision on that statutory question makes it unnecessary to reach the First Amendment claim raised by Conestoga and the Hahns.

The judgment of the Tenth Circuit in No. 13–354 is affirmed; the judgment of the Third Circuit in No. 13–356 is reversed, and that case is remanded for further proceedings consistent with this opinion.

It is so ordered.

Justice KENNEDY, concurring.

It seems to me appropriate, in joining the Court's opinion, to add these few remarks. At the outset it should be said that the Court's opinion does not have the breadth and sweep ascribed to it by the respectful and powerful dissent. The Court and the dissent disagree on the proper interpretation of the Religious Freedom and Restoration Act of 1993 (RFRA), but do agree on the purpose of that statute. 42 U.S.C. § 2000bb et seq. It is to ensure that interests in religious freedom are protected.

In our constitutional tradition, freedom means that all persons have the right to believe or strive to believe in a divine creator and a divine law. For those who choose this course, free exercise is essential in preserving their own dignity and in striving for a self-definition shaped by their religious precepts. Free exercise in this sense implicates more than just freedom of belief. See Cantwell v. Connecticut, 310 U.S. 296, 303, 1213 (1940). It means, too, the right to express those beliefs and to establish one's religious (or nonreligious) self-definition in the political, civic, and economic life of our larger community. But in a complex society and an era of pervasive governmental regulation, defining the proper realm for free exercise can be difficult. In these cases the plaintiffs deem it necessary to exercise their religious beliefs within the context of their own closely held, for-profit corporations. They claim protection under RFRA, the federal statute discussed with care and in detail in the Court's opinion.

As the Court notes, under our precedents, RFRA imposes a "stringent test." The Government must demonstrate that the application of a substantial burden to a person's exercise of religion "(1) is in furtherance of a compelling governmental interest; and (2) is the least restrictive means of furthering that compelling governmental interest." § 2000bb–1(b).

As to RFRA's first requirement, the Department of Health and Human Services (HHS) makes the case that the mandate serves the Government's compelling interest in providing insurance coverage that is necessary to protect the health of female employees, coverage that is significantly more costly than for a male employee. There are many medical conditions for which pregnancy is contraindicated. It is important to confirm that a premise of the Court's opinion is its assumption that the HHS regulation here at issue furthers a legitimate and compelling interest in the health of female employees.

But the Government has not made the second showing required by RFRA, that the means it uses to regulate is the least restrictive way to further its interest. As the Court's opinion explains, the record in these cases shows that there is an existing, recognized, workable, and already-implemented framework to provide coverage. That framework is one that HHS has itself devised, that the plaintiffs have not criticized with a specific objection that has been considered in detail by the courts in this litigation, and that is less restrictive than the means challenged by the plaintiffs in these cases.

The means the Government chose is the imposition of a direct mandate on the employers in these cases. But in other instances the Government has allowed the same contraception coverage in issue here to be provided to employees of nonprofit religious organizations, as an accommodation to the religious objections of those entities. The accommodation works by requiring insurance companies to cover, without cost sharing, contraception coverage for female employees who wish it. That accommodation equally furthers the Government's interest but does not impinge on the plaintiffs' religious beliefs.

On this record and as explained by the Court, the Government has not met its burden of showing that it cannot accommodate the plaintiffs' similar religious objections under this established framework. RFRA is inconsistent with the insistence of an agency such as HHS on distinguishing between different religious believers—burdening one while accommodating the other—when it may treat both equally by offering both of them the same accommodation.

The parties who were the plaintiffs in the District Courts argue that the Government could pay for the methods that are found objectionable. In discussing this alternative, the Court does not address whether the proper response to a legitimate claim for freedom in the health care arena is for the Government to create an additional program. The Court properly does not resolve whether one freedom should be protected by creating incentives for additional government constraints. In these cases, it is the Court's understanding that an accommodation may be made to the employers without imposition of a whole new program or burden on the Government. As the Court makes clear, this is not a case where it can be established that it is difficult to accommodate the government's interest, and in fact the mechanism for doing so is already in place.

"[T]he American community is today, as it long has been, a rich mosaic of religious faiths." Town of Greec v. Galloway, 572 U.S. __, __ (2014) (KAGAN, J., dissenting). Among the reasons the United States is so open, so tolerant, and so free is that no person may be restricted or demeaned by government in exercising his or her religion. Yet neither may that same exercise unduly restrict other persons, such as employees, in protecting their own interests, interests the law deems compelling. In these cases the means to reconcile those two priorities are at hand in the existing accommodation the Government has designed, identified, and used for circumstances closely parallel to those presented here. RFRA requires the Government to use this less restrictive means. As the Court explains, this existing model, designed precisely for this problem, might well suffice to distinguish the instant cases from many others in which it is more difficult and expensive to accommodate a governmental program to countless religious claims based on an alleged statutory right of free exercise.

For these reasons and others put forth by the Court, I join its opinion.

Justice GINSBURG, with whom Justice Sotomayor joins, and with whom Justice Breyer and Justice KAGAN join as to all but Part III–C–1, dissenting.

In a decision of startling breadth, the Court holds that commercial enterprises, including corporations, along with partnerships and sole proprietorships, can opt out of any law (saving only tax laws) they judge incompatible with their sincerely held religious beliefs. Compelling governmental interests in uniform compliance with the law, and disadvantages that religion-based opt-outs impose on others, hold no sway, the Court decides, at least when there is a "less restrictive alternative." And such an alternative, the Court suggests, there always will be whenever, in lieu of tolling an enterprise claiming a religion-based exemption, the government, i.e., the general public, can pick up the tab.

The Court does not pretend that the First Amendment's Free Exercise Clause demands religion-based accommodations so extreme, for our decisions leave no doubt on that score. Instead, the Court holds that Congress, in the Religious Freedom Restoration Act of 1993 (RFRA), 42 U.S.C. § 2000bb et seq., dictated the extraordinary religion-based exemptions today's decision endorses. In the Court's view, RFRA demands accommodation of a for-profit corporation's religious beliefs no matter the impact that accommodation may have on third parties who do not share the corporation owners' religious faith—in these cases, thousands of women employed by Hobby Lobby and Conestoga or dependents of persons those corporations employ. Persuaded that Congress enacted RFRA to serve a far less radical purpose, and mindful of the havoc the Court's judgment can introduce, I dissent.

I

"The ability of women to participate equally in the economic and social life of the Nation has been facilitated by their ability to control their reproductive lives." Planned Parenthood of Southeastern Pa. v. Casey, 505 U.S. 833, 856 (1992). Congress acted on that understanding when, as part of a nationwide insurance program intended to be comprehensive, it called for coverage of preventive care responsive to women's needs. Carrying out Congress' direction, the Department of Health and Human Services (HHS), in consultation with public health experts, promulgated regulations requiring group health plans to cover all forms of contraception approved by the Food and Drug Administration (FDA). The genesis of this coverage should enlighten the Court's resolution of these cases.

A

The Affordable Care Act (ACA), in its initial form, specified three categories of preventive care that health plans must cover at no added cost to the plan participant or beneficiary. Particular services were to be recommended by the U.S. Preventive Services Task Force, an independent panel of experts. The scheme had a large gap, however; it left out preventive services that "many women's health advocates and medical professionals believe are critically important." 155 Cong. Rec. 28841 (2009) (statement of Sen. Boxer). To correct this oversight, Senator Barbara Mikulski introduced the Women's Health Amendment, which added to the ACA's minimum coverage requirements a new category of preventive services specific to women's health.

Women paid significantly more than men for preventive care, the amendment's proponents noted; in fact, cost barriers operated to block many women from obtaining needed care at all. And increased access to contraceptive services, the sponsors comprehended, would yield important public health gains.

As altered by the Women's Health Amendment's passage, the ACA requires new insurance plans to include coverage without cost sharing of "such additional preventive care and screenings. . .as provided for in comprehensive guidelines supported by the Health Resources and Services Administration (HRSA)," a unit of HHS. 42 U.S.C. § 300gg–13(a)(4). Thus charged, the HRSA developed recommendations in consultation with the Institute of Medicine (IOM). See 77 Fed. Reg. 8725–8726 (2012).[3] The IOM convened a group of independent experts, including "specialists in disease prevention [and] women's health"; those experts prepared a report evaluating the efficacy of a number of preventive services. IOM, Clinical Prevention Services for Women: Closing the Gaps 2 (2011) (hereinafter IOM Report). Consistent with the findings of "[n]umerous health professional associations" and other organizations, the IOM experts determined that preventive coverage should include the "full range" of FDA-approved contraceptive methods. Id. at 10.

* * *

In line with the IOM's suggestions, the HRSA adopted guidelines recommending coverage of "all FDA-approved contraceptive methods, sterilization procedures, and patient education and counseling for all

---

[3] The IOM is an arm of the National Academy of Sciences, an organization Congress established "for the explicit purpose of furnishing advice to the Government." Public Citizen v. Department of Justice, 491 U.S. 440, 460, n. 11 (1989).

women with reproductive capacity." Thereafter, HHS, the Department of Labor, and the Department of Treasury promulgated regulations requiring group health plans to include coverage of the contraceptive services recommended in the HRSA guidelines, subject to certain exceptions. * * *

* * *

II

Any First Amendment Free Exercise Clause claim Hobby Lobby or Conestoga might assert is foreclosed by this Court's decision in *Employment Division, Department of Human Resources of Oregon v. Smith,* 494 U.S. 872 (1990). In *Smith,* two members of the Native American Church were dismissed from their jobs and denied unemployment benefits because they ingested peyote at, and as an essential element of, a religious ceremony. Oregon law forbade the consumption of peyote, and this Court, relying on that prohibition, rejected the employees' claim that the denial of unemployment benefits violated their free exercise rights. The First Amendment is not offended, *Smith* held, when "prohibiting the exercise of religion. . .is not the object of [governmental regulation] but merely the incidental effect of a generally applicable and otherwise valid provision." Id. at 878; see id. at 878–879 ("an individual's religious beliefs [do not] excuse him from compliance with an otherwise valid law prohibiting conduct that the State is free to regulate"). The ACA's contraceptive coverage requirement applies generally, it is "otherwise valid," it trains on women's well being, not on the exercise of religion, and any effect it has on such exercise is incidental.

Even if *Smith* did not control, the Free Exercise Clause would not require the exemption Hobby Lobby and Conestoga seek. Accommodations to religious beliefs or observances, the Court has clarified, must not significantly impinge on the interests of third parties.

III

A

Lacking a tenable claim under the Free Exercise Clause, Hobby Lobby and Conestoga rely on RFRA * * *.

C

* * *

2

Even if Hobby Lobby and Conestoga were deemed RFRA "person[s]," to gain an exemption, they must demonstrate that the contraceptive coverage requirement "substantially burden[s] [their] exercise of religion." 42 U.S.C. § 2000bb–1(a). * * *

The Court barely pauses to inquire whether any burden imposed by the contraceptive coverage requirement is substantial. Instead, it rests on the Greens' and Hahns' "belie[f] that providing the coverage demanded by the HHS regulations is connected to the destruction of an embryo in a way that is sufficient to make it immoral for them to provide the coverage." I agree with the Court that the Green and Hahn families' religious convictions regarding contraception are sincerely held. But those beliefs, however deeply held, do not suffice to sustain a RFRA claim. RFRA, properly understood, distinguishes between "factual allegations that [plaintiffs'] beliefs are sincere and of a religious nature," which a court must accept as true, and the "legal conclusion. . .that [plaintiffs'] religious exercise is substantially burdened," an inquiry the court must undertake.

Undertaking the inquiry that the Court forgoes, I would conclude that the connection between the families' religious objections and the contraceptive coverage requirement is too attenuated to rank as substantial. The requirement carries no command that Hobby Lobby or Conestoga purchase or provide the contraceptives they find objectionable. Instead, it calls on the companies covered by the requirement to direct money into undifferentiated funds that finance a wide variety of benefits under comprehensive health plans. Those plans, in order to comply with the ACA, must offer contraceptive coverage without cost sharing, just as they must cover an array of other preventive services.

Importantly, the decisions whether to claim benefits under the plans are made not by Hobby Lobby or Conestoga, but by the covered employees and dependents, in consultation with their health care providers. Should an employee of Hobby Lobby or Conestoga share the religious beliefs of the Greens and Hahns, she is of course under no compulsion to use the contraceptives in question. * * * It is doubtful that Congress, when it specified that burdens must be "substantia[l]," had in mind a linkage thus interrupted by independent decisionmakers (the woman and her health counselor) standing between the challenged government action and the religious exercise claimed to be infringed. Any decision to use contraceptives made by a woman covered under Hobby Lobby's or Conestoga's plan will not be propelled by the Government, it will be the woman's autonomous choice, informed by the physician she consults.

3

Even if one were to conclude that Hobby Lobby and Conestoga meet the substantial burden requirement, the Government has shown that the contraceptive coverage for which the ACA provides furthers compelling interests in public health and women's well being. Those interests are concrete, specific, and demonstrated by a wealth of empirical evidence. * * *

* * *

Stepping back from its assumption that compelling interests support the contraceptive coverage requirement, the Court notes that small employers and grandfathered plans are not subject to the requirement. If there is a compelling interest in contraceptive coverage, the Court suggests, Congress would not have created these exclusions.

Federal statutes often include exemptions for small employers, and such provisions have never been held to undermine the interests served by these statutes. See, e.g., Family and Medical Leave Act of 1993, 29 U.S.C. § 2611(4)(A)(i) (applicable to employers with 50 or more employees); Age Discrimination in Employment Act of 1967, 29 U.S.C. § 630(b) (originally exempting employers with fewer than 50 employees, 81 Stat. 605, the statute now governs employers with 20 or more employees); Americans With Disabilities Act, 42 U.S.C. § 12111(5)(A) (applicable to employers with 15 or more employees); Title VII, 42 U.S.C. § 2000e(b) (originally exempting employers with fewer than 25 employees, see Arbaugh v. Y & H Corp., 546 U.S. 500, 505, n. 2 (2006), the statute now governs employers with 15 or more employees).

The ACA's grandfathering provision allows a phasing-in period for compliance with a number of the Act's requirements (not just the contraceptive coverage or other preventive services provisions). Once specified changes are made, grandfathered status ceases. Hobby Lobby's own situation is illustrative. By the time this litigation commenced, Hobby Lobby did not have grandfathered status. Asked why by the District Court, Hobby Lobby's counsel explained that the "grandfathering requirements mean that you can't make a whole menu of changes to your plan that involve things like the amount of co-pays, the amount of co-insurance, deductibles, that sort of thing." Counsel acknowledged that, "just because of economic realities, our plan has to shift over time. I mean, insurance plans, as everyone knows, shif[t] over time." The percentage of employees in grandfathered plans is steadily declining, having dropped from 56% in 2011 to 48% in 2012 to 36% in 2013. Kaiser Family Foundation & Health Research & Educ. Trust, Employer Benefits 2013 Annual Survey 7, 196. In short, far from ranking as a categorical exemption, the grandfathering provision is "temporary, intended to be a means for gradually transitioning employers into mandatory coverage." Gilardi v. United States Dept. of Health & Human Servs., 733 F.3d 1208, 1241 (D.C. Cir. 2013) (Edwards, J., concurring in part and dissenting in part).

4

After assuming the existence of compelling government interests, the Court holds that the contraceptive coverage requirement fails to satisfy RFRA's least restrictive means test. But the Government has shown that there is no less restrictive, equally effective means that would both (1) satisfy the challengers' religious objections to providing insurance coverage for certain contraceptives (which they believe cause abortions); and (2) carry out the objective of the ACA's contraceptive coverage requirement, to ensure that women employees receive, at no cost to them, the preventive care needed to safeguard their health and well being. A "least restrictive means" cannot require employees to relinquish benefits accorded them by federal law in order to ensure that their commercial employers can adhere unreservedly to their religious tenets.

Then let the government pay (rather than the employees who do not share their employer's faith), the Court suggests. "The most straightforward [alternative]," the Court asserts, "would be for the Government to assume the cost of providing. . .contraceptives. . .to any women who are unable to obtain them under their health insurance policies due to their employers' religious objections." The ACA, however, requires coverage of preventive services through the existing employer-based system of health insurance "so that employees face minimal logistical and administrative obstacles." 78 Fed. Reg. 39888.* * *

And where is the stopping point to the "let the government pay" alternative? Suppose an employer's sincerely held religious belief is offended by health coverage of vaccines, or paying the minimum wage, or according women equal pay for substantially similar work? Does it rank as a less restrictive alternative to require the government to provide the money or benefit to which the employer has a religion-based objection? Because the Court cannot easily answer that question, it proposes something else: Extension to commercial enterprises of the accommodation already afforded to nonprofit religion-based organizations. * * *

* * *

In sum, in view of what Congress sought to accomplish, i.e., comprehensive preventive care for women furnished through employer-based health plans, none of the proffered alternatives would satisfactorily serve the compelling interests to which Congress responded.

IV

* * *

Would the exemption the Court holds RFRA demands for employers with religiously grounded objections to the use of certain contraceptives extend to employers with religiously grounded objections to blood transfusions (Jehovah's Witnesses); antidepressants (Scientologists); medications derived from pigs, including anesthesia, intravenous fluids, and pills coated with gelatin (certain Muslims, Jews, and Hindus); and vaccinations (Christian Scientists, among others)? According to counsel for Hobby Lobby, "each one of these cases. . .would have to be evaluated on its own. . .apply [ing] the compelling interest-least restrictive alternative test." Tr. of Oral Arg. 6. Not much help there for the lower courts bound by today's decision.

The Court, however, sees nothing to worry about. Today's cases, the Court concludes, are "concerned solely with the contraceptive mandate. Our decision should not be understood to hold that an insurance-coverage mandate must necessarily fall if it conflicts with an employer's religious beliefs. Other coverage requirements, such as immunizations, may be supported by different interests (for example, the need to combat the spread of infectious diseases) and may involve different arguments about the least restrictive means of providing them." But the Court has assumed, for RFRA purposes, that the interest in women's health and well being is compelling and has come up with no means adequate to serve that interest, the one motivating Congress to adopt the Women's Health Amendment.

There is an overriding interest, I believe, in keeping the courts "out of the business of evaluating the relative merits of differing religious claims," Lee, 455 U.S. at 263, n. 2 (Stevens, J., concurring in judgment), or the sincerity with which an asserted religious belief is held. Indeed, approving some religious claims while deeming others unworthy of accommodation could be "perceived as favoring one religion over another," the very "risk the Establishment Clause was designed to preclude." Id. The Court, I fear, has ventured into a minefield, cf. Spencer v. World Vision, Inc., 633 F.3d 723, 730 (9th Cir. 2010) (O'Scannlain, J., concurring), by its immoderate reading of RFRA. I would confine religious exemptions under that Act to organizations formed "for a religious purpose," "engage[d] primarily in carrying out that religious purpose," and not "engaged. . .substantially in the exchange of goods or services for money beyond nominal amounts." See id. at 748 (Kleinfeld, J., concurring).

* * *

For the reasons stated, I would reverse the judgment of the Court of Appeals for the Tenth Circuit and affirm the judgment of the Court of Appeals for the Third Circuit.

NOTES AND QUESTIONS

1. *Defining a Person.* ERISA expressly defines a "person" as including a corporation. See ERISA § 3(9). Why did Congress fail to expressly define a "person" for purposes of the RFRA? Is reliance on the dictionary's definition appropriate when the context is protecting the free exercise of religion?

2. *Determining a Substantial Burden.* Amici in *Hobby Lobby Stores* argued that the contraceptive mandate did not impose a substantial burden on the plaintiffs because they would be better off financially by not offering any health insurance coverage to their employees and paying the play or pay

penalty under Code Section 4980H(a) instead. This argument suggests that the play or pay penalty amount ($2,000 per full-time employee on an annual basis) is too low to incentivize employers to sponsor group health plans. What are the off-setting nonfinancial incentives for an employer to offer health insurance coverage to its full-time employees?

3. *Future Implications.* In *Hobby Lobby Stores*, the federal government already had an accommodation mechanism in place for non-profit corporations who objected to the contraceptive mandate on religious grounds. Thus, expanding this accommodation mechanism to for-profit, closely-held corporations presented a less restrictive alternative means of achieving the government's compelling interest in ensuring that women have access to all FDA-approved contraceptives without cost-sharing. Does the majority opinion suggest that contraceptive coverage is unique in this regard? Or are other types of coverage requirements under the ACA similarly susceptible to challenges on religious grounds, as suggested by the dissenting opinion?

QUESTIONS ON THE ACA

1. *Comparing Legislative Approaches to National Health Care Policy.* Congress embraced an incremental legislative approach to health care reform between 1996 and 2008 by enacting a series of targeted requirements for group health plans aimed at resolving discrete issues. The Affordable Care Act represents a far more ambitious legislative approach that attempts to simultaneously resolve multiple and interrelated issues. Which legislative approach to reform do you prefer?

2. *The Individual Coverage Mandate and the Problem of Adverse Selection.* One of the criticisms of the ACA is that the tax penalty for individuals who fail to obtain minimum essential coverage may be insufficient to prevent *adverse selection.* The potential for adverse selection arises because all group health plans and health care insurance policy issuers must enroll an individual in the plan or policy without preexisting condition coverage exclusions. If individuals who are healthy wait to obtain health insurance coverage until they have a significant health issue that requires expensive treatment, then the pool of persons covered under the plan or insurance policy will consist of individuals who incur higher than anticipated medical expenses on an actuarial basis. As a result, it may become difficult for the plan to estimate its expenses, and the premiums for coverage increase dramatically to reflect the fact that the pool of participants includes a higher than average percentage of individuals who need expensive medical care. Group health plans mitigate the problem of adverse selection by generally allowing current employees to enroll for coverage only once per year during an open enrollment period. (Enrollment through a policy sold through the Exchange system also is limited to an annual enrollment period, unless an exception applies.) If you were a healthy individual, would you choose to

enroll in your employer's group health plan, or would you pay the tax penalty under Code Section 5000A?

3.   *International Economic Competition and the Burden on Employers.* Given that large employers today often compete in a global economy, is the economic burden imposed by the employer mandate too great? Are the penalties imposed on large employers who do not offer affordable group health plan coverage to their full-time workers sufficient to deter large employers from terminating their plans altogether? Can universal health insurance coverage be accomplished *without* group health plans sponsored by large employers?

4.   *The Exchanges and Price Competition.* One of the criticisms of the ACA is that the law relies on price competition through the Exchange system to make health insurance policies for individuals more affordable. Critics question whether competition among for-profit insurance companies will result in a fair price for the individual health insurance policies sold through an Exchange. Should a public option—the ability by an individual to purchase minimum essential coverage directly from the federal government—be added to the Exchange system to encourage greater price competition?

5.   *Implications of the ACA for Worker Mobility.* Prior to the enactment of the ACA, an employer who sponsored a group health plan had to enroll a new employee in the plan without any coverage exclusions for a preexisting health condition if the employee had at least 12 months of prior creditable coverage and did not incur a gap in coverage of more than 63 consecutive days. See generally ERISA § 701. The same rules prohibiting preexisting condition coverage exclusions applied to the spouse and dependents of the employee. These pre-ACA requirements provided a measure of portability for employer-based health insurance coverage.

Post-ACA, in future years both large and small employers may choose not to sponsor group health plans and rely instead on the Exchange system to provide health insurance coverage for their workers. One of the key cost-containment features of the least expensive policies sold on the Exchange system is a limited network (both in area and number) of health care providers. This limited provider network is coupled with an absence of coverage for out-of-network medical expenses (except for emergency care services, which are deemed to be in-network), and the exclusion of out-of-network expenses from the policy's out-of-pocket maximum limit. In addition, the premium price of an Exchange policy may vary dramatically based on location because such policies are priced on a community rating system. How might these features affect the mobility of workers, particularly unemployed workers, in the future? Do the cost-containment mechanisms of policies offered through the Exchange system provide an incentive for employers to continue to offer group health plans as a means of attracting and retaining employees?

5. ENFORCEMENT OF THE FEDERAL REQUIREMENTS FOR GROUP HEALTH PLANS

The federal requirements for group health care plans contained in Part 7 of Title I of ERISA, including all of the provisions of the ACA that are incorporated by reference in ERISA Section 715, are enforced through a nondeductible excise tax penalty imposed on the employer who sponsors the group health plan. The penalty amount is $100 per day (indexed for inflation), per individual affected, for failure to comply with a Part 7 requirement. See Code §§ 4980D; 9801–02, 9811–12, 9815 (added by ACA § 1562). For an unintentional failure "due to reasonable cause and not due to wilful neglect," the maximum excise tax amount that can be assessed in a taxable year for a single employer plan cannot exceed the lesser of: (1) 10% of the employer's group health plan expenses in the prior year; or (2) $500,000. See Code § 4980D(b)(3). This limitation does not apply if the employer *knowingly* refuses to comply with a requirement without "reasonable cause." Thus, as explained by the Supreme Court in *Burwell v. Hobby Lobby Stores, Inc.,* 134 S.Ct. 2751 (2014), the maximum penalty amount of $100 per day, per individual employee, is imposed for an employer who refuses to comply with one of the ACA's coverage requirements.

Group health plan participants or beneficiaries may bring a private civil action under ERISA Section 502(a)(3) to enforce the federal requirements for group health care plans. Claims under ERISA Section 502(a)(3) are discussed in Chapter Six of the casebook.

E. AMENDING OR TERMINATING WELFARE BENEFIT PLANS

Under the settlor function doctrine, "[e]mployers or other plan sponsors are generally free under ERISA, for any reason at any time, to adopt, modify, or terminate welfare plans." Curtiss-Wright Corp. v. Schoonejongen, 514 U.S. 73, 78 (1995). In *McGann v. H & H Music Co.,* the plaintiff attempted to challenge an amendment to the employer's group health plan that imposed a $5,000 lifetime maximum on benefits payable due to AIDS-related claims. As you read the Fifth Circuit's opinion, notice how the court relies upon the settlor function doctrine to reject the plaintiff's claim.

McGANN v. H & H MUSIC CO.

United States Court of Appeals, Fifth Circuit, 1991.
946 F.2d 401.

GARWOOD, CIRCUIT JUDGE.

Plaintiff-appellant John McGann (McGann) filed this suit under section 510 of the Employee Retirement Income Security Act of 1974 (ERISA), against defendants-appellees H & H Music Company (H & H Music), Brook Mays Music Company (Brook Mays) and General American Life Insurance Company (General American) (collectively defendants) claiming that they discriminated against McGann, an employee of H & H Music, by reducing benefits available to H & H Music's group medical plan beneficiaries for treatment for acquired immune deficiency syndrome (AIDS) and related illnesses. The district court granted defendants' motion for summary judgment on the ground that an employer has an absolute right to alter the terms of medical coverage available to plan beneficiaries. We affirm.

FACTS AND PROCEEDINGS BELOW

McGann, an employee of H & H Music, discovered that he was afflicted with AIDS in December 1987. Soon thereafter, McGann submitted his first claims for reimbursement under H & H Music's group medical plan, provided through Brook Mays, the plan administrator, and issued by General American, the plan insurer, and informed his employer that he had AIDS. McGann met with officials of H & H Music in March 1988, at which time they discussed McGann's illness. Before the change in the terms of the plan, it provided for lifetime medical benefits of up to $1,000,000 to all employees.

In July 1988, H & H Music informed its employees that, effective August 1, 1988, changes would be made in their medical coverage. These changes included, but were not limited to, limitation of benefits payable for AIDS-related claims to a lifetime maximum of $5,000.[1] No limitation was placed on any other catastrophic illness. H & H Music became self-insured under the new plan and General American became the plan's administrator. By January 1990, McGann had exhausted the $5,000 limit on coverage for his illness.

In August 1989, McGann sued H & H Music, Brook Mays and General American under section 510 of ERISA, which provides, in part, as follows:

It shall be unlawful for any person to discharge, fine, suspend, expel, discipline, or discriminate against a participant or beneficiary for exercising any right to which he is entitled under

---

[1] Other changes included increased individual and family deductibles, elimination of coverage for chemical dependency treatment, adoption of a preferred provider plan and increased contribution requirements.

the provisions of an employee benefit plan, . . . or for the purpose of interfering with the attainment of any right to which such participant may become entitled under the plan. . . .

McGann claimed that defendants discriminated against him in violation of both prohibitions of section 510. He claimed that the provision limiting coverage for AIDS-related expenses was directed specifically at him in retaliation for exercising his rights under the medical plan and for the purpose of interfering with his attainment of a right to which he may become entitled under the plan.

Defendants, conceding the factual allegations of McGann's complaint, moved for summary judgment. These factual allegations include no assertion that the reduction of AIDS benefits was intended to deny benefits to McGann for any reason which would not be applicable to other beneficiaries who might then or thereafter have AIDS, but rather that the reduction was prompted by the knowledge of McGann's illness, and that McGann was the only beneficiary then known to have AIDS.[4] On June 26, 1990, the district court granted defendants' motion on the ground that they had an absolute right to alter the terms of the plan, regardless of their intent in making the alterations. The district court also held that even if the issue of discriminatory motive were relevant, summary judgment would still be proper because the defendants' motive was to ensure the future existence of the plan and not specifically to retaliate against McGann or to interfere with his exercise of future rights under the plan.

DISCUSSION

McGann contends that defendants violated both clauses of section 510 by discriminating against him for two purposes: (1) "for exercising any right to which [the beneficiary] is entitled," and (2) "for the purpose of interfering with the attainment of any right to which such participant may become entitled." In order to preclude summary judgment in defendants' favor, McGann must make a showing sufficient to establish the existence of a genuine issue of material fact with respect to each material element on which he would carry the burden of proof at trial.

At trial, McGann would bear the burden of proving the existence of defendants' specific discriminatory intent as an essential element of either of his claims. Thus, in order to survive summary judgment McGann must make a showing sufficient to establish that a genuine issue exists as to defendants' specific intent to retaliate against McGann for filing claims for AIDS-related treatment or to interfere with McGann's attainment of any right to which he may have become entitled.

---

[4] We assume, for purposes of this appeal that the defendants' knowledge of McGann's illness was a motivating factor in their decision to reduce coverage for AIDS-related expenses, that this knowledge was obtained either through McGann's filing of claims or his meetings with defendants, and that McGann was the only plan beneficiary then known to have AIDS.

Although we assume there was a connection between the benefits reduction and either McGann's filing of claims or his revelations about his illness, there is nothing in the record to suggest that defendants' motivation was other than as they asserted, namely to avoid the expense of paying for AIDS treatment (if not, indeed, also for other treatment), no more for McGann than for any other present or future plan beneficiary who might suffer from AIDS. McGann concedes that the reduction in AIDS benefits will apply equally to all employees filing AIDS-related claims and that the effect of the reduction will not necessarily be felt only by him. He fails to allege that the coverage reduction was otherwise specifically intended to deny him particularly medical coverage except "in effect." He does not challenge defendants' assertion that their purpose in reducing AIDS benefits was to reduce costs.

Furthermore, McGann has failed to adduce evidence of the existence of "any right to which [he] may become entitled under the plan." The right referred to in the second clause of section 510 is not simply any right to which an employee may conceivably become entitled, but rather any right to which an employee may become entitled pursuant to an existing, enforceable obligation assumed by the employer. "Congress viewed [section 510] as a crucial part of ERISA because, without it, employers would be able to circumvent the provision of *promised* benefits." Ingersoll-Rand Co. v. McClendon, 498 U.S. 133 (1990) (emphasis added).

McGann's allegations show no *promised* benefit, for there is nothing to indicate that defendants ever promised that the $1,000,000 coverage limit was permanent. The H & H Music plan expressly provides: "Termination or Amendment of Plan: The Plan Sponsor may terminate or amend the Plan at any time or terminate any benefit under the Plan at any time." There is no allegation or evidence that any oral or written representations were made to McGann that the $1,000,000 coverage limit would never be lowered. Defendants broke no promise to McGann. The continued availability of the $1,000,000 limit was not a right to which McGann may have become entitled for the purposes of section 510. To adopt McGann's contrary construction of this portion of section 510 would mean that an employer could not effectively reserve the right to amend a medical plan to reduce benefits respecting subsequently incurred medical expenses, as H & H Music did here, because such an amendment would obviously have as a purpose preventing participants from attaining the right to such future benefits as they otherwise might do under the existing plan absent the amendment. But this is plainly not the law, and ERISA does not require such "vesting" of the right to a continued level of the same medical benefits once those are ever included in a welfare plan.

McGann appears to contend that the reduction in AIDS benefits alone supports an inference of specific intent to retaliate against him or to interfere with his future exercise of rights under the plan. McGann characterizes as evidence of an individualized intent to discriminate the fact that AIDS was the only catastrophic illness to which the $5,000 limit was applied and the fact that McGann was the only employee known to have AIDS. He contends that if defendants reduced AIDS coverage because they learned of McGann's illness through his exercising of his rights under the plan by filing claims, the coverage reduction therefore could be "retaliation" for McGann's filing of the claims. Under McGann's theory, any reduction in employee benefits would be impermissibly discriminatory if motivated by a desire to avoid the anticipated costs of continuing to provide coverage for a particular beneficiary. McGann would find an implied promise not to discriminate for this purpose; it is the breaking of this promise that McGann appears to contend constitutes interference with a future entitlement.

* * *

McGann effectively contends that section 510 was intended to prohibit any discrimination in the alteration of an employee benefits plan that results in an identifiable employee or group of employees being treated differently from other employees. The First Circuit rejected a somewhat similar contention in *Aronson v. Servus Rubber, Div. of Chromalloy,* 730 F.2d 12 (1st Cir. 1984). In *Aronson,* an employer eliminated a profit sharing plan with respect to employees at only one of two plants. The disenfranchised employees sued their employer under section 510, claiming that partial termination of the plan with respect to employees at one plant and not at the other constituted illegal discrimination. The court rejected the employees' discrimination claim, stating in part:

> [Section 510] relates to discriminatory conduct directed against individuals, not to actions involving the plan in general. The problem is with the word "discriminate." An overly literal interpretation of this section would make illegal any partial termination, since such terminations obviously interfere with the attainment of benefits by the terminated group, and, indeed, are expressly intended so to interfere. . . . This is not to say that a plan could not be discriminatorily modified, intentionally benefitting, or injuring, certain identified employees or a certain group of employees, but a partial termination cannot constitute discrimination per se. A termination that cuts along independently established lines—here separate divisions—and that has a readily apparent business justification, demonstrates no invidious intent. Id. at 16 (citation omitted).

The Supreme Court has observed in dictum: "ERISA does not mandate that employers provide any particular benefits, and does not itself proscribe discrimination in the provision of employee benefits." Shaw v. Delta Air Lines, Inc., 463 U.S. 85 (1983). See also Moore v.

Reynolds Metals Co. Retirement Program for Salaried Employees, 740 F.2d 454, 456 (6th Cir.1984) (*Reynolds Metals*). To interpret "discrimination" broadly to include defendants' conduct would clearly conflict with Congress's intent that employers remain free to create, modify and terminate the terms and conditions of employee benefits plans without governmental interference.

The Sixth Circuit, in rejecting a challenge to an employer's freedom to choose the terms of its employee pension plan, stated that:

> [i]n enacting ERISA, Congress continued its reliance on *voluntary* action by employers by granting substantial tax advantages for the creation of qualified retirement programs. Neither Congress nor the courts are involved in either the decision to establish a plan or in the decision concerning which benefits a plan should provide. In particular, courts have no authority to decide which benefits employers must confer upon their employees; these are decisions which are more appropriately influenced by forces in the marketplace and, when appropriate, by federal legislation. Absent a violation of federal or state law, a federal court may not modify a substantive provision of a pension plan.

Reynolds Metals, 740 F.2d at 456 (citation omitted) (emphasis in original).

The Sixth Circuit has subsequently declared that "the principle articulated in [*Reynolds Metals*] applies with at least as much force to welfare plans. . . ." Musto v. American General Corp., 861 F.2d 897, 912 (6th Cir.1988).[9]

As persuasively explained by the Second Circuit, the policy of allowing employers freedom to amend or eliminate employee benefits is particularly compelling with respect to medical plans:

> With regard to an employer's right to change medical plans, Congress evidenced its recognition of the need for flexibility in rejecting the automatic vesting of welfare plans. Automatic vesting was rejected because the costs of such plans are subject to fluctuating and unpredictable variables. Actuarial decisions concerning fixed annuities are based on fairly stable data, and vesting is appropriate. In contrast, medical insurance must take account of inflation, changes in medical practice and technology, and increases in the costs of treatment independent of inflation.

---

[9] *Musto* involved an ERISA claim by retirees that their former employer violated contractual and fiduciary duties by changing the terms of their medical coverage. The court rejected plaintiffs' claim that they had a vested interest in the terms of their medical coverage. *Musto*, like *Reynolds Metals*, noted that "[t]here is a world of difference between administering a welfare plan in accordance with its terms and deciding what those terms are to be. A company acts as a fiduciary in performing the first task, but not the second." Musto, 861 F.2d at 911.

These unstable variables prevent accurate predictions of future needs and costs. Moore v. Metropolitan Life Ins. Co., 856 F.2d 488, 492 (2d Cir.1988) (*Metropolitan Life*).

In *Metropolitan Life,* the court rejected an ERISA claim by retirees that their employer could not change the level of their medical benefits without their consent. The court stated that limiting an employer's right to change medical plans increased the risk of "decreas[ing] protection for future employees and retirees." Id. at 492; see also Reynolds Metals, 740 F.2d at 457 ("judicial interference into the establishment of pension plan provisions . . . would serve only to discourage employers from creating voluntary pension plans").

McGann's claim cannot be reconciled with the well-settled principle that Congress did not intend that ERISA circumscribe employers' control over the content of benefits plans they offered to their employees. McGann interprets section 510 to prevent an employer from reducing or eliminating coverage for a particular illness in response to the escalating costs of covering an employee suffering from that illness. Such an interpretation would, in effect, change the terms of H & H Music's plan. Instead of making the $1,000,000 limit available for medical expenses on an as-incurred basis only as long as the limit remained in effect, the policy would make the limit *permanently* available for all medical expenses as they might thereafter be incurred because of a single event, such as the contracting of AIDS. Under McGann's theory, defendants would be effectively proscribed from reducing coverage for AIDS once McGann had contracted that illness and filed claims for AIDS-related expenses. If a federal court could prevent an employer from reducing an employee's coverage limits for AIDS treatment once that employee contracted AIDS, the boundaries of judicial involvement in the creation, alteration or termination of ERISA plans would be sorely tested.

As noted, McGann has failed to adduce any evidence of defendants' specific intent to engage in conduct proscribed by section 510. A party against whom summary judgment is ordered cannot raise a fact issue simply by stating a cause of action where defendants' state of mind is a material element. There must be some indication that he can produce the requisite quantum of evidence. * * *

Proof of defendants' specific intent to discriminate among plan beneficiaries on grounds not proscribed by section 510 does not enable McGann to avoid summary judgment. ERISA does not broadly prevent an employer from "discriminating" in the creation, alteration or termination of employee benefits plans; thus, evidence of such intentional discrimination cannot alone sustain a claim under section 510. That section does not prohibit welfare plan discrimination between or among categories of diseases. Section 510 does not mandate that if some, or most, or virtually all catastrophic illnesses are covered, AIDS (or any other particular catastrophic illness) must be among them. It does not prohibit an employer from electing not to cover or continue to cover AIDS, while covering or continuing to cover other catastrophic illnesses, even though the employer's decision in this respect may stem from some "prejudice" against AIDS or its victims generally. The same, of course, is true of any other disease and its victims. That sort of "discrimination" is simply not addressed by section 510. Under section 510, the asserted discrimination is illegal only if it is motivated by a desire to retaliate against an employee or to deprive an employee of an existing right to which he may become entitled. The district court's decision to grant summary judgment to defendants therefore was proper. Its judgment is accordingly

AFFIRMED.

NOTES AND QUESTIONS

1.   Do you find the Fifth Circuit's rationale for rejecting the plaintiff's claim that the plan amendment violated ERISA Section 510 persuasive? Or can the settlor function doctrine operate as a subterfuge for prohibited interference with a participant's right to plan benefits?

2.   Under the Fifth Circuit's analysis in *H & H Music*, what types of evidence could the plaintiff present to support the allegation that the employer intended to discriminate by amending the benefits provided by the plan? How likely is it that the participant will be able to present evidence contradicting the employer's assertion that the motivating factor behind the plan amendment merely was to reduce the costs of the plan?

3.   *Constraints on the Settlor Function Doctrine.* Today, the requirements of the Affordable Care Act constrain the plan sponsor's ability to alter or amend the benefits provided by a group health plan under the settlor function doctrine. Other federal laws, which are not preempted by ERISA, similarly may constrain the employer's ability to amend other types of employee benefit plans. For example, the Americans With Disabilities Act, 42 U.S.C. §§ 12101 et seq. (ADA) generally prohibits discrimination against an individual with a disability in regard to compensation and other terms and conditions of employment, which include employee benefit plans. (Note: The ADA became effective in 1992, long after the employer in *H & H Music* had amended its health care plan). The ADA and other federal laws that may impact the design and administration of employee benefit plans are discussed in Section F of Chapter Four.

F.   WELFARE BENEFIT PLANS AND OTHER FEDERAL LAWS

ERISA does not preempt other federal laws. See ERISA § 514(d). Consequently, the design and administration of an employer's welfare benefit plan may be subject to regulation under a number of federal laws that regulate the employer-employee relationship. Other federal laws that are commonly encountered in the context of designing and administering a welfare benefit plan are:

- The Americans With Disabilities Act, 42 U.S.C. §§ 12101 et seq.
- Title VII of the Civil Rights Act, as amended by the Pregnancy Discrimination Act, 42 U.S.C. §§ 2000e(k).
- The Family and Medical Leave Act, 29 U.S.C. §§ 2601 et seq.
- The federal Medicare as secondary payer rules, 42 U.S.C. §§ 1395y et seq.
- The Uniformed Services Employment and Reemployment Rights Act, 38 U.S.C. §§ 4301 et seq.
- The Age Discrimination in Employment Act, 29 U.S.C. §§ 621 et seq.

The reading material in Section F provides an overview of these laws. The purpose of Section F is to highlight the more prominent points of intersection between ERISA and these federal laws in the context of employee benefit plans.

1. AMERICANS WITH DISABILITIES ACT

Title I of the Americans With Disabilities Act (ADA) regulates employers engaged in interstate commerce who have fifteen or more employees. Under Title I of the ADA, it is unlawful for an employer to discriminate on the basis of disability against a qualified individual with a disability in regard to "job application procedures, the hiring, advancement, or discharge of employees, employee compensation, job training, and other terms, conditions, and privileges of employment." 42 U.S.C. § 12112(a). Employee benefits are included as part of the employer's "other terms, conditions, and privileges of employment." Consequently, employment decisions cannot be motivated by concerns about the impact of an individual's disability on the employer's plans, or by concerns over the impact on the employer's plans of the known disability of someone with whom the individual has a family, business, social or other relationship.

Under the ADA, a disability is defined as a physical or mental impairment that substantially limits one or more of the person's major life activities. In the ADA Amendments Act of 2008, Pub. L. No. 110–325, § 2, 122 Stat. 3553, Congress directed the federal courts to construe the definition of a disability broadly in favor of coverage of an individual under the ADA. The ADA Amendments Act specifically rejected earlier Supreme Court decisions that narrowly construed the definition of a disability. See Toyota Motor Mfg., Inc. v. Williams, 534 U.S. 184 (2002); Sutton v. United Air Lines, 527 U.S. 471 (1999).

The ADA intersects with an employer's ERISA plan when the plan makes a *disability-based distinction* concerning benefits. A disability-based distinction arises when an ERISA plan provides a lesser level of benefits, or a different type of benefit, due to the disability of a plan participant.

In enacting the ADA, Congress recognized that sometimes employee benefit plans necessarily must take into account the risks and costs associated with health conditions in designing and funding the plan's benefits. See S. Rep. No. 116, 101st Cong., 1st Sess. 85–86 (1989); H.R. Rep. No. 485, pt. 2, 101st Cong., 2d Sess. 137–38 (1990). Accordingly, the ADA provides for a safe harbor for disability-based distinctions in employee benefit plans. If a provision in the employer's plan is disability-based (such as the AIDS-based benefit limit at issue in *H & H Music*), the provision nevertheless is not prohibited under the ADA if the employer's plan falls within the ADA's safe harbor. To qualify for the ADA's safe harbor, the employer must demonstrate that both of the following two requirements are satisfied:

- The plan is a "bona fide" insured or self-insured plan, and the challenged plan provision is "based on underwriting risks, classifying risks, or administering such risks that are based on or not inconsistent with State law." 42 U.S.C. § 12201(c)(2)–(3).

- The disability-based plan provision is not being used as a "subterfuge" to intentionally violate the ADA. 42 U.S.C. § 12201(c)(2).

The Equal Employment Opportunity Commission (EEOC) is the federal agency charged with enforcement of the ADA. The EEOC defines a "subterfuge" under the second requirement above as disability-based disparate treatment that is not justified by the risks or costs associated with the disability. Subterfuge is determined under the totality of the circumstances.

Prior to the enactment of the Affordable Care Act, group health plans commonly imposed restrictions on coverage and benefits. Some of these restrictions arguably were disability-based distinctions under the ADA. See EEOC INTERIM GUIDANCE ON THE APPLICATION OF THE ADA TO HEALTH INSURANCE (June 8, 1993). The Affordable Care Act reduces the potential for disability-based distinctions in group health plans by mandating that any essential health benefit offered by the plan cannot be subject to an annual or lifetime dollar limit. In addition, the Mental Health Parity and Addiction Equity Act (MHPAEA) requires that if a group health plan offers coverage for mental health care and substance abuse treatment, then such coverage must be equal to the plan's coverage of health care services for physical health conditions. Consequently, federal requirements for group health plans today make it difficult for a group health plan to contain a disability-based distinction in terms of coverage and benefits.

Although ADA challenges to group health plans are less likely due to the ACA and the MHPAEA, plan participants may challenge disability-based distinctions in pension plans and other types of welfare benefit plans. See generally EEOC COMPLIANCE MANUAL, CHAP. 3, EMPLOYEE BENEFITS (Oct. 3, 2000). Consider the following hypothetical example:

> An employer sponsors a pension plan that provides for pension benefits payable at the earlier of attainment of normal retirement age under the plan or upon completing twenty years of service. The employer also sponsors a disability retirement plan that provides for the payment of disability retirement benefits immediately if an illness or injury prevents the participant from working and the disabled individual has attained age 50 with ten years of service. The pension benefit is an annuity equal to 35% of the participant's final average compensation. The disability retirement benefit is an annuity equal to 25% of the participant's final average compensation.

Does this arrangement violate the ADA? See EEOC COMPLIANCE MANUAL, CHAP. 3, ADA Issues, Part V (2000) ("[T]he ADA does not require that service retirement and disability retirement plans provide the same level of benefits, because they are two separate benefits which serve two difference purposes."). Suppose the employer requires that a participant who qualifies for both a pension and disability retirement benefits must take the disability retirement benefits? See id. (ADA violation).

Another area of ADA litigation involves challenges to disability income plans where the plan imposes a limit—typically a maximum of two years—on the duration of benefits for participants with a mental disability, but imposes no time limit on the payment of benefits for participants with a physical disability. (Recall that the Mental Health Parity and Addiction Equity Act applies only to benefits provided by group health plans.) The federal courts have universally rejected these claims under the ADA, either because all employees (both disabled and nondisabled) were subject to the same restrictions, or because the plaintiffs were former employees and therefore lacked standing to bring an ADA claim against the employer. See, e.g., McKnight v. General Motors Corp., 550 F.3d 519 (6th Cir. 2008); EEOC v. Staten Island Sav. Bank, 207 F.3d 144 (2d Cir. 2000); Weyer v. Twentieth Century Fox Film Corp., 198 F.3d 1104 (9th Cir. 2000); EEOC v. Aramark, 208 F.3d 266 (D.C. Cir. 2000); Parker v. Metropolitan Life Ins. Co., 121 F.3d 1006 (6th Cir. 1997).

2. TITLE VII AND THE PREGNANCY DISCRIMINATION ACT

Title VII of the Civil Rights Act of 1964 (Title VII) regulates employers engaged in interstate commerce who have at least fifteen employees for each working day in at least twenty weeks in the current or preceding calendar year. Under Title VII, it is an unlawful employment practice for an employer to discriminate "on the basis of race, color, religion, sex, or national origin" with respect to an employee's "compensation, terms, conditions, or privileges of employment." 42 U.S.C. § 2000e–2(a)(1). The Pregnancy Discrimination Act of 1978 (PDA) amended Title VII to clarify that:

> [t]he terms "because of sex" or "on the basis of sex" include, but are not limited to, because of or on the basis of pregnancy, childbirth, or related medical condition; and women affected by pregnancy, childbirth, or related medical conditions shall be treated the same for all employment-related purposes, including receipt of benefits under fringe benefit programs, as other persons not so affected but similar in their ability or inability to work.

42 U.S.C. § 2000e(k).

As a result of the PDA amendments to Title VII, employers today are required to treat pregnancy, childbirth, and related medical conditions on the same basis as all other disabilities and medical conditions for employment-related purposes, including entitlement to accrued sick leave or vacation time or the payment of benefits under an employer's short-term or long-term disability plan. For example, if the employer offers a short-term disability plan for its employees, it may not pay a lesser level of benefits, or pay benefits for a shorter period of time, for physical disability following childbirth than the plan pays for other types of short-term physical disabilities. The employer also cannot limit plan benefits for pregnancy-related conditions to married employees. See generally 29 C.F.R. § 1604, Appendix. If the employer's group health plan covers the medical expenses of spouses of female employees, the employer's group health plan must cover the medical expenses of spouses of male employees, including those arising from pregnancy-related conditions, on the same terms and conditions. See Newport News Shipbuilding & Dry Dock Co. v. EEOC, 462 U.S. 669 (1983). An employer's group health plan is not required to provide coverage of abortion procedures unless the life of the mother is endangered if the fetus is carried to term, or where medical complications have arisen from an abortion. See 42 U.S.C. § 2000e(k).

3. FAMILY AND MEDICAL LEAVE ACT

The Family and Medical Leave Act (FMLA) applies to employers engaged in interstate commerce who employ fifty or more employees on each working day during twenty or more calendar work weeks in the current or preceding calendar year. Congress enacted the FMLA to enable workers to better balance the demands of the workplace with the needs of families, to promote the stability and economic security of their families, and to promote the national interest in preserving the integrity of the family.

The FMLA allows an eligible employee of the employer to take a leave of absence from work for up to a total of twelve working weeks in any twelve month period for any one or a combination of the following reasons:

(1) For the birth of a child and to care for the newborn child;

(2) Because of the placement of a child with the employee for adoption or foster care;

(3) Because the employee is needed to care for a family member (defined as a child, spouse, or parent) with a serious health condition;

(4) Because the employee's own serious health condition makes the employee unable to perform the functions of the employee's job; or

(5) For any qualifying exigency arising out of the fact that a family member is serving on active duty in the Armed Forces, or has been called to active duty as a member of the National Guard or the Reserves. Department of Labor regulations define a "qualifying exigency" as including short-notice deployment and post-deployment activities, military events and related activities, childcare and school activities, financial and legal arrangements, and counseling, rest and recuperation.

Department of Labor regulations provide detailed guidance concerning the five permissible reasons listed above for taking FMLA leave. See generally 29 C.F.R. §§ 825.100 et seq. FMLA leave may be taken on an intermittent basis rather than all at once, or the employee may take FMLA leave in the form of a part-time schedule.

The FMLA also provides for military caregiver leave. Under the FMLA's military caregiver provisions, a child, parent or next of kin may take up to 26 weeks of leave to provide care for a member of the Armed Forces, National Guard, or the Reserves who is undergoing medical treatment, recuperation or therapy for a serious medical injury or illness. Expanded military caregiver leave applies if the person requiring care was a member of the Armed Forces, National Guard, or the Reserves at any time during the five year period before medical treatment, recuperation or therapy begins.

An employee who takes FMLA leave generally has the right to return to work at the same position or an equivalent position with equivalent working conditions and benefits. 29 C.F.R. § 825.100(c). The employer has the right to advance notice from the employee who desires to take FMLA leave, if providing such notice to the employer is practicable. The employer may require an employee to submit a certification from a health care provider to document that a requested FMLA leave is due to the serious health condition of the employee or the employee's family member. Failure to comply with these employer notice and documentation requirements may delay the start of the employee's FMLA leave. 29 C.F.R. § 825.100(d).

To be eligible for FMLA leave, the employee must have been employed by the employer for at least twelve months and had at least 1,250 hours of service during the twelve month period immediately preceding commencement of the FMLA leave. The employee does not have to work twelve consecutive months to satisfy the FMLA requirement of twelve months of employment. For purposes of determining an employee's eligibility for FMLA leave, hours of service are measured according to the principles established under the federal Fair Labor Standards Act.

The FMLA does not require that FMLA leave must be paid. Normally, FMLA leave is unpaid. 29 C.F.R. § 825.207(a). The FMLA permits the employer to require an employee to substitute and consume other types of accrued paid leave for FMLA leave. For example, if the FMLA leave relates to the birth or adoption of a child, or the FMLA leave is for the purpose of allowing the employee to care for a spouse, child, or parent who has a serious health condition, the employer may require the employee to substitute and consume accrued paid vacation leave for FMLA leave. This type of substitution does not, however, extend the employee's entitlement to a total of only twelve weeks of FMLA leave. If the FMLA leave relates to the employee's own serious health condition, the employer may require the employee to substitute and consume accrued paid vacation leave or accrued paid sick leave. Again, this substitution does not extend the duration of the employee's FMLA leave beyond twelve weeks.

Short-term disability leave for the birth of a child is treated for purposes of the FMLA as leave because of the employee's own serious health condition. Often the period of physical disability following childbirth is paid under the employer's short-term disability income plan. The employer may designate the short-term disability leave as FMLA leave so that the entitlement periods for short-term disability plan benefits and FMLA leave run concurrently rather than consecutively. If the employer designates the short-term disability leave following childbirth as FMLA leave, the employee's FMLA leave, including the period of short-term disability leave, is limited to a total of twelve weeks.

In instances where an employee uses some form of accrued paid leave under circumstances that do not qualify for FMLA leave, the employee's leave is not counted toward the overall twelve week limit for FMLA leave. For example, if the employee uses paid sick leave for a condition that does not meet the FMLA's criteria for a serious health condition, then the sick leave time cannot be counted as FMLA leave. Similarly, if the employee uses paid vacation leave time, and then later the employee desires to take FMLA leave, the previous period of paid vacation time cannot reduce the employee's entitlement to twelve weeks of FMLA leave. Normally, the consequence of using paid leave prior to taking FMLA leave is merely financial. Consuming paid accrued leave prior to taking FMLA leave reduces the remaining amount of paid leave time available to be substituted for unpaid FMLA leave.

The FMLA and COBRA

When a participant in the employer's group health plan takes FMLA leave, the normal requirements of COBRA are suspended. The Treasury Department and the Department of Labor have both issued regulations that address how the taking of FMLA leave changes the application of COBRA's requirements. See generally Treas. Reg. § 54.4980B–10; DOL Reg. § 825.209.

When an employee takes FMLA leave, the resulting absence from work or reduction in the employee's hours may render the employee eligible for participation in the employer's group health care plan. In this situation, the taking of leave under the FMLA cannot trigger a qualifying event under COBRA. When an employee who is participating in the employer's group health plan takes FMLA leave, the employer is required to maintain the employee's coverage under the group health plan "on the same conditions as coverage would have been provided if the employee had been continuously employed during the entire leave period." 29 C.F.R. § 825.209(a). If the employee had family coverage under the group health plan, the employer must maintain the family coverage during the FMLA leave period.

An employee on FMLA leave must be given the option of either continuing coverage under the group health plan or discontinuing coverage during the FMLA leave period. A qualifying event under COBRA is not triggered when an employee declines coverage under a group health plan while on FMLA leave, or elects to continue coverage under the plan but later allows the coverage to lapse by not paying the required premium. See Treas. Reg. § 54.4980B–10, Q & A–1, Q & A–3.

If the employee elects to continue coverage under the group health plan during FMLA leave, any share of the premium that had been paid by the employee prior to FMLA leave must continue to be paid by the employee during the FMLA leave period. Thus, if the employer subsidizes part of the premium costs for employees to participate in the plan, the employer must continue to subsidize the employee's premium while on FMLA leave. This represents a significant advantage for the employee over the normal rules for continuation coverage under COBRA, which do not require the employer to continue to subsidize COBRA premium payments. If the premium amount for all employees who participate in the group health plan is raised or lowered for active employees while the employee is on leave, the employee must pay the new premium rate.

Several premium payment options are possible for an employee on FMLA leave who desires to continue coverage under the group health care plan. These options depend on whether the employee's FMLA leave is designated as paid or unpaid leave. If the employee's FMLA leave is paid, the employee's share of the premium must be paid by the method normally used during any paid leave (most likely payroll deduction). For the portion, if any, of the employee's FMLA leave that is unpaid, the employer has several options for collecting premium payments from the employee, so long as the employer does not impose payment requirements for an employee who is on unpaid FMLA leave that are less favorable than the requirements the employer imposes on other employees who are on unpaid leave. See 29 C.F.R. § 825.210(b)–(e).

If the employee elects to discontinue coverage under the employer's group health plan while absent from work due to FMLA leave, once the employee returns from FMLA leave the employee must be immediately reinstated as a participant in the group health plan "on the same terms as prior to taking the leave, including family or dependent coverages, without any qualifying period, physical examination, [or] exclusion of preexisting conditions." 29 C.F.R. § 825.209(e). If the employee's coverage under the health plan lapsed during the FMLA leave because the employee did not pay the required premium,

> upon the employee's return from FMLA leave the employer must still restore the employee to coverage/benefits equivalent to those the employee would have had if leave had not been taken and the premium payment(s) had not been missed, including family or dependent coverage. In such case, an employee may not be required to meet any qualification requirements imposed by the plan, including any new preexisting condition waiting period, to wait for an open [enrollment date], or to pass a medical examination to obtain reinstatement of coverage.

29 C.F.R. § 825.212(c).

An employer's obligation to restore the employee's prior coverage and benefits under the group health plan ceases "if and when the employment relationship would have terminated if the employee had not taken FMLA leave." 29 C.F.R. § 209(f). For purposes of COBRA, a qualifying event occurs at the earlier of: (1) the time when the employee informs the employer that the employee does not intend to return to work once the FMLA leave period has expired; or (2) the time when the FMLA leave period expires. In other words, the qualifying event occurs on the day the employer learns that the employee does not intend to return to work after the FMLA leave period has expired. Treasury Department regulations provide the following examples of how COBRA applies in the context of FMLA leave.

> *Example 1*: Employee B is covered under the group health plan of Employer X on January 31, 2001. B takes FMLA leave beginning February 1, 2001. B's last day of FMLA leave is twelve weeks later, on April 25, 2001, and B does not return to work with Employer X at the end of the FMLA leave. If B does not elect COBRA continuation coverage, B will not be covered under the group health plan of Employer X as of April 26, 2001.
>
> B experiences a qualifying event on April 25, 2001, and the maximum coverage period is measured from that date. (This is the case even if, for part or all of the FMLA leave, B fails to pay the employee portion of premiums for coverage under the group health plan of Employer X and is not covered under Employer X's plan.)
>
> *Example 2*: Employee C and C's spouse are covered under the group health plan of Employer Y on August 15, 2001. C takes FMLA leave beginning August 16, 2001. C informs Employer Y less than twelve weeks later, on September 28, 2001, that C will not be returning to work. * * *
>
> C and C's spouse experience a qualifying event on September 28, 2001, and the maximum coverage period (generally eighteen months) is measured from that date. (This is the case even if, for part or all of the FMLA leave, C fails to pay the employee portion of premiums for coverage under the group health plan of Employer Y and C or C's spouse is not covered under Employer Y's plan.)

Treas. Reg. § 54.4980B–10, Q & A–2, Examples 1 & 2.

PROBLEMS ON FMLA, PDA AND COBRA

The Machine Shop (Employer), a small manufacturing business with thirty-five full-time employees, has the following short-term disability policy concerning its employees.

Short-term Disability Policy

If you are unable to work due to an injury or medical disability, the Machine Shop will continue to pay your regular salary and will "hold" your position for you for twelve weeks. If you do not return to work at the end of this twelve week period, your employment will be terminated.

If you are disabled due to pregnancy or childbirth, you will receive unpaid maternity leave for eight weeks. At the end of your eight weeks of maternity leave, you must return to work your normal schedule or your employment may be terminated at the discretion of the Employer.

The Machine Shop sponsors a group health plan for its employees. The group health plan offers maternity benefits. Each employee pays 30% of the premium cost for coverage under the group health plan, and the Employer pays the other 70% of the premium cost. Employees pay their premiums for coverage under the group health plan through payroll deduction.

Nancy Nillow has worked as a full-time employee of the Employer for two years. Nancy is unmarried and becomes pregnant. Nancy is a participant in the Employer's group health plan.

Eight months into her pregnancy, on March 1st Nancy becomes physically disabled and is ordered by her physician to stay at home in bed until she delivers her baby. Alice Appleton, the office manager of the Machine Shop and the plan administrator for both the Short-Term Disability Policy and the group health plan, tells Nancy that in order to maintain her coverage under the group health plan, Nancy must "pay the entire premium, including the Employer's share, up front for coverage for the next eight weeks." As instructed by Alice, Nancy pays the full premium for two months of coverage under the group health plan in advance. The Employer imposes this advance payment requirement only for employees who are on maternity leave.

Nancy delivers her baby by cesarean section five weeks later. Three weeks after the birth of her child, the Employer sends Nancy the following letter:

Dear Nancy,

Your maternity leave period of eight weeks under the Machine Shop's Short-Term Disability Policy has expired. You must report to work next Monday or your employment and health care coverage will be terminated.

Best Regards,

The Machine Shop

Nancy, who is still physically disabled from childbirth (and, according to her physician, will continue to be physically disabled until six weeks postpartum), does not report to work on Monday. The Employer terminates Nancy's employment and cancels her coverage under the group health plan.

Alice Appleton fails to send Nancy a COBRA notice. When Nancy asks Alice about continuing her health insurance coverage, Alice tells Nancy that "you should be grateful that you were paid short-term disability for eight weeks."

Nancy comes to you for legal advice with respect to the following questions:

A. Did the Employer's actions violate the Family and Medical Leave Act? Explain.

B. Does the Machine Shop's Short-Term Disability Policy violate the Pregnancy Discrimination Act? How much paid leave is Nancy legally entitled to receive under the terms of the Short-Term Disability Policy?

C. Is Nancy entitled to a COBRA notice? At what point did a COBRA qualifying event occur?

D. Assume that the Machine Shop has ninety-eight full-time employees. How would your answer to Question A above change?

4. MEDICARE AS SECONDARY PAYER RULES

Individuals who qualify for Social Security benefits are eligible for health care coverage under the federal Medicare program. Such individuals may still be working and therefore are eligible for coverage under both their employer's group health care plan and Medicare. Persons in this situation are known as the *working aged*. As a general principle, the federal Medicare program prohibits discrimination against individuals who are eligible for participation in the employer's group health plan because such individuals also are eligible for health care coverage under Medicare. In implementing this general principle, federal Medicare law draws a sharp distinction between the working aged and retired employees.

The Working Aged and the Medicare As Secondary Payer Rules

The *Medicare as secondary payer* (MSP) rules apply to the working aged. The MSP rules are codified at 42 U.S.C. § 1395y. The MSP rules apply to any employer who has at least twenty employees and who sponsors a group health plan. Under these rules, the health plan is required to offer employees age sixty-five and older who have *current employment status* and their spouses the same health care coverage under the plan as the plan offers to younger workers. An individual has current employment status for the purpose of the MSP rules if the individual is "an employee, is the employer, or is associated with the employer in a business relationship." 42 U.S.C. § 1395y(b)(1)(E)(ii).

If an employee who is subject to the MSP rules is a participant in the employer's group health care plan, the employer's plan must be the primary payer of claims for the employee. Medicare acts as the secondary payer of the individual's claims. As a secondary payer, Medicare pays only the individual's health care expenses that are not covered under the employer's plan, but are covered by Medicare.

An employer's group health plan violates the MSP rules if the plan:

(1) improperly takes Medicare eligibility or entitlement to Medicare coverage into account when determining eligibility for participation in the plan or benefits provided under the plan;

(2) fails to provide the same benefits to Medicare-eligible participants as the plan provides to younger participants;

(3) fails to refund a claim payment made by Medicare that should have been paid by the plan as the primary payer; or

(4) fails to provide information to Medicare on the plan's obligations as primary payer and thereby leads Medicare improperly to make a primary payment.

If the employer's group health care plan violates the MSP rules, the employer is subject to a nondeductible excise tax equal to 25% of *all* of the expenses of the group health plan (not just expenses incurred for the working aged and their eligible spouses that are subject to the MSP rules). See Code § 5000. In addition, the federal government has broad authority to recover double the amount of an improper Medicare payment as liquidated damages for violation of the MSP rules from any and all entities who were required, or who were directly or indirectly responsible, for an improper Medicare payment that should have been made by a plan as the primary payer. See 42 U.S.C. §§ 1395y(b)(2)(B)(iii). Persons potentially liable under this double damages penalty include the plan, an insurer for the plan, the employer who sponsors the plan, the employer as the self-insurer of its own plan, and any third party claims administrator for the plan.

Retirees and Retiree Group Health Plans

The MSP rules do not apply to retired employees. As a result, employers who sponsor group health care plans or prescription drug plans for retired employees typically coordinate the benefits provided by these plans with Medicare coverage. Retiree health care or prescription drug plans generally are designed so that Medicare is the primary payer of claims, with the employer's plan paying for expenses that are not covered by Medicare.

The Medicare Prescription Drug Improvement and Modernization Act of 2003, Pub. L. No. 108–173, 117 Stat. 2066 (Medicare Act of 2003), added a prescription drug benefit for individuals covered by Medicare. To encourage employers to continue to sponsor prescription drug plans for retirees, the Medicare Act of 2003 provided employers with a direct subsidy for each retiree covered under the employer's plan. In 2010, the amount of the subsidy payment was 28% of the actual retiree prescription drug costs of the plan that were more than $310 and less than $6,300.

From the perspective of corporate income taxation, the retiree prescription drug subsidy under the Medicare Act of 2003 was unusual in that corporations were not required to report the subsidy payments as income, yet were permitted to take a deduction for the full cost of the retiree prescription drug plan (even though a portion of that cost had been reimbursed by the federal subsidy payment). To illustrate, under the Medicare Act of 2003, if a company had $100 in retiree drug expenses, the company would receive a tax-free federal subsidy payment of $28, and also would take an income tax deduction for the full $100 of retiree drug expenses.

The Affordable Care Act changed this unusual corporate income tax treatment of the federal subsidy for retiree prescription drug plans. Beginning in 2013, corporate employers only may deduct the *unsubsidized* expenses of a retiree prescription drug plan. See ACA § 9012, as amended by HCRA § 1407 (adding Code § 139A). The Joint Committee on Taxation explained this change with the following example:

> [A]ssume a company receives a subsidy of $28 with respect to eligible retiree drug expenses of $100. The $28 is excludable from income under Code Section 139A, and the amount otherwise allowable as a deduction is reduced by the $28. Thus, if the company otherwise meets the requirements of the Code for ordinary business expenses] with respect to its eligible retiree drug expenses, it would be entitled to an ordinary business expense deduction of $72.

See JOINT COMM. ON TAXATION, 111TH CONG., TECHNICAL EXPLANATION OF THE REVENUE PROVISIONS OF THE "RECONCILIATION ACT OF 2010," AS AMENDED, IN COMBINATION WITH THE "PATIENT PROTECTIONS AND AFFORDABLE CARE ACT" (Comm. Print 2010).

As a direct result of this change, numerous public companies who sponsored retiree prescription drug plans took charges against earnings for the first quarter of 2010. These charges, which were required under the accounting rules for public companies, indicated the economic value of the subsidy prior to its modification by the Affordable Care Act. For example, AT&T announced a $1 billion charge against earnings. Caterpillar and 3M announced charges against earnings of $100 million and $90 million, respectively. Experts predict that the reduction in the federal subsidy for retiree prescription drug plans will accelerate the long-term trend of declining retiree prescription drug coverage.

5. UNIFORMED SERVICES EMPLOYMENT AND REEMPLOYMENT RIGHTS ACT

The Uniformed Services Employment and Reemployment Rights Act (USERRA) is designed to protect the employee benefits of employees who are called to active military service. Like the FMLA, the USERRA suspends the normal requirements of COBRA.

When an employee who is a participant in a group health plan is absent due to active military service for a period that does not exceed thirty-one days, the group health plan must continue to offer coverage to the employee (including dependent coverage). During this thirty-one day period, the plan cannot charge the employee a higher premium for coverage under the group health plan than the premium amount the plan charges to active employees of the employer. See 38 U.S.C. § 4317. As a result, during this initial thirty-one day period a COBRA qualifying event does not occur and the employee continues to benefit from any employer subsidy for coverage under the employer's group health plan.

If the employee's absence due to active military service extends beyond this initial thirty-one day period, the plan must continue to offer coverage (including dependent coverage) to the employee for a maximum period that is the lesser of twenty-four months or the period of military service (measured beginning on the date the absence from work begins and ending on the day after the employee fails to apply for reemployment). After a thirty-one day absence, the plan may charge the employee not more than 102% of the full premium amount (i.e., without any employer subsidy provided for active employees) for coverage under the group health plan. See 38 U.S.C. § 4317.

6. AGE DISCRIMINATION IN EMPLOYMENT ACT

The Age Discrimination in Employment Act (ADEA) applies to employers engaged in interstate commerce who employ at least twenty employees on each working day for at least twenty calendar weeks in the current or preceding calendar year. Congress enacted the ADEA to promote the employment of older persons by making it unlawful for employers "to fail or refuse to hire or to discharge any individual or otherwise discriminate against any individual with respect to his compensation, terms, conditions, or privileges of employment, because of such individual's age." 29 U.S.C. § 623(a)(1). An individual who is age forty or older is protected under the ADEA.

The ADEA's protections concerning "terms, conditions, or privileges of employment" include participation in employee benefit plans. In the Older Workers Benefit Protection Act of 1990, Pub. L. No. 101–433, 104 Stat. 978 (OWBPA), Congress amended the provisions of the ADEA to indicate Congress's intention that if the employer's plan provides a lesser level of benefits based on an individual's age, the lesser level of benefits must be justified under the ADEA on the basis of the employer's cost to provide the benefits. As amended by the OWBPA, the ADEA provides the following rule for when an employer's plan may provide lesser benefits to individuals on the basis of age.

> It shall not be unlawful for an employer . . . to observe the terms of a bona fide employee benefit plan where, for each benefit or benefit package, the actual amount of payment made or cost incurred on behalf of an older worker is no less than that made or incurred on behalf of a younger worker, as permissible under section 1625.10, title 29, Code of Federal Regulations (as in effect on June 22, 1989).

29 U.S.C. § 623(f)(2)(B). The statutory reference to the Code of Federal Regulations in the above paragraph incorporates regulations that were previously promulgated by the federal Equal Employment Opportunity Commission (EEOC). These regulations provide that if the employer's plan provides lesser benefits to older workers, the employer bears the burden of proving that the cost of providing the lesser level of benefits to older individuals under the plan nevertheless is equal to the employer's costs of providing benefits under the plan to younger workers. This rule under the ADEA is known as the *equal cost principle*.

The ADEA applies to both employee pension and employee welfare benefit plans. With respect to welfare benefit plans, issues under the ADEA typically arise in the context of life insurance plans, long-term disability income plans and retiree health care plans. For example, assume that an employer sponsors a life insurance or long-term disability income plan for its employees. If the plan is insured, for a given level or amount of benefits provided under the plan, the insurer will charge the employer more for an older worker than for a younger worker. Pursuant to the equal cost principle, the employer's plan will not violate the ADEA if the plan provides a lesser amount of benefits to the older worker, so long as the employer's costs for the older worker and the younger worker under the plan are equal. Detailed regulations promulgated by the EEOC provide guidance concerning how the employer may justify different levels or amounts of welfare plan benefits provided to older and younger workers using the equal cost principle. See generally 29 C.F.R. § 1625.

The concept of prohibited discrimination "because of an individual's age" under the ADEA can be difficult to apply in the context of an employee pension plan. For example, in *Kentucky Retirement Systems v. EEOC*, 554 U.S. 135 (2008), the Supreme Court held that Kentucky's pension plan for public sector employees in hazardous occupations (e.g., police officers and firefighters) did not violate the ADEA. The Kentucky plan imputed unearned years of service as a means of boosting the years of service used to compute benefits for eligible workers who became disabled before reaching normal retirement age under the plan. The Kentucky plan did not, however, similarly impute additional unearned years of service for workers who attained normal retirement age under the plan and then became disabled. The effect of this provision was to provide more generous benefits for younger disabled workers than for older disabled workers. The purpose of the provision was to make the benefits for disabled workers consistent, regardless of whether the worker became disabled early or late in the worker's career.

The Supreme Court held that the different treatment of older and younger workers under the Kentucky plan was not "actually motivated by age." The Court further reasoned that age and pension status (i.e., eligibility for benefits based on attaining normal retirement age) were "analytically distinct" concepts, and that pension status is not a "proxy for age." The reasoning in *Kentucky Retirement Systems* has been criticized by ERISA experts, who describe the application of the ADEA to retirement plan benefits as a "question [that] will never be answered" and one that qualifies "for inclusion in our Mysteries of ERISA file." *Supreme Court Once Again Divides Over How the ADEA Applies to Employee Benefits*, ERISA LITIG. REP. (Glasser Legal Works), vol. 16, no. 4, at 11 (Aug./Sept. 2008).

Retiree Health Care Plans and the ADEA

The ADEA does not prohibit an employer from engaging in so-called "reverse" discrimination on the basis of age in providing plan benefits to employees who are age forty or older. For example, it is not a violation of the ADEA for the employer to continue to provide retiree health care plan benefits to current workers who are age fifty or older, but terminate the retiree health care plan benefits of current workers who are ages forty to forty-nine. See General Dynamics Land Systems, Inc. v. Cline, 540 U.S. 581 (2004) (statutory language, purpose and legislative history show that the ADEA does not prohibit an employer from providing more favorable benefits to an older employee than to a younger one).

The ADEA has proven particularly controversial in the context of retiree health care plans. In a retiree health care plan, it is common for the plan to be designed so that retirees who are eligible for Medicare coverage receive a package of benefits that is coordinated with Medicare benefits. As a result, the retiree health care plan only pays for health care expenses that Medicare does not cover.

For example, assume that the employer's plan requires all Medicare-eligible participants to receive their health care benefits through a HMO. Participants in the plan who are under age sixty-five (and therefore not yet eligible for Medicare) receive health care benefits through a traditional insured health care plan. This was the plan design that was successfully challenged by the plaintiffs as a violation of the ADEA in

Erie County Retirees Association v. County of Erie, 220 F.3d 193 (3d Cir. 2000). As a result of the Third Circuit's ruling in *Erie County*, the EEOC reacted by creating an ADEA exemption that permits employers who sponsor retiree health care plans to alter, reduce, or eliminate benefits when the participant becomes eligible for Medicare. See 72 Fed. Reg. 72,938 (Dec. 26, 2007) (codified at 29 C.F.R. § 1625).

G. RETIREE HEALTH CARE PLANS AND ERISA LITIGATION

1. THE IMPACT OF FINANCIAL ACCOUNTING STANDARDS ON RETIREE HEALTH CARE PLANS

Health care benefits for retired workers historically have been offered by large public companies. The origins of the decline in retiree health care plans offered by public companies can be traced back to two changes in the financial accounting standards for how such companies must report liabilities for retiree health care benefits on the company's financial statements.

In 1990, the Financial Accounting Standards Board (FASB) issued Financial Accounting Standard No. 106, entitled "Employers' Accounting for Postretirement Benefits Other Than Pensions" (FAS 106). FAS 106 was a dramatic accounting standard change for public companies that offered retiree health care benefits. Prior to FAS 106, companies did not prefund retiree health care benefits, but rather paid for these benefits as they were incurred. Company financial statements only reported that the company provided retiree health care benefits and disclosed the amount of *current* payments for those benefits. After FAS 106, companies were required to estimate and disclose *future* accrued unfunded liabilities for retiree health care benefits on their balance sheets. The financial impact was immediate and dramatic. For example, to comply with FAS 106 General Motors reported a one-time $20.8 billion charge in the footnotes to its balance sheet in 1992. Ford Motor Company reported a $7.5 billion charge in that same year.

The issuance of FAS 106 coincided with a rapid escalation of health care costs during the 1990s that affected all employer-sponsored health care plans, but particularly impacted retiree health care plans. Employers responded by either terminating their retiree health benefits, or imposing cost controls such as absolute dollar caps on amounts the employer would spend annually on retiree health benefits, eliminating certain benefits, or requiring retirees to bear an increased share of the cost of benefits. These actions spawned waves of ERISA litigation as retirees challenged the legality of retiree health plan terminations or the modification of retiree health benefits.

In 2006, the FASB issued FAS No. 158, entitled "Employers' Accounting for Defined Benefit Pension and Other Postretirement Plans" (FAS 158). FAS 158 required that companies not only must estimate and disclose the true value of unfunded accrued liabilities for retiree health benefits in the footnotes to their balance sheets, but that these liabilities must be treated as *current* expenses on income statements. Again, the immediate impact on the profits reported by public companies was dramatic.

To remove the legacy cost of retiree health care benefits off of their financial statements, in 2007 General Motors, Ford Motor Company, and Chrysler (collectively, the "Big Three") negotiated a historic agreement with the United Automobile Workers (UAW). The Big Three agreed to contribute billions of dollars, partly in cash and partly in company stock and debt instruments, to a particular type of tax-favored trust known as a voluntary employees' beneficiary association (VEBA). In return, the VEBA would assume all future liabilities for retiree health benefits for union workers that had been negotiated in prior collective bargaining agreements between the Big Three and the UAW.

Although the benefits of the VEBA arrangements to the Big Three were obvious, the VEBA arrangements provided two significant benefits to union workers and retirees. First, the workers and retirees obtained a measure of control through the VEBAs of future changes or modifications to their retiree health benefits. Second, unlike pension benefits that are insured by the PBGC, retiree health benefits are not insured in the event of employer insolvency. By transferring corporate assets to a VEBA, these assets became the property of the VEBA beneficiaries and thus became sheltered from the claims of corporate creditors in the event of a future bankruptcy filing by the companies.

Although highlighted in news reports, the VEBAs established by the Big Three and the UAW are not a general solution to the problem of funding and accounting for retiree health benefits. Ideally, employers would fund future accrued liabilities for retiree health benefits on an actuarially sound basis, as pension plan benefits are funded, by making present contributions to a VEBA. Under Code Sections 419 and 419A, however, employers are significantly constrained in their ability to prefund future accrued VEBA benefits. These constraints do not apply to a VEBA established pursuant to a collective bargaining agreement. Thus, the VEBA solution is available only as an option for employers with union workers who eventually will be entitled to retiree health care benefits.

2. THE EVOLUTION OF RETIREE HEALTH CARE PLAN CLAIMS IN ERISA LITIGATION

During the 1970s and 1980s, many large employers in traditional manufacturing industries suffered from declining revenues and rising health care plan costs for retired workers. In response, employers attempted to control the costs associated with retiree health care plans. Retirees whose health care plan benefits were reduced or eliminated responded by bringing claims under ERISA.

Many of the early cases involved collective bargaining agreements where the terms of the agreement were silent concerning whether the retiree health care benefits would continue after the agreement expired. The leading case in this early era, *United Automobile Workers v. Yard-Man*, 716 F.2d 1476 (6th Cir. 1983), illustrates the common fact pattern found in many collective bargaining agreement cases. In *Yard-Man*, the employer and the union entered into a collective bargaining agreement for the period 1974–1977. Under the terms of the collective bargaining agreement, the employer agreed to pay for health care insurance benefits for retired workers age sixty-five and older that were equal to the benefits received by active employees. The employer's manufacturing plant closed in 1975, and the employer terminated the employment of its active employees at the facility. The employer continued to pay for health care insurance benefits for retired workers at the closed plant until 1977, when the collective bargaining agreement expired. When the collective bargaining agreement expired in 1977, the employer ceased paying for health care insurance benefits for the retired workers.

The union, acting on behalf of the retired workers, challenged the employer's actions as a breach of the collective bargaining agreement. The collective bargaining agreement did not address explicitly how long retiree health care benefits would continue. The agreement did, however, contain a general duration clause (typically found in all collective bargaining agreements) that provided the employer's obligations under the agreement did not extend beyond the duration of the agreement. The Sixth Circuit concluded that the language of the collective bargaining agreement was ambiguous, and held that under the circumstances an inference was created that the benefits under the retiree health care plan had "vested" and therefore could not be reduced or eliminated by the employer once the collective bargaining agreement expired. The Sixth Circuit justified drawing this inference in part based on the unique nature of retiree health care benefits:

> [R]etiree benefits are in a sense status benefits which, as such carry with them an inference that they continue so long as the prerequisite status is maintained. Thus, when the parties contract for benefits which accrue upon achievement of retiree status, there is an inference that the parties likely intended those benefits to continue as long as the beneficiary remains a retiree. This is not to say that retiree insurance benefits are necessarily interminable by their nature. Nor does any federal labor policy identified to this Court presumptively favor the

> finding of interminable rights to retiree insurance benefits when
> the collective bargaining agreement is silent. Rather, as part of
> the context from which collective bargaining agreement arose,
> the nature of such benefits simply provides another inference of
> intent. Standing alone, this factor would be insufficient to find
> an intent to create interminable benefits. In the present case,
> however, this contextual factor buttresses the already sufficient
> evidence of such intent in the language of this agreement itself.

Id. at 1482. The Sixth Circuit's statements in *Yard-Man* became the
inspiration for subsequent claims based on a "vested rights" theory of
retiree health care benefits. Although *Yard-Man* has never been
overruled by the Sixth Circuit, the persuasive power of the inference that
retiree health benefits granted under a collective bargaining agreement
are vested appears to have been diminished in more recent Sixth Circuit
cases. For example, in *Yolton v. El Paso Tennessee Pipeline Co.*, 435 F.3d
571 (6th Cir. 2006), the Sixth Circuit declared:

> Under *Yard-Man* we may *infer* an intent to vest from the context
> and already sufficient evidence of such intent. Absent such other
> evidence, we do not start our analysis presuming anything. If
> *Yard-Man* required a *presumption*, the burden of rebutting that
> presumption would fall on the defendants. However, under *Yard-*
> *Man*, there is no legal presumption that benefits vest and that
> the burden of proof rests on plaintiffs. This Court has never
> inferred an intent to vest benefits in the absence of either
> explicit contractual language or extrinsic evidence indicating
> such an intent. Rather, the inference functions more to provide a
> contextual understanding about the nature of labor-management
> negotiations over retirement benefits. That is, because
> retirement health care benefits are not mandatory or required to
> be included in an agreement, and because they are typically
> understood as a form of delayed compensation or reward for past
> services, it is unlikely that they would be left to the
> contingencies of future negotiations. When other contextual
> factors so indicate, Yard-Man simply provides another inference
> of intent. All that *Yard-Man* and subsequent cases instruct is
> that the Court should apply ordinary principles of contract
> interpretation.

Id. at 579–80 (emphasis in original, quotations and citations omitted); see
also Winnett v. Caterpillar, Inc., 553 F.3d 1000 (6th Cir. 2009) (holding
that the language of a collective bargaining agreement was unambiguous
in permitting the employer to unilaterally modify retiree health benefits
for active workers who became eligible for such retiree benefits while the
agreement was still in effect, but who did not retire under after the
agreement expired).

When the disputed retiree health benefits are promised as part of a collective bargaining agreement, the First, Fourth, and Eleventh Circuits apply the *Yard-Man* inference in favor of vesting. See United Steelworkers v. Textron, Inc., 836 F.2d 6 (1st Cir. 1987); Keffer v. H.K. Porter Co., 872 F.2d 60 (4th Cir. 1989); United Steelworkers v. Connors Steel Co., 855 F.2d 1499 (11th Cir. 1988). The Third, Fifth, Seventh and Eighth Circuits reject the *Yard-Man*. See United Automobile Workers Int'l Union v. Skinner Engine Co., 188 F.3d 130 (3d Cir. 1999); International Ass'n of Machinists & Aerospace Workers v. Masonite Corp., 122 F.3d 228 (5th Cir. 1997); Rossetto v. Pabst Brewing Co., 217 F.3d 539 (7th Cir. 2000); Anderson v. Alpha Portland Indus., 836 F.2d 1512 (8th Cir. 1988).

Outside of the collective bargaining agreement context, the vested rights theory of retiree health plan benefits often is paired with a claim that the employer is estopped from amending or terminating the retiree health care plan. Estoppel claims typically arise when the employer or the plan administrator has made representations to an employee concerning the availability of retiree health care benefits. Often these representations are made as an inducement to encourage the employee to accept an early retirement offer as part of a program to downsize the employer's workforce. The basic elements of such an estoppel claim are discussed in the Note on Estoppel Claims in Chapter Two of the casebook.

Employers today are keenly aware of possible legal challenges under ERISA to changes in a retiree health plan. In anticipation of a legal challenge, the plan typically contains language that reserves to the employer the right to amend or terminate the retiree health care benefits provided by the employer's plan at any time. *Bland v. Fiataliss North America, Inc.* illustrates this type of ERISA litigation.

BLAND V. FIATALLIS NORTH AMERICA, INC.
United States Court of Appeals, Seventh Circuit, 2005.
401 F.3d 779.

CUDAHY, CIRCUIT JUDGE.

A "lifetime" can be a slippery concept in the context of retiree benefits litigation under the Employee Retirement Income Security Act ("ERISA"). This case asks us to consider, on the heels of *Vallone v. CNA Financial Corporation,* 375 F.3d 623 (7th Cir.2004), whether designating retiree benefits as "lifetime" really means "for life." Unlike previous cases, where the interpretation of explicit "lifetime" language was constrained by reservation of rights clauses allowing an employer to modify or terminate retiree welfare benefits, the plan documents at issue here contain no such limiting language. Accordingly, we find that the "lifetime" language, as used here, is ambiguous as to vesting, and so we reverse the grant of summary judgment to the defendant and remand this case for further proceedings.

I.

The plaintiffs in the present case are former retired salaried and hourly employees of Fiatallis North America, Inc. ("FANA"), who retired in the late 1970s through 1988 and their surviving spouses. Most are at least eighty years of age and are presumably on fixed incomes. Before or upon their retirement, each of the plaintiffs received documents known as summary plan descriptions ("SPDs") that described the medical and dental benefits that they would receive and that allegedly contained explicit promises that retirees and their spouses would continue to receive these benefits at little or no cost until their death.

Of the five SPDs at issue in this case, three refer to salaried employees, and two address hourly employees. We will discuss the SPDs in the chronological order of their issuance. An SPD related to a "Benefit for Retired Salaried Employees Plan," which covers retired salaried employees who retired after Dec. 31, 1976, provides that health insurance and dental " . . . coverage remains in effect as long as you or your surviving spouse are living." The SPD related to a "Group Health Plan for Salaried Active Employees," dated January of 1978 and distributed to active salaried employees, states in pertinent part that upon retirement "benefits continue to be paid for by the Company," and that employees who wish to continue major medical coverage must "continue to pay [their] share of the cost."[1] With respect to retirees' spouses, the plan document states that the "spouse and any eligible dependents . . . can continue the protection" until the spouse "dies, remarries, or is covered by another employee's group plan"; spouses are "required to make monthly payments for both Basic and Major Medical coverage." The two plan documents applicable to hourly employees are essentially identical. The "Health Benefits Plan" and "Benefits for Retired Hourly Employees Plan" documents, created in January of 1978 and distributed to hourly employees at FANA's Carol Stream and Deerfield plants, both state that ". . . [b]enefits are provided to help you meet the expense of illness, injury, and other similar emergencies within your family" and that "[i]f a retired employee dies, the surviving spouse will have basic coverage continued for his or her lifetime at no cost." Finally, plan documents dated March and April of 1985, titled "Benefit Fact Sheets,"[2] that were provided to salaried employees affected by the shutdown of FANA's Springfield plant, state that "[s]alaried employees for retirement will have the retired

---

[1] Plaintiffs contend that this SPD was in effect for active salaried employees from January of 1978 through March or April of 1985.

[2] These documents were never designated by FANA as SPDs.

employee benefits in effect prior to March 1, 1985."[3] None of these documents contain express reservation of rights clauses.

In the mid-1980s, FANA and its Italian parent corporation sought advice from three outside law firms as to whether these retiree plan benefits were vested. The employer had in mind an "onion solution" to deal with rising insurance costs, under which retiree benefits would be gradually peeled away. Lou Bland, a named retiree plaintiff, who served as a former vice-president and member of the Employee Benefits Committee, received copies of documents discussing the onion solution in the course of his employment, and retained these documents upon retirement.

In 1989, FANA published another SPD for active employees that altered the description of plan benefits and expressly reserved the right to amend benefits; this document did not state that these changes were effective with respect to retirees, and no plaintiff received it. Late in 2000, however, the plaintiffs received plan documents containing new benefit descriptions, which stated that costs for medical and dental coverage would dramatically increase as of February 1, 2001, and warned that benefits could be modified even after retirement.[4]

Angered by these modifications, plaintiffs filed suit in Illinois state court, contending that FANA had unilaterally reduced vested benefits by greatly increasing the cost to retirees. The case was then removed by FANA to federal district court. After discovery began, the plaintiffs uncovered documents discussing the "onion solution," and turned the documents over to defense counsel on the grounds that the documents might be privileged. FANA then requested a protective order claiming that the documents were privileged as attorney-client communications or work product and moved for the appointment of a magistrate judge to determine privilege issues. After conducting an *in camera* review, the magistrate judge entered a recommendation that most of the documents, including portions discussing the onion solution, were protected and inadmissible since they contained communications including attorney advice and relating exclusively to amendment or termination of the plan.

---

[3]   Plaintiffs assert that the Benefit Fact sheets referenced the benefits described in the Benefit for Retired Salaried Employees Plan.

[4]   The new "BenefitSelect" Medical Plan implemented on February 1, 2001, increased retiree cost-sharing features. While it contained hospitalization, X-ray, ambulance, emergency room, and office visit coverages similar to those in the pre-1989 plans, it implemented a preferred provider network system. Non-Medicare-eligible retirees were offered PPO, POS, HMO, and basic protection, and Medicare-eligible retirees were offered a non-network plan. Retirees who elected PPO in-network benefits had many of the same coverage levels for many items as provided under the pre-1989 plan, with costs being covered at rates of 90 to 100 percent and with co-payments between $10 and $25. The POS and HMO plans varied in coverage levels and deductibles, depending on residence. Finally, the non-network plan contained a $500 annual deductible and covered 70% of the expenses found in the network plan. The new BenefitSelect Dental Plan changed the percentage of covered expenses depending on whether retirees elected the PPO or the traditional plan, with some levels of coverage (such as for dentures, bridgework, fillings, and crowns) remaining the same or substantially similar.

The magistrate also rejected the plaintiffs' claims that numerous exceptions to the privilege applied.

After the district court accepted the magistrate's recommendations, the plaintiffs filed an amended complaint alleging that FANA had established a new health plan less favorable to plaintiffs in February of 2001 in breach of ERISA contract obligations and that FANA had made oral and written promises vesting health benefits that had been breached, thus violating ERISA fiduciary duties and the principles of estoppel. The plaintiffs never sought to certify any class under Fed.R.Civ.P. 23. The parties then filed cross-motions for judgment on the pleadings as to the alleged breach of the ERISA contract obligations claim. The district court awarded judgment on the pleadings to FANA, and the plaintiffs then voluntarily dismissed their other claims without prejudice in order to pursue an appeal of the ruling relating to the alleged breach of ERISA contract obligations. After the district court questioned whether these matters were in fact ripe for appeal, the plaintiffs agreed to voluntarily dismiss their breach of fiduciary duty and estoppel claims with prejudice. Thus, the only issues before us are whether the plan documents contain language that unambiguously vested ERISA contract rights or that is so ambiguous as to require a trial on the issue of vesting. There is a further question whether the district court erred in not admitting certain documents into evidence under exceptions to the privilege doctrine.

We review the decision to grant FANA's motion for judgment on the pleadings de novo. Forseth v. Village of Sussex, 199 F.3d 363, 368 (7th Cir.2000).

II.

A.

Today's employment market is heavily impacted by the abruptly rising cost of health care, and the ensuing increases in health insurance premiums. The plan documents in the present case, created in the 1970s and 1980s, likely were the product of a social reality different from that now prevailing. Before 1980, employers in many cases, in granting health benefits, did not consider a possible need to modify them in the future. Only later with "spiraling medical costs, heightened foreign competition, epidemic corporate take-overs and the declining bargaining power of labor" was thought given to modifying benefits granted to retirees. See Bidlack v. Wheelabrator Corp., 993 F.2d 603, 613 (7th Cir.1993) (Cudahy, J., concurring). Thus, at the time the relevant plan documents were created, there may not have been much thought given to any language affecting possible future changes in benefits. This expectation has now changed, and many courts have rejected retirees' attempts to show that their benefits have vested under the language of plan documents. Meanwhile, retirees living on limited fixed incomes can be squeezed by unanticipated increases in medical costs. It is with this historical context in mind that we turn to the question whether the FANA plan documents vested retiree health benefits here.

Under ERISA, employee benefit plans are classified either as welfare benefit plans or as pension plans. * * * While pension benefits are subject to strict vesting requirements, welfare benefits such as health and life insurance are vested only if the plan contract so provides. Thus, employers are "generally free . . . for any reason at any time, to adopt, modify or terminate welfare plans." Curtiss-Wright Corp. v. Schoonejongen, 514 U.S. 73, 78 (1995).

Welfare benefits may vest, however, when employers elect to enter into a private contract with employees as set forth in benefit plan documents. If welfare benefits "vest at all, they do so under the terms of a particular contract." Vallone v. CNA Financial Corp., 375 F.3d 623, 632 (7th Cir.2004). An ERISA plan is a contract. Therefore, "[t]he question before us is essentially one of contract interpretation," and so federal principles of contract construction apply. Diehl v. Twin Disc, Inc., 102 F.3d 301, 305 (7th Cir.1996). Under these rules, a document should be read as a whole with all its parts given effect, and related documents must be read together. Murphy v. Keystone Steel & Wire Co., 61 F.3d 560, 565 (7th Cir.1995). In addition, "we will give contract terms their 'ordinary and popular sense' and avoid resort to extrinsic evidence when faced with unambiguous language." Diehl, 102 F.3d at 305. "Contract language is unambiguous if it is susceptible to only one reasonable interpretation." Murphy, 61 F.3d at 566. Only if the language of the plan document is ambiguous and these ambiguities are not clarified elsewhere in the document may we consider evidence of the parties' intent that is extrinsic to the writing. Vallone, 375 F.3d at 632–33.

Upon vesting, benefits become forever unalterable, and because employers are not legally required to vest benefits, the intention to vest must be found in "clear and express language" in plan documents. Plan language should be read "in an ordinary and popular sense," construed as if by a "person of average intelligence and experience." Grun v. Pneumo Abex Corp., 163 F.3d 411, 420 (7th Cir.1998).

We have rejected the position that documents must use the word "vest" or some variant of it, or that the relevant writings must "state unequivocally" that the employer is creating rights that will not expire, since a court should not refuse to enforce a contract simply because the parties fail to use the "prescribed formula." Bidlack v. Wheelabrator Corp., 993 F.2d 603, 607 (7th Cir. 1993). In addition, the same principles apply to a vesting analysis whether the retiree benefits are provided under a collective bargaining agreement or under summary plan documents, since "the same underlying considerations are present irrespective of the particular type of document at issue." UAW v. Skinner

Engine Co., 188 F.3d 130, 139 (3d Cir. 1999). See also Rossetto v. Pabst Brewing Co., Inc., 217 F.3d 539, 541 (7th Cir.2000) (stating that the issue in *Rossetto* was "when a right to health benefits that is granted to retired workers by a collective bargaining agreement (*or an ERISA plan*, but that is not this case) survives the termination of the agreement.") (emphasis added).

This circuit has held that there is a presumption against vesting when there is "silence" that "indicates that welfare benefits are not vested." Vallone, 375 F.3d at 632. * * *

B.

As Judge Posner remarked in *Rossetto*, the presumption against vesting is defeated by "any positive indication of ambiguity, something to make you scratch your head." 217 F.3d at 544. The language contained in the plan documents before us certainly makes us scratch our heads.

"Lifetime" language is found in three plan documents. Thus, the "Benefit for Retired Salaried Employees Plan" document covering retired salaried employees who retired after Dec. 31, 1976, provides that health insurance and dental ". . . coverage remains in effect as long as you or your surviving spouse are living." In addition, the "Health Benefits Plan" and "Benefits for Retired Hourly Employees Plan" documents distributed to hourly employees at FANA's Carol Stream and Deerfield plants state that "[i]f a retired employee dies, the surviving spouse will have basic coverage continued for his or her lifetime at no cost." Finally, the "Benefit Fact Sheets" provided to salaried employees affected by shutdown of FANA's Springfield plant state that employees would have "the retired employee benefits in effect prior to March 1, 1985," which plaintiffs contend were those established in the "Benefit for Retired Salaried Employees Plan," noted above.

But other language in the plan documents is comparatively weak. The January 1978 "Group Health Plan for Active Salaried Employees" document simply assures active salaried employees that "benefits continue to be paid for by the company," and that spouses and dependents "can continue the protection." And the two plan documents directed to hourly employees merely state that "benefits are provided" for retirees. Significantly, there is no express reservation of rights clause in any of the plan documents.

To further complicate the matter, the question arises whether the "Benefits for Retired Salaried Employees Plan" document may be applied to employees who retired after the "Group Health Plan for Active Salaried Employees" was established. The district court found that the "Benefits for Retired Salaried Employees" Plan governed only the claims of salaried employees who retired in 1977 and later stated that this plan was replaced in January of 1978 by the "Group Health Plan for Active

Salaried Employees." The district court also concluded with respect to the 1985 "Benefit Fact Sheets" that they referenced only the January 1978 "Group Health Plan For Active Salaried Employees," and not the "Benefits for Retired Salaried Employees Plan" of 1976 vintage. We are doubtful, however, that such conclusions can be reached on summary judgment.

Whatever plans were in effect at any given time, the "life-time" language in the plan documents leads us to conclude that they are not silent as to vesting, but merely somewhat vague; however, they are clear enough to vitiate the presumption against vesting. The absence of a reservation of rights clause distinguishes this case from *Vallone,* and the "lifetime" language used in the plan documents is stronger and more explicit than language in comparable cases. See Senn v. United Dominion Indus., Inc., 951 F.2d 806, 816 (7th Cir.1992) (holding that language stating welfare benefits "will continue" did not create ambiguity as to vesting). See also Skinner Engine Co., 188 F.3d at 141, 143 (holding that plan language stating that health benefits "will continue" and life insurance "shall remain" at the same level did not unambiguously express an intent to vest benefits for life because there was no durational language, and the language was not ambiguous because it merely indicated a continuation of prior practice and policies). And the language before us is either similar to or more explicit than language that we and other courts have found to be at least ambiguous with respect to vesting. See Rossetto, 217 F.3d at 546 (finding latent ambiguity in collective bargaining agreements conferring benefits upon retirees consisting either of medigap insurance or in line with the coverage given to active employees and stating that benefits would continue for retirees' dependents until the sixth month after the retirees' death); Diehl, 102 F.3d at 306 (holding that a separate agreement containing "lifetime" benefits language stating that retirees would be "entitled [to health benefits] for the lifetime of the petitioner" modified a reservation of rights clause incorporated from another agreement and that retirees were thus entitled to welfare benefits for their lifetimes); Bidlack, 993 F.2d at 606 (construing as ambiguous collective bargaining agreement language providing that retired employees "will have the full cost" of health insurance coverage "paid by the Company" after age 65 and that benefits "shall be continued" for spouses after the retirees' deaths, and finding ambiguity in plan language stating that retirees and spouses "will be covered for the remainder of your lives" at no cost); Int'l Assoc. of Machinists and Aerospace Workers, Woodworkers Division, AFL-CIO v. Masonite, 122 F.3d 228, 233 (5th Cir.1997) (construing as ambiguous language incorporated into collective bargaining agreement stating that retirees were entitled to comprehensive medical benefits "until the death of the retired employee"); UAW v. Yard-Man, Inc., 716 F.2d 1476 (6th Cir.1983) (construing as ambiguous the statement that the "Company will provide insurance benefits equal to the active group benefits for retirees and their spouses"). *Diehl* goes so far as to intimate that "lifetime" language may be *unambiguous,* since such language "stands apart from language we have considered in similar cases in recent years" in which "we are more commonly asked to find an intent to create lifetime entitlements despite terms that are ambiguous or completely silent on the issue." 102 F.2d at 306.

Further, in the absence of a reservation of rights clause, we are convinced (not surprisingly) that in the case before us "lifetime" is durational, meaning "for life." In *Vallone,* we acknowledged alternatively that "lifetime" in the context of "lifetime benefits" could be construed as "good for life unless revoked or modified." 375 F.3d at 633. However, we also noted that this construction of "lifetime" was most plausible if the plan documents included a reservation of rights clause, as was the case in *Vallone.* Id. This is because the presence of a reservation of rights clause fundamentally alters the interpretation of "lifetime" language; both the clause and the "lifetime" language must be read together, creating a tension that is best relieved by finding that retirees are entitled to benefits for life, but that this entitlement is subject to change at the employer's will. See UAW v. Rockford Powertrain, Inc., 350 F.3d 698, 704 (7th Cir.2003) ("We must resolve the tension between the lifetime benefits clause, and the plan termination and reservation of rights clauses, by giving meaning to all of them. Reading the document in its entirety, the clauses explain that although the plan . . . entitles retirees to health coverage for the duration of their lives . . . the terms of the plan—including the plan's continued existence—are subject to change at the will of" the employer). In the absence of a reservation of rights clause, interpreting "lifetime" as being limited by the employer's continuing willingness to provide benefits is unreasonable. In fact, *Vallone* appears to limit the interpretation of "lifetime" as "lifetime subject to change" to cases in which there is a reservation of rights clause. Id. at 634 (stating that "the 'lifetime' nature of a welfare benefit does not operate to vest that benefit *if the employer reserved the right to amend or terminate the benefit.*") (emphasis added).

We thus hold that, under *Vallone* and its antecedents, the presence of "lifetime" language in several of the FANA plan documents—language uncontradicted by the agreement read in its entirety—defeats summary judgment. Vallone, 375 F.3d at 637 (quoting Rossetto, 217 F.3d at 547) ("If there is language in the agreement to suggest a grant of lifetime benefits, and the suggestion is not negated by the agreement read as a whole, the plaintiff is entitled to a trial."). * * *

III.

In holding that the language of several of the plan documents is ambiguous as to vesting, of course we open the door to consideration of extrinsic evidence. However, considerations of privilege may not allow that door to open very far, since the opening may be constrained by the magistrate judge's conclusion that most of the documents to which plaintiffs seek to gain access are protected by the attorney-client and/or work-product privileges.

A.

The appropriate standard of review of a district court's findings of fact regarding claims of attorney-client privilege is the clearly erroneous standard. On appeal, the plaintiffs seek to undermine the claims of attorney-client privilege by relying on two exceptions to that privilege doctrine. The plaintiffs first argue that they should be permitted access to the privileged documents under the breach of fiduciary duty exception. Under that exception, a fiduciary of an ERISA plan "must make available to the beneficiary, upon request, any communications with an attorney that are intended to assist in the administration of the plan." In re Long Island Lighting Co., 129 F.3d 268, 272 (2d Cir.1997). This exception is premised on the theory that the attorney-client privilege should not be used as a shield to prevent disclosure of information relevant to an alleged breach of fiduciary duty.

The magistrate judge determined that the fiduciary exception was not available here since the amendment or termination of plan benefits is not a fiduciary action. Initially, it is questionable whether the fiduciary exception is even applicable, since the plaintiffs voluntarily dismissed their breach of fiduciary duty claim with prejudice, and thus should perhaps not get the benefit of the exception. In any event, we cannot find that the magistrate judge erred in concluding that an employer acts as a fiduciary only when it undertakes plan management or administration. An employer acts in a dual capacity as both the manager of its business and as a fiduciary with respect to unaccrued welfare benefits, is free to alter or eliminate such benefits without considering employees' interests and does not owe its employees a fiduciary duty when it amends or abolishes unaccrued benefits. Young v. Standard Oil, Inc., 849 F.2d 1039, 1045 (7th Cir.1988). Decisions relating to the plan's amendment or termination are not fiduciary decisions. See Hughes Aircraft Co. v. Jacobsen, 525 U.S. 432, 443–44 (1999) (stating that since "employers or other plan sponsors are generally free under ERISA, for any reason at any time, to adopt, modify, or terminate welfare plans," "[w]hen employers undertake those actions, they do not act as fiduciaries, but are analogous to the settlors of a trust."). Plan management, after all, consists of such activities as "investment of pension funds and communications to employees about plan administration." King v.

National Human Resource Committee, 218 F.3d 719, 724 (7th Cir.2000). In addition, we have previously held that amending plan benefits, such as by spinning off plan assets to a new plan, does not implicate fiduciary responsibilities. Id.

B.

The plaintiffs also seek to obviate the work-product doctrine through two exceptions: a "crime/fraud" exception and an "extraordinary need" exception. The magistrate judge stated that the plaintiffs had dropped the crime/fraud exception in their sur-reply, and so did not address that argument. For this reason, we deem this argument waived.

The plaintiffs also assert that they have a substantial need for the documents protected as work-product, claiming that these documents prove that FANA knew its medical benefits were vested as of 1984, and that the plaintiffs would encounter substantial hardship in obtaining the material through alternative means under Fed.R.Civ.P. 26(b)(3). See Hickman v. Taylor, 329 U.S. 495 (1947). The magistrate judge has not yet addressed these issues. We are not unsympathetic to these concerns, and would ask the district court to carefully consider them.

IV.

We therefore hold that the "lifetime" language in several of the FANA plan documents is at least ambiguous as to whether some or all of the retiree benefits are vested. Here, there is no reservation of rights clause to constrain the interpretation of explicit "lifetime" language. If any retiree benefits are in fact vested, then additional determinations will have to be made with respect to which benefits are vested, or whether the 2001 modifications to retiree benefits effectively cut off retirees' rights. Accordingly, we REVERSE the grant of summary judgment to the defendant and REMAND this case for further proceedings consistent with this opinion.

NOTES AND QUESTIONS

1. *"Lifetime" Versus "Vested" Benefits.* The dispute in *Bland* centered around whether a promise of "lifetime" retiree health care benefits should be interpreted to mean that the benefits provided by the plan were "vested" and therefore were not subject to subsequent amendment or modification by the employer. The Seventh Circuit in *Bland* concluded that because the summary plan description documents distributed to the plaintiffs did not expressly reserve to the employer the right to amend or terminate the benefits provided by the plan, the term "lifetime" benefits was sufficiently ambiguous concerning vesting to survive a motion for summary judgment.

In an earlier case, *Vallone v. CNA Financial Corp.*, 375 F.3d 623 (7th Cir. 2004), the Seventh Circuit was faced with similar "lifetime" retiree health care benefits language, but the employer's plan document contained a reservation of rights clause. The Seventh Circuit in *Vallone* determined that under these circumstances the phrase "lifetime" benefits did not connote "vested" benefits.

> We start from the premise that "[e]mployers. . . . are generally free under ERISA, for any reason at any time, to adopt, modify, or terminate welfare plans." Curtiss-Wright Corp. v. Schoonejongen, 514 U.S. 73, 78 (1995). For this reason, if ERISA welfare benefits "vest" at all, they do so under the terms of a particular contract. Pabst Brewing Co. v. Corrao, 161 F.3d 434, 439 (7th Cir. 1998). * * * Given our presumption against the vesting of welfare benefits, silence indicates that welfare benefits are not vested. * * *
>
> The problem for the plaintiffs is that "lifetime" may be construed as "good for life unless revoked or modified." This construction is particularly plausible if the contract documents include a reservation of rights clause (which, as will be shown, is the case here). As laypersons, the plaintiffs' confusion on this issue is understandable; it is also very unfortunate, if it was a basis for their accepting the [early retirement] package. But in the perhaps beady eyes of the law, the "lifetime" nature of a welfare benefit does not operate to vest that benefit if the employer reserved the right to amend or terminate the benefit * * *.

375 F.3d at 632–34. How likely is it that participants will recognize the implications of a reservation of rights clause for their "lifetime" retiree health care benefits? Should the "beady eyes of the law" require that the employer who uses "lifetime" language in describing retiree health care benefits also clearly state whether or not such benefits are "vested"?

2. *Breach of Fiduciary Duty Claims in Lieu of Estoppel.* Employers are highly sensitive to legal challenges resulting from the amendment or termination of a health care or other welfare benefit plan. In response to the threat of potential litigation, employers routinely insert a reservation of rights clause and other relevant language in the plan document and the summary plan description to prevent possible claims based on a vested rights or estoppel theory.

As employers have become more sophisticated in preventing estoppel claims, plaintiffs attempting to challenge an employer's amendment or termination of plan benefits have instead asserted a breach of the fiduciary duty to accurately and fully inform participants about their plan benefits. Such "duty to inform" claims typically allege a misrepresentation by the plan administrator or another plan fiduciary in responding to a participant's questions about the benefits offered under the plan. The plan fiduciary's responses may have conveyed inaccurate information, or may have conveyed incomplete information that was misleading due to the omitted information. The fiduciary's misstatements may have been oral or contained in letters and other informal written communications outside of the plan document and the summary plan description. Duty to inform claims, which are brought under

Section 502(a)(3) of ERISA, are discussed in detail later in Chapter Six of the casebook.

In the specific context of communications concerning retiree health care benefits, the federal courts of appeals are divided over the degree of fiduciary culpability necessary to establish a duty to inform claim. The Seventh Circuit requires that the fiduciary's misrepresentation must have been intentional. See Vallone v. CNA Financial Corp., 375 F.3d 623, 640–42 (7th Cir. 2004); Frahm v. Equitable Life Assurance Soc'y, 137 F.3d 955, 959–60 (7th Cir. 1998). The Second, Third, and Sixth Circuits require only a showing that the fiduciary was negligent in communicating inaccurate or incomplete information. See Abbruscato v. Empire Blue Cross & Blue Shield, 274 F.3d 90, 102–03 (2d Cir. 2001); In re Unisys Corp. Retiree Med. Benefit "ERISA" Litig., 57 F.3d 1255, 1266–67 (3d Cir. 1995); James v. Pirelli Armstrong Tire Corp., 305 F.3d 439, 455–56 (6th Cir. 2002). Notably, in the *Abbruscato*, *Unisys* and *Pirelli Tire* cases the summary plan description contained a reservation of rights clause.

H. DISCUSSION QUESTIONS FOR CHAPTER FOUR

QUESTION ONE

As a matter of public policy, do you favor the reforms enacted by the Affordable Care Act? Why or why not? If you could amend the ACA, which requirements would you retain? Which requirements would you repeal or change?

QUESTION TWO

The Mental Health Parity and Addiction Equity Act is limited in its application to benefits provided by group health plans. Should parity be extended to disability income plans, too?

QUESTION THREE

Has federal regulation of group health plans become as complex as the regulation of qualified retirement plans? Is simplification needed so that employers will not be deterred from sponsoring group health plans? Should Congress simplify the law by eliminating all distinctions between grandfathered and non-grandfathered health care plans? Between insured and self-insured plans?

QUESTION FOUR

As a matter of public policy, is the trend toward consumer-directed health care desirable? Should the federal government do more to educate consumers about health care spending and treatment decisions? Or should employers be required to provide more information so that participants in their health care plans can make more informed choices concerning their health care?

CHAPTER 5

FIDUCIARY DUTIES AND PROHIBITED TRANSACTIONS

■ ■ ■

fiduciary = §3(21)(A)

A. OVERVIEW OF ERISA'S FIDUCIARY RESPONSIBILITY PROVISIONS

ERISA's fiduciary responsibility provisions center around the concept of a fiduciary. ERISA § 3(21)(A). The legal duties and potential liability associated with fiduciary status under this definition are significant. Fiduciaries are subject to ERISA's rules concerning fiduciary and co-fiduciary duties. ERISA §§ 404; 405. Fiduciaries also are subject to the prohibited transaction rules, which prohibit broad categories of transactions between an ERISA fiduciary and an employee benefit plan. ERISA § 406(a)–(b). The prohibited transaction rules also regulate, in a limited fashion, how a fiduciary may invest the assets of an employee benefit plan. ERISA § 407.

In contrast, ERISA imposes relatively few constraints on the conduct of persons who are not fiduciaries. ERISA's fiduciary and co-fiduciary duties do not apply to persons who are not fiduciaries. Although ERISA's prohibited transaction rules prohibit certain transactions between an employee benefit plan and some persons who are not fiduciaries, such transactions are much more likely to qualify for an exemption. ERISA § 408.

Section B of this chapter examines who is a fiduciary for purposes of ERISA. Section C describes the fiduciary responsibilities that ERISA imposes on fiduciaries. ERISA's prohibited transaction rules are discussed in Section D of the chapter. Chapter Five concludes by exploring some of the emerging fiduciary issues associated with 401(k) plans in Section E.

B. WHO IS AN ERISA FIDUCIARY?

ERISA requires that every plan document identify at least one named plan fiduciary. ERISA § 402(a). If plan assets are held in trust, the plan must have at least one trustee. ERISA § 403(a). The named plan fiduciary and the plan's trustee obviously are ERISA fiduciaries. Many employee benefit plans, however, have multiple fiduciaries beyond a named plan fiduciary and a trustee.

ERISA Section 3(21)(A) defines who is a fiduciary. The statutory definition is based on the functions actually performed by the person, rather than on the person's official title. DOL Reg. § 2509.75–8, Questions D–3–D–5. Moreover, a person can be a fiduciary under ERISA without knowing or intending to be a fiduciary. See Freund v. Marshall & Ilsley Bank, 485 F.Supp. 629, 635 (W.D. Wis. 1979) ("It is apparent from the evidence that many of these persons were confused about the nature of their fiduciary duties and indeed unsure whether they were fiduciaries with respect to the Plan. . . . Their state of mind, however, does not determine their fiduciary status under ERISA.").

ERISA Section 3(21)(A) expressly limits fiduciary status "to the extent" the person performs fiduciary functions. This limitation means that the same person can act as an ERISA fiduciary when performing some functions, and yet not be an ERISA fiduciary when performing other nonfiduciary tasks. There are three main categories of fiduciary functions under Section 3(21)(A):

(1) Persons who have discretionary authority over administration and management of the plan;

(2) Persons who have any authority (whether discretionary or not) over the assets of the plan; or,

(3) Persons who render investment advice concerning assets held by the plan for compensation, regardless of whether the compensation is paid out of plan assets and whether the compensation is direct or indirect.

There are four well-recognized exceptions to fiduciary status. First, persons who assist in plan administration or management, but who perform only *ministerial functions*, are not plan fiduciaries. DOL Reg. § 2509.75–8, Questions D–2, D–3. Second, professionals such as attorneys, accountants, actuaries, and other consultants who assist in the administration and management of the plan by rendering *professional services* ordinarily are not considered to be fiduciaries of the plan. DOL Reg. § 2509.75–5, Question D–1. Third, persons who *provide investment education* (as opposed to investment advice for compensation) are not fiduciaries. DOL Reg. § 2509.96–1. Finally, an employer does not act as a plan fiduciary when it performs certain actions known as *settlor functions*. Settlor functions of the employer include establishing, designing, terminating, or amending an employee benefit plan. The settlor function doctrine, a judicially created exception, is discussed in *Curtiss-Wright Corp. v. Schoonejongen,* reproduced in Chapter Two, and in *Lockheed Corporation v. Spink,* reproduced in Section D of Chapter Five.

Fiduciary status is a crucial (and hotly contested) threshold issue in much of ERISA litigation. Whether or not a defendant is an ERISA fiduciary often is determinative of the defendant's liability. The Supreme

Court's opinions in *Varity Corporation v. Howe*, reproduced below, and *Pegram v. Herdrich,* reproduced after *Varity*, illustrate this situation. As you read these two decisions, compare how the Supreme Court applied the statutory definition of a fiduciary to the particular facts of each case.

VARITY CORPORATION V. HOWE

United States Supreme Court, 1996.
516 U.S. 489, 116 S.Ct. 1065, 134 L.Ed.2d 130.

JUSTICE BREYER delivered the opinion of the Court.

A group of beneficiaries of a firm's employee welfare benefit plan, protected by the Employee Retirement Income Security Act of 1974 (ERISA), have sued their plan's administrator, who was also their employer. They claim that the administrator, through trickery, led them to withdraw from the plan and to forfeit their benefits. They seek, among other things, an order that, in essence, would reinstate each of them as a participant in the employer's ERISA plan. The lower courts entered judgment in the employees' favor, and we agreed to review that judgment.

In conducting our review, we do not question the lower courts' findings of serious deception by the employer, but instead consider three legal questions. First, in the factual circumstances (as determined by the lower courts), was the employer acting in its capacity as an ERISA "fiduciary" when it significantly and deliberately misled the beneficiaries? Second, in misleading the beneficiaries, did the employer violate the fiduciary obligations that ERISA § 404 imposes upon plan administrators? Third, does ERISA § 502(a)(3) authorize ERISA plan beneficiaries to bring a lawsuit, such as this one, that seeks relief for individual beneficiaries harmed by an administrator's breach of fiduciary obligations?

We answer each of these questions in the beneficiaries' favor, and we therefore affirm the judgment of the Court of Appeals.

I

The key facts, as found by the District Court after trial, include the following: Charles Howe, and the other respondents, used to work for Massey-Ferguson, Inc., a farm equipment manufacturer, and a wholly owned subsidiary of the petitioner, Varity Corporation. (Since the lower courts found that Varity and Massey-Ferguson were "alter egos," we shall refer to them interchangeably.) These employees all were participants in, and beneficiaries of, Massey-Ferguson's self-funded employee welfare benefit plan—an ERISA-protected plan that Massey-Ferguson itself administered. In the mid-1980's, Varity became concerned that some of Massey-Ferguson's divisions were losing too much money and developed a business plan to deal with the problem.

The business plan—which Varity called "Project Sunshine"—amounted to placing many of Varity's money-losing eggs in one financially rickety basket. It called for a transfer of Massey-Ferguson's money-losing divisions, along with various other debts, to a newly created, separately incorporated subsidiary called Massey Combines. The plan foresaw the possibility that Massey Combines would fail. But it viewed such a failure, from Varity's business perspective, as closer to a victory than to a defeat. That is because Massey Combine's failure would not only eliminate several of Varity's poorly performing divisions, but it would also eradicate various debts that Varity would transfer to Massey Combines, and which, in the absence of the reorganization, Varity's more profitable subsidiaries or divisions might have to pay.

the deception

Among the obligations that Varity hoped the reorganization would eliminate were those arising from the Massey-Ferguson benefit plan's promises to pay medical and other nonpension benefits to employees of Massey-Ferguson's money-losing divisions. Rather than terminate those benefits directly (as it had retained the right to do), Varity attempted to avoid the undesirable fallout that could have accompanied cancellation by inducing the failing divisions' employees to switch employers and thereby voluntarily release Massey-Ferguson from its obligation to provide them benefits (effectively substituting the new, self-funded Massey Combines benefit plan for the former Massey-Ferguson plan). Insofar as Massey-Ferguson's employees did so, a subsequent Massey Combines failure would eliminate—simply and automatically, without distressing the remaining Massey-Ferguson employees—what would otherwise have been Massey-Ferguson's obligation to pay those employees their benefits.

To persuade the employees of the failing divisions to accept the change of employer and benefit plan, Varity called them together at a special meeting and talked to them about Massey Combines' future business outlook, its likely financial viability, and the security of their employee benefits. The thrust of Varity's remarks was that the employees' benefits would remain secure if they voluntarily transferred to Massey Combines. As Varity knew, however, the reality was very different. Indeed, the District Court found that Massey Combines was insolvent from the day of its creation and that it hid a $46 million negative net worth by overvaluing its assets and underestimating its liabilities.

After the presentation, about 1,500 Massey-Ferguson employees accepted Varity's assurances and voluntarily agreed to the transfer. * * * Unfortunately for these employees, Massey Combines ended its first year with a loss of $88 million, and ended its second year in a receivership, under which its employees lost their nonpension benefits. Many of those employees * * * brought this lawsuit, seeking the benefits they would have been owed under their old, Massey-Ferguson plan, had they not transferred to Massey Combines.

After trial, the District Court found, among other things, that Varity and Massey-Ferguson, acting as ERISA fiduciaries, had harmed the plan's beneficiaries through deliberate deception. The court held that Varity and Massey-Ferguson thereby violated an ERISA-imposed fiduciary obligation to administer Massey-Ferguson's benefit plan "solely in the interest of the participants and beneficiaries" of the plan. ERISA § 404(a). The court added that ERISA § 502(a)(3) gave the former Massey-Ferguson employees a right to "appropriate equitable relief . . . to redress" the harm that this deception had caused them individually. Among other remedies the court considered "appropriate equitable relief" was an order that Massey-Ferguson reinstate its former employees into its own plan (which had continued to provide benefits to employees of Massey-Ferguson's profitable divisions). * * *

dist. ct.
findings

We granted certiorari in this case primarily because the Courts of Appeals have disagreed about the proper interpretation of ERISA § 502(a)(3), the provision the District Court held authorized the lawsuit and relief in this case. Some Courts of Appeals have held that this section, when applied to a claim of breach of fiduciary obligation, does not authorize awards of relief to individuals, but instead only authorizes suits to obtain relief for the *plan* (as, for example, when a beneficiary sues in a representative capacity, seeking to compel a dishonest fiduciary to return embezzled funds to the plan). Other Courts of Appeals, such as the Eighth Circuit in this case, have not read any such limitation into the statute.

reason cert
who granted

Varity has raised two additional issues. First, Varity points out that the relevant ERISA section imposes liability only upon plan *fiduciaries;* and it argues that it was acting only as an *employer* and not as a plan *fiduciary* when it deceived its employees. Second, it argues that, in any event, its conduct did not violate the fiduciary standard that ERISA imposes.

issues raised
by Varity

We consider all three issues to be fairly within the scope of the questions that Varity posed in its petition for certiorari. * * *

II

ERISA protects employee pensions and other benefits by providing insurance (for vested pension rights, see ERISA § 4001 et seq.), specifying certain plan characteristics in detail (such as when and how pensions vest, see ERISA §§ 201–211), and by setting forth certain general fiduciary duties applicable to the management of both pension and nonpension benefit plans. See ERISA § 404. In this case, we interpret and apply these general fiduciary duties and several related statutory provisions. In doing so, we recognize that these fiduciary duties draw

[handwritten margin note: fiduciary obligations of ERISA stem from TRUST law]

much of their content from the common law of trusts, the law that governed most benefit plans before ERISA's enactment.

. We also recognize, however, that trust law does not tell the entire story. After all, ERISA's standards and procedural protections partly reflect a congressional determination that the common law of trusts did not offer completely satisfactory protection. See ERISA § 2(a). And, even with respect to the trust-like fiduciary standards ERISA imposes, Congress "expected that the courts will interpret this prudent man rule (and the other fiduciary standards) bearing in mind the special nature and purpose of employee benefit plans," as they "develop a 'federal common law of rights and obligations under ERISA-regulated plans.'" Firestone Tire & Rubber Co. v. Bruch, 489 U.S. 101, 110–111 (1989) (quoting Pilot Life Ins. Co. v. Dedeaux, 481 U.S. 41, 56 (1987)).

Consequently, we believe that the law of trusts often will inform, but will not necessarily determine the outcome of, an effort to interpret ERISA's fiduciary duties. In some instances, trust law will offer only a starting point, after which courts must go on to ask whether, or to what extent, the language of the statute, its structure, or its purposes require departing from common law trust requirements. And, in doing so, courts may have to take account of competing congressional purposes, such as Congress' desire to offer employees enhanced protection for their benefits, on the one hand, and, on the other, its desire not to create a system that is so complex that administrative costs, or litigation expenses, unduly discourage employers from offering welfare benefit plans in the first place. Compare ERISA § 2 with Curtiss-Wright Corp. v. Schoonejongen, 514 U.S. 73, 78–81 (1995), and with Mertens v. Hewitt Associates, 508 U.S. 248, 262–263 (1993).

We have followed this approach when interpreting, and applying, the statutory provisions here before us.

A

[handwritten margin note: definition of fiduciary under ERISA]

We begin with the question of Varity's fiduciary status. In relevant part, the statute says that a "person is a fiduciary with respect to a plan," and therefore subject to ERISA fiduciary duties, "to the extent" that he or she "exercises any discretionary authority or discretionary control respecting management" of the plan, or "has any discretionary authority or discretionary responsibility in the administration" of the plan. ERISA § 3(21)(A).

Varity was *both* an employer *and* the benefit plan's administrator, as ERISA permits. Compare ERISA § 3(16) (employer is, in some circumstances, the default plan administrator) with NLRB v. Amax Coal Co., 453 U.S. 322, 329–30 (1981) (common law of trusts prohibits fiduciaries from holding positions that create conflict of interest with trust beneficiaries). But, obviously, not all of Varity's business activities involved plan management or administration. Varity argues that when it communicated with its Massey-Ferguson workers about transferring to Massey Combines, it was not administering or managing the plan; rather, it was acting only in its capacity as an *employer* and not as a plan *administrator.*

[handwritten margin note: Varity argument]

The District Court, however, held that when the misrepresentations regarding employee benefits were made, Varity was wearing its "fiduciary," as well as its "employer," hat. In reviewing this legal conclusion, we give deference to the factual findings of the District Court, recognizing its comparative advantage in understanding the specific context in which the events of this case occurred. We believe that these factual findings (which Varity does not challenge) adequately support the District Court's holding that Varity was exercising "discretionary authority" respecting the plan's "management" or "administration" when it made these misrepresentations. * * *

[handwritten margin note: deference to fact findings]

The relevant factual circumstances include the following: In the spring of 1986, Varity summoned the employees of Massey-Ferguson's money-losing divisions to a meeting at Massey-Ferguson's corporate headquarters for a 30-minute presentation. The employees saw a 90-second videotaped message from Mr. Ivan Porter, a Varity vice president and Massey Combines' newly appointed president. They also received four documents:

(a) a several-page, detailed comparison between the employee benefits offered by Massey-Ferguson and those offered by Massey Combines;

(b) a question-and-answer sheet;

(c) a transcript of the Porter videotape; and

(d) a cover letter with an acceptance form.

Each of these documents discussed employee benefits and benefit plans, some briefly in general terms, and others at length and in detail:

(a) The longest document, the side-by-side benefits comparison, contained a fairly detailed description of the benefit plans. Its object was to show that after transfer, the employees' benefits would remain the same. It says, for example, that, under Massey-Ferguson's plan, "diagnostic x-ray and laboratory expenses will be paid on the basis of reasonable and customary charges for such services." It then repeats the same sentence in describing Massey Combines' "diagnostic x-ray and laboratory expenses" benefits. It describes about 20 different benefits in this way.

(b) The eight questions and answers on the question-and-answer sheet include three that relate to welfare benefits or to the ERISA pension plan Varity also administered:

Q.   3. What happens to my benefits, pension, etc.?

A.   3. When you transfer to MCC [Massey Combines], pay levels and benefit programmes will remain unchanged. There will be no loss of seniority or pensionable service.

Q.   4. Do you expect the terms and conditions of employment to change?

A.   4. Employment conditions in the future will depend on our ability to make Massey Combines Corporation a success and if changes are considered necessary or appropriate, they will be made.

* * *

Q.   8. Are the pensions protected under MCC?

A.   8. Responsibility for pension benefits earned by employees transferring to Massey Combines Corporation is being assumed by the Massey Combines Corporation Pension Plan.

The assets which are held in the Massey Ferguson Pension Plan to fund such benefits, as determined by actuarial calculations, are being transferred to the Massey Combines Corporation Plan. Such benefits and assets will be protected by the same legislation that protects the Massey Ferguson Pension Plan.

There will be no change in pension benefits as a result of your transfer to Massey Combines Corporation.

(c) The transcript of the 90-second videotape message repeated much of the information in the question-and-answer sheet, adding assurances about Massey Combines' viability:

This financial restructuring created Massey Combines Corporation and will provide the funds necessary to ensure its future viability. I believe that with the continued help and support of you we can make Massey Combines Corporation the kind of successful business enterprise which we all want to work for. . . .

When you transfer your employment to the Massey Combines Corporation, pay levels and benefit programs will remain unchanged. There will be no loss of seniority or pensionable service. Employment conditions in the future will depend on the success of the Massey Combines Corporation and should changes be deemed appropriate or necessary, they will be made. . . .

Finally, despite the depression which persists in the North American economy, I am excited about the future of Massey Combines Corporation.

(d) The cover letter, in five short paragraphs, repeated verbatim these benefit-related assurances:

To enable us to accept you as an employee of Massey Combines Corporation and to continue to process the payment of benefits to you, we require that you complete the information below and return this letter. . . .

When you accept employment with Massey Combines Corporation, pay levels and benefit programs will remain unchanged. There will be no loss of seniority or pensionable service. Employment conditions in the future will depend on our ability to make Massey Combines Corporation a success, and if changes are considered necessary or appropriate, they will be made.

We are all very optimistic that our new company, has a bright future, and are excited by the new challenges facing all of us. . . .

In order to ensure uninterrupted continuation of your pay and benefits, please return this signed acceptance of employment. . . .

Given this record material, the District Court determined, as a factual matter, that the key meeting, to a considerable extent, was about benefits, for the documents described them in detail, explained the similarity between past and future plans in principle, and assured the employees that they would continue to receive similar benefits in practice. The District Court concluded that the basic message conveyed to the employees was that transferring from Massey-Ferguson to Massey Combines would not significantly undermine the security of their benefits. And, given this view of the facts, we believe that the District Court reached the correct legal conclusion, namely, that Varity spoke, in significant part, in its capacity as plan administrator.

To decide whether Varity's actions fall within the statutory definition of "fiduciary" acts, we must interpret the statutory terms which limit the scope of fiduciary activity to discretionary acts of plan "management" and "administration." ERISA § 3(21)(A). These words are not self-defining, and the activity at issue here neither falls clearly within nor outside of the common understanding of these words. The dissent looks to the dictionary for interpretive assistance. Though dictionaries sometimes help in such matters, we believe it more important here to look to the common law, which, over the years, has given to terms such as "fiduciary" and trust "administration" a legal meaning to which, we normally presume, Congress meant to refer. See, e.g., Nationwide Mut. Ins. Co. v. Darden, 503 U.S. 318, 322 (1992). The ordinary trust law understanding of fiduciary "administration" of a trust is that to act as an administrator is to perform the duties imposed, or exercise the powers conferred, by the trust documents. See Restatement (Second) of Trusts § 164 (1957). The law of trusts also understands a trust document to implicitly confer "such powers as are necessary or appropriate for the carrying out of the purposes" of the trust. 3 A. Scott & W. Fratcher, Law of Trusts § 186, p. 6 (4th ed.1988). See also G. Bogert & G. Bogert, Law of Trusts and Trustees § 551, p. 41 (rev. 2d ed. 1992). Conveying information about the likely future of plan benefits, thereby permitting beneficiaries to make an informed choice about continued participation, would seem to be an exercise of a power "appropriate" to carrying out an important plan purpose. After all, ERISA itself specifically requires administrators to give beneficiaries certain information about the plan. See, e.g., ERISA §§ 102; 104(b)(1); 105(a). And administrators, as part of their administrative responsibilities, frequently offer beneficiaries more than the minimum information that the statute requires—for example, answering beneficiaries' questions about the meaning of the terms of a plan so that those beneficiaries can more easily obtain the plan's benefits. To offer beneficiaries detailed plan information in order to help them decide whether to remain with the plan is essentially the same kind of plan-related activity. Cf. Restatement (Second) of Agency § 229(1) (1957) (determining whether an activity is within the "scope of . . . employment" in part by examining whether it is "of the same general nature as that authorized").

Moreover, as far as the record reveals, Mr. Porter's letter, videotape, and the other documents came from those within the firm who had authority to communicate as fiduciaries with plan beneficiaries. Varity does not claim that it authorized only special individuals, not connected with the meeting documents, to speak as plan administrators. See ERISA § 402(b)(2) (a plan may describe a "procedure under the plan for the allocation of responsibilities for the operation and administration of the plan").

Finally, reasonable employees, in the circumstances found by the District Court, could have thought that Varity was communicating with them *both* in its capacity as employer *and* in its capacity as plan administrator. Reasonable employees might not have distinguished consciously between the two roles. But they would have known that the employer was their plan's administrator and had expert knowledge about how their plan worked. The central conclusion ("your benefits are secure") could well have drawn strength from their awareness of that expertise, and one could reasonably believe that the employer, aware of the importance of the matter, so intended.

We conclude, therefore, that the factual context in which the statements were made, combined with the plan-related nature of the activity, engaged in by those who had plan-related authority to do so, together provide sufficient support for the District Court's legal conclusion that Varity was acting as a fiduciary.

Varity raises three contrary arguments. First, Varity argues that it was not engaged in plan administration because neither the specific disclosure provisions of ERISA, nor the specific terms of the plan instruments *required* it to make these statements. But that does not mean Varity was not engaging in plan administration in making them, as the dissent seems to suggest. There is more to plan (or trust) administration than simply complying with the specific duties imposed by the plan documents or statutory regime; it also includes the activities that are "ordinary and natural means" of achieving the "objective" of the plan. Bogert & Bogert, supra, § 551, at 41–52. Indeed, the primary function of the fiduciary duty is to constrain the exercise of *discretionary* powers which are controlled by no other specific duty imposed by the trust instrument or the legal regime. If the fiduciary duty applied to nothing more than activities already controlled by other specific legal duties, it would serve no purpose.

[handwritten margin note: Varity's argument, ERISA did not require the disclosures made]

Second, Varity says that when it made the statements that most worried the District Court—the statements about Massey Combines' "bright future"—it must have been speaking only as employer (and not as fiduciary), for statements about a new subsidiary's financial future have virtually nothing to do with administering benefit plans. But this argument parses the meeting's communications too finely. The ultimate message Varity intended to convey—"your benefits are secure"—depended in part upon its repeated assurances that benefits would remain "unchanged," in part upon the detailed comparison of benefits, and in part upon assurances about Massey Combines' "bright" financial future. Varity's workers would not necessarily have focused upon each underlying supporting statement separately, because what primarily interested them, and what primarily interested the District Court, was the truthfulness of the ultimate conclusion that transferring to Massey Combines would not adversely affect the security of their benefits. And, in the present context Varity's statements about the security of benefits amounted to an act of plan administration. That Varity intentionally communicated its conclusion through a closely linked set of statements (some directly concerning plan benefits, others concerning the viability of the corporation) does not change this conclusion.

[handwritten margin note: Sec., Varity argument]

We do not hold, as the dissent suggests, that Varity acted as a fiduciary simply because it made statements about its expected financial condition or because "an ordinary business decision turn[ed] out to have an adverse impact on the plan." Instead, we accept the undisputed facts found, and factual inferences drawn, by the District Court, namely, that Varity *intentionally* connected its statements about Massey Combines' financial health to statements it made about the future of benefits, so that its intended communication about the security of benefits was rendered materially misleading. And we hold that making intentional representations about the future of plan benefits in that context is an act of plan administration.

Varity's third argument

Third, Varity says that an employer's decision to amend or terminate a plan (as Varity had the right to do) is not an act of plan administration. See Curtiss-Wright Corp., 514 U.S. at 78–81. How then, it asks, could conveying information about the likelihood of termination be an act of plan administration? While it may be true that amending or terminating a plan (or a common-law trust) is beyond the power of a plan administrator (or trustee)—and, therefore, cannot be an act of plan "management" or "administration"—it does not follow that making statements about the likely future of the plan is also beyond the scope of plan administration. As we explained above, plan administrators often have, and commonly exercise, discretionary authority to communicate with beneficiaries about the future of plan benefits.

B

The second question—whether Varity's deception violated ERISA-imposed fiduciary obligations—calls for a brief, affirmative answer. ERISA requires a "fiduciary" to "discharge his duties with respect to a plan solely in the interest of the participants and beneficiaries." ERISA § 404(a). To participate knowingly and significantly in deceiving a plan's beneficiaries in order to save the employer money at the beneficiaries' expense is not to act "solely in the interest of the participants and beneficiaries." As other courts have held, "[l]ying is inconsistent with the duty of loyalty owed by all fiduciaries and codified in Section 404(a)(1) of ERISA." Peoria Union Stock Yards Co. v. Pennsylvania Mut. Life Ins. Co., 698 F.2d 320, 326 (7th Cir. 1983). Because the breach of this duty is sufficient to uphold the decision below, we need not reach the question whether ERISA fiduciaries have any fiduciary duty to disclose truthful information on their own initiative, or in response to employee inquiries.

We recognize, as mentioned above, that we are to apply common-law trust standards "bearing in mind the special nature and purpose of employee benefit plans." H.R. Conf. Rep. No. 93–1280, p. 302 (1973). But we can find no adequate basis here, in the statute or otherwise, for any special interpretation that might insulate Varity, acting as a fiduciary, from the legal consequences of the kind of conduct (intentional misrepresentation) that often creates liability even among strangers.

We are aware, as *Varity* suggests, of one possible reason for a departure from ordinary trust law principles. In arguing about ERISA's remedies for breaches of fiduciary obligation, Varity says that Congress intended ERISA's fiduciary standards to protect only the financial integrity of the plan, not individual beneficiaries. This intent, says Varity, is shown by the fact that Congress did not provide remedies for individuals harmed by such breaches; rather, Congress limited relief to remedies that would benefit only the plan itself. This argument fails, however, because, in our view, Congress *did* provide remedies for individual beneficiaries harmed by breaches of fiduciary duty, as we shall next discuss.

C

The remaining question before us is whether or not the remedial provision of ERISA that the beneficiaries invoked, ERISA § 502(a)(3), authorizes this lawsuit for individual relief. * * *

[The remainder of Part C of the majority opinion is reproduced in Chapter Six of the casebook.—Ed.]

JUSTICE THOMAS, with whom JUSTICE O'CONNOR and JUSTICE SCALIA join, dissenting.

* * *

II

Even assuming that ERISA authorizes recovery for breach of fiduciary duty by individual plan participants, I cannot agree with the majority that Varity committed any breach of fiduciary duty cognizable under ERISA. Section 3(21)(A) of the Act explicitly defines the extent to which a person will be considered a fiduciary under ERISA. In place of the statutory language, the majority creates its own standard for determining fiduciary status. But constrained, as I am, to follow the command of the statute, I conclude that Varity's conduct is not actionable as a fiduciary breach under the Act.

A

Under ERISA, an employer is permitted to act both as plan sponsor and plan administrator. § 408(c)(3). Employers who choose to administer their own plans assume responsibilities to both the company and the plan, and, accordingly, owe duties of loyalty and care to both entities. In permitting such arrangements, which ordinary trust law generally forbids due to the inherent potential for conflict of interest, Congress understood that the interests of the plan might be sacrificed if an employer were forced to choose between the company and the plan. Hence, Congress imposed on plan administrators a duty of care that requires them to "discharge [their] duties with respect to a plan solely in the interest of the participants and beneficiaries." ERISA § 404(a)(1). Congress also understood, however, that virtually every business decision an employer makes can have an adverse impact on the plan, and that an employer would not be able to run a company profitably if every business decision had to be made in the best interests of plan participants.

. In defining the term "fiduciary" in § 3(21)(A) of ERISA, Congress struck a balance that it believed would protect plan participants without impinging on the ability of employers to make business decisions. In recognition that ERISA allows trustee-beneficiary arrangements that the common law of trusts generally forbids, Congress "define[d] 'fiduciary' not in terms of formal trusteeship, but in *functional* terms of control and authority over the plan." Mertens v. Hewitt Assoc., 508 U.S. 248, 262 (1993). Accordingly, under ERISA, a person "is a fiduciary with respect to a plan" only "to the extent" that "he has any discretionary authority or discretionary responsibility in the administration of such plan." ERISA § 3(21)(A)(iii). This "artificial definition of 'fiduciary,' " Mertens, supra, at 255 n.5, is designed, in part, so that an employer that administers its own plan is not a fiduciary to the plan for all purposes and at all times, but only to the extent that it has discretionary authority to administer the plan. When the employer is not acting as plan administrator, it is not a fiduciary under the Act, and the fiduciary duty of care codified in § 404 is not activated.

Though we have recognized that Congress borrowed from the common law of trusts in enacting ERISA, Firestone Tire & Rubber Co. v. Bruch, 489 U.S. 101, 111 (1989), we must not forget that ERISA is a statute, and in "every case involving construction of a statute," the "starting point . . . is the language itself." Ernst & Ernst v. Hochfelder, 425 U.S. 185, 197 (1976). We should be particularly careful to abide by the statutory text in this case, since, as explained, ERISA's statutory definition of a fiduciary departs from the common law in an important respect. The majority, however, tells us that the "starting point" in determining fiduciary status under ERISA is the common law of trusts. According to the majority, it is only "after" courts assess the common law that they may "go on" to consider the statutory definition, and even then the statutory inquiry is only "to ask whether, or to what extent, the language of the statute, its structure, or its purposes require departing from common-law trust requirements." This is a novel approach to statutory construction, one that stands our traditional approach on its head.

To determine whether an employer acts as a fiduciary under ERISA, I begin with the text of § 3(21)(A)(iii). To "administer" a plan is to "manage or supervise the execution . . . or conduct of" the plan. Webster's Ninth New Collegiate Dictionary 57 (1991). Essentially, to administer the plan is to implement its provisions and to carry out plan duties imposed by the Act. The question in this case is whether Varity was carrying out discretionary responsibilities over management or implementation of the plan, when, as respondents argued below, it "made misrepresentations to the class plaintiffs about MCC's business prospects and about the anticipated effect of the employment transfers on plaintiffs' benefits." Although representations of this sort may well affect plan participants' assessment of the security of their benefits, I disagree with the majority that such communications qualify as "plan administration" under the Act.

In the course of running a business, an employer that administers its own benefits plan will make countless business decisions that affect the plan. Congress made clear in § 3(21)(A), however, that "ERISA does not require that day-to-day corporate business transactions, which may have a collateral effect on prospective, contingent employee benefits, be performed solely in the interest of plan participants." Adams v. Avondale Indus., Inc., 905 F.2d 943, 947 (6th Cir. 1990). Thus, ordinary business decisions, such as whether to pay a dividend or to incur debt, may be made without fear of liability for breach of fiduciary duty under ERISA, even though they may turn out to have negative consequences for plan participants. Even business decisions that directly affect the plan and plan participants, such as the decision to modify or terminate welfare benefits, are not governed by ERISA's fiduciary obligations because they do not involve discretionary administration of the plan. See Curtiss-Wright Corp. v. Schoonejongen, 514 U.S. 73, 78 (1995). In contrast, the discretionary interpretation of a plan term, or the discretionary determination that the plan does not authorize a certain type of procedure, would likely qualify as plan administration by a fiduciary. There is no claim in this case, however, that Varity failed to implement the plan according to its terms, since respondents actually received all of the benefits to which they were entitled under the plan, as the courts below found.

An employer will also make countless representations in the course *fiduciary obl.* of managing a business about the current and expected financial *do not apply* condition of the corporation. Similarly, an employer may make *when making* representations that either directly or impliedly evince an intention to *representations* increase, decrease, or maintain employee welfare benefits. Like the decision to terminate or modify welfare benefits, the decision to make, or not to make, such representations is made in the employer's "corporate nonfiduciary capacity as plan sponsor or settlor," Borst v. Chevron Corp., 36 F.3d 1308, 1323 n.28 (5th Cir. 1994), and ERISA's fiduciary rules do not apply. Such communications simply are not made in the course of implementing the plan or executing its terms. Rather, they are the necessary incidents of conducting a business, and Congress determined that employers would not be burdened with fiduciary obligations to the plan when engaging in such conduct. See ERISA § 3(21)(A)(iii).

To be sure, ERISA does impose a "comprehensive set of 'reporting and disclosure' requirements," which is part of "an elaborate scheme . . .

for enabling beneficiaries to learn their rights and obligations at any time." Curtiss-Wright Corp. v. Schoonejongen, supra, at 83; see ERISA §§ 101–111. But no provision of ERISA requires an employer to keep plan participants abreast of the plan sponsor's financial security or of the sponsor's future intentions with regard to terminating or reducing the level of benefits. And to the extent that ERISA does impose disclosure obligations, the Act already provides for civil liability and penalties for disclosure violations wholly apart from ERISA's provisions governing fiduciary duties. See ERISA §§ 502(a)(1)(A); 502(c). Though "[t]his may not be a foolproof informational scheme, . . . it is quite thorough." Curtiss-Wright Corp., supra, at 84. Congress' decision not to include the types of representations at issue in this case within the Act's extensive disclosure requirements is strong evidence that Congress did not consider such statements to qualify as "plan administration."

Because an employer's representations about the company's financial prospects or about the possible impact of ordinary business transactions on the security of unvested welfare benefits do not involve execution or implementation of duties imposed by the plan or the Act, and because these are the types of representations employers regularly make in the ordinary course of running a business, I would not hold that such communications involve plan administration. The untruthfulness of a statement cannot magically transform it from a nonfiduciary representation into a fiduciary one; the determinative factor is not truthfulness but the capacity in which the statement is made.

* * *

The majority confirms that the statutory text is largely irrelevant under its approach by indulging the notion that a plan participant's subjective understanding of the employers' conduct is relevant in determining whether an employer's actions qualify as "plan administration" under ERISA. The majority concludes that Varity was engaged in plan administration in part on the ground that "reasonable employees . . . could have thought" that Varity was administering the plan. ERISA does not make a person a fiduciary to the extent reasonable employees believe him to be a fiduciary, but rather to the extent "he has any discretionary authority or discretionary responsibility in the administration of such plan." ERISA § 3(21)(A)(iii). Under ERISA, an act either involves plan administration, or it does not; whether the employees have a subjective belief that the employer is acting as a fiduciary cannot matter. A rule turning on the subjective perceptions of plan participants is simply inconsistent with ERISA's fundamental structure, which is built not upon perceptions, but "around reliance on the face of written plan documents." Curtiss-Wright Corp., 514 U.S. at 83.

* * *

III

I do not read the Court's opinion to extend fiduciary liability to all instances in which the Court's rationale would logically apply. Indeed, the Court's awkward articulation of its holding confirms that this case is quite limited.

If not limited to cases involving facts similar to those presented in this case, the Court's expansion of recovery for fiduciary breach to individuals and its substantial broadening of the definition of fiduciary will undermine the careful balance Congress struck in enacting ERISA. See Pilot Life Ins. Co. v. Dedeaux, 481 U.S. 41, 54 (1987). Although Congress sought to guarantee that employees receive the welfare benefits promised by employers, Congress was also aware that if the cost of providing welfare benefits rose too high, employers would not provide them at all. Application of the Court's holding in the many cases in which it may logically apply could result in significantly increased liability, or at the very least heightened litigation costs, and an eventual reduction in plan benefits to accommodate those costs. Fortunately, the import of the Court's holdings appears to be far more modest, and courts should not feel compelled to bind employers to the strict fiduciary standards of ERISA just because an ordinary business decision turns out to have an adverse impact on the plan.

I respectfully dissent.

NOTES AND QUESTIONS

1. How did a majority of the Supreme Court in *Varity* define the terms "management" and "administration" under ERISA Section 3(21)(A)? What sources of law did the majority look to in defining these terms? What other factors did the majority consider in determining that Varity Corporation and its officers were fiduciaries? How would the dissenting Justices in *Varity* define these terms? Which approach do you think is more consistent with Congress's goals in enacting ERISA?

2. Describe Varity Corporation's three arguments as to why it was not an ERISA fiduciary. Why did a majority of the Supreme Court reject each of these arguments? Do you find the majority's reasoning persuasive? Why or why not?

3. Why did the employer Varity Corporation choose this scheme rather than simply terminating the welfare benefit plans offered to employees of Massey Combines? Do you find the purported business rationale for the scheme—to avoid distressing the remaining Massey-Ferguson employees— credible? How would you have advised Varity Corporation in this situation?

4. *Communications with Plan Participants.* One of the most controversial aspects of *Varity* is the lack of guidance to employers concerning

communications with employees about their employee benefit plans. Although intentionally misleading communications with employees clearly violate ERISA's fiduciary duty of loyalty, *Varity* did not address the scope of a fiduciary's affirmative duty to provide information to employees beyond the statutory reporting and disclosure requirements contained in Part 1 of Title I of ERISA. These issues are discussed in more detail in the Note on the Duty to Inform in Section C of Chapter Five.

5.   *Mutual Fund Companies and Insurance Companies as Fiduciaries.* Under the definition of a fiduciary in ERISA Section 3(21)(A), a person who exercises any authority concerning the management or disposition of plan assets is a fiduciary. This definition raises potential issues for mutual fund companies who manage and invest the mutual funds offered as investment options under a plan, and for insurance companies who supply insurance policies that are part of the plan's benefits.

ERISA Section 401(b)(1) provides that when a plan invests in a mutual fund, the plan "asset" is deemed to be the shares of the mutual fund itself, not the underlying assets held in the fund and managed by the mutual fund company. Thus, a mutual fund company is not deemed to be a plan fiduciary simply by virtue of managing and investing the underlying assets of the mutual fund.

ERISA Section 401(b)(2) provides that "[i]n the case of a plan to which a guaranteed benefit policy is issued by an insurer, the assets of such plan shall be deemed to include such policy, but shall not, solely by reason of the issuance of such policy, be deemed to include any assets of such insurer." In *John Hancock Mutual Life Insurance Co. v. Harris Trust & Savings Bank,* 510 U.S. 86 (1993), the Supreme Court interpreted this provision, which had been generally understood by the insurance industry as excluding assets held in an insurance company's general account as "plan" assets. *John Hancock* held that, contrary to the common understanding and practice of the insurance industry, under certain circumstances the assets held in the insurance company's general account could be "plan" assets, thereby making the insurance company a potential fiduciary of the plan with respect to the management and investment of the assets held in the general account.

In response to the *John Hancock* decision, Congress enacted ERISA Section 401(c), which directed the Department of Labor to issue regulations providing guidance concerning the circumstances when assets held in an insurance company's general account would be deemed to be "plan" assets in situations where an insurance company has issued an insurance policy to or for the benefit of an employee benefit plan and the insurance policy is supported by assets held in the insurance company's general account. The Department of Labor regulations generally negate the fiduciary status of insurance companies with respect to managing the assets held in a general account by providing that where an insurer has issued an insurance policy to or for the benefit of an employee benefit plan, the plan's asset is normally deemed to be the insurance policy itself, rather than the assets in the insurance company's general account that support the insurance company's financial obligations under the policy. This rule applies only if the insurance company complies with various conditions and notice and disclosure requirements listed in the regulation. See DOL Reg. § 2550.401c–1.

PEGRAM V. HERDRICH

United States Supreme Court, 2000.
530 U.S. 211, 120 S.Ct. 2143, 147 L.Ed.2d 164.

JUSTICE SOUTER delivered the opinion of the Court.

The question in this case is whether treatment decisions made by a health maintenance organization, acting through its physician employees, are fiduciary acts within the meaning of the Employee Retirement Income Security Act of 1974 (ERISA). We hold that they are not.

I

Petitioners, Carle Clinic Association, P.C., Health Alliance Medical Plans, Inc., and Carle Health Insurance Management Co., Inc. (collectively Carle), function as a health maintenance organization (HMO) organized for profit. Its owners are physicians providing prepaid medical services to participants whose employers contract with Carle to provide such coverage. Respondent, Cynthia Herdrich, was covered by Carle through her husband's employer, State Farm Insurance Company.

The events in question began when a Carle physician, petitioner Lori Pegram, examined Herdrich, who was experiencing pain in the midline area of her groin. Six days later, Dr. Pegram discovered a six by eight centimeter inflamed mass in Herdrich's abdomen. Despite the noticeable inflammation, Dr. Pegram did not order an ultrasound diagnostic procedure at a local hospital, but decided that Herdrich would have to wait eight more days for an ultrasound, to be performed at a facility staffed by Carle more than 50 miles away. Before the eight days were over, Herdrich's appendix ruptured, causing peritonitis.

Herdrich sued Pegram and Carle in state court for medical malpractice, and she later added two counts charging state-law fraud. Carle and Pegram responded that ERISA preempted the new counts, and removed the case to federal court, where they then sought summary judgment on the state-law fraud counts. The District Court granted their motion as to the second fraud count but granted Herdrich leave to amend the one remaining. This she did by alleging that provision of medical services under the terms of the Carle HMO organization, rewarding its physician owners for limiting medical care, entailed an inherent or anticipatory breach of an ERISA fiduciary duty, since these terms created an incentive to make decisions in the physicians' self-interest, rather than the exclusive interests of plan participants.

Herdrich sought relief under ERISA § 409(a), which provides that [a]ny person who is a fiduciary with respect to a plan who breaches any of the responsibilities, obligations, or duties imposed upon fiduciaries by this subchapter shall be personally liable to make good to such plan any losses to the plan resulting from each such breach, and to restore to such plan any profits of such fiduciary which have been made through use of assets of the plan by the fiduciary, and shall be subject to such other equitable or remedial relief as the court may deem appropriate, including removal of such fiduciary.

When Carle moved to dismiss the ERISA count for failure to state a claim upon which relief could be granted, the District Court granted the motion, accepting the Magistrate Judge's determination that Carle was not "involved [in these events] as" an ERISA fiduciary. The original malpractice counts were then tried to a jury, and Herdrich prevailed on both, receiving $35,000 in compensation for her injury. She then appealed the dismissal of the ERISA claim to the Court of Appeals for the Seventh Circuit, which reversed. The court held that Carle was acting as a fiduciary when its physicians made the challenged decisions and that Herdrich's allegations were sufficient to state a claim:

> Our decision does not stand for the proposition that the existence of incentives *automatically* gives rise to a breach of fiduciary duty. Rather, we hold that incentives can *rise* to the level of a breach where, as pleaded here, the fiduciary trust between plan participants and plan fiduciaries no longer exists (i.e., where physicians delay providing necessary treatment to, or withhold administering proper care to, plan beneficiaries for the sole purpose of increasing their bonuses). 154 F.3d at 373.

We granted certiorari and now reverse the Court of Appeals.

II

Whether Carle is a fiduciary when it acts through its physician owners as pleaded in the ERISA count depends on some background of fact and law about HMOs, medical benefit plans, fiduciary obligation, and the meaning of Herdrich's allegations.

A

Traditionally, medical care in the United States has been provided on a "fee-for-service" basis. A physician charges so much for a general physical exam, a vaccination, a tonsillectomy, and so on. The physician bills the patient for services provided or, if there is insurance and the doctor is willing, submits the bill for the patient's care to the insurer, for payment subject to the terms of the insurance agreement. In a fee-for-service system, a physician's financial incentive is to provide more care, not less, so long as payment is forthcoming. The check on this incentive is a physician's obligation to exercise reasonable medical skill and judgment in the patient's interest.

Beginning in the late 1960's, insurers and others developed new models for health care delivery, including HMOs. The defining feature of an HMO is receipt of a fixed fee for each patient enrolled under the terms of a contract to provide specified health care if needed. The HMO thus assumes the financial risk of providing the benefits promised: if a participant never gets sick, the HMO keeps the money regardless, and if a participant becomes expensively ill, the HMO is responsible for the treatment agreed upon even if its cost exceeds the participant's premiums.

Like other risk-bearing organizations, HMOs take steps to control costs. At the least, HMOs, like traditional insurers, will in some fashion make coverage determinations, scrutinizing requested services against the contractual provisions to make sure that a request for care falls within the scope of covered circumstances (pregnancy, for example), or that a given treatment falls within the scope of the care promised (surgery, for instance). They customarily issue general guidelines for their physicians about appropriate levels of care. And they commonly require utilization review (in which specific treatment decisions are reviewed by a decisionmaker other than the treating physician) and approval in advance (precertification) for many types of care, keyed to standards of medical necessity or the reasonableness of the proposed treatment. These cost controlling measures are commonly complemented by specific financial incentives to physicians, rewarding them for decreasing utilization of health care services, and penalizing them for what may be found to be excessive treatment. Hence, in an HMO system, a physician's financial interest lies in providing less care, not more. The check on this influence (like that on the converse, fee-for-service incentive) is the professional obligation to provide covered services with a reasonable degree of skill and judgment in the patient's interest.

The adequacy of professional obligation to counter financial self-interest has been challenged no matter what the form of medical organization. HMOs became popular because fee-for-service physicians were thought to be providing unnecessary or useless services; today, many doctors and other observers argue that HMOs often ignore the individual needs of a patient in order to improve the HMOs' bottom lines. In this case, for instance, one could argue that Pegram's decision to wait before getting an ultrasound for Herdrich, and her insistence that the ultrasound be done at a distant facility owned by Carle, reflected an interest in limiting the HMO's expenses, which blinded her to the need for immediate diagnosis and treatment.

B

Herdrich focuses on the Carle scheme's provision for a "year-end distribution" to the HMO's physician owners. She argues that this particular incentive device of annually paying physician owners the profit resulting from their own decisions rationing care can distinguish Carle's organization from HMOs generally, so that reviewing Carle's decisions under a fiduciary standard as pleaded in Herdrich's complaint would not open the door to like claims about other HMO structures. While the Court of Appeals agreed, we think otherwise, under the law as now written.

Although it is true that the relationship between sparing medical treatment and physician reward is not a subtle one under the Carle scheme, no HMO organization could survive without some incentive connecting physician reward with treatment rationing. The essence of an HMO is that salaries and profits are limited by the HMO's fixed membership fees. This is not to suggest that the Carle provisions are as socially desirable as some other HMO organizational schemes; they may not be. But whatever the HMO, there must be rationing and inducement to ration.

Since inducement to ration care goes to the very point of any HMO scheme, and rationing necessarily raises some risks while reducing others (ruptured appendixes are more likely; unnecessary appendectomies are less so), any legal principle purporting to draw a line between good and bad HMOs would embody, in effect, a judgment about socially acceptable medical risk. A valid conclusion of this sort would, however, necessarily turn on facts to which courts would probably not have ready access: correlations between malpractice rates and various HMO models, similar correlations involving fee-for-service models, and so on. And, of course, assuming such material could be obtained by courts in litigation like this, any standard defining the unacceptably risky HMO structure (and consequent vulnerability to claims like Herdrich's) would depend on a judgment about the appropriate level of expenditure for health care in light of the associated malpractice risk. But such complicated factfinding and such a debatable social judgment are not wisely required of courts unless for some reason resort cannot be had to the legislative process, with its preferable forum for comprehensive investigations and judgments of social value, such as optimum treatment levels and health care expenditure. Cf. Patsy v. Board of Regents of Fla., 457 U.S. 496, 513 (1982) ("[T]he relevant policy considerations do not invariably point in one direction, and there is vehement disagreement over the validity of the assumptions underlying many of them. The very difficulty of these policy considerations, and Congress' superior institutional competence to pursue this debate, suggest that legislative not judicial solutions are preferable.").

We think, then, that courts are not in a position to derive a sound legal principle to differentiate an HMO like Carle from other HMOs. For that reason, we proceed on the assumption that the decisions listed in Herdrich's complaint cannot be subject to a claim that they violate fiduciary standards unless all such decisions by all HMOs acting through their owner or employee physicians are to be judged by the same standards and subject to the same claims.

C

We turn now from the structure of HMOs to the requirements of ERISA. A fiduciary within the meaning of ERISA must be someone acting in the capacity of manager, administrator, or financial adviser to a "plan," see ERISA §§ 3(21)(A)(i)–(iii), and Herdrich's ERISA count accordingly charged Carle with a breach of fiduciary duty in discharging its obligations under State Farm's medical plan. ERISA's definition of an employee welfare benefit plan is ultimately circular: "any plan, fund, or program . . . to the extent that such plan, fund, or program was established . . . for the purpose of providing . . . through the purchase of insurance or otherwise . . . medical, surgical, or hospital care or benefits." ERISA § 3(1)(A). One is thus left to the common understanding of the word "plan" as referring to a scheme decided upon in advance, see Webster's New International Dictionary 1879 (2d ed.1957). Here the scheme comprises a set of rules that define the rights of a beneficiary and provide for their enforcement. Rules governing collection of premiums, definition of benefits, submission of claims, and resolution of disagreements over entitlement to services are the sorts of provisions that constitute a plan. Thus, when employers contract with an HMO to provide benefits to employees subject to ERISA, the provisions of documents that set up the HMO are not, as such, an ERISA plan; but the agreement between an HMO and an employer who pays the premiums may, as here, provide elements of a plan by setting out rules under which beneficiaries will be entitled to care.

D

As just noted, fiduciary obligations can apply to managing, advising, and administering an ERISA plan, the fiduciary function addressed by Herdrich's ERISA count being the exercise of "discretionary authority or discretionary responsibility in the administration of [an ERISA] plan." ERISA § 3(21)(A)(iii). And as we have already suggested, although Carle is not an ERISA fiduciary merely because it administers or exercises discretionary authority over its own HMO business, it may still be a fiduciary if it administers the plan.

* * *

E

The allegations of Herdrich's ERISA count that identify the claimed fiduciary breach are difficult to understand. In this count, Herdrich does not point to a particular act by any Carle physician owner as a breach. She does not complain about Pegram's actions, and at oral argument her counsel confirmed that the ERISA count could have been brought, and would have been no different, if Herdrich had never had a sick day in her life.

What she does claim is that Carle, acting through its physician owners, breached its duty to act solely in the interest of beneficiaries by making decisions affecting medical treatment while influenced by the terms of the Carle HMO scheme, under which the physician owners ultimately profit from their own choices to minimize the medical services provided. She emphasizes the threat to fiduciary responsibility in the Carle scheme's feature of a year-end distribution to the physicians of profit derived from the spread between subscription income and expenses of care and administration.

The specific payout detail of the plan was, of course, a feature that the employer as plan sponsor was free to adopt without breach of any fiduciary duty under ERISA, since an employer's decisions about the content of a plan are not themselves fiduciary acts. Lockheed Corp. v. Spink, 517 U.S. 882, 887 (1996) ("Nothing in ERISA requires employers to establish employee benefit plans. Nor does ERISA mandate what kind of benefits employers must provide if they choose to have such a plan.").[7] Likewise it is clear that there was no violation of ERISA when the incorporators of the Carle HMO provided for the year-end payout. The HMO is not the ERISA plan, and the incorporation of the HMO preceded its contract with the State Farm plan. See ERISA § 409(b) (no fiduciary liability for acts preceding fiduciary status).

The nub of the claim, then, is that when State Farm contracted with Carle, Carle became a fiduciary under the plan, acting through its physicians. At once, Carle as fiduciary administrator was subject to such influence from the year-end payout provision that its fiduciary capacity was necessarily compromised, and its readiness to act amounted to anticipatory breach of fiduciary obligation.

---

[7]   It does not follow that those who administer a particular plan design may not have difficulty in following fiduciary standards if the design is awkward enough. A plan might lawfully provide for a bonus for administrators who denied benefits to every tenth beneficiary, but it would be difficult for an administrator who received the bonus to defend against the claim that he had not been solely attentive to the beneficiaries' interests in carrying out his administrative duties. The important point is that Herdrich is not suing the employer, State Farm, and her claim cannot be analyzed as if she were.

F

The pleadings must also be parsed very carefully to understand what acts by physician owners acting on Carle's behalf are alleged to be fiduciary in nature. It will help to keep two sorts of arguably administrative acts in mind. What we will call pure "eligibility decisions" turn on the plan's coverage of a particular condition or medical procedure for its treatment. "Treatment decisions," by contrast, are choices about how to go about diagnosing and treating a patient's condition: given a patient's constellation of symptoms, what is the appropriate medical response?

These decisions are often practically inextricable from one another, as amici on both sides agree. This is so not merely because, under a scheme like Carle's, treatment and eligibility decisions are made by the same person, the treating physician. It is so because a great many and possibly most coverage questions are not simple yes-or-no questions, like whether appendicitis is a covered condition (when there is no dispute that a patient has appendicitis), or whether acupuncture is a covered procedure for pain relief (when the claim of pain is unchallenged). The more common coverage question is a when-and-how question. Although coverage for many conditions will be clear and various treatment options will be indisputably compensable, physicians still must decide what to do in particular cases. The issue may be, say, whether one treatment option is so superior to another under the circumstances, and needed so promptly, that a decision to proceed with it would meet the medical necessity requirement that conditions the HMO's obligation to provide or pay for that particular procedure at that time in that case. The Government in its brief alludes to a similar example when it discusses an HMO's refusal to pay for emergency care on the ground that the situation giving rise to the need for care was not an emergency. In practical terms, these eligibility decisions cannot be untangled from physicians' judgments about reasonable medical treatment, and in the case before us, Dr. Pegram's decision was one of that sort. She decided (wrongly, as it turned out) that Herdrich's condition did not warrant immediate action; the consequence of that medical determination was that Carle would not cover immediate care, whereas it would have done so if Dr. Pegram had made the proper diagnosis and judgment to treat. The eligibility decision and the treatment decision were inextricably mixed, as they are in countless medical administrative decisions every day.

The kinds of decisions mentioned in Herdrich's ERISA count and claimed to be fiduciary in character are just such mixed eligibility and treatment decisions: physician's conclusions about when to use diagnostic tests; about seeking consultations and making referrals to physicians and facilities other than Carle's; about proper standards of care, the experimental character of a proposed course of treatment, the reasonableness of a certain treatment, and the emergency character of a medical condition.

We do not read the ERISA count, however, as alleging fiduciary breach with reference to a different variety of administrative decisions, those we have called pure eligibility determinations, such as whether a plan covers an undisputed case of appendicitis. Nor do we read it as claiming breach by reference to discrete administrative decisions separate from medical judgments; say, rejecting a claim for no other reason than the HMO's financial condition. The closest Herdrich's ERISA count comes to stating a claim for a pure, unmixed eligibility decision is her general allegation that Carle determines "which claims are covered under the Plan and to what extent." But this vague statement, difficult to interpret in isolation, is given content by the other elements of the complaint, all of which refer to decisions thoroughly mixed with medical judgment. Any lingering uncertainty about what Herdrich has in mind is dispelled by her brief, which explains that this allegation, like the others, targets medical necessity determinations.

III

A

Based on our understanding of the matters just discussed, we think Congress did not intend Carle or any other HMO to be treated as a fiduciary to the extent that it makes mixed eligibility decisions acting through its physicians. We begin with doubt that Congress would ever have thought of a mixed eligibility decision as fiduciary in nature. At common law, fiduciary duties characteristically attach to decisions about managing assets and distributing property to beneficiaries. Trustees buy, sell, and lease investment property, lend and borrow, and do other things to conserve and nurture assets. They pay out income, choose beneficiaries, and distribute remainders at termination. Thus, the common law trustee's most defining concern historically has been the payment of money in the interest of the beneficiary.

Mixed eligibility decisions by an HMO acting through its physicians have, however, only a limited resemblance to the usual business of traditional trustees. To be sure, the physicians (like regular trustees) draw on resources held for others and make decisions to distribute them in accordance with entitlements expressed in a written instrument (embodying the terms of an ERISA plan). It is also true that the objects of many traditional private and public trusts are ultimately the same as the ERISA plans that contract with HMOs. Private trusts provide medical care to the poor; thousands of independent hospitals are privately held and publicly accountable trusts, and charitable foundations make grants to stimulate the provision of health services. But beyond this point the resemblance rapidly wanes. Traditional trustees administer a medical trust by paying out money to buy medical care, whereas physicians making mixed eligibility decisions consume the money as well. Private trustees do not make treatment judgments, whereas treatment judgments are what physicians reaching mixed decisions do make, by definition. Indeed, the physicians through whom HMOs act make just the sorts of decisions made by licensed medical practitioners millions of times every day, in every possible medical setting: HMOs, fee-for-service proprietorships, public and private hospitals, military field hospitals, and so on. The settings bear no more resemblance to trust departments than a decision to operate turns on the factors controlling the amount of a quarterly income distribution. Thus, it is at least questionable whether Congress would have had mixed eligibility decisions in mind when it provided that decisions administering a plan were fiduciary in nature. Indeed, when Congress took up the subject of fiduciary responsibility under ERISA, it concentrated on fiduciaries' financial decisions, focusing on pension plans, the difficulty many retirees faced in getting the payments they expected, and the financial mismanagement that had too often deprived employees of their benefits. See, e.g., S. Rep. No. 93–127, p. 5 (1973); S. Rep. No. 93–383, p. 17 (1973). Its focus was far from the subject of Herdrich's claim.

Our doubt that Congress intended the category of fiduciary administrative functions to encompass the mixed determinations at issue here hardens into conviction when we consider the consequences that would follow from Herdrich's contrary view.

B

First, we need to ask how this fiduciary standard would affect HMOs if it applied as Herdrich claims it should be applied, not directed against any particular mixed decision that injured a patient, but against HMOs that make mixed decisions in the course of providing medical care for profit. Recovery would be warranted simply upon showing that the profit incentive to ration care would generally affect mixed decisions, in derogation of the fiduciary standard to act solely in the interest of the patient without possibility of conflict. Although Herdrich is vague about the mechanics of relief, the one point that seems clear is that she seeks the return of profit from the pockets of the Carle HMO's owners, with the money to be given to the plan for the benefit of the participants. Since the provision for profit is what makes the HMO a proprietary organization, her remedy in effect would be nothing less than elimination of the for-profit HMO. Her remedy might entail even more than that, although we are in no position to tell whether and to what extent nonprofit HMO schemes would ultimately survive the recognition of Herdrich's theory.[11] It is enough to recognize that the Judiciary has no warrant to precipitate

---

[11] Herdrich's theory might well portend the end of nonprofit HMOs as well, since those HMOs can set doctors' salaries. A claim against a nonprofit HMO could easily allege that salaries were excessively high because they were funded by limiting care, and some nonprofits actually use incentive schemes similar to that challenged here.

the upheaval that would follow a refusal to dismiss Herdrich's ERISA claim. The fact is that for over 27 years the Congress of the United States has promoted the formation of HMO practices. The Health Maintenance Organization Act of 1973, 42 U.S.C. § 300e et seq., allowed the formation of HMOs that assume financial risks for the provision of health care services, and Congress has amended the Act several times, most recently in 1996. See 42 U.S.C. § 300e. If Congress wishes to restrict its approval of HMO practice to certain preferred forms, it may choose to do so. But the Federal Judiciary would be acting contrary to the congressional policy of allowing HMO organizations if it were to entertain an ERISA fiduciary claim portending wholesale attacks on existing HMOs solely because of their structure, untethered to claims of concrete harm.

C

The Court of Appeals did not purport to entertain quite the broadside attack that Herdrich's ERISA claim thus entails, see 154 F.3d at 373, and the second possible consequence of applying the fiduciary standard that requires our attention would flow from the difficulty of extending it to particular mixed decisions that on Herdrich's theory are fiduciary in nature.

The fiduciary is, of course, obliged to act exclusively in the interest of the beneficiary, but this translates into no rule readily applicable to HMO decisions or those of any other variety of medical practice. While the incentive of the HMO physician is to give treatment sparingly, imposing a fiduciary obligation upon him would not lead to a simple default rule, say, that whenever it is reasonably possible to disagree about treatment options, the physician should treat aggressively. After all, HMOs came into being because some groups of physicians consistently provided more aggressive treatment than others in similar circumstances, with results not perceived as justified by the marginal expense and risk associated with intervention; excessive surgery is not in the patient's best interest, whether provided by fee-for-service surgeons or HMO surgeons subject to a default rule urging them to operate. Nor would it be possible to translate fiduciary duty into a standard that would allow recovery from an HMO whenever a mixed decision influenced by the HMO's financial incentive resulted in a bad outcome for the patient. It would be so easy to allege, and to find, an economic influence when sparing care did not lead to a well patient, that any such standard in practice would allow a factfinder to convert an HMO into a guarantor of recovery.

These difficulties may have led the Court of Appeals to try to confine the fiduciary breach to cases where "the sole purpose" of delaying or withholding treatment was to increase the physician's financial reward. But this attempt to confine mixed decision claims to their most egregious examples entails erroneous corruption of fiduciary obligation and would simply lead to further difficulties that we think fatal. While a mixed decision made solely to benefit the HMO or its physician would violate a fiduciary duty, the fiduciary standard condemns far more than that, in its requirement of "an eye single" toward beneficiaries' interests. Donovan v. Bierwirth, 680 F.2d 263, 271 (2d Cir. 1982). But whether under the Court of Appeals's rule or a straight standard of undivided loyalty, the defense of any HMO would be that its physician did not act out of financial interest but for good medical reasons, the plausibility of which would require reference to standards of reasonable and customary medical practice in like circumstances. That, of course, is the traditional standard of the common law. See W. Keeton, D. Dobbs, R. Keeton, & D. Owens, Prosser & Keeton on Torts, § 32, pp. 188–89 (5th ed. 1984). Thus, for all practical purposes, every claim of fiduciary breach by an HMO physician making a mixed decision would boil down to a malpractice claim, and the fiduciary standard would be nothing but the malpractice standard traditionally applied in actions against physicians.

What would be the value to the plan participant of having this kind of ERISA fiduciary action? It would simply apply the law already available in state courts and federal diversity actions today, and the formulaic addition of an allegation of financial incentive would do nothing but bring the same claim into a federal court under federal question jurisdiction. It is true that in States that do not allow malpractice actions against HMOs the fiduciary claim would offer a plaintiff a further defendant to be sued for direct liability, and in some cases the HMO might have a deeper pocket than the physician. But we have seen enough to know that ERISA was not enacted out of concern that physicians were too poor to be sued, or in order to federalize malpractice litigation in the name of fiduciary duty for any other reason. It is difficult, in fact, to find any advantage to participants across the board, except that allowing them to bring malpractice actions in the guise of federal fiduciary breach claims against HMOs would make them eligible for awards of attorney's fees if they won. See ERISA § 502(g)(1). But, again, we can be fairly sure that Congress did not create fiduciary obligations out of concern that state plaintiffs were not suing often enough, or were paying too much in legal fees.

The mischief of Herdrich's position would, indeed, go further than mere replication of state malpractice actions with HMO defendants. For not only would an HMO be liable as a fiduciary in the first instance for its own breach of fiduciary duty committed through the acts of its physician employee, but the physician employee would also be subject to liability as a fiduciary on the same basic analysis that would charge the HMO. The physician who made the mixed administrative decision would be exercising authority in the way described by ERISA and would therefore be deemed to be a fiduciary. Hence the physician, too, would be subject to suit in federal court applying an ERISA standard of reasonable medical skill. This result, in turn, would raise a puzzling issue of preemption. On its face, federal fiduciary law applying a malpractice standard would seem to be a prescription for preemption of state malpractice law, since the new ERISA cause of action would cover the subject of a state law malpractice claim. * * * We could struggle with this problem, but first it is well to ask, again, what would be gained by opening the federal courthouse doors for a fiduciary malpractice claim, save for possibly random fortuities such as more favorable scheduling, or the ancillary opportunity to seek attorney's fees. And again, we know that Congress had no such haphazard boons in prospect when it defined the ERISA fiduciary, nor such a risk to the efficiency of federal courts as a new fiduciary malpractice jurisdiction would pose in welcoming such unheard-of fiduciary litigation.

IV

We hold that mixed eligibility decisions by HMO physicians are not fiduciary decisions under ERISA. Herdrich's ERISA count fails to state an ERISA claim, and the judgment of the Court of Appeals is reversed.

NOTES AND QUESTIONS

1.   The patient in *Pegram v. Herdrich*, Cynthia Herdrich, recovered $35,000 for personal injury on her state law medical malpractice claim against the treating physician, Dr. Lori Pegram, and the Carle HMO. The issue before the Supreme Court in *Pegram* was whether Herdrich also could sue the Carle HMO as a fiduciary under ERISA for breach of fiduciary duty. The attorney for Herdrich at oral argument before the Supreme Court admitted that "the ERISA count could have been brought, and would have been no different, if Herdrich had never had a sick day in her life." Given that Herdrich was compensated for her personal injury, what were the economic incentives for the plaintiff to pursue the ERISA fiduciary claims against the Carle HMO?

2.   The Carle HMO's bonus system was unusual in that it sought directly to link physician compensation with physician incentives to minimize the use of patient diagnostic tests and the referral of patients to physicians and facilities for medical services that were not part of the Carle HMO network. The Seventh Circuit in *Pegram* had focused in part on the unusual characteristics of the Carle HMO bonus system to arrive at its narrowly tailored holding that such "incentives can rise to the level of a [fiduciary] breach where physicians delay providing necessary treatment to, or withhold administering proper care to, plan beneficiaries for the sole purpose of increasing their bonuses." Herdrich v. Pegram, 154 F.3d 362, 373 (7th Cir. 1998). Why did the Supreme Court reject the Seventh Circuit's approach and instead determine that it was necessary to have a "bright-line" rule governing all HMOs, regardless of their physician compensation structure and their status as for-profit or non-profit entities? Which approach do you prefer? Which approach represents the better public policy?

3.   For the Carle HMO to be a fiduciary under ERISA, it had to engage in the administration or management of an employee benefit plan. What did the Supreme Court determine to be the "plan" at issue in *Pegram*?

4.   According to *Pegram*, what is an "eligibility" decision? A "treatment" decision? A "mixed" decision? Why did the Supreme Court conclude that Congress never intended for ERISA's fiduciary administration functions to include mixed decisions in the context of an HMO? What legal authority and social policy factors did the Supreme Court use to support its conclusion that the Carle HMO was not an ERISA fiduciary? How does the Supreme Court's analysis of fiduciary status in *Pegram* compare with the Court's analysis of this issue in *Varity*? Do you find the Supreme Court's reasoning in *Pegram* to be persuasive?

The status of a HMO as a possible fiduciary under ERISA frequently arises when state law claims are asserted against the HMO. The HMO's defense usually is that ERISA preempts the plaintiff's state law claims. ERISA preemption of state law claims against HMOs, health care plans and health care providers is discussed in Section D of Chapter Seven of the casebook.

C. FIDUCIARY AND CO-FIDUCIARY RESPONSIBILITIES

1. LEGISLATIVE HISTORY

Congress modeled ERISA's statutory framework governing the conduct of fiduciaries after the common law of trusts, but with certain modifications for employee benefit plans. As you read ERISA's legislative history below, notice those instances where Congress deemed the common law of trusts to be inadequate. How does ERISA change the common law of trusts?

House of Representatives Report No. 93–533 (1973)

The fiduciary responsibility section, in essence, codifies and makes applicable to these fiduciaries certain principles developed in the evolution of the law of trusts. The section was deemed necessary for several reasons.

First, a number of plans are structured in such a way that it is unclear whether the traditional law of trusts is applicable. Predominantly, these are plans, such as insured plans, which do not use the trust form as their mode of funding. Administrators and others exercising control functions in such plans under the [Welfare and Pension Plans Disclosure Act of 1958, as amended] are subject only to minimal restrictions and the applicability of present State law to employee benefit plans is sometimes unclear. Second, even where the funding mechanism of the plan is in the form of a trust, reliance on conventional trust law often is insufficient to adequately protect the interests of plan participants and beneficiaries. This is because trust law had developed in the context of testamentary and inter vivos trusts (usually designed to pass designated property to an individual or small group of persons) with an attendant emphasis on carrying out the instructions of the settler. Thus, if the settler includes in the trust document an exculpatory clause under which the trustee is relieved from liability for certain actions which would otherwise constitute a breach of duty, or if the settler specifies that the trustee shall be allowed to make investments which might otherwise be considered imprudent, the trust law in many states will be interpreted to allow the deviation. In the absence of a fiduciary responsibility section in the [Welfare and Pension Plans Disclosure Act of 1958, as amended], courts applying trust law to employee benefit plans have allowed the same kinds of deviations, even though the typical employee benefit plan, covering hundreds or even thousands of participants, is quite different from the testamentary trust both in purpose and in nature.

Third, even assuming that the law of trusts is applicable, without detailed information about the plan, access to the courts, and without standards by which a participant can measure the fiduciary's conduct he is not equipped to safeguard either his own rights or the plan assets. Furthermore, a fiduciary standard embodied in Federal legislation is considered desirable because it will bring a measure of uniformity in an area where decisions under the same set of facts may differ from state to state. It is expected that courts will interpret the prudent man rule and other fiduciary standards bearing in mind the special nature and purposes of employee benefit plans intended to be effectuated by [ERISA].

Finally, it is evident that the operations of employee benefit plans are increasingly interstate. The uniformity of decision which [ERISA] is designed to foster will help administrators, fiduciaries and participants to predict the legality of proposed actions without the necessity of reference to varying state laws.

2. ILLUSTRATIONS OF FIDUCIARY AND CO-FIDUCIARY RESPONSIBILITIES

a. Overview of Fiduciary Duties

As described in Chapter One of the casebook, Congress enacted ERISA in response to well-publicized instances of fiduciary misconduct and misuse of plan assets. The heart of ERISA's civil enforcement scheme lies in the statute's fiduciary responsibility provisions, which apply to both pension and welfare benefit plans. ERISA § 401(a). These rules impose fiduciary duties (ERISA § 404) and co-fiduciary duties (ERISA § 405) on plan fiduciaries. The fiduciary duties of Section 404 consist of four primary duties:

- ERISA Section 404(a)(1)(A)—the *duty of loyalty* to plan participants (also known as the *exclusive benefit rule*);
- ERISA Section 404(a)(1)(B)—the *duty of prudence*;
- ERISA Section 404(a)(1)(C)—the *duty of prudent diversification* of plan assets; and
- ERISA Section 404(a)(1)(D)—the *duty to follow plan terms* (but only to the extent that the terms of the plan are consistent with the provisions of Titles I and IV of ERISA).

[handwritten: 4 fiduciary obligations]

Several special rules apply concerning the investment of plan assets. Indicia of ownership of plan assets must be maintained within the jurisdiction of the federal district courts of the United States. ERISA § 404(b). Individual account plans that hold qualifying employer securities or qualifying employer real property are exempt from the duty of prudent diversification of plan assets. ERISA § 404(a)(2). ERISA Section 404(c)(1) exempts plan fiduciaries from liability for investment losses in individual account plans where the plan participants exercise investment control over their own accounts. Participant-directed retirement plans (known as *404(c) plans*) are discussed in Section E of Chapter Five.

The co-fiduciary duties of ERISA Section 405 impose liability on one fiduciary (the co-fiduciary) for a breach of fiduciary responsibility by another plan fiduciary if the co-fiduciary:

- knowingly participates in, or undertakes to conceal, the fiduciary's breach;
- enables the fiduciary to commit the breach through the co-fiduciary's own breach of the duty of prudence; or
- has knowledge of the fiduciary's breach and fails to make reasonable efforts to remedy the fiduciary's breach.

[handwritten: when co-fid will be held liable]

ERISA § 405(a)(1)–(3). Special co-fiduciary rules apply to co-trustees of a plan, ERISA § 405(b), and to investment managers, ERISA § 405(d). ERISA Section 405(c) provides that the plan document may establish a procedure for allocating fiduciary responsibilities among fiduciaries and delegating fiduciary tasks to other persons. The trustee of an employee benefit plan generally is assumed to have discretion over the management and investment of the assets held in the plan's trust. A trustee's fiduciary responsibility for the investment of plan assets may be allocated by the plan document to an investment manager or managers. See ERISA § 405(d).

The plan document also may identify another fiduciary or fiduciaries who provide directions to the trustee concerning how the trustee shall invest plan assets. See ERISA § 403(a)(1). The fiduciary or fiduciaries who direct the trustee may include the employer or the plan's participants, who direct the investment of assets held in their individual

directed
mvke *vihahon*

accounts. In these *directed trustee* situations, the trustee's fiduciary responsibilities concerning the investment of plan assets are limited to determining whether the direction is "proper" and "not contrary to the terms of the plan." See ERISA § 403(a)(1); DOL Field Assistance Bulletin No. 2004–03 (describing the fiduciary duties of directed trustees); Colleen E. Medill, *The Law of Directed Trustees Under ERISA: A Proposed Blueprint for the Federal Courts*, 61 MO.L.REV. 825 (1996).

ERISA Section 412(a) generally requires that plan fiduciaries and other persons who handle plan funds or property must be bonded. Corporations, trust companies, insurance companies, banks, and other regulated financial institutions are exempt from this bonding requirement. ERISA § 412(a)(2).

co-fids subject
to joint and
severable
liability

Plan fiduciaries are personally liable for a breach of the fiduciary responsibility provisions contained in Part 4 of Title I of ERISA. ERISA § 409(a). Unless fiduciary duties have been properly allocated under ERISA Section 405, breaching co-fiduciaries are subject to joint and several liability. See, e.g. Leister v. Dovetail, Inc., 546 F.3d 875, 878 (7th Cir. 2008); LaScala v. Scrufari, 479 F.3d 213 (2d Cir. 2007). The Department of Labor's Voluntary Fiduciary Correction Program (VFCP) is available to fiduciaries who desire to self-correct certain common fiduciary violations. Plan fiduciaries who utilize the VFCP may avoid civil enforcement actions by the Department of Labor and the related imposition of civil money penalties for fiduciary violations under ERISA Section 502(*l*).

A plan fiduciary is not liable for a breach of fiduciary duty if the breach was committed before the person became a fiduciary or after the person ceased to be a fiduciary. ERISA § 409(b). Although exculpatory clauses relieving fiduciaries from liability are void as against public policy, plan fiduciaries may, and oftentimes do, purchase fiduciary liability insurance. ERISA § 410(a)–(b). Fiduciary liability, claims and remedies under ERISA are discussed in Chapter Six of the casebook.

b.   The Duty of Loyalty (Exclusive Benefit Rule)

ERISA Section 404(a)(1)(A) requires that a fiduciary must act "solely in the interest" of plan participants and beneficiaries, and must act for the exclusive purposes of "providing benefits to participants and their beneficiaries" and "defraying reasonable expenses of administering the plan." In addition, ERISA Section 403(c)(1) requires that the assets of the plan "shall be held for the exclusive purposes of providing benefits to participants in the plan and their beneficiaries." These "solely in the interest" and "exclusive purpose" standards are derived loosely from the duty of loyalty imposed by the common law upon a trustee. See Eaves v. Penn, 587 F.2d 453, 457 (10th Cir. 1978). ERISA's fiduciary duty of loyalty under Section 404(a)(1)(A) has a long and well-established parentage in the common law of trusts.

ERISA as a whole is a complex statute, but the concepts which underlie its fiduciary provisions are straightforward and have long formed the basis of the law of trusts. At the heart of the fiduciary relationship is the duty of complete and undivided loyalty to the beneficiaries of the trust. In the classic description of then-Judge Cardozo:

> Many forms of conduct permissible, in a workaday world for those acting at arm's length, are forbidden to those bound by fiduciary ties. A trustee is held to something stricter than the morals of the market place. Not honesty alone, but the punctilio of an honor the most sensitive, is then the standard of behavior.

Cardozo on fiduciary

Freund v. Marshall & Ilsley Bank, 485 F.Supp. 629, 639 (W.D. Wis. 1979) (quoting Meinhard v. Salmon, 249 N.Y. 458, 164 N.E. 545 (1928)).

The duty of loyalty imposed upon fiduciaries by ERISA is an objective standard. In evaluating whether a fiduciary's actions are consistent with the duty of loyalty, the subjective good faith of the fiduciary is irrelevant. "Good faith is not a defense to an ERISA fiduciary's breach of the duty of loyalty." Leigh v. Engle, 727 F.2d 113, 124 (7th Cir. 1984).

objective good faith, not a defense

The common law imposed a stringent duty of loyalty upon the trustee that categorically barred the trustee from self-dealing with trust assets or engaging in transactions using trust property where the trustee's judgment was potentially influenced or tainted by the trustee's personal interests. One of the modifications ERISA made to the common law of trusts was to permit officers, employees, agents or other representatives of the plan sponsor also to serve as plan fiduciaries—thereby potentially placing these individuals in a position of divided loyalties between the plan participants and the plan sponsor. See ERISA § 408(c)(3).

Although ERISA does not prohibit an officer or employee of the employer also from serving in a fiduciary capacity, such dual role fiduciaries "remain subject to the general requirements of Section 404." Donovan v. Cunningham, 716 F.2d 1455, 1467 (5th Cir. 1983). If a conflict of interest arises, ERISA's duty of loyalty under Section 404(a)(1)(A) requires that the fiduciary must act with an "eye single" to the interests of the plan's participants and beneficiaries. Donovan v. Bierwirth, 680 F.2d 263, 271 (2d Cir. 1982). So long as the fiduciary's actions are prudent and, viewed objectively, in the best interests of the plan participants, it is not a breach of the duty of loyalty if the fiduciary's decision results in an "incidental benefit" to the employer. See Trenton v. Scott Paper Co., 832 F.2d 806, 809 (3d Cir. 1987).

By modifying the undivided duty of loyalty imposed by the common law of trusts, ERISA permits an employer to operate as a fiduciary under the cloud of a potential conflict of interest. This potential conflict of interest has proven particularly problematic for the federal courts in several situations. First, where the fiduciary is charged with approving or denying claims for plan benefits, a denied claim may be motivated by the employer's desire to reduce the costs of the plan. These conflict of interest situations in the context of claims for plan benefits are discussed in Chapter Six of the casebook. Second, where the fiduciary makes investment decisions concerning company stock held as a plan asset, these decisions may have been made for the benefit of the employer rather than for the exclusive benefit of the plan's participants. The problems associated with company stock as a plan investment are discussed in Section E of Chapter Five. For further discussion of the tensions that arise as a result of ERISA's modified duty of loyalty, see Daniel Fischel & John H. Langbein, *ERISA's Fundamental Contradiction: The Exclusive Benefit Rule*, 55 U. CHI. L. REV. 1105 (1988).

Brock v. Hendershott, 840 F.2d 339 (6th Cir. 1988), provides a classic illustration of the sort of fiduciary self-dealing that ERISA's duty of loyalty prohibits. In *Brock v. Hendershott*, the Secretary of Labor claimed that two local union representatives, Kenneth Hendershott and Edgar Platel had violated the fiduciary duty provisions of ERISA. Hendershott and Platel had set up a corporation, known as ISI, to solicit business for a group of dentists (Southmoor group). Hendershott and Platel received a profit for every dental contract with an employee benefit plan that the Southmoor group received.

During the events at issue in the case, Hendershott was the highest-ranking union official in Ohio for the United Paperworkers International Union (Union). Platel was a Union representative and Hendershott's assistant. The Secretary of Labor claimed that Hendershott, with the assistance of Platel, had used his influence over the local Union bargaining units to demand dental plan benefits from various employers and to propose the Southmoor group as the dental group of choice for these dental plans. The court of appeals found that the defendants had violated ERISA, and ordered Hendershott and Platel to disgorge the profits they had received from ISI whenever a collective bargaining unit dental plan chose the Southmoor group to provide dental benefits.

The requirement that a plan fiduciary must act for the exclusive benefit of the plan participants and beneficiaries extends beyond situations where the fiduciary has a personal conflict of interest. *Donovan v. Mazzola*, 716 F.2d 1226 (9th Cir. 1983), illustrates a situation where the court found that the plan fiduciaries had violated the exclusive benefit rule of ERISA Section 404(a)(1)(A), even though the fiduciaries were not involved in personal self-dealing. In *Donovan v. Mazzola*, a local union operated a pension fund and a convalescent fund for its members. The convalescent fund owned and operated a hotel, a summer camp, and a retirement housing project. During the events at issue in the case, the same individuals served as trustees of both the pension fund and the convalescent fund. Although the contributing employers and the participants in the pension fund and the convalescent fund were substantially the same, they were not identical, and the eligibility requirements of the two funds were different.

Beginning in December of 1975, the trustees of the pension fund authorized the pension fund to make a series of loans to the convalescent fund. At the time of the loans, the convalescent fund was in poor financial condition and was unable to make the payments on an outstanding bank loan and on previous loans made by the pension fund prior to the enactment of ERISA. The pension fund loans to the convalescent fund were at below-market interest rates and on terms that were not commercially reasonable. The Secretary of Labor claimed that the trustees of the pension fund had violated their fiduciary duties, including the duty to act for the exclusive benefit of the pension fund participants, by authorizing the pension fund to make the loans to the convalescent fund. The court agreed, and ordered that the individual trustees of the pension fund were jointly and severally liable to make restitution to the pension fund for the losses the pension fund suffered as a result of receiving a below-market interest rate on the loans to the convalescent fund.

The exclusive benefit rule has been asserted by the Department of Labor as prohibiting the trustees of a multiemployer defined benefit plan from expending plan assets to inform plan participants about proposals to reform Social Security, and from making decisions on the hiring and firing of plan service providers based on their opinions concerning proposals for Social Security reform. The broader policy implication of the Department of Labor's position is that plan assets cannot be expended for the purpose of influencing public debate or to favor service providers who take a particular side in a public policy debate. The Department of Labor's position, which was asserted in response to an inquiry by the general counsel for the AFL-CIO, is reproduced below. Can you think of other public policy issues today that plan fiduciaries may want to advocate for or against using plan assets?

Letter from Employee Benefit Security Administration to Jonathan P. Hiatt, General Counsel, AFL-CIO, dated May 3, 2005

The Department is very concerned about the potential use of plan assets to promote particular policy positions. Under Section 404(a)(1)(A) of ERISA, plan fiduciaries must act solely in the interest of participants and beneficiaries and for the exclusive purpose of paying benefits and defraying reasonable administrative expenses. In our view, plan fiduciaries are not complying with the exclusive purpose rule when they expend plan assets to communicate with plan participants to advocate a particular result in the current Social Security debate or to disseminate their views on matters of broad public policy such as Social Security reform. Fiduciaries must prudently manage plan assets to ensure that they are available to pay promised benefits. A fiduciary may never increase a plan's expenses, sacrifice the security of promised benefits, or reduce the return on plan assets, in order to promote its views on Social Security or any other broad policy issue.

a fiduciary may never...

1. The use of plan assets to express views or provide information on Social Security policy.

The Department disagrees with any suggestion that plan fiduciaries may expend plan assets on efforts to promote a particular point of view, or to advise, plan participants about the current Social Security debate. Such expenditures are neither for the payment of benefits nor for plan administration, and accordingly fall outside the limited scope of expenditures permitted by ERISA, even if, as the AFL-CIO asserts, current Social Security proposals could have a significant impact on the national economy, financial markets, and plan investments.

Plans are important participants in the national economy, and are generally affected by legislation, regulations, actions, and events which affect the economy as a whole, such as Social Security policy. This simple fact does not convert every legislative or regulatory proposal concerning the economy into a rationale for spending plan assets on the policy debate. If a fiduciary could characterize an "educational" expense as "plan administration" merely by positing some connection between the particular policy at issue and the broad economic interests of ERISA-covered plans, there would be virtually no limit to the range of such expenses that would be permissible. Federal policies concerning public debt, trade, exchange rates, interest rates, housing, the environment, labor, tax law, antitrust law, bankruptcy law, criminal law, civil rights, and myriad other matters have important effects on the economy and economic actors such as ERISA-covered benefit plans. The Department rejects a construction of ERISA which would render the Act's tight limits on the use of plan assets illusory, and which would permit plan fiduciaries to tap into ERISA trusts to promote myriad public policy preferences, rather than to pay benefits and engage in plan administration with undivided loyalty.

In certain very narrow circumstances, such as where a legislative proposal is near enactment and closely tied to plan issues, a fiduciary could decide to spend plan assets to educate participants about the need to take the legislation into account in making particular decisions about their options under the plan. If, for example, proposed changes to the tax code would have specific tax consequences for participants who are choosing between particular investment or distribution options, and such changes are reasonably believed by plan fiduciaries to be imminent, it may be appropriate for the plan's fiduciaries to advise participants of the potential consequences so that they could choose wisely. In such circumstances, plan administration appropriately includes educating participants about the information they need to make sensible decisions under the plan. See, e.g., DOL Reg. § 2509.96–1. Giving plan participants information directly relevant to particular plan choices, however, is very different from expressing views or providing information concerning broad issues of public policy like Social Security reform.

exception to department's general stance

2. Consideration of service providers' views on Social Security as a factor in selection and retention decisions.

Section 404 imposes on plan fiduciaries the duty to act prudently measured against the highest standard of care and with an "eye single to the interests of the participants and beneficiaries." Donovan v. Bierwirth, 680 F.2d 263, 271 (2d Cir. 1982). Fiduciaries cannot subordinate the interests of the participants and beneficiaries to unrelated objectives. DOL Reg. § 2509.94–1.

Under ERISA's stringent standards of prudence and loyalty, it would be unlawful for a plan fiduciary to review the plan's service providers based, not upon the quality and expense of their services, but rather upon their views on Social Security or any other broad area of public policy. Although your [general] counsel's opinion points out that a fiduciary may consider such collateral factors only when choosing a service provider that is better than or equal to alternative providers (see also DOL Reg. § 2509.94–1), the Department is concerned that fiduciaries may nevertheless view the AFL-CIO's recent attention to the question as an invitation to judge service providers first for their positions on Social Security and only second for their ability to meet plans' particular needs.

For this reason, the Department reiterates its view that plan fiduciaries may not increase expenses, sacrifice investment returns, or reduce the security of plan benefits in order to promote collateral goals. A fiduciary's reconsideration of its current service providers based solely upon the service provider's views on Social Security would raise grave concerns about the prudence and loyalty of the fiduciaries' actions. Similarly, a fiduciary could not, consistent with the duties of prudence and loyalty, simply exclude qualified service providers from consideration in hiring based solely upon their views on Social Security policy.

Letter from Employee Benefit Security Administration to Jonathan P. Hiatt, General Counsel, AFL-CIO, dated May 3, 2005.

c. The Duties of Prudence and Prudent Diversification of Plan Assets

ERISA Section 404(a)(1)(B) requires that a fiduciary must act with the "care, skill, prudence and diligence under the circumstances then prevailing that a prudent man acting in a like capacity and familiar with such matters would use in the conduct of an enterprise of a like character and with like aims." As ERISA's legislative history indicates, this standard is derived from the prudent person standard developed under the common law of trusts. In applying ERISA's duty of prudence the federal courts are to apply the standard in a flexible manner, bearing in mind "the special nature and purpose of employee benefit plans." See Donovan v. Mazzola, 716 F.2d 1226, 1231 (9th Cir. 1983).

The prudence of the fiduciary's conduct is evaluated based on the circumstances at the time the decision is made, and not "from the vantage point of hindsight." See Katsaros v. Cody, 744 F.2d 270, 279 (2d Cir. 1984). The duty of prudence is not concerned with results, but rather with the process the fiduciary used in making his decision. See Roth v. Sawyer-Cleator Lumber Co., 16 F.3d 915, 918 (8th Cir. 1994). Thus, the fact that the fiduciary's decision ultimately resulted in an undesirable outcome for the plan or its participants does not establish that a breach of the duty of prudence occurred. Conversely, a successful outcome resulting from the fiduciary's decision will not absolve the fiduciary's breach of the duty of prudence. "Luck or good fortune is no substitute for a trustee's duty of inquiry." Donovan v. Bierwirth, 538 F.Supp. 463, 471 (E.D.N.Y. 1981).

Like ERISA's duty of loyalty, the fiduciary duty of prudence is an objective standard that emphasizes the necessity of careful investigation before a fiduciary embarks upon a course of action. A fiduciary's subjective good faith—a "pure heart and an empty head"—is not a defense to a breach of the duty of prudence. See Donovan v. Cunningham, 716 F.2d 1455, 1467 (5th Cir. 1983). Such careful investigation may require the fiduciary to engage the help of outside experts to assist in the investigative process.

Whenever a plan fiduciary uses plan assets to pay for expenses associated with administering the plan, the plan fiduciary must determine that the expense is "reasonable." The plan fiduciary also must follow a prudent decision making procedure. *Donovan v. Mazzola*, 716 F.2d 1226 (9th Cir. 1983), described previously, illustrates the fiduciary duty of prudence in the context of hiring and paying for the services of an outside consultant using plan assets. In *Donovan v. Mazzola*, the pension fund trustees determined that they needed a feasibility study to determine the most profitable use of the hotel property that was held as an asset by the convalescent fund. The pension trustees selected Dr. Schwartz, who was a personal acquaintance of several of the pension fund trustees, to perform the study. The pension fund trustees never inquired as to Dr. Schwartz's qualifications to prepare the study. In fact, Dr. Schwartz had never performed a feasibility study, had never made a written report on the potential markets and customers for a recreational facility, and had never specialized in advising owners of recreational resorts how to manage and operate their facilities. The pension trustees did not solicit alternate bids for the feasibility study and paid Dr. Schwartz $250,000 (out of pension fund assets) in advance for the study. Dr. Schwartz's price for the feasibility study was approximately $200,000 more than the going market rate for similar studies prepared by individuals with the appropriate experience and credentials.

The court found that under these circumstances the pension fund trustees' conduct in hiring Dr. Schwartz violated ERISA's fiduciary duty of prudence. According to the court, to satisfy the duty of prudence the pension fund trustees should have obtained written bids and proposals from several consultants, inquired into the consultants' qualifications, and withheld payment of part of the consulting fee until the consultant had satisfactorily completed the written report.

Although ERISA's duties of loyalty and prudence are separate duties, sometimes the court will allow evidence of an imprudent course of conduct to support the additional allegation that a breach of the duty of loyalty has occurred. For example, in *Bussian v. RJR Nabisco, Inc.*, 223 F.3d 286 (5th Cir. 2000), the employer-fiduciary, RJR Nabisco, Inc. (RJR), selected the lowest bidder, Executive Life Insurance Co. (Executive Life), to provide annuities to satisfy the pension obligations under the company's terminated pension plan. When Executive Life later declared bankruptcy and defaulted on its annuity obligations, the plan participants sued, alleging that RJR had breached its ERISA duties of loyalty and prudence in selecting Executive Life. The Fifth Circuit reversed the district court's grant of summary judgment for RJR, finding that a reasonable trier of fact could conclude that the selection of

Executive Life was imprudent based on the insurance company's risky investment strategy. The Fifth Circuit further found that RJR's selection of Executive Life as the plan's annuity provider was motivated by its own interest in maximizing the reversion of plan assets to the company rather than selecting a fiscally sound annuity provider for the plan's participants.

ERISA's duty of prudence is closely associated with plan administration. In the course of administering the plan, the fiduciary may act carelessly in processing a participant's claim, or may make mistakes in calculating or paying plan benefits. The fiduciary also may act carelessly in response to a plan participant's question concerning the plan or plan benefits and fail to provide the participant with complete and accurate information. This particular category of breach of fiduciary duty cases is discussed in the Note on the Duty to Inform in Section C.3 of Chapter Five.

The duty of prudence further requires that the fiduciary must exercise care when delegating fiduciary tasks to co-fiduciaries, when selecting and overseeing persons who provide services to the plan and its participants, or when selecting a menu of investment options for a plan where the participants direct the investment of their own accounts. See DOL Reg. §§ 2509.75–8, FR–14–FR–17; 2509.96–1(e); Final Regulation Regarding Participant Directed Individual Account Plans, 57 Fed. Reg. 46,906, 46,922 (Oct. 13, 1992). This obligation, known as the *duty to monitor,* has received close attention by the Department of Labor in the context of 401(k) plans, particularly when the fees associated with the plan's menu of investment options are deducted from participant accounts and paid to the plan's service providers. Department of Labor regulations require that a plan service provider must disclose any fees that result in direct or indirect compensation to the service provider in conjunction with investment advisory services, recordkeeping services or brokerage services provided to the plan. The fee disclosure regulations apply only for pension plans. Disclosure is required if the plan service provider expects to receive direct or indirect compensation related to plan investments of at least $1,000. See generally Final Regulation Relating to Service Provider Disclosures Under Section 408(b)(2), 77 Fed. Reg. 5632 (Feb. 3, 2012).

The fee disclosure rules provide plan fiduciaries with the information they need to determine whether the contracts or arrangements they enter into with plan service providers are prudent. Disclosure enables plan fiduciaries to evaluate whether the total compensation received by a service provider in connection with the services provided to the plan is reasonable. The fee disclosure requirements also permit plan fiduciaries to determine whether a potential conflict of interest may affect the quality of the plan services performed by the service provider under the contract or arrangement. See id. at 41,609. Fees and expenses in participant-directed plans are discussed in more detail in Section E of Chapter Five.

Another plan administration issue that invokes the fiduciary duty of prudence concerns the timely forwarding of employee salary deferral contributions to the trustee of the employer's 401(k) plan. Department of Labor regulations require that amounts the employer withholds from wages as employee salary deferral contributions to a 401(k) plan must be forwarded to the trustee of the 401(k) plan on the earliest date that the contributions reasonably can be segregated from the employer's general assets. In no event may employee salary deferral contributions be forwarded to the trustee of the 401(k) plan later than the fifteenth business day of the month following the month in which the participant contributions to the 401(k) plan were received by the employer. See DOL Reg. § 2510.3–102(b)(1).

The duty of prudence frequently arises in the context of plan investment decisions. Often the duty of prudence is paired with a claim that the fiduciary who made the investment decision also violated ERISA's duty of prudent diversification of plan assets. ERISA Section 404(a)(1)(C) describes the fiduciary's duty of prudent diversification of plan assets as the duty to diversify "the investments of the plan so as to minimize the risk of large losses, unless under the circumstances, it is clearly prudent not to do so."

The legislative history of ERISA indicates that the duty of prudent diversification is designed to prevent the fiduciary from concentrating the investment of the plan's assets in a single type of investment, geographic location, or industry.

The [legislation] requires fiduciaries to diversity plan assets to minimize the risk of large losses, unless under the circumstances it is clearly prudent not to do so. It is not intended that a more stringent standard of prudence be established with the use of the term "clearly prudent." Instead, by using this term it is intended that in an action for plan losses based on breach of the diversification requirement, the plaintiff's initial burden will be to demonstrate that there has been a failure to diversify. The defendant then is to have the burden of demonstrating that this failure to diversify was prudent. The [legislation] places these relative burdens on the parties in this matter, because the basic policy is to require diversification, and if diversification on its face does not exist, then the burden of justifying failure to follow this general policy should be on the fiduciary who engages in this conduct.

The degree of investment concentration that would violate this requirement to diversify cannot be stated as a fixed percentage because a prudent fiduciary must consider the facts and circumstances of each case. The factors to be considered include:

(1) the purposes of the plan;

(2) the amount of the plan assets;

(3) financial and industrial conditions;

(4) the type of investment, whether mortgages, bonds or shares of stock or otherwise;

(5) distribution as to geographical location;

(6) distribution as to industries; and

(7) the dates of maturity.

A fiduciary usually should not invest the whole or an unreasonably large proportion of the trust property in a single security. Ordinarily the fiduciary should not invest the whole or an unduly large proportion of the trust property in one type of security or in various types of securities dependent upon the success of one enterprise or upon conditions in one locality, since the effect is to increase the risk of large losses. Thus, although the fiduciary may be authorized to invest in industrial stocks, he should not invest a disproportionate amount of the plan assets in the shares of corporations engaged in a particular industry. If he is investing in mortgages on real property he should not invest a disproportionate amount of the trust in mortgages in a particular district or on a particular class of property so that a decline in property values in that district or of that class might cause a large loss.

The assets of many pension plans are managed by one or more investment managers. For example, one investment manager, A, may be responsible for 10% of the assets of a plan and instructed by the named fiduciary or trustee to invest solely in bonds; another investment manager, B, may be responsible for a different 10% of the assets of the same plan and instructed to invest solely in equities. Such arrangements often result in investment returns which are quite favorable to the plan, its participants, and its beneficiaries. In these circumstances, A would invest solely in bonds in accordance with his instructions and would diversify the bond investments in accordance with the diversification standard, the prudent man standard, and all other provisions applicable to A as a fiduciary. Similarly, B would invest solely in equities in accordance with his instructions and these standards. Neither A nor B would incur any liability for diversifying assets subject to their management in accordance with their instructions.

The conferees intend that, in general, whether the plan assets are sufficiently diversified is to be determined by examining the ultimate investment of the plan assets. For example, the conferees understand that for efficiency and economy plans may invest all their assets in a single bank or other pooled investment fund, but that the pooled fund itself could have diversified investments. It is intended that, in this case, the diversification rule is to be applied to the plan by examining the diversification of the investments in the pooled fund. The same is true with respect to investments in a mutual fund. Also, generally a plan may be invested wholly in insurance or annuity contracts without violating the diversification rules, since generally an insurance company's assets are to be invested in a diversified manner.

H.R. CONF. REP. NO. 93–1280 (1973).

GIW Industries, Inc. v. Trevor, Stewart, Burton & Jacobsen, Inc., 895 F.2d 729 (11th Cir. 1990), illustrates an investment decision that violated both the duty of prudence and the duty of prudent diversification. In *GIW Industries,* the plan's investment manager invested 70% of the plan's assets in U.S. government bonds with a single maturity date, and invested an additional 15% in zero coupon bonds with a different maturity date. Prior to making these investment decisions, the investment manager failed to investigate the historical cash flow requirements of the plan and did not attempt to ascertain what withdrawals from the plan might be anticipated in the future. The Eleventh Circuit affirmed the district court's ruling that this investment strategy violated ERISA's fiduciary duties of prudence and prudent diversification, despite the fact that the principal amount invested in the bonds was guaranteed. The court reasoned that the lack of liquidity resulting from tying up almost all of the plan's assets in interest rate sensitive bonds with only two maturity dates exposed the plan to an unreasonable risk of loss in the event the plan had to liquidate the investment prior to maturity in order to pay benefits to the plan participants.

Modern Portfolio Theory and FAS 158

The Department of Labor interprets ERISA's duty of prudence concerning plan investments as consistent with the *prudent investor standard* that incorporates the modern portfolio theory of investments. See DOL Reg. § 2550.404a–1; Laborers Nat'l Pension Fund v. Northern Trust Quantitative Advisors, 173 F.3d 313 (5th Cir. 1999); Meyer v. Berkshire Life Ins. Co., 250 F.Supp.2d 544 (D. Md. 2003). Historically, the common law of trusts applied the "prudent person" standard to a trustee's investment decisions. Under the common law prudent person standard, the trustee was required to evaluate the prudence of each trust investment individually. See AMY MORRIS HESS, ET AL., THE LAW OF TRUSTS AND TRUSTEES § 612 (3d ed. 2000). Today, the common law of trusts uses the prudent investor standard and modern portfolio theory to evaluate a trustee's investment decisions. See id. Modern portfolio theory also is used to determine the asset allocation strategy used by defined benefit plans. Modern portfolio theory focuses the fiduciary's attention on the overall diversification of the trust's assets, and requires the fiduciary to analyze the diversification and risk of each individual investment in light of the trust's complete investment portfolio.

For public companies who sponsor defined benefit plans, the financial accounting rules related to pension funding also may play a role in the plan's investment strategy. Under Financial Accounting Standard 158 (FAS 158), publicly traded companies must recognize a defined benefit plan's funding status as an asset or a liability on the company's balance sheet. Consequently, market fluctuations in the value of the defined benefit plan's assets can affect the company's net worth. To stabilize plan asset values, employers may desire to manage the risk of stock market volatility by investing a greater proportion of plan assets in fixed income investments and a corresponding lesser proportion of plan assets in equities.

Such a change in investment strategy raises issues under both the exclusive benefit rule and the duty of prudent diversification. By managing the plan's investment portfolio to reduce stock market volatility, the employer who funds the plan receives the potential "benefit" of reduced volatility in the employer's net worth as reported in public financial statements, and further reduces the year-to-year volatility in the employer's required minimum funding contributions. To provide guidance to employers and investment managers in this area, the Department of Labor has opined that "plan fiduciaries have broad discretion in defining investment strategies appropriate to their plans," and that a plan fiduciary would not violate its fiduciary duties solely by implementing "an investment strategy for a plan that takes into account the liability obligations of the plan and the risks associated with such liabilities and that results in reduced volatility in the plan's funding requirements." DOL Op. Ltr. 2006–08A. Whether a particular investment strategy is prudent "depends on all the facts and circumstances involved." Id. According to the Department of Labor, relevant facts and circumstances that the fiduciary should consider in designing an investment allocation strategy for the plan include:

> (A) a determination by the fiduciary that the particular investment or investment course of action is reasonably designed, as part of the portfolio (or, where applicable, that portion of the plan portfolio with respect to which the fiduciary has investment duties) to further the purposes of the plan,

taking into consideration the risk of loss and the opportunity for gain (or other return) associated with the investment or investment course of action; and

(B) consideration of the following factors as they relate to such portion of the portfolio:

  (i)   the composition of the portfolio with regard to diversification;

  (ii) the liquidity and current return of the portfolio relative to the anticipated cash flow requirement of the plan; and

  (iii) the projected return of the portfolio relative to the funding objectives of the plan.

DOL Op. Ltr. 2006–08A.

Individual Account Plans and the Duty of Prudent Diversification

ERISA exempts individual account plans from the duty of prudent diversification with respect to the acquisition or holding of qualifying employer securities as a plan asset. See ERISA §§ 404(a)(2); 407(d)(5). Such plans also are exempt from the duty of prudence, but "only to the extent that it requires diversification." See ERISA § 404(a)(2). Similarly, individual account plans are exempt from ERISA's prohibited transaction rule that limits an investment in employer securities to no more than 10% of the plan's assets. See ERISA § 407(b)(1). These exemptions make it possible for participants in individual account plans to hold high concentrations of company stock in their plan accounts. Section E of Chapter Five explores the unique issues associated with significant concentrations of company stock held as an asset in individual account plans.

d. Fiduciary Responsibilities and Social Investing

The term *social investing* refers to the practice of making investment decisions concerning plan assets that are designed to achieve social or political goals rather than making investment decisions that are based solely on the anticipated investment return to the plan. The practice of social investing is much more common in defined benefit plans sponsored by governmental employers than in plans subject to ERISA's fiduciary responsibility provisions.

In the context of plans regulated by ERISA, an investment that confers a collateral economic or social benefit on others in addition to the investment return the plan receives from the investment is known as an *economically targeted investment*. See DOL Reg. § 2509.94–1. Examples of economically targeted investments include investing in the development of affordable housing, investing in a construction project that will be built using only union labor, investing in redevelopment of a blighted area, or investing only in the stock of companies that conform to certain labor or environmental standards in conducting the company's domestic or international business operations.

When an ERISA plan fiduciary is considering whether to make an economically targeted investment, several of ERISA's fiduciary responsibilities are implicated. The extent to which the plan fiduciary may consider the collateral benefits of the economically targeted investment implicates the exclusive benefit rule under ERISA's duty of loyalty. In addition, ERISA's general fiduciary duties of prudence and the prudent diversification of plan assets apply to the plan fiduciary who directs the investment of plan assets. The Department of Labor's position concerning economically targeted investments of ERISA plan assets is set forth in Interpretive Bulletin 94–1, DOL Reg. § 2509.94–1. Interpretive Bulletin 94–1, reproduced below, takes the position that a fiduciary for an ERISA plan must evaluate an economically targeted investment using the same general fiduciary standards that apply to any other type of plan investment.

Interpretive Bulletin 94–1: The Fiduciary Standard Under ERISA in Considering Economically Targeted Investments

This Interpretive Bulletin sets forth the Department of Labor's interpretation of Sections 403 and 404 of the Employee Retirement Income Security Act of 1974 (ERISA), as applied to employee benefit plan investments in economically targeted investments (ETIs). Sections 403 and 404, in part, require that a fiduciary of a plan act prudently, and to diversify plan investments so as to minimize the risk of large losses, unless under the circumstances it is clearly prudent not to do so. In addition, these sections require that a fiduciary act solely in the interest of the plan's participants and beneficiaries and for the exclusive purpose of providing benefits to participants and beneficiaries. The Department has construed the requirements that a fiduciary act solely in the interest of, and for the exclusive purpose of providing benefits to, participants and beneficiaries as prohibiting a fiduciary from subordinating the interests of participants and beneficiaries in their retirement income to unrelated objectives.

With regard to investing plan assets, the Department has issued a regulation, DOL Reg. § 2550.404a–1, interpreting the prudence requirements of ERISA as they apply to the investment duties of fiduciaries of employee benefit plans. The regulation provides that the prudence requirements of Section 404(a)(1)(B) are satisfied if (1) the fiduciary making an investment or engaging in an investment course of action has given appropriate consideration to those facts and circumstances that, given the scope of the fiduciary's investment duties, the fiduciary knows or should know are relevant, and (2) the fiduciary acts accordingly. This includes giving appropriate consideration to the role that the investment or investment course of action plays (in terms of such factors as diversification, liquidity and risk/return characteristics) with respect to that portion of the plan's investment portfolio within the scope of the fiduciary's responsibility.

Other facts and circumstances relevant to an investment or investment course of action would, in the view of the Department, include consideration of the expected return on alternative investments with similar risks available to the plan. It follows that, because every investment necessarily causes a plan to forgo other investment opportunities, an investment will not be prudent if it would be expected to provide a plan with a lower rate of return than available alternative investments with commensurate degrees of risk or is riskier than alternative available investments with commensurate rates of return.

The fiduciary standards applicable to ETIs—that is, investments selected for the economic benefits they confer on others apart from their investment return to the employee benefit plan—are no different than the standards applicable to plan investments generally. Therefore, if the above requirements are met, the selection of an ETI, or the engaging in an investment course of action intended to result in the selection of ETIs, will not violate Section 404(a)(1)(A) and (B) and the exclusive purpose requirements of Section 403.

e. The Duty to Follow (or Disregard) Plan Terms

ERISA Section 404(a)(1)(D) requires that a fiduciary must discharge his duties "in accordance with the documents and instruments governing the plan insofar as such documents and instruments are consistent with the provisions of [ERISA]." The fiduciary duty created by ERISA Section 404(a)(1)(D) is in essence a two-edged sword—the fiduciary must follow the terms of the plan, but also must disregard the plan's terms if following the terms of the plan would violate the fiduciary's duties and responsibilities under the statute.

The statutory language of ERISA Section 404(a)(1)(D) serves to modify the rule under the common law of trusts that a trustee's fiduciary duties could be limited, altered, or eliminated by the settlor who established the trust through appropriate language in the trust agreement. The principle embedded in ERISA Section 404(a)(1)(D)—that a fiduciary under ERISA is first and foremost obligated to comply with the fiduciary duties imposed by the statute—is further reinforced by ERISA Section 410(a). Section 410(a) voids exculpatory language in a plan document that purports to relieve an ERISA fiduciary from the obligation to comply with any of the fiduciary responsibility provisions contained in Part 4 of Title I of ERISA.

Cases involving an alleged violation of ERISA Section 404(a)(1)(D) arise in a variety of contexts. For example, in *Marshall v. Teamsters Local 282 Pension Trust Fund*, 458 F.Supp. 986, 991 (E.D.N.Y. 1978), the court found a violation of ERISA Section 404(a)(1)(D) because the trustees failed to follow the plan's requirement that they must make a specific determination that any single investment which exceeded 25% of the total value of the plan's assets was prudent. *Herman v. NationsBank Trust Co.*, 126 F.3d 1354 (11th Cir. 1997), illustrates a situation where the court found that the plan fiduciary was obligated to disregard the terms of the plan in order to satisfy the fiduciary's statutory duties under ERISA. In *Herman v. NationsBank Trust Co.*, the court found that the trustee of an employee stock ownership plan could not blindly follow the plan's requirement that the trustee must vote unallocated shares of company stock in the same proportion as participants voted their allocated shares. Rather, in voting the unallocated shares the trustee was bound by ERISA's statutory duty of prudence and had to exercise independent judgment concerning how to vote the unallocated shares.

Best v. Cyrus, 310 F.3d 932 (6th Cir. 2002), provides an example of a situation where ERISA's statutory duties may require a fiduciary to take action *beyond* the duties described in the plan document. In *Best v. Cyrus*, the defendant, Ronald J. Cyrus, served as the trustee of the Kentucky State AFL-CIO Money Purchase Pension Plan (Plan) from 1984 through 1998. During this period, Cyrus also served as the Executive Secretary-Treasurer of the Plan's sponsoring employer, which was the Kentucky State AFL-CIO. Under the terms of the Plan, the employer was required to contribute 15.5% of participants' annual salaries to the Plan. The Plan also permitted participants to borrow funds from their own Plan accounts and repay the loans through payroll deductions.

While Cyrus was serving as both trustee of the Plan and as the Executive Secretary-Treasurer of the employer, the employer experienced financial difficulties and stopped making the required contributions to the Plan. During this period of economic difficulty, Cyrus failed to credit loan repayments made by the Plan participants to their accounts. Instead, the participants' loan repayments apparently were used to pay for the operating and payroll expenses of the employer. Eventually, the National AFL-CIO assumed control over the financial operations of the employer. In reviewing and overseeing the daily operations of the employer, the National AFL-CIO discovered that Cyrus had not taken steps to secure the missing contributions from the employer and had failed to credit loan repayments to participant accounts. The National AFL-CIO removed Cyrus as the Plan's trustee and installed two new trustees.

The new trustees of the Plan, a Plan participant, and the Plan itself all sued Cyrus for breach of his fiduciary duties under ERISA. Cyrus claimed that the scope of his fiduciary duties as the Plan's trustee was determined solely by the description of his responsibilities as trustee in the Plan document. The Plan document provided that the trustee "shall be responsible for the administration of investments" held in the Plan, and that the trustee's responsibilities included "receiving contributions" under the terms of the Plan, "making distributions" from the Plan, and "keeping accurate records" to reflect the administration of the Plan. The Plan document further stated that the trustee's duties "shall be limited to those described."

The district court granted summary judgment for Cyrus on the ground that the Plan document alone governed the trustee's fiduciary duties. Under the terms of the Plan document, Cyrus as trustee had no duty to act regarding the employer's missing contributions or the crediting of loan repayments. The Sixth Circuit reversed, and found that Cyrus's fiduciary duties as trustee of the Plan under ERISA went beyond the description of his responsibilities in the Plan document.

> We think the district court erred when it concluded that, as a matter of law, Cyrus's duties were limited to those described in the plan document. The plaintiffs argue that, quite aside from the language of the plan document, ERISA and ordinary trust law imposed an obligation upon Cyrus to act in the interest of the plan's beneficiaries. We agree. Fiduciary duties under ERISA "draw much of their content from the common law of trusts." Varity Corp. v. Howe, 516 U.S. 489, 496 (1996). Under ordinary trust law, to administer a trust is to perform the duties imposed, or exercise the powers conferred, by the trust document. Id. at 502. A trust document implicitly confers "such powers as are necessary or appropriate for the carrying out of the purposes of the trust." Id. Cyrus had the power and corresponding duty to act in the interest of the plan's beneficiaries, that is, to take necessary and appropriate action with respect to the required contributions and missing repayments.

> "There is more to plan (or trust) administration than simply complying with the specific duties imposed by the plan documents or statutory regime; it also includes the activities that are ordinary and natural means of achieving the objective of the plan." Id. at 504. Here, taking some action with respect to the funds would have been an ordinary means of achieving the plan's objective of benefitting its participants. Cyrus had duties beyond those specified in the plan document because "trust documents cannot excuse trustees from their duties under ERISA, and . . . trust documents must generally be construed in light of ERISA's policies." Central States, Southeast & Southwest Areas Pension Fund v. Central Transp., Inc., 472 U.S. 559, 568 (1985). The plan document must be construed to require

the trustee to act in the interest of the plan's beneficiaries. Because Cyrus could not be "excuse[d]" from his fiduciary duties under ERISA, the language of the plan document could not absolve him of a duty to secure the contributions and repayments.

Cyrus had a specific duty to secure the contributions and repayments because "ERISA clearly assumes that trustees will act to ensure that a plan receives all funds to which it is entitled, so that those funds can be used on behalf of participants and beneficiaries." Id. at 571. Cyrus was aware that contributions were not being made and, according to Parker, Cyrus was also aware that repayments were not being deposited. Therefore, Cyrus knew that the plan was not receiving all the funds to which it was entitled. In circumstances similar to those faced by Cyrus, trustees have had a duty to act in the interest of a plan's beneficiaries. A trustee's failure to attempt to collect contributions owed to a plan has been a breach of the duty to ensure that the plan receives the funds to which it is entitled. A trustee's failure to forward a plan's assets to the plan can likewise create liability for a breach of fiduciary duty. * * * Accordingly, ERISA, along with the law of trusts incorporated into the statute, defines the limits of Cyrus's fiduciary duties. The contributions and repayments must fall within this scope because, as trustee, Cyrus was responsible for the plan's assets. The district court erred when it concluded that he did not have a duty to secure those funds.

Best v. Cyrus, 310 F.3d at 935–36 (citations and internal quotations omitted).

f.   Co-Fiduciary Duties

The legislative history of ERISA, reproduced below, illustrates the variety of contexts in which co-fiduciary duties under Section 405 may arise.

House of Representatives Conference Report No. 93–1280 (1973)

Under Section 405(a) of the legislation, a fiduciary of a plan is to be liable for the breach of fiduciary responsibility by another fiduciary of the plan if he knowingly participates in a breach of duty committed by the other fiduciary. Under this rule, the fiduciary must know the other person is a fiduciary with respect to the plan, and must know that he participated in the act that constituted a breach, and must know that it was a breach. For example, A and B are co-trustees, and the terms of the trust provide that they are not to invest in commodity futures. If A suggests to B that B invest part of the plan assets in commodity futures, and if B does so, A, as well as B, is to be liable for the breach.

In addition, a fiduciary is to be liable for the breach of fiduciary responsibility by another fiduciary of the plan if he knowingly undertakes to conceal a breach committed by the other. For the first fiduciary to be liable, he must know that the other is a fiduciary with regard to the plan, must know of the act, and must know that it is a breach. For example, A and B are co-trustees, and B invests in commodity futures in violation of the trust instrument. If B tells his co-trustee A of this investment, A would be liable with B for breach of fiduciary responsibility if he concealed this investment.

Also, if a fiduciary knows that another fiduciary of the plan has committed a breach, and the first fiduciary knows that this is a breach, the first fiduciary must take reasonable steps under the circumstances to remedy the breach. In the second example above, if A has the authority to do so, and if it is prudent under the circumstances, A may be required to dispose of the commodity futures acquired by B. Alternatively, the most appropriate steps in the circumstances may be to notify the plan sponsor of the breach, or to proceed to an appropriate Federal court for instructions, or bring the matter to the attention of the Secretary of Labor. The proper remedy is to be determined by the facts and circumstances of the particular case, and it may be affected by the relationship of the fiduciary to the plan and to the co-fiduciary, the duties and responsibilities of the fiduciary in question, and the nature of the breach.

A fiduciary also is to be liable for the loss caused by the breach of fiduciary responsibility by another fiduciary of the plan if he enables the other fiduciary to commit a breach through his failure to exercise prudence (or otherwise comply with the basic fiduciary rules of the bill) in carrying out his specific responsibilities. For example, A and B are co-trustees and are to jointly manage the plan assets. A improperly allows B to have the sole custody of the plan assets and makes no inquiry as to his conduct. B is thereby enabled to sell the property and to embezzle the proceeds. A is to be liable for a breach of fiduciary responsibility.

Allocation of Duties of Co-Trustees

Under the legislation, if the plan assets are held by co-trustees, then each trustee has the duty to manage and control those assets. For example, shares of stock held in trust by several trustees generally should be registered in the name of all the trustees, or in the name of the trust. In addition each trustee is to use reasonable care to prevent his co-trustee from committing a breach of fiduciary duty.

Although generally each trustee must manage and control the plan assets, nevertheless, under [Section 405(b) of] the legislation specific duties and responsibilities with respect to the management of plan assets may be allocated among co-trustees by the trust instrument. For example, the trust instrument may provide that trustee A is to manage and control one-half of the plan assets, and trustee B is to manage and control the other half of the plan assets.

Also, the trust instrument may provide that specific duties may be allocated by agreement among the co-trustees. In this case, however, the conferees intend that the trust instrument is to specifically delineate the duties that may be allocated by agreement of the co-trustees and is to specify a procedure for such allocation. Also, the trustees must act prudently in implementing such an allocation procedure.

If duties are allocated among co-trustees in accordance with the legislation, a trustee to whom duties have not been allocated is not to be liable for any loss that arises from acts or omissions of the co-trustee to whom such responsibilities have been allocated.

However, a co-trustee will be liable notwithstanding allocation [of co-trustee duties] if he individually fails to comply with the other fiduciary standards of Section 404. For example, a co-trustee would be liable on account of his own acts if he did not act in accordance with the prudent man standard and thereby caused the plan to suffer a loss. In addition, the general rules of co-fiduciary liability are to apply [under Section 405(a)]. Therefore, for example, if a trustee had knowledge of a breach by a co-trustee, he would be liable unless he made reasonable efforts to remedy the breach.

Investment Managers and Investment Committees

Under Section 405(d) of the legislation, if the plan so provides, a person who is a named fiduciary with respect to the control or management of plan assets may appoint a qualified investment manager to manage all or part of the plan assets.

(However, in choosing an investment manager, the named fiduciary must act prudently and in the interests of participants and beneficiaries, and also must act in this manner in continuing the use of an investment manager.) In this case, the plan trustee would no longer have responsibility for managing the assets controlled by the qualified investment manager, and the trustee would not be liable for the acts or omissions of the investment manager.

g. Indemnification of Fiduciaries and Fiduciary Liability Insurance

Personal fiduciary liability under Section 409(a) can be significant, particularly given that co-fiduciaries are jointly and severally liable for damages resulting from a breach of fiduciary duty. See Cavalieri v. General Elec. Co., 47 Empl. Benefits Cas. (BNA) 2719 (N.D.N.Y. 2009) (approving settlement of $40.15 million in damages and $10 million in attorneys' fees); In re Delphi Corp. Sec., Deriv. and ERISA Litig., 248 F.R.D. 483, 491 (E.D. Mich. 2008) (approving settlement for $47 million in damages); In re Healthsouth Corp. ERISA Litig., 2006 WL 2109484 (N.D. Ala. 2006) (approving settlement of $28 million in damages). Given the large damages awards or settlement amounts that may result from fiduciary litigation, ERISA-savvy individuals who are asked to serve as fiduciaries usually insist upon indemnification, fiduciary liability insurance coverage, or both as a prerequisite to serving as a fiduciary.

In order to indemnify a fiduciary against liability or purchase fiduciary insurance coverage, the employer who sponsors the plan must navigate the provisions of Section 410(a). Recall that under Section 410(a), any attempt to relieve a fiduciary from liability by inserting an exculpatory clause in a plan document or instrument generally is void as against public policy. The Department of Labor interprets Section 410(a) as further prohibiting the indemnification of a fiduciary using *plan assets* because"[s]uch an arrangement would have the same result as an exculpatory clause in that it would, in effect, relieve the fiduciary of responsibility and liability to the plan by abrogating the plan's right to recovery from the fiduciary for breaches of fiduciary obligations." DOL Reg. § 2509.75–4.

It is permissible, however, for a fiduciary to be contractually indemnified using the *corporate assets* of the employer who sponsors the plan:

> The Department of Labor interprets Section 410(a) to permit indemnification agreements which do not relieve a fiduciary of responsibility or liability under Part 4 of Title I. Indemnification provisions which leave the fiduciary fully responsible and liable, but merely permit another party to satisfy any liability incurred

by the fiduciary in the same manner as insurance purchased under Section 410(b)(3), are therefore not void under Section 410(a).

DOL Reg. § 2509.75–4; contra Johnson v. Couturier, 572 F.3d 1067 (9th Cir. 2009) (affirming district court's grant of a preliminary injunction prohibiting 100% ESOP-owned company from advancing defense costs pursuant to indemnification agreement with ESOP fiduciaries).

Although plan assets may not be used to indemnify a fiduciary, plan assets may be used to purchase fiduciary liability insurance so long as the policy permits recourse by the insurer against the fiduciary if a court finds that a breach of fiduciary duty has occurred. See ERISA § 410(b)(1). This restriction—that the insurer must have a right of recourse against the fiduciary—does not apply if the fiduciary personally purchases the insurance policy, or if the employer who sponsors the plan purchases the insurance policy for the fiduciary. See ERISA §§ 1110(b)(2)–(3). Another option is for the fiduciary to personally purchase a rider to the plan's policy waiving the right of recourse.

Given the very high hourly rates charged by ERISA litigation attorneys, the defense costs associated with fiduciary litigation are significant. In general, the plan may advance the fiduciary's defense costs. If the litigation establishes that a breach of fiduciary duty has occurred, then the fiduciary personally must pay the defense costs. E.g., Leigh v. Engle, 727 F.2d 113 (7th Cir. 1984). If the fiduciary litigation is settled, the plan may pay the defense and settlement costs associated with the litigation if legal counsel has opined that no breach of fiduciary duty has occurred. See DOL Adv. Op. Ltr. No. 77–66A (June 2, 1976).

The combination of ERISA's prohibition on exculpatory clauses and the restrictions on using plan assets to insure or indemnify breaching fiduciaries addresses the problem of moral hazard that may arise when the risk of a breaching fiduciary's insolvency is high. Section 410 attempts to strike the appropriate balance between protecting the assets of the plan and promoting service by fiduciaries who act in compliance with their statutory fiduciary responsibilities.

3. NOTE ON THE DUTY TO INFORM

In *Varity Corporation v. Howe*, 516 U.S. 489 (1996), the Supreme Court acknowledged that a fiduciary may have a duty to provide relevant information to individual plan participants beyond the statutory disclosure requirements found in Part 1 of Title I of ERISA. The federal courts have struggled to determine the exact parameters of this fiduciary duty, which is commonly referred to as the *duty to inform*.

Duty to inform cases fall into two general categories. The first category involves everyday situations where a plan administrator communicates with a plan participant concerning plan benefits. In these *participant communication* cases, the participant ask questions of the plan administrator seeking either clarification of ambiguous language in a summary plan description, assistance in complying with the plan's procedure for a benefits claim, or advice concerning the participant's benefits under the plan. The participant relies on the plan administrator's statements and other representations, which later turn out to be either misleading, incomplete, inaccurate, or false. As a result of relying on the plan administrator's communications, the participant suffers some economic injury, typically either by receiving a lesser amount of plan benefits or by losing the benefits under the plan entirely.

The second category of duty to inform cases arises in the specific factual context of a company's reduction in its workforce. Rather than laying off workers, the company decides to induce workers to terminate their employment voluntarily. This inducement takes the form of an enhanced early retirement or severance benefit package that is available only to those employees who voluntarily terminate employment within a certain time frame, or "window." If this first window of opportunity for enhanced benefits expires and the company's workforce has not been sufficiently reduced in number, the company may consider whether to offer a second round of enhanced benefits. This second round of enhanced benefits may be even more generous than the enhanced benefits provided under the first window. When the company offers a second round of enhanced benefits, those employees who terminated employment and accepted the less generous benefits in the first round, or who terminated employment after the first window closed, but before the second window of opportunity for enhanced benefits opened, typically claim that the company breached its fiduciary duty to them by failing to disclose that a second round of enhanced benefits was under consideration. These cases are known as *serious consideration* cases because most, but not all, of the federal circuit courts of appeals take the position that a fiduciary's duty to disclose a proposed, but not yet finalized, second round of enhanced benefits is triggered once the proposal is under "serious consideration" by the employer.

Participant Communication Cases

The plan administrator's fiduciary duty to inform in the context of communications with plan participants is derived from the general fiduciary duty of prudence. See ERISA § 404(a)(1)(B). The duty to inform requires the plan administrator not only to be accurate when responding to participant inquiries, but also to provide complete information and not to mislead the participant by omitting material information. The duty to inform imposes an affirmative duty upon the plan fiduciary to disclose all material facts or other information to the plan participant in response to participant questions. See Krohn v. Huron Mem. Hosp., 173 F.3d 542,

547–48 (6th Cir. 1999). The duty to inform includes an affirmative duty to speak up when the plan fiduciary knows that silence itself might be misleading. See Harte v. Bethlehem Steel Corp., 214 F.3d 446, 452 (3d Cir. 2000). The plan fiduciary must convey complete and accurate information that is material to the participant's circumstances, even if the participant has not made a specific inquiry concerning such information. See Shea v. Esensten, 107 F.3d 625, 629 (8th Cir. 1997).

The District of Columbia Court of Appeals was the first federal circuit to recognize the fiduciary's duty to inform in *Eddy v. Colonial Life Insurance Co.*, 919 F.2d 747 (D.C. Cir. 1990). In *Eddy*, the plan participant, James Eddy, had been diagnosed as HIV-positive. Eddy received a memo from his employer less than one week before a previously scheduled surgery notifying him that the company had terminated its group health insurance plan. The memo informed Eddy that due to the termination of the employer's group health plan, he would be personally responsible for paying the expenses of his upcoming surgery. Eddy called the plan's fiduciary, Colonial Life, and inquired about the status of his health insurance coverage. At trial, the parties disputed whether in this telephone call Eddy asked about "continuing" his employer's group health plan coverage or "converting" it to an individual policy. (Eddy did not have continuation rights under COBRA because the employer had terminated the group health plan. He did, however, have a contractual right to convert his group coverage to an individual policy.) Eddy testified he was told that he did not have the right to "convert" his group coverage to an individual policy. He subsequently incurred several thousand dollars' worth of medical expenses, and eventually sued Colonial Life for breach of fiduciary duty based on the allegedly inaccurate information conveyed to him in the telephone conversation.

The district court ruled for Colonial Life on Eddy's breach of fiduciary duty claim, reasoning that Eddy failed to prove that he had used the word "convert" or otherwise properly communicated to the plan's fiduciary his desire to convert his group health plan coverage to an individual policy. The court of appeals reversed, finding that the district court's view of a plan fiduciary's duty when communicating with plan participants was too narrow.

> The duty to disclose material information is the core of a fiduciary's responsibility, animating the common law of trusts long before the enactment of ERISA. At the request of a beneficiary (and in some circumstances upon his own initiative), a fiduciary must convey complete and correct material information to a beneficiary. * * * A fiduciary's duty, however, is not discharged simply by the issuance and dissemination of [documents and notices required by statute under Part 1 of Title I of ERISA]. Instead, that duty carries through in all of the

fiduciary's dealings with beneficiaries; in general, a fiduciary may not materially mislead those to whom the duties of loyalty and prudence are owed. * * * A beneficiary, about to plunge into a ruinous course of dealing, may be betrayed by silence as well as by the spoken word. * * * [R]efraining from imparting misinformation is only *part* of the fiduciary's duty. Once Eddy presented his predicament, Colonial Life was required to do more than simply *not misinform.* Colonial Life also had an affirmative obligation to *inform*—to provide complete and correct material information on Eddy's status and options.

imposition of affirmative duty

Eddy, 919 F.2d at 750–51 (emphasis in original) (quotations and citations omitted).

Since *Eddy,* the duty to inform has been widely recognized in various forms by other circuits. E.g., Becker v. Eastman Kodak Co., 120 F.3d 5 (2d Cir. 1997); Bixler v. Central Pa. Teamsters Health & Welfare Fund, 12 F.3d 1292 (3d Cir. 1993); Griggs v. E.I. DuPont de Nemours & Co., 237 F.3d 371 (4th Cir. 2001); Switzer v. Wal-Mart Stores, Inc., 52 F.3d 1294 (5th Cir. 1995); Krohn v. Huron Mem. Hosp., 173 F.3d 542 (6th Cir. 1999); Bowerman v. Wal-Mart Stores, Inc., 226 F.3d 574 (7th Cir. 2000); Shea v. Esensten, 107 F.3d 625 (8th Cir. 1997); Barker v. American Mobile Power Corp., 64 F.3d 1397, 1403 (9th Cir. 1995).

The federal courts also recognize that the scope of the duty to inform is subject to limitations. *Barrs v. Lockheed Martin Corp.,* 287 F.3d 202 (1st Cir. 2002), illustrates the reluctance of the federal courts to extend the duty to situations involving personalized counseling or advice to a plan participant based on the individual's unique circumstances. In *Barrs,* the plaintiff, Nancy Barrs, was the ex-wife of an employee who was covered by two employer-sponsored life insurance policies, a "basic" policy and an "optional" policy. The property settlement order issued by the divorce court required the employee to designate the plaintiff as the beneficiary of both of the life insurance policies and to continue to make all necessary premium payments so that the life insurance policies would remain in effect.

The employer, Lockheed Martin Corporation (Lockheed Martin), was informed of the divorce court's order and promised Barrs in a letter that Lockheed Martin would notify her by registered mail within twenty-four hours if her ex-husband's employment was terminated. Significantly, the divorce court's order referred only to the two life insurance policies that were in effect at the time of the divorce, and did not apply to life insurance policies that might be issued later by a different insurance carrier.

Lockheed Martin later replaced the optional policy with a different insurance carrier. The employee named his fiancée as the beneficiary of the new optional policy. Lockheed Martin did not notify Barrs that the optional policy had been changed and that she was no longer the beneficiary. When the employee later terminated employment, Lockheed Martin sent the promised letter to Barrs informing her of the termination and advising her that she could convert the basic policy (of which she was still the beneficiary) to an individual policy. This letter was sent via certified mail to the most current address that Lockheed Martin had on file for Barrs. Barrs never received the Lockheed Martin letter because she had moved. It was only when her ex-husband died that Barrs learned for the first time that she had no benefits under either of the two life insurance policies.

Barrs sued Lockheed Martin for failing to provide her with the promised notice of her ex-husband's termination, and for breach of fiduciary duty in failing to notify her that the optional policy had been replaced. The court of appeals rejected Barrs's notice claim because Lockheed Martin's agreement was merely to furnish the notice, not to ensure receipt of it. Concerning the breach of the duty to inform claim, Barrs argued that "the obvious intent of the divorce decree was to maintain her interest in her husband's life insurance, and thus Lockheed had to notify her as an assignee-beneficiary of events that eliminated her benefits under an existing policy." Barrs, 287 F.3d at 207. The court of appeals rejected Barrs's fiduciary duty claim, stating:

> Absent a promise or misrepresentation, the courts have almost uniformly rejected claims by plan participants or beneficiaries that an ERISA administrator has to volunteer individualized information taking account of their particular circumstances. This view reflects ERISA's focus on limited and general reporting and disclosure requirements, and also reflects the enormous burdens an obligation to proffer individualized advice would inflict on plan administrators. In general, increased burdens necessarily increase costs, discourage employers from offering plans, and reduce benefits to employees.

[handwritten: policy argument]

Barrs, 287 F.3d at 207–08 (footnotes and citations omitted).

Serious Consideration Cases

The serious consideration line of cases began with *Berlin v. Michigan Bell Telephone Co.*, 858 F.2d 1154 (6th Cir. 1988). In *Berlin*, the company offered a first round of severance plan benefits and medical plan benefits as an incentive to induce management-level employees to retire. This incentive benefits package was called the Management Income Protection Plan (MIPP). After the period of time to retire and receive the incentive MIPP benefits had expired, it became apparent that some management employees were delaying their retirement in hopes of a second MIPP offer. The company allegedly made misrepresentations to the plaintiffs that the MIPP was a one-time offering and that a second round of MIPP benefits would not be available in the future. The plaintiffs terminated employment or retired after the first MIPP window closed and before a second MIPP window opened, thus losing the opportunity to qualify for the second round of MIPP benefits.

The company argued that because amending a plan to offer enhanced benefits was a business decision and not a fiduciary act by the employer, communications by the plan administrator to employees concerning whether the company was considering adopting a plan amendment in the future (here, the amendment to the MIPP opening a second window for eligibility) could not be fiduciary conduct. The district court agreed and granted the company's motion for summary judgment on the plaintiffs' breach of fiduciary duty claim. The court of appeals reversed, stating that "when serious consideration was given by [the company] to implementing MIPP by making a second offering (a question of material fact), then the plan administrator had a fiduciary duty not to make misrepresentations, either negligently or intentionally, to potential plan participants concerning the second offering." Berlin, 858 F.2d at 1163–64.

The key factual question in serious consideration cases is determining when "serious consideration" begins. The test most widely adopted by the federal courts of appeals was first articulated in *Fischer v. Philadelphia Electric Co.*, 96 F.3d 1533 (3d Cir. 1996) (*Fischer II*). In *Fischer II*, the Third Circuit adopted a three-factor test for determining when the employer has begun serious consideration of a proposed future change in plan benefits. Under this test, "[s]erious consideration of a change in plan benefits exists when (1) a specific proposal (2) is being discussed for purposes of implementation (3) by senior management with the authority to implement the change." Fischer II, 96 F.3d at 1539. This test seeks to balance the competing policy purposes that underlie ERISA.

The concept of "serious consideration" recognizes and moderates the tension between an employee's right to information and an employer's need to operate on a day-to-day basis. Every business must develop strategies, gather information, evaluate options, and make decisions. Full disclosure of each step in this process is a practical impossibility. Moreover, as counsel for [the company] emphasized at oral argument, large corporations regularly review their benefit packages as part of an on-going process of cost-monitoring and personnel management. The various levels of management are constantly considering changes in corporate benefit plans. A corporation could not function if ERISA required complete disclosure of every facet of these on-going activities. * * *

Equally important, serious consideration protects employees. Every employee has a need for material information on which that employee can rely in making employment decisions. Too low a standard could result in an avalanche of notices and disclosures. For employees at a large company like [the defendant], which regularly reviews its benefits plans, truly material information could easily be missed if the flow of information was too great. The warning that a change in benefits was under consideration would become meaningless if cried too often.

Fischer II, 96 F.3d at 1539.

The serious consideration test attempts to draw a clear rule that defines an employer's fiduciary duty to provide information to employees concerning possible changes in plan benefits available in the future. Prior to the time serious consideration of a change in plan benefits begins, the plan administrator has no duty to say anything at all to plan participants about the availability of future plan benefits. After serious consideration has begun, the plan administrator has a fiduciary duty not to make material misrepresentations to plan participants in response to their inquiries about the availability of future plan benefits. The practical difficulty in implementing this rule is that the point in time at which "serious consideration" begins is a legal conclusion, known definitively only once the parties are in litigation and a federal court makes this determination.

The *Fischer II* test has been adopted by the First, Sixth, Seventh, Ninth and Tenth Circuits. See Vartanian v. Monsanto Co., 131 F.3d 264, 268 (1st Cir. 1997); McAuley v. International Business Machines Corp., Inc., 165 F.3d 1038, 1043 (6th Cir. 1999); Beach v. Commonwealth Edison Co., 382 F.3d 656, 660 (7th Cir. 2004); Bins v. Exxon Co. U.S.A., 220 F.3d 1042, 1047 (9th Cir. 2000); Hockett v. Sun Co., Inc., 109 F.3d 1515, 1522 (10th Cir. 1997). The Second Circuit and the Fifth Circuit do not follow the *Fischer II* test, but rather rely on a case-by-case analysis of the circumstances to determine whether there is a substantial likelihood that a reasonable plan participant would have considered the information allegedly misrepresented by the fiduciary to be important in the participant's decision to retire. See Ballone v. Eastman Kodak Co., 109 F.3d 117 (2d Cir. 1997); Pocchia v. NYNEX Corp., 81 F.3d 275 (2d Cir. 1996); Martinez v. Schlumberger, Ltd., 338 F.3d 407 (5th Cir. 2003).

QUESTION

One of the routine responsibilities of the plan's administrator is to respond to questions from participants concerning the operation of the plan and the benefits provided by the plan. In light of the duty to inform, how comprehensively should a plan administrator respond to questions from plan participants? Under what circumstances might the plan administrator be required to do more than simply review the relevant provisions of the plan's summary plan description with the participant?

PROBLEMS ON FIDUCIARY AND CO-FIDUCIARY RESPONSIBILITIES

PROBLEM ONE

Treetop Company sponsors a profit sharing plan (Retirement Plan) for its employees. The named plan fiduciary for the Retirement Plan is Treetop Company. John Jason, the human resources manager, is responsible for the administration of the Retirement Plan. The paperwork for the Retirement Plan is handled by Joan Bixby, the assistant human resources manager.

A. Treetop Company acquires a subsidiary, Greenleaf Company. *[handwritten: in house lawyer]* The board of directors for Treetop Company decides that it is in the *[handwritten: likely exempted]* best interests of the shareholders of Treetop Company to keep the company's costs of sponsoring the Retirement Plan as low as possible. Consequently, the board of directors decides that the employees of Greenleaf Company should be excluded from participating in the Retirement Plan. Accordingly, John Jason (the plan administrator) directs the in-house lawyer for Treetop Company to prepare an amendment to the Retirement Plan that excludes the employees of Greenleaf Company from participating in the Retirement Plan. The amendment is properly adopted by the board of directors of Treetop Company pursuant to the procedure for plan amendments specified in the Retirement Plan. In deciding to exclude the employees of Greenleaf Company from participation in the Retirement Plan, has Treetop Company committed a breach of fiduciary duty? Why or why not?

B. Sally Haverty, an employee of Treetop Company and a *[handwritten: duty to inform]* participant in the Retirement Plan, terminates employment. Joan *[handwritten: question]* Bixby, who is the assistant human resources manager for Treetop Company, forgets to give Sally the explanation required under the Internal Revenue Code that describes the tax consequences of electing to receive a distribution rather than electing a direct rollover of Sally's nonforfeitable accrued benefit under the Retirement Plan. When Sally asks Joan Bixby about the possible tax consequences of receiving a distribution, Joan tells Sally, "Don't worry, it's only a 10% tax." Relying on Joan's erroneous remark, Sally elects to receive a lump sum distribution from the Retirement Plan. Sally later discovers she owes $5,500 in additional income tax (much more than 10%) due to the inclusion of the distribution in her gross income for the year. Sally is upset about the additional taxes she owes and comes to you for legal advice. Sally wants to know if Joan Bixby has committed a breach of fiduciary duty under ERISA. How will you advise Sally?

PROBLEM TWO

Digital Company, the named plan fiduciary, sponsors a participant-directed 401(k) plan for its employees. The 401(k) plan is administered by First Bank, and the plan assets are held by First Trust Company, who serves as the plan's directed trustee.

Digital Company experiences cash flow difficulties due to its inability to collect on overdue accounts receivable from the company's customers. Rather than immediately forwarding the employee contributions to the 401(k) plan to First Trust Company, as had regularly been done in the past, Digital Company uses the money instead to purchase raw materials used in the company's manufacturing business.

First Trust Company immediately notifies First Bank that it has not received the usual employee 401(k) plan contributions from Digital Company. The client account representative of First Bank calls the president of Digital Company concerning the late payment. The president of Digital Company tells the First Bank account representative that "business is slow" and that "the money is coming."

Three weeks later, one of the company's customers pays a large, long overdue bill. Digital Company uses the money to pay the overdue employee contributions to the 401(k) plan.

Discuss the potential fiduciary and co-fiduciary duties of Digital Company (and its president), First Bank (including the customer account representative), and First Trust Company in this situation. What fiduciary duties have been breached?

D. PROHIBITED TRANSACTIONS AND EXEMPTIONS

The concept of a prohibited transaction is rooted in the historical abuse of plan assets that preceded the enactment of ERISA. To eliminate such misconduct, ERISA generally prohibits fiduciaries and other persons closely associated with the plan from engaging in transactions that involve plan assets. The purpose of ERISA's prohibited transaction rules is to "make illegal per se the types of transactions that experience had shown to entail a high potential for abuse." Donovan v. Cunningham, 716 F.2d 1455, 1464–65 (5th Cir. 1983).

In theory, the concept of a prohibition on certain types of transaction involving plan assets is a simple one. In application, the devil (as always) is in the details. The body of statutory and regulatory law that codifies and interprets ERISA's prohibited transaction rules is notoriously detailed and difficult. Section D of Chapter Five presents a brief overview and summary of the prohibited transaction rules and highlights several of the more prominent judicial decisions in the area.

1. OVERVIEW OF THE PROHIBITED TRANSACTION RULES

ERISA Section 406 creates two sets of prohibited transaction rules. Section 406(a) lists the types of transactions prohibited for a party in interest (*party in interest prohibited transactions*). Section 406(b) describes additional transactions that are prohibited for a plan fiduciary (*fiduciary prohibited transactions*).

a. Definition of a Party in Interest

The underlying rationale for the party in interest prohibited transactions is that a party in interest has some connection, either with the plan or the plan's sponsor, that potentially could influence the plan fiduciary's decision to authorize the transaction. ERISA Section 3(14) defines a party in interest as:

- Any plan fiduciary, legal counsel to the plan, or employee of the plan;
- Any person who provides services to the plan (a *service provider*);
- An employer or employee organization whose employees or members are covered by the plan;
- Any person who owns 50% or more of an employer or employee organization which itself is a party in interest;
- Any relative of an individual who is a party in interest;
- Any entity which is owned 50% or more by a party in interest; and
- Any employee, officer, director, or 10% owner of an entity that is a party in interest.

Of this list, the most easily recognized parties in interest are plan fiduciaries, service providers to the plan, the plan's sponsor (either an employer or an employee organization) and persons directly associated with the plan's sponsor, such as employees, officers, and directors.

b. Party in Interest Prohibited Transactions

The party in interest prohibited transactions contained in ERISA Section 406(a) are loosely based upon principles developed under the common law of trusts. Under the common law of trusts, a transaction involving trust assets could be set aside if the trustee was improperly influenced by the other party to the transaction or if the trustee allowed the trust to engage in a transaction on terms that were less than arms' length. The common law of trusts required that before a transaction involving trust assets could be set aside, undue influence, bad faith, or detriment to the trust had to be demonstrated.

ERISA Section 406(a) modifies the common law of trusts by creating broad categories of transactions with a plan involving plan assets that are illegal per se based solely on the identity of the party or parties involved in the transaction. The effect of the party in interest prohibited transactions is to eliminate the need to prove that a particular transaction was detrimental to the plan, or that the plan fiduciary who authorized the transaction was unduly influenced or acted in bad faith.

ERISA Section 406(a)(1) describes the various categories of party in interest prohibited transactions as follows:

> A fiduciary with respect to a plan shall not cause the plan to engage in a transaction, if he knows or should know that such transaction constitutes a direct or indirect—
>
> (A) sale or exchange, of any property between the plan and a party in interest;
>
> (B) lending of money or other extension of credit between the plan and a party in interest;
>
> (C) furnishing of goods, services, or facilities between the plan and a party in interest;
>
> (D) transfer to, or use by or for the benefit of, a party in interest, of any assets of the plan; or
>
> (E) acquisition, on behalf of the plan, of any employer security or employer real property in violation of Section 407(a).

c. Fiduciary Prohibited Transactions

The three fiduciary prohibited transactions described in ERISA Section 406(b) are based on the principle developed under the common law of trusts that a trustee has an undivided duty of loyalty to the trust for which the trustee acts. See DOL Reg. § 2550.408b–2(e)(1); Morton Klevan, *The Fiduciary's Duty of Loyalty Under ERISA Section 406(b)(1)*, 23 REAL PROP. PROB. & TR. J. 561, 561–64 (1988). First, a fiduciary cannot engage in a self-dealing transaction using plan assets. ERISA § 406(b)(1). Second, a fiduciary cannot engage in a transaction, in either an individual or representative capacity, where a conflict of interest exists between the fiduciary and the plan or the plan's participants. ERISA § 406(b)(2). Third, a fiduciary cannot receive a "kickback" from a third party who is engaged in a transaction involving plan assets. ERISA § 406(b)(3).

The fiduciary prohibited transaction rules of ERISA Section 406(b) are construed strictly by the federal courts. Under the rules of ERISA Section 406(b), a transaction between the plan and a plan fiduciary is prohibited even where there is "no taint of scandal, no hint of self-dealing, no trace of bad faith." Cutaiar v. Marshall, 590 F.2d 523, 528 (3d Cir. 1979).

Of course, some prohibited transaction violations by fiduciaries *are* scandalous and involve intentional self-dealing. The actions of NFL quarterback Michael Vick illustrate exactly the sort of misuse of plan assets that the fiduciary prohibited transaction rules were designed to deter. Michael Vick's personal marketing company, MV7, sponsored a defined benefit pension plan for its employees. Vick served as the trustee for the plan. According to the Department of Labor's complaint, Vick withdrew money from the plan's trust in 2007 for his personal benefit and used the money to pay his attorney's fees and the restitution penalty that resulted from his criminal conviction for illegal dog fighting. A consent judgment was entered in the case in 2009 ordering Vick to pay $416,461.10 in restitution to the plan. See Employee Benefit Security Administration, News Release (Sept. 30, 2009).

d.   Prohibited Transactions Involving Qualified Plans

The party in interest and fiduciary prohibited transactions of ERISA Section 406 are incorporated into the Internal Revenue Code and made applicable to transactions involving qualified retirement plans. See Code § 4975(c). When a prohibited transaction involves the assets of a qualified retirement plan, the prohibited transaction rules of Code Section 4975(c) govern. These Code provisions substitute the term *disqualified person* for ERISA's term, *party in interest*. The definition of a disqualified person is identical to the definition of a party in interest, but with one minor exception. A disqualified person includes only those employees who earn 10% or more of the yearly wages of an employer, whereas a party in interest includes all employees of the employer. Compare Code § 4975(e)(2)(H) with ERISA § 3(14)(H). The Code and ERISA definitions of a fiduciary are identical. Compare Code § 4975(e)(3) with ERISA § 3(21)(A).

Although the prohibited transaction rules of ERISA Section 406 and Code Section 4975 are similar, their enforcement mechanisms are distinctly different. For prohibited transactions involving the assets of a qualified plan, enforcement under the Code is through an excise tax penalty imposed by the Internal Revenue Service on the disqualified person who has engaged in the prohibited transaction. See Code § 4975(a)–(b); ERISA § 502(i). For all other types of employee benefit plans, the prohibited transaction rules of ERISA govern. The prohibited transaction rules of ERISA are enforced by the Secretary of Labor, who may impose a civil money penalty on the party in interest who engages in a prohibited transaction. See ERISA § 502(i). For both qualified plans and other types of employee benefit plans, a plan fiduciary who authorizes the plan to engage in a prohibited transaction has committed a breach of fiduciary duty and is subject to personal liability under ERISA Section 409(a). Under ERISA Section 409(a), the authorizing fiduciary is responsible for restoring any losses to the plan that occurred as a result of the prohibited transaction, and must disgorge any profits obtained through the use of plan assets. ERISA's legislative history, reproduced later in Section D of Chapter Five, explains the rationale for the different enforcement mechanisms for prohibited transactions used for qualified plans under the Code and other types of employee benefit plans under ERISA.

e. Restrictions on Plan Investments Involving Employer Securities or Employer Real Property

ERISA Section 407 contains additional rules concerning the types of investments that are prohibited for employee benefit plans. An employee benefit plan may hold employer securities or employer real property as an investment only if the securities or real property satisfy certain statutory criteria. See ERISA § 407(d)(4) (defining *qualifying real property*); § 407(d)(5) (defining a *qualifying employer security*). If the plan acquires qualifying employer securities or qualifying employer real property, immediately after the acquisition the aggregate fair market value of all employer securities and employer real property investments held by the plan cannot exceed 10% of the fair market value of the total assets of the plan. ERISA § 407(a). This 10% limitation does not apply to individual account plans. As a result, a 401(k) plan can hold much more than 10% of its assets in company stock. The unique issues associated with company stock as an investment option in 401(k) plans are explored in Section E of Chapter Five.

f. Exemptions

The prohibited transaction rules of ERISA Section 406 sweep so broadly that Congress found it necessary to create a number of statutory exemptions. These statutory exemptions are listed in ERISA Section 408(b). The most commonly encountered exemptions are for loans by the plan to participants or beneficiaries and the payment of "reasonable" compensation to plan service providers (e.g., attorneys, accountants, and actuaries) using plan assets. See ERISA § 408(b)(1)–(2); DOL Reg. §§ 2550.408b–1 (loans); 2550.408c–2 (compensation for services).

The Department of Labor has authority to issue administrative exemptions to the prohibited transaction rules. ERISA § 408(a). Significantly, a statutory or administrative exemption from the prohibited transactions rules does not relieve the plan's fiduciary from its general fiduciary and co-fiduciary responsibilities under ERISA Sections 404 and 405 concerning the administration and management of the plan and its assets.

The Department of Labor has long taken the position that the list of statutory exemptions contained in ERISA Section 408(b) does *not* apply to fiduciary prohibited transactions. See DOL Reg. § 2550.408b–2(a), (e).

But see Harley v. Minnesota Mining and Mfg. Co., 284 F.3d 901 (8th Cir. 2002) (holding that ERISA Section 408(b) exempts fiduciary self-dealing under Section 406(b) so long as the compensation paid to the fiduciary was reasonable). As a result of the Department of Labor's position, ERISA lawyers generally advise their clients that a plan fiduciary can engage in a prohibited transaction that involves plan assets only if the terms and conditions of the transaction qualify for an administrative exemption issued by the Department of Labor.

Although the fiduciary prohibited transaction rules of ERISA Section 406(b) would appear to prohibit an officer, employee, agent, or other representative of the plan's sponsoring employer from serving as a plan fiduciary due to a conflict of interest, ERISA Section 408(c)(3) expressly states that the prohibited transaction rules do not bar such individuals from serving as plan fiduciaries. When such a dual role fiduciary acts in a fiduciary capacity, the individual remains subject to the general fiduciary and co-fiduciary duties of ERISA Sections 404 and 405, including the duty to act for the exclusive benefit of the plan and its participants and beneficiaries.

2. LEGISLATIVE HISTORY

House of Representatives Conference Report No. 93–1280 (1973)

The legislation prohibits plan fiduciaries and parties in interest from engaging in a number of specific transactions. Prohibited transaction rules are included both in the labor and tax provisions of the legislation. Under the labor provisions of Title I of ERISA, the fiduciary is the main focus of the prohibited transaction rules. This corresponds to the traditional focus of trust law and of civil enforcement of fiduciary responsibilities through the courts. On the other hand, the tax provisions focus on the disqualified person. * * *

The prohibited transactions, and exceptions therefrom, are nearly identical in the labor and tax provisions. However, the labor and tax provisions differ somewhat in establishing liability for violation of prohibited transactions. Under the labor provisions, a fiduciary will only be liable if he knew or should have known that he engaged in a prohibited transaction. Such a knowledge requirement is not included in the tax provisions. This distinction conforms to the distinction in present law in the private foundation provisions (where a foundation's manager generally is subject to a tax on self-dealing if he acted with knowledge, but a disqualified person is subject to tax without proof of knowledge).

Under the labor provisions a fiduciary will be liable for losses to a plan from a prohibited transaction in which he engaged if he would have known the transaction involving the particular party in interest was prohibited if he had acted as a prudent man. The type of investigation that will be needed to satisfy the test of prudence will depend upon the particular facts and circumstances of the case. In the case of a significant transaction, generally for a fiduciary to be prudent he must make a thorough investigation of the other party's relationship to the plan to determine if he is a party in interest. In the case of a normal and insubstantial day-to-day transaction, it may be sufficient to check the identity of the other party against a roster of parties in interest that is periodically updated.

In general, it is expected that a transaction will not be a prohibited transaction (under either the labor or tax provisions) if the transaction is an ordinary "blind" purchase or sale of securities through an exchange where neither buyer nor seller (nor the agent of either) knows the identity of the other party involved. In this case, there is no reason to impose a sanction on a fiduciary (or party in interest) merely because, by chance, the other party turns out to be a party in interest (or plan).

Party in Interest Transactions

Under the legislation, the direct or indirect sale, exchange, or leasing of any property between the plan and a party in interest (with exceptions subsequently noted) is a prohibited transaction. Under this rule, the transaction is prohibited whether or not the property involved is owned by the plan or party in interest, and the prohibited transaction includes sales, etc., from the party in interest to the plan, and also from the plan to the party in interest. Also, following the private foundation rules of the tax law, a transfer of property by a party in interest to a plan is treated as a sale or exchange if the property is subject to a mortgage or a similar lien which the party in interest placed on the property * * * or if the plan assumes a mortgage or similar lien placed on the property by a party in interest. * * * This rule prevents circumvention of the prohibition on sale by mortgaging the property before transfer to the plan.

The legislation also generally prohibits the direct or indirect lending of money or other extension of credit between a plan and parties in interest. For example, a prohibited transaction generally will occur if a loan to a plan is guaranteed by a party in interest, unless it comes within the special exemption for employee stock ownership plans.

With certain exceptions described below, the direct or indirect furnishing of goods or services or facilities between a plan and a party in interest also is prohibited. This would apply, for example, to the furnishing of personal living quarters to a party in interest.

The legislation prohibits the direct or indirect transfer of any plan income or assets to or for the benefit of a party in interest. It also prohibits the use of plan income or assets by or for the benefit of any party in interest. As in other situations, this prohibited transaction may occur even though there has not been a transfer of money or property between the plan and a party in interest. For example, securities purchases or sales by a plan to manipulate the price of the security to the advantage of a party in interest constitutes a use by or for the benefit of a party in interest of assets of the plan.

The labor provisions and the tax provisions differ slightly on the wording with respect to this latter prohibition. The labor provision prohibits such use of the plan's "assets," and the tax provision prohibits use of the plan's "income or assets." (This same difference appears with respect to other prohibited transactions, as well.) The conferees intend that the labor and tax provisions are to be interpreted in the same way and both are to apply to income and assets. The different wordings are used merely because of different usages in the labor and tax laws. In addition, even though the term "income" is used in the tax law, it is intended that this is not to imply in any way that investment in growth assets (which may provide little current income) is to be prohibited where such investment would otherwise meet the prudent man and other rules of the legislation.

Additional Prohibitions

The legislation generally prohibits a fiduciary from dealing with the income or assets of a plan in his own interest or for his own account. However, this does not prohibit the fiduciary from dealings where he has an account in the plan and the dealings apply to all plan accounts without discrimination.

The legislation also prohibits a fiduciary from receiving consideration for his own personal account from any party dealing with the plan in connection with the transaction involving the income or assets of the plan. This prevents, e.g., "kickbacks" to a fiduciary.

In addition, the labor provisions (but not the tax provisions) prohibit a fiduciary from acting in any transaction involving the plan on behalf of a person (or representing a party) whose interests are adverse to the interests of the plan or of its participants or beneficiaries. This prevents a fiduciary from being put in a position where he has dual loyalties, and, therefore, he cannot act exclusively for the benefit of a plan's participants and beneficiaries. (This prohibition is not included in the tax provisions because of the difficulty in determining an appropriate measure for an excise tax.)

Administrative Exemptions or Variances

The conferees recognize that some transactions that are prohibited (and for which there are no statutory exemptions) nevertheless should be allowed in order not to disrupt the established business practices of financial institutions, which often perform fiduciary functions in connection with these plans consistent with adequate safeguards to protect employee benefit plans. For example, while brokerage houses generally would be prohibited from providing, either directly or through affiliates, both discretionary investment management and brokerage services to the same plan, the conferees expect that the Secretary of Labor and Secretary of the Treasury would grant a variance with respect to these services (and other services traditionally rendered by such institutions), provided that they can show that such a variance will be administratively feasible and that the type of transaction for which an exemption is sought is in the interest of and protective of the rights of plan participants and beneficiaries.

In addition, the conferees recognize that some individual transactions between a plan and party in interest may provide substantial independent safeguards for the plan participants and beneficiaries and may provide substantial benefit to the community as a whole, so that the transaction should be allowed under a variance.

Under the legislation, variances may be conditional or unconditional and may exempt a transaction from all or part of the prohibited transaction rules. In addition, variances may be for a particular transaction or for a class of transactions, and may be allowed pursuant to rulings or regulations. A variance from the prohibited transaction rules is to have no effect with respect to the basic fiduciary responsibility rules requiring prudent action, diversification of investments, actions exclusively for the benefit of participants and beneficiaries, etc. (This is the case with respect to all statutory exemptions from the prohibited transaction rules as well.)

Employer Securities and Employer Real Property in Eligible Individual Account Plans

The labor provisions of the legislation generally limit the acquisition and holding by a plan of employer securities and of employer real property (combined) to 10% of plan assets. (Employer securities are securities issued by an employer with employees covered by the plan or its affiliates. Employer real property is real property which is leased by a plan to an employer (or its affiliates) with employees covered by the plan.)

However, a special rule is provided for individual account plans which are profit sharing plans, stock bonus plans, employee stock ownership plans, or thrift or savings plans, since these plans commonly provide for substantial investments in employer securities or real property. In recognition of the special purpose of these individual account plans, the 10% limitation with respect to the acquisition or holding of employer securities or employer real property does not apply to such plans if they explicitly provide for greater investment in these assets. In addition, the diversification requirements of the legislation and any diversification principle that may develop in the application of the prudent man rule are not to restrict investments by eligible individual account plans in qualifying employer securities or qualifying employer real property.

Civil Liability: Fiduciaries

Under the labor provisions (but not the tax provisions), a fiduciary who breaches the fiduciary requirements of the bill is to be personally liable for any losses to the plan resulting from this breach. Such a fiduciary is also to be liable for restoring to the plan any profits which he has made through the use of any plan asset. In addition, such a fiduciary is to be subject to other appropriate relief (including removal) as ordered by a court.

Civil Liability: Party in Interest

A party in interest who engages in a prohibited transaction with respect to a plan that is not qualified (at the time of the transaction) under the Internal Revenue Code may be subject to a civil penalty of up to 5% of the amount involved in the transaction. If the transaction is not corrected after notice from the Secretary of Labor, the penalty may be up to 100% of the transaction.

Excise Tax on Prohibited Transactions

The legislation establishes an excise tax on disqualified persons who participate in specific prohibited transactions respecting a qualified retirement plan.

The tax is at least two levels; initially, disqualified persons who participate in a prohibited transaction are to be subject to a tax of 5%[a] of the amount involved in the transaction per year. A second tax of 100% is imposed if the transaction is not corrected after notice from the Internal Revenue Service that the 5% tax is due.

The first-level tax is owed for each taxable year (or part of a year) in the period that begins with the date when the prohibited transaction occurs and ends on the earlier of the date of collection or the date of mailing of a deficiency notice for the first-level tax. The first-level tax is imposed automatically without regard to whether the violation was inadvertent.

To correct a prohibited transaction, the transaction must be undone to the extent possible, but in any case the final position of the plan must be no worse than it would have been if the disqualified person were acting under the highest fiduciary standards. The higher valuation to be used in computing any second-level tax that might be applicable is also the valuation to be used in correcting the transaction. In other words,

---

[a]   Under current law, this amount is set at 15% under Code Section 4975(a). The Pension Protection Act of 2006 authorized a 14-day grace period for the penalty-free correction of prohibited transactions that involve the purchase or sale of any commodity or security (excluding employer securities). The grace period begins on the date that the prohibited transaction is or reasonably should have been discovered. See Code §§ 4975(d)(23); 4975(f)(11).—Ed.

correction requires that the plan receive the benefit of whatever bargain turns out to have been involved in the transaction.

NOTES AND QUESTIONS

1. *Lowen v. Tower Asset Management, Inc.,* 829 F.2d 1209 (2d Cir. 1987), illustrates the sweeping nature of the prohibited transaction rules concerning transactions between the plan and a fiduciary. In *Lowen v. Tower Asset Management*, three individual defendants personally owned and controlled an investment management company (Tower Asset), an investment banking corporation (Tower Capital), and a registered securities broker-dealer (Tower Securities). Tower Asset, acting as the fiduciary investment manager for two pension plans, invested $30 million in plan assets in several risky ventures involving companies in the maritime industry. The plans ultimately lost $20 million as a result of these investments.

The defendants owned substantial equity interests in some of the maritime companies that also were plan investments. The court found that under these circumstances ERISA Section 406(b)(1) prohibited the investment of plan assets in the maritime companies. Many of the maritime companies had agreed to pay Tower Capital or Tower Securities commissions, fees and other compensation for investment banking services, which included raising investment capital. The court found that, in causing the plans to invest in these companies, Tower Asset violated ERISA Section 406(b)(3) because Tower Capital or Tower Securities received compensation "in connection with" the investment of the plans' funds. The court concluded that the three individual defendants, along with Tower Capital and Tower Securities, were jointly and severally liable with Tower Asset for the prohibited transaction violations because they had acted in concert with Tower Asset in causing the prohibited transactions. For purposes of assessing joint and several liability, the court stated that it was "irrelevant" whether the individual defendants, Tower Capital or Tower Securities were plan fiduciaries.

> The parties have expended much effort in the district court and on appeal in debating whether Tower Capital, Tower Securities and the individual defendants are fiduciaries of the Plans. * * * Neither the separate corporate status of the three corporations nor the general principle of limited shareholder liability afford protection where exacting obeisance to the corporate form is inconsistent with ERISA's remedial purposes. Parties may not use shell-game-like maneuvers to shift fiduciary obligations to one legal entity while channeling profits from self-dealing to a separate legal entity under their control.

Tower Asset Management, 829 F.2d at 1220 (citations omitted). The defendants were ordered to disgorge $1,087,787 in fees and other compensation and pay this amount to the two pension plans as restitution.

2. *Regulatory Authority to Interpret the Prohibited Transactions Rules.* Consistent with the dual labor/tax nature of the prohibited transaction rules, Congress originally gave the Department of Labor and the Treasury Department dual jurisdiction over interpretation of the prohibited transaction rules of ERISA and the Code. When this dual jurisdiction scheme resulted in conflicting interpretations by the regulatory agencies, sole interpretive authority over the prohibited transaction rules was transferred to the Department of Labor. See Presidential Reorganization Plan No. 4 of 1978, § 102(a), 43 Fed. Reg. 47,713 (1978).

3. *Administrative Exemptions from the Prohibited Transactions Rules.* ERISA Section 408(a) gives the Department of Labor authority to issue administrative exemptions from the prohibited transaction rules. To issue an administrative exemption, the Department of Labor must find that three statutory criteria are satisfied: (1) the exemption must be administratively feasible; (2) the exemption must be in the interests of the plan, its participants and its beneficiaries; and (3) the exemption must be protective of the rights of plan participants and beneficiaries. Administrative exemptions may be issued for a generic class of transactions, or for an individual transaction. Class prohibited transaction exemptions are collected and described in DONALD J. MEYERS AND MICHAEL B. RICHMAN, ERISA CLASS EXEMPTIONS (2d ed. 1996).

3. SUPREME COURT INTERPRETATIONS

COMMISSIONER V. KEYSTONE CONSOLIDATED INDUSTRIES, INC.

United States Supreme Court, 1993.
508 U.S. 152, 113 S.Ct. 2006, 124 L.Ed.2d 71.

In this case, we are concerned with the legality of an employer's contributions of unencumbered property to a defined benefit pension plan. Specifically, we must address the question whether such a contribution, when applied to the employer's funding obligation, is a prohibited "sale or exchange" under Code § 4975 so that the employer thereby incurs the substantial excise taxes imposed by the statute.

* * *

II

The facts that are pertinent for resolving the present litigation are not in dispute. During its taxable years ended June 30, 1983, through June 30, 1988, inclusive, respondent Keystone Consolidated Industries, Inc., a Delaware corporation with principal place of business in Dallas, Texas, maintained several tax-qualified defined benefit pension plans. These were subject to the minimum funding requirements prescribed by § 302 of the Employee Retirement Income Security Act of 1974 (ERISA).

Respondent funded the plans by contributions to the Keystone Consolidated Master Pension Trust.

On March 8, 1983, respondent contributed to the Pension Trust five truck terminals having a stated fair market value of $9,655,454 at that time. Respondent credited that value against its minimum funding obligation to its defined benefit pension plans for its fiscal years 1982 and 1983. On March 13, 1984, respondent contributed to the Pension Trust certain Key West, Florida, real property having a stated fair market value of $5,336,751 at that time. Respondent credited that value against its minimum funding obligation for its fiscal year 1984. The truck terminals were not encumbered at the times of their transfers. Neither was the Key West property. Their respective stated fair market values are not challenged here.

Respondent claimed deductions on its federal income tax returns for the fair market values of the five truck terminals and the Key West property. It also reported as taxable capital gain the difference between its income tax basis in each property and that property's stated fair market value. Thus, for income tax purposes, respondent treated the disposal of each property as a "sale or exchange" of a capital asset. See Code § 1222.

Section 4975 of the Internal Revenue Code was added by § 2003(a) of ERISA. It imposes a two-tier excise tax on specified "prohibited transactions" between a pension plan and a "disqualified person." Among the "disqualified persons" listed in the statute is the employer of employees covered by the pension plan. See Code § 4975(e)(2)(C). Among the transactions prohibited is "any direct or indirect . . . sale or exchange . . . of any property between a plan and a disqualified person." See Code § 4975(c)(1)(A).

The Commissioner of Internal Revenue, who is the petitioner here, ruled that respondent's transfers to the Pension Trust of the five truck terminals and the Key West property were sales or exchanges prohibited under § 4975(c)(1)(A). This ruling resulted in determined deficiencies in respondent's first-tier excise tax liability of $749,610 for its fiscal year 1984 and of $482,773 for each of its fiscal years 1983 and 1985–1988, inclusive. The Commissioner also determined that respondent incurred second-tier excise tax liability in the amount of $9,655,454 for its fiscal year 1988.

Respondent timely filed a petition for redetermination with the United States Tax Court. That court, with an unreviewed opinion on cross-motions for summary judgment, ruled in respondent's favor. 60 T.C.M. 1423 (1990), ¶ 90,628 P-H Memo TC.

The Tax Court acknowledged that "there is a potential for abuse by allowing unencumbered property transfers to plans in satisfaction of minimum funding requirements." Id. at 1424, ¶ 90,628 P-H Memo TC, p.90–3071. Nonetheless, it did not agree that the transfers in this case constituted sales or exchanges under § 4975. It rejected the Commissioner's attempt to analogize the property transfers to the recognition of income for income tax purposes, for it considered the issue whether a transfer is a prohibited transaction under § 4975 to be "separate and distinct from income tax recognition." Id. at 1425, ¶ 90,628 P-H Memo TC, p. 90–3071.

In drawing this distinction, the Tax Court cited Code § 4975(f)(3). That section specifically states that a transfer of property "by a disqualified person to a plan shall be treated as a sale or exchange if the property is subject to a mortgage or similar lien." The court observed: "Since section 4975(f)(3) specifically describes certain transfers of real or personal property to a plan by a disqualified person as a sale or exchange for purposes of section 4975, the definitional concerns of 'sale or exchange' are removed from the general definitions found in other areas of the tax law." 60 T.C.M., at 1425, ¶ 90–628 P-H Memo TC, p. 90–3072. The Tax Court thus seemed to say that § 4975(f)(3) limits the reach of § 4975(c)(1)(A), so that only transfers of *encumbered* property are prohibited.

The Tax Court also rejected the Commissioner's argument that by contributing noncash property to its plan, the employer was in a position to exert unwarranted influence over the Pension Trust's investment policy. The court's answer was that the trustee "can dispose of" the property. Id. at 1425, ¶ 90–628 P-H memo, p. 90–3072. The court noted that it earlier had rejected the Commissioner's distinction between transfers of property that satisfy a funding obligation and transfers of *encumbered* property, whether or not the latter transfers fulfill a funding obligation, in *Wood v. Commissioner*, 95 T.C. 364 (1990) rev'd, 955 F.2d 908 (4th Cir. 1992).

The United States Court of Appeals for the Fifth Circuit affirmed. 951 F.2d 76 (1992). It read § 4975(f)(3) as "implying that unless it is encumbered by a mortgage or lien, a transfer of property is not to be treated as if it were a sale or exchange." Id. at 78. It rejected the Commissioner's argument that § 4975(f)(3) was intended to expand the definition of "sale or exchange" to include transfers of encumbered property that do not fulfill funding obligations; in the court's view, "there is no basis for this distinction between involuntary and voluntary transfers anywhere in the Code." Id. The court reasoned: "If all transfers of property to a plan were to be treated as a sale or exchange" under § 4975(c)(1)(A), then § 4975(f)(3) "would be superfluous." Id. That a transfer of property in satisfaction of an obligation is treated as a "sale or exchange" of property for income tax purposes is "irrelevant," because "[s]ection 4975 was not enacted to measure economic income." Id. at 79.

The Court of Appeals ruled that the Commissioner's views were not entitled to deference, despite the fact that both the Internal Revenue Service and the Department of Labor administer ERISA's prohibited transaction provisions. This was because the Commissioner's views had not been set out in a formal regulation, and because the Department of Labor's views were set out in an advisory opinion that was binding "only on the parties thereto, and has no precedential effect." Id.

In view of the acknowledged conflict between the Fourth Circuit's decision in *Wood,* 955 F.2d at 913, and the Fifth Circuit's decision in the present litigation, cases decided within two weeks of each other, we granted certiorari.

III

The statute with which we are concerned is a complicated one. But when much of its language, not applicable to the present case, is set to one side, the issue before us comes into better focus. Respondent acknowledges that it is a "disqualified person" with respect to the Pension Trust. It also acknowledges that the trust qualifies as a plan under § 4975. Our task, then, is only to determine whether the transfers of the terminals and of the Key West property were sales or exchanges within the reach of § 4975(c)(1)(A) and therefore were prohibited transactions.

A

It is well established for income tax purposes that the transfer of property in satisfaction of a monetary obligation is usually a "sale or exchange" of the property. See, e.g., Helvering v. Hammel, 311 U.S. 504 (1941). It seems clear, therefore, that respondent's contribution of the truck terminals and the Key West property constituted, under the income tax laws, sales of those properties to the Pension Trust. The Fourth Circuit, in *Wood,* 955 F.2d at 913, observed: "[W]e are aware of no instance when the term 'sale or exchange' has been used or interpreted not to include transfers of property in satisfaction of indebtedness." 955 F.2d at 913.

This logic applied in income tax cases is equally applicable under § 4975(c)(1)(A). The phrase "sale or exchange" had acquired a settled judicial and administrative interpretation over the course of a half century before Congress enacted in § 4975 the even broader statutory language of "any direct or indirect ... sale or exchange." Congress presumptively was aware when it enacted § 4975 that the phrase "sale or exchange" consistently had been construed to include the transfer of property in satisfaction of a monetary obligation. See Albernaz v. United States, 450 U.S. 333, 340–43 (1981). It is a "normal rule of statutory construction," Sorenson v. Secretary of the Treasury, 475 U.S. 851, 860 (1986), that "identical words used in different parts of the same act are intended to have the same meaning." Atlantic Cleaners & Dyers, Inc. v.

United States, 286 U.S. 427, 433 (1932). Further, "the Code must be given as great an internal symmetry and consistency as its words permit." Commissioner v. Lester, 366 U.S. 299, 304 (1961). Accordingly, when we construe § 4975(c)(1)(A), it is proper to accept the already settled meaning of the phrase "sale or exchange."

Even if this phrase had not possessed a settled meaning, it still would be clear that § 4975(c)(1)(A) prohibits the transfer of property in satisfaction of a debt. Congress barred not merely a "sale or exchange." It prohibited something more, namely, "any direct or indirect . . . sale or exchange." The contribution of property in satisfaction of a funding obligation is at least both an indirect type of sale and a form of exchange, since the property is exchanged for diminution of the employer's funding obligation.

B

We note, too, that this construction of the statute's broad language is necessary to accomplish Congress's goal. Before ERISA's enactment in 1974, the measure that governed a transaction between a pension plan and its sponsor was the customary arm's length standard of conduct. This provided an open door for abuses such as the sponsor's sale of property to the plan at an inflated price or the sponsor's satisfaction of a funding obligation by contribution of property that was overvalued or nonliquid. Congress's response to these abuses included the enactment of ERISA's § 406(a)(1)(A) and the addition of § 4975 to the Internal Revenue Code.

Congress's goal was to bar categorically a transaction that was likely to injure the pension plan. S. Rep. No. 93–383, pp. 95–96 (1973). The transfer of encumbered property may jeopardize the ability of the plan to pay promised benefits. See Wood v. Commissioner, supra. Such a transfer imposes upon the trust the primary obligation to pay the encumbrance, and thus frees cash for the employer by restricting the use of cash by the trust. Overvaluation, the burden of disposing of the property, and the employer's substitution of its own judgment as to investment policy, are other obvious considerations. Although the burden of an encumbrance is unique to the contribution of encumbered property, concerns about overvaluation, disposal of property, and the need to maintain an independent investment policy animate any contribution of property that satisfies a funding obligation, regardless of whether or not the property is encumbered. This is because as long as a pension fund is giving up an account receivable in exchange for property, the fund runs the risk of giving up more than it is getting in return if the property is either less valuable or more burdensome than a cash contribution would have been.

These potential harmful effects are illustrated by the facts of the present case, even though the properties at issue were unencumbered and not overvalued at the times of their respective transfers. There were exclusive sales-listing agreements respondent had made with respect to two of the truck terminals; these agreements called for sales commissions. The presence of this requirement demonstrates that it is neither easy nor costless to dispose of such properties. The Chicago truck terminal, for example, was not sold for 3½ years after it was listed for sale by the Pension Trust.

These problems are not solved, as the Court of Appeals suggested, by the mere imposition of excise taxes by § 4971. It is § 4975 that prevents the abuses.

C

We do not agree with the Court of Appeals' conclusion that § 4975(f)(3) limits the meaning of "sale or exchange," as that phrase appears in § 4975(c)(1)(A). Section 4975(f)(3) states that a transfer of property "by a disqualified person to a plan shall be treated as a sale or exchange if the property is subject to a mortgage or similar lien." The Court of Appeals read this language as implying that unless property "is encumbered by a mortgage or lien, a transfer of property is not to be treated as if it were a sale or exchange." 951 F.2d at 78. We feel that by this language Congress intended § 4975(f)(3) to expand, not limit, the scope of the prohibited transaction provision. It extends the reach of "sale or exchange" in § 4975(c)(1)(A) to include contributions of encumbered property that do not satisfy funding obligations. See H.R. Conf. Rep. No. 93–1280, p. 307 (1974). Congress intended by § 4975(f)(3) to provide additional protection, not to limit the protection already provided by § 4975(c)(1)(A).

We feel that the Commissioner's construction of § 4975 is a sensible one. A transfer of encumbered property, like the transfer of unencumbered property to satisfy an obligation, has the potential to burden a plan, while a transfer of property that is neither encumbered nor satisfies a debt presents far less potential for causing loss to the plan.

IV

The judgment of the Court of Appeals is reversed.

NOTE

In *Keystone,* the employer contributed unencumbered real property to a defined benefit plan to satisfy the employer's minimum funding obligation under Part 3 of Title I of ERISA. The Supreme Court held that because the employer's property was contributed to the plan *in satisfaction of the employer's legal obligation under the minimum funding rules*, a prohibited "sale or exchange" under Code Section 4975 had occurred. What are the implications of *Keystone* if the plan is a defined contribution plan that is not subject to the minimum funding rules? In a footnote to the *Keystone* opinion, the Supreme Court provided the following summary of the practical impact of its decision in this situation.

Assume that an employer with no outstanding funding obligations wishes to contribute property to a pension fund to reward its employees for an especially productive year of service. Under our analysis, the property contribution is permissible if the property is unencumbered, because it will not be "exchanged" for a diminution in funding obligations and therefore does not fall within the prohibition of § 4975(c)(1)(A). On the other hand, the property contribution is impermissible if the property is encumbered, because § 4975(f)(3) specifically prohibits all contributions of encumbered property.

508 U.S. at 161 n.2.

LOCKHEED CORPORATION v. SPINK

United States Supreme Court, 1996.
517 U.S. 882, 116 S.Ct. 1783, 135 L.Ed.2d 153.

JUSTICE THOMAS delivered the opinion of the Court.

In this case, we decide whether the payment of benefits pursuant to an early retirement program conditioned on the participants' release of employment-related claims constitutes a prohibited transaction under the Employee Retirement Income Security Act of 1974 (ERISA).

* * *

I

Respondent Paul Spink was employed by petitioner Lockheed Corporation from 1939 until 1950, when he left to work for one of Lockheed's competitors. In 1979, Lockheed persuaded Spink to return. Spink was 61 years old when he resumed employment with Lockheed. At that time, the terms of the Lockheed Retirement Plan for Certain Salaried Individuals (Plan), a defined benefit plan, excluded from participation employees who were over the age of 60 when hired. This was expressly permitted by ERISA. See ERISA § 202(a)(2)(B) (1982 ed.).

Congress subsequently passed the Omnibus Budget Reconciliation Act of 1986 (OBRA). Section 9203(a)(1) of OBRA repealed the age-based exclusion provision of ERISA, and the statute now flatly mandates that "[n]o pension plan may exclude from participation (on the basis of age) employees who have attained a specified age." ERISA § 202(a)(2). Sections 9201 and 9202 of OBRA amended ERISA and the Age Discrimination in Employment Act of 1967 (ADEA) to prohibit age-based cessations of benefit accruals and age-based reductions in benefit accrual rates. See ERISA § 204(b)(1)(H)(i); 29 U.S.C. § 623(i)(1) (ADEA).

In an effort to comply with these new laws, Lockheed ceased its prior practice of age-based exclusion from the Plan, effective December 25,

1988. As of that date, all employees, including Spink, who had previously been ineligible to participate in the Plan due to their age at the time of hiring became members of the Plan. Lockheed made clear, however, that it would not credit those employees for years of service rendered before they became members.

When later faced with the need to streamline its operations, Lockheed amended the Plan to provide financial incentives for certain employees to retire early. Lockheed established two programs, both of which offered increased pension benefits to employees who would retire early, payable out of the Plan's surplus assets. Both programs required as a condition of the receipt of benefits that participants release any employment-related claims they might have against Lockheed. Though Spink was eligible for one of the programs, he declined to participate because he did not wish to waive any ADEA or ERISA claims. He then retired, without earning any extra benefits for doing so.

Spink brought this suit, in his individual capacity and on behalf of others similarly situated, against Lockheed and several of its directors and officers. Among other things, the complaint alleged that Lockheed and the members of the board of directors violated ERISA's duty of care and prohibited transaction provisions by amending the Plan to create the retirement programs. Relatedly, the complaint alleged that the members of Lockheed's Retirement Committee, who implemented the Plan as amended by the board, violated those same parts of ERISA. * * * For these alleged ERISA violations, Spink sought monetary, declaratory, and injunctive relief pursuant to §§ 502(a)(2) and (3) of ERISA's civil enforcement provisions. Lockheed moved to dismiss the complaint for failure to state a claim, and the District Court granted the motion.

The Court of Appeals for the Ninth Circuit reversed in relevant part. 60 F.3d 616 (1995). The Court of Appeals held that the amendments to the Plan were unlawful under ERISA § 406(a)(1)(D), which prohibits a fiduciary from causing a plan to engage in a transaction that transfers plan assets to a party in interest or involves the use of plan assets for the benefit of a party in interest. The court reasoned that because the amendments offered increased benefits in exchange for a release of employment claims, they constituted a use of Plan assets to "purchase" a significant benefit for Lockheed. 60 F.3d at 624. Though the court found a violation of § 406(a)(1)(D), it decided that there was no need to address Lockheed's status as a fiduciary. Id. at 623 n.5. * * *

II

Nothing in ERISA requires employers to establish employee benefits plans. Nor does ERISA mandate what kind of benefits employers must provide if they choose to have such a plan. Shaw v. Delta Air Lines, Inc., 463 U.S. 85, 91 (1983); Alessi v. Raybestos-Manhattan, Inc., 451 U.S. 504, 511 (1981). ERISA does, however, seek to ensure that employees will not be left empty-handed once employers have guaranteed them certain benefits. As we said in *Nachman Corp. v. Pension Benefit Guaranty Corporation,* 446 U.S. 359 (1980), when Congress enacted ERISA it "wanted to . . . mak[e] sure that if a worker has been promised a defined pension benefit upon retirement-and if he has fulfilled whatever conditions are required to obtain a vested benefit—he actually will receive it." Id. at 375. Accordingly, ERISA tries to "make as certain as possible that pension fund assets [will] be adequate" to meet expected benefits payments. Id.

To increase the chances that employers will be able to honor their benefits commitments—that is, to guard against the possibility of bankrupt pension funds—Congress incorporated several key measures into ERISA. Section 302 of ERISA sets minimum annual funding levels for all covered plans and creates tax liens in favor of such plans when those funding levels are not met. Sections 404 and 409 of ERISA impose respectively a duty of care with respect to the management of existing trust funds, along with liability for breach of that duty, upon plan fiduciaries. Finally, § 406 of ERISA prohibits fiduciaries from involving the plan and its assets in certain kinds of business deals. It is this last feature of ERISA that is at issue today.

Congress enacted § 406 "to bar categorically a transaction that [is] likely to injure the pension plan." Commissioner v. Keystone Consol. Industries, Inc., 508 U.S. 152, 160 (1993). That section mandates, in relevant part, that "[a] fiduciary with respect to a plan shall not cause the plan to engage in a transaction, if he knows or should know that such transaction constitutes a direct or indirect . . . transfer to, or use by or for the benefit of a party in interest, of any assets of the plan." ERISA § 406(a)(1)(D). The question here is whether this provision of ERISA prevents an employer from conditioning the receipt of early retirement benefits upon the participants' waiver of employment claims. For the following reasons, we hold that it does not.

III

Section 406(a)(1) regulates the conduct of plan fiduciaries, placing certain transactions outside the scope of their lawful authority. When a fiduciary violates the rules set forth in § 406(a)(1), § 409 of ERISA renders him personally liable for any losses incurred by the plan, any ill-gotten profits, and other equitable and remedial relief deemed appropriate by the court. But in order to sustain an alleged transgression of § 406(a), a plaintiff must show that a fiduciary caused the plan to engage in the allegedly unlawful transaction. Unless a plaintiff can make that showing, there can be no violation of § 406(a)(1) to warrant relief under the enforcement provisions. The Court of Appeals erred by not asking whether fiduciary status existed in this case before it found a violation of § 406(a)(1)(D).

A

We first address the allegation in Spink's complaint that Lockheed and the board of directors breached their fiduciary duties when they adopted the amendments establishing the early retirement programs. Plan sponsors who alter the terms of a plan do not fall into the category of fiduciaries. As we said with respect to the amendment of welfare benefit plans in *Curtiss-Wright Corp. v. Schoonejongen*, 514 U.S. 73 (1995), "[e]mployers or other plan sponsors are generally free under ERISA, for any reason at any time, to adopt, modify, or terminate welfare plans." Id. at 78. When employers undertake those actions, they do not act as fiduciaries, but are analogous to the settlors of a trust.

This rule is rooted in the text of ERISA's definition of fiduciary. As the Second Circuit has observed, "only when fulfilling certain defined functions, including the exercise of discretionary authority or control over plan management or administration," does a person become a fiduciary under § 3(21)(A). Siskind v. Sperry Retirement Program, Unisys, 47 F.3d 498, 505 (2d Cir. 1995). "[B]ecause [the] defined functions [in the definition of fiduciary] do not include plan design, an employer may decide to amend an employee benefit plan without being subject to fiduciary review." Id. We recently recognized this very point, noting that "it may be true that amending or terminating a plan . . . cannot be an act of plan 'management' or 'administration.'" Varity Corp. v. Howe, 516 U.S. 489, 505 (1996). As noted above, we in fact said as much in *Curtiss-Wright,* see 514 U.S. at 78, at least with respect to welfare benefit plans.

We see no reason why the rule of *Curtiss-Wright* should not be extended to pension benefit plans. Indeed, there are compelling reasons to apply the same rule to cases involving both kinds of plans, as most Courts of Appeals have done. The definition of fiduciary makes no distinction between persons exercising authority over welfare benefit plans and those exercising authority over pension plans. It speaks simply of a "fiduciary with respect to a plan," ERISA § 3(21)(A), and of "management" and "administration" of "such plan." Id. And ERISA defines a "plan" as being either a welfare or pension plan, or both. See ERISA § 3(3). Likewise, the fiduciary duty provisions of ERISA are phrased in general terms and apply with equal force to welfare and pension plans. See, e.g., ERISA § 404(a). Given ERISA's definition of fiduciary and the applicability of the duties that attend that status, we think that the rules regarding fiduciary capacity—including the settlor-fiduciary distinction—should apply to pension and welfare plans alike.

Lockheed acted not as a fiduciary but as a settlor when it amended the terms of the Plan to include the retirement programs. Thus, § 406(a)'s requirement of fiduciary status is not met. While other portions of ERISA govern plan amendments, see, e.g., ERISA § 204(a), the act of amending a pension plan does not trigger ERISA's fiduciary provisions.

B

Spink also alleged that the members of Lockheed's Retirement Committee who implemented the amended Plan violated § 406(a)(1)(D). As with the question whether Lockheed and the board members can be held liable under ERISA's fiduciary rules, the Court of Appeals erred in holding that the Retirement Committee members violated the prohibited transaction section of ERISA without making the requisite finding of fiduciary status. It is not necessary for us to decide the question whether the Retirement Committee members acted as fiduciaries when they paid out benefits according to the terms of the amended Plan, however, because we do not think that they engaged in any conduct prohibited by § 406(a)(1)(D).

The "transaction" in which fiduciaries may not cause a plan to engage is one that "constitutes a direct or indirect . . . transfer to, or use by or for the benefit of a party in interest, of any assets of the plan." ERISA § 406(a)(1)(D). Spink reads § 406(a)(1)(D) to apply in cases where the benefit received by the party in interest—in this case, the employer— is not merely a "natural inciden[t] of the administration of pension plans." Lockheed, on the other hand, maintains that a plan administrator's payment of benefits to plan participants and beneficiaries pursuant to the terms of an otherwise lawful plan is wholly outside the scope of § 406(a)(1)(D). We agree with Lockheed.

Section 406(a)(1)(D) does not in direct terms include the payment of benefits by a plan administrator. And the surrounding provisions suggest that the payment of benefits is in fact not a "transaction" in the sense that Congress used that term in § 406(a). Section 406(a) prohibits fiduciaries from engaging the plan in the "sale," "exchange," or "leasing" of property, the "lending of money" or "extension of credit," the "furnishing of goods, services, or facilities," and the "acquisition . . . of any employer security or employer real property" with a party in interest. These are commercial bargains that present a special risk of plan underfunding because they are struck with plan insiders, presumably not at arm's length. See Commissioner v. Keystone Consol. Industries, Inc., 508 U.S. at 160. What the "transactions" identified in § 406(a) thus have in common is that they generally involve uses of plan assets that are potentially harmful to the plan. Cf. id. at 160–61 (reasoning that a transfer of unencumbered property to the plan by the employer for the purpose of applying it toward the employer's funding obligation fell within § 406(a)(1)'s companion tax provision, Code § 4975, because it could "jeopardize the ability of the plan to pay promised benefits"). The payment of benefits conditioned on performance by plan participants cannot reasonably be said to share that characteristic.

According to Spink and the Court of Appeals, however, Lockheed's early retirement programs were prohibited transactions within the meaning of § 406(a)(1)(D) because the required release of employment-related claims by participants created a "significant benefit" for Lockheed. 60 F.3d at 624. Spink concedes, however, that among the "incidental" and thus legitimate benefits that a plan sponsor may receive from the operation of a pension plan are attracting and retaining employees, paying deferred compensation, settling or avoiding strikes, providing increased compensation without increasing wages, increasing employee turnover, and reducing the likelihood of lawsuits by encouraging employees who would otherwise have been laid off to depart voluntarily.

We do not see how obtaining waivers of employment-related claims can meaningfully be distinguished from these admittedly permissible objectives. Each involves, at bottom, a quid pro quo between the plan sponsor and the participant: that is, the employer promises to pay increased benefits in exchange for the performance of some condition by the employee. By Spink's admission, the employer can ask the employee to continue to work for the employer, to cross a picket line, or to retire early. The execution of a release of claims against the employer is functionally no different; like these other conditions, it is an act that the employee performs for the employer in return for benefits. Certainly, there is no basis in § 406(a)(1)(D) for distinguishing a valid from an invalid quid pro quo. Section 406(a)(1)(D) simply does not address what an employer can and cannot ask an employee to do in return for benefits. See generally Alessi v. Raybestos-Manhattan, Inc., 451 U.S. at 511 (ERISA "leaves th[e] question" of the content of benefits "to the private parties creating the plan. . . . [T]he private parties, not the Government, control the level of benefits.").[6] Furthermore, if an employer can avoid litigation that might result from laying off an employee by enticing him to retire early, as Spink concedes, it stands to reason that the employer can

---

[6]   Indeed, federal law expressly approves the use of early retirement incentives conditioned upon the release of claims. The Older Workers Benefit Protection Act, Pub. L. 101–433, 104 Stat. 983 (1990), establishes requirements for the enforceability of employee waivers of ADEA claims made in exchange for early retirement benefits. See 29 U.S.C. § 626(f). Of course, the enforceability of a particular waiver under this and other applicable laws, including state law, is a separate issue from the question whether such an arrangement violates ERISA's prohibited transaction rules. But absent clearer indication than what we have in § 406(a)(1)(D), we would be reluctant to infer that ERISA bars conduct affirmatively sanctioned by other federal statutes.

also protect itself from suits arising out of that retirement by asking the employee to release any employment-related claims he may have.[7]

In short, whatever the precise boundaries of the prohibition in § 406(a)(1)(D), there is one use of plan assets that it cannot logically encompass: a quid pro quo between the employer and plan participants in which the plan pays out benefits to the participants pursuant to its terms. When § 406(a)(1)(D) is read in the context of the other prohibited transaction provisions, it becomes clear that the payment of benefits in exchange for the performance of some condition by the employee is not a "transaction" within the meaning of § 406(a)(1). A standard that allows some benefits agreements but not others, as Spink suggests, lacks a basis in § 406(a)(1)(D); it also would provide little guidance to lower courts and those who must comply with ERISA. We thus hold that the payment of benefits pursuant to an amended plan, regardless of what the plan requires of the employee in return for those benefits, does not constitute a prohibited transaction.[8]

JUSTICE BREYER, with whom JUSTICE SOUTER joins, concurring in part and dissenting in part.

I join the Court's opinion except for its conclusion in Part III-B that "the payment of benefits pursuant to an amended plan, regardless of what the plan requires of the employee in return for those benefits, does not constitute a prohibited transaction." The legal question addressed in Part III-B is a difficult one, which we need not here answer and which would benefit from further development in the lower courts, where interested parties who are experienced in these highly technical, important matters could present their views. Accordingly, I would follow the suggestion of the Solicitor General that the Court not reach the issue in this case.

---

[7]   Spink's amicus the United States suggests that § 406(a)(1)(D) is not violated so long as the employer provides benefits as compensation for the employee's labor, not for other things such as a release of claims. But the Government contradicts its own rule with the examples it gives of lawful plans. For instance, the Government recognizes that "[a]n employer may provide increased pension benefits as an incentive for early retirement." While retirement benefits themselves may be defined as deferred wages, an *increase* in retirement benefits as part of an early retirement plan does not compensate the employee so much for services rendered as for the distinct act of leaving the company sooner than planned. The standard offered by the Government is thus of little help in identifying transactions prohibited by § 406(a)(1)(D).

[8]   If the benefits payment were merely a sham transaction, meant to disguise an otherwise unlawful transfer of assets to a party in interest, or involved a kickback scheme, that might present a different question from the one before us. Spink does not suggest that Lockheed's payment was a cover for an illegal scheme, only that payment of the benefits conditioned on the release was itself violative of § 406(a)(1)(D).

NOTES AND QUESTIONS

1.   *Lockheed Corporation v. Spink* was followed three years later by *Hughes Aircraft Co. v. Jacobson*, 525 U.S. 432 (1999). The plaintiffs in *Jacobson* claimed in part that the amendments to the benefit formula of the employer's pension plan violated the fiduciary duties of ERISA Section 404 and the prohibited transaction rules of ERISA Section 406. The Supreme Court rejected these claims based upon its earlier ruling in *Spink*, stating:

> In general, an employer's decision to amend a pension plan concerns the composition or design of the plan itself and does not implicate the employer's fiduciary duties, which consist of such actions as the administration of the plan's assets. ERISA's fiduciary duty requirement simply is not implicated where Hughes Aircraft Co., acting as the plan's settlor, makes a decision regarding the form or structure of the plans such as who is entitled to receive plan benefits and in what amounts, or how such benefits are calculated. * * * Respondents' three fiduciary duty claims are directly foreclosed by *Spink*'s holding that, without exception, "[p]lan sponsors who alter the terms of a plan do not fall into the category of fiduciaries."

Hughes Aircraft Co. v. Jacobson, 525 U.S. at 444–45.

Curtiss-Wright Corp. v. Schoonejongen, 514 U.S. 73 (1995) (reproduced in Chapter Two of the casebook), *Lockheed Corporation v. Spink*, and *Hughes Aircraft Co. v. Jacobson* form a trilogy of Supreme Court decisions defining the scope of the settlor function doctrine. These cases are discussed collectively in Dana M. Muir, *The Plan Amendment Trilogy: Settling the Scope of the Settlor Doctrine*, 15 LAB. LAW. 205 (1999).

2.   Do you agree with the Supreme Court's holding in *Spink* that, short of a sham transaction designed to disguise an illegal scheme, the payment of benefits pursuant to an amended plan, regardless of what the plan requires of the employee in return for those benefits, does not constitute a prohibited transaction? Recall that one of the purposes of ERISA's vesting rules is to eliminate plan provisions that result in an employee's forfeiture of accrued benefits if the employee engages in behavior, such as going to work for a competitor, that the employer finds undesirable. From a policy perspective, what is the difference between a prohibited forfeiture clause and the employer's conditioning of enhanced pension benefits on some act or conduct by the employee that the employer desires?

3.   *Pension Plan Benefits and Age Discrimination.* In addition to making a prohibited transaction claim under ERISA, Paul Spink also claimed that the employer's plan amendment violated certain parallel amendments made to ERISA, the Code, and the Age Discrimination in Employment Act of 1967 (ADEA) by the Omnibus Budget Reconciliation Act of 1986, Pub. L. No. 99–509, 100 Stat. 1874. See ERISA § 204(b)(1)(H); Code § 411(b)(1)(H); ADEA, 29 U.S.C. § 623(i) (collectively, the "1986 amendments"). The 1986 amendments prohibit age-based benefit accruals in pension plans. The Supreme Court dismissed Spink's claim of age discrimination on the ground

that the 1986 amendments applied prospectively, not retroactively, to the employer's pension plan.

As originally enacted in 1967, the ADEA permitted an employee pension plan to impose mandatory retirement at age sixty-five. The Omnibus Budget Reconciliation Act of 1986 eliminated mandatory retirement provisions in employee pension plans by extending the protections of the ADEA to any individual who is age forty or older, with no upper age limit. See ERISA § 202(a)(2) ("No pension plan may exclude from participation (on the basis of age) employees who have attained a specified age."); Code § 410(a)(2) ("A trust shall not constitute a qualified trust under Section 401(a) if the plan of which it is a part excludes from participation (on the basis of age) employees who have attained a specified age.").

In 1990, Congress again amended the ADEA by enacting the Older Workers Benefit Protection Act of 1990, Pub. L. No. 101–433, 104 Stat. 978 (OWBPA). The requirements of the ADEA, as amended by the OWBPA, are discussed in Chapter Four of the casebook. As a general principle, the OWBPA provides that if the employer's plan provides a lesser level of benefits based on an individual's age, the lesser level of benefits must be justified on the basis of the employer's cost to provide the benefits. See 29 U.S.C. § 623(f)(2)(B). This rule, known as the *equal cost principle*, arises frequently in the context of enhanced retirement benefits offered as an incentive to employees to volunteer for early retirement. Early retirement incentives usually are subsidized more heavily by the employer for younger workers to entice them to volunteer for early retirement. If the plan's early retirement incentive benefit does not fit within one of three statutory safe harbors established under ADEA, the plan must show that an early retirement incentive provision does not result in arbitrary age discrimination under the equal cost principle. See generally 29 U.S.C. § 623(*l*) (statutory exceptions for common practices concerning retirement benefits). A limited exception, enacted by Congress in 1998, permits age-based reductions in retirement incentives for tenured faculty members at universities if certain criteria are satisfied. See 29 U.S.C. § 623(m).

4. *"Voluntary" Early Retirement Incentives and ADEA Waivers.* When an employer offers enhanced early retirement benefits for employees who "volunteer" for early retirement, it is common for the employer to require the employee to waive all potential age discrimination claims under the ADEA as a condition for receiving enhanced early retirement benefits. The ADEA outlines numerous statutory requirements and procedures that must be satisfied for the waiver to be "knowing and voluntary." See generally 29 U.S.C. § 626(f); 29 C.F.R. § 1625.22 (EEOC regulations implementing the ADEA waiver standards and procedures).

PROBLEM ON FIDUCIARY DUTIES AND PROHIBITED TRANSACTIONS

Wholesale Granite Company sponsors a defined benefit plan for its employees (Retirement Plan). The named plan fiduciary for the Retirement

Plan is the Administrative Committee, which consists of three members: Joe Jones (who is the company president), the chief financial officer, and the human resources manager for the company.

Which of the following actions of the Administrative Committee constitute:

- A breach of fiduciary duty?

- A prohibited transaction?

A. The Committee uses Retirement Plan assets to purchase new equipment to modernize the Company's manufacturing plant. This purchase saves the jobs of 1,000 Company employees, all of whom are participants in the Retirement Plan.

B. The Committee agrees to make a loan to the Company out of Retirement Plan assets to enable the Company to purchase new equipment. The loan is secured by a promissory note and bears a market rate of interest.

C. The Committee agrees to pledge the assets of the Retirement Plan as additional collateral for a loan from Small Bank to the Company to enable the Company to purchase new equipment.

D. The Company president, Joe Jones, urges the Committee to invest some of the Plan assets in Start-Up, Inc., a new high-technology company. Joe does not tell the other members of the Committee that he is personally a secret investor in the venture. Relying solely on Joe's assertion that the investment is a "good deal," the Committee invests $100,000 in Plan assets in Start-Up, Inc. One year later, Start-Up, Inc. fails and the Plan loses its entire investment.

E. EMERGING FIDUCIARY ISSUES IN 401(k) PLANS

1. COMPANY STOCK AND 401(k) PLANS

Like the Studebaker incident in 1963, the spectacular collapse of Enron Corporation (Enron) in 2001 and the resulting financial devastation for participants in Enron's 401(k) plan brought national attention to the investment risk associated with holding company stock in one's 401(k) plan account. Enron was a prominent publicly traded company that sponsored a 401(k) plan for its employees. Enron made matching contributions to its 401(k) plan in the form of Enron stock. The plan required participants to hold the matching contribution in the form of Enron stock until age fifty, when they could sell the Enron stock and diversify into other investments. When the share price of Enron's stock fell, those participants who were unable to sell their Enron stock eventually saw the value of their matching contribution accounts reduced to zero.

Although Enron's 401(k) plan offered participants a menu of well-diversified mutual funds from which to select, many participants voluntarily chose to invest their 401(k) salary deferral contributions in Enron stock. A significant number of these participants chose to hold their Enron stock rather than sell it when the stock began its steep decline. These participants then became trapped when the company prohibited sales and purchases of Enron stock from October 27 to November 12, 2001, while the 401(k) plan changed administrators. Prior to this lockdown period, the share price of Enron stock had already fallen from around $80 per share in early 2001 to $15.40 on October 26, 2001. When the lockdown period ended on November 13, the price of Enron stock was $9.98 per share.

Much of the subsequent public scrutiny of Enron's 401(k) plan was focused on the investment losses incurred by the plan participants as a result of the lockdown period. Less attention given to the more fundamental question of why so many Enron 401(k) plan participants voluntarily selected Enron stock as a retirement investment, and why they chose not to sell their Enron stock prior to the lockdown period despite the already steep decline in the stock's price over a period of several months.

Clearly, many of Enron's 401(k) plan participants did not understand the concept of investment risk. In his testimony before Congress, Professor John H. Langbein described the importance of investment diversification and the risks associated with holding company stock as a retirement plan investment.

> The importance of diversification is by far the most important finding in the entire field of financial economics. Over the past 40 years, we have had a stream of empirical and theoretical studies, which have led so far to six Nobel prizes in economics, conclusively showing that there are large and essentially costless gains to diversifying an investment portfolio thoroughly.

> Investment risk has three distinct components: market risk, industry risk, and firm risk. Market risk is common to all securities; it reflects general economic and political conditions, interest rates, and so forth; hence it cannot be eliminated. Industry risk, by contrast, is specific to all the firms in each industry or industry grouping. Firm risk refers to factors that affect the fortunes only of the particular firm. My favorite illustration is the example of the international oil companies. All of them suffered from the 1973 Arab embargo (industry risk). By

contrast, only Exxon incurred the liabilities arising from the great Alaskan oil spill of March 1989 (firm risk). Holding shares in other industries helped prudent investors to offset the decline of the oils in 1973; holding shares of other oils helped offset the decline in Exxon.

Only about 30 percent of the risk of security ownership is market risk, that is, risk that cannot be eliminated by diversification. By contrast, industry risk amounts to about 50 percent of investment risk, and firm risk comprises the remaining 20 percent. Thus, effective diversification can eliminate roughly 70 percent of investment risk. And that is why, from the standpoint of good investment practice, a portfolio such as the Enron pension fund, so heavily concentrated in a single stock, any stock, is pure folly. But there are many plans sitting out there with even more employer stock than Enron. For example, as of January 2000, Proctor and Gamble had a DC plan with 96 percent in employer stock, Pfizer has one with 88 percent, and Abbot Laboratories has one with 87 percent.

* * *

A pension fund portfolio holding a massive part of its assets in any one stock is bad; but holding such a concentration in the stock of the employer is worse. For the employees of any firm, diversification away from the stock of that employer is even more important. The simple reason is that the employee is already horrifically underdiversified by having his or her human capital tied up with the employer. The employee is necessarily exposed to the risks of the employer by virtue of the employment relationship. The last thing in the world that the employee needs is to magnify the intrinsic underdiversification of the employment relationship, by taking his or her diversifiable investment capital and tying that as well to the fate of the employer.

The Enron debacle illustrates this point poignantly. Just when many of the employees have lost their jobs, they have also lost their pension savings, which in a 401(k) plan they could have borrowed against (or with a penalty, withdrawn) in order to tide them over.

John H. Langbein, Testimony Before the U.S. Senate Committee on Governmental Affairs, The Enron Pension Investment Catastrophe: Why It Happened and How Congress Should Fix It (Jan. 24, 2002), reprinted in ENRON: CORPORATE FIASCOS AND THEIR IMPLICATIONS 487–94 (Nancy B. Rapaport & Bala G. Dharan eds., Foundation Press 2004).

In the Pension Protection Act of 2006, Congress enacted two significant reforms concerning company stock as an investment option in defined contribution plans. Rather than setting a maximum limit on the percentage of company stock that participants in 401(k) plans could hold in their plan accounts, Congress opted to enhance the written disclosures given to participants concerning the importance of investment diversification, and to enhance the ability of participants to diversify account assets invested in company stock.

Today, each participant in a plan that permits participants to direct the investment of their account must receive an annual benefit statement that provides an explanation, written in a manner calculated to be understood by the average plan participant, of the importance of a well-balanced and diversified investment portfolio. The statement must provide a notice directing the participant to the Internet web site sponsored by the Department of Labor for additional information on retirement investing. The statement must contain an explicit warning that concentrating more than 20% of the participant's plan investments in a single investment, such as employer securities, may result in a plan account that is not adequately diversified. See ERISA § 105(a)(2)(B). These enhanced disclosure requirements are in response to research studies concerning the investment behavior of participants in 401(k) plans.

In addition, participants in defined contribution plans today have the right to diversify immediately any salary deferral contributions to a 401(k) plan that are invested in company stock. Once the participant has attained at least three years of service, the participant is permitted to diversify all employer contributions to the participant's plan account that are invested in company stock. See Code § 401(a)(35); ERISA § 204(j). These enhanced diversification rights are described in more detail in Chapter Three of the casebook.

In enacting these reforms as part of the Pension Protection Act of 2006, Congress attempted to respond to potential problems with the investment activities of participants in 401(k) plans. The next subsection describes the history and evolution of the participant-directed 401(k) plan and describes the results of research concerning participant financial literacy and participant investment choices in 401(k) plans. As you read the material in the next subsection, consider whether the reforms enacted by the Pension Protection Act of 2006 are sufficient, or whether additional reforms may be necessary to strengthen the 401(k) plan as a means for workers to achieve retirement income security.

2. PARTICIPANT INVESTMENT BEHAVIOR IN 401(k) PLANS[b]

a. The History and Evolution of the Participant-Directed 401(k) Plan

The rise to prominence of the 401(k) plan in the pension system began in 1992, when the Department of Labor issued final regulations under ERISA Section 404(c) governing 401(k) and other individual account plans in which the participants direct the investment of their own individual plan accounts. These regulations are commonly known as the *404(c) Regulations*. See DOL Reg. § 2550.404c–1. The 404(c) Regulations provide that if the employer's plan is structured to comply with these regulations, the employer will not be liable for investment losses resulting from a participant's investment directions. There are two general requirements under the 404(c) Regulations. These requirements concern the information that the employer must provide to plan participants and the types of plan investment options that the employer must make available to plan participants.

The 404(c) Regulations require that participants must receive general information concerning the plan and specific financial information concerning the plan's investment options. Financial information concerning the plan's investment options is provided in the form of (and at the sophistication level of) a securities prospectus as required under federal securities laws. Significantly, the 404(c) Regulations do not require the employer to provide investment education or investment advice to the 401(k) plan participants.

The 404(c) Regulations require that the plan must offer at least three investment options. The employer who sponsors the plan is responsible for selecting these investment options. In performing this task, the employer acts as a fiduciary and is subject to two ERISA fiduciary duties. These duties are the duty of prudence and the duty to act exclusively for the benefit of the plan participants (also known as the fiduciary duty of loyalty).

The range of investment alternatives offered by the plan must offer materially different risk and return characteristics, and must provide participants, even those with small account balances, the opportunity to diversify their investments and minimize the risk of large investment losses. Most employers select a set of three core mutual funds—a stock fund, a bond fund, and a money market fund—to satisfy these

---

[b] Portions of this subsection are reprinted with permission from Colleen E. Medill, Enron and the Pension System, in ENRON: CORPORATE FIASCOS AND THEIR IMPLICATIONS 478–80 (Nancy B. Rapaport & Bala G. Dharan eds., Foundation Press 2004), and Colleen E. Medill, *Transforming the Role of the Social Security System*, 92 CORNELL L.J. 323 (2007). Parts of the original text have been modified to conform to the casebook style and format, and some information has been updated.

requirements. Other investment options, such as more specialized industrial sector mutual funds, employer company stock, or even a brokerage feature allowing the participant to invest in the individual stock of other companies, can be added to this group of core funds.

In recent years, employers who sponsor 401(k) plans have expanded the number of investment options available to plan participants. In their book, *Coming Up Short*, Alicia H. Munnell and Annika Sundén describe the trend toward more participant investment choices.

> Today, sponsors of 401(k) plans have dramatically increased the number of options available to participants. For example, in plans managed by Fidelity Investments, which represents $400 billion in assets (or 18 percent of the holdings of defined contribution plans), the number of investment options has more than doubled over the period 1995–2000. Plans with 10,000 participants or more now offer an average of thirty-eight investment options, up from fourteen in 1995; even plans with 5,000–10,000 participants average twenty-two options, up from nine in 1995. But this is not a phenomenon limited to a few large plans. Roughly half of participants in the Fidelity sample are in plans that provide more than sixteen options. These include money market funds; guaranteed investment contracts; short-term, intermediate, and long-term bonds, high-yield bonds; large cap and small cap domestic equities; global equities; and equities from emerging markets. Fidelity plans may be at the high end in terms of options, but they are representative of the trend toward more choice.

ALICIA H. MUNNELL AND ANNIKA SUNDÉN, COMING UP SHORT 70–71 (2004).

If the company stock of the plan's sponsoring employer is publicly traded on the NYSE or the NASDAQ, the 404(c) Regulations expressly permit such company stock to be included as a permissible investment option in the employer's 401(k) plan. To offer company stock as an investment option, the plan must provide for certain additional safeguards against improper employer influence over the participant's investment decisions concerning company stock. The plan must have some procedure in place to protect the confidentiality of participants who buy and sell company stock. The plan also must designate a fiduciary to monitor compliance with these confidentiality procedures. If necessary, a third-party independent fiduciary must be appointed to handle 401(k) plan transactions in company stock. This situation typically arises when the company is engaged in a merger or acquisition, or when there is a contested election of company directors.

b. Research Studies Concerning Financial Literacy and Investment Decisions

To take full advantage of 401(k) plans, workers must assume significant individual responsibility. They must decide how much to save to fund the 401(k) plan account and how to invest the funds in the account. These tasks require both the motivation and the financial literacy necessary to save and invest successfully.

Numerous research studies have assessed the financial illiteracy of the American public, albeit with somewhat discouraging results. For example, in 2012 the United States Department of the Treasury conducted the National Financial Capability Study, which was a nation-wide, scientific on-line survey of over 25,000 American adults. The study consisted of the following five questions. Try answering these questions yourself.[c]

1.   Suppose you have $100 in a savings account earning 2 percent a year. After five years, how much would you have?

- More than $102
- Exactly $102
- Less than $102
- Don't Know

2.   Suppose that the interest rate on your savings account is 1 percent per year and inflation is 2 percent a year. After one year, would the money in the account buy more than it does today, exactly the same, or less than today?

- More
- Same
- Less
- Don't Know

3.   If interest rates rise, what will typically happen to bond prices? Rise, fall, stay the same, or is there no relationship?

- Rise
- Fall
- Stay the Same
- No Relationship

4.   True or False: A 15-year mortgage requires higher monthly payments than a 30-year mortgage but the total interest over the life of the loan will be less.

- True

---

[c]   The answers are: (1) more than $102; (2) less than today; (3) fall; (4) true; and (5) false.

- False
- Don't Know

5. True or false: Buying a single company stock usually provides a safer return than a stock mutual fund.

- True
- False
- Don't Know

Of the 25,509 persons surveyed, only 14% of the respondents were able to answer all five questions correctly. The results for each question are presented in the table below.

Results from the 2012 National Financial Capability Study

	Correct	Incorrect	Don't Know
1. Interest rate question	75%	13%	11%
2. Inflation question	61%	17%	20%
3. Bond price question	28%	33%	37%
4. Mortgage question	75%	9%	15%
5. Risk question	48%	9%	42%

The study also found that there were considerable demographic differences in financial literacy levels. Males, older respondents, White and Asian respondents, and those with college or higher education levels were more likely to answer the five questions correctly.

In theory, actuarial simulations show that financially knowledgeable workers can accumulate sufficient assets for retirement using 401(k) plans. E.g., ALICIA H. MUNNELL AND ANNIKA SUDÉN, COMING UP SHORT 28–34 (2004). But in reality, many individuals are not saving nearly enough for retirement. Research by social scientists in the fields of psychology and economics explains why many individuals—who could otherwise afford to save for retirement—often fail to do so.

Saving through a 401(k) plan or an individual account involves a complex, multi-step decision making process. Decision making theory posits that to make a "good" decision, a decision maker must first establish a goal. Next, the decision maker must gather information concerning the various options for attaining that goal. Finally, the decision maker must evaluate those options and select the one best suited for attaining the goal.[d]

A perfectly rational actor would correctly execute each of these steps. Not surprisingly, however, research by psychologists and behavioral

---

[d] See Barry Schwartz, The Paradox of Choice 47–48 (2004).

economists demonstrates that psychological biases and high information costs are likely to adversely affect each of these decision making steps.

How Psychological Biases Affect Retirement Financial Planning[e]

Researchers have identified several psychological biases that impede retirement financial planning. First, people naturally tend to overly discount the future by placing a greater value on the present than a rational economic actor would. As a result, individuals have shorter than optimal planning horizons, resulting in a tendency to overconsume today and undersave for tomorrow.

In forecasting the future, individuals also tend to be overly confident and excessively optimistic. These psychological biases are particularly evident when the task involves saving and investing for retirement. A further psychological bias that adversely affects retirement financial planning is the tendency to procrastinate, particularly when making a decision that involves difficult choices. The psychological bias toward procrastination is especially pernicious in the context of 401(k) plans. One of the most significant reasons individuals fail to achieve retirement income security is that they do not consistently save for retirement beginning early in their working careers. Economic simulations show that a worker who postpones saving for retirement through a 401(k) plan until age fifty will have only 26% of the retirement wealth of a similarly situated worker who has participated in a 401(k) plan since age thirty. The tendency to procrastinate is particularly acute among workers under the age of thirty, who are significantly less likely to participate in their employers' 401(k) plans than older workers, either because they are not eligible to participate in the plans or because they choose not to participate.

The tendency to procrastinate is closely related to inertia, also known as the problem of "sticky" defaults.[f] In the 401(k) plan context, the problem of sticky defaults explains why participation rates in 401(k) plans can be improved dramatically by changing the "default" option from nonparticipation to participation in the plan through an automatic enrollment feature.[g] It also explains why workers who are automatically enrolled in 401(k) plans tend to "stick" at the contribution levels assigned by their employers rather than increasing their contribution levels over

---

[e] See generally Victor Ricciari, The Psychology of Risk: The Behavioral Finance Perspective, in 2 The Handbook of Finance 85–111 (Frank J. Fabozzi, ed. 2008)(summarizing the scholarly literature).

[f] See Richard H. Thaler & Cass R. Sunstein, Nudge 103–17 (2008); Brigitte C. Madrian & Dennis F. Shea, *The Power of Suggestion: Inertia in* 401(k) *Participation and Savings Behavior*, 116 Q.J. ECON. 1149, 1149–59 (2001); James J. Choi et al., *Passive Decisions and Potent Defaults* (NAT'L BUREAU OF ECON. RESEARCH, Working Paper No. 9917, 2003); James J. Choi et.al., *For Better or for Worse: Default Effects and* 401(k) *Savings Behavior* (NAT'L BUREAU OF ECON. RESEARCH, Working Paper No. 8651, 2001).

[g] See Madrian & Shea, supra, at 1158–60 (enrollment rates for new workers increased from 50% to 85%).

time as their wages increase, and tend to remain in the default investment option assigned by their employers.[h] Changing these defaults to a "save more tomorrow" feature that automatically increases contributions when earnings increase, or to a life-cycle fund, can help overcome these inertia effects. But until all employers who sponsor 401(k) plans voluntarily adopt these features, there will remain many workers who need to make their own decisions concerning participation, contribution levels, and investment options.

How High Information Costs Affect Retirement

Financial Planning

Retirement financial planning involves high information costs in determining and assessing available options, and then using those options to manage various types of financial risks. Gathering and evaluating the necessary information can be overwhelming. Choice overload—when individuals face an excessive number of choices—is one problem associated with high information costs. This problem lessens an individual's motivation to choose and reduces his or her ability to commit to making a choice. Thus, choice overload reinforces the psychological biases in favor of procrastination and inertia.

Individuals cope with high information costs by employing a number of mental shortcuts, known as heuristics, to simplify their decision-making process. Heuristics are examples of bounded rationality in which the real world decisions of individuals differ from the rational actor due to an inability to gather and process all of the relevant information. Studies of 401(k) plan participants' investment behavior indicate that several types of heuristics may negatively influence investment decisions.

- The endorsement effect leads some participants to invest heavily in company stock.[i]

- Risk or loss aversion explains why some participants tend to overinvest in lower-earning fixed income investments and underinvest in higher-earning diversified portfolios of equity investments.[j]

- Framing effects lead some individuals to allocate their 401(k) plan account assets proportionately among their plans' investment options (a $1/n$ allocation scheme in which n is the number of investment options), even though such a proportionate allocation may result in investment portfolios

---

[h]   See id. at 1170–71 (noting that three-quarters of automatically enrolled employees remained in the default investment option).

[i]   See generally Shlomo Benartzi, *Excessive Extrapolation and the Allocation of 401(k) Accounts to Company Stock*, 56 J. FIN. 1747, 1747–49 (2001); Gur Huberman, *Familiarity Breeds Investment*, 14 REV. FIN. STUD. 659, 659–61 (2001).

[j]   See generally Daniel Kahneman & Amos Iversky, *Prospect Theory: An Analysis of Decision Under Risk*, 42 ECONOMETRICIA 263, 263–65 (1979).

that are either disproportionately susceptible to investment losses, low investment earnings, or both.[k]

In the context of investment behavior, the above heuristics are harmful. These research studies of investment behavior by participants in 401(k) plans show that heuristics lead them to invest in ways that are contrary to modern portfolio theory, which seeks to maximize investment earnings over time while minimizing the risk of disproportionate investment losses.

d. The Role of Financial Education in Improving Retirement Saving

Numerous research studies have found that even when controlling for disparities in income levels, there is a strong positive correlation between the level of financial literacy and the amount of personal retirement savings.[l] The causal link between the two centers on the planning process. Researchers hypothesize that greater financial literacy improves retirement savings because it counters psychological biases and improves the cognitive ability of individuals to collect and evaluate information concerning their options. Significantly, researchers have shown that improved financial literacy correlates with higher levels of retirement savings by all workers, not just those with high incomes.

> Much of the explanation for low participation rates [in 401(k) plans] among young and low-income workers rests on factors such as short planning horizons and lack of financial knowledge. These characteristics make participation and contribution decisions overwhelming, and young and low-income workers often simply put off making a decision. All these factors can be affected by financial education.

MUNNELL & SUNDÉN, supra, at 65. How do workers today acquire the knowledge they need to save and invest for retirement? The most likely source of financial education is from an employer who sponsors a 401(k) plan. Employers are not required to provide investment education materials to 401(k) plan participants, and many employers do not. When employers do provide such educational materials, the quality is uneven. Recent research also suggests that employer-provided education materials are geared toward individuals who are natural "planners" and

---

[k] See generally Shlomo Benartzi & Richard Thaler, *Naive Diversification Strategies in Retirement Savings Plans*, 91 AM. ECON. REV. 79 (2001).

[l] See Robert L. Clark et al., *Sex Differences, Financial Education, and Retirement Goals*, in PENSION DESIGN AND STRUCTURE 185–92 (Olivia S. Mitchell & Stephen P. Utkus, eds., 2004); Annamaria Lusardi, *Saving and the Effectiveness of Financial Education*, in PENSION DESIGN AND STRUCTURE, supra, at 157, 157–68.

that these materials do not appeal to the approximately 50% of the working population that is not planning-oriented.[m]

From the perspective of national retirement policy, low financial literacy is troubling. Relying solely on private sector employers voluntarily to provide investment education to the working population appears to be producing an information gap that primarily affects young and low-income workers—the very individuals who could arguably benefit the most from retirement financial education.

QUESTION

Should the law require employers who sponsor 401(k) plans to provide investment education or investment advice to their workers? Does the employer have a moral or ethical obligation to go beyond the minimum legal requirements to assist financially illiterate workers in achieving retirement income security? Alternatively, should the federal government assume this responsibility?

3.   FEES AND EXPENSES IN 401(k) PLANS

Investment management fees are the single largest expense for participants in the typical 401(k) plan. Investment management fees compensate the manager of a mutual fund for its services in managing and investing the assets of the mutual fund. Because investment management fees are deducted directly from the assets of the mutual fund, such fees reduce the rate of investment return earned by the mutual fund. As the reading material below from the Employee Benefits Security Administration demonstrates, the subtle impact of investment management fees over time on a participant's account balance at retirement can be dramatic.

Employee Benefits Security Administration

A Look at 401(k) Plan Fees for Employees

More and more employees are investing in their futures through 401(k) plans. Employees who participate in 401(k) plans assume responsibility for their retirement income by contributing part of their salary and, in many instances, by directing their own investments.

If you are among those who direct your investments, you will need to consider the investment objectives, the risk and return characteristics, and the performance over time of each investment option offered by your plan in order to make sound investment decisions.

---

[m] See Donna M. McFarland, et al., *"Money Attitudes" and Retirement Plan Design: One Size Does Not Fit All*, in PENSION DESIGN AND STRUCTURE, supra, at 117–18.

Why Consider Fees?

In a 401(k) plan, your account balance will determine the amount of retirement income you will receive from the plan. Although contributions to your account and the earnings on your investments will increase your retirement income, fees and expenses paid by your plan may substantially reduce the growth in your account. The following example demonstrates how fees and expenses can impact your account.

> Assume that you are an employee with thirty-five years until retirement and a current 401(k) account balance of $25,000. If returns on investments in your account over the next thirty-five years average 7% and fees and expenses reduce your average returns by 0.5%, your account balance will grow to $227,000 at retirement, even if there are no further contributions to your account. If fees and expenses are 1.5%, however, your account balance will grow to only $163,000. The 1% difference in fees and expenses would reduce your account balance at retirement by 28%.

In recent years, there has been a dramatic increase in the number of investment options typically offered under 401(k) plans as well as the level and types of services provided to participants. These changes give today's employees who direct their 401(k) investments greater opportunity than ever before to affect their retirement savings. As a participant you may welcome the variety of investment alternatives and the additional services, but you may not be aware of their cost. As shown above, the cumulative effect of the fees and expenses on your retirement savings can be substantial.

You should be aware that your employer also has a specific obligation to consider the fees and expenses paid by your plan. ERISA requires employers to follow certain rules in managing 401(k) plans. Employers are held to a high standard of care and diligence and must discharge their duties solely in the interest of the plan participants and their beneficiaries. Among other things, this means that employers must:

- Establish a prudent process for selecting investment alternatives and service providers;
- Ensure that fees paid to service providers and other expenses of the plan are reasonable in light of the level and quality of services provided;
- Select investment alternatives that are prudent and adequately diversified; and
- Monitor investment alternatives and service providers once selected to see that they continue to be appropriate choices.

What Are 401(k) Plan Fees and Who Pays for Them?

If you want to know how fees affect your retirement savings, you will need to know about the different types of fees and expenses and the different ways in which they are charged. Plan fees and expenses for 401(k) plans generally fall into three categories.

- Plan Administration Fees: The day-to-day operation of a 401(k) plan involves expenses for basic administrative services—such as plan record keeping, accounting, legal and trustee services—that are necessary for administering the plan as a whole. Today, a 401(k) plan also may offer a host of additional services, such as telephone voice response systems, access to a customer service representative, educational seminars, retirement planning software, investment advice, electronic access to plan information, daily valuation and on-line transactions.

- In some instances, the costs of administrative services will be covered by investment fees that are deducted directly from investment returns. Otherwise, if administrative costs are separately charged, they will be borne either by your employer or charged directly against the assets of the plan. When paid directly by the plan, administrative fees are either allocated among individual accounts in proportion to each account balance (i.e., participants with larger account balances pay more of the allocated expenses) or passed through as a flat fee against each participant's account. Either way, generally the more services provided, the higher the fees.

- Investment Fees: By far the largest component of 401(k) plan fees and expenses is associated with managing plan investments. Fees for investment management and other investment-related services generally are assessed as a percentage of assets invested. You should pay attention to these fees. You pay for them in the form of an indirect charge against your account because they are deducted directly from your investment returns. Your net total return is your return after these fees have been deducted. For this reason, these fees, which are not specifically identified on statements of investments, may not be immediately apparent.

- Individual Service Fees: In addition to overall administrative expenses, there may be individual service fees associated with optional features offered under a 401(k) plan. Individual service fees are charged separately to the accounts of individuals who choose to take advantage of a particular plan feature. For example, individual service fees may be charged to a participant for taking a loan from the plan or for executing participant investment directions.

Plan investments and services for a 401(k) plan may be provided through a variety of arrangements.

- Employers may directly provide, or separately negotiate for, some or all of the various services and investment alternatives offered under their 401(k) plans (sometimes referred to as an unbundled arrangement). The expenses of each provider (i.e., investment manager, trustee, recordkeeper, communications firm) are charged separately.

- In many plans, some or all of the various services and investment alternatives may be offered by one provider for a fee paid to that provider (sometimes referred to as a bundled arrangement). The provider will then pay out of that fee any other service providers with whom it may have contracted to provide the services.

- Some plans may use an arrangement that combines a single provider for certain services, such as administrative services, with a number of providers for investment options.

- Fees need to be evaluated keeping in mind the cost of all covered services.

What Fees Are Associated with My Investment Choices in a 401(k) Plan?

Apart from fees charged for administration of the plan itself, there are three basic types of fees that may be charged in connection with investment alternatives in a 401(k) plan. These fees, which can be referred to by different terms, include:

- Sales charges (also known as loads or commissions): These are basically transaction costs for the buying and selling of shares. They may be computed in different ways, depending upon the particular investment product.

- Management fees (also known as investment advisory fees or account maintenance fees): These are ongoing charges for managing the assets of the investment fund. They are generally stated as a percentage of the amount of assets invested in the fund. Sometimes management fees may be used to cover administrative expenses. You should know that the level of management fees can vary widely, depending on the investment manager and the nature of the investment product. Investment products that require significant management, research and monitoring services generally will have higher fees.

- Other fees: This category covers services, such as record keeping, furnishing statements, toll-free telephone numbers and investment advice, involved in the day-to-day management of investment products. They may be stated either as a flat fee or as a percentage of the amount of assets invested in the fund.

In addition, there are some fees that are unique to specific types of investments. Following are brief descriptions of some of the more common investments offered under 401(k) plans and explanations of some of the different terminology or unique fees associated with them.

Some Common Investments and Related Fees

Most investments offered under 401(k) plans today pool the money of a large number of individual investors. Pooling money makes it possible for individual participants to diversify investments, to benefit from economies of scale and to lower their transaction costs. These funds may invest in stocks, bonds, real estate and other investments. Larger plans, by virtue of their size, are more likely to pool investments on their own— for example, by using a separate account held with a financial institution. Smaller plans generally invest in commingled pooled investment vehicles offered by financial institutions, such as banks, insurance companies or mutual funds. Generally, investment-related fees, usually charged as a percentage of assets invested, are paid by the participant.

- Mutual Funds: Mutual funds pool and invest the money of many people. Each investor owns shares in the mutual fund that represent a part of the mutual fund's holdings. The portfolio of securities held by a mutual fund is managed by a professional investment adviser following a specific investment policy.

- Some mutual funds assess sales charges (see above for a discussion of sales charges). These charges may be paid when you invest in a fund (known as a front-end load) or when you sell shares (known as a back-end load, deferred sales charge or redemption fee). A front-end load is deducted up front and, therefore, reduces the amount of your initial investment. A back-end load is determined by how long you keep your investment. There are various types of back-end loads, including some that decrease and eventually disappear over time. A back-end load is paid when the shares are sold (i.e., if you decide to sell a fund share when a back-end load is in effect, you will be charged the load).

- Mutual funds also may charge what are known as Rule 12b–1 fees, which are ongoing fees paid out of fund assets. Rule 12b–1 fees may be used to pay commissions to brokers and other salespersons, to pay for advertising and other costs of promoting the fund to investors and to pay various service providers to a 401(k) plan pursuant to a bundled services arrangement. Rule 12b–1 fees are usually between 0.25% and 1.00% of assets annually.

- Some mutual funds may be advertised as "no load" funds. This can mean that there is no front-or back-end load. However, there may be a small 12b–1 fee.

- Collective Investment Funds: A collective investment fund is a trust fund managed by a bank or trust company that pools investments of 401(k) plans and other similar investors. Each investor has a proportionate interest in the trust fund assets. For example, if a collective investment fund holds $10 million in assets and your investment in the fund is $10,000, you have a 0.1% interest in the fund. Like mutual funds, collective investment funds may have different investment objectives. There are no front or back-end fees associated with a collective investment fund, but there are investment management and administrative fees.

- Variable Annuities: Insurance companies frequently offer a range of investment alternatives for 401(k) plans through a group variable annuity contract between an insurance company and an employer on behalf of a plan. The variable annuity contract "wraps" around investment alternatives, often a number of mutual funds. Participants select from among the investment alternatives offered, and the returns to their individual accounts vary with their choice of investments. Variable annuities also include one or more insurance elements that are not present in other investment alternatives. Generally, these elements include an annuity feature, interest and expense guarantees, and any death benefit provided during the term of the contract. In addition to investment management fees and administration fees, you may find these additional fees.

- Insurance-related charges are associated with investment alternatives that include an insurance component. They include items such as sales expenses, mortality risk charges and the cost of issuing and administering contracts.

- Surrender and transfer charges are fees an insurance company may charge when an employer terminates a contract (in other words, withdraws the plan's investment) before the term of the contract expires or if you withdraw an amount from the contract. This fee may be imposed if these events occur before the expiration of a stated period and commonly decrease and disappear over time. It is similar to an early withdrawal penalty on a bank certificate of deposit or to a back-end load or redemption fee charged by some mutual funds.

- Pooled Guaranteed Investment Contract (GIC) Funds: A common fixed income investment option, a pooled GIC fund generally includes a number of contracts issued by an insurance company or bank paying an interest rate that blends the fixed interest rates of each of the GICs included in the pool. There are investment management and administrative fees associated with the pooled GIC fund.

Although the investments described above are common, 401(k) plans also may offer other investments which are not described here (such as employer securities).

Is There a Checklist I Can Use to Review My 401(k) Plan's Fees?

There is an array of investment options and services offered under today's 401(k) plans. Even though there is no easy way to calculate the fees and expenses paid by your 401(k) plan due to the number of variables involved, you can begin by asking yourself questions and, if you cannot find the answers, by asking your plan administrator. Answers to the following ten questions will help in gathering information about the fees and expenses paid by your plan:

- What investment options are offered under your company's 401(k) plan?
- Do you have all available documentation about the investment choices under your plan and the fees charged to your plan?
- What types of investment education are available under your plan?
- What arrangement is used to provide services under your plan (i.e., are any or all of the services or investment alternatives provided by a single provider)?
- Do you and other participants use most or all of the optional services offered under your 401(k) plan, such as participant loan programs and insurance coverages?
- If administrative services are paid separately from investment management fees, are they paid for by the plan or your employer or are they shared?
- Are the investment options tracking an established market index or is there a higher level of investment management services being provided?
- Do any of the investment options under your plan include sales charges (such as loads or commissions)?
- Do any of the investment options under your plan include any fees related to specific investments, such as 12b–1 fees,

insurance charges or surrender fees, and what do they cover?

- Does your plan offer any special funds or special classes of stock (generally sold to larger group investors)?

Keep in mind that the law requires the fees charged to a 401(k) plan must be "reasonable" rather than setting a specific level of fees that are permissible. Therefore, the reasonableness of fees must be determined in each case.

In Conclusion

When you consider the fees in your 401(k) plan and their impact on your retirement income, remember that all services have costs. If your employer has selected a bundled program of services and investments, compare all services received with the total cost.

Remember, too, that higher investment management fees do not necessarily mean better performance. Nor is cheaper necessarily better. Compare the net returns relative to the risks among available investment options.

And, finally, don't consider fees in a vacuum. They are only one part of the bigger picture including investment risk and returns and the extent and quality of services provided.

QUESTION

Have you participated in a 401(k) plan? If so, could you answer the questions contained in the above checklist concerning 401(k) plan fees and investment options?

4.   TRENDS IN 401(K) PLAN LITIGATION

Virtually all 401(k) plans today are designed as 404(c) plans that allow participants to direct the investment of their individual plan accounts. To comply with the 404(c) Regulations, 401(k) plans use mutual funds as investment options. In addition, public companies who sponsor a 401(k) plan usually offer company stock as an additional investment option. These plan investment choices—mutual funds and company stock—have sparked two trends in 401(k) plan litigation.

As the importance of 401(k) plans in providing retirement income security has grown, the scrutiny of fees and expenses assessed against mutual fund investment options accordingly has increased. In asserting *excessive fee claims*, the plan participants challenge the fees associated with the plan's mutual fund investment options using a variety of breach of fiduciary duty theories. The plaintiffs may allege that the selection of a mutual fund was imprudent because the fees that are deducted from the assets of the mutual fund are unreasonable and excessive. Under this theory, the plan participants contend that the plan's mutual fund fees are being assessed at an imprudent "retail" level instead of at a lower "wholesale" or "institutional" level. Another prominent theory is that the employer breached its fiduciary duty to inform participants by entering into an undisclosed arrangement with the mutual fund company to share in the revenues generated by the fees paid from the plan's mutual fund investment options.

In excessive fee cases, the employer typically asserts two defenses. First, employers usually counter that the fees associated with the plan's mutual fund investment options are reasonable and not imprudent in light of the services provided. Here, some federal courts have looked for guidance to the standard for excessive fees under Section 36(b) of the Investment Company Act of 1940, 15 U.S.C. § 80a–35(b), which is the federal statute that regulates mutual fund companies. E.g., Young v. General Motors Inv. Mgmt. Corp., 325 Fed. Appx. 31 (2d Cir. 2009); cf. Jones v. Harris Assocs. L.P., 130 S.Ct. 1418 (2010) (excessive fee under § 36(b) of the Investment Company Act is one that, under all of the circumstances, is so disproportionately large that it bears no reasonable relationship to the services rendered and could not have been the product of arm's length bargaining). Other federal courts have applied ERISA's fiduciary standards of loyalty and prudence under Section 404(a). Compare Hecker v. Deere & Co., 556 F.3d 575 (7th Cir.) (Hecker I), pet. for reh'g and reh'g en banc denied, 569 F.3d 708 (7th Cir. 2009) (Hecker II) (affirming summary judgment for plan fiduciary) and Taylor v. United Technologies Corp., 46 Empl. Benefits Cas. (BNA) 1935 (D. Conn. 2009) (granting summary judgment for plan fiduciary), judgment aff'd, 48 Empl. Benefits Cas. (BNA) 1193 (2d Cir. 2009), with Braden v. Wal-Mart Stores, Inc., 588 F.3d 585 (8th Cir. 2009) (reversing district court's dismissal of plaintiffs' claims under Rule 12(b)(6)).

Second, employers have argued that if the plan complies with the 404(c) Regulations, the employer is immune from claims of breach of fiduciary duty associated with the plan's investment options. The federal courts disagree concerning the scope of protection from breach of fiduciary duty claims that the 404(c) Regulations provide to an employer who sponsors a participant-directed 401(k) plan. Some courts have suggested that the 404(c) Regulations provide a complete defense to claims that the employer has breached its ERISA fiduciary duties in selecting or retaining a plan investment option. See Hecker I, 556 F.3d 575, pet. for reh'g and reh'g en banc denied, Hecker II, 569 F.3d 708 (narrowing sweeping statements concerning the scope of protection afforded by the 404(c) Regulations in *Hecker I*); Langbecker v. Electronic Data Sys., Inc., 476 F.3d 299 (5th Cir. 2007) (404(c) Regulations provide a defense against allegations of company stock as an imprudent investment option). Other courts and the Secretary of Labor view the selection and retention of the investment options for a 404(c) plan as a fiduciary function that is not protected by the 404(c) Regulations. See DiFelice v. U.S. Airways, Inc., 497 F.3d 410 (4th Cir. 2007); Hecker II, 569 F.3d 708 (describing the DOL's position); DOL Op. Ltr. No. 98–04A, n. 1 (the selection of investment options for plans is always a fiduciary decision that is not subject to participant control); Final Regulations Regarding Participant Directed Individual Account Plains, 57 Fed. Reg. 46,906, 46,924 n. 27 (Oct. 13, 1992) (selection and retention of investment options is a fiduciary obligation not protected by the 404(c) Regulations).

The other recent litigation trend, known as *stock drop claims*, involves a public company that offers company stock as one of the investment options in the company's 401(k) plan. If the company stock suddenly drops in value, the plan participants may claim that the plan's fiduciaries (who are typically company officers or employees) breached their fiduciary duties. Stock drop claims under ERISA often are intertwined with federal securities law claims because the plaintiffs typically allege that the company fiduciaries made material misrepresentations or failed to disclose material information about the company's operations. E.g., In re Enron Corp. Sec., Derivative & ERISA Litig., 284 F.Supp.2d 511 (S.D. Tex. 2003). In a garden variety stock drop case, the plaintiffs claim that the plan's fiduciaries knew or should have known that the company stock was an imprudent investment option and breached their fiduciary duties by retaining the company stock as a plan investment option. E.g., In re Washington Mut., Inc., Sec., Derivative & ERISA Litig., 47 Empl. Benefits Cas. (BNA) 2505 (W.D. Wash. 2009) (denying defendant fiduciaries motion to dismiss); In re Harley-Davidson, Inc. Sec. Litig., 660 F.Supp.2d 953 (E.D. Wis. 2009) (granting defendants motion to dismiss). In a *reverse stock drop claim*, the plaintiffs claim that the plan's fiduciaries acted imprudently in *selling* the company stock held by the plan at an undervalued price. E.g., Bunch v. W.R. Grace & Co., 555 F.3d 1 (1st Cir. 2009).

When defending against breach of fiduciary duty claims in stock drop cases, employers argued that plan fiduciaries were entitled to a "presumption of prudence" regarding decisions to buy or sell company stock as a plan asset. In *Fifth Third Bancorp v. Dudenhoeffer*, the Supreme Court rejected this defense and described the standards by which the federal courts must evaluate claims of breach of fiduciary duty involving company stock.

FIFTH THIRD BANCORP V. DUDENHOEFFER

United States Supreme Court, 2014.
134 S. Ct. 2459.

Justice BREYER delivered the opinion of the Court.

The Employee Retirement Income Security Act of 1974 (ERISA) requires the fiduciary of a pension plan to act prudently in managing the plan's assets. § 404(a)(1)(B). This case focuses upon that duty of prudence as applied to the fiduciary of an "employee stock ownership plan" (ESOP), a type of pension plan that invests primarily in the stock of the company that employs the plan participants.

We consider whether, when an ESOP fiduciary's decision to buy or hold the employer's stock is challenged in court, the fiduciary is entitled to a defense-friendly standard that the lower courts have called a "presumption of prudence." The Courts of Appeals that have considered the question have held that such a presumption does apply, with the presumption generally defined as a requirement that the plaintiff make a showing that would not be required in an ordinary duty of prudence case, such as that the employer was on the brink of collapse.

We hold that no such presumption applies. Instead, ESOP fiduciaries are subject to the same duty of prudence that applies to ERISA fiduciaries in general, except that they need not diversify the fund's assets. § 404(a)(2).

I

Petitioner Fifth Third Bancorp, a large financial services firm, maintains for its employees a defined contribution retirement savings plan. Employees may choose to contribute a portion of their compensation to the Plan as retirement savings, and Fifth Third provides matching contributions of up to 4% of an employee's compensation. The Plan's assets are invested in 20 separate funds, including mutual funds and an ESOP. Plan participants can allocate their contributions among the funds however they like. Fifth Third's matching contributions, on the other hand, are always invested initially in the ESOP, though the participant can then choose to move them to another fund. The Plan requires the ESOP's funds to be "invested primarily in shares of common stock of Fifth Third."

Respondents, who are former Fifth Third employees and ESOP participants, filed this putative class action in Federal District Court in Ohio. They claim that petitioners, Fifth Third and various Fifth Third officers, were fiduciaries of the Plan and violated the duties of loyalty and prudence imposed by ERISA. See §§ 409(a), 502(a)(2). We limit our review to the duty of prudence claims.

The complaint alleges that by July 2007, the fiduciaries knew or should have known that Fifth Third's stock was overvalued and excessively risky for two separate reasons. First, publicly available information such as newspaper articles provided early warning signs that subprime lending, which formed a large part of Fifth Third's business, would soon leave creditors high and dry as the housing market collapsed and subprime borrowers became unable to pay off their mortgages. Second, nonpublic information (which petitioners knew because they were

Fifth Third insiders) indicated that Fifth Third officers had deceived the market by making material misstatements about the company's financial prospects. Those misstatements led the market to overvalue Fifth Third stock—the ESOP's primary investment—and so petitioners, using the participants' money, were consequently paying more for that stock than it was worth.

The complaint further alleges that a prudent fiduciary in petitioners' position would have responded to this information in one or more of the following ways: (1) by selling the ESOP's holdings of Fifth Third stock before the value of those holdings declined, (2) by refraining from purchasing any more Fifth Third stock, (3) by canceling the Plan's ESOP option, and (4) by disclosing the inside information so that the market would adjust its valuation of Fifth Third stock downward and the ESOP would no longer be overpaying for it.

Rather than follow any of these courses of action, petitioners continued to hold and buy Fifth Third stock. Then the market crashed, and Fifth Third's stock price fell by 74% between July 2007 and September 2009, when the complaint was filed. Since the ESOP's funds were invested primarily in Fifth Third stock, this fall in price eliminated a large part of the retirement savings that the participants had invested in the ESOP. (The stock has since made a partial recovery to around half of its July 2007 price.)

The District Court dismissed the complaint for failure to state a claim. The court began from the premise that where a lawsuit challenges ESOP fiduciaries' investment decisions, "the plan fiduciaries start with a presumption that their 'decision to remain invested in employer securities was reasonable.'" 757 F.Supp. 2d 753, 758 (S.D. Ohio 2010) (quoting Kuper v. Iovenko, 66 F.3d 1447, 1459 (6th Cir. 1995)). The court next held that this rule is applicable at the pleading stage and then concluded that the complaint's allegations were insufficient to overcome it.

The Court of Appeals for the Sixth Circuit reversed. Although it agreed that ESOP fiduciaries are entitled to a presumption of prudence, it took the view that the presumption is evidentiary only and therefore does not apply at the pleading stage. Thus, the Sixth Circuit simply asked whether the allegations in the complaint were sufficient to state a claim for breach of fiduciary duty. It held that they were.

In light of differences among the Courts of Appeals as to the nature of the presumption of prudence applicable to ESOP fiduciaries, we granted the fiduciaries' petition for certiorari. Compare In re Citigroup ERISA Litigation, 662 F.3d 128, 139–140 (2d Cir. 2011) (presumption of prudence applies at the pleading stage and requires the plaintiff to establish that the employer was "in a 'dire situation' that was objectively unforeseeable by the settlor" (quoting Edgar v. Avaya, Inc., 503 F.3d 340, 348 (3d Cir. 2007))), with Pfeil v. State Street Bank & Trust Co., 671 F.3d

585, 592–596 (6th Cir. 2012) (presumption of prudence applies only at summary judgment and beyond and only requires the plaintiff to establish that " 'a prudent fiduciary acting under similar circumstances would have made a different investment decision' " (quoting Kuper, supra, at 1459)).

II

A

In applying a "presumption of prudence" that favors ESOP fiduciaries' purchasing or holding of employer stock, the lower courts have sought to reconcile congressional directives that are in some tension with each other. On the one hand, ERISA itself subjects pension plan fiduciaries to a duty of prudence. . . .

On the other hand, Congress recognizes that ESOPs are "designed to invest primarily in" the stock of the participants' employer, § 407(d)(6)(A), meaning that they are *not* prudently diversified. And it has written into law its "interest in encouraging" their use. * * *

In addition * * * Congress has given ESOP fiduciaries a statutory exemption from some of the duties imposed on ERISA fiduciaries. ERISA specifically provides that, in the case of ESOPs and other eligible individual account plans, "the diversification requirement of § 404(a)(1)(C) and the prudence requirement (only to the extent that it requires diversification) of § 404(a)(1)(B) [are] not violated by acquisition or holding of employer stock." § 404(a)(2).

Thus, an ESOP fiduciary is not obliged under § 404(a)(1)(C) to "diversif[y] the investments of the plan so as to minimize the risk of large losses" or under § 404(a)(1)(B) to act "with the care, skill, prudence, and diligence" of a "prudent man" insofar as that duty "requires diversification."

B

Several Courts of Appeals have gone beyond ERISA's express provision that ESOP fiduciaries need not diversify by giving ESOP fiduciaries a "presumption of prudence" when their decisions to hold or buy employer stock are challenged as imprudent. Thus, the Third Circuit has held that "an ESOP fiduciary who invests the ESOP's assets in employer stock is entitled to a presumption that it acted consistently with ERISA" in doing so. Moench v. Robertson, 62 F.3d 553, 571 (3d Cir. 1995). The Ninth Circuit has said that to "overcome the presumption of prudent investment, plaintiffs must. . .make allegations that clearly implicate the company's viability as an ongoing concern or show a precipitous decline in the employer's stock. . .combined with evidence that the company is on the brink of collapse or is undergoing serious mismanagement." Quan v. Computer Sciences Corp., 623 F.3d 870, 882 (9th Cir. 2010). And the

Seventh Circuit has described the presumption as requiring plaintiffs to "allege and ultimately prove that the company faced 'impending collapse' or 'dire circumstances' that could not have been foreseen by the founder of the plan." White v. Marshall & Ilsley Corp., 714 F.3d 980, 989 (7th Cir. 2013).

The Sixth Circuit agreed that some sort of presumption favoring an ESOP fiduciary's purchase of employer stock is appropriate. But it held that this presumption is an evidentiary rule that does not apply at the pleading stage. It further held that, to overcome the presumption, a plaintiff need not show that the employer was on the "brink of collapse" or the like. Rather, the plaintiff need only show that " 'a prudent fiduciary acting under similar circumstances would have made a different investment decision.' " Dudenhoeffer v. Fifth Third Bancorp, 692 F.3d 410, 418 (6th Cir. 2012) (quoting Kuper, 66 F.3d at 1459).

Petitioners argue that the lower courts are right to apply a presumption of prudence, that it should apply from the pleading stage onward, and that the presumption should be strongly in favor of ESOP fiduciaries' purchasing and holding of employer stock.

In particular, petitioners propose a rule that a challenge to an ESOP fiduciary's decision to hold or buy company stock "cannot prevail unless extraordinary circumstances, such as a serious threat to the employer's viability, mean that continued investment would substantially impair the purpose of the plan." In petitioners' view, the "purpose of the plan," in the case of an ESOP, is promoting employee ownership of the employer's stock over the long-term. And, petitioners assert, that purpose is "substantially impair[ed]"—rendering continued investment imprudent— only when "a serious threat to the employer's viability" makes it likely that the employer will go out of business. This is because the goal of employee ownership will be substantially impaired only if the employer goes out of business, leaving the employees with no company to own.

We must decide whether ERISA contains some such presumption.

III

A

In our view, the law does not create a special presumption favoring ESOP fiduciaries. Rather, the same standard of prudence applies to all ERISA fiduciaries, including ESOP fiduciaries, except that an ESOP fiduciary is under no duty to diversify the ESOP's holdings. This conclusion follows from the pertinent provisions of ERISA, which are set forth above.

Section 404(a)(1)(B) "imposes a 'prudent person' standard by which to measure fiduciaries' investment decisions and disposition of assets." Massachusetts Mut. Life Ins. Co. v. Russell, 473 U.S. 134, 143, n. 10

(1985). Section 404(a)(1)(C) requires ERISA fiduciaries to diversify plan assets. And § 404(a)(2) establishes the extent to which those duties are loosened in the ESOP context to ensure that employers are permitted and encouraged to offer ESOPs. Section 404(a)(2) makes no reference to a special "presumption" in favor of ESOP fiduciaries. It does not require plaintiffs to allege that the employer was on the "brink of collapse," under "extraordinary circumstances," or the like. Instead, § 404(a)(2) simply modifies the duties imposed by § 404(a)(1) in a precisely delineated way: It provides that an ESOP fiduciary is exempt from § 404(a)(1)(C)'s diversification requirement and also from § 404(a)(1)(B)'s duty of prudence, but *only to the extent that it requires diversification.* § 404(a)(2) (emphasis added).

Thus, ESOP fiduciaries, unlike ERISA fiduciaries generally, are not liable for losses that result from a failure to diversify. But aside from that distinction, because ESOP fiduciaries are ERISA fiduciaries and because § 404(a)(1)(B)'s duty of prudence applies to all ERISA fiduciaries, ESOP fiduciaries are subject to the duty of prudence just as other ERISA fiduciaries are.

B

Petitioners make several arguments to the contrary. First, petitioners argue that the special purpose of an ESOP—investing participants' savings in the stock of their employer—calls for a presumption that such investments are prudent. Their argument is as follows: ERISA defines the duty of prudence in terms of what a prudent person would do "in the conduct of an enterprise of a like character and with like aims." § 404(a)(1)(B). The "character" and "aims" of an ESOP differ from those of an ordinary retirement investment, such as a diversified mutual fund. An ordinary plan seeks (1) to maximize retirement savings for participants while (2) avoiding excessive risk. But an ESOP also seeks (3) to promote employee ownership of employer stock. For instance, Fifth Third's Plan requires the ESOP's assets to be "invested primarily in shares of common stock of Fifth Third." In light of this additional goal, an ESOP fiduciary's decision to buy more shares of employer stock, even if it would be imprudent were it viewed solely as an attempt to secure financial retirement benefits while avoiding excessive risk, might nonetheless be prudent if understood as an attempt to promote employee ownership of employer stock, a goal that Congress views as important. Thus, a claim that an ESOP fiduciary's investment in employer stock was imprudent as a way of securing retirement savings should be viewed unfavorably because, unless the company was about to go out of business, that investment was advancing the additional goal of employee ownership of employer stock.

We cannot accept the claim that underlies this argument, namely, that the content of ERISA's duty of prudence varies depending upon the specific nonpecuniary goal set out in an ERISA plan, such as what petitioners claim is the nonpecuniary goal here. Taken in context, § 404(a)(1)(B)'s reference to "an enterprise of a like character and with like aims" means an enterprise with what the immediately preceding provision calls the "exclusive purpose" to be pursued by all ERISA fiduciaries: "providing benefits to participants and their beneficiaries" while "defraying reasonable expenses of administering the plan." §§ 404(a)(1)(A)(i), (ii). Read in the context of ERISA as a whole, the term "benefits" in the provision just quoted must be understood to refer to the sort of *financial* benefits (such as retirement income) that trustees who manage investments typically seek to secure for the trust's beneficiaries. Cf. § 3(2)(A) (defining "employee pension benefit plan" and "pension plan" to mean plans that provide employees with "retirement income" or other "deferral of income"). The term does not cover nonpecuniary benefits like those supposed to arise from employee ownership of employer stock.

Consider the statute's requirement that fiduciaries act "in accordance with the documents and instruments governing the plan *insofar as such documents and instruments are consistent with the provisions of this subchapter.*" § 1104(a)(1)(D) (emphasis added). This provision makes clear that the duty of prudence trumps the instructions of a plan document, such as an instruction to invest exclusively in employer stock even if financial goals demand the contrary. See also § 410(a) (With irrelevant exceptions, "any provision in an agreement or instrument which purports to relieve a fiduciary from responsibility. . .for any. . .duty under this part shall be void as against public policy"). This rule would make little sense if, as petitioners argue, the duty of prudence is defined by the aims of the particular plan as set out in the plan documents, since in that case the duty of prudence could never conflict with a plan document.

Consider also § 404(a)(2), which exempts an ESOP fiduciary from § 404(a)(1)(B)'s duty of prudence but "only to the extent that it requires diversification." What need would there be for this specific provision were the nature of § 404(a)(1)(B)'s duty of prudence altered anyway in the case of an ESOP in light of the ESOP's aim of promoting employee ownership of employer stock?

Petitioners are right to point out that *Congress,* in seeking to permit and promote ESOPs, was pursuing purposes other than the financial security of plan participants. Congress pursued those purposes by promoting ESOPs with tax incentives. See 26 U.S.C. §§ 402(e)(4), 404(k), 1042. And it also pursued them by exempting ESOPs from ERISA's diversification requirement, which otherwise would have precluded their creation. § 404(a)(2). But we are not convinced that Congress *also* sought to promote ESOPs by further relaxing the duty of prudence as applied to ESOPs with the sort of presumption proposed by petitioners.

Second, and relatedly, petitioners contend that the duty of prudence should be read in light of the rule under the common law of trusts that "the settlor can reduce or waive the prudent man standard of care by specific language in the trust instrument." G. Bogert & G. Bogert, Law of Trusts and Trustees § 541, p. 172 (rev. 2d ed. 1993); see also Restatement (Second) of Trusts § 174, Comment *d* (1957) ("By the terms of the trust the requirement of care and skill may be relaxed or modified"). The argument is that, by commanding the ESOP fiduciary to invest primarily in Fifth Third stock, the plan documents waived the duty of prudence to the extent that it comes into conflict with investment in Fifth Third stock—at least unless "extraordinary circumstances" arise that so threaten the goal of employee ownership of Fifth Third stock that the fiduciaries must assume that the settlor would want them to depart from that goal under the common law "deviation doctrine." See id. § 167. This argument fails, however, in light of this Court's holding that, by contrast to the rule at common law, "trust documents cannot excuse trustees from their duties under ERISA." Central States, Southeast & Southwest Areas Pension Fund, 472 U.S. at 559, 568 (1985); see also §§ 404(a)(1)(D), 410(a).

Third, petitioners argue that subjecting ESOP fiduciaries to a duty of prudence without the protection of a special presumption will lead to conflicts with the legal prohibition on insider trading. The potential for conflict arises because ESOP fiduciaries often are company insiders and because suits against insider fiduciaries frequently allege, as the complaint in this case alleges, that the fiduciaries were imprudent in failing to act on inside information they had about the value of the employer's stock.

This concern is a legitimate one. But an ESOP-specific rule that a fiduciary does not act imprudently in buying or holding company stock unless the company is on the brink of collapse (or the like) is an ill-fitting means of addressing it. While ESOP fiduciaries may be more likely to have insider information about a company that the fund is investing in than are other ERISA fiduciaries, the potential for conflict with the securities laws would be the same for a non-ESOP fiduciary who had relevant inside information about a potential investment. And the potential for conflict is the same for an ESOP fiduciary whose company is on the brink of collapse as for a fiduciary who is invested in a healthier company. (Surely a fiduciary is not obligated to break the insider trading laws even if his company is about to fail.) The potential for conflict therefore does not persuade us to accept a presumption of the sort adopted by the lower courts and proposed by petitioners. We discuss alternative means of dealing with the potential for conflict in Part IV, infra.

Finally, petitioners argue that, without some sort of special presumption, the threat of costly duty of prudence lawsuits will deter companies from offering ESOPs to their employees, contrary to the stated intent of Congress. ESOP plans instruct their fiduciaries to invest in company stock, and § 404(a)(1)(D) requires fiduciaries to follow plan documents so long as they do not conflict with ERISA. Thus, in many cases an ESOP fiduciary who fears that continuing to invest in company stock may be imprudent finds himself between a rock and a hard place: If he keeps investing and the stock goes down he may be sued for acting imprudently in violation of § 404(a)(1)(B), but if he stops investing and the stock goes up he may be sued for disobeying the plan documents in violation of § 404(a)(1)(D). Petitioners argue that, given the threat of such expensive litigation, ESOPs cannot thrive unless their fiduciaries are granted a defense-friendly presumption.

Petitioners are basically seeking relief from what they believe are meritless, economically burdensome lawsuits. We agree that Congress sought to encourage the creation of ESOPs. And we have recognized that "ERISA represents a careful balancing between ensuring fair and prompt enforcement of rights under a plan and the encouragement of the creation of such plans.'" Conkright v. Frommert, 559 U.S. 506, 517 (2010); see also Varity Corp. v. Howe, 516 U.S. 489, 497 (1996) (In "interpret[ing] ERISA's fiduciary duties," "courts may have to take account of competing congressional purposes, such as Congress' desire to offer employees enhanced protection for their benefits, on the one hand, and, on the other, its desire not to create a system that is so complex that administrative costs, or litigation expenses, unduly discourage employers from offering welfare benefit plans in the first place").

At the same time, we do not believe that the presumption at issue here is an appropriate way to weed out meritless lawsuits or to provide the requisite "balancing." The proposed presumption makes it impossible for a plaintiff to state a duty of prudence claim, no matter how meritorious, unless the employer is in very bad economic circumstances. Such a rule does not readily divide the plausible sheep from the meritless goats. That important task can be better accomplished through careful, context-sensitive scrutiny of a complaint's allegations. We consequently stand by our conclusion that the law does not create a special presumption of prudence for ESOP fiduciaries.

IV

We consider more fully one important mechanism for weeding out meritless claims, the motion to dismiss for failure to state a claim. That mechanism, which gave rise to the lower court decisions at issue here, requires careful judicial consideration of whether the complaint states a claim that the defendant has acted imprudently. See Fed. Rule Civ. Proc. 12(b)(6); Ashcroft v. Iqbal, 556 U.S. 662, 677–680 (2009); Bell Atlantic

Corp. v. Twombly, 550 U.S. 544, 554–563 (2007). Because the content of the duty of prudence turns on "the circumstances. . .prevailing" at the time the fiduciary acts, § 404(a)(1)(B), the appropriate inquiry will necessarily be context specific.

The District Court in this case granted petitioners' motion to dismiss the complaint because it held that respondents could not overcome the presumption of prudence. The Court of Appeals, by contrast, concluded that no presumption applied. And we agree with that conclusion. The Court of Appeals, however, went on to hold that respondents had stated a plausible duty of prudence claim. The arguments made here, along with our review of the record, convince us that the judgment of the Court of Appeals should be vacated and the case remanded. On remand, the Court of Appeals should apply the pleading standard as discussed in *Twombly* and *Iqbal* in light of the following considerations.

A

Respondents allege that, as of July 2007, petitioners knew or should have known in light of publicly available information, such as newspaper articles, that continuing to hold and purchase Fifth Third stock was imprudent. The complaint alleges, among other things, that petitioners "continued to allow the Plan's investment in Fifth Third Stock even during the time that the stock price was declining in value as a result of the collapse of the housing market" and that "a prudent fiduciary facing similar circumstances would not have stood idly by as the Plan's assets were decimated."

In our view, where a stock is publicly traded, allegations that a fiduciary should have recognized from publicly available information alone that the market was over- or under-valuing the stock are implausible as a general rule, at least in the absence of special circumstances. Many investors take the view that " 'they have little hope of outperforming the market in the long run based solely on their analysis of publicly available information,' " and accordingly they " 'rely on the security's market price as an unbiased assessment of the security's value in light of all public information.' " Halliburton Co. v. Erica P. John Fund, Inc. 134 S.Ct. 2398 (2014) (quoting Amgen Inc. v. Connecticut Retirement Plans and Trust Funds, 133 S.Ct. 1184, 1192 (2013)). ERISA fiduciaries, who likewise could reasonably see "little hope of outperforming the market. . .based solely on their analysis of publicly available information," id., may, as a general matter, likewise prudently rely on the market price.

In other words, a fiduciary usually "is not imprudent to assume that a major stock market. . .provides the best estimate of the value of the stocks traded on it that is available to him." Summers v. State Street Bank & Trust Co., 453 F.3d 404, 408 (7th Cir. 2006); see also White, 714 F.3d at 992 (A fiduciary's "failure to outsmart a presumptively efficient market. . .is. . .not a sound basis for imposing liability"); cf. Quan, 623

F.3d at 881 ("Fiduciaries are not expected to predict the future of the company stock's performance").

We do not here consider whether a plaintiff could nonetheless plausibly allege imprudence on the basis of publicly available information by pointing to a special circumstance affecting the reliability of the market price as " 'an unbiased assessment of the security's value in light of all public information,' " Halliburton Co., supra, (quoting Amgen Inc., supra), that would make reliance on the market's valuation imprudent. In this case, the Court of Appeals held that the complaint stated a claim because respondents "allege that Fifth Third engaged in lending practices that were equivalent to participation in the subprime lending market, that Defendants were aware of the risks of such investments by the start of the class period, and that such risks made Fifth Third stock an imprudent investment." The Court of Appeals did not point to any special circumstance rendering reliance on the market price imprudent. The court's decision to deny dismissal therefore appears to have been based on an erroneous understanding of the prudence of relying on market prices.

B

Respondents also claim that petitioners behaved imprudently by failing to act on the basis of *nonpublic* information that was available to them because they were Fifth Third insiders. In particular, the complaint alleges that petitioners had inside information indicating that the market was overvaluing Fifth Third stock and that they could have used this information to prevent losses to the fund by (1) selling the ESOP's holdings of Fifth Third stock; (2) refraining from future stock purchases (including by removing the Plan's ESOP option altogether); or (3) publicly disclosing the inside information so that the market would correct the stock price downward, with the result that the ESOP could continue to buy Fifth Third stock without paying an inflated price for it.

To state a claim for breach of the duty of prudence on the basis of inside information, a plaintiff must plausibly allege an alternative action that the defendant could have taken that would have been consistent with the securities laws and that a prudent fiduciary in the same circumstances would not have viewed as more likely to harm the fund than to help it. The following three points inform the requisite analysis.

First, in deciding whether the complaint states a claim upon which relief can be granted, courts must bear in mind that the duty of prudence, under ERISA as under the common law of trusts, does not require a fiduciary to break the law. Cf. Restatement (Second) of Trusts § 166, comment *a* ("The trustee is not under a duty to the beneficiary to do an act which is criminal or tortious"). Federal securities laws "are violated when a corporate insider trades in the securities of his corporation on the basis of material, nonpublic information." United States v. O'Hagan, 521 U.S. 642, 651–652 (1997). As every Court of Appeals to address the question has held, ERISA's duty of prudence cannot require an ESOP fiduciary to perform an action—such as divesting the fund's holdings of the employer's stock on the basis of inside information—that would violate the securities laws. See, e.g., Rinehart v. Akers, 722 F.3d 137, 146–147 (2d Cir. 2013); Kirschbaum v. Reliant Energy, Inc., 526 F.3d 243, 256 (5th Cir. 2008); White, supra, at 992; Quan, supra, at 881–882, and n. 8; Lanfear v. Home Depot, Inc., 679 F.3d 1267, 1282 (11th Cir. 2012). To the extent that the Sixth Circuit denied dismissal based on the theory that the duty of prudence required petitioners to sell the ESOP's holdings of Fifth Third stock, its denial of dismissal was erroneous.

Second, where a complaint faults fiduciaries for failing to decide, on the basis of the inside information, to refrain from making additional stock purchases or for failing to disclose that information to the public so that the stock would no longer be overvalued, additional considerations arise. The courts should consider the extent to which an ERISA-based obligation either to refrain on the basis of inside information from making a planned trade or to disclose inside information to the public could conflict with the complex insider trading and corporate disclosure requirements imposed by the federal securities laws or with the objectives of those laws. Cf. § 514(d) "Nothing in this subchapter [which includes § 404] shall be construed to alter, amend, modify, invalidate, impair, or supersede any law of the United States. . .or any rule or regulation issued under any such law"); Black & Decker Disability Plan v. Nord, 538 U.S. 822, 831 (2003) ("Although Congress 'expect[ed]' courts would develop 'a federal common law of rights and obligations under ERISA-regulated plans,' the scope of permissible judicial innovation is narrower in areas where other federal actors are engaged;" (quoting Pilot Life Ins. Co. v. Dedeaux, 481 U.S. 41, 56 (1987)); Varity Corp., 516 U.S. at 506 (reserving the question "whether ERISA fiduciaries have any fiduciary duty to disclose truthful information on their own initiative, or in response to employee inquiries"). The U.S. Securities and Exchange Commission has not advised us of its views on these matters, and we believe those views may well be relevant.

Third, lower courts faced with such claims should also consider whether the complaint has plausibly alleged that a prudent fiduciary in the defendant's position could not have concluded that stopping purchases—which the market might take as a sign that insider fiduciaries viewed the employer's stock as a bad investment—or publicly disclosing negative information would do more harm than good to the fund by causing a drop in the stock price and a concomitant drop in the value of the stock already held by the fund.

We leave it to the courts below to apply the foregoing to the complaint in this case in the first instance. The judgment of the Court of

Appeals for the Sixth Circuit is vacated and the case is remanded for further proceedings consistent with this opinion.

NOTES AND QUESTIONS

1.   At the end of Part III.A of *the Fifth Third Bancorp* opinion, the Supreme Court states that ERISA fiduciaries are "not liable for losses that result from a failure to diversify." How does the duty of prudence in Section 404(a)(1)(B) differ from the duty of prudent diversification in Section 404(a)(1)(C)? After *Fifth Third Bancorp*, what actions should an ESOP fiduciary take to demonstrate prudence when making decisions to buy, hold, or sell company stock?

2.   What are the arguments made by the ESOP fiduciaries in *Fifth Third Bancorp* to support a presumption of prudence regarding employer stock held as a plan asset? Why did the Supreme Court reject these arguments? Did the Supreme Court effectively substitute a new presumption of prudence by holding that ESOP fiduciaries may, as a general matter, prudently rely on the market price of publicly traded employer stock when making decisions to buy or continue to hold that stock as a plan asset?

3.   *"Deep Pocket" Trustees.* Occasionally, the defendant employer in a stock drop case is insolvent. In this situation, the plan's participants are likely to seek out another "deep pocket" defendant, who typically is the financial institution that served as the directed trustee for the employer's plan. In a 401(k) plan, a directed trustee is used to execute the investment directions of the plan's participants. A directed trustee also may be used to execute the investment directions of another fiduciary (again, typically company officers and employees). If the trustee follows directions to invest employer matching contributions to the 401(k) plan in company stock, and the company stock later suddenly drops in value, the participants may sue the directed trustee in an attempt to recoup their investment losses. The participants' claim is that the directed trustee was obligated under ERISA Section 403(a)(1) to ignore directions to invest contributions to the plan in company stock, and instead should have either frozen investments in the company stock or liquidated the company stock held in the 401(k) plan. E.g., In re WorldCom, Inc. ERISA Litigation, 354 F.Supp.2d 423 (S.D.N.Y. 2005); see generally DOL Field Assistance Bull. No. 2004–03.

4.   *Class Actions and the ERISA Bar.* The relative ease by which class certification can be obtained for the plaintiffs in cases alleging excessive fees or the imprudent handling of company stock as a plan asset has led to the emergence of an increasingly sophisticated ERISA plaintiffs' bar. The world of ERISA class action litigation is exceedingly complex. In the past, the ERISA defense bar held the upper hand in fiduciary litigation simply because defense attorneys had more repeat business, and with those repetitions came greater expertise. In the future, the litigation playing field is likely to be more equal as the plaintiffs' bar gains experience in complex ERISA litigation. Chapter Six of the casebook explores ERISA's statutory scheme of

claims and remedies, and the landmark Supreme Court decisions interpreting these statutory provisions.

F. DISCUSSION QUESTIONS FOR CHAPTER FIVE

QUESTION ONE

The fiduciary status of a person who responds to an inquiry from a plan participant concerning the plan or its benefits may be unclear, both to the person who responds to the inquiry and to the plan participant. In these situations, should ERISA permit the person who responds to an inquiry from a plan participant expressly to disclaim fiduciary status? Why or why not?

QUESTION TWO

The individual account plans of many publicly traded companies hold company stock. Should Congress make ERISA Section 407(a), which prohibits defined benefit plans from investing more than 10% of their assets in qualifying employer securities, applicable to individual account plans? Or is there a legitimate policy basis for distinguishing between defined benefit plans and individual account plans concerning the plan's investment concentration in company stock?

QUESTION THREE

The fiduciary prohibited transaction rules of ERISA Section 406(b) overlap with the fiduciary duties of ERISA Section 404(a). The regulatory approach of these two sections, however, is distinctly different. ERISA's fiduciary duties represent a flexible regulatory scheme where the rules are applied on a case-by-case basis according to the particular facts and circumstances of the situation. In contrast, absent an administrative exemption, the prohibited transaction rules categorically bar certain types of transactions between a plan and a fiduciary, even those transactions that are entered into in good faith and that are economically beneficial to the plan. Are both sets of rules necessary or desirable as a matter of public policy? Do the prohibited transaction rules provide a needed layer of additional protection for the plan and its participants? Or are the prohibited transaction rules simply a trap for the unwary?

QUESTION FOUR

If the underlying rationale for the prohibited transaction rules is to prohibit situations where the potential for undue influence exists, why are dual role fiduciaries expressly permitted under ERISA Section 408(c)(3)? Do the general fiduciary provisions of ERISA Section 404(a) provide an adequate safeguard against undue employer influence of a dual role fiduciary? Is it realistic to expect that an officer or director of the plan's sponsoring employer who also serves as a plan fiduciary will be able to make fiduciary decisions based solely on the interests of the plan's participants and beneficiaries, particularly if company stock is one of the plan's assets?

CHAPTER 6

CIVIL ENFORCEMENT ACTIONS

■ ■ ■

A. OVERVIEW OF ERISA'S CIVIL ENFORCEMENT PROVISIONS

Chapter Six focuses primarily on civil actions brought by private parties or the Secretary of Labor in ERISA litigation. To put you in the appropriate frame of mind to study the material in Chapter Six, consider the following statement, written by a federal appellate judge who was faced with resolving several complex ERISA claims:

> Throughout his judicial career [Oliver Wendell] Holmes relished challenging cases. While on Massachusetts' highest court he confessed to a friend that although none of the cases he had handled that year had been of universal interest, "there is always the pleasure of unraveling a difficulty." A decade and a half later, while on the Supreme Court, he told the same friend that he had few cases of general interest that term, but "there is always the fun of untying a knot and trying to do it in good compact form." It is a pity that Holmes did not live to see ERISA cases.

Gilley v. Monsanto Co., Inc., 490 F.3d 848, 852 (11th Cir. 2007) (Carnes, J.).

Untying the "knot" of ERISA civil litigation begins with Section 502(a), which lists the various types of civil enforcement actions authorized under the statute. These claims fall into three broad general categories.

First, under ERISA Section 502(a)(1)(B) a plan participant or beneficiary may bring a claim to recover benefits due under the terms of the plan or to clarify rights to future benefits under the plan. This type of claim typically is brought after the plan's administrator has denied a claim for benefits and the participant or beneficiary has exhausted the plan's administrative appeal procedure for denied benefits claims.

Second, a plan participant, a beneficiary, or a plan fiduciary may bring a claim under ERISA Section 502(a)(2) against another plan fiduciary seeking relief under ERISA Section 409(a) for a breach of fiduciary duty. A similar claim also may be brought by the Secretary of Labor under ERISA Section 502(a)(2).

Third, a plan participant, a beneficiary, or a plan fiduciary may bring a claim under ERISA Section 502(a)(3) to enjoin any act or practice that violates either Title I of ERISA or the terms of the plan, or to obtain appropriate equitable relief to remedy such a violation. The Secretary of Labor is authorized to bring a similar claim for injunctive or equitable relief under ERISA Section 502(a)(5). This third category of civil claims, known as the "catch-all" category because of its broad scope, has been the subject of numerous Supreme Court cases.

Section B of Chapter Six describes some of the procedural issues that are unique to ERISA civil litigation. Section C examines claims for plan benefits brought under ERISA Section 502(a)(1)(B) and the appropriate standard of judicial review. Breach of fiduciary duty claims brought under ERISA Section 502(a)(2) are discussed in Section D. Finally, Section E of Chapter Six explores the different types of claims that may be brought under ERISA's catch-all claims category, Section 502(a)(3).

Although Chapter Six focuses on the three general categories of claims authorized by Section 502(a), other types of ERISA claims are authorized for specific situations. A statutory penalty claim may be brought by a plan participant or beneficiary or by the Secretary of Labor against a plan administrator for violations of ERISA's various notice and reporting requirements. See ERISA §§ 502(a)(1)(A); 502(a)(6). Section 502(a)(7) authorizes claims by state agencies to enforce qualified medical child support orders. ERISA Section 502(a)(9) authorizes a claim and relief in connection with the purchase of annuity or insurance contracts used to provide annuity benefits to plan participants or beneficiaries. Section 502(a)(9) claims are brought in the unique circumstance where the insurance company who sold the contract becomes financially insolvent or is otherwise unable to continue the payments provided for under the contract.

B. THE "NUTS AND BOLTS" OF ERISA LITIGATION

The attorney who represents a potential plaintiff in ERISA civil litigation must first determine whether the client has a claim under ERISA. This initial determination is made by analyzing the client's circumstances in light of the three components of a civil action under ERISA Section 502(a):

(1) Does the client have *standing* to bring a claim?

(2) Is the *type of claim* the client may bring appropriate for the client's situation?

(3) Is the *remedy* available under the statute for the client's claim satisfactory to the client?

In addition to the three components necessary for a successful civil action brought under ERISA, there are a number of other practical questions that potentially impact litigation strategy. These include such questions as:

- Should this claim be filed in state court or federal court?
- If the claim is filed in state court, can it be removed to federal court?
- Is the claim barred by the statute of limitations?
- Is a jury trial available?
- Will attorney's fees be awarded?

Issues that commonly arise under the standing component of a claim brought under ERISA Section 502(a) are discussed below. The other practical questions that impact ERISA litigation strategy are addressed in the remainder of this section.

Standing to Bring a Claim

Plan participants and beneficiaries, plan fiduciaries, and the Secretary of Labor all have standing to bring claims under ERISA Section 502(a). Standing issues often arise because the statutory definitions of who qualifies as a "participant," a "beneficiary," and a "fiduciary" are both circular and vague.

ERISA Section 3(7) defines a participant as an "employee or former employee . . . who is or may become eligible to receive a benefit" from an employee benefit plan. A beneficiary is defined as a person designated by a participant "who is or may become entitled to a benefit" from an employee benefit plan. ERISA § 3(8). The clarity of these definitions obviously leaves much to be desired.

One common standing issue involves so-called "former" participants. Objections to standing by former plan participants can arise in different contexts. One typical situation involves a termination of employment that has resulted in the loss of the participant's right to participate in, or receive benefits from, the employer's plan. The Supreme Court's discussion in *Firestone Tire & Rubber Co. v. Bruch*, reproduced in the Notes following *Nationwide Mutual Insurance Co. v. Darden* in Chapter Two of the casebook, provides guidance for determining when such former plan participants or beneficiaries have standing to bring an ERISA claim.

Determining whether an individual has standing to bring a claim as a plan participant is particularly difficult in the context of alleged violations of ERISA Section 510, which prohibits employers from interfering with the exercise or attainment of rights under an employee benefit plan. These Section 510 cases may present a sort of standing Catch-22, because the plaintiff's claim often is that the employer terminated the individual's employment to prevent the individual from becoming a participant and thereby attaining the right to benefits under the employer's plan. Section 510 claims are discussed in detail in Section E of Chapter Six.

A variation on the "former participant" theme involves a group of individuals who were participants in an employer's defined contribution plan, but who received a distribution of their entire vested account balance. The federal courts have ruled that former "cashed-out" participants have standing to bring a breach of fiduciary duty claim if the alleged breach of fiduciary duty reduced the value of their accounts and caused the former participants to receive a lesser distribution amount. E.g., In re Mut. Funds Inv. Litig., 529 F.3d 207 (4th Cir. 2008); Harzewski v. Guidant Corp., 489 F.3d 799 (7th Cir. 2007). On a related note, the Eighth Circuit has ruled that a current individual participant in an employer's 401(k) plan has Article III standing to bring breach of fiduciary duty claims on behalf of *all* of the participants in the plan, based on the allegation that a fiduciary's breach of duty has reduced the value of the participant's own individual account. See Braden v. Wal-Mart Stores, Inc., 588 F.3d 585 (8th Cir. 2009).

Another that raises potential standing issues occurs in the context of a claim for benefits under a health care plan. Before providing medical treatment, health care providers generally require the patient to assign all rights under the patient's health care plan for payment for treatment to the health care provider. If the plan later refuses to pay for the treatment (technically, denies the participant's claim for health care plan benefits), this assignment of rights allows the health care provider to bring a claim against the plan for payment on the patient's behalf under ERISA Section 502(a)(1)(B). The patient's plan may be sued as an entity, and service of process is made by serving the plan's administrator or trustee. ERISA § 502(d)(1). In these cases, the health care provider acquires *derivative standing* to bring the claim against the plan by virtue of the patient's assignment of rights. Some early judicial decisions indicated that the federal courts were reluctant to recognize derivative standing. E.g., Northeast Dept. ILGWU Health and Welfare Fund v. Teamsters Local Union No. 229 Welfare Fund, 764 F.2d 147, 153–54 & n.6 (3d Cir. 1985). The modern trend, however, is to allow derivative standing and permit the health care provider to sue on the patient's behalf pursuant to the assignment of rights under the health care plan. E.g., Dallas County Hosp. Distr. v. Associates' Health and Welfare Plan, 293 F.3d 282, 285–86 (5th Cir. 2002); City of Hope Nat. Med. Ctr. v. HealthPlus, Inc., 156 F.3d 223, 225–26 (1st Cir. 1998); Cagle v. Bruner, 112 F.3d 1510, 1514–16 (11th Cir. 1997). If the health care plan document itself prohibits participants from assigning their rights under the plan, then the health care provider cannot acquire derivative standing, and the participant must bring the claim for benefits against the plan's administrator.

1. FEDERAL COURT JURISDICTION AND REMOVAL

The federal courts have jurisdiction over any claim brought under Section 502(a) of ERISA. ERISA § 502(e)(1). The federal and state courts share dual jurisdiction over claims for plan benefits under Section 502(a)(1)(B) and claims by state agencies to enforce qualified medical child support orders under Section 502(a)(7). ERISA § 502(e)(1). The federal courts have *exclusive* jurisdiction over all other claims brought under Section 502(a). ERISA § 502(e)(1).

The plaintiff has several choices for venue when filing a claim under ERISA Section 502(a). The claim may be filed in the district where the plan is administered, where an alleged breach of fiduciary duty occurred, or where a defendant resides. ERISA § 502(e)(2). Nationwide service of process is authorized by the statute. ERISA § 502(e)(2).

If the plaintiff takes advantage of ERISA's dual jurisdiction provision and files a claim for plan benefits in state court under Section 502(a)(1)(B) of ERISA, a federal question is presented on the face of the complaint. Under the Federal Rules of Civil Procedure, the defendant may automatically remove the case to federal court. See 28 U.S.C. § 1441(a).

What happens, however, if the plaintiff's complaint does not make a claim under ERISA, but instead asserts various state law theories for relief in connection with a denied claim for benefits from an ERISA plan? Can the defendant still remove the plaintiff's case to federal court, even though a federal question under ERISA does not present itself on the face of the plaintiff's complaint? The Supreme Court answered this important jurisdictional question in *Metropolitan Life Insurance Co. v. Taylor*.

METROPOLITAN LIFE INSURANCE CO. V. TAYLOR

United States Supreme Court, 1987.
481 U.S. 58, 107 S.Ct. 1542, 95 L.Ed.2d 55.

JUSTICE O'CONNOR delivered the opinion of the Court.

In *Pilot Life Insurance Co. v. Dedeaux,* 481 U.S. 41 (1987), the Court held that state common law causes of action asserting improper processing of a claim for benefits under an employee benefit plan regulated by the Employee Retirement Income Security Act of 1974 (ERISA) are preempted by the Act. ERISA § 514(a). The question presented by this litigation is whether these state common law claims are not only preempted by ERISA, but also displaced by ERISA's civil enforcement provision, ERISA § 502(a)(1)(B), to the extent that complaints filed in state courts purporting to plead such state common law causes of action are removable to federal court.

I

General Motors Corporation, a Delaware corporation whose principal place of business is in Michigan, has set up an employee benefit plan subject to the provisions of ERISA for its salaried employees. The plan pays benefits to salaried employees disabled by sickness or accident and is insured by the Metropolitan Life Insurance Company (Metropolitan).

General Motors employed Michigan resident Arthur Taylor as a salaried employee from 1959–1980. In 1961 Taylor was involved in a job-related automobile accident and sustained a back injury. Taylor filed a workers' compensation claim for this injury, and he eventually returned to work. In May 1980, while embroiled in a divorce and child custody dispute, Taylor took a leave of absence from his work on account of severe emotional problems. Metropolitan began paying benefits under General Motors' employee benefit plan, but asked Taylor to submit to a psychiatric examination by a designated psychiatrist. He did so and the psychiatrist determined that Taylor was emotionally unable to work. Six weeks later, after a follow up examination, however, Metropolitan's psychiatrist determined that Taylor was now fit for work; Metropolitan stopped making payments as of July 30, 1980.

Meanwhile, Taylor had filed a supplemental claim for benefits alleging that his back injuries disabled him from continuing his work. Metropolitan again sent Taylor to be examined, this time by an orthopedist. The physician found no orthopedic problems and Metropolitan subsequently denied the supplemental disability claim. On October 31, General Motors requested that Taylor report to its medical department for an examination. That examination took place on November 5 and a General Motors physician concluded that Taylor was not disabled. When Taylor nevertheless refused to return to work, General Motors notified him that his employment had been terminated.

Six months later Taylor filed suit against General Motors and Metropolitan in Michigan state court praying for judgment for "compensatory damages for money contractually owed Plaintiff, compensation for mental anguish caused by breach of this contract, as well as immediate reimplementation of all benefits and insurance coverages Plaintiff is entitled to." Taylor also asserted claims for wrongful termination of his employment and for wrongfully failing to promote him in retaliation for the 1961 worker's compensation claim. General Motors and Metropolitan removed the suit to federal court alleging federal question jurisdiction over the disability benefits claim by virtue of ERISA and pendent jurisdiction over the remaining claims. The District Court found the case properly removable and granted General Motors and Metropolitan summary judgment on the merits.

The Court of Appeals reversed on the ground that the District Court lacked removal jurisdiction. Noting a split in authority on the question among the federal courts, the Court of Appeals found that Taylor's complaint stated only state law causes of action subject to the federal defense of ERISA preemption, and that the "well-pleaded complaint" rule of *Louisville & Nashville R. Co. v. Mottley,* 211 U.S. 149 (1908), precluded removal on the basis of a federal defense. The Court of Appeals further held that the established doctrine permitting the removal of cases purporting to state only state law causes of action in labor cases preempted by § 301 of the Labor Management Relations Act of 1947 (LMRA) did not apply to this case. We granted certiorari and now reverse.

II

Under our decision in *Pilot Life Insurance Co. v. Dedeaux,* Taylor's common law contract and tort claims are preempted by ERISA. This lawsuit "relate[s] to [an] employee benefit plan." ERISA § 514(a). It is based upon common law of general application that is not a law regulating insurance. See Pilot Life Ins. Co. v. Dedeaux, 481 U.S. at 48–51. Accordingly, the suit is preempted by § 514(a) and is not saved by § 514(b)(2)(A). Moreover, as a suit by a beneficiary to recover benefits from a covered plan, it falls directly under ERISA § 502(a)(1)(B) of ERISA, which provides an exclusive federal cause of action for resolution of such disputes.

III

The century-old jurisdictional framework governing removal of federal question cases from state into federal courts is described in Justice Brennan's opinion for a unanimous Court in *Franchise Tax Board of California v. Construction Laborers Vacation Trust for Southern California,* 463 U.S. 1 (1983). By statute "any civil action brought in a State court of which the district courts of the United States have original jurisdiction, may be removed by the defendant or the defendants, to the district court of the United States for the district and division embracing the place where such action is pending." 28 U.S.C. § 1441(a). One category of cases over which the district courts have original jurisdiction are "federal question" cases; that is, those cases "arising under the Constitution, laws, or treaties of the United States." 28 U.S.C. § 1331. It is long settled law that a cause of action arises under federal law only when the plaintiff's well-pleaded complaint raises issues of federal law. Gully v. First National Bank, 299 U.S. 109 (1936); Louisville & Nashville R. Co. v. Mottley, supra. The "well-pleaded complaint rule" is the basic principle marking the boundaries of the federal question jurisdiction of the federal district courts. Franchise Tax Board, 463 U.S. at 9–12.

Federal preemption is ordinarily a federal defense to the plaintiff's suit. As a defense, it does not appear on the face of a well-pleaded complaint, and, therefore, does not authorize removal to federal court. One corollary of the well-pleaded complaint rule developed in the case law, however, is that Congress may so completely preempt a particular area that any civil complaint raising this select group of claims is necessarily federal in character. For 20 years, this Court has singled out claims preempted by § 301 of the LMRA for such special treatment. Avco Corp. v. Machinists, 390 U.S. 557 (1968).

> The necessary ground of decision [in *Avco*] was that the preemptive force of § 301 is so powerful as to displace entirely any state cause of action "for violation of contracts between an employer and a labor organization." Any such suit is purely a creature of federal law, notwithstanding the fact that state law would provide a cause of action in the absence of § 301.

Franchise Tax Board, 463 U.S. at 23.

There is no dispute in this litigation that Taylor's complaint, although preempted by ERISA, purported to raise only state law causes of action. The question therefore resolves itself into whether or not the *Avco* principle can be extended to statutes other than the LMRA in order to recharacterize a state law complaint displaced by § 502(a)(1)(B) as an action arising under federal law. In *Franchise Tax Board,* the Court held that ERISA preemption, without more, does not convert a state claim into an action arising under federal law. Franchise Tax Board, 463 U.S. at 25–27. The court suggested, however, that a state action that was not only preempted by ERISA, but also came "within the scope of § 502(a) of ERISA" might fall within the *Avco* rule. The claim in this case, unlike the state tax collection suit in *Franchise Tax Board,* is within the scope of ERISA § 502(a) and we therefore must face the question specifically reserved by *Franchise Tax Board.*

In the absence of explicit direction from Congress, this question would be a close one. As we have made clear today in *Pilot Life Insurance Co. v. Dedeaux,* 481 U.S. at 54, "[t]he policy choices reflected in the inclusion of certain remedies and the exclusion of others under the federal scheme would be completely undermined if ERISA plan participants and beneficiaries were free to obtain remedies under state law that Congress rejected in ERISA." Even with a provision such as § 502(a)(1)(B) that lies at the heart of a statute with the unique preemptive force of ERISA, however, we would be reluctant to find that extraordinary preemptive power, such as has been found with respect to § 301 of the LMRA, that converts an ordinary state common law complaint into one stating a federal claim for purposes of the well-pleaded complaint rule. But the language of the jurisdictional subsection of ERISA's civil enforcement provisions closely parallels that of § 301 of the LMRA. Section 502(f) says:

> The district courts of the United States shall have jurisdiction, without respect to the amount in controversy or the citizenship of the parties, to grant the relief provided for in subsection (a) of this section in any action.

ERISA § 502(f). Cf. § 301(a) of the LMRA. The presumption that similar language in two labor law statutes has a similar meaning is fully confirmed by the legislative history of ERISA's civil enforcement provisions. The Conference Report on ERISA describing the civil enforcement provisions of § 502(a) says:

> [W]ith respect to suits to enforce benefit rights under the plan or to recover benefits under the plan which do not involve application of the title I provisions, they may be brought not only in U.S. district courts but also in State courts of competent jurisdiction. *All such actions in Federal or State courts are to be regarded as arising under the laws of the United States in similar fashion to those brought under section 301 of the Labor Management Relations Act of 1947.*

H.R. Conf. Rep. No. 93–1280, p. 327 (1974) (emphasis added).

No more specific reference to the *Avco* rule can be expected and the rest of the legislative history consistently sets out this clear intention to make § 502(a)(1)(B) suits brought by participants or beneficiaries federal questions for the purposes of federal court jurisdiction in like manner as § 301 of the LMRA.

* * *

Accordingly, this suit, though it purports to raise only state law claims, is necessarily federal in character by virtue of the clearly manifested intent of Congress. It, therefore, "arise[s] under the . . . laws . . . of the United States," 28 U.S.C. § 1331, and is removable to federal court by the defendants. 28 U.S.C. § 1441(b). The judgment of the Court of Appeals is

Reversed.

NOTES AND QUESTIONS

1. *The Doctrine of Complete Preemption.* Complete preemption operates as an exception to the general rule that a defendant may remove a case filed in state court to the federal court system based on federal question jurisdiction only if the face of the plaintiff's complaint presents a claim that arises under federal law. In the ERISA context, there are two requirements that must be satisfied before the plaintiff's case may be removed from state court to federal court under the doctrine of complete preemption. The first requirement is that the state law upon which the claim is based must be preempted by ERISA's general preemption clause, Section 514(a). This first requirement is known as *ordinary preemption.* Ordinary preemption alone does not justify *removing* the plaintiff's case to federal court. The second requirement for complete preemption is that Section 502(a) of ERISA must provide a substitute federal claim. It is the availability of this substitute federal claim under Section 502(a) that makes preemption of the plaintiff's

state law-based claim "complete" and justifies removing the case to federal court. In essence, the doctrine of complete preemption is a legal fiction. Complete preemption operates to rewrite the plaintiff's complaint to present the claim under ERISA Section 502(a) that the plaintiff *should* have asserted in the complaint.

Once removed, the federal district court has discretion either to retain the entire case and exercise supplemental jurisdiction over any remaining state law claims, or to remand the remaining state law claims back to the state court. 28 U.S.C. §§ 1441(c); 1367. Often, the federal district court exercises supplemental jurisdiction over the remaining state law claims, only to subsequently dismiss them on the basis of ordinary preemption under ERISA Section 514(a).

2. *Complete Preemption and ERISA Litigation Strategy.* Complete preemption is commonly used as a legal strategy by defendants in ERISA litigation. Conventional wisdom holds that the defendant in an ERISA action is better off in federal court because the federal judiciary is more familiar than state court judges with ERISA's limitations on claims and remedies and with the defense to state law claims provided by ordinary preemption under ERISA Section 514(a). From the defendant's perspective, the doctrine of complete preemption is particularly effective when a plaintiff's lawyer files various state law claims—typically breach of contract, tort, and insurance law claims—in state court against a welfare benefit plan that has denied the plaintiff's claim for benefits. The defense response is immediately to remove the entire case to federal court, followed by a motion to dismiss all of the plaintiff's state law claims on the ground of ordinary preemption. *Aetna Health Inc. v. Davila*, 542 U.S. 200 (2004), illustrates use of the doctrine of complete preemption as a defensive strategy in the context of state law claims brought against an HMO as the administrator of the employer's health care plan. *Davila* is reproduced in Section D of Chapter Seven of the casebook.

The plaintiff's tactical response to removal on the basis of complete preemption is a motion to remand the case back to the state court. If the federal court determines that federal question jurisdiction (based on a theory of complete preemption under ERISA) does not exist, the case is remanded back to state court. In this situation, an order of remand by the federal district court, even if clearly erroneous, cannot be appealed. See 28 U.S.C. § 1447(d).

3. *The Policy Basis for Complete Preemption.* The traditional policy basis for the doctrine of complete preemption has been described as follows:

> Because the practical effect of complete preemption is that the defendant gets a federal forum for what is essentially a preemption defense, we assume that there must be a reason why defendants with this specific preemption defense are given access to the federal courts. Normally, we take the risk that state courts will sometimes get the preemption question wrong and will allow a suit to continue

under state law. The justification for preemption removal must be that, in some areas of regulation, the consequences of wrongly allowing a party to obtain relief under state law are unusually severe. We therefore allow the defendant to make the preemption argument in federal court because we are less willing to take a chance that the state court will wrongly decide the preemption issue.

Robert A. Cohen, *Understanding Preemption Removal Under ERISA § 502*, 72 N.Y.U. L. REV. 578, 586–87 (1997). What are the possible "severe consequences" of a wrong decision by a state court that justify the doctrine of complete preemption in the ERISA context?

4.   *The Scope of Complete Preemption.* Should complete preemption be limited only to claims, such as the one in *Metropolitan Life*, that may be recharacterized as a claim for plan benefits under ERISA Section 502(a)(1)(B)? Or is removal on the basis of complete preemption available whenever a state law claim can be recharacterized as an ERISA claim under Section 502(a)? This issue potentially arises when state law claims are made in state court against plan fiduciaries or nonfiduciary plan service providers alleging misconduct that could be recharacterized as a breach of fiduciary duty, a violation of Title I of ERISA, or a violation of the terms of the plan. The lower federal courts are divided over this issue. Compare Anderson v. Electronic Data Systems Corp., 11 F.3d 1311 (5th Cir. 1994) (complete preemption exists for claims under ERISA Section 502(a)(2) and (3)), and Wood v. Prudential Ins. Co. of Am., 207 F.3d 674 (3d Cir. 2000) (complete preemption exists for wrongful termination claim under ERISA Section 510), with Lupo v. Human Affairs Int'l, Inc., 28 F.3d 269 (2d Cir. 1994) (complete preemption exists only for claims under ERISA Section 502(a)(1)(B)). Does ERISA Section 502(e)(1), which grants the federal courts exclusive jurisdiction over all ERISA claims except for claims under Section 502(a)(1)(B), suggest how the issue should be resolved?

2. STATUTE OF LIMITATIONS, RIGHT TO JURY TRIAL AND ATTORNEY'S FEES

Statute of Limitations for ERISA Claims

ERISA's statute of limitations, found in Section 413, applies only to claims against fiduciaries for a breach or other violation of the fiduciary responsibility provisions found in Part 4 of Title I. Section 413 provides as a general rule that the plaintiff must commence an action against a fiduciary within the earlier of:

(1)   three years from the date the plaintiff had actual knowledge of the breach or violation; or

(2)   for affirmative actions that constitute a breach or violation, six years of the last action that was part of ongoing breach or violation; or

(3) for omissions that constitute a breach or violation, six years
     of the latest date the fiduciary could have acted to cure the
     breach or violation.

If concealment or fraud has occurred, this general rule does not apply.
Instead, ERISA Section 413 substitutes a six year statute of limitations
for cases involving concealment or fraud, measured from the date the
breach or violation is discovered. Litigation issues arising under Section
413 typically involve factual questions such as whether (and if so, when)
the plaintiff had actual knowledge of the breach or violation, whether
concealment or fraud has occurred, or when the last breach or
opportunity to cure occurred.

ERISA Section 413 does not provide a statute of limitations for
claims for plan benefits brought under Section 502(a)(1)(B), or for claims
brought under Section 510 for unlawful interference with a participant's
right to attain plan benefits. In these cases, the federal court determines
what the most analogous claim would be under the law of the state where
the federal court sits, and then applies the state law statute of limitations
for the analogous state law claim. E.g., Dameron v. Sinai Hosp. of
Baltimore, Inc., 815 F.2d 975 (4th Cir. 1987). In claims for plan benefits
under Section 502(a)(1)(B), the federal courts typically characterize the
participant's claim as a breach of contract claim. E.g., Corsini v. United
HealthCare Servs., Inc., 145 F.Supp.2d 184 (D.R.I. 2001). Where the plan
document itself specifies a statute of limitations period for claims, the
federal courts will enforce the plan's statute of limitations if the period is
reasonable. See Heimeshoff v. Hartford Life & Accident Ins. Co., 134 S.
Ct. 604 (2013) (upholding dismissal of a denial of benefits claim under
ERISA Section 502(a)(1)(B) based on a three year statute of limitations
provision set forth in the plan document). If the participant's claim under
ERISA Section 510 involves a termination of employment, the federal
courts usually characterize the participant's claim as one for wrongful
termination under state law. E.g., Muldoon v. C.J. Muldoon & Sons, 278
F.3d 31 (1st Cir. 2002).

Right to Jury Trial

ERISA does not expressly provide for the right to a jury trial for any
of the claims authorized under Section 502(a). When a federal statute is
silent concerning the right to a jury trial, the federal courts must
determine whether such a right nevertheless exists under the Seventh
Amendment to the United States Constitution, which guarantees the
right to a jury trial "in suits at common law." To determine whether the
right to a jury trial exists under the Seventh Amendment, the federal
courts look to whether the nature of the federal statutory right is
analogous to a claim that could have been brought in an English court of
common law, and, most importantly, whether the remedies provided by

the federal statute are legal or equitable in nature. See Granfinanciera, S.A. v. Nordberg, 492 U.S. 33 (1989).

The federal courts almost always rule that there is no right to a jury trial for claims brought under ERISA. Although the specific rationale for denying the right to a jury trial varies by the type of claim brought under ERISA Section 502(a), the federal courts generally view claims brought under ERISA as not triable by jury because ERISA's statutory rights and remedies are derived from the common law of trusts and, therefore, are quintessentially equitable in nature. E.g., Calamia v. Spivey, 632 F.2d 1235 (5th Cir. 1980); Wardle v. Central States, Southeast and Southwest Areas Pension Fund, 627 F.2d 820 (7th Cir. 1980). The absence of a jury trial right is often perceived as a strategic disadvantage for the ERISA plaintiff, who would prefer to have the merits of the claim, usually accompanied by dire personal circumstances, determined by a sympathetic jury rather than by a federal judge.

Attorney's Fees

The federal district courts have broad discretion to award reasonable attorney's fees and costs to either party in any action brought by a participant, beneficiary, or fiduciary under Title I of ERISA. In *Hardt v. Reliance Standard Life Insurance Co.*, 130 S.Ct. 2149 (2010), the Supreme Court held that it is not necessary to be a "prevailing party" in the litigation to be eligible to recover attorney's fees under Section 502(g)(1) of ERISA. Rather, the district court has discretion to award fees and costs under Section 502(g)(1) "to either party" so long as the fee claimant has achieved some degree of success on the merits.

Hardt illustrates a situation where the plaintiff achieved some degree of success on the merits and ultimately was awarded attorney's fees and costs. After exhausting administrative remedies, the plan participant in *Hardt* brought a claim under ERISA contesting the denial of her claim for benefits under the employer's long-term disability plan. After completing discovery, the district court denied cross-motions for summary judgment made by both the plaintiff and the plan administrator. In so doing the court found that the plan administrator's denial of the claim was not based on substantial evidence and that "compelling evidence" supported the participant's claim. The district court remanded the case back to the plan administrator to "remedy the deficiencies in its approach" because "the plan administrator has failed to comply with the ERISA guidelines" in reviewing the participant's claim for benefits. The district court warned the plan administrator to reconsider all the evidence in support of the plaintiff's claim for benefits and render a decision within 30 days or else judgment would be entered for the participant.

After conducting this review, the plan administrator determined that the participant was eligible for long-term disability benefits and paid the participant $55,250 in accrued, past-due benefits. The participant then moved for an award of attorney's fees and costs, which the district court granted. Based on these facts, the Supreme Court found that the participant had achieved some degree of success on the merits of her claim and affirmed the district court's award of attorneys' fees and costs.

In determining whether to award fees and costs, the federal courts focus on the following five factors:

(1) the degree of the offending party's culpability or bad faith;

(2) the degree of the ability of the offending party to personally satisfy an award of attorney fees;

(3) whether or not an award of attorney's fees against the offending party would deter other persons acting under similar circumstances;

(4) the amount of benefit conferred on members of the plan as a whole; and

(5) the relative merits of the parties' positions.

Eaves v. Penn, 587 F.2d 453, 465 (10th Cir. 1978). The federal district court judges have wide latitude under these factors to achieve a result that they believe is fair to the parties. Naturally, awards of attorney's fees and costs can vary greatly depending on the unique circumstances of each case.

Unlike claims brought under the federal Civil Rights Act, the majority of the federal courts of appeals do not presume automatically that the prevailing plaintiff in an ERISA action is entitled to an award of attorney's fees and costs. The Seventh and Ninth Circuits are exceptions. See Little v. Cox's Supermarkets, 71 F.3d 637, 644 (7th Cir. 1995) (employing a "modest presumption"); McElwaine v. US West, Inc., 176 F.3d 1167, 1172 (9th Cir. 1999) (a successful ERISA plaintiff "should ordinarily recover an attorney's fee unless special circumstances would render such an award unjust"). In extraordinary circumstances, a prevailing defendant has been awarded attorney's fees and costs. E.g., Seitzman v. Sun Life Assurance Co., 311 F.3d 477 (2d Cir. 2002) (awarding defendant more than one-half of its requested $208,000 fee award).

In awarding attorney's fees to a prevailing plaintiff, several circuits limit the fee award to work performed in conjunction with court litigation and exclude work performed as part of the administrative claims process the participant must pursue before filing a claim for plan benefits in federal court. See Peterson v. Continental Cas. Co., 282 F.3d 112 (2d Cir. 2002); Anderson v. Procter & Gamble Co., 220 F.3d 449 (6th Cir. 2000); Cann v. Carpenters' Pension Trust Fund, 989 F.2d 313 (9th Cir. 1993).

Claims for plan benefits are discussed in Section C of Chapter Six. As you read Section C, notice how this limitation on an award of attorney's fees potentially disadvantages the plan participant whose claim for benefits has been denied by the plan administrator.

C. SECTION 502(a)(1)(B) CLAIMS: JUDICIAL REVIEW OF CLAIMS FOR PLAN BENEFITS

In terms of the sheer number of cases filed, the bulk of ERISA litigation involves disputed claims for plan benefits brought by plan participants under ERISA Section 502(a)(1)(B). ERISA requires that every employee benefit plan must establish reasonable procedures governing: (1) the filing of claims by participants and beneficiaries for benefits under the plan; (2) the plan administrator's review of claims for benefits; and (3) appeals of adverse decisions by the plan administrator concerning claims for benefits. ERISA § 503; DOL Reg. § 2560.503–1. These claims procedures are described in the summary plan description for the plan. If the plan administrator initially denies the claim for benefits, the claimant generally must exhaust the administrative appeal procedures under the plan before filing a claim in court. Failure to exhaust the plan's administrative appeals procedures before filing a claim in court may result in dismissal of the plaintiff's case with prejudice. E.g., Harrow v. Prudential Ins. Co., 279 F.3d 244 (3d Cir. 2002); Diaz v. United Agricultural Employee Welfare Benefit Plan & Trust, 50 F.3d 1478 (9th Cir. 1995).

This exhaustion requirement serves two public policy purposes. First, it potentially reduces litigation by allowing the plan administrator an opportunity to reconsider an adverse decision in light of additional evidence submitted by the claimant through the appeal process. Second, in the event that the plan administrator denies the claimant's appeal, the exhaustion requirement serves to fully develop an administrative record for judicial review that documents the reasons for the plan administrator's decision.

Consistent with these two public policy purposes, the federal courts recognize several exceptions to the exhaustion requirement. The exhaustion requirement has been waived in cases where:

- the plan's appeal procedure had been abolished, e.g., Lee v. California Butchers' Pension Trust Fund, 154 F.3d 1075, 1080 (9th Cir. 1998);

- the plaintiff demonstrated an immediate danger of irreparable harm, e.g., Henderson v. Bodine Aluminum, Inc., 70 F.3d 958, 961 (8th Cir. 1995);

- the plaintiff demonstrated that pursuing the plan's claim procedures would have been futile, e.g., McGraw v. Prudential Ins. Co., 137 F.3d 1253, 1264 (10th Cir. 1998);

- the plaintiff was denied meaningful access to an appeal procedure, e.g., Wilczynski v. Lumbermens Mut. Cas. Co., 93 F.3d 397, 402–04 (7th Cir. 1996); or

- the document language describing the appeal procedure reasonably could be interpreted as making the appeal procedure optional, e.g., Watts v. Bellsouth Telecommunications, Inc., 316 F.3d 1203, 1209–10 (11th Cir. 2003).

1.   DEPARTMENT OF LABOR REGULATIONS GOVERNING CLAIMS PROCEDURES

Section 503 of ERISA governs plan claims procedures. Section 503 requires that every employee benefit plan must:

(1)   provide adequate notice in writing to any participant or beneficiary whose claim for benefits under the plan has been denied, setting forth the specific reasons for such denial and written in a manner calculated to be understood by the participant.

(2)   afford a reasonable opportunity to any participant whose claim for benefits has been denied for a full and fair review of the decision denying the claim by the appropriate named plan fiduciary.

Department of Labor regulations implementing the statutory requirements of Section 503 were issued originally in 1977 and later, modified in 2000 for claims arising under health care and disability plans.

The 1977 Regulations

The Department of Labor issued its first set of regulations governing plan claims procedures under ERISA Section 503 in 1977. 42 Fed. Reg. 27,426 (May 27, 1977) (1977 regulations). The 1977 regulations established uniform time limits for the administrative appeal process, regardless of whether the claim was for pension, health care, or other welfare plan benefits. Under the 1977 regulations, the plan administrator was required to notify the claimant of an adverse benefits decision within 90 days after receipt of the claim. The plan administrator could receive an additional 90 days to decide the claim by notifying the claimant that an extension of time was required. This notice had to be provided to the claimant in writing prior to the time the initial 90-day period expired and indicate the special circumstances justifying the request for an extension of time. If the plan administrator denied the claim, the 1977 regulations required the plan to give the claimant at least 60 days to appeal the decision. The plan administrator was required to decide the appeal within 60 days of receiving the claimant's request for review of the denied claim. The plan administrator could receive an additional 60 days to determine the appeal by notifying the claimant in writing that an extension of time was required and stating the special circumstances warranting an extension of time.

In the years following 1977, the health care industry and the structure of health care plans sponsored by employers changed dramatically. Rather than providing medical care first and worrying about payment later, health care providers began to require that the patient's health care plan certify that payment would be made by the patient's health care plan for the medical treatment. This pre-certification or pre-approval of payment by the patient's health care plan was required before medical treatment would be rendered. Participants in managed care plans were required to wait for treatment while the plan's utilization review administrator determined that the treatment was medically necessary.

During this period, disability plans also became increasingly popular as an employee benefit. A delay in processing a claim for disability benefits often resulted in economic hardship for the disabled claimant. As the number of disputed claims under health care and disability plans grew, the public perception arose that the claims procedures under the 1977 regulations were both too slow and procedurally unfair to the claimant.

The 2000 Regulations

Responding to public dissatisfaction, the Department of Labor adopted new regulations in 2000 to improve the claim review process and strengthen the procedural protections for plan participants and beneficiaries. See 42 Fed. Reg. 70,246 (Nov. 21, 2000) (codified as DOL Reg. § 2560.503–1) (2000 regulations). The 2000 regulations established new standards for the processing of claims under health care and disability plans. The old standards established by the 1977 regulations remain in effect for processing claims under plans other than health care and disability plans.

For health care plans, the 2000 regulations created three categories of claims and assigned each category a specific time period for administrative review. Under the 2000 regulations, *urgent care claims* generally must be decided as soon as possible consistent with the medical exigencies involved, but in no event later than 72 hours. If the claimant's treating physician determines that the claim is urgent, the plan must defer to the opinion of the treating physician and treat the claim as urgent. *Pre-service claims* (defined as claims for treatment that must be approved in advance by the plan) generally must be decided within 15 days. These rules for urgent care claims continue to apply under the Affordable Care Act. See generally Group Health Plans and Health Insurance Issuers: Rules Relating to Internal Claims and Appeals and External Review Processes, 76 Fed. Reg. 37,208 (June 24, 2011). *Post-service claims* generally must be decided within 30 days. The plan administrator is allowed one 15 day extension of time to consider pre-and post-service claims. The time limit for the claimant to appeal a denied claim is extended to 180 days. For appeals of denied claims for health care plan benefits, the plan administrator generally has 72 hours to determine an appeal of an urgent care claim, 30 days for a pre-service claim, and 60 days for a post-service claim.

For disability plan claims, the 2000 regulations require that the plan administrator must decide an initial claim within 45 days, with the possibility of up to two 30-day extensions. An appeal of a denied claim for disability benefits must be decided within 45 days, with the possibility of one 45-day extension.

The 2000 regulations also revised the procedures for claims review to make the process more fair to plan participants. Most significantly, the 2000 regulations require that the decision maker who reviews the appeal of a claim for health plan benefits that has been denied must be different from the person who denied the original claim. The 2000 regulations also prohibite plans from imposing fees or other costs as a prerequisite to filing a claim or appealing a denied claim.

2. ILLUSTRATIONS OF CLAIMS LITIGATION

The majority of cases filed under ERISA Section 502(a)(1)(B) involve disputed claims under welfare benefit plans. The case summaries below illustrate the variety of procedural and substantive issues that arise in litigation over disputed claims for plan benefits. As you read these case summaries, pay particular attention to the language in the plan document that is the focus of the lawsuit. Could this language in the plan document be rewritten to eliminate the potential for future lawsuits? If so, how would you rewrite the disputed plan terms?

Health Care Plans

Health care plans commonly provide benefits only for treatment that is "medically necessary" and may expressly exclude coverage of medical treatments that are "experimental." Disputes over whether the health care plan will pay for the participant's medical treatment often turn on both the plan language defining these terms and the current state of the art in the medical profession.

Killian v. Healthsource Provident Administrators, Inc., 152 F.3d 514 (6th Cir. 1998), provides an example of this situation. In *Killian*, the plaintiff was diagnosed with breast cancer. After three rounds of standard dosage chemotherapy proved unsuccessful, the plaintiff's physician recommended that she undergo a procedure known as high-dose chemotherapy with peripheral stem cell rescue (HDC/PSCR).

The plaintiff's health care plan provided coverage only for treatment deemed "medically necessary," which was defined in the plan document as:

> Medically Necessary and/or Medical Necessity-Services or supplies provided by a: (1) Hospital, (2) Physician, or (3) other qualified provider . . . are Medically Necessary if they are:
>
> (1) required for the diagnosis and/or treatment of the particular condition, disease, injury or illness; and
>
> (2) consistent with the symptom or diagnosis and treatment of the condition, disease, injury, or illness; and
>
> (3) commonly and usually noted throughout the medical field as proper to treat the diagnosed condition, disease, injury, or illness; and
>
> (4) the most fitting supply or level of service which can safely be given.

See id. at 516. The plaintiff's treating physician submitted a pre-authorization request to the health care plan for the HDC/PSCR treatment and estimated the cost of the treatment at $70,000. The plan submitted the pre-authorization request to two outside oncologists for review, who concluded that the proposed treatment was not medically necessary as defined by the plan's terms. The treating physician disagreed with the outside reviewers. The plaintiff appealed and eventually submitted affidavits from fifty oncologists opining that HDC/PSCR was the best and most effective treatment for the plaintiff's advanced breast cancer. The plan administrator refused to consider the additional affidavits on the basis that the affidavits were not timely filed and denied the appeal.

The plaintiff filed suit under ERISA Section 502(a)(1)(B). During the course of litigation, the plaintiff died and the plaintiff's claim was pursued by the executor of her estate.

The federal district court held that the plan administrator should have considered the participant's additional affidavit evidence. Reviewing the additional affidavit evidence along with the rest of the administrative record, the federal district court found that the plan administrator's denial of the pre-authorization request was arbitrary and capricious. The court of appeals agreed that the plan administrator's refusal to consider the additional affidavit evidence was arbitrary and capricious. See id. at 521. The court of appeals determined that district court erred, however, when it conducted its own review of the plaintiff's additional evidence and granted summary judgment in favor of the plaintiff. See id. at 522. The court of appeals held that the appropriate procedure was for the district court to allow the plan administrator to review the additional affidavit evidence first and decide whether, in light of this additional evidence, the plaintiff's requested treatment was "medically necessary" within the meaning of the plan's definition. See id.

Another coverage exclusion commonly found in health care plans is for cosmetic procedures. Like beauty itself, whether a procedure is considered cosmetic often lies in the eye of the beholder. *Bynum v. Cigna Healthcare of North Carolina, Inc.*, 287 F.3d 305 (4th Cir. 2002), illustrates a dispute over an allegedly cosmetic procedure. The plaintiff in *Bynum*, who was a nine month old infant, was covered as a dependent under the health care plan sponsored by the mother's employer. The infant was born with a severely twisted neck and an abnormally asymmetrical head. The infant's pediatrician referred the mother to a pediatric neurosurgeon, who recommended that the infant be treated with a medical procedure known as dynamic orthotic cranioplasty (DOC). The DOC procedure involved creating a custom orthotic device to be worn over the infant's head for twenty-three hours each day. The average treatment time was estimated to be four months, and the procedure was estimated to cost approximately $3,000. The purpose of the DOC procedure, according to the infant's pediatric neurosurgeon, was to correct the infant's misshapen head because "head shape abnormalities or asymmetry of the skull base can lead to further deformities or physical impairments of the facial region, such as malocclusion of the mandible." (Malocclusion of the mandible is a serious condition affecting the teeth, jaw and facial structure. It involves the malposition of teeth, which results in pain, degeneration, and jaw clicking. If left untreated, the condition can affect a person's ability to eat, speak and maintain good oral hygiene.)

The pediatric neurosurgeon submitted a claim to the plan for coverage of the DOC procedure. The next day, the plan administrator denied the claim on the ground that "cosmetic services are not covered." The plan document itself simply stated a list of coverage exclusions, which included "all cosmetic procedures or surgery." The plan did not contain a definition for the terms "cosmetic" or "cosmetic services."

The claim denial was appealed by the infant's mother and further written documentation from the treating neurosurgeon was submitted for review. In this additional documentation, the neurosurgeon explained how the DOC procedure would benefit the infant, and stated that although correction of the physical defect may lead to a more pleasant appearance, "it is the functional significance of the defect that compels the treatment" and that "it is clearly not treatment of a cosmetic deformity." Id. at 309. The plan administrator again denied the claim for failing to substantiate the medical necessity for the procedure. The claim was submitted again for a final appeal. Both the neurosurgeon and the infant's pediatrician submitted written documentation substantiating that the DOC procedure was for treatment of a serious medical condition and not for cosmetic purposes. In support of the claim, the mother submitted a medical article on the DOC procedure, the official definition of reconstructive surgery from the American Medical Association, and a newsletter from the American Orthotic and Prosthetic Association showing that the Food and Drug Administration had approved the DOC procedure for treatment of the medical condition. The plan administrator denied the appeal, stating in the written denial letter that the decision was based on the "Section 5.0 . . . Exclusion . . . All cosmetic procedures or surgery are considered non-covered." The final denial letter did not define "cosmetic" procedures or surgery. See id. at 309.

The mother filed suit on the infant's behalf under ERISA Section 502(a)(1)(B). The district court found that the DOC procedure was covered under the terms of the plan. The court of appeals agreed, concluding that the plan administrator's denial of the claim as a "cosmetic" procedure was "objectively unreasonable." Id. at 314. The court of appeals affirmed the district court's ruling that the plan could not exclude coverage of the DOC procedure.

Disability Plans

Disputes over claims for benefits under disability plans often involve whether the plaintiff is "disabled" under the terms of the plan. The outcome in these cases depends heavily on the particular circumstances of the plaintiff's condition, the medical evidence, and the plan's definition of a "disability." Other disputes concern technical or procedural defects in the plaintiff's claim, such as failing to notify the plan of the disability within the time limits for submitting a claim.

Lauder v. First Unum Life Insurance Co., 284 F.3d 375 (2d Cir. 2002), illustrates a dispute over disability plan benefits where the basis for the denial was not the plaintiff's physical condition, but rather her technical status as an "employee" covered under the disability plan's insurance policy. In Lauder, the employer (Coach) sponsored a disability plan, the benefits of which were provided by a group long-term disability insurance policy. The insurance policy provided long-term disability benefits for those employees who were engaged in "active employment" at the onset of the disability. Active employment was defined in the policy as working for the employer on a full-time basis for a minimum of thirty hours per week.

The plaintiff, who had been a full-time employee of the employer for many years, entered into a termination of employment agreement with the employer. This agreement stated that the plaintiff's employment "shall terminate" effective November 1, 1996, which was a Friday. The plaintiff's last day of work was Thursday, October 31, 1996. Late in the afternoon of November 1, 1996, the plaintiff slipped and fell in the parking lot of a convenience store, injuring her neck. On January 21, 1998, the plaintiff applied for disability benefits due to her neck injury.

The insurance company investigated the plaintiff's application for disability benefits by calling the employer to find out the last day the plaintiff had worked. The employer stated that was the plaintiff's last day of work was October 31, 1996. The insurance company also requested the plaintiff's medical records, but then canceled the request a few days later because it did not want to incur the expense of investigating the plaintiff's medical condition. The insurance company denied the plaintiff's request for disability benefits, stating that her coverage was in effect through October 31, 1996, and that she was no longer in the eligible class of employees when her accident occurred on November 1, 1996. The plaintiff appealed the denial by submitting a letter from her employer's benefits manager, dated December 5, 1996, which stated that her last day worked was November 1, 1996, and that her long-term disability coverage would terminate at the end of November. The insurance company denied the appeal, stating:

> Our review of the documents contained in your claim file indicate that you last worked at Coach on October 31, 1996. * * * While we do understand that your employment separation with Coach was not effective until November 1, 1996, your coverage for the purposes of your long-term disability insurance is in effect only if you meet the "active employment" requirements found in the policy.

Id. at 378. The plaintiff filed suit under ERISA Section 502(a)(1)(B). The district court found that the plaintiff was an "active employee" of the employer on November 1, 1996, and therefore within the policy's defined class of eligible employees on the date of her injury. The district court also found that the insurance company had waived its right to assert that the plaintiff was not "disabled" within the meaning of the policy's definition because the company had chosen not to pursue the issue. The court of appeals agreed that the plaintiff was an "active employee" at the time of her injury, stating:

> We do not credit First UNUM's argument that Lauder was not actively employed, and therefore ineligible for coverage, because her accident occurred after she had left Coach on her termination date. According to First UNUM's policy, Lauder was actively employed if she was working for Coach on a full-time basis for a minimum number of thirty hours per week. First UNUM has not argued that Lauder worked less than thirty

> hours, or was not a full-time employee, in the week ending on
> Friday, November 1, 1996. We do not think it twists logic to
> conclude that Lauder's coverage continued through the whole of
> her last day of active employment, rather than ending when she
> walked out of Coach's door for the last time. Indeed, First
> UNUM's proposed coverage cut-off point seems the less
> reasonable construction of the policy, albeit the one most
> favorable to it.

Id. at 380. The court of appeals also found that the insurance company
had waived its right to contest whether the plaintiff was disabled.

> This case raises the concern that plan administrators like First
> UNUM will try the easiest and least expensive means of denying
> a claim while holding in reserve another, perhaps stronger,
> defense should the first one fail. In light of ERISA's remedial
> purpose of protecting plan beneficiaries, we are unwilling to
> endorse manipulative strategies that attempt to take advantage
> of beneficiaries in this manner. * * * "[C]andid" statements by
> the insurer should be encouraged. First UNUM here chose to
> proceed on the questionable—but cheapest—argument of lack of
> coverage when it could easily have investigated the merits of
> Lauder's claim. It should not now get another proverbial bite at
> the apple.

Id. at 382.

Accidental Death Plans

Accidental death plans pay benefits to the surviving spouse and
dependents of the employee when the employee's death is the result of an
injury caused by an accident. Accidental death policies typically exclude
coverage for situations where the insured's death is the result of physical
sickness, where death is caused during the commission of a felony, or
where the injury resulting in the insured's death was self-inflicted.
Disputed claims for benefits under accidental death plans often center
around whether the injury that caused the death should be characterized
as accidental or as falling within one of the plan's coverage exclusions.
Like disability plans, the outcome in these cases depends heavily on the
particular circumstances of the insured's death and the precise language
of the plan document.

Stamp v. Metropolitan Life Insurance Co., 531 F.3d 84 (1st Cir. 2008),
illustrates a dispute over whether an insured's death was accidental. In
Stamp, the employee was killed in a single-car accident when his car
went off the road and struck a tree. According to the police report, the
road conditions at the time of the collision were dry and the traffic was
light. At the time of his death, the employee's blood alcohol level was

.265%, which was more than three times the legal limit under Rhode Island law.

The accident occurred several hours after the employee had left a day-long company meeting at a resort. The meeting ended with a boat cruise and a dinner. The employee consumed several alcoholic beverages during the cruise and at dinner, but several witnesses testified that he did not appear intoxicated when he left the meeting.

The employee's widow filed a claim for accidental death benefits under two employer-sponsored accidental death plans that were administered and insured by Metropolitan Life Insurance Company (Met Life). One plan document provided that accidental death benefits were to be paid if the insured was "physically injured as a result of an accident and die[s] within 90 days as a result of that injury or accident." The other plan document provided that accidental death benefits were to be paid if the insured's death occurred "within one year as a result of an injury caused by an occupational accident while at work." The term "accident" was not defined in either plan.

Both claims were denied by Met Life as the plan's administrator. The written explanation for the denials stated in part:

> [T]he purpose of the plan is to protect participants from risks that are outside of their control. The risks flowing from driving while intoxicated are completely within the control of the participant. While it is true that certain behavior that increases risk (such as skiing or horseback riding) would not result in loss of coverage, [driving while intoxicated] can be distinguished because it unreasonably increases the risk associated with a normally safe activity by interfering with an individual's ability to perceive and respond to risk. To impose the costs of such unreasonable risk-taking on the plan would result in an unanticipated cost.

The claim denial letter further explained that "[t]he fact that the coroner's report and the police report use the term 'accident' does not govern the proper interpretation under the plan." Id. at 87.

The widow filed suit under ERISA Section 502(a)(1)(B). The district court granted summary judgment in favor of the plan administrator. The First Circuit, in a split 2–1 decision, affirmed the grant of summary judgment. The majority concluded that "it is not arbitrary and capricious [for the plan administrator] to conclude that a reasonable person would view death or serious injury as a highly likely outcome of driving while so drunk that one may need help to stand or walk and is likely to black out." Id. at 91.

3. THE STANDARD OF JUDICIAL REVIEW

Once the plan administrator has issued a final denial of a claim for plan benefits, the only recourse left to the claimant is to ask a court to overturn the plan administrator's decision. How much deference should the court give to the plan administrator's decision to deny the claim for plan benefits? Should the court scrutinize the decision more closely if the plan administrator is operating under a conflict of interest? The Supreme Court addressed these issues first in *Firestone Tire & Rubber Co. v. Bruch*, and later in *Metropolitan Life Insurance Co. v. Glenn*, which follows *Firestone*.

FIRESTONE TIRE & RUBBER CO. V. BRUCH

United States Supreme Court, 1989.
489 U.S. 101, 109 S.Ct. 948, 103 L.Ed.2d 80.

JUSTICE O'CONNOR delivered the opinion of the Court.

This case presents two questions concerning the Employee Retirement Income Security Act of 1974 (ERISA). First, we address the appropriate standard of judicial review of benefit determinations by fiduciaries or plan administrators under ERISA. * * *

I

Late in 1980, petitioner Firestone Tire and Rubber Company (Firestone) sold, as going concerns, the five plants composing its Plastics Division to Occidental Petroleum Company (Occidental). Most of the approximately 500 salaried employees at the five plants were rehired by Occidental and continued in their same positions without interruption and at the same rates of pay. At the time of the sale, Firestone maintained three pension and welfare benefit plans for its employees: a termination pay plan, a retirement plan, and a stock purchase plan. Firestone was the sole source of funding for the plans and had not established separate trust funds out of which to pay the benefits from the plans. All three of the plans were either "employee welfare benefit plans" or "employee pension benefit plans" governed (albeit in different ways) by ERISA. By operation of law, Firestone itself was the administrator and fiduciary of each of these "unfunded" plans. At the time of the sale of its Plastics Division, Firestone was not aware that the termination pay plan was governed by ERISA, and therefore had not set up a claims procedure nor complied with ERISA's reporting and disclosure obligations with respect to that plan.

Respondents, six Firestone employees who were rehired by Occidental, sought severance benefits from Firestone under the termination pay plan. In relevant part, that plan provides as follows:

If your service is discontinued prior to the time you are eligible for pension benefits, you will be given termination pay if released because of a reduction in work force or if you become physically or mentally unable to perform your job.

The amount of termination pay you will receive will depend on your period of credited company service.

Several of the respondents also sought information from Firestone regarding their benefits under all three of the plans pursuant to certain ERISA disclosure provisions. See ERISA §§ 104(b)(4); 105(a). Firestone denied respondents severance benefits on the ground that the sale of the Plastics Division to Occidental did not constitute a "reduction in work force" within the meaning of the termination pay plan. * * *

Respondents then filed a class action on behalf of "former, salaried, nonunion employees who worked in the five plants that comprised the Plastics Division of Firestone." The action was based on § 502(a)(1), which provides that a "civil action may be brought . . . by a participant or beneficiary [of a covered plan] . . . (A) for the relief provided for in [§ 502(c)], [and] (B) to recover benefits due to him under the terms of his plan." In Count I of their complaint, respondents alleged that they were entitled to severance benefits because Firestone's sale of the Plastics Division to Occidental constituted a "reduction in work force" within the meaning of the termination pay plan. * * *

The District Court granted Firestone's motion for summary judgment. With respect to Count I, the District Court held that Firestone had satisfied its fiduciary duty under ERISA because its decision not to pay severance benefits to respondents under the termination pay plan was not arbitrary or capricious. * * *

The Court of Appeals reversed the District Court's grant of summary judgment. * * * 828 F.2d 134 (3d Cir. 1987). With respect to Count I, the Court of Appeals acknowledged that most federal courts have reviewed the denial of benefits by ERISA fiduciaries and administrators under the arbitrary and capricious standard. Id. at 138. It noted, however, that the arbitrary and capricious standard had been softened in cases where fiduciaries and administrators had some bias or adverse interest. Id. at 139–40. The Court of Appeals held that where an employer is itself the fiduciary and administrator of an unfunded benefit plan, its decision to deny benefits should be subject to de novo judicial review. It reasoned that in such situations deference is unwarranted given the lack of assurance of impartiality on the part of the employer. Id. at 137–45. * * *

We granted certiorari to resolve the conflicts among the Courts of Appeals as to the appropriate standard of review in actions under § 502(a)(1)(B). * * *.

II

ERISA provides "a panoply of remedial devices" for participants and beneficiaries of benefit plans. Massachusetts Mutual Life Ins. Co. v. Russell, 473 U.S. 134 (1985). Respondents' action asserting that they were entitled to benefits because the sale of Firestone's Plastics Division constituted a "reduction in work force" within the meaning of the termination pay plan was based on the authority of § 502(a)(1)(B). That provision allows a suit to recover benefits due under the plan, to enforce rights under the terms of the plan, and to obtain a declaratory judgment of future entitlement to benefits under the provisions of the plan contract. The discussion which follows is limited to the appropriate standard of review in § 502(a)(1)(B) actions challenging denials of benefits based on plan interpretations. We express no view as to the appropriate standard of review for actions under other remedial provisions of ERISA.

A

Although it is a "comprehensive and reticulated statute," Nachman Corp. v. Pension Benefit Guaranty Corp., 446 U.S. 359, 361 (1980), ERISA does not set out the appropriate standard of review for actions under § 502(a)(1)(B) challenging benefit eligibility determinations. To fill this gap, federal courts have adopted the arbitrary and capricious standard developed under 61 Stat. 157, 29 U.S.C. § 186(c), a provision of the Labor Management Relations Act, 1947 (LMRA). In light of Congress' general intent to incorporate much of LMRA fiduciary law into ERISA, see NLRB v. Amax Coal Co., 453 U.S. 322, 332 (1981), and because ERISA, like the LMRA, imposes a duty of loyalty on fiduciaries and plan administrators, Firestone argues that the LMRA arbitrary and capricious standard should apply to ERISA actions. A comparison of the LMRA and ERISA, however, shows that the wholesale importation of the arbitrary and capricious standard into ERISA is unwarranted.

In relevant part, 29 U.S.C. § 186(c) authorizes unions and employers to set up pension plans jointly and provides that contributions to such plans be made "for the sole and exclusive benefit of the employees . . . and their families and dependents." The LMRA does not provide for judicial review of the decisions of LMRA trustees. Federal courts adopted the arbitrary and capricious standard both as a standard of review and, more importantly, as a means of asserting jurisdiction over suits by beneficiaries of LMRA plans who were denied benefits by trustees. Unlike the LMRA, ERISA explicitly authorizes suits against fiduciaries and plan administrators to remedy statutory violations, including breaches of fiduciary duty and lack of compliance with benefit plans. See ERISA §§ 502(a); 502(f). See generally Pilot Life Ins. Co. v. Dedeaux, 481 U.S. 41 (1987). Thus, the raison d'etre for the LMRA arbitrary and capricious standard—the need for a jurisdictional basis in suits against trustees—is not present in ERISA. Without this jurisdictional analogy, LMRA principles offer no support for the adoption of the arbitrary and capricious standard insofar as § 502(a)(1)(B) is concerned.

B

ERISA abounds with the language and terminology of trust law. ERISA's legislative history confirms that the Act's fiduciary responsibility provisions "codif[y] and mak[e] applicable to [ERISA] fiduciaries certain principles developed in the evolution of the law of trusts." H.R. Rep. No. 93–533, p. 11 (1973). Given this language and history, we have held that courts are to develop a "federal common law of rights and obligations under ERISA-regulated plans." Pilot Life Ins. Co., 481 U.S. at 56. See also Franchise Tax Board v. Construction Laborers Vacation Trust, 463 U.S. 1, 24 n.26 (1983) ("[A] body of Federal substantive law will be developed by the courts to deal with issues involving rights and obligations under private welfare and pension plans."). In determining the appropriate standard of review for actions under § 502(a)(1)(B), we are guided by principles of trust law. Central States, Southeast and Southwest Areas Pension Fund v. Central Transport, Inc., 472 U.S. 559, 570 (1985).

Trust principles make a deferential standard of review appropriate when a trustee exercises discretionary powers. See Restatement (Second) of Trusts § 187 (1959) ("[w]here discretion is conferred upon the trustee with respect to the exercise of a power, its exercise is not subject to control by the court except to prevent an abuse by the trustee of his discretion"). See also G. Bogert & G. Bogert, Law of Trusts and Trustees § 560, pp. 193–208 (2d rev. ed. 1980). A trustee may be given power to construe disputed or doubtful terms, and in such circumstances the trustee's interpretation will not be disturbed if reasonable. Id. § 559, at 169–71. Whether "the exercise of a power is permissive or mandatory depends upon the terms of the trust." 3 W. Fratcher, Scott on Trusts § 187, p. 14 (4th ed. 1988). Hence, over a century ago we remarked that "[w]hen trustees are in existence, and capable of acting, a court of equity will not interfere to control them in the exercise of a *discretion vested in them by the instrument* under which they act." Nichols v. Eaton, 91 U.S. 716, 724–25 (1875) (emphasis added). Firestone can seek no shelter in these principles of trust law, however, for there is no evidence that under Firestone's termination pay plan the administrator has the power to construe uncertain terms or that eligibility determinations are to be given deference.

Finding no support in the language of its termination pay plan for the arbitrary and capricious standard, Firestone argues that as a matter of trust law the interpretation of the terms of a plan is an inherently discretionary function. But other settled principles of trust law, which point to de novo review of benefit eligibility determinations based on plan interpretations, belie this contention. As they do with contractual provisions, courts construe terms in trust agreements without deferring to either party's interpretation. "The extent of the duties and powers of a trustee is determined by the rules of law that are applicable to the situation, and not the rules that the trustee or his attorney believes to be applicable, and by the terms of the trust *as the court may interpret them*, and not as they may be interpreted by the trustee himself or by his attorney." 3 W. Fratcher, Scott on Trusts § 201, at 221 (emphasis added). A trustee who is in doubt as to the interpretation of the instrument can protect himself by obtaining instructions from the court. Bogert & Bogert, supra, § 559, at 162–168; Restatement (Second) of Trusts § 201, Comment b (1959). The terms of trusts created by written instruments are "determined by the provisions of the instrument as interpreted in light of all the circumstances and such other evidence of the intention of the settlor with respect to the trust as is not inadmissible." Id. at Comment d (1959).

The trust law de novo standard of review is consistent with the judicial interpretation of employee benefit plans prior to the enactment of ERISA. Actions challenging an employer's denial of benefits before the enactment of ERISA were governed by principles of contract law. If the plan did not give the employer or administrator discretionary or final authority to construe uncertain terms, the court reviewed the employee's claim as it would have any other contract claim—by looking to the terms of the plan and other manifestations of the parties' intent.

Despite these principles of trust law pointing to a de novo standard of review for claims like respondents', Firestone would have us read ERISA to require the application of the arbitrary and capricious standard to such claims. ERISA defines a fiduciary as one who "exercises any discretionary authority or discretionary control respecting management of [a] plan or exercises any authority or control respecting management or disposition of its assets." ERISA § 3(21)(A)(i). A fiduciary has "authority to control and manage the operation and administration of the plan," ERISA § 402(a)(1), and must provide a "full and fair review" of claim denials, ERISA § 503(2). From these provisions, Firestone concludes that an ERISA plan administrator, fiduciary, or trustee is empowered to exercise *all* his authority in a discretionary manner subject only to review for arbitrariness and capriciousness. But the provisions relied upon so heavily by Firestone do not characterize a fiduciary as one who exercises entirely discretionary authority or control. Rather, one is a fiduciary to the extent he exercises any discretionary authority or control.

ERISA was enacted "to promote the interests of employees and their beneficiaries in employee benefit plans," Shaw v. Delta Air Lines, Inc., 463 U.S. 85, 90 (1983), and "to protect contractually defined benefits." Massachusetts Mutual Life Ins. Co. v. Russell, 473 U.S. at 148. Adopting Firestone's reading of ERISA would require us to impose a standard of review that would afford less protection to employees and their beneficiaries than they enjoyed before ERISA was enacted. Nevertheless, Firestone maintains that congressional action after the passage of ERISA indicates that Congress intended ERISA claims to be reviewed under the arbitrary and capricious standard. At a time when most federal courts had adopted the arbitrary and capricious standard of review, a bill was introduced in Congress to amend § 502 by providing de novo review of decisions denying benefits. See H.R. 6226, 97th Cong., 2d Sess. (1982). Because the bill was never enacted, Firestone asserts that we should conclude that Congress was satisfied with the arbitrary and capricious standard. We do not think that this bit of legislative inaction carries the day for Firestone. Though "instructive," failure to act on the proposed bill is not conclusive of Congress' views on the appropriate standard of review. Bowsher v. Marck & Co., 460 U.S. 824, 837 n.12 (1983). The bill's demise may have been the result of events that had nothing to do with Congress' view on the propriety of de novo review. Without more, we cannot ascribe to Congress any acquiescence in the arbitrary and capricious standard. "[T]he views of a subsequent Congress form a hazardous basis for inferring the intent of an earlier one." United States v. Price, 361 U.S. 304, 313 (1960).

Firestone and its amici also assert that a de novo standard would contravene the spirit of ERISA because it would impose much higher administrative and litigation costs and therefore discourage employers from creating benefit plans. Because even under the arbitrary and capricious standard an employer's denial of benefits could be subject to judicial review, the assumption seems to be that a de novo standard would encourage more litigation by employees, participants, and beneficiaries who wish to assert their right to benefits. Neither general principles of trust law nor a concern for impartial decisionmaking, however, forecloses parties from agreeing upon a narrower standard of review. Moreover, as to both funded and unfunded plans, the threat of increased litigation is not sufficient to outweigh the reasons for a de novo standard that we have already explained.

As this case aptly demonstrates, the validity of a claim to benefits under an ERISA plan is likely to turn on the interpretation of terms in the plan at issue. Consistent with established principles of trust law, we hold that a denial of benefits challenged under § 502(a)(1)(B) is to be reviewed under a de novo standard unless the benefit plan gives the administrator or fiduciary discretionary authority to determine eligibility for benefits or to construe the terms of the plan. Because we do not rest our decision on the concern for impartiality that guided the Court of Appeals, we need not distinguish between types of plans or focus on the motivations of plan administrators and fiduciaries. Thus, for purposes of actions under § 502(a)(1)(B), the de novo standard of review applies regardless of whether the plan at issue is funded or unfunded and regardless of whether the administrator or fiduciary is operating under a possible or actual conflict of interest. Of course, if a benefit plan gives discretion to an administrator or fiduciary who is operating under a conflict of interest, that conflict must be weighed as a "facto[r] in determining whether there is an abuse of discretion." Restatement (Second) of Trusts § 187 comment d (1959).

The Supreme Court's opinion in *Firestone* immediately was criticized by one prominent ERISA scholar as "doctrinal hash" that "garbles long-settled principles of trust law, confuses trust and contract rubrics, and invites plan drafters to defeat the stated objectives of the decision." John H. Langbein, *The Supreme Court Flunks Trusts*, 1990 S. Ct. Rev. 207, 228. In response to *Firestone*, as predicted plan sponsors amended their plan documents to obtain deferential judicial review by giving plan administrators the discretionary authority to determine eligibility for benefits and to construe the terms of the plan.

Today, *Firestone* stands for the proposition that, for plans containing the requisite *Firestone* language, the plan administrator's denial of a claim for plan benefits is subject to judicial review under an abuse of discretion standard. Given that many denied claims for benefits turn on the administrator's interpretation of language in the plan, the abuse of discretion standard gives the plan administrator a significant strategic advantage in claims litigation under ERISA Section 502(a)(1)(B).

The Supreme Court's concluding statement in *Firestone*, "if a benefit plan gives discretion to an administrator or fiduciary who is operating under a conflict of interest, that conflict must be weighed as a factor in determining whether there is an abuse of discretion," proved difficult for the federal courts to apply. In the words of one federal judge, "[s]ince *Firestone*, courts have struggled to give effect to this delphic statement, and to determine both what constitutes a conflict of interest and how a conflict should affect the scrutiny of an administrator's decision to deny benefits." Pinto v. Reliance Standard Life Ins. Co., 214 F.3d 377, 383 (3d Cir. 2000) (Becker, J.).

Two types of structural conflict of interest arrangements in particular proved troublesome for the federal courts. First, the employer may both fund and administer the plan. This structural arrangement is typical for pension and severance pay plans, and also is used when the employer self-insures a health care plan. A variation on this arrangement occurs when the employer hires an independent third party to review and administer claims, but the employer retains the final authority to approve or deny claims. Second, the employer's plan may consist of a group insurance policy contract. Such insured plans are typical for disability, life insurance, and accidental death plans, and for the health care plans of employers who are unwilling or unable to self-insure. In both situations, the insurance company operates under a conflict of interest due to the financial incentive to deny claims for plan benefits under the policy.

Nineteen years after deciding *Firestone*, the Supreme Court addressed these conflict of interest situations in *Metropolitan Life Insurance Co. v. Glenn*. As you read the opinion in *Glenn*, imagine that you are a federal district court judge. After *Glenn*, what are the legal principles you must apply in reviewing a denied claim for plan benefits? Did *Glenn* change the standard of judicial review in situations where the plan administrator is laboring under a structural conflict of interest?

<hr />

METROPOLITAN LIFE INSURANCE CO. V. GLENN

United States Supreme Court, 2008.
554 U.S. 105, 128 S.Ct. 2343, 171 L.Ed.2d 299.

JUSTICE BREYER delivered the opinion of the Court.

The Employee Retirement Income Security Act of 1974 (ERISA) permits a person denied benefits under an employee benefit plan to challenge that denial in federal court. Often the entity that administers the plan, such as an employer or an insurance company, both determines whether an employee is eligible for benefits and pays benefits out of its own pocket. We here decide that this dual role creates a conflict of interest; that a reviewing court should consider that conflict as a factor in determining whether the plan administrator has abused its discretion in denying benefits; and that the significance of the factor will depend upon the circumstances of the particular case. See Firestone Tire & Rubber Co. v. Bruch, 489 U.S. 101, 115 (1989).

I

Petitioner Metropolitan Life Insurance Company (MetLife) serves as both an administrator and the insurer of Sears, Roebuck & Company's long-term disability insurance plan, an ERISA-governed employee benefit plan. The plan grants MetLife (as administrator) discretionary authority to determine whether an employee's claim for benefits is valid; it simultaneously provides that MetLife (as insurer) will itself pay valid benefit claims.

Respondent Wanda Glenn, a Sears employee, was diagnosed with severe dilated cardiomyopathy, a heart condition whose symptoms include fatigue and shortness of breath. She applied for plan disability benefits in June 2000, and MetLife concluded that she met the plan's standard for an initial 24 months of benefits, namely, that she could not "perform the material duties of her own job." MetLife also directed Glenn to a law firm that would assist her in applying for federal Social Security disability benefits (some of which MetLife itself would be entitled to receive as an offset to the more generous plan benefits). In April 2002, an Administrative Law Judge found that Glenn's illness prevented her not only from performing her own job but also "from performing any jobs [for which she could qualify] existing in significant numbers in the national economy." The Social Security Administration consequently granted Glenn permanent disability payments retroactive to April 2000. Glenn herself kept none of the backdated benefits: three-quarters went to MetLife, and the rest (plus some additional money) went to the lawyers.

To continue receiving Sears plan disability benefits after 24 months, Glenn had to meet a stricter, Social-Security-type standard, namely, that her medical condition rendered her incapable of performing not only her own job but of performing "the material duties of any gainful occupation for which" she was "reasonably qualified." MetLife denied Glenn this extended benefit because it found that she was "capable of performing full-time sedentary work."

After exhausting her administrative remedies, Glenn brought this federal lawsuit, seeking judicial review of MetLife's denial of benefits. The District Court denied relief. Glenn appealed to the Court of Appeals for the Sixth Circuit. Because the plan granted MetLife "discretionary authority to determine benefits," the Court of Appeals reviewed the administrative record under a deferential standard. In doing so, it treated "as a relevant factor" a "conflict of interest" arising out of the fact that MetLife was "authorized both to decide whether an employee is eligible for benefits and to pay those benefits."

The Court of Appeals ultimately set aside MetLife's denial of benefits in light of a combination of several circumstances: (1) the conflict of interest; (2) MetLife's failure to reconcile its own conclusion that Glenn could work in other jobs with the Social Security Administration's conclusion that she could not; (3) MetLife's focus upon one treating physician report suggesting that Glenn could work in other jobs at the expense of other, more detailed treating physician reports indicating that she could not; (4) MetLife's failure to provide all of the treating physician reports to its own hired experts; and (5) MetLife's failure to take account of evidence indicating that stress aggravated Glenn's condition.

MetLife sought certiorari, asking us to determine whether a plan administrator that both evaluates and pays claims operates under a conflict of interest in making discretionary benefit determinations. The Solicitor General suggested that we also consider " 'how' " any such conflict should " 'be taken into account on judicial review of a discretionary benefit determination.' " We agreed to consider both questions.

II

In *Firestone Tire & Rubber Co. v. Bruch,* 489 U.S. 101 (1989), this Court addressed "the appropriate standard of judicial review of benefit determinations by fiduciaries or plan administrators under" § 502(a)(1)(B), the ERISA provision at issue here. Id. at 105. *Firestone* set forth four principles of review relevant here.

(1) In "determining the appropriate standard of review," a court should be "guided by principles of trust law"; in doing so, it should analogize a plan administrator to the trustee of a common-law trust; and it should consider a benefit determination to be a fiduciary act (i.e., an act in which the administrator owes a special duty of loyalty to the plan beneficiaries). Id. at 111–113.

(2) Principles of trust law require courts to review a denial of plan benefits "under a de novo standard" unless the plan provides to the contrary. Id. at 115.

(3) Where the plan provides to the contrary by granting "the administrator or fiduciary *discretionary authority* to determine eligibility for benefits," id. (emphasis added), "[t]rust principles make a *deferential standard* of review appropriate," id. at 111 (emphasis added).

(4) If "a benefit plan gives discretion to an administrator or fiduciary who *is operating under a conflict of interest,* that conflict must be *weighed as a 'factor* in determining whether there is an abuse of discretion.' "

Id. at 115 (emphasis added). The questions before us, while implicating the first three principles, directly focus upon the application and the meaning of the fourth.

III

The first question asks whether the fact that a plan administrator both evaluates claims for benefits and pays benefits claims creates the kind of "conflict of interest" to which *Firestone's* fourth principle refers. In our view, it does.

That answer is clear where it is the employer that both funds the plan and evaluates the claims. In such a circumstance, "every dollar provided in benefits is a dollar spent by . . . the employer; and every dollar saved is a dollar in the employer's pocket." Bruch v. Firestone Tire & Rubber Co., 828 F.2d 134, 144 (3d Cir. 1987). The employer's fiduciary interest may counsel in favor of granting a borderline claim while its immediate financial interest counsels to the contrary. Thus, the employer has an "interest conflicting with that of the beneficiaries," the type of conflict that judges must take into account when they review the discretionary acts of a trustee of a common-law trust. Restatement

(Second) of Trusts § 187, Comment d (1959) (hereinafter Restatement); see also Firestone, 489 U.S. at 115; cf. Black's Law Dictionary 319 (8th ed. 2004) ("conflict of interest" is a "real or seeming incompatibility between one's private interests and one's public or fiduciary duties").

Indeed, *Firestone* itself involved an employer who administered an ERISA benefit plan and who both evaluated claims and paid for benefits. And thus that circumstance quite possibly was what the Court had in mind when it mentioned conflicted administrators. The *Firestone* parties, while disagreeing about other matters, agreed that the dual role created a conflict of interest of some kind in the employer.

MetLife points out that an employer who creates a plan that it will both fund and administer foresees, and implicitly approves, the resulting conflict. But that fact cannot change our conclusion. At trust law, the fact that a settlor (the person establishing the trust) approves a trustee's conflict does not change the legal need for a judge later to take account of that conflict in reviewing the trustee's discretionary decisionmaking. See Restatement § 107, Comment f (discretionary acts of trustee with settlor-approved conflict subject to "careful scrutiny"); id. § 107, Comment f, Illustration 1 (conflict is "a factor to be considered by the court in determining later whether" there has been an "abuse of discretion"); id. § 187, Comment d (same).

MetLife also points out that we need not follow trust law principles where trust law is "inconsistent with the language of the statute, its structure, or its purposes." Hughes Aircraft Co. v. Jacobson, 525 U.S. 432, 447 (1999). MetLife adds that to find a conflict here is inconsistent (1) with ERISA's efforts to avoid complex review proceedings, see Varity Corp. v. Howe, 516 U.S. 489, 497 (1996); (2) with Congress' efforts not to deter employers from setting up benefit plans, see id.; and (3) with an ERISA provision specifically allowing employers to administer their own plans, see ERISA § 408(c)(3).

But we cannot find in these considerations any significant inconsistency. As to the first, we note that trust law functions well with a similar standard. As to the second, we have no reason, empirical or otherwise, to believe that our decision will seriously discourage the creation of benefit plans. As to the third, we have just explained why approval of a conflicted trustee differs from review of that trustee's conflicted decisionmaking. As to all three taken together, we believe them outweighed by "Congress' desire to offer employees enhanced protection for their benefits." Varity, 516 U.S. at 497 (discussing "competing congressional purposes" in enacting ERISA).

The answer to the conflict question is less clear where (as here) the plan administrator is not the employer itself but rather a professional insurance company. Such a company, MetLife would argue, likely has a much greater incentive than a self-insuring employer to provide accurate claims processing. That is because the insurance company typically charges a fee that attempts to account for the cost of claims payouts, with the result that paying an individual claim does not come to the same extent from the company's own pocket. It is also because the marketplace (and regulators) may well punish an insurance company when its products, or ingredients of its products, fall below par. And claims processing, an ingredient of the insurance company's product, falls below par when it seeks a biased result, rather than an accurate one. Why, MetLife might ask, should one consider an insurance company *inherently* more conflicted than any other market participant, say, a manufacturer who might earn more money in the short run by producing a product with poor quality steel or a lawyer with an incentive to work more slowly than necessary, thereby accumulating more billable hours?

Conceding these differences, we nonetheless continue to believe that for ERISA purposes a conflict exists. For one thing, the employer's own conflict may extend to its selection of an insurance company to administer its plan. An employer choosing an administrator in effect buys insurance for others and consequently (when compared to the marketplace customer who buys for himself) may be more interested in an insurance company with low rates than in one with accurate claims processing. Cf. John H. Langbein, Trust Law as Regulatory Law, 101 Nw. U. L. Rev. 1315, 1323–1324 (2007) (observing that employees are rarely involved in plan negotiations).

For another, ERISA imposes higher-than-marketplace quality standards on insurers. It sets forth a special standard of care upon a plan administrator, namely, that the administrator "discharge its duties" in respect to discretionary claims processing "solely in the interests of the participants and beneficiaries" of the plan, ERISA § 404(a)(1); it simultaneously underscores the particular importance of accurate claims processing by insisting that administrators "provide a 'full and fair review' of claim denials," Firestone, 489 U.S. at 113 (quoting ERISA § 503(2)); and it supplements marketplace and regulatory controls with judicial review of individual claim denials, see ERISA § 502(a)(1)(B).

Finally, a legal rule that treats insurance company administrators and employers alike in respect to the *existence* of a conflict can nonetheless take account of the circumstances to which MetLife points so far as it treats those, or similar, circumstances as diminishing the *significance* or *severity* of the conflict in individual cases.

IV

We turn to the question of "how" the conflict we have just identified should "be taken into account on judicial review of a discretionary benefit.

In doing so, we elucidate what this Court set forth in *Firestone,* namely, that a conflict should" be weighed as a "'factor in determining whether there is an abuse of discretion.'" 489 U.S. at 115 (quoting Restatement § 187, Comment d).

We do not believe that *Firestone's* statement implies a change in the *standard* of review, say, from deferential to de novo review. Trust law continues to apply a deferential standard of review to the discretionary decisionmaking of a conflicted trustee, while at the same time requiring the reviewing judge to take account of the conflict when determining whether the trustee, substantively or procedurally, has abused his discretion. See Restatement § 187, Comments d-j; id. § 107, Comment f. We see no reason to forsake *Firestone's* reliance upon trust law in this respect.

Nor would we overturn *Firestone* by adopting a rule that in practice could bring about near universal review by judges de novo—i.e., without deference—of the lion's share of ERISA plan claims denials. Had Congress intended such a system of review, we believe it would not have left to the courts the development of review standards but would have said more on the subject. See Firestone, 489 U.S. at 109 ("ERISA does not set out the appropriate standard of review for actions under § 502(a)(1)(B)"); cf. Whitman v. American Trucking Ass'n., Inc., 531 U.S. 457, 468 (2001) (Congress does not "hide elephants in mouseholes").

Neither do we believe it necessary or desirable for courts to create special burden-of-proof rules, or other special procedural or evidentiary rules, focused narrowly upon the evaluator/payor conflict. In principle, as we have said, conflicts are but one factor among many that a reviewing judge must take into account. Benefits decisions arise in too many contexts, concern too many circumstances, and can relate in too many different ways to conflicts—which themselves vary in kind and in degree of seriousness—for us to come up with a one-size-fits-all procedural system that is likely to promote fair and accurate review. Indeed, special procedural rules would create further complexity, adding time and expense to a process that may already be too costly for many of those who seek redress.

We believe that *Firestone* means what the word "factor" implies, namely, that when judges review the lawfulness of benefit denials, they will often take account of several different considerations of which a conflict of interest is one. This kind of review is no stranger to the judicial system. Not only trust law, but also administrative law, can ask judges to determine lawfulness by taking account of several different, often case-specific, factors, reaching a result by weighing all together. See Restatement § 187, Comment d; cf. Citizens to Preserve Overton Park, Inc. v. Volpe, 401 U.S. 402, 415–417 (1971) (review of governmental decision for abuse of discretion); Universal Camera Corp. v. NLRB, 340 U.S. 474 (1951) (review of agency factfinding).

In such instances, any one factor will act as a tiebreaker when the other factors are closely balanced, the degree of closeness necessarily depending upon the tiebreaking factor's inherent or case-specific importance. The conflict of interest at issue here, for example, should prove more important (perhaps of great importance) where circumstances suggest a higher likelihood that it affected the benefits decision, including, but not limited to, cases where an insurance company administrator has a history of biased claims administration. See Langbein, 101 Nw. U. L. Rev. at 1317–1321 (detailing such a history for one large insurer). It should prove less important (perhaps to the vanishing point) where the administrator has taken active steps to reduce potential bias and to promote accuracy, for example, by walling off claims administrators from those interested in firm finances, or by imposing management checks that penalize inaccurate decision making irrespective of whom the inaccuracy benefits.

The Court of Appeals' opinion in the present case illustrates the combination-of-factors method of review. The record says little about MetLife's efforts to assure accurate claims assessment. The Court of Appeals gave the conflict weight to some degree; its opinion suggests that, in context, the court would not have found the conflict alone determinative. The court instead focused more heavily on other factors. In particular, the court found questionable the fact that MetLife had encouraged Glenn to argue to the Social Security Administration that she could do no work, received the bulk of the benefits of her success in doing so (the remainder going to the lawyers it recommended), and then ignored the agency's finding in concluding that Glenn could in fact do sedentary work. This course of events was not only an important factor in its own right (because it suggested procedural unreasonableness), but also would have justified the court in giving more weight to the conflict (because MetLife's seemingly inconsistent positions were both financially advantageous). And the court furthermore observed that MetLife had emphasized a certain medical report that favored a denial of benefits, had deemphasized certain other reports that suggested a contrary conclusion, and had failed to provide its independent vocational and medical experts with all of the relevant evidence. All these serious concerns, taken together with some degree of conflicting interests on MetLife's part, led the court to set aside MetLife's discretionary decision. We can find nothing improper in the way in which the court conducted its review.

Finally, we note that our elucidation of *Firestone's* standard does not consist of a detailed set of instructions. In this respect, we find pertinent this Court's comments made in a somewhat different context, the context of court review of agency factfinding. See Universal Camera Corp., 340 U.S. 474. In explaining how a reviewing court should take account of the agency's reversal of its own examiner's factual findings, this Court did not lay down a detailed set of instructions. It simply held that the reviewing judge should take account of that circumstance as a factor in determining the ultimate adequacy of the record's support for the agency's own factual conclusion. Id. at 492–497. In so holding, the Court noted that it had not enunciated a precise standard. See, e.g., id. at 493. But it warned against creating formulas that will "falsif[y] the actual process of judging" or serve as "instrument[s] of futile casuistry." Id. at 489. The Court added that there "are no talismanic words that can avoid the process of judgment." Id. It concluded then, as we do now, that the "want of certainty" in judicial standards "partly reflects the intractability of any formula to furnish definiteness of content for all the impalpable factors involved in judicial review." Id. at 477.

We affirm the decision of the Court of Appeals.

CHIEF JUSTICE ROBERTS, concurring in part and concurring in the judgment.

I join all but Part IV of the Court's opinion. I agree that a third-party insurer's dual role as a claims administrator and plan funder gives rise to a conflict of interest that is pertinent in reviewing claims decisions. I part ways with the majority, however, when it comes to *how* such a conflict should matter. The majority would accord weight, of varying and indeterminate amount, to the existence of such a conflict in every case where it is present. The majority's approach would allow the bare existence of a conflict to enhance the significance of other factors already considered by reviewing courts, even if the conflict is not shown to have played any role in the denial of benefits. The end result is to increase the level of scrutiny in every case in which there is a conflict—that is, in many if not most ERISA cases—thereby undermining the deference owed to plan administrators when the plan vests discretion in them.

I would instead consider the conflict of interest on review only where there is evidence that the benefits denial was motivated or affected by the administrator's conflict. No such evidence was presented in this case. I would nonetheless affirm the judgment of the Sixth Circuit, because that court was justified in finding an abuse of discretion on the facts of this case-conflict or not.

* * *

The conflict of interest at issue here is a common feature of ERISA plans. The majority acknowledges that the "lion's share of ERISA plan claims denials" are made by administrators that both evaluate and pay claims. For this reason, the majority is surely correct in concluding that it is important to retain deferential review for decisions made by conflicted administrators, in order to avoid "near universal review by judges de novo."

But the majority's approach does not do so. Saying that courts should consider the mere existence of a conflict in every case, without focusing that consideration in any way, invites the substitution of judicial discretion for the discretion of the plan administrator. Judicial review under the majority's opinion is less constrained, because courts can look to the bare presence of a conflict as authorizing more exacting scrutiny.

This problem is exacerbated because the majority is so imprecise about how the existence of a conflict should be treated in a reviewing court's analysis. The majority is forthright about this failing. In a triumph of understatement, the Court acknowledges that its approach "does not consist of a detailed set of instructions." The majority tries to transform this vice into a virtue, pointing to the practice of courts in reviewing agency determinations. The standard of review for agency determinations has little to nothing to do with the appropriate test for identifying ERISA benefits decisions influenced by a conflict of interest. In fact, we have rejected this analogy before, see Firestone, 489 U.S. at 109–110 (rejecting the arbitrary and capricious standard of review under the Labor Management Relations Act for claims brought under ERISA § 502(a)(1)(B)), and not even the Solicitor General, whose position the majority accepts, endorses it.

Pursuant to the majority's strained analogy, *Universal Camera Corp. v. NLRB*, 340 U.S. 474 (1951), makes an unexpected appearance on stage. The case is cited for the proposition that the lack of certainty in judicial standards " 'partly reflects the intractability of any formula to furnish definiteness of content for all the impalpable factors involved in judicial review.' " Maybe. But certainty and predictability are important criteria under ERISA, and employers considering whether to establish ERISA plans can have no notion what it means to say that a standard feature of such plans will be one of the "impalpable factors involved in judicial review" of benefits decisions. The Court leaves the law more uncertain, more unpredictable than it found it. Cf. O. Holmes, The Common Law 101 (M. Howe ed.1963) ("[T]he tendency of the law must always be to narrow the field of uncertainty").

JUSTICE KENNEDY, concurring in part and dissenting in part.

The Court sets forth an important framework for the standard of review in ERISA cases, one consistent with our holding in *Firestone Tire & Rubber Co. v. Bruch,* 489 U.S. 101 (1989). In my view this is correct, and I concur in those parts of the Court's opinion that discuss this framework. In my submission, however, the case should be remanded so that the Court of Appeals can apply the standards the Court now explains to these facts.

JUSTICE SCALIA, with whom JUSTICE THOMAS joins, dissenting.

I agree with the Court that petitioner Metropolitan Life Insurance Company (hereinafter petitioner) has a conflict of interest. A third-party insurance company that administers an ERISA-governed disability plan and that pays for benefits out of its own coffers profits with each benefits claim it rejects. I see no reason why the Court must volunteer, however, that *an employer* who administers its own ERISA-governed plan "clearly" has a conflict of interest. At least one Court of Appeals has thought that while the insurance company administrator has a conflict, the employer-administrator does not. See Colucci v. Agfa Corp. Severance Pay Plan, 431 F.3d 170, 179 (4th Cir. 2005). I would not resolve this question until it has been presented and argued, and the Court's unnecessary and uninvited resolution must be regarded as dictum.

The more important question is how the existence of a conflict should bear upon judicial review of the administrator's decision, and on that score I am in fundamental disagreement with the Court. Even if the choice were mine as a policy matter, I would not adopt the Court's totality-of-the-circumstances (so-called) "test," in which the existence of a conflict is to be put into the mix and given some (unspecified) "weight." This makes each case unique, and hence the outcome of each case unpredictable—not a reasonable position in which to place the administrator that has been explicitly given discretion by the creator of the plan, despite the existence of a conflict. More importantly, however, this is not a question to be solved by this Court's policy views; our cases make clear that it is to be governed by the law of trusts. Under that law, a fiduciary with a conflict does not abuse its discretion unless the conflict *actually* and *improperly motivates* the decision. There is no evidence of that here.

I

Our opinion in *Firestone Tire & Rubber Co. v. Bruch,* 489 U.S. 101 (1989), does not provide the answer to the all-important question in this case, but it does direct us to the answer. It held that federal courts hearing § 502(a)(1)(B) claims should review the decisions of ERISA-plan administrators the same way that courts have traditionally reviewed decisions of trustees. In trust law, the decision of a trustee who was not vested with discretion would be reviewed de novo. Citing the Restatement of Trusts current at the time of ERISA's enactment, *Firestone* acknowledged that courts traditionally would defer to trustees vested with discretion, but rejected that course in the case at hand because, among other reasons, the *Firestone* plan did not vest its administrator with discretion. Accordingly, *Firestone* had no occasion to consider the scope of, or limitations on, the deference accorded to fiduciaries with discretion. But in sheer dictum quoting a portion of one comment of the Restatement, our opinion said, "of course, if a benefit plan gives discretion to an administrator or fiduciary who is operating under a conflict of interest, that conflict must be weighed as a 'factor in determining whether there is an abuse of discretion.'" Id. at 115 (quoting Restatement (Second) of Trusts § 187, Comment d).

The Court takes that throwaway dictum literally and builds a castle upon it. But the dictum cannot bear that weight, and the Court's "elucidation" of the sentence does not reveal trust-law practice as much as it reveals the Justices' fondness for a judge-liberating totality-of-the-circumstances "test." The Restatement does indeed list in Comment d certain circumstances (including conflict of interest) that "may be relevant" to deciding whether a trustee has abused his discretion. It does *not,* however, suggest that they should all be chucked into a brown paper bag and shaken up to determine the answer. * * *

Instead of taking the pain to reconcile the entirety of the Restatement section with the *Firestone* dictum, the Court treats the dictum like a statutory command, and makes up a standard (if one can call it that) to make sense of the dictum. The opinion is painfully opaque, despite its promise of elucidation. It variously describes the object of judicial review as "determining whether the trustee, substantively or procedurally, has abused his discretion," determining "the lawfulness of benefit denials," and as tantamount to "review of agency factfinding." How a court should go about conducting this review is unclear. The opinion is rife with instruction on what a court should *not* do. In the final analysis, the Court seems to advance a gestalt reasonableness standard (a "combination-of-factors method of review," the opinion calls it) by which a reviewing court, mindful of being deferential, should nonetheless consider all the circumstances, weigh them as it thinks best, then divine whether a fiduciary's discretionary decision should be overturned. Notwithstanding the Court's assurances to the contrary, that is nothing but de novo review in sheep's clothing. * * *

NOTES AND QUESTIONS

1. Firestone *Language in Plan Documents.* What plan document language suffices to obtain deferential judicial review under *Firestone* and *Glenn*? In an attempt to create a uniform national standard, the Seventh Circuit has proposed that plan sponsors incorporate the following language in their plan documents: "Benefits under this plan will be paid only if the plan administrator decides in his discretion that the applicant is entitled to them." Herzberger v. Standard Ins. Co., 205 F.3d 327, 331 (7th Cir. 2000). Should this statement also be required as part of the contents of the plan's summary description? As a plan participant, what would be your reaction if you read this statement in your summary plan description?

As a practical matter, professionally prepared ERISA plans always incorporate *Firestone* language. But occasionally the employer may not realize that a policy or plan (such as the termination pay policy in *Firestone*) is governed by ERISA, or an insured plan may simply incorporate the insurance contract and fail to include *Firestone* language. For a survey of these issues, see Kathryn J. Kennedy, *Judicial Standard of Review in ERISA Benefit Claim Cases*, 50 AM. U. L. REV. 1083, 1119–29 (2001).

2. *Arbitrary and Capricious Versus Abuse of Discretion (or De Novo) Judicial Review.* In its amicus brief, the Department of Labor in *Glenn* argued that part of the confusion generated by *Firestone* was the proper interpretation of the "abuse of discretion" standard of judicial review:

> Some courts have equated abuse of discretion review and arbitrary and capricious review and held, under the latter, that the court need only be satisfied that "substantial evidence" supports the plan administrator's decision. In the administrative law context, the "substantial evidence" standard for reviewing agency factual findings is even more deferential than the "clearly erroneous" standard of appellate review, and it is satisfied if the evidence would justify, in a jury trial, a refusal to take a decision away from the jury. And the arbitrary and capricious standard more generally requires only a "rational" foundation for the agency decision. Those standards are specifically identified in the Administrative Procedure Act itself, 5 U.S.C. §§ 706(2)(A) and (E), and they reflect a special measure of deference rooted in the separation of powers and statutory allocations of governmental power.

> ERISA's statutory cause of action to recover benefits under a plan does not incorporate those standards. It rather looks to the distinct body of private trust law, which imposes special fiduciary duties of loyalty, prudence, and care and assigns reviewing responsibilities to courts under a more general standard of reasonableness that traditionally has required especially careful scrutiny in the case of a self-interested trustee. There are other key differences between ERISA and the administrative law context. "Decisions in the ERISA context involve the interpretation of

contractual entitlements; they are not discretionary in the sense, familiar from administrative law, of decisions that make policy under a broad grant of delegated powers," and "the individuals who occupy the position of ERISA fiduciaries are less well-insulated from outside pressures than are decision makers at government agencies." Brown v. Blue Cross & Blue Shield of Ala., Inc., 898 F.2d 1556, 1564 n. 7 (11th Cir. 1990).

Brief for the United States as Amicus Curiae Supporting Respondent, p. 29–30 n. 3 (other citations omitted).

Does the reference by the majority in *Glenn* to *Universal Camera Corp. v. NLRB*, 340 U.S. 474 (1951), a case decided under the Administrative Procedures Act, support the interpretation of *Firestone*'s abuse of discretion standard as synonymous with the highly deferential standard of judicial review for administrative agency decisions? Or, do the references to the Restatement (Second) of Trusts in *Glenn*'s majority opinion mean that the "reasonableness" standard under the common law of trusts should be used to evaluate whether an abuse of discretion has occurred in denying a claim for plan benefits? Or, does *Glenn*'s general instruction to "weigh" the conflict in light of the totality of the circumstances effectively permit de novo judicial review, if the district court is so inclined?

3.   Glenn *and the Lower Federal Courts.* Given *Firestone*'s cryptic instruction that the federal courts were to "weigh" a conflict of interest, it is not surprising that different circuit approaches had emerged prior to *Glenn*. *Glenn* swept these circuit-specific distinctions away. Post-*Glenn*, the lower federal courts view the existence of a conflict of interest as one factor to be weighed in determining whether the plan administrator has wrongfully denied the participant's claim. See, e.g., Holland v. International Paper Co. Retirement Plan, 576 F.3d 240, 246–49 (5th Cir. 2009); Jenkins v. Price Waterhouse Long-term Disability Plan, 564 F.3d 856, 861–62 (7th Cir. 2009); Champion v. Black & Decker, Inc., 550 F.3d 353, 359 (4th Cir. 2008); Wakkinen v. UNUM Life Ins. Co., 531 F.3d 575, 581 (8th Cir. 2008); Doyle v. Liberty Life Assurance Co., 542 F.3d 1352, 1357 (11th Cir. 2008). If the plan contains *Firestone* language, then the standard of judicial review remains abuse of discretion, even if the plan administrator operated under a conflict of interest in deciding to deny the claim.

Although the lower federal courts dutifully have implemented *Glenn*'s instructions, the decision has generated criticism. Consider the reaction of Judge Richard Posner of the Seventh Circuit to *Glenn*:

> [*Glenn*] sounds like a balancing test in which unweighted factors mysteriously are weighed. Such a test is not conducive to providing guidance to courts or plan administrators. Multifactor tests with no weight assigned to any factor are bad enough from the standpoint of providing an objective basis for a judicial decision; multifactor tests when none of the factors is concrete are worse.

Marrs v. Motorola, Inc., 577 F.3d 783, 789 (7th Cir. 2009) (quotations and citations omitted) (characterizing *Glenn* as a potentially "rudderless" balancing test).

4. *State Regulation of Insured Plans and* Firestone *Language.* In 2002, the National Association of Insurance Commissioners (NAIC) adopted the Prohibition on the Use of Discretionary Clauses Model Act (NAIC Model Act). The NAIC Model Act proposed statutory language prohibiting clauses in insurance contracts that give discretion to the insurance company to interpret the terms of the contract. The purpose of the NAIC Model Act was to require de novo judicial review of denied claims for insured plan benefits under *Firestone.*

In the wake of the NAIC Model Act, various states adopted similar language through legislation, or achieved the same result through regulatory interpretation of existing state insurance laws. For example, in 2004 the Unum/Provident insurance company asked the California Department of Insurance to opine whether the following standard *Firestone* clause in a disability insurance contract was valid under California insurance law.

> When making a benefit determination under the policy, the insurer has the discretionary authority to determine your eligibility for benefits and to interpret the terms and provisions of the policy.

Relying in part on the underlying purpose of the NAIC Model Act, the California Department of Insurance concluded that "all such discretionary clauses in disability insurance contracts violate California law and deprive insured of protections to which they are entitled," and "render the contract 'fraudulent or unsound insurance'" under California insurance law. See California Department of Insurance, Letter Opinion per CIC § 12921.9: Discretionary Clauses, dated February 26, 2004. In rendering its opinion, the California Department of Insurance reasoned that:

> Discretionary clauses have great legal significance because they act to nullify the bargained contract provisions and create an illusory contract. In the ERISA context, they place a severe burden on insureds and effectively shield insurers who deny meritorious claims. Under ERISA law, state insurance regulation is exempt from federal preemption; thereby permitting states to prohibit discretionary clauses if they violate state law.

Id. After several challenges were made through the courts to this regulatory position, the State of California enacted legislation in 2012 that banned provisions in insurance policies that reserve discretionary authority to the insurer to determine eligibility for benefits or coverage. See Cal. Ins. Code § 10110.6.

As of 2012, eighteen states had either adopted legislation restricting the use of or had imposed significant regulatory restrictions on such clauses in group insurance contracts offering health, disability, accidental death and life insurance benefits. Additional states are considering enacting legislative bans or implementing regulatory restrictions. See America's Health

Insurance Plans, Limitations on the Use of Discretionary Clauses: Summary of State Laws (Aug. 2012). The federal courts currently are divided over whether such bans or restrictions are enforceable as state laws regulating insurance, or are unenforceable due to preemption by ERISA. Compare *Standard Ins. Co. v. Morrison*, 584 F.3d 837 (9th Cir. 2009) (Montana ban enforceable) and *American Council of Life Insurers v. Ross*, 558 F.3d 600 (6th Cir. 2009) (Michigan ban enforceable) with *Hancock v. Metropolitan Life Ins. Co.*, 590 F.3d 1141 (10th Cir. 2009) (Utah restriction preempted).

5. Firestone *Deference and "Mistaken" Interpretations by the Plan Administrator.* Assume that the plan administrator must interpret a complex and ambiguous provision of the plan to calculate a participant's retirement benefit. The participant successfully challenges the administrator's interpretation as an abuse of discretion under Section 502(a)(1)(B). If the federal district court remands the case and orders the plan administrator to reinterpret the plan ("try again") and recalculate the retirement benefit, must the federal court apply the deferential *Firestone* standard of judicial review to the administrator's second attempt at plan interpretation? Or, may the district court apply de novo review and decide the appropriate calculation of the participant's retirement benefit?

The Supreme Court answered this question in *Conkright v. Frommert*, 559 U.S. 506 (2010). In *Frommert*, the Court held that *Glenn* requires the district court to continue to apply deferential *Firestone* review to the plan administrator's new proposed interpretation. The majority in *Frommert* reasoned that "the interests in efficiency, predictability, and uniformity—and the manner in which they are promoted by deference to reasonable plan construction by administrators—do not suddenly disappear simply because a plan administrator has made a single honest mistake." Id. at 517.

In a dissenting opinion, Justice Breyer argued that the district court had the equitable power to craft a remedy and therefore was not required to defer to the administrator's second proposed method of calculating the participant's retirement benefit. Justice Breyer harshly criticized the majority's ruling as undermining ERISA's primary policy of protecting the promised benefits of plan participants:

> [T]he majority's approach creates incentives for administrators to take "one free shot" at employer-favorable plan interpretations and to draft ambiguous retirement plans in the first instance with the expectation that they will have repeated opportunities to interpret (and possibly reinterpret) the ambiguous terms. I thus fail to see how the majority's "one free honest mistake" approach furthers ERISA's core purpose of promoting the interests of employees and their beneficiaries in employee benefit plans.
>
> The majority does identify ERISA-related factors—e.g., promoting predictability and uniformity, encouraging employers to adopt strong plans—that it believes favor giving more power to plan administrators. But, in my view, these factors are, at the least,

offset by the factors discussed above—e.g., discouraging administrators from writing opaque plans and interpreting them aggressively—that argue to the contrary. At best, the policies at issue—some arguing in one direction, some the other—are far less able than trust law to provide a "guiding principle." Thus, I conclude that here, as elsewhere, trust law ultimately provides the best way for courts to approach the administration and interpretation of ERISA. And trust law here, as I have said, leaves to the supervising court the decision as to how much weight to give to a plan administrator's remedial opinion.

Id. at 535–36. (Breyer, J., dissenting) (citations omitted). Do you believe, as Justice Breyer suggests, that some employers may *purposefully* draft ambiguous plan language and then interpret that language aggressively against a plan participant?

4. PRACTICAL CONSIDERATIONS IN CLAIMS LITIGATION

The starting point for evaluation of a potential claim for denied plan benefits under Section 502(a)(1)(B) is the governing language of the plan document and the summary plan description. The defendant already will possess these documents. As discussed in Chapter Two, the plaintiff easily can acquire them by making a request to the plan administrator under Section 104(b)(4).

Assuming that the plan document language is consistent with the claim for benefits, there are several strategic questions, unique to ERISA claims litigation, that the attorney who represents either the plaintiff or the defendant should consider in evaluating the plaintiff's case:

- What is the scope of judicial review?
- Will the court permit discovery to supplement the administrative record that was the basis for the plan administrator's denial of the claim?
- If a medical opinion is involved, what weight will the court give to the opinion of the claimant's treating physician?
- Is monetary relief available if the court determines that the claim for benefits was improperly denied?

The answers to these questions will determine the strategy for both the plaintiff and the defendant in claims litigation under Section 502(a)(1)(B).

The Scope of Judicial Review and Discovery

When *Firestone* language is absent from the plan document, the standard of judicial review is de novo. Under a de novo standard of judicial review, the scope of judicial review is the same as for any trial. See Krolnik v. Prudential Ins. Co., 570 F.3d 841, 843 (7th Cir. 2009). In reviewing the plan administrator's decision, the court will consider evidence obtained through discovery and presented at trial in addition to the administrative record that was developed during the claims appeal process. E.g., Jebian v. Hewlett-Packard Co. Employee Benefits Org. Income Protection Plan, 349 F.3d 1098, 1110 (9th Cir. 2003) (limitation on judicial review to the administrative record does not apply when the standard of judicial review is de novo); Elliott v. Sara Lee Corp., 190 F.3d 601, 608 & n. 6 (4th Cir. 1999) (when judicial review is de novo, a court may consider extra-judicial evidence).

Most plans, however, incorporate *Firestone* language that results in deferential judicial review of the plan administrator's decision under the abuse of discretion standard. Prior to the Supreme Court's decision in *Glenn*, when deferential judicial review applied under *Firestone* the courts generally limited the scope of judicial review to the evidence that was presented to the plan administrator during the claims appeal process. E.g., Abatie v. Alta Health & Life Ins. Co., 458 F.3d 955, 970 (9th Cir. 2006) (under an abuse of discretion standard, judicial review is limited to the record before the plan administrator); Urbania v. Central States, Southeast & Southwest Areas Pension Fund, 421 F.3d 580, 586 (7th Cir. 2005) (deferential review of an administrative decision means review on the administrative record); Kosiba v. Merck & Co., 384 F.3d 58, 67 n. 5 (3d Cir. 2004) (the record for arbitrary and capricious review of a denied claim for benefits generally is the record made before the plan administrator); Fought v. UNUM Life Ins. Co., 379 F.3d 997, 1003 (10th Cir. 2004) (in reviewing a plan administrator's decision under the arbitrary and capricious standard, the federal courts are limited to the administrative record compiled by the plan administrator in the course of making his decision); Zervos v. Verizon N.Y., Inc., 252 F.3d 163, 173 (2d Cir. 2001) (when judicial review is for abuse of discretion, the record consists of the administrative record).

Courts developed limited exceptions to the general rule that the scope of judicial review is limited to the evidence in the administrative record. For example, expert testimony is admissible to assist the district court in understanding medical terminology. See Quesinberry v. Life Insurance Co. of North America, 987 F.2d 1017, 1027 (4th Cir. 1993). Notably, one pre-*Glenn* exception involved situations of alleged bias or a conflict of interest on the part of the plan administrator. E.g., Wilkins v. Baptist Healthcare System, Inc., 150 F.3d 609, 619 (6th Cir. 1998) (Gilman, J., concurring) (evidence may be admitted to support a procedural challenge to the administrator's decision on the grounds of lack of due process or alleged bias); Abatie, 458 F.3d at 970 (evidence outside of the administrative record may be admitted to establish that the plan administrator had a conflict of interest that would affect the standard of judicial review); Kosiba, 384 F.3d at 67 n. 5 (same).

Post-*Glenn*, the federal courts have become more willing to permit the plaintiff to engage in discovery related to a conflict of interest by the plan administrator. As the district court in *Pemberton v. Reliance Standard Life Insurance Co.* explained:

> Even though the Supreme Court [Justices in *Glenn*] did not expressly alter the rules for discovery in an ERISA conflict of interest case, they effectively did so by recognizing the inherent conflict and requiring courts to consider it as a factor when deciding whether the plan administrator abused its discretion. Without discovery, plaintiffs would be severely hindered in their ability to obtain evidence to show the significance of the conflict of interest. Therefore, it is logical to assume that the Supreme Court meant for lower courts to allow some discovery beyond the administrative record when a conflict of interest is present.

46 Empl. Benefits Cas. (BNA) 1017, 2009 WL 89696 (E.D. Ky. 2009). In *Pemberton*, the dispute arose when the insurance company decided to terminate the participant's benefits under a long-term disability plan. The court permitted discovery of the compensation arrangements between the insurance company and its outside medical reviewers for the prior ten years, statistical data on the number of claims reviewed, and the number of resulting denials. Ultimately, the district court remanded the case back to the plan administrator for further consideration, with this admonishment:

> Taken as a whole, the factors support remanding this case for further consideration. Reliance failed to consider [the Social Security Administration's] determination [of permanent disability] at each stage of its decision-making process. This failure increases the significance of Reliance's conflict of interest inherent in its determining eligibility and also being the entity that pays benefits. The fact that the second [residual employability analysis] was based on insufficient information further undermines the integrity of Reliance's decision-making process. And although the medical evidence may ultimately support Reliance's decision, the explanation provided failed to sufficiently address ambiguities in the record. For these reasons, the court will remand this case to Reliance for further consideration.

Pemberton v. Reliance Standard Life Ins. Co., 2010 WL 60088 (E.D. Ky. 2010). Other courts have permitted limited discovery concerning the existence of conflict-ameliorating procedures utilized by the plan administrator, internal manuals instructing reviewers how to process claims, or whether the plan administrator actually read the professional credentials of the external medical reviewers whose opinions were relied upon by the plan administrator. E.g., Denmark v. Liberty Life Assurance

Co., 566 F.3d 1 (1st Cir. 2009) (conflict-ameliorating procedures); Jacoby v. Hartford Life & Accident Ins. Co., 254 F.R.D. 477 (S.D.N.Y. 2009) (internal manuals); Keller v. AT & T Disability Income Plan, 2009 WL 1438802 (W.D. Tex. 2009) (credentials of external reviewers).

In addition to the scope of judicial review, other practical obstacles exist for the plaintiff who seeks to overturn the plan administrator's decision through a claim filed under Section 502(a)(1)(B). These obstacles frequently present traps for the legally unsophisticated plan participant, and challenges for the participant's attorney.

First, limiting the scope of judicial review to the administrative record (even with narrow discovery related to a conflict of interest) places a high premium on fully developing and documenting the basis for the plaintiff's claim during the administrative appeal process. Unsophisticated participants are unlikely to seek legal counsel until after the administrative appeal procedure under the plan has been exhausted and the administrative record has closed. Thus, as a practical matter the attorney who files the plaintiff's claim may be constrained severely by the lack of supporting evidence in the administrative record before the court.

Second, gathering the documentation necessary to develop an adequate administrative record is especially difficult if the participant is seeking approval of an urgent care claim under a health care plan. Although the expedited period for administrative review allows the participant quickly to exhaust her administrative remedies and proceed to court for judicial review, the short time frame may result in an inadequate or incomplete administrative record. In this sense, the expedited claims process for urgent care claims presents a two-edged sword for the plan participant and her attorney.

Third, if the participant does seek the assistance of legal counsel at the administrative appeal stage, the cost may be borne by the participant. Several courts have denied the plaintiff's request for attorney's fees for legal work performed at the administrative appeal stage of the process, notwithstanding the fact that the participant ultimately prevailed in the litigation. See Peterson v. Continental Cas. Co., 282 F.3d 112 (2d Cir. 2002); Anderson v. Procter & Gamble Co., 220 F.3d 449 (6th Cir. 2000); Cann v. Carpenters' Pension Trust Fund, 989 F.2d 313 (9th Cir. 1993).

Expert Medical Opinion Evidence

The task of developing the administrative record becomes more daunting if the basis for the claim turns on expert medical opinion evidence, which is often the case for claims involving health care or disability benefits. In such situations, typically the claimant relies on the medical opinion of a treating physician. In *Black & Decker Disability Plan v. Nord*, 538 U.S. 822 (2003), the Supreme Court held that "plan administrators are not obliged to accord special deference to the opinions of treating physicians." Id. at 825. As a practical matter, this means that the participant may need to buttress the opinion of her treating physician with additional written evaluations prepared by other medical experts. Collecting these additional medical opinions can be both time-consuming and costly for the plan participant.

Remedies Available Under Section 502(a)(1)(B)

Even if the plaintiff 's claim under Section 502(a)(1)(B) is successful, the available remedy may be less than satisfactory. In general, the remedy available under Section 502(a)(1)(B) is limited to a court order directing the plan to provide the claimed benefit under the terms of the plan. If the benefit sought under the terms of the plan consists of the payment of money, either as a promised disability income benefit or as reimbursement for medical care already received, then relief under Section 502(a)(1)(B) is likely to be satisfactory. In addition, the court will award prejudgment interest on the amount of the benefit claim that was wrongfully denied as restitution designed to prevent unjust enrichment of the plan at the participant's expense. E.g., Rivera v. Benefit Trust Life Ins. Co., 921 F.2d 692 (7th Cir. 1991) (awarding prejudgment interest under Section 502(a)(1)(B)); Dunnigan v. Metropolitan Life Ins. Co., 277 F.3d 223 (2d Cir. 2002) (awarding prejudgment interest under Section 502(a)(3)).

Where the claimed benefit under the plan has not yet been provided to the participant (as is often the case in claims for health care plan benefits provided by a managed care entity, or claims for medical treatment that require preapproval by the plan), then the plan only must provide the benefit that is due in accordance with the terms of the plan. If the benefit due under a health care plan is for a particular type of medical treatment, but the plaintiff has died or is no longer a viable candidate for the medical treatment or the plaintiff has suffered irreparable injury as a result of the initial decision to deny the claim, then the plaintiff (or the plaintiff's estate) cannot recover compensatory damages under Section 502(a)(1)(B). Under some circumstances, the plaintiff (or the plaintiff's estate) may receive additional monetary "equitable relief" under Section 502(a)(3). The nature of "equitable relief" available under Section 502(a)(3) is explored later in Section E of Chapter Six.

QUESTION

Recall from Chapter Four that one of the reforms enacted by the Affordable Care Act was to give plan participants the option of submitting denied claims for benefits under a group health care plan to an independent external review process, rather than litigating their claims under Section 502(a)(1)(B). This federal independent external review requirement applies only to grandfathered group health care plans. For participants in an insured group health plan, an independent external review process for denied claims may be authorized under state law. In light of the obstacles to a successful appeal of a denied claim presented by Section 502(a)(1)(B), would you ever advise a plan participant to litigate a denied claim for group health care plan benefits if the alternative of independent external review is available? What are the strategic advantages and disadvantages of each process?

D. SECTION 502(a)(2) CLAIMS: BREACH OF FIDUCIARY DUTY

ERISA Section 409(a) states that a plan fiduciary is personally liable for, and must make good to the plan, any losses to the plan that result from the fiduciary's breach of "any of the responsibilities, obligations, or duties imposed upon fiduciaries by this title." Section 409(a) also requires that the fiduciary must restore to the plan any profits obtained by the fiduciary through the fiduciary's use of plan assets. In addition to these remedies, the federal courts have discretionary authority under Section 409(a) to order other appropriate equitable or remedial relief and to remove the breaching fiduciary. Relief under Section 409(a) for a breach of fiduciary responsibility is obtained through a claim brought under ERISA Section 502(a)(2). Section 502(a)(2) authorizes three types of plaintiffs—the Secretary of Labor, a plan participant or beneficiary, or another plan fiduciary—to bring a breach of fiduciary duty claim under Section 502(a)(2) for relief under Section 409(a).

The brevity of Sections 409(a) and 502(a)(2) belie their significance and potential breadth. Although the fiduciary's responsibilities, obligations, and duties are found throughout Title I of ERISA, cases brought under Section 502(a)(2) usually are based on violations of the fiduciary responsibility provisions found in Part 4 of Title I of ERISA. These fiduciary responsibilities include the fiduciary duties contained in Section 404, the co-fiduciary duties contained in Section 405, and the prohibited transaction rules contained in Sections 406 and 407.

The personal liability of plan fiduciaries under Section 409(a) is significant for several reasons. First, the plan fiduciary cannot avoid personal liability by incorporating an exculpatory clause in the plan purporting to relieve the fiduciary from liability. ERISA § 410. Second, in the co-fiduciary context the impact of potential personal liability is heightened because breaching co-fiduciaries are jointly and severally liable. Under the common law of trusts, in joint and several liability situations one co-fiduciary could assert a claim for contribution or indemnification against another, more culpable, co-fiduciary. See Restatement (Second) of Trusts § 258. ERISA does not expressly authorize claims for contribution or indemnification, and the federal courts of appeals are divided over whether a claim is possible under

ERISA for contribution or indemnification by a less culpable fiduciary against a more culpable co-fiduciary. See, e.g., Travelers Cas. & Sur. Co. v. IADA Servs, Inc., 497 F.3d 862 (8th Cir. 2007) (no right of contribution under ERISA); Summers v. State Street Bank & Trust Co. 453 F.3d 404 (7th Cir. 2006) (noting circuit split); Smith v. Local 819 I.B.T. Pension Plan, 291 F.3d 236 (2d Cir. 2002) (permitting equitable claim for contribution/indemnification under ERISA); Kim v. Fujikawa, 871 F2d 1427 (9th Cir. 1989) (not permitting equitable claim for contribution/indemnification under ERISA). A third reason fiduciaries under ERISA are concerned with liability under Section 409(a) is that actual knowledge of a violation by the fiduciary may not be required to impose liability. Rather, the fiduciary may be liable if the court determines the fiduciary failed to act prudently, see ERISA § 404(a)(1)(B), "should have known" of the violation, see ERISA § 406(a)(1), or failed prudently to select and monitor other co-fiduciaries, see ERISA § 405(a)(2).

1. FIDUCIARY LIABILITY

Even though a fiduciary's potential liability under ERISA Section 409(a) is significant, it could have been far more so, but for the Supreme Court's decision in *Massachusetts Mutual Life Insurance Co. v. Russell*. In *Russell*, the Court was asked to interpret the scope of relief available under Section 409(a). The justices in *Russell* were unanimous in their judgment that the plaintiff as an individual could not recover compensatory damages in a claim brought under ERISA Section 502(a)(2) for relief under Section 409(a). The majority and concurring opinions in *Russell*, however, revealed the deep divisions among the justices in their philosophical approach to the civil enforcement provisions of Section 502(a). These divisions became explicit in the Supreme Court's later decisions interpreting the scope of "equitable relief" available for claims filed under Section 502(a)(3) of ERISA. Section 502(a)(3) claims are the subject of Section E of Chapter Six.

As you read the majority and concurring opinions in *Russell*, examine the statutory language of Sections 409(a), 502(a)(2) and 502(a)(3). Do you find the statutory interpretation analysis contained in the majority opinion persuasive? Or, is the interpretation proposed by Justice Brennan in the concurring opinion preferable?

MASSACHUSETTS MUTUAL LIFE INSURANCE CO.
v. RUSSELL

United States Supreme Court, 1985.
473 U.S. 134, 105 S.Ct. 3085, 87 L.Ed.2d 96.

JUSTICE STEVENS delivered the opinion of the Court.

The question presented for decision is whether, under the Employee Retirement Income Security Act of 1974 (ERISA), a fiduciary to an employee benefit plan may be held personally liable to a plan participant or beneficiary for extra-contractual compensatory or punitive damages caused by improper or untimely processing of benefit claims.

Respondent Doris Russell, a claims examiner for petitioner Massachusetts Mutual Life Insurance Company (hereafter petitioner), is a beneficiary under two employee benefit plans administered by petitioner for eligible employees. Both plans are funded from the general assets of petitioner and both are governed by ERISA.

In May 1979 respondent became disabled with a back ailment. She received plan benefits until October 17, 1979, when, based on the report of an orthopedic surgeon, petitioner's disability committee terminated her benefits. On October 22, 1979, she requested internal review of that decision and, on November 27, 1979, submitted a report from her own psychiatrist indicating that she suffered from a psychosomatic disability with physical manifestations rather than an orthopedic illness. After an examination by a second psychiatrist on February 15, 1980, had confirmed that respondent was temporarily disabled, the plan administrator reinstated her benefits on March 11, 1980. Two days later retroactive benefits were paid in full.

Although respondent has been paid all benefits to which she is contractually entitled, she claims to have been injured by the improper refusal to pay benefits from October 17, 1979, when her benefits were terminated, to March 11, 1980, when her eligibility was restored. Among other allegations, she asserts that the fiduciaries administering petitioner's employee benefit plans are high-ranking company officials who (1) ignored readily available medical evidence documenting respondent's disability, (2) applied unwarrantedly strict eligibility standards, and (3) deliberately took 132 days to process her claim, in violation of regulations promulgated by the Secretary of Labor. The interruption of benefit payments allegedly forced respondent's disabled husband to cash out his retirement savings which, in turn, aggravated the psychological condition that caused respondent's back ailment. Accordingly, she sued petitioner in the California Superior Court pleading various causes of action based on state law and on ERISA.

Petitioner removed the case to the United States District Court for the Central District of California and moved for summary judgment. The

District Court granted the motion, holding that the state law claims were preempted by ERISA and that "ERISA bars any claims for extra-contractual damages and punitive damages arising out of the original denial of plaintiff's claims for benefits under the Salary Continuance Plan and the subsequent review thereof."

On appeal, the United States Court of Appeals for the Ninth Circuit affirmed in part and reversed in part. 722 F.2d 482 (9th Cir. 1983). Although it agreed with the District Court that respondent's state law causes of action were preempted by ERISA, it held that her complaint alleged a cause of action under ERISA. Id. at 487–92. The court reasoned that the 132 days petitioner took to process respondent's claim violated the fiduciary's obligation to process claims in good faith and in a fair and diligent manner. Id. at 488. The court concluded that this violation gave rise to a cause of action under § 409(a) that could be asserted by a plan beneficiary pursuant to § 502(a)(2). Id. at 489–90. It read the authorization in § 409(a) of "such other equitable or remedial relief as the court may deem appropriate" as giving it "wide discretion as to the damages to be awarded," including compensatory and punitive damages. Id. at 490–91.

According to the Court of Appeals, the award of compensatory damages shall "remedy the wrong and make the aggrieved individual whole," which meant not merely contractual damages for loss of plan benefits, but relief "that will compensate the injured party for all losses and injuries sustained as a direct and proximate cause of the breach of fiduciary duty," including "damages for mental or emotional distress." Id. at 490. Moreover, the liability under § 409(a) "is against the fiduciary personally, not the plan." Id. at 490 n.8.

The Court of Appeals also held that punitive damages could be recovered under § 409(a), although it decided that such an award is permitted only if the fiduciary "acted with actual malice or wanton indifference to the rights of a participant or beneficiary." Id. at 492. The court believed that this result was supported by the text of § 409(a) and by the congressional purpose to provide broad remedies to redress and prevent violations of the Act.

We granted certiorari to review both the compensatory and punitive components of the Court of Appeals' holding that § 409 authorizes recovery of extracontractual damages. Respondent defends the judgment of the Court of Appeals both on its reasoning that § 409 provides an express basis for extracontractual damages, as well as by arguing that in any event such a private remedy should be inferred under the analysis employed in *Cort v. Ash*, 422 U.S. 66, 78 (1975). We reject both arguments.

I

As its caption implies, § 409(a) establishes "LIABILITY FOR BREACH OF FIDUCIARY DUTY."[1] Specifically, it provides:

> (a) Any person who is a fiduciary with respect to a plan who breaches any of the responsibilities, obligations, or duties imposed upon fiduciaries by this title shall be personally liable to make good to such plan any losses to the plan resulting from each such breach, and to restore to such plan any profits of such fiduciary which have been made through use of assets of the plan by the fiduciary, and shall be subject to such other equitable or remedial relief as the court may deem appropriate, including removal of such fiduciary. A fiduciary may also be removed for a violation of section 411 of this Act.

Sections 501 and 502 authorize, respectively, criminal and civil enforcement of the Act. While the former section provides for criminal penalties against any person who willfully violates any of the reporting and disclosure requirements of the Act, the latter section identifies six types of civil actions that may be brought by various parties. Most relevant to our inquiry is § 502(a), which provides in part:

> A civil action may be brought—
>
> (1) by a participant or beneficiary—
>
>   (A) for the relief provided for in subsection (c) of this section, or
>
>   (B) to recover benefits due to him under the terms of his plan, to enforce his rights under the terms of the plan, or to clarify his rights to future benefits under the terms of the plan;
>
> (2) by the Secretary, or by a participant, beneficiary or fiduciary for appropriate relief under section 409. . . .

There can be no disagreement with the Court of Appeals' conclusion that § 502(a)(2) authorizes a beneficiary to bring an action against a fiduciary who has violated § 409. Petitioner contends, however, that recovery for a violation of § 409 inures to the benefit of the plan as a whole. We find this contention supported by the text of § 409, by the statutory provisions defining the duties of a fiduciary, and by the provisions defining the rights of a beneficiary.

The Court of Appeals' opinion focused on the reference in § 409 to "such other equitable or remedial relief as the court may deem appropriate." But when the entire section is examined, the emphasis on

---

[1] Because respondent relies entirely on § 409(a), and expressly disclaims reliance on § 502(a)(3), we have no occasion to consider whether any other provision of ERISA authorizes recovery of extracontractual damages.

the relationship between the fiduciary and the plan as an entity becomes apparent. Thus, not only is the relevant fiduciary relationship characterized at the outset as one "with respect to a plan," but the potential personal liability of the fiduciary is "to make good *to such plan* any losses *to the plan* . . . and to restore *to such plan* any profits of such fiduciary which have been made through use of assets *of the plan*. . . ."

To read directly from the opening clause of § 409(a), which identifies the proscribed acts, to the "catchall" remedy phrase at the end—skipping over the intervening language establishing remedies benefitting, in the first instance, solely the plan—would divorce the phrase being construed from its context and construct an entirely new class of relief available to entities other than the plan. This "blue pencil" method of statutory interpretation-omitting all words not part of the clauses deemed pertinent to the task at hand—impermissibly ignores the relevant context in which statutory language subsists. In this case, this mode of interpretation would render superfluous the preceding clauses providing relief singularly to the plan, and would slight the language following after the phrase "such other equitable or remedial relief." Congress specified that this remedial phrase includes "removal of such fiduciary"—an example of the kind of "plan-related" relief provided by the more specific clauses it succeeds. A fair contextual reading of the statute makes it abundantly clear that its draftsmen were primarily concerned with the possible misuse of plan assets, and with remedies that would protect the entire plan, rather than with the rights of an individual beneficiary.

It is of course true that the fiduciary obligations of plan administrators are to serve the interest of participants and beneficiaries and, specifically, to provide them with the benefits authorized by the plan. But the principal statutory duties imposed on the trustees relate to the proper management, administration, and investment of fund assets, the maintenance of proper records, the disclosure of specified information, and the avoidance of conflicts of interest. Those duties are described in Part 4 of Title 1 of the Act, which is entitled "FIDUCIARY RESPONSIBILITY," see §§ 401–414, whereas the statutory provisions relating to claim procedures are found in Part 5, dealing with "ADMINISTRATION AND ENFORCEMENT." ERISA §§ 502(a); 503. The only section that concerns review of a claim that has been denied—§ 503—merely specifies that every plan shall comply with certain regulations promulgated by the Secretary of Labor.

* * *

Significantly, the statutory provision explicitly authorizing a beneficiary to bring an action to enforce his rights under the plan—§ 502(a)(1)(B)—says nothing about the recovery of extracontractual damages, or about the possible consequences of delay in the plan administrators' processing of a disputed claim. Thus, there really is nothing at all in the statutory text to support the conclusion that such a delay gives rise to a private right of action for compensatory or punitive relief. And the entire text of § 409 persuades us that Congress did not intend that section to authorize any relief except for the plan itself. In short, unlike the Court of Appeals, we do not find in § 409 express authority for an award of extracontractual damages to a beneficiary.[12]

II

Relying on the four-factor analysis employed by the Court in *Cort v. Ash*, 422 U.S. at 78, respondent argues that a private right of action for extracontractual damages should be implied even if it is not expressly authorized by ERISA. Two of the four *Cort* factors unquestionably support respondent's claim: respondent is a member of the class for whose benefit the statute was enacted and, in view of the preemptive effect of ERISA, there is no state law impediment to implying a remedy. But the two other factors—legislative intent and consistency with the legislative scheme—point in the opposite direction. And "unless this congressional intent can be inferred from the language of the statute, the statutory structure, or some other source, the essential predicate for implication of a private remedy simply does not exist." Northwest Airlines, Inc. v. Transport Workers, 451 U.S. 77, 94 (1981). "The federal judiciary will not engraft a remedy on a statute, no matter how salutary, that Congress did not intend to provide." California v. Sierra Club, 451 U.S. 287, 297 (1981).

The voluminous legislative history of the Act contradicts respondent's position. It is true that an early version of the statute contained a provision for "legal or equitable" relief that was described in both the Senate and House Committee Reports as authorizing "the full range of legal and equitable remedies available in both state and federal courts." H.R. Rep. No. 93–533, p. 17 (1973); S. Rep. No. 93–127, p. 35 (1973). But that language appeared in Committee Reports describing a version of the bill before the debate on the floor and before the Senate-House Conference Committee had finalized the operative language. In the bill passed by the House of Representatives and ultimately adopted by the Conference Committee the reference to legal relief was deleted. The language relied on by respondent and by the Court of Appeals below, therefore, is of little help in understanding whether Congress intended to make fiduciaries personally liable to beneficiaries for extracontractual damages.

The six carefully integrated civil enforcement provisions found in § 502(a) of the statute as finally enacted, however, provide strong evidence that Congress did not intend to authorize other remedies that it simply forgot to incorporate expressly. The assumption of inadvert

---

[12] In light of this holding, we do not reach any question concerning the extent to which § 409 may authorize recovery of extracontractual compensatory or punitive damages from a fiduciary by a *plan*.

omission is rendered especially suspect upon close consideration of ERISA's interlocking, interrelated, and interdependent remedial scheme, which is in turn part of a "comprehensive and reticulated statute." Nachman Corp. v. Pension Benefit Guaranty Corp., 446 U.S. 359, 361 (1980). If in this case, for example, the plan administrator had adhered to his initial determination that respondent was not entitled to disability benefits under the plan, respondent would have had a panoply of remedial devices at her disposal. To recover the benefits due her, she could have filed an action pursuant to § 502(a)(1)(B) to recover accrued benefits, to obtain a declaratory judgment that she is entitled to benefits under the provisions of the plan contract, and to enjoin the plan administrator from improperly refusing to pay benefits in the future. If the plan administrator's refusal to pay contractually authorized benefits had been willful and part of a larger systematic breach of fiduciary obligations, respondent in this hypothetical could have asked for removal of the fiduciary pursuant to §§ 502(a)(2) and 409. Finally, in answer to a possible concern that attorney's fees might present a barrier to maintenance of suits for small claims, thereby risking underenforcement of beneficiaries' statutory rights, it should be noted that ERISA authorizes the award of attorney's fees. See ERISA § 502(g).

We are reluctant to tamper with an enforcement scheme crafted with such evident care as the one in ERISA. As we stated in *Transamerica Mortgage Advisors, Inc. v. Lewis*, 444 U.S. 11, 19 (1979): "[W]here a statute expressly provides a particular remedy or remedies, a court must be chary of reading others into it." See also Touche Ross & Co. v. Redington, 442 U.S. 560, 571–74 (1979). "The presumption that a remedy was deliberately omitted from a statute is strongest when Congress has enacted a comprehensive legislative scheme including an integrated system of procedures for enforcement." Northwest Airlines, Inc. v. Transport Workers, 451 U.S. at 97.

In contrast to the repeatedly emphasized purpose to protect contractually defined benefits, there is a stark absence—in the statute itself and in its legislative history—of any reference to an intention to authorize the recovery of extracontractual damages.[17] Because "neither the statute nor the legislative history reveals a congressional intent to create a private right of action . . . we need not carry the *Cort v. Ash* inquiry further." Northwest Airlines, Inc. v. Transport Workers, 451 U.S. at 94.

III

Thus, the relevant text of ERISA, the structure of the entire statute, and its legislative history all support the conclusion that in § 409(a)

---

[17] Indeed, Congress was concerned lest the cost of federal standards discourage the growth of private pension plans. See, e.g., H.R. Rep. No. 93–533, 1, 9 (1973); 120 Cong. Rec. 29949 (1974); 20 Cong. Rec. 29210–29211 (1974).

Congress did not provide, and did not intend the judiciary to imply, a cause of action for extra-contractual damages caused by improper or untimely processing of benefit claims.

The judgment of the Court of Appeals is therefore

Reversed.

———————

JUSTICE BRENNAN, with whom JUSTICE WHITE, JUSTICE MARSHALL, and JUSTICE BLACKMUN join, concurring in the judgment.

Section 502(a) of the Employee Retirement Income Security Act of 1974 (ERISA) provides a wide array of measures to employee benefit plan participants and beneficiaries by which they may enforce their rights under ERISA and under the terms of their plans. A participant or beneficiary may file a civil action, for example, (1) "to recover benefits due to him under the terms of his plan, to enforce his rights under the terms of the plan, or to clarify his rights to future benefits under the terms of the plan," § 502(a)(1)(B); (2) "for appropriate relief under section 409," § 502(a)(2); and (3) "to enjoin any act or practice which violates any provision of this title or the terms of the plan, or . . . to obtain *other appropriate equitable relief . . . to redress such violations.*" § 502(a)(3) (emphasis added).

This case presents a single, narrow question: whether the § 409 "appropriate relief" referred to in § 502(a)(2) includes individual recovery by a participant or beneficiary of extra-contractual damages for breach of fiduciary duty. The Court of Appeals for the Ninth Circuit held that, because § 409 broadly authorizes "such other equitable or remedial relief as the court may deem appropriate," participants and beneficiaries may recover such damages under that section. I agree with the Court's decision today that § 409 is more fairly read in context as providing "remedies that would protect the entire plan" rather than individuals and that participants and beneficiaries accordingly must look elsewhere in ERISA for personal relief. Indeed, since § 502(a)(3) already provides participants and beneficiaries with "other appropriate equitable relief . . . to redress [ERISA] violations," there is no reason to construe § 409 expansively in order to bring these individuals under the penumbra of "equitable or remedial relief."

This does not resolve, of course, whether and to what extent extracontractual damages are available under § 502(a)(3). This question was not addressed by the courts below and was not briefed by the parties and amici. Thus the Court properly emphasizes that "we have no occasion to consider whether any other provision of ERISA authorizes recovery of extracontractual damages." Accordingly, we save for another day the questions (1) to what extent a fiduciary's mishandling of a claim might

constitute an actionable breach of the fiduciary duties set forth in
§ 404(a), and (2) the nature and extent of the "appropriate equitable relief
. . . to redress" such violations under § 502(a)(3).

There is dicta in the Court's opinion, however, that could be
construed as sweeping more broadly than the narrow ground of resolution
set forth above. Although the Court takes care to limit the binding effect
of its decision to the terms of § 409, its opinion at some points seems to
speak generally of whether fiduciaries ever may be held personally liable
to beneficiaries for extracontractual damages. Moreover, some of the
Court's remarks are simply incompatible with the structure, legislative
history, and purposes of ERISA. The Court's ambiguous discussion is
certainly subject to different readings, and in any event is without
controlling significance beyond the question of relief under § 409. I write
separately to outline what I believe is the proper approach for courts to
take in construing ERISA's provisions and to emphasize the issues left
open under today's decision.

Fiduciary Duties in Claims Administration

There is language in the Court's opinion that might be read as
suggesting that the fiduciary duties imposed by ERISA on plan
administrators for the most part run only to the plan itself, as opposed to
individual beneficiaries. The Court apparently thinks there might be
some significance in the fact that an administrator's fiduciary duties "are
described in Part 4 of Title 1 of the Act . . . whereas the statutory
provisions relating to claim procedures are found in Part 5." Accordingly,
the Court seems to believe that the duties and remedies associated with
claims processing might be restricted to those explicitly spelled out in
§§ 502(a)(1)(B) and 503.

To the extent the Court suggests that administrators might not be
fully subject to strict fiduciary duties to participants and beneficiaries in
the processing of their claims and to traditional trust law remedies for
breaches of those duties, I could not more strongly disagree. As the Court
acknowledges, * * * § 404(a) sets forth the governing standard that "a
fiduciary shall discharge his duties with respect to a plan solely in the
interest of the participants and beneficiaries and—(A) for the exclusive
purpose of: (i) providing benefits to participants and their beneficiaries."
That section also provides that, in carrying out these duties, a fiduciary
shall exercise "the care, skill, prudence, and diligence" of a "prudent man
acting in like capacity." The legislative history demonstrates that
Congress intended by § 404(a) to incorporate the fiduciary standards of
trust law into ERISA,[6] and it is black letter trust law that fiduciaries owe

---

[6]   See, e.g., H.R. Rep. No. 93–533, p. 11 (1973) ("The fiduciary responsibility section, in
essence, codifies and makes applicable to . . . fiduciaries certain principles developed in the
evolution of the law of trusts"); id. at 13.

   The principles of fiduciary conduct are adopted from existing trust law, but with
   modifications appropriate for employee benefit plans. These salient principles place a

strict duties running directly to beneficiaries in the administration and payment of trust benefits. The legislative history also shows that Congress intended these fiduciary standards to govern the ERISA claims-administration process.[8]

Moreover, the Court's suggestion concerning the distinction between Parts 4 and 5 of Title I is thoroughly unconvincing. Section 502(a)(3) authorizes the award of "appropriate equitable relief" directly to a participant or beneficiary to "redress" "*any* act or practice which violates any provision of this title or the terms of the plan." This section and § 404(a)'s fiduciary duty standards both appear in Title I, which is entitled "PROTECTION OF EMPLOYEE BENEFIT RIGHTS." A beneficiary therefore may obtain "appropriate equitable relief" whenever an administrator breaches the fiduciary duties set forth in § 404(a).[10] Accordingly, an administrator's claims-processing duties and a beneficiary's corresponding remedies are not at all necessarily limited to the terms of §§ 502(a)(1)(B) and 503. In light of the Court's narrow holding further consideration of these important issues remains open for another day when the disposition of a controversy might really turn on them.

Judicial Construction of ERISA

Russell argues that a private right of action for beneficiaries and participants should be read into § 409. Because the Court has concluded

---

twofold duty on every fiduciary: to act in his relationship to the plan's fund as a prudent man in a similar situation and under like conditions would act, and to act consistently with the principles of administering the trust for the exclusive purposes previously enumerated, and in accordance with the documents and instruments governing the fund unless they are inconsistent with the fiduciary principles of the section.

See also S. Rep. No. 93–127, pp. 28–29 (1973); H.R. Conf. Rep. No. 93–1280, p. 303 (1974) ("[T]he assets of the employee benefit plan are to be held for the exclusive benefit of participants and beneficiaries"); 120 Cong. Rec. 29932 (1974) (remarks of Sen. Williams); Central States Pension Fund v. Central Transport, Inc., 472 U.S. 559, 570 (1985) ("Congress invoked the common law of trusts to define the general scope of [fiduciary] authority and responsibility"); NLRB v. Amax Coal Co., 453 U.S. 322, 329 (1981) ("Where Congress uses terms that have accumulated settled meaning under either equity or the common law, a court must infer, unless the statute otherwise dictates, that Congress means to incorporate the established meaning of these terms.").

[8] See, e.g., 120 Cong. Rec. 29929 (1974) (remarks of Sen. Williams) (emphasis added) (ERISA imposes "strict fiduciary obligations upon those who exercise management or control over the assets or *administration* of an employee pension or welfare plan"); H.R. Conf. Rep. No. 93–1280, at 301, and n.1 (procedures for delegating fiduciary duties, including "allocation or delegation of duties with respect to payment of benefits").

[10] Trust law remedies are equitable in nature, and include provision of monetary damages. See, e.g., G. Bogert & G. Bogert, Law of Trusts and Trustees § 862 (2d ed. 1982) (hereinafter Bogert & Bogert, Trusts and Trustees); Restatement (Second) of Trusts §§ 199; 205 (1959). Thus while a given form of monetary relief may be unavailable under ERISA for other reasons it cannot be withheld simply because a beneficiary's remedies under ERISA are denominated "equitable." See also Restatement (Second) of Torts § 874, Comment b (1979) ("Violation of Fiduciary Duty") (although "[t]he remedy of a beneficiary against a defaulting or negligent trustee is ordinarily in equity," the beneficiary is entitled to all redress "for harm caused by the breach of a duty arising from the relation").

that Congress' intent and ERISA's overall structure restrict the scope of § 409 to recovery on behalf of a plan, such a private right is squarely barred under the standards set forth in *Cort v. Ash*, 422 U.S. 66 (1975).

In disposing of this relatively straightforward issue, the Court makes some observations about the role of courts generally in construing and enforcing ERISA. The Court suggests, for example, that Congress "crafted" ERISA with "carefully integrated" remedies so as to create an "interlocking, interrelated, and interdependent remedial scheme" that courts should not "tamper with."

The Court's discussion, I say respectfully, is both unnecessary and to some extent completely erroneous. The Court may or may not be correct as a general matter with respect to implying private rights of action under ERISA; as the respondent has sought such an implied right only under § 409, we of course cannot purport to resolve this question in the many other contexts in which it might arise under the statute. Moreover, the Court's remarks about the constrictive judicial role in enforcing ERISA's remedial scheme are inaccurate insofar as Congress provided in § 502(a)(3) that beneficiaries could recover, in addition to the remedies explicitly set forth in that section, "other appropriate equitable relief . . . to redress" ERISA violations. Congress already had instructed that beneficiaries could recover benefits, obtain broad injunctive and declaratory relief for their own personal benefit or for the benefit of their plans, and secure attorney's fees, so this additional provision can only be read precisely as authorizing federal courts to "fine-tune" ERISA's remedial scheme. Thus while it may well be that courts generally may not find implied private remedies in ERISA, the Court's remarks have little bearing on how courts are to go about construing the private remedy that Congress explicitly provided in § 502(a)(3).

The legislative history demonstrates that Congress intended federal courts to develop federal common law in fashioning the additional "appropriate equitable relief." In presenting the Conference Report to the full Senate, for example, Senator Javits, ranking minority member of the Senate Committee on Labor and Public Welfare and one of the two principal Senate sponsors of ERISA, stated that "[i]t is also intended that a body of Federal substantive law will be developed by the courts to deal with issues involving rights and obligations under private welfare and pension plans." 120 Cong. Rec. 29942 (1974). Senator Williams, the Committee's Chairman and the Act's other principal Senate sponsor, similarly emphasized that suits involving beneficiaries' rights "will be regarded as arising under the laws of the United States, in similar fashion to those brought under section 301 of the Labor Management Relations Act." Id. at 29943. Section 301, of course, "authorizes federal courts to fashion a body of federal law" in the context of collective-bargaining agreements, to be derived by "looking at the policy of the legislation and fashioning a remedy that will effectuate that policy." Textile Workers v. Lincoln Mills, 353 U.S. 448, 451 (1957). ERISA's legislative history also demonstrates beyond question that Congress intended to engraft trust law principles onto the enforcement scheme, and a fundamental concept of trust law is that courts "will give to the beneficiaries of a trust such remedies as are necessary for the protection of their interests."[16] Thus ERISA was not so "carefully integrated" and "crafted" as to preclude further judicial delineation of appropriate rights and remedies; far from barring such a process, the statute explicitly directs that courts shall undertake it.

The Court today expressly reserves the question whether extra-contractual damages might be one form of "other appropriate relief" under § 502(a)(3). I believe that, in resolving this and other questions concerning appropriate relief under ERISA, courts should begin by ascertaining the extent to which trust and pension law as developed by state and federal courts provide for recovery by the beneficiary above and beyond the benefits that have been withheld; this is the logical first step, given that Congress intended to incorporate trust law into ERISA's equitable remedies. If a requested form of additional relief is available under state trust law, courts should next consider whether allowance of such relief would significantly conflict with some other aspect of the ERISA scheme. In addition, courts must always bear in mind the ultimate consideration whether allowance or disallowance of particular relief would best effectuate the underlying purposes of ERISA-enforcement of strict fiduciary standards of care in the administration of all aspects of pension plans and promotion of the best interests of participants and beneficiaries.

I concur in the judgment of the Court.

NOTES AND QUESTIONS

1. *The Significance of* Russell. The majority opinion in *Russell* profoundly influenced the development of federal law concerning the remedies available under ERISA. In the aftermath of *Russell*, the federal courts consistently ruled that compensatory (extra-contractual) damages are not available under *either* Section 502(a)(2) *or* Section 502(a)(3) of ERISA. In other words, the dicta in *Russell* evolved into the "rule" that compensatory damages not available to an individual plaintiff under ERISA. Over 25 years later, the Supreme Court in *Cigna Corp. v. Amara*, 131 S.Ct. 1866 (2011), directly addressed the issue of whether monetary compensation is available under Section 502(a)(3) as "equitable" relief. The Court's opinion in *Amara* is reproduced in Section E of Chapter Six.

---

[16] 3 A. Scott, Law of Trusts § 199, p. 1638 (1967). See also Restatement (Second) of Trusts § 205, and Comment a (1959) (beneficiary entitled to a remedy "which will put him in the position in which he would have been if the trustee had not committed the breach of trust"); Bogert & Bogert, Trusts and Trustees § 862.

2. *Comparing the Remedies Available Under Sections 409(a) and 502(a)(3).* The remedies available under ERISA Sections 409(a) and 502(a)(3) differ significantly. Under Section 409(a), the breaching fiduciary must pay monetary damages for losses suffered by the plan and restore all ill-gotten profits to the plan. In contrast, the recovery under Section 502(a)(3) against a breaching fiduciary is limited to injunctive or "other appropriate equitable relief." The plaintiff in *Russell* brought her claim under Section 502(a)(2), seeking a remedy under Section 409(a), rather than under Section 502(a)(3), because she sought compensatory damages rather than "equitable" relief. *Russell* makes clear that the remedies authorized by Section 409(a) are available only to the plan itself. Individual plan participants who suffer a personal financial loss due to a fiduciary's breach of duty *must* bring their claims under Section 502(a)(3), and frame the relief sought as "equitable" in nature. The Supreme Court's opinion in *Amara*, see supra Note 1, lays out the framework for pleading a claim for "equitable" monetary relief under Section 502(a)(3).

3. *Punitive Damages Awards and ERISA Public Policy.* Under the common law of trusts, punitive damages may be awarded against a breaching trustee if the court believes that a punitive damage award would serve as a desirable deterrent to future violations. In footnote 12 of the majority opinion in *Russell*, the Supreme Court expressly reserved the question of whether a *plan* might recover punitive damages against a breaching fiduciary under ERISA Section 409(a). Should a plan be able to recover punitive damages against a plan fiduciary? If so, under what circumstances should the federal courts award punitive damages against a breaching fiduciary? What are the public policy arguments for and against allowing punitive damages to be awarded to an ERISA plan?

Unlike a defined benefit plan, in a defined contribution plan each participant has an individual account. Many defined contribution plans, particularly 401(k) plans, permit each participant to direct and control the investment of the funds in the participant's plan account. After *Russell*, it was unclear whether *all* of the participants in a defined contribution plan must have been injured by a fiduciary's breach of duty to assert a claim for "plan-wide" relief under Section 502(a)(2), or whether the claim must be brought under Section 502(a)(3). The Supreme Court resolved this issue in *LaRue v. DeWolff, Boberg & Associates, Inc.*

LaRue v. DeWolff, Boberg & Associates, Inc.

United States Supreme Court, 2008.
552 U.S. 248, 128 S.Ct. 1020, 169 L.Ed.2d 847.

JUSTICE STEVENS delivered the opinion of the Court.

In *Massachusetts Mutual Life Insurance Co. v. Russell*, 473 U.S. 134 (1985), we held that a participant in a disability plan that paid a fixed level of benefits could not bring suit under § 502(a)(2) of the Employee Retirement Income Security Act of 1974 (ERISA) to recover consequential damages arising from delay in the processing of her claim. In this case we consider whether that statutory provision authorizes a participant in a defined contribution pension plan to sue a fiduciary whose alleged misconduct impaired the value of plan assets in the participant's individual account. Relying on our decision in *Russell*, the Court of Appeals for the Fourth Circuit held that § 502(a)(2) "provides remedies only for entire plans, not for individuals. Recovery under this subsection must 'inure to the benefit of the plan *as a whole*,' not to particular persons with rights under the plan." 450 F.3d 570, 572–573 (4th Cir. 2006) (quoting *Russell*, 473 U.S. at 140). While language in our *Russell* opinion is consistent with that conclusion, the rationale for *Russell*'s holding supports the opposite result in this case.

I

Petitioner filed this action in 2004 against his former employer, DeWolff, Boberg & Associates (DeWolff), and the ERISA-regulated 401(k) retirement savings plan administered by DeWolff (Plan). The Plan permits participants to direct the investment of their contributions in accordance with specified procedures and requirements. Petitioner alleged that in 2001 and 2002 he directed DeWolff to make certain changes to the investments in his individual account, but DeWolff never carried out these directions. Petitioner claimed that this omission "depleted" his interest in the Plan by approximately $150,000, and amounted to a breach of fiduciary duty under ERISA. The complaint sought " 'make-whole' or other equitable relief as allowed by § 502(a)(3)," as well as "such other and further relief as the court deems just and proper."

Respondents filed a motion for judgment on the pleadings, arguing that the complaint was essentially a claim for monetary relief that is not recoverable under § 502(a)(3). Petitioner countered that he "did not wish for the court to award him any money, but simply wanted the plan to properly reflect that which would be his interest in the plan, but for the breach of fiduciary duty." The District Court concluded, however, that since respondents did not possess any disputed funds that rightly belonged to petitioner, he was seeking damages rather than equitable relief available under § 502(a)(3). Assuming, *arguendo*, that respondents had breached a fiduciary duty, the District Court nonetheless granted their motion.

On appeal, petitioner argued that he had a cognizable claim for relief under §§ 502(a)(2) and 502(a)(3) of ERISA. The Court of Appeals stated that petitioner had raised his § 502(a)(2) argument for the first time on appeal, but nevertheless rejected it on the merits.

Section 502(a)(2) provides for suits to enforce the liability-creating provisions of § 409, concerning breaches of fiduciary duties that harm plans. The Court of Appeals cited language from our opinion in *Russell* suggesting that these provisions "protect the entire plan, rather than the rights of an individual beneficiary." 473 U.S. at 142. It then characterized the remedy sought by petitioner as "personal" because he "desires recovery to be paid into his plan account, an instrument that exists specifically for his benefit," and concluded:

> We are therefore skeptical that plaintiff's individual remedial interest can serve as a legitimate proxy for the plan in its entirety, as § 502(a)(2) requires. To be sure, the recovery plaintiff seeks could be seen as accruing to the plan in the narrow sense that it would be paid into plaintiff's plan *account*, which is part of the plan. But such a view finds no license in the statutory text, and threatens to undermine the careful limitations Congress has placed on the scope of ERISA relief.

The Court of Appeals also rejected petitioner's argument that the make-whole relief he sought was "equitable" within the meaning of § 502(a)(3). Although our grant of certiorari, encompassed the § 502(a)(3) issue, we do not address it because we conclude that the Court of Appeals misread § 502(a)(2).

As the case comes to us we must assume that respondents breached fiduciary obligations defined in § 409(a), and that those breaches had an adverse impact on the value of the plan assets in petitioner's individual account. Whether petitioner can prove those allegations and whether respondents may have valid defenses to the claim are matters not before us.[3] Although the record does not reveal the relative size of petitioner's account, the legal issue under § 502(a)(2) is the same whether his account includes 1% or 99% of the total assets in the plan.

As we explained in *Russell,* and in more detail in our later opinion in *Varity Corp. v. Howe,* 516 U.S. 489, 508–512 (1996), § 502(a) of ERISA identifies six types of civil actions that may be brought by various parties. The second, which is at issue in this case, authorizes the Secretary of

---

[3] For example, we do not decide whether petitioner made the alleged investment directions in accordance with the requirements specified by the Plan, whether he was required to exhaust remedies set forth in the Plan before seeking relief in federal court pursuant to § 502(a)(2), or whether he asserted his rights in a timely fashion.

Labor as well as plan participants, beneficiaries, and fiduciaries, to bring actions on behalf of a plan to recover for violations of the obligations defined in § 409(a). The principal statutory duties imposed on fiduciaries by that section "relate to the proper management, administration, and investment of fund assets," with an eye toward ensuring that "the benefits authorized by the plan" are ultimately paid to participants and beneficiaries. Russell, 473 U.S. at 142; see also Varity, 516 U.S. at 511–512 (noting that § 409's fiduciary obligations "relate to the plan's financial integrity" and "reflect a special congressional concern about plan asset management"). The misconduct alleged by the petitioner in this case falls squarely within that category.[4]

The misconduct alleged in *Russell,* by contrast, fell outside this category. The plaintiff in *Russell* received all of the benefits to which she was contractually entitled, but sought consequential damages arising from a delay in the processing of her claim. 473 U.S. at 136–137. In holding that § 502(a)(2) does not provide a remedy for this type of injury, we stressed that the text of § 409(a) characterizes the relevant fiduciary relationship as one "with respect to a plan," and repeatedly identifies the "plan" as the victim of any fiduciary breach and the recipient of any relief. See id. at 140. The legislative history likewise revealed that "the crucible of congressional concern was misuse and mismanagement of plan assets by plan administrators." Id. at 141, n. 8. Finally, our review of ERISA as a whole confirmed that §§ 502(a)(2) and 409 protect "the financial integrity of the plan," id. at 142, n. 9, whereas other provisions specifically address claims for benefits. See id. at 143–144 (discussing §§ 502(a)(1)(B) and 503). We therefore concluded: "A fair contextual reading of the statute makes it abundantly clear that its draftsmen were primarily concerned with the possible misuse of plan assets, and with remedies that would protect the entire plan, rather than with the rights of an individual beneficiary." Id. at 142.

Russell's emphasis on protecting the "entire plan" from fiduciary misconduct reflects the former landscape of employee benefit plans. That landscape has changed.

Defined contribution plans dominate the retirement plan scene today. In contrast, when ERISA was enacted, and when *Russell* was decided, "the [defined benefit] plan was the norm of American pension practice." J. Langbein, S. Stabile, & B. Wolk, Pension and Employee

---

[4]   The record does not reveal whether the alleged $150,000 injury represents a decline in the value of assets that DeWolff should have sold or an increase in the value of assets that DeWolff should have purchased. Contrary to respondents' argument, however, § 502(a)(2) encompasses appropriate claims for "lost profits." Under the common law of trusts, which informs our interpretation of ERISA's fiduciary duties, see Varity, 516 U.S. at 496–497, trustees are "chargeable with any profit which would have accrued to the trust estate if there had been no breach of trust," including profits forgone because the trustee "fails to purchase specific property which it is his duty to purchase." Restatement (Second) Trusts § 205, and Comment i, § 211 (1959).

Benefit Law 58 (4th ed.2006); see also Zelinsky, The Defined Contribution Paradigm, 114 Yale L.J. 451, 471 (2004) (discussing the "significant reversal of historic patterns under which the traditional defined benefit plan was the dominant paradigm for the provision of retirement income"). Unlike the defined contribution plan in this case, the disability plan at issue in *Russell* did not have individual accounts; it paid a fixed benefit based on a percentage of the employee's salary.

The "entire plan" language in *Russell* speaks to the impact of § 409 on plans that pay defined benefits. Misconduct by the administrators of a defined benefit plan will not affect an individual's entitlement to a defined benefit unless it creates or enhances the risk of default by the entire plan. It was that default risk that prompted Congress to require defined benefit plans (but not defined contribution plans) to satisfy complex minimum funding requirements, and to make premium payments to the Pension Benefit Guaranty Corporation for plan termination insurance. See Zelinsky, 114 Yale L. J. at 475–478.

For defined contribution plans, however, fiduciary misconduct need not threaten the solvency of the entire plan to reduce benefits below the amount that participants would otherwise receive. Whether a fiduciary breach diminishes plan assets payable to all participants and beneficiaries, or only to persons tied to particular individual accounts, it creates the kind of harms that concerned the draftsmen of § 409. Consequently, our references to the "entire plan" in *Russell,* which accurately reflect the operation of § 409 in the defined benefit context, are beside the point in the defined contribution context.

Other sections of ERISA confirm that the "entire plan" language from *Russell,* which appears nowhere in § 409 or § 502(a)(2), does not apply to defined contribution plans. Most significant is § 404(c), which exempts fiduciaries from liability for losses caused by participants' exercise of control over assets in their individual accounts. See also 29 CFR § 2550.404c–1 (2007). This provision would serve no real purpose if, as respondents argue, fiduciaries never had any liability for losses in an individual account.

We therefore hold that although § 502(a)(2) does not provide a remedy for individual injuries distinct from plan injuries, that provision does authorize recovery for fiduciary breaches that impair the value of plan assets in a participant's individual account. Accordingly, the judgment of the Court of Appeals is vacated, and the case is remanded for further proceedings consistent with this opinion.[5]

---

[5] After our grant of certiorari respondents filed a motion to dismiss the writ, contending that the case is moot because petitioner is no longer a participant in the Plan. While his withdrawal of funds from the Plan may have relevance to the proceedings on remand, we denied their motion because the case is not moot. A plan "participant," as defined by § 3(7) of ERISA, may include a former employee with a colorable claim for benefits. See, e.g., Harzewski v. Guidant Corp., 489 F.3d 799 (7th Cir. 2007).

It is so ordered.

<hr>

CHIEF JUSTICE ROBERTS, with whom JUSTICE KENNEDY joins, concurring in part and concurring in the judgment.

In the decision below, the Fourth Circuit concluded that the loss to LaRue's individual plan account did not permit him to "serve as a legitimate proxy for the plan in its entirety," thus barring him from relief under § 502(a)(2) of the Employee Retirement Income Security Act of 1974 (ERISA). The Court today rejects that reasoning. I agree with the Court that the Fourth Circuit's analysis was flawed, and join the Court's opinion to that extent.

The Court, however, goes on to conclude that § 502(a)(2) does authorize recovery in cases such as the present one. It is not at all clear that this is true. LaRue's right to direct the investment of his contributions was a right granted and governed by the plan. In this action, he seeks the benefits that would otherwise be due him if, as alleged, the plan carried out his investment instruction. LaRue's claim, therefore, is a claim for benefits that turns on the application and interpretation of the plan terms, specifically those governing investment options and how to exercise them.

It is at least arguable that a claim of this nature properly lies only under § 502(a)(1)(B) of ERISA. That provision allows a plan participant or beneficiary "to recover benefits due to him under the terms of his plan, to enforce his rights under the terms of the plan, or to clarify his rights to future benefits under the terms of the plan." It is difficult to imagine a more accurate description of LaRue's claim. And in fact claimants have filed suit under § 502(a)(1)(B) alleging similar benefit denials in violation of plan terms. See, e.g., Hess v. Reg-Ellen Machine Tool Corp., 423 F.3d 653, 657 (7th Cir. 2005) (allegation made under § 502(a)(1)(B) that a plan administrator wrongfully denied instruction to move retirement funds from employer's stock to a diversified investment account).

If LaRue may bring his claim under § 502(a)(1)(B), it is not clear that he may do so under § 502(a)(2) as well. Section 502(a)(2) provides for "appropriate" relief. Construing the same term in a parallel ERISA provision, we have held that relief is not "appropriate" under § 502(a)(3) if another provision, such as § 502(a)(1)(B), offers an adequate remedy. See Varity Corp. v. Howe, 516 U.S. 489, 515 (1996). Applying the same rationale to an interpretation of "appropriate" in § 502(a)(2) would accord with our usual preference for construing the "same terms [to] have the same meaning in different sections of the same statute," Barnhill v. Johnson, 503 U.S. 393, 406 (1992), and with the view that ERISA in particular is a " 'comprehensive and reticulated statute' " with "carefully integrated civil enforcement provisions," Massachusetts Mut. Life Ins. Co.

v. Russell, 473 U.S. 134, 146 (1985) (quoting Nachman Corp. v. Pension Benefit Guaranty Corporation, 446 U.S. 359, 361 (1980)). In a variety of contexts, some Courts of Appeals have accordingly prevented plaintiffs from recasting what are in essence plan-derived benefit claims that should be brought under § 502(a)(1)(B) as claims for fiduciary breaches under § 502(a)(2). See, e.g., Coyne & Delany Co. v. Blue Cross & Blue Shield of Va., Inc., 102 F.3d 712, 714 (4th Cir. 1996). Other Courts of Appeals have disagreed with this approach. See, e.g., Graden v. Conexant Systems Inc., 496 F.3d 291, 301 (3d Cir. 2007).

The significance of the distinction between a § 502(a)(1)(B) claim and one under § 502(a)(2) is not merely a matter of picking the right provision to cite in the complaint. Allowing a § 502(a)(1)(B) action to be recast as one under § 502(a)(2) might permit plaintiffs to circumvent safeguards for plan administrators that have developed under § 502(a)(1)(B). Among these safeguards is the requirement, recognized by almost all the Courts of Appeals, see Fallick v. Nationwide Mut. Ins. Co., 162 F.3d 410, 418, n. 4 (6th Cir. 1998) (citing cases), that a participant exhaust the administrative remedies mandated by ERISA § 503 before filing suit under § 502(a)(1)(B). Equally significant, this Court has held that ERISA plans may grant administrators and fiduciaries discretion in determining benefit eligibility and the meaning of plan terms, decisions that courts may review only for an abuse of discretion. Firestone Tire & Rubber Co. v. Bruch, 489 U.S. 101, 115 (1989).

These safeguards encourage employers and others to undertake the voluntary step of providing medical and retirement benefits to plan participants, see Aetna Health Inc. v. Davila, 542 U.S. 200, 215 (2004), and have no doubt engendered substantial reliance interests on the part of plans and fiduciaries. Allowing what is really a claim for benefits under a plan to be brought as a claim for breach of fiduciary duty under § 502(a)(2), rather than as a claim for benefits due "under the terms of the plan," § 502(a)(1)(B), may result in circumventing such plan terms.

I do not mean to suggest that these are settled questions. They are not. Nor are we in a position to answer them. LaRue did not rely on § 502(a)(1)(B) as a source of relief, and the courts below had no occasion to address the argument, raised by an amicus in this Court, that the availability of relief under § 502(a)(1)(B) precludes LaRue's fiduciary breach claim. I simply highlight the fact that the Court's determination that the present claim may be brought under § 502(a)(2) is reached without considering whether the possible availability of relief under § 502(a)(1)(B) alters that conclusion. In matters of statutory interpretation, where principles of stare decisis have their greatest effect, it is important that we not seem to decide more than we do. I see nothing in today's opinion precluding the lower courts on remand, if they determine that the argument is properly before them, from considering the contention that LaRue's claim may proceed only under § 502(a)(1)(B). In any event, other courts in other cases remain free to consider what we have not—what effect the availability of relief under § 502(a)(1)(B) may have on a plan participant's ability to proceed under § 502(a)(2).

———————————

JUSTICE THOMAS, with whom JUSTICE SCALIA joins, concurring in the judgment.

I agree with the Court that petitioner alleges a cognizable claim under § 502(a)(2) of the Employee Retirement Income Security Act of 1974 (ERISA), but it is ERISA's text and not "the kind of harms that concerned ERISA's draftsmen" that compels my decision. * * *

Although I agree with the majority's holding, I write separately because my reading of §§ 409 and 502(a)(2) is not contingent on trends in the pension plan market. Nor does it depend on the ostensible "concerns" of ERISA's drafters. Rather, my conclusion that petitioner has stated a cognizable claim flows from the unambiguous text of §§ 409 and 502(a)(2) as applied to defined contribution plans. Section 502(a)(2) states that "a civil action may be brought" by a plan "participant, beneficiary or fiduciary," or by the Secretary of Labor, to obtain "appropriate relief" under § 409. Section 409(a) provides that "any person who is a fiduciary with respect to a *plan* shall be personally liable to make good to such *plan* any losses to the *plan* resulting from each fiduciary breach, and to restore to such *plan* any profits of such fiduciary which have been made through use of assets of the *plan* by the fiduciary." ERISA § 409(a) (emphasis added).

The plain text of § 409(a), which uses the term "plan" five times, leaves no doubt that § 502(a)(2) authorizes recovery only for the plan. Likewise, Congress' repeated use of the word "any" in § 409(a) clarifies that the key factor is whether the alleged losses can be said to be losses "to the plan," not whether they are otherwise of a particular nature or kind. On their face, §§ 409(a) and 502(a)(2) permit recovery of *all* plan losses caused by a fiduciary breach.

The question presented here, then, is whether the losses to petitioner's individual 401(k) account resulting from respondents' alleged breach of their fiduciary duties were losses "to the plan." In my view they were, because the assets allocated to petitioner's individual account were plan assets. ERISA requires the assets of a defined contribution plan (including "gains and losses" and legal recoveries) to be allocated for bookkeeping purposes to individual accounts within the plan for the beneficial interest of the participants, whose benefits in turn depend on the allocated amounts. Thus, when a defined contribution plan sustains losses, those losses are reflected in the balances in the plan accounts of the affected participants, and a recovery of those losses would be allocated to one or more individual accounts.

The allocation of a plan's assets to individual accounts for bookkeeping purposes does not change the fact that all the assets in the plan remain plan assets. A defined contribution plan is not merely a collection of unrelated accounts. Rather, ERISA requires a plan's combined assets to be held in trust and legally owned by the plan trustees. In short, the assets of a defined contribution plan under ERISA constitute, at the very least, the sum of all the assets allocated for bookkeeping purposes to the participants' individual accounts. Because a defined contribution plan is essentially the sum of its parts, losses attributable to the account of an individual participant are necessarily "losses to the plan" for purposes of § 409(a). Accordingly, when a participant sustains losses to his individual account as a result of a fiduciary breach, the plan's aggregate assets are likewise diminished by the same amount, and § 502(a)(2) permits that participant to recover such losses on behalf of the plan.[1]

NOTES AND QUESTIONS

1.   *Comparing* LaRue *with* Russell. Why did the Supreme Court reject the plaintiff's claim under Section 502(a)(2) in *Russell*, but allow the claim in *LaRue*? Does the current retirement trend toward individual account plans justify a reinterpretation of *Russell's* language that a claim under Section 502(a)(2) must provide for a remedy to the "entire" plan? Or, is the result in *LaRue* better grounded in Justice Thomas's reasoning that any loss involving plan assets is a loss "to the plan" within the meaning of Section 502(a)(2)?

2.   *Section 502(a)(1)(B) Claims After* LaRue. The concurring opinion in *LaRue* by Chief Justice Roberts suggests that the plaintiff's claim may have been more appropriately brought under Section 502(a)(1)(B). Why would a plaintiff like LaRue prefer to bring a claim under Section 502(a)(2) than under Section 502(a)(1)(B)?

3.   *Remedies Available Under Section 502(a)(2) and Section 502(a)(3).* In footnote 4 of the *LaRue* majority opinion, the Supreme Court stated that relief is available under Section 502(a)(2) for "lost profits" to a plan (including to an individual's plan account) resulting from a fiduciary's breach of duty. The standard by which lost profits to the plan are measured for claims under Section 502(a)(2) is discussed in the next case, *Donovan v. Bierwirth*.

4.   *Restorative Payments to the Plan's Trustee.* As discussed by Justice Thomas in his concurring opinion in *LaRue*, the trustee of the plan is the legal owner of the plan's assets. Therefore, "plan-wide" relief to a defined contribution plan is awarded by a payment to the plan's trustee and not by a direct payment to the individual plaintiff-participants.

---

[1]   Of course, a participant suing to recover benefits on behalf of the plan is not entitled to monetary relief payable directly to him; rather, any recovery must be paid to the plan.

If an employer breaches its fiduciary responsibilities under ERISA, the employer may be required to make a *restorative payment* to the employer's plan. Restorative payments can be substantial in amount, particularly when the alleged breach of fiduciary duty involves company stock held as a plan asset. See, e.g., In re Delphi Corp. Secs., Derivative & ERISA Litig., 248 F.R.D. 483 (E.D. Mich. 2008) (approving settlement for $47 million in damages). A restorative payment may be the product of a court ordered remedy or a court approved settlement agreement resulting from ERISA fiduciary litigation. The employer also may decide voluntarily to make a restorative payment to the plan after learning that the participants are considering filing a lawsuit against the employer and reasonably determining that, if such a lawsuit is filed, the employer has a reasonable risk of liability for breach of its fiduciary duties under ERISA.

Restorative payments made to a qualified plan generally are not counted for purposes of the individual or employer deduction limits under the Code for employer contributions. See Rev. Rul. 2002–45. But a settlement of litigation that involves a restorative payment to the plan is potentially subject to ERISA's prohibited transaction rules of ERISA Section 406. See Class Exemption for the Release of Claims and Extensions of Credit in Connection with Litigation, 68 Fed. Reg. 75,632, 75,635 (Dec. 31, 2003), Harris v. Koenig, 602 F.Supp.2d 39, 55 & nn. 19–20 (D.D.C. 2009). Therefore, the terms of the settlement must be structured to comply with a class exemption from the prohibited transaction rules, see Prohibited Transaction Exemption 2003–39, or the litigants may need to obtain an individual administrative exemption before the settlement can be finalized, see ERISA § 408(a).

2. MEASURING INVESTMENT LOSSES

The statutory language of ERISA Section 409(a) provides that the breaching fiduciary must make good to the plan any "losses" resulting from the fiduciary's misconduct. In footnote 4 of the *LaRue* majority opinion, the Supreme Court indicated that the relief available under Section 502(a)(2) includes "lost profits" (sometimes referred to as a "lost investment opportunity") that result from a fiduciary's breach of duty. How should the federal courts measure the investment "losses" incurred by the plan? *Donovan v. Bierwirth* addressed this question.

DONOVAN V. BIERWIRTH

United States Court of Appeals, Second Circuit, 1985.
754 F.2d 1049.

PIERCE, CIRCUIT JUDGE.

Before us on these consolidated appeals are: the Secretary of the United States Department of Labor ("Secretary") and Robert J. Lawrence, plaintiffs-appellants, and John C. Bierwirth, Robert G. Freese, and Carl A. Paladino, defendants-appellees, who are the trustees ("Trustees") of the Grumman Corporation Pension Plan ("Plan"). The Secretary and Lawrence appeal from judgments entered February 28, 1984, in the United States District Court for the Eastern District of New York, * * * after a joint trial of both plaintiffs' actions. The complaints alleged that the defendant Trustees violated their fiduciary responsibilities by improperly buying Grumman securities on behalf of the Plan. The plaintiffs sought, inter alia, recovery of any losses suffered by the Plan as a result of the Trustees' alleged breach. On February 21, 1984, the district court concluded that no losses were sustained by the Plan. We reverse and remand the question of loss to the district court for findings of fact as to what the Plan would have earned but for the Trustees' purchase of the Grumman stock.

I.   BACKGROUND

[On September 24, 1981, the LTV Corporation ("LTV") made a tender offer for a controlling interest in Grumman Corporation at a price of $45 per share. At that time, the Plan held approximately 525,000 shares of Grumman stock. The Trustees, who were also high ranking officials of Grumman, determined not to tender any of these shares. On October 12 and 13, the Trustees directed the Plan to purchase 1,158,000 additional shares of Grumman stock at the prevailing market price in an effort to defeat the tender offer. The day before the tender offer was announced, Grumman stock sold for $26.75 per share. The next day, after announcement of the tender offer, the price rose to $35.88 per share. On October 12 and 13, when the Trustees made the purchases, Grumman stock was selling at $36 to $39.34 per share. The tender offer ultimately failed, and the price of Grumman stock dropped in the next month to approximately $23 per share.

Approximately seventeen months after the Grumman stock was purchased, the Trustees sold the stock, together with some of the previously-held Grumman shares, for $47.55 per share. Including dividends, the amount earned by the Plan on the shares purchased during the tender offer was, net of commissions, $11.41 per share (selling price of $47.55 per share, plus dividends of $2.20 per share, less an average purchase price of $38.34 per share). The total amount earned by the Plan due to its investment in the Grumman stock was $13,212,780.

The district court found that the market price of Grumman stock on October 12 and 13, 1981, was distorted by the pending tender offer and that the fair market value of the stock at that time was only $23 per share. Nevertheless, the district court dismissed the complaint because the Court found that the Plan had not suffered a "loss" within the meaning of ERISA Section 409(a).]

* * *

The chief issue presented for our review concerns the applicable measure of damages. Specifically, if securities are purchased in breach of trust but are later sold at a price exceeding the purchase price, is there a "loss" within the meaning of ERISA section 409?

II. DISCUSSION

In resolving the question whether the Plan sustained a "loss," we bear in mind that the Trustees, if ultimately found to have breached their fiduciary duties, will be liable personally for any such "loss" pursuant to section 409. ERISA does not define "loss" as that term is used in section 409. The Act's legislative history, however, indicates that Congress' intent was "to provide the full range of legal and equitable remedies available in both state and federal courts." H.R. Rep. No. 533, 93d Cong., 2d Sess. (1974). Measuring damages involves the application of law to fact; the proper formula for calculating damages is essentially a question of law. * * *

[The Court considered and rejected the ways to measure a "loss" under ERISA Section 409(a) that were proposed by the defendant-Trustees, the Secretary of Labor, and the district court judge.]

Since we have rejected the three measures of loss proposed to us [by the parties], our task is to determine what the measure of loss in this case ought to be. Because section 409 speaks in terms of "losses . . . resulting from [a] breach," we assume for purposes of resolving this question that a breach of fiduciary duty has been established, as indeed it was for purposes of preliminary relief. We recognize that state law has been preempted by ERISA. See ERISA § 514(a). Nevertheless, it is "clear that Congress intended to provide the courts with broad remedies for redressing the interests of participants and beneficiaries when they have been adversely affected by breaches of a fiduciary duty." Eaves v. Penn, 587 F.2d 453, 462 (10th Cir. 1978). We thus look to principles developed under the common law of trusts, which in large measure remain applicable under ERISA. Leigh v. Engle, 727 F.2d 113, 122–23 (7th Cir. 1984). Still, we recognize, as the Secretary points out, that ERISA standards were intended to be construed in light of the nature of modern employee benefit plans. One characteristic of these plans is that they control large pools of capital, which are frequently partly invested in the securities markets. Fiduciaries of such plans may be called upon to make decisions regarding tender offers and other contests for corporate control. Clearly, there is a need to deter abuses in these areas, where the temptation to misuse funds often may be especially strong. Brink v. DaLesio, 667 F.2d 420, 427 (4th Cir. 1982).

Fiduciary abuses may be deterred in various ways. One method is to impose personal liability upon trustees for losses sustained by pension plans as a result of such abuses. Additionally, for certain statutorily-enumerated types of fiduciary misconduct, Congress has legislated penalty provisions in the nature of surcharges and excises. See ERISA §§ 406; 502(a)(6). The Act also provides criminal penalties for "willful" violations of its provisions. ERISA § 501. Although such penalties are not claimed to be at issue here, Congress' enactment both of penalty provisions and provisions requiring losses suffered by a pension plan to be repaid suggests that the two kinds of provisions have different aims. Section 409, by providing for the recovery of losses, primarily seeks to undo harm that may have been caused a pension plan by virtue of the fiduciaries' acts.

One appropriate remedy in cases of breach of fiduciary duty is the restoration of the trust beneficiaries to the position they would have occupied but for the breach of trust. Restatement (Second) of Trusts § 205(c) (1959); see Eaves v. Penn, 587 F.2d at 463. In view of the intent expressed by Congress in providing for the recovery of "losses," and in the absence of evidence of congressional intent to penalize, as such, violations of section 409, we hold that the measure of loss applicable under ERISA section 409 requires a comparison of what the Plan actually earned on the Grumman investment with what the Plan would have earned had the funds been available for other Plan purposes. If the latter amount is greater than the former, the loss is the difference between the two; if the former is greater, no loss was sustained.

In determining what the Plan would have earned had the funds been available for other Plan purposes, the district court should presume that the funds would have been treated like other funds being invested during the same period in proper transactions. Where several alternative investment strategies were equally plausible, the court should presume that the funds would have been used in the most profitable of these. The burden of proving that the funds would have earned less than that amount is on the fiduciaries found to be in breach of their duty. Any doubt or ambiguity should be resolved against them. This is nothing more than application of the principle that, once a breach of trust is established, uncertainties in fixing damages will be resolved against the wrongdoer.

Determining what portfolios are to be compared, however, does not end our inquiry. The value of each portfolio is likely to vary every business day. The question then remains, as of what date should the portfolios be valued? Herein, there was an actual sale of the Grumman securities, and therefore the amount realized on the sale should be compared with the earnings, if any, that would have been realized through alternative investment over the same period of time. In the event there were no sale, breaching fiduciaries might argue that they should be given indefinite extensions of time in which to hold the improperly purchased property, because it might appreciate in value, thereby reducing their personal liability. * * *

[T]he court might properly select a date for valuation between the date suit was filed and the date of the entry of judgment. The value of the improper investment on that date could then be compared with the performance of the portfolio in which the improperly used funds would have been invested but for the breach of fiduciary duty, with the burden of proof on the trustees to show that the funds would have been put to less than their most profitable use.

* * *

Of importance, however, is the need to ensure that trustees who misuse funds not be permitted to delay determinations of loss indefinitely in the hope of avoiding a statutory "loss." The trial court must have discretion to fix a reasonable time at which the actual performance of the improper investment will be measured and compared with the earnings performance which would have been realized but for the breach.

Such a determination is of necessity somewhat arbitrary. Without the benefit of hindsight, it is indeed difficult to know what the ideal amount is at which to evaluate plan performances. Still, we do not believe the problem to be incapable of resolution. The trial court, in its sound discretion, must pick a date on which the relative performance of the plan and the improper investment may fairly be compared. Without purporting to catalogue the relevant factors exhaustively, they include at least: (1) market conditions and abnormalities affecting the price of the improperly purchased stock; (2) such conditions as they affect the price of other assets of the plan at issue; (3) the court's determination of the relative price advantages to the plan of selling or holding the stock; and (4) the interests of the beneficiaries of the plan.

Any incentive to delay on the part of trustees in breach should be mitigated by the possibility that the improperly purchased stock may decline in value, and that a comparison will be made with the performance of the other plan assets. While the improperly purchased stock may increase in value in a rising market, very likely so will the other plan assets. The advantages of delaying the determination of damages are thus minimized.

Accordingly, we reverse the judgment of the district court and remand the cause for disposition consistent with the foregoing.

NOTES AND QUESTIONS

1.   *Methods of Measuring an Investment Loss.* In *Donovan v. Bierwirth*, the Second Circuit adopted a measure of damages based on the potential lost investment earnings of the plan. Under this lost investment opportunity approach, it was possible for the pension plan to suffer a "loss" within the

meaning of Section 409(a), despite the fact that the plan earned $13,212,780 when it ultimately sold the Grumman stock. Applying the Second Circuit's measure of damages on remand, the district court found that the amount the Plan funds would have earned had they been available for other investments was $4,519,476 *less* than what the Plan actually earned though its investment in Grumman stock. Therefore, the district court ultimately concluded that no "loss" had occurred. See Ford v. Bierwirth, 636 F.Supp. 540, 542 (E.D.N.Y. 1986). For an analysis and critique of the Second Circuit's decision in *Donovan v. Bierwirth*, see Daniel Fischel & John H. Langbein, *ERISA's Fundamental Contradiction: The Exclusive Benefit Rule*, 55 U. CHICAGO L. REV. 1105, 1138–42 (1988).

The lost investment opportunity measure of damages in *Donovan v. Bierwirth* has been followed in other cases involving a restorative payment to a defined benefit plan for losses resulting from an alleged breach of the fiduciary's duty of loyalty. See GIW Indus. v. Trevor, Stewart, Burton & Jacobsen, Inc., 895 F.2d 729, 733 (11th Cir. 1990); Dardaganis v. Grace Capital Inc., 889 F.2d 1237, 1243–44 (2d Cir. 1989). In challenging this measure of the loss to the plan, defendant-fiduciaries have argued that focusing on the investment return for a single plan investment is inconsistent with the theoretical premise of modern portfolio theory, which focuses on the entirety of the plan's investment portfolio and the role that each individual investment plays in furthering the plan's overall investment strategy. In cases where the investment has resulted from a breach of the fiduciary's duty of loyalty, the courts have rejected this argument. See Leigh v. Engle, 858 F.2d 361, 368 (7th Cir. 1988) ("where fiduciaries breach their duty of loyalty by making individual investments with an eye toward some goal other than the creation of a proper portfolio for their clients, a court may return the favor, viewing the investments in isolation to determine damages").

In *California Ironworkers Field Pension Trust v. Loomis Sayles & Co.,* 259 F.3d 1036 (9th Cir. 2001), the Ninth Circuit addressed the appropriate measure of damages where the plan fiduciary's investment decision was not tainted by a breach of the fiduciary's duty of loyalty, but rather was merely imprudent because an excessive percentage of the defined benefit plan's funds (30% of trust assets) were placed in a single investment. The Ninth Circuit adopted a measure of damages where "the [fiduciary] is liable only for such loss as results from the investment of the excess beyond the amount which it would have been proper to invest." Id. at 1046 (quoting Restatement (Third) of Trusts, § 205, comment f). The Ninth Circuit justified this measure of damages on the grounds that "[i]t would be both illogical and unjust to require a fiduciary to pay damages resulting from the entire amount of an investment when only a portion of the investment was imprudent." Id. at 1047.

The federal circuit courts also have endorsed the *Donovan v. Bierwirth* measure of damages where the fiduciary's breach of duty adversely affected the assets held by individual participants in a defined contribution plan:

Benefits are benefits; in a defined contribution plan they are the value of the retirement account when the employee retires, and a breach of fiduciary duty that diminishes that value gives rise to a claim for benefits measured by the difference between what the retirement account was worth when the employee retired and cashed it out and what it would have been worth then had it not been for the breach of fiduciary duty.

Harzewski v. Guidant Corp., 489 F.3d 799, 807 (7th Cir. 2007); accord Graden v. Conexant Sys. Inc., 496 F.3d 291, 297 (3d Cir. 2007).

2. *Breach of Fiduciary Duty and Disgorgement of Profits.* The Seventh Circuit's opinion in *Leigh v. Engle*, 727 F.2d 113 (7th Cir. 1984), addresses the disgorgement remedy available under Section 409(a). The plaintiffs in *Leigh v. Engle* were vested participants in the Reliable Manufacturing Corporation Profit Sharing Plan (Plan). In March of 1978, the trustees of the Plan invested approximately 30% of the Plan's assets in the stock of three companies. Prior to March of 1978, all of the assets of the Plan had been invested in fixed income money market investments. The plaintiffs alleged that the trustees of the Plan caused the Plan to make these investments to aid the defendants in their attempt to either win control of the three target companies or to earn a substantial control premium on their personal investments in the stock of the three target companies.

The Plan's investment in the stock of the three target companies was successful, producing an aggregate return on investment of 72%, exclusive of dividends. Id. at 121. Because the Plan did not suffer an investment loss from the challenged transactions, the district court concluded that the plaintiffs could not bring a claim for breach of fiduciary duty under ERISA Sections 502(a)(2) and 409(a). The Seventh Circuit reversed, stating:

> The nature of the breach of fiduciary duty alleged here is not the *loss* of plan assets but instead the *risking* of the trust assets at least in part to aid the defendants in their acquisition program. ERISA expressly prohibits the use of assets for purposes other than the best interests of the beneficiaries, and the language of [Section 409(a)] providing for disgorgement of profits from improper use of trust assets is the appropriate remedy. On the record before us, we are unable to determine the extent of the defendants' total profits, and we certainly cannot measure the extent, if any, to which any profits resulted from the defendants' use of the trust assets. However, those questions are relevant only in measuring damages. At this point in the analysis, we need only say that plaintiffs are not required to show that the trust lost money as a result of the alleged breaches of fiduciary duties. If ERISA fiduciaries breach their duties by risking trust assets for their own purposes, beneficiaries may recover the fiduciaries' profits made by misuse of the plan's assets.

Id. at 122 (emphasis in original). The district court on remand found that the defendant fiduciaries had met their burden of proving that the personal profits each defendant received from investing in the stock of the three target companies were not attributable to the use of trust assets. See Leigh v. Engle, 669 F.Supp. 1390, 1404–05 (N.D. Ill. 1987), aff'd by 858 F.2d 361, 366–67 (7th Cir. 1988).

3. *"Losses" in a Defined Benefit Plan with a Funding Surplus.* Can a defined benefit pension plan that has a funding surplus nevertheless suffer a "loss" under Section 409(a)? In *Harley v. Minnesota Mining and Manufacturing Co.*, 284 F.3d 901 (8th Cir. 2002), the employer 3M sponsored a defined benefit plan. 3M's pension asset committee, which was charged with the responsibility of investing plan assets, directed that the plan invest $20 million in a hedge fund that consisted primarily of collateralized mortgage securities. Four years later, the hedge fund became bankrupt, causing the plan to lose its entire $20 million investment. Despite this loss, the 3M plan maintained a funding surplus.

The plan's participants sued the members of the 3M pension asset committee for breach of fiduciary duty in failing prudently to investigate and monitor the plan's investment in the hedge fund. The district court granted summary judgment for the plan fiduciaries on the ground that the plan still maintained a surplus and therefore did not suffer a "loss" under Section 409(a). On appeal, the Secretary of Labor as amicus curiae urged the Eighth Circuit to reverse the district court's ruling, arguing that the decision was contrary to the Department of Labor's longstanding interpretation of Section 409(a) and would "have a substantial impact on the ability of the Secretary to enforce [ERISA]." Id. at 905. The Eighth Circuit appeared to agree with the Secretary of Labor that the district court had incorrectly interpreted Section 409(a), but nevertheless affirmed the grant of summary judgment on the ground that the participants lacked standing to bring the suit under Article III of the United States Constitution because they had not suffered a concrete injury as required by Article III. Id. at 906–07. According to the Eighth Circuit, "absence of adequate surplus is an element of plaintiffs' standing under [ERISA § 502(a)(2)]—proof they are suing to redress a loss to the Plan that is an actual injury *to themselves.*" Id. at 908 (emphasis in original).

The Eighth Circuit's ruling in *Harley* conflicts with several other circuit decisions. See Financial Institutions Retirement Fund v. Office of Thrift Supervision, 964 F.2d 142 (2d Cir. 1992); Amalgamated Clothing & Textile Workers Union v. Murdock, 861 F.2d 1406 (9th Cir. 1988); Brink v. DaLesio, 667 F.2d 420 (4th Cir. 1981); see also Olsen v. Hegarty, 180 F.Supp.2d 552 (D.N.J. 2001). *Harley* also seems inconsistent with ERISA's primary purpose, described by the Supreme Court in *LaRue*, of protecting against the mismanagement of plan assets. See LaRue v. DeWolff, Boberg & Associates, Inc., 552 U.S. 248, 254 (2008) ("the crucible of congressional concern was misuse and mismanagement of plan assets by plan administrators"). Do you agree with the Eighth Circuit's conclusion that the participants in a defined benefit plan that suffers an investment loss, but nevertheless maintains a funding surplus, cannot suffer a sufficient injury-in-fact to acquire Article III standing? What injury have the plan participants suffered?

4. *Proof of Causal Connection.* Even in situations where a clear breach of fiduciary duty has occurred, there still must be a causal connection between the breach of fiduciary duty and a loss incurred by the plan, or between the breach of fiduciary duty and ill-gotten profits obtained by the fiduciaries through the use of plan assets. *Wsol v. Fiduciary Management Associates, Inc.,* 266 F.3d 654 (7th Cir. 2001), illustrates the causal connection requirement. In *Wsol,* the trustees of a pension fund sponsored by the Teamsters Union hired Fiduciary Management Associates, Inc. (FMA) as a broker for the fund's investments. FMA used another entity, East West, to act as an intermediary between the pension fund and a broker who executed the trades for the fund. East West paid kickbacks to one of the trustees of the plan. This crooked trustee pressured FMA to use East West as the intermediary between the pension fund and the broker. FMA appeased the crooked trustee by hiring East West and, incidentally, by providing the crooked trustee with numerous paid golf outings. (The crooked trustee was later indicted and convicted on criminal charges.)

When the crooked trustee's conduct came to light, the honest trustees of the pension fund sued FMA for breach of fiduciary duty. The Seventh Circuit affirmed the district court's ruling that neither damages nor disgorgement was available as a remedy where the breach of fiduciary duty did not result in a loss to the pension plan and did not produce a profit for FMA through the use of plan assets. According to the Seventh Circuit, "surprising as this may seem, the shady operation that was East West appears to have given the fund all the benefits it would have received had FMA either retained a reputable introducing broker or dealt directly with the executing brokers." Even if "FMA hired a choir of heavenly angels as introducing brokers" for the fund, the fund would not have fared better. Id. at 657–58. In short, "[i]f no misuse of the funds occurs, if no losses are incurred or profits obtained that differ from what they would have been had there been no breach of fiduciary duty, there is no remedy." Id. at 658.

Should the plaintiff bear the burden of proof on the loss causation element? The federal circuit courts are divided on the issue. One view is that the plaintiff bears the burden of establishing that the alleged breach of fiduciary duty caused a loss to the plan. See Holdeman v. Devine, 572 F.3d 1190, 1193 (10th Cir. 2009); Silverman v. Mutual Ben. Life Ins. Co., 138 F.3d 98, 105 (2d Cir. 1998). The other view is that "once the ERISA plaintiff has proved a breach of fiduciary duty and a prima facie case of loss to the plan or ill-gotten profit to the fiduciary, the burden of persuasion shifts to the fiduciary to prove that the loss was not caused by, or his profit was not attributable to, the breach of duty." Martin v. Feilen, 965 F.2d 660, 671 (8th Cir. 1992).

E. SECTION 502(a)(3) CLAIMS: THE "CATCH-ALL" CATEGORY

ERISA Section 502(a)(3) authorizes a plan participant, beneficiary, or fiduciary to bring a civil action:

(A) to enjoin any act or practice which violates any provision of Title I of ERISA or the terms of the plan, or

(B) to obtain other appropriate equitable relief (i) to redress such violations or (ii) to enforce any provisions of Title I of ERISA or the terms of the plan.

The statutory language of Section 502(a)(3) offers a flexible "catch-all" remedial mechanism for the federal courts to address claims and remedies concerning employee benefit plans that Congress did not anticipate when it enacted ERISA. Indeed, the statutory language of Section 502(a)(3) on its face "admits of no limit (aside from the 'appropriate equitable relief' caveat * * *) on the universe of possible defendants." Harris Trust & Sav. Bank v. Salomon Smith Barney, 530 U.S. 238, 246 (2000).

Section 502(a)(3) has perplexed the Supreme Court, which has struggled to define the parameters of "appropriate equitable relief." The Court's opinions addressing this issue have been harshly criticized for failing to provide meaningful guidance to the lower federal courts concerning "one of the critical issues that dominates much of ERISA litigation." Robert N. Eccles and David E. Gordon, *Under the Radar*, 9 ERISA LITIG. REP. (Glasser Legal Works), no. 4, at 1–2 (Oct. 2001).

The divisions among the Supreme Court justices concerning Section 502(a)(3), first revealed in the Court's majority and concurring opinions in *Massachusetts Mutual Life Insurance Co. v. Russell*, resurfaced when the Court addressed the scope of appropriate equitable relief available under Section 502(a)(3) directly in *Mertens v. Hewitt Associates*, 508 U.S. 248 (1993). *Mertens* was followed, in chronological order, by *Varity Corporation v. Howe* (1996), *Harris Trust and Savings Bank v. Solomon Smith Barney* (2000), *Great-West Life and Annuity Insurance Co. v. Knudson* (2002), *Sereboff v. Mid Atlantic Medical Services, Inc.* (2006), *Cigna Corp. v. Amara* (2011), and *US Airways, Inc. v. McCuthchen* (2013).

Rather than presenting these Supreme Court decisions in chronological order, Section E of Chapter Six organizes the cases according to the nature of the claim and remedy sought under Section 502(a)(3) and the type of defendant. Section E.1, entitled Claims Against Nonfiduciaries, contains *Mertens* and *Harris Trust*. In both of these cases, a plan fiduciary brought a claim against a nonfiduciary plan service provider seeking "equitable" monetary relief. Section E.2, entitled Claims to Enforce a Plan Reimbursement Clause, contains *Great-West*, *Sereboff*, and *McCutchen*. In these cases, the terms of the employer's health care plan required reimbursement to the plan for any medical expenses paid by the plan if an injured participant ultimately recovered from a third party tortfeasor who caused the participant's injuries. In each case, the plan administrator brought a claim for equitable relief against a plan participant to enforce the terms of the plan's reimbursement clause.

Sections E.3 and E.4 contain decisions where the Supreme Court determined that the participant had a valid claim under Section 502(a)(3), but the Court did not explicitly address the scope of appropriate equitable relief available as a remedy. *Inter-Modal Rail Employees Association v. Atchison, Topeka & Santa Fe Railway Co.* is reproduced in Section E.3, which is entitled Claims for Retaliation in Violation of Section 510. In *Inter-Modal*, the Supreme Court ruled that the employer's conduct could constitute a violation of ERISA Section 510, which prohibits retaliatory action against a plan participant to prevent the participant from attaining or exercising rights under an employee benefit plan. Section 510 violations are remedied through a claim brought under ERISA Section 502(a)(3). Although *Inter-Modal* does not address the types of remedies available under Section 502(a)(3) for a claim of a prohibited retaliation under Section 510, a footnote in the majority opinion in *Great-West* suggests that the equitable remedy of back pay may not be available to a participant whose employment has been wrongfully terminated in violation of Section 510.

Section E.4, entitled Claims for Individual Relief for Breach of Fiduciary Duty, contains the last part of the Supreme Court's opinion in *Varity Corporation* and *Amara*. In Parts A and B of the *Varity* opinion, which are reproduced in Chapter Five of the casebook, the Supreme Court held that the employer's agents were plan fiduciaries, and that their intentional misrepresentations to the plan's participants concerning their benefits constituted a breach of fiduciary duty. In Part C of the *Varity* opinion, reproduced at the end of Chapter Six, the Supreme Court concluded that the plan participants as individuals could bring a claim for breach of fiduciary duty under Section 502(a)(3). The *Varity* Court did not elaborate on the nature of equitable relief available under Section 502(a)(3), however, because the employer in *Varity* previously had conceded that the participants' requested relief was equitable. In *Amara*, the Supreme Court finally addressed the types of equitable relief available under Section 502(a)(3) when an individual plan participant has been injured by a fiduciary's breach of duty.

As you read these Supreme Court decisions, consider the underlying (and sometimes conflicting) public policies that are triggered by the nature of the claim, the requested remedy, and the type of defendant in the case. In each situation, do you think that the Supreme Court's definition of equitable relief under Section 502(a)(3) was appropriate in light of ERISA's underlying policies? If not, can you think of a better "rule" for defining the scope of equitable relief available under Section 502(a)(3) for each situation?

1. CLAIMS AGAINST NONFIDUCIARIES

MERTENS V. HEWITT ASSOCIATES

United States Supreme Court, 1993.
508 U.S. 248, 113 S.Ct. 2063, 124 L.Ed.2d 161.

JUSTICE SCALIA delivered the opinion of the Court.

The question presented is whether a nonfiduciary who knowingly participates in the breach of a fiduciary duty imposed by the Employee Retirement Income Security Act of 1974 (ERISA) is liable for losses that an employee benefit plan suffers as a result of the breach.

I

According to the complaint, the allegations of which we take as true, petitioners represent a class of former employees of the Kaiser Steel Corporation (Kaiser) who participated in the Kaiser Steel Retirement Plan, a qualified pension plan under ERISA. Respondent was the plan's actuary in 1980, when Kaiser began to phase out its steel-making operations, prompting early retirement by a large number of plan participants. Respondent did not, however, change the plan's actuarial assumptions to reflect the additional costs imposed by the retirements. As a result, Kaiser did not adequately fund the plan, and eventually the plan's assets became insufficient to satisfy its benefit obligations, causing the Pension Benefit Guaranty Corporation (PBGC) to terminate the plan pursuant to ERISA § 4041. Petitioners now receive only the benefits guaranteed by ERISA, see ERISA § 4022, which are in general substantially lower than the fully vested pensions due them under the plan.

Petitioners sued the fiduciaries of the failed plan, alleging breach of fiduciary duties. See Mertens v. Black, 948 F.2d 1105 (9th Cir. 1991). They also commenced this action against respondent, alleging that it had caused the losses by allowing Kaiser to select the plan's actuarial assumptions, by failing to disclose that Kaiser was one of its clients, and by failing to disclose the plan's funding shortfall. Petitioners claimed that these acts and omissions violated ERISA by effecting a breach of respondent's "professional duties" to the plan, for which they sought, inter alia, monetary relief. In opposing respondent's motion to dismiss, petitioners fleshed out this claim, asserting that respondent was liable (1) as an ERISA fiduciary that committed a breach of its own fiduciary duties, (2) as a nonfiduciary that knowingly participated in the plan fiduciaries' breach of their fiduciary duties, and (3) as a nonfiduciary that committed a breach of nonfiduciary duties imposed on actuaries by

ERISA. The District Court for the Northern District of California dismissed the complaint and the Court of Appeals for the Ninth Circuit affirmed in relevant part. 948 F.2d 607 (1991).

Petitioners sought certiorari only on the question whether ERISA authorizes suits for money damages against nonfiduciaries who knowingly participate in a fiduciary's breach of fiduciary duty. We agreed to hear the case.

II

ERISA is, we have observed, a "comprehensive and reticulated statute," the product of a decade of congressional study of the Nation's private employee benefit system. Nachman Corp. v. Pension Benefit Guaranty Corporation, 446 U.S. 359, 361 (1980). The statute provides that not only the persons named as fiduciaries by a benefit plan, see ERISA § 402(a), but also anyone else who exercises discretionary control or authority over the plan's management, administration, or assets, see ERISA § 3(21)(A), is an ERISA "fiduciary." Fiduciaries are assigned a number of detailed duties and responsibilities, which include "the proper management, administration, and investment of [plan] assets, the maintenance of proper records, the disclosure of specified information, and the avoidance of conflicts of interest." Massachusetts Mut. Life Ins. Co. v. Russell, 473 U.S. 134, 142–143 (1985); see ERISA § 404(a). Section 409(a) makes fiduciaries liable for breach of these duties, and specifies the remedies available against them: The fiduciary is personally liable for damages ("to make good to [the] plan any losses to the plan resulting from each such breach"), for restitution ("to restore to [the] plan any profits of such fiduciary which have been made through use of assets of the plan by the fiduciary"), and for "such other equitable or remedial relief as the court may deem appropriate," including removal of the fiduciary. Section 502(a)(2)—the second of ERISA's "six carefully integrated civil enforcement provisions," Russell, supra,—allows the Secretary of Labor or any plan beneficiary, participant, or fiduciary to bring a civil action "for appropriate relief under section [409]."

The above described provisions are, however, limited by their terms to fiduciaries. The Court of Appeals decided that respondent was not a fiduciary, and petitioners do not contest that holding. Lacking equivalent provisions specifying nonfiduciaries as potential defendants, or damages as a remedy available against them, petitioners have turned to § 502(a)(3), which authorizes a plan beneficiary, participant, or fiduciary to bring a civil action:

> (A) to enjoin any act or practice which violates any provision of [ERISA] or the terms of the plan, or

(B) to obtain other appropriate equitable relief (i) to redress such violations or (ii) to enforce any provisions of [ERISA] or the terms of the plan. . . .

See also ERISA § 502(a)(5) (providing, in similar language, for civil suits by the Secretary based upon violation of ERISA provisions). Petitioners contend that requiring respondent to make the Kaiser plan whole for the losses resulting from its alleged knowing participation in the breach of fiduciary duty by the Kaiser plan's fiduciaries would constitute "other appropriate equitable relief" within the meaning of § 502(a)(3).

We note at the outset that it is far from clear that, even if this provision does make money damages available, it makes them available for the actions at issue here. It does not, after all, authorize "appropriate equitable relief" *at large*, but only "appropriate equitable relief" for the purpose of "redress[ing any] violations or . . . enforc[ing] any provisions" of ERISA or an ERISA plan. No one suggests that any term of the Kaiser plan has been violated, nor would any be enforced by the requested judgment. And while ERISA contains various provisions that can be read as imposing obligations upon nonfiduciaries, including actuaries,[4] no provision explicitly requires them to avoid participation (knowing or unknowing) in a fiduciary's breach of fiduciary duty. It is unlikely, moreover, that this was an oversight, since ERISA *does* explicitly impose "knowing participation" liability on cofiduciaries. See ERISA § 405(a). That limitation appears all the more deliberate in light of the fact that "knowing participation" liability on the part of *both* cotrustees and third persons was well established under the common law of trusts. See 3 A. Scott & W. Fratcher, Law of Trusts § 224.1, p. 404 (4th ed. 1988) (hereinafter Scott & Fratcher) (cotrustees); 4 Scott & Fratcher § 326, p. 291 (third persons). In *Russell* we emphasized our unwillingness to infer causes of action in the ERISA context, since that statute's carefully crafted and detailed enforcement scheme provides "strong evidence that Congress did not intend to authorize other remedies that it simply forgot to incorporate expressly." 473 U.S. at 146–47. All of this notwithstanding, petitioners and their amicus the United States seem to assume that respondent's alleged action (or inaction) violated ERISA, and address their arguments almost exclusively to what forms of relief are available. And respondent, despite considerable prompting by its amici, expressly disclaims reliance on this preliminary point. Thus, although we acknowledge the oddity of resolving a dispute over remedies where it is unclear that a remediable wrong has been alleged, we decide this case on

---

[4] For example, a person who provides services to a plan is a "party in interest," ERISA § 3(14)(B), and may not offer his services or engage in certain other transactions with the plan, ERISA § 406(a), for more than reasonable compensation, ERISA § 408(b)(2). See also ERISA § 103(d)(8) (annual reports must include certification by enrolled actuary); ERISA § 302(c)(3) (minimum funding standards for plan to be based on "reasonable" actuarial assumptions).

the narrow battlefield the parties have chosen, and reserve decision of that antecedent question.[5]

Petitioners maintain that the object of their suit is "appropriate *equitable* relief" under § 502(a)(3) (emphasis added). They do not, however, seek a remedy traditionally viewed as "equitable," such as injunction or restitution. (The Court of Appeals held that restitution was unavailable, and petitioners have not challenged that.) Although they often dance around the word, what petitioners in fact seek is nothing other than compensatory *damages*—monetary relief for all losses their plan sustained as a result of the alleged breach of fiduciary duties. Money damages are, of course, the classic form of *legal* relief. Curtis v. Loether, 415 U.S. 189, 196 (1974); Teamsters v. Terry, 494 U.S. 558, 570–71(1990); D. Dobbs, Remedies § 1.1, p. 3 (1973). And though we have never interpreted the precise phrase "other appropriate equitable relief," we have construed the similar language of Title VII of the Civil Rights Act of 1964 (before its 1991 amendments)—"any other equitable relief as the court deems appropriate," 42 U.S.C. § 2000e–5(g)—to preclude "awards for compensatory or punitive damages." United States v. Burke, 504 U.S. 229, 238 (1992).

Petitioners assert, however, that this reading of "equitable relief" fails to acknowledge ERISA's roots in the common law of trusts, see Firestone Tire & Rubber Co. v. Bruch, 489 U.S. 101, 110–11 (1989). "[A]lthough a beneficiary's action to recover losses resulting from a breach of duty superficially resembles an action at law for damages," the Solicitor General suggests, "such relief traditionally has been obtained in courts of equity" and therefore "is, by definition, 'equitable relief.' " It is true that, at common law, the courts of equity had exclusive jurisdiction over virtually all actions by beneficiaries for breach of trust. See Lessee of Smith v. McCann, 24 How. 398, 407, 16 L. Ed. 714 (1861); 3 Scott & Fratcher § 197, p. 188. It is also true that money damages were available in those courts against the trustee, see United States v. Mitchell, 463 U.S. 206, 226 (1983); G. Bogert & G. Bogert, Law of Trusts and Trustees § 701, p. 198 (rev. 2d ed. 1982) (hereinafter Bogert & Bogert), and against third persons who knowingly participated in the trustee's breach, see Seminole Nation v. United States, 316 U.S. 286, 296–97 (1942); Scott, Participation in a Breach of Trust, 34 Harv. L. Rev. 454 (1921).

At common law, however, there were many situations—not limited to those involving enforcement of a trust—in which an equity court could

---

[5]   The dissent expresses its certitude that "the statute clearly does not bar such a suit." That, of course, is not the issue. The issue is whether the statute affirmatively authorizes such a suit. To meet that requirement, it is not enough to observe that "trust beneficiaries clearly had such a remedy [against nonfiduciaries who actively assist in the fiduciary's breach] at common law." They had such a *remedy* because nonfiduciaries had a *duty* to the beneficiaries not to assist in the fiduciary's breach. A similar duty is set forth in ERISA; but as we have noted, only *some* common law "nonfiduciaries" are made subject to it, namely, those who fall within ERISA's artificial definition of "fiduciary."

"establish purely legal rights and grant legal remedies which would otherwise be beyond the scope of its authority." 1 J. Pomeroy, Equity Jurisprudence § 181, p. 257 (5th ed. 1941). The term "equitable relief" can assuredly mean, as petitioners and the Solicitor General would have it, whatever relief a court of equity is empowered to provide in the particular case at issue. But as indicated by the foregoing quotation—which speaks of "legal remedies" granted by an equity court—"equitable relief" can also refer to those categories of relief that were *typically* available in equity (such as injunction, mandamus, and restitution, but not compensatory damages). As memories of the divided bench, and familiarity with its technical refinements, recede further into the past, the former meaning becomes, perhaps, increasingly unlikely; but it remains a question of interpretation in each case which meaning is intended.

In the context of the present statute, we think there can be no doubt. Since *all* relief available for breach of trust could be obtained from a court of equity, limiting the sort of relief obtainable under § 502(a)(3) to "equitable relief" in the sense of "whatever relief a common-law court of equity could provide in such a case" would limit the relief *not at all*.[7] We will not read the statute to render the modifier superfluous. Regarding "equitable" relief in § 502(a)(3) to mean "all relief available for breach of trust at common law" would also require us either to give the term a different meaning there than it bears elsewhere in ERISA, or to deprive of all meaning the distinction Congress drew between "equitable" and "remedial" relief in § 409(a),[8] and between "equitable" and "legal" relief in the very same section of ERISA, see ERISA § 502(g)(2)(E); in the same subchapter of ERISA, see ERISA § 104(a)(5)(C); and in the ERISA subchapter dealing with the PBGC, see ERISA §§ 4003(e)(1); 4301(a)(1). Neither option is acceptable. The authority of courts to develop a "federal common law" under ERISA, see Firestone, 489 U.S. at 110, is not the authority to revise the text of the statute.

Petitioners point to ERISA § 502(*l*), which was added to the statute in 1989, see Omnibus Budget Reconciliation Act of 1989 (OBRA), Pub.L. 101–239, § 2101, 103 Stat. 2123, and provides as follows:

---

[7] The dissent argues that it would limit the relief by rendering punitive damages unavailable. The notion that concern about punitive damages motivated Congress is a classic example of projecting current attitudes upon the helpless past. Unlike the availability of money damages, which always has been a central concern of courts and legislatures in fashioning causes of action, the availability of punitive damages is a major issue today, but was not in 1974, when ERISA was enacted. That is particularly so for breach of trust cases. * * * But even if Congress had been concerned about "extracompensatory forms of relief," it would have been foolhardy to believe that excluding "legal" relief was the way to prohibit them (while still permitting *other* forms of monetary relief) in breach of trust cases. The dissent's confident assertion that punitive damages "were not available" in equity simply does not correspond to the state of the law when ERISA was enacted. * * *

[8] We agree with the dissent, that the distinction between "equitable" and "remedial" relief is artless, but do not agree that we are therefore free to consider it meaningless. "Equitable" relief must mean *something* less than *all* relief. Congress has, it may be noted, used the same language ("other equitable or remedial relief") elsewhere. See 5 U.S.C. § 8477(e)(1)(A).

(1) In the case of—

    (A) any breach of fiduciary responsibility under (or other violation of) part 4 by a fiduciary, or

    (B) any knowing participation in such a breach or violation by any other person,

the Secretary shall assess a civil penalty against such fiduciary or other person in an amount equal to 20 percent of the applicable recovery amount.

ERISA § 502(*l*)(1) (1988 ed., Supp. III).

The Secretary may waive or reduce this penalty if he believes that "the fiduciary or other person will [otherwise] not be able to restore all losses to the plan without severe financial hardship." ERISA § 502(*l*)(3)(B). "[A]pplicable recovery amount" is defined (in § 502(*l*)(2)(B)) as "any amount . . . ordered by a court to be paid by such fiduciary or other person to a plan or its participants or beneficiaries in a judicial proceeding instituted by the Secretary under [§§ 502](a)(2) or (a)(5)." It will be recalled that the latter subsection, § 502(a)(5), authorizes relief in actions by the Secretary on the same terms ("appropriate equitable relief") as in the private party actions authorized by § 502(a)(3). Petitioners argue that § 502(*l*) confirms that § 502(a)(5)—and hence, since it uses the same language, § 502(a)(3)—allows actions for damages, since otherwise there could be no "applicable recovery amount" against some "other person" than the fiduciary, and the Secretary would have no occasion to worry about whether any such "other person" would be able to "restore all losses to the plan" without financial hardship.

We certainly agree with petitioners that language used in one portion of a statute (§ 502(a)(3)) should be deemed to have the same meaning as the same language used elsewhere in the statute (§ 502(a)(5)). Indeed, we are even more zealous advocates of that principle than petitioners, who stop short of applying it directly to the term "equitable relief." We cannot agree, however, that § 502(*l*) establishes the existence of a damages remedy under § 502(a)(5)—i.e., that it is otherwise so inexplicable that we must give the term "equitable relief" the expansive meaning "all relief available for breach of trust." For even in its more limited sense, the "equitable relief" awardable under § 502(a)(5) includes restitution of ill-gotten plan assets or profits, providing an "applicable recovery amount" to use to calculate the penalty, which the Secretary may waive or reduce if paying it would prevent the restoration of those gains to the plan; and even assuming nonfiduciaries are not liable at all for knowing participation in a fiduciary's breach of duty, cofiduciaries expressly are, see ERISA § 405(a), so there are some "other person[s]" than fiduciaries-in-breach liable under § 502(*l*)(1)(B). These applications of § 502(*l*) give it meaning and scope without resort to the strange interpretation of "equitable relief" in § 502(a)(3) that petitioners propose. The Secretary's initial interpretation of § 502(*l*) accords with our view. The prologue of the proposed regulation implementing § 502(*l*), to be codified at 29 CFR § 2560.502l–1, states that when a court awards "equitable relief"—as opposed to "monetary damages"—a § 502(*l*) penalty will be assessed only if the award involves the transfer to the plan of money or property. 55 Fed. Reg. 25288, 25289, and n.9 (1990).

In the last analysis, petitioners and the United States ask us to give a strained interpretation to § 502(a)(3) in order to achieve the "purpose of ERISA to protect plan participants and beneficiaries." They note, as we have, that before ERISA nonfiduciaries were generally liable under state trust law for damages resulting from knowing participation in a trustees's breach of duty, and they assert that such actions are now preempted by ERISA's broad preemption clause, ERISA § 514(a), see Ingersoll-Rand Co. v. McClendon, 498 U.S. 133, 139–40 (1990). Thus, they contend, our construction of § 502(a)(3) leaves beneficiaries like petitioners with *less* protection than existed before ERISA, contradicting ERISA's basic goal of "promot[ing] the interests of employees and their beneficiaries in employee benefit plans," Shaw v. Delta Air Lines, Inc., 463 U.S. 85, 90 (1983). See Firestone Tire & Rubber Co. v. Bruch, 489 U.S. at 114.

Even assuming (without deciding) that petitioners are correct about the preemption of previously available state court actions, vague notions of a statute's "basic purpose" are nonetheless inadequate to overcome the words of its text regarding the *specific* issue under consideration. See Pension Benefit Guaranty Corporation v. LTV Corp., 496 U.S. 633, 646–47 (1990). This is especially true with legislation such as ERISA, an enormously complex and detailed statute that resolved innumerable disputes between powerful competing interests—not all in favor of potential plaintiffs. See, e.g., Pilot Life Ins. Co. v. Dedeaux, 481 U.S. 41, 54–56 (1987). The text that we have described is certainly not nonsensical; it allocates liability for plan-related misdeeds in reasonable proportion to respective actors' power to control and prevent the misdeeds. Under traditional trust law, although a beneficiary could obtain damages from third persons for knowing participation in a trustee's breach of fiduciary duties, only the trustee had fiduciary duties. See 1 Scott & Fratcher § 2.5, p. 43. ERISA, however, defines "fiduciary" not in terms of formal trusteeship, but in *functional* terms of control and authority over the plan, see ERISA § 3(21)(A), thus expanding the universe of persons subject to fiduciary duties—and to damages—under § 409(a). Professional service providers such as actuaries become liable for damages when they cross the line from advisor to fiduciary; must disgorge assets and profits obtained through participation as parties-in-interest in transactions prohibited by § 406, and pay related civil penalties, see ERISA § 502(i), or excise taxes, see 26 U.S.C. § 4975; and (assuming nonfiduciaries can be sued under § 502(a)(3)) may be enjoined from participating in a fiduciary's breaches, compelled to make restitution, and subjected to other equitable decrees. All that ERISA has eliminated, on these assumptions, is the common law's joint and several liability, for *all* direct and consequential damages suffered by the plan, on the part of persons who had no real power to control what the plan did. Exposure to that sort of liability would impose high insurance costs upon persons who regularly deal with and offer advice to ERISA plans, and hence upon ERISA plans themselves. There is, in other words, a "tension between the primary [ERISA] goal of benefiting employees and the subsidiary goal of containing pension costs." Alessi v. Raybestos-Manhattan, Inc., 451 U.S. 504, 515 (1981); see also Russell, 473 U.S. at 148 n.17. We will not attempt to adjust the balance between those competing goals that the text adopted by Congress has struck.

* * *

The judgment of the Court of Appeals is Affirmed.

JUSTICE WHITE, with whom THE CHIEF JUSTICE, JUSTICE STEVENS and JUSTICE O'CONNOR join, dissenting.

The majority candidly acknowledges that it is plausible to interpret the phrase "appropriate equitable relief" as used in § 502(a)(3) at least standing alone, as meaning that relief which was available in the courts of equity for a breach of trust. The majority also acknowledges that the relief petitioners seek here—a compensatory monetary award—*was* available in the equity courts under the common law of trusts, not only against trustees for breach of duty, but also against nonfiduciaries knowingly participating in a breach of trust. Finally, there can be no dispute that ERISA was grounded in this common law experience and that "we are [to be] guided by principles of trust law" in construing the terms of the statute. Firestone Tire & Rubber Co. v. Bruch, 489 U.S. 101, 111 (1989). Nevertheless, the majority today holds that in enacting ERISA Congress stripped ERISA trust beneficiaries of a remedy against trustees and third parties that they enjoyed in the equity courts under common law. Although it is assumed that a cause of action against a third party such as respondent is provided by ERISA, the remedies available are limited to the "traditional" equitable remedies, such as injunction and restitution, and do not include compensatory damages—"the classic form of *legal* relief." Because I do not believe that the statutory language requires this result and because we have elsewhere recognized the anomaly of construing ERISA in a way that "would afford *less* protection to employees and their beneficiaries than they enjoyed before ERISA was enacted," Firestone, 489 U.S. at 114, I must dissent.

I

Concerned that many pension plans were being corruptly or ineptly mismanaged and that American workers were losing their financial security in retirement as a result, Congress in 1974 enacted ERISA, "declar[ing] [it] to be the policy of [the statute] to protect . . . the interests of participants in employee benefit plans and their beneficiaries, by requiring the disclosure and reporting to participants and beneficiaries of financial and other information with respect [to the plans], by establishing standards of conduct, responsibility, and obligation for fiduciaries of employee benefit plans, and by providing for appropriate remedies, sanctions, and ready access to the Federal courts." ERISA § 2(b).

As we have noted previously, "ERISA's legislative history confirms that the Act's fiduciary responsibility provisions codif[y] and mak[e] applicable to [ERISA] fiduciaries certain principles developed in the evolution of the law of trusts'." Firestone, 489 U.S. at 110 (quoting H.R. Rep. No. 93–533, p. 11 (1973)). ERISA, we have explained, "abounds with the language and terminology of trust law" and must be construed against the background of the common law of trusts. Firestone, 489 U.S. at 110–11; see also Central States, Southeast and Southwest Areas Pension Fund v. Central Transport, Inc., 472 U.S. 559, 570–71(1985). Indeed, absent some express statutory departure-such as ERISA's broader definition of a responsible "fiduciary"—Congress intended that the courts would look to the settled experience of the common law in giving shape to a "federal common law of rights and obligations under ERISA-regulated plans." Firestone, 489 U.S. at 110; see also H.R. Rep. No. 93–533, supra, at 11; S. Rep. No. 93–127, p. 29 (1973).

Accordingly, it is to the common law of trusts that we must look in construing the scope of the "appropriate equitable relief" for breaches of trust contemplated by § 502(a)(3).[1] As the majority notes, at common law

---

[1] As an initial matter, the majority expresses some uncertainty about whether § 502(a)(3) affords a cause of action and *any* sort of remedy against nonfiduciaries who participate in a fiduciary's breach of duty under the statute. In my view, however, the statute clearly does not bar such a suit. Section 502(a)(3) gives a cause of action to any participant, beneficiary, or fiduciary of an ERISA governed plan "to redress . . . violations" of the statute. There can be no dispute that when an ERISA fiduciary breaches his or her duty of care in managing the plan, there has been a violation of the statute. See ERISA § 404. The only question then is whether the remedies provided by § 502(a)(3) "to redress such [a] violatio[n]" must stop with the breaching fiduciary or may extend to nonfiduciaries who actively assist in the fiduciary's breach. Section 502(a)(3) does not expressly provide for such a limitation and it does not seem appropriate to import one given that trust beneficiaries clearly had such a remedy at common law and that ERISA is grounded in that common law and was intended, above all, to protect the interests of beneficiaries. Moreover, the amendment of the statute in 1989, adding § 502(*l*), seems clearly to reflect Congress' understanding that ERISA provides such a remedy. As the majority notes, § 502(*l*) empowers the Secretary of Labor to assess a civil penalty against nonfiduciaries who "knowing[ly] participat[e]" in a fiduciary's breach of trust. ERISA § 502(*l*)(1)(B). The subsection further provides that this penalty shall be "equal to 20 percent of the applicable recovery amount" obtained from the nonfiduciary in a proceeding under § 502(a)(5), which provides a cause of action to the Secretary that parallels that provided to beneficiaries under § 502(a)(3).

the courts of equity were the predominant forum for beneficiaries' claims arising from a breach of trust. These courts were not, however, the exclusive forum. In some instances, there was jurisdiction both in law and in equity and it was generally (although not universally) acknowledged that the beneficiary could elect between her legal and equitable remedies. Indeed, the Restatement of Trusts sets out in separate, successive sections the "legal" and "equitable" remedies available to beneficiaries under the common law of trusts. See Restatement (Second) of Trusts §§ 198; 199 (1959).

The traditional "equitable remedies" available to a trust beneficiary included compensatory damages. Equity "endeavor[ed] as far as possible to replace the parties in the same situation as they would have been in, if no breach of trust had been committed." J. Hill, Trustees *522; see also J. Tiffany & E. Bullard, Law of Trusts and Trustees 585–86 (1862). This included, where necessary, the payment of a monetary award to make the victims of the breach whole.

Given this history, it is entirely reasonable in my view to construe § 502(a)(3)'s reference to "appropriate equitable relief" to encompass what was equity's routine remedy for such breaches—a compensatory monetary award calculated to make the victims whole, a remedy that was available against both fiduciaries and participating nonfiduciaries. Construing the statute in this manner also avoids the anomaly of interpreting ERISA so as to leave those Congress set out to protect—the participants in ERISA-governed plans and their beneficiaries—with "less protection . . . than they enjoyed before ERISA was enacted." Firestone, 489 U.S. at 114. Indeed, this is precisely how four Justices of this Court read § 502(a)(3)'s reference to "appropriate equitable relief" in *Russell*. See 473 U.S., at 154, and n.10 (Brennan, J., joined by White, Marshall, and Blackmun, JJ., concurring in judgment).

II

The majority, however, struggles to find on the face of the statute evidence that § 502(a)(3) is to be more narrowly construed. First, it observes that ERISA elsewhere uses the terms "remedial relief" and "legal relief" and reasons that Congress must therefore have intended to differentiate between these concepts and "equitable relief." Second, it is noted that the crucial language of § 502(a)(3) describes the available relief as *equitable* relief. It is then asserted that "[s]ince *all* relief available for breach of trust could be obtained from a court of equity, limiting the sort of relief obtainable under § 502(a)(3) to 'equitable relief' in the sense of

---

This provision clearly contemplates that some remedy may be had under § 502(a)(5)—and, by necessary implication, under § 502(a)(3)—against nonfiduciaries for "knowing participation" in a fiduciary's "breach of fiduciary responsibilit[ies]." Given that this understanding accords with well-established common law trust principles undergirding ERISA and that it is also compatible with the language of § 502(a)(3), I see no basis for doubting the validity of petitioners' cause of action.

'whatever relief a common law court of equity could provide in such a case' would limit the relief *not at all*," rendering Congress' imposition of the modifier "equitable" a nullity. Searching for some way in which to give "appropriate equitable relief" a limiting effect, the majority feels compelled to read the phrase as encompassing only "those categories of relief that were *typically* available" in the broad run of equity cases, without regard to the particular equitable remedies available in trust cases. This would include injunction and restitution, for example, but not money damages. As I see it, however, the words "appropriate equitable relief" are no more than descriptive and simply refer to all remedies available in equity under the common law of trusts, whether or not they were or are the exclusive remedies for breach of trust.

I disagree with the majority's inference that by using the term "legal ... relief" elsewhere in ERISA, Congress demonstrated a considered judgment to constrict the relief available under § 502(a)(3). To be sure, § 502(g)(2)(E) of the statute empowers courts to award appropriate "legal or equitable relief" where a fiduciary successfully sues an employer for failing to make required contributions to a multiemployer plan. ERISA § 502(g)(2)(E). Likewise, § 104(a)(5)(C) authorizes the Secretary of Labor to bring "a civil action for such legal or equitable relief as may be appropriate" to force the administrator of an employee benefit plan to file certain plan documents with the Secretary. ERISA § 104(a)(5)(C). And, finally, §§ 4003(e)(1) and 4301(a)(1) of the statute, also cited by the majority, empower courts to dispense "appropriate relief, legal or equitable or both," in actions brought by the Pension Benefit Guaranty Corporation (PBGC) or by plan fiduciaries, participants, or beneficiaries with respect to the peculiar statutory duties relating to the PBGC. Significantly, however, none of the causes of action described in these sections—relating to the financing of multiemployer plans, administrative filing requirements, and the PBGC—had any discernible analogue in the common law of trusts. Accordingly, there being no common law tradition either in law or in equity to which Congress might direct the courts, it is not at all surprising that Congress would refer to both legal and equitable relief in making clear that the courts are free to craft whatever relief is most appropriate. It seems to me a treacherous leap to draw from these sections a congressional intention to foreclose compensatory monetary awards under § 502(a)(3) notwithstanding that such awards had always been considered "appropriate equitable relief" for breach of trust at common law.[4]

---

[4] Moreover, if the text of the statute reflects Congress' careful differentiation between "legal" and "equitable" relief, as the majority posits, it presumably must also reflect a careful differentiation between "equitable" and "remedial" relief and, for that matter, between "legal" and "remedial" relief. See ERISA § 409(a) (breaching fiduciary "shall be subject to such other equitable or remedial relief as the court may deem appropriate"). What limiting principle Congress could have intended to convey by this latter term I cannot readily imagine. "Remedial," after all, simply means "intended as a remedy," Webster's Ninth New Collegiate Dictionary 996

Even accepting, however, that "equitable" relief is to be distinguished from "legal" relief under the statute, the majority is wrong in supposing that the former concept swallows the latter if § 502(a)(3)'s reference to "appropriate equitable relief" is understood to encompass those remedies that were traditionally available in the equity courts for breach of trust. The fact of the matter is that not all forms of relief were available in the common law courts of equity for a breach of trust. Although the equity courts could award monetary relief to make the victim of a breach of trust whole, extracompensatory forms of relief, such as punitive damages, were not available. As this Court has long recognized, courts of equity would not—absent some express statutory authorization—enforce penalties or award punitive damages. See Tull v. United States, 481 U.S. 412, 422, and n.7 (1987); Stevens v. Gladding, 17 How. 447, 454–55 (1855); Livingston v. Woodworth, 15 How. 546, 559–60 (1854). As Justice Kennedy has observed, this limitation on equitable relief applied in the trust context as well, where plaintiffs could recover compensatory monetary relief for a breach of trust, but not punitive or exemplary damages. See Teamsters v. Terry, 494 U.S. 558, 587 (1990) (dissenting opinion).[5]

By contrast, punitive damages were among the "legal remedies" available in common law trust cases. In those trust cases that historically could have been brought as actions at law—such as where a trustee is under an immediate and unconditional duty to pay over funds to a beneficiary—it has been acknowledged that the beneficiary may recover punitive as well as compensatory damages. Moreover, while the majority of courts adhere to the view that equity courts, even in trust cases, cannot award punitive damages, a number of courts in more recent decades have drawn upon their "legal" powers to award punitive damages even in cases that historically could have been brought only in equity. While

---

(1983), and "relief" is commonly understood to be a synonym for "remedy," id. at 995. At the very least, Congress' apparent imprecision in this regard undermines my confidence in the strong inferences drawn by the majority from Congress' varying phraseology concerning relief under ERISA.

[5]   Justice Kennedy's observation is well grounded in legal history. In crafting a remedy for a breach of trust the exclusive aim of the common law equity courts was to make the victim whole, "endeavor[ing] as far as possible to replace the parties in the same situation as they would have been in, if no breach of trust had been committed." Historically, punitive damages were unavailable in any equitable action on the theory that "the Court of Chancery as the Equity Court is a court of conscience and will permit only what is just and right with no element of vengeance." Thus, even "where, in equitable actions, it becomes necessary to award damages, only compensatory damages should be allowed."

The majority denigrates this traditional rule by citing to Professor Dobbs' 1973 treatise on remedies. That treatise noted a "modern" trend among some courts (on the eve of ERISA's enactment) to allow punitive damages in equity cases, but it also noted that the majority rule remained otherwise. Moreover, the trend Professor Dobbs identified was driven in large part by the "modern" merger of law and equity and by the consequent belief that there is no longer any reason to disallow "legal" remedies in what traditionally were "equitable" actions. Accordingly, the majority's observation in no way undermines the validity of the traditional rule—well ensconced at the time of ERISA's enactment—that punitive damages were not an appropriate *equitable* remedy, even in trust cases.

acknowledging the traditional bar against such relief in equity, these courts have concluded that the merger of law and equity authorizes modern courts to draw upon both legal and equitable powers in crafting an appropriate remedy for a breach of trust. Because some forms of "legal" relief in trust cases were thus not available at equity, limiting the scope of relief under § 502(a)(3) to the sort of relief historically provided by the equity courts for a breach of trust provides a meaningful limitation and, if one is needed, a basis for distinguishing "equitable" from "legal" relief. Accordingly, the statutory text does not compel the majority's rejection of the reading of "appropriate equitable relief" advanced by petitioners and the Solicitor General—a reading that the majority acknowledges is otherwise plausible.[7]

III

Although the trust beneficiary historically had an equitable suit for damages against a fiduciary for breach of trust, as well as against a participating nonfiduciary, the majority today construes § 502(a)(3) as not affording such a remedy against any fiduciary or participating third party on the ground that damages are not "appropriate equitable relief." The majority's conclusion, as I see it, rests on transparently insufficient grounds. The text of the statute supports a reading of § 502(a)(3) that would permit a court to award compensatory monetary relief where necessary to make an ERISA beneficiary whole for a breach of trust. Such a reading would accord with the established equitable remedies available under the common law of trusts, to which Congress has directed us in construing ERISA, and with Congress' primary goal in enacting the statute, the protection of beneficiaries' financial security against corrupt or inept plan mismanagement. Finally, such a reading would avoid the perverse and, in this case, entirely needless result of construing ERISA so as to *deprive* beneficiaries of remedies they enjoyed prior to the statute's enactment. For these reasons, I respectfully dissent.

NOTES AND QUESTIONS

1. *Equitable Relief Under* Mertens. The precise question before the Supreme Court in *Mertens* was whether a remedy of money damages was available against the actuary, a nonfiduciary, who knowingly participated in a fiduciary's breach of duty under ERISA. The plan participants and the Solicitor General in *Mertens* argued that, given ERISA's basis in the common law of trusts, equitable relief under Section 502(a)(3) should consist of all

---

[7] The majority faults "[t]he notion that concern about punitive damages motivated Congress" in drafting ERISA on the grounds that the availability of punitive damages was not "a major issue" in 1974. Neither, of course, is there anything to suggest that the availability of *compensatory* damages was a "major issue" in 1974, although the majority does not hesitate to attribute this concern to the 93d Congress. In any event, it seems to me considerably less fanciful to suppose that Congress was motivated by a desire to limit the availability of punitive damages than that it was moved by a desire to take from the statute's intended beneficiaries their traditional and possibly their only means of make whole relief.

relief available for breach of a common law trust that could have been obtained in a court of equity. Such relief historically included money damages to remedy a breach of trust. The majority in *Mertens* rejected this argument because it failed to limit, and thereby differentiate, equitable relief under Section 502(a)(3) from the "legal" and "remedial" relief available under other sections of ERISA. *Mertens* today stands for the principle that when a claim is brought against a non-fiduciary, the scope of equitable relief under Section 502(a)(3) is limited to "those categories of relief that were *typically* available in equity (such as injunction, mandamus, and restitution)" and excludes monetary relief because "[m]oney damages are, of course, the classic form of *legal* relief." Mertens, 508 U.S. at 255–56 (emphasis in original).

In the aftermath of *Mertens*, many lower federal courts have read *Mertens* as holding that injunction, mandamus, and restitution were the *only* remedies available under Section 502(a)(3), irrespective of the nature of the plaintiff's claim and requested remedy or the status of the defendant. E.g., Armstrong v. Jefferson Smurfit Corp., 30 F.3d 11, 13 (1st Cir. 1994); Buckley Dement v. Travelers Plan Admin., 39 F.3d 784, 788 (7th Cir. 1994); Slice v. Sons of Norway, 34 F.3d 630, 633 (8th Cir. 1994); Hein v. F.D.I.C., 88 F.3d 210, 224 (3d Cir. 1996); Watkins v. Westinghouse Hanford Co. 12 F.3d 1517, 1527–28 (9th Cir. 1993). In addition, the lower federal courts struggled with the concept of "equitable" restitution. Judge Richard Posner of the Seventh Circuit Court of Appeals pointedly criticized the concept of restitution as articulated in *Mertens*, calling it "an unfortunate and surely unintended dictum because restitution is *both* a legal *and* an equitable remedy." Health Cost Controls of Illinois v. Washington, 187 F.3d 703, 710 (7th Cir. 1999) (emphasis in original).

2. *Questioning* Mertens' *Distinction Between Legal and Equitable Relief.* The majority opinion in *Mertens* held that Congress must have intended the reference to "equitable relief" to limit the remedies available under Section 502(a)(3) to those remedies that historically were awarded by a court of equity in the bygone days of a divided bench. Justice White, writing for the four dissenting justices in *Mertens,* disagreed with the majority's assumption that Congress must have purposefully used the phrase "equitable relief" to distinguish, and thereby limit, the remedies available under Section 502(a)(3). Justice White instead proposed an alternative interpretation of the statutory language, namely that Congress intended the distinction between equitable and legal relief to exclude *punitive* damages from the scope of equitable relief available under Section 502(a)(3). 508 U.S. at 270–73.

Justice White's alternative interpretation has been corroborated by the eyewitness account of the late Michael S. Gordon, who was appointed by Senator Jacob Javits to serve as minority counsel to the Senate Committee on Labor and Public Welfare from 1970 to 1975, the period during which ERISA was formulated and enacted. In a letter written to the editors of the *ERISA Litigation Reporter*, Mr. Gordon stated that:

> In *Mertens*, Scalia derides the notion that Congress wrote Section 502(a) the way it did because it was concerned about

punitive damages. He is wrong. In *Russell*, Stevens notes that the Senate version of ERISA referred to both legal and equitable remedies, but the last version passed by the House and accepted in the ERISA Conference deleted the reference to legal remedies, the implication being—since ERISA is a "comprehensive and reticulated" statute—that punitive damages were being excluded. He is also wrong; the matter was being fudged. Why was the matter being fudged? * * *

Certain key legislators in both the Senate and House felt that if ERISA automatically provided access to punitive damages relief, it would send a signal that Congress thought the [Age Discrimination in Employment Act] should provide the same relief and that Congress would overturn any court decision that ruled otherwise. Of course, that possibility would create another cross for ERISA to bear as opponents of ERISA were, as we know, looking for any opportunity at hand to stop the bill's enactment. This meant that the references in Section 502(a) to "legal" relief had to be deleted.

However, from the viewpoint of Senator Javits (and yours truly), the deletion of "legal" relief did not mean there would never be access to punitive damages under ERISA. In New York, then regarded as the most important jurisdiction in terms of state jurisprudential leadership, the merger of law and equity had proceeded quite rapidly and the highest New York appellate court had ruled that punitive damages could be awarded by a court of equity in appropriate cases. The New York position could be harmonized with the political imperative of avoiding embroiling the ERISA conferees in yet another potentially ruinous dispute. * * * [To] those who understood the trend toward the law-equity merger, it meant that they would not be totally abandoning their desire to preserve access to punitive damages relief; it only meant that access to such relief would be provided infrequently and only under the most compelling circumstances. There was nothing wrong with that. Even with Scalia's views on legislative history and the role of staff, none of the foregoing has any official standing or legal significance. But it does unofficially reinforce the suspicion that Scalia is off the mark in holding fast to the myth that the ERISA authors only intended to enact "typical" equitable remedies and that they rejected the law-equity merger process, then at its peak.

Robert N. Eccles and David E. Gordon, *Great-West Life & Annuity Ins. Co. v. Knudson: Supreme Court Announces That It Was Not Kidding in Mertens v. Hewitt Associates*, 9 ERISA LITIG. REP. (Glasser Legal Works) no. 6, at 6–8 (Feb. 2002) (citations omitted).

3. Mertens *and Department of Labor Claims Under Section 502(a)(5).* The Department of Labor has argued that *Mertens* should be limited to claims brought against nonfiduciaries by private parties under Section 502(a)(3), and should not apply to suits brought against nonfiduciaries by the

Department of Labor under Section 502(a)(5), which contains language identical to the remedies authorized by Section 502(a)(3). The lower federal courts have rejected this argument and held that the *Mertens* definition of equitable relief applies with equal force to suits brought by the Department of Labor under Section 502(a)(5). See Reich v. Rowe, 20 F.3d 25, 28–29 (1st Cir. 1994); Reich v. Continental Cas. Co., 33 F.3d 754, 757–58 (7th Cir. 1994).

4. *Competing Public Policies in* Mertens. The public policy basis for the majority's decision in *Mertens* was that Congress had purposely restructured the common law by expanding the concept of a fiduciary in exchange for limiting the common law liability of nonfiduciaries under the statute. The majority perceived this reallocation of liability as a policy compromise designed to resolve the "tension between the primary [ERISA] goal of benefitting employees and the subsidiary goal of containing pension costs" by reducing the liability of those persons who assist the employer in operating its plan. 508 U.S. at 262–63. Given this policy compromise, the majority in *Mertens* was unwilling to award a remedy against a nonfiduciary that effectively would "adjust the balance between those competing goals that the text adopted by Congress has struck." Id. at 263.

Do you think *Mertens* strikes the correct balance between the competing public policies that underlie ERISA? Why or why not?

Although technically dicta in the opinion, the lower federal courts subsequently read *Mertens* as "go[ing] out of its way to throw cold water on the idea of an implied liability of nonfiduciaries for knowing participation in fiduciaries' misconduct." Reich v. Continental Cas. Co., 33 F.3d 754, 757–58 (7th Cir. 1994). In the wake of *Mertens*, conventional wisdom held that the combined effect of ERISA's broad preemption of state law claims, together with the Supreme Court's pointed comments at the beginning of the *Mertens* opinion questioning whether ERISA even permitted a claim against a nonfiduciary, effectively insulated nonfiduciary plan service providers from liability under both state and federal law. The Supreme Court's subsequent decision in *Harris Trust & Savings Bank v. Salomon Smith Barney* makes clear that Section 502(a)(3) *does* permit a claim against a nonfiduciary who participates in a prohibited transaction involving plan assets.

HARRIS TRUST & SAVINGS BANK V. SALOMON SMITH BARNEY

United States Supreme Court, 2000.
530 U.S. 238, 120 S.Ct. 2180, 147 L.Ed.2d 187.

JUSTICE THOMAS delivered the opinion of the Court.

Section 406(a) of the Employee Retirement Income Security Act of 1974 (ERISA) bars a fiduciary of an employee benefit plan from causing the plan to engage in certain transactions with a "party in interest." Section 502(a)(3) authorizes a "participant, beneficiary, or fiduciary" of a plan to bring a civil action to obtain "appropriate equitable relief" to redress violations of ERISA Title I. The question is whether that authorization extends to a suit against a nonfiduciary "party in interest" to a transaction barred by § 406(a). We hold that it does.

I

Responding to deficiencies in prior law regulating transactions by plan fiduciaries, Congress enacted ERISA § 406(a)(1), which supplements the fiduciary's general duty of loyalty to the plan's beneficiaries, ERISA § 404(a), by categorically barring certain transactions deemed "likely to injure the pension plan," Commissioner v. Keystone Consol. Indus., Inc., 508 U.S. 152, 160 (1993). Section 406(a)(1) provides, among other things, that "[a] fiduciary with respect to a plan shall not cause the plan to engage in a transaction, if he knows or should know that such transaction constitutes a direct or indirect . . . sale or exchange . . . of any property between the plan and a party in interest." Congress defined "party in interest" to encompass those entities that a fiduciary might be inclined to favor at the expense of the plan's beneficiaries. See ERISA § 3(14). Section 406's prohibitions are subject to both statutory and regulatory exemptions. See ERISA §§ 408(a); (b).

This case comes to us on the assumption that an ERISA pension plan (the Ameritech Pension Trust (APT)) and a party in interest (respondent Salomon Smith Barney (Salomon)) entered into a transaction prohibited by § 406(a) and not exempted by § 408. APT provides pension benefits to employees and retirees of Ameritech Corporation and its subsidiaries and affiliates. Salomon, during the late 1980's, provided broker-dealer services to APT, executing nondiscretionary equity trades at the direction of APT's fiduciaries, thus qualifying itself (we assume) as a "party in interest." See ERISA § 3(14)(B) (defining "party in interest" as "a person providing services to [an employee benefit] plan"). During the same period, Salomon sold interests in several motel properties to APT for nearly $21 million. APT's purchase of the motel interests was directed by National Investment Services of America (NISA), an investment manager to which Ameritech had delegated investment discretion over a portion of the plan's assets, and hence a fiduciary of APT, see ERISA § 3(21)(A)(i).

This litigation arose when APT's fiduciaries—its trustee, petitioner Harris Trust and Savings Bank, and its administrator, petitioner Ameritech Corporation—discovered that the motel interests were nearly worthless. Petitioners maintain that the interests had been worthless all along; Salomon asserts, to the contrary, that the interests declined in value due to a downturn in the motel industry. Whatever the true cause, petitioners sued Salomon in 1992 under § 502(a)(3), which authorizes a "participant, beneficiary, or fiduciary" to bring a civil action "to enjoin any act or practice which violates any provision of [ERISA Title I] . . . or . . . to obtain other appropriate equitable relief . . . to redress such violations."

Petitioners claimed, among other things, that NISA, as plan fiduciary, had caused the plan to engage in a per se prohibited transaction under § 406(a) in purchasing the motel interests from Salomon, and that Salomon was liable on account of its participation in the transaction as a nonfiduciary party in interest. Specifically, petitioners pointed to § 406(a)(1)(A), which prohibits a "sale or exchange . . . of any property between the plan and a party in interest," and § 406(a)(1)(D), which prohibits a "transfer to . . . a party in interest . . . of any assets of the plan." Petitioners sought rescission of the transaction, restitution from Salomon of the purchase price with interest, and disgorgement of Salomon's profits made from use of the plan assets transferred to it.

Salomon moved for summary judgment, arguing that § 502(a)(3), when used to remedy a transaction prohibited by § 406(a), authorizes a suit only against the party expressly constrained by § 406(a)—the fiduciary who caused the plan to enter the transaction—and not against the counterparty to the transaction. See ERISA § 406(a)(1) ("A *fiduciary* with respect to a plan shall not cause the plan to engage in a transaction, if he knows or should know that such transaction . . ." (emphasis added)). The District Court denied the motion, holding that ERISA does provide a private cause of action against nonfiduciaries who participate in a prohibited transaction, but granted Salomon's subsequent motion for certification of the issue for interlocutory appeal under 28 U.S.C. § 1292(b).

The Court of Appeals for the Seventh Circuit reversed. 184 F.3d 646 (1999). It began with the observation that § 406(a), by its terms and like several of its neighboring provisions, e.g., ERISA § 404, governs only the conduct of fiduciaries, not of counterparties or other nonfiduciaries. See id. at 650. The court next posited that "where ERISA does not expressly impose a duty, there can be no cause of action," id., relying upon dictum in our decision in *Mertens v. Hewitt Associates*, 508 U.S. 248, 254 (1993), that § 502(a)(3) does not provide a private cause of action against a nonfiduciary for knowing participation in a fiduciary's breach of duty. The Seventh Circuit saw no distinction between the *Mertens* situation (involving § 404) and the instant case (involving § 406), explaining that neither section expressly imposes a duty on nonfiduciaries. Finally, in the Seventh Circuit's view, Congress' decision to authorize the Secretary of Labor to impose a civil penalty on a nonfiduciary "party in interest" to a § 406 transaction, see ERISA § 502(i), simply confirms that Congress deliberately selected one enforcement tool (a civil penalty imposed by the Secretary) instead of another (a civil action under § 502(a)(3)). Accordingly, the Seventh Circuit held that a nonfiduciary cannot be liable under § 502(a)(3) for participating in a § 406 transaction and entered summary judgment in favor of Salomon.

In doing so, the Seventh Circuit departed from the uniform position of the Courts of Appeals that § 502(a)(3)—and the similarly worded § 502(a)(5), which authorizes civil actions by the Secretary—does authorize a civil action against a nonfiduciary who participates in a transaction prohibited by § 406(a)(1). We granted certiorari, and now reverse.

II

We agree with the Seventh Circuit's and Salomon's interpretation of § 406(a). They rightly note that § 406(a) imposes a duty only on the fiduciary that causes the plan to engage in the transaction. See ERISA § 406(a)(1) ("A *fiduciary* with respect to a plan shall not cause the plan to engage in a transaction, if he knows or should know that such transaction . . ." (emphasis added)). We reject, however, the Seventh Circuit's and Salomon's conclusion that, absent a substantive provision of ERISA expressly imposing a duty upon a nonfiduciary party in interest, the nonfiduciary party may not be held liable under § 502(a)(3), one of ERISA's remedial provisions. Petitioners contend, and we agree, that § 502(a)(3) itself imposes certain duties, and therefore that liability under that provision does not depend on whether ERISA's substantive provisions impose a specific duty on the party being sued.

Section 502(a) provides:

A civil action may be brought—

> . . .
>
> (3) by a participant, beneficiary, or fiduciary (A) to enjoin any act or practice which violates any provision of [ERISA Title I] or the terms of the plan, or (B) to obtain other appropriate equitable relief (i) to redress such violations or (ii) to enforce any provisions of this title or the terms of the plan.

This language, to be sure, "does not . . . authorize 'appropriate equitable relief' *at large,* but only 'appropriate equitable relief' for the purpose of 'redress[ing any] violations or . . . enforc[ing] any provisions' of ERISA or an ERISA plan." Peacock v. Thomas, 516 U.S. 349, 353 (1996) (quoting Mertens, 508 U.S. at 253). But § 502(a)(3) admits of no limit (aside from the "appropriate equitable relief" caveat, which we address infra) on the universe of possible defendants. Indeed, § 502(a)(3) makes no mention at all of which parties may be proper defendants—the focus, instead, is on redressing the "*act or practice* which violates any provision of [ERISA Title I]." ERISA § 502(a)(3) (emphasis added). Other provisions of ERISA, by contrast, do expressly address who may be a defendant. See, e.g.,

§ 409(a) (stating that "*[a]ny person who is a fiduciary* with respect to a plan who breaches any of the responsibilities, obligations, or duties imposed upon fiduciaries by this subchapter shall be personally liable" (emphasis added)); ERISA § 502(*l*) (authorizing imposition of civil penalties only against a "fiduciary" who violates part 4 of Title I or "any other person" who knowingly participates in such a violation). And § 502(a) itself demonstrates Congress' care in delineating the universe of *plaintiffs* who may bring certain civil actions. See, e.g., § 502(a)(3) ("A civil action may be brought . . . *by a participant, beneficiary, or fiduciary* . . ." (emphasis added)); ERISA § 502(a)(5) ("A civil action may be brought . . . *by the Secretary* . . ." (emphasis added)).

In light of Congress' precision in these respects, we would ordinarily assume that Congress' failure to specify proper defendants in § 502(a)(3) was intentional. But ERISA's "comprehensive and reticulated" scheme warrants a cautious approach to inferring remedies not expressly authorized by the text, Massachusetts Mut. Life Ins. Co. v. Russell, 473 U.S. 134, 146 (1985), especially given the alternative and intuitively appealing interpretation, urged by Salomon, that § 502(a)(3) authorizes suits only against defendants upon whom a duty is imposed by ERISA's substantive provisions. In this case, however, § 502(*l*) resolves the matter—it compels the conclusion that defendant status under § 502(a)(3) may arise from duties imposed by § 502(a)(3) itself, and hence does not turn on whether the defendant is expressly subject to a duty under one of ERISA's substantive provisions.

Section 502(*l*) provides in relevant part:

(1) In the case of—

> (A) any breach of fiduciary responsibility under (or other violation of) part 4 of this subtitle by a fiduciary, or
>
> (B) any knowing participation in such a breach or violation by any other person,

the Secretary shall assess a civil penalty against such fiduciary or other person in an amount equal to 20 percent of the applicable recovery amount.

(2) For purposes of paragraph (1), the term "applicable recovery amount" means any amount which is recovered from a fiduciary or other person with respect to a breach or violation described in paragraph (1)—

> (A) pursuant to any settlement agreement with the Secretary, or
>
> (B) ordered by a court to be paid by such fiduciary or other person to a plan or its participants and beneficiaries in a judicial proceeding instituted by the Secretary under subsection (a)(2) or (a)(5) of this section.

Section 502(*l*) contemplates civil penalty actions by the Secretary against two classes of defendants, fiduciaries and "other person[s]." The latter class concerns us here. Paraphrasing, the Secretary shall assess a civil penalty against an "other person" who "knowing[ly] participat[es] in" "any . . . violation of . . . part 4 . . . by a fiduciary." And the amount of such penalty is defined by reference to the amount "ordered by a court to be paid by such . . . other person to a plan or its participants and beneficiaries in a judicial proceeding instituted by the Secretary under subsection (a)(2) or *(a)(5)*." Id. (emphasis added). The plain implication is that the Secretary may bring a civil action under § 502(a)(5) against an "other person" who "knowing[ly] participat[es]" in a fiduciary's violation; otherwise, there could be no "applicable recovery amount" from which to determine the amount of the civil penalty to be imposed on the "other person." This § 502(a)(5) action is available notwithstanding the absence of any ERISA provision explicitly imposing a duty upon an "other person" not to engage in such "knowing participation." And if the Secretary may bring suit against an "other person" under subsection (a)(5), it follows that a participant, beneficiary, or fiduciary may bring suit against an "other person" under the similarly worded subsection (a)(3). See Mertens, 508 U.S. at 260. Section 502(*l*), therefore, refutes the notion that § 502(a)(3) (or (a)(5)) liability hinges on whether the particular defendant labors under a duty expressly imposed by the substantive provisions of ERISA Title I.

Salomon invokes *Mertens* as articulating an alternative, more restrictive reading of § 502(*l*) that does not support the inference we have drawn. In *Mertens,* we suggested, in dictum, that the "other person[s]" in § 502(*l*) might be limited to the "cofiduciaries" made expressly liable under § 405(a) for knowingly participating in another fiduciary's breach of fiduciary responsibility. Id. at 261. So read, § 502(*l*) would be consistent with the view that liability under § 502(a)(3) depends entirely on whether the particular defendant violated a duty expressly imposed by the substantive provisions of ERISA Title I. But the *Mertens* dictum did not discuss—understandably, since we were merely flagging the issue, see 508 U.S. at 255, 260–61—that ERISA defines the term "person" without regard to status as a cofiduciary (or, for that matter, as a fiduciary or party in interest), see ERISA § 3(9). Moreover, § 405(a) indicates that a cofiduciary is *itself* a fiduciary, see ERISA § 405(a) ("[A] fiduciary . . . shall be liable for a breach of fiduciary responsibility of another fiduciary . . ."), and § 502(*l*) clearly distinguishes between a "fiduciary," ERISA § 502(*l*)(1)(A), and an "other person," § 502(*l*)(1)(B).

III

Notwithstanding the text of § 502(a)(3) (as informed by § 502(*l*)), Salomon protests that it would contravene common sense for Congress to have imposed civil liability on a party, such as a nonfiduciary party in interest to a § 406(a) transaction, that is not a "wrongdoer" in the sense of violating a duty expressly imposed by the substantive provisions of ERISA Title I. Salomon raises the specter of § 502(a)(3) suits being brought against innocent parties—even those having no connection to the allegedly unlawful "act or practice"—rather than against the true wrongdoer, i.e., the fiduciary that caused the plan to engage in the transaction.

But this reductio ad absurdum ignores the limiting principle explicit in § 502(a)(3): that the retrospective relief sought be "appropriate equitable relief." The common law of trusts, which offers a "starting point for analysis [of ERISA] . . . [unless] it is inconsistent with the language of the statute, its structure, or its purposes," Hughes Aircraft Co. v. Jacobson, 525 U.S. 432, 447 (1999), plainly countenances the sort of relief sought by petitioners against Salomon here. As petitioners and amicus curiae the United States observe, it has long been settled that when a trustee in breach of his fiduciary duty to the beneficiaries transfers trust property to a third person, the third person takes the property subject to the trust, unless he has purchased the property for value and without notice of the fiduciary's breach of duty. The trustee or beneficiaries may then maintain an action for restitution of the property (if not already disposed of) or disgorgement of proceeds (if already disposed of), and disgorgement of the third person's profits derived therefrom. See, e.g., Restatement (Second) of Trusts §§ 284; 291; 294; 295; 297 (1957). As we long ago explained in the analogous situation of property obtained by fraud:

> Whenever the legal title to property is obtained through means or under circumstances "which render it unconscientious for the holder of the legal title to retain and enjoy the beneficial interest, equity impresses a constructive trust on the property thus acquired in favor of the one who is truly and equitably entitled to the same, although he may never, perhaps, have had any legal estate therein; and a court of equity has jurisdiction to reach the property either in the hands of the original wrongdoer, or in the hands of any subsequent holder, until a purchaser of it in good faith and without notice acquires a higher right and takes the property relieved from the trust." Moore v. Crawford, 130 U.S. 122, 128 (1889) (quoting 2 J. Pomeroy, Equity Jurisprudence § 1053, pp. 628–629 (1886)).

Importantly, that a transferee was not "the original wrongdoer" does not insulate him from liability for restitution. It also bears emphasis that the common law of trusts sets limits on restitution actions against defendants other than the principal "wrongdoer." Only a transferee of ill-gotten trust assets may be held liable, and then only when the transferee (assuming he has purchased for value) knew or should have known of the existence of the trust and the circumstances that rendered the transfer in breach of the trust. Translated to the instant context, the transferee must be demonstrated to have had actual or constructive knowledge of the circumstances that rendered the transaction unlawful. Those circumstances, in turn, involve a showing that the *plan fiduciary,* with actual or constructive knowledge of the facts satisfying the elements of a § 406(a) transaction, caused the plan to engage in the transaction. Lockheed Corp. v. Spink, 517 U.S. 882, 888–89 (1996).

* * *

But Salomon advances a more fundamental critique of the common law analogy, reasoning that the antecedent violation here—a violation of § 406(a)'s per se prohibitions on transacting with a party in interest—was unknown at common law, and that common law *liability* should not attach to an act that does not violate a common law *duty*. While Salomon accurately characterizes § 406(a) as expanding upon the common law's arm's length standard of conduct, see Keystone Consol. Indus., 508 U.S. at 160, we reject Salomon's unsupported suggestion that remedial principles of the common law are tethered to the precise contours of common law duty.

* * *

IV

We turn, finally, to two nontextual clues cited by Salomon and amici. First, Salomon urges us to consider, as the Seventh Circuit did, the Conference Committee's rejection of language from the Senate bill that would have expressly imposed a duty on nonfiduciary parties to § 406(a) transactions. Second, Salomon and amici submit that the policy consequences of recognizing a § 502(a)(3) action in this case could be devastating—counterparties, faced with the prospect of liability for dealing with a plan, may charge higher rates or, worse, refuse altogether to transact with plans.

We decline these suggestions to depart from the text of § 502(a)(3). In ERISA cases, "[a]s in any case of statutory construction, our analysis begins with the language of the statute. . . . And where the statutory language provides a clear answer, it ends there as well." Hughes Aircraft, 525 U.S. at 438. Section 502(a)(3), as informed by § 502(*l*), satisfies this standard.

Accordingly, we reverse the Seventh Circuit's judgment and remand the case for further proceedings consistent with this opinion.

NOTES AND QUESTIONS

1. *Speculation Concerning the Scope of* Harris Trust. *Harris Trust* involved ERISA's prohibited transaction rules, a technical subject that

usually interests only ERISA tax lawyers. The precise legal question presented in *Harris Trust*, whether Section 502(a)(3) authorized a claim against a nonfiduciary defendant who engaged in a prohibited transaction, was one that had divided the lower federal courts in the wake of *Mertens*. In a unanimous opinion, the Supreme Court held in *Harris Trust* that this type of claim could be brought under Section 502(a)(3).

Professor Susan J. Stabile has argued that *Harris Trust* should not be read as limited to claims against nonfiduciaries who participate in a violation of ERISA's prohibited transaction rules, but rather the federal courts also should recognize a cause of action under Section 502(a)(3) against any nonfiduciary who participates in a fiduciary's breach of duty under Section 404. See Susan J. Stabile, *Breach of ERISA Fiduciary Responsibilities: Who's Liable Anyway?*, 5 EMPLOYEE. RTS. & EMP. POL'Y J. 135 (2001). Do you agree? Is there an argument, based on the plain language of Sections 404, 406, and 409, that nonfiduciaries should *not* be liable under ERISA for participating in a fiduciary's breach of duty under Section 404? Which rule would best promote ERISA's underlying public policies?

2. *Attorney Liability After* Harris Trust. Although an attorney who performs only the usual professional services for the plan or the plan's administrator normally is not considered to be an ERISA fiduciary, *Harris Trust* suggests that a nonfiduciary attorney who assists a plan fiduciary in committing a breach of fiduciary duty may be liable for the resulting injury to the plan or the plan's participants. The predictable reaction of malpractice insurance providers to *Harris Trust* was to reexamine and revise the scope of coverage offered to attorneys who practiced in the ERISA area. See, e.g., Ronald E. Mallen & Paul E. Vallone, *Attorney Liability Under ERISA: Myth or Reality?*, 68 DEFENSE COUNS. J. 435 (2001).

2. CLAIMS TO ENFORCE A PLAN REIMBURSEMENT CLAUSE

The claims in *Great-West Life & Annuity Insurance Co. v. Knudson, Sereboff v. Mid Atlantic Medical Services, Inc.*, and *US Airways, Inc. v. McCutchen* are distinctly different from *Mertens* and *Harris Trust*. These cases all involve a claim brought under Section 502(a)(3) to enforce the terms of an employee benefit plan.

In *Great-West*, the plaintiff who asserted the claim was the stop-loss insurance carrier for employer's self-insured health care plan. The defendants in *Great-West* were a plan beneficiary, Janette Knudson, and her husband. The plan contained a feature found in all employer self-insured health care plans that is known as a *reimbursement clause*. A reimbursement clause requires the plan's participants and beneficiaries to reimburse the plan for any medical benefits paid by the plan for injuries to the participant or beneficiary if he or she later recovers against the third party who was responsible for causing the injury.

Janette Knudson suffered a catastrophic injury in an automobile accident and later recovered a settlement of $650,000 in a state law tort action against the automobile manufacturer and other tortfeasors involved in the accident. To preserve Knudson's eligibility for Medicaid under the income and asset eligibility criteria established by California law, the disbursement of the settlement proceeds was structured so that Knudson did not personally receive any of the proceeds from the settlement. Part of the settlement proceeds were paid to and controlled by the trustee of a unique type of trust, known as a special needs trust, that was established for the benefit of Knudson. Under California law, the trustee of the special needs trust could use the trust assets only to pay for expenses or other items for Knudson that were not covered by the state's Medicaid program. The purpose of the special needs trust was to maintain Knudson's continued eligibility for Medicaid benefits while at the same time providing a source of funds to pay for other things that Knudson might need or desire to make her life more comfortable.

Rather than bringing a claim against the trustee of the special needs trust, the plaintiff brought a claim under Section 502(a)(3) against Knudson personally to enforce the plan's reimbursement clause. The issue before the Supreme Court in *Great-West* was whether the remedy sought by the plaintiff—essentially a payment of money out of Knudson's personal assets—could properly be characterized as "appropriate equitable relief."

As you read *Great-West*, bear in mind that the settlement proceeds were disbursed to the trustee of the special needs trust and not to Knudson personally. How does this fact influence the analysis in the majority opinion? How would the majority's analysis apply if, as in a typical settlement, the plan participant personally received a portion of the tort settlement proceeds?

GREAT-WEST LIFE & ANNUITY INSURANCE CO. V. KNUDSON

United States Supreme Court, 2002.
534 U.S. 204, 122 S.Ct. 708, 151 L.Ed.2d 635.

JUSTICE SCALIA delivered the opinion of the Court.

The question presented is whether § 502(a)(3) of the Employee Retirement Income Security Act of 1974 (ERISA) authorizes this action by petitioners to enforce a reimbursement provision of an ERISA plan.

I

Respondent Janette Knudson was rendered quadriplegic by a car accident in June 1992. Because her then-husband, respondent Eric Knudson, was employed by petitioner Earth Systems, Inc., Janette was covered by the Health and Welfare Plan for Employees and Dependents of

Earth Systems, Inc. (Plan). The Plan covered $411,157.11 of Janette's medical expenses, of which all except $75,000 was paid by petitioner Great-West Life & Annuity Insurance Co. pursuant to a "stop-loss" insurance agreement with the Plan.

The Plan includes a reimbursement provision that is the basis for the present lawsuit. This provides that the Plan shall have "the right to recover from the [beneficiary] any payment for benefits" paid by the Plan that the beneficiary is entitled to recover from a third party. Specifically, the Plan has "a first lien upon any recovery, whether by settlement, judgment or otherwise," that the beneficiary receives from the third party, not to exceed "the amount of benefits paid [by the Plan] . . . [or] the amount received by the [beneficiary] for such medical treatment. . . ." If the beneficiary recovers from a third party and fails to reimburse the Plan, "then he will be personally liable to [the Plan] . . . up to the amount of the first lien." Pursuant to an agreement between the Plan and Great-West, the Plan "assign[ed] to Great-West all of its rights to make, litigate, negotiate, settle, compromise, release or waive" any claim under the reimbursement provision.

In late 1993, the Knudsons filed a tort action in California state court seeking to recover from Hyundai Motor Company, the manufacturer of the car they were riding in at the time of the accident, and other alleged tortfeasors. The parties to that action negotiated a $650,000 settlement, a notice of which was mailed to Great-West. This allocated $256,745.30 to a Special Needs Trust under Cal. Prob.Code Ann. § 3611 (West 1991 and Supp.1993) to provide for Janette's medical care; $373,426 to attorney's fees and costs; $5,000 to reimburse the California Medicaid program (Medi-Cal); and $13,828.70 (the portion of the settlement attributable to past medical expenses) to satisfy Great-West's claim under the reimbursement provision of the Plan.

The day before the hearing scheduled for judicial approval of the settlement, Great-West, calling itself a defendant and asserting that the state court action involved federal claims related to ERISA, filed in the United States District Court for the Central District of California a notice of removal pursuant to 28 U.S.C. § 1441. That court concluded that Great-West was not a defendant and could not remove the case, and therefore remanded to the state court, which approved the settlement. The state court's order provided that the defendants would pay the settlement amount allocated to the Special Needs Trust directly to the trust, and the remaining amounts to respondents' attorney, who, in turn, would tender checks to Medi-Cal and Great-West.

Great-West, however, never cashed the check it received from respondents' attorney. Instead, at the same time that Great-West sought to remove the state law tort action, it filed this action in the same federal court (the United States District Court for the Central District of

California), seeking injunctive and declaratory relief under § 502(a)(3) to enforce the reimbursement provision of the Plan by requiring the Knudsons to pay the Plan $411,157.11 of any proceeds recovered from third parties. Great-West subsequently filed an amended complaint adding Earth Systems and the Plan as plaintiffs and seeking a temporary restraining order against continuation of the state court proceedings for approval of the settlement. The District Court denied the temporary restraining order, a ruling that petitioners did not appeal. After the state court approved the settlement and the money was disbursed, the District Court granted summary judgment to the Knudsons. It held that the language of the Plan limited its right of reimbursement to the amount received by respondents from third parties *for past medical treatment,* an amount that the state court determined was $13,828.70. The United States Court of Appeals for the Ninth Circuit affirmed on different grounds. Citing *FMC Medical Plan v. Owens,* 122 F.3d 1258 (9th Cir. 1997), it held that judicially decreed reimbursement for payments made to a beneficiary of an insurance plan by a third party is not equitable relief and is therefore not authorized by § 502(a)(3). We granted certiorari.

II

We have observed repeatedly that ERISA is a "comprehensive and reticulated statute, the product of a decade of congressional study of the Nation's private employee benefit system." Mertens v. Hewitt Associates, 508 U.S. 248, 251 (1993). We have therefore been especially "reluctant to tamper with [the] enforcement scheme" embodied in the statute by extending remedies not specifically authorized by its text. Massachusetts Mut. Life Ins. Co. v. Russell, 473 U.S. 134, 147 (1985). Indeed, we have noted that ERISA's "carefully crafted and detailed enforcement scheme provides 'strong evidence that Congress did *not* intend to authorize other remedies that it simply forgot to incorporate expressly.'" Mertens, 508 U.S. at 254 (quoting Russell, 473 U.S. at 146–47).

Section 502(a)(3) authorizes a civil action:

> by a participant, beneficiary, or fiduciary (A) to enjoin any act or practice which violates . . . the terms of the plan, or (B) to obtain other appropriate equitable relief (i) to redress such violations or (ii) to enforce any provisions of . . . the terms of the plan.

As we explained in *Mertens,* " '[e]quitable' relief must mean *something less than all* relief." 508 U.S. at 258 n.8. Thus, in *Mertens,* we rejected a reading of the statute that would extend the relief obtainable under § 502(a)(3) to whatever relief a court of equity is empowered to provide in the particular case at issue (which could include legal remedies that would otherwise be beyond the scope of the equity court's authority). Such a reading, we said, would "limit the relief *not at all*" and "render the modifier ['equitable'] superfluous." Id. at 257–258. Instead, we held that the term "equitable relief" in § 502(a)(3) must refer to "those categories of relief that were *typically* available in equity. . . ." Id. at 256.

Here, petitioners seek, in essence, to impose personal liability on respondents for a contractual obligation to pay money—relief that was not typically available in equity. "A claim for money due and owing under a contract is 'quintessentially an action at law.'" Wal-Mart Stores, Inc. v. Wells, 213 F.3d 398, 401 (7th Cir. 2000) (Posner, J.). "Almost invariably . . . suits seeking (whether by judgment, injunction, or declaration) to compel the defendant to pay a sum of money to the plaintiff are suits for 'money damages,' as that phrase has traditionally been applied, since they seek no more than compensation for loss resulting from the defendant's breach of legal duty." Bowen v. Massachusetts, 487 U.S. 879, 918–919 (1988) (Scalia, J., dissenting). And "[m]oney damages are, of course, the classic form of *legal* relief." Mertens, 508 U.S. at 255.

Nevertheless, petitioners, along with their amicus the United States, struggle to characterize the relief sought as "equitable" under the standard set by *Mertens*. We are not persuaded.

A

First, petitioners argue that they are entitled to relief under § 502(a)(3)(A) because they seek "to enjoin a[n] act or practice"— respondents' failure to reimburse the Plan—"which violates . . . the terms of the plan." But an injunction to compel the payment of money past due under a contract, or specific performance of a past due monetary obligation, was not typically available in equity. See, e.g., 3 Restatement (Second) of Contracts § 359 (1979); 3 D. Dobbs, Law of Remedies § 12.8(2), p. 199 (2d ed. 1993) (hereinafter Dobbs); 5 A. Corbin, Contracts § 1142, p. 119 (1964) (hereinafter Corbin). Those rare cases in which a court of equity would decree specific performance of a contract to transfer funds were suits that, unlike the present case, sought to prevent future losses that were either incalculable or would be greater than the sum awarded. For example, specific performance might be available to enforce an agreement to lend money "when the unavailability of alternative financing would leave the plaintiff with injuries that are difficult to value; or to enforce an obligor's duty to make future monthly payments, after the obligor had consistently refused to make past payments concededly due, and thus threatened the obligee with the burden of bringing multiple damages actions." Bowen, supra, at 918. See also 3 Dobbs § 12.8(2) at 200; 5A Corbin § 1142, at 117–18. Typically, however, specific performance of a contract to pay money was not available in equity.

* * *

B

Second, petitioners argue that their suit is authorized by § 502(a)(3)(B) because they seek restitution, which they characterize as a form of equitable relief. However, not all relief falling under the rubric of restitution is available in equity. In the days of the divided bench, restitution was available in certain cases at law, and in certain others in equity. Thus, "restitution is a legal remedy when ordered in a case at law and an equitable remedy . . . when ordered in an equity case," and whether it is legal or equitable depends on "the basis for [the plaintiff's] claim" and the nature of the underlying remedies sought. Reich v. Continental Casualty Co., 33 F.3d 754, 756 (7th Cir. 1994) (Posner, J.).

In cases in which the plaintiff "could *not* assert title or right to possession of particular property, but in which nevertheless he might be able to show just grounds for recovering money to pay for some benefit the defendant had received from him," the plaintiff had a right to restitution *at law* through an action derived from the common law writ of assumpsit. 1 Dobbs § 4.2(1), at 571. In such cases, the plaintiff's claim was considered legal because he sought "to obtain a judgment imposing a merely personal liability upon the defendant to pay a sum of money." Restatement of Restitution § 160, Comment a, pp. 641–642 (1936). Such claims were viewed essentially as actions at law for breach of contract (whether the contract was actual or implied).

In contrast, a plaintiff could seek restitution *in equity,* ordinarily in the form of a constructive trust or an equitable lien, where money or property identified as belonging in good conscience to the plaintiff could clearly be traced to particular funds or property in the defendant's possession. See 1 Dobbs § 4.3(1), at 587–88; Restatement of Restitution, supra, § 160, Comment a, at 641–42; 1 G. Palmer, Law of Restitution § 1.4, p. 17; § 3.7, p.262 (1978). A court of equity could then order a defendant to transfer title (in the case of the constructive trust) or to give a security interest (in the case of the equitable lien) to a plaintiff who was, in the eyes of equity, the true owner. But where "the property [sought to be recovered] or its proceeds have been dissipated so that no product remains, [the plaintiff's] claim is only that of a general creditor," and the plaintiff "cannot enforce a constructive trust of or an equitable lien upon other property of the [defendant]." Restatement of Restitution § 215, Comment a, at 867. Thus, for restitution to lie in equity, the action generally must seek not to impose personal liability on the defendant, but to restore to the plaintiff particular funds or property in the defendant's possession.

Here, the funds to which petitioners claim an entitlement under the Plan's reimbursement provision—the proceeds from the settlement of respondents' tort action—are not in respondents' possession. As the order of the state court approving the settlement makes clear, the disbursements from the settlement were paid by two checks, one made payable to the Special Needs Trust and the other to respondents' attorney (who, after deducting his own fees and costs, placed the remaining funds in a client trust account from which he tendered checks to respondents' other creditors, Great-West and Medi-Cal). The basis for petitioners' claim is not that respondents hold particular funds that, in good conscience, belong to petitioners, but that petitioners are contractually entitled to *some* funds for benefits that they conferred. The kind of restitution that petitioners seek, therefore, is not equitable—the imposition of a constructive trust or equitable lien on particular property—but legal—the imposition of personal liability for the benefits that they conferred upon respondents.

Admittedly, our cases have not previously drawn this fine distinction between restitution at law and restitution in equity, but neither have they involved an issue to which the distinction was relevant. In *Mertens,* we mentioned in dicta that "injunction, mandamus, and *restitution*" are categories of relief that were typically available in equity. 508 U.S. at 256 (emphasis added). *Mertens,* however, did not involve a claim for restitution at all; rather, we addressed the question whether a nonfiduciary who knowingly participates in the breach of a fiduciary duty imposed by ERISA is liable to the plan for compensatory damages. Id. at 249–250. Thus, as courts and commentators have noted, "all the [Supreme] Court meant [in *Mertens* and other cases] was that restitution, in contrast to damages, is a remedy commonly ordered in equity cases and therefore an equitable remedy in a sense in which damages, though *occasionally* awarded in equity cases, are not." Reich v. Continental Casualty Co., 33 F.3d at 756. *Mertens* did not purport to change the well-settled principle that restitution is "not an *exclusively* equitable remedy," and whether it is legal or equitable in a particular case (and hence whether it is authorized by § 502(a)(3)) remains dependent on the nature of the relief sought. 33 F.3d at 756.

* * *

Justice Stevens [in his dissenting opinion] finds it "difficult . . . to understand why Congress would not have wanted to provide recourse in federal court for the plan violation disclosed by the record in this case." It is, however, not our job to find reasons for what Congress has plainly done; and it *is* our job to avoid rendering what Congress has plainly done (here, limit the available relief) devoid of reason and effect. If, as Justice Ginsburg surmises [in her dissenting opinion that] Congress meant to rule out nothing more than "compensatory and punitive damages," it could simply have said that. That Congress sought to achieve this result by subtle reliance upon the dissenters' novel and expansive view of equity is most implausible.

Respecting Congress's choice to limit the relief available under § 502(a)(3) to "equitable relief" requires us to recognize the difference between legal and equitable forms of restitution.[4] Because petitioners seek only the former, their suit is not authorized by § 502(a)(3).

* * *

JUSTICE STEVENS, dissenting.

In her lucid dissent, which I join, Justice Ginsburg has explained why it is fanciful to assume that in 1974 Congress intended to revive the obsolete distinctions between law and equity as a basis for defining the remedies available in federal court for violations of the terms of a plan under the Employee Retirement Income Security Act of 1974 (ERISA). She has also convincingly argued that the relief sought in the present case is permissible even under the Court's favored test for determining what qualifies as "equitable relief" under § 502(a)(3)(B) of ERISA. I add this postscript because I am persuaded that Congress intended the word "enjoin," as used in § 502(a)(3)(A), to authorize any appropriate order that prohibits or terminates a violation of an ERISA plan, regardless of whether a precedent for such an order can be found in English Chancery cases.

I read the word "other" in § 502(a)(3)(B) as having been intended to enlarge, not contract, a federal judge's remedial authority. Consequently,

---

[4] In support of its argument that Congress intended all restitution to be "equitable relief" under § 502(a)(3), Justice Ginsburg's dissent asserts that Congress has treated backpay, "a type of restitution," as equitable for purposes of Title VII of the Civil Rights Act of 1964. The authorities of this Court cited for the proposition that backpay is a type of restitution are *Curtis v. Loether,* 415 U.S. 189, 197 (1974), and *Teamsters v. Terry,* 494 U.S. 558, 572 (1990). It is notable, however, that these cases do not say that *since* it is restitutionary, it is *therefore* equitable. *Curtis,* in fact, explicitly refuses to do so. 415 U.S. at 197 ("Whatever may be the merit of the 'equitable' characterization [of backpay] in Title VII cases . . ." (footnote omitted)). And in *Terry,* while we noted that "we have characterized damages as equitable where they are restitutionary," 494 U.S. at 570, we did not (and could not) say that *all* forms of restitution are equitable.

Congress "treated [backpay] as equitable" in Title VII (opinion of GINSBURG, J.), only in the narrow sense that it allowed backpay to be awarded *together with* equitable relief:

[T]he court may . . . order such affirmative action as may be appropriate, which may include, but is not limited to, *reinstatement or hiring of employees, with or without back pay* . . ., or any other equitable relief as the court deems appropriate. 42 U.S.C. § 2000e–5(g)(1) (emphasis added).

If the referent of "other equitable relief" were "back pay," it could be said, in a sense relevant here, that Congress "treated" backpay as equitable relief. In fact, however, the referent is "reinstatement or hiring of employees," which is modified by the phrase "with or without back pay." *Curtis* recognized that courts of appeals had treated Title VII backpay as equitable because § 2000e–5(g)(1) had made backpay "an integral part of an equitable remedy," 415 U.S. at 197.

The statement in *Terry* on which Justice Ginsburg relies—that "Congress specifically characterized backpay under Title VII as a form of 'equitable relief,' " 494 U.S. at 572—is plainly inaccurate unless it is understood to mean that Title VII backpay was "specifically" made part of an equitable remedy. That is the only sense which the *Terry* discussion requires, and is reinforced by the immediately following citation of the portion of *Curtis* that called Title VII backpay "an integral part of an equitable remedy," Curtis, 415 U.S. at 197. See Terry, 494 U.S. at 572. The restitution sought here by Great-West is not that, but a freestanding claim for money damages. Title VII has nothing to do with this case.

and contrary to the Court's view in *Mertens v. Hewitt Associates,* 508 U.S. 248, 256. (1993), I would neither read § 502(a)(3)(B) as placing a *limitation* on a judge's authority under § 502(a)(3)(A), nor shackle an analysis of what constitutes "equitable relief" under § 502(a)(3)(B) to the sort of historical analysis that the Court has chosen.

* * *

JUSTICE GINSBURG, with whom JUSTICE STEVENS, JUSTICE SOUTER, and JUSTICE BREYER join, dissenting.

Today's holding, the majority declares, is compelled by "Congress's choice to limit the relief available under § 502(a)(3)." In the Court's view, Congress' placement of the word "equitable" in that provision signaled an intent to exhume the "fine distinction[s]" borne of the "days of the divided bench;" to treat as dispositive an ancient classification unrelated to the substance of the relief sought; and to obstruct the general goals of ERISA by relegating to state court (or to no court at all) an array of suits involving the interpretation of employee health plan provisions. Because it is plain that Congress made no such "choice," I dissent.

I

The Court purports to resolve this case by determining the "nature of the relief" Great-West seeks. The opinion's analysis, however, trains on the question, deemed subsidiary, whether the disputed claim could have been brought in an equity court "[i]n the days of the divided bench." To answer that question, the Court scrutinizes the form of the claim and contrasts its features with the technical requirements that once governed the jurisdictional divide between the premerger courts. Finding no clear match on the equitable side of the line, the Court concludes that Great-West's claim is beyond the scope of § 502(a)(3) and therefore outside federal jurisdiction.

The rarified rules underlying this rigid and time-bound conception of the term "equity" were hardly at the fingertips of those who enacted § 502(a)(3). By 1974, when ERISA became law, the "days of the divided bench" were a fading memory, for that era had ended nearly 40 years earlier with the advent of the Federal Rules of Civil Procedure. Those rules instruct: "There shall be one form of action" cognizable in the federal courts. Fed. Rule Civ. Proc. 2. Except where reference to historical practice might be necessary to preserve a right established before the merger, the doctrinal rules delineating the boundaries of the divided courts had receded. See 4 C. Wright & A. Miller, Federal Practice and Procedure § 1041, p. 135 (1987); C. Wright, Handbook on Law of Federal Courts § 67, p. 282 (2d ed. 1970) ("[I]nstances in which the old distinctions continue to rule from their graves are quite rare.").

It is thus fanciful to attribute to members of the 93d Congress familiarity with those "needless and obsolete distinctions," much less a deliberate "choice" to resurrect and import them wholesale into the modern regulatory scheme laid out in ERISA. "[T]here is nothing to suggest that ERISA's drafters wanted to embed their work in a time warp." Health Cost Controls of Ill. v. Washington, 187 F.3d 703, 711 (7th Cir. 1999) (Posner, J.); cf. Mertens v. Hewitt Associates, 508 U.S. 248, 257 n.7 (1993) (meaning of "equitable relief" in § 502(a)(3) must be determined based on "the state of the law when ERISA was enacted").

That Congress did not intend to strap § 502(a)(3) with the anachronistic rules on which the majority relies is corroborated by the anomalous results to which the supposed legislative "choice" leads. Although the Court recognizes that it need not decide the issue, its opinion surely contemplates that a constructive trust claim would lie; hence, the outcome of this case would be different if Great-West had sued the trustee of the Special Needs Trust, who has "possession" of the requested funds, instead of the Knudsons, who do not. Under that view, whether relief is "equitable" would turn entirely on the designation of the defendant, even though the substance of the relief Great-West could have obtained in a suit against the trustee—a judgment ordering the return of wrongfully withheld funds—is identical to the relief Great-West in fact sought from the Knudsons. Unlike today's majority, I resist this rule unjustified in reason, which produces different results for breaches of duty in situations that cannot be differentiated in policy.

* * *

It is particularly ironic that the majority acts in the name of equity as it sacrifices congressional intent and statutory purpose to archaic and unyielding doctrine. "Equity eschews mechanical rules; it depends on flexibility." Holmberg v. Armbrecht, 327 U.S. 392, 396 (1946). And "[a]s this Court long ago recognized, 'there is inherent in the Courts of Equity a jurisdiction to . . . give effect to the policy of the legislature.'" Mitchell v. Robert DeMario Jewelry, Inc., 361 U.S. 288, 291–92 (1960) (quoting Clark v. Smith, 13 Pet. 195, 203 (1839)).

II

* * *

More important, if one's concern is to follow the Legislature's will, Congress itself has treated as equitable a type of restitution substantially similar to the relief Great-West seeks here. Congress placed in Title VII of the Civil Rights Act of 1964 the instruction that, to redress violations of the Act, courts may award, inter alia, "appropriate . . . equitable relief," including "reinstatement or hiring of employees, with or without back pay." 42 U.S.C. § 2000e–5(g)(1). Interpreting this provision, we have recognized that backpay is "a form of restitution," Curtis v. Loether, 415

U.S. 189, 197 (1974); see Teamsters v. Terry, 494 U.S. 558, 572 (1990), and that "Congress specifically characterized backpay under Title VII as a form of 'equitable relief,'" id. The *Mertens* majority used Title VII's "equitable relief" provision as the touchstone for its interpretation of § 502(a)(3); today's majority declares [in footnote 4], with remarkable inconsistency, that "Title VII has nothing to do with this case." The Court inexplicably fails to offer any reason why Congress did not intend "equitable relief" in § 502(a)(3) to include a plaintiff's "recover[y of] money to pay for some benefit the defendant had received from him," but did intend those words to encompass such relief in a measure (Title VII) enacted years earlier.

I agree that "not *all* relief falling under the rubric of restitution [was] available in equity"; restitution was also available in claims brought at law, and the majority may be correct that in such cases restitution would have been termed "legal." But that in no way affects the answer to the question at the core of this case. Section 502(a)(3) as interpreted in *Mertens* encompasses those "categories of relief that were *typically* available in equity," not those that were *exclusively* so. Restitution plainly fits that bill. By insisting that § 502(a)(3) embraces only those *claims* that, in the circumstances of the particular case, could be brought in chancery in times of yore, the majority labors against the holding of that case. * * *

* * *

That the import of the term "equity" might depend on context does not signify a "rolling revision of its content," but rather a recognition that equity, characteristically, was and should remain an evolving and dynamic jurisprudence. As courts in the common law realm have reaffirmed: "Principles of equity, we were all taught, were introduced by Lord Chancellors and their deputies . . . in order to provide relief from the inflexibility of common law rules." Medforth v. Blake, [1993] 3 All E.R. 97, 110 (C.A.). This Court's equation of "equity" with the rigid application of rules frozen in a bygone era, I maintain, is thus "unjustifiabl[e]" even as applied to a law grounded in that era. Grupo Mexicano, 527 U.S. at 336 (GINSBURG, J., dissenting). As applied to a statute like ERISA, however, such insistence is senseless.

* * *

Today's decision needlessly obscures the meaning and complicates the application of § 502(a)(3). The Court's interpretation of that provision embroils federal courts in "recondite controversies better left to legal historians," Terry, 494 U.S. at 576, and yields results that are demonstrably at odds with Congress' goals in enacting ERISA. Because in my view Congress cannot plausibly be said to have "carefully crafted" such confusion, I dissent.

NOTES AND QUESTIONS

1. How did the majority in *Great-West* interpret "equitable" relief under ERISA Section 502(a)(3)? According to the majority opinion, what common law requirement for imposing a constructive trust remedy was lacking in *Great-West*? How does Justice Ginsburg's proposed approach to determining "equitable" relief differ from the majority's approach? Which approach to determining the remedies available under Section 502(a)(3) do you prefer? Why?

2. *Reimbursement Clauses Versus Subrogation Clauses.* Reimbursement clauses are the corollary in the self-insured health care plan context to the typical subrogation clause found in an insured health care plan. See THOMAS H. LAWRENCE & JOHN M. RUSSELL, ERISA SUBROGATION: ENFORCING RECOUPMENT PROVISIONS IN ERISA—COVERED HEALTH AND DISABILITY PLANS 4 (2000). There are, however, important distinctions in how a subrogation clause and a reimbursement clause function. In an insured plan, a subrogation clause authorizes the insurer to "step into the shoes" of the injured participant who has received health care benefits under the plan and sue any party the participant could have sued to recover for the participant's injuries. See generally 6 COUCH ON INSURANCE § 222 (3d ed. 2000). In contrast, the typical self-insured health care plan does not authorize the plan's sponsoring employer to assert the participant's potential claims against a third party tortfeasor. Rather, the reimbursement clause is a contractual term of the plan providing that, *if* the participant sues and recovers from the third party, *then* the participant must reimburse the plan for the cost of the health care benefits provided by the plan. See FMC Medical Plan v. Owens, 122 F.3d 1258, 1260 & n.1 (9th Cir. 1997).

Importantly, many reimbursement clauses are written broadly so that the plan must be reimbursed for the benefits provided to the participant out of *all* funds recovered from the third party, not just for that portion of the tort recovery allocated to cover the participant's medical costs. As a result, the participant's lawyer (who usually takes the case on a contingency fee) may be required to disgorge part or all of his or her attorney's fees to the plan in accordance with the plan's reimbursement clause. Compare Greenwood Mills, Inc. v. Burris, 130 F.Supp.2d 949 (M.D. Tenn. 2001) (attorney and his law firm held jointly and severally liable to reimburse the plan under Section 502(a)(3) where attorney knowingly distributed settlement funds to participant and himself in violation of plan's reimbursement clause and counseled participant to lie to the plan administrator about the amount of money recovered in the lawsuit) with Hotel Employees & Restaurant Employees Int'l Union Welfare Fund v. Gentner, 50 F.3d 719 (9th Cir. 1995) (absent commitment to comply with plan reimbursement clause, attorney was not liable under Section 502(a)(3) for reimbursement to the plan of the fees paid to the attorney).

Unlike *Great-West*, *Sereboff v. Mid Atlantic Medical Services, Inc.* involved a more typical situation where the plaintiffs-participants personally received a portion of the tort litigation recovery. As you read *Sereboff*, consider how the disposition of the damages award from the tort litigation may have influenced the Supreme Court's analysis.

SEREBOFF V. MID ATLANTIC MEDICAL SERVICES, INC.

United States Supreme Court, 2006.
547 U.S. 356, 126 S.Ct. 1869, 164 L.Ed.2d 612.

CHIEF JUSTICE ROBERTS delivered the opinion of the Court.

In this case we consider again the circumstances in which a fiduciary under the Employee Retirement Income Security Act of 1974 (ERISA) may sue a beneficiary for reimbursement of medical expenses paid by the ERISA plan, when the beneficiary has recovered for its injuries from a third party.

I

Marlene Sereboff's employer sponsors a health insurance plan administered by respondent Mid Atlantic Medical Services, Inc., and covered by ERISA. Marlene Sereboff and her husband Joel are beneficiaries under the plan. The plan provides for payment of certain covered medical expenses and contains an "Acts of Third Parties" provision. This provision "applies when [a beneficiary is] sick or injured as a result of the act or omission of another person or party," and requires a beneficiary who "receives benefits" under the plan for such injuries to "reimburse [Mid Atlantic]" for those benefits from "[a]ll recoveries from a third party (whether by lawsuit, settlement, or otherwise)." The provision states that "[Mid Atlantic's] share of the recovery will not be reduced because [the beneficiary] has not received the full damages claimed, unless [Mid Atlantic] agrees in writing to a reduction."

The Sereboffs were involved in an automobile accident in California and suffered injuries. Pursuant to the plan's coverage provisions, the plan paid the couple's medical expenses. The Sereboffs filed a tort action in state court against several third parties, seeking compensatory damages for injuries suffered as a result of the accident. Soon after the suit was commenced, Mid Atlantic sent the Sereboffs' attorney a letter asserting a lien on the anticipated proceeds from the suit for the medical expenses Mid Atlantic paid on the Sereboffs' behalf. On several occasions over the next 2 1/2 years, Mid Atlantic sent similar correspondence to the attorney and to the Sereboffs, repeating its claim to a lien on a portion of the Sereboffs' recovery, and detailing the medical expenses as they accrued and were paid by the plan.

The Sereboffs' tort suit eventually settled for $750,000. Neither the Sereboffs nor their attorney sent any money to Mid Atlantic in satisfaction of its claimed lien which, after Mid Atlantic completed its payments on the Sereboffs' behalf, totaled $74,869.37.

Mid Atlantic filed suit in District Court under § 502(a)(3) of ERISA seeking to collect from the Sereboffs the medical expenses it had paid on their behalf. Since the Sereboffs' attorney had already distributed the settlement proceeds to them, Mid Atlantic sought a temporary restraining order and preliminary injunction requiring the couple to retain and set aside at least $74,869.37 from the proceeds. The District Court approved a stipulation by the parties, under which the Sereboffs agreed to "preserve $74,869.37 of the settlement funds" in an investment account, "until the [District] Court rules on the merits of this case and all appeals, if any, are exhausted."

On the merits, the District Court found in Mid Atlantic's favor and ordered the Sereboffs to pay Mid Atlantic the $74,869.37, plus interest, with a deduction for Mid Atlantic's share of the attorney's fees and court costs the Sereboffs had incurred in state court. The Sereboffs appealed and the Fourth Circuit affirmed in relevant part. 407 F.3d 212 (2005). The Fourth Circuit observed that the Courts of Appeal are divided on the question whether § 502(a)(3) authorizes recovery in these circumstances. We granted certiorari to resolve the disagreement.

II

A

A fiduciary may bring a civil action under § 502(a)(3) of ERISA "(A) to enjoin any act or practice which violates any provision of this subchapter or the terms of the plan, or (B) to obtain other appropriate equitable relief (i) to redress such violations or (ii) to enforce any provisions of this subchapter or the terms of the plan." There is no dispute that Mid Atlantic is a fiduciary under ERISA and that its suit in District Court was to "enforce . . . the terms of" the "Acts of Third Parties" provision in the Sereboffs' plan. The only question is whether the relief Mid Atlantic requested from the District Court was "equitable" under § 502(a)(3)(B).

This is not the first time we have had occasion to clarify the scope of the remedial power conferred on district courts by § 502(a)(3)(B). In *Mertens v. Hewitt Associates*, 508 U.S. 248 (1993), we construed the provision to authorize only "those categories of relief that were *typically* available in equity," and thus rejected a claim that we found sought "nothing other than compensatory *damages*." Id. at 255–256. We elaborated on this construction of § 502(a)(3)(B) in *Great-West Life & Annuity Ins. Co. v. Knudson*, 534 U.S. 204 (2002), which involved facts similar to those in this case. Much like the "Acts of Third Parties" provision in the Sereboffs' plan, the plan in *Knudson* reserved " 'a first lien upon any recovery, whether by settlement, judgment or otherwise,' that the beneficiary receives from [a] third party." Id. at 207. After Knudson was involved in a car accident, Great-West paid medical bills on her behalf and, when she recovered in tort from a third party for her injuries, Great-West sought to collect from her for the medical bills it had paid. Id. at 207–209.

In response to the argument that Great-West's claim in *Knudson* was for "restitution" and thus equitable under § 502(a)(3)(B) and *Mertens,* we noted that "not all relief falling under the rubric of restitution [was] available in equity." 534 U.S. at 212. To decide whether the restitutionary relief sought by Great-West was equitable or legal, we examined cases and secondary legal materials to determine if the relief would have been equitable "[i]n the days of the divided bench." Id. We explained that one feature of equitable restitution was that it sought to impose a constructive trust or equitable lien on "particular funds or property in the defendant's possession." Id. at 213. That requirement was not met in *Knudson* because "the funds to which petitioners claim[ed] an entitlement" were not in Knudson's possession, but had instead been placed in a "Special Needs Trust" under California law. Id. at 207. The kind of relief Great-West sought, therefore, was "not equitable—the imposition of a constructive trust or equitable lien on particular property—but legal—the imposition of personal liability for the benefits that [Great-West] conferred upon [Knudson]." Id. at 214. We accordingly determined that the suit could not proceed under § 502(a)(3). Id.

That impediment to characterizing the relief in *Knudson* as equitable is not present here. As the Fourth Circuit explained below, in this case Mid Atlantic sought "specifically identifiable" funds that were "within the possession and control of the Sereboffs"—that portion of the tort settlement due Mid Atlantic under the terms of the ERISA plan, set aside and "preserved [in the Sereboffs'] investment accounts." 407 F.3d at 218. Unlike Great-West, Mid Atlantic did not simply seek "to impose personal liability . . . for a contractual obligation to pay money." Knudson, 534 U.S. at 210. It alleged breach of contract and sought money, to be sure, but it sought its recovery through a constructive trust or equitable lien on a specifically identified fund, not from the Sereboffs' assets generally, as would be the case with a contract action at law. ERISA provides for equitable remedies *to enforce plan terms,* so the fact that the action involves a breach of contract can hardly be enough to prove relief is not equitable; that would make § 502(a)(3)(B)(ii) an empty promise. This Court in *Knudson* did not reject Great-West's suit out of hand because it alleged a breach of contract and sought money, but because Great-West did not seek to recover a particular fund from the defendant. Mid Atlantic does.

B

While Mid Atlantic's case for characterizing its relief as equitable thus does not falter because of the nature of the recovery it seeks, Mid Atlantic must still establish that the basis for its claim is equitable. See Knudson, 534 U.S. at 213 (whether remedy "is legal or equitable depends on 'the basis for [the plaintiff's] claim' and the nature of the underlying remedies sought"). Our case law from the days of the divided bench confirms that Mid Atlantic's claim is equitable. In *Barnes v. Alexander*, 232 U.S. 117 (1914), for instance, attorneys Street and Alexander performed work for Barnes, another attorney, who promised them "one-third of the contingent fee" he expected in the case. Id. at 119. In upholding their equitable claim to this portion of the fee, Justice Holmes recited "the familiar rul[e] of equity that a contract to convey a specific object even before it is acquired will make the contractor a trustee as soon as he gets a title to the thing." Id. at 121. On the basis of this rule, he concluded that Barnes' undertaking "create[d] a lien" upon the portion of the monetary recovery due Barnes from the client, which Street and Alexander could "follow . . . into the hands of . . . Barnes," "as soon as [the fund] was identified." Id. at 121–23.

Much like Barnes' promise to Street and Alexander, the "Acts of Third Parties" provision in the Sereboffs' plan specifically identified a particular fund, distinct from the Sereboffs' general assets—"[a]ll recoveries from a third party (whether by lawsuit, settlement, or otherwise)"—and a particular share of that fund to which Mid Atlantic was entitled—"that portion of the total recovery which is due [Mid Atlantic] for benefits paid." Like Street and Alexander in *Barnes*, therefore, Mid Atlantic could rely on a "familiar rul[e] of equity" to collect for the medical bills it had paid on the Sereboffs' behalf. Barnes, 232 U.S. at 121. This rule allowed them to "follow" a portion of the recovery "into the [Sereboffs'] hands" "as soon as [the settlement fund] was identified," and impose on that portion a constructive trust or equitable lien. 232 U.S. at 123.

The Sereboffs object that Mid Atlantic's suit would not have satisfied the conditions for "equitable restitution" at common law, particularly the "strict tracing rules" that allegedly accompanied this form of relief. When an equitable lien was imposed as restitutionary relief, it was often the case that an asset belonging to the plaintiff had been improperly acquired by the defendant and exchanged by him for other property. A central requirement of equitable relief in these circumstances, the Sereboffs argue, was the plaintiff's ability to " 'trac[e]' the asset into its products or substitutes," or "trace his money or property to some particular funds or assets." 1 D. Dobbs, Law of Remedies § 4.3(2), pp. 591, n. 10, 592 (2d ed.1993).

But as the Sereboffs themselves recognize, an equitable lien sought as a matter of restitution, and an equitable lien "by agreement," of the sort at issue in *Barnes,* were different species of relief. See 1 Dobbs, supra, § 4.3(3), at 601; 1 G. Palmer, Law of Restitution § 1.5, p. 20 (1978). *Barnes* confirms that no tracing requirement of the sort asserted by the Sereboffs applies to equitable liens by agreement or assignment: The plaintiffs in *Barnes* could not identify an asset they originally possessed, which was improperly acquired and converted into property the defendant held, yet that did not preclude them from securing an equitable lien. To the extent Mid Atlantic's action is proper under *Barnes,* therefore, its asserted inability to satisfy the "strict tracing rules" for "equitable restitution" is of no consequence.

The Sereboffs concede as much, stating that they "do not contend—and have never suggested—that any tracing was historically required when an equitable lien was imposed *by agreement*." Their argument is that such tracing was required when an equitable lien was "predicated on a theory of *equitable restitution*." The Sereboffs appear to assume that *Knudson* endorsed application of all the restitutionary conditions-including restitutionary tracing rules—to every action for an equitable lien under § 502(a)(3). This assumption is inaccurate. *Knudson* simply described in general terms the conditions under which a fiduciary might recover when it was seeking equitable restitution under a provision like that at issue in this case. There was no need in *Knudson* to catalog all the circumstances in which equitable liens were available in equity; Great-West claimed a right to recover in restitution, and the Court concluded only that equitable restitution was unavailable because the funds sought were not in Knudson's possession. 534 U.S. at 214.

* * *

C

Shifting gears, the Sereboffs contend that the lower courts erred in allowing enforcement of the "Acts of Third Parties" provision without imposing various limitations that they say would apply to "truly equitable relief grounded in principles of subrogation." According to the Sereboffs, they would in an equitable *subrogation* action be able to assert certain equitable defenses, such as the defense that subrogation may be pursued only after a victim had been made whole for his injuries. Such defenses should be available against Mid Atlantic's action, the Sereboffs claim, despite the plan provision that "[Mid Atlantic's] share of the recovery will not be reduced because [the beneficiary] has not received the full damages claimed, unless [Mid Atlantic] agrees in writing to a reduction."

But Mid Atlantic's claim is not considered equitable because it is a subrogation claim. As explained, Mid Atlantic's action to enforce the "Acts of Third Parties" provision qualifies as an equitable remedy because it is indistinguishable from an action to enforce an equitable lien established by agreement of the sort epitomized by our decision in *Barnes*. See 4 Palmer, Law of Restitution § 23.18(d), at 470 (A subrogation lien "is not an express lien based on agreement, but instead is an equitable lien impressed on moneys on the ground that they ought to go to the insurer."). Mid Atlantic need not characterize its claim as a freestanding action for equitable subrogation. Accordingly, the parcel of equitable defenses the Sereboffs claim accompany any such action are beside the point.

Under the teaching of *Barnes* and similar cases, Mid Atlantic's action in the District Court properly sought "equitable relief" under § 502(a)(3); the judgment of the Fourth Circuit is affirmed in relevant part.

NOTES AND QUESTIONS

1. *The Requirement of a Separate and Identifiable Fund.* After *Sereboff*, is the existence of a separate and identifiable fund from which recovery is sought by the plan administrator a prerequisite to enforcement of a plan reimbursement clause? If so, when must the separate and identifiable fund exist? At the time the plan administrator files a claim to enforce the plan reimbursement clause? At the time the federal court rules in favor of the plan administrator's claim? Can the defendant thwart enforcement of the reimbursement clause by simply commingling or dissipating the assets of what was once a separate and identifiable fund?

Longaberger Co. v. Kolt, 586 F.3d 459 (6th Cir. 2009), provides an interesting illustration of these post-*Sereboff* questions. In *Longaberger Co.*, an attorney represented a client who had been injured in an automobile accident. The client's medical expenses were paid by the employer's self-insured health care plan, which contained a reimbursement clause. The attorney settled the case for $135,000 and initially placed the settlement funds in his trust account, but later disbursed all but $1,000 of the settlement proceeds by paying himself $45,000 in attorney's fees and $86,000 to the client. When the employer's plan sued the attorney for taking his fee out of the settlement funds, the attorney argued that there was no longer a specifically identifiable fund on which a *Sereboff*-like equitable lien could be imposed. The Sixth Circuit rejected the attorney's argument and ruled that the plan had an enforceable equitable lien on the settlement proceeds, including the sums that the attorney had disbursed to himself as attorney's fees.

2. *Equitable Defenses After* Sereboff. In footnote 2 of the *Sereboff* opinion, the Supreme Court acknowledged the possibility that, given the equitable nature of the relief sought by the plan under Section 502(a)(3), the participant may be able to counter with various equitable defenses, such as the "make whole" doctrine. Unfortunately for the Sereboffs, their legal counsel failed to make this argument at either the district court or appellate court stages of the litigation. Consequently, the Supreme Court refused to consider the issue of possible equitable defenses when it was raised for the

first time before the Court. See Sereboff v. Mid Atlantic Med. Servs., Inc. 547 U.S. 356, 368–69, n. 2 (2006). Seven years later, the Supreme Court addressed the issue of equitable defenses that it had successfully dodged in *Sereboff* in the next principal case.

The Supreme Court's ruling in *Sereboff* was a blow to the plaintiffs' tort bar, who continued in subsequent litigation to assert a "parcel of equitable defenses" whenever an ERISA plan sought to enforce a reimbursement clause. In *US Airways, Inc. v. McCutchen*, the Supreme Court described when these equitable defenses would apply under the federal common law of ERISA. As you read *McCutchen*, consider the similarities to *Firestone Tire & Rubber Co. v. Bruch*, 489 U.S. 101 (1989), which is reproduced in Section C of Chapter Six. How are employers who sponsor self-insured group health plans likely to respond to *McCutchen*?

US AIRWAYS, INC. V. MCCUTCHEN
United States Supreme Court, 2013.
133 S. Ct. 1537.

JUSTICE KAGAN delivered the opinion of the Court.

Respondent James McCutchen participated in a health benefits plan that his employer, petitioner U.S. Airways, established under the Employee Retirement Income Security Act of 1974 (ERISA), 29 U.S.C. § 1001 et seq. That plan obliged U.S. Airways to pay any medical expenses McCutchen incurred as a result of a third party's actions—for example, another person's negligent driving. The plan in turn entitled U.S. Airways to reimbursement if McCutchen later recovered money from the third party.

This Court has held that a health-plan administrator like U.S. Airways may enforce such a reimbursement provision by filing suit under § 502(a)(3) of ERISA. See Sereboff v. Mid Atlantic Medical Services, Inc., 547 U.S. 356 (2006). That section authorizes a civil action "to obtain . . . appropriate equitable relief . . . to enforce . . . the terms of the plan." We here consider whether in that kind of suit, a plan participant like McCutchen may raise certain equitable defenses deriving from principles of unjust enrichment. In particular, we address one equitable doctrine limiting reimbursement to the amount of an insured's "double recovery" and another requiring the party seeking reimbursement to pay a share of the attorney's fees incurred in securing funds from the third party. We hold that neither of those equitable rules can override the clear terms of a plan. But we explain that the latter, usually called the common-fund doctrine, plays a role in interpreting U.S. Airways' plan because the plan is silent about allocating the costs of recovery.

I

In January 2007, McCutchen suffered serious injuries when another driver lost control of her car and collided with McCutchen's. At the time, McCutchen was an employee of U.S. Airways and a participant in its self-funded health plan. The plan paid $66,866 in medical expenses arising from the accident on McCutchen's behalf.

McCutchen retained attorneys, in exchange for a 40% contingency fee, to seek recovery of all his accident-related damages, estimated to exceed $1 million. The attorneys sued the driver responsible for the crash, but settled for only $10,000 because she had limited insurance coverage and the accident had killed or seriously injured three other people. Counsel also secured a payment from McCutchen's own automobile insurer of $100,000, the maximum amount available under his policy. McCutchen thus received $110,000—and after deducting $44,000 for the lawyer's fee, $66,000.

On learning of McCutchen's recovery, U.S. Airways demanded reimbursement of the $66,866 it had paid in medical expenses. In support of that claim, U.S. Airways relied on the following statement in its summary plan description:

> If [US Airways] pays benefits for any claim you incur as the result of negligence, willful misconduct, or other actions of a third party,. . .[y]ou will be required to reimburse [US Airways] for amounts paid for claims out of any monies recovered from [the] third party, including, but not limited to, your own insurance company as the result of judgment, settlement, or otherwise.[1]

McCutchen denied that U.S. Airways was entitled to any reimbursement, but his attorneys placed $41,500 in an escrow account pending resolution of the dispute. That amount represented U.S. Airways' full claim minus a proportionate share of the promised attorney's fees.

U.S. Airways then filed this action under § 502(a)(3), seeking "appropriate equitable relief" to enforce the plan's reimbursement provision. The suit requested an equitable lien on $66,866—the $41,500 in the escrow account and $25,366 more in McCutchen's possession. McCutchen countered by raising two defenses relevant here. First, he maintained that U.S. Airways could not receive the relief it sought because he had recovered only a small portion of his total damages; absent over-recovery on his part, U.S. Airways'

---

[1] We have made clear that the statements in a summary plan description "communicat[e] with beneficiaries *about* the plan, but. . .do not themselves constitute the *terms* of the plan." CIGNA Corp. v. Amara, 131 S. Ct. 1866, 1878 (2011). Nonetheless, the parties litigated this case, and both lower courts decided it, based solely on the language quoted above. Only in this Court, in response to a request from the Solicitor General, did the plan itself come to light. That is too late to affect what happens here. Because everyone in this case has treated the language from the summary description as though it came from the plan, we do so as well.

right to reimbursement did not kick in. Second, he contended that U.S. Airways at least had to contribute its fair share to the costs he incurred to get his recovery; any reimbursement therefore had to be marked down by 40%, to cover the promised contingency fee. The District Court rejected both arguments, granting summary judgment to U.S. Airways on the ground that the plan "clear[ly] and unambiguous[ly]" provided for full reimbursement of the medical expenses paid.

The Court of Appeals for the Third Circuit vacated the District Court's order. The Third Circuit reasoned that in a suit for "appropriate equitable relief" under § 502(a)(3), a court must apply any "equitable doctrines and defenses" that traditionally limited the relief requested. 663 F.3d 671, 676 (3rd Cir. 2011). And here, the court continued, " 'the principle of unjust enrichment' " should " 'serve to limit the effectiveness' " of the plan's reimbursement provision. See id. at 677 (quoting 4 G. Palmer, Law of Restitution § 23.18, p. 472–473 (1978)). Full reimbursement, the Third Circuit thought, would "leav[e] [McCutchen] with less than full payment" for his medical bills; at the same time, it would provide a "windfall" to U.S. Airways given its failure to "contribute to the cost of obtaining the third-party recovery." 663 F.3d at 679. The Third Circuit then instructed the District Court to determine what amount, shy of the entire $66,866, would qualify as "appropriate equitable relief."

We granted certiorari to resolve a circuit split on whether equitable defenses can so override an ERISA plan's reimbursement provision.[2] We now vacate the Third Circuit's decision.

II

A health-plan administrator like U.S. Airways may bring suit under § 502(a)(3) for "appropriate equitable relief. . .to enforce. . .the terms of the plan." That provision, we have held, authorizes the kinds of relief "typically available in equity" in the days of "the divided bench," before law and equity merged. Mertens v. Hewitt Associates, 508 U.S. 248, 256 (1993) (emphasis deleted).

In *Sereboff v. Mid Atlantic Medical Services,* we allowed a health-plan administrator to bring a suit just like this one under § 502(a)(3). Mid Atlantic had paid medical expenses for the Sereboffs after they were injured in a car crash. When they settled a tort suit against the other driver, Mid Atlantic

---

[2] Compare 663 F.3d 671, 673 (3rd Cir. 2011) (case below) (holding that equitable doctrines can trump a plan's terms); CGI Technologies & Solutions Inc. v. Rose, 683 F.3d 1113, 1124 (9th Cir. 2012) (same), with Zurich Am. Ins. Co. v. O'Hara, 604 F.3d 1232, 1237 (11th Cir. 2010) (holding that they cannot do so); Administrative Comm. of Wal-Mart Stores, Inc. v. Shank, 500 F.3d 834, 838 (8th Cir. 2007) (same); Moore v. CapitalCare, Inc., 461 F.3d 1, 9–10 and n. 10 (D.C. Cir. 2006) (same); Bombardier Aerospace Employee Welfare Benefits Plan v. Ferrer, Poirot, & Wansbrough, 354 F.3d 348, 362 (5th Cir. 2003) (same); Administrative Comm. of Wal-Mart Stores, Inc. v. Varco, 338 F.3d 680, 692 (7th Cir. 2003) (same).

claimed a share of the proceeds, invoking the plan's reimbursement clause. We held that Mid Atlantic's action sought "equitable relief," as §502(a)(3) requires. See 547 U.S. at 369. The "nature of the recovery" requested was equitable because Mid Atlantic claimed "specifically identifiable funds" within the Sereboffs' control—that is, a portion of the settlement they had gotten. Id. at 362–363. And the "basis for [the] claim" was equitable too, because Mid Atlantic relied on " 'the familiar rul[e] of equity that a contract to convey a specific object' " not yet acquired " 'create[s] a lien' " on that object as soon as " 'the contractor. . .gets a title to the thing.' " Id. at 363–364 (quoting Barnes v. Alexander, 232 U.S. 117, 121(1914)). Mid Atlantic's claim for reimbursement, we determined, was the modern-day equivalent of an action in equity to enforce such a contract-based lien—called an "equitable lien by agreement." 547 U.S. at 364–365. Accordingly, Mid Atlantic could bring an action under § 502(a)(3) seeking the funds that its beneficiaries had promised to turn over. And here, as all parties agree, U.S. Airways can do the same thing.

The question in this case concerns the role that equitable defenses alleging unjust enrichment can play in such a suit. As earlier noted, the Third Circuit held that "the principle of unjust enrichment" overrides U.S. Airways' reimbursement clause if and when they come into conflict. 663 F.3d at 677. McCutchen offers a more refined version of that view, alleging that two specific equitable doctrines meant to "prevent unjust enrichment" defeat the reimbursement provision. First, he contends that in equity, an insurer in U.S. Airways' position could recoup no more than an insured's "double recovery"—the amount the insured has received from a third party to compensate for the same loss the insurance covered. That rule would limit U.S. Airways' reimbursement to the share of McCutchen's settlements paying for medical expenses; McCutchen would keep the rest (e.g., damages for loss of future earnings or pain and suffering), even though the plan gives U.S. Airways first claim on the whole third-party recovery. Second, McCutchen claims that in equity the common-fund doctrine would have operated to reduce any award to U.S. Airways. Under that rule, "a litigant or a lawyer who recovers a common fund for the benefit of persons other than himself or his client is entitled to a reasonable attorney's fee from the fund as a whole." Boeing Co. v. Van Gemert, 444 U.S. 472, 478 (1980). McCutchen urges that this doctrine, which is designed to prevent freeloading, enables him to pass on a share of his lawyer's fees to U.S. Airways, no matter what the plan provides.

We rejected a similar claim in *Sereboff,* though without altogether foreclosing McCutchen's position. The Sereboffs argued, among other things, that the lower courts erred in enforcing Mid Atlantic's reimbursement clause "without imposing various limitations" that would "apply to truly equitable relief grounded in principles of subrogation." 547 U.S. at 368. In particular, the Sereboffs contended that a variant of the double-recovery rule, called the make-whole doctrine, trumped the plan's terms. We rebuffed that argument, explaining that the Sereboffs were improperly mixing and matching rules from different equitable boxes. The Sereboffs asserted a "parcel of equitable defenses" available when an out-of-pocket insurer brought a "freestanding action for equitable subrogation," not founded on a contract, to succeed to an insured's judgment against a third party. Id. But Mid Atlantic's reimbursement claim was "considered equitable," we replied, because it sought to enforce a "lien based on agreement"—*not* a lien imposed independent of contract by virtue of equitable subrogation. Id. In light of that fact, we viewed the Sereboffs' equitable defenses—which again, closely resemble McCutchen's—as "beside the point." Id. And yet, we left a narrow opening for future litigants in the Sereboffs' position to make a like claim. In a footnote, we observed that the Sereboffs had forfeited a "distinct assertion" that the contract-based relief Mid Atlantic requested, although "equitable," was not "appropriate" under § 502(a)(3) because "it contravened principles like the make-whole doctrine." Id. at 368–369 n. 2. Enter McCutchen, to make that basic argument.

In the end, however, *Sereboff* 's logic dooms McCutchen's effort. U.S. Airways, like Mid Atlantic, is seeking to enforce the modern-day equivalent of an "equitable lien by agreement." And that kind of lien—as its name announces—both arises from and serves to carry out a contract's provisions. So enforcing the lien means holding the parties to their mutual promises. Conversely, it means declining to apply rules—even if they would be "equitable" in a contract's absence—at odds with the parties' expressed commitments. McCutchen therefore cannot rely on theories of unjust enrichment to defeat U.S. Airways' appeal to the plan's clear terms. Those principles, as we said in *Sereboff,* are "beside the point" when parties demand what they bargained for in a valid agreement. See Restatement (Third) of Restitution and Unjust Enrichment § 2(2), p. 15 (2010) ("A valid contract defines the obligations of the parties as to matters within its scope, displacing to that extent any inquiry into unjust enrichment"). In those circumstances, hewing to the parties' exchange yields "appropriate" as well as "equitable" relief.

We have found nothing to the contrary in the historic practice of equity courts. McCutchen offers us a slew of cases in which those courts applied the double-recovery or common-fund rule to limit insurers' efforts to recoup funds from their beneficiaries' tort judgments. But his citations are not on point. In some of McCutchen's cases, courts apparently applied equitable doctrines in the absence of any relevant contract provision. In others, courts found those rules to comport with the applicable contract term. For example, in *Svea Assurance Co. v. Packham,* 92 Md. 464, 48 A. 359 (1901)—the case McCutchen calls his best, see Tr. of Oral Arg. 47–48—the court viewed the double-recovery rule as according with "the intention" of the contracting parties; "[b]road as [the] language is," the court explained, the agreement "cannot be construed to" give the insurer any greater recovery. 92 Md. at 478, 48 A. at 362. But in none of these cases—nor in any other we can find—did an equity court apply the double-recovery or common-fund rule to override a plain contract term. That is, in none did an equity court do what McCutchen asks of us.

Nevertheless, the United States, appearing as amicus curiae, claims that the common-fund rule has a special capacity to trump a conflicting contract. The Government begins its brief foursquare with our (and *Sereboff* 's) analysis: In a suit like this one, to enforce an equitable lien by agreement, "the agreement, not general restitutionary principles of unjust enrichment, provides the measure of relief due." Brief for United States 6. Because that is so, the Government (naturally enough) concludes, McCutchen cannot invoke the double-recovery rule to defeat the plan. But then the Government takes an unexpected turn. "When it comes to the costs incurred" by a beneficiary to obtain money from a third party, "the terms of the plan do not control." Id. at 21. An equity court, the Government contends, has "inherent authority" to apportion litigation costs in accord with the "longstanding equitable common-fund doctrine," even if that conflicts with the parties' contract. Id. at 22.

But if the agreement governs, the agreement governs. The reasons we have given (and the Government mostly accepts) for looking to the contract's terms do not permit an attorney's fees exception. We have no doubt that the common-fund doctrine has deep roots in equity. See Sprague v. Ticonic Nat. Bank, 307 U.S. 161, 164 (1939) (tracing equity courts' authority over fees to the First Judiciary Act). Those roots, however, are set in the soil of unjust enrichment. To allow "others to obtain full benefit from the plaintiff's efforts without contributing. . .to the litigation expenses," we have often noted, "would be to enrich the others unjustly at the plaintiff's expense." Mills v. Electric Auto-Lite Co., 396 U.S. 375, 392 (1970). And as we have just explained, principles of unjust enrichment give way when a court enforces an equitable lien by agreement. The agreement itself becomes the measure of the parties' equities; so if a contract abrogates the common-fund doctrine, the insurer is not unjustly enriched by claiming the benefit of its bargain. That is why the Government, like McCutchen, fails to produce a single case in which an equity court applied the common-fund rule (any more than the double-recovery rule) when a contract provided to the contrary. Even in equity, when a party sought to enforce a lien by agreement, all provisions of that agreement controlled. So too, then, in a suit like this one.

The result we reach, based on the historical analysis our prior cases prescribe, fits lock and key with ERISA's focus on what a plan provides. The section under which this suit is brought "does not, after all, authorize 'appropriate equitable relief' *at large*," Mertens, 508 U.S. at 253 (quoting § 502(a)(3)); rather, it countenances only such relief as will enforce "*the terms of the plan*" or the statute, § 502(a)(3) (emphasis added). That limitation reflects ERISA's principal function: to "protect contractually defined benefits." Massachusetts Mut. Life Ins. Co. v. Russell, 473 U.S. 134, 148 (1985). The statutory scheme, we have often noted, "is built around reliance

on the face of written plan documents." Curtiss-Wright Corp. v.
Schoonejongen, 514 U.S. 73, 83 (1995). "Every employee benefit plan shall be
established and maintained pursuant to a written instrument," § 402(a)(1),
and an administrator must act "in accordance with the documents and
instruments governing the plan" insofar as they accord with the statute,
§ 404(a)(1)(D). The plan, in short, is at the center of ERISA. And precluding
McCutchen's equitable defenses from overriding plain contract terms helps it
to remain there.

<h2 style="text-align:center">III</h2>

Yet McCutchen's arguments are not all for naught. If the equitable
rules he describes cannot trump a reimbursement provision, they still
might aid in properly construing it. And for U.S. Airways' plan, the
common-fund doctrine (though not the double-recovery rule) serves that
function. The plan is silent on the allocation of attorney's fees, and in
those circumstances, the common-fund doctrine provides the appropriate
default. In other words, if U.S. Airways wished to depart from the well-
established common-fund rule, it had to draft its contract to say so—and
here it did not.[7]

Ordinary principles of contract interpretation point toward this
conclusion. Courts construe ERISA plans, as they do other contracts, by
"looking to the terms of the plan" as well as to "other manifestations of
the parties' intent." Firestone Tire & Rubber Co. v. Bruch, 489 U.S. 101,
113 (1989). The words of a plan may speak clearly, but they may also
leave gaps. And so a court must often "look outside the plan's written
language" to decide what an agreement means. CIGNA Corp. v. Amara,
131 S. Ct. 1866, 1877; see Curtiss-Wright, 514 U.S. at 80–81. In
undertaking that task, a court properly takes account of background legal
rules—the doctrines that typically or traditionally have governed a given
situation when no agreement states otherwise. See Wal-Mart Stores, Inc.
Assoc. Health & Welfare Plan v. Wells, 213 F.3d 398, 402 (7th Cir. 2000)
(Posner, J.) ("[C]ontracts. . .are enacted against a background of common-
sense understandings and legal principles that the parties may not have
bothered to incorporate expressly but that operate as default rules to
govern in the absence of a clear expression of the parties' [contrary]

---

[7]   The dissent faults us for addressing this issue, but we think it adequately preserved and
presented. The language the dissent highlights in McCutchen's brief in opposition, indicating
that the plan clearly abrogates the common-fund doctrine, comes from his description of U.S.
Airways' claim in the District Court. McCutchen's argument in that court urged the very position
we adopt—that the common-fund doctrine applies because the plan is silent. To be sure,
McCutchen shifted ground on appeal because the District Court ruled that Third Circuit
precedent foreclosed his contract-based argument; the Court of Appeals' decision then put front-
and-center his alternative contention that the common-fund rule trumps a contract. But both
claims have the same basis (the nature and function of the common-fund doctrine), which the
parties have disputed throughout this litigation. And similarly, the question we decide here is
included in the question presented. The principal clause of that question asks whether a court
may use "equitable principles to rewrite contractual language." We answer "not rewrite, but
inform"—a reply well within the question's scope.

intent"); 11 R. Lord, Williston on Contracts § 31:7 (4th ed.2012); Restatement (Second) of Contracts § 221 (1979). Indeed, ignoring those rules is likely to frustrate the parties' intent and produce perverse consequences.

The reimbursement provision at issue here precludes looking to the double-recovery rule in this manner. Both the contract term and the equitable principle address the same problem: how to apportion, as between an insurer and a beneficiary, a third party's payment to recompense an injury. But the allocation formulas they prescribe differ markedly. According to the plan, U.S. Airways has first claim on the entire recovery—as the plan description states, on "any monies recovered from [the] third party"; McCutchen receives only whatever is left over (if anything). By contrast, the double-recovery rule would give McCutchen first dibs on the portion of the recovery compensating for losses that the plan did not cover (e.g., future earnings or pain and suffering); U.S. Airways' claim would attach only to the share of the recovery for medical expenses. The express contract term, in short, contradicts the background equitable rule; and where that is so, for all the reasons we have given, the agreement must govern.

By contrast, the plan provision here leaves space for the common-fund rule to operate. That equitable doctrine, as earlier noted, addresses not how to allocate a third-party recovery, but instead how to pay for the costs of obtaining it. And the contract, for its part, says nothing specific about that issue. The District Court below thus erred when it found that the plan clearly repudiated the common-fund rule. To be sure, the plan's allocation formula—first claim on the recovery goes to U.S. Airways— *might* operate on every dollar received from a third party, even those covering the beneficiary's litigation costs. But alternatively, that formula could apply to only the true recovery, after the costs of obtaining it are deducted. (Consider, for comparative purposes, how an income tax is levied on net, not gross, receipts.) See Dawson, Lawyers and Involuntary Clients: Attorney Fees From Funds, 87 Harv. L. Rev. 1597, 1606–1607 (1974) ("[T]he claim for legal services is a first charge on the fund and must be satisfied before any distribution occurs"). The plan's terms fail to select between these two alternatives: whether the recovery to which U.S. Airways has first claim is every cent the third party paid or, instead, the money the beneficiary took away.

Given that contractual gap, the common-fund doctrine provides the best indication of the parties' intent. No one can doubt that the common-fund rule would govern here in the absence of a contrary agreement. This Court has "recognized consistently" that someone "who recovers a common fund for the benefit of persons other than himself" is due "a reasonable attorney's fee from the fund as whole." Boeing Co., 444 U.S. at 478. We have understood that rule as "reflect[ing] the traditional practice in courts of equity." Id. And we have applied it in a wide range of circumstances as part of our inherent authority. State courts have done the same; the "overwhelming majority" routinely use the common-fund rule to allocate the costs of third-party recoveries between insurers and beneficiaries. A party would not typically expect or intend a plan saying nothing about attorney's fees to abrogate so strong and uniform a background rule. And that means a court should be loath to read such a plan in that way.

The rationale for the common-fund rule reinforces that conclusion. Third-party recoveries do not often come free: To get one, an insured must incur lawyer's fees and expenses. Without cost sharing, the insurer free rides on its beneficiary's efforts—taking the fruits while contributing nothing to the labor. Odder still, in some cases—indeed, in this case—the beneficiary is made worse off by pursuing a third party. Recall that McCutchen spent $44,000 (representing a 40% contingency fee) to get $110,000, leaving him with a real recovery of $66,000. But U.S. Airways claimed $66,866 in medical expenses. That would put McCutchen $866 in the hole; in effect, he would pay for the privilege of serving as U.S. Airways' collection agent. We think McCutchen would not have foreseen that result when he signed on to the plan. And we doubt if even U.S. Airways should want it. When the next McCutchen comes along, he is not likely to relieve U.S. Airways of the costs of recovery. See Blackburn v. Sundstrand Corp., 115 F.3d 493, 496 (7th Cir. 1997) (Easterbrook, J.) ("[I]f. . .injured persons could not charge legal costs against recoveries, people like [McCutchen] would in the future have every reason" to make different judgments about bringing suit, "throwing on plans the burden and expense of collection"). The prospect of generating those strange results again militates against reading a general reimbursement provision—like the one here—for more than it is worth. Only if U.S. Airways' plan expressly addressed the costs of recovery would it alter the common-fund doctrine.

IV

Our holding today has two parts, one favoring U.S. Airways, the other McCutchen. First, in an action brought under § 502(a)(3) based on an equitable lien by agreement, the terms of the ERISA plan govern. Neither general principles of unjust enrichment nor specific doctrines reflecting those principles—such as the double-recovery or common-fund rules—can override the applicable contract. We therefore reject the Third Circuit's decision. But second, the common-fund rule informs interpretation of U.S. Airways' reimbursement provision. Because that term does not advert to the costs of recovery, it is properly read to retain the common-fund doctrine. We therefore also disagree with the District Court's decision. In light of these rulings, we vacate the judgment below and remand the case for further proceedings consistent with this opinion.

Justice SCALIA, with whom THE CHIEF JUSTICE, Justice THOMAS, and Justice ALITO join, dissenting.

I agree with Parts I and II of the Court's opinion, which conclude that equity cannot override the plain terms of the contract.

The Court goes on in Parts III and IV, however, to hold that the terms are *not* plain and to apply the "common-fund" doctrine to fill that "contractual gap." The problem with this is that we granted certiorari on a question that presumed the contract's terms were unambiguous—namely, "where the plan's terms give it an absolute right to full reimbursement." Respondents interpreted "full reimbursement" to mean what it plainly says— reimbursement of *all* the funds the Plan had expended. In their brief in opposition to the petition they conceded that, under the contract, "a beneficiary is required to reimburse the Plan for any amounts it has paid out of any monies the beneficiary recovers from a third-party, *without any contribution to attorney's fees and expenses.*" Brief in Opposition 5 (emphasis added). All the parties, as well as the Solicitor General, have treated that concession as valid. The Court thus has no business deploying against petitioner an argument that was neither preserved, nor fairly included within the question presented.

I would reverse the judgment of the Third Circuit.

QUESTIONS

1. *Clear or Ambiguous Terms?* Do you find the reimbursement clause language quoted in *McCutchen* to be ambiguous? How would you amend this language to preclude application of the common-fund doctrine and other equitable defenses?

2. *Federal Common Law and the Written Instrument Rule.* The Supreme Court's emphasis in *McCutchen* on the language in the written instrument that establishes the employer's plan echoes a theme introduced earlier in Chapter Two of the casebook. Namely, the federal courts are to defer to the written plan document language so long as that language is not contrary to the statutory provisions of ERISA. Thus, the role of federal common law in plan interpretation appears to be limited to a gap-filler function, to be used only when the plan's language is ambiguous. Do ERISA's statutory provisions regarding participant rights and remedies provide sufficient protection against misuse of the written instrument rule by employers?

3. *Future Implications for Personal Injury Litigation.* If you were a plaintiff's trial lawyer, after *McCutchen* how will you proceed when presented with a potential personal injury claim? What information concerning the client's health care insurance will you need to obtain before deciding whether to pursue the claim? How will you obtain that information?

---

3. CLAIMS FOR INTERFERENCE WITH PROTECTED RIGHTS UNDER SECTION 510

Section 510 of ERISA was introduced in Chapter Four of the casebook in connection with the employer's right to terminate or amend the benefits under a health care plan. A careful parsing of the statutory language of Section 510 reveals that this section protects against several different types of interference with the exercise of rights associated with ERISA. Section 510 prohibits:

- the disruption of employment privileges to punish the exercise of rights under an employee benefit plan;
- the disruption of employment privileges to prevent the vesting or enjoyment of rights under an employee benefit plan; and
- the disruption of employment privileges to prevent or punish a person who gives testimony in any proceeding related to ERISA.

See Teumer v. General Motors Corp., 34 F.3d 542, 547 (7th Cir. 1994). Although Section 510 does not limit the universe of potential defendants, the typical Section 510 violation is asserted against the employer. A violation of Section 510 is remedied by a claim brought under Section 502(a)(3) of ERISA. Ingersoll-Rand Co. v. McClendon, 498 U.S. 133, 142–44 (1990).

Congress designed Section 510 to reinforce ERISA's vesting and benefit accrual rules and to prevent "unscrupulous employers from discharging or harassing employees in order to keep them from obtaining vested pension rights." West v. Butler, 621 F.2d 240, 245 (6th Cir. 1980). *Gavalik v. Continental Can Co.*, 812 F.2d 834 (3d Cir. 1987), illustrates the unscrupulous employer conduct that Section 510 prohibits. In *Continental Can*, the employer, who was a manufacturer of steel cans, experienced a steady decline in business during the 1970s. The employer's collective bargaining agreement with the United Steelworkers of America provided for two special pension benefit plans for eligible employees who experienced a two-year break in service as a result of a plant closing or layoff. Faced with having to close plants and lay off workers, the employer initiated a "liability avoidance program" designed to minimize the pension liability costs associated with downsizing the company. This liability avoidance program was, in fact, an elaborate scheme designed to identify those employees who had not yet satisfied the eligibility requirements for the special pension plan benefits and lay them off before they could satisfy those service requirements.

The Third Circuit found that the employer's liability avoidance program was the proverbial smoking gun—direct evidence of the employer's discriminatory motivation under ERISA Section 510. The court concluded that "if Continental's liability avoidance scheme does not constitute direct proof of discrimination under § 510, we are hard pressed to imagine a set of facts that would." Id. at 856.

To establish a violation of ERISA Section 510, the plaintiff must prove that the defendant acted with the specific intent to interfere with rights protected under Section 510. Direct proof of an employer's discriminatory intent, as in *Continental Can*, is rare. The plaintiff usually must rely on circumstantial evidence to prove the employer's discriminatory motive. The question of intent is further complicated because the employer may have had mixed motives—both illegal and legitimate reasons—for the adverse employment action taken against the plaintiff.

Where evidence of discriminatory intent under ERISA Section 510 is circumstantial, the federal courts apply the same three-step analytical framework used to prove discriminatory employer intent under Title VII of the Civil Rights Act. This analytical framework was first articulated by the Supreme Court in *McDonnell Douglas Corp. v. Green*, 411 U.S. 792 (1973). The plaintiff first must establish a prima facie case under Section 510. At this initial stage, the plaintiff need only show that the employer's actions give rise to an inference of discriminatory intent under Section 510. If the plaintiff successfully establishes a prima facie case, the burden shifts to the employer to produce a legitimate, nondiscriminatory reason or reasons for the action that interfered with the plaintiff's rights under Section 510. If the employer satisfies its burden of producing a legitimate reason or reasons for the employer's action, then the burden shifts back to the plaintiff to prove, by a preponderance of the evidence, that the legitimate reason or reasons offered by the employer were not the true motivations for the employer's conduct, but rather serve as a pretext for conduct prohibited by Section 510.

Although Congress enacted Section 510 in response to employer interference with vested pension plan benefits, the statutory language of Section 510 protects the rights associated with any type of employee benefit plan. In *Inter-Modal Rail Employees Association v. Atchison, Topeka & Santa Fe Railway Co.*, the Supreme Court concluded that, consistent with the statutory language, Section 510 also protects rights associated with welfare benefit plans.

INTER-MODAL RAIL EMPLOYEES ASSOCIATION V. ATCHISON, TOPEKA & SANTA FE RAILWAY CO.

United States Supreme Court, 1997.
520 U.S. 510, 117 S.Ct. 1513, 137 L.Ed.2d 763.

JUSTICE O'CONNOR delivered the opinion of the Court.

Section 510 of the Employee Retirement Income Security Act of 1974 (ERISA) makes it unlawful to "discharge, fine, suspend, expel, discipline, or discriminate against a participant or beneficiary [of an employee benefit plan] for the purpose of interfering with the attainment of any right to which such participant may become entitled under the plan." The Court of Appeals for the Ninth Circuit held that § 510 only prohibits interference with the attainment of rights that are capable of "vesting," as that term is defined in ERISA. We disagree.

I

The individual petitioners are former employees of respondent Santa Fe Terminal Services, Inc. (SFTS), a wholly owned subsidiary of respondent the Atchison, Topeka and Santa Fe Railway Co. (ATSF), which was responsible for transferring cargo between railcars and trucks at ATSF's Hobart Yard in Los Angeles, California. While petitioners were employed by SFTS, they were entitled to retirement benefits under the Railroad Retirement Act of 1974, and to pension, health, and welfare benefits under collective bargaining agreements involving SFTS and the Teamsters Union. SFTS provided its workers with pension, health, and welfare benefits through employee benefit plans subject to ERISA's comprehensive regulations.

In January 1990, ATSF entered into a formal "Service Agreement" with SFTS to have SFTS do the same "inter-modal" work it had done at the Hobart Yard for the previous 15 years without a contract. Seven weeks later, ATSF exercised its right to terminate the newly formed agreement and opened up the Hobart Yard work for competitive bidding. Respondent In-Terminal Services (ITS) was the successful bidder, and SFTS employees who declined to continue employment with ITS were terminated. ITS, unlike SFTS, was not obligated to make contributions to the Railroad Retirement Account under the Railroad Retirement Act. ITS also provided fewer pension and welfare benefits under its collective bargaining agreement with the Teamsters Union than had SFTS. Workers who continued their employment with ITS "lost their Railroad Retirement Act benefits" and "suffered a substantial reduction in Teamsters benefits."

Petitioners sued respondents SFTS, ATSF, and ITS in the United States District Court for the Central District of California, alleging that respondents had violated § 510 of ERISA by "discharg[ing]" petitioners "for the purpose of interfering with the attainment of. . .right[s] to which" they would have "become entitled" under the ERISA pension and welfare plans adopted pursuant to the SFTS-Teamsters collective bargaining agreement. Had SFTS remained their employer, petitioners contended, they would have been entitled to assert claims for benefits under the SFTS-Teamsters benefit plans, at least until the collective bargaining agreement that gave rise to those plans expired. The substitution of ITS for SFTS, however, precluded them from asserting those claims and relegated them to asserting claims under the less generous ITS-Teamsters benefit plans. According to petitioners, the substitution "interfer[ed] with the attainment" of their "right" to assert those claims and violated § 510. Respondents moved to dismiss these § 510 claims, and the District Court granted the motion.

The Court of Appeals for the Ninth Circuit affirmed in part and reversed in part. The court reinstated petitioners' claim under § 510 for interference with their *pension* benefits, concluding that § 510 "protects plan participants from termination motivated by an employer's desire to prevent a pension from vesting." But the Court of Appeals affirmed the dismissal of petitioners' claim for interference with their *welfare* benefits. "Unlike pension benefits," the Court of Appeals observed, "welfare benefits do not vest." As a result, the Court of Appeals noted, "employers remain free to unilaterally amend or eliminate [welfare] plans," and "employees have no present 'right' to future, anticipated welfare benefits." Because the "existence of a present 'right' is [a] prerequisite to section 510 relief," the Court of Appeals concluded that § 510 did not state a cause of action for interference with welfare benefits. We granted certiorari to resolve a conflict among the Courts of Appeals on this issue, and now vacate the decision below and remand.

II

The Court of Appeals' holding that § 510 bars interference only with vested rights is contradicted by the plain language of § 510. As noted above, that section makes it unlawful to "discharge. . .a [plan] participant or beneficiary. . .for the purpose of interfering with the *attainment of any right* to which such participant may become entitled under *the plan.*" ERISA § 510 (emphasis added). ERISA defines a "plan" to include both "an employee welfare benefit plan [and] an employee pension benefit plan," ERISA § 3(3), and specifically exempts "employee welfare benefit plan[s]" from its stringent vesting requirements, see ERISA § 201(1). Because a "plan" includes an "employee welfare benefit plan," and because welfare plans offer benefits that do not "vest" (at least insofar as ERISA is concerned), Congress' use of the word "plan" in § 510 all but forecloses the argument that § 510's interference clause applies only to "vested" rights. Had Congress intended to confine § 510's protection to "vested" rights, it could have easily substituted the term "pension plan," see ERISA § 3(2), for "plan," or the term "nonforfeitable" right, see ERISA

§ 3(19), for "any right." But § 510 draws no distinction between those rights that "vest" under ERISA and those that do not.

The right that an employer or plan sponsor may enjoy in some circumstances to unilaterally amend or eliminate its welfare benefit plan does not, as the Court of Appeals apparently thought, justify a departure from § 510's plain language. It is true that ERISA itself "does not regulate the substantive content of welfare-benefit plans." Metropolitan Life Ins. Co. v. Massachusetts, 471 U.S. 724, 732 (1985). Thus, unless an employer contractually cedes its freedom, it is "generally free under ERISA, for any reason at any time, to adopt, modify, or terminate [its] welfare pla[n]." Curtiss-Wright Corp. v. Schoonejongen, 514 U.S. 73, 78 (1995).

The flexibility an employer enjoys to amend or eliminate its welfare plan is not an accident; Congress recognized that "requir[ing] the vesting of these ancillary benefits would seriously complicate the administration and increase the cost of plans." S. Rep. No. 93–383, p. 51 (1973). Giving employers this flexibility also encourages them to offer more generous benefits at the outset, since they are free to reduce benefits should economic conditions sour. If employers were locked into the plans they initially offered, "they would err initially on the side of omission." Heath v. Varity Corp., 71 F.3d 256, 258 (7th Cir. 1995). Section 510 counterbalances this flexibility by ensuring that employers do not "circumvent the provision of promised benefits." Ingersoll-Rand Co. v. McClendon, 498 U.S. 133 (1990) (citing S. Rep. No. 93–127, pp. 35–36 (1973); H. R. Rep. No. 93–533, p. 17 (1973)). In short, "§ 510 helps to make promises credible." Heath, 71 F.3d at 258. An employer may, of course, retain the unfettered right to alter its promises, but to do so it must follow the formal procedures set forth in the plan. See ERISA § 402(b)(3)(requiring plan to "provide a procedure for amending such plan"); Schoonejongen, 514 U.S. at 78 (observing that the "cognizable claim [under ERISA] is that the company did not [amend its welfare benefit plan] in a permissible manner"). Adherence to these formal procedures "increases the likelihood that proposed plan amendments, which are fairly serious events, are recognized as such and given the special consideration they deserve." Schoonejongen, 514 U.S. at 82. The formal amendment process would be undermined if § 510 did not apply because employers could "informally" amend their plans one participant at a time. Thus, the power to amend or abolish a welfare benefit plan does not include the power to "discharge, fine, suspend, expel, discipline, or discriminate against" the plan's participants and beneficiaries "for the purpose of interfering with [their] attainment of. . .right[s]. . .under the plan." To be sure, when an employer acts without this purpose, as could be the case when making fundamental business decisions, such actions are not barred by § 510. But in the case where an employer acts with a purpose that triggers the protection of § 510, any tension that might exist between an employer's power to amend the plan and a participant's rights under § 510 is the product of a careful balance of competing interests, and is most surely not the type of "absurd or glaringly unjust" result that would warrant departure from the plain language of § 510.

Respondents argue that the Court of Appeals' decision must nevertheless be affirmed because § 510, when applied to benefits that do not "vest," only protects an employee's right to cross the "threshold of eligibility" for welfare benefits. In other words, argue respondents, an employee who is eligible to receive benefits under an ERISA welfare benefit plan has already "attain[ed]" her "right[s]" under the plan, so that any subsequent actions taken by an employer cannot, by definition, "interfer[e]" with the "attainment of. . .right[s]" under the plan. According to respondents, petitioners were eligible to receive welfare benefits under the SFTS-Teamsters plan at the time they were discharged, so they cannot state a claim under § 510. The Court of Appeals' approach precluded it from evaluating this argument, and others presented to us, and we see no reason not to allow it the first opportunity to consider these matters on remand.

We therefore vacate the judgment of the Court of Appeals and remand the case for further proceedings consistent with this opinion.

NOTES AND QUESTIONS

1. *Outsourcing, the Settlor Function Doctrine, and Section 510 Claims.* The facts of *Inter-Modal* illustrate how the outsourcing of work to a third party contractor can trigger a claim under Section 510 that the employer's motive is to reduce the costs of the company's employee benefit plans. Even if the company's outsourced employees are hired by the third party contractor and continue to perform the same jobs, often the outsourced employees end up with less generous pension and health care benefits under their new employer.

For another example where the monetary savings to the employer from terminating a group of employees and outsourcing their work was an alleged motivating factor giving rise to a Section 510 claim, see *Register v. Honeywell Federal Manufacturing & Technologies, LLC*, 397 F.3d 1130 (8th Cir. 2005) (summary judgment granted to employer on Section 510 claim). For an example of a corporate spin-off that triggered a Section 510 claim based on the employer's restrictive rehiring policies that were allegedly designed to preserve the employer's pension cost savings from the corporate spin-off, see *Eichorn v. AT&T Corp.*, 484 F.3d 644 (3d Cir. 2007) (granting employer's motion for summary judgment on Section 510 claim because relief sought by plaintiffs was not available under Section 502(a)(3)). For an example where a plant closure triggered a Section 510 claim, see *Alexander v. Bosch Automotive Systems, Inc.*, 232 Fed.Appx. 491 (6th Cir. 2007) (reversing grant of summary judgment for plaintiffs on Section 510 claim because relief sought by plaintiffs was not available under Section 502(a)(3)).

To what extent should the settlor function doctrine immunize the employer from claims under Section 510 when the employer makes a business decision to reduce its labor costs (which include the costs of employee benefit plans) by outsourcing work performed by current employees, reducing the employer's workforce, selling a subsidiary or division of the employer, or closing an entire facility?

2. *Remedies Available Under Section 502(a)(3) for a Violation of Section 510.* Prior to the Supreme Court's decision in *Great-West Life & Annuity Insurance Co. v. Knudson*, 534 U.S. 204 (2002), several federal courts determined that reinstatement, back pay and front pay were all appropriate equitable remedies under Section 502(a)(3) for a violation of Section 510. See Schwartz v. Gregori, 45 F.3d 1017 (6th Cir. 1995); Warner v. Buck Creek Nursery, Inc., 149 F.Supp.2d 246 (W.D. Va. 2001) (following *Schwartz*); Russell v. Northrop Grumman Corp., 921 F.Supp. 143 (E.D.N.Y. 1996) (following *Schwartz*). In footnote four of the majority opinion in *Great-West*, the Supreme Court suggested that back pay may not be "equitable relief" for purposes of Section 502(a)(3). After *Great-West,* the federal courts have ruled that back pay and front pay are not available as equitable under Section 502(a)(3) where the plaintiff's employment has been terminated in violation of Section 510. See, e.g., Millsap v. McDonnell Douglas Corp., 368 F.3d 1246 (10th Cir. 2004) (backpay not available); Serpa v. SBC Tele Comms., Inc., 318 F.Supp.2d 865 (N.D. Cal. 2004) (front pay not available).

From a policy perspective, what are the arguments for and against awarding back pay or front pay as equitable relief available under Section 502(a)(3) as a remedy for a Section 510 violation?

3. *Plant Closings and Section 510 Claims.* In *Millsap v. McDonnell Douglas Corporation*, 368 F.3d 1246 (10th Cir. 2004), the plaintiffs were former workers at an aircraft manufacturing facility located in Tulsa, Oklahoma. The plaintiffs alleged that their employer decided to close the plant in 1993 for the illegal purpose under Section 510 of preventing employees who worked at the plant from attaining eligibility for benefits under their retirement and health care plans. The district court found that the employer violated Section 510 when deciding to close the plant. A key piece of evidence in the case was a cost savings estimate, prepared by the company's accounting firm, showing that by closing the Tulsa plant the employer would save an estimated $18 million in pension funding liabilities and $7 million in medical plan liabilities.

After the district court's ruling, the parties entered into a settlement agreement that awarded the plaintiffs $36 million for their pension and health care benefits that were lost due to the plant closing. The district court also awarded attorneys' fees in the total amount of $8.75 million and costs in the amount of $1 million to counsel for the class of plaintiffs.

Under the terms of the settlement agreement, the employer was allowed to appeal the district court's ruling that back pay also was available as a remedy for the Section 510 violation. The Tenth Circuit later ruled, in a divided panel opinion, that after *Great-West* back pay was not available as "appropriate equitable relief" for the plaintiffs under Section 502(a)(3). Id. at 1260. In reversing the district court, the majority panel opinion emphasized that Congress did not specifically include back pay as part of the equitable relief available under Section 502(a)(3). The majority panel opinion also rejected the argument that the remedial purpose of Section 502(a)(3) was to make the aggrieved plan participants "whole."

The dissenting judge on the Tenth Circuit panel strenuously objected on public policy grounds to the reversal of the district court's ruling that back pay was an available remedy.

> Under the majority's result, the class plaintiffs are entitled to neither reinstatement nor back pay. Not only does the majority's holding fail to deter ERISA violations, it also encourages employers who violate ERISA to delay proceedings as long as possible, "lead[ing] to the strange result that . . . the most egregious offenders could be subject to the least sanctions." Pollard v. E.I. du Pont de Nemours & Co., 532 U.S. 843, 853 (2001). Because I disagree that Congress intended this result or that precedent demands it, I respectfully dissent. * * *

> The majority's result is similarly disconcerting. Here, reinstatement would have been an appropriate equitable remedy had [the defendants] not so delayed proceedings as to make reinstatement impossible [due to the fact that the plant had been closed for over ten years]. Thus, through no fault of their own, the class plaintiffs find themselves devoid of the undeniably appropriate equitable remedy of reinstatement. Back pay, which was integral to the relief sought by the plaintiffs at the onset of this litigation, provides an appropriate equitable alternative.

Id. at 1261 (Lucero, J., dissenting).

4.   *Interference with Protected Rights Under Health Care Plans.* As discussed in Chapter Four, ERISA's vesting rules do not apply to health care plan benefits. Given this limitation, what protection does Section 510 offer to participants in health care plans?

Section 510 clearly prevents the employer from *firing* an individual because the individual (or a family member covered under the plan) has or is likely to incur high medical costs under the employer's health care plan. *Folz v. Marriott Corp.*, 594 F.Supp. 1007 (W.D. Mo. 1984), illustrates this situation. In *Folz*, the plaintiff was a long-time employee of the Marriott Corporation (Marriott) who had become a hotel manager. In 1981, the plaintiff was diagnosed with multiple sclerosis. Upon learning of the plaintiff's condition, the plaintiff's immediate supervisor and the vice-president of Marriott decided to place him on probation and terminate his employment, despite the plaintiff's satisfactory performance record. The plaintiff asserted that Marriott's conduct violated Section 510.

After a bench trial, the district court found that the termination of the plaintiff's employment was motivated "solely by the realization that plaintiff's disease could lead to increased illness and possible incapacity, and the desire to avoid the adverse economic impact which that disease could have under Marriott's employee benefit plans," which included Marriott's self-insured health care plan. The district court ordered Marriott to pay the plaintiff both back pay and front pay (calculated to retirement at age 65). The district court further ordered Marriott to reinstate the plaintiff, "with the seniority status plaintiff would have achieved had he not been discharged from his employment" in Marriott's pension and profit sharing plans, stock option programs, medical benefits program, sick leave plan, long-term disability and salary continuation plan, and life insurance program.

Recall that *Folz* was decided before the Supreme Court's decision in *Great-West*, which cast doubt on back pay and front pay as forms of "equitable relief" available under Section 502(a)(3). *Millar v. Lakin Law Firm*, 2010 WL 1325182 (S.D. Ill. 2010), illustrates the potential chilling effect of *Great-West* on retaliation claims under Section 510 based on the plaintiff's exercise of rights under a group health care plan. *Millar* was decided on a motion to dismiss; therefore, the description of the facts below is based on the plaintiff's allegations in the complaint.

In *Millar*, the plaintiff worked as the supervisory attorney for the class action litigation department of a law firm. The plaintiff's son had an extremely rare metabolic condition that required him to take oral neurotransmitter precursor medications six times a day. The son's medication was expensive and difficult to obtain, but also necessary to prevent brain damage or possible death. The law firm's group health plan insurance provider covered the medication.

In November of 2007, the law firm changed its health insurance provider to United Healthcare, which initially refused to cover the son's medication. After the plaintiff threatened litigation against United Healthcare, the insurance company began covering the son's medications in February of 2008, but at considerable additional expense to the group health plan. Shortly thereafter, the law firm began to falsely accuse the plaintiff of excessive absenteeism and faltering work performance. The plaintiff eventually was fired in December of 2008.

Not surprisingly given his background, the plaintiff sued the law firm, alleging among other claims prohibited retaliation under Section 510. The plaintiff sought reinstatement, back pay and front pay, and restitution of forfeited employee benefits as equitable relief under Section 502(a)(3). The district court granted the law firm's motion to dismiss the plaintiff's Section 510 claim based on the lack of a viable remedy. Although acknowledging that reinstatement was an equitable remedy, the court ruled that reinstatement was not "appropriate" under the circumstances due to the lack of trust between the parties. The court rejected back pay and front pay based on *Great-West*. Finally, the court rejected the plaintiff's proposed restitution remedy because the plaintiff did not assert a constructive trust or an equitable lien against specific identifiable funds held by the law firm, as required by *Great-West*.

Congress pointedly did not address the lack of an effective remedy in situations such as *Millar* when it enacted the Affordable Care Act. Congress also did not address whether Section 510 prohibits an employer from *refusing to hire* an individual due to the likelihood that the employer or a family member of the employee is likely to incur high medical expenses that will increase the costs of the employer's health care plan. This issue continues to divide the federal courts of appeals. Compare Fleming v. Ayers & Assocs., 948 F.2d 993 (6th Cir. 1991) (employer violated Section 510 by refusing to hire nurse whose infant child suffered from hydrocephalus) with Becker v. Mack Trucks, Inc., 281 F.3d 372 (3d Cir. 2002) (Section 510 applies only in the context of an ongoing employer-employee relationship). Should Congress have addressed these issues as part of the Affordable Care Act?

4. CLAIMS FOR INDIVIDUAL RELIEF FOR BREACH OF FIDUCIARY DUTY

Varity Corporation v. Howe involved a claim brought by a class of plan participants who alleged that the fiduciary's breach of duty injured the plaintiffs personally as individuals, rather than harming the plan itself. In Parts A and B of the majority opinion, reproduced in Chapter Five of the casebook, the Supreme Court held that the employer had acted in its fiduciary capacity when it purposefully made misleading statements concerning the availability and security of future plan benefits to the participants. The Supreme Court concluded that "[l]ying is inconsistent with the duty of loyalty owed by all fiduciaries and codified in Section 404(a)(1) of ERISA." Varity, 516 U.S. at 506. In Part C of the majority opinion, reproduced below, the Supreme Court held that the plan participants as individuals could bring a claim for breach of fiduciary duty under ERISA Section 502(a)(3).

VARITY CORPORATION V. HOWE
United States Supreme Court, 1996.
516 U.S. 489, 116 S.Ct. 1065, 134 L.Ed.2d 130.

* * *

C

The remaining question before us is whether or not the remedial provision of ERISA that the beneficiaries invoked, ERISA § 502(a)(3), authorizes this lawsuit for remedial relief. That subsection is the third of six subsections contained within ERISA's "Civil Enforcement" provision (as it stood at the times relevant to this lawsuit):

Sec. 502. (a) A civil action may be brought—

(1) by a participant or beneficiary—

(A) for the relief provided for in subsection (c) of this section [providing for liquidated damages for failure to provide certain information on request], or

(B) to recover benefits due to him under the terms of his plan, to enforce his rights under the terms of the plan, or to clarify his rights to future benefits under the terms of the plan;

(2) by the Secretary, or by a participant, beneficiary or fiduciary for appropriate relief under section 409 [entitled "Liability for Breach of Fiduciary Duty"];

(3) *by a participant, beneficiary, or fiduciary (A) to enjoin any act or practice which violates any provision of this title or the terms of the plan, or (B) to obtain other appropriate equitable relief (i) to redress such violations or (ii) to enforce any provisions of this title or the terms of the plan;*

* * *

The District Court held that the third subsection, which we have italicized, authorized this suit and the relief awarded. Varity concedes that the plaintiffs satisfy most of this provision's requirements, namely, that the plaintiffs are plan "participants" or "beneficiaries," and that they are suing for "equitable" relief to "redress" a violation of § 404(a), which is a "provision of this title." Varity does not agree, however, that this lawsuit seeks equitable relief that is "appropriate." In support of this conclusion, Varity makes a complicated, four-step argument:

Step One: Section 502(a)'s second subsection says that a plaintiff may bring a civil action "for appropriate relief under section 409."

Step Two: Section 409(a), in turn, reads:

Liability for Breach of Fiduciary Duty

Sec. 409.(a) Any person who is a fiduciary with respect to a plan who breaches any of the responsibilities, obligations, or duties imposed upon fiduciaries by this title shall be personally liable *to make good to such plan* any losses to the plan resulting from each such breach, and *to restore to such plan* any profits of such fiduciary which have been made through use of assets of the plan by the fiduciary, and shall be subject to such *other equitable or remedial relief* as the court may deem appropriate, including removal of such fiduciary. . . . (emphasis added).

Step Three: In *Massachusetts Mutual Life Insurance Co. v. Russell*, 473 U.S. 134 (1985), this Court pointed to the above-italicized language in § 409 and concluded that this section (and its companion remedial provision, subsection (2)) did not authorize the plaintiff's suit for compensatory and punitive damages against an administrator who had wrongfully delayed payment of her benefit claim. The first two italicized phrases, the Court said, show that § 409's "draftsmen were primarily concerned with the possible misuse of plan assets, and with remedies that would protect the entire plan, rather than with the rights of an individual beneficiary." Id. at 142 (emphasis added). The Court added that, in this context, the last italicized phrase ("other equitable or remedial relief") does not "authorize any relief except for the plan itself." Id. at 144.

Step Four: In light of *Russell*, as well as ERISA's language, structure, and purposes, one cannot read the third subsection (the subsection before us) as including (as "appropriate") the very kind of action—an action for individual, rather than plan, relief—that this Court found Congress excluded in subsection (2). It is at this point, however, that we must disagree with Varity. We have reexamined *Russell*, as well as the relevant statutory language, structure, and purpose. And, in our view, they support the beneficiaries' view of the statute, not Varity's.

First, *Russell* discusses § 502(a)'s second subsection, not its third subsection, and the language that the Court found limiting appears in a statutory section (§ 409) that the second subsection, not the third, cross-references. *Russell's* plaintiff expressly disavowed reliance on the third subsection, perhaps because she was seeking compensatory and punitive damages and subsection (3) authorizes only "equitable" relief. See Mertens, 508 U.S. at 255, 256–58, and n.8 (compensatory and punitive damages are not "equitable relief" within the meaning of subsection (3)); ERISA § 409(a) (authorizing "other equitable *or remedial* relief") (emphasis added). Further, *Russell* involved a complicating factor not present here, in that another remedial provision (subsection (1)) already provided specific relief for the sort of injury the plaintiff had suffered (wrongful denial of benefits), but said "nothing about the recovery of extracontractual damages, or about the possible consequences of delay in the plan administrators' processing of a disputed claim." Russell, 473 U.S. at 144. These differences lead us to conclude that *Russell* does not control, either implicitly or explicitly, the outcome of the case before us.

Second, subsection (3)'s language does not favor Varity. The words of subsection (3)—"appropriate equitable relief" to "redress" any "act or practice which violates any provision of this title"—are broad enough to cover individual relief for breach of a fiduciary obligation. Varity argues that the title of § 409—"Liability for Breach of Fiduciary Duty"—means that § 409 (and its companion, subsection (2)) cover all such liability. But that is not what the title or the provision says. And other language in the statute suggests the contrary. Section 502(*l*), added in 1989, calculates a certain civil penalty as a percentage of the sum "ordered by a court to be paid by such fiduciary . . . to a plan or its participants and beneficiaries" under subsection (5). Subsection (5) is identical to subsection (3), except that it authorizes suits by the Secretary, rather than the participants and beneficiaries. Compare § 502(a)(3) with § 502(a)(5). This new provision, therefore, seems to foresee instances in which the sort of relief provided by both subsection (5) and, by implication, subsection (3), would include an award to "participants and beneficiaries," rather than to the "plan," for breach of fiduciary obligation.

Third, the statute's structure offers Varity little support. Varity notes that the second subsection refers specifically through its § 409 (cross-reference) to breaches of fiduciary duty, while the third subsection refers, as a kind of "catchall," to all ERISA Title One violations. And it argues that a canon of statutory construction, namely "the specific governs over the general," means that the more specific *second* (fiduciary breach) subsection makes the more general *third* (catchall) subsection inapplicable to claims of fiduciary breach. Canons of construction, however, are simply "rules of thumb" which will sometimes "help courts determine the meaning of legislation." Connecticut Nat. Bank v. Germain, 503 U.S. 249, 253 (1992). To apply a canon properly one must understand its rationale. This Court has understood the present canon ("the specific governs the general") as a warning against applying a general provision when doing so would undermine limitations created by a more specific provision. See, e.g., Morales v. Trans World Airlines, Inc., 504 U.S. 374, 384–85 (1992). Yet, in this case, why should one believe that Congress intended the specific remedies in § 409 as a *limitation*?

To the contrary, one can read § 409 as reflecting a special congressional concern about plan asset management without also finding that Congress intended that section to contain the exclusive set of remedies for every kind of fiduciary breach. After all, ERISA makes clear that a fiduciary has obligations other than, and in addition to, managing plan assets. See § 3(21)(A) (defining "fiduciary" as one who "exercises any discretionary authority . . . respecting management of such plan *or* . . . respecting management or disposition of its assets") (emphasis added). For example, as the dissent concedes, a plan administrator engages in a fiduciary act when making a discretionary determination about whether a claimant is entitled to benefits under the terms of the plan documents. See § 404(a)(1)(D); DOL Reg. § 2509.75–8. ("[A] plan employee who has the final authority to authorize or disallow benefit payments in cases where a dispute exists as to the interpretation of plan provisions . . . would be a fiduciary"). And, as the Court pointed out in *Russell*, ERISA specifically provides a remedy for breaches of fiduciary duty with respect to the interpretation of plan documents and the payment of claims, one that is outside the framework of the *second* subsection and cross-referenced § 409, and one that runs directly to the injured beneficiary. ERISA § 502(a)(1)(B). See also Firestone, 489 U.S. at 108. Why should we not conclude that Congress provided yet other remedies for yet other breaches of other sorts of fiduciary obligation in another, "catchall" remedial section?

Such a reading is consistent with § 502's overall structure. Four of that section's six subsections focus upon specific areas, i.e., the first (wrongful denial of benefits and information), the second (fiduciary obligations related to the plan's financial integrity), the fourth (tax registration), and the sixth (civil penalties). The language of the other two subsections, the third and the fifth, creates two "catchalls," providing "appropriate equitable relief" for "any" statutory violation. This structure suggests that these "catchall" provisions act as a safety net, offering appropriate equitable relief for injuries caused by violations that § 502 does not elsewhere adequately remedy. And, contrary to Varity's argument, there is nothing in the legislative history that conflicts with this interpretation. See S. Rep. No. 93–127, p. 35 (1973) (describing Senate version of enforcement provisions as intended to "provide both the Secretary and participants and beneficiaries with broad remedies for redressing or preventing violations of [ERISA]"); H.R. Rep. No. 93–533, at 17 (describing House version in identical terms).

Fourth, ERISA's basic purposes favor a reading of the *third* subsection that provides the plaintiffs with a remedy. The statute itself says that it seeks

> to protect. . .the interests of participants. . .and. . .beneficiaries . . .by establishing standards of conduct, responsibility, and obligation for fiduciaries. . .and. . .providing for appropriate remedies. . .and ready access to the Federal courts.

ERISA § 2(b). Section 404(a), in furtherance of this general objective, requires fiduciaries to discharge their duties "solely in the interest of the participants and beneficiaries." Given these objectives, it is hard to imagine why Congress would want to immunize breaches of fiduciary obligation that harm individuals by denying injured beneficiaries a remedy.

Amici supporting Varity find a strong contrary argument in an important, subsidiary congressional purpose—the need for a sensible administrative system. They say that holding that the Act permits individuals to enforce fiduciary obligations owed directly to them as individuals threatens to increase the cost of welfare benefit plans and thereby discourage employers from offering them. Consider a plan administrator's decision not to pay for surgery on the ground that it falls outside the plan's coverage. At present, courts review such decisions with a degree of deference to the administrator, provided that "the benefit plan gives the administrator or fiduciary discretionary authority to determine eligibility for benefits or to construe the terms of the plan." Firestone, 489 U.S. at 115. But what will happen, ask amici, if a beneficiary can repackage his or her "denial of benefits" claim as a claim for "breach of fiduciary duty?" Wouldn't a court, they ask, then have to forgo deference and hold the administrator to the "rigid level of conduct" expected of fiduciaries? And, as a consequence, would there not then be two "incompatible legal standards for courts hearing benefit claim disputes" depending upon whether the beneficiary claimed simply "denial of benefits," or a virtually identical "breach of fiduciary duty?" Consider, too, they add, a medical review board trying to decide whether certain proposed surgery is medically necessary. Will the board's awareness of a "duty of loyalty" to the surgery-seeking beneficiary not risk inadequate attention to the countervailing, but important, need to constrain costs in order to preserve the plan's funds?

Thus, amici warn that a legally enforceable duty of loyalty that extends beyond plan asset management to individual beneficiaries will risk these and other adverse consequences. Administrators will tend to interpret plan documents as requiring payments to individuals instead of trying to preserve plan assets; nonexpert courts will try to supervise too closely, and second guess, the often technical decisions of plan administrators; and, lawyers will complicate ordinary benefit claims by dressing them up in "fiduciary duty" clothing. The need to avoid these consequences, they conclude, requires us to accept Varity's position.

The concerns that amici raise seem to us unlikely to materialize, however, for several reasons. First, a fiduciary obligation, enforceable by beneficiaries seeking relief for themselves, does not necessarily favor payment over nonpayment. The common law of trusts recognizes the need to preserve assets to satisfy future, as well as present, claims and requires a trustee to take impartial account of the interests of all beneficiaries. See Restatement (Second) of Trusts § 183 (discussing duty of impartiality); id. § 232 (same).

Second, characterizing a denial of benefits as a breach of fiduciary duty does not necessarily change the standard a court would apply when reviewing the administrator's decision to deny benefits. After all, *Firestone*, which authorized deferential court review when the plan itself gives the administrator discretionary authority, based its decision upon the same common-law trust doctrines that govern standards of fiduciary conduct. See Restatement (Second) of Trusts § 187 ("Where discretion is conferred upon the trustee with respect to the exercise of a power, its exercise is not subject to control by the court, except to prevent an abuse by the trustee of his discretion") (as quoted in Firestone, 489 U.S. at 111).

Third, the statute authorizes "appropriate" equitable relief. We should expect that courts, in fashioning "appropriate" equitable relief, will keep in mind the "special nature and purpose of employee benefit plans," and will respect the "policy choices reflected in the inclusion of certain remedies and the exclusion of others." Pilot Life Ins. Co., 481 U.S. at 54. See also Russell, 473 U.S. at 147; Mertens, 508 U.S. at 263–64. Thus, we should expect that where Congress elsewhere provided adequate relief for a beneficiary's injury, there will likely be no need for further equitable relief, in which case such relief normally would not be "appropriate." Cf. Russell, 473 U.S. at 144.

But that is not the case here. The plaintiffs in this case could not proceed under the *first* subsection because they were no longer members of the Massey-Ferguson plan and, therefore, had no "benefits due [them] under the terms of [the] plan." ERISA § 502(a)(1)(B). They could not proceed under the *second* subsection because that provision, tied to § 409, does not provide a remedy for individual beneficiaries. Russell, 473 U.S. at 144. They must rely on the *third* subsection or they have no remedy at all. We are not aware of any ERISA-related purpose that denial of a remedy would serve. Rather, we believe that granting a remedy is consistent with the literal language of the statute, the Act's purposes, and pre-existing trust law.

For these reasons, the judgment of the Court of Appeals is

Affirmed.

JUSTICE THOMAS, with whom JUSTICE O'CONNOR and JUSTICE SCALIA join, dissenting.

* * *

[T]hough the majority finds *Russell* to be irrelevant, it is all but dispositive. We analyzed in that case all of the provisions the Court today holds to be enforceable through § 502(a)(3). We considered these provisions as part of our "contextual reading" of § 409, and only when we read § 409 in conjunction with these surrounding provisions did it become "abundantly clear that [§ 409's] draftsmen were primarily concerned with the possible misuse of plan assets, and with remedies that would protect the entire plan, rather than with the rights of an individual beneficiary." Russell, 473 U.S. at 142. This is not to say that Congress did not intend to protect plan participants from fiduciary breach; it surely did. Congress chose, however, to protect individuals by creating a single remedy on behalf of the plan rather than authorizing piecemeal suits for individual relief.

Given Congress' apparent intent to allow suit for breach of fiduciary duty exclusively under §§ 409 and 502(a)(2), and given the abundant evidence of Congress' intent to authorize only relief on behalf of the plan, I would hold that individual relief for fiduciary breach is unavailable under § 502(a)(3).

NOTES AND QUESTIONS

1. *The Significance of* Varity. *Varity* opened the federal courthouse doors to a new generation of breach of fiduciary duty claims by holding that a plaintiff could assert a claim for individual relief under Section 502(a)(3) for a

fiduciary's breach of duty. One of the new claims that emerged following *Varity* was the so called "duty to inform" claim. Duty to inform claims challenge a plan fiduciary's failure to fully and accurately communicate with a plan participant or beneficiary concerning plan benefits. Since *Varity*, individual plaintiffs generally have preferred the duty to inform theory over a theory of equitable estoppel when bringing a claim based on alleged misrepresentations by a plan fiduciary. A duty to inform theory often is strategically superior to equitable estoppel due to the federal courts' reluctance to allow oral or informal written communications to amend the terms of the written plan document.

2.   *Denial of Benefits Claims and Relief Under ERISA Section 502(a)(3).* One of the concerns expressed by amici counsel in *Varity* was that the plan participants would attempt to recharacterize their claims against plan administrators for denied plan benefits under ERISA Section 502(a)(1)(B) as breach of fiduciary duty claims under ERISA Section 502(a)(3). Such recharacterization, if successful, would allow participants to circumvent the deferential abuse of discretion standard of judicial review commonly afforded to plan administrators in the wake of *Firestone* because breach of fiduciary duty claims are subject to a de novo standard of judicial review.

The lower federal courts have followed the Supreme Court's guidance in *Varity* that "where Congress elsewhere provided adequate relief for a beneficiary's injury, there will likely be no need for further equitable relief" under ERISA Section 502(a)(3). See Varity, 516 U.S. at 515. Where the participant brings a claim for denial of benefits under ERISA Section 502(a)(1)(B), or the participant's claim can be properly recharacterized as a claim for denial of benefits, the participant generally cannot plead an alternative claim under ERISA Section 502(a)(3) based on an alleged breach of fiduciary duty. See LaRocca v. Borden, 276 F.3d 22, 28–29 (1st Cir. 2002) (collecting cases).

Even though *Varity* held that an individual could bring a claim for "appropriate equitable relief" under Section 502(a)(3), the federal courts subsequently limited such relief to the three types of traditional equitable relief—restitution, injunction and mandamus—originally identified by the Supreme Court in *Mertens*. In *Cigna Corp. v. Amara*, the Supreme Court suggested that other types of equitable relief may be available to an individual who brings a breach of fiduciary duty claim under Section 502(a)(3).

CIGNA CORP. V. AMARA

United States Supreme Court, 2011.
131 S. Ct. 1866.

JUSTICE BREYER delivered the opinion of the Court.

In 1998, petitioner CIGNA Corporation changed the nature of its basic pension plan for employees. Previously, the plan provided a retiring employee with a defined benefit in the form of an annuity calculated on the basis of his preretirement salary and length of service. The new plan provided most retiring employees with a (lump sum) cash balance calculated on the basis of a defined annual contribution from CIGNA as increased by compound interest. Because many employees had already earned at least some old-plan benefits, the new plan translated already-earned benefits into an opening amount in the employee's cash balance account.

Respondents, acting on behalf of approximately 25,000 beneficiaries of the CIGNA Pension Plan (which is also a petitioner here), challenged CIGNA's adoption of the new plan. They claimed in part that CIGNA had failed to give them proper notice of changes to their benefits, particularly because the new plan in certain respects provided them with less generous benefits. See Employee Retirement Income Security Act of 1974 (ERISA) §§ 102(a), 104(b), 204(h).

The District Court agreed that the disclosures made by CIGNA violated its obligations under ERISA. In determining relief, the court found that CIGNA's notice failures had caused the employees "likely harm." The Court then reformed the new plan and ordered CIGNA to pay benefits accordingly. It found legal authority for doing so in ERISA § 502(a)(1)(B) (authorizing a plan "participant or beneficiary" to bring a "civil action" to "recover benefits due to him under the terms of his plan").

We agreed to decide whether the District Court applied the correct legal standard, namely, a "likely harm" standard, in determining that CIGNA's notice violations caused its employees sufficient injury to warrant legal relief. To reach that question, we must first consider a more general matter—whether the ERISA section just mentioned (ERISA's recovery-of-benefits-due provision, § 502(a)(1)(B)) authorizes entry of the relief the District Court provided. We conclude that it does not authorize this relief. Nonetheless, we find that a different equity-related ERISA provision, to which the District Court also referred, authorizes forms of relief similar to those that the court entered. § 502(a)(3).

Section 502(a)(3) authorizes "appropriate equitable relief" for violations of ERISA. Accordingly, the relevant standard of harm will depend upon the equitable theory by which the District Court provides relief. We leave it to the District Court to conduct that analysis in the first instance, but we identify equitable principles that the court might apply on remand.

I

Because our decision rests in important part upon the circumstances present here, we shall describe those circumstances in some detail. We still simplify in doing so. But the interested reader can find a more thorough description in two District Court opinions, which set forth that court's findings reached after a lengthy trial. See 559 F.Supp.2d 192 (D.Conn.2008); 534 F. Supp. 2d 288 (D. Conn. 2008).

A

Under CIGNA's pre-1998 defined-benefit retirement plan, an employee with at least five years of service would receive an annuity annually paying an amount that depended upon the employee's salary and length of service. Depending on when the employee had joined CIGNA, the annuity would equal either: (1) 2 percent of the employee's average salary over his final three years with CIGNA, multiplied by the number of years worked (up to 30); or (2) 1 2/3 percent of the employee's average salary over his final five years with CIGNA, multiplied by the number of years worked (up to 35). Calculated either way, the annuity would approach 60 percent of a longtime employee's final salary. A well-paid longtime employee, earning, say, $160,000 per year, could receive a retirement annuity paying the employee about $96,000 per year until his death. The plan offered many employees at least one other benefit: They could retire early, at age 55, and receive an only-somewhat-reduced annuity.

In November 1997, CIGNA sent its employees a newsletter announcing that it intended to put in place a new pension plan. The new plan would substitute an "account balance plan" for CIGNA's pre-existing defined-benefit system. The newsletter added that the old plan would end on December 31, 1997, that CIGNA would introduce (and describe) the new plan sometime during 1998, and that the new plan would apply retroactively to January 1, 1998.

Eleven months later CIGNA filled in the details. Its new plan created an individual retirement account for each employee. (The account consisted of a bookkeeping entry backed by a CIGNA-funded trust.) Each year CIGNA would contribute to the employee's individual account an amount equal to between 3 percent and 8.5 percent of the employee's salary, depending upon age, length of service, and certain other factors. The account balance would earn compound interest at a rate equal to the return on 5-year treasury bills plus one-quarter percent (but no less than 4.5 percent and no greater than 9 percent). Upon retirement the employee would receive the amount then in his or her individual account—in the form of either a lump sum or whatever annuity the lump sum then would buy. As promised, CIGNA would open the accounts and begin to make contributions as of January 1, 1998.

But what about the retirement benefits that employees had already earned prior to January 1, 1998? CIGNA promised to make an initial contribution to the individual's account equal to the value of that employee's already earned benefits. And the new plan set forth a method for calculating that initial contribution. The method consisted of calculating the amount as of the employee's (future) retirement date of the annuity to which the employee's salary and length of service already (i.e., as of December 31, 1997) entitled him and then discounting that sum to its present (i.e., January 1, 1998) value.

An example will help: Imagine an employee born on January 1, 1966, who joined CIGNA in January 1991 on his 25th birthday, and who (during the five years preceding the plan changeover) earned an average salary of $100,000 per year. As of January 1, 1998, the old plan would have entitled that employee to an annuity equal to $100,000 times 7 (years then worked) times 1 2/3 percent, or $11,667 per year—when he retired in 2031 at age 65. The 2031 price of an annuity paying $11,667 per year until death depends upon interest rates and mortality assumptions at that time. If we assume the annuity would pay 7 percent until the holder's death (and we use the mortality assumptions used by the plan, then the 2031 price of such an annuity would be about $120,500. And CIGNA should initially deposit in this individual's account on January 1, 1998, an amount that will grow to become $120,500, 33 years later, in 2031, when the individual retires. If we assume a 5 percent average interest rate, then that amount presently (i.e., as of January 1, 1998) equals about $24,000. And that is the amount, more or less, that the new plan's transition rules would have required CIGNA initially to deposit. Then CIGNA would make further annual deposits, and all the deposited amounts would earn compound interest. When the employee retired, he would receive the resulting lump sum.

The new plan also provided employees a guarantee: An employee would receive upon retirement either (1) the amount to which he or she had become entitled as of January 1, 1998, or (2) the amount then in his or her individual account, whichever was greater. Thus, the employee in our example would receive (in 2031) no less than an annuity paying $11,667 per year for life.

B

1

The District Court found that CIGNA's initial descriptions of its new plan were significantly incomplete and misled its employees. In November 1997, for example, CIGNA sent the employees a newsletter that said the new plan would "significantly enhance" its "retirement program," would produce "an overall improvement in. . .retirement benefits," and would provide "the same benefit security" with "steadier benefit growth." CIGNA also told its employees that they would "see the growth in [their] total retirement benefits from CIGNA every year," that its initial deposit "represent[ed] the full value of the benefit [they] earned for service before 1998," and that "[o]ne advantage the company *will not* get from the retirement program changes is cost savings."

In fact, the new plan saved the company $10 million annually (though CIGNA later said it devoted the savings to other employee benefits). Its initial deposit did not "represen[t] the full value of the benefit" that employees had "earned for service before 1998." And the plan made a significant number of employees worse off in at least the following specific ways:

First, the initial deposit calculation ignored the fact that the old plan offered many CIGNA employees the right to retire early (beginning at age 55) with only somewhat reduced benefits. This right was valuable. For example, as of January 1, 1998, respondent Janice Amara had earned vested age 55 retirement benefits of $1,833 per month, but CIGNA's initial deposit in her new plan individual retirement account (ignoring this benefit) would have allowed her at age 55 to buy an annuity benefit of only $900 per month.

Second, as we previously indicated but did not explain, the new plan adjusted CIGNA's initial deposit downward to account for the fact that, unlike the old plan's lifetime annuity, an employee's survivors would receive the new plan's benefits (namely, the amount in the employee's individual account) even if the employee died before retiring. The downward adjustment consisted of multiplying the otherwise-required deposit by the probability that the employee would live until retirement— a 90 percent probability in the example of our 32-year-old. And that meant that CIGNA's initial deposit in our example—the amount that was supposed to grow to $120,500 by 2031—would be less than $22,000, not $24,000 (the number we computed). The employee, of course, would receive a benefit in return—namely, a form of life insurance. But at least some employees might have preferred the retirement benefit and consequently could reasonably have thought it important to know that the new plan traded away one-tenth of their already-earned benefits for a life insurance policy that they might not have wanted.

Third, the new plan shifted the risk of a fall in interest rates from CIGNA to its employees. Under the old plan, CIGNA had to buy a retiring employee an annuity that paid a specified sum irrespective of whether falling interest rates made it more expensive for CIGNA to pay for that annuity. And falling interest rates also meant that any sum CIGNA set aside to buy that annuity would grow more slowly over time, thereby requiring CIGNA to set aside more money to make any specific sum available at retirement. Under the new plan CIGNA did not have to buy a retiring employee an annuity that paid a specific sum. The employee would simply receive whatever sum his account contained. And falling interest rates meant that the account's lump sum would earn less money each year after the employee retired. Annuities, for example, would become more expensive (any fixed purchase price paying for less annual income). At the same time falling interest rates meant that the individual account would grow more slowly over time, leaving the employee with less money at retirement.

Of course, interest rates might rise instead of fall, leaving CIGNA's employees better off under the new plan. But the latter advantage does not cancel out the former disadvantage, for most individuals are risk averse. And that means that most of CIGNA's employees would have preferred that CIGNA, rather than they, bear these risks.

The amounts likely involved are significant. If, in our example, interest rates between 1998 and 2031 averaged 4 percent rather than the 5 percent we assumed, and if in 2031 annuities paid 6 percent rather than the 7 percent we assumed, then CIGNA would have had to make an initial deposit of $35,500 (not $24,000) to assure that employee the $11,667 annual annuity payment to which he had already become entitled. Indeed, that $24,000 that CIGNA would have contributed (leaving aside the life-insurance problem) would have provided enough money to buy (in 2031) an annuity that assured the employee an annual payment of only about $8,000 (rather than $11,667).

We recognize that the employee in our example (like others) might have continued to work for CIGNA after January 1, 1998; and he would thereby eventually have earned a pension that, by the time of his retirement, was worth far more than $11,667. But that is so because CIGNA made an *additional* contribution for each year worked *after* January 1, 1998. If interest rates fell (as they did), it would take the employee several additional years of work simply to catch up (under the new plan) to where he had already been (under the old plan) as of January 1, 1998—a phenomenon known in pension jargon as "wear away," see 534 F. Supp. 2d, at 303–304 (referring to respondents' requiring 6 to 10 years to catch up).

The District Court found that CIGNA told its employees nothing about any of these features of the new plan—which individually and together made clear that CIGNA's descriptions of the plan were incomplete and inaccurate. The District Court also found that CIGNA intentionally misled its employees. A focus group and many employees asked CIGNA, for example, to " '[d]isclose details' " about the plan, to provide " 'individual comparisons,' " or to show " '[a]n actual projection for retirement.' " But CIGNA did not do so. Instead (in the words of one internal document), it " 'focus[ed] on NOT providing employees before and after samples of the Pension Plan changes.' "

The District Court concluded, as a matter of law, that CIGNA's representations (and omissions) about the plan, made between November 1997 (when it announced the plan) and December 1998 (when it put the plan into effect) violated:

> (a) ERISA § 204(h), implemented by Treas. Reg. § 1.411(d)–6, 26 CFR §1.411(d)–6 (2000), which (as it existed at the relevant time) forbade an amendment of a pension plan that would "provide for a significant reduction in the rate of future benefit accrual" unless the plan administrator also sent a "written notice" that provided either the text of the amendment or summarized its likely effects; and

> (b) ERISA §§ 102(a) and 104(b), which require a plan administrator to provide beneficiaries with summary plan descriptions and with summaries of material modifications, "written in a manner calculated to be understood by the average plan participant," that are "sufficiently accurate and comprehensive to reasonably apprise such participants and beneficiaries of their rights and obligations under the plan."

2

The District Court then turned to the remedy. First, the court agreed with CIGNA that only employees whom CIGNA's disclosure failures had harmed could obtain relief. But it did not require each individual member of the relevant CIGNA employee class to show individual injury. Rather, it found (1) that the evidence presented had raised a presumption of "likely harm" suffered by the members of the relevant employee class, and (2) that CIGNA, though free to offer contrary evidence in respect to some or all of those employees, had failed to rebut that presumption. It concluded that this unrebutted showing was sufficient to warrant class-applicable relief.

Second, the court noted that § 204(h) had been interpreted by the Second Circuit to permit the invalidation of plan amendments not preceded by a proper notice, prior to the 2001 amendment that made this power explicit. 559 F.Supp.2d, at 207 (citing *Frommert v. Conkright,* 433 F.3d 254, 263 (2006)); see 29 U.S.C. § 1054(h)(6) (2006 ed.) (entitling participants to benefits "without regard to [the] amendment" in case of an "egregious failure"). But the court also thought that granting this relief here would harm, not help, the injured employees. That is because the notice failures all concerned the new plan that took effect in December 1998. The court thought that the notices in respect to the freezing of old-plan benefits, effective December 31, 1997, were valid. To strike the new plan while leaving in effect the frozen old plan would not help CIGNA's employees.

The court considered treating the November 1997 notice as a sham or treating that notice and the later 1998 notices as part and parcel of a single set of related events. But it pointed out that respondents "ha[d] argued none of these things." And it said that the court would "not make these arguments now on [respondents'] behalf."

Third, the court reformed the terms of the new plan's guarantee. It erased the portion that assured participants who retired the greater of "A" (that which they had already earned as of December 31, 1997, under the old plan, $11,667 in our example) *or* "B" (that which they would earn via CIGNA's annual deposits under the new plan, *including* CIGNA's initial deposit). And it substituted a provision that would guarantee each employee "A" (that which they had already earned, as of December 31, 1997, under the old plan) *plus* "B" (that which they would earn via CIGNA's annual deposits under the new plan, *excluding* CIGNA's initial deposit). In our example, the District Court's remedy would no longer force our employee to choose upon retirement *either* an $11,667 annuity *or* his new plan benefits (including both CIGNA's annual deposits and CIGNA's initial deposit). It would give him an $11,667 annuity *plus* his new plan benefits (with CIGNA's annual deposits but without CIGNA's initial deposit).

Fourth, the court "order[ed] and enjoin[ed] the CIGNA Plan to reform its records to reflect that all class members. . .now receive [the just described] 'A + B' benefits," and that it pay appropriate benefits to those class members who had already retired.

Fifth, the court held that ERISA § 502(a)(1)(B) provided the legal authority to enter this relief. That provision states that a "civil action may be brought" by a plan "participant or beneficiary. . .to recover benefits due to him under the terms of his plan." The court wrote that its orders in effect awarded "benefits under the terms of the plan" as reformed.

At the same time the court considered whether ERISA § 502(a)(3) also provided legal authority to enter this relief. That provision states that a civil action may be brought

> by a participant, beneficiary, or fiduciary (A) to enjoin any act or practice which violates any provision of this subchapter or the terms of the plan, or (B) to obtain other *appropriate equitable relief* (i) to redress such violations or (ii) to enforce any provisions of this subchapter or the terms of the plan. (emphasis added).

The District Court decided not to answer this question because (1) it had just decided that the same relief was available under § 502(a)(1)(B), regardless, cf. Varity Corp. v. Howe, 516 U.S. 489, 515 (1996); and (2) the

Supreme Court has "issued several opinions. . .that have severely curtailed the kinds of relief that are available under § 502(a)(3)," 559 F.Supp.2d at 205 (citing Sereboff v. Mid Atlantic Medical Services, Inc., 547 U.S. 356 (2006); Great-West Life & Annuity Ins. Co. v. Knudson, 534 U.S. 204 (2002); and Mertens v. Hewitt Associates, 508 U.S. 248 (1993)).

3

The parties cross-appealed the District Court's judgment. The Court of Appeals for the Second Circuit issued a brief summary order, rejecting all their claims, and affirming "the judgment of the district court for substantially the reasons stated" in the District Court's "well-reasoned and scholarly opinions." The parties filed cross-petitions for writs of certiorari in this Court. We granted the request in CIGNA's petition to consider whether a showing of "likely harm" is sufficient to entitle plan participants to recover benefits based on faulty disclosures.

II

CIGNA in the merits briefing raises a preliminary question. It argues first and foremost that the statutory provision upon which the District Court rested its orders, namely, the provision for recovery of plan benefits, § 502(a)(1)(B), does not in fact authorize the District Court to enter the kind of relief it entered here. And for that reason, CIGNA argues, whether the District Court did or did not use a proper standard for determining harm is beside the point. We believe that this preliminary question is closely enough related to the question presented that we shall consider it at the outset.

A

The District Court ordered relief in two steps. Step 1: It ordered the terms of the plan reformed (so that they provided an "A plus B," rather than a "greater of A or B" guarantee). Step 2: It ordered the plan administrator (which it found to be CIGNA) to enforce the plan as reformed. One can fairly describe step 2 as consistent with § 502(a)(1)(B), for that provision grants a participant the right to bring a civil action to "recover benefits due. . .under the terms of his plan." And step 2 orders recovery of the benefits provided by the "terms of [the] plan" *as reformed*.

But what about step 1? Where does § 502(a)(1)(B) grant a court the power to *change* the terms of the plan as they previously existed? The statutory language speaks of *"enforc[ing]* " the "terms of the plan," not of *changing* them. The provision allows a court to look outside the plan's written language in deciding what those terms are, i.e., what the language means. See UNUM Life Ins. Co. of America v. Ward, 526 U.S. 358, 377–379 (1999) (permitting the insurance terms of an ERISA-governed plan to be interpreted in light of state insurance rules). But we have found nothing suggesting that the provision authorizes a court to alter those terms, at least not in present circumstances, where that change, akin to the reform of a contract, seems less like the simple enforcement of a contract as written and more like an equitable remedy.

Nor can we accept the Solicitor General's alternative rationale seeking to justify the use of this provision. The Solicitor General says that the District Court did enforce the plan's terms as written, adding that the "plan" includes the disclosures that constituted the summary plan descriptions. In other words, in the view of the Solicitor General, the terms of the summaries are terms of the plan.

Even if the District Court had viewed the summaries as plan "terms" (which it did not), however, we cannot agree that the terms of statutorily required plan summaries (or summaries of plan modifications) necessarily may be enforced (under § 502(a)(1)(B)) as the terms of the plan itself. For one thing, it is difficult to square the Solicitor General's reading of the statute with ERISA § 102(a), the provision that obliges plan administrators to furnish summary plan descriptions. The syntax of that provision, requiring that participants and beneficiaries be advised of their rights and obligations "under the plan," suggests that the information *about* the plan provided by those disclosures is not itself *part of* the plan. Nothing in § 502(a)(1)(B) (or, as far as we can tell, anywhere else) suggests the contrary.

Nor do we find it easy to square the Solicitor General's reading with the statute's division of authority between a plan's sponsor and the plan's administrator. The plan's sponsor (e.g., the employer), like a trust's settlor, creates the basic terms and conditions of the plan, executes a written instrument containing those terms and conditions, and provides in that instrument "a procedure" for making amendments. § 402. The plan's administrator, a trustee-like fiduciary, manages the plan, follows its terms in doing so, and provides participants with the summary documents that describe the plan (and modifications) in readily understandable form. §§ 3(21)(A), 101(a), 102, 104. Here, the District Court found that the same entity, CIGNA, filled both roles. But that is not always the case. Regardless, we have found that ERISA carefully distinguishes these roles. See, e.g., Varity Corp., 516 U.S. at 498. And we have no reason to believe that the statute intends to mix the responsibilities by giving the administrator the power to set plan terms indirectly by including them in the summary plan descriptions. See Curtiss-Wright Corp. v. Schoonejongen, 514 U.S. 73, 81–85 (1995).

Finally, we find it difficult to reconcile the Solicitor General's interpretation with the basic summary plan description objective: clear, simple communication. See §§ 2(a), 102(a). To make the language of a plan summary legally binding could well lead plan administrators to sacrifice simplicity and comprehensibility in order to describe plan terms in the language of lawyers. Consider the difference between a will and the summary of a will or between a property deed and its summary. Consider, too, the length of Part I of this opinion, and then consider how much longer Part I would have to be if we had to include all the qualifications and nuances that a plan drafter might have found important and feared to omit lest they lose all legal significance. The District Court's opinions take up 109 pages of the Federal Supplement. None of this is to say that plan administrators can avoid providing complete and accurate summaries of plan terms in the manner required by ERISA and its implementing regulations. But we fear that the Solicitor General's rule might bring about complexity that would defeat the fundamental purpose of the summaries.

For these reasons taken together we conclude that the summary documents, important as they are, provide communication with beneficiaries *about* the plan, but that their statements do not themselves constitute the *terms* of the plan for purposes of § 502(a)(1)(B). We also conclude that the District Court could not find authority in that section to reform CIGNA's plan as written.

B

If § 502(a)(1)(B) does not authorize entry of the relief here at issue, what about nearby § 502(a)(3)? That provision allows a participant, beneficiary, or fiduciary "to obtain other *appropriate equitable relief*" to redress violations of (here relevant) parts of ERISA "or the terms of the plan." (emphasis added). The District Court strongly implied, but did not directly hold, that it would base its relief upon this subsection were it not for (1) the fact that the preceding "plan benefits due" provision, § 502(a)(1)(B), provided sufficient authority; and (2) certain cases from this Court that narrowed the application of the term "appropriate equitable relief," see, e.g., Mertens, 508 U.S. 248; Great-West, 534 U.S. 204. Our holding in Part II-A removes the District Court's first obstacle. And given the likelihood that, on remand, the District Court will turn to and rely upon this alternative subsection, we consider the court's second concern. We find that concern misplaced.

We have interpreted the term "appropriate equitable relief" in § 502(a)(3) as referring to " 'those categories of relief' " that, traditionally speaking (i.e., prior to the merger of law and equity) " 'were *typically* available in equity.' " Sereboff, 547 U.S. at 361 (quoting Mertens, 508 U.S. at 256). In *Mertens,* we applied this principle to a claim seeking money damages brought by a beneficiary against a private firm that provided a trustee with actuarial services. We found that the plaintiff sought "nothing other than compensatory damages" against a nonfiduciary. Id. at 253, 255 (emphasis deleted). And we held that such a claim, traditionally speaking, was legal, not equitable, in nature. Id. at 255.

In *Great-West,* we considered a claim brought by a fiduciary against a tort-award-winning beneficiary seeking monetary reimbursement for medical outlays that the plan had previously made on the beneficiary's behalf. We noted that the fiduciary sought to obtain a lien attaching to (or a constructive trust imposed upon) money that the beneficiary had received from the tort-case defendant. But we noted that the money in question was not the "particular" money that the tort defendant had paid. And, traditionally speaking, relief that sought a lien or a constructive trust was legal relief, not equitable relief, unless the funds in question were *particular* funds or property in the defendant's possession." 534 U.S. at 213 (emphasis added).

The case before us concerns a suit by a beneficiary against a plan fiduciary (whom ERISA typically treats as a trustee) about the terms of a plan (which ERISA typically treats as a trust). See LaRue v. DeWolff, Boberg & Associates, Inc., 552 U.S. 248, 253, n. 4 (2008); Varity Corp., 516 U.S. at 496–497. It is the kind of lawsuit that, before the merger of law and equity, respondents could have brought only in a court of equity, not a court of law. 4 A. Scott, W. Fratcher, & M. Ascher, Trusts § 24.1, p. 1654 (5th ed.2007) (hereinafter Scott & Ascher) ("Trusts are, and always have been, the bailiwick of the courts of equity"); Duvall v. Craig, 2 Wheat. 45, 56, 4 L.Ed. 180 (1817) (a trustee was "only suable in equity").

With the exception of the relief now provided by § 502(a)(1)(B), Restatement (Second) of Trusts §§ 198(1)–(2) (1957) (hereinafter Second Restatement); 4 Scott & Ascher § 24.2.1, the remedies available to those courts of equity were traditionally considered equitable remedies, see Second Restatement § 199; J. Adams, Doctrine of Equity: A Commentary on the Law as Administered by the Court of Chancery 61 (7th Am. ed. 1881) (hereinafter Adams); 4 Scott & Ascher § 24.2.

The District Court's affirmative and negative injunctions obviously fall within this category. Mertens, supra, at 256 (identifying injunctions, mandamus, and restitution as equitable relief). And other relief ordered by the District Court resembles forms of traditional equitable relief. That is because equity chancellors developed a host of other "distinctively equitable" remedies—remedies that were "fitted to the nature of the primary right" they were intended to protect. 1 S. Symons, Pomeroy's Equity Jurisprudence § 108, pp. 139–140 (5th ed.1941) (hereinafter Pomeroy). See generally 1 J. Story, Commentaries on Equity Jurisprudence § 692 (12th ed. 1877) (hereinafter Story). Indeed, a maxim of equity states that "[e]quity suffers not a right to be without a remedy." R. Francis, Maxims of Equity 29 (1st Am. ed. 1823). And the relief entered here, insofar as it does not consist of injunctive relief, closely resembles three other traditional equitable remedies.

First, what the District Court did here may be regarded as the reformation of the terms of the plan, in order to remedy the false or misleading information CIGNA provided. The power to reform contracts (as contrasted with the power to enforce contracts as written) is a traditional power of an equity court, not a court of law, and was used to prevent fraud. See Baltzer v. Raleigh & Augusta R. Co., 115 U.S. 634, 645 (1885) ("[I]t is well settled that equity would reform the contract, and enforce it, as reformed, if the mistake or fraud were shown"); Hearne v. Marine Ins. Co., 20 Wall. 488, 490, 22 L.Ed. 395 (1874) ("The reformation of written contracts for fraud or mistake is an ordinary head of equity jurisdiction"); Bradford v. Union Bank of Tenn., 13 How. 57, 66, 14 L.Ed. 49 (1852); J. Eaton, Handbook of Equity Jurisprudence § 306, p. 618 (1901) (hereinafter Eaton) (courts of common law could only void or enforce, but not reform, a contract); 4 Pomeroy § 1375, at 1000 (reformation "chiefly occasioned by fraud or mistake," which were themselves concerns of equity courts); 1 Story §§ 152–154; see also 4 Pomeroy § 1375, at 999 (equity often considered reformation a "preparatory step" that "establishes the real contract").

Second, the District Court's remedy essentially held CIGNA to what it had promised, namely, that the new plan would not take from its employees benefits they had already accrued. This aspect of the remedy resembles estoppel, a traditional equitable remedy. See, e.g., E. Merwin, Principles of Equity and Equity Pleading § 910 (H. Merwin ed. 1895); 3 Pomeroy § 804. Equitable estoppel "operates to place the person entitled to its benefit in the same position he would have been in had the representations been true." Eaton § 62, at 176. And, as Justice Story long ago pointed out, equitable estoppel "forms a very essential element in. . .fair dealing, and rebuke of all fraudulent misrepresentation, which it is the boast of courts of equity constantly to promote." 2 Story § 1533, at 776.

Third, the District Court injunctions require the plan administrator to pay to already retired beneficiaries money owed them under the plan as reformed. But the fact that this relief takes the form of a money payment does not remove it from the category of traditionally equitable relief. Equity courts possessed the power to provide relief in the form of monetary "compensation" for a loss resulting from a trustee's breach of duty, or to prevent the trustee's unjust enrichment. Restatement (Third) of Trusts § 95, and Comment a (Tent. Draft No. 5, Mar. 2, 2009) (hereinafter Third Restatement); Eaton §§ 211–212, at 440. Indeed, prior to the merger of law and equity this kind of monetary remedy against a trustee, sometimes called a "surcharge," was "exclusively equitable." Princess Lida of Thurn and Taxis v. Thompson, 305 U.S. 456, 464 (1939); Third Restatement § 95, and Comment a; G. Bogert & G. Bogert, Trusts and Trustees § 862 (rev.2d ed.1995) (hereinafter Bogert); 4 Scott & Ascher §§ 24.2, 24.9, at 1659–1660, 1686; Second Restatement § 197; see also Manhattan Bank of Memphis v. Walker, 130 U.S. 267, 271 (1889) ("The suit is plainly one of equitable cognizance, the bill being filed to charge the defendant, as a trustee, for a breach of trust"); 1 J. Perry, A Treatise on the Law of Trusts and Trustees § 17, p. 13 (2d ed. 1874) (common-law attempts "to punish trustees for a breach of trust in damages,. . .w[ere] soon abandoned").

The surcharge remedy extended to a breach of trust committed by a fiduciary encompassing any violation of a duty imposed upon that fiduciary. See Second Restatement § 201; Adams 59; 4 Pomeroy § 1079; 2 Story §§ 1261, 1268. Thus, insofar as an award of make-whole relief is concerned, the fact that the defendant in this case, unlike the defendant in *Mertens,* is analogous to a trustee makes a critical difference. See 508 U.S. at 262–263. In sum, contrary to the District Court's fears, the types of remedies the court entered here fall within the scope of the term "appropriate equitable relief" in § 502(a)(3).

III

Section 502(a)(3) invokes the equitable powers of the District Court. We cannot know with certainty which remedy the District Court understood itself to be imposing, nor whether the District Court will find it appropriate to exercise its discretion under § 502(a)(3) to impose that remedy on remand. We need not decide which remedies are appropriate on the facts of this case in order to resolve the parties' dispute as to the appropriate legal standard in determining whether members of the relevant employee class were injured.

The relevant substantive provisions of ERISA do not set forth any particular standard for determining harm. They simply require the plan administrator to write and to distribute written notices that are "sufficiently accurate and comprehensive to reasonably apprise" plan participants and beneficiaries of "their rights and obligations under the plan." § 102(a); see also §§ 104(b), 204(h). Nor can we find a definite standard in the ERISA provision, § 502(a)(3) (which authorizes the court to enter "appropriate equitable relief" to redress ERISA "violations"). Hence any requirement of harm must come from the law of equity.

Looking to the law of equity, there is no general principle that "detrimental reliance" must be proved before a remedy is decreed. To the extent any such requirement arises, it is because the specific remedy being contemplated imposes such a requirement. Thus, as CIGNA points out, when equity courts used the remedy of *estoppel,* they insisted upon a showing akin to detrimental reliance, i.e., that the defendant's statement "in truth, influenced the conduct of" the plaintiff, causing "prejudic[e]." Eaton § 61, at 175; see 3 Pomeroy § 805. Accordingly, when a court exercises its authority under § 502(a)(3) to impose a remedy equivalent to estoppel, a showing of detrimental reliance must be made.

But this showing is not always necessary for other equitable remedies. Equity courts, for example, would reform contracts to reflect the mutual understanding of the contracting parties where "fraudulent suppression[s], omission[s], or insertion[s]," 1 Story § 154, at 149, "material[ly]. . .affect[ed]" the "substance" of the contract, even if the "complaining part[y]" was negligent in not realizing its mistake, as long as its negligence did not fall below a standard of "reasonable prudence" and violate a legal duty. 3 Pomeroy §§ 856, 856b, at 334, 340–341; see Baltzer, 115 U.S. at 645; Eaton § 307(b).

Nor did equity courts insist upon a showing of detrimental reliance in cases where they ordered "surcharge." Rather, they simply ordered a trust or beneficiary made whole following a trustee's breach of trust. In such instances equity courts would "mold the relief to protect the rights of the beneficiary according to the situation involved." Bogert § 861, at 4. This flexible approach belies a strict requirement of "detrimental reliance."

To be sure, just as a court of equity would not surcharge a trustee for a nonexistent harm, 4 Scott & Ascher § 24.9, a fiduciary can be surcharged under § 502(a)(3) only upon a showing of actual harm—proved (under the default rule for civil cases) by a preponderance of the evidence. That actual harm may sometimes consist of detrimental reliance, but it might also come from the loss of a right protected by ERISA or its trust-law antecedents. In the present case, it is not difficult to imagine how the failure to provide proper summary information, in violation of the statute, injured employees even if they did not themselves act in reliance on summary documents—which they might not themselves have seen—for they may have thought fellow employees, or informal workplace discussion, would have let them know if, say, plan changes would likely prove harmful. We doubt that Congress would have wanted to bar those employees from relief.

The upshot is that we can agree with CIGNA only to a limited extent. We believe that, to obtain relief by surcharge for violations of §§ 102(a) and 104(b), a plan participant or beneficiary must show that the violation injured him or her. But to do so, he or she need only show harm and causation. Although it is not always necessary to meet the more rigorous standard implicit in the words "detrimental reliance," actual harm must be shown.

We are not asked to reassess the evidence. And we are not asked about the other prerequisites for relief. We are asked about the standard of prejudice. And we conclude that the standard of prejudice must be borrowed from equitable principles, as modified by the obligations and injuries identified by ERISA itself. Information-related circumstances, violations, and injuries are potentially too various in nature to insist that harm must always meet that more vigorous "detrimental harm" standard when equity imposed no such strict requirement.

IV

We have premised our discussion in Part III on the need for the District Court to revisit its determination of an appropriate remedy for the violations of ERISA it identified. Whether or not the general principles we have discussed above are properly applicable in this case is for it or the Court of Appeals to determine in the first instance. Because the District Court has not determined if an appropriate remedy may be imposed under §502(a)(3), we must vacate the judgment below and remand this case for further proceedings consistent with this opinion.

It is so ordered.

JUSTICE SOTOMAYOR took no part in the consideration or decision of this case.

JUSTICE SCALIA, with whom JUSTICE THOMAS joins, concurring in the judgment.

I agree with the Court that § 502(a)(1)(B) of the Employee Retirement Income Security Act of 1974 (ERISA), does not authorize relief for misrepresentations in a summary plan description (SPD). I do not join the Court's opinion because I see no need and no justification for saying anything more than that.

Section 502(a)(1)(B) of ERISA states that a plan participant or beneficiary may bring a civil action "to recover benefits due to him under the terms of his plan, to enforce his rights under the terms of the plan, or to clarify his rights to future benefits under the terms of the plan." ERISA defines the word "plan" as "an employee welfare benefit plan or an employee pension benefit plan or a plan which is both," and it requires that a "plan" "be established and maintained pursuant to a written instrument," § 402(a)(1). An SPD, in contrast, is a disclosure meant "to reasonably apprise [plan] participants and beneficiaries of their rights and obligations under the plan." § 102(a). It would be peculiar for a document meant to "apprise" participants of their rights *under the plan* to be itself part of the "plan." Any doubt that it is not is eliminated by ERISA's repeated differentiation of SPDs from the "written instruments" that constitute a plan, and ERISA's assignment to different entities of responsibility for drafting and amending SPDs on the one hand and plans on the other. An SPD, moreover, would not fulfill its purpose of providing an easily accessible summary of the plan if it were an authoritative part of the plan itself; the minor omissions appropriate for a summary would risk revising the plan.

Nothing else needs to be said to dispose of this case. The District Court based the relief it awarded upon ERISA § 502(a)(1)(B), and that provision alone. It thought that the "benefits" due "under the terms of the plan," § 502(a)(1)(B), could derive from an SPD, either because the SPD is part of the plan or because it is capable of somehow modifying the plan. Under either justification, that conclusion is wrong. An SPD is separate from a plan, and cannot amend a plan unless the plan so provides. See Curtiss-Wright Corp. v. Schoonejongen, 514 U.S. 73, 79, 85, (1995). I would go no further.

* * *

I agree with the Court that an SPD is not part of an ERISA plan, and that, as a result, a plan participant or beneficiary may not recover for misrepresentations in an SPD under §502(a)(1)(B). Because this is the only question properly presented for our review, and the only question briefed and argued before us, I concur only in the judgment.

NOTES AND QUESTIONS

1.   Why did the *Amara* Court reject reformation as a remedy under Section 502(a)(1)(B)? Do you agree with the Supreme Court's determination that excluding the summary plan description as part of the "plan" under Section 502(a)(1)(B) is consistent with the policy objectives that underlie ERISA's reporting and disclosure requirements?

2.   In a breach of fiduciary duty case, according to *Amara* what circumstances are required for a federal court to order reformation of the plan as an equitable remedy? To order equitable estoppel? To surcharge the breaching fiduciary and order a monetary payment? How is surcharge different from the equitable remedy of restitution as described by the Supreme Court in *Great-West*?

3.   In interpreting a "modern" (circa 1974) statute such as ERISA, should the Supreme Court rely on sources of law that date from the early 1900's (or even earlier)? Or, should the Court give greater deference to the underlying public policies that Congress intended to implement when interpreting the statutory language of ERISA?

4.   *Monetary Relief as Equitable Restitution.* In the years leading up to the Supreme Court's decision in *Amara*, the federal courts struggled to determine when monetary relief could be characterized as "equitable" restitution under *Mertens*. This characterization issue arose because "[e]quity sometimes awards monetary relief, or the equivalent, and restitution is both a legal and an equitable remedy that is monetary yet is distinct from damages." Clair v. Harris Trust & Savings Bank, 190 F.3d 495, 498 (7th Cir. 1999); see also Kerr v. Charles F. Vatterott & Co., 184 F.3d 938, 944 (8th Cir. 1999) ("Though we sometimes speak of restitution in generic terms, restitution may be either equitable or compensatory.").

In the wake of *Mertens*, two distinct judicial approaches to equitable restitution emerged. Under the unjust enrichment approach, restitution focused on the wrongful conduct of the fiduciary and sought to prevent a fiduciary's unjust enrichment. *Kerr v. Charles F. Vatterott & Co.*, 184 F.3d 938 (8th Cir. 1999), illustrates how the unjust enrichment approach distinguished between restitution and compensatory damages.

> The basic distinction between equitable restitution and compensation focuses on the genesis of the award sought by the plaintiff. A restitutionary award focuses on the defendant's wrongfully obtained gain while a compensatory award focuses on the plaintiff's loss at the defendant's hands. Restitution seeks to punish the wrongdoer by taking his ill-gotten gains, thus removing his incentive to perform the wrongful act again. Compensatory damages, on the other hand, focus on the plaintiff's losses and seek to recover in money the value of the harm done to him.

Id. at 944. See also Fotta v. United Mine Workers of America, Health & Retirement Fund, 165 F.3d 209, 214 (3d Cir. 1998) (monetary payment characterized as restitution when necessary to prevent unjust enrichment). Prior to *Amara*, the Supreme Court's characterization of restitution in *Great-West* and *Sereboff* appeared to support this unjust enrichment approach.

A second judicial approach to restitution focused on the injury suffered by the plan participant as a result of the fiduciary's breach of duty and attempted to make the participant whole for the loss suffered. For example, in *Varity* the district court had ordered that monetary payments be made to the individual plaintiffs and not to the plan itself. The Eighth Circuit in *Varity* affirmed this monetary remedy as equitable restitution.

> The relief awarded includes payments of money that plaintiffs would have received if they had remained members of the [Massey-Ferguson] Plan, but we do not think these payments can properly be characterized as "damages," and thus unavailable under Section 502(a)(3). Rather, we view the payments as restitution. Equity will treat that as done which ought to have been done. Or, to put it in words that fit the present cases more precisely, equity will disregard that which ought not to have been done. Plaintiffs should never have been lured away from [Massey-Ferguson] into the financially shaky [Massey Combines]. The payments we are ordering are exactly what plaintiffs would have gotten if they had remained at [Massey-Ferguson]. They are restored to their rightful position.

Howe v. Varity Corporation, 36 F.3d 746, 756 (8th Cir. 1994). The make-whole judicial perspective on restitution intellectually is rooted in the common law of trusts, where monetary make-whole relief routinely was awarded by courts of equity to a trust beneficiary who had been injured by a trustee's breach of fiduciary duty. See generally John H. Langbein, What ERISA Means by "Equitable": The Supreme Court's Trail of Error in *Russell*, *Mertens*, and *Great-West*, 103 Colum. L. Rev. 1317 (2003).

The Supreme Court's description in *Amara* of "surcharge" as a form of equitable relief under Section 502(a)(3) bridges these two judicial approaches to monetary restitution. In Part II.B of the *Amara* opinion, the Court describes the surcharge remedy as within the power of the equity courts "to provide relief in the form of monetary 'compensation' for a loss resulting from a trustee's breach of duty, or to prevent the trustee's unjust enrichment." Thus, a surcharge remedy appears to be available when a monetary payment is necessary to make the individual plaintiff whole for a loss caused by the fiduciary's breach of duty, even though the fiduciary may not have been personally enriched by the breach.

F. DISCUSSION QUESTIONS FOR CHAPTER SIX

QUESTION ONE

Florence Bell is a participant in her employer's self-insured health care plan (Plan). The Plan has a utilization review feature that requires a participant to obtain approval from the plan for hospital stays within twenty-four hours of being admitted to the hospital, and to obtain prior approval for certain types of medical procedures. This utilization review function is performed by the Plan's third-party administrator, Quality Care (QC). If the participant does not follow the utilization review approval procedures, the Plan will not pay the participant's claim.

Florence becomes pregnant. Three months before her due date, Florence's blood pressure becomes dangerously high. Her physician orders her to have complete bed rest for the final months of her pregnancy. On October 1, four weeks before her delivery date, Florence's physician recommends that she be admitted to the hospital for twenty-four hour fetal monitoring. Florence's physician seeks approval of the hospital stay from QC in accordance with the Plan's utilization review procedures. The next day, QC denies Florence's request for approval of the hospital stay despite the treating physician's recommendation. Instead, the Plan authorizes ten hours a day of fetal monitoring at home, which is performed by a home health nurse. Three weeks later, during a period of time while the nurse is not on duty, Florence's unborn child goes into fetal distress as a result of Florence's high blood pressure and dies.

> **A.** Assume that Florence comes to you on October 2 for legal advice. She is upset that QC has denied her physician's request for twenty-four hour fetal monitoring at the hospital. Explain Florence's legal options under ERISA. What course of action would you recommend to Florence? Would your legal advice depend on whether or not the Plan is a grandfathered plan under the Affordable Care Act?

B. Assume that Florence comes to you after the death of her unborn child seeking legal advice. Explain Florence's potential claims and remedies under ERISA Section 502(a).

QUESTION TWO

Josh Jackson is employed as a cook at Brown's Grill. He is a participant in his employer's health care plan (Plan), which is insured through First Insurance Company. The Plan's administrator is the owner of Brown's Grill, Todd Thompson. The Plan lists both of the local hospitals, Hospital A and Hospital B, as participating providers under the Plan. The Plan does not require prior approval for medical services that do not require an overnight hospital stay, but does require that all medical treatment (except for emergency services) must be rendered by health care providers on the Plan's list of approved providers.

On January 1, the Plan's insurer is changed to Second Insurance Company in an effort to reduce the costs of the Plan. Hospital A is not on the list of health care providers approved by Second Insurance Company. Although Thompson did notify his employees sixty days prior to the change that the insurance company for the Plan would change, he fails to provide the Plan's participants with the new list of health care providers approved by Second Insurance Company.

On March 1, Josh injures his right knee playing softball. His physician recommends that he have non-emergency surgery, which is performed on an out-patient basis. The surgery is performed two days later at Hospital A, which is an approved health care provider according to the now-outdated list of approved providers previously furnished to the Plan participants by Thompson. On March 10, Thompson furnishes the new list of approved health care providers to the Plan's participants, accompanied by a written statement that there has been a "material reduction in Plan benefits in order to reduce the costs of the Plan." The written statement "urges Plan participants to consult the revised list of approved health care providers before seeking medical treatment."

In accordance with the terms of the Plan, Second Insurance Company initially denies Josh's claim for the services of Hospital A. Josh appeals, and again the claim is denied.

Josh comes to you for legal advice. Discuss Josh's potential claims and remedies under ERISA Section 502(a).

QUESTION THREE

Wholesale Granite Company (Company) sponsors a defined benefit plan for its employees (Retirement Plan). The named plan fiduciary for the Retirement Plan is the Administrative Committee (Committee), which consists of three members: Joe Jones, who is the Company president, and the chief financial officer and the human resources manager for the Company.

For each of the following transactions, discuss whether the Retirement Plan participants have a cause of action under ERISA Section 502(a). If so, what is the participants' remedy? In answering these questions, what additional facts would you want to know?

A. The Committee uses Retirement Plan assets to purchase new equipment to modernize the Company's manufacturing plant and thereby saves the jobs of 1,000 Company employees, all of whom are participants in the Retirement Plan.

B. The Committee agrees to make a loan to the Company out of Retirement Plan assets to enable the Company to purchase new equipment. The loan is secured by a promissory note and bears a market rate of interest. The loan was repaid in full by the Company in accordance with the terms of the promissory note.

C. The Committee agrees to pledge the assets of the Retirement Plan as additional collateral for a loan from Small Bank to the Company to enable the Company to purchase new equipment.

D. The Company president, Joe Jones, urges the Committee to invest some of the Plan assets in Start-Up, Inc., a new high-technology company. Joe does not tell the other members of the Committee that he is personally a secret investor in the venture. Relying solely on Joe's assertion that the investment is a "good deal," the Committee invests $100,000 in Plan assets in Start-Up, Inc. Start-Up, Inc. uses the Committee's $100,000 investment to immediately repay Joe Jones $25,000 that he personally loaned to Start-Up, Inc. as a secret investor to cover the business's initial costs. One year later, Start-Up, Inc. fails and the Plan loses its entire investment.

QUESTION FOUR

Big Red Company (Employer) sponsors a self-insured health care plan (Plan) for its employees. Under the terms of the Plan, each employee pays a portion of the monthly premium for coverage under the Plan.

Trudent Plan Administration (TPA) serves as the third party claims administrator for the Plan. The Plan's assets are held in an account administered by TPA. Employee premium payments to the Plan are deducted by the Employer directly from each employee's wages and forwarded to TPA's trust account for the Plan.

Employer suffers a decline in business and stops forwarding the Employer's share of the monthly premium to TPA, even though the Employer continues to deduct the employee premium payments from the wages of its employees. After not receiving any payments from the Employer for several months, TPA contacts Employer and warns that the trust account balance is approaching zero. The Employer assures TPA that "the money is on its way." Once the funds in the Plan's trust account are exhausted, TPA stops processing claims for Plan benefits, but takes no further action against Employer.

Six months later, the Employer is insolvent and files for bankruptcy. Fifty employees who were participants in the Plan and who, according to their payroll statements from the Employer, dutifully paid their Plan premiums, have unpaid claims pending with TPA. These employees have come to you for legal advice. Discuss the potential claims and remedies these employees may have under ERISA Section 502(a) against TPA.

QUESTION FIVE

For each of the situations described below, discuss whether a violation of ERISA Section 510 has occurred. If so, what are the plaintiff's possible remedies under ERISA Section 502(a)(3)? In each instance, what additional facts would you want to know?

A. Employer sponsors a disability plan for its employees that provides up to six weeks of full pay for an absence due to sickness or short-term disability. An absence from work that qualifies for disability plan benefits is deemed an excused absence. The Employer also has a "no fault" attendance policy that requires an employee to be placed on probation after five absences from work during a twelve month period. All absences from work, including excused absences due to disability, are counted for purposes of this attendance policy.

Over a period of several months, Employee X calls in sick for sixteen days. These sick days are counted as excused absences under the short-term disability plan and each time the Employee X receives short-term disability plan benefits for the absence. After five excused absences, the Employer places Employee X on probation, with a written warning that Employee X could be discharged if attendance does not improve. After Employee X's sixteenth absence, Employer terminates Employee, citing a violation of the attendance policy.

B. Employee X, who works for a subsidiary business of Employer, injures her spine due to a work-related injury. Following spinal surgery, Employee X goes on workers' compensation leave, but remains covered as a participant in the subsidiary's health care plan and receives benefits under the subsidiary's disability plan. According to Employee X's physician, the prognosis for Employee X's return to full-time employment is "poor."

Six months later, Employer enters into an agreement with Buyer to sell all of the assets of Employer's subsidiary business. To ensure that there is no disruption in the ongoing operation of the business, Buyer agrees to continue to employ all employees of the subsidiary who are actively at work on the date of the sale, or who are actively employed but absent from work on the sale date due to a non-medical reason. All such transferred employees automatically become participants in the Buyer's self-insured health and disability plans, with no disruption of their benefits. Under the terms of the agreement between Employer and Buyer, if a subsidiary employee was on medical, disability, or workers' compensation leave on the sale date, Buyer is not obligated to hire the employee. Pursuant to this provision in the agreement, Employee X is not transferred to Buyer's workforce. After the sale of the subsidiary business, Employer terminates the medical and disability plans of the subsidiary, causing Employee X to lose her benefits.

QUESTION SIX

For each of the situations described below, discuss the potential claims and remedies under ERISA Section 502(a).

A. Digital Company, the named plan fiduciary, sponsors a participant-directed 401(k) plan for its employees. The 401(k) plan is administered by First Bank. The plan assets are held by First Trust Company, who serves as the plan's directed trustee. Julia Jones is a participant in the 401(k) plan.

Digital Company experiences cash flow difficulties due to its inability to collect on overdue accounts receivable from the company's customers. Rather than immediately forwarding the employee contributions to the 401(k) plan to First Trust Company, as it has regularly done in the past, Digital Company uses the money instead to purchase raw materials used in the company's manufacturing business.

First Trust Company immediately notifies First Bank that it has not received the usual employee 401(k) plan contributions from Digital Company. The client account representative of First Bank calls the president of Digital Company concerning the late payment. The president of Digital Company tells the First Bank account representative that "business is slow" and that "the money is coming."

Three weeks later, one of the company's customers pays a large, long overdue bill. Digital Company uses the money to pay the overdue employee contributions to the 401(k) plan. During this three week period, however, the stock market experienced an unprecedented rise in value. Julia Jones estimates that she personally "lost" $10,000 during this three week period because her 401(k) plan contributions were not invested in a timely manner.

Discuss the claims and remedies available to Julia Jones under ERISA Section 502(a).

B.   Treetop Company sponsors a profit sharing plan (Retirement Plan) for its employees. The named plan fiduciary for the Retirement Plan is Treetop Company. John Jason, the human resources manager, is responsible for the administration of the Retirement Plan. The paperwork for the Retirement Plan is handled by Joan Bixby, the assistant human resources manager.

Sally Haverty, an employee of Treetop Company and a participant in the Retirement Plan, terminates employment. Joan Bixby forgets to give Sally an explanation of the tax consequences of failing to elect a direct rollover of Sally's plan account. As a result, Sally takes a lump sum distribution from the Retirement Plan. Sally later discovers she owes $5,500 in additional income tax due to the inclusion of the distribution in her gross income for the year. Sally is upset about the additional taxes she owes and wants her employer, Treetop Company, to "make her whole."

Discuss the claims and remedies available to Sally Haverty under ERISA Section 502(a).

C.   Jon Martinez applies for a $500,000 supplemental life insurance policy through his Employer. Jon dutifully completes the application form and submits the form to Employer's human resources manager by May 1. Jon names his wife Isabelle as the beneficiary of the policy. The human resources manager is negligent in processing the application and fails to forward the application to the insurance company in a timely manner. Consequently, instead of a June 1 effective date, the supplemental life insurance coverage does not become effective until the first day of the following month, July 1. On June 26, Jon suddenly dies of a massive heart attack.

Discuss the claims and remedies available to Jon's wife Isabelle as the named beneficiary of the life insurance policy under ERISA Section 502(a).

CHAPTER 7

PREEMPTION OF STATE LAW

■ ■ ■

A. OVERVIEW OF ERISA PREEMPTION OF STATE LAW

1. STATUTORY PROVISIONS AND LEGISLATIVE HISTORY

The statutory provisions of ERISA governing preemption of state law, found in Section 514, repeatedly have been criticized by the Supreme Court as being far from a model of clear drafting. See New York State Conference of Blue Cross & Blue Shield Plans v. Travelers Ins. Co., 514 U.S. 645, 655 (1995); Pilot Life Ins. Co. v. Dedeaux, 481 U.S. 41, 46 (1987); Metropolitan Life Ins. Co. v. Massachusetts, 471 U.S. 724, 739 (1985). As a result, the Supreme Court has addressed preemption of state law under Section 514 more frequently than any other statutory provision of ERISA.

ERISA Section 514(a), known as the general preemption clause, states that "the provisions of this title . . . shall supersede any and all State laws insofar as they may now or hereafter relate to any employee benefit plan." For purposes of this provision, "State laws" are defined broadly as including "all laws, decisions, rules, regulations, or other State action having the effect of law, of any State." ERISA § 514(c)(1). The term "State" includes "a State, any political subdivisions thereof, or any agency or instrumentality" of either a State or its political subdivision. ERISA § 514(c)(2).

ERISA Section 514(b)(2)(A), known as the savings clause, preserves from ERISA preemption state laws that regulate insurance, banking, or securities. ERISA Section 514(b)(2)(B), known as the deemer clause, provides that an employee benefit plan shall not be deemed to be an insurance company, bank, trust company, or investment company that is subject to regulation under state laws regulating insurance, banking, or securities. The Supreme Court's early precedents interpreting the savings and deemer clauses in the context of health care plans, *Metropolitan Life Insurance Co. v. Massachusetts*, 471 U.S. 724 (1985), and *FMC Corp. v. Holliday*, 498 U.S. 52 (1990), were introduced in Chapter Four of the casebook.

The legislative history surrounding ERISA's general preemption clause, Section 514(a), and its key words—"relate to"—are mysterious. The bill passed by the United States House of Representatives provided that ERISA would supersede "any and all laws of the States and of the political subdivisions thereof insofar as they may now or hereafter relate to the reporting and disclosure responsibilities and fiduciary responsibilities of persons acting on behalf of any employee benefit plan to which part 1 applies." H.R. 2, 93d Cong., 2d Sess., § 514(a) (1974). The United States Senate adopted the language contained in an earlier draft of the House bill, which provided that ERISA would preempt "any and all laws of the States and of any political subdivision thereof insofar as they may now or hereafter relate to the subject matters regulated by this Act or the Welfare and Pension Plans Disclosure Act." H.R. 2, 93d Cong., 1st Sess., § 699(a) (1973). The Conference Committee was charged with reconciling the different provisions of the House and Senate bills, including the statutory language governing preemption of state laws. During the Conference Committee, the language of ERISA Section 514(a) was changed to its present form. The Conference Committee Report itself does not explain why the language of Section 514(a) was changed. See H.R. Conf. Rep. No. 1280, 93d Cong., 2d Sess., 383 (1974). The remarks of individual Senators and Representatives are inconclusive concerning what the Conference Committee members intended to accomplish by changing the preemption language in the final version of the enacted legislation.

The late Michael Gordon, an eyewitness to the political process that produced Section 514(a) in its final form, described the drafting change made by the Conference Committee as a political compromise.

> The House and Senate versions of preemption brought to conference in 1974 were considerably less sweeping than the version that ultimately emerged. These penultimate versions were designed to preempt only what was federally regulated, leaving the states free to experiment in the employee benefit field where ERISA stopped short. It was just these heuristic possibilities that unsettled a number of the key business, labor, and other groups who had otherwise determined that they could live with ERISA's substantive reforms. The potential burdens threatened by non-uniform state regulation where ERISA left off made the price for supporting ERISA seem too high to pay.
>
> In theory many of the conferees thought it more reasonable to preempt only what was federally regulated in order not to deprive participants and beneficiaries of additional protections that might be offered by state regulation. But the same conferees also recognized that many states might not take as carefully balanced an approach to regulation as Congress had in enacting

ERISA. In the welfare plan area, which was not as extensively regulated under ERISA as pension plans, there had been some adverse experience in this regard. Accordingly, notwithstanding some misgivings, the conferees adopted a broad preemption provision of the type urged by the concerned groups. The preemption provision has been criticized [by the Supreme Court] as not being "a model of legislative drafting," but this criticism overlooks the thorny nature of the drafting dilemma then presented. To develop a less ambiguous and more discriminating preemption provision would have required a sophisticated agreement on the types of state laws to be preserved and the types to be canceled. Obtaining such an agreement would have compelled many more months of effort with no certainty that such an agreement could be reached. Even if such an agreement had been reached, the outcome may not have been any more authoritative than that produced after a decade and more of Supreme Court litigation.

Although this litigation has exposed more effectively than could any congressional study the flaws in ERISA's preemption methodology, it remains to be seen whether the attitudes that precipitated present preemption policy have been sufficiently altered to induce a congressional reexamination of the subject. Many of the groups that united behind ERISA may still see sweeping preemption as the only basis for their unqualified support of the law.[a]

2. THE EVOLUTION OF ERISA PREEMPTION ANALYSIS

The Supreme Court has described federal preemption of state law in general terms as consisting of several categories of judicial analysis.

A fundamental principle of the Constitution is that Congress has the power to preempt state law. Even without an express provision for preemption, we have found that state law must yield to a congressional Act in at least two circumstances. When Congress intends federal law to occupy the field, state law in that area is preempted. And even if Congress has not occupied the field, state law is naturally preempted to the extent of any conflict with a federal statute.

We recognize, of course, that the categories of preemption are not rigidly distinct. Because a variety of state laws and regulations may conflict with a federal statute, whether because a private party cannot comply with both sets of provisions or because the objectives of the federal statute are frustrated, field preemption may be understood as a species of conflict preemption.

We will find preemption where it is impossible for a private party to comply with both state and federal law, and where under the circumstances of a particular case, the challenged state law stands as an obstacle to the accomplishment and execution of the full purposes and objectives of Congress. What is a sufficient obstacle is a matter of judgment, to be informed by examining the federal statute as a whole and identifying its purpose and intended effects.

Crosby v. National Foreign Trade Council, 530 U.S. 363, 372–73 (2000) (quotations and citations omitted) (footnote 6 inserted).

Viewed in historical perspective, the Supreme Court's preemption jurisprudence under ERISA has evolved from a broad field preemption approach in the Court's early preemption decisions to a more narrowly tailored conflict preemption analysis today. Section B of Chapter Seven focuses on the Supreme Court's early preemption decisions, *Shaw v. Delta Air Lines, Inc.*, 463 U.S. 85 (1983), *Pilot Life Insurance Co. v. Dedeaux*, 481 U.S. 41 (1987), and *Ingersoll-Rand Co. v. McClendon*, 498 U.S. 133 (1990). In these early preemption cases, the Supreme Court read the legislative history of Section 514(a) as an indication that Congress had rejected a more narrow conflict preemption approach and instead intended ERISA broadly to preempt all state laws, excepting only state laws that affected an employee benefit plan "in too tenuous, remote, or peripheral a manner to warrant a finding that the law 'relates to' the plan." Shaw, 463 US. at 100 n.21.

In 1995, the Supreme Court ushered in the modern era of ERISA preemption analysis with its landmark opinion in *New York State Conference of Blue Cross & Blue Shield Plans v. Travelers Insurance Co.*, 514 U.S. 645 (1995) (*Travelers*). Section C of Chapter Seven focuses on the *Travelers* approach to preemption analysis. Under *Travelers*, a rebuttable presumption exists that Congress did not intend ERISA to preempt traditional areas of state law regulation. The other Supreme Court decision reproduced in Section C, *Egelhoff v. Egelhoff*, 530 U.S. 1242 (2000), illustrates how the Supreme Court has applied the *Travelers* approach to preemption of state law.

The Supreme Court's preemption jurisprudence has proven particularly troublesome when applied to state laws that attempt to regulate group health care plans and health care providers. Section D of

Chapter Seven examines the Supreme Court's preemption decisions concerning state law efforts to regulate and reform the health care system. Chapter Seven concludes with a discussion of state and local initiatives to increase the scope of employer-sponsored health care plan coverage.

B. THE EARLY PREEMPTION CASES: BROAD PREEMPTION OF STATE LAW

In *Shaw v. Delta Air Lines, Inc.*, the Supreme Court articulated a two-pronged test for the lower federal courts to use in determining whether a state law "relates to" an employee benefit plan within the meaning of ERISA Section 514(a). Under the *Shaw* test, a state law "relates to" an employee benefit plan if the state law has *a connection with* an employee benefit plan, or the state law has a *reference to* an employee benefit plan. Subsequent Supreme Court preemption decisions have continued to rely on the *Shaw* test as the starting point for judicial preemption analysis under Section 514(a).

SHAW V. DELTA AIR LINES, INC.
United States Supreme Court, 1983.
463 U.S. 85, 103 S.Ct. 2890, 77 L.Ed.2d 490.

JUSTICE BLACKMUN delivered the opinion of the Court.

New York's Human Rights Law forbids discrimination in employment, including discrimination in employee benefit plans on the basis of pregnancy. The State's Disability Benefits Law requires employers to pay sick-leave benefits to employees unable to work because of pregnancy or other nonoccupational disabilities. The question before us is whether these New York laws are preempted by the federal Employee Retirement Income Security Act of 1974 (ERISA).

I

A

The Human Rights Law is a comprehensive anti-discrimination statute prohibiting, among other practices, employment discrimination on the basis of sex. The New York Court of Appeals has held that a private employer whose employee benefit plan treats pregnancy differently from other nonoccupational disabilities engages in sex discrimination within the meaning of the Human Rights Law. Brooklyn Union Gas Co. v. New York State Human Rights Appeal Board, 41 N.Y.2d 84, 390 N.Y.S.2d 884, 359 N.E.2d 393 (1976). In contrast, two weeks before the decision in *Brooklyn Union Gas*, this Court ruled that discrimination based on pregnancy was not sex discrimination under Title VII of the Civil Rights Act of 1964, 42 U.S.C. § 2000e et seq. General Electric Co. v. Gilbert, 429

U.S. 125 (1976). Congress overcame the *Gilbert* ruling by enacting § 1 of the Pregnancy Discrimination Act of 1978, which added subsection (k) to § 701 of the Civil Rights Act of 1964.[3] Until that Act took effect on April 29, 1979, the Human Rights Law in this respect had a reach broader than Title VII.

The Disability Benefits Law requires employers to pay certain benefits to employees unable to work because of nonoccupational injuries or illness. Disabled employees generally are entitled to receive the lesser of $95 per week or one-half their average weekly wage, for a maximum of 26 weeks in any one-year period. Until August 1977, the Disability Benefits Law provided that employees were not entitled to benefits for pregnancy-related disabilities. From August 1977 to June 1981, employers were required to provide eight weeks of benefits for pregnancy-related disabilities. This limitation was repealed in 1981, and the Disability Benefits Law now requires employers to provide the same benefits for pregnancy as for any other disability.

* * *

II

Appellees in this litigation, Delta Air Lines, Inc., and other airlines (Airlines), Burroughs Corporation (Burroughs), and Metropolitan Life Insurance Company (Metropolitan), provided their employees with various medical and disability benefits through welfare plans subject to ERISA. These plans, prior to the effective date of the Pregnancy Discrimination Act, did not provide benefits to employees disabled by pregnancy as required by the New York Human Rights Law and the State's Disability Benefits Law. Appellees brought three separate federal declaratory judgment actions against appellant state agencies and officials, alleging that the Human Rights Law was preempted by ERISA. The Airlines in their action alleged that the Disability Benefits Law was similarly preempted.

* * *

III

In deciding whether a federal law preempts a state statute, our task is to ascertain Congress' intent in enacting the federal statute at issue. "Preemption may be either express or implied, and is compelled whether Congress' command is explicitly stated in the statute's language or

---

[3] Subsection (k) provides in relevant part:

The terms 'because of sex' or 'on the basis of sex' include, but are not limited to, because of or on the basis of pregnancy, childbirth, or related medical conditions; and women affected by pregnancy, childbirth, or related medical conditions shall be treated the same for all employment-related purposes, including receipt of benefits under fringe benefit programs, as other persons not so affected but similar in their ability or inability to work, and nothing in section 703(h) of this title shall be interpreted to permit otherwise.

implicitly contained in its structure and purpose." Fidelity Federal Sav. &
Loan Ass'n v. De la Cuesta, 458 U.S. 141, 152–53 (1982). In this case, we
address the scope of several provisions of ERISA that speak expressly to
the question of preemption. The issues are whether the Human Rights
Law and Disability Benefits Law "relate to" employee benefit plans
within the meaning of § 514(a), and, if so, whether any exception in
ERISA saves them from preemption.

We have no difficulty in concluding that the Human Rights Law and
Disability Benefits Law "relate to" employee benefit plans. The breadth of
§ 514(a)'s preemptive reach is apparent from that section's language. A
law "relates to" an employee benefit plan, in the normal sense of the
phrase, if it has a connection with or reference to such a plan. Employing
this definition, the Human Rights Law, which prohibits employers from
structuring their employee benefit plans in a manner that discriminates
on the basis of pregnancy, and the Disability Benefits Law, which
requires employers to pay employees specific benefits, clearly "relate to"
benefit plans. We must give effect to this plain language unless there is
good reason to believe Congress intended the language to have some more
restrictive meaning.

In fact, however, Congress used the words "relate to" in § 514(a) in
their broad sense. To interpret § 514(a) to preempt only state laws
specifically designed to affect employee benefit plans would be to ignore
the remainder of § 514. It would have been unnecessary to exempt
generally applicable state criminal statutes from preemption in § 514(b),
for example, if § 514(a) applied only to state laws dealing specifically with
ERISA plans.

Nor, given the legislative history, can § 514(a) be interpreted to
preempt only state laws dealing with the subject matters covered by
ERISA—reporting, disclosure, fiduciary responsibility, and the like. The
bill that became ERISA originally contained a limited preemption clause,
applicable only to state laws relating to the specific subjects covered by
ERISA. The Conference Committee rejected these provisions in favor of
the present language, and indicated that the section's preemptive scope
was as broad as its language. See H.R. Conf. Rep. No. 93–1280, p. 383
(1974); S. Conf. Rep. No. 93–1090, p. 383 (1974). Statements by the bill's
sponsors during the subsequent debates stressed the breadth of federal
preemption. Representative Dent, for example, stated:

> Finally, I wish to make note of what is to many the crowning
> achievement of this legislation, the reservation to Federal
> authority the sole power to regulate the field of employee benefit
> plans. With the preemption of the field, we round out the
> protection afforded participants by eliminating the threat of
> conflicting and inconsistent State and local regulation. 120 Cong.
> Rec. 29197 (1974).

Senator Williams echoed these sentiments:

> It should be stressed that with the narrow exceptions specified in the bill, the substantive and enforcement provisions of the conference substitute are intended to preempt the field for Federal regulations, thus eliminating the threat of conflicting or inconsistent State and local regulation of employee benefit plans. This principle is intended to apply in its broadest sense to all actions of State or local governments, or any instrumentality thereof, which have the force or effect of law. Id. at 29933.

Given the plain language of § 514(a), the structure of the Act, and its legislative history, we hold that the Human Rights Law and the Disability Benefits Law "relate to any employee benefit plan" within the meaning of ERISA's § 514(a).[21]

* * *

NOTES AND QUESTIONS

1.   How did the Supreme Court in *Shaw* interpret the scope of ERISA Section 514(a) in light of the legislative history? Do you find the Court's interpretation of the legislative history of ERISA Section 514(a) persuasive?

2.   *ERISA Preemption and Other Federal Laws.* ERISA Section 514(d) provides that "[n]othing in this title shall be construed to alter, amend, modify, invalidate, impair, or supersede any law of the United States . . . or any rule or regulation issued under any such law." In an omitted portion of the Supreme Court's opinion in *Shaw*, the Court held that state fair employment laws that were necessary for federal enforcement of Title VII of the Civil Rights Act of 1964 were not preempted by ERISA due to Section 514(d). State laws that prohibit employment practices that *are* lawful under Title VII are preempted, however, insofar as the state law "relates to" an employee benefit plan.

3.   *State Laws Requiring Benefits for Same-Sex Spouses.* Based on the reasoning in *Shaw*, prior to the Supreme Court's decision in *United States v. Windsor*, 133 S. Ct. 2675 (2013), the courts routinely held that ERISA Section 514(a) preempted any state law or municipal ordinance that required, either directly or indirectly, an employer to extend ERISA plan benefits to same-sex spouse or domestic partner of an employee. See, e.g., Council of City of New York v. Bloomberg, 6 N.Y.3d 380, 846 N.E.2d 433 (N.Y. 2006) (city ordinance prohibiting municipal agencies from contracting with companies that failed to provide equal domestic partner benefits held preempted); Catholic Charities of Maine, Inc. v. City of Portland, 304 F.Supp.2d 77 (D. Me. 2004) (city ordinance requiring employers who receive city funds to provide equal

---

[21]   Some state actions may affect employee benefit plans in too tenuous, remote, or peripheral a manner to warrant a finding that the law "relates to" the plan. The present litigation plainly does not present a borderline question, and we express no views about where it would be appropriate to draw the line.

domestic partner benefits held preempted); Air Transport v. City and County of San Francisco, 992 F. Supp. 1149 (N.D. Cal. 1998) (city ordinance prohibiting city from contracting with companies that failed to provide equal domestic partner benefits held preempted). After the Supreme Court's ruling in *Windsor*, as interpreted by the Department of Labor ERISA plans must offer benefits to same-sex spouses on the same terms and conditions as benefits that are offered to opposite-sex spouses. ERISA plans are not, however, required to offer benefits to the domestic partner of an employee. State laws requiring ERISA plans to offer benefits to domestic partners remain preempted.

4. *ERISA Preemption and State Workers' Compensation Laws.* Title I of ERISA does not apply to a plan that is "maintained solely for the purpose of complying with applicable workers compensation laws or unemployment, compensation or disability insurance laws." ERISA §4(b)(3). State workers compensation laws, however, may be preempted by ERISA Section 514(a) to the extent the state law establishes requirements for employee benefit plans that are subject to ERISA. For example, a state workers' compensation law that requires the employer to offer health care plan benefits to employees who are receiving workers' compensation benefits is preempted. See District of Columbia v. Greater Washington Board of Trade, 506 U.S. 125 (1992).

PILOT LIFE INSURANCE CO. V. DEDEAUX

United States Supreme Court, 1987.
481 U.S. 41, 107 S.Ct. 1549, 95 L.Ed.2d 39.

JUSTICE O'CONNOR delivered the opinion of the Court.

This case presents the question whether the Employee Retirement Income Security Act of 1974 (ERISA) preempts state common law tort and contract actions asserting improper processing of a claim for benefits under an insured employee benefit plan.

I

In March 1975, in Gulfport, Mississippi, respondent Everate W. Dedeaux injured his back in an accident related to his employment for Entex, Inc. (Entex). Entex had at this time a long-term disability employee benefit plan established by purchasing a group insurance policy from petitioner, Pilot Life Insurance Co. (Pilot Life). Entex collected and matched its employees' contributions to the plan and forwarded those funds to Pilot Life; the employer also provided forms to its employees for processing disability claims, and forwarded completed forms to Pilot Life. Pilot Life bore the responsibility of determining who would receive disability benefits. Although Dedeaux sought permanent disability benefits following the 1975 accident, Pilot Life terminated his benefits after two years. During the following three years Dedeaux's benefits were reinstated and terminated by Pilot Life several times.

In 1980, Dedeaux instituted a diversity action against Pilot Life in the United States District Court for the Southern District of Mississippi. Dedeaux's complaint contained three counts: "Tortious Breach of Contract"; "Breach of Fiduciary Duties"; and "Fraud in the Inducement." Dedeaux sought "[d]amages for failure to provide benefits under the insurance policy in a sum to be determined at the time of trial," "[g]eneral damages for mental and emotional distress and other incidental damages in the sum of $250,000.00," and "[p]unitive and exemplary damages in the sum of $500,000.00." Dedeaux did not assert any of the several causes of action available to him under ERISA.

At the close of discovery, Pilot Life moved for summary judgment, arguing that ERISA preempted Dedeaux's common law claim for failure to pay benefits on the group insurance policy. The District Court granted Pilot Life summary judgment, finding all Dedeaux's claims preempted.

The Court of Appeals for the Fifth Circuit reversed, primarily on the basis of this Court's decision in *Metropolitan Life Insurance Co. v. Massachusetts*, 471 U.S. 724 (1985). We granted certiorari, and now reverse.

II

In ERISA, Congress set out to:

> protect ... participants in employee benefit plans and their beneficiaries, by requiring the disclosure and reporting to participants and beneficiaries of financial and other information with respect thereto, by establishing standards of conduct, responsibility, and obligation for fiduciaries of employee benefit plans, and by providing for appropriate remedies, sanctions, and ready access to the Federal courts. ERISA § 2.

ERISA comprehensively regulates, among other things, employee welfare benefit plans that, "through the purchase of insurance or otherwise," provide medical, surgical, or hospital care, or benefits in the event of sickness, accident, disability, or death. ERISA § 3(1).

Congress capped off the massive undertaking of ERISA with three provisions relating to the preemptive effect of the federal legislation:

> Except as provided in subsection (b) of this section [the saving clause], the provisions of this subchapter and subchapter III of this chapter shall supersede any and all State laws insofar as they may now or hereafter relate to any employee benefit plan. .... ERISA § 514(a) (preemption clause).

> Except as provided in subparagraph (B) [the deemer clause], nothing in this subchapter shall be construed to exempt or

relieve any person from any law of any State which regulates insurance, banking, or securities. ERISA § 514(b)(2)(A) (saving clause).

Neither an employee benefit plan . . . nor any trust established under such a plan, shall be deemed to be an insurance company or other insurer, bank, trust company, or investment company or to be engaged in the business of insurance or banking for purposes of any law of any State purporting to regulate insurance companies, insurance contracts, banks, trust companies, or investment companies. ERISA § 514(b)(2)(B) (deemer clause).

To summarize the pure mechanics of the provisions quoted above: If a state law "relate[s] to . . . employee benefit plan[s]," it is preempted. ERISA § 514(a). The saving clause excepts from the preemption clause laws that "regulat[e] insurance." ERISA § 514(b)(2)(A). The deemer clause makes clear that a state law that "purport[s] to regulate insurance" cannot deem an employee benefit plan to be an insurance company. ERISA § 514(b)(2)(B).

* * *

In *Metropolitan Life*, this Court, noting that the preemption and saving clauses "perhaps are not a model of legislative drafting," 471 U.S. at 739, interpreted these clauses in relation to a Massachusetts statute that required minimum mental health care benefits to be provided Massachusetts residents covered by general health insurance policies. The appellants in *Metropolitan Life* argued that the state statute, as applied to insurance policies purchased by employee health care plans regulated by ERISA, was preempted.

The Court concluded, first, that the Massachusetts statute did "relate to . . . employee benefit plan[s]," thus placing the state statute within the broad sweep of the preemption clause, § 514(a). However, the Court held that, because the state statute was one that "regulate[d] insurance," the saving clause prevented the state law from being preempted. * * *

Given the "statutory complexity" of ERISA's three preemption provisions, as well as the wide variety of state statutory and decisional law arguably affected by the federal preemption provisions, it is not surprising that we are again called on to interpret these provisions.

III

There is no dispute that the common law causes of action asserted in Dedeaux's complaint "relate to" an employee benefit plan and therefore fall under ERISA's express preemption clause, § 514(a). In both *Metropolitan Life* and *Shaw v. Delta Air Lines, Inc.*, we noted the expansive sweep of the preemption clause. In both cases "[t]he phrase 'relate to' was given its broad common-sense meaning, such that a state law 'relate[s] to' a benefit plan 'in the normal sense of the phrase, if it has a connection with or reference to such a plan.' " Metropolitan Life, 471 U.S. at 739 (quoting Shaw v. Delta Air Lines, Inc., 463 U.S. at 97). In particular we have emphasized that the preemption clause is not limited to "state laws specifically designed to affect employee benefit plans." Shaw v. Delta Air Lines, 463 U.S. at 98. The common law causes of action raised in Dedeaux's complaint, each based on alleged improper processing of a claim for benefits under an employee benefit plan, undoubtedly meet the criteria for preemption under § 514(a).

Unless these common law causes of action fall under an exception to § 514(a), therefore, they are expressly preempted. Although Dedeaux's complaint pleaded several state common law causes of action, before this Court Dedeaux has described only one of the three counts—called "tortious breach of contract" in the complaint, and "the Mississippi law of bad faith" in respondent's brief—as protected from the preemptive effect of § 514(a). The Mississippi law of bad faith, Dedeaux argues, is a law "which regulates insurance," and thus is saved from preemption by § 514(b)(2)(A).

* * *

As early as 1915 the Mississippi Supreme Court had recognized that punitive damages were available in a contract case when "the act or omission constituting the breach of the contract amounts also to the commission of a tort." See Hood v. Moffett, 109 Miss. 757, 767, 69 So. 664, 666 (1915) (involving a physician's breach of a contract to attend to a woman at her approaching "accouchement"). * * * Recently the Mississippi Supreme Court stated that "[w]e have come to term an insurance carrier which refuses to pay a claim when there is no reasonably arguable basis to deny it as acting in 'bad faith,' and a lawsuit based upon such an arbitrary refusal as a 'bad faith' cause of action." Blue Cross & Blue Shield of Mississippi, Inc. v. Campbell, 466 So.2d 833, 842 (1984).

Certainly a common sense understanding of the phrase "regulates insurance" does not support the argument that the Mississippi law of bad faith falls under the saving clause. A common-sense view of the word "regulates" would lead to the conclusion that in order to regulate insurance, a law must not just have an impact on the insurance industry, but must be specifically directed toward that industry. Even though the Mississippi Supreme Court has identified its law of bad faith with the insurance industry, the roots of this law are firmly planted in the general principles of Mississippi tort and contract law. Any breach of contract, and not merely breach of an insurance contract, may lead to liability for punitive damages under Mississippi law.

* * *

In the present case, moreover, we are obliged in interpreting the saving clause to consider not only the factors by which we were guided in *Metropolitan Life*, but also the role of the saving clause in ERISA as a whole. On numerous occasions we have noted that "[i]n expounding a statute, we must not be guided by a single sentence or member of a sentence, but look to the provisions of the whole law, and to its object and policy." Kelly v. Robinson, 479 U.S. 36, 43 (1986). Because in this case, the state cause of action seeks remedies for the improper processing of a claim for benefits under an ERISA-regulated plan, our understanding of the saving clause must be informed by the legislative intent concerning the civil enforcement provisions provided by ERISA § 502(a).

The Solicitor General, for the United States as amicus curiae, argues that Congress clearly expressed an intent that the civil enforcement provisions of ERISA § 502(a) be the exclusive vehicle for actions by ERISA-plan participants and beneficiaries asserting improper processing of a claim for benefits, and that varying state causes of action for claims within the scope of § 502(a) would pose an obstacle to the purposes and objectives of Congress. We agree. The conclusion that § 502(a) was intended to be exclusive is supported, first, by the language and structure of the civil enforcement provisions, and second, by legislative history in which Congress declared that the preemptive force of § 502(a) was modeled on the exclusive remedy provided by § 301 of the Labor Management Relations Act, 1947 (LMRA), 29 U.S.C. § 185.

* * * Under the civil enforcement provisions of § 502(a), a plan participant or beneficiary may sue to recover benefits due under the plan, to enforce the participant's rights under the plan, or to clarify rights to future benefits. Relief may take the form of accrued benefits due, a declaratory judgment on entitlement to benefits, or an injunction against a plan administrator's improper refusal to pay benefits. A participant or beneficiary may also bring a cause of action for breach of fiduciary duty, and under this cause of action may seek removal of the fiduciary. ERISA §§ 502(a)(2); 409. In *Massachusetts Mutual Life Insurance Co. v. Russell*, we concluded that ERISA's breach of fiduciary duty provision, § 409(a), provided no express authority for an award of punitive damages to a beneficiary. Moreover, we declined to find an implied cause of action for punitive damages in that section, noting that "[t]he presumption that a remedy was deliberately omitted from a statute is strongest when Congress has enacted a comprehensive legislative scheme including an integrated system of procedures for enforcement." Russell, 473 U.S. 134, 147 (1985). Our examination of these provisions made us "reluctant to tamper with an enforcement scheme crafted with such evident care as the one in ERISA." Id.

In sum, the detailed provisions of § 502(a) set forth a comprehensive civil enforcement scheme that represents a careful balancing of the need for prompt and fair claims settlement procedures against the public interest in encouraging the formation of employee benefit plans. The policy choices reflected in the inclusion of certain remedies and the exclusion of others under the federal scheme would be completely undermined if ERISA-plan participants and beneficiaries were free to obtain remedies under state law that Congress rejected in ERISA. "The six carefully integrated civil enforcement provisions found in § 502(a) of the statute as finally enacted. . .provide strong evidence that Congress did *not* intend to authorize other remedies that it simply forgot to incorporate expressly." Russell, 473 U.S. at 146 (emphasis in original).

The deliberate care with which ERISA's civil enforcement remedies were drafted and the balancing of policies embodied in its choice of remedies argue strongly for the conclusion that ERISA's civil enforcement remedies were intended to be exclusive. This conclusion is fully confirmed by the legislative history of the civil enforcement provision. The legislative history demonstrates that the preemptive force of § 502(a) was modeled after § 301 of the LMRA.

The Conference Report on ERISA describing the civil enforcement provisions of § 502(a) says:

> Under the conference agreement, civil actions may be brought by a participant or beneficiary to recover benefits due under the plan, to clarify rights to receive future benefits under the plan, and for relief from breach of fiduciary responsibility. . . . [W]ith respect to suits to enforce benefit rights under the plan or to recover benefits under the plan which do not involve application of the title I provisions, they may be brought not only in U.S. district courts but also in State courts of competent jurisdiction. *All such actions in Federal or State courts are to be regarded as arising under the laws of the United States in similar fashion to those brought under section 301 of the Labor-Management Relations Act of 1947.* H.R. Conf. Rep. No. 93–1280, p. 327 (1974) (emphasis added).

Congress was well aware that the powerful preemptive force of § 301 of the LMRA displaced all state actions for violation of contracts between an employer and a labor organization, even when the state action purported to authorize a remedy unavailable under the federal provision. Section 301 preempts any "state-law claim [whose resolution] is substantially dependent upon the analysis of the terms of an agreement made between the parties in a labor contract." Allis-Chalmers Corp. v. Lueck, 471 U.S. at 220. * * *

Congress' specific reference to § 301 of the LMRA to describe the civil enforcement scheme of ERISA makes clear its intention that all suits brought by beneficiaries or participants asserting improper processing of claims under ERISA-regulated plans be treated as federal questions governed by § 502(a). * * * The expectations that a federal common law of rights and obligations under ERISA-regulated plans would develop, indeed, the entire comparison of ERISA's § 502(a) to § 301 of the LMRA, would make little sense if the remedies available to ERISA participants and beneficiaries under § 502(a) could be supplemented or supplanted by varying state laws.

In *Metropolitan Life Ins. Co. v. Massachusetts*, 471 U.S. at 746, this Court rejected an interpretation of the saving clause of ERISA's express preemption provisions, § 514(b)(2)(A), that saved from preemption "only state regulations unrelated to the substantive provisions of ERISA," finding that "[n]othing in the language, structure, or legislative history of the Act" supported this reading of the saving clause. *Metropolitan Life*, however, did not involve a state law that conflicted with a substantive provision of ERISA. Therefore the Court's general observation—that state laws related to ERISA may also fall under the saving clause—was not focused on any particular relationship or conflict between a substantive provision of ERISA and a state law. In particular, the Court had no occasion to consider in *Metropolitan Life* the question raised in the present case: whether Congress might clearly express, through the structure and legislative history of a particular substantive provision of ERISA, an intention that the federal remedy provided by that provision displace state causes of action. Our resolution of this different question does not conflict with the Court's earlier general observations in *Metropolitan Life*.

Considering the common-sense understanding of the saving clause, * * * and, most importantly, the clear expression of congressional intent that ERISA's civil enforcement scheme be exclusive, we conclude that Dedeaux's state law suit asserting improper processing of a claim for benefits under an ERISA-regulated plan is not saved by § 514(b)(2)(A), and therefore is preempted by § 514(a). Accordingly, the judgment of the Court of Appeals is

Reversed.

NOTES

1.   *The Legacy of* Pilot Life. In *Pilot Life*, the Supreme Court reasoned that the plaintiff's claim was preempted by ERISA on two grounds. First, the Court determined that the plaintiff's claim was not derived from a law that regulated insurance under ERISA's savings clause. Second (and of far greater importance in later cases), the Court concluded that preemption of the plaintiff's claim was consistent with Congressional intent, stating that "[t]he deliberate care with which ERISA's civil enforcement remedies were drafted and the balancing of policies embodied in its choice of remedies argue

strongly for the conclusion that ERISA's civil enforcement remedies were intended to be exclusive." 481 U.S. at 54. In the aftermath of *Pilot Life*, the lower federal courts consistently have ruled that state law claims brought under various legal theories against a plan administrator for wrongfully denying or delaying claims made under an employee benefit plan are preempted by ERISA. These decisions have rested primarily on the above-quoted language from *Pilot Life* and the Court's conclusion that Congress intended such claims to be brought exclusively under ERISA Section 502(a)(1)(B) as claims for plan benefits.

The combined effect of ERISA preemption of state law claims under *Pilot Life* and the limited private civil remedies available under ERISA Section 502(a)(1)(B) has proven frustrating, both for plan participants and the federal judiciary. E.g., Bast v. Prudential Ins. Co., 150 F.3d 1003 (9th Cir. 1998); Cannon v. Group Health Service of Okla., Inc., 77 F.3d 1270 (10th Cir. 1996); Andrews-Clarke v. Travelers Ins. Co., 984 F.Supp. 49 (D. Mass. 1997). This frustration has been particularly acute in the context of wrongful death claims under state law based on a denial or delay in authorizing medical treatment under the plan's utilization review system.

Corcoran v. United HealthCare, Inc., 965 F.2d 1321 (5th Cir. 1992), dramatically illustrates the perceived problems with ERISA preemption of state law claims based on benefit decisions made by the plan's utilization reviewer. Florence Corcoran, an employee of South Central Bell Telephone Company (Bell), became pregnant in early 1989. Her physician recommended that she have complete bed rest during the final months of pregnancy. As Corcoran neared her delivery date, her obstetrician ordered her hospitalized so that he could monitor her unborn child around the clock.

Corcoran was a participant in Bell's self-insured health care plan (Plan). The Plan required that a participant must obtain advance approval for overnight hospital admissions. United Healthcare, Inc. (United Healthcare), a service provider to the Plan, reviewed pre-authorization requests for overnight hospital admissions. When Corcoran's obstetrician requested approval from the Plan for her hospital stay, United Healthcare denied the request and authorized instead ten hours per day of home nursing care with fetal monitoring. During a period of time when the home health nurse was not on duty, Corcoran's unborn child went into distress and died.

Corcoran and her husband filed several state law claims in Louisiana state court against United Healthcare as the utilization reviewer, alleging that the defendant's negligence resulted in the wrongful death of their unborn child. They sought damages under state law for their child's death, loss of consortium and emotional distress. Relying on the Supreme Court's decision in *Pilot Life*, the Fifth Circuit reluctantly concluded that the Corcorans' state law claims were preempted by ERISA, despite the significant policy ramifications of this conclusion.

> The result ERISA compels us to reach means that the
> Corcorans have no remedy, state or federal, for what may have been

a serious mistake. This is troubling for several reasons. First, it eliminates an important check on the thousands of medical decisions routinely made in the burgeoning utilization review system. With liability rules generally inapplicable, there is theoretically less deterrence of substandard medical decision making. Moreover, if the cost of compliance with a standard of care (reflected either in the cost of prevention or the cost of paying judgments) need not be factored into utilization review companies' cost of doing business, bad medical judgments will end up being cost-free to the plans that rely on these companies to contain medical costs. ERISA plans, in turn, will have one less incentive to seek out the companies that can deliver both high quality services and reasonable prices.

Second, in any plan benefit determination, there is always some tension between the interest of the beneficiary in obtaining quality medical care and the interest of the plan in preserving the pool of funds available to compensate all beneficiaries. In a prospective review context, with its greatly increased ability to deter the beneficiary (correctly or not) from embarking on a course of treatment recommended by the beneficiary's physician, the tension between interest of the beneficiary and that of the plan is exacerbated. A system which would, at least in some circumstances, compensate the beneficiary who changes course based upon a wrong call for the costs of that call might ease the tension between the conflicting interests of the beneficiary and the plan.

Finally, cost containment features such as the one at issue in this case did not exist when Congress passed ERISA. While we are confident that the result we have reached is faithful to Congress's intent neither to allow state law causes of action that relate to employee benefit plans nor to provide beneficiaries in the Corcorans' position with a remedy under ERISA, the world of employee benefit plans has hardly remained static since 1974. Fundamental changes such as the widespread institution of utilization review would seem to warrant a reevaluation of ERISA so that it can continue to serve its noble purpose of safeguarding the interests of employees. Our system, of course, allocates this task to Congress, not the courts, and we acknowledge our role today by interpreting ERISA in a manner consistent with the expressed intentions of its creators.

Id. at 1338–39 (footnote omitted). When faced with life-or-death situations, courts occasionally will grant a preliminary injunction and order the plan administrator to provide or pre-authorize the treatment sought by the plan participant. E.g., Kopicki v. Fitzgerald Auto. Family Employee Benefits Plan, 121 F.Supp.2d 467 (D. Md. 2000); Velez v. Prudential Health Care Plan of New York, 943 F.Supp. 332 (S.D.N.Y. 1996); Marro v. K-III Communic'ns Corp., 943 F.Supp. 247 (E.D.N.Y. 1996); Mattive v. Healthsource of

Savannah, Inc., 893 F.Supp. 1559 (S.D. Ga. 1995); Dozsa v. Crum & Forster Ins. Co., 716 F.Supp. 131 (D. N.J. 1989).

2.   *State Health Care Reform Laws and* Pilot Life. The Supreme Court's analysis in *Pilot Life* has played a prominent role in subsequent Supreme Court decisions addressing ERISA preemption of state laws designed to regulate health care plans and health care providers. In *Rush Prudential HMO, Inc. v. Moran*, 536 U.S. 355 (2002), the Supreme Court held that an alternative mechanism established under state law to appeal a denied claim for plan benefits by a plan administrator was not preempted by ERISA, even though the state law mechanism overlapped with a claim for denial of plan benefits under ERISA Section 502(a)(1)(B). In *Kentucky Association of Health Plans, Inc. v. Miller*, 538 U.S. 329 (2003), the Supreme Court revisited the *Pilot Life* issue of when a state law "regulates insurance" within the meaning of ERISA's savings clause, Section 514(b)(2)(A). Finally, in *Aetna Health Inc. v. Davila*, 542 U.S. 200 (2004), the Supreme Court relied on its earlier analysis in *Pilot Life* in finding that an alternative tort claim and remedy established under state law against a health maintenance organization was preempted by ERISA. *Moran*, *Miller* and *Davila* are reproduced later in Section D of Chapter Seven.

INGERSOLL-RAND CO. V. MCCLENDON

United States Supreme Court, 1990.
498 U.S. 133, 111 S.Ct. 478, 112 L.Ed.2d 474.

JUSTICE O'CONNOR delivered the opinion of the Court.

This case presents the question whether the Employee Retirement Income Security Act of 1974 (ERISA) preempts a state common law claim that an employee was unlawfully discharged to prevent his attainment of benefits under a plan covered by ERISA.

I

Petitioner Ingersoll-Rand Company employed respondent Perry McClendon as a salesman and distributor of construction equipment. In 1981, after McClendon had worked for the company for nine years and eight months, the company fired him citing a company-wide reduction in force. McClendon sued the company in Texas state court, alleging that his pension would have vested in another four months and that a principal reason for his termination was the company's desire to avoid making contributions to his pension fund. McClendon did not realize that * * * he had already been credited with sufficient service to vest his pension under the plan's 10-year requirement. McClendon sought compensatory and punitive damages under various tort and contract theories; he did not assert any cause of action under ERISA. After a period of discovery, the company moved for, and obtained, summary judgment on all claims. The

State Court of Appeals affirmed, holding that McClendon's employment was terminable at will.

In a 5-to-4 decision, the Texas Supreme Court reversed and remanded for trial. The majority reasoned that notwithstanding the traditional employment-at-will doctrine, public policy imposes certain limitations upon an employer's power to discharge at-will employees. * * *

Because this issue has divided state and federal courts, we granted certiorari, and now reverse.

II

"ERISA is a comprehensive statute designed to promote the interests of employees and their beneficiaries in employee benefit plans." Shaw v. Delta Air Lines, Inc., 463 U.S. 85, 90 (1983). * * * As part of this closely integrated regulatory system Congress included various safeguards to preclude abuse and "to completely secure the rights and expectations brought into being by this landmark reform legislation." S. Rep. No. 93–127, p. 36 (1973). Prominent among these safeguards are three provisions of particular relevance to this case: § 514(a), ERISA's broad preemption provision; § 510, which proscribes interference with rights protected by ERISA; and § 502(a), a "carefully integrated" civil enforcement scheme that "is one of the essential tools for accomplishing the stated purposes of ERISA." Pilot Life Ins. Co. v. Dedeaux, 481 U.S. 41, 52, 54 (1987).

We must decide whether these provisions, singly or in combination, preempt the cause of action at issue in this case. * * *

A

Where, as here, Congress has expressly included a broadly worded preemption provision in a comprehensive statute such as ERISA, our task of discerning congressional intent is considerably simplified. In § 514(a) of ERISA, Congress provided:

> Except as provided in subsection (b) of this section, the provisions of this subchapter and subchapter III of this chapter shall supersede any and all State laws insofar as they may now or hereafter relate to any employee benefit plan described in section 1003(a) of this title and not exempt under section 1003(b) of this title.

"The preemption clause is conspicuous for its breadth." FMC Corp. v. Holliday, 498 U.S. 52, 58 (1990). Its "deliberately expansive" language was "designed to establish pension plan regulation as exclusively a federal concern." Pilot Life, 481 U.S. at 46. The key to § 514(a) is found in the words "relate to." Congress used those words in their broad sense, rejecting more limited preemption language that would have made the clause "applicable only to state laws relating to the specific subjects covered by ERISA." Shaw, 463 U.S. at 98. Moreover, to underscore its intent that § 514(a) be expansively applied, Congress used equally broad language in defining the "State law" that would be preempted. Such laws include "all laws, decisions, rules, regulations, or other State action having the effect of law." § 514(c)(1).

"A law 'relates to' an employee benefit plan, in the normal sense of the phrase, if it has a connection with or reference to such a plan." Shaw, 463 U.S. at 96–97. Under this "broad common-sense meaning," a state law may "relate to" a benefit plan, and thereby be preempted, even if the law is not specifically designed to affect such plans, or the effect is only indirect. Pilot Life, 481 U.S. at 47. Preemption is also not precluded simply because a state law is consistent with ERISA's substantive requirements. Metropolitan Life Ins. Co. v. Massachusetts, 471 U.S. 724, 739 (1985).

* * *

We have no difficulty in concluding that the cause of action which the Texas Supreme Court recognized here—a claim that the employer wrongfully terminated plaintiff primarily because of the employer's desire to avoid contributing to, or paying benefits under, the employee's pension fund—"relate[s] to" an ERISA-covered plan within the meaning of § 514(a), and is therefore preempted.

"[W]e have virtually taken it for granted that state laws which are 'specifically designed to affect employee benefit plans' are preempted under § 514(a)." Mackey v. Lanier Collection Agency & Service, 486 U.S. 825, 829 (1988). In Mackey, the statute's express reference to ERISA plans established that it was so designed; consequently, it was preempted. The facts here are slightly different but the principle is the same: The Texas cause of action makes specific reference to, and indeed is premised on, the existence of a pension plan. In the words of the Texas court, the cause of action "allows recovery when the plaintiff proves that the principal reason for his termination was the employer's desire to avoid contributing to or paying benefits under the employee's pension fund." Thus, in order to prevail, a plaintiff must plead, and the court must find, that an ERISA plan exists and the employer had a pension-defeating motive in terminating the employment. Because the court's inquiry must be directed to the plan, this judicially created cause of action "relate[s] to" an ERISA plan.

* * *

The conclusion that the cause of action in this case is preempted by § 514(a) is supported by our understanding of the purposes of that provision. Section 514(a) was intended to ensure that plans and plan sponsors would be subject to a uniform body of benefits law; the goal was to minimize the administrative and financial burden of complying with conflicting directives among States or between States and the Federal

Government. Otherwise, the inefficiencies created could work to the detriment of plan beneficiaries. Allowing state based actions like the one at issue here would subject plans and plan sponsors to burdens not unlike those that Congress sought to foreclose through § 514(a). Particularly disruptive is the potential for conflict in substantive law. It is foreseeable that state courts, exercising their common law powers, might develop different substantive standards applicable to the same employer conduct, requiring the tailoring of plans and employer conduct to the peculiarities of the law of each jurisdiction. Such an outcome is fundamentally at odds with the goal of uniformity that Congress sought to implement.

B

Even if there were no express preemption in this case, the Texas cause of action would be preempted because it conflicts directly with an ERISA cause of action. McClendon's claim falls squarely within the ambit of ERISA § 510, which provides:

> It shall be unlawful for any person to discharge, fine, suspend, expel, discipline, or discriminate against a participant or beneficiary for exercising any right to which he is entitled under the provisions of an employee benefit plan . . . *or for the purpose of interfering with the attainment of any right to which such participant may become entitled* under the plan. . . . ERISA § 510 (emphasis added).

By its terms § 510 protects plan participants from termination motivated by an employer's desire to prevent a pension from vesting. Congress viewed this section as a crucial part of ERISA because, without it, employers would be able to circumvent the provision of promised benefits. S. Rep. No. 93–127, pp. 35–36 (1973); H. R. Rep. No. 93–533, p. 17 (1973). We have no doubt that this claim is prototypical of the kind Congress intended to cover under § 510.

[The Supreme Court determined, based on its prior decisions in *Pilot Life Insurance Co. v. Dedeaux*, 481 U.S. 41 (1987), and *Metropolitan Life Insurance Co. v. Taylor*, 481 U.S. 58 (1987), that Congress intended Section 502(a)(3) to provide the exclusive remedy for violations of Section 510.]

* * *

The judgment of the Texas Supreme Court is reversed.

NOTES AND QUESTIONS

1.   Why did the Supreme Court in *Ingersoll-Rand* determine that the plaintiff's claim of wrongful discharge under Texas state law had a "reference to" an employee benefit plan?

2. *State Garnishment Laws and ERISA Preemption.* The Supreme Court's opinion in *Ingersoll-Rand* refers to the Court's earlier decision in *Mackey v. Lanier Collection Agency & Service,* 486 U.S. 825 (1988). *Mackey* addressed the intersection of state garnishment laws and ERISA's anti-alienation rule. The anti-alienation rule of ERISA Section 206(d)(1) generally prohibits the assignment or alienation of a participant's benefits from an employee pension plan. Code Section 401(a)(13) incorporates the anti-alienation rule as a requirement for qualified retirement plans. Chapter Three of the casebook discusses the anti-alienation rule and its statutory exceptions in the context of qualified retirement plans.

The practical effect of ERISA Section 206(d)(1) is to prevent creditors of a plan participant from using a state law garnishment proceeding as a method to collect a judgment from the participant's pension plan. Significantly, ERISA Section 206(d)(1) does not apply to the assignment or alienation of benefits from a participant's *welfare benefit* plan. In *Mackey*, the Supreme Court addressed whether state garnishment proceedings can be used to collect a judgment obtained by a creditor against a participant in a welfare benefit plan.

Mackey involved two distinct provisions of the Georgia state garnishment statute. The first provision, Georgia Code Section 18–4–22.1, stated:

> Funds or benefits of a pension, retirement, or employee benefit plan or program subject to the provisions of the federal Employee Retirement Income Security Act of 1974, as amended, shall not be subject to the process of garnishment * * * unless such garnishment is based upon a judgment for alimony or for child support. * * *

The Supreme Court in *Mackey* ruled that Section 18–4–22.1 was preempted as a state law that "relates to" an employee benefit plan under ERISA Section 514(a). The Supreme Court reasoned that Section 18–4–22.1 had an explicit "reference to" employee benefit plans under the *Shaw* test for preemption. The fact that the Georgia legislature had enacted Section 18–4–22.1 to *promote* ERISA's underlying purpose was not sufficient to save the statute from preemption. 486 U.S. at 829.

The plan participants in *Mackey* further argued that, assuming Section 18–4–22.1 was preempted (and therefore did not bar the collection agency's garnishment action against the plan and its participants under Georgia state law), Georgia's *general* garnishment statute, Georgia Code Section 18–4–10, also was preempted by ERISA. The Supreme Court rejected the argument that ERISA Section 514(a) preempted Georgia's general garnishment procedures. The *Mackey* Court reasoned that Section 514(a) did not preempt the procedures provided by a state's general garnishment law for collecting a judgment obtained against an employee benefit plan as an entity, such as an action for unpaid rent or unpaid attorney fees owed by the plan to the debtor. Consequently, if ERISA Section 514(a) permitted a debtor to use the garnishment procedure provided under state law to collect a judgment against the plan itself, the Supreme Court in *Mackey* saw no principled basis for prohibiting the creditor of a participant in a welfare benefit plan from using the same garnishment procedure to collect a judgment obtained against a participant in a welfare benefit plan.

The Supreme Court justified the seemingly incongruous result in *Mackey*—holding that ERISA Section 514(a) preempted one section of the Georgia garnishment statute but not the other—in a footnote to the opinion.

> It is not incongruous to find that [Georgia Code §] 18–4–20, which provides for garnishment of ERISA welfare benefit plans, escapes preemption under ERISA, while striking down § 18–4–22.1—an exception to the general state law provision—as preempted. While we believe that state law garnishment procedures are not preempted by § 514(a), we also conclude that *any* state law which singles out ERISA plans, by express reference, for special treatment is preempted. It is this "singling out" that preempts the Georgia anti-garnishment exception.

486 U.S. at 838 n.12.

3.   *Recharacterizing* Ingersoll-Rand. In *Rush Prudential HMO, Inc. v. Moran*, 536 U.S. 355 (2002), the Supreme Court later recharacterized the basis for its decision in *Ingersoll-Rand*.

> Since *Pilot Life*, we have found only one other state law to "conflict" with § 502(a) in providing a prohibited alternative remedy. In *Ingersoll-Rand Co. v. McClendon*, we had no trouble finding that Texas's tort of wrongful discharge, turning on an employer's motivation to avoid paying pension benefits, conflicted with ERISA enforcement. While state law duplicated the elements of a claim available under ERISA, it converted the remedy from an equitable one under § 502(a)(3) (available exclusively in federal district courts) into a legal one for money damages (available in a state tribunal). Thus, *Ingersoll-Rand* fit within the category of state laws *Pilot Life* had held to be incompatible with ERISA's enforcement scheme; the law provided a form of ultimate relief in a judicial forum that added to the judicial remedies provided by ERISA. Any such provision patently violates ERISA's policy of inducing employers to offer benefits by assuring a predictable set of liabilities, under uniform standards of primary conduct and a uniform regime of ultimate remedial orders and awards when a violation has occurred.

536 U.S. at 379.

C. MODERN PREEMPTION JURISPRUDENCE

In *New York State Conference of Blue Cross and Blue Shield Plans v. Travelers Insurance Co.*, the State of New York had enacted a law requiring hospitals to bill their patients different amounts for the same services based on the patient's health care insurance coverage. Additional amounts that were assessed over the base rate payable under insurance coverage provided by Blue Cross and Blue Shield of New York for a particular service were called a "surcharge." The New York law required hospitals to surcharge patients covered by a commercial insurer 24% more than patients who were covered by health care insurance through Blue Cross and Blue Shield of New York. Patients whose health insurance coverage was through an employer's self-insured plan were billed at a 13% surcharge rate. The goal of the New York law was to increase the cost of health care coverage for commercial insurers and self-insured plans in order to provide an economic incentive for employers to obtain health insurance plan coverage for their employees through Blue Cross and Blue Shield of New York, which was struggling financially due to its policy of enrolling individuals without imposing preexisting condition coverage exclusion.

The plaintiffs in *Travelers* challenged the New York law as preempted by ERISA. Given the prior Supreme Court precedents of *Shaw*, *Pilot Life*, and *Ingersoll-Rand*, it seemed likely that the Supreme Court would rule the New York law was preempted by ERISA Section 514(a). Instead, the *Travelers* Court embarked on a new approach to ERISA's general preemption clause—the rebuttable presumption *against* preemption of traditional areas of state law regulation.

NEW YORK STATE CONFERENCE OF BLUE CROSS & BLUE SHIELD PLANS v. TRAVELERS INSURANCE CO.

United States Supreme Court, 1995.
514 U.S. 645, 115 S.Ct. 1671, 131 L.Ed.2d 695.

JUSTICE SOUTER delivered the opinion of the Court.

A New York statute requires hospitals to collect surcharges from patients covered by a commercial insurer but not from patients insured by a Blue Cross/Blue Shield plan, and it subjects certain health maintenance organizations (HMO's) to surcharges that vary with the number of Medicaid recipients each enrolls. These cases call for us to decide whether the Employee Retirement Income Security Act of 1974 (ERISA) preempts the state provisions for surcharges on bills of patients whose commercial insurance coverage is purchased by employee health care plans governed by ERISA, and for surcharges on HMO's insofar as their membership fees are paid by an ERISA plan. We hold that the provisions for surcharges do not "relate to" employee benefit plans within the meaning of ERISA's preemption provision, ERISA § 514(a), and accordingly suffer no preemption.

I

A

New York's Prospective Hospital Reimbursement Methodology (NYPHRM) regulates hospital rates for all in-patient care, except for services provided to Medicare beneficiaries. The scheme calls for patients to be charged not for the cost of their individual treatment, but for the average cost of treating the patient's medical problem, as classified under one or another of 794 Diagnostic Related Groups (DRG's). The charges allowable in accordance with DRG classifications are adjusted for a specific hospital to reflect its particular operating costs, capital investments, bad debts, costs of charity care, and the like.

Patients with Blue Cross/Blue Shield coverage, Medicaid patients, and HMO participants are billed at a hospital's DRG rate. Others, however, are not. Patients served by commercial insurers providing in-patient hospital coverage on an expense-incurred basis, by self-insured funds directly reimbursing hospitals, and by certain workers' compensation, volunteer firefighters' benefit, ambulance workers' benefit, and no-fault motor vehicle insurance funds, must be billed at the DRG rate plus a 13% surcharge to be retained by the hospital. For the year ending March 31, 1993, moreover, hospitals were required to bill commercially insured patients for a further 11% surcharge to be turned over to the State, with the result that these patients were charged 24% more than the DRG rate.

New York law also imposes a surcharge on HMO's, which varies depending on the number of eligible Medicaid recipients an HMO has enrolled, but which may run as high as 9% of the aggregate monthly charges paid by an HMO for its members' in-patient hospital care. This assessment is not an increase in the rates to be paid by an HMO to hospitals, but a direct payment by the HMO to the State's general fund.

* * *

C

On the claimed authority of ERISA's general preemption provision, several commercial insurers, acting as fiduciaries of ERISA plans they administer, joined with their trade associations to bring actions against state officials in United States District Court seeking to invalidate the 13%, 11%, and 9% surcharge statutes [on the grounds that the statutes were preempted by Section 514(a).] * * *

The Court of Appeals determined that the surcharges were meant to increase the costs of certain insurance and health care by HMO's, and held that this "purpose[ful] interfer[ence] with the choices that ERISA plans make for health care coverage ... is sufficient to constitute [a] 'connection with' ERISA plans" triggering preemption. The court's conclusion, in sum, was that "the three surcharges 'relate to' ERISA because they impose a significant economic burden on commercial insurers and HMOs" and therefore "have an impermissible impact on ERISA plan structure and administration." In the light of its conclusion that the surcharge statutes were not otherwise saved by any applicable exception, the court held them preempted. It recognized the apparent conflict between its conclusion and the decision of the Third Circuit in *United Wire, Metal and Machine Health and Welfare Fund v. Morristown Memorial Hospital*, 995 F.2d 1179, 1191 (3d Cir. 1993), which held that New Jersey's similar rate setting statute "does not relate to the plans in a way that triggers ERISA's preemption clause." We granted certiorari to resolve this conflict, and now reverse and remand.

II

Our past cases have recognized that the Supremacy Clause, U.S. Const., Art. VI, may entail preemption of state law either by express provision, by implication, or by a conflict between federal and state law. And yet, despite the variety of these opportunities for federal preeminence, we have never assumed lightly that Congress has derogated state regulation, but instead have addressed claims of preemption with the starting presumption that Congress does not intend to supplant state law. Indeed, in cases like this one, where federal law is said to bar state action in fields of traditional state regulation, we have worked on the "assumption that the historic police powers of the States were not to be superseded by the Federal Act unless that was the clear and manifest purpose of Congress." Rice v. Santa Fe Elevator Corp., 331 U.S. 218, 230 (1947).

Since preemption claims turn on Congress's intent, we begin as we do in any exercise of statutory construction with the text of the provision in question, and move on, as need be, to the structure and purpose of the Act in which it occurs. The governing text of ERISA is clearly expansive. Section 514(a) marks for preemption "all state laws insofar as they. . .relate to any employee benefit plan" covered by ERISA, and one might be excused for wondering, at first blush, whether the words of limitation ("insofar as they. . .relate") do much limiting. If "relate to" were taken to extend to the furthest stretch of its indeterminacy, then for all practical purposes preemption would never run its course, for "[r]eally, universally, relations stop nowhere," H. James, Roderick Hudson xli (New York ed., World's Classics 1980). But that, of course, would be to read Congress's words of limitation as mere sham, and to read the presumption against preemption out of the law whenever Congress speaks to the matter with generality. That said, we have to recognize that our prior attempt to construe the phrase "relate to" does not give us much help drawing the line here.

In *Shaw v. Delta Air Lines, Inc.*, we explained that "[a] law 'relates to' an employee benefit plan, in the normal sense of the phrase, if it has a connection with or reference to such a plan." 463 U.S. 85, 96–97 (1983). The latter alternative, at least, can be ruled out. The surcharges are imposed upon patients and HMO's, regardless of whether the commercial coverage or membership, respectively, is ultimately secured by an ERISA plan, private purchase, or otherwise, with the consequence that the surcharge statutes cannot be said to make "reference to" ERISA plans in any manner. But this still leaves us to question whether the surcharge laws have a "connection with" the ERISA plans, and here an uncritical literalism is no more help than in trying to construe "relate to." For the same reasons that infinite relations cannot be the measure of preemption, neither can infinite connections. We simply must go beyond the unhelpful text and the frustrating difficulty of defining its key term, and look instead to the objectives of the ERISA statute as a guide to the scope of the state law that Congress understood would survive.

A

As we have said before, § 514 indicates Congress's intent to establish the regulation of employee welfare benefit plans "as exclusively a federal concern." Alessi v. Raybestos-Manhattan, Inc., 451 U.S. 504, 523 (1981). We have found that in passing § 514(a), Congress intended "to ensure that plans and plan sponsors would be subject to a uniform body of benefits law; the goal was to minimize the administrative and financial burden of complying with conflicting directives among States or between States and the Federal Government . . ., [and to prevent] the potential for conflict in substantive law . . . requiring the tailoring of plans and employer conduct to the peculiarities of the law of each jurisdiction." Ingersoll-Rand Co. v. McClendon, 498 U.S. 133, 142 (1990).

This objective was described in the House of Representatives by a sponsor of the Act, Representative Dent, as being to "eliminat[e] the threat of conflicting and inconsistent State and local regulation." 120 Cong. Rec. 29197 (1974). Senator Williams made the same point, that "with the narrow exceptions specified in the bill, the substantive and enforcement provisions . . . are intended to preempt the field for Federal regulations, thus eliminating the threat of conflicting or inconsistent State and local regulation of employee benefit plans." Id. at 29933. The basic thrust of the preemption clause, then, was to avoid a multiplicity of regulation in order to permit the nationally uniform administration of employee benefit plans.

Accordingly in *Shaw*, for example, we had no trouble finding that New York's "Human Rights Law, which prohibit[ed] employers from structuring their employee benefit plans in a manner that discriminate[d] on the basis of pregnancy, and [New York's] Disability Benefits Law, which require[d] employers to pay employees specific benefits, clearly 'relate[d] to' benefit plans." 463 U.S. at 97. These mandates affecting coverage could have been honored only by varying the subjects of a plan's benefits whenever New York law might have applied, or by requiring every plan to provide all beneficiaries with a benefit demanded by New York law if New York law could have been said to require it for any one beneficiary. Similarly, Pennsylvania's law that prohibited "plans from. . .requiring reimbursement [from the beneficiary] in the event of recovery from a third party" related to employee benefit plans within the meaning of § 514(a). FMC Corp. v. Holliday, 498 U.S. 52, 60 (1990). The law "prohibit[ed] plans from being structured in a manner requiring reimbursement in the event of recovery from a third party" and "require[d] plan providers to calculate benefit levels in Pennsylvania based on expected liability conditions that differ from those in States that have not enacted similar antisubrogation legislation," thereby "frustrat[ing] plan administrators' continuing obligation to calculate uniform benefit levels nationwide." Id. Pennsylvania employees who recovered in negligence actions against tort-feasors would, by virtue of the state law, in effect have been entitled to benefits in excess of what plan administrators intended to provide, and in excess of what the plan provided to employees in other States. Along the same lines, New Jersey could not prohibit plans from setting workers' compensation payments off against employees' retirement benefits or pensions, because doing so would prevent plans from using a method of calculating benefits permitted by federal law. Alessi, 451 U.S. at 524. In each of these cases, ERISA preempted state laws that mandated employee benefit structures or their administration. Elsewhere, we have held that state laws providing alternative enforcement mechanisms also relate to ERISA plans, triggering preemption. See Ingersoll-Rand, 498 U.S. 133.

B

Both the purpose and the effects of the New York surcharge statute distinguish it from the examples just given. The charge differentials have been justified on the ground that the Blues pay the hospitals promptly and efficiently and, more importantly, provide coverage for many subscribers whom the commercial insurers would reject as unacceptable risks. The Blues' practice, called open enrollment, has consistently been cited as the principal reason for charge differentials, whether the differentials resulted from voluntary negotiation between hospitals and payers as was the case prior to the NYPHRM system, or were created by the surcharges as is the case now. Since the surcharges are presumably passed on at least in part to those who purchase commercial insurance or HMO membership, their effects follow from their purpose. Although there is no evidence that the surcharges will drive every health insurance consumer to the Blues, they do make the Blues more attractive (or less unattractive) as insurance alternatives and thus have an indirect economic effect on choices made by insurance buyers, including ERISA plans.

An indirect economic influence, however, does not bind plan administrators to any particular choice and thus function as a regulation of an ERISA plan itself; commercial insurers and HMO's may still offer more attractive packages than the Blues. Nor does the indirect influence of the surcharges preclude uniform administrative practice or the provision of a uniform interstate benefit package if a plan wishes to provide one. It simply bears on the costs of benefits and the relative costs of competing insurance to provide them. It is an influence that can affect a plan's shopping decisions, but it does not affect the fact that any plan will shop for the best deal it can get, surcharges or no surcharges.

There is, indeed, nothing remarkable about surcharges on hospital bills, or their effects on overall cost to the plans and the relative attractiveness of certain insurers. Rate variations among hospital providers are accepted examples of cost variation, since hospitals have traditionally "attempted to compensate for their financial shortfalls by adjusting their price . . . schedules for patients with commercial health insurance." Thorpe, Does All-Payer Rate Setting Work? The Case of the New York Prospective Hospital Reimbursement Methodology, 12 J. Health Politics, Policy & Law, 391, 394 (1987). Charge differentials for commercial insurers, even prior to state regulation, "varied dramatically across regions, ranging from 13 to 36 percent," presumably reflecting the geographically disparate burdens of providing for the uninsured. Id. at 400.

If the common character of rate differentials even in the absence of state action renders it unlikely that ERISA preemption was meant to bar such indirect economic influences under state law, the existence of other common state action with indirect economic effects on a plan's costs leaves the intent to preempt even less likely. Quality standards, for example, set by the State in one subject area of hospital services but not another would affect the relative cost of providing those services over others and, so, of providing different packages of health insurance benefits. Even basic regulation of employment conditions will invariably affect the cost and price of services.

Quality control and workplace regulation, to be sure, are presumably less likely to affect premium differentials among competing insurers, but that does not change the fact that such state regulation will indirectly affect what an ERISA or other plan can afford or get for its money. Thus, in the absence of a more exact guide to intended preemption than § 514, it is fair to conclude that mandates for rate differentials would not be preempted unless other regulation with indirect effects on plan costs would be superseded as well. The bigger the package of regulation with indirect effects that would fall on the respondents' reading of § 514, the less likely it is that federal regulation of benefit plans was intended to eliminate state regulation of health care costs.

Indeed, to read the preemption provision as displacing all state laws affecting costs and charges on the theory that they indirectly relate to ERISA plans that purchase insurance policies or HMO memberships that would cover such services would effectively read the limiting language in § 514(a) out of the statute, a conclusion that would violate basic principles of statutory interpretation and could not be squared with our prior pronouncement that "[p]reemption does not occur . . . if the state law has only a tenuous, remote, or peripheral connection with covered plans, as is the case with many laws of general applicability." District of Columbia v. Greater Washington Bd. of Trade, 506 U.S. at 130 n.1. While Congress's extension of preemption to all "state laws relating to benefit plans" was meant to sweep more broadly than "state laws dealing with the subject matters covered by ERISA [,] reporting, disclosure, fiduciary responsibility, and the like," Shaw, 463 U.S. at 98, and n.19, nothing in the language of the Act or the context of its passage indicates that Congress chose to displace general health care regulation, which historically has been a matter of local concern.

In sum, cost uniformity was almost certainly not an object of preemption, just as laws with only an indirect economic effect on the relative costs of various health insurance packages in a given State are a far cry from those "conflicting directives" from which Congress meant to insulate ERISA plans. See Ingersoll-Rand, 498 U.S. at 142. Such state laws leave plan administrators right where they would be in any case, with the responsibility to choose the best overall coverage for the money. We therefore conclude that such state laws do not bear the requisite "connection with" ERISA plans to trigger preemption.

C

* * *

The commercial challengers counter by invoking the earlier case of *Metropolitan Life Insurance Co. v. Massachusetts*, 471 U.S. 724 (1985), which considered whether a State could mandate coverage of specified minimum mental-health-care benefits by policies insuring against hospital and surgical expenses. Because the regulated policies included those bought by employee welfare benefit plans, we recognized that the law "directly affected" such plans. Id. at 732. Although we went on to hold that the law was ultimately saved from preemption by the insurance saving clause, § 514(b)(2)(A), respondents proffer the first steps in our decision as support for their argument that all laws affecting ERISA plans through their impact on insurance policies "relate to" such plans and are preempted unless expressly saved by the statute. The challengers take *Metropolitan Life* too far, however.

The Massachusetts statute applied not only to "[a]ny blanket or general policy of insurance . . . or any policy of accident and sickness insurance" but also to "any employees' health and welfare fund which provide[d] hospital expense and surgical expense benefits." 471 U.S. at 730 n.11. In fact, the State did not even try to defend its law as unrelated to employee benefit plans for the purpose of § 514(a). As a result, there was no reason to distinguish with any precision between the effects on insurers that are sufficiently connected with employee benefit plans to "relate to" the plans and those effects that are not. It was enough to address the distinction bluntly, saying on the one hand that laws like the one in *Metropolitan Life* relate to plans since they "bea[r] indirectly but substantially on all insured benefit plans,. . .requir[ing] them to purchase the mental-health benefits specified in the statute when they purchase a certain kind of common insurance policy," id. at 739, but saying on the other that "laws that regulate only the insurer, or the way in which it may sell insurance, do not 'relate to' benefit plans," id. at 741. Even this basic distinction recognizes that not all regulations that would influence the cost of insurance would relate to employee benefit plans within the meaning of § 514(a). If, for example, a State were to regulate sales of insurance by commercial insurers more stringently than sales by insurers not for profit, the relative cost of commercial insurance would rise; we would nonetheless say, following *Metropolitan Life*, that such laws "do not 'relate to' benefit plans in the first instance." Id. And on the same authority we would say the same about the basic tax exemption enjoyed by nonprofit insurers like the Blues since the days long before ERISA; and yet on respondents' theory the exemption would necessarily be preempted as affecting insurance prices and plan costs.

In any event, *Metropolitan Life* cannot carry the weight the commercial insurers would place on it. The New York surcharges do not impose the kind of substantive coverage requirement binding plan administrators that was at issue in *Metropolitan Life*. Although even in the absence of mandated coverage there might be a point at which an exorbitant tax leaving consumers with a Hobson's choice would be treated as imposing a substantive mandate, no showing has been made here that the surcharges are so prohibitive as to force all health insurance consumers to contract with the Blues. As they currently stand, the surcharges do not require plans to deal with only one insurer, or to insure against an entire category of illnesses they might otherwise choose to leave without coverage.

D

It remains only to speak further on a point already raised, that any conclusion other than the one we draw would bar any state regulation of hospital costs. The basic DRG system (even without any surcharge), like any other interference with the hospital services market, would fall on a theory that all laws with indirect economic effects on ERISA plans are preempted under § 514(a). This would be an unsettling result and all the more startling because several States, including New York, regulated hospital charges to one degree or another at the time ERISA was passed. And yet there is not so much as a hint in ERISA's legislative history or anywhere else that Congress intended to squelch these state efforts.

* * *

III

That said, we do not hold today that ERISA preempts only direct regulation of ERISA plans, nor could we do that with fidelity to the views expressed in our prior opinions on the matter. See, e.g., Ingersoll-Rand, 498 U.S. at 139; Pilot Life Ins. Co. v. Dedeaux, 481 U.S. 41, 47–48, (1987); Shaw, 463 U.S. at 98. We acknowledge that a state law might produce such acute, albeit indirect, economic effects, by intent or otherwise, as to force an ERISA plan to adopt a certain scheme of substantive coverage or effectively restrict its choice of insurers, and that such a state law might indeed be preempted under § 514. But as we have shown, New York's surcharges do not fall into either category; they affect only indirectly the relative prices of insurance policies, a result no different from myriad state laws in areas traditionally subject to local regulation, which Congress could not possibly have intended to eliminate.

The judgment of the Court of Appeals is therefore reversed, and the cases are remanded for further proceedings consistent with this opinion.

NOTES AND QUESTIONS

1.   How does the Supreme Court's approach in *Travelers* to ERISA's general preemption clause differ from the Court's earlier preemption opinions? Does the preemption analysis articulated by the Supreme Court in *Travelers* provide meaningful guidelines for the lower federal courts to follow when deciding ERISA preemption cases? To state lawmakers when drafting state laws of general application that may affect employee benefit plans?

2.   *State Taxation of Medical Facilities Held as Plan Assets.* In *Travelers*, the Supreme Court ruled that the state law at issue was not preempted because the law had only an indirect economic effect on an employer's health care plan. Two years after *Travelers*, the Supreme Court ruled in *De Buono v. NYSA-ILA Medical and Clinical Services Fund*, 520 U.S. 806 (1997), that a state tax imposed on medical centers that were held as assets by a health care plan was not preempted by ERISA. The plaintiffs in

De Buono were the trustees of the NYSA-ILA Medical and Clinical Services Fund (Fund). The Fund was a self-insured multiemployer welfare benefit plan for longshore workers, retirees, and their dependents. The Fund owned three medical centers, two of which were located in New York. The Fund's medical centers provided medical, dental, and other health care benefits to the Fund's participants.

In 1990, the State of New York was faced with either curtailing its Medicaid program or generating additional revenues to fund the program's deficit. The New York legislature chose to raise additional revenues for the Medicaid program and enacted a state tax on the gross receipts for patient services at various types of health care facilities, including the two New York medical centers owned and operated by the Fund.

After initially paying a tax of $7,066 to the State of New York under the new law, the trustees of the Fund sought an injunction against future tax assessments and a refund of the $7,066 tax payment that had been made by the Fund. The basis for the trustees' action was that the New York law was preempted by ERISA because, as applied to the medical centers owned and operated by the Fund, the law "related to" an employee benefit plan by imposing a tax on plan assets. According to the trustees, the New York tax reduced the amount of the Fund's assets that otherwise would be available to provide benefits to the Fund's participants, and thereby could cause the Fund to either limit benefits to participants or to charge Fund members higher fees to participate in the plan. The Supreme Court held that the New York law was not preempted by ERISA.

> A consideration of the actual operation of the state statute leads us to the conclusion that the [New York law] is one of "myriad state laws" of general applicability that impose some burdens on the administration of ERISA plans but nevertheless do not "relate to" them within the meaning of the governing statute. The [New York law] is a tax on hospitals. Most hospitals are not owned or operated by ERISA funds. This particular ERISA fund has arranged to provide medical benefits for its plan beneficiaries by running hospitals directly, rather than by purchasing the same services at independently run hospitals. If the Fund had made the other choice, and had purchased health care services from a hospital, that facility would have passed the expense of the [tax] onto the Fund and its plan beneficiaries through the rates it set for the services provided. The Fund would then have had to decide whether to cover a more limited range of services for its beneficiaries, or perhaps to charge plan members higher rates. Although the tax in such a circumstance would be "indirect," its impact on the Fund's decisions would be in all relevant respects identical to the "direct" impact felt here. Thus, the supposed difference between direct and indirect impact—upon which the Court of Appeals relied in distinguishing this case from *Travelers*—cannot withstand scrutiny. Any state tax, or other law, that increases the cost of providing benefits to covered

employees will have some effect on the administration of ERISA plans, but that simply cannot mean that every state law with such an effect is preempted by the federal statute.

520 U.S. at 815–16 (citations omitted).

3.   Shaw's *"Reference to" Test After* Dillingham Construction. In another 1997 decision, *California Division of Labor Standards Enforcement v. Dillingham Construction, Inc.,* 519 U.S. 316 (1997), the Supreme Court narrowed the potential reach of the "reference to" prong of the *Shaw* test for preemption. In *Dillingham Construction,* the Supreme Court ruled unanimously that ERISA did not preempt a California wage statute that required contractors on state public works projects to pay an apprentice the higher prevailing journeyman wage unless the apprentice was enrolled in an apprenticeship training program approved by the State of California. If the apprentice was enrolled in an apprenticeship program approved by the State of California, the state wage statute permitted the contractor to pay the apprentice the lesser apprentice wage.

ERISA Section 3(1) expressly includes "apprenticeship or other training programs" within the definition of an employer welfare benefit plan subject to regulation under ERISA. The apprenticeship program at issue in *Dillingham Construction* was one of 175 such construction apprenticeship programs in California that were jointly sponsored by labor and management under the Taft-Hartley Act. The parties agreed that all of these jointly sponsored apprenticeship programs were subject to regulation under ERISA as welfare benefit plans. California also had thirteen other state-approved apprenticeship programs that were not Taft-Hartley Act plans. Some of these other apprenticeship programs may not have been ERISA plans under Department of Labor regulations because their funding was out of the general assets of the employer, rather than from a separate fund. See DOL Reg. § 2510.3–1(b), (k).

The Supreme Court concluded that under these circumstances the California wage statute did not have a "reference to" an ERISA plan because no party had established conclusively that *all* of the California apprenticeship programs approved by the State of California were subject to regulation under Title I of ERISA. 519 U.S. at 329 n.5. According to the Supreme Court, the mere possibility that the California wage statute could apply to an apprenticeship program that was not subject to regulation under ERISA allowed the California state law to escape preemption under the "reference to" prong of the *Shaw* test.

[The California wage statute] "functions irrespective of. . .the existence of an ERISA plan." Ingersoll-Rand Co., 498 U.S. at 139. An apprenticeship program meeting the substantive standards * * * can be approved [by the State of California] whether or not its funding apparatus is of a kind as to bring it under ERISA. [The California wage statute] is indifferent to the funding, and attendant ERISA coverage, of apprenticeship programs. Accordingly,

California's prevailing wage statute does not make reference to ERISA plans.

519 U.S. at 328 (citations omitted).

After *Dillingham Construction*, how would you advise a state lawmaker to define the types of employer plans, funds, or programs that are potentially subject to regulation under a proposed state law?

4. Shaw's *"Connection with" Test and "Indirect Economic Influence" on ERISA Plans.* Immediately following *Travelers*, it was unclear whether the Supreme Court's interpretation—that mere indirect economic influence on an ERISA plan did not constitute a connection with the plan under the *Shaw* test—would be subsequently limited by the Court to state laws concerning health care finance. The Supreme Court's decision in *Dillingham Construction* further signaled that the Court would apply the *Travelers* interpretation of the "connection with" test beyond the realm of health care finance.

> We think that, in every relevant respect, California's prevailing wage statute is indistinguishable from New York's surcharge program. At the outset, we note that apprenticeship standards and the wages paid on state public works have long been regulated by the States. * * *

> That the States traditionally regulated these areas would not alone immunize their efforts; ERISA certainly contemplated the preemption of substantial areas of traditional state regulation. The wages to be paid on public works projects and the substantive standards to be applied to apprenticeship training programs are, however, quite remote from the areas with which ERISA is expressly concerned—reporting, disclosure, fiduciary responsibility and the like. * * *

> Like New York's surcharge requirement, the apprenticeship portion of the prevailing wage statute does not bind ERISA plans to anything. No apprenticeship program is required by California law to meet California's standards. If a contractor chooses to hire apprentices for a public works project, it need not hire them from an approved program (although if it does not, it must pay these apprentices journeyman wages). So, apprenticeship programs that have not gained [State] approval may still supply public works contractors with apprentices. * * * The effect of [the California wage statute] on ERISA apprenticeship programs, therefore, is merely to provide some measure of economic incentive to comport with the State's requirements, at least to the extent that those programs seek to provide apprentices who can work on public works projects at a lower wage.

* * *

The effect of the prevailing wage statute on ERISA-covered apprenticeship programs in California is substantially similar to the effect of New York law on ERISA plans choosing whether to provide health insurance benefits in New York through the Blues, or through a commercial carrier. The prevailing wage statute alters the incentives, but does not dictate the choices, facing ERISA plans. In this regard, it is "no different from myriad state laws in areas traditionally subject to local regulation, which Congress could not possibly have intended to eliminate." Travelers, 514 U.S. at 668. We could not hold preempted a state law in an area of traditional state regulation based on so tenuous a relation without doing grave violence to our presumption that Congress intended nothing of the sort. We thus conclude that California's prevailing wage laws and apprenticeship standards do not have a "connection with," and therefore do not "relate to," ERISA plans.

Dillingham Construction, 519 U.S. at 330–34 (citations and footnote omitted).

State laws governing the probate of a decedent's estate are a traditional area of state regulation. In *Egelhoff v. Egelhoff*, the Supreme Court determined that, notwithstanding the *Travelers* presumption against preemption of traditional areas of state regulation, a provision of the Washington Probate Code had an impermissible "connection with" the employer's life insurance and pension plans. As you read *Egelhoff*, notice how the majority opinion frames the potential conflict between the Washington statute and the administration of the employer's plans. ERISA §

EGELHOFF V. EGELHOFF
United States Supreme Court, 2001.
532 U.S. 141, 121 S.Ct. 1322, 149 L.Ed.2d 264.

JUSTICE THOMAS delivered the opinion of the Court.

A Washington statute provides that the designation of a spouse as the beneficiary of a nonprobate asset is revoked automatically upon divorce. We are asked to decide whether the Employee Retirement Income Security Act of 1974 (ERISA) preempts that statute to the extent it applies to ERISA plans. We hold that it does.

I

Petitioner Donna Rae Egelhoff was married to David A. Egelhoff. Mr. Egelhoff was employed by the Boeing Company, which provided him with a life insurance policy and a pension plan. Both plans were governed by ERISA, and Mr. Egelhoff designated his wife as the beneficiary under both. In April 1994, the Egelhoffs divorced. Just over two months later,

Mr. Egelhoff died intestate following an automobile accident. At that time, Mrs. Egelhoff remained the listed beneficiary under both the life insurance policy and the pension plan. The life insurance proceeds, totaling $46,000, were paid to her.

Respondents Samantha and David Egelhoff, Mr. Egelhoff's children by a previous marriage, are his statutory heirs under state law. They sued petitioner in Washington state court to recover the life insurance proceeds. Respondents relied on a Washington statute that provides:

> If a marriage is dissolved or invalidated, a provision made prior to that event that relates to the payment or transfer at death of the decedent's interest in a nonprobate asset in favor of or granting an interest or power to the decedent's former spouse is revoked. A provision affected by this section must be interpreted, and the nonprobate asset affected passes, as if the former spouse failed to survive the decedent, having died at the time of entry of the decree of dissolution or declaration of invalidity. Wash. Rev. Code § 11.07.010(2)(a) (1994).

language of Wash Stat

That statute applies to "all nonprobate assets, wherever situated, held at the time of entry by a superior court of this state of a decree of dissolution of marriage or a declaration of invalidity." § 11.07.010(1). It defines "nonprobate asset" to include "a life insurance policy, employee benefit plan, annuity or similar contract, or individual retirement account." § 11.07.010(5)(a).

definition of nonprobate asset

Respondents argued that they were entitled to the life insurance proceeds because the Washington statute disqualified Mrs. Egelhoff as a beneficiary, and in the absence of a qualified named beneficiary, the proceeds would pass to them as Mr. Egelhoff's heirs. In a separate action, respondents also sued to recover the pension plan benefits. Respondents again argued that the Washington statute disqualified Mrs. Egelhoff as a beneficiary and they were thus entitled to the benefits under the plan.

Respondent's argument

The trial courts, concluding that both the insurance policy and the pension plan "should be administered in accordance" with ERISA, granted summary judgment to petitioner in both cases. The Washington Court of Appeals consolidated the cases and reversed. It concluded that the Washington statute was not preempted by ERISA. Applying the statute, it held that respondents were entitled to the proceeds of both the insurance policy and the pension plan.

Trial ct. holding

ct. of App. reversed

The Supreme Court of Washington affirmed. It held that the state statute, although applicable to "employee benefit plan[s]," does not "refe[r] to" ERISA plans to an extent that would require preemption, because it "does not apply immediately and exclusively to an ERISA plan, nor is the existence of such a plan essential to operation of the statute." It also held that the statute lacks a "connection with" an ERISA plan that

Washington Supreme Court

Washington Supreme Court's reasoning

would compel preemption. It emphasized that the statute "does not alter the nature of the plan itself, the administrator's fiduciary duties, or the requirements for plan administration." Nor, the court concluded, does the statute conflict with any specific provision of ERISA, including the antialienation provision, ERISA § 206(d)(1), because it "does not operate to divert benefit plan proceeds from distribution under terms of the plan documents," but merely alters "the underlying circumstances to which the distribution scheme of [the] plan must be applied."

Courts have disagreed about whether statutes like that of Washington are preempted by ERISA. To resolve the conflict, we granted certiorari.

II

Petitioner's argument

SCOTUS holding

Petitioner argues that the Washington statute falls within the terms of ERISA's express preemption provision and that it is preempted by ERISA under traditional principles of conflict preemption. Because we conclude that the statute is expressly preempted by ERISA, we address only the first argument.

ERISA's preemption section, § 514(a), states that ERISA "shall supersede any and all State laws insofar as they may now or hereafter relate to any employee benefit plan" covered by ERISA. We have observed repeatedly that this broadly worded provision is "clearly expansive." New York State Conference of Blue Cross & Blue Shield Plans v. Travelers Ins. Co., 514 U.S. 645, 655 (1995). But at the same time, we have recognized that the term "relate to" cannot be taken "to extend to the furthest stretch of its indeterminacy," or else "for all practical purposes preemption would never run its course." Travelers, 514 U.S. at 655.

We have held that a state law relates to an ERISA plan "if it has a connection with or reference to such a plan." Shaw v. Delta Air Lines, Inc., 463 U.S. 85, 97 (1983). Petitioner focuses on the "connection with" part of this inquiry. Acknowledging that "connection with" is scarcely more restrictive than "relate to," we have cautioned against an "uncritical literalism" that would make preemption turn on "infinite connections." Travelers, 514 U.S. at 656. Instead, "to determine whether a state law has the forbidden connection, we look both to the objectives of the ERISA statute as a guide to the scope of the state law that Congress understood would survive, as well as to the nature of the effect of the state law on ERISA plans." California Div. of Labor Standards Enforcement v. Dillingham Constr., N. A., Inc., 519 U.S. 316, 325 (1997).

Applying this framework, petitioner argues that the Washington statute has an impermissible connection with ERISA plans. We agree. The statute binds ERISA plan administrators to a particular choice of rules for determining beneficiary status. The administrators must pay benefits to the beneficiaries chosen by state law, rather than to those

State law binds ERISA plan administrators

identified in the plan documents. The statute thus implicates an area of core ERISA concern. In particular, it runs counter to ERISA's commands that a plan shall "specify the basis on which payments are made to and from the plan," ERISA § 402(b)(4), and that the fiduciary shall administer the plan "in accordance with the documents and instruments governing the plan," ERISA § 404(a)(1)(D), making payments to a "beneficiary" who is "designated by a participant, or by the terms of [the] plan." ERISA § 3(8).[1] In other words, unlike generally applicable laws regulating "areas where ERISA has nothing to say," Dillingham, 519 U.S. at 330, which we have upheld notwithstanding their incidental effect on ERISA plans, this statute governs the payment of benefits, a central matter of plan administration.

The Washington statute also has a prohibited connection with ERISA plans because it interferes with nationally uniform plan administration. One of the principal goals of ERISA is to enable employers "to establish a uniform administrative scheme, which provides a set of standard procedures to guide processing of claims and disbursement of benefits." Fort Halifax Packing Co. v. Coyne, 482 U.S. 1, 9 (1987). Uniformity is impossible, however, if plans are subject to different legal obligations in different States.

The Washington statute at issue here poses precisely that threat. Plan administrators cannot make payments simply by identifying the beneficiary specified by the plan documents. Instead they must familiarize themselves with state statutes so that they can determine whether the named beneficiary's status has been "revoked" by operation of law. And in this context the burden is exacerbated by the choice-of-law problems that may confront an administrator when the employer is located in one State, the plan participant lives in another, and the participant's former spouse lives in a third. In such a situation, administrators might find that plan payments are subject to conflicting legal obligations.

To be sure, the Washington statute protects administrators from liability for making payments to the named beneficiary unless they have

---

[1]   One can of course escape the conflict between the plan documents (which require making payments to the named beneficiary) and the statute (which requires making payments to someone else) by calling the statute an "invalidation" of the designation of the named beneficiary, and by observing that the plan documents are silent on whether "invalidation" is to occur upon divorce. The dissent employs just such an approach. Reading a clear statement as an ambiguous metastatement enables one to avoid all kinds of conflicts between seemingly contradictory texts. Suppose, for example, that the statute required that all pension benefits be paid to the Governor of Washington. That seems inconsistent with the plan documents (and with ERISA), but the inconsistency disappears if one calls the statute an "invalidation" of the principal and alternate beneficiary designations. After all, neither the plan nor ERISA actually *says* that beneficiaries *cannot* be invalidated in favor of the Governor. This approach exploits the logical inability of any text to contain a complete set of instructions for its own interpretation. It has the vice—or perhaps the virtue, depending upon one's point of view—of draining all language of its meaning.

"actual knowledge of the dissolution or other invalidation of marriage," Wash. Rev. Code § 11.07.010(3)(a) (1994), and it permits administrators to refuse to make payments until any dispute among putative beneficiaries is resolved, § 11.07.010(3)(b). But if administrators do pay benefits, they will face the risk that a court might later find that they had "actual knowledge" of a divorce. If they instead decide to await the results of litigation before paying benefits, they will simply transfer to the beneficiaries the costs of delay and uncertainty.[3] Requiring ERISA administrators to master the relevant laws of 50 States and to contend with litigation would undermine the congressional goal of "minimiz[ing] the administrative and financial burden[s]" on plan administrators— burdens ultimately borne by the beneficiaries. Ingersoll-Rand Co. v. McClendon, 498 U.S. 133, 142 (1990).

We recognize that all state laws create some potential for a lack of uniformity. But differing state regulations affecting an ERISA plan's "system for processing claims and paying benefits" impose "precisely the burden that ERISA preemption was intended to avoid." Fort Halifax, 482 U.S. at 10. And as we have noted, the statute at issue here directly conflicts with ERISA's requirements that plans be administered, and benefits be paid, in accordance with plan documents. We conclude that the Washington statute has a "connection with" ERISA plans and is therefore preempted.

particularly egregious state laws

III

Darling of Respondent's Arg

Respondents suggest several reasons why ordinary ERISA preemption analysis should not apply here. First, they observe that the Washington statute allows employers to opt out. According to respondents, the statute neither regulates plan administration nor impairs uniformity because it does not apply when "[t]he instrument governing disposition of the nonprobate asset expressly provides otherwise." Wash. Rev. Code § 11.07.010(2)(b)(I) (1994). We do not believe that the statute is saved from preemption simply because it is, at least in a broad sense, a default rule.

first argument

Even though the Washington statute's cancellation of private choice may itself be trumped by specific language in the plan documents, the statute does "dictate the choice[s] facing ERISA plans" with respect to matters of plan administration. Dillingham, 519 U.S. at 334. Plan administrators must either follow Washington's beneficiary designation scheme or alter the terms of their plan so as to indicate that they will not follow it. The statute is not any less of a regulation of the terms of ERISA plans simply because there are two ways of complying with it. Of course,

---

[3] The dissent observes that the Washington statute permits a plan administrator to avoid resolving the dispute himself and to let courts or parties settle the matter. This observation only presents an example of how the costs of delay and uncertainty can be passed on to beneficiaries, thereby thwarting ERISA's objective of efficient plan administration.

simple noncompliance with the statute is not one of the options available to plan administrators. Their only choice is one of timing, i.e., whether to bear the burden of compliance ex post, by paying benefits as the statute dictates (and in contravention of the plan documents), or ex ante, by amending the plan.[4]

Respondents emphasize that the opt-out provision makes compliance with the statute less burdensome than if it were mandatory. That is true enough, but the burden that remains is hardly trivial. It is not enough for plan administrators to opt out of this particular statute. Instead, they must maintain a familiarity with the laws of all 50 States so that they can update their plans as necessary to satisfy the opt-out requirements of other, similar statutes. They also must be attentive to changes in the interpretations of those statutes by state courts. This "tailoring of plans and employer conduct to the peculiarities of the law of each jurisdiction" is exactly the burden ERISA seeks to eliminate. Ingersoll-Rand, 498 U.S. at 142.

Second, respondents emphasize that the Washington statute involves both family law and probate law, areas of traditional state regulation. There is indeed a presumption against preemption in areas of traditional state regulation such as family law. But that presumption can be overcome where, as here, Congress has made clear its desire for preemption. Accordingly, we have not hesitated to find state family law preempted when it conflicts with ERISA or relates to ERISA plans. See, e.g., Boggs v. Boggs, 520 U.S. 833 (1997) (holding that ERISA preempts a state community property law permitting the testamentary transfer of an interest in a spouse's pension plan benefits).

Finally, respondents argue that if ERISA preempts this statute, then it also must preempt the various state statutes providing that a murdering heir is not entitled to receive property as a result of the killing. In the ERISA context, these "slayer" statutes could revoke the beneficiary status of someone who murdered a plan participant. Those statutes are not before us, so we do not decide the issue. We note, however, that the principle underlying the statutes—which have been adopted by nearly every State—is well established in the law and has a long historical pedigree predating ERISA. See, e.g., Riggs v. Palmer, 115 N.Y. 506, 22 N.E. 188 (1889). And because the statutes are more or less uniform nationwide, their interference with the aims of ERISA is at least debatable.

---

[4]   Contrary to the dissent's suggestion that the resolution of this case depends on one's view of federalism, we are called upon merely to interpret ERISA. And under the text of ERISA, the fiduciary "shall" administer the plan "in accordance with the documents and instruments governing the plan," ERISA § 404(a)(1)(D). The Washington statute conflicts with this command because under this statute, the only way the fiduciary can administer the plan according to its terms is to change the very terms he is supposed to follow.

The judgment of the Supreme Court of Washington is reversed, and the case is remanded for further proceedings not inconsistent with this opinion.

JUSTICE SCALIA, with whom JUSTICE GINSBURG joins, concurring.

I join the opinion of the Court, since I believe that the "relate to" preemptive provision of the Employee Retirement Income Security Act of 1974 (ERISA) is assuredly triggered by a state law that contradicts ERISA. As the Court notes, "the statute at issue here directly conflicts with ERISA's requirements that plans be administered, and benefits be paid, in accordance with plan documents." I remain unsure (as I think the lower courts and everyone else will be) as to what else triggers the "relate to" provision, which—if it is interpreted to be anything other than a reference to our established jurisprudence concerning conflict and field preemption—has no discernible content that would not pick up every ripple in the pond, producing a result "that no sensible person could have intended." California Div. of Labor Standards Enforcement v. Dillingham Constr., N.A., Inc., 519 U.S. 316, 336 (1997) (Scalia, J., concurring). I persist in the view that we can bring some coherence to this area, and can give the statute both a plausible and precise content, only by interpreting the "relate to" clause as a reference to our ordinary preemption jurisprudence.

JUSTICE BREYER, with whom JUSTICE STEVENS joins, dissenting.

Like Justice Scalia, I believe that we should apply normal conflict preemption and field preemption principles where, as here, a state statute covers ERISA and non-ERISA documents alike. Our more recent ERISA cases are consistent with this approach. And I fear that our failure to endorse this "new approach" explicitly will continue to produce an "avalanche of litigation," as courts struggle to interpret a clause that lacks any "discernible content," threatening results that Congress could not have intended.

I do not agree with Justice Scalia or with the majority, however, that there is any plausible preemption principle that leads to a conclusion that ERISA preempts the statute at issue here. No one could claim that ERISA preempts the entire *field* of state law governing inheritance—though such matters "relate to" ERISA broadly speaking. See Travelers, 514 U.S. at 655. Neither is there any direct conflict between the Washington statute and ERISA, for the one nowhere directly contradicts the other.

The Court correctly points out that ERISA requires a fiduciary to make payments to a beneficiary "in accordance with the documents and instruments governing the plan." ERISA § 404(a)(1)(D). But nothing in the Washington statute requires the contrary. Rather, the state statute simply sets forth a default rule for interpreting documentary silence. The statute specifies that a nonprobate asset will pass at A's death "as if" A's "former spouse" had died first—*unless the "instrument governing disposition of the nonprobate asset expressly provides otherwise."* Wash. Rev. Code § 11.07.010(2)(b)(I) (1994) (emphasis added). This state law rule is a rule of interpretation, and it is designed to carry out, not to conflict with, the employee's likely intention as revealed in the plan documents.

There is no direct conflict or contradiction between the Washington statute and the terms of the plan documents here at issue. David Egelhoff's investment plan provides that when a "beneficiary designation" is "invalid," the "benefits will be paid" to a "surviving spouse," or "if there is no surviving spouse," to the "children in equal shares." The life insurance plan is silent about what occurs when a beneficiary designation is invalid. The Washington statute fills in these gaps, i.e., matters about which the documents themselves say nothing. Thus, the Washington statute specifies that a beneficiary designation—here "Donna R. Egelhoff wife" in the pension plan—is invalid where there is no longer any such person as Donna R. Egelhoff, wife. And the statute adds that in such instance the funds would be paid to the children, who themselves are potential pension plan beneficiaries.

The Court's "direct conflict" conclusion rests upon its claim that "administrators must pay benefits to the beneficiaries chosen by state law, rather than to those identified in the plan documents." But the Court cannot mean "identified *anywhere* in the plan documents," for the Egelhoff children were "identified" as recipients in the pension plan documents should the initial designation to "Donna R. Egelhoff wife" become invalid. And whether that initial designation became invalid upon divorce is a matter about which the plan documents are silent.

To refer to state law to determine whether a given name makes a designation that is, or has become, invalid makes sense where background property or inheritance law is at issue, say, for example, where a written name is potentially ambiguous, where it is set forth near, but not in, the correct space, where it refers to a missing person perhaps presumed dead, where the name was written at a time the employee was incompetent, or where the name refers to an individual or entity disqualified by other law, say, the rule against perpetuities or rules prohibiting a murderer from benefitting from his crime. Why would Congress want the courts to create an ERISA-related federal property law to deal with such problems? Regardless, to refer to background state law in such circumstances does not *directly* conflict with any explicit ERISA provision, for no provision of ERISA forbids reading an instrument or document in light of state property law principles. In any event, in this case the plan documents *explicitly* foresee that a beneficiary designation may become "invalid," but they do not specify the invalidating circumstances. To refer to state property law to fill in that blank cannot possibly create any direct conflict with the plan documents.

The majority simply denies that there is any blank to fill in and suggests that the plan documents require the plan to pay the designated beneficiary under all circumstances. But there is nonetheless an open question, namely, whether a designation that (here explicitly) refers to a wife remains valid after divorce. The question is genuine and important (unlike the imaginary example in the majority's footnote 1). The plan documents themselves do not answer the question any more than they describe what is to occur in a host of other special circumstances (e.g., mental incompetence, intoxication, ambiguous names, etc.). To determine whether ERISA permits state law to answer such questions requires a careful examination of the particular state law in light of ERISA's basic policies. We should not short-circuit that necessary inquiry simply by announcing a "direct conflict" where none exists.

The Court also complains that the Washington statute restricts the plan's choices to "two." But it is difficult to take this complaint seriously. After all, the two choices that Washington gives the plan are (1) to comply with Washington's rule or (2) not to comply with Washington's rule. What other choices could there be? A state statute that asks a plan to choose whether it intends to comply is not a statute that directly conflicts with a plan. Quite obviously, it is possible, not "impossible," to comply with both the Washington statute and federal law.

The more serious preemption question is whether this state statute "stands as an obstacle to the accomplishment and execution of the full purposes and objectives of Congress." In answering that question, we must remember that petitioner has to overcome a strong presumption *against* preemption. That is because the Washington statute governs family property law—a "field of traditional state regulation," where courts will not find federal preemption unless such was the "clear and manifest purpose of Congress," Travelers, 514 U.S. at 655, or the state statute does "major damage to clear and substantial federal interests," Hisquierdo v. Hisquierdo, 439 U.S. 572, 581 (1979). No one can seriously argue that Congress has *clearly* resolved the question before us. And the only damage to federal interests that the Court identifies consists of the added administrative burden the state statute imposes upon ERISA plan administrators.

The Court claims that the Washington statute "interferes with nationally uniform plan administration" by requiring administrators to "familiarize themselves with state statutes." But administrators have to familiarize themselves with state law in any event when they answer such routine legal questions as whether amounts due are subject to garnishment, Mackey v. Lanier Collection Agency & Service, Inc., 486 U.S. 825, 838 (1988), who is a "spouse," who qualifies as a "child," or when an employee is legally dead. And were that "familiarizing burden" somehow overwhelming, the plan could easily avoid it by resolving the divorce revocation issue in the plan documents themselves, stating expressly that state law does not apply. The "burden" thus reduces to a one-time requirement that would fall primarily upon the few who draft model ERISA documents, not upon the many who administer them. So meager a burden cannot justify preempting a state law that enjoys a presumption against preemption.

* * *

In this case, "field preemption" is not at issue. There is no "direct" conflict between state and federal statutes. The state statute poses no significant obstacle to the accomplishment of any federal objective. Any effort to squeeze some additional preemptive force from ERISA's words (i.e., "relate to") is inconsistent with the Court's recent case law. And the state statute before us is one regarding family property-a "field of traditional state regulation," where the interpretive presumption against preemption is particularly strong. Travelers, 514 U.S. at 655. For these reasons, I disagree with the Court's conclusion. And, consequently, I dissent.

NOTES AND QUESTIONS

1.   Do you agree with the majority's characterization of the Washington statute as creating a *direct* conflict with the provisions of ERISA concerning plan administration? Why or why not?

2.   As a general principle, should the federal courts require a plan administrator to comply with a state law when it is possible to do so without contradicting the terms of the written plan document? Or should ERISA's federal goal of minimizing the burden of plan administration through preemption of conflicting state laws always trump state law policy objectives? Should it matter whether the state law permits ERISA plans to "opt out" of the law's requirements?

3.   *State Community Property Laws and ERISA Preemption. Boggs v. Boggs*, 520 U.S. 833 (1997), cited in the majority opinion in *Engelhoff,* is a significant decision for estate planning attorneys who practice in community property law states. *Boggs* involved a dispute over the decedent's pension plan benefits. In *Boggs*, the decedent's surviving second wife claimed she was entitled to receive all of the decedent's pension plan benefits as the plan's designated beneficiary. The sons of the decedent's predeceased first wife

claimed they were entitled to a portion of the decedent's pension benefits under Louisiana community property law.

The Fifth Circuit in *Boggs* ruled that ERISA Section 514(a) did not preempt Louisiana community property law and awarded a share of the decedent's pension plan benefits to the two sons. See Boggs v. Boggs, 82 F.3d 90 (5th Cir. 1996). The Fifth Circuit's decision in *Boggs* conflicted with an earlier Ninth Circuit decision, *Ablamis v. Roper*, 937 F.2d 1450 (9th Cir. 1991), which held that ERISA Section 514(a) preempted an interest in pension plan benefits created under state community property law.

Recognizing the potential significance of state community property laws for benefits provided by ERISA plans, the Supreme Court granted certiorari in *Boggs* to resolve the circuit conflict created by the Fifth Circuit's decision. The Supreme Court resolved the circuit split in *Boggs* by holding that state community property laws creating a property interest in plan benefits are preempted by ERISA.

4. *State Laws Governing Probate and Nonprobate Transfers and ERISA Preemption.* The Supreme Court's decision in *Egelhoff* suggests that other state laws governing probate and nonprobate transfers of a decedent's property may be preempted by ERISA. The implications of the Court's analysis in *Egelhoff* for state laws addressing issues of property succession in circumstances of simultaneous deaths, lapsed gifts to predeceased beneficiaries under the decedent's will, a surviving spouse's elective share rights under state law, and revocation by homicide are discussed in T.P. Gallanis, *ERISA and the Law of Succession*, 65 OHIO ST. L.J. 185 (2004).

5. *Slayer Statutes.* The majority in *Egelhoff* did not decide whether Section 514(a) preempts so-called "slayer" statutes. State law slayer statutes typically provide that the felonious and intentional killing of a decedent automatically revokes the disposition or appointment of property made by the decedent to the killer in a governing document or instrument. In the ERISA context, a slayer statute potentially comes into play when the killer has been designated by the decedent as the designated beneficiary of the decedent's pension or insurance plan benefits. The principle that underlies slayer statutes also has long been recognized as a matter of federal common law. See Mutual Life Ins. Co. v. Armstrong, 117 U.S. 591, 600 (1886) (as a matter of equity a person should not benefit from his wrongs).

In *Nale v. Ford Motor Co. UAW Retirement Plan*, 703 F.Supp.2d 714 (E.D. Mich. 2010), Fayette Nale was convicted of voluntary manslaughter after fatally stabbing her husband Michael during a domestic dispute. Michael Nale, who was a participant in his employer's defined benefit plan, had named Fayette as his surviving spouse under the plan's qualified joint and survivor annuity provisions. After being sentenced to a minimum of 34 months and a maximum of 15 years in prison for the crime, Fayette filed a claim for pension benefits as a surviving spouse while she was incarcerated. The plan administrator denied the claim based on both Michigan's slayer statute and analogous federal common law principles.

Fayette brought suit against the plan, alleging that the plan administrator had wrongfully denied her claim for plan benefits under Section 502(a)(1)(B). The district court upheld the plan administrator's decision to deny the claim, reasoning:

> Although it seems reasonably clear that the application of a state slayer statute may alter the distribution of benefits under an employee benefit plan, there is some debate among federal courts as to whether ERISA preempts state slayer statutes. Many courts have simply declined to resolve the issue because federal common law, which encompasses the equitable principle that a person should not benefit from his wrongs, almost universally produces the same result as state law. * * * Because voluntary manslaughter is an intentional killing under Michigan law and because Plaintiff was convicted of voluntary manslaughter, Plaintiff is subject to both Michigan's slayer statute and the federal common law "slayer's rule." Neither state nor federal law, which are made applicable to the Plan through Article IX, allow Plaintiff to recover her husband's benefits.

Id. at 722–23.

PROBLEM ON ERISA PREEMPTION OF STATE LAW

Elisa Employee is a participant in the Tiara Company Profit Sharing Plan (Plan). Elisa has been diagnosed with a brain tumor and must undergo life-threatening surgery immediately. Prior to surgery, Elisa visited her estate planning lawyer and revised her will so that in the event of her death Elisa's estate would go to a trust for the benefit of her two young children. Elisa also executed a durable general power of attorney under state law naming her best friend Betty as Elisa's agent in the event that Elisa becomes incapacitated (another possible outcome of the brain tumor surgery).

Elisa divorced her husband Harry two months prior to the discovery of her brain tumor. Harry is still the designated beneficiary for Elisa's account under the Plan in the event of her death. Elisa's estate planner advised her that she should change this beneficiary designation so that in the event of her death, the Plan account balance would be paid to her estate. By changing the Plan beneficiary designation in this manner, Elisa's Plan account balance would, under the terms of her revised will, become part of the corpus of the trust for the benefit of her two young children.

The night before her surgery, Elisa remembered that she had not changed her beneficiary designation under the Plan as instructed by her estate planner. Elisa called Betty and directed Betty to use her authority as Elisa's agent under the durable general power of attorney to contact Tiara Company and change the Plan beneficiary designation for Elisa.

Betty visited the Plan administrator the next morning, presented the durable general power of attorney to the administrator, and requested the form necessary to change Elisa's beneficiary designation under the Plan. The Plan administrator refused to recognize Betty's authority under state law as Elisa's agent pursuant to the durable general power of attorney. Consequently, Elisa's beneficiary designation was not changed.

Elisa's brain tumor surgery was unsuccessful and she now is unable to move or speak. Betty has brought a claim in federal court against the Plan administrator under ERISA Section 502(a)(1)(B) to "enforce Elisa's right to change her beneficiary designation under the Plan." Betty claims that the Plan administrator must allow Betty to change Elisa's beneficiary designation under the Plan pursuant to Betty's authority as Elisa's agent pursuant to the durable general power of attorney. The power of attorney document expressly authorizes Betty to "change any and all beneficiary designations that have been executed prior to the onset of [Elisa's] incapacity." This provision of the power of attorney is valid and enforceable under state law. The Plan document states only that "a Plan Participant may change the designated beneficiary for the Participant's Plan benefits at any time by completing the appropriate change of beneficiary designation form."

Assume that the federal court has determined that Betty has standing to bring this claim on behalf of Elisa as a participant in the Plan. Should the federal court order the Plan administrator to allow Betty to make the change of beneficiary designation pursuant to Betty's authority under state law as Elisa's agent? Or should the federal court rule that state law, which gives authority to Betty to act on behalf of Elisa, is preempted by ERISA?

D. STATE LAWS REGULATING HEALTH CARE PLANS AND HEALTH CARE PROVIDERS

1. SUPREME COURT DECISIONS

Public dissatisfaction with the health care system has led state and local lawmakers to enact various reform measures aimed at health care plans and health care providers. These health care reform laws are often challenged as preempted by ERISA.

The Supreme Court's more recent preemption decisions have focused on state law efforts at health care reform. In two of the decisions reproduced in Section D, *Rush Prudential HMO, Inc. v. Moran* and *Kentucky Association of Health Care Plans v. Miller*, the Supreme Court determined that the state law was not preempted by ERISA. In the third decision, *Aetna Health Inc. v. Davila*, the Supreme Court found that ERISA preempted the state law. As you read *Moran*, *Miller*, and *Davila*, compare the principles that underlie the Supreme Court's preemption analysis in each case. Why does the challenged state law survive ERISA preemption in *Moran* and *Miller?*—Why is the outcome different in *Davila?*

In *Moran*, an Illinois state law gave participants in any health maintenance organization (HMO) the right to an independent external review of a claim for benefits that was denied by the HMO based on a lack of medical necessity. As you read *Moran*, focus on the following two questions. First, how does the Supreme Court characterize an HMO for purposes of state laws that regulate insurance (and thus are saved from ERISA preemption)? Second, when (if ever) can a state law right or remedy be substituted for ERISA's civil enforcement scheme under Section 502?

RUSH PRUDENTIAL HMO, INC. v. MORAN

United States Supreme Court, 2002.
536 U.S. 355, 122 S.Ct. 2151, 153 L.Ed.2d 375.

JUSTICE SOUTER delivered the opinion of the Court.

Section 4–10 of Illinois's Health Maintenance Organization Act provides recipients of health coverage by such organizations with a right to independent medical review of certain denials of benefits. The issue in this case is whether the statute, as applied to health benefits provided by a health maintenance organization under contract with an employee welfare benefit plan, is preempted by the Employee Retirement Income Security Act of 1974 (ERISA). We hold it is not.

I

Petitioner, Rush Prudential HMO, Inc., is a health maintenance organization (HMO) that contracts to provide medical services for employee welfare benefit plans covered by ERISA. Respondent Debra Moran is a beneficiary under one such plan, sponsored by her husband's employer. Rush's "Certificate of Group Coverage," issued to employees who participate in employer-sponsored plans, promises that Rush will provide them with "medically necessary" services. The terms of the certificate give Rush the "broadest possible discretion" to determine whether a medical service claimed by a beneficiary is covered under the certificate. The certificate specifies that a service is covered as "medically necessary" if Rush finds:

> (a) [The service] is furnished or authorized by a Participating Doctor for the diagnosis or the treatment of a Sickness or Injury or for the maintenance of a person's good health.

> (b) The prevailing opinion within the appropriate specialty of the United States medical profession is that [the service] is safe and effective for its intended use, and that its omission would adversely affect the person's medical condition.

[handwritten marginal note: HMO provides medical services for ERISA EEs]

(c) It is furnished by a provider with appropriate training, experience, staff and facilities to furnish that particular service or supply.

As the certificate explains, Rush contracts with physicians "to arrange for or provide services and supplies for medical care and treatment" of covered persons. Each covered person selects a primary care physician from those under contract to Rush, while Rush will pay for medical services by an unaffiliated physician only if the services have been "authorized" both by the primary care physician and Rush's medical director.

In 1996, when Moran began to have pain and numbness in her right shoulder, Dr. Arthur LaMarre, her primary care physician, unsuccessfully administered "conservative" treatments such as physiotherapy. In October 1997, Dr. LaMarre recommended that Rush approve surgery by an unaffiliated specialist, Dr. Julia Terzis, who had developed an unconventional treatment for Moran's condition. Although Dr. LaMarre said that Moran would be "best served" by that procedure, Rush denied the request and, after Moran's internal appeals, affirmed the denial on the ground that the procedure was not "medically necessary." Rush instead proposed that Moran undergo standard surgery, performed by a physician affiliated with Rush.

In January 1998, Moran made a written demand for an independent medical review of her claim, as guaranteed by § 4–10 of Illinois's HMO Act, which provides:

> Each Health Maintenance Organization shall provide a mechanism for the timely review by a physician holding the same class of license as the primary care physician, who is unaffiliated with the Health Maintenance Organization, jointly selected by the patient . . ., primary care physician and the Health Maintenance Organization in the event of a dispute between the primary care physician and the Health Maintenance Organization regarding the medical necessity of a covered service proposed by a primary care physician. In the event that the reviewing physician determines the covered service to be medically necessary, the Health Maintenance Organization shall provide the covered service.

Text of the HMO Act

* * *

When Rush failed to provide the independent review, Moran sued in an Illinois state court to compel compliance with the state Act. Rush removed the suit to Federal District Court, arguing that the cause of action was "completely preempted" under ERISA.

While the suit was pending, Moran had surgery by Dr. Terzis at her own expense and submitted a $94,841.27 reimbursement claim to Rush.

Rush treated the claim as a renewed request for benefits and began a new inquiry to determine coverage. The three doctors consulted by Rush said the surgery had been medically unnecessary.

Meanwhile, the federal court remanded the case back to state court on Moran's motion, concluding that because Moran's request for independent review under § 4–10 would not require interpretation of the terms of an ERISA plan, the claim was not "completely preempted" so as to permit removal under 28 U.S.C. § 1441. The state court enforced the state statute and ordered Rush to submit to review by an independent physician. The doctor selected was a reconstructive surgeon at Johns Hopkins Medical Center, Dr. A. Lee Dellon. Dr. Dellon decided that Dr. Terzis's treatment had been medically necessary, based on the definition of medical necessity in Rush's Certificate of Group Coverage, as well as his own medical judgment. Rush's medical director, however, refused to concede that the surgery had been medically necessary, and denied Moran's claim in January 1999.

Moran amended her complaint in state court to seek reimbursement for the surgery as "medically necessary" under Illinois' HMO Act, and Rush again removed to federal court, arguing that Moran's amended complaint stated a claim for ERISA benefits and was thus completely preempted by ERISA's civil enforcement provisions, ERISA § 502, as construed by this Court in *Metropolitan Life Insurance Co. v. Taylor*, 481 U.S. 58 (1987). The District Court treated Moran's claim as a suit under ERISA, and denied the claim on the ground that ERISA preempted Illinois's independent review statute.

The Court of Appeals for the Seventh Circuit reversed. Although it found Moran's state law reimbursement claim completely preempted by ERISA so as to place the case in federal court, the Seventh Circuit did not agree that the substantive provisions of Illinois' HMO Act were so preempted. The court noted that although ERISA broadly preempts any [*7th Cir. holding*] state laws that "relate to" employee benefit plans, state laws that "regulat[e] insurance" are saved from preemption, § 514(b)(2)(A). * * * The Seventh Circuit rejected the contention that Illinois' independent review requirement constituted a forbidden "alternative remedy" under [*alternative remedy prohibition*] this Court's holding in *Pilot Life Insurance Co. v. Dedeaux*, 481 U.S. 41 (1987), and emphasized that § 4–10 does not authorize any particular form of relief in state courts; rather, with respect to any ERISA health plan, the judgment of the independent reviewer is only enforceable in an action brought under ERISA's civil enforcement scheme, ERISA § 502(a).

Because the decision of the Court of Appeals conflicted with the Fifth Circuit's treatment of a similar provision of Texas law in *Corporate Health Insurance, Inc. v. Texas Dept. of Insurance*, 215 F.3d 526 (2000), we granted certiorari. We now affirm.

II

Text of ERISA

To "safeguard . . . the establishment, operation, and administration" of employee benefit plans, ERISA sets "minimum standards . . . assuring the equitable character of such plans and their financial soundness," § 2(a), and contains an express preemption provision that ERISA "shall supersede any and all State laws insofar as they may now or hereafter relate to any employee benefit plan. . . ." § 514(a). A saving clause then reclaims a substantial amount of ground with its provision that "nothing in this subchapter shall be construed to exempt or relieve any person from any law of any State which regulates insurance, banking, or securities." § 514(b)(2)(A). The "unhelpful" drafting of these antiphonal clauses, New York Conference of Blue Cross & Blue Shield Plans v. Travelers Ins. Co., 514 U.S. 645, 656 (1995), occupies a substantial share of this Court's time. In trying to extrapolate congressional intent in a case like this, when congressional language seems simultaneously to preempt everything and hardly anything, we "have no choice" but to temper the assumption that "the ordinary meaning . . . accurately expresses the legislative purpose," id. at 740, with the qualification "that the historic police powers of the States were not [meant] to be superseded by the Federal Act unless that was the clear and manifest purpose of Congress." Id.

It is beyond serious dispute that under existing precedent § 4–10 of the Illinois HMO Act "relates to" employee benefit plans within the meaning of § 514(a). The state law bears "indirectly but substantially on all insured benefit plans," Metropolitan Life v. Massachusetts, 471 U.S. 724, 739 (1985), by requiring them to submit to an extra layer of review for certain benefit denials if they purchase medical coverage from any of the common types of health care organizations covered by the state law's definition of HMO. As a law that "relates to" ERISA plans under § 514(a), § 4–10 is saved from preemption only if it also "regulates insurance" under § 514(b)(2)(A). Rush insists that the Act is not such a law.

A

In *Metropolitan Life v. Massachusetts*, we said that in deciding whether a law "regulates insurance" under ERISA's saving clause, we start with a "common sense view of the matter," 471 U.S. at 740, under which "a law must not just have an impact on the insurance industry, but must be specifically directed toward that industry." Pilot Life Ins. Co. v. Dedeaux, 481 U.S. at 50. * * *

1

The common sense inquiry focuses on "primary elements of an insurance contract[, which] are the spreading and underwriting of a policyholder's risk." Group Life & Health Ins. Co. v. Royal Drug Co., 440 U.S. 205, 211 (1979). The Illinois statute addresses these elements by defining "health maintenance organization" by reference to the risk that it bears. See 215 Ill. Comp. Stat., ch. 125, § 1–2(9) (2000) (an HMO "provide[s] or arrange[s] for . . . health care plans under a system which causes any part of the risk of health care delivery to be borne by the organization or its providers").

Rush contends that seeing an HMO as an insurer distorts the nature *Rush's Argument* of an HMO, which is, after all, a health care provider, too. This, Rush argues, should determine its characterization, with the consequence that regulation of an HMO is not insurance regulation within the meaning of ERISA.

The answer to Rush is, of course, that an HMO is both: it provides health care, and it does so as an insurer. Nothing in the saving clause requires an either-or choice between health care and insurance in deciding a preemption question, and as long as providing insurance fairly accounts for the application of state law, the saving clause may apply. There is no serious question about that here, for it would ignore the whole purpose of the HMO-style of organization to conceive of HMOs * * * without their insurance element.

"The defining feature of an HMO is receipt of a fixed fee for each patient enrolled under the terms of a contract to provide specified health care if needed." Pegram v. Herdrich, 530 U.S. 211, 218 (2000). "The HMO thus assumes the financial risk of providing the benefits promised: if a participant never gets sick, the HMO keeps the money regardless, and if a participant becomes expensively ill, the HMO is responsible for the treatment. . . ." Id. at 218–219. The HMO design goes beyond the simple truism that all contracts are, in some sense, insurance against future fluctuations in price, because HMOs actually underwrite and spread risk among their participants, a feature distinctive to insurance.

So Congress has understood from the start, when the phrase "Health *Congressional* Maintenance Organization" was established and defined in the HMO Act *recognition of* of 1973. The Act was intended to encourage the development of HMOs as *HMOs* a new form of health care delivery system, see S. Rep. No. 93–129, pp. 7–9 (1973), and when Congress set the standards that the new health delivery organizations would have to meet to get certain federal benefits, the terms included requirements that the organizations bear and manage risk. * * *

This conception has not changed in the intervening years. Since passage of the federal Act, States have been adopting their own HMO enabling acts, and today, at least 40 of them, including Illinois, regulate HMOs primarily through the States' insurance departments, see Aspen Health Law and Compliance Center, Managed Care Law Manual 31–32 (Supp. 6, Nov. 1997), although they may be treated differently from traditional insurers, owing to their additional role as health care providers. Finally, this view shared by Congress and the States has passed into common understanding. HMOs (broadly defined) have "grown explosively in the past decade and [are] now the dominant form of health plan coverage for privately insured individuals." Gold & Hurley, The Role of Managed Care "Products" in Managed Care "Plans," in Contemporary Managed Care 47 (M. Gold ed.1998). While the original form of the HMO was a single corporation employing its own physicians, the 1980s saw a variety of other types of structures develop even as traditional insurers altered their own plans by adopting HMO-like cost control measures. The dominant feature is the combination of insurer and provider and "an observer may be hard pressed to uncover the differences among products that bill themselves as HMOs, [preferred provider organizations], or managed care overlays to health insurance." Managed Care Law Manual, supra, at 1. Thus, virtually all commentators on the American health care system describe HMOs as a combination of insurer and provider, and observe that in recent years, traditional "indemnity" insurance has fallen out of favor. Rush cannot checkmate common sense by trying to submerge HMOs' insurance features beneath an exclusive characterization of HMOs as providers of health care.

2

On a second tack, Rush and its amici dispute that § 4–10 is aimed specifically at the insurance industry. They say the law sweeps too broadly with definitions capturing organizations that provide no insurance, and by regulating noninsurance activities of HMOs that do. Rush points out that Illinois law defines HMOs to include organizations that cause the risk of health care delivery to be borne by the organization itself, or by "its providers." 215 Ill. Comp. Stat., ch. 125, § 1–2(9) (2000). In Rush's view, the reference to "its providers" suggests that an organization may be an HMO under state law (and subject to § 4–10) even if it does not bear risk itself, either because it has "devolve[d]" the risk of health care delivery onto others, or because it has contracted only to provide "administrative" or other services for self-funded plans.

These arguments, however, are built on unsound assumptions. Rush's first contention assumes that an HMO is no longer an insurer when it arranges to limit its exposure, as when an HMO arranges for capitated contracts to compensate its affiliated physicians with a set fee for each HMO patient regardless of the treatment provided. Under such an arrangement, Rush claims, the risk is not borne by the HMO at all. In a similar vein, Rush points out that HMOs may contract with third-party insurers to protect themselves against large claims.

The problem with Rush's argument is simply that a reinsurance contract does not take the primary insurer out of the insurance business and capitation contracts do not relieve the HMO of its obligations to the beneficiary. The HMO is still bound to provide medical care to its members, and this is so regardless of the ability of physicians or third party insurers to honor their contracts with the HMO.

* * *

In sum, prior to ERISA's passage, Congress demonstrated an awareness of HMOs as risk-bearing organizations subject to state insurance regulation, the state Act defines HMOs by reference to risk bearing, HMOs have taken over much business formerly performed by traditional indemnity insurers, and they are almost universally regulated as insurers under state law. That HMOs are not traditional "indemnity" insurers is no matter; "we would not undertake to freeze the concepts of insurance. . .into the mold they fitted when these Federal Acts were passed." SEC v. Variable Annuity Life Ins. Co., 359 U.S. 65, 71 (1959). Thus, the Illinois HMO Act is a law "directed toward" the insurance industry, and an "insurance regulation" under a "common sense" view.

all reasons to consider HMO's insurers

* * *

III

Given that § 4–10 regulates insurance, ERISA's mandate that "nothing in this subchapter shall be construed to exempt or relieve any person from any law of any State which regulates insurance," ERISA § 514(b)(2)(A), ostensibly forecloses preemption. See Metropolitan Life v. Massachusetts, 471 U.S. at 746. ("If a state law 'regulates insurance,' . . . it is not preempted"). Rush, however, does not give up. It argues for preemption anyway, emphasizing that the question is ultimately one of congressional intent, which sometimes is so clear that it overrides a statutory provision designed to save state law from being preempted.

In ERISA law, we have recognized one example of this sort of overpowering federal policy in the civil enforcement provisions, ERISA § 502(a), authorizing civil actions for six specific types of relief. In *Massachusetts Mutual Life Insurance Co. v. Russell*, 473 U.S. 134 (1985), we said those provisions amounted to an "interlocking, interrelated, and interdependent remedial scheme," which *Pilot Life* described as "represent[ing] a careful balancing of the need for prompt and fair claims settlement procedures against the public interest in encouraging the formation of employee benefit plans," 481 U.S. at 54. So, we have held, the civil enforcement provisions are of such extraordinarily preemptive power that they override even the "well-pleaded complaint" rule for establishing the conditions under which a cause of action may be removed to a federal forum. Metropolitan Life Ins. Co. v. Taylor, 481 U.S. at 63–64.

civil enforcement provisions → preemption very strong

A

Although we have yet to encounter a forced choice between the congressional policies of exclusively federal remedies and the "reservation of the business of insurance to the States," we have anticipated such a

alternate remedies

conflict, with the state insurance regulation losing out if it allows plan participants "to obtain remedies. . .that Congress rejected in ERISA." *Pilot Life*, 481 U.S. at 54.

* * *

But this case addresses a state regulatory scheme that provides no new cause of action under state law and authorizes no new form of ultimate relief. While independent review under § 4–10 may well settle the fate of a benefit claim under a particular contract, the state statute does not enlarge the claim beyond the benefits available in any action brought under § 502(a). And although the reviewer's determination would presumably replace that of the HMO as to what is "medically necessary" under this contract, the relief ultimately available would still be what ERISA authorizes in a suit for benefits under § 502(a). This case therefore does not involve the sort of additional claim or remedy exemplified in *Pilot Life*, *Russell*, and *Ingersoll-Rand*[.]

* * *

In deciding what to make of these facts and conclusions, it helps to go back to where we started and recall the ways States regulate insurance in looking out for the welfare of their citizens. Illinois has chosen to regulate insurance as one way to regulate the practice of medicine, which we have previously held to be permissible under ERISA, see Metropolitan Life v. Massachusetts, 471 U.S. at 741. While the statute designed to do this undeniably eliminates whatever may have remained of a plan sponsor's option to minimize scrutiny of benefit denials, this effect of eliminating an insurer's autonomy to guarantee terms congenial to its own interests is the stuff of garden variety insurance regulation through the imposition of standard policy terms. See id. at 742 ("[S]tate laws regulating the substantive terms of insurance contracts were commonplace well before the mid-70's"). It is therefore hard to imagine a reservation of state power to regulate insurance that would not be meant to cover restrictions of the insurer's advantage in this kind of way. And any lingering doubt about the reasonableness of § 4–10 in affecting the application of § 502(a) may be put to rest by recalling that regulating insurance tied to what is medically necessary is probably inseparable from enforcing the quintessentially state law standards of reasonable medical care. See Pegram v. Herdrich, 530 U.S. at 236. "[I]n the field of health care, a subject of traditional state regulation, there is no ERISA preemption without clear manifestation of congressional purpose." Id. at 237. To the extent that benefits litigation in some federal courts may have to account for the effects of § 4–10, it would be an exaggeration to hold that the objectives of § 502(a) are undermined. The saving clause is entitled to prevail here, and we affirm the judgment.

JUSTICE THOMAS, with whom THE CHIEF JUSTICE, JUSTICE SCALIA, and JUSTICE KENNEDY join, dissenting.

This Court has repeatedly recognized that ERISA's civil enforcement provision, § 502 of the Employee Retirement Income Security Act of 1974 (ERISA), provides the exclusive vehicle for actions asserting a claim for benefits under health plans governed by ERISA, and therefore that state laws that create additional remedies are preempted. See, e.g., Pilot Life Ins. Co. v. Dedeaux, 481 U.S. 41, 52 (1987); Massachusetts Mutual Life Ins. Co. v. Russell, 473 U.S. 134, 146–147 (1985). Such exclusivity of remedies is necessary to further Congress' interest in establishing a uniform federal law of employee benefits so that employers are encouraged to provide benefits to their employees: "To require plan providers to design their programs in an environment of differing state regulations would complicate the administration of nationwide plans, producing inefficiencies that employers might offset with decreased benefits." FMC Corp. v. Holliday, 498 U.S. 52, 60 (1990).

Of course, the "expectations that a federal common law of rights and obligations under ERISA-regulated plans would develop. . .would make little sense if the remedies available to ERISA participants and beneficiaries under § 502(a) could be supplemented or supplanted by varying state laws." Pilot Life, 481 U.S. at 56. Therefore, as the Court concedes even a state law that "regulates insurance" may be preempted if it supplements the remedies provided by ERISA, despite ERISA's saving clause, § 514(b)(2)(A). See Silkwood v. Kerr-McGee Corp., 464 U.S. 238, 248 (1984) (noting that state laws that stand as an obstacle to the accomplishment of the full purposes and objectives of Congress are preempted). Today, however, the Court takes the unprecedented step of allowing respondent Debra Moran to short-circuit ERISA's remedial scheme by allowing her claim for benefits to be determined in the first instance through an arbitral-like procedure provided under Illinois law, and by a decisionmaker other than a court. This decision not only conflicts with our precedents, it also eviscerates the uniformity of ERISA remedies Congress deemed integral to the "careful balancing of the need for prompt and fair claims settlement procedures against the public interest in encouraging the formation of employee benefit plans." Pilot Life, 481 U.S. at 54. I would reverse the Court of Appeals' judgment and remand for a determination of whether Moran was entitled to reimbursement absent the independent review conducted under § 4–10.

* * *

In addressing the relationship between ERISA's remedies under § 502(a) and a state law regulating insurance, the Court has observed that "[t]he policy choices reflected in the inclusion of certain remedies and the exclusion of others under the federal scheme would be completely undermined if ERISA-plan participants and beneficiaries were free to obtain remedies under state law that Congress rejected in ERISA." Id. at 54. Thus, while the preeminent federal interest in the uniform administration of employee benefit plans yields in some instances to varying state regulation of the business of insurance, the exclusivity and uniformity of ERISA's enforcement scheme remains paramount. "Congress intended § 502(a) to be the exclusive remedy for rights guaranteed under ERISA." Ingersoll-Rand Co., 498 U.S. at 144. In accordance with ordinary principles of conflict preemption, therefore, even a state law "regulating insurance" will be preempted if it provides a separate vehicle to assert a claim for benefits outside of, or in addition to, ERISA's remedial scheme. See, e.g., Pilot Life, 481 U.S. at 54 (citing Russell, 473 U.S. at 146).

III

The question for the Court, therefore, is whether § 4–10 provides such a vehicle. Without question, Moran had a "panoply of remedial devices," available under § 502 of ERISA when petitioner denied her claim for benefits. Section 502(a)(1)(B) of ERISA provided the most obvious remedy: a civil suit to recover benefits due under the terms of the plan. But rather than bring such a suit, Moran sought to have her right to benefits determined outside of ERISA's remedial scheme through the arbitral-like mechanism available under § 4–10.

Section 4–10 cannot be characterized as anything other than an alternative state law remedy or vehicle for seeking benefits. In the first place, § 4–10 comes into play only if the HMO and the claimant dispute the claimant's entitlement to benefits; the purpose of the review is to determine whether a claimant is entitled to benefits. Contrary to the majority's characterization of § 4–10 as nothing more than a state law regarding medical standards, it is in fact a binding determination of whether benefits are due: "In the event that the reviewing physician determines the covered service to be medically necessary, the [HMO] *shall provide* the covered service." 215 Ill. Comp. Stat., ch. 125, § 4–10 (2000) (emphasis added). Section 4–10 is thus most precisely characterized as an arbitration-like mechanism to settle benefits disputes.

There is no question that arbitration constitutes an alternative remedy to litigation. Consequently, although a contractual agreement to arbitrate—which does not constitute a "State law" relating to "any employee benefit plan"—is outside § 514(a) of ERISA's preemptive scope, States may not circumvent ERISA preemption by mandating an alternative arbitral-like remedy as a plan term enforceable through an ERISA action.

* * *

Section 4–10 constitutes an arbitral-like state remedy through which plan members may seek to resolve conclusively a disputed right to benefits. Some 40 other States have similar laws, though these vary as to applicability, procedures, standards, deadlines, and consequences of independent review. Allowing disparate state laws that provide inconsistent external review requirements to govern a participant's or beneficiary's claim to benefits under an employee benefit plan is wholly destructive of Congress' expressly stated goal of uniformity in this area. Moreover, it is inimical to a scheme for furthering and protecting the "careful balancing of the need for prompt and fair claims settlement procedures against the public interest in encouraging the formation of employee benefit plans," given that the development of a federal common law under ERISA-regulated plans has consistently been deemed central to that balance.[8] Pilot Life, 481 U.S. at 54, 56. While it is true that disuniformity is the inevitable result of the Congressional decision to save local insurance regulation, this does not answer the altogether different question before the Court today, which is whether a state law "regulating insurance" nonetheless provides a separate vehicle to assert a claim for benefits outside of, or in addition to, ERISA's remedial scheme. If it does, the exclusivity and uniformity of ERISA's enforcement scheme must remain paramount and the state law is preempted in accordance with ordinary principles of conflict preemption.[9]

For the reasons noted by the Court, independent review provisions may sound very appealing. Efforts to expand the variety of remedies available to aggrieved beneficiaries beyond those set forth in ERISA are obviously designed to increase the chances that patients will be able to receive treatments they desire, and most of us are naturally sympathetic

---

[8] The Court suggests that a state law's impact on cost is not relevant after *New York State Conference of Blue Cross & Blue Shield Plans v. Travelers Insurance Co.*, 514 U.S. 645, 662 (1995), which holds that a state law providing for surcharges on hospital rates did not, based solely on their indirect economic effect, "bear the requisite 'connection with' ERISA plans to trigger preemption." But *Travelers* addressed only the question whether a state law "relates to" an ERISA plan so as to fall within § 514(a)'s broad preemptive scope in the first place and is not relevant to the inquiry here. The Court holds that "[i]t is beyond serious dispute," that § 4–10 does "relate to" an ERISA plan; § 4–10's economic effects are necessarily relevant to the extent that they upset the object of § 502(a). See *Ingersoll-Rand Co. v. McClendon*, 498 U.S. 133, 142 (1990) ("Section 514(a) was intended to ensure that plans and plan sponsors would be subject to a uniform body of benefits law; the goal was to minimize the administrative and financial burden of complying with conflicting directives among States or between States and the Federal Government. Otherwise, the inefficiencies created could work to the detriment of plan beneficiaries").

[9] The Court isolates the "plan" from the HMO and then concludes that the independent review provision "does not threaten the object of ERISA § 502" because it does not affect the plan, but only the HMO. To my knowledge such a distinction is novel. Cf. *Pegram*, 530 U.S. at 223 (recognizing that the agreement between an HMO and an employer may provide elements of a plan by setting out the rules under which care is provided). Its application is particularly novel here, where the Court appears to view the HMO as the plan administrator, leaving one to wonder how the myriad state independent review procedures can help but have an impact on plan administration.

to those suffering from illness who seek further options. Nevertheless, the Court would do well to remember that no employer is required to provide any health benefit plan under ERISA and that the entire advent of managed care, and the genesis of HMOs, stemmed from spiraling health costs. To the extent that independent review provisions such as § 4–10 make it more likely that HMOs will have to subsidize beneficiaries' treatments of choice, they undermine the ability of HMOs to control costs, which, in turn, undermines the ability of employers to provide health care coverage for employees.

As a consequence, independent review provisions could create a disincentive to the formation of employee health benefit plans, a problem that Congress addressed by making ERISA's remedial scheme exclusive and uniform. While it may well be the case that the advantages of allowing States to implement independent review requirements as a supplement to the remedies currently provided under ERISA outweigh this drawback, this is a judgment that, pursuant to ERISA, must be made by Congress. I respectfully dissent.

NOTES AND QUESTIONS

1.   The majority in *Moran* fundamentally characterized the Illinois statute as a law that regulated insurance. How did the dissent in *Moran* characterize the Illinois statute? Which characterization is more persuasive to you?

2.   The plaintiff in *Moran* could have brought a claim for denial of plan benefits under ERISA Section 502(a)(1)(B). Why would a plan participant prefer to proceed through a state-based independent external review procedure rather than bring a claim under ERISA Section 502(a)(1)(B)?

3.   *Independent External Review Requirements Under the ACA.* The Affordable Care Act requires that participants in non-grandfathered health plans must have the opportunity to obtain independent external review of denied claims. As a practical matter, this requirement has the greatest impact on self-insured plans. Before the enactment of the ACA, self-insured plans were not subject to state-based independent external review programs, such as the Illinois program at issue in *Moran*, by virtue of preemption under ERISA's deemer clause. See ERISA § 514(b)(2)(B); FMC Corp. v. Holliday, 498 U.S. 52 (1990). Under the ACA, all non-grandfathered self-insured plans must offer independent external review of denied claims for plan benefits as an alternative procedural mechanism to Section 502(a)(1)(B) claims. In addition, the ACA requires that all states must operate an independent external review program for denied claims under non-grandfathered insured plans that satisfies the consumer protection standards established by the ACA. These ACA requirements are described in detail in Chapter Four of the casebook.

Section 514(b)(2)(A) of ERISA saves from federal preemption "any law of any State that regulates insurance * * *." The Affordable Care Act increases the significance of ERISA's insurance savings clause because it relies heavily on state-regulated insurance issuers to provide health insurance policies to both individuals and employer-based groups. As a result, state legislatures are likely to continue to be active in regulating health insurance policy issuers and health care providers. *Kentucky Association of Health Care Plans, Inc. v. Miller* illustrates this type of state-insurance regulation.

Prior to *Miller*, in interpreting Section 514(b)(2)(A) the Supreme Court had relied on judicial interpretations of similar statutory language under the McCarran-Ferguson Act, which provides that "[n]o Act of Congress shall be construed to invalidate, impair, or supersede any law enacted by any State for the purpose of regulating the business of insurance." 15 U.S.C. § 1012(b). In *Miller*, the Supreme Court abandoned its prior test based on the McCarran-Ferguson Act and created a new test for determining when a state law "regulates insurance" under ERISA Section 514(b)(2)(A). Does the new *Miller* test expand or contract the scope of state insurance regulation that is saved from ERISA preemption under Section 514(b)(2)(A)?

KENTUCKY ASSOCIATION OF HEALTH PLANS, INC. V. MILLER

United States Supreme Court, 2003.
538 U.S. 329, 123 S.Ct. 1471, 155 L.Ed.2d 468.

SCALIA, J., delivered the opinion for a unanimous Court.

Kentucky law provides that "[a] health insurer shall not discriminate against any provider who is located within the geographic coverage area of the health benefit plan and who is willing to meet the terms and conditions for participation established by the health insurer, including the Kentucky state Medicaid program and Medicaid partnerships." Ky. Rev. Stat. Ann. § 304.17A–270. Moreover, any "health benefit plan that includes chiropractic benefits shall...[p]ermit any licensed chiropractor who agrees to abide by the terms, conditions, reimbursement rates, and standards of quality of the health benefit plan to serve as a participating primary chiropractic provider to any person covered by the plan." § 304.17A171(2). We granted certiorari to decide whether the Employee Retirement Income Security Act of 1974 (ERISA) preempts either, or both, of these "Any Willing Provider" (AWP) statutes.

[handwritten margin note: kentucky laws @ issue]

I

Petitioners include several health maintenance organizations (HMOs) and a Kentucky-based association of HMOs. In order to control the quality and cost of health care delivery, these HMOs have contracted with selected doctors, hospitals, and other health care providers to create exclusive "provider networks." Providers in such networks agree to render health care services to the HMOs' subscribers at discounted rates and to comply with other contractual requirements. In return, they receive the benefit of patient volume higher than that achieved by nonnetwork providers who lack access to petitioners' subscribers.

Kentucky's AWP statutes impair petitioners' ability to limit the number of providers with access to their networks, and thus their ability to use the assurance of high patient volume as the quid pro quo for the discounted rates that network membership entails. Petitioners believe that AWP laws will frustrate their efforts at cost and quality control, and will ultimately deny consumers the benefit of their cost-reducing arrangements with providers.

In April 1997, petitioners filed suit against respondent, the Commissioner of Kentucky's Department of Insurance, in the United States District Court for the Eastern District of Kentucky, asserting that ERISA preempts Kentucky's AWP laws. * * *

II

To determine whether Kentucky's AWP statutes are saved from preemption, we must ascertain whether they are "law[s] . . . which regulat[e] insurance" under § 514(b)(2)(A).

It is well established in our case law that a state law must be "specifically directed toward" the insurance industry in order to fall under ERISA's savings clause; laws of general application that have some bearing on insurers do not qualify. Pilot Life Ins. Co. v. Dedeaux, 481 U.S. 41, 50 (1987); see also Rush Prudential HMO, Inc. v. Moran, 536 U.S. 355, 366 (2002); FMC Corp. v. Holliday, 498 U.S. 52, 61(1990). At the same time, not all state laws "specifically directed toward" the insurance industry will be covered by § 514(b)(2)(A), which saves laws that regulate *insurance*, not insurers. As we explained in *Rush Prudential*, insurers must be regulated "with respect to their insurance practices," 536 U.S. at 366. Petitioners contend that Kentucky's AWP laws fall outside the scope of § 514(b)(2)(A) for two reasons. First, because Kentucky has failed to "specifically direc[t]" its AWP laws towards the insurance industry; and second, because the AWP laws do not regulate an insurance practice. We find neither contention persuasive.

A

Petitioners claim that Kentucky's statutes are not "specifically directed toward" insurers because they regulate not only the insurance industry but also doctors who seek to form and maintain limited provider networks with HMOs. That is to say, the AWP laws equally prevent *providers* from entering into limited network contracts with *insurers*, just as they prevent insurers from creating exclusive networks in the first place. We do not think it follows that Kentucky has failed to specifically direct its AWP laws at the insurance industry.

Neither of Kentucky's AWP statutes, by its terms, imposes any prohibitions or requirements on health care providers. See Ky. Rev. Stat. Ann. § 304.17A–270 (imposing obligations only on "health insurer[s]" not to discriminate against any willing provider); § 304.17A171 (imposing obligations only on "health benefit plan[s] that include chiropractic benefits"). And Kentucky health care providers are still capable of entering exclusive networks with insurers who conduct business outside the Commonwealth of Kentucky or who are otherwise not covered by §§ 304.17A–270 or 304.17A–171. Kentucky's statutes are transgressed only when a "health insurer," or a "health benefit plan that includes chiropractic benefits," excludes from its network a provider who is willing and able to meet its terms.

It is of course true that as a *consequence* of Kentucky's AWP laws, entities outside the insurance industry (such as health care providers) will be unable to enter into certain agreements with Kentucky insurers. But the same could be said about the state laws we held saved from preemption in *FMC Corp.* and *Rush Prudential.* Pennsylvania's law prohibiting insurers from exercising subrogation rights against an insured's tort recovery, see FMC Corp., supra, at 55 n.1, also prevented insureds from entering into enforceable contracts with insurers allowing subrogation. Illinois' requirement that HMOs provide independent review of whether services are "medically necessary," Rush Prudential, supra, at 372, likewise excluded insureds from joining an HMO that would have withheld the right to independent review in exchange for a lower premium. Yet neither case found the effects of these laws on noninsurers, significant though they may have been, inconsistent with the requirement that laws saved from preemption by § 514(b)(2)(A) be "specifically directed toward" the insurance industry. Regulations "directed toward" certain entities will almost always disable other entities from doing, with the regulated entities, what the regulations forbid; this does not suffice to place such regulation outside the scope of ERISA's savings clause.

B

Petitioners claim that the AWP laws do not regulate insurers with respect to an insurance practice because, unlike the state laws we held saved from preemption in *Metropolitan Life Insurance Co. v. Massachusetts,* 471 U.S. 724 (1985), *UNUM* [*Life Insurance Co. of America v. Ward,* 526 U.S. 358 (1999),] and *Rush Prudential,* they do not control the actual terms of insurance policies. Rather, they focus upon the relationship between an insurer and *third party providers*—which in petitioners' view does not constitute an "insurance practice."

P's 2nd argument

* * *

III

Our prior decisions construing § 514(b)(2)(A) have relied, to varying degrees, on our cases interpreting §§ 2(a) and 2(b) of the McCarran-Ferguson Act. In determining whether certain practices constitute "the *business of* insurance" under the McCarran-Ferguson Act, our cases have looked to three factors: "*first*, whether the practice has the effect of transferring or spreading a policyholder's risk; *second*, whether the practice is an integral part of the policy relationship between the insurer and the insured; and *third*, whether the practice is limited to entities within the insurance industry." United Labor Life Ins. Co. v. Pireno, 458 U.S. 119, 129 (1982).

We believe that our use of the McCarran-Ferguson case law in the ERISA context has misdirected attention, failed to provide clear guidance to lower federal courts, and, as this case demonstrates, added little to the relevant analysis. That is unsurprising, since the statutory language of § 514(b)(2)(A) differs substantially from that of the McCarran-Ferguson Act. Rather than concerning itself with whether certain practices constitute "[t]he business of insurance," 15 U.S.C. § 1012(a), or whether a state law was "enacted . . . *for the purpose of* regulating the business of insurance," § 1012(b), ERISA § 514(b)(2)(A) asks merely whether a state law is a "law . . . which regulates insurance, banking, or securities." What is more, the McCarran-Ferguson factors were developed in cases that characterized *conduct* by private actors, not state laws. * * * Today we make a clean break from the McCarran-Ferguson factors and hold that for a state law to be deemed a "law . . . which regulates insurance" under § 514(b)(2)(A), it must satisfy two requirements. First, the state law must be specifically directed toward entities engaged in insurance. See Pilot Life, 481 U.S. at 50; UNUM, 526 U.S. at 368; Rush Prudential, 536 U.S. at 366. Second, * * * the state law must substantially affect the risk pooling arrangement between the insurer and the insured. Kentucky's law satisfies each of these requirements.

For these reasons, we affirm the judgment of the Sixth Circuit.

NOTES AND QUESTIONS

1.   Miller's *"Specifically Directed" Prong.* In support of the first prong of the *Miller* test—whether the state law is "specifically directed" at the insurance industry— the Supreme Court cited in support its prior decision in *UNUM Life Insurance Co. of America v. Ward*, 526 U.S. 358 (1999). In *UNUM*, the plaintiff Ward was a participant in his employer's long-term disability plan, which was insured through a group policy. The policy required that a claim for disability benefits had to be provided to the insurance company no later than one year and 180 days after the onset of the disability. Ward became permanently disabled, but did not submit a claim for

benefits under the plan to the insurance company until five months after the policy deadline had expired. When the insurance company denied Ward's claim as untimely, he brought suit under Section 502(a)(1)(B).

In support of the timeliness of his claim, Ward relied upon a line of California state court decisions that established the "notice-prejudice" rule. Under the notice-prejudice rule, an insurer cannot avoid payment of a claim as untimely unless the delay in presenting the claim created actual prejudice to the insurer. The Supreme Court ruled in *UNUM* that the notice-prejudice rule was saved from ERISA preemption as a state law that regulated insurance under Section 514(b)(2)(A). Fundamentally, the Supreme Court viewed California's notice-prejudice rule, unlike the plaintiff's Mississippi common law claim in *Pilot Life*, as unique to the insurance industry. The key distinguishing factor was that the insurance company was unable to point to *any* California authority outside of the insurance industry context where the notice-prejudice rule had been applied. It was this fact that convinced the Supreme Court that the Mississippi common law claim in *Pilot Life* was distinguishable from the notice-prejudice rule at issue in *UNUM*.

2. Miller's *"Risk Pooling Arrangement" Prong.* In an omitted part of the opinion, the Supreme Court elaborated on the intended meaning of the second prong of the *Miller* test:

> We emphasize that conditions on the right to engage in the business of insurance must also substantially affect the risk pooling arrangement between the insurer and the insured to be covered by ERISA's savings clause. Otherwise, any state law aimed at insurance companies could be deemed a law that "regulates insurance." * * * A state law requiring all insurance companies to pay their janitors twice the minimum wage would not "regulate insurance," even though it would be a prerequisite to engaging in the business of insurance, because it does not substantially affect the risk pooling arrangement undertaken by insurer and insured. Petitioners contend that Kentucky's AWP statutes fail this test as well, since they do not alter or affect the terms of insurance policies, but concern only the relationship between insureds and third-party providers. We disagree. We have never held that state laws must alter or control the actual terms of insurance policies to be deemed "laws ... which regulat[e] insurance" under § 514(b)(2)(A); it suffices that they substantially affect the risk pooling arrangement between insurer and insured. By expanding the number of providers from whom an insured may receive health services, AWP laws alter the scope of permissible bargains between insurers and insureds in a manner similar to the mandated-benefit laws we upheld in *Metropolitan Life*, the notice-prejudice rule we sustained in *UNUM*, and the independent-review provisions we approved in *Rush Prudential*. No longer may Kentucky insureds seek insurance from a closed network of health care providers in exchange for a lower

premium. The AWP prohibition substantially affects the type of risk pooling arrangements that insurers may offer.

538 U.S. 329 (2003) (footnote omitted).

In *Aetna Health Inc. v. Davila*, the plaintiffs were participants in their respective employers' health care plans. Claims for benefits under each employer's plan were administered by a HMO. As with all health care plans today, each employer's plan contained a medical necessity clause that limited coverage under the plan to medical treatments that were found by the plan's HMO administrator to be medically necessary. The plaintiffs alleged that they each suffered injuries as a result of the HMO administrator's decision to deny coverage of the medical treatment recommended by the participant's treating physician as not medically necessary. Rather than bringing a claim under ERISA, each plaintiff sued the plan's HMO administrator under a Texas statute that imposed a duty on a HMO to exercise ordinary care where making health care treatment decisions.

The Supreme Court held in *Davila* that the plaintiffs' claims under Texas law were properly dismissed by the federal district court as completely preempted by ERISA Section 502(a)(1)(B). As you read the opinion in *Davila*, focus on the Supreme Court's characterization of the plaintiffs' claims as claims for health care plan benefits that were denied by the plan administrator. Do you find the Court's characterization of the plaintiffs' claims persuasive?

AETNA HEALTH INC. V. DAVILA

United States Supreme Court, 2004.
542 U.S. 200, 124 S.Ct. 2488, 159 L.Ed.2d 312.

JUSTICE THOMAS delivered the opinion of the Court.

In these consolidated cases, two individuals sued their respective health maintenance organizations (HMOs) for alleged failures to exercise ordinary care in the handling of coverage decisions, in violation of a duty imposed by the Texas Health Care Liability Act (THCLA). We granted certiorari to decide whether the individuals' causes of action are completely pre-empted by the "interlocking, interrelated, and interdependent remedial scheme," Massachusetts Mut. Life Ins. Co. v. Russell, 473 U.S. 134, 146 (1985), found at § 502(a) of the Employee Retirement Income Security Act of 1974 (ERISA). We hold that the causes of action are completely pre-empted and hence removable from state to federal court. The Court of Appeals, having reached a contrary conclusion, is reversed.

I

A

Respondent Juan Davila is a participant, and respondent Ruby Calad is a beneficiary, in ERISA-regulated employee benefit plans. Their respective plan sponsors had entered into agreements with petitioners, Aetna Health Inc. and CIGNA Healthcare of Texas, Inc., to administer the plans. Under Davila's plan, for instance, Aetna reviews requests for coverage and pays providers, such as doctors, hospitals, and nursing homes, which perform covered services for members; under Calad's plan sponsor's agreement, CIGNA is responsible for plan benefits and coverage decisions.

Respondents both suffered injuries allegedly arising from Aetna's and CIGNA's decisions not to provide coverage for certain treatment and services recommended by respondents' treating physicians. Davila's treating physician prescribed Vioxx to remedy Davila's arthritis pain, but Aetna refused to pay for it. Davila did not appeal or contest this decision, nor did he purchase Vioxx with his own resources and seek reimbursement. Instead, Davila began taking Naprosyn, from which he allegedly suffered a severe reaction that required extensive treatment and hospitalization. Calad underwent surgery, and although her treating physician recommended an extended hospital stay, a CIGNA discharge nurse determined that Calad did not meet the plan's criteria for a continued hospital stay. CIGNA consequently denied coverage for the extended hospital stay. Calad experienced postsurgery complications forcing her to return to the hospital. She alleges that these complications would not have occurred had CIGNA approved coverage for a longer hospital stay.

Respondents brought separate suits in Texas state court against petitioners. Invoking [the THCLA], respondents argued that petitioners' refusal to cover the requested services violated their "duty to exercise ordinary care when making health care treatment decisions," and that these refusals "proximately caused" their injuries. Petitioners removed the cases to Federal District Courts, arguing that respondents' causes of action fit within the scope of, and were therefore completely pre-empted by, ERISA § 502(a). The respective District Courts agreed, and declined to remand the cases to state court. Because respondents refused to amend their complaints to bring explicit ERISA claims, the District Courts dismissed the complaints with prejudice.

B

Both Davila and Calad appealed the refusals to remand to state court. The United States Court of Appeals for the Fifth Circuit consolidated their cases with several others raising similar issues. * * * After examining the causes of action available under § 502(a), the Court of Appeals determined that respondents' claims could possibly fall under only two: § 502(a)(1)(B), which provides a cause of action for the recovery of wrongfully denied benefits, and § 502(a)(2), which allows suit against a plan fiduciary for breaches of fiduciary duty to the plan.

[handwritten margin note: where these claims would've fallen under ERISA]

Analyzing § 502(a)(2) first, the Court of Appeals concluded that, under Pegram v. Herdrich, 530 U.S. 211 (2000), the decisions for which petitioners were being sued were "mixed eligibility and treatment decisions" and hence were not fiduciary in nature. The Court of Appeals next determined that respondents' claims did not fall within § 502(a)(1)(B)'s scope. It found significant that respondents "assert tort claims," while § 502(a)(1)(B) "creates a cause of action for breach of contract," and also that respondents "are not seeking reimbursement for benefits denied them," but rather request "tort damages" arising from "an external, statutorily imposed duty of 'ordinary care.'" From *Rush Prudential HMO, Inc. v. Moran,* 536 U.S. 355 (2002), the Court of Appeals derived the principle that complete pre-emption is limited to situations in which "States . . . duplicate the causes of action listed in ERISA § 502(a)," and concluded that "[b]ecause the THCLA does not provide an action for collecting benefits," it fell outside the scope of § 502(a)(1)(B).

II

A

Under the removal statute, "any civil action brought in a State court of which the district courts of the United States have original jurisdiction, may be removed by the defendant" to federal court. 28 U.S.C. § 1441(a). One category of cases of which district courts have original jurisdiction are "federal question" cases: cases "arising under the Constitution, laws, or treaties of the United States." § 1331. We face in these cases the issue whether respondents' causes of action arise under federal law.

Ordinarily, determining whether a particular case arises under federal law turns on the "well-pleaded complaint" rule. Franchise Tax Bd. of Cal. v. Construction Laborers Vacation Trust, 463 U.S. 1, 9–10 (1983). The Court has explained that

> whether a case is one arising under the Constitution or a law or treaty of the United States, in the sense of the jurisdictional statute[,]. . .must be determined from what necessarily appears in the plaintiff's statement of his own claim in the bill or declaration, unaided by anything alleged in anticipation of

avoidance of defenses which it is thought the defendant may interpose. Taylor v. Anderson, 234 U.S. 74, 75–76 (1914).

In particular, the existence of a federal defense normally does not create statutory "arising under" jurisdiction, Louisville & Nashville R. Co. v. Mottley, 211 U.S. 149 (1908), and "a defendant may not [generally] remove a case to federal court unless the *plaintiff's* complaint establishes that the case 'arises under' federal law." Franchise Tax Bd., supra, at 10. There is an exception, however, to the well-pleaded complaint rule. "[W]hen a federal statute wholly displaces the state-law cause of action through complete pre-emption," the state claim can be removed. Beneficial Nat. Bank v. Anderson, 539 U.S. 1, 8 (2003). This is so because "[w]hen the federal statute completely pre-empts the state-law cause of action, a claim which comes within the scope of that cause of action, even if pleaded in terms of state law, is in reality based on federal law." Id. ERISA is one of these statutes.

B

Congress enacted ERISA to "protect. . .the interests of participants in employee benefit plans and their beneficiaries" by setting out substantive regulatory requirements for employee benefit plans and to "provid[e] for appropriate remedies, sanctions, and ready access to the Federal courts." ERISA § 2(b). The purpose of ERISA is to provide a uniform regulatory regime over employee benefit plans. To this end, ERISA includes expansive pre-emption provisions, see ERISA § 514, which are intended to ensure that employee benefit plan regulation would be "exclusively a federal concern." Alessi v. Raybestos-Manhattan, Inc., 451 U.S. 504, 523 (1981).

ERISA's "comprehensive legislative scheme" includes "an integrated system of procedures for enforcement." Russell, 473 U.S. at 147. This integrated enforcement mechanism, ERISA § 502(a), is a distinctive feature of ERISA, and essential to accomplish Congress' purpose of creating a comprehensive statute for the regulation of employee benefit plans. As the Court said in *Pilot Life Ins. Co. v. Dedeaux,* 481 U.S. 41 (1987):

> [T]he detailed provisions of § 502(a) set forth a comprehensive civil enforcement scheme that represents a careful balancing of the need for prompt and fair claims settlement procedures against the public interest in encouraging the formation of employee benefit plans. The policy choices reflected in the inclusion of certain remedies and the exclusion of others under the federal scheme would be completely undermined if ERISA-plan participants and beneficiaries were free to obtain remedies under state law that Congress rejected in ERISA. "The six carefully integrated civil enforcement provisions found in § 502(a) of the statute as finally enacted . . . provide strong

evidence that Congress did *not* intend to authorize other remedies that it simply forgot to incorporate expressly." Id. at 54 (quoting Russell, supra, at 146).

Therefore, any state-law cause of action that duplicates, supplements, or supplants the ERISA civil enforcement remedy conflicts with the clear congressional intent to make the ERISA remedy exclusive and is therefore pre-empted. See 481 U.S. at 54–56; see also Ingersoll-Rand Co. v. McClendon, 498 U.S. 133, 143–145 (1990).

The pre-emptive force of ERISA § 502(a) is still stronger. In *Metropolitan Life Ins. Co. v. Taylor,* 481 U.S. 58, 65–66 (1987), the Court determined that the similarity of the language used in the Labor Management Relations Act, 1947 (LMRA), and ERISA, combined with the "clear intention" of Congress "to make § 502(a)(1)(B) suits brought by participants or beneficiaries federal questions for the purposes of federal court jurisdiction in like manner as § 301 of the LMRA," established that ERISA § 502(a)(1)(B)'s pre-emptive force mirrored the pre-emptive force of LMRA § 301. Since LMRA § 301 converts state causes of action into federal ones for purposes of determining the propriety of removal, see Avco Corp. v. Machinists, 390 U.S. 557, (1968), so too does ERISA § 502(a)(1)(B). Thus, the ERISA civil enforcement mechanism is one of those provisions with such "extraordinary pre-emptive power" that it "converts an ordinary state common law complaint into one stating a federal claim for purposes of the well-pleaded complaint rule." Metropolitan Life, 481 U.S. at 65–66. Hence, "causes of action within the scope of the civil enforcement provisions of § 502(a) [are] removable to federal court." Id. at 66.

civil enforcement
ERISA

III

A

ERISA § 502(a)(1)(B) provides:

> A civil action may be brought—(1) by a participant or beneficiary— . . . (B) to recover benefits due to him under the terms of his plan, to enforce his rights under the terms of the plan, or to clarify his rights to future benefits under the terms of the plan. 29 U.S.C. § 1132(a)(1)(B).

This provision is relatively straightforward. If a participant or beneficiary believes that benefits promised to him under the terms of the plan are not provided, he can bring suit seeking provision of those benefits. A participant or beneficiary can also bring suit generically to "enforce his rights" under the plan, or to clarify any of his rights to future benefits. Any dispute over the precise terms of the plan is resolved by a court under a *de novo* review standard, unless the terms of the plan "giv[e] the administrator or fiduciary discretionary authority to determine eligibility for benefits or to construe the terms of the plan." Firestone Tire & Rubber Co. v. Bruch, 489 U.S. 101, 115 (1989).

It follows that if an individual brings suit complaining of a denial of coverage for medical care, where the individual is entitled to such coverage only because of the terms of an ERISA-regulated employee benefit plan, and where no legal duty (state or federal) independent of ERISA or the plan terms is violated, then the suit falls "within the scope of" ERISA § 502(a)(1)(B). Metropolitan Life, supra, at 66. In other words, if an individual, at some point in time, could have brought his claim under ERISA § 502(a)(1)(B), and where there is no other independent legal duty that is implicated by a defendant's actions, then the individual's cause of action is completely pre-empted by ERISA § 502(a)(1)(B).

To determine whether respondents' causes of action fall "within the scope" of ERISA § 502(a)(1)(B), we must examine respondents' complaints, the statute on which their claims are based (the THCLA), and the various plan documents. Davila alleges that Aetna provides health coverage under his employer's health benefits plan. Davila also alleges that after his primary care physician prescribed Vioxx, Aetna refused to pay for it. The only action complained of was Aetna's refusal to approve payment for Davila's Vioxx prescription. Further, the only relationship Aetna had with Davila was its partial administration of Davila's employer's benefit plan.

Similarly, Calad alleges that she receives, as her husband's beneficiary under an ERISA-regulated benefit plan, health coverage from CIGNA. She alleges that she was informed by CIGNA, upon admittance into a hospital for major surgery, that she would be authorized to stay for only one day. She also alleges that CIGNA, acting through a discharge nurse, refused to authorize more than a single day despite the advice and recommendation of her treating physician. Calad contests only CIGNA's decision to refuse coverage for her hospital stay. And, as in Davila's case, the only connection between Calad and CIGNA is CIGNA's administration of portions of Calad's ERISA-regulated benefit plan.

It is clear, then, that respondents complain only about denials of coverage promised under the terms of ERISA-regulated employee benefit plans. Upon the denial of benefits, respondents could have paid for the treatment themselves and then sought reimbursement through a § 502(a)(1)(B) action, or sought a preliminary injunction.

Respondents contend, however, that the complained-of actions violate legal duties that arise independently of ERISA or the terms of the employee benefit plans at issue in these cases. Both respondents brought suit specifically under the THCLA, alleging that petitioners "controlled, influenced, participated in and made decisions which affected the quality of the diagnosis, care, and treatment provided" in a manner that violated "the duty of ordinary care set forth in [the THCLA]." Respondents contend that this duty of ordinary care is an independent legal duty. * * *

The duties imposed by the THCLA in the context of these cases, however, do not arise independently of ERISA or the plan terms. The THCLA does impose a duty on managed care entities to "exercise ordinary care when making health care treatment decisions," and makes them liable for damages proximately caused by failures to abide by that duty. However, if a managed care entity correctly concluded that, under the terms of the relevant plan, a particular treatment was not covered, the managed care entity's denial of coverage would not be a proximate cause of any injuries arising from the denial. Rather, the failure of the plan itself to cover the requested treatment would be the proximate cause.[3] More significantly, the THCLA clearly states that "[t]he standards in Subsections (a) and (b) create no obligation on the part of the health insurance carrier, health maintenance organization, or other managed care entity to provide to an insured or enrollee treatment which is not covered by the health care plan of the entity." Hence, a managed care entity could not be subject to liability under the THCLA if it denied coverage for any treatment not covered by the health care plan that it was administering.

Thus, interpretation of the terms of respondents' benefit plans forms an essential part of their THCLA claim, and THCLA liability would exist here only because of petitioners' administration of ERISA-regulated benefit plans. Petitioners' potential liability under the THCLA in these cases, then, derives entirely from the particular rights and obligations established by the benefit plans. * * *

Hence, respondents bring suit only to rectify a wrongful denial of benefits promised under ERISA-regulated plans, and do not attempt to remedy any violation of a legal duty independent of ERISA. We hold that respondents' state causes of action fall "within the scope of" ERISA § 502(a)(1)(B), Metropolitan Life, 481 U.S. at 66, and are therefore completely pre-empted by ERISA § 502 and removable to federal district court.

B

The Court of Appeals came to a contrary conclusion for several reasons, all of them erroneous. First, the Court of Appeals found significant that respondents "assert a tort claim for tort damages" rather than "a contract claim for contract damages," and that respondents "are not seeking reimbursement for benefits denied them." But, distinguishing between pre-empted and non-pre-empted claims based on the particular

---

[3] To take a clear example, if the terms of the health care plan specifically exclude from coverage the cost of an appendectomy, then any injuries caused by the refusal to cover the appendectomy are properly attributed to the terms of the plan itself, not the managed care entity that applied those terms.

label affixed to them would "elevate form over substance and allow parties to evade" the pre-emptive scope of ERISA simply "by relabeling their contract claims as claims for tortious breach of contract." Allis-Chalmers Corp. v. Lueck, 471 U.S. 202, 211 (1985). Nor can the mere fact that the state cause of action attempts to authorize remedies beyond those authorized by ERISA § 502(a) put the cause of action outside the scope of the ERISA civil enforcement mechanism. In *Pilot Life, Metropolitan Life,* and *Ingersoll-Rand,* the plaintiffs all brought state claims that were labeled either tort or tort-like. See Pilot Life, 481 U.S. at 43 (suit for, inter alia, "Tortious Breach of Contract"); Metropolitan Life, 481 U.S. at 61–62 (suit requesting damages for "mental anguish caused by breach of [the] contract"); Ingersoll-Rand, 498 U.S. at 136 (suit brought under various tort and contract theories). And, the plaintiffs in these three cases all sought remedies beyond those authorized under ERISA. See Pilot Life, supra, at 43 (punitive damages); Metropolitan Life, supra, at 61 (mental anguish); Ingersoll-Rand, supra, at 136 (punitive damages, mental anguish). And, in all these cases, the plaintiffs' claims were pre-empted. The limited remedies available under ERISA are an inherent part of the "careful balancing" between ensuring fair and prompt enforcement of rights under a plan and the encouragement of the creation of such plans. Pilot Life, supra, at 55.

Second, the Court of Appeals believed that "the wording of [respondents'] plans is immaterial" to their claims, as "they invoke an external, statutorily imposed duty of 'ordinary care'." But as we have already discussed, the wording of the plans is certainly material to their state causes of action, and the duty of "ordinary care" that the THCLA creates is not external to their rights under their respective plans.

Ultimately, the Court of Appeals rested its decision on one line from *Rush Prudential.* There, we described our holding in *Ingersoll-Rand* as follows: "[W]hile state law duplicated the elements of a claim available under ERISA, it converted the remedy from an equitable one under § 1132(a)(3) (available exclusively in federal district courts) into a legal one for money damages (available in a state tribunal)." 536 U.S. at 379. The point of this sentence was to describe why the state cause of action in *Ingersoll-Rand* was pre-empted by ERISA § 502(a): It was pre-empted because it attempted to convert an equitable remedy into a legal remedy. Nowhere in *Rush Prudential* did we suggest that the pre-emptive force of ERISA § 502(a) is limited to the situation in which a state cause of action precisely duplicates a cause of action under ERISA § 502(a).

Nor would it be consistent with our precedent to conclude that only strictly duplicative state causes of action are pre-empted. Frequently, in order to receive exemplary damages on a state claim, a plaintiff must prove facts beyond the bare minimum necessary to establish entitlement to an award. Cf. Allis-Chalmers, 471 U.S. at 217 (bad-faith refusal to honor a claim needed to be proved in order to recover exemplary damages). In order to recover for mental anguish, for instance, the plaintiffs in *Ingersoll-Rand* and *Metropolitan Life* would presumably have had to prove the existence of mental anguish; there is no such element in an ordinary suit brought under ERISA § 502(a)(1)(B). See Ingersoll-Rand, supra, at 136; Metropolitan Life, supra, at 61. This did not save these state causes of action from pre-emption. Congress' intent to make the ERISA civil enforcement mechanism exclusive would be undermined if state causes of action that supplement the ERISA § 502(a) remedies were permitted, even if the elements of the state cause of action did not precisely duplicate the elements of an ERISA claim.

C

Respondents also argue—for the first time in their brief to this Court—that the THCLA is a law that regulates insurance, and hence that ERISA § 514(b)(2)(A) saves their causes of action from pre-emption (and thereby from complete pre-emption). This argument is unavailing. The existence of a comprehensive remedial scheme can demonstrate an "overpowering federal policy" that determines the interpretation of a statutory provision designed to save state law from being pre-empted. Rush Prudential, 536 U.S. at 375. ERISA's civil enforcement provision is one such example. See id.

As this Court stated in *Pilot Life,* "our understanding of [§ 514(b)(2)(A)] must be informed by the legislative intent concerning the civil enforcement provisions provided by ERISA § 502(a)." 481 U.S. at 52. The Court concluded that "[t]he policy choices reflected in the inclusion of certain remedies and the exclusion of others under the federal scheme would be completely undermined if ERISA-plan participants and beneficiaries were free to obtain remedies under state law that Congress rejected in ERISA." Id. at 54. The Court then held, based on

> the common-sense understanding of the saving clause, the McCarran-Ferguson Act factors defining the business of insurance, and, *most importantly,* the clear expression of congressional intent that ERISA's civil enforcement scheme be exclusive, ... that [the plaintiffs'] state law suit asserting improper processing of a claim for benefits under an ERISA-regulated plan is not saved by § 514(b)(2)(A). Id. at 57 (emphasis added).

Pilot Life's reasoning applies here with full force. Allowing respondents to proceed with their state-law suits would "pose an obstacle to the purposes and objectives of Congress." Id. at 52. As this Court has recognized in both *Rush Prudential* and *Pilot Life,* ERISA § 514(b)(2)(A) must be interpreted in light of the congressional intent to create an exclusive federal remedy in ERISA § 502(a). Under ordinary principles of conflict pre-emption, then, even a state law that can arguably be characterized as "regulating insurance" will be pre-empted if it provides a separate vehicle to assert a claim for benefits outside of, or in addition to, ERISA's remedial scheme.

IV

Respondents, their amici, and some Courts of Appeals have relied heavily upon *Pegram v. Herdrich,* 530 U.S. 211 (2000), in arguing that ERISA does not pre-empt or completely pre-empt state suits such as respondents'. They contend that *Pegram* makes it clear that causes of action such as respondents' do not "relate to [an] employee benefit plan," ERISA § 514(a), and hence are not pre-empted. See Cicio v. Does, 321 F.3d 83, 100–104 (2d Cir. 2003); see also Land v. CIGNA Healthcare, 339 F.3d 1286, 1292–1294 (11th Cir. 2003).

Pegram cannot be read so broadly. In *Pegram,* the plaintiff sued her physician-owned-and-operated HMO (which provided medical coverage through plaintiff's employer pursuant to an ERISA-regulated benefit plan) and her treating physician, both for medical malpractice and for a breach of an ERISA fiduciary duty. The plaintiff's treating physician was also the person charged with administering plaintiff's benefits; it was she who decided whether certain treatments were covered. We reasoned that the physician's "eligibility decision and the treatment decision were inextricably mixed." Id. at 229. We concluded that "Congress did not intend [the defendant HMO] or any other HMO to be treated as a fiduciary to the extent that it makes mixed eligibility decisions acting through its physicians." Id. at 231.

A benefit determination under ERISA, though, is generally a fiduciary act. See Bruch, 489 U.S. at 111–113. "At common law, fiduciary duties characteristically attach to decisions about managing assets and distributing property to beneficiaries." Pegram, supra, at 231; cf. 2A A. Scott & W. Fratcher, Law of Trusts §§ 182; 183 (4th ed.1987); G. Bogert & G. Bogert, Law of Trusts & Trustees § 541 (rev.2d ed.1993). Hence, a benefit determination is part and parcel of the ordinary fiduciary responsibilities connected to the administration of a plan. See Varity Corp. v. Howe, 516 U.S. 489, 512 (1996) (relevant plan fiduciaries owe a "fiduciary duty with respect to the interpretation of plan documents and the payment of claims"). The fact that a benefits determination is infused with medical judgments does not alter this result.

Pegram itself recognized this principle. *Pegram,* in highlighting its conclusion that "mixed eligibility decisions" were not fiduciary in nature, contrasted the operation of "[t]raditional trustees administer[ing] a medical trust" and "physicians through whom HMOs act." 530 U.S. at 231–232. A traditional medical trust is administered by "paying out money to buy medical care, whereas physicians making mixed eligibility decisions consume the money as well." Id. And, significantly, the Court stated that "[p]rivate trustees do not make treatment judgments." Id. at

232. But a trustee managing a medical trust undoubtedly must make administrative decisions that require the exercise of medical judgment. Petitioners are not the employers of respondents' treating physicians and are therefore in a somewhat analogous position to that of a trustee for a traditional medical trust.[6]

ERISA itself and its implementing regulations confirm this interpretation. ERISA defines a fiduciary as any person "to the extent . . . he has any discretionary authority or discretionary responsibility in the administration of [an employee benefit] plan." § 3(21)(A)(iii). When administering employee benefit plans, HMOs must make discretionary decisions regarding eligibility for plan benefits, and, in this regard, must be treated as plan fiduciaries. See Varity Corp., supra, at 511 (plan administrator "engages in a fiduciary act when making a discretionary determination about whether a claimant is entitled to benefits under the terms of the plan documents"). Also, ERISA § 503, which specifies minimum requirements for a plan's claim procedure, requires plans to "afford a reasonable opportunity to any participant whose claim for benefits has been denied for a full and fair review by the appropriate named fiduciary of the decision denying the claim." ERISA § 503(2). This strongly suggests that the ultimate decisionmaker in a plan regarding an award of benefits must be a fiduciary and must be acting as a fiduciary when determining a participant's or beneficiary's claim. The relevant regulations also establish extensive requirements to ensure full and fair review of benefit denials. These regulations, on their face, apply equally to health benefit plans and other plans, and do not draw distinctions between medical and nonmedical benefits determinations. Indeed, the regulations strongly imply that benefits determinations involving medical judgments are, just as much as any other benefits determinations, actions by plan fiduciaries. Classifying any entity with discretionary authority over benefits determinations as anything but a plan fiduciary would thus conflict with ERISA's statutory and regulatory scheme.

Since administrators making benefits determinations, even determinations based extensively on medical judgments, are ordinarily acting as plan fiduciaries, it was essential to *Pegram*'s conclusion that the decisions challenged there were truly "mixed eligibility and treatment decisions," 530 U.S. at 229, i.e., medical necessity decisions made by the plaintiff's treating physician *qua* treating physician and *qua* benefits administrator. Put another way, the reasoning of *Pegram* "only make[s] sense where the underlying negligence also plausibly constitutes medical maltreatment by a party who can be deemed to be a treating physician or

---

[6] Both *Pilot Life* and *Metropolitan Life* support this understanding. The plaintiffs in *Pilot Life* and *Metropolitan Life* challenged disability determinations made by the insurers of their ERISA-regulated employee benefit plans. See Pilot Life Ins. Co. v. Dedeaux, 481 U.S. 41, 43 (1987); Metropolitan Life Ins. Co. v. Taylor, 481 U.S. 58, 61 (1987). A disability determination often involves medical judgments. Yet, in both *Pilot Life* and *Metropolitan Life,* the Court held that the causes of action were pre-empted. * * *

such a physician's employer." Cicio, 321 F.3d at 109 (Calabresi, J., dissenting in part). Here, however, petitioners are neither respondents' treating physicians nor the employers of respondents' treating physicians. Petitioners' coverage decisions, then, are pure eligibility decisions, and *Pegram* is not implicated.

V

We hold that respondents' causes of action, brought to remedy only the denial of benefits under ERISA-regulated benefit plans, fall within the scope of, and are completely pre-empted by, ERISA § 502(a)(1)(B), and thus removable to federal district court. The judgment of the Court of Appeals is reversed, and the cases are remanded for further proceedings consistent with this opinion.

* * *

NOTES AND QUESTIONS

1.   Do you agree with the majority's characterization in *Davila* of the plaintiffs' claims under the Texas Health Care Liability Act (THCLA) as claims for health care plan benefits that were denied by the plan's HMO administrator? Why or why not?

2.   If you represented a plan participant and were presented with the same facts as in *Davila*, how would you draft the complaint to bring a claim under ERISA in light of the Supreme Court's subsequent decision in *Cigna Corp. v. Amara*? What remedies under ERISA Section 502 would you seek?

3.   In *Varity Corporation v. Howe*, the Supreme Court stated that "we should expect that where Congress elsewhere provided adequate relief for a beneficiary's injury, there will likely be no need for further equitable relief, in which case such relief normally would not be 'appropriate.'" 516 U.S. 489, 515 (1996) (citation omitted). Given this statement, what would be your defense if you represented the defendant HMO in a case today and were presented with the same facts as in *Davila*?

4.   Can the Supreme Court's preemption analysis in *Davila* be reconciled with the Court's earlier opinion in *Rush Prudential HMO, Inc. v. Moran*, 536 U.S. 355 (2002)? Can *Davila* be reconciled with the Supreme Court's discussion in *Pegram v. Herdrich*, 530 U.S. 211 (2000), regarding when a HMO acts as a fiduciary for purposes of ERISA?

5.   *"Mixed" Decisions and Medical Necessity Clauses.* Judge Becker, writing a separate concurring opinion in *DiFelice v. Aetna U.S. Healthcare*, 346 F.3d 442 (3d Cir. 2003), described the practical difficulties inherent in characterizing a "mixed" decision by a HMO as either a treatment decision or an eligibility decision when eligibility for a proscribed course of treatment is based upon a medical necessity clause.

I write separately * * * to make clear my concern that the opinion masks extraordinary subtleties and complexities of this area of the law that cry out for clarification by the Congress, or, failing that, by the Supreme Court. In fact, I believe that the fundamental distinction upon which federal caselaw currently relies—between * * * eligibility and treatment decisions—is untenable, and that the blurring is becoming more severe, not less. To the extent we insist on categorizing every HMO decision as *either* an eligibility *or* a treatment decision, we contort ourselves into parsing terms that are conceptually indistinguishable, and we fail to come to terms with the realities of modern health coverage.

* * *

The case at bar makes evident the impossibility that any such simple rule can adequately reflect the Byzantine complexities of modern-day health care. Aetna's policy explicitly equated its coverage (i.e., eligibility) based on an assessment of medical necessity. But the medical necessity clause, which attempts to convert medical decisions into eligibility decisions, compounds the problem I address herein.* * *

DiFelice v. Aetna U.S. Healthcare, 346 F.3d at 461–62 (emphasis in original).

PROBLEM ON *ERISA* PREEMPTION AND STATE INSURANCE LAWS

Paul Plaintiff became disabled with a back injury and filed a claim for disability income payments under his employer's long-term disability plan (Plan). The Plan is insured through ABC Insurance Company (ABC). ABC initially delayed payment under the Plan for six months, and then made disability payments to Paul for four months. ABC stopped making payments to Paul after four months because Paul refused to supply additional documentation of continued disability. Paul refused to supply the additional documentation requested by ABC because under the terms of the Plan, such additional documentation is only required every twelve months.

Paul has filed a claim in state court against ABC pursuant to a state statute, which provides an insured with a statutory claim for treble damages if an insurance company wrongfully denies or delays payment to the insured of benefits provided under an insurance policy. (Assume that the facts of Paul's situation would give rise to a valid claim under the state statute.)

Is Paul's claim under the state statute preempted by ERISA?

PROBLEM ON COMPLETE PREEMPTION AND STATE LAW CLAIMS

Josephine Plaintiff, a participant in her employer's health care plan (Plan), was diagnosed with cancer. After unsuccessfully undergoing standard chemotherapy treatment for six months, Josephine's treating oncologist wrote a letter to the Plan administrator "requesting insurance approval for treatment of Josephine Plaintiff with high dose chemotherapy supported with peripheral tandem blood stem cell transplantation." The oncologist's letter described in detail Josephine's clinical history and prior treatment, and explained why Josephine would be a "good candidate" for the requested treatment. In particular, the letter stated that:

> The treatment of Ms. Plaintiff's cancer by high dose chemotherapy accompanied by a tandem ("double") stem cell transplantation is a well-established method of treatment with a superior response rate, complete response rate, post therapy disease-free interval, and possibly even a long-term cure in some patients, as compared to standard chemotherapy treatment. Although these facts are true for single transplant methodologies, the statistical response rate is further improved with double transplantation.

You are the Plan administrator. The Plan document provides that "only Medically Necessary Services are provided as benefits under the Plan." The Plan defines "Medically Necessary Services" as excluding "any procedure or service which is experimental or is not generally recognized to be effective for a particular condition, diagnosis, or body area." The Plan's Medical Director has reviewed the oncologist's letter and other information concerning Josephine's condition, and has recommended to you that the Plan deny the oncologist's requested double transplantation treatment on the ground that the treatment is not a "Medically Necessary Service." The Medical Director has recommended that the Plan should approve a single transplant treatment, which is a less costly treatment.

As the Plan administrator, you have the authority to:

A.   Approve the double transplantation treatment as requested by the treating oncologist.

B.   Deny the double transplantation treatment requested by the treating oncologist, but approve the single transplantation treatment recommended by the Plan's Medical Director.

What types of claims, under both ERISA and state law, may be brought against you in your capacity as the Plan administrator, depending on the course of action you choose and the outcome of Josephine's medical treatment?

2.   STATE LAWS EXPANDING HEALTH INSURANCE COVERAGE

Prior to the enactment of the Affordable Care Act in 2010, several states and municipalities had enacted laws designed to expand the scope of health care insurance coverage. Even after the employer mandate under the Affordable Care Act is fully implemented, the public policy goal of ensuring universal access to health care services may remain elusive, particularly for part-time workers. States and municipalities may seek to fill these coverage "gaps" through legislation. The two pre-Affordable Care Act cases presented in this subsection provide insights into the possible future role of state law in achieving more universal health care insurance coverage.

In *Retail Industry Leaders Association v. Fielder*, the Fourth Circuit held in a 2–1 decision that ERISA preempted the Maryland Fair Share Health Care Fund Act. In *Golden Gate Restaurant Association v. City and County of San Francisco*, reproduced following *Fielder*, the Ninth Circuit held that ERISA did not preempt the San Francisco Health Care Security Ordinance. In so ruling, the Ninth Circuit in *Golden Gate* proclaimed that "[w]e see no inconsistency between the Fourth Circuit's holding in *Fielder* and our holding in this case." 546 F.3d 639, 659 (9th Cir. 2008).

As you read *Fielder* and *Golden Gate*, consider first the immediate issue. Do you agree with the Ninth Circuit's statement quoted above, or does *Golden Gate* effectively create a circuit split with *Fielder*? Next, consider the broader implications of *Fielder* and *Golden Gate* for the future of state-level reforms. Could a state require an employer to spend a certain percentage of its total payroll on health insurance for employees, their dependents, and their spouses? Could a city or county require an employer to contribute a certain amount per hour worked toward health care insurance coverage for all employees, including part-time employees? If challenged on the ground of ERISA preemption, would the Supreme Court be more or less likely to uphold or strike down these types of state laws?

RETAIL INDUSTRY LEADERS ASSOCIATION V. FIELDER
United States Court of Appeals, Fourth Circuit, 2007.
475 F.3d 180.

NIEMEYER, CIRCUIT JUDGE.

On January 12, 2006, the Maryland General Assembly enacted the Fair Share Health Care Fund Act, which requires employers with 10,000 or more Maryland employees to spend at least 8% of their total payrolls on employees' health insurance costs or pay the amount their spending falls short to the State of Maryland. Resulting from a nationwide campaign to force Wal-Mart Stores, Inc., to increase health insurance benefits for its 16,000 Maryland employees, the Act's minimum spending provision was crafted to cover just Wal-Mart. The Retail Industry Leaders Association, of which Wal-Mart is a member, brought suit against James D. Fielder, Jr., the Maryland Secretary of Labor, Licensing, and Regulation, to declare that the Act is preempted by the Employee Retirement Income Security Act of 1974 ("ERISA") and to enjoin the Act's enforcement. On cross-motions for summary judgment, the district court entered judgment declaring that the Act is preempted by ERISA and therefore not enforceable, and this appeal followed.

Because Maryland's Fair Share Health Care Fund Act effectively requires employers in Maryland covered by the Act to restructure their employee health insurance plans, it conflicts with ERISA's goal of permitting uniform nationwide administration of these plans. We conclude therefore that the Maryland Act is preempted by ERISA and accordingly affirm.

I

Before enactment of the Fair Share Health Care Fund Act ("Fair Share Act"), the Maryland General Assembly heard extensive testimony about the rising costs of the Maryland Medical Assistance Program (Medicaid and children's health programs). It learned that between fiscal years 2003 and 2006, annual expenditures on the Program increased from $3.46 billion to $4.7 billion. The General Assembly also perceived that Wal-Mart Stores, Inc., a particularly large employer, provided its employees with a substandard level of healthcare benefits, forcing many Wal-Mart employees to depend on state-subsidized healthcare programs.* * *

In response, the General Assembly enacted the Fair Share Act in January 2006, to become effective January 1, 2007. The Act applies to employers that have at least 10,000 employees in Maryland and imposes spending and reporting requirements on such employers. The core provision provides:

> An employer that is not organized as a nonprofit organization and does not spend up to 8% of the total wages paid to employees in the State on health insurance costs shall pay to the Secretary an amount equal to the difference between what the employer spends for health insurance costs and an amount equal to 8% of the total wages paid to employees in the State.

An employer that fails to make the required payment is subject to a civil penalty of $250,000.

* * *

Any payments collected by the Secretary are directed to the Fair Share Health Care Fund, which is held by the Treasurer of the State and accounted for by the State Comptroller like all other state funds. The funds so collected, however, may be used only to support the Maryland Medical Assistance Program, which consists of Maryland's Medicaid and children's health programs.

The record discloses that only four employers have at least 10,000 employees in Maryland: Johns Hopkins University, Giant Food, Northrop Grumman, and Wal-Mart. The Fair Share Act subjected Johns Hopkins, as a nonprofit organization, to a lower 6% spending threshold which Johns Hopkins already satisfies. Giant Food, which employs unionized workers, spends over the 8% threshold on health insurance and lobbied in support of the Fair Share Act. Northrop Grumman, a defense contractor, was subject to the minimum spending requirement in an earlier version of the Act, but the General Assembly included an amendment that effectively excluded Northrop Grumman. Because Northrop Grumman has many high-salaried employees in Maryland, the General Assembly was able to exclude it by an amendment that permits an employer, in calculating its total wages paid, to exempt compensation paid to employees in excess of the median household income in Maryland. The parties agree that only Wal-Mart, who employs approximately 16,000 in Maryland, is currently subject to the Act's minimum spending requirements. Wal-Mart representatives testified that it spends about 7 to 8% of its total payroll on healthcare, falling short of the Act's 8% threshold.

* * *

Shortly after enactment of the Fair Share Act, the Retail Industry Leaders Association ("RILA") commenced this action against the Maryland Secretary of Labor, Licensing, and Regulation to declare the Act preempted by ERISA and to enjoin the Secretary from enforcing it. RILA is a trade association whose members are major companies from all segments of retailing, including Wal-Mart, as well as many of Wal-Mart's competitors, such as Best Buy Company, Target Corporation, Lowe's Companies, and IKEA. Many of these competitors are represented on RILA's board, which voted unanimously to authorize RILA to prosecute this action.

RILA's complaint alleged that the Fair Share Act was preempted by ERISA § 514.* * *

* * *

III

On the merits of whether ERISA preempts the Fair Share Act, the Secretary contends that the district court misunderstood the nature and effect of the Fair Share Act, erroneously finding that the Act mandates an employer's provision of healthcare benefits and therefore "relates to" ERISA plans. The Secretary offers a different characterization of the Fair Share Act—one with which ERISA is not concerned. He describes the Act as "part of the State's comprehensive scheme for planning, providing, and financing health care for its citizens." In his view, the Act imposes a payroll tax on covered employers and offers them a credit against that tax for their healthcare spending. The revenue from this tax funds a Fair Share Health Care Fund, which is used to offset the costs of Maryland's Medical Assistance Program.

To resolve the question whether ERISA preempts the Fair Share Act, we consider first the scope of ERISA's preemption provision, ERISA § 514(a), and then the nature and effect of the Fair Share Act to determine whether it falls within the scope of ERISA's preemption.

A

* * *

The primary objective of ERISA was to "provide a uniform regulatory regime over employee benefit plans." Aetna Health Inc. v. Davila, 542 U.S. 200, 208 (2004); see also Shaw, 463 U.S. at 98–100 (reviewing the legislative history of ERISA's preemption provision). To accomplish this objective, § 514(a) of ERISA broadly preempts "any and all State laws insofar as they may now or hereafter *relate to* any employee benefit plan" covered by ERISA. This preemption provision aims "to minimize the administrative and financial burden of complying with conflicting directives among States or between States and the Federal Government" and to reduce "the tailoring of plans and employer conduct to the peculiarities of the law of each jurisdiction." Ingersoll-Rand Co. v. McClendon, 498 U.S. 133, 142 (1990).

The language of ERISA's preemption provision—covering all laws that "relate to" an ERISA plan—is "clearly expansive." New York Conference of Blue Cross & Blue Shields Plans v. Travelers, 514 U.S. 645, 655 (1995). The Supreme Court has focused judicial analysis by explaining that a state law "relates to" an ERISA plan "if it has a *connection with* or *reference to* such a plan." Shaw, 463 U.S. at 97. But even these terms, "taken to extend to the furthest stretch of [their] indeterminacy," would have preemption "never run its course." Travelers, 514 U.S. at 655. Accordingly, we do not rely on "uncritical literalism" but attempt to ascertain whether Congress would have expected the Fair Share Act to be preempted. See id. at 656; California Div. of Labor Standards Enforcement v. Dillingham Constr., 519 U.S. 316, 325 (1997). * * *

A state law that directly regulates the structuring or administration of an ERISA plan is not saved by inclusion of a means for opting out of its requirements. See Egelhoff v. Egelhoff, 532 U.S. 141, 150–51 (2001). In *Egelhoff,* the Court held that ERISA preempted a Washington statute that voided the designation of a spouse as a beneficiary of a nonprobate asset, including ERISA-governed life insurance policies. Its effect was to require plan administrators to "pay benefits to the beneficiaries chosen by state laws, rather than to those identified in the plan documents." Id. at 147. Even though the statute permitted employers to opt out of the law with specific plan language, the Court struck the law down under ERISA's preemption provision because it still mandated that plan administrators "either follow Washington's beneficiary designation scheme or alter the terms of their plans so as to indicate that they will not follow it." Id. at 150. Additionally, a proliferation of laws like Washington's would have undermined ERISA's objective of sparing plan administrators the task of monitoring the laws of all 50 States and modifying their plan documents accordingly.

In sum, a state law has an impermissible "connection with" an ERISA plan if it directly regulates or effectively mandates some element of the structure or administration of employers' ERISA plans. On the other hand, a state law that creates only indirect economic incentives that affect but do not bind the choices of employers or their ERISA plans is generally not preempted. See Travelers, 514 U.S. at 658. In deciding which of these principles is applicable, we assess the effect of a state law on the ability of ERISA plans to be administered uniformly nationwide. Even if a state law provides a route by which ERISA plans can avoid the state law's requirements, taking that route might still be too disruptive of uniform plan administration to avoid preemption. See Egelhoff, 532 U.S. at 151.

B

We now consider the nature and effect of the Fair Share Act to determine whether it falls within ERISA's preemption. At its heart, the Fair Share Act requires every employer of 10,000 or more Maryland employees to pay to the State an amount that equals the difference between what the employer spends on "health insurance costs" (which includes any costs "to provide health benefits") and 8% of its payroll. As Wal-Mart noted by way of affidavit, it would not pay the State a sum of money that it could instead spend on its employees' healthcare. This would be the decision of any reasonable employer. Healthcare benefits are a part of the total package of employee compensation an employer gives in consideration for an employee's services. An employer would gain from increasing the compensation it offers employees through improved retention and performance of present employees and the ability to attract more and better new employees. In contrast, an employer would gain nothing in consideration of paying a greater sum of money to the State. Indeed, it might suffer from lower employee morale and increased public condemnation.

In effect, the only rational choice employers have under the Fair Share Act is to structure their ERISA healthcare benefit plans so as to meet the minimum spending threshold. The Act thus falls squarely under Shaw's prohibition of state mandates on how employers structure their ERISA plans. Because the Fair Share Act effectively mandates that employers structure their employee healthcare plans to provide a certain level of benefits, the Act has an obvious "connection with" employee benefit plans and so is preempted by ERISA.

* * *

It is a stretch to claim, as the Secretary does, that the Fair Share Act is a revenue statute of general application. When it was enacted, the General Assembly knew that it applied, and indeed intended that it apply, to one employer in Maryland—Wal-Mart. The General Assembly designed the statute to avoid applying the 8% level to Johns Hopkins University; it knew that Giant Food was unionized and already was providing more than 8%; and it amended the statute to avoid including Northrop Grumman. Even as the statute is written, the category of employers employing 10,000 employees in Maryland includes only four persons in Maryland and therefore could hardly be intended to function as a revenue act of general application.

While the Secretary argues that the Fair Share Act is designed to collect funds for medical care under the Maryland Medical Assistance Program, the core provision of the Act aims at requiring covered employers to provide medical benefits to employees. The effect of this provision will force employers to structure their recordkeeping and healthcare benefit spending to comply with the Fair Share Act. Functioning in that manner, the Act would disrupt employers' uniform administration of employee benefit plans on a nationwide basis. As Wal-Mart officials averred, Wal-Mart does not presently allocate its contributions to ERISA plans or other healthcare spending by State, and so the Fair Share Act would require it to segregate a separate pool of expenditures for Maryland employees.

This problem would not likely be confined to Maryland. As a result of similar efforts elsewhere to pressure Wal-Mart to increase its healthcare spending, other States and local governments have adopted or are considering healthcare spending mandates that would clash with the Fair Share Act. For example, two New York counties recently adopted provisions to require Wal-Mart to spend an amount on healthcare to be determined annually by an administrative agency. See N.Y.C. Admin. Code § 22–506(c)(2); Suffolk County, N.Y., Reg. Local Laws § 325–3. * * * If permitted to stand, these laws would force Wal-Mart to tailor its healthcare benefit plans to each specific State, and even to specific cities and counties. This is precisely the regulatory balkanization that Congress sought to avoid by enacting ERISA's preemption provision.

The Secretary argues that the Act is not mandatory and therefore does not, for preemption purposes, have a "connection with" employee benefit plans because it gives employers two options to avoid increasing benefits to employees. An employer can, under the Fair Share Act, (1) increase healthcare spending on employees in ways that do not qualify as ERISA plans; or (2) refuse to increase benefits to employees and pay the State the amount by which the employer's spending falls short of 8%. Because employers have these choices, the Secretary argues, the Fair

Share Act does not preclude Wal-Mart from continuing its uniform administration of ERISA plans nationwide. He maintains that the Fair Share Act is more akin to the laws upheld in *Travelers,* 514 U.S. at 658–59, and *Dillingham,* 519 U.S. at 319, which merely created economic incentives that affected employers' choices while not effectively dictating their choice. This argument fails for several reasons.

First, the laws involved in *Travelers* and *Dillingham* are inapposite because they dealt with regulations that only *indirectly* regulated ERISA plans. In *Travelers,* a New York law required hospitals to add a surcharge to the fees they demanded from most insurance companies, but the law exempted Blue Cross and Blue Shield from having to pay the surcharge. The effect of the law was to make Blue Cross and Blue Shield a cheaper and more attractive option for ERISA-covered healthcare plans to purchase. The Supreme Court upheld the law because it did not act *directly upon employers or their plans* but merely created "an indirect economic influence" on plans. 514 U.S. at 659. The New York law did not "bind plan administrators to any particular choice." Id. Nor did this incentive to choose Blue Cross/Blue Shield "preclude uniform administrative practice" on a nationwide basis. Id. The Court acknowledged, however, that a state law could produce such "acute, albeit indirect, economic effects. . .as to force an ERISA plan to adopt a certain scheme of substantive coverage or effectively restrict its choice of insurers" and therefore be preempted by ERISA. Id. at 668. In short, while the state law in *Travelers* directly regulated *hospitals'* charges to insurance companies, it only *indirectly* affected the prices ERISA plans would pay for insurance policies.

Likewise, in *Dillingham,* a California law directly regulated wages that contractors paid to apprentices on public construction projects, which only indirectly affected ERISA-covered apprenticeship programs' incentives to obtain state certification. 519 U.S. at 332–34. The law permitted contractors to pay apprentices a lower-than-prevailing wage if the apprentices participated in a state-certified apprentice program. The effect of the law was to create an *indirect* incentive for ERISA-governed programs to obtain state certification. Id. at 332–33. This incentive, the Court concluded, was not so strong that it effectively eliminated the programs' choice as to whether to seek state certification. Id. Noncertified apprentice programs were still free to supply apprentices for private projects at no disadvantage and to supply apprentices for public projects with just a slight disadvantage. Accordingly, the Court upheld the prevailing wage law as more akin to the law in *Travelers* than to the law in *Shaw.* Id. at 334.

In contrast, to *Travelers* and *Dillingham,* the Fair Share Act *directly* regulates employers' structuring of their employee health benefit plans. This tighter causal link between the regulation and employers' ERISA plans makes the Fair Share Act much more analogous to the regulations at issue in *Shaw* and *Egelhoff*, both of which were found to be preempted by ERISA.

* * *

Further, the Fair Share Act and a proliferation of similar laws in other jurisdictions would force Wal-Mart or any employer like it to monitor these varying laws and manipulate its healthcare spending to comply with them, whether by increasing contributions to its ERISA plans or navigating the narrow regulatory channel between the Fair Share Act's definition of healthcare spending and ERISA's definition of an employee benefit plan. In this way, the Fair Share Act is directly analogous to the Washington State statute in *Egelhoff* that revoked a spouse's beneficiary designation upon divorce. Even though the Washington statute included an opt-out provision, the Court held the law to be preempted because it required plan administrators to "maintain a familiarity with the laws of all 50 States so that they can update their plans as necessary to satisfy the opt-out requirements of other, similar statutes." The Fair Share Act likewise would deny Wal-Mart the uniform nationwide administration of its healthcare plans by requiring it to keep an eye on conflicting state and local minimum spending requirements and adjust its healthcare spending accordingly.

* * * [T]he Secretary relies most heavily on its argument that the Fair Share Act gives employers the choice of paying the State rather than altering their healthcare spending. The Secretary contends that, in certain circumstances, it would be rational for an employer to choose to do so. It conceives that an employer, whose healthcare spending comes close to the 8% threshold, may find it more cost-effective to pay the State the required amount rather than incur the costs of altering the administration of its healthcare plans. The existence of this stylized scenario, however, does nothing to refute the fact that in *most* scenarios, the Act would cause an employer to alter the administration of its healthcare plans. Indeed, identifying the narrow conditions under which the Act would not force an employer to increase its spending on healthcare plans only reinforces the conclusion that the overwhelming effect of the Act is to mandate spending increases. This conclusion is further supported by the fact that Wal-Mart representatives averred that Wal-Mart would in fact increase healthcare spending rather than pay the State.

In short, the Fair Share Act leaves employers no reasonable choices except to change how they structure their employee benefit plans.

Because the Act directly regulates employers' provision of healthcare benefits, it has a "connection with" covered employers' ERISA plans and accordingly is preempted by ERISA.

* * *

V

The Maryland General Assembly, in furtherance of its effort to require Wal-Mart to spend more money on employee health benefits and thus reduce Wal-Mart's employees' reliance on Medicaid, enacted the Fair Share Act. Not disguised was Maryland's purpose to require Wal-Mart to change, at least in Maryland, its employee benefit plans and how they are administered. This goal, however, directly clashes with ERISA's preemption provision and ERISA's purpose of authorizing Wal-Mart and others like it to provide uniform health benefits to its employees on a nationwide basis.

Were we to approve Maryland's enactment solely for its noble purpose, we would be leading a charge against the foundational policy of ERISA, and surely other States and local governments would follow. As sensitive as we are to the right of Maryland and other States to enact laws of their own choosing, we are also bound to enforce ERISA as the "supreme Law of the Land." U.S. Const. art. VI.

The judgment of the district court is AFFIRMED.

MICHAEL, CIRCUIT JUDGE, dissenting:

Maryland, like most states, is wrestling with explosive growth in the cost of Medicaid. Innovative ideas for solving the funding crisis are required, and the federal government, as the co-sponsor of Medicaid, has consistently called upon the states to function as laboratories for developing workable solutions. In response to this call and its own funding predicament, Maryland enacted the Fair Share Health Care Fund Act (Maryland Act or Act) in 2006 to require very large employers, such as Wal-Mart Stores, Inc., to assume greater responsibility for employee health insurance costs that are now shunted to Medicaid. I respectfully dissent from the majority's opinion that the Maryland Act is preempted by ERISA. The Act offers a covered employer the option to pay an assessment into a state fund that will support Maryland's Medicaid program. Thus, the Act offers a means of compliance that does not impact ERISA plans, and it is not preempted.

* * *

GOLDEN GATE RESTAURANT ASSOCIATION V. CITY AND COUNTY OF SAN FRANCISCO

United States Court of Appeals, Ninth Circuit, 2008.
546 F.3d 639.

WILLIAM A. FLETCHER, CIRCUIT JUDGE:

Plaintiff Golden Gate Restaurant Association ("the Association") challenges the employer spending requirements of the newly enacted San Francisco Health Care Security Ordinance ("the Ordinance"). The Association argues that the federal Employee Retirement Income Security Act of 1974 ("ERISA") preempts the employer spending requirements of the Ordinance * * *.

* * * We hold that ERISA does not preempt the Ordinance.

* * *

III. THE ORDINANCE

The Ordinance mandates that covered employers make "required health care expenditures to or on behalf of" certain employees each quarter. "Covered employers" are employers engaging in business within the City that have an average of at least twenty employees performing work for compensation during a quarter, and nonprofit corporations with an average of at least fifty employees performing work for compensation during a quarter. "Covered employees" are individuals who (1) work in the City, (2) work at least ten hours per week, (3) have worked for the employer for at least ninety days, and (4) are not excluded from coverage by other provisions of the Ordinance.

The Ordinance sets the required health care expenditure for employers based on the Ordinance's "health care expenditure rate. For-profit employers with between twenty and ninety-nine employees and non-profit employers with fifty or more employees must make health care expenditures at a rate of $1.17 per hour. For-profit employers with one hundred or more employees must make expenditures at a rate of $1.76 per hour. Under the Ordinance, "[t]he required health care expenditure for a covered employer shall be calculated by multiplying the total number of hours paid for each of its covered employees during the quarter. . .by the applicable health care expenditure rate."

Regulations implementing the Ordinance specify that "[a] health care expenditure is any amount paid by a covered employer to its covered employees or to a third party on behalf of its covered employees for the purpose of providing health care services for covered employees or reimbursing the cost of such services for its covered employees." A "covered employer has discretion as to the type of health care expenditure it chooses to make for its covered employees." * * * [T]he Ordinance specifies that the definition of health care expenditure includ[es], but [is] not limited to

(a) contributions by [a covered] employer on behalf of its covered employees to a health savings account as defined under section 223 of the United States Internal Revenue Code * * *;

(b) reimbursement by such covered employer to its covered employees for expenses incurred in the purchase of health care services;

(c) payments by a covered employer to a third party for the purpose of providing health care services for covered employees;

(d) costs incurred by a covered employer in the direct delivery of health care services to its covered employees; and

(e) payments by a covered employer to the City to be used on behalf of covered employees. The City may use these payments to:

(i) fund membership in the [HAP] for uninsured San Francisco residents; and

(ii) establish and maintain reimbursement accounts for covered employees, whether or not those covered employees are San Francisco residents.

If an employer does not make required health care expenditures on behalf of employees in some other way, it may meet its spending requirement by making payments directly to the City * * *. We refer to this option as the City-payment option. If an employer elects the City-payment option, its covered employees who satisfy age and income requirements and are "uninsured San Francisco residents" may enroll in the HAP, and its other covered employees will be eligible for medical reimbursement accounts with the City. Covered employees may enroll in the HAP free of charge or at reduced rates. * * *

The Ordinance requires covered employers to "maintain accurate records of health care expenditures, required health care expenditures, and proof of such expenditures made each quarter each year," but it does not require them "to maintain such records in any particular form." Employers must provide the City with "reasonable access to such records." If an employer fails to comply with these requirements, the City will "presume[] that the employer did not make the required health expenditures for the quarter for which records are lacking, absent clear and convincing evidence otherwise."

The Ordinance includes a special provision for employers with self-insured health plans. An employer providing "health coverage to some or all of its covered employees through a self-funded/self-insured plan" will "comply with the spending requirement . . . if the preceding year's average expenditure rate per employee meets or exceeds the applicable expenditure rate" for the employer. Such employers do not need to keep track of their actual expenditures for each employee.

Relevant to our analysis, there are five categories of employers under the Ordinance. First are employers that have no ERISA plans ("No Coverage Employers"). Second are employers that have ERISA plans for all employees, and that spend at least as much as the Ordinance's required health care expenditure per employee ("Full High Coverage Employers"). Third are employers that have ERISA plans for some, but not all, employees, and that spend at least as much as the Ordinance's required health care expenditure per employee for employees under the ERISA plan ("Selective High Coverage Employers"). Fourth are employers that have ERISA plans for all employees, but that spend less than the Ordinance's required health care expenditure per employee ("Full Low Coverage Employers"). Fifth are employers that have ERISA plans for some, but not all, employees, and that spend less than the Ordinance's required health care expenditure per employee for employees under the ERISA plan ("Selective Low Coverage Employers").

No Coverage Employers may choose to continue without any ERISA plans. In that event, they can make their required health care expenditures directly to the City. If these employers choose, instead, to establish an ERISA plan, the Ordinance requires only that they make the required level of health care expenditures. They can do so by paying the full amount to the plan, or by paying part to the plan and part to the City. The Ordinance does not dictate which employees must be eligible for the plan, or what benefits a plan must provide.

Full High Coverage Employers may choose to leave their ERISA plans intact and unaltered. So long as they maintain records to show that they are making the required health care expenditures, they comply with the Ordinance.

Selective High Coverage Employers may choose to leave their ERISA plans intact and unaltered. In that event, for employees not covered by their ERISA plans, they can comply with the Ordinance by making the required health care expenditures to the City.

Full Low Coverage Employers may choose to leave their ERISA plans intact and unaltered. In that event, they can comply with the Ordinance by making payments to the City in an amount equal to the difference between their expenditures for the ERISA plans and the required health care expenditures under the Ordinance.

Selective Low Coverage Employers may choose to leave their ERISA plans intact and unaltered. In that event, they can comply with the Ordinance for employees enrolled in their ERISA plans by paying to the City the difference between their expenditures for the plans and the required health care expenditures under the Ordinance, and for employees not enrolled in their ERISA plans by paying to the City the full amount of the required health care expenditures.

We make two observations about the Ordinance. First, the Ordinance does not require employers to establish their own ERISA plans or to make any changes to any existing ERISA plans. Employers may choose to make up the difference between their existing health care expenditures and the minimum expenditures required by the Ordinance either by altering existing ERISA plans or by establishing new ERISA plans. However, they need not do so. The City-payment option allows employers to make payments directly to the City, if they so choose, without requiring them to establish, or to alter existing, ERISA plans. If employers choose to pay the City, the employees for whom those payments are made are entitled to receive either discounted enrollment in the HAP or medical reimbursement accounts with the City.

Second, the Ordinance is not concerned with the nature of the health care benefits an employer provides its employees. It is only concerned with the dollar amount of the payments an employer makes toward the provision of such benefits. An employer can satisfy its spending requirements by paying the City; it can satisfy those requirements by funding exclusively preventive care; it can satisfy those requirements by setting up an on-site clinic and reimbursing employees for the purchase of over-the-counter medications; or it can satisfy those requirements in some other manner, such as funding a traditional ERISA plan. The Ordinance does not look beyond the dollar amount spent, and it does not evaluate benefits derived from those dollars.

IV. DISCUSSION

* * *

Crafted as a compromise between employers and employees, ERISA has two primary purposes. First, from the perspective of employees and other beneficiaries of ERISA plans, "ERISA was passed by Congress in 1974 to safeguard employees from the abuse and mismanagement of funds that had been accumulated to finance various types of employee benefits." Massachusetts v. Morash, 490 U.S. 107, 112 (1989). "In enacting ERISA, Congress' primary concern was with the mismanagement of funds accumulated to finance employee benefits and the failure to pay employees benefits from accumulated funds. To that end, it established extensive reporting, disclosure, and fiduciary duty requirements to insure against the possibility that the employee's expectation of the benefit would be defeated through poor management by the plan administrator." Id. at 115. Second, from the perspective of employers, "[t]he purpose of ERISA is to provide a uniform regulatory regime over employee benefit plans." Aetna Health Inc. v. Davila, 542 U.S. 200, 208 (2004). Uniformity of regulation eases the administrative burdens on employers and plan administrators, thereby reducing costs to employers.

A.   PRESUMPTION AGAINST PREEMPTION

We begin by noting that state and local laws enjoy a presumption against preemption when they "clearly operate[ ] in a field that has been traditionally occupied by the States." De Buono v. NYSA-ILA Med. & Clinical Servs. Fund, 520 U.S. 806, 814 (1997). This presumption informs our preemption analysis. The presumption against preemption applies in ERISA cases. "[N]othing in the language of [ERISA] or the context of its passage indicates that Congress chose to displace general health care regulation, which historically has been a matter of local concern." N.Y. State Conference of Blue Cross & Blue Shield Plans v. Travelers Ins. Co., 514 U.S. 645, 661 (1995). * * *

The field in which the Ordinance operates is the provision of health care services to persons with low or moderate incomes. State and local governments have traditionally provided health care services to such persons. See Paul Star, The Social Transformation of American Medicine 185 (1982) (noting that other than the four-year period from 1879 to 1883, when there was a National Board of Health, "public health remained almost entirely a state and local responsibility"); id. at 181–82 (describing "the role of public dispensaries in treating the sick poor"); id. at 169 (describing the first phase of the hospital system in the United States, spanning 1751 to 1850, in which there were charitable hospitals "and public hospitals, descended from almshouses and operated by municipalities [and] by counties"); id. at 171 (noting that "[p]ublic hospitals generally treated the poor [and] relied on government appropriations rather than fees"). The Ordinance uses a novel approach to the provision of health services to such persons, but operates in a field that has long been the province of state and local governments, thereby "implement[ing] policies and values lying within the traditional domain of the States." Boggs, 520 U.S. at 840.

B.   PREEMPTION UNDER ERISA

* * *

The Association and the amicus, the Secretary of Labor, make two central arguments. First, they argue that the City-payment option under the Ordinance creates an ERISA plan. * * * Second, they argue that even if the City-payment option does not establish an ERISA plan, an employer's obligation to make payments at a certain level—whether or not the payments are made to the City—"relates to" the ERISA plans of covered employers and is thus preempted. We address these arguments in turn.

1.   THE CITY-PAYMENT OPTION DOES NOT CREATE AN ERISA "PLAN"

If the City-payment option does not create an "employee welfare benefit plan" within the meaning of ERISA, the first argument fails. The district court concluded that employers' payments to the City do not create an ERISA plan. * * * [W]e agree with the district court and hold that the City-payment option does not create an ERISA plan * * *.

* * *

2.   "RELATES TO" EMPLOYERS' ERISA PLANS

The Association's and the Secretary of Labor's second argument is that, even if the City-payment option does not create an ERISA plan, the Ordinance is preempted because it "relates to" *employers'* ERISA plans. ERISA § 514(a).

* * *

a.   "CONNECTION WITH" A PLAN

In *New York State Conference of Blue Cross & Blue Shield Plans v. Travelers Insurance Co.,* 514 U.S. 645, 655 (1995), the Court acknowledged the difficulty of interpreting § 514(a):

> If "relate to" were taken to extend to the furthest stretch of its indeterminacy, then for all practical purposes pre-emption would never run its course. . . . But that, of course, would be to read Congress's words of limitation as mere sham, and to read the presumption against pre-emption out of the law whenever Congress speaks to the matter with generality.

Likewise, the Court recognized that the two-part inquiry it had adopted to interpret § 514(a) did not provide much additional guidance in cases hinging on a law's "connection with" an employee benefit plan. "For the same reasons that infinite relations cannot be the measure of pre-emption, neither can infinite connections." Id. at 656.

We read *Travelers* as narrowing the Court's interpretation of the scope of § 514(a).The Court reasoned it had to "go beyond the unhelpful text and the frustrating difficulty of defining [§ 514(a)'s] key term, and look instead to the objectives of the ERISA statute as a guide to the scope of the state law that Congress understood would survive." Id. In this light, we employ a "holistic analysis guided by congressional intent." Dishman v. UNUM Life Ins. Co. of Am., 269 F.3d 974, 981 n. 15 (9th Cir.2001); see e.g., Egelhoff v. Egelhoff, 532 U.S. 141, 147 (2001).

As noted above, one "purpose of ERISA is to provide a uniform regulatory regime over employee benefit plans." Davila, 542 U.S. at 208. The purpose of ERISA's preemption provision is to "ensure [ ] that the administrative practices of a benefit plan will be governed by only a single set of regulations." Fort Halifax Packing Co., 482 U.S. 1, 11 (1987). In *Ingersoll-Rand Co. v. McClendon,* 498 U.S. 133, 142 (1990), the Court explained that

> Section 514(a) was intended to ensure that plans and plan sponsors would be subject to a uniform body of benefits law; the goal was to minimize the administrative and financial burden of complying with conflicting directives among States or between States and the Federal Government. Otherwise, the inefficiencies created could work to the detriment of plan beneficiaries.

In furtherance of ERISA's goal of ensuring that "plans and plan sponsors [are] subject to a uniform body of benefits laws," the Court in *Egelhoff v. Egelhoff,* 532 U.S. 141 (2001), struck down a Washington State law that directed a choice of beneficiary that conflicted with the choice provided in an ERISA plan. The Court held that a state or local law has an impermissible "connection with" ERISA plans where it "binds ERISA plan administrators to a particular choice of rules for determining beneficiary status[,] . . . rather than [allowing administrators to pay the benefits] to those identified in the plan documents." Id. at 147. Similarly, in *Shaw v. Delta Air Lines,* 463 U.S. 85, 97–100 (1983), the Court held that ERISA preempts state laws "which prohibit[ ] employers from structuring their employee benefit plans" in a particular manner or "which require employers to pay employees specific benefits."

* * *

The Ordinance in this case stands in stark contrast to the laws struck down in *Egelhoff* and *Shaw* * * *. The Ordinance does not require any employer to adopt an ERISA plan or other health plan. Nor does it require any employer to provide specific benefits through an existing ERISA plan or other health plan. Any employer covered by the Ordinance may fully discharge its expenditure obligations by making the required level of employee health care expenditures, whether those expenditures are made in whole or in part to an ERISA plan, or in whole or in part to the City. The Ordinance thus preserves ERISA's "uniform regulatory regime." See Davila, 542 U.S. at 208. The Ordinance also has no effect on "the administrative practices of a benefit plan," Fort Halifax, 482 U.S. at 11, unless an employer voluntarily elects to change those practices.

A covered employer may choose to adopt or to change an ERISA plan in lieu of making the required health care expenditures to the City. An employer may be influenced by the Ordinance to do so because, when faced with an unavoidable obligation to make a payment at a certain level, it may prefer to make that payment to an ERISA plan. However, as *Travelers* makes clear, such influence is entirely permissible.

In *Travelers,* a New York statute required hospitals to collect surcharges from patients covered by commercial insurance companies, including those administering ERISA plans, but not from patients covered by Blue Cross/Blue Shield plans. The difference in treatment was justified on the ground that "the Blues pay the hospitals promptly and efficiently and, more importantly, provide coverage for many subscribers whom the commercial insurers would reject as unacceptable risks." Travelers, 514 U.S. at 658. The Court recognized that the surcharge might influence "choices made by insurance buyers, including ERISA plans." But such an influence was not fatal to the New York statute: "An indirect economic influence . . . does not bind plan administrators to any particular choice and thus function as a regulation of an ERISA plan itself[.] . . . Nor does the indirect influence of the surcharges preclude uniform administrative practice [.]" Id. at 659–60.

In this case, the influence exerted by the Ordinance is even less direct than the influence in *Travelers.* In *Travelers,* the required surcharge on benefits provided under ERISA plans administered by commercial insurers inescapably changed the cost structure for those plans' health care benefits and thereby exerted economic pressure on the manner in which the plans would be administered. Here, by contrast, the Ordinance does not regulate benefits or charges for benefits provided by ERISA plans. Its only influence is on the employer who, because of the Ordinance, may choose to make its required health care expenditures to an ERISA plan rather than to the City.

Further, the Ordinance does not "bind[ ] ERISA plan administrators to a particular choice of rules" for determining plan eligibility or entitlement to particular benefits. See Egelhoff, 532 U.S. at 147. Employers may "structur[e] their employee benefit plans" in a variety of ways and need not "pay employees specific benefits." See Shaw, 463 U.S. at 97. The Ordinance affects employers, but it "leave[s] plan administrators right where they would be in any case." Travelers, 514 U.S. at 662.

Finally, the Ordinance does not impose on plan administrators any "administrative [or] financial burden of complying with conflicting directives" relating to benefits law. Ingersoll-Rand, 498 U.S. at 142. The Ordinance does impose an administrative burden on covered employers, for they must keep track of their obligations to make expenditures on behalf of covered employees and must maintain records to show that they have complied with the Ordinance. But these burdens exist whether or not a covered employer has an ERISA plan. Thus, they are burdens on the employer rather than on an ERISA plan.

* * *

C. *RETAIL INDUSTRY LEADERS ASSOCIATION V. FIELDER*

Finally, the Association contends that the Ordinance is preempted under the analysis set forth in *Retail Industry Leaders Association v. Fielder,* 475 F.3d 180, 183 (4th Cir.2007). The Association contends that we will create a circuit split if we uphold the Ordinance. We disagree. We see no inconsistency between the Fourth Circuit's holding in *Fielder* and our holding in this case.

We neither adopt nor reject the analysis of the Fourth Circuit in *Fielder.* The panel majority in that case held a Maryland law preempted over a forceful dissent. For purposes of argument, however, we assume that the panel majority in *Fielder* was correct. But even under the reasoning of the panel majority, San Francisco's Ordinance is valid.

The Maryland law at issue in *Fielder* required "employers with 10,000 or more Maryland employees to spend at least 8% of their total payrolls on employees' health insurance costs or pay the amount their spending falls short to the State of Maryland." The Maryland law gave nothing in return—either to an employer or its employees—for the employer's payment to the State.

Wal-Mart was the only employer in Maryland affected by the law's minimum spending requirements. On the face of the law, Wal-Mart appeared to have two options. To reach the required spending level of 8%, it could either increase contributions to its own ERISA plan, or it could pay money to the State of Maryland. But the Fourth Circuit concluded that, in practical fact, Wal-Mart had no choice. The court wrote that Wal-Mart had "noted by way of affidavit [that] it would not pay the State a sum of money that it could instead spend on its employees' healthcare." * * *

In stark contrast to the Maryland law in *Fielder,* the City-payment option under the San Francisco Ordinance offers employers a meaningful alternative that allows them to preserve the existing structure of their ERISA plans. If an employer elects to pay the City, that employer's employees are eligible for free or discounted enrollment in the HAP, or for medical reimbursement accounts. In contrast to the Maryland law, the San Francisco Ordinance provides tangible benefits to employees when their employers choose to pay the City rather than to establish or alter ERISA plans. In its motion for summary judgment, the Association provided no evidence to demonstrate that San Francisco employers are, in practical fact, compelled to alter or establish ERISA plans rather than to make payments to the City.

Because the City-payment option offers San Francisco employers a realistic alternative to creating or altering ERISA plans, the Ordinance does not "effectively mandate[ ] that employers structure their employee healthcare plans to provide a certain level of benefits." See Fielder, 475 F.3d at 193. * * * Unlike the Maryland law, the San Francisco Ordinance provides employers with a legitimate alternative to establishing or altering ERISA plans. See Travelers, 514 U.S. at 664 (stating that if the New York surcharges had been "an exorbitant tax," they might leave ERISA plan purchasers "with a Hobson's choice," thereby amounting to an impermissible substantive mandate, but concluding that there was no evidence "that the surcharges are so prohibitive as to force all health insurance consumers to contract with the Blues"). We therefore conclude that the San Francisco Ordinance does not compel covered employers to establish or to alter ERISA plans.

CONCLUSION

There may be better ways to provide health care than to require employers in the City of San Francisco to foot the bill. But our task is a narrow one, and it is beyond our province to evaluate the wisdom of the Ordinance now before us. We are asked only to decide whether § 514(a) of ERISA preempts the employer spending requirements of the Ordinance. We hold that it does not. The spending requirements do not establish an ERISA plan; nor do they have an impermissible connection with employers' ERISA plans, or make an impermissible reference to such plans.

We therefore REVERSE the judgment of the district court and REMAND with instructions to enter summary judgment in favor of the City * * *.

NOTES AND QUESTIONS

1.   *Comparing* Fielder *with* Golden Gate. At the end of its opinion in *Golden Gate*, the Ninth Circuit asserts that "[w]e see no inconsistency between the Fourth Circuit's holding in *Fielder* and our holding in this case." Do you agree?

2.   *Postscript*. Golden Gate Restaurant Association filed a petition for a writ of certiorari in the Supreme Court on June 8, 2009, arguing that the Ninth Circuit's opinion conflicted with the Fourth Circuit's decision in *RILA v. Fielder*. The City of San Francisco responded by denying that a circuit split existed, and further arguing that "the question presented by the petition may be mooted by national health care reform, so granting certiorari would not be a good use of the Court's resources." Brief for Respondent in Opposition, at 39. The Supreme Court invited the Solicitor General to present the views of the Obama Administration on the case. Previously, the Bush Administration had filed briefs in support of the position advanced by the Golden Gate Restaurant Association. This time, however, the Solicitor General's views differed. The Solicitor General urged the Supreme Court to deny the petition, arguing that "the intervening enactment of comprehensive federal health

care legislation has dramatically changed the landscape governing payment for health care, substantially reducing the importance of the question whether ERISA preempts state or local requirements and also giving rise to additional legal issues that have not been addressed by the federal Departments responsible for implementing the new legislation or by the courts. Accordingly, this Court's review of the ERISA preemption issue is not warranted at this time." Brief for the United States as Amicus Curiae, at 21. On June 28, 2010, the Supreme Court denied the Golden Gate Restaurant Association's petition for writ of certiorari without further comment.

E. DISCUSSION QUESTIONS FOR CHAPTER SEVEN

QUESTION ONE

How does ERISA's preemption of state law in combination with ERISA's claims and remedies scheme operate to limit the protections available to plan participants? To limit the costs to employers of sponsoring employee benefit plans? Are ERISA's provisions preempting state law claims and remedies consistent with Congress's policy objectives in enacting ERISA?

QUESTION TWO

In rendering preemption decisions under ERISA, to what extent should the Supreme Court be concerned with the potential implications for patients, health care providers, and national health care policy? Will the option of independent external review of denied claims for health care benefits by non-grandfathered plans significantly change the status quo for employers and plan participants?

QUESTION THREE

The plaintiffs in *Davila* argued that the Texas statute under which their claims were brought was saved from ERISA preemption as a state law regulating insurance. In rejecting this argument, the Supreme Court stated: "Under ordinary principles of conflict preemption, then, even a state law that can arguable be characterized as 'regulating insurance' will be preempted if it provides a separate vehicle to assert a claim for benefits outside of, or in addition to, ERISA's remedial scheme." Aetna Health, Inc. v. Davila, 542 U.S. 200, 217–18 (2004).

The federal courts usually apply conflict preemption principles when a federal statute overlaps with the provisions of state law, but the federal statute itself is silent concerning the scope of preemption of state law. E.g., Crosby v. National Foreign Trade Council, 530 U.S. 363, 372–73 & n. 6 (2000). In contrast, ERISA Section 514(b)(2)(A) expressly "saves" state laws regulating insurance from preemption by ERISA. In light of the express statutory language of ERISA Section 514(b)(2)(A), is it appropriate for the federal courts to apply "ordinary" conflict preemption principles when determining whether a state law that regulates insurance is preempted by ERISA? How much deference should the federal courts give to Congress's intent, as indicated by the express statutory language of ERISA Section 514(b)(2)(A), that state laws regulating insurance are to be "saved" from preemption by ERISA?

QUESTION FOUR

How do the provisions of the Affordable Care Act differ from the Maryland Fair Share Health Care Fund Act and the San Francisco Health Care Security Ordinance? What are the advantages and disadvantages of each statutory approach to health care reform?

APPENDIX A

ADOPTION AGREEMENT FOR SUNGARD BUSINESS SYSTEMS LLC NON-STANDARDIZED 401(K) PROFIT SHARING PLAN*

■ ■ ■

Non-Standardized 401(k) Profit Sharing Plan

ADOPTION AGREEMENT FOR

SUNGARD BUSINESS SYSTEMS LLC
NON STANDARDIZED 401(K) PROFIT SHARING PLAN

CAUTION: Failure to properly fill out this Adoption Agreement may result in disqualification of the Plan.

EMPLOYER INFORMATION
(An amendment to the Adoption Agreement is not needed solely to reflect a change in this Employer Information Section.)

1.   EMPLOYER'S NAME, ADDRESS, TELEPHONE NUMBER, TIN AND FISCAL YEAR

Name: _____

Address: _____
                        Street

_____   _____   _____
   City   State   Zip

Telephone: _____

Taxpayer Identification Number (TIN): _____

Employer's Fiscal Year ends: _____

2.   TYPE OF ENTITY
    a. [ ] Corporation (including tax-exempt or non-profit Corporation)
    b. [ ] Professional Service Corporation
    c. [ ] S Corporation
    d. [ ] Limited Liability Company that is taxed as:
          1. [ ] a partnership or sole proprietorship
          2. [ ] a Corporation
          3. [ ] an S Corporation
    e. [ ] Sole Proprietorship
    f. [ ] Partnership (including limited liability)
    g. [ ] Other: _____ (must be a legal entity recognized under federal income tax laws)

3.   AFFILIATED EMPLOYERS/PARTICIPATING EMPLOYERS (Plan Sections 1.7 and 1.61). Is the Employer an Affiliated Employer (i.e., a member of a controlled group or an affiliated service group (within the meaning of Code §414(b), (c), (m) or (o)))?
    a. [ ] No
    b. [ ] Yes, the Employer is a member of (select one or both of 1. - 2. AND select one of 3. - 4. below):
          1. [ ] A controlled group
          2. [ ] An affiliated service group

          AND, will any of the Affiliated Employers adopt the Plan as Participating Employers?
          3. [ ] Yes (Complete a participation agreement for each Participating Employer.)
          4. [ ] No (The Plan could fail to satisfy the Code §410(b) coverage rules.)

    MULTIPLE EMPLOYER PLAN (Plan Article XIV). Will any Employers who are not Affiliated Employers adopt this Plan as part of a multiple employer plan (MEP) arrangement?
    c. [ ] No
    d. [ ] Yes (Complete a participation agreement for each Participating Employer.)

PLAN INFORMATION
(An amendment to the Adoption Agreement is not needed solely to reflect a change in the information in Questions 9. through 11.)

4.   PLAN NAME:

_____

Non-Standardized 401(k) Profit Sharing Plan

5. PLAN STATUS
  a. [ ] New Plan
  b. [ ] Amendment and restatement of existing Plan
    PPA RESTATEMENT (leave blank if not applicable)
    1. [ ] This is an amendment and restatement to bring a plan into compliance with the Pension Protection Act of 2006 ("PPA") and other legislative and regulatory changes (i.e., the 6-year pre-approved plan restatement).

6. EFFECTIVE DATE (Plan Section 1.25) (complete a. if new plan; complete a. AND b. if an amendment and restatement)
  Initial Effective Date of Plan

  a. _____ (enter month day, year) (hereinafter called the "Effective Date" unless 6.b. is entered below)

  Restatement Effective Date. If this is an amendment and restatement, the effective date of the restatement (hereinafter called the "Effective Date") is:

  b. _____ (enter month day, year, may enter a restatement date that is the first day of the current Plan Year. Plan contains appropriate retroactive effective dates with respect to provisions for appropriate laws.)

7. PLAN YEAR (Plan Section 1.65) means, except as otherwise provided in d. below:
  a. [ ] the calendar year
  b. [ ] the twelve-month period ending on ___ (e.g., June 30th)
  c. [ ] other:_____ (e.g., a 52/53 week year ending on the date nearest the last Friday in December).

  SHORT PLAN YEAR (Plan Section 1.76). Select below if there is a Short Plan Year (if the effective date of participation is based on a Plan Year, then coordinate with Question 15) (leave blank if not applicable):
  d. [ ] beginning on _____ (enter month day, year; e.g., July 1, 2013)
    and ending on _____ (enter month day, year).

8. VALUATION DATE (Plan Section 1.86) means:
  a. [ ] every day that the Trustee (or Insurer), any transfer agent appointed by the Trustee (or Insurer) or the Employer, and any stock exchange used by such agent are open for business (daily valuation)
  b. [ ] the last day of each Plan Year
  c. [ ] the last day of each Plan Year half (semi-annual)
  d. [ ] the last day of each Plan Year quarter
  e. [ ] other (specify day or days): _____ (must be at least once each Plan Year)
  NOTE: The Plan always permits interim valuations.

9. PLAN NUMBER assigned by the Employer
  a. [ ] 001
  b. [ ] 002
  c. [ ] Other: _____

10. TRUSTEE(S) OR INSURER(S) (Plan Sections 1.44 and 1.84):
  a. [ ] **Insurer.** This Plan is funded exclusively with Contracts and the name of the Insurer(s) is:

    (1) _____ (2) _____ (if more than 2, add names to signature page).

  b. [ ] **Individual Trustee(s).** Individual Trustee(s) who serve as Trustee(s) over assets not subject to control by a corporate Trustee. (add additional Trustees as necessary)

  Name(s)   Title(s)

  _____ _____

  _____ _____

  _____ _____

Non-Standardized 401(k) Profit Sharing Plan

Address and telephone number
1. [ ] Use Employer address and telephone number
2. [ ] Use address and telephone number below:

Address: _____
Street

_____
City   State   Zip

Telephone: _____

c. [ ] **Corporate Trustee(s)** (add additional Trustees as necessary)

Name: _____

Address: _____
Street

_____
City   State   Zip

Telephone: _____

Directed/Discretionary Trustee. Unless otherwise specified below, if there is a corporate Trustee, it will serve as a Directed (nondiscretionary) Trustee (Plan Section 1.21) and if there is an individual Trustee, he or she will serve as a Discretionary Trustee (Plan Section 1.22) over all Plan assets (select all that apply; leave blank if defaults apply)

d. [ ] Directed Trustee exceptions (leave blank if no exceptions):
     Directed Trustee over specified Plan assets (select all that apply; leave blank if none apply)
     1. [ ] The corporate Trustee will serve as Directed Trustee over the following assets: _____
     2. [ ] The individual Trustee(s) will serve as Directed Trustee over the following assets: _____
     Individual Trustee will serve as Directed Trustee (may not be selected with d.1. or d.2.)
     3. [ ] over all Plan assets

e. [ ] Discretionary Trustee exceptions (leave blank if no exceptions):
     Discretionary Trustee over specified Plan assets (select all that apply; leave blank if none apply)
     1. [ ] The individual Trustee(s) will serve as Discretionary Trustee over the following assets: _____
     2. [ ] The corporate Trustee will serve as Discretionary Trustee over the following assets: _____
     Corporate Trustee will serve as Discretionary Trustee (may not be selected with e.1. or e.2.)
     3. [ ] over all Plan assets

NOTE: Appendix A to the Adoption Agreement (Special Effective Dates and Other Permitted Elections) or a separate agreement may be used to appoint a special Trustee for purposes of collecting delinquent contributions. If no such appointment is made, then except as provided in Plan Section 7.3(c), the Trustee will have such responsibility.

Separate trust. Will a separate trust agreement that is approved by the IRS for use with this Plan be used?
f. [ ] No
g. [ ] Yes

NOTE: If Yes is selected, an executed copy of the trust agreement between the Trustee and the Employer must be attached to this Plan. The Plan and trust agreement will be read and construed together. The responsibilities, rights and powers of the Trustee will be those specified in the trust agreement.

11.   ADMINISTRATOR'S NAME, ADDRESS AND TELEPHONE NUMBER
     (If none is named, the Employer will be the Administrator (Plan Section 1.5).)
     a. [ ] Employer (use Employer address and telephone number)
     b. [ ] Other:

Name: _____

Address: _____
Street

_____
City   State   Zip

Telephone: _____

Non-Standardized 401(k) Profit Sharing Plan

12. CONTRIBUTION TYPES
The selections made below must correspond with the selections made under the Contributions and Allocations Section of this Adoption Agreement.
FROZEN PLAN OR CONTRIBUTIONS HAVE BEEN SUSPENDED (Plan Section 4.1(c)) (optional)
a. [ ] This is a frozen Plan (i.e., all contributions cease) (if this is a temporary suspension, select a.2):
    1. [ ] All contributions ceased as of, or prior to, the effective date of this amendment and restatement and the prior Plan provisions are not reflected in this Adoption Agreement (may enter effective date at 3. below and/or select contributions at b. - h. (optional), skip questions 13-19 and 23-31)
    2. [ ] All contributions ceased or were suspended and the prior Plan provisions are reflected in this Adoption Agreement (must enter effective date at 3. below and select contributions at b. - h.)

    Effective date
    3. [ ] as of_____ (effective date is optional unless a.2. has been selected above or this is the amendment or restatement to freeze the Plan).

CONTRIBUTIONS
The Plan permits the following contributions (select one or more):
b. [ ] **Elective Deferrals** (Question 25). Also select below if Roth Elective Deferrals are permitted.
    1. [ ] Roth Elective Deferrals (Plan Section 1.73)
c. [ ] **401(k) "ADP test safe harbor contributions"** (Question 27)
    1. [ ] **401(k) "ADP test safe harbor contributions"** (other than QACA "ADP test safe harbor contributions") (Match, Nonelective)
    2. [ ] **QACA "ADP test safe harbor contributions"**
d. [ ] **Employer matching contributions** (Question 28)
e. [ ] **Employer profit sharing contributions** (includes "prevailing wage contributions") (Questions 29-30)
f. [ ] **Rollover contributions** (Question 46)
g. [ ] **After-tax voluntary Employee contributions** (Question 47)
h. [ ] **SIMPLE 401(k) contributions** (Plan Section 13.1) (may not be selected with 12.c., 12.d., 12.e. or 12.g.)

ELIGIBILITY REQUIREMENTS

13. ELIGIBLE EMPLOYEES (Plan Section 1.28) means all Employees (including Leased Employees) EXCEPT those Employees who are excluded below or elsewhere in the Plan:
a. [ ] **No excluded Employees.** There are no additional excluded Employees under the Plan (skip to Question 14).
b. [ ] **Exclusions - same for all contribution types.** The following Employees are not Eligible Employees for all contribution types (select one or more of e. - k. below; also select 1. for each exclusion selected at e. - j.):
c. [ ] **Exclusions - different exclusions apply.** The following Employees are not Eligible Employees for the designated contribution types (select one or more of d. - k. below; also select 1. OR all that apply of 2. - 4. for each exclusion selected at d. - j.):

NOTE: Unless otherwise specified in this Section, Elective Deferrals include Roth Elective Deferrals, after-tax voluntary Employee contributions, and rollover contributions; Matching includes QMACs; and Nonelective Profit Sharing includes QNECs. **"ADP test safe harbor contributions" (SH) (including those made pursuant to a QACA) and SIMPLE 401(k) contributions are subject to the exclusions for Elective Deferrals except as provided in Question 27.**

Exclusions	All Contributions		Elective Deferrals/SH	Matching	Nonelective Profit Sharing
d. No exclusions	N/A		2. [ ]	3. [ ]	4. [ ]
e. Union Employees (as defined in Plan Section 1.28)	1. [ ]	OR	2. [ ]	3. [ ]	4. [ ]
f. Nonresident aliens (as defined in Plan Section 1.28)	1. [ ]	OR	2. [ ]	3. [ ]	4. [ ]
g. Highly Compensated Employees (Plan Section 1.41)	1. [ ]	OR	2. [ ]	3. [ ]	4. [ ]
h. Leased Employees (Plan Section 1.49)	1. [ ]	OR	2. [ ]	3. [ ]	4. [ ]
i. Part-time/temporary/seasonal Employees. A part-time, temporary or seasonal Employee is an Employee whose regularly scheduled service is less than _____ Hours of Service in the relevant eligibility computation period (as defined in Plan Section 1.88). However, if any such excluded Employee actually completes a Year of Service, then such Employee will no longer be part of this excluded class.	1. [ ]	OR	2. [ ]	3. [ ]	4. [ ]

Non-Standardized 401(k) Profit Sharing Plan

j. Other: _____   1.[ ]   **OR**   2. [ ]   3. [ ]   4. [ ]

(must be definitely determinable, may not be based on age or length
of service (except in a manner consistent with i. above) or level of
Compensation, and, if using the average benefits test to satisfy Code
§410(b) coverage testing, must be a reasonable classification)

k. [ ] Other: _____ (must (1) specify contributions to which exclusions apply,
(2) be definitely determinable and not based on age or length of service (except in a manner consistent with i. above) or
level of Compensation, and, (3) if using the average benefits test to satisfy Code §410(b) coverage testing, be a
reasonable classification).

14. CONDITIONS OF ELIGIBILITY (Plan Section 3.1)

a. [ ] **No age or service required.** No age or service required for all contribution types (skip to Question 15).

b. [ ] **Eligibility - same for all contribution types.** An Eligible Employee will be eligible to participate in the Plan for all
contribution types upon satisfaction of the following (select one or more of e. - n. below; also select 1. (All
Contributions) for each condition selected at e. - m.):

c. [ ] **Eligibility - different conditions apply.** An Eligible Employee will be eligible to participate in the Plan upon
satisfaction of the following either for all contribution types or to the designated contribution type (select one or more
of d. - n. below; also select 1. OR all that apply of 2. - 4. for each condition selected at d. - m.):

NOTE: Unless otherwise specified in this Section, Elective Deferrals include Roth Elective Deferrals, after-tax voluntary
Employee contributions, and rollover contributions (unless otherwise selected at Question 46); Matching includes
QMACs; and Nonelective Profit Sharing includes QNECs. **"ADP test safe harbor contributions" (SH) (including
those made pursuant to a QACA) and SIMPLE 401(k) contributions are subject to the conditions for Elective
Deferrals except as provided in Question 27.**

Eligibility Conditions	All Contributions		Elective Deferrals/SH	Matching	Nonelective Profit Sharing
d. No age or service required	N/A		2. [ ]	3. [ ]	4. [ ]
e. Age 20 1/2	1.[ ]	**OR**	2. [ ]	3. [ ]	4. [ ]
f. Age 21	1.[ ]	**OR**	2. [ ]	3. [ ]	4. [ ]
g. Age _____ (may not exceed 21)	1.[ ]	**OR**	2. [ ]	3. [ ]	4. [ ]
h. _____ (not to exceed 12) months of service (elapsed time)	1.[ ]	**OR**	2. [ ]	3. [ ]	4. [ ]
i. 1 Year of Service	1.[ ]	**OR**	2. [ ]	3. [ ]	4. [ ]
j. 2 Years of Service	N/A	**OR**	N/A	3. [ ]	4. [ ]
k. _____ (not to exceed 12) consecutive month period from the Eligible Employee's employment commencement date and during which at least _____ (not to exceed 1,000) Hours of Service are completed. If an Employee does not complete the stated Hours of Service during the specified time period, the Employee is subject to the 1 Year of Service requirement in i. above.	1.[ ]	**OR**	2. [ ]	3. [ ]	4. [ ]
l. _____ (not to exceed 12) consecutive months of employment from the Eligible Employee's employment commencement date. If an Employee does not complete the stated number of months, the Employee is subject to the 1 Year of Service requirement in i. above.	1.[ ]	**OR**	2. [ ]	3. [ ]	4. [ ]
m. Other: _____	1.[ ]	**OR**	2. [ ]	3. [ ]	4. [ ]

(e.g., date on which 1,000 Hours of Service is completed within
the computation period) (must satisfy the Notes below)

n. [ ] Other: _____ (e.g., date on which 1,000 Hours of Service is completed within the
computation period) (must specify contributions to which conditions apply and satisfy the Notes below)

NOTE: If m. or n. is selected, the condition must be an age or service requirement that is definitely determinable and may not
exceed age 21 and for Elective Deferrals, 1 Year of Service; for Employer matching and/or Nonelective profit sharing
contributions, may not exceed 2 Years of Service. If more than 1 Year of Service is required for Employer matching
and/or Nonelective profit sharing contributions, 100% immediate vesting is required.

Non-Standardized 401(k) Profit Sharing Plan

NOTE: If the service requirement is or includes a fractional year, then, except in a manner consistent with k., an Employee will not be required to complete any specified number of Hours of Service to receive credit for such fractional year. If expressed in months of service, then an Employee will not be required to complete any specified number of Hours of Service in a particular month, unless selected in k. above. In both cases, the Plan must use the elapsed time method to determine service, except that the Hours of Service method will be used for the 1 Year of Service override (e.g., options k. and l.). In such case, select the Hours of Service method at Question 17.

NOTE: Year of Service means Period of Service if elapsed time method is chosen.

Waiver of conditions. The service and/or age requirements specified above will be waived in accordance with the following (leave blank if there are no waivers of conditions):

Requirements waived	All Contributions		Elective Deferrals/SH	Matching	Nonelective Profit Sharing
o. [ ] If employed on _____ the following requirements, and the entry date requirement, will be waived. The waiver applies to any Eligible Employee unless c. selected below. Such Employees will enter the Plan as of such date (select a. and/or b. AND c. if applicable; also select 1. OR all that apply of 2. - 4.):	1. [ ]	OR	2. [ ]	3. [ ]	4. [ ]
a. [ ] service requirement (may let part-time Eligible Employees into the Plan)					
b. [ ] age requirement					
c. [ ] waiver is for: _____ (e.g., Employees of a specific division or Employees covered by a Code §410(b)(6)(C) acquisition)					
p. [ ] If employed on _____ the following requirements, and the entry date requirement, will be waived. The waiver applies to any Eligible Employee unless c. selected below. Such Employees will enter the Plan as of such date (select a. and/or b. AND c. if applicable; also select 1. OR all that apply of 2. - 4.):	1. [ ]	OR	2. [ ]	3. [ ]	4. [ ]
a. [ ] service requirement (may let part-time Eligible Employees into the Plan)					
b. [ ] age requirement					
c. [ ] waiver is for: _____ (e.g., Employees of a specific division or Employees covered by a Code §410(b)(6)(C) acquisition)					

Amendment or restatement to change eligibility requirements

q. [ ] This amendment or restatement (or a prior amendment and restatement) modified the eligibility requirements and the prior eligibility conditions continue to apply to the Eligible Employees specified below. If this option is NOT selected, then all Eligible Employees must satisfy the eligibility conditions set forth above.

  1. [ ] The eligibility conditions above only apply to Eligible Employees who were not Participants as of the effective date of the modification.

  2. [ ] The eligibility conditions above only apply to individuals who were hired on or after the effective date of the modification.

15. EFFECTIVE DATE OF PARTICIPATION (ENTRY DATE) (Plan Section 3.2)

  a. [ ] **Entry date same for all contribution types.** An Eligible Employee who has satisfied the eligibility requirements will become a Participant in the Plan for all contribution types as of the entry date selected below (select one of c. - g., j. or k. below; also select 1. (All Contributions) for entry date selected at c. - g. or j.):

  b. [ ] **Entry date - different dates apply.** An Eligible Employee who has satisfied the eligibility requirements will become a Participant in the Plan for the designated contribution type as of the entry dates selected below (select one or more of c. - k. below; also select all that apply of 2. - 4. for each entry date selected at c. - j.).

NOTE: Option g. below can only be selected when eligibility for Elective Deferral purposes is six months of service or less and age is 20 1/2 or less. Options g.3. and g.4. may be selected when eligibility is 1 1/2 Years of Service or less and age is 20 1/2 or less and the Plan provides for 100% vesting.

NOTE: Unless otherwise specified in this Section or any other Section, Elective Deferrals include Roth Elective Deferrals, after-tax voluntary Employee contributions, and rollover contributions (unless otherwise selected at Question 46); Matching includes QMACs; and Nonelective Profit Sharing includes QNECs. **"ADP test safe harbor contributions" (SH) (including those made pursuant to a QACA) and SIMPLE 401(k) contributions are subject to the provisions for Elective Deferrals except as provided in Question 27.**

Entry Date	All Contributions		Elective Deferrals/SH	Matching	Nonelective Profit Sharing
c. Date requirements met	1. [ ]	OR	2. [ ]	3. [ ]	4. [ ]
d. First day of the month coinciding with or next following date requirements met	1. [ ]	OR	2. [ ]	3. [ ]	4. [ ]

Non-Standardized 401(k) Profit Sharing Plan

e.	First day of the Plan Year quarter coinciding with or next following date requirements met	1.[ ] **OR**	2. [ ]	3. [ ]	4. [ ]
f.	First day of Plan Year or first day of 7th month of Plan Year coinciding with or next following date requirements met	1.[ ] **OR**	2. [ ]	· 3. [ ]	4. [ ]
g.	First day of Plan Year coinciding with or next following date requirements met	1.[ ] **OR**	2. [ ]	3. [ ]	4. [ ]
h.	First day of Plan Year in which requirements met	N/A	N/A	3. [ ]	4. [ ]
i.	First day of Plan Year nearest date requirements met	N/A	N/A	3. [ ]	4. [ ]
j.	Other:	1.[ ] **OR**	2. [ ]	3. [ ]	4. [ ]

(must be definitely determinable and satisfy Note below)

k. [ ] Other: _____ (must specify contributions to which the conditions apply and must be definitely determinable and satisfy Note below)

NOTE: If j. or k. above is selected, then it must be completed in a manner that ensures an Eligible Employee who has satisfied the maximum age (21) and service requirements (1 Year (or Period) of Service (or more than 1 year if full and immediate vesting)) and who is otherwise entitled to participate, will become a Participant not later than the earlier of (a) 6 months after such requirements are satisfied, or (b) the first day of the first Plan Year after such requirements are satisfied, unless the Employee separates from service before such participation date.

SERVICE

16.   RECOGNITION OF SERVICE WITH OTHER EMPLOYERS (Plan Sections 1.62 and 1.88)

      a. [ ] No service with other employers is recognized except as otherwise required by law (e.g., the Plan already provides for the recognition of service with Employers who have adopted this Plan as well as service with Affiliated Employers and predecessor Employers who maintained this Plan; skip to Question 17).

      b. [ ] Prior service with the designated employers is recognized as follows (answer c. and select one or more of c.1. - 3.; select d. - g. as applicable) (if more than 3 employers, attach an addendum to the Adoption Agreement or complete option l. under Section B of Appendix A to the Adoption Agreement (Special Effective Dates and Other Permitted Elections)):

Other Employer	Eligibility	Vesting	Contribution Allocation
c. [ ] Employer name:	1. [ ]	2. [ ]	3. [ ]
d. [ ] Employer name:	1. [ ]	2. [ ]	3. [ ]
e. [ ] Employer name:	1. [ ]	2. [ ]	3. [ ]
f. [ ] Any entity the Employer acquires whether by asset or stock purchase, but only with respect to individuals who are employees of the acquired entity at the time of the acquisition	1. [ ]	2. [ ]	3. [ ]

Limitations

	Eligibility	Vesting	Contribution Allocation
g. [ ] The following provisions or limitations apply with respect to the recognition of prior service: _____ (e.g., credit service with X only on/following 1/1/13 or credit all service with entities the Employer acquires after 12/31/12)	1. [ ]	2. [ ]	3. [ ]

NOTE: If the other Employer(s) maintained this qualified Plan, then Years (and/or Periods) of Service with such Employer(s) must be recognized pursuant to Plan Sections 1.62 and 1.88 regardless of any selections above.

Non-Standardized 401(k) Profit Sharing Plan

17.   SERVICE CREDITING METHOD (Plan Sections 1.62 and 1.88)

NOTE: The provisions set forth in the definition of Year of Service in Plan Section 1.88 will apply, including the following defaults, except as otherwise elected below:
1. A Year of Service means completion of at least 1,000 Hours of Service during the applicable computation period.
2. Hours of Service (Plan Section 1.43) will be based on actual Hours of Service.
3. For eligibility purposes, the computation period will be as defined in Plan Section 1.88 (i.e., shift to the Plan Year if the eligibility condition is one (1) Year of Service or less).
4. For vesting and allocation purposes, the computation period will be the Plan Year.
5. The one-year hold-out rule after a 1-Year Break in Service will not be used.

a. [ ] **Elapsed time method.** (Period of Service applies instead of Year of Service) Instead of Hours of Service, elapsed time will be used for:
   1. [ ] all purposes (skip to Question 18)
   2. [ ] the following purposes (select one or more):
      a. [ ] eligibility to participate
      b. [ ] vesting
      c. [ ] sharing in allocations or contributions

b. [ ] **Alternative definitions for the Hours of Service method.** Instead of the defaults, the following alternatives will apply for the Hours of Service method (select one or more):
   1. [ ] **Eligibility computation period.** Instead of shifting to the Plan Year, the eligibility computation period after the initial eligibility computation period will be based on each anniversary of the date the Employee first completes an Hour of Service
   2. [ ] **Vesting computation period.** Instead of the Plan Year, the vesting computation period will be the date an Employee first performs an Hour of Service and each anniversary thereof.
   3. [ ] **Equivalency method.** Instead of using actual Hours of Service, an equivalency method will be used to determine Hours of Service for:
      a. [ ] all purposes
      b. [ ] the following purposes (select one or more):
         1. [ ] eligibility to participate
         2. [ ] vesting
         3. [ ] sharing in allocations or contributions

      Such method will apply to:
      c. [ ] all Employees
      d. [ ] Employees for whom records of actual Hours of Service are not maintained or available (e.g., salaried Employees)
      e. [ ] other: _____ (e.g., per-diem Employees only)

      Hours of Service will be determined on the basis of:
      f. [ ] days worked (10 hours per day)
      g. [ ] weeks worked (45 hours per week)
      h. [ ] semi-monthly payroll periods worked (95 hours per semi-monthly pay period)
      i. [ ] months worked (190 hours per month)
      j. [ ] bi-weekly payroll periods worked (90 hours per bi-weekly pay period)
      k. [ ] other: _____ (e.g., option f. is used for per-diem Employees and option g. is used for on-call Employees)

   4. [ ] **Number of Hours of Service required.** Instead of 1,000 Hours of Service, Year of Service means the applicable computation period during which an Employee has completed at least _____ (not to exceed 1,000) Hours of Service for:
      a. [ ] all purposes
      b. [ ] the following purposes (select one or more):
         1. [ ] eligibility to participate
         2. [ ] vesting
         3. [ ] sharing in allocations or contributions

Non-Standardized 401(k) Profit Sharing Plan

VESTING

18.   VESTING OF PARTICIPANT'S INTEREST (Plan Section 6.4(b))

     a.   [ ]   N/A (no Employer Nonelective profit sharing contributions (other than "prevailing wage contributions"), matching contributions or QACA "ADP test safe harbor contributions"; skip to Question 20)

     b.   [ ]   The vesting provisions selected below apply to all Participants unless otherwise selected below. In addition, option m. under Section B of Appendix A to the Adoption Agreement (Special Effective Dates and Other Permitted Elections) can be used to specify any exceptions to the provisions below.

        Vesting waiver. Employees who were employed on the date(s) indicated below and were Participants as of such date are 100% Vested. For Participants who enter the Plan after such date, the vesting provisions selected below apply (leave blank if no waiver applies):

        1.   [ ]   For all contributions. The vesting waiver applies to all contributions if employed on _____ (enter date)

        2.   [ ]   For designated contributions. The vesting waiver applies to (select one or more):

            a.   [ ]   Employer Nonelective profit sharing contributions if employed on _____

            b.   [ ]   Employer matching contributions if employed on _____

            c.   [ ]   QACA "ADP test safe harbor contributions" if employed on _____

Vesting for Employer Nonelective profit sharing contributions

     c.   [ ]   N/A (no Employer Nonelective profit sharing contributions (other than "prevailing wage contributions"); skip to f.)

     d.   [ ]   100% vesting. Participants are 100% Vested in Employer Nonelective profit sharing contributions upon entering Plan (required if eligibility requirement is greater than one (1) Year (or Period) of Service).

     e.   [ ]   The following vesting schedule, based on a Participant's Years of Service (or Periods of Service if the elapsed time method is selected), applies to Employer Nonelective profit sharing contributions:

        1.   [ ]   6 Year Graded: 0-1 year-0%;   2 years-20%;   3 years-40%;   4 years-60%;   5 years-80%;   6 years-100%

        2.   [ ]   4 Year Graded: 1 year-25%;   2 years-50%;   3 years-75%;   4 years-100%

        3.   [ ]   5 Year Graded: 1 year-20%;   2 years-40%;   3 years-60%;   4 years-80%;   5 years-100%

        4.   [ ]   3 Year Cliff: 0-2 years-0%; 3 years-100%

        5.   [ ]   Other - Must be at least as liberal as either 1. or 4. above in each year without switching between the two schedules:

Years (or Periods) of Service	Percentage
_____	_____%
_____	_____%
_____	_____%
_____	_____%
_____	_____%
_____	_____%

Vesting for Employer matching contributions

     f.   [ ]   N/A (no Employer matching contributions; skip to j.)

     g.   [ ]   The schedule above will also apply to Employer matching contributions.

     h.   [ ]   100% vesting. Participants are 100% Vested in Employer matching contributions upon entering Plan. (required if eligibility requirement is greater than 1 Year (or Period) of Service)

     i.   [ ]   The following vesting schedule, based on a Participant's Years of Service (or Periods of Service if the elapsed time method is selected), applies to Employer matching contributions:

        1.   [ ]   6 Year Graded: 0-1 year-0%;   2 years-20%;   3 years-40%;   4 years-60%;   5 years-80%;   6 years-100%

        2.   [ ]   4 Year Graded: 1 year-25%;   2 years-50%;   3 years-75%;   4 years-100%

        3.   [ ]   5 Year Graded: 1 year-20%;   2 years-40%;   3 years-60%;   4 years-80%;   5 years-100%

        4.   [ ]   3 Year Cliff: 0-2 years-0%; 3 years-100%

        5.   [ ]   Other - must be at least as liberal as either 1. or 4. above in each year without switching between the two schedules:

Years (or Periods) of Service	Percentage
_____	_____%
_____	_____%
_____	_____%
_____	_____%
_____	_____%
_____	_____%

Non-Standardized 401(k) Profit Sharing Plan

Vesting for QACA safe harbor contributions

j. [ ] N/A (no QACA "ADP test safe harbor contributions"; skip to Question 19)

k. [ ] 100% vesting. Participants are 100% Vested in QACA "ADP test safe harbor contributions" upon entering Plan (skip to Question 19).

l. [ ] The following vesting schedule, based on a Participant's Years of Service (or Periods of Service if the elapsed time method is selected), applies to the Participant's Qualified Automatic Contribution Safe Harbor Account:

    1. [ ] 100% after two years: 0-1 year-0%; 2 years-100%

    2. [ ] Other - Must be at least as liberal as 1. above in each year:

Years (or Periods) of Service	Percentage
Less than 1	_____%
1	_____%
2	100%

19. VESTING OPTIONS

Excluded vesting service. The following Years of Service will be disregarded for vesting purposes (select all that apply; leave blank if none apply):

a. [ ] Service prior to the initial Effective Date of the Plan or a predecessor plan (as defined in Regulations §1.411(a)-5(b)(3))

b. [ ] Service prior to the computation period in which an Employee has attained age 18

Vesting for death, Total And Permanent Disability and Early Retirement Date. Regardless of the vesting schedule, a Participant will become fully Vested upon (select all that apply; leave blank if none apply):

c. [ ] Death

d. [ ] Total and Permanent Disability

e. [ ] Early Retirement Date

NOTE: Unless otherwise elected at option v. under Section B of Appendix A to the Adoption Agreement (Special Effective Dates and Other Permitted Elections), the options above apply to QACA "ADP test safe harbor contributions," if any, as well as to Employer Nonelective profit sharing contributions and matching contributions.

RETIREMENT AGES

20. NORMAL RETIREMENT AGE ("NRA") (Plan Section 1.55) means:

a. [ ] **Specific age.** The date a Participant attains age _____ (see Note below).

b. [ ] **Age/participation.** The later of the date a Participant attains age _____ (see Note below) or the _____ (not to exceed 5th) anniversary of the first day of the Plan Year in which participation in the Plan commenced.

NOTE: A Participant's age specified above may not exceed 65 and, if this Plan includes transferred pension assets, may not be less than age 62 unless the Employer has evidence that the representative typical retirement age for the adopting Employer's industry is a lower age, but may be no less than age 55.

21. NORMAL RETIREMENT DATE (Plan Section 1.56) means, with respect to any Participant, the:

a. [ ] date on which the Participant attains "NRA"

b. [ ] first day of the month coinciding with or next following the Participant's "NRA"

c. [ ] first day of the month nearest the Participant's "NRA"

d. [ ] Anniversary Date coinciding with or next following the Participant's "NRA"

e. [ ] Anniversary Date nearest the Participant's "NRA"

f. [ ] Other: _____ (e.g., first day of the month following the Participant's "NRA").

22. EARLY RETIREMENT DATE (Plan Section 1.23)

a. [ ] N/A (no early retirement provision provided)

b. [ ] Early Retirement Date means the:

    1. [ ] date on which a Participant satisfies the early retirement requirements

    2. [ ] first day of the month coinciding with or next following the date on which a Participant satisfies the early retirement requirements

    3. [ ] Anniversary Date coinciding with or next following the date on which a Participant satisfies the early retirement requirements

Early retirement requirements

    4. [ ] Participant attains age _____

        AND, completes.... (leave blank if not applicable)

        a. [ ] at least _____ Years (or Periods) of Service for vesting purposes

        b. [ ] at least _____ Years (or Periods) of Service for eligibility purposes

Non-Standardized 401(k) Profit Sharing Plan

COMPENSATION

23.   COMPENSATION with respect to any Participant is defined as follows (Plan Sections 1.18 and 1.40).

Base definition
a. [ ] Wages, tips and other compensation on Form W-2
b. [ ] Code §3401(a) wages (wages for withholding purposes)
c. [ ] 415 safe harbor compensation

NOTE: Plan Sections 1.18(d) and 1.40 provide that the base definition of Compensation includes deferrals that are not included in income due to Code §§401(k), 125, 132(f)(4), 403(b), 402(h)(1)(B)(SEP), 414(h)(2), & 457.

Determination period. Compensation will be based on the following "determination period" (this will also be the Limitation Year unless otherwise elected at option i. under Section B of Appendix A to the Adoption Agreement (Special Effective Dates and Other Permitted Elections)):

d. [ ] the Plan Year
e. [ ] the Fiscal Year coinciding with or ending within the Plan Year
f. [ ] the calendar year coinciding with or ending within the Plan Year

Adjustments to Compensation (for Plan Section 1.18). Compensation will be adjusted by:

g. [ ] **No adjustments.** No adjustments to Compensation for all contribution types (skip to v. below).
h. [ ] **Adjustments - same for all contribution types.** The following Compensation adjustments apply to all contribution types (select one or more of l. - u. below; also select 1. (All Contributions) for each adjustment selected at l. - t.):
i. [ ] **Adjustments - different adjustments apply.** The following Compensation adjustments for the designated contribution type (select one or more of j. - u. below; also select 1. OR all that apply 2. - 5. for each adjustment selected at j. - t.):

NOTE: Elective Deferrals include Roth Elective Deferrals, Matching includes QMACs and matching "ADP test safe harbor contributions" (including those made pursuant to a QACA), and Nonelective Profit Sharing includes QNECs unless specified otherwise. ADP Safe Harbor Nonelective includes nonelective "ADP test safe harbor contributions" (including those made pursuant to a QACA).

Adjustments	All Contributions		Elective Deferrals	Matching	Nonelective Profit Sharing	ADP Safe Harbor Nonelective
j. no Adjustments	N/A		2. [ ]	3. [ ]	4. [ ]	5. [ ]
k. excluding salary reductions (401(k), 125, 132(f)(4), 403(b), SEP, 414(h)(2) pickup, & 457)	N/A		N/A	N/A	4. [ ]	5. [ ]
l. excluding reimbursements or other expense allowances, fringe benefits (cash or non-cash), moving expenses, deferred compensation (other than deferrals specified in k. above) and welfare benefits.	1. [ ]	OR	2. [ ]	3. [ ]	4. [ ]	5. [ ]
m. excluding Compensation paid during the "determination period" while not a Participant in the component of the Plan for which the definition applies.	1. [ ]	OR	2. [ ]	3. [ ]	4. [ ]	5. [ ]
n. excluding Compensation paid during the "determination period" while not a Participant in *any* component of the Plan for which the definition applies.	1. [ ]	OR	2. [ ]	3. [ ]	4. [ ]	5. [ ]
o. excluding Military Differential Pay	1. [ ]	OR	2. [ ]	3. [ ]	4. [ ]	5. [ ]
p. excluding overtime	1. [ ]	OR	2. [ ]	3. [ ]	4. [ ]	5. [ ]
q. excluding bonuses	1. [ ]	OR	2. [ ]	3. [ ]	4. [ ]	5. [ ]
r. excluding commissions	1. [ ]	OR	2. [ ]	3. [ ]	4. [ ]	5. [ ]
s. excluding Compensation paid by an Affiliated Employer that has not adopted this Plan.	1. [ ]	OR	2. [ ]	3. [ ]	4. [ ]	5. [ ]
t. other: _____	1. [ ]	OR	2. [ ]	3. [ ]	4. [ ]	5. [ ]

(e.g., describe Compensation from the elections
available above or a combination thereof as to a Participant group
(e.g., no exclusions as to Division A Employees and exclude
bonuses as to Division B Employees); and/or describe another
exclusion (e.g., exclude shift differential pay))

Non-Standardized 401(k) Profit Sharing Plan

u. other: _____ (e.g., describe Compensation from the elections available above or a combination thereof as to a contribution source and Participant group (e.g., no exclusions as to Division A Employees and exclude bonuses as to Division B Employees); and/or describe another exclusion (e.g., exclude shift differential pay)).

NOTE: If p., q., r., s., t. or u. is selected, the definition of Compensation could violate the nondiscrimination rules. In addition, p., q., r., s., t. or u. are not recommended if the Plan is using the ADP/ACP safe harbor provisions.

Military Differential Pay special effective date (leave blank if not applicable)

v. [ ] If this is a PPA restatement and the provisions above regarding Military Differential Pay (included unless o. is selected) have a later effective date than Plan Years beginning after December 31, 2008, then enter the date such provisions were first effective: _____ (may not be earlier than January 1, 2009; for Plan Years beginning prior to January 1, 2009, Military Differential Pay is treated in accordance with the post-severance compensation provisions in the following Question).

24. POST-SEVERANCE COMPENSATION (415 REGULATIONS)

The following optional provision of the 415 Regulations will apply to Limitation Years beginning on or after July 1, 2007 unless otherwise elected below:

415 Compensation (post-severance compensation adjustments) (select all that apply at a. - b.; leave blank if none apply)

NOTE: Unless otherwise elected under a. below, the following defaults apply: 415 Compensation will **include** (to the extent provided in Plan Section 1.40), post-severance regular pay, leave cash-outs and payments from nonqualified unfunded deferred compensation plans.

a. [ ] The defaults listed above apply except for the following (select one or more):
    1. [ ] Leave cash-outs will be **excluded**
    2. [ ] Nonqualified unfunded deferred compensation will be **excluded**
    3. [ ] Military Differential Pay will be **included** (Plan automatically includes for Limitation Years beginning after December 31, 2008)
    4. [ ] Disability continuation payments will be **included** for:
        a. [ ] Nonhighly Compensated Employees only
        b. [ ] all Participants and the salary continuation will continue for the following fixed or determinable period: _____

b. [ ] The last paycheck ("administrative delay") rule will be applied (amounts paid in the first few weeks of a Limitation Year due to administrative delay relate back to the prior Limitation Year).

Plan Compensation (post-severance compensation adjustments)

c. [ ] **Defaults apply.** For all contribution types, Compensation will **include** (to the extent provided in Plan Section 1.18 and to the extent such amounts would be included in Compensation if paid prior to severance of employment) post-severance regular pay, leave cash-outs, and payments from nonqualified unfunded deferred compensation plans (skip to n. below).

d. [ ] **Exclude all post-severance compensation.** Exclude all post-severance compensation for all contribution types (skip to n. below).

e. [ ] **Post-severance adjustments - same for all contribution types.** The defaults listed at c. apply except for the following for all contribution types (select one or more of i. - m. below; also select 1. (All Contributions) for each adjustment selected):

f. [ ] **Post-severance adjustments - different adjustments apply.** The defaults listed at c. apply except for the following for the designated contribution type (select one or more of g. - m. below; also select 1. OR all that apply of 2. - 5. for each adjustment selected):

Adjustments	All Contributions	Elective Deferrals	Matching	Nonelective Profit Sharing	ADP Safe Harbor Nonelective
g. Defaults apply	N/A	2.[ ]	3.[ ]	4.[ ]	5.[ ]
h. Exclude all post-severance compensation (may violate the nondiscrimination requirements)	N/A	2.[ ]	3.[ ]	4.[ ]	5.[ ]
i. Regular pay will be **excluded** (may violate the nondiscrimination requirements)	1.[ ] OR	2.[ ]	3.[ ]	4.[ ]	5.[ ]
j. Leave cash-outs will be **excluded**	1.[ ] OR	2.[ ]	3.[ ]	4.[ ]	5.[ ]
k. Nonqualified unfunded deferred compensation will be **excluded**	1.[ ] OR	2.[ ]	3.[ ]	4.[ ]	5.[ ]
l. Military Differential Pay will be **included**	1.[ ] OR	2.[ ]	3.[ ]	4.[ ]	5.[ ]
m. Disability continuation payments will be **included** for:	1.[ ] OR	2.[ ]	3.[ ]	4.[ ]	5.[ ]

    a. [ ] Nonhighly Compensated Employees only
    b. [ ] all Participants and the salary continuation will continue for the following fixed or determinable period: _____

Non-Standardized 401(k) Profit Sharing Plan

NOTE: The above treatment of Military Differential Pay only applies to Plan Years beginning prior to January 1, 2009. For Plan Years beginning after such date, Military Differential Pay is not considered post-severance compensation and the provisions of Question 23 apply.

Post-severance compensation special effective date (leave blank if not applicable)

n. [ ] If this is a PPA restatement and the post-severance compensation adjustments above for 415 Compensation or Plan Compensation applied other than the first day of the Plan Year beginning on or after July 1, 2007, then enter the date such provisions were first effective: _____

CONTRIBUTIONS AND ALLOCATIONS

25.   SALARY DEFERRAL ARRANGEMENT - ELECTIVE DEFERRALS (Plan Section 12.2) (skip if Elective Deferrals NOT selected at Question 12.b.) (Roth Elective Deferrals are permitted if selected at Question 12.b.1)

   A.   **Elective Deferral limit.** Each Participant may elect to have Compensation deferred by:

     a. [ ]   up to _____%

     b. [ ]   from _____% (may not be less than 1%) to _____%

     c. [ ]   up to the maximum amount allowed by law (i.e., Code §§402(g) and 415)

   B.   **Additional Elective Deferral limits.** Regardless of the above limits (if any), the following apply (select all that apply; leave blank if none apply):

     d. [ ]   If a. or b. above is selected, a Participant may make a separate election to defer up to _____% of any irregular pay (e.g., bonus) regardless of the limitation in a. or b. above

     e. [ ]   For Participants who are HCEs determined as of the beginning of a Plan Year, then instead of 25.A. applying, the Elective Deferral limit is (must be equal to or lower than limit selected in 25.A.; may not be selected if HCEs are excluded at 13.g.1 or 13.g.2):

       1. [ ]   _____% of Compensation

       2. [ ]   the percentage equal to the Elective Deferral limit in effect under Code §402(g)(3) for the calendar year that begins with or within the Plan Year divided by the annual compensation limit in effect for the Plan Year under Code §401(a)(17)

       3. [ ]   other: _____ (e.g., must be a specific limit that only applies to some or all HCEs)

   C.   **Catch-Up Contributions** (Plan Section 1.15). May eligible Participants make Catch-Up Contributions?

     f. [ ]   No (skip to D. below)

     g. [ ]   Yes, and the following provisions apply:

       Matching Catch-Up Contributions. Will Catch-Up Contributions be taken into account in applying any matching contribution under the Plan?

       1. [ ]   Yes

       2. [ ]   No (may not be selected if this Plan provides for matching "ADP test safe harbor contributions" or "ACP test safe harbor matching contributions")

       Special effective date (may be left blank if effective date is same as the Plan or Restatement Effective Date)

       3. [ ]   The effective date of the Catch-Up Contribution provisions is _____ (enter special effective date)

       Applying limits. If the amount of Elective Deferrals that may be made to the Plan is limited in A. and/or B. above, are Catch-Up Contributions aggregated with other Elective Deferrals in applying such limits?

       4. [ ]   No or N/A (there are no limits or Catch-Up Contributions may be made in addition to any imposed limits)

       5. [ ]   Yes (if selected, the limits in A. and/or B. must not be less than 75% of Compensation)

   D.   **Elective Deferral special effective date** (may be left blank if effective date is same as the Plan or Restatement Effective Date)

     h. [ ]   The effective date of the Elective Deferral component of the Plan is _____ (enter month day, year; may not be earlier than the date on which the Employer first adopts the Elective Deferral component of the Plan).

26.   AUTOMATIC CONTRIBUTION ARRANGEMENT (Plan Section 12.2 and 12.9) (skip if Elective Deferrals are NOT selected at Question 12.b.)

   A.   **Automatic Deferral provisions.** Will the Plan include Automatic Deferral provisions?

     a. [ ]   No (skip to Question 27)

     b. [ ]   Yes, this Plan includes (select one):

       1. [ ]   A traditional Automatic Contribution Arrangement (not an Eligible Automatic Contribution Arrangement (EACA) or a Qualified Automatic Contribution Arrangement (QACA))

       2. [ ]   An Eligible Automatic Contribution Arrangement (EACA) but not a Qualified Automatic Contribution Arrangement (QACA)

       3. [ ]   A Qualified Automatic Contribution Arrangement (QACA) (a QACA, by definition, satisfies the requirements of an Eligible Automatic Contribution Arrangement (EACA)) (must be selected if QACA safe harbor contributions is selected at 12.c.2.)

Non-Standardized 401(k) Profit Sharing Plan

B. **Participants subject to the Automatic Deferral provisions.** The Automatic Deferral provisions apply to Employees who become Participants on or after the effective date of the Automatic Deferral provisions, except as otherwise provided herein.

Application to existing Participants. For Employees who became Participants prior to the effective date of the Automatic Deferral provisions (if an EACA and not a QACA, see the Note below; skip if new Plan):

c. [ ] Provisions do not apply to existing Participants (may not be selected with QACA)

d. [ ] Provisions apply to existing Participants in accordance with the following (select one):

    1. [ ] **All Participants.** All Participants, regardless of any prior Salary Deferral Agreement.

    2. [ ] **Affirmative Election of at least Automatic Deferral amount.** All Participants, except those who have an Affirmative Election in effect on the effective date of the Automatic Deferral provisions that is at least equal to the Automatic Deferral amount and except as otherwise provided below with respect to the escalation of deferral provisions.

    3. [ ] **No existing Affirmative Election.** All Participants, except those who have an Affirmative Election in effect on the effective date of the Automatic Deferral provisions and except as otherwise provided below with respect to the escalation of deferral provisions.

    4. [ ] **Escalation only.** Escalation provisions in Part D. below apply to all Participants, including those who become Participants on or after the effective date of the escalation provisions, who have an Affirmative Elections. No other Automatic Deferral provisions apply. If selected, complete 26.f. under Part C. below with the percentage at which escalation applies and complete 26.j. under Part D. (may not be selected with QACA)

e. [ ] Other (may not be used if a QACA): _____ (must be definitely determinable in accordance with Regulation §1.401-1(b)(1)(ii)).

NOTE: Option E.k.3. may be used to exclude other Participants from the Automatic Deferral provisions.

NOTE: If an EACA and not a QACA and c. is selected (i.e., EACA does not apply to existing Participants), then the six-month period for relief from the excise tax under Code §4979(f)(1) will not apply. In addition, effective for Plan Years beginning on or after January 1, 2010, the six-month period for relief from the excise tax will only apply if all HCEs and NHCEs are covered Employees under the EACA for the entire Plan Year (or for the portion of the Plan Year that such Employees are Eligible Employees under the Plan within the meaning of Code §410(b)).

C. **Automatic Deferral amount.** Unless a Participant makes an Affirmative Election, the Employer will withhold the following Automatic Deferral amount (only select one):

f. [ ] _____ % of Compensation for each payroll period (if a QACA, must not be more than 10% and may not be less than 3% if escalation provisions used in j. below or 6% if no escalation provisions are selected)

g. [ ] $_____ for each payroll period (may not be selected if a QACA or EACA)

h. [ ] **QACA statutory minimum schedule** (may select even if Plan is not a QACA). Unless a modified QACA statutory schedule is selected below, the Employer will withhold from a Participant's Compensation each payroll period the percentage of Compensation set forth in the following, which is based on the Plan Year of application to a Participant: 1–2 years–3%; 3 years–4%; 4 years–5%; 5 or more–6%. (if selected, skip D.)

    1. [ ] The following modified QACA statutory schedule will apply:

Plan Year of application to a Participant	Automatic Deferral Percentage
1 - 2	_____ % (not less than 3)
3	_____ % (not less than 4)
4	_____ % (not less than 5)
5	_____ % (not less than 6 and not more than 10)
6 and thereafter	_____ % (not less than 6 and not more than 10)

NOTE: If Plan only applies escalation provisions to Participants with Affirmative Elections then select f. above and enter the percentage at which escalation applies (e.g., if escalation only applies to Participants who have an Affirmative Election of 3% or greater, then enter 3%).

D. **Escalation of Automatic Deferral amount** (may not be selected with 26.h.)

i. [ ] No escalation

j. [ ] **Scheduled increases.** The initial Automatic Deferral amount will increase as selected below (may not be selected with h. above):

    1. [ ] by _____ % of Compensation up to a maximum of _____ % of Compensation (may not be selected if a QACA)

    2. [ ] by $_____ up to a maximum of $_____ (may not be selected if a QACA or EACA)

    3. [ ] other: _____ (in order to satisfy the QACA requirements (if applicable), an alternative Automatic Deferral amount schedule (i) must be uniform based on the number of years, or portions of years, since the beginning of the initial period for a Participant, (ii) must satisfy the minimum percentage requirement in h. above throughout the Plan Year, and (iii) must not exceed 10% of Compensation)

Timing of escalation

    4. [ ] N/A (entry at j.3. includes timing provision)

    5. [ ] The escalation provision above will apply as of:

        a. [ ] each anniversary of the Participant's date of hire

        b. [ ] each anniversary of the Participant's Entry Date

Non-Standardized 401(k) Profit Sharing Plan

c. [ ]   the first day of each Plan Year
d. [ ]   the first day of each calendar year
e. [ ]   other: _____ (must be a specified date that occurs at least annually
after the Plan Year in which the Participant is first subject to the Automatic Contribution
Arrangement).

First period of application. Unless selected below, the escalation provision above will apply as of the
second period specified above that begins after the period in which the Participant first has contributions
made pursuant to a default election.

f. [ ]   The escalation provision will apply as of the first period after the Participant first has contributions
made pursuant to a default election (or the date of Affirmative Election if 6. or 7. below is
selected).

Application to Participants with Affirmative Elections
Unless selected below, the escalation provisions will not apply to Participants with an Affirmative Election.

6. [ ]   The escalation provisions apply to Participants with an Affirmative Election of at least _____ % of
Compensation.
7. [ ]   The escalation provisions apply to Participants with an Affirmative Election in accordance with the following
rules: _____ (must be definitely determinable in accordance with
Regulation §1.401-1(b)(1)(ii) and if an EACA, must be uniform).

E.   **Other Automatic Deferral elections** (leave blank if none apply)
k. [ ]   **Optional elections** (select one or more)
Type of Elective Deferral. The Automatic Deferral is a Pre-Tax Elective Deferral unless selected below (may only be
selected if Roth Elective Deferrals are selected at 12.b.1.):
1. [ ]   the Automatic Deferral is a Roth Elective Deferral
2. [ ]   other: _____ (e.g., 50% Pre-Tax and 50% Roth Elective
Deferrals)

Excluded Participants. If this is not a QACA, then the following Participants are excluded from the Automatic
Deferral provisions:
3. [ ]   _____ (must be definitely determinable; e.g., union Employees or Participants employed in Division A)
(may not be selected if a QACA). If this option is elected and the Plan is an EACA, then the six-month period
for relief from the excise tax under Code §4979(f)(1) will not apply.

F.   **EACA elections** (skip if NOT a QACA or EACA)

Permissible withdrawals. Does the Plan permit Participant permissible withdrawals (as described in Plan Section 12.2(b)(4)) within
90 days (or less) of first Automatic Deferral?
l. [ ]   No
m. [ ]   Yes, within 90 days of first Automatic Deferral
n. [ ]   Yes, within: _____ days (may not be less than 30 nor more than 90 days)

Affirmative Election. For Plan Years beginning on or after January 1, 2010, will Participants who make an Affirmative Election
continue to be covered by the EACA provisions (i.e., their Affirmative Election will remain intact but they must receive an
annual notice)? (skip if a QACA)
o. [ ]   Yes (if selected, then the annual notice must be provided to Participants)
p. [ ]   No (if selected, then the Plan cannot use the six-month period for relief from the excise tax of Code §4979(f)(1))

G.   **Special effective date** (may be left blank if the effective date is the same as the Effective Date)
q. [ ]   The Automatic Deferral provisions are effective for Plan Years beginning after _____ (if using an EACA or QACA
and this is a PPA restatement and the provisions were effective prior to the Restatement Effective Date, then enter the
date such provisions were first effective; may not be earlier than December 31, 2007)
r. [ ]   Other: _____ (If using an EACA or QACA and this is a PPA restatement and the
provisions were effective prior to the Restatement Effective Date, then enter the date such provisions were first
effective; may not be earlier than December 31, 2007. If there are multiple retroactive special effective dates (e.g., for a
PPA restatement), complete this Question 26 based on the current Plan provisions and then duplicate this Question 26
and attach as an Appendix to indicate the special retroactive effective dates and provisions that applied.)

27.   401(k) ADP TEST SAFE HARBOR PROVISIONS (Plan Sections 12.8 and 12.9) (skip if "ADP test safe harbor contributions"
are NOT selected at Question 12.c.)

NOTE: If the Employer wants the discretion to determine whether the provisions will apply on a year-by-year basis, then the
Employer may select 27.a. or b. and 27.d.3.

A.   **ADP and ACP test safe harbor.** For any Plan Year in which any type of matching contribution is made, will the "ADP and ACP
test safe harbor" provisions be used?
a. [ ]   No. Only the "ADP (and NOT the ACP) test safe harbor" provisions will be used.
b. [ ]   Yes. Both the "ADP and ACP test safe harbor" provisions will be used for any Plan Year in which any type of
matching contribution is made. (If selected, complete the provisions of the Adoption Agreement relating to Employer

matching contributions (i.e., Question 28) that will apply in addition to any selections made in c. below. Also, no allocation conditions may be imposed at 28.E. unless no HCEs are eligible to receive the matching contribution)

B. **Safe harbor contribution.** The Employer will make the following "ADP test safe harbor contribution" for the Plan Year:

NOTE: The "ACP test safe harbor" is automatically satisfied if the only matching contribution made to the Plan is either, as described below, (1) a basic matching contribution (traditional or QACA) or (2) an enhanced matching contribution (traditional or QACA) that does not provide a match on Elective Deferrals in excess of 6% of Compensation.

c. [ ] **Safe harbor matching contribution** (select one of 1. - 4. **AND** one of 5. - 9.). The Employer will make matching "ADP test safe harbor contributions" to the Account of each "eligible Participant" as elected below.

1. [ ] **Traditional basic matching contribution** (may not be selected if a QACA). The Employer will contribute an amount equal to the sum of 100% of the amount of the Participant's Elective Deferrals that do not exceed 3% of the Participant's Compensation, plus 50% of the amount of the Participant's Elective Deferrals that exceed 3% of the Participant's Compensation but do not exceed 5% of the Participant's Compensation.

2. [ ] **Traditional enhanced matching contribution** (may not be selected if a QACA). The Employer will contribute an amount equal to the sum of:

    a. [ ] ____% (may not be less than 100%) of the Participant's Elective Deferrals that do not exceed ____% (may not be less than 3%; if over 6% or if left blank, the ACP test will still apply) of the Participant's Compensation, plus

    b. [ ] ____% of the Participant's Elective Deferrals that exceed ____% (must be the same % entered at a.) of the Participant's Compensation but do not exceed ____% (if over 6% or if left blank, the ACP test will still apply) of the Participant's Compensation, plus

    c. [ ] ____% of the Participant's Elective Deferrals that exceed ____% (must be the same % entered at b.) of the Participant's Compensation but do not exceed ____% (if over 6% or if left blank, the ACP test will still apply) of the Participant's Compensation.

    NOTE: a., b. and c. must be completed so that, at any rate of Elective Deferrals, the matching contribution is at least equal to what the matching contribution would be if the Employer were making basic matching contributions (as defined in 27.c.1. above), but the rate of match cannot increase as Elective Deferrals increase. For example, if a. is completed to provide a matching contribution equal to 100% of Elective Deferrals up to 4% of Compensation, then b. and c. need not be completed.

3. [ ] **QACA basic matching contribution.** The Employer will contribute an amount equal to the sum of 100% of a Participant's Elective Deferrals that do not exceed 1% of Participant's Compensation, plus 50% of the Participant's Elective Deferrals that exceed 1% of the Participant's Compensation but do not exceed 6% of the Participant's Compensation.

4. [ ] **QACA enhanced matching contribution.** The Employer will contribute an amount equal to the sum of:

    a. [ ] ____% (may not be less than 100%) of the Participant's Elective Deferrals that do not exceed ____% (may not be less than 1%; if over 6% or if left blank, the ACP test will still apply) of the Participant's Compensation, plus

    b. [ ] ____% of the Participant's Elective Deferrals that exceed ____% (must be the same % entered at a.) of the Participant's Compensation but do not exceed ____% (if over 6% or if left blank, the ACP test will still apply) of the Participant's Compensation, plus

    c. [ ] ____% of the Participant's Elective Deferrals that exceed ____% (must be the same % entered at b.) of the Participant's Compensation but do not exceed ____% (if over 6% or if left blank, the ACP test will still apply) of the Participant's Compensation.

    NOTE: a., b. and c. must be completed so that, at any rate of Elective Deferrals, the matching contribution is at least equal to what the matching contribution would be if the Employer were making QACA basic matching contributions (as defined in 27.c.3. above), but the rate of match cannot increase as Elective Deferrals increase. For example, if a. is completed to provide a matching contribution equal to 100% of Elective Deferrals up to 4% of Compensation, then b. and c. need not be completed.

Determination period. The matching "ADP test safe harbor contribution" above will be applied on the following basis (and Elective Deferrals and any Compensation or dollar limitation used in determining the matching contribution will be based on the applicable period):

5. [ ] the Plan Year
6. [ ] each payroll period
7. [ ] each month
8. [ ] each Plan Year quarter
9. [ ] each payroll unit (e.g., hour)

d. [ ] **Safe harbor nonelective contributions** (select one)

1. [ ] **3% contribution.** The Employer will make a nonelective "ADP test safe harbor contribution" for the Plan Year to the Account of each "eligible Participant" in an amount equal to 3% of each Participant's Compensation.

Non-Standardized 401(k) Profit Sharing Plan

    2. [ ]   **Stated contribution.** The Employer will make a nonelective "ADP test safe harbor contribution" to the Account of each "eligible Participant" in an amount equal to _____% (may not be less than 3%) of each Participant's Compensation.

    3. [ ]   **"Maybe" election.** The Employer may elect to make a nonelective "ADP test safe harbor contribution" after a Plan Year has commenced in accordance with the provisions of Plan Section 12.8(h). If this option d.3. is selected, the nonelective "ADP test safe harbor contribution" will be required only for a Plan Year for which the Plan is amended to provide for such contribution and the appropriate supplemental notice is provided to Participants.

  e. [ ]   **Safe harbor contribution to another Plan.** The Employer will make a nonelective or matching "ADP test safe harbor contribution" to another defined contribution plan maintained by the Employer (specify the name of the other plan): _____.

C.   **Excluded Participants.** For purposes of the "ADP test safe harbor contribution," the term "eligible Participant" means any Participant who is eligible to make Elective Deferrals unless otherwise excluded below (leave blank if no exclusions):

  f. [ ]   Exclusions (select one or more):

    1. [ ]   Highly Compensated Employees (HCEs). The Employer may, however, make a discretionary "ADP test safe harbor contribution" for the HCEs in a percentage that does not exceed the amount (or in the case of a matching "ADP test safe harbor contribution," the rate) provided to the NHCEs.

    2. [ ]   Employees who have not satisfied the greatest minimum age and service conditions permitted under Code §410(a) (i.e., age 21 and 1 Year of Service), with the following deemed effective date of participation:

      a. [ ]   the earlier of the first day of the first month or the first day of the seventh month of the Plan Year immediately following the date such conditions are satisfied

      b. [ ]   the first day of the Plan Year in which the requirements are met

      c. [ ]   other: _____ (not later than the earlier of (a) 6 months after such requirements are satisfied, or (b) the first day of the first Plan Year after such requirements are satisfied)

    3. [ ]   Union Employees (as defined in Plan Section 1.28)

    4. [ ]   Other: _____ (must be an HCE or an Employee who can be excluded under the permissive or mandatory disaggregation rules of Regulations §§1.401(k)-1(b)(4) and 1.401(m)-1(b)(4); e.g., Employees who have not completed 6 months of service)

D.   **Special effective dates** (may be left blank if no special effective dates need to be specified in this Plan)

  g. [ ]   **Safe harbor provisions (other than QACA).** The "ADP and ACP test safe harbor" provisions are effective for Plan Years beginning on and after: _____ (enter the first day of the Plan Year for which the provisions are effective and, if necessary, enter any other special effective dates that apply with respect to the provisions).

  h. [ ]   **QACA provisions.** The QACA provisions are effective for Plan Years beginning after: _____ (if this is a PPA restatement and the provisions were effective prior to the Restatement Effective Date, then enter the date such provisions were first effective; may not be earlier than December 31, 2007)

  i. [ ]   **Other:** _____ (If there are multiple retroactive special effective dates (e.g., for a PPA restatement), complete this Question 27 based on the current Plan provisions and then duplicate this Question 27 and attach as an Appendix to indicate the special retroactive effective dates and provisions that applied.)

E.   **Elective Deferrals considered for matching contribution.** If a matching contribution is selected above, then the Plan will disregard a Participant's Elective Deferrals that are made prior to the date the matching contribution component of the Plan is effective with respect to such Participant unless otherwise elected below.

  j. [ ]   The Plan will include a Participant's Elective Deferrals that are made prior to the date the matching contribution component of the Plan is effective with respect to such Participant.

28.   EMPLOYER MATCHING CONTRIBUTIONS (Plan Section 12.1(a)(2)) (skip if matching contributions are NOT selected at Question 12.d.)

If the "ACP test safe harbor" provisions are being used (i.e., Question 27.b. is selected), then the Plan will only take into account Elective Deferrals up to 6% of Compensation in applying the matching contribution set forth below and the maximum discretionary matching contribution that may be made on behalf of any Participant is 4% of Compensation.

A.   **Matching formula.**

  a. [ ]   Employer matching contribution as follows (select 1. or 2.):

    1. [ ]   **Discretionary.** The Employer may make matching contributions equal to a discretionary percentage, to be determined by the Employer, of the Participant's Elective Deferrals.

      a. [ ]   **Discretionary based on business units or location.** The Employer may determine a separate discretionary matching contribution for Participants working in different business units or locations.

    2. [ ]   **Fixed - uniform rate/amount.** The Employer will make matching contributions equal to _____% (e.g., 50) of the Participant's Elective Deferrals, plus (select a. or leave blank if not applicable):

      a. [ ]   an additional matching contribution of a discretionary percentage determined by the Employer,

        1. [ ]   but not to exceed _____% of Compensation (leave blank if not applicable)

Non-Standardized 401(k) Profit Sharing Plan

Matching limit on Elective Deferrals. In determining the Employer matching contribution above, only the following will be matched. Elective Deferrals up to (select 3. OR 4.; leave blank if not applicable):

3. [ ] the percentage or dollar amount specified below (select one or both)

     a. [ ] _____% of a Participant's Compensation.

     b. [ ] $_____.

4. [ ] a discretionary percentage of a Participant's Compensation or a discretionary dollar amount, the percentage or dollar amount to be determined by the Employer on a uniform basis for all Participants.

b. [ ] **Discretionary - tiered.** The Employer may make matching contributions equal to a discretionary percentage of a Participant's Elective Deferrals, to be determined by the Employer, of each tier, to be determined by the Employer. The tiers may be based on the rate of a Participant's Elective Deferrals or Years of Service.

c. [ ] **Fixed - tiered.** The Employer will make matching contributions equal to a uniform percentage of each tier of each Participant's Elective Deferrals, determined as follows:

NOTE: Fill in only percentages or dollar amounts, but not both. If percentages are used, each tier represents the amount of the Participant's applicable contributions that equals the specified percentage of the Participant's Compensation (add additional tiers if necessary):

Tiers of Contributions (indicate $ or %)	Matching Percentage
First _____	_____%
Next _____	_____%
Next _____	_____%
Next _____	_____%

d. [ ] **Fixed - Years of Service.** The Employer will make matching contributions equal to a uniform percentage of each Participant's Elective Deferrals based on the Participant's Years of Service (or Periods of Service if the elapsed time method is selected), determined as follows (add additional tiers if necessary):

Years (or Periods) of Service	Matching Percentage
_____	_____%
_____	_____%
_____	_____%

For purposes of the above matching contribution formula, a Year (or Period) of Service means a Year (or Period) of Service for:

1. [ ] vesting purposes

2. [ ] eligibility purposes

In determining the Employer matching contribution above, only Elective Deferrals up to the percentage or dollar amount specified below will be matched (select all that apply; leave blank if not applicable):

3. [ ] _____% of a Participant's Compensation.

4. [ ] $_____.

e. [ ] Other: _____ (the formula described must satisfy the definitely determinable requirement under Reg. §1.401-1(b). If the formula is non-uniform, it is not a design-based safe harbor for nondiscrimination purposes.)

NOTE: If b., c., d. or e. above is selected, the Plan may violate the Code §401(a)(4) nondiscrimination requirements if the rate of matching contributions increases as a Participant's Elective Deferrals or Years (or Periods) of Service increase.

Maximum matching contribution. The matching contribution made on behalf of any Participant for any Plan Year will not exceed (leave blank if no limit on matching contribution):

f. [ ] $_____.

g. [ ] _____% of Compensation.

B. **Elective Deferrals considered for matching contribution.** The Plan will disregard a Participant's Elective Deferrals that are made prior to the date the matching contribution component of the Plan is effective with respect to such Participant unless otherwise elected below.

h. [ ] The Plan will include a Participant's Elective Deferrals that are made prior to the date the matching contribution component of the Plan is effective with respect to such Participant.

C. **Period of determination.** The matching contribution formula will be applied on the following basis (and Elective Deferrals and any Compensation or dollar limitation used in determining the matching contribution will be based on the applicable period):

i. [ ] the Plan Year

j. [ ] each payroll period

k. [ ] each month

l. [ ] each Plan Year quarter

m. [ ] each payroll unit (e.g., hour)

n. [ ] N/A (Plan only provides for discretionary matching contributions; i.e., a.1. or b. is selected above)

Non-Standardized 401(k) Profit Sharing Plan

NOTE: For any discretionary match, the Employer will determine the calculation methodology at the time the matching contribution is determined.

D.   **QMACs** (Plan Section 1.69). The matching contributions will NOT be Qualified Matching Contributions (QMACs) unless otherwise selected below (leave blank if not applicable).
  o. [ ]   The matching contributions will be QMACs (fully Vested and subject to restrictions on withdrawals as set forth in the Plan). Such contributions may be used in either the ADP or ACP test.

E.   **Allocation conditions** (Plan Section 12.3). Select p. OR q. and all that apply of r. - x. (**Note:** If the "ACP test safe harbor" provisions are being used (Question 27.b.), option p. below (no conditions) must be selected, unless no HCEs are eligible to receive the matching contribution.)
  p. [ ]   **No conditions.** All Participants share in the allocations regardless of service completed during the Plan Year or employment status on the last day of the Plan Year (skip r. - x.).
  q. [ ]   **Allocation conditions apply** (select one of 1. -5. AND one of 6. - 9. below):
  Conditions for Participants NOT employed on the last day of the Plan Year.
  1. [ ]   A Participant must complete more than _____ (not to exceed 500) Hours of Service (or _____ (not to exceed 3) months of service if the elapsed time method is selected).
  2. [ ]   A Participant must complete a Year of Service (or Period of Service if the elapsed time method is selected). (could cause the Plan to violate coverage requirements under Code §410(b))
  3. [ ]   Participants will NOT share in the allocations, regardless of service. (could cause the Plan to violate coverage requirements under Code §410(b))
  4. [ ]   Participants will share in the allocations, regardless of service.
  5. [ ]   Other: _____ (must be definitely determinable, not subject to Employer discretion and may not require more than one Year of Service (or Period of Service if the elapsed time method is selected))

  Conditions for Participants employed on the last day of the Plan Year (options 7., 8. and 9. could cause the Plan to violate coverage requirements under Code §410(b))
  6. [ ]   No service requirement.
  7. [ ]   A Participant must complete a Year of Service (or Period of Service if the elapsed time method is selected).
  8. [ ]   A Participant must complete at least _____ (not to exceed 1,000) Hours of Service during the Plan Year.
  9. [ ]   Other: _____ (must be definitely determinable, not subject to Employer discretion and may not require more than one Year of Service (or Period of Service if the elapsed time method is selected)).

  Waiver of conditions for Participants NOT employed on the last day of the Plan Year. If q.1., 2., 3., or 5. is selected, Participants who are not employed on the last day of the Plan Year in which one of the following events occur will be eligible to share in the allocations regardless of the above conditions (select all that apply; leave blank if none apply):
  r. [ ]   Death
  s. [ ]   Total and Permanent Disability
  t. [ ]   Termination of employment on or after Normal Retirement Age
      1. [ ]   or Early Retirement Date

  Code §410(b) fail-safe. If q.2., 3., 5. and/or q.7., 8. or 9. is selected, the Code §410(b) ratio percentage fail-safe provisions (Plan Section 12.3(f)) will NOT apply unless selected below (leave blank if not applicable or fail-safe will not be used):
  u. [ ]   The Plan will use the Code §410(b) fail-safe provisions and must satisfy the "ratio percentage test" of Code §410(b).

  Conditions based on period other than Plan Year. The allocation conditions above will be applied based on the Plan Year unless otherwise selected below. If selected, the above provisions will be applied by substituting the term Plan Year with the specified period (e.g., if Plan Year quarter is selected below and the allocation condition is 250 Hours of Service per quarter, enter 250 hours (not 1000) at q.8. above). (may not be selected with q.2. or q.7.)
  v. [ ]   The Plan Year quarter.
  w. [ ]   Payroll period.
  x. [ ]   Other: _____ (must be definitely determinable and not subject to Employer discretion and may not be longer than a twelve month period).

F.   **Additional matching contributions.** No additional matching contribution may be made unless otherwise selected below (leave blank if not applicable).
  y. [ ]   Additional matching contributions may be made (e.g., a matching contribution made on a periodic basis as well as a matching contribution based on the end of the Plan Year). Specify the additional matching contribution by attaching an addendum to the Adoption Agreement that duplicates this entire Question 28. If selected, the additional matching contribution applies to all Participants eligible to share in matching contributions except as otherwise specified in the addendum or below.
      1. [ ]   The additional matching contribution only applies to the following Participants: _____ (must be definitely determinable). (If the additional matching contribution is in lieu of the matching contribution set forth in 28A – E above then use Eligible Employee question to exclude these Participants from such matching contribution).

G. **True-up contributions.** Under Period of determination above, if j. – m. is selected, does the Employer have the discretion to true-up the Employer matching contribution (i.e., apply the Employer matching contribution on a Plan Year basis)? (leave blank if not applicable).

    z. [ ] Yes (may not be elected if the "ADP and/or ACP test safe harbor" provisions are being used).

29.   EMPLOYER PROFIT SHARING CONTRIBUTIONS (Plan Section 12.1(a)(3)) (skip Questions 29 and 30 if Employer profit sharing contributions are NOT selected at Question 12.e.)

  A. **Profit sharing formula** (c. may be selected in addition to a., b. or d.)

    a. [ ] **Discretionary.** Discretionary contribution, to be determined by the Employer.

      1. [ ] **Discretionary based on business units or location.** The Employer may determine a separate discretionary contribution for Participants working in different business units or locations.

    b. [ ] **Fixed.** Fixed contribution equal to _____% of Compensation of Participants eligible to share in allocations.

    c. [ ] **Prevailing wage contribution.** The Employer will make a "prevailing wage contribution" on behalf of each Participant who performs services subject to the Service Contract Act, Davis-Bacon Act or similar federal, state, or municipal prevailing wage statutes. The "prevailing wage contribution" will be an amount equal to the remaining balance of the prevailing wage defined bona-fide fringe benefit amount, based on the Participant's employment classification as designated on the appropriate prevailing wage determination, after the application of other prevailing wage defined bona-fide fringe payments. Specify the "prevailing wage contribution" by attaching an appendix to the Adoption Agreement that indicates the contribution rate(s) applicable to the prevailing wage employment/job classification(s). The "prevailing wage contribution" will not be subject to any age or service requirements set forth in Question 14, entry date provisions at Question 15, nor to any service or employment conditions set forth in Question 30 and will be 100% Vested.

      Additional "prevailing wage contribution" provisions (select all that apply; leave blank if none apply)

      1. [ ] **Offset.** The "prevailing wage contribution" made on behalf of a Participant for a Plan Year will reduce (offset) other Employer contributions allocated or contributed on behalf of such Participant for the Plan.

      2. [ ] **Exclude Highly Compensated Employees.** Highly Compensated Employees will be excluded from receiving a "prevailing wage contribution."

      3. [ ] **QNEC.** The "prevailing wage contribution" is considered a Qualified Nonelective Contribution (QNEC).

    d. [ ] Other: _____ (the formula described must satisfy the definitely determinable requirement under Reg. §1.401-1(b). If the formula is non-uniform, it is not a design-based safe harbor for nondiscrimination purposes.)

  B. **Contribution allocations.** If a., b., or d. above is selected, the Employer Nonelective profit sharing contribution for a Plan Year will be allocated as follows:

    e. [ ] **INCORPORATION OF CONTRIBUTION FORMULA.** In accordance with the contribution formula specified above (may only be selected if b. or d. above is selected).

    f. [ ] **NON-INTEGRATED ALLOCATION**

      1. [ ] in the same ratio as each Participant's Compensation bears to the total of such Compensation of all Participants

      2. [ ] in the same dollar amount to all Participants (per capita)

      3. [ ] in the same dollar amount per Hour of Service completed by each Participant

      4. [ ] in the same proportion that each Participant's points bears to the total of such points of all Participants. A Participant's points with respect to any Plan Year will be computed as follows (select all that apply):

        a. [ ] _____ point(s) will be allocated for each Year of Service (or Period of Service).

        However, the maximum Years (or Periods if elapsed time method is selected) of Service taken into account will not exceed:

        1. [ ] _____ (leave blank if no limit on service applies).

        Year of Service (or Period of Service if applicable), means:

        2. [ ] service for eligibility purposes

        3. [ ] service for vesting purposes

        b. [ ] _____ point(s) will be allocated for each full $_____ (may not exceed $200) of Compensation

        c. [ ] _____ point(s) will be allocated for each year of age as of the last day of the Plan Year

    g. [ ] **INTEGRATED (PERMITTED DISPARITY) ALLOCATION**

    In accordance with Plan Section 4.3(b)(2) based on a Participant's Compensation in excess of:

      1. [ ] the Taxable Wage Base

      2. [ ] _____% (not to exceed 100%) of the Taxable Wage Base (see Note below)

      3. [ ] 80% of the Taxable Wage Base plus $1.00

      4. [ ] $_____ (not greater than the Taxable Wage Base) (see Note below)

    NOTE: The integration percentage of 5.7% will be reduced to:

      1. 4.3% if 2. or 4. above is more than 20% and less than or equal to 80% of the Taxable Wage Base.

      2. 5.4% if 3. is selected or if 2. or 4. above is more than 80% of the Taxable Wage Base.

Non-Standardized 401(k) Profit Sharing Plan

h. [ ] **NON-SAFE HARBOR ALLOCATION METHODS**

    1. [ ] **Grouping method.** Pursuant to Plan Section 4.3(b)(3)(vi), the classifications are (select a. or b.):

       a. [ ] Each Participant constitutes a separate classification.

       b. [ ] Participants will be divided into the following classifications with the allocation methods indicated under each classification.

       Definition of classifications. Define each classification and specify the method of allocating the contribution among members of each classification. Classifications specified below must be clearly defined in a manner that will not violate the definitely determinable allocation requirement of Regulation §1.401-1(b)(1)(ii). The design of the groups cannot be such that the only NHCEs benefiting under the Plan are those with the lowest amount of Compensation and/or the shortest periods of service and who may represent the minimum number of these Employees necessary to satisfy coverage under Code §410(b).

       Classification A will consist of _____

       The allocation method will be: [ ] pro rata based on Compensation

                                     [ ] equal dollar amounts (per capita)

       Classification B will consist of _____

       The allocation method will be: [ ] pro rata based on Compensation

                                       [ ] equal dollar amounts (per capita)

       Classification C will consist of _____

       The allocation method will be: [ ] pro rata based on Compensation

                                       [ ] equal dollar amounts (per capita)

       Classification D will consist of _____

       The allocation method will be: [ ] pro rata based on Compensation

                                       [ ] equal dollar amounts (per capita)

       Additional classifications: _____ (specify the classifications and which of the above allocation methods (pro rata or per capita) will be used for each classification).

       NOTE: In the case of Self-Employed Individuals (i.e., sole proprietors or partners), the requirements or Regulation §1.401(k)-1(a)(6) continue to apply and the allocation method should not be such that a cash or deferred election is created for a Self-Employed Individual as a result of application of the allocation method.

       NOTE: If more than four (4) classifications, the additional classifications and allocation methods may be attached as an addendum to the Adoption Agreement or may be entered under Additional Classifications above.

       Determination of applicable group. If a Participant shifts from one classification to another during a Plan Year, then unless selected below, the Participant is in a classification based on the Participant's status as of the last day of the Plan Year, or if earlier, the date of termination of employment. If selected below, the Administrator will apportion the Participant's allocation during a Plan Year based on the following:

       1.   [ ] Beginning of Plan Year. The classification will be based on the Participant's status as of the beginning of the Plan Year.

       2.   [ ] Months in each classification. Pro rata based on the number of months the Participant spent in each classification.

       3.   [ ] Days in each classification. Pro rata based on the number of days the Participant spent in each classification.

       4.   [ ] One classification only. The Employer in a nondiscriminatory manner will direct the Administrator to place the Participant in only one classification for the entire Plan Year during which the shift occurs.

    2. [ ] **Age-weighted method.** The Schedule of Age-Weighted Allocation Factors is set forth in attached Exhibit A (which is hereby incorporated by reference and made a part of the Plan) and will be based on the following interest rate (if no selection is made, c. will be deemed to have been selected):

       a. [ ]   7.5% interest

       b. [ ]   8.0% interest

       c. [ ]   8.5% interest

    3. [ ] **Other:** _____ (the formula described must satisfy the definitely determinable requirement under Reg. §1.401-1(b). If the formula is non-uniform, it is not a design-based safe harbor for nondiscrimination purposes.)

Non-Standardized 401(k) Profit Sharing Plan

30. ALLOCATION CONDITIONS (Plan Section 12.3). Requirements to share in allocations of Employer Nonelective profit sharing contributions and QNECs (as permitted by Plan Section 12.1(a)(4)) (select a. OR b. and all that apply of c. - f.)

    a. [ ] **No conditions.** All Participants share in the allocations regardless of service completed during the Plan Year or employment status on the last day of the Plan Year (skip to Question 31).

    b. [ ] **Allocation conditions apply** (select one of 1. -5. AND one of 6. - 9. below)

        Conditions for Participants NOT employed on the last day of the Plan Year

        1. [ ] A Participant must complete more than _____ (not to exceed 500) Hours of Service (or _____ (not to exceed 3) months of service if the elapsed time method is selected).

        2. [ ] A Participant must complete a Year of Service (or Period of Service if the elapsed time method is selected). (could cause the Plan to violate coverage requirements under Code §410(b))

        3. [ ] Participants will NOT share in the allocations, regardless of service. (could cause the Plan to violate coverage requirements under Code §410(b))

        4. [ ] Participants will share in the allocations, regardless of service.

        5. [ ] Other: _____ (must be definitely determinable, not subject to Employer discretion and may not require more than one Year of Service (or Period of Service if the elapsed time method is selected)).

        Conditions for Participants employed on the last day of the Plan Year (options 7., 8. and 9. could cause the Plan to violate coverage requirements under Code §410(b))

        6. [ ] No service requirement.

        7. [ ] A Participant must complete a Year of Service (or Period of Service if the elapsed time method is selected).

        8. [ ] A Participant must complete at least _____ (not to exceed 1,000) Hours of Service during the Plan Year.

        9. [ ] Other: _____ (must be definitely determinable, not subject to Employer discretion and may not require more than one Year of Service (or Period of Service if the elapsed time method is selected)).

    Waiver of conditions for Participants NOT employed on the last day of the Plan Year. If b.1., 2., 3., or 5. is selected, Participants who are not employed on the last day of the Plan Year in which one of the following events occur will be eligible to share in the allocations regardless of the above conditions (select all that apply; leave blank if none apply):

    c. [ ] Death

    d. [ ] Total and Permanent Disability

    e. [ ] Termination of employment on or after Normal Retirement Age

        1. [ ] or Early Retirement Date

    Code §410(b) fail-safe. If b.2., 3., 5. and/or b.7., 8. or 9. is selected, the Code §410(b) ratio percentage fail-safe provisions will NOT apply (Plan Section 4.3(m)) unless selected below (leave blank if not applicable or fail-safe will not be used):

    f. [ ] The Plan will use the Code §410(b) fail-safe provisions and must satisfy the ratio percentage test of Code §410(b).

31. FORFEITURES (Plan Sections 1.37 and 4.3(e))

    Except as provided in Plan Section 1.37, a Forfeiture will occur:

    a. [ ] N/A (may only be selected if all contributions are fully Vested (default provisions at Plan Section 4.3(e) apply); skip to Question 32)

    b. [ ] As of the earlier of (1) the last day of the Plan Year in which the former Participant incurs five (5) consecutive 1-Year Breaks in Service, or (2) the distribution of the entire Vested portion of the Participant's Account.

    c. [ ] As of the last day of the Plan Year in which the former Participant incurs five (5) consecutive 1-Year Breaks in Service.

    NOTE: (1) Forfeitures are disposed of in accordance with Employer direction that is consistent with Section 4.3(e).

        (2) Effective for Plan Years beginning after the Plan Year in which this Plan document is adopted, Forfeitures may not be used to reduce Employer contributions which are required pursuant to the Code to be fully Vested when contributed to the Plan (such as QMACs, QNECs and "ADP test safe harbor contributions" other than QACA "ADP test safe harbor contributions"). The reallocation of Forfeitures could affect the Plan's top-heavy exemption (see Plan Section 12.8(f)). One approach to avoid this result is to provide for a discretionary matching contribution that satisfies the "ACP test safe harbor" provisions (i.e., select Question 27A.b. and select a discretionary matching contribution at Question 28) and then allocate Forfeitures as a matching contribution.

32. ALLOCATION OF EARNINGS (Plan Section 4.3(c))

    Allocation of earnings with respect to amounts which are not subject to Participant investment direction and which are contributed to the Plan after the previous Valuation Date will be determined:

    a. [ ] N/A (all assets in the Plan are subject to Participant investment direction)

    b. [ ] by using a weighted average based on the amount of time that has passed between the date a contribution or distribution is made and the prior Valuation Date

    c. [ ] by treating one-half of all such contributions as being a part of the Participant's nonsegregated Account balance as of the previous Valuation Date

    d. [ ] by using the method specified in Plan Section 4.3(c) (balance forward method)

    e. [ ] other: _____ (must be a definite predetermined formula that is not based on Compensation, that satisfies the nondiscrimination requirements of Regulation §1.401(a)(4)-4, and that is applied uniformly to all Participants)

Non-Standardized 401(k) Profit Sharing Plan

33.   TOP-HEAVY MINIMUM ALLOCATION

The minimum allocation requirements for any Top-Heavy Plan Year will be applied only to Non-Key Employee Participants unless selected below:

a. [ ] The Top-Heavy minimum will be provided to both Key and Non-Key Employee Participants.

DISTRIBUTIONS

34.   FORM OF DISTRIBUTIONS (Plan Sections 6.5 and 6.6)

Distributions under the Plan may be made in (select all that apply; must select at least one from a. - e. unless g. is selected below)

a. [ ] lump-sums

b. [ ] substantially equal installments

c. [ ] partial withdrawals, provided the minimum withdrawal is $_____ (leave blank if no minimum)

d. [ ] partial withdrawals or installments are only permitted for Participants or Beneficiaries who must receive required minimum distributions under Code §401(a)(9) except for the following (e.g., partial is not permitted for death benefits; leave blank if no exceptions):

      1. [ ] _____

e. [ ] other: _____ (must be definitely determinable and not subject to Employer discretion)

NOTE: Regardless of the above, a Participant is not required to request a withdrawal of his or her total Account for an in-service distribution, a hardship distribution, or a distribution from the Participant's Rollover Account.

Annuities. Is the annuity form of distribution the normal form of distribution?

NOTE: If this Plan includes transferred pension assets, f.1. or g. below must be selected.

f. [ ] **Annuities are not allowed or are not the normal form of distribution** (except as indicated below). Plan Section 6.13(b) will apply and the joint and survivor rules of Code §§401(a)(11) and 417 will not apply to the Plan.

    Special rules. An annuity form of distribution is available to certain Participants and/or with respect to only a portion of the Plan assets according to the following: (select all that apply)

    1. [ ] **Pension assets.** Annuities are the normal form of distribution for assets that are transferred pension assets (Plan Section 6.13(a)).

    2. [ ] **Annuity selected by Participant.** Plan Section 6.13(c) will apply and the joint and survivor rules of Code §§401(a)(11) and 417 will apply only if an annuity form of distribution is selected by a Participant.

      However, the Participant may only select an annuity distribution according to the following:

      a. [ ] _____ (leave blank if no conditions apply).

g. [ ] **Annuities are the normal form of distribution.** The qualified Joint and Survivor Annuity and Qualified Pre-Retirement Survivor Annuity provisions apply (Plan Section 6.13 will not apply and the joint and survivor rules of Code §§401(a)(11) and 417 will automatically apply).

Pre-Retirement Survivor Annuity

If the Plan permits an annuity form of payment under option f.1. or g. above, the Pre-Retirement Survivor Annuity (minimum Spouse's death benefit) will be equal to 50% of a Participant's interest in the Plan unless a different percentage is selected below (leave blank if default applies)

h. [ ] 100% of a Participant's interest in the Plan.

i. [ ] _____% (may not be less than 50%) of a Participant's interest in the Plan.

Cash or property. Distributions may be made in:

j. [ ] cash only, except for (select all that apply; leave blank if none apply):

    1. [ ] insurance Contracts

    2. [ ] annuity Contracts

    3. [ ] Participant loans

    4. [ ] property in an open brokerage window or similar arrangement

k. [ ] cash or property, except that the following limitation(s) apply: (leave blank if there are no limitations on property distributions):

    1. [ ] _____

35.   CONDITIONS FOR DISTRIBUTIONS UPON SEVERANCE OF EMPLOYMENT. Distributions upon severance of employment pursuant to Plan Section 6.4(a) will not be made unless the following conditions have been satisfied:

A. **Accounts in excess of $5,000**

a. [ ] Distributions may be made as soon as administratively feasible following severance of employment.

b. [ ] Distributions may be made as soon as administratively feasible after the Participant has incurred _____ 1-Year Break(s) in Service (or Period(s) of Severance if the elapsed time method is selected).

c. [ ] Distributions may be made as soon as administratively feasible after the last day of the Plan Year coincident with or next following severance of employment.

d. [ ] Distributions may be made as soon as administratively feasible after the last day of the Plan Year quarter coincident with or next following severance of employment.

Non-Standardized 401(k) Profit Sharing Plan

e. [ ] Distributions may be made as soon as administratively feasible after the Valuation Date coincident with or next following severance of employment.

f. [ ] Distributions may be made as soon as administratively feasible after _____ months have elapsed following severance of employment.

g. [ ] No distributions may be made until a Participant has reached Early or Normal Retirement Date.

h. [ ] Other: _____ (must be objective conditions which are ascertainable and are not subject to Employer discretion except as otherwise permitted in Regulation §1.411(d)-4 and may not exceed the limits of Code §401(a)(14) as set forth in Plan Section 6.7)

B. **Accounts of $5,000 or less**

i. [ ] Same as above

j. [ ] Distributions may be made as soon as administratively feasible following severance of employment.

k. [ ] Distributions may be made as soon as administratively feasible after the Participant has incurred _____ 1-Year Break(s) in Service (or Period(s) of Severance if the elapsed time method is selected).

l. [ ] Distributions may be made as soon as administratively feasible after the last day of the Plan Year coincident with or next following severance of employment.

m. [ ] Other: _____ (must be objective conditions which are ascertainable and are not subject to Employer discretion except as otherwise permitted in Regulation §1.411(d)-4 and may not exceed the limits of Code §401(a)(14) as set forth in Plan Section 6.7)

C. **Timing after initial distributable event.** If a distribution is not made in accordance with the above provisions upon the occurrence of the distributable event, then a Participant may elect a subsequent distribution at any time after the time the amount was first distributable (assuming the amount is still distributable), unless otherwise selected below (may not be selected with 35.g. and 35.i.):

n. [ ] Other: _____ (e.g., a subsequent distribution request may only be made in accordance with l. above (i.e., the last day of another Plan Year); must be objective conditions which are ascertainable and are not subject to Employer discretion except as otherwise permitted in Regulation §1.411(d)-4 and may not exceed the limits of Code §401(a)(14) as set forth in Plan Section 6.7)

D. **Participant consent (i.e., involuntary cash-outs).** Should Vested Account balances less than a certain dollar threshold be automatically distributed without Participant consent (mandatory distributions)?

NOTE: The Plan provides that distributions of amounts of $5,000 or less do not require spousal consent and are only paid as lump-sums.

o. [ ] No, Participant consent is required for all distributions.

p. [ ] Yes, Participant consent is required only if the distribution is over:

     1. [ ] $5,000

     2. [ ] $1,000

     3. [ ] $_____ (less than $1,000)

     NOTE: If 2. or 3. is selected, rollovers will be included in determining the threshold for Participant consent.

     Automatic IRA rollover. With respect to mandatory distributions of amounts that are $1,000 or less, if a Participant makes no election, the amount will be distributed as a lump-sum unless selected below.

     4. [ ] If a Participant makes no election, then the amount will be automatically rolled over to an IRA provided the amount is at least $_____ (e.g., $200).

E. **Rollovers in determination of $5,000 threshold.** Unless otherwise elected below, amounts attributable to rollover contributions (if any) will be **included** in determining the $5,000 threshold for timing of distributions, form of distributions or consent rules.

q. [ ] Exclude rollovers (rollover contributions will be **excluded** in determining the $5,000 threshold)

NOTE: Regardless of the above election, if the Participant consent threshold is $1,000 or less, then the Administrator must include amounts attributable to rollovers for such purpose. In such case, an election to exclude rollovers above will apply for purposes of the timing and form of distributions.

F. **Mandatory distribution at Normal Retirement Age.** Regardless of the above elections other than any mandatory distributions provided for in p. above, unless otherwise selected below, a Participant who has severed employment may elect to delay a distribution beyond the later of age 62 or the Participant's Normal Retirement Age (subject to Plan Section 6.8).

r. [ ] A Participant who has severed employment may not elect to delay a distribution beyond the later of age 62 or the Participant's Normal Retirement Age.

36. DISTRIBUTIONS UPON DEATH (Plan Section 6.8(b)(2))

Distributions upon the death of a Participant prior to the "required beginning date" will:

a. [ ] be made pursuant to the election of the Participant or "designated Beneficiary"

b. [ ] begin within 1 year of death for a "designated Beneficiary" and be payable over the life (or over a period not exceeding the "life expectancy") of such Beneficiary, except that if the "designated Beneficiary" is the Participant's Spouse, begin prior to December 31st of the year in which the Participant would have attained age 70 1/2

Non-Standardized 401(k) Profit Sharing Plan

    c. [ ] be made within 5 (or if lesser _____) years of death for all Beneficiaries
    d. [ ] be made within 5 (or if lesser _____) years of death for all Beneficiaries, except that if the "designated Beneficiary" is the Participant's Spouse, begin prior to December 31st of the year in which the Participant would have attained age 70 1/2 and be payable over the life (or over a period not exceeding the "life expectancy") of such "surviving Spouse"

NOTE: The elections above must be coordinated with the Form of distributions (e.g., if the Plan only permits lump-sum distributions, then options a., b. and d. would not be applicable).

37.   HARDSHIP DISTRIBUTIONS (Plan Sections 6.12 and/or 12.10)
    a. [ ] Hardship distributions are NOT permitted (skip to Question 38).
    b. [ ] Hardship distributions are permitted from the following Participant Accounts:
       1. [ ] all Accounts
       2. [ ] only from the following Accounts (select one or more):
          a. [ ] Pre-Tax Elective Deferral Account
          b. [ ] Roth Elective Deferral Account
          c. [ ] Account(s) attributable to Employer matching contributions
          d. [ ] Account attributable to Employer Nonelective profit sharing contributions
          e. [ ] Rollover Account
          f. [ ] Transfer Account (other than amounts attributable to a money purchase pension plan)
          g. [ ] Other: _____ (specify Account(s) and conditions in a manner that is definitely determinable and not subject to Employer discretion)

NOTE: Distributions from a Participant's Elective Deferral Account are limited to the portion of such Account attributable to such Participant's Elective Deferrals (and earnings attributable thereto up to December 31, 1988). Hardship distributions are NOT permitted from a Participant's Qualified Nonelective Contribution Account, Qualified Matching Contribution Account, Accounts attributable to "ADP test safe harbor contributions" or Transfer Account attributable to pension assets (e.g., from a money purchase pension plan).

Additional limitations. The following limitations apply to hardship distributions:
    3. [ ] N/A (no additional limitations)
    4. [ ] Additional limitations (select one or more):
         a. [ ] The minimum amount of a distribution is $_____ (may not exceed $1,000).
         b. [ ] No more than _____ distribution(s) may be made to a Participant during a Plan Year.
         c. [ ] Distributions may only be made from Accounts which are fully Vested.
         d. [ ] A Participant does not include a Former Employee at the time of the hardship distribution.
         e. [ ] Hardship distributions may be made subject to the following provisions: _____ (must be definitely determinable and not subject to Employer discretion).

Beneficiary Hardship. Hardship distributions for Beneficiary expenses are NOT allowed unless otherwise selected below.
    5. [ ] Hardship distributions for expenses of Beneficiaries are allowed
        Special effective date (may be left blank if effective date is same as the Plan or Restatement Effective Date; select a. and, if applicable, b.)
         a. [ ] effective as of _____ (if this is a PPA restatement and the provisions were effective prior to the Restatement Effective Date, then enter the date such provisions were first effective; may not be earlier than August 17, 2006)
         b. [ ] eliminated effective as of _____.

Safe harbor hardship rules. Will the safe harbor hardship rules of Plan Section 12.10 apply to hardship distributions from all Accounts? (Note: The safe harbor hardship rules automatically apply to hardship distributions of Elective Deferrals.)
    6. [ ] Yes. The provisions of Plan Section 12.10 apply to all hardship distributions.
    7. [ ] No. The provisions of Plan Section 6.12 apply to hardship distributions from all Accounts other than a Participant's Elective Deferral Account.

38.   IN-SERVICE DISTRIBUTIONS (Plan Section 6.11)
    a. [ ] In-service distributions are NOT permitted (except as otherwise selected for Hardship Distributions).
    b. [ ] In-service distributions may be made to a Participant who has not separated from service provided any of the following conditions have been satisfied (select one or more):
       1. [ ] Age
          a. [ ] the Participant has attained age _____
          b. [ ] the Participant has reached Normal Retirement Age
       2. [ ] the Participant has been a Participant in the Plan for at least _____ years (may not be less than five (5))
       3. [ ] the amounts being distributed have accumulated in the Plan for at least 2 years
       4. [ ] other: _____ (must satisfy the definitely determinable requirement under Regulations §401-1(b); may not be subject to Employer discretion; must be nondiscriminatory; and must be limited to a combination of items b.1. – b.3. or a Participant's disability)

More than one condition. If more than one condition is selected above, then a Participant only needs to satisfy one of the conditions, unless selected below:

　5. [ ]　A Participant must satisfy each condition

NOTE:　Regardless of any elections above, distributions from a Participant's Elective Deferral Account, Qualified Matching Contribution Account, Qualified Nonelective Contribution Account and Accounts attributable to "ADP test safe harbor contributions" are subject to restrictions and generally may not be distributed prior to age 59 1/2. Distributions from a Transfer Account attributable to a money purchase pension plan are not permitted prior to age 62.

Account restrictions. In-service distributions are permitted from the following Participant Accounts:

　6. [ ]　all Accounts
　7. [ ]　only from the following Accounts (select one or more):
　　　a. [ ]　Pre-Tax Elective Deferral Account
　　　b. [ ]　Roth Elective Deferral Account
　　　c. [ ]　Account(s) attributable to Employer matching contributions (includes matching "ADP test safe harbor contributions")
　　　d. [ ]　Account attributable to Employer Nonelective profit sharing contributions
　　　e. [ ]　Qualified Nonelective Contribution Account (includes nonelective "ADP test safe harbor contributions")
　　　f. [ ]　Rollover Account
　　　g. [ ]　Transfer Account attributable to (select one or both):
　　　　　1. [ ]　non-pension assets
　　　　　2. [ ]　pension assets (e.g., from a money purchase pension plan)
　　　h. [ ]　Other: _____ (specify Account(s) and conditions in a manner that is definitely determinable and not subject to Employer discretion)

Limitations. The following limitations apply to in-service distributions:

　8. [ ]　N/A (no additional limitations)
　9. [ ]　Additional limitations (select one or more):
　　　a. [ ]　The minimum amount of a distribution is $_____ (may not exceed $1,000).
　　　b. [ ]　No more than _____ distribution(s) may be made to a Participant during a Plan Year.
　　　c. [ ]　Distributions may only be made from Accounts which are fully Vested.
　　　d. [ ]　Distributions from the Roth Elective Deferral Account (38.b.6. or 38.b.7.b. selected), may only be made if the distribution is a "qualified distribution."
　　　e. [ ]　In-service distributions may be made subject to the following provisions: _____ (must be definitely determinable and not subject to discretion).

39.　AGE 62 IN-SERVICE DISTRIBUTIONS FOR TRANSFERRED MONEY PURCHASE ASSETS (Plan Section 6.11) In-service distributions at age 62 will NOT be allowed (except as otherwise permitted under the Plan without regard to this provision) unless selected below (applies only for Transfer Accounts from a money purchase pension plan):

　a. [ ]　In-service distributions will be allowed for Participants at age 62.
　　　Special effective date. If this is a PPA restatement and the provision applied other than as of the first day of the 2007 Plan Year, then enter the date such provision was first effective: (leave blank if not applicable)
　　　1. [ ]　_____ (may not be earlier than the first day of the 2007 Plan Year).

　　　Limitations. The following limitations apply to these in-service distributions:
　　　2. [ ]　The Plan already provides for in-service distributions and the restrictions set forth in the Plan (e.g., minimum amount of distributions or frequency of distributions) are applicable to in-service distributions at age 62.
　　　3. [ ]　N/A (no limitations)
　　　4. [ ]　The following elections apply to in-service distributions at age 62 (select one or more):
　　　　　a. [ ]　The minimum amount of a distribution is $_____ (may not exceed $1,000).
　　　　　b. [ ]　No more than _____ distribution(s) may be made to a Participant during a Plan Year.
　　　　　c. [ ]　Distributions may only be made from Accounts which are fully Vested.
　　　　　d. [ ]　In-service distributions may be made subject to the following provisions: _____ (must be definitely determinable and not subject to discretion).

40.　IN-PLAN ROTH ROLLOVER CONTRIBUTIONS (Plan Section 12.11) (skip if Roth Elective Deferrals NOT selected at Question 12.b.1.)

　a. [ ]　In-Plan Roth rollover contributions are NOT permitted (skip to Question 41).
　b. [ ]　In-Plan Roth rollover contributions are permitted according to the following provisions.
　　　Special effective date. (may be left blank if same as Plan or Restatement Effective Date)
　　　1. [ ]　_____ (if this is a PPA restatement and the provisions were effective prior to the Restatement Effective Date, then enter the date such provisions were first effective; may not be earlier than September 28, 2010)

Non-Standardized 401(k) Profit Sharing Plan

Eligibility and type of rollover. Any Participant may elect an in-Plan Roth rollover contribution by direct rollover except as selected below (select all that apply; leave blank if none apply):

c. [ ]   **In-service distribution only.** Only Participants who are Employees may elect an in-Plan Roth rollover contribution. (if not selected, Terminated Participants may make an in-Plan Roth rollover contribution but only when entitled to an actual cash distribution)

d. [ ]   **No transfer of loans.** Loans may not be distributed as part of an in-Plan Roth rollover contribution. (if not selected, any loans may be transferred)

In-service distribution provisions. The Employer elects the following regarding in-service distributions from the Plan solely for purposes of making an in-Plan Roth rollover contribution:

e. [ ]   N/A (Plan's existing in-service distribution provisions apply) (may only be selected if Plan permits in-service distributions; skip to Question 41)

f. [ ]   In-service distribution provisions. The Employer elects to permit in-service distributions as follows solely for purposes of making an in-Plan Roth rollover contribution (select one or more):

     1. [ ]   the Participant has attained age _____

     2. [ ]   the Participant has _____ months of participation (specify minimum of 60 months)

     3. [ ]   the amounts being distributed have accumulated in the Plan for at least _____ years (at least 2)

     4. [ ]   other (describe): _____ (must satisfy the definitely determinable requirement under Regulations §401-1(b); may not be subject to Employer discretion; must be nondiscriminatory; and must be limited to a combination of items f.1. – f.3. or a Participant's disability)

More than one condition. If more than one condition is selected above, then a Participant only needs to satisfy one of the conditions, unless selected below:

     5. [ ]   A Participant must satisfy each condition

NOTE: Regardless of any election above to the contrary, in-Plan Roth rollover contributions are not permitted from a Participant's Elective Deferral Account, Qualified Matching Contribution Account, Qualified Nonelective Contribution Account and Accounts attributable to "ADP test safe harbor contributions" prior to age 59 1/2. Distributions from a Transfer Account attributable to a money purchase pension plan are not permitted prior to age 62.

Source of in-Plan Roth rollover contribution. Plan permits a direct rollover from the following qualifying sources:

     6. [ ]   all Accounts

     7. [ ]   only from the following qualifying sources (select one or more):

         a. [ ]   Pre-Tax Elective Deferral Account

         b. [ ]   Account(s) attributable to Employer matching contributions (includes any matching "ADP test safe harbor contributions")

         c. [ ]   Account attributable to Employer Nonelective profit sharing contributions

         d. [ ]   Qualified Nonelective Contribution Account (includes any nonelective "ADP test safe harbor contributions")

         e. [ ]   Rollover Account

         f. [ ]   Transfer Account

         g. [ ]   Other: _____ (specify Account(s) and conditions in a manner that is definitely determinable and not subject to Employer discretion; e.g., a Participant's Pre-Tax Deferral Account or Matching Contribution Account, but not the Participant's Nonelective Contribution Account)

Other limitations on direct in-Plan Roth rollover contribution (leave blank if none apply)

     8. [ ]   The following limitations apply (select one or more):

         a. [ ]   The minimum amount that may be rolled over is $_____ (may not exceed $1,000).

         b. [ ]   Distributions may only be made from Accounts which are fully Vested.

         c. [ ]   In-service distributions may be made subject to the following provisions: _____ (describe - must be definitely determinable and not subject to discretion).

Withholding. If the Plan does not permit an actual distribution upon the event triggering the right to elect the in-Plan Roth rollover contribution, then a Participant may not elect to have a portion of the amount that may be distributed as an in-Plan Roth rollover contribution distributed for tax withholding purposes unless selected below (leave blank if not applicable):

     9. [ ]   **Distribution for withholding.** A Participant may elect to have a portion of the amount that may be distributed as an in-Plan Roth rollover contribution distributed solely for purposes of federal or state income tax withholding related to the in-Plan Roth rollover contribution.

41.   QUALIFIED RESERVIST DISTRIBUTIONS (Plan Section 6.18)

     a. [ ]   Qualified reservist distributions are NOT permitted

     b. [ ]   Qualified reservist distributions are permitted

         Special effective date (may be left blank if same as Plan or Restatement Effective Date)

         1. [ ]   _____ (if this is a PPA restatement and the provisions were effective prior to the Restatement Effective Date, then enter the date such provisions were first effective; may not be earlier than September 12, 2001)

42.　HEART ACT PROVISIONS (Plan Section 6.18)
Continued benefit accruals.
a.　[ ]　Continued benefit accruals will NOT apply
b.　[ ]　Continued benefit accruals will apply

Special effective date. If this is a PPA restatement and the provision applied other than as of the first day of the 2007 Plan Year, then enter the date such provision was first effective: (leave blank if not applicable)
c.　[ ]　_____ (may not be earlier than the first day of the 2007 Plan Year)

Distributions for deemed severance of employment
d.　[ ]　The Plan does NOT permit distributions for deemed severance of employment
e.　[ ]　The Plan permits distributions for deemed severance of employment
　　Special effective date (may be left blank if same as Plan or Restatement Effective Date)
　　1.　[ ]　_____ (if this is a PPA restatement and the provisions were effective prior to the Restatement Effective Date, then enter the date such provisions were first effective; may not be earlier than January 1, 2007)

NONDISCRIMINATION TESTING

43.　HIGHLY COMPENSATED EMPLOYEE (Plan Section 1.41)
Top-Paid Group election and calendar year data election are not used unless selected below (the selections made for the latest year will continue to apply to subsequent Plan Years unless the Plan is amended) (select all that apply; leave blank if none apply):
a.　[ ]　**Top-Paid Group election** will be used.
b.　[ ]　**Calendar year data election** will be used (only applicable to non-calendar year Plan Year).

44.　ADP AND ACP TESTS (Plan Sections 12.4 and 12.6)
NOTE:　The selections made below for the latest year will continue to apply to subsequent Plan Years unless the Plan is amended. Also, the prior method will not apply if the Employer uses the discretionary nonelective "ADP test safe harbor contribution" described in Section 12.8(h) or if the Plan is amended during a Plan Year to eliminate an "ADP test safe harbor contribution."
ADP test. If applicable, the ADP ratio for NHCEs will be based on the current year ratio unless prior year testing method is selected below (leave blank if current year testing method is being used):
a.　[ ]　**Prior year testing method.** The prior year ratio will be used. If this selection is made for the first year the Code §401(k) feature is added to this Plan (unless this Plan is a successor plan), then for the first Plan Year only, the amount taken into account as the ADP of Nonhighly Compensated Employees for the preceding Plan Year will be the greater of 3% or the actual percentage for the initial Plan Year.

ACP test. If applicable, the ACP ratio for NHCEs will be based on the current year ratio unless prior year testing method is selected below (leave blank if current year testing method is being used):
b.　[ ]　**Prior year testing method.** The prior year ratio will be used. If this selection is made for the first year the Code §401(m) feature is added to this Plan (unless this Plan is a successor plan), then for the first Plan Year only, the amount taken into account as the ACP of NHCEs for the preceding Plan Year will be the greater of 3% or the actual percentage for the initial Plan Year.

Effective dates. (optional)
c.　[ ]　**Current year testing method.** If the current year testing method is currently being used, enter the date it was first effective (used for purposes of applying the five year restriction on amending to the prior year testing method):
　　1.　[ ]　ADP test: _____ (may not be selected with 44.a.)
　　2.　[ ]　ACP test: _____ (may not be selected with 44.b.)

MISCELLANEOUS

45.　LOANS TO PARTICIPANTS (Plan Section 7.6)
a.　[ ]　New loans are NOT permitted.
b.　[ ]　New loans are permitted.
NOTE:　Regardless of whether new loans are permitted, if the Plan permits rollovers, then the Administrator may, in a uniform and nondiscriminatory manner, accept rollovers of loans into this Plan.

46.　ROLLOVERS (Plan Section 4.6) (skip if rollover contributions are NOT selected at 12.f.)
Eligibility. Rollovers may be accepted from all Participants who are Employees as well as the following (select all that apply; leave blank if not applicable):
a.　[ ]　Any Eligible Employee, even prior to meeting eligibility conditions to be a Participant
b.　[ ]　Participants who are Former Employees

Distributions. When may distributions be made from a Participant's Rollover Account?

c. [ ] At any time

d. [ ] Only when the Participant is otherwise entitled to a distribution under the Plan

47. AFTER-TAX VOLUNTARY EMPLOYEE CONTRIBUTIONS (Plan Section 4.8) (skip if after-tax voluntary Employee contributions NOT selected at Question 12.g.)

Matching after-tax voluntary Employee contributions. There are no Employer matching contributions on after-tax voluntary Employee contributions unless elected below.

a. [ ] After-tax voluntary Employee contributions are aggregated with Elective Deferrals for purposes of applying any matching contributions under the Plan.

PPA TRANSITION RULES

The following questions only apply if this is a PPA restatement (i.e., Question 5.b.1. is selected). If this is not a PPA restatement, then this Plan will not be considered an individually designed plan merely because the following questions are deleted from the Adoption Agreement.

NOTE: The following provisions are designed to be left unanswered if the selections do not apply to the Plan.

48. PRIOR VESTING SCHEDULE FOR EMPLOYER NONELECTIVE PROFIT SHARING CONTRIBUTIONS. The vesting schedule for amounts attributable to Employer Nonelective profit sharing contributions made prior to Plan Years beginning after December 31, 2006, is (leave blank if not applicable):

a. [ ] _____ (enter the vesting schedule that applied prior to the Plan Year beginning in 2007; such schedule must satisfy 5-year cliff or 7-year graded and, if applicable, must provide for a top-heavy minimum schedule)

49. WRERA - RMD WAIVERS FOR 2009 (Plan Section 6.8(f))

Suspension/continuation of RMDs. Unless otherwise elected below, required minimum distributions (RMDs) for 2009 were suspended unless a Participant or Beneficiary elected to receive such distributions:

a. [ ] RMDs for 2009 were suspended for any Participant or Beneficiary who was scheduled to receive his/her first RMD for 2009 or who did not make a continuing election prior to 2009 to receive his/her RMD (unless the Participant or Beneficiary made an election to receive such distribution). RMDs for 2009 were continued for any Participant or Beneficiary who had made a continuing election to receive an RMD prior to 2009 (unless the Participant or Beneficiary made an election to suspend such distribution).

b. [ ] RMDs continued unless otherwise elected by a Participant or Beneficiary.

c. [ ] RMDs continued in accordance with the terms of the Plan (i.e., no election available to Participants or Beneficiaries).

d. [ ] Other: _____

Direct rollovers. The Plan also treated the following as "eligible rollover distributions" in 2009 (If no election is made, then a "direct rollover" was only offered for "2009 RMDs"):

e. [ ] "2009 RMDs" and "Extended 2009 RMDs."

f. [ ] "2009 RMDs" but only if paid with an additional amount that is an "eligible rollover distribution" without regard to Code §401(a)(9)(H).

50. NON-SPOUSAL ROLLOVERS (Plan Section 6.15(d)). Non-spousal rollovers are permitted effective for distributions after December 31, 2006 unless an alternative effective date is selected at a. below:

a. [ ] Non-spousal rollovers are allowed effective _____ (may not be earlier than January 1, 2007 and not later than January 1, 2010; the Plan already provides for non-spousal rollovers effective as of January 1, 2010)

Non-Standardized 401(k) Profit Sharing Plan

The adopting Employer may rely on an opinion letter issued by the Internal Revenue Service as evidence that the Plan is qualified under Code §401 only to the extent provided in Rev. Proc. 2011-49 or subsequent guidance.

The Employer may not rely on the opinion letter in certain other circumstances or with respect to certain qualification requirements, which are specified in the opinion letter issued with respect to the Plan and in Rev. Proc. 2011-49 or subsequent guidance. In order to have reliance in such circumstances or with respect to such qualification requirements, application for a determination letter must be made to Employee Plans Determinations of the Internal Revenue Service.

This Adoption Agreement may be used only in conjunction with basic Plan document #10. This Adoption Agreement and the basic Plan document will together be known as SunGard Business Systems LLC Non-Standardized 401(k) Profit Sharing Plan #10-005.

The adoption of this Plan, its qualification by the IRS, and the related tax consequences are the responsibility of the Employer and its independent tax and legal advisors.

SunGard Business Systems LLC will notify the Employer of any amendments made to the Plan or of the discontinuance or abandonment of the Plan. Furthermore, in order to be eligible to receive such notification, the Employer agrees to notify SunGard Business Systems LLC of any change in address. In addition, this Plan is provided to the Employer either in connection with investment in a product or pursuant to a contract or other arrangement for products and/or services. Upon cessation of such investment in a product or cessation of such contract or arrangement, as applicable, the Employer is no longer considered to be an adopter of this Plan and SunGard Business Systems LLC no longer has any obligations to the Employer that relate to the adoption of this Plan.

With regard to any questions regarding the provisions of the Plan, adoption of the Plan, or the effect of an opinion letter from the IRS, call or write (this information must be completed by the sponsor of this Plan or its designated representative):

Name: _____

Address: _____

_____

Telephone: _____

The Employer and Trustee (or Insurer), by executing below, hereby adopt this Plan:

EMPLOYER: [name of Employer]

By: _____   _____
                                                         DATE SIGNED

TRUSTEE (OR INSURER):

[ ] The signature of the Trustee or Insurer appears on a separate agreement or Contract.

OR (add additional Trustee signature lines as necessary)
[name of Trustee]

_____   _____
               TRUSTEE OR INSURER   DATE SIGNED

Non-Standardized 401(k) Profit Sharing Plan

APPENDIX A
SPECIAL EFFECTIVE DATES AND OTHER PERMITTED ELECTIONS

A.   **Special effective dates/spin-offs/mergers** (the following elections are optional; select any that apply):

   a.   [   ]   **Employer matching contributions.** The Employer matching contribution provisions under Question 28. are effective: _____.

   b.   [   ]   **Employer profit sharing contributions.** The Employer profit sharing contribution provisions under Questions 29. and 30. are effective: _____.

   c.   [   ]   **Distribution elections.** The distribution elections under Questions _____ (Choose 34. - 42. as applicable) are effective: _____.

   d.   [   ]   **Other special effective date(s):** _____.
For periods prior to the specified special effective date(s), the Plan terms in effect prior to its restatement under this Adoption Agreement will control for purposes of the designated provisions. A special effective date may not result in the delay of a Plan provision beyond the permissible effective date under any applicable law.

   e.   [   ]   **Spin-off.** The Plan was a spin-off from the _____ (enter name of plan), which was originally effective _____ (enter effective date of original plan).

   f.   [   ]   **Merged plans.** The following plan(s) are merged into this Plan (enter applicable information; attach addendum if more than 4 merged plans):

	Name of merged plan	Merger date	Original effective date of merged plan
1.	_____	_____	_____
2.	_____	_____	_____
3.	_____	_____	_____
4.	_____	_____	_____

B.   **Other permitted elections** (the following elections are optional):

   a.   [   ]   **No other permitted elections**

   The following elections apply (select one or more):

   b.   [   ]   **Deemed 125 compensation** (Plan Section 1.40). Deemed 125 compensation will be included in Compensation and 415 Compensation.

   c.   [   ]   **Reemployed after five (5) 1-Year Breaks in Service ("rule of parity" provisions)** (Plan Section 3.5(d)). The "rule of parity" provisions in Plan Section 3.5(d) will not apply for (select one or both):
      1.   [   ]   eligibility purposes
      2.   [   ]   vesting purposes

   d.   [   ]   **The "one-year hold-out" rule** described in Plan Section 3.5(e) will apply to (select one or both):
      1.   [   ]   determine eligibility (for all contributions types except Elective Deferrals)
      2.   [   ]   determine vesting

   e.   [   ]   **Normal form of annuity.** If the Plan permits an annuity form of payment (e.g., if 34.f.1., f.2. or g. is selected), instead of a joint and 50% survivor annuity, the normal form of the qualified Joint and Survivor Annuity will be:
      1.   [   ]   joint and 100% survivor annuity
      2.   [   ]   joint and 75% survivor annuity
      3.   [   ]   joint and 66 2/3% survivor annuity

   f.   [   ]   **Beneficiary if no beneficiary elected by Participant** (Plan Section 6.2(e)). In the event no valid designation of Beneficiary exists, then in lieu of the order set forth in Plan Section 6.2(e), the following order of priority will be used: _____ (specify an order of beneficiaries; e.g., children per stirpes, parents, and then step-children).

   g.   [   ]   **Common, collective or pooled trust funds** (Plan Sections 7.2(c)(5) and/or 7.3(b)(6)). The name(s) of the common, collective or pooled trust funds available under the Plan is (are): _____.

   h.   [   ]   **"Section 411(d)(6) protected benefits"** (Plan Section 8.1(b)). The following are Code §411(d)(6) protected benefits that are preserved under this Plan: _____ (specify the protected benefits and the accrued benefits that are subject to the protected benefits).

   i.   [   ]   **Limitation Year** (Plan Section 1.50). The Limitation Year for Code §415 purposes will be _____ (must be a consecutive twelve month period) instead of the "determination period" for Compensation.

   j.   [   ]   **415 Limits when 2 or more defined contribution plans are maintained** (Plan Section 4.4). If any Participant is covered under another qualified defined contribution plan maintained by the Employer or an Affiliated Employer, or if the Employer or an Affiliated Employer maintains a welfare benefit fund, as defined in Code §419(e), or an individual medical account, as defined in Code §415(l)(2), under which amounts are treated as "annual additions" with respect to any Participant in this Plan, then the provisions of Plan Section 4.4(b) will apply unless otherwise specified below:

Non-Standardized 401(k) Profit Sharing Plan

1. [ ]   Specify, in a manner that precludes Employer discretion, the method under which the plans will limit total "annual additions" to the "maximum permissible amount" and will properly reduce any "excess amounts": _____

k. [ ]   **Top-heavy duplications** (select one or more)
    1. [ ]   **Top-heavy duplications when 2 or more defined contribution plans are maintained** (Plan Section 4.3(f)). When a Non-Key Employee is a Participant in this Plan and another defined contribution plan maintained by the Employer that is subject to the top-heavy rules, indicate which method will be utilized to avoid duplication of top-heavy minimum benefits:
        a. [ ]   The full top-heavy minimum will be provided in each plan.
        b. [ ]   A minimum, non-integrated contribution of 3% of each Non-Key Employee's 415 Compensation will be provided in the Money Purchase Plan (or other plan subject to Code §412).
        c. [ ]   Specify the method under which the plans will provide top-heavy minimum benefits for Non-Key Employees that will preclude Employer discretion and avoid inadvertent omissions, including any adjustments required under Code §415: _____
        NOTE: If b. or c. is selected then (1) an Employer may not rely on the opinion letter issued by the Internal Revenue Service with respect to the requirements of Code §416, and (2), if the plans do not benefit the same Participants, the uniformity requirement of the Regulations under Code §401(a)(4) may be violated.
    2. [ ]   **Top-heavy duplications when a defined benefit plan is maintained** (Plan Section 4.3(i)). When a Non-Key Employee is a Participant in this Plan and a non-frozen defined benefit plan maintained by the Employer that is subject to the top-heavy rules, indicate which method will be utilized to avoid duplication of top-heavy minimum benefits: (select one of a. - d. AND complete e. or select f.)
        a. [ ]   The full top-heavy minimum will be provided in each plan (if selected, Plan Section 4.3(i) will not apply).
        b. [ ]   5% defined contribution minimum
        c. [ ]   2% defined benefit minimum will be made in the _____ (enter the name of the other plan)
        d. [ ]   Specify the method under which the plans will provide top-heavy minimum benefits for Non-Key Employees that will preclude Employer discretion and avoid inadvertent omissions: _____
        NOTE: If b., c., or d. is selected then (1) an Employer may not rely on the opinion letter issued by the Internal Revenue Service with respect to the requirements of Code §416, and (2), if the plans do not benefit the same Participants, the uniformity requirement of the Regulations under Code §401(a)(4) may be violated.
        AND, the "present value" (Plan Section 9.2) for top-heavy purposes will be based on:
        e. [ ]   Interest Rate: _____

        Mortality Table: _____
        f. [ ]   The interest rate and mortality table specified to determine "present value" for top-heavy purposes in the defined benefit plan.

        AND, a Participant must be employed on the last day of the Plan Year in order to receive the top-heavy minimum (Plan Section 4.3(h)) unless elected below.
        g. [ ]   A Participant is not required to be employed by the Employer on the last day of the Plan Year.

l. [ ]   **Recognition of Service with other employers** (Plan Sections 1.62 and 1.88). Service with the following employers (in addition to those specified at Question 16) will be recognized as follows (select one or more; if more than 6 employers, attach an addendum to the Adoption Agreement):

		Eligibility	Vesting	Contribution Allocation
1. [ ]	Employer name: _____	a. [ ]	b. [ ]	c. [ ]
2. [ ]	Employer name: _____	a. [ ]	b. [ ]	c. [ ]
3. [ ]	Employer name: _____	a. [ ]	b. [ ]	c. [ ]
4. [ ]	Employer name: _____	a. [ ]	b. [ ]	c. [ ]
5. [ ]	Employer name: _____	a. [ ]	b. [ ]	c. [ ]
6. [ ]	Employer name: _____	a. [ ]	b. [ ]	c. [ ]

Non-Standardized 401(k) Profit Sharing Plan

Limitations

7. [ ] The following provisions or limitations apply with respect to the   a. [ ]   b. [ ]   c. [ ]
recognition of prior service: _____
(e.g., credit service with X only on/following 1/1/13 or credit all service with entities the Employer acquires after 12/31/12)

m. [ ] **Other vesting provisions.** The following vesting provisions apply to the Plan (select one or more):

1. [ ] **Special vesting provisions.** The following special provisions apply to the vesting provisions of the Plan:
_____ (must be definitely determinable, non-discriminatory under Code §401(a)(4) and otherwise satisfy the parameters set forth in Questions 18 and 19 and Plan Section 6.4.; e.g., rather than the schedule specified at Question 18, the 5-year graded schedule applies to amounts merged into the Plan from the XYZ Plan.)

2. [ ] **Pre-amendment vesting schedule.** (Plan Section 6.4(h)). If the vesting schedule has been amended and a different vesting schedule other than the schedule at Question 18 applies to any Participants, then the following provisions apply (must select one of a. - d. AND complete e.):
Applicable Participants. The vesting schedules in Question 18 only apply to:

   a. [ ] Participants who are Employees as of _____ (enter date).
   b. [ ] Participants in the Plan who have an Hour of Service on or after _____ (enter date).
   c. [ ] Participants (even if not an Employee) in the Plan on or after _____ (enter date).
   d. [ ] Other: _____ (e.g., Participants in division A)

Vesting schedule

   e. The schedule that applies to Participants not subject to the vesting schedule in Question 18 is:

Years (or Periods) of Service	Percentage
_____	_____ %
_____	_____ %
_____	_____ %
_____	_____ %
_____	_____ %
_____	_____ %

3. [ ] **Prior vesting schedule for Employer matching contributions.** The vesting schedule for amounts attributable to Employer matching contributions made prior to Plan Years beginning after December 31, 2001 is:
_____ (enter the vesting schedule that applied prior to the Plan Year beginning in 2002; such schedule must satisfy 5-year cliff or 7-year graded and, if applicable, must provide for a top-heavy minimum schedule)

n. [ ] **Top-heavy vesting schedule** (Plan Section 6.4(e)).
Instead of any other vesting schedules set forth in the Plan, if this Plan becomes a Top-Heavy Plan, the following vesting schedule, based on number of Years of Service (or Periods of Service if the elapsed time method is selected) will apply:

1. [ ] 6 Year Graded: 0-1 year-0%;   2 years-20%;   3 years-40%;   4 years-60%;   5 years-80%;   6 years-100%
2. [ ] 3 Year Cliff: 0-2 years-0%;   3 years-100%
3. [ ] Other - Must be at least as liberal as either 1. or 2. above in each year without switching between the two schedules. (if a different top-heavy schedule applies to different contribution sources, attach an addendum specifying the schedule that applies to each source):

Years (or Periods) of Service	Percentage
_____	_____ %
_____	_____ %
_____	_____ %
_____	_____ %
_____	_____ %
_____	_____ %

NOTE: This Section does not apply to the Account balance of any Participant who does not have an Hour of Service after the Plan has initially become top-heavy. Such Participant's Vested Account balance will be determined without regard to this Section.

o. [ ] **Leased Employees** (Plan Section 1.49)

1. [ ] **Offset of contributions to leasing organization plan.** The Employer will reduce allocations to this Plan for any Leased Employee to the extent that the leasing organization contributes to or provides benefits under a leasing organization plan to or for the Leased Employee and which are attributable to the Leased Employee's services for the Employer.

2. [ ] **Disregard one year requirement.** The definition of Leased Employee shall be applied by disregarding the requirement of performing services for at least one year, for the following contributions (select a. or all that apply of b.1. – b.3.) (Elective Deferrals include Roth Elective Deferrals, "ADP test safe harbor contributions" (including those made pursuant to a QACA) and SIMPLE 401(k) contributions, after-tax voluntary Employee contributions, and rollover contributions; Matching includes QMACs; and Nonelective Profit Sharing includes QNECs):

   a. [ ] All contributions

   b. [ ] The following contributions (select all that apply)

     1. [ ] Elective Deferrals

     2. [ ] Matching contributions

     3. [ ] Nonelective Profit Sharing contributions

p. [ ] **Minimum distribution transitional rules** (Plan Section 6.8(e)(5))

  NOTE: This Section does not apply to (1) a new Plan, (2) an amendment or restatement of an existing Plan that never contained the provisions of Code §401(a)(9) as in effect prior to the amendments made by the Small Business Job Protection Act of 1996 (SBJPA), or (3) a Plan where the transition rules below do not affect any current Participants.

  The "required beginning date" for a Participant who is not a "five percent (5%) owner" is:

  1. [ ] April 1st of the calendar year following the year in which the Participant attains age 70 1/2. (pre-SBJPA rules continue to apply)

  2. [ ] April 1st of the calendar year following the later of the year in which the Participant attains age 70 1/2 or retires (the post-SBJPA rules), with the following exceptions (select one or both; leave blank if both applied effective as of January 1, 1996):

    a. [ ] A Participant who was already receiving required minimum distributions under the pre-SBJPA rules as of _____ (may not be earlier than January 1, 1996) was allowed to stop receiving distributions and have them recommence in accordance with the post-SBJPA rules. Upon the recommencement of distributions, if the Plan permits annuities as a form of distribution then the following apply:

      1. [ ] N/A (annuity distributions are not permitted)

      2. [ ] Upon the recommencement of distributions, the original Annuity Starting Date will be retained.

      3. [ ] Upon the recommencement of distributions, a new Annuity Starting Date is created.

    b. [ ] A Participant who had not begun receiving required minimum distributions as of _____ (may not be earlier than January 1, 1996) may elect to defer commencement of distributions until retirement. The option to defer the commencement of distributions (i.e., to elect to receive in-service distributions upon attainment of age 70 1/2) applies to all such Participants unless selected below:

      1. [ ] The in-service distribution option was eliminated with respect to Participants who attained age 70 1/2 in or after the calendar year that began after the later of (1) December 31, 1998, or (2) the adoption date of the restatement to bring the Plan into compliance with the SBJPA.

q. [ ] **Other spousal provisions** (select one or more)

  1. [ ] **One-year marriage rule.** For purposes of the Plan, other than for purposes of determining eligible hardship distribution expenses, an individual is treated as Spouse only if such individual was married throughout the one year period ending on the earlier of the Annuity Starting Date or the date of the Participant's death.

  2. [ ] **Definition of Spouse.** The term Spouse includes a spouse under federal law as well as the following:

    _____

  3. [ ] **Automatic revocation of spousal designation** (Plan Section 6.2(f)). The automatic revocation of a spousal Beneficiary designation in the case of divorce does not apply.

  4. [ ] **Timing of QDRO payment.** A distribution to an Alternate Payee shall not be permitted prior to the time a Participant would be entitled to a distribution.

r. [ ] **Applicable law.** Instead of using the applicable laws set forth in Plan Section 10.4(a), the Plan will be governed by the laws of: _____

s. [ ] **Total and Permanent Disability.** Instead of the definition at Plan Section 1.83, Total and Permanent Disability means: _____ (must be definitely determinable).

t. [ ] **Other Trust provisions** (select any that apply)

  1. [ ] **Special Trustee for collection of contributions.** The Employer appoints the following Special Trustee with the responsibility to collect delinquent contributions pursuant to Plan Section 7.1(b):

    Name: _____

    Title

    a. [ ] _____

    Address and telephone number

    b. [ ] Use Employer address and telephone number

    c. [ ] Use address and telephone number below:

    Address: _____

           Street

    _____ _____ _____

     City   State   Zip

    Telephone: _____

  NOTE: The Trustee named above is hereby appointed as a Trustee for the Plan, and is referred to as the Special Trustee. The sole responsibility of the Special Trustee is to collect contributions the Employer owes to

Non-Standardized 401(k) Profit Sharing Plan

the Plan. No other Trustee has any duty to ensure that the contributions received comply with the provisions of the Plan or is obliged to collect any contributions from the Employer. No Trustee, other than the Special Trustee, is obliged to ensure that funds deposited are deposited according to the provisions of the Plan. The Special Trustee must accept its position and agree to its obligations hereunder.

2. [ ] **Permissible Trust (or Custodian) modifications.** The Employer makes the following modifications to the Trust (or Custodial) provisions as permitted under Rev. Proc. 2011-49 (or subsequent IRS guidance) (select one or more of a. - c. below):

NOTE: Any elections below must not: (i) conflict with any Plan provision unrelated to the Trust or Trustee; or (ii) cause Plan to violate Code §401(a). In addition, this may not be used to substitute all of the Trust provisions in the Plan.

a. [ ] **Investments.** The Employer amends the Trust provisions relating to Trust investments as follows: _____

b. [ ] **Duties.** The Employer amends the Trust provisions relating to Trustee (or Custodian) duties as follows: _____

c. [ ] **Other administrative provisions.** The Employer amends the other administrative provisions of the Trust as follows: _____

u. [ ] **Other provisions for matching contributions** (select one or more)

1. [ ] **Match applied to elective deferrals to 403(b) arrangement.** In applying any matching contributions in this Plan, elective deferrals to a Code §403(b) arrangement will be aggregated with Elective Deferrals to this Plan.

2. [ ] **Matching contributions not used to satisfy top-heavy contribution** (Plan Section 4.3(j)). Employer matching contributions will NOT be taken into account for purposes of satisfying the minimum contribution requirements of Code §416(c)(2) and the Plan.

v. [ ] **QACA safe harbor contributions vesting options.** The vesting options selected at Question 19 on the Adoption Agreement also apply to the Participant's Qualified Automatic Contribution Safe Harbor Account unless otherwise selected below (select all that apply):

Excluded service prior to initial Effective Date of Plan or a predecessor plan (as defined in Regulations §1.411(a)-5(b)(3))

1. [ ] applies
2. [ ] does not apply

Excluded service prior to the computation period in which an Employee has attained age 18

3. [ ] applies
4. [ ] does not apply

Full vesting upon death

5. [ ] applies
6. [ ] does not apply

Full vesting upon Total and Permanent Disability

7. [ ] applies
8. [ ] does not apply

Non-Standardized 401(k) Profit Sharing Plan

EXHIBIT A
ONLY APPLICABLE IF 29.h.2. IS SELECTED
Age-Weighted Allocation Factors
Assumption: UP84 mortality

Table I -Normal Retirement Age

Age	Interest Assumptions		
	7.5%	8.0%	8.5%
55	124.24	119.46	115.01
56	122.23	117.61	113.31
57	120.15	115.70	111.54
58	118.01	113.72	109.71
59	115.81	111.69	107.83
60	113.55	109.59	105.89
61	111.23	107.44	103.88
62	108.86	105.23	101.83
63	106.44	102.98	99.72
64	103.98	100.68	97.57
65	101.49	98.35	95.38
66	98.97	95.98	93.16
67	96.44	93.60	90.92
68	93.89	91.21	88.66
69	91.31	88.78	86.37
70	88.70	86.30	84.03
71	86.04	83.79	81.65
72	83.35	81.24	79.22
73	80.64	78.66	76.77
74	77.91	76.06	74.29
75	75.18	73.45	71.80
76	72.45	70.85	69.31
77	69.75	68.26	66.83
78	67.07	65.70	64.37
79	64.42	63.14	61.92
80	61.78	60.61	59.48

Table II - Number of Years prior to Normal Retirement Age

Years prior to NRA	Interest Assumptions		
	7.5%	8.0%	8.5%
45	0.038603	0.031328	0.025448
44	0.041498	0.033834	0.027612
43	0.044610	0.036541	0.029959
42	0.047956	0.039464	0.032505
41	0.051553	0.042621	0.035268
40	0.055419	0.046031	0.038266
39	0.059576	0.049713	0.041518
38	0.064044	0.053690	0.045047
37	0.068847	0.057986	0.048876
36	0.074011	0.062624	0.053031
35	0.079562	0.067634	0.057539
34	0.085529	0.073045	0.062429
33	0.091943	0.078889	0.067736
32	0.098839	0.085200	0.073493
31	0.106252	0.092016	0.079740
30	0.114221	0.099377	0.086518
29	0.122787	0.107327	0.093872
28	0.131997	0.115914	0.101851
27	0.141896	0.125187	0.110509
26	0.152538	0.135202	0.119902
25	0.163979	0.146018	0.130094
24	0.176277	0.157699	0.141152
23	0.189498	0.170315	0.153150
22	0.203710	0.183940	0.166167
21	0.218989	0.198656	0.180291
20	0.235413	0.214548	0.195616
19	0.253069	0.231712	0.212244
18	0.272049	0.250249	0.230284
17	0.292453	0.270269	0.249859
16	0.314387	0.291890	0.271097
15	0.337966	0.315242	0.294140
14	0.363313	0.340461	0.319142
13	0.390562	0.367698	0.346269
12	0.419854	0.397114	0.375702
11	0.451343	0.428883	0.407636
10	0.485194	0.463193	0.442285
9	0.521583	0.500249	0.479880
8	0.560702	0.540269	0.520669
7	0.602755	0.583490	0.564926
6	0.647961	0.630169	0.612945
5	0.696558	0.680583	0.665045
4	0.748800	0.735030	0.721574
3	0.804960	0.793832	0.782908
2	0.865333	0.857339	0.849455
1	0.930233	0.925926	0.921659
0	1.000000	1.000000	1.000000
past NRA	1.000000	1.000000	1.000000

1

APPENDIX B

SAMPLE FORM 5500

■ ■ ■

Form **5500** Department of the Treasury Internal Revenue Service Department of Labor Employee Benefit Security Administration Pension Benefit Guaranty Corporation	**Annual Return/Report of Employee Benefit Plan** This form is required to be filed for employee benefit plans under sections 104 and 4065 of the Employee Retirement Income Security Act of 1974 (ERISA) and sections 6047(e), 6057(b), and 6058(a) of the Internal Revenue Code (the Code). ▶ **Complete all entries in accordance with the instructions to the Form 5500.**	OMB Nos. 1210-0110 1210-0089 **2013** This Form is Open to Public Inspection

Part I — Annual Report Identification Information

For calendar plan year 2013 or fiscal plan year beginning _____ and ending _____

A This return/report is for: ☐ a multiemployer plan;   ☐ a multiple-employer plan; or
                             ☐ a single-employer plan;   ☐ a DFE (specify) ____

B This return/report is: ☐ the first return/report;   ☐ the final return/report;
                            ☐ an amended return/report;   ☐ a short plan year return/report (less than 12 months).

C If the plan is a collectively-bargained plan, check here. . . . . ▶ ☐

D Check box if filing under: ☐ Form 5558;   ☐ automatic extension;   ☐ the DFVC program;
                            ☐ special extension (enter description) _____

Part II — Basic Plan Information—enter all requested information

1a Name of plan

	1b Three-digit plan number (PN) ▶
	1c Effective date of plan

2a Plan sponsor's name and address; include room or suite number (employer, if for a single-employer plan)

	2b Employer Identification Number (EIN)
	2c Sponsor's telephone number
	2d Business code (see instructions)

Caution: A penalty for the late or incomplete filing of this return/report will be assessed unless reasonable cause is established.

Under penalties of perjury and other penalties set forth in the instructions, I declare that I have examined this return/report, including accompanying schedules, statements and attachments, as well as the electronic version of this return/report, and to the best of my knowledge and belief, it is true, correct, and complete.

SIGN HERE	Signature of plan administrator	Date	Enter name of individual signing as plan administrator
SIGN HERE	Signature of employer/plan sponsor	Date	Enter name of individual signing as employer or plan sponsor
SIGN HERE	Signature of DFE	Date	Enter name of individual signing as DFE
Preparer's name (including firm name, if applicable) and address; include room or suite number. (optional)			Preparer's telephone number (optional)

For Paperwork Reduction Act Notice and OMB Control Numbers, see the Instructions for Form 5500.   Form **5500** (2013)
v. 130118

Form 5500 (2013)   Page **2**

3a Plan administrator's name and address ☐ Same as Plan Sponsor Name ☐ Same as Plan Sponsor Address	**3b** Administrator's EIN	
	3c Administrator's telephone number	

4 If the name and/or EIN of the plan sponsor has changed since the last return/report filed for this plan, enter the name, EIN and the plan number from the last return/report:	**4b** EIN	
a Sponsor's name	**4c** PN	

5 Total number of participants at the beginning of the plan year	**5**	
6 Number of participants as of the end of the plan year (welfare plans complete only lines 6a, 6b, 6c, and 6d).		
a Active participants	**6a**	
b Retired or separated participants receiving benefits	**6b**	
c Other retired or separated participants entitled to future benefits	**6c**	
d Subtotal. Add lines 6a, 6b, and 6c	**6d**	
e Deceased participants whose beneficiaries are receiving or are entitled to receive benefits	**6e**	
f Total. Add lines 6d and 6e	**6f**	
g Number of participants with account balances as of the end of the plan year (only defined contribution plans complete this item)	**6g**	
h Number of participants that terminated employment during the plan year with accrued benefits that were less than 100% vested	**6h**	
7 Enter the total number of employers obligated to contribute to the plan (only multiemployer plans complete this item).........	**7**	

8a If the plan provides pension benefits, enter the applicable pension feature codes from the List of Plan Characteristics Codes in the instructions:

b If the plan provides welfare benefits, enter the applicable welfare feature codes from the List of Plan Characteristics Codes in the instructions:

9a Plan funding arrangement (check all that apply)		**9b** Plan benefit arrangement (check all that apply)	
(1) ☐ Insurance		**(1)** ☐ Insurance	
(2) ☐ Code section 412(e)(3) insurance contracts		**(2)** ☐ Code section 412(e)(3) insurance contracts	
(3) ☐ Trust		**(3)** ☐ Trust	
(4) ☐ General assets of the sponsor		**(4)** ☐ General assets of the sponsor	

10 Check all applicable boxes in 10a and 10b to indicate which schedules are attached, and, where indicated, enter the number attached. (See instructions)

a Pension Schedules		**b** General Schedules	
(1) ☐ R (Retirement Plan Information)		**(1)** ☐ H (Financial Information)	
(2) ☐ MB (Multiemployer Defined Benefit Plan and Certain Money Purchase Plan Actuarial Information) - signed by the plan actuary		**(2)** ☐ I (Financial Information – Small Plan)	
		(3) __ A (Insurance Information)	
		(4) ☐ C (Service Provider Information)	
(3) ☐ SB (Single-Employer Defined Benefit Plan Actuarial Information) - signed by the plan actuary		**(5)** ☐ D (DFE/Participating Plan Information)	
		(6) ☐ G (Financial Transaction Schedules)	

SCHEDULE R (Form 5500)	Retirement Plan Information	OMB No. 1210-0110
Department of the Treasury Internal Revenue Service Department of Labor Employee Benefits Security Administration Pension Benefit Guaranty Corporation	This schedule is required to be filed under section 104 and 4065 of the Employee Retirement Income Security Act of 1974 (ERISA) and section 6058(a) of the Internal Revenue Code (the Code). ▶ File as an attachment to Form 5500.	**2013** This Form is Open to Public Inspection.

For calendar plan year 2013 or fiscal plan year beginning _____ and ending _____

A Name of plan	B Three-digit plan number (PN) ▶
C Plan sponsor's name as shown on line 2a of Form 5500	D Employer Identification Number (EIN)

Part I   Distributions

All references to distributions relate only to payments of benefits during the plan year.

1. Total value of distributions paid in property other than in cash or the forms of property specified in the instructions.............................. | 1 |

2. Enter the EIN(s) of payor(s) who paid benefits on behalf of the plan to participants or beneficiaries during the year (if more than two, enter EINs of the two payors who paid the greatest dollar amounts of benefits):

    EIN(s): _____

    Profit-sharing plans, ESOPs, and stock bonus plans, skip line 3.

3. Number of participants (living or deceased) whose benefits were distributed in a single sum, during the plan year.............................. | 3 |

Part II   Funding Information (if the plan is not subject to the minimum funding requirements of section of 412 of the Internal Revenue Code or ERISA section 302, skip this Part)

4. Is the plan administrator making an election under Code section 412(d)(2) or ERISA section 302(d)(2)?.................. ☐ Yes ☐ No ☐ N/A

    If the plan is a defined benefit plan, go to line 8.

5. If a waiver of the minimum funding standard for a prior year is being amortized in this plan year, see instructions and enter the date of the ruling letter granting the waiver. **Date:** Month _____ Day _____ Year _____

    If you completed line 5, complete lines 3, 9, and 10 of Schedule MB and do not complete the remainder of this schedule.

6. a   Enter the minimum required contribution for this plan year (include any prior year accumulated funding deficiency not waived)............................ | 6a |

   b   Enter the amount contributed by the employer to the plan for this plan year............... | 6b |

   c   Subtract the amount in line 6b from the amount in line 6a. Enter the result (enter a minus sign to the left of a negative amount)............................ | 6c |

    If you completed line 6c, skip lines 8 and 9.

7. Will the minimum funding amount reported on line 6c be met by the funding deadline?.................. ☐ Yes ☐ No ☐ N/A

8. If a change in actuarial cost method was made for this plan year pursuant to a revenue procedure or other authority providing automatic approval for the change or a class ruling letter, does the plan sponsor or plan administrator agree with the change?.................. ☐ Yes ☐ No ☐ N/A

Part III   Amendments

9. If this is a defined benefit pension plan, were any amendments adopted during this plan year that increased or decreased the value of benefits? If yes, check the appropriate box. If no, check the "No" box.............................. ☐ Increase ☐ Decrease ☐ Both ☐ No

Part IV   ESOPs (see instructions). If this is not a plan described under Section 409(a) or 4975(e)(7) of the Internal Revenue Code, skip this Part.

10. Were unallocated employer securities or proceeds from the sale of unallocated securities used to repay any exempt loan?.................. ☐ Yes ☐ No

11. a   Does the ESOP hold any preferred stock?.............................. ☐ Yes ☐ No

   b   If the ESOP has an outstanding exempt loan with the employer as lender, is such loan part of a "back-to-back" loan? (See instructions for definition of "back-to-back" loan.).................. ☐ Yes ☐ No

12. Does the ESOP hold any stock that is not readily tradable on an established securities market?.................. ☐ Yes ☐ No

For Paperwork Reduction Act Notice and OMB Control Numbers, see the Instructions for Form 5500.   Schedule R (Form 5500) 2013   v. 130118

Schedule R (Form 5500) 2013   Page **2 -** ☐

Part V	Additional Information for Multiemployer Defined Benefit Pension Plans

13   Enter the following information for each employer that contributed more than 5% of total contributions to the plan during the plan year (measured in dollars). See instructions. *Complete as many entries as needed to report all applicable employers.*

a   Name of contributing employer

b   EIN   **c**   Dollar amount contributed by employer

d   Date collective bargaining agreement expires *(If employer contributes under more than one collective bargaining agreement, check box* ☐ *and see instructions regarding required attachment. Otherwise, enter the applicable date.)* Month _____ Day _____ Year _____

e   Contribution rate information *(If more than one rate applies, check this box* ☐ *and see instructions regarding required attachment. Otherwise, complete lines 13e(1) and 13e(2).)*
     (1)   Contribution rate (in dollars and cents) _____
     (2)   Base unit measure: ☐ Hourly   ☐ Weekly   ☐ Unit of production   ☐ Other (specify): _____

a   Name of contributing employer

b   EIN   **c**   Dollar amount contributed by employer

d   Date collective bargaining agreement expires *(If employer contributes under more than one collective bargaining agreement, check box* ☐ *and see instructions regarding required attachment. Otherwise, enter the applicable date.)* Month _____ Day _____ Year _____

e   Contribution rate information *(If more than one rate applies, check this box* ☐ *and see instructions regarding required attachment. Otherwise, complete lines 13e(1) and 13e(2).)*
     (1)   Contribution rate (in dollars and cents) _____
     (2)   Base unit measure: ☐ Hourly   ☐ Weekly   ☐ Unit of production   ☐ Other (specify): _____

a   Name of contributing employer

b   EIN   **c**   Dollar amount contributed by employer

d   Date collective bargaining agreement expires *(If employer contributes under more than one collective bargaining agreement, check box* ☐ *and see instructions regarding required attachment. Otherwise, enter the applicable date.)* Month _____ Day _____ Year _____

e   Contribution rate information *(If more than one rate applies, check this box* ☐ *and see instructions regarding required attachment. Otherwise, complete lines 13e(1) and 13e(2).)*
     (1)   Contribution rate (in dollars and cents) _____
     (2)   Base unit measure: ☐ Hourly   ☐ Weekly   ☐ Unit of production   ☐ Other (specify): _____

a   Name of contributing employer

b   EIN   **c**   Dollar amount contributed by employer

d   Date collective bargaining agreement expires *(If employer contributes under more than one collective bargaining agreement, check box* ☐ *and see instructions regarding required attachment. Otherwise, enter the applicable date.)* Month _____ Day _____ Year _____

e   Contribution rate information *(If more than one rate applies, check this box* ☐ *and see instructions regarding required attachment. Otherwise, complete lines 13e(1) and 13e(2).)*
     (1)   Contribution rate (in dollars and cents) _____
     (2)   Base unit measure: ☐ Hourly   ☐ Weekly   ☐ Unit of production   ☐ Other (specify): _____

a   Name of contributing employer

b   EIN   **c**   Dollar amount contributed by employer

d   Date collective bargaining agreement expires *(If employer contributes under more than one collective bargaining agreement, check box* ☐ *and see instructions regarding required attachment. Otherwise, enter the applicable date.)* Month _____ Day _____ Year _____

e   Contribution rate information *(If more than one rate applies, check this box* ☐ *and see instructions regarding required attachment. Otherwise, complete lines 13e(1) and 13e(2).)*
     (1)   Contribution rate (in dollars and cents) _____
     (2)   Base unit measure: ☐ Hourly   ☐ Weekly   ☐ Unit of production   ☐ Other (specify): _____

a   Name of contributing employer

b   EIN   **c**   Dollar amount contributed by employer

d   Date collective bargaining agreement expires *(If employer contributes under more than one collective bargaining agreement, check box* ☐ *and see instructions regarding required attachment. Otherwise, enter the applicable date.)* Month _____ Day _____ Year _____

e   Contribution rate information *(If more than one rate applies, check this box* ☐ *and see instructions regarding required attachment. Otherwise, complete lines 13e(1) and 13e(2).)*
     (1)   Contribution rate (in dollars and cents) _____
     (2)   Base unit measure: ☐ Hourly   ☐ Weekly   ☐ Unit of production   ☐ Other (specify): _____

Schedule R (Form 5500) 2013   Page **3**

14 Enter the number of participants on whose behalf no contributions were made by an employer as an employer of the participant for:

a The current year	**14a**	
b The plan year immediately preceding the current plan year	**14b**	
c The second preceding plan year	**14c**	

15 Enter the ratio of the number of participants under the plan on whose behalf no employer had an obligation to make an employer contribution during the current plan year to:

a The corresponding number for the plan year immediately preceding the current plan year	**15a**	
b The corresponding number for the second preceding plan year	**15b**	

16 Information with respect to any employers who withdrew from the plan during the preceding plan year:

a Enter the number of employers who withdrew during the preceding plan year	**16a**	
b If line 16a is greater than 0, enter the aggregate amount of withdrawal liability assessed or estimated to be assessed against such withdrawn employers	**16b**	

17 If assets and liabilities from another plan have been transferred to or merged with this plan during the plan year, check box and see instructions regarding supplemental information to be included as an attachment. ☐

Part VI	Additional Information for Single-Employer and Multiemployer Defined Benefit Pension Plans

18 If any liabilities to participants or their beneficiaries under the plan as of the end of the plan year consist (in whole or in part) of liabilities to such participants and beneficiaries under two or more pension plans as of immediately before such plan year, check box and see instructions regarding supplemental information to be included as an attachment ☐

19 If the total number of participants is 1,000 or more, complete lines (a) through (c)

   a Enter the percentage of plan assets held as:

     Stock: _____ %   Investment-Grade Debt: _____ %   High-Yield Debt: _____ %   Real Estate: _____ %   Other: _____ %

   b Provide the average duration of the combined investment-grade and high-yield debt:

     ☐ 0-3 years   ☐ 3-6 years   ☐ 6-9 years   ☐ 9-12 years   ☐ 12-15 years   ☐ 15-18 years   ☐ 18-21 years   ☐ 21 years or more

   c What duration measure was used to calculate line 19(b)?

     ☐ Effective duration   ☐ Macaulay duration   ☐ Modified duration   ☐ Other (specify): _____

APPENDIX C

VALUE TABLES

■ ■ ■

TABLE C.1
PRESENT VALUE OF $1 TOMORROW

Year	1%	2%	3%	4%	5%	6%	7%	8%	10%	15%	20%
1	0.9901	0.9804	0.9709	0.9615	0.9524	0.9434	0.9346	0.9259	0.9091	0.8696	0.8333
2	0.9803	0.9612	0.9426	0.9246	0.9070	0.8900	0.8734	0.8573	0.8264	0.7561	0.6944
3	0.9706	0.9423	0.9151	0.8890	0.8638	0.8396	0.8163	0.7938	0.7513	0.6575	0.5787
4	0.9610	0.9238	0.8885	0.8548	0.8227	0.7921	0.7629	0.7350	0.6830	0.5718	0.4823
5	0.9515	0.9057	0.8626	0.8219	0.7835	0.7473	0.7130	0.6806	0.6209	0.4972	0.4019
6	0.9420	0.8880	0.8375	0.7903	0.7462	0.7050	0.6663	0.6302	0.5645	0.4323	0.3349
7	0.9327	0.8706	0.8131	0.7599	0.7107	0.6651	0.6227	0.5835	0.5132	0.3759	0.2791
8	0.9235	0.8535	0.7894	0.7307	0.6768	0.6274	0.5820	0.5403	0.4665	0.3269	0.2326
9	0.9143	0.8368	0.7664	0.7026	0.6446	0.5919	0.5439	0.5002	0.4241	0.2843	0.1938
10	0.9053	0.8203	0.7441	0.6756	0.6139	0.5584	0.5083	0.4632	0.3855	0.2472	0.1615
11	0.8963	0.8043	0.7224	0.6496	0.5847	0.5268	0.4751	0.4289	0.3505	0.2149	0.1346
12	0.8874	0.7885	0.7014	0.6246	0.5568	0.4970	0.4440	0.3971	0.3186	0.1869	0.1122
13	0.8787	0.7730	0.6810	0.6006	0.5303	0.4688	0.4150	0.3677	0.2897	0.1625	0.0935
14	0.8700	0.7579	0.6611	0.5775	0.5051	0.4423	0.3878	0.3405	0.2633	0.1413	0.0779
15	0.8613	0.7430	0.6419	0.5553	0.4810	0.4173	0.3624	0.3152	0.2394	0.1229	0.0649
16	0.8528	0.7284	0.6232	0.5339	0.4581	0.3936	0.3387	0.2919	0.2176	0.1069	0.0541
17	0.8444	0.7142	0.6050	0.5134	0.4363	0.3714	0.3166	0.2703	0.1978	0.0929	0.0451
18	0.8360	0.7002	0.5874	0.4936	0.4155	0.3503	0.2959	0.2502	0.1799	0.0808	0.0376
19	0.8277	0.6864	0.5703	0.4746	0.3957	0.3305	0.2765	0.2317	0.1635	0.0703	0.0313
20	0.8195	0.6730	0.5537	0.4564	0.3769	0.3118	0.2584	0.2145	0.1486	0.0611	0.0261
25	0.7798	0.6095	0.4776	0.3751	0.2953	0.2330	0.1842	0.1460	0.0923	0.0304	0.0105
30	0.7419	0.5521	0.4120	0.3083	0.2314	0.1741	0.1314	0.0994	0.0573	0.0151	0.0042
40	0.6717	0.4529	0.3066	0.2083	0.1420	0.0972	0.0668	0.0460	0.0221	0.0037	0.0007
45	0.6391	0.4102	0.2644	0.1712	0.1113	0.0727	0.0476	0.0313	0.0137	0.0019	0.0003
50	0.6080	0.3715	0.2281	0.1407	0.0872	0.0543	0.0339	0.0213	0.0085	0.0009	0.0001

TABLE C.2
COMPOUND AMOUNT OF $1

Year	1%	2%	3%	4%	5%	6%	7%	8%	10%
1	1.0100	1.0200	1.0300	1.0400	1.0500	1.0600	1.0700	1.0800	1.1000
2	1.0201	1.0404	1.0609	1.0816	1.1025	1.1236	1.1449	1.1664	1.2100
3	1.0303	1.0612	1.0927	1.1249	1.1576	1.1910	1.2250	1.2597	1.3310
4	1.0406	1.0824	1.1255	1.1699	1.2155	1.2625	1.3108	1.3605	1.4641
5	1.0510	1.1041	1.1593	1.2167	1.2763	1.3382	1.4026	1.4693	1.6105
6	1.0615	1.1262	1.1941	1.2653	1.3401	1.4185	1.5007	1.5869	1.7716
7	1.0721	1.1487	1.2299	1.3159	1.4071	1.5036	1.6058	1.7138	1.9487
8	1.0829	1.1717	1.2668	1.3686	1.4775	1.5938	1.7182	1.8509	2.1436
9	1.0937	1.1951	1.3048	1.4233	1.5513	1.6895	1.8385	1.9990	2.3579
10	1.1046	1.2190	1.3439	1.4802	1.6289	1.7908	1.9672	2.1589	2.5937
11	1.1157	1.2434	1.3842	1.5395	1.7103	1.8983	2.1049	2.3316	2.8531
12	1.1268	1.2682	1.4258	1.6010	1.7959	2.0122	2.2522	2.5182	3.1384
13	1.1381	1.2936	1.4685	1.6651	1.8856	2.1329	2.4098	2.7196	3.4523
14	1.1495	1.3195	1.5126	1.7317	1.9799	2.2609	2.5785	2.9372	3.7975
15	1.1610	1.3459	1.5580	1.8009	2.0789	2.3966	2.7590	3.1722	4.1772
16	1.1726	1.3728	1.6047	1.8730	2.1829	2.5404	2.9522	3.4259	4.5950
17	1.1843	1.4002	1.6528	1.9479	2.2920	2.6928	3.1588	3.7000	5.0545
18	1.1961	1.4282	1.7024	2.0258	2.4066	2.8543	3.3799	3.9960	5.5599
19	1.2081	1.4568	1.7535	2.1068	2.5270	3.0256	3.6165	4.3157	6.1159
20	1.2202	1.4859	1.8061	2.1911	2.6533	3.2071	3.8697	4.6610	6.7275
25	1.2824	1.6406	2.0938	2.6658	3.3864	4.2919	5.4274	6.8485	10.8347
30	1.3478	1.8114	2.4273	3.2434	4.3219	5.7435	7.6123	10.0627	17.4494
40	1.4889	2.2080	3.2620	4.8010	7.0400	10.2857	14.9745	21.7245	45.2593
45	1.5648	2.4379	3.7816	5.8412	8.9850	13.7646	21.0025	31.9204	72.8905
50	1.6446	2.6916	4.3839	7.1067	11.4674	18.4202	29.4570	46.9016	117.3909

TABLE C.3
PRESENT VALUE OF ANNUITY OF $1

Year	1%	2%	3%	4%	5%	6%	7%	8%	10%	15%
1	0.9901	0.9804	0.9709	0.9615	0.9524	0.9434	0.9346	0.9259	0.9091	0.8696
2	1.9704	1.9416	1.9135	1.8861	1.8594	1.8334	1.8080	1.7833	1.7355	1.6257
3	2.9410	2.8839	2.8286	2.7751	2.7232	2.6730	2.6243	2.5771	2.4869	2.2832
4	3.9020	3.8077	3.7171	3.6299	3.5460	3.4651	3.3872	3.3121	3.1699	2.8550
5	4.8534	4.7135	4.5797	4.4518	4.3295	4.2124	4.1002	3.9927	3.7908	3.3522
6	5.7955	5.6014	5.4172	5.2421	5.0757	4.9173	4.7665	4.6229	4.3553	3.7845
7	6.7282	6.4720	6.2303	6.0021	5.7864	5.5824	5.3893	5.2064	4.8684	4.1604
8	7.6517	7.3255	7.0197	6.7327	6.4632	6.2098	5.9713	5.7466	5.3349	4.4873
9	8.5660	8.1622	7.7861	7.4353	7.1078	6.8017	6.5152	6.2469	5.7590	4.7716
10	9.4713	8.9826	8.5302	8.1109	7.7217	7.3601	7.0236	6.7101	6.1446	5.0188
11	10.3676	9.7868	9.2526	8.7605	8.3064	7.8869	7.4987	7.1390	6.4951	5.2337
12	11.2551	10.5753	9.9540	9.3851	8.8633	8.3838	7.9427	7.5361	6.8137	5.4206
13	12.1337	11.3484	10.6350	9.9856	9.3936	8.8527	8.3577	7.9038	7.1034	5.5831
14	13.0037	12.1062	11.2961	10.5631	9.8986	9.2950	8.7455	8.2442	7.3667	5.7245
15	13.8651	12.8493	11.9379	11.1184	10.3797	9.7122	9.1079	8.5595	7.6061	5.8474
16	14.7179	13.5777	12.5611	11.6523	10.8378	10.1059	9.4466	8.8514	7.8237	5.9542
17	15.5623	14.2919	13.1661	12.1657	11.2741	10.4773	9.7632	9.1216	8.0216	6.0472
18	16.3983	14.9920	13.7535	12.6593	11.6896	10.8276	10.0591	9.3719	8.2014	6.1280
19	17.2260	15.6785	14.3238	13.1339	12.0853	11.1581	10.3356	9.6036	8.3649	6.1982
20	18.0456	16.3514	14.8775	13.5903	12.4622	11.4699	10.5940	9.8181	8.5136	6.2593
25	22.0232	19.5235	17.4131	15.6221	14.0939	12.7834	11.6536	10.6748	9.0770	6.4641
30	25.8077	22.3965	19.6004	17.2920	15.3725	13.7648	12.4090	11.2578	9.4269	6.5660
40	32.8347	27.3555	23.1148	19.7928	17.1591	15.0463	13.3317	11.9246	9.7791	6.6418
45	36.0945	29.4902	24.5187	20.7200	17.7741	15.4558	13.6055	12.1084	9.8628	6.6543
50	39.1961	31.4236	25.7298	21.4822	18.2559	15.7619	13.8007	12.2335	9.9148	6.6605

APPENDIX D

SAMPLE FORM 5300

■ ■ ■

Form 5300
(Rev. December 2013)
Department of the Treasury
Internal Revenue Service

Application for Determination for Employee Benefit Plan

(Under section 401(a) and 501(a) of the Internal Revenue Code)
► Information about Form 5300 and its instructions is at *www.irs.gov/form5300.*

OMB No. 1545-0197

Review instructions and the Procedural Requirements Checklist before completing this application.

For Internal Use Only

Complete lines 1j-1m and 2h-2k only if you have a foreign address, see instructions.

1a Name of plan sponsor (employer if single-employer plan)

b Address of plan sponsor

c City

d State

e Zip code

f Employer identification number (EIN)

g Telephone number

h Fax number

i Employer's tax year end (MM)

j City or town

k Country name

l Province/country

m Foreign postal code

2a Person to contact. If a Power of Attorney is attached, mark box, and do not complete this line. ☐
Contact person's name

b Contact person's address

c City

d State

e Zip code

f Telephone number

g Fax number

h City or town

i Country name

j Province/country

k Foreign postal code

If more space is needed for any item, attach additional sheets the same size as this form. Identify each additional sheet with the plan sponsor's name and EIN and identify each item.

Under penalties of perjury, I declare that I have examined this application, including accompanying statements and schedules, and to the best of my knowledge and belief, it is true, correct, and complete.

SIGN HERE ►

Date ►

Type or print name

Type or print title

For Privacy Act and Paperwork Reduction Act Notice, see the separate instructions.   Cat. No. 11740X   Form **5300** (Rev. 12-2013)

Form 5300 (Rev. 12-2013)   Page **2**

3a (1) Determination requested for (enter applicable number in box):

        ☐ **1** – Initial Qualification – New Plan

        2 – Initial Qualification – Existing Plan

        3 – Request after initial qualification

(2) Enter applicable number (4-7) in box for special rulings, if applicable.

        ☐ **4** – Affiliated Service Group (ASG) status (section 414(m))

        5 – Leased employee status (section 414(n))

        6 – Partial termination

        7 – Termination of multiemployer collectively bargained or multiple employer plan covered by Pension Benefit Guaranty Corporation (PBGC) insurance.

b   If line 3a(1) is "1" or "2," enter the date the plan was initially adopted.

c   If line 3a(2) is "6," enter the date of the partial termination.

d   If line 3a(2) is "7," enter the effective date of termination.

e (1) **Yes** **No**

      ☐   ☐   Is the plan being filed "on-cycle" pursuant to section 13 or 14 of Rev. Proc. 2007-44, 2007-28 I.R.B. 54? If "Yes," complete lines 3e(2) and 3e(3) below.

(2) Provide the submission cycle indicator pursuant to section 13 or 14 or Rev. Proc. 2007-44. ☐

      A. Cycle A   **C.** Cycle C   **E.** Cycle E   **G.** Pre-approved DB plans

      B. Cycle B   **D.** Cycle D   **F.** Pre-approved DC plans

(3) Provide the cycle reason. ☐

        1. The last digit of the EIN, or

        2. A multiple employer plan, or

        3. A governmental plan including governmental multiple employer plan, or

        4. A multiemployer plan, or

        5. A DC pre-approved plan, or an individually designed DC plan that is eligible for the six-year remedial amendment cycle (RAC), filing in the two-year window, or

        6. A DB pre-approved plan, or an individually designed DB plan that is eligible for the six-year RAC, filing in the two-year window, or

        7. EIN of the parent company, jointly trusteed single employer collectively bargained plan (if the plan sponsor is the Joint Board of Trustees include the EIN used on the Form 5500 filing) or centralized organization if that organization administers and operates the plan, or

        8. New plan exception, or

        9. Cycle changing event (include the date and explanation of the cycle changing event), or

      10. Cycle A controlled group election, ASG election or centralized group election. Attach a copy of the election. Also, attach a statement showing in detail:

          a. All members of the group (including their EIN),

          b. The type(s) of plan(s) each member has, and

          c. Plans common to all members.

      11. Urgent business need, or

      12. Other, attach an explanation.

    See Rev. Proc. 2007-44 for details, including sections 10, 11 and 16.

Form **5300** (Rev. 12-2013)

Form 5300 (Rev. 12-2013)   Page **3**

(Line 3 continued)

If line 3e(2) is "A" through "E," skip to line 3g.
If line 3e(2) is "F" or "G," go to line 3f.

    Yes **No**

f (1) ☐ ☐   Is the plan a pre-approved Master & Prototype (M&P) plan?

  (2) ☐ ☐   Is the plan a pre-approved Volume Submitter plan (VS)?

    (i) Name of sponsor or practitioner

    (ii) Date of opinion/advisory letter

    (iii) Serial # of opinion/advisory letter

    Yes **No**

g (1) ☐ ☐   Is this form being filed because it is a pre-approved plan required to file on a Form 5300?

  (2) If "Yes," mark each applicable box. (More than one box may be checked, if applicable.)

    ☐ ☐   **1** – Multiple employer plan, or

    ☐ ☐   **2** – Request required pursuant to published guidance by Service (such as minimum funding waiver), or

    ☐ ☐   **3** – Section 415 and 416 added to an M&P plan due to required aggregation, or

    ☐ ☐   **4** – The normal retirement age in the M&P or VS pension plan is earlier than age 62.

    If this is a pre-approved plan that does not meet one of the requirements above, attach an explanation why the Form 5300 is being filed.

h ☐ ☐   If the plan is not a pre-approved plan, is the plan an individually designed plan that is eligible for the six-year RAC?

i (1) ☐ ☐   If this is a VS plan, did the VS practitioner have the authority to amend on behalf of adopting employers for the entire prior RAC?

  (2) ☐ ☐   If this is a VS plan, does the VS practitioner have the authority to amend on behalf of adopting employers for the entire current RAC?

j ☐ ☐   Was the plan sponsor entitled to rely on a favorable opinion or advisory letter as an "identical adopter" of a pre-approved plan for the plan's RAC immediately preceding the cycle in which the application is submitted?
        If "Yes," complete j(i), (ii) and (iii).
        If "No," go to line 3k.

    (i) Name of sponsor or practitioner

    (ii) Date of opinion/advisory letter

    (iii) Serial # of opinion/advisory letter

    Yes **No**

k ☐ ☐   Does the plan have a determination letter (DL) for the plan's RAC immediately preceding the cycle in which the application is filed?
        If "Yes," complete line k (i), (ii), and (iii).
        If "No," go to line 3l.

Form **5300** (Rev. 12-2013)

Form 5300 (Rev. 12-2013)   Page **4**

(Line 3 continued)

(i) Date the letter was issued [   ]

(ii) Year of the Cumulative List considered in the letter [   ]

(iii) Expiration date of the letter [   ]

    Yes   No

l   [ ]   [ ]   Do any amendments not considered in a prior DL have any discretionary provisions?

                 If "Yes," and the amendment contains only discretionary provisions, mark an "X" in column (v) in the table.

                 If "Yes," and the amendment contains both interim and discretionary provisions, mark an "X" in columns (iv) and (v) in the table.

m   Complete the following table (for (iv), (v), and (vi) mark with an "X" in the applicable boxes). If additional space is needed, attach a separate sheet of paper the same size, label it "Attachment to 3m" using the same format as below.

| | **(i)** Amendment ID | **(ii)** Effective Date (MMDDYYYY) | **(iii)** Adoption Date (MMDDYYYY) | Type of Amendment | | **(vi)** Power to Amend on Behalf of | **(vii)** Due Date of Tax Return (including extensions) (MMDDYYYY) |
				(iv) Interim Amnd.	**(v)** Discr. Amnd.		
3m(1)							
3m(2)							
3m(3)							
3m(4)							
3m(5)							
3m(6)							
3m(7)							
3m(8)							
3m(9)							
3m(10)							

n   Enter total number of amendments on line 3m. [   ]

o   Designate the specific tax return that the employer uses to file its return. [   ]

Form **5300** (Rev. 12-2013)

Form 5300 (Rev. 12-2013)   Page **5**

4a Name of plan (plan name cannot exceed 70 characters, including spaces):

b Enter 3-digit plan number   **c** Enter the month on which the plan year ends (MM)

d Enter plan's original effective date   **e** Enter number of participants
       If 100 or less, complete line 4f. Otherwise, go to line 5a.

Yes   No

f Does the plan sponsor have no more than 100 employees who received at least $5,000 of compensation for the preceding year?
       If "Yes," go to line 4g.
       If "No," go to line 5a.

g Is at least one employee a non highly compensated employee?

5a Indicate the type of plan by entering the number from the list below.
        (Use the lowest number from the list below applicable to the plan.)

    1 – Pension Equity Plan (PEP)   5 – ESOP   9 – 401(k)
    2 – cash balance conversion   6 – money purchase   10 – profit sharing plan
    3 – cash balance (not converted)   7 – target benefit
    4 – defined benefit but not cash balance   8 – stock bonus

Yes   No

b (1) If the response to 5a was "1," "2," "3," "4," "6," or "7," was the plan's normal retirement age below 62 any time after 5/22/07?
           If "Yes," go to line 5b(2).
           If "No," go to line 5c(1).

(2) Has the employer (or trustees, if this is a multiemployer plan) made a good faith determination that the plan's normal retirement age is not lower than an age that reasonably represents the typical retirement age for the industry in which the covered workforce is employed? If "Yes," attach required statement. Governmental plans see instructions.

c (1) If the response to 5a was "5," mark the box to indicate whether the plan sponsor is an S Corporation or a C Corporation.

           ☐ C Corp.   ☐ S Corp.

(2) If there has been a change to the corporate status from C to S or S to C (election/revocation), provide the effective date of such change.

Yes   No

6a (1) Is the plan sponsor a member of an ASG, controlled group of corporations, or a group of trades or businesses under common control within the meaning of section 414(b) or (c)?
            If "Yes," attach the required statement.

(2) Is the plan sponsor a foreign entity or is the plan sponsor a member of an ASG, controlled group of corporations, or a group of trades or businesses under common control within the meaning of section 414(b) or (c) that includes a foreign entity?

b Is this a governmental plan under section 414(d)?

c (1) Is this a church plan under section 414(e)?
           If "Yes," go to line 6c(2).
           If "No," go to line 6d.

Form **5300** (Rev. 12-2013)

Form 5300 (Rev. 12-2013)   Page **6**

(Line 6 continued)

	Yes	No	
(2)	☐	☐	Was an election made by the church to have participation, vesting, funding, etc. provisions apply in accordance with section 410(d)?
d	☐	☐	Does this plan benefit any collectively bargained employees under Regulations section 1.410(b)-6(d)(2)?
e	☐	☐	Is this an insurance contract plan under section 412(e)(3)?
f	☐	☐	Is this a multiemployer plan under section 414(f)?
g	☐	☐	Is this a request for a ruling under section 401(h)?
h	☐	☐	Is this a request for ruling under section 420?
i (1)	☐	☐	Is this a multiple employer plan under section 413(c)? If "Yes," complete lines 6i(2) through 6i(5). If "No," go to line 7.

(2) Enter the total number of participating employers.   ☐

(3) Enter the number of participating employers submitting a Form 5300 concurrent with this application.   ☐

(4) Enter the EIN of the employer submitting the controlling plan.   ☐

(5) Enter the 3-digit plan number of the controlling plan.   ☐

7	☐	☐	Have interested parties been given the required notification of this application?
8	☐	☐	Is a separate DL application for this plan currently pending before the IRS?
9a	☐	☐	Does this plan satisfy one of the design-based safe harbor requirements for contributions or benefits under Regulations section 1.401(a)(4)-2(b) or 3(b)? If "Yes," go to line 9b. If "No," go to line 10a.

	Yes	No	
b	☐	☐	Is this an election for a determination regarding a design-based safe harbor? If "Yes," complete lines 9c through 9e. If "No," go to line 10a.
c	☐		Enter the letter ("A" - "E") from the list below that identifies the safe harbor intended to be satisfied. **A** = 1.401(a)(4)-2(b)(2) defined contribution (DC) plan with uniform allocation formula **B** = 1.401(a)(4)-3(b)(3) unit credit defined benefit (DB) plan **C** = 1.401(a)(4)-3(b)(4)(i)(C)(1) unit credit DB fractional rule plan **D** = 1.401(a)(4)-3(b)(4)(i)(C)(2) flat benefit DB plan **E** = 1.401(a)(4)-3(b)(5) insurance contract plan
d	☐	☐	Does this plan satisfy one of the safe harbor definitions of compensation under Regulation sections 1.414(s)-1(c)(2) or (3)?

Form **5300** (Rev. 12-2013)

Form 5300 (Rev. 12-2013)   Page **7**

(Line 9 continued)

e   List the plan section(s) that satisfy the design-based safe harbor (including, if applicable, the permitted disparity requirements):

        Yes   No

10a   ☐   ☐   Does this plan have a cash or deferred arrangement (CODA)?
                      If "Yes," go to line 10b(1).
                      If "No," go to line 10e.

b (1)   ☐   ☐   Does the CODA satisfy a safe harbor?
                      If "Yes," go to line 10b(2).
                      If "No," go to line 10d.

(2)   Indicate by using the corresponding number the type of section 401(k) safe harbor that was satisfied.   ☐
                      1. 401(k)(12)(B)
                      2. 401(k)(12)(C)
                      3. 401(m)(11)(B)

c   ☐   ☐   Does this plan contain a qualified automatic contribution arrangement (QACA) within the meaning of section 401(k)(13)?

d   ☐   ☐   Does this plan contain an eligible automatic contribution arrangement (EACA) within the meaning of section 414(w)?

e   ☐   ☐   Does this plan have matching contributions within the meaning of section 401(m)?
                      If "Yes," go to line 10f.
                      If "No," go to line 10g.

        Yes   No

f   ☐   ☐   Does this plan satisfy the 401(m) safe harbor?

g   ☐   ☐   Does this plan have after-tax employee voluntary contributions within the meaning of section 401(m)?

11   ☐   ☐   Does this plan utilize the permitted disparity rules of section 401(l)?

12   ☐   ☐   Is this plan part of an offset arrangement with any other plans?
                      If "Yes," attach the required statement.

13   ☐   ☐   Is this plan part of an eligible combined plan arrangement within the meaning of section 414(x)?
                      If "Yes," include the EIN and Plan # of the other plan.
                      EIN: _____   Plan #: _____

14   ☐   ☐   Has this plan been involved in a merger, consolidation, spinoff, or a transfer of plan assets or liabilities
                      that was not considered under a previous DL?
                      If "Yes," submit the required attachment.

15a   ☐   ☐   Has the plan been amended or restated to change the plan type?
                      If "Yes," go to line 15b.
                      If "No," go to line 16a.

b   ☐   ☐   Was the change considered in a prior DL?
                      If "No," attach a statement explaining the change.

                                                                        Form **5300** (Rev. 12-2013)

Form 5300 (Rev. 12-2013)   Page **8**

	Yes	No	
16a	☐	☐	Does the plan sponsor maintain any other qualified plans under section 401(a)?

If "Yes," attach required statement and complete lines 16b and 16c.
If "No," go to line 17.

| **b (1)** | ☐ | ☐ | Does the plan sponsor maintain another plan of the same type (for example, both this plan and the other plan are DC plans or both are DB plans) that covers non-key employees who are also covered under this plan? |

If "No," go to line 16c(1).

If "Yes," when the plan is top-heavy, do non-key employees covered under both plans receive the top-heavy minimum contribution or benefit under:

(2)	☐	☐	This plan, or
(3)	☐	☐	The other plan?
c (1)	☐	☐	If this is a DC plan, does the plan sponsor maintain a DB plan (or if this is a DB plan, does the plan sponsor maintain a DC plan) that covers non-key employees who are also covered under this plan?

If "No," go to line 17.
If "Yes," when the plan is top-heavy, do non-key employees covered under both plans receive:

(2)	☐	☐	The top-heavy minimum benefit under the DB plan,
(3)	☐	☐	At least a 5% minimum contribution under the DC plan,
(4)	☐	☐	The minimum benefit offset by benefits provided by the DC plan, or
(5)	☐	☐	Benefits under both plans, using a comparability analysis, at least equal to the minimum benefit.
17	☐	☐	Does any amendment to this plan reduce or eliminate any section 411(d)(6) protected benefit?

If "Yes," attach the required statement.

	Yes	No	NA	
18	☐	☐	☐	If this is a DC plan, are trust earnings and losses allocated on the basis of account balances?

If "No," attach a statement explaining how they are allocated.

	Yes	No	
19	☐	☐	Is any issue involving this plan currently pending or has any issue related to this plan been resolved during the current RAC by:

(1) Internal Revenue Service,
(2) Department of Labor,
(3) PBGC,
(4) Any court (including bankruptcy), or
(5) The Voluntary Correction Program of the Employee Plans Compliance Resolution System.
If "Yes," attach a statement with the contact person's name (IRS Agent, DOL Investigator, etc.) and telephone number.

Form **5300** (Rev. 12-2013)

Form 5300 (Rev. 12-2013)   Page **9**

20   Indicate the regular (non top-heavy) vesting provisions of the plan by entering the letter from the list below:

       a – Full and immediate   **d** – Full vesting after 5 years of service   **f** – 3 to 6 year graded vesting

       b – Full vesting after 2 years of service   **e** – 2 to 6 year graded vesting   **g** – Other

       c – Full vesting after 3 years of service

21   For DB plans – method for determining accrued benefit:

       a(1) Benefit formula at early retirement age is:

       a(2) Benefit formula at normal retirement age is:

       a(3) Normal form of retirement benefit is:

22   For DB plans – enter the letter of the accrual rule satisfied by the plan:

       A = Regulations section 1.411(b)-1(b)(1) – 3 percent method

       B = Regulations section 1.411(b)-1(b)(2) – 133 1/3 percent rule

       C = Regulations section 1.411(b)-1(b)(3) – Fractional rule

23   For DC plans – Employer contributions:

       a(1) Profit sharing or stock bonus plan contributions are determined under (mark box):

            ☐ A definite formula   ☐ A discretionary formula   ☐ Both

       Indicate the plan section where the above formula is located in the plan document:

       (2) Matching contributions are determined under (mark box):

            ☐ A definite formula   ☐ A discretionary formula   ☐ Both

       Indicate the plan section where the above formula is located in the plan document:

       (3) Money purchase plan – Enter rate of contribution:

       Indicate the plan section where the above formula is located in the plan document:

       (4) Target benefit plan formula is:

       Indicate the plan section where the above formula is located in the plan document:

Yes   No   NA

24a   ☐   ☐   ☐   For DC plans—Is this an applicable DC plan as defined in Regulations section 1.401(a)(35)-1(f)(2)?

b   If this is an applicable DC plan enter the section of the plan that contains the diversification language.

c   If the plan satisfies one of the exceptions noted in line 24 of the instructions, enter the relevant section(s) of the plan.

Form **5300** (Rev. 12-2013)

Form 5300 (Rev. 12-2013)   Page **10**

Procedural Requirements Checklist

Use this list to ensure that your submitted package is complete. Failure to supply the appropriate information may result in a delay in the processing of the application.

	Yes	No	
1.	☐	☐	Is Form 8717, User Fee for Employee Plan Determination Letter Request, attached to your submission?
2.	☐	☐	Is the appropriate user fee for your submission attached to Form 8717?
3.	☐	☐	If appropriate, is Form 2848, Power of Attorney and Declaration of Representative, Form 8821, Tax Information Authorization, or a privately designed authorization attached? (For more information, see the Disclosure Request by Taxpayer in the instructions and Rev. Proc. 2013-4, 2013-1 I.R.B. 126, updated annually.)
4.	☐	☐	Is a copy of your plan's latest DL, if any, attached?
5.	☐	☐	Have you included a copy of the plan, trust, and all amendments adopted or effective during the current RAC?
6.	☐	☐	Is the EIN of the plan sponsor/employer (NOT the trust's EIN) entered on line 1f?
7.	☐	☐	If you are requesting a determination for an ASG Status, have you included the information requested in the instructions?
8.	☐	☐	For Partial Termination Requests: Have you included the required information as specified in the instructions?
9.	☐	☐	If line 3g is "Yes" and does not meet one of the exceptions, have you attached an explanation of why the Form 5300 is being filed?
10.	☐	☐	If line 5b (2) is "Yes," is the required statement attached?
11.	☐	☐	If you answered "Yes" to line(s) 6a, have you included the information requested in the instructions?
12.	☐	☐	For Multiple Employer Plans: Have you included the required information as specified in the instructions?
13.	☐	☐	Have interested parties been given the required notification of this application? Make sure line 7 is completed.
14.	☐	☐	If line 12 is "Yes," have you attached the required statement?
15.	☐	☐	If line 14 is "Yes," have you attached the required statement?
16.	☐	☐	If line 15b is "No," have you attached the required statement?
17.	☐	☐	If line 16a is "Yes," have you attached the required statement?
18.	☐	☐	If line 17 is "Yes," have you attached the required statement?
19.	☐	☐	If line 18 is "No," have you attached the required statement?
20.	☐	☐	If line 19 is "Yes," have you attached the required statement?
21.	☐	☐	Is the application signed and dated? (Stamped signatures are not acceptable; see Rev. Proc. 2013-4 updated annually.)

Form **5300** (Rev. 12-2013)

Appendix E

Limits on Contributions and Benefits (2014)

■ ■ ■

Maximum annual benefit payable from a defined benefit plan (Code § 415(b)(i)(A))	$210,000
Maximum annual contribution amount (including forfeitures) to a participant's defined contribution plan account (Code § 415(c)(i)(A))	$52,000
Maximum amount for traditional and safe harbor 401(k) plan elective salary deferral contributions (Code § 402(g)(1))	$17,500
Maximum amount for traditional and safe harbor 401(k) plan catch-up contributions for participants age 50 or older (Code § 414(v)(2)(B)(i))	$5,500
Maximum amount for SIMPLE 401(k) plan elective salary deferral contributions (Code § 408(p)(2))	$12,000
Maximum amount for SIMPLE 401(k) plan catch-up contributions for participants age 50 or older (Code § 414(v)(2)(B)(ii))	$2,500
Limit on compensation amount used to determine plan contributions or benefits (Code § 401(a)(17))	$260,000
Highly compensated employee ("HCE") status (Code § 414(q))	$115,000

Key employee status for top heavy testing	
1% owner (Code § 416(i)(1)(A)(iii))	$150,000
Officer (Code § 416(i)(1)(A)(i))	$170,000
Social Security taxable wage base	$117,000
Health savings accounts (Code §223)	
Minimum HDHP deductible amount for individual/family coverage	$1,250/$2,500
Maximum annual contribution to a HSA for individual/family coverage	$3,300/$6,550
Maximum annual catch-up contribution (age 55 and older)	$1,000
Maximum annual out-of-pocket amount for individual/family coverage under a HDHP	$6,350/$12,700

Appendix F

Sample QDRO

■ ■ ■

IN THE CIRCUIT COURT OF [_____] COUNTY, [_____]
[_____] JUDICIAL DISTRICT OF [_____] AT [_____],
[_____]

In Re The Marriage Of:)	
)	
[Name] and [Name])	
)	Case No. [_____]
[Name],)	
)	Division No. [_____]
Petitioner,)	
)	
and)	
)	
[Name],)	
)	
Respondent.)	

QUALIFIED DOMESTIC RELATIONS ORDER

[Revise introductory language as appropriate]

THIS CAUSE having come on for a hearing and the Court having simultaneously herewith entered a Decree of Dissolution of Marriage, the Court hereby makes the following findings of fact:

WHEREAS, the parties to this action have entered into a [title] Agreement dated [_____] (the "Agreement"); and the Court incorporated

the Agreement into its Decree of Dissolution of Marriage dated [_____].
[Revise as appropriate for a contested proceeding.]

WHEREAS, the Court intends this order to be a Qualified Domestic Relations Order ("QDRO") within the meaning of Section 414(p) of the Internal Revenue Code of 1986 ("Code").

WHEREAS, this QDRO applies to the _____ (the "Plan"); and [Name] ("Participant") is a participant in the Plan; and [Name] ("Alternate Payee") is the alternate payee for purposes of this QDRO.

WHEREAS, this QDRO does not require the Plan to provide any type or form of benefit the Plan does not otherwise provide, or to provide increased benefits.

WHEREAS, this QDRO does not require the Plan to pay any benefit which another order previously determined to be a qualified domestic relations order requests the Plan to pay another alternate payee.

WHEREAS, the Participant's name, social security number, date of birth, and mailing address are:

WHEREAS, the Alternate Payee's name, social security number, date of birth, and mailing address are:

NOW, THEREFORE, IT IS HEREBY ORDERED, ADJUDGED AND DECREED:

The Alternate Payee shall receive from the Plan [___%] [$_____] of the Participant's accrued benefit as of the valuation date immediately preceding the date of this QDRO (the "QDRO Distribution"). The QDRO Distribution shall be paid pro rata from the Participant's accounts under the Plan. The QDRO Distribution shall be made as soon as administratively practicable in accordance with the terms of the Plan after the date of this QDRO. The QDRO Distribution shall be made in the form of [a lump sum payment.]

IT IS FURTHER ORDERED: (1) that this QDRO does not require the Alternate Payee's consent to the QDRO Distribution, and the Plan may distribute the QDRO Distribution without obtaining any further consent from the Alternate Payee; (2) after payment of the amount required by this QDRO, the Alternate Payee shall have no further claim against the Participant's interest in the Plan; (3) the Alternate Payee assumes sole responsibility for the tax consequences of the QDRO Distribution; (4) the Plan shall treat this QDRO in accordance with Code Section 414(p)(7); (5) an attested copy of this QDRO shall be served upon the Plan Administrator; and (6) the Plan Administrator shall determine the qualified status of the QDRO and shall notify the Participant and the Alternate Payee of the determination within a reasonable period of time after receipt of this QDRO.

IT IS FURTHER ORDERED, that this QDRO shall take effect immediately as of this ____ day of _____, and shall remain in effect until further order of this Court.

_____   _____

Dated: Circuit Court Judge

APPENDIX G

TIMELINE OF AFFORDABLE CARE ACT REFORMS

■ ■ ■

The Affordable Care Act contains multiple effective dates for reforms impacting group health plans. To simplify the timeline presented below, these effective dates assume that the group health plan operates on a calendar plan year.

2011

- Group health plans generally are required to offer coverage to an adult child of a plan participant through age 26, regardless of the child's marital status, full-time student status, or financial support by the parent. Grandfathered plans are not required to extend coverage to adult children if the adult child is eligible for coverage under another employer-sponsored group health care plan. (This exception for grandfathered plans expired January 1, 2014.)

- All group health plans are prohibited from rescinding coverage once an individual is enrolled in the plan, unless the individual has engaged in fraud or intentional misrepresentation in enrolling in the plan.

- Group health plans generally are prohibited from imposing lifetime and annual dollar limits on any essential health benefits offered by the plan. (Until January 1, 2014, grandfathered plans were allowed to impose reasonable annual dollar limits on any essential health benefit offered by the plan.)

- All group health plans are prohibited from imposing preexisting condition coverage exclusions for children under age 19.

- Employers with more than 200 full-time equivalent employees who sponsor a group health plan must automatically enroll new full-time employees in the plan. (Enforcement of this requirement has been suspended until further regulatory guidance is issued.)

- Non-grandfathered plan: (1) must pay the entire cost of immunizations and preventive care services; (2) cannot require pre-authorization for emergency services and must treat all emergency services as in-network; (3) must permit participants to see a gynecologist or obstetrician without a referral, and to select a pediatrician as a child's primary care physician; and (4) must permit independent external review of denied claims for plan benefits.

- Insured group health plans generally are subject to the same nondiscrimination requirements applicable to self-insured plans under Code Section 105(h)(2). (Enforcement of this requirement has been suspended until further regulatory guidance is issued.)

2012

- Plan administrators and insurers for all group health plans must provide plan participants with a concise explanation of the plan's benefits and coverage provisions prior to enrollment in the plan. The summary must be written in a culturally and linguistically appropriate manner utilizing terminology that is understandable by the average plan participant. The format of the concise explanation must conform to regulatory standards.

- Plan administrators and insurers for all group health plans must provide notice of a material modification to the plan's benefits no later than 60 days prior to the effective date of the modification.

- Employers who sponsor group health plans must begin reporting the total cost of employer-provided coverage (both employer costs and employee-paid premiums) on IRS Form W-2 for the 2011 calendar year. (Enforcement of this requirement has been suspended for employers who file fewer than 250 Form W-2s until further regulatory guidance is issued. Employers who file 250 or more Form W-2s were not required to comply with this requirement for calendar year 2011, but are required to comply for calendar year 2012 and subsequent years.)

2013

- Employers who receive a federal tax subsidy for prescription drug coverage under a group health plan for retirees no longer can deduct the amount of the tax subsidy on corporate income tax returns.

2014

- Individuals must have minimum essential coverage through a federal or state program, an employer-sponsored group health plan, or an individual insurance policy. Individuals who fail to obtain and maintain minimum essential coverage must pay a tax penalty under Code Section 5000A.

- Individual insurance policies providing coverage in 2014 may be purchased through the American Health Benefits Exchanges. Premium assistance tax credits become available to qualifying individuals and families based on income levels, but only if coverage is purchased through an Exchange. Medicaid coverage is expanded voluntarily in some states so that individuals and households with incomes of up to 133% of the federal poverty level are eligible for Medicaid coverage.

- All group health plans are prohibited from imposing preexisting condition coverage exclusions on adults or waiting periods for longer than 90 days. Non-grandfathered plans must limit the out-of-pocket expenses of the plan participants.

- Private insurance companies are subject to guaranteed issue and guaranteed renewability requirements for group health insurance policies. Insurance companies are not restricted, however, in the amount of the premium that may be charged for the issuance or renewal of a group health insurance policy.

2015

- Employers with 100 or more full-time equivalent employees must offer a group health plan that provides minimum essential coverage to at least 70% of their full-time employees and their dependents, or else pay a nondeductible excise tax penalty under Code Section 4980H. The coverage offered must be affordable and provide minimum value in accordance with federal regulations.

2016

- Employers with 50 or more full-time equivalent employees must offer a group health plan that provides minimum essential coverage to at least 95% of their full-time employees and their dependents, or else pay a nondeductible excise tax penalty under Code Section 4980H. The coverage offered must be affordable and provide minimum value in accordance with federal regulations.

2018

- A 40 percent nondeductible excise tax is imposed on health care plans that have annual premiums in excess of $10,200 for single coverage or $27,5000 for family coverage. The tax is assessed only on the portion of the annual coverage that exceeds these dollar limits, and is indexed for inflation in future years.

APPENDIX H

LIST OF ACRONYMS

■ ■ ■

ADA	Americans with Disabilities Act of 1990
ADEA	Age Discrimination in Employment Act of 1967
ACP	actual contribution percentage
ADP	actual deferral percentage
Audit CAP	Audit Closing Agreement Program
COBRA	Consolidated Omnibus Budget Reconciliation Act of 1985
DB	defined benefit
DC	defined contribution
DFVCP	Delinquent Filer Voluntary Compliance Program
DOL	Department of Labor
EBSA	Employee Benefit Security Administration
EEOC	Equal Employment Opportunity Commission
EGTRRA	Economic Growth and Tax Relief Reconciliation Act of 2001
EPCRS	Employee Plans Compliance Resolution System
ERISA	Employee Retirement Income Security Act of 1974
ESOP	employee stock ownership plan
ETI	economically targeted investment
FAB	Field Assistance Bulletin
FAS	Financial Accounting Standard
FASB	Financial Accounting Standards Board
FMLA	Family and Medical Leave Act of 1993

GINA	Genetic Information Nondiscrimination Act
HCE	highly compensated employee
HCRA	Health Care and Education Reconciliation Act of 2010
HDHP	high-deductible health plan
HIPAA	Health Insurance Portability and Accountability Act of 1996
HMO	Health Maintenance Organization Act of 1973 or health maintenance organization
HSA	health savings account
IRA	individual retirement account
IRO	Independent review organization
IRS	Internal Revenue Service
LMRA	Labor Management Relations Act of 1947
MEWA	Multiple Employer Welfare Arrangement
MHPA	Mental Health Parity Act of 1996
MHPAEA	Mental Health Parity and Addiction Equity Act of 2008
MPPAA	Multiemployer Pension Plan Amendments Act of 1980
MSP	Medicare as secondary payer
MEWA	multiple employer welfare arrangement
NLRA	National Labor Relations Act of 1935
NLRB	National Labor Relations Board
NMHPA	Newborns' and Mothers' Health Protection Act of 1996
OBRA	Omnibus Budget Reconciliation Act of 1993
OWBPA	Older Workers Benefit Protection Act of 1990
PBGC	Pension Benefit Guaranty Corporation
PDA	Pregnancy Discrimination Act of 1978
PHSA	Public Health Services Act

POS	point of service
PPA	Pension Protection Act of 2006
ACA	Affordable Care Act
PPO	preferred provider organization
QDRO	qualified domestic relations order
QJSA	qualified joint and survivor annuity
QMCSO	qualified medical child support order
QPSA	qualified preretirement survivor annuity
QSLOB	qualified separate line of business
REA	Retirement Equity Act of 1984
RMD	required minimum distribution
SAR	summary annual report
SEP	simplified employee pension plan
SEPPA	Single Employer Pension Plan Amendments Act of 1986
SMM	summary of material modifications
SPD	summary plan description
USERRA	Uniformed Services Employment and Reemployment Rights Act
VCP	Voluntary Correction Program
WHCRA	Women's Health and Cancer Rights Act of 1998
WPPDA	Welfare and Pension Plans Disclosure Act of 1958

INDEX

References are to Pages